HARDY

HARDY

MARTIN SEYMOUR-SMITH

St. Martin's Press
New York

Pictures reproduced by kind permission of the Trustees of the Thomas
Hardy Memorial Collection in the Dorset County Museum, Dorchester,
Dorset, with the exception of those on pages 5, 7, 8, 9, 10 *top*, 11, 12, 13
and 15 (Mary Evans Picture Library)

Library of Congress Cataloging-in-Publication Data

Seymour-Smith, Martin.
Hardy / Martin Seymour-Smith.
p.   cm.
ISBN 0-312-11819-8
1. Hardy, Thomas, 1840-1928—Biography.   2. Authors, English—19th
century—Biography.   3. Authors, English—20th century—Biography.
I. Title.
PR4753.S49   1994
823\.8—dc20
[B]   94-35466   CIP

First published in Great Britain by Bloomsbury Publishing Limited

First U.S. Edition: December 1994
10 9 8 7 6 5 4 3 2 1

TO ROBERT NYE

Contents

Acknowledgements

M y greatest debt is to Ann Wilson. Well knowing, from previous experience with my books, the difficulties that would be involved, she nevertheless consented, when I asked her, to edit this one. Circumstances prevented her from working on more than about a quarter of it, but this crucial part she helped me to get into shape – to the extent of substantial rewriting. Often she understood what I wanted to say better than I did myself. My debt to her is incalculable.

When Ann could not continue, Esther Jagger took over the job, at very short notice; I am grateful to her, too, for her speed and expertise.

Among those others to whom I am grateful, pride of place must go to my friend of thirty-seven years, Robert Nye, to whom this volume is dedicated. Throughout the long and often difficult period of its composition he cajoled me, threatened me, teased me, attacked me, defended me, besieged me and studiously ignored me when I was not getting on with it as I should. Most vital of all, he discussed with me, at great length and in great detail, Hardy's poetry. I have had much from him, and can only hope that this book pays back some of my debt.

My wife always wanted me to write a book on Hardy; I early learned from her of a few bad misconceptions I had. Here it is, with thanks for her suggestions – and for sharing so much of his work with me for so long.

While I cannot emulate the genius of Joseph Conrad, I can endorse his description of what it feels like to get a grant from the Royal Literary Fund when all else seems to have failed: 'miracles', he wrote. I could not have finished this book without two such grants, and I thank everyone concerned for their courtesy and sensitivity.

I am grateful, as always, to the London Library and to the East Sussex County Library here at Bexhill-on-Sea. I am grateful, too, to those who drew my attention to the fact that much of the Hardy material housed in the County Museum at Dorchester is also stored on microfilm, and who made the facilities for viewing it available to me. In addition, I would like to thank Christine Bernstein, who under huge pressure of time compiled the index; and I am very happy to acknowledge the help of Clare Hulton and Suzy Lucas, at Bloomsbury, unobtrusively given though this has always been: their kindly persistence has smoothed over many an apparently hopeless situation.

Two others who helped, and whom I now thank, are Nicholas Dyer and Valentinus Softon-Doidge. Last, but not least, I thank my long-suffering publishers for their support.

Martin Seymour-Smith
November 1993

1

Family and Boyhood

At eight o'clock in the morning, on Tuesday, 2 June 1840, the infant who was to become known throughout the world as Thomas Hardy was cast aside as dead by the doctor who delivered him. 'Had it not been for the common sense of the estimable woman who attended as monthly nurse,' he said, writing of himself in the third person some eighty years later, 'he might never have walked the earth.' For this nurse exclaimed, 'Dead! Stop a minute: he's alive enough, sure!' Thus was the beginning of the smallish man – five feet six and a half inches – often diffident in manner, whose obstinate intimations of doomed mortality would be so dramatic, so passionate and so persuasive as to shock his contemporaries, even some of his closest friends, into a protest almost as strong as the eagerness with which they devoured his unwelcome but irresistible books.

The event took place in a cottage at Bockhampton in Dorset, 'in a lonely and silent spot between woodland and heathland', a spot from which he would seldom be far away for long. It was on the edge of that 'sullen . . . mass of dark heath-land', 'a tract in pain', which stretched, little interrupted, from Dorchester in the west to Bournemouth in the east, and which would become known to the world as Egdon Heath. In 'Domicilium', a poem he wrote between the ages of seventeen and twenty, and did not publish until 1916, Hardy imagined 'with obvious and naive fidelity' the cottage as it had been in 1790. Despite the youthful, and what he called the 'Wordsworthian', nature of the lines, he managed to make a pun on his own name, with reference to that wild and independent part of himself so in love with the heath and its nature:

> Red roses, lilacs, variegated box
> Are there in plenty, and such hardy flowers
> As flourish best untrained . . .
> Behind, the scene is wilder. Heath and furze

1

Are everything that seems to grow and thrive
Upon the uneven ground. A stunted thorn
Stands here and there, indeed; and from a pit
An oak uprises, springing from a seed
Dropped by some bird a hundred years ago.

The older and famous Thomas Hardy, not the boy or the author of this poem (sparked off by the death in 1857 of his much loved paternal grandmother – who is mentioned in it as 'now/Blest with the blest') – was fascinated by the history of his name. He liked to think that he sprang from a Jersey family called Le Hardy and that he had some collateral association with such men as Thomas Hardye of Frampton, who had endowed Hardye School in Dorchester in 1579, and Vice-Admiral Sir Thomas Masterton Hardy, by whose side Nelson so famously died.

He was perhaps right in assuming this connection, although most of the (quite numerous) people called Hardy in that area had similarly plausible claims; it was in any case a Victorian habit to advance them. This was an age in which even enlightened people manufactured pedigrees, and faked 'Norman' prefixes to their names. The practice was not confined to Great Britain: in Maupassant's *Bel Ami* the upstart seducer and crook Georges Duroy, army NCO and son of peasants, became Baron Du Roy de Cantel. Hardy's occasional interest in his family name was motivated not by snobbery (he deals with such pretensions convincingly and comically in *Tess*) but by his liking for the notion that his forebears 'had all the characteristics of spent energies'; 'the Thomas Hardy of this memoir', he wrote in the *Life*, his disguised autobiography, '. . . never cared to take advantage of the many worldly opportunities that his popularity and esteem as an author afforded him.' On the whole, and given the exception of one or two women with whom he would have liked to have an affair – and Florence Dugdale, with whom he did – this was true. But he needed to feel that by the time of his birth his 'family had declined'. It appealed to his cast of mind, as did the morbid Victorian interest in heredity and its terrible implications. He was always, although never uncritically, a student of the French naturalist movement and its crown, the novels of Emile Zola.

The charge that Hardy 'invented' such family connections, even that they were part of a 'delusion', is unfair, even if he did resent emphasis being put, by newspaper writers, on the 'lowness' of his origins. Few like to believe that their origins are 'low'. But it would be fanciful to pursue (as has been done) the question of his ancestry as if it could be securely established. It cannot.

His father, paternal grandfather and great-grandfather were all enterprising men. Perhaps his father's enterprise has been somewhat underplayed, in the interests of presenting him as dominated by his wife, and thus, in turn, building up a picture of young Thomas as a child over-dependent on his mother. That she was formidable is certain. But that she over-dominated her son is unlikely. He was, in his quieter way, more than a match for her.

The paternal great-great-grandfather, John Hardy of Overmoigne (Hardy's Nether Moynton), who died in 1807, married an Elizabeth Swyre, said to have been Irish, in 1746. His son, also John (1756–1822), married a Jane Knight (1758–1825) in 1777. This John is reputed, no doubt falsely, to have turned up from nowhere, with a bag of tools, in eighteenth-century Puddletown. His son was Thomas (1778–1837), the poet's grandfather, and a lover and player of church music. He married Mary Head of Fawley (Hardy's Marygreen, and Jude's surname) in Berkshire. She was born in 1772.

Hardy had especially tender memories of this grandmother, Mary Head. He was fascinated by what she told him of her Berkshire youth. She might or might not have been the Mary Head who had an illegitimate daughter in Reading at the age of twenty-four (probably not); she was certainly not the one who was sentenced in 1797, at the same place, for the theft of a copper kettle. It is understandable that writers eager to establish originals for Hardy's characters should be attracted by such investigations. But such 'originals' seldom exactly resemble a novelist's characters. It is enough to say that Hardy's imagination was caught by his grandmother's early struggles, and by what she told him of them when he was a boy. She was sixty-eight when he was born, and eighty-five when she died, and from the oddly poignant retrospective freedom with which the elderly often speak, a sensitive child, especially one of such reminiscent habit as Hardy, may later construct essential truths.

Mary and Thomas Hardy had five children before Thomas (II), Hardy's father (1811–92), was born: Martha (1800), John (1803), James (1805), Mary (1807) and Jane (1809), who died in infancy. A second Jane was born after Thomas, in 1815. Of these aunts and uncles Hardy himself knew Martha (wife of a butcher called Levi Groves, of Upwey, near Weymouth), John, James and Jane (who married a thatcher, brother to Levi Groves, also of Upwey).

John, James and Thomas II were all independent masons and brick-layers, a trade their own father passed on to them. The John Hardy who is supposed to have turned up in Puddletown from nowhere leased an acre and a half of land (from the Morton Pitt family, for whom he had presumably done some building work) in one of the hamlets, New Bockhampton, lying within the parish of Stinsford (Hardy's Mellstock). It was on this land that in 1801, following the marriage of his son Thomas I (Hardy's grandfather) to the orphaned Mary Head in 1799, at the early age of twenty-one, John built the cottage where Hardy would be born. In those days, as in Hardy's own, the heath stretched right up to it.

Thomas I operated his building business from this cottage, a substantial one for the time, made of cob (clay mixed with gravel and straw) and thatch. He made some extra money by allowing it to be used for the unofficial trade in spirits, then quite freely carried on despite continual government opposition. Traders would carry tubs of brandy from the nearby coast to the back-porches of this and other store-houses, flicking their whips against the windows as they delivered. Thomas, who stored the strong-smelling tubs under the stairs, had a small window built into the front porch to look out for any snooper from the Excise, which was even more despised than it is today. The Dorset novel *Moonfleet* (1898), by John Meade Falkner (whom Hardy knew well), contains many authentic details of this trade, and of the sometimes disastrous interference from the Excise into its conduct – the romance of which largely derived from the fact that it was an act of defiance. Smuggling became increasingly risky, and in 1805, doubtless at the behest of his wife, Thomas gave it up.

Bockhampton itself already existed when New Bockhampton came into being. The 'New' Bockhampton (only later 'Higher') reflected the need for housing for a population that in 1800 was rapidly rising. In Hardy's childhood Higher Bockhampton consisted of only a row of houses, known as 'Veterans' Valley' or 'Cherry Alley': the first because a few retired military men had settled there, and the second because the 'lane or street leading through it' was 'planted with an avenue of cherries'. It was the wife of an 'old militiaman', Elizabeth Downton, who, in his own words, 'assisted Thomas Hardy into the world'.

Hardy's disguised autobiography, written in the third person as if by his second wife, Florence (Dugdale), is in part an ironic and selective work. It should be read between the lines, with some respect for Hardy's intellect, and with the recognition that it was written by a man in his extreme, although canny, old age, and that it had too to

4

be filtered through the unhappy temperament of his conventionally minded second wife. It remains, however, by far the most knowing guide to the psychological life of its subject. A considerable work of art, it is often a quiet send-up of the 'official' (and therefore false) 'lives' of which its author had read so many. It is alive with clues to the initiated – meaning simply those who are not misled into believing that Hardy wrote fiction and poetry with his left hand, while his right represented a mean and fundamentally stupid old peasant whose 'gloomy philosophy of life' must be repudiated at all costs. It is true that his story as he told it must be treated with some caution, for it was largely a defensive act by a hypersensitive man, but in the *Life* are the pointers to much of what was important to him.

Because of his second wife's, and his brother's and surviving sister's standing in the neighbourhood, Hardy did not much emphasize that his family on his mother's side had at one time been poverty-stricken, or that he himself had been the occasion of a shotgun wedding. It was not, as some biographers have claimed, that he was unable to bring himself to mention the poverty, or the fact that he had been conceived outside wedlock: there were other, more important tasks, such as to establish the character of his mother, Jemima, and of her mother, Betty. Such matters as sex outside wedlock in rural England are in any case run-of-the-mill to realists, if not to moralists. Polite society, however, has never been able to treat private matters with quite such *sang froid*. Hardy knew that if he mentioned that he had been conceived outside wedlock, then Florence, or her advisors (Sir James Barrie, Sydney Cockerell), or his publishers, would have removed the detail. The book must, after all, seem to be 'by' Florence Hardy, children's writer and, after her eminent husband's death, distinguished critical biographer. Only Hardy knew that she was incapable, by reasons of health as well as understanding, of competently putting any biography together.

Hardy's maternal grandmother, Elizabeth (Betty) Swetman, was the fourth child of John Swetman, a small land proprietor or 'yeoman' of Melbury Osmund (Hardy's King's Hintock), and his wife Maria, *née* Childs. We know little about Swetman, except that Hardy called him a 'severe and unyielding parent', who refused to speak again to Betty when, a couple of years after his wife's death, she married George Hand (or, as Hardy himself suggests, Hadd). The thirty-five-year-old Hand, a 'servant', shepherd, gardener and probably odd-job man, was of bad repute in the district. Hardy says that the marriage, on 27 December 1804, was 'clandestine'. But, although a daughter, Maria (later Sparks), was born only eight days afterwards, the ceremony took place in Melbury Osmund Church and was regular enough, the banns having been published three times by the vicar, the Rev. Jenkins. By 'clandestine marriage' Hardy may have meant that Betty managed to conceal from her father that the banns had been read in the prescribed manner – and thus that the wedding was to take place at all. Alternatively, there may already have been an elopement.

Hardy's late poem 'In Sherborne Abbey' concerns an abduction, and has at its foot the note '*A Family tradition*', and at its head a bracketed '17—', which is perhaps an attempt to lead readers away from the occasion of the poem. But 1799 would have been very early for an elopement by Betty and George Hand: their marriage took place in late 1804. However, the date is possible, had the association been of long standing and subject to Swetman's constant censure. The woman of the poem is an 'heiress', and she and her abductor sit in Sherborne Abbey surrounded by figures 'chiselled in frigid stone':

'Why did you make me ride in your front?' says she.
'To outwit the law. That was my strategy.
　　As I was borne off on the pillion behind you,
　　Th'abductor was you, Dearest, let me remind you;
　　The seizure of me by an heiress is no felony,
　　Whatever to do with me as the seizer may be.'

In the last stanza the outcome is not seen as promising:

Another silence sinks. And a cloud comes over the moon:
The print of the panes upon them enfeebles, as fallen in a swoon,
　　Until they are left in darkness unbroke and profound,
　　As likewise are left their chill and chiselled neighbours around.

Swetman died at the age of eighty-nine in 1822, and George Hand soon followed him. Betty insisted that her husband be buried by the side of a woman who had been his mistress – possibly the subject of another poem, 'Her Late Husband'. This poem, from Hardy's second collection, *Poems of the Past and the Present* (1901), is headed 'King's Hintock, 182–', which is certainly a right date as far as it goes, though it cannot be checked because the gravestones are no longer readable.

'No – not where I shall make my own;
    But dig his grave just by
The woman's with the initialed stone –
    As near as he can lie –
After whose death he seemed to ail,
    Though none considered why.

'And when I also claim a nook,
    And your feet tread me in,
Bestow me, in my maiden name,
    Among my kith and kin,
That strangers gazing may not dream
    I did a husband win.'

'Widow, your wish shall be obeyed:
    Though, thought I, certainly
You'd lay him where your folk are laid,
    And your grave, too, will be,
As custom hath it; you to right,
    And on the left hand he.'

'Aye, sexton; such the Hintock rule,
    And none has said it nay;
But now you find a native here
    Eschews that ancient way . . .
And it may be, some Christmas night,
    When angels walk, they'll say:

' "O strange interment! Civilized lands
    Afford few types thereof;
Here is a man who takes his rest
    Beside his very Love,
Beside the one who was his wife
    In our sight up above!" '

Hand had been a difficult husband for Betty, and a bad father to their seven children. The marriage must have been disastrous from early in its course; Hand was steadfastly anti-Christian and a violent drunkard, whose children had to be baptized out of his enraged sight. Stories of this grandfather told to him by his mother certainly contributed to some of Hardy's books, although, since he did not know him, perhaps not to any

7

significant extent. Another maternal relative, John Antell, shoemaker of Puddletown and husband to his aunt Mary, had some resemblance to Hand; but in this case it is known for certain that he was devoted not only to drinking bouts, and to beating up his wife, but also to the acquirement of knowledge.

Hardy may not have emphasized his grandmother's poverty, but he did not, as has so often been charged, shirk its recording. He wrote:

> Not so long after the death of this stern father of Elizabeth's – Hardy's maternal great-grandfather – her husband also died, leaving her with several children, the youngest only a few months old [in fact, unless an unrecorded child died in infancy, Martin, the youngest, was aged six or seven]. Her father, though in comfortable circumstances, had bequeathed her nothing, and she was at her wit's end to maintain herself and family, if ever widow was. Among Elizabeth's children there was one, a girl, of unusual ability and judgement, and an energy that might have carried her to incalculable issues. This was the child Jemima, the mother of Thomas Hardy. By reason of her parent's bereavement and consequent poverty under the burden of a young family, Jemima saw during girlhood and young womanhood some very stressful experiences of which she would never speak in her maturer years without pain.

In this explicit account Hardy omits any discussion of the character of George Hand, which – drunkenness and fierce dislike of Christianity apart – remains enigmatic. He may have had another side to his nature, or even have been involved with 'agitators', the sort of people in that area whose views contributed to the agricultural riots in Puddletown of 1830, and in 1834 to the famous incident of the transportation of the Tolpuddle Martyrs (Tolpuddle is a few miles down the road from Puddletown). The interesting questions remain. Why did Betty marry him? What attracted her in the first place to the extent that she, a cut above him socially, became pregnant by him? From where did his strong anti-Christian bias, if it was not part of a general bloody-mindedness, arise?

Betty was well known in Melbury Osmund as the daughter of a reasonably well-to-do man who had married beneath her. Hardy mentions her striking looks, and says that she knew the 'writings of Addison, Steele, and others . . . almost by heart, was familiar with Richardson and Fielding, and, of course, with such standard works as

Paradise Lost and *The Pilgrim's Progress'*. She also, having a knowledge of herbal medicine, 'doctored half the village'. From a roughly punctuated letter she wrote in 1842 to her daughter Mary, complaining of her poverty, it might be supposed that Hardy exaggerated the extent of her reading, and doubt has been cast upon the degree of literacy of her daughter Jemima. But in those days writing was usually taught only after reading skills had been mastered, and many good readers had little writing practice, or need to write. Betty's book knowledge is thus not incongruous with the fact that her one surviving letter is poorly written.

After her husband's death Betty was forced to go 'on the parish'; as Hardy wrote, making no attempt to conceal the poverty into which she was brought, she was 'at her wit's end . . . if ever widow was'. Her grievance, expressed in the words 'I should not have been poor if right had took its place' (i.e. if she had inherited), doubtless transmitted itself to her daughter, and through her to her grandson, who liked to play with the notion that his family had once been mighty, and had now fallen. However, the size of Betty's inheritance would not have been large, and he must have known that, too. Besides, the notion provides such tragi-comic material in *Tess* that it is clear that Hardy could laugh at himself over such aspirations. His literary executor, Sydney Cockerell, recorded that, in complaining that there were Dorchester people too snobbish to speak to him, Hardy commented that his had been a county family, too, 'if only they knew'. He also mentioned the family crest to which he thought he was entitled, though he chose not to display it – and it has been suggested that 'to have a family crest but not to use it was intricately pleasurable in itself'. That may be over-subtle. It seems more probable that Hardy wished to avoid the vulgarity implicit in suddenly, as a famous man, coming forward with a family crest.

Of his mother, Jemima Hand, born in 1813, few details of her early history can be established. There was no money, and many children, and she went into service, probably at the age of thirteen. Hardy tells us that she became an expert cook, and that she was good at 'tambouring' – ornamenting – gloves. She went into service with the 3rd Earl of Ilchester's uncle, the Rev. Charles Fox-Strangways, vicar of Maiden Newton. When this society parson went up to London for the season, she joined the household, and probably made a few friends in the city. Fox-Strangways died in 1836, when Jemima was twenty-four. She must have been valued, for she went to Stinsford House, owned by the same family. Edward Murray, vicar of Stinsford and brother-in-law to the

Earl of Ilchester, lived there. Early on, or in the meantime, she may have been elsewhere: her son mentions that she had 'lived in London, Weymouth and other towns'.

Lady Susan, daughter of the 1st Earl of Ilchester, had died in Stinsford House in 1827. She had famously eloped with the actor-dramatist William O'Brien in 1764, and the affair always caught Hardy's imagination. In the *Life* he quotes Horace Walpole's comment: 'Even a footman was preferable, I could not have believed that Lady Susan would have stooped so low.' He adds that O'Brien's career was 'annihilated' because Ilchester, faced with the *fait accompli*, would on no account allow him to continue on the stage. He mentions the 'coincidence that both his maternal and his paternal grandmothers had seen and admired him in the theatre', and that 'his great-grandfather and grandfather had known him well'. The latter had 'constructed the vault for him and his wife . . . had been asked by her to "make it just large enough for our two selves only" ': this 'lent the occupants of the little vault in the chancel a romantic interest in the boy's mind at an early age'.

Murray, the vicar, was, says Hardy, an 'ardent musician and performer on the violin'. The two sons of Thomas I who helped him to run his business, James and Thomas II (the eldest, John, removed himself to Fordington, in Dorchester, and largely cut himself off from the family), both played the violin, and were both as enthusiastic as their father. They went about the churches playing on Sundays, and also hired themselves out for social occasions such as weddings, harvest suppers, dances, Christmas carolling, and the like.

It is obvious from his novels that Hardy knew a great deal about drink and its consequences, although he never drank to excess, and what he did not pick up in London in his days there as an architect, he must have learned from the festivities he attended as a boy. There are one or two stories of his father's drinking heavily, but this could not have been a habit with him, or there would have been more; the chief of the tales suggested Hardy's story 'Interlopers at the Knap'.

Hardy in old age still believed in the 'easy superiority' of the Stinsford musicians: 'Puddletown west-gallery . . . could boast of eight players, and Maiden Newton of nine, these included wood-wind and leather – that is to say, clarionets and serpents – which were apt to be a little too sonorous, when zealously blown. But the few and well-practised violists of Stinsford were never unduly emphatic, according to tradition.' Owing to Murray's departure in 1837 and to Thomas III's sudden death in that year, Thomas II abandoned with 'some relief' all connection with

10

the Stinsford choir, which packed up in 1841–2. It did not 'assist' the brothers' 'building business' (do we see the hand of Jemima here?). But the music-making continued, whether it was approved or not.

When Jemima married Thomas II, she was two or three months pregnant, but, for all the importance that some commentators have attached to Hardy's alleged 'reticence' on this matter, there is no reason to suppose that Jemima's unmarried pregnancy attracted much interest. (What other attitude could he anyway have taken at that time?) Jemima was simply following (with rather more chronological discretion) in her mother's footsteps. Such affairs were so common in rural Dorset as to arouse little talk, unless there was some social differentiation between the couple, as there had been between Betty Swetman and the already disreputable George Hand. But in that case Betty may have deliberately become pregnant in order to defy her father.

Hardy's own carefully composed description of his parents cannot be bettered:

The second Thomas Hardy . . . was a man who in his prime could be, and was, called handsome. To the courtesy of his manners there was much testimony among the local county-ladies with whom he came into contact as a builder . . . He was about five feet nine in height, of good figure, with dark Vandyke-brown hair, and a beard which he wore cut back all round in the custom of his date; with teeth that were white and regular to nearly the last years of his life, and blue eyes that never faded grey; a quick step, and a habit of bearing his head a little to one side as he walked. He carried no stick or umbrella till past middle-life, and was altogether an open-air liver, and a great walker always. He was good, too, when young, at hornpipes and jigs, and other folk-dances, performing them with all the old movements of leg-crossing and hop, to the delight of his children, till warned by his wife that this fast perishing style might tend to teach them what it was not quite necessary they should be familiar with, the more genteel 'country-dance' having superseded the former.

Mrs Hardy once described him to her son as he was when she first set eyes on him . . . appearing to her more travelled glance . . . and somewhat satirical vision 'rather amusingly old-fashioned, in spite of being decidedly good-looking – wearing the blue swallow-tailed coat with gilt embossed buttons then customary, a red and black flowered waistcoat, Wellington boots, and French-blue trousers'.

The second sentence of the description is Hardy's ironic way of telling his readers that his father had been more than just a lady's man – although the 'family tradition' of his seeing Jemima and seducing her on the spot should not be treated seriously. There is a hint here, too, of his mother's severity. It may have become more pronounced after she suffered a severe miscarriage soon after the birth, in 1841, of Hardy's much loved sister Mary. She had to be nursed by her sister and was delirious for some months, probably due to post-puerperal fever, common at the time. In Hardy's portrait:

Mrs Hardy herself was rather below the middle height with chestnut hair and grey eyes, and a trim and upright figure. Her movement also in walking being buoyant through life, strangers approaching her from behind imagined themselves, even when she was nearly seventy, about to overtake quite a young woman. The Roman nose and countenance inherited from her mother would better have suited a taller build. Like her mother, too, she read omnivorously. She sang songs of the date . . . The children had a quaint old piano for their practice, over which she would sigh because she could not play it herself.

Mary's birth the year after Thomas was followed ten years later by that of Henry and, in 1856, Katherine (Kate), by which time Jemima was forty-three. Kate, who lived until 1940, was the sibling Hardy knew least well, and the one who knew him least well; they shared no childhood years together, whereas he grew up with Mary, and looked after Henry as a younger brother for some five or six years. He could have had little to do with the infant Kate, born sixteen years after him. What the Hardy household was like in the 1840s and 1850s cannot be known, but Hardy would never really feel as much at home as with this family – except, probably, in the very early years of his first marriage. Not so long after that marriage he built Max Gate, within a mile or two of his birthplace, where both his parents were still living.

Hardy's account of his eight pre-school years is brief, but carefully written. It is unlikely that the details he gives of his actual birth are 'apocryphal'. True, the story of being cast aside at birth is suspiciously Hardyan, but then who is it about? However, supposing that the *Life* is read as that kind of Aristotelian story which is 'truer' than history itself, then what could be more appropriate than this reminder of fate's capriciousness? Hardy was always grateful to his neighbour, Elizabeth Downton, the 'estimable woman' who interceded for him at the start of his existence.

The page and a half which follows the account of Hardy's birth is highly selective, but full of significant detail. First, the infant is seen sleeping with a snake! The event is described as a 'curious fact': 'on his mother's returning from out-of-doors one hot afternoon, to him asleep in his cradle, she found a large snake curled upon his breast, comfortably asleep like himself'. Thus the author who shocked and appalled most of his contemporaries, and received fame and eventually honour by reason of it, is seen as initially so intimate with that holder of poisonous and forbidden knowledge, the devil, as to sleep 'comfortably' with him. (It was in fact a harmless grass snake.)

The next paragraph establishes some essential characteristics of the man – characteristics which were present at birth and were hardly changed by experiences of failure and success. Much has been made of Hardy's weakness and fragility as an infant, and reasonably so: he remarks that his parents 'till his fifth year hardly supposed he would survive to grow up'. And his grandmother Hand, in the 1842 letter to her daughter Mary, wrote: 'I hope she [Mary, Hardy's new sister] will not be so tiresome as Tomey'. By 'tiresome' she probably meant 'anxiety-making' rather than 'noisy and naughty', which Hardy seems not to have been at this stage. His parents were nonplussed by him (as everyone else has been), and they did, as he tells us, worry.

Later he drew as much philosophical satisfaction from this early weakness – though he asserts that he was 'healthy' – as he did from the fact that he had almost not been born at all, something which was always his obstinately stated ideal. At one of the most unhappy periods of his life, when he had just passed his mid-fifties, he wrote the three poems forming the sequence 'In Tenebris'. The third, under the rubric of St Jerome's Latin version of Psalm 119 ('Woe to me that my dwelling is prolonged! I have dwelt with the inhabitants of Cedar. My soul has been a long dweller'), recalls his childhood more lyrically and emotionally than in the *Life*:

There have been times when I well might have passed and the
   ending have come –
Points in my path when the dark might have stolen on me, artless,
   unrueing –
Ere I had learnt that the world was a welter of futile doing:
Such had been times when I well might have passed, and the ending
   have come!

Say, on the noon when the half-sunny hours told that April was
   nigh,
And I upgathered and cast forth the snow from the crocus-border,
Fashioned and furbished the soil into a summer-seeming order,
Glowing in gladsome faith that I quickened the year thereby.

Or that loneliest of eves when afar and benighted we stood,
She who upheld me and I, in the midmost of Egdon together,
Confident I in her watching and ward through the blackening
   heather,
Deeming her matchless in might and with measureless scope endued.

Or on that winter-wild night when, reclined by the chimney-nook
   quoin,
Slowly a drowse overgat me, the smallest and feeblest of folk there,
Weak from my baptism of pain; when at times and anon I awoke
   there –
Heard of a world wheeling on, with no listing or longing to join.

Even then! while unweeting that vision could vex or that knowledge
   could numb,
That sweets to the mouth in the belly are bitter, and tart, and
   untoward,
Then, on some dim-coloured scene should my briefly raised curtain
   have lowered,
Then might the Voice that is law have said 'Cease!' and the ending
   have come.

The late J.O. Bailey, the industrious American annotator of every
one of Hardy's poems (*The Poetry of Thomas Hardy*, 1970), regards
the third stanza as alluding to Hardy's 'happiness with his mother'
'somewhere on Egdon', confident of her 'watching and ward' as the
evening darkened into night. He believes that 'The Roman Road', a
poem included in *Time's Laughingstocks*, refers to the same incident.
But there is nothing to connect the two poems except that they both

allude to their author's being with his mother on Egdon, which after all bordered on the Bockhampton cottage. One can read into the 'In Tenebris' stanza more than Bailey cares to: surely it is about being lost and frightened (not 'happy') on Egdon, but then confident in mother's 'scope' to see him safely home.

This heath – actually a series of heaths – is now forested, but at that time it was largely a bleak and bare expanse where people could easily lose their sense of direction. The implication, in the sad context of a life of 'futile doing' and 'pain', is that while he was a child frightened of being lost on the heath Hardy could look to his mother, 'matchless in might'; as an adult he is alone. It was at all events with the heath that he most associated his mother (one of the most original aspects of his technique was association of landscapes with events and people), for certainly Mrs Yeobright of *The Return of the Native* has affinities with her, as he himself stated. And certainly he had real, not fictional, recollections of being labelled delicate as an infant: 'the smallest and feeblest of folk there'. That memory of home included his sister Mary, who, though younger, must have been regarded as less frail. But in pointing out that he was 'healthy', he implies that his 'weakness' was less physical than mental:

> Though healthy he was fragile, and precocious to a degree, being able to read almost before he could walk, and to tune a violin when of quite tender years. He was of ecstatic temperament, extraordinarily sensitive to music, and among the endless jigs, hornpipes, reels, waltzes and country-dances that his father played of an evening in his early married years, and to which the boy danced a *pas seul* in the middle of the room, there were three or four that moved the child to tears, though he strenuously tried to hide them . . . This peculiarity in himself troubled the mind of 'Tommy' as he was called, and set him wondering at a phenomenon to which he ventured not to confess. He used to say in later life that, like Calantha in Ford's *Broken Heart*, he danced on at these times to conceal his weeping. He was not over four years of age at this date.

He seems here to be ascribing the fragility, the lack of hope in his parents for his survival, not to poor health, but to a temperament which was at one and the same time 'ecstatic' and melancholy ('weeping'). Calantha in Ford's play *The Broken Heart* is revelling; she then hears three items of disastrous news. She says, with an involved bitter irony not unlike that which Hardy himself would develop:

How dull this music sounds! Strike up more sprightly;
Our footings are not active like our heart,
Which treads the nimbler measure.

After that a character, Bassanes, comments:

She has a masculine spirit;
And wherefore should I pale, and, like a girl,
Put finger in the eye? let's be all toughness,
Without distinction between sex and sex.

Having told us of the trouble his 'peculiarity' caused in his own mind
– to be moved to tears and then to dance, even 'ecstatic' dance – he
goes on to point out two further 'characteristics of personality at this
childhood-time'. One is his habit of awaiting the evening sun's addition
of 'intensity' to the Venetian red walls of the Bockhampton staircase,
and of his then reciting Isaac Watts' hymn 'And now another day is
done', 'because the scene suited the lines' rather than 'for any religious
reason'. He then draws our attention to another, connected, emotional
habit: his 'dramatic sense of the church services'. When the family, which
was punctilious about church attendance (at Stinsford), could not get to
church because it was wet, he would, he says, dress himself up in the
tablecloth and be the vicar reading the morning prayer and delivering a
sermon reminiscent of all the others he had heard. An unspecified cousin
(he had many) acted as clerk, and his grandmother the congregation.

A boy who dresses up as the vicar, who forces his cousin and his
grandmother to be his audience, who dances a *pas seul* in the middle of
the room, is not 'passive', as some insist. Indeed, whilst one might well
attribute a strategy of passivity to him, it is hard to see so successful a man
as Hardy as essentially passive. Rather, he was sporadically a dramatic
and dominant boy, getting and holding attention. His 'peculiarity',
though, was certainly of concern to his mother as well as himself.
'Everybody said that Tommy would have to be a parson, being
obviously no good for any practical pursuit; which remark caused
his mother many misgivings.' This theme of his mother's misgivings
is taken up again after the following famous passage:

One event of this date or a little later stood out, he used to say, more
distinctly than any. He was lying on his back in the sun, thinking how
useless he was, and covered his face with his straw hat. The sun's

16

rays streamed through the interstices of the straw, the lining having disappeared. Reflecting on his experience of the world so far as he had got it, he came to the conclusion that he did not wish to grow up. Other boys were always talking of when they would be men; he did not want at all to be a man, or to possess things, but to remain as he was, in the same spot, and to know no more people than he already knew (about half a dozen). Yet this early evidence of that lack of social ambition which followed him through life was shown when he was in perfect health and happy circumstances.

Afterwards he told his mother of his conclusions on existence, thinking she would enter into his views. But to his great surprise she was very much hurt, which was natural enough considering she had been near death's door in bringing him forth. And she never forgot what he had said, a source of much regret to him in after years.

The incident of the sunlight streaming through the hat remained with him for the whole of his life. It came into passages in *Jude* and the late poem 'Childhood Among the Ferns':

> The sun then burst, and brought forth a sweet breath
> From the limp ferns as they dried underneath:
> I said: 'I could live on here thus till death;'
>
> And queried in the green rays as I sate:
> 'Why should I have to grow to man's estate,
> And this afar-noised World perambulate?'

There is also the image of life as a 'latticed hearse' in that other very late poem, almost his last, 'We Are Getting to the End'. So these tendencies were with him lifelong. Such thoughts distressed his mother even when he was of a very tender age. Neither good fortune – 'happy circumstances' – nor 'perfect health', both of which he experienced, did anything to dispel them.

Hardy, always formal in his behaviour – sometimes even coldly so – to all but his closest friends, played his cards close to his chest for the whole of his life. The 'essence' of him, the innate character over which a 'personality' is formed by external circumstances, was not often clearly glimpsed by strangers (servants, interviewers, press men and so on), and was most nearly seen when he was in the bosom of his family.

The masks with which Hardy chose to confront the world – his fellow pupils at school, his fellow workers in architecture, his publishers, his fellow writers, the society people who in time craved to know him – were consciously turned on for the occasion, then abruptly turned off. Behind all his masks, from early on, lay a determined resolve, but in early childhood and adolescence that determination could not take coherent intellectual shape. What predominated then was the driving force of the basic character. And what does Hardy tell us about that? That he did not want to grow up. That he was 'dramatic', 'ecstatic', melancholy – so melancholy that he would wait for the most appropriate time of day in order to express himself through the doleful words of Isaac Watts. If this, unlike dressing up as the parson, was unusual (some would call it distinctly 'morbid' – and morbidity, despite the apparently unpromising condition of humanity, is always to be frowned upon), then Hardy the man can hardly be described as particularly usual, either. It was the very young boy's way of contemplating the meaning of existence, if indeed existence had a meaning. He already wanted to know. This became an admittedly 'gloomy', though hardly pointless habit with him. He would never be able to state, unequivocally, that life had no meaning – as would so many writers after him – and he could only ever go as far as to say that he was unaware of a coherent purpose to existence. But he always suspected, as he showed by the persistence with which he pursued the theme of death, that an intrinsic part of any meaning that existence might have would contain the fact of its end. That is something which few really accept.

2

School

Tom, as Hardy called himself with his intimates, did not grow up in affluent circumstances, and the family (so he told Florence) went through periods of 'bitter poverty'. Business fluctuated, sometimes wildly. When Tom was eleven, his father was listed by the census-taker as a bricklayer employing two men. Later the number of employees went up, and in the early 1880s, when Thomas II and his younger son Henry – an expansive and extroverted man, with the broad Dorset accent Tom eschewed – were operating the business, it became relatively prosperous. It is evident that the Hardys did reliable work, and that much of this was undertaken for the nearby Kingston Maurward estate. The poverty Tom claimed to have known in the 1840s, while 'bitter', consisted of shortage of ready money; the Bockhampton cottage was self-sufficient, and there was always enough to eat. For Hardy's family, like most of the other people living in the cottages of Higher Bockhampton, were not of the lowest class: they worked for themselves, not for someone else, and Thomas II held his house for life. This was an important distinction.

Until Tom reached his teens – he himself later estimated the time of change at about 1851 – the lot of the labourer was atrocious. Dorset was, as it still is, an intensely conservative county, and those who owned the land were no less greedy or short-sighted than they are anywhere else. It was Dorset intransigence which threw up the Tolpuddle Martyrs in 1834. Legislation of 1819 had set the minimum working age at nine years, but in practice this was ignored; farmers generally expected that an employee would put the whole of his family to work in the fields when tasks were to be performed. Tom, with his lifelong eye for the macabre, remembered a shepherd's boy who starved to death and whose stomach was found to contain nothing but raw turnip. Some farmers were of course more humane than others.

But the society of the second half of the nineteenth century slowly but surely became less deferential. The George Hands of rural society were becoming more numerous. The Whig clergyman and wit Sydney

19

Smith had been right to laugh at the expectations aroused by the Reform Bill (rejected by the Lords in 1831, but passed by them in the following year after William IV agreed to create new peers): 'All young ladies will imagine . . . that they will instantly be married. Schoolboys will believe that gerunds and supines will be abolished . . . bad poets will expect a demand for their epics.' But the Bill did enfranchise the upper-middle classes, and it did encourage a mood of radicalism, for all that the governments were long able to play radical factions against one another. In 1834 a cruel set of farmers could still transport George Loveless and his five friends, of Tolpuddle, to Australia, and Lord Melbourne could still refuse to receive a petition signed by a quarter of a million people, although in 1836 the government had to pardon them.

Melbourne was still in office when Tom was born, but in September of the following year he was succeeded by Sir Robert Peel, a more 'modern-minded' man, who, for all the verbal comfort he offered to high Tories about 'resisting radicalism', well knew that what had to be done would include some actions that would be anathema to them. And the Poor Laws, which for all their shortcomings did offer the first real reform since Elizabethan times, had come into effect in 1834.

There is no doubt where the liberal (but not radical) Hardy family stood on the matter of the Corn Laws, since Tom records a memory of himself dipping a toy wooden sword, made for him by his father, into the blood of a freshly killed pig, and dancing about with it in the garden crying 'Free Trade or blood!'. Peel, although originally pledged to preserve them, repealed the Corn Laws in 1846, but promptly lost office when Disraeli engineered the fall of his government on another issue.

It was once accepted that one of the main themes in Hardy's work was sorrow for the passing of old rural ways. This over-simplified view mistook an acknowledged subjective nostalgia, a normal attachment to the environment one knows earliest of all, as an intellectual and polemical political stance. The confusion is understandable. Kipling, for example, whose mind was never as clear as Hardy's, confused his emotional attachment to the India he knew as a small boy with his political wishes for India itself, and was consequently unrealistic. It is evident from what he said to various people in his old age that Tom, although no believer in 'progress', recognized that the changes in Dorset rural society throughout the nineteenth century had led to less misery amongst the poorest classes. He never regarded labourers (not their own word for themselves) as 'children', and took the view that

Kipling had been spoiled when 'the imperialists got hold of him'. Some of Tom's own relatives were labourers, although he does not mention this in the *Life*. But why should he? He had already drawn attention to his grandmother's and mother's poverty. His eldest paternal uncle, John, who went away to live in Fordington, the half-slum district that lay around three-quarters of Dorchester, may have been an 'ordinary labourer'; but John in any case seems to have isolated himself from his family, and little is known of him.

Tom, by his own and others' account, could read before he was three. Allowing for family pride in literary achievement and the usual exaggeration, it is likely that he did learn to read very early (writers seem to develop this sometimes useful skill either very early or very late). He certainly knew the illustrated *Cries of London* – 'Cherry Ripe', 'The Sweep', 'A Live Lobster', and so on – very early on, for his copy survives. It is usually assumed that Jemima long expected her eldest son to follow in his father's footsteps as a mason; but she may have harboured ambitions for him. He was only eight when she gave him Dryden's *Vergil*, Johnson's *Rasselas* and the novel *Paul and Virginia*, a French Rousseauist tale, by Bernadine de Saint-Pierre, which first appeared in *Etudes de la Nature* (1787) and was translated into many languages. It may have had some influence on young Tom, who at that age was engaged on what may fairly be called the first love affair of his life. It tells of two children brought up in idyllic surroundings on a tropical island (Mauritius). Then the girl, Virginie, is called back to the mainland, where she is unhappy. She returns to the island and 'Nature', but drowns as she reaches it – refusing, owing to the corruption of her instincts on the mainland, to jump into the water to be rescued by a naked sailor.

Tom's 'affair' was with Julia Augusta Martin, the wife of the owner of the Kingston Maurward estate. The childless Mrs Martin took a fancy to the boy, grew, in his words, 'passionately fond of Tommy almost from his infancy – he is said to have been an attractive little fellow at the time – when she had been accustomed to take him into her lap and kiss him until he was quite a big child'. One does not have to be a Freudian to see what the frustrated Julia was unconsciously up to.

The emotions aroused in the child were not unusual in themselves, although Tom supercharged his memory of them with erotic significance. This has attracted much wondering attention, as if there were something abnormal about his interest in sexual matters. Yet he does no more than draw attention to an aspect of childhood feeling that is perfectly normal, but seldom recorded. Tom retained an interest in the affair with the lady of the manor because for him it represented the first adumbrations of conscious sexual feeling – 'the thrilling "frou-frou" of her four gray silk flounces', as he retrospectively put it. Robert Gittings in his two-volume biography of Hardy offers no evidence for his assertion that 'in his eighties Hardy still indulged himself in day-dreams about love-passages with her'; but such 'day-dreams' are in any case more 'normal' than otherwise. Also, when he was recollecting all this, alone in his study, at an advanced age, he had, in his wife Florence, one who was far more 'averse to sexual intercourse' than he had himself learned to be. Small wonder if he dwelled erotically upon all aspects of his past.

But is the erotic speculation of Thomas Hardy mere fantasy, or is it something else? In 'The Clock of the Years' he wrote:

> And the Spirit said,
> 'I can make the clock of the years go backward,
> But am loth to stop it where you will.'
> And I cried, 'Agreed
> To that. Proceed:
> It's better than dead!'
>
> He answered, 'Peace;'
> And called her up – as last before me;
> Then younger, younger she freshed, to the year
> I first had known
> Her woman-grown,
> And I cried, 'Cease! –
>
> Thus far is good –
> It is enough – let her stay thus always!'
> But alas for me – He shook his head:
> No stop was there;
> And she waned child-fair,
> And to babyhood.
>
> Still less in mien
> To my great sorrow became she slowly,
> And smalled till she was nought at all
> In his checkless griff;
> And it was as if
> She had never been.

SCHOOL

'Better,' I plained,
'She were dead as before! The memory of her
Had lived in me; but it cannot now!'
       And coldly his voice:
       'It was your choice
       To mar the ordained.'

This poem is perhaps not 'about' any particular woman, let alone
Julia Augusta Martin; but it suggests that the processes of memory
in Thomas Hardy are best left free from orthodox disapproval, for
they are subtle, self-critical (specifically, of the self-regarding nature
and potential destructiveness of this habit of contemplating the beloved),
truthful and far from merely 'pessimistic' ('better than dead').

Mrs Martin paid for the building of a Church of England ('National')
school for the parish, on property bought by her husband in 1844. There
was already a dame school in Lower Bockhampton (about a mile from
Higher Bockhampton), but it was to the new school in 1848 that Tom
was sent, some time after his eighth birthday. It was run by a Thomas
Fuller (and his wife), of whom Tom later wrote that, while he was
more learned than a schoolmaster in his position needed to be, he was a
'drunkard'. This must have been a disappointment both to Mrs Martin,
who had endowed the school, and his wife; but perhaps his lessons were
none the worse for it.

It is clear from the phrase 'almost in his infancy' that the unusual
and contemplative little boy from Higher Bockhampton had caught
the attention of Mrs Martin long before he attended 'her' school, and
she later even claimed, in a letter to him written in 1887, when he
was well known, that she taught him his letters. By that she must
have meant that she helped him learn to write. He did well at her
school, but his parents nevertheless decided to send him to another:
the Dorchester British School, run by Isaac Last. This decision was
wise, perhaps obvious; the school at Dorchester was the right place
for one who had gone late to the village school but had progressed
well there. Isaac Last, Tom wrote, 'his mother had learned to be
an exceptionally able man, and a good teacher of Latin, which was
quite enough to leave her to waive the fact that the school was
Nonconformist'.

But the decision led to a quarrel between Mrs Martin and Jemima,
although the feeling seems to have come more from the former. Tom's
removal from Bockhampton school

seriously wounded the lady of the manor who had erected it, though she must have guessed that he had only been sent there until sturdy enough to go further. To his mother this came as an unpleasant misunderstanding. While not wishing to be uncivil she had, naturally, not consulted the other at all in taking him away, considering his interests only, the Hardys being comparatively independent of the manor, as their house and the adjoining land were a family freehold, and the estate-work forming only part of Mr Hardy's business. That the school to which he was removed was not a Church-of-England one was another rock of offence to this too sensitive lady, though, as has been stated, it was an accident as unwished by the boy's mother as by the squire's wife . . . Moreover, under her dignity lay a tender heart . . . Shortly before or after the boy's removal the estate-building work was taken out of the hands of Tommy's father, who went farther afield to replace it . . . Thomas Hardy the youngest, however, secretly mourned the loss of his friend . . . to whom he had grown more attached than he cared to own. In fact, although he was only nine or ten and she must have been nearly forty, his feeling for her was almost that of a lover . . . He so much longed to see her that he jumped at the offer of a young woman of the village to take him to a harvest-supper at which he knew she would be present . . . [She] called for young Thomas on the afternoon of the festivity. Together they went off, his mother being away from home, though they left word where he had gone. The 'Supper', an early meal at that date, probably about four o'clock, was over by the time they reached the barn . . . Presently the manor-lady, her husband, and a house-party arrived to lead off some dances. As soon as she saw little Thomas – who had no business whatever there – she came up to him and said reproachfully: 'O Tommy, how is this? I thought you had deserted me!'

Tommy assured her through his tears that he had not deserted her, and never would desert her: and then the dance went on . . . In spite of his lover-like promise of fidelity to her ladyship, the two never met again till he was a young man of twenty-two, and she quite an elderly woman; though it was not his fault, her husband selling the estate shortly after and occupying a house in London.

Tom, while he was recollecting all this, wrote:

Thus, though their eyes never met again after his call on her in London, nor their lips from the time when she held him in her arms, who can say that both occurrences might not have been in the order of things, if he had developed their reacquaintance earlier, now that she was in her widowhood [her husband died in 1892], with nothing to hinder her mind from rolling back upon her past?

Before Tom attended Last's school, Jemima took him on a visit to her sister Martha in Hertfordshire, far away from home. Martha was pregnant, which was why Jemima was going to stay with her; but it seems possible that Jemima also felt that Julia Augusta Martin might be exerting a bad influence on her son – one she might well have thought of as 'morbid', and wanted to counter – and that she took this opportunity of temporarily removing him entirely from the sphere of Mrs Martin's influence. Jemima, being a humorous and 'still attractive' woman, assured him that she had taken him on this journey for her 'protection'. However, the 'affair' remained in Tom's mind, and gave him some emotionally charged material for his first (unpublished) novel, *The Poor Man and the Lady*. Also, the poem 'In Her Precincts', published in *Moments of Vision* (1917), which has the words '*Kingston Maurward Park*' at its foot, seems to refer to it.

His aunt Martha impressed him, and would be one of the models for Bathsheba of *Far From the Madding Crowd*. She was married to an ex-army officer, John Brereton Sharpe, who was employed by the Marquess of Salisbury as a bailiff on his Hatfield estate. This Sharpe, recollections of whose manner gave Tom some ideas for the villainous Sergeant Troy, was a restless man who would emigrate in 1851 to Canada, where he ended as a schoolteacher. Tom might have intuited even then that there was something wrong with the marriage, or that Sharpe would lead his wife into ill fortune (which to some extent he did).

En route to Hertfordshire Tom made his first visit to London, and he remembered Hyde Park and, in particular, the horrors and cruelties of Smithfield. While at Martha's he was also sent for a few weeks 'to a private school, which appears to have been somewhat on the Squeers model. Since, however, he was only a day-scholar this did not affect him much, though he was mercilessly tyrannized over by the bigger boys whom he could beat hollow in arithmetic and geography.'

At home, there seems to have been no unusual tension within the Hardy household, although Tom, with his dramatic, hypersensitive nature, might already have seen the situation otherwise and made the most of such unhappinesses as there were. He experienced the usual fears of small boys, especially of those who have to walk to and from isolated rural dwellings. But the dwelling was not, in itself, solitary: besides his parents, there were Mary (and later Henry), his grandmother Head, and a constant stream of callers, relatives and otherwise. Indeed his childhood, given the peculiarities of its rural nature and the awkward position of his home, was a fairly ordinary one. At times, he tells us, his mother made moves to take

> more commodious premises nearer to or in the town, but Thomas Hardy the Second had not the tradesman's soul. Instead of waylaying possible needers of brick and stone in the market-place or elsewhere, he liked going alone in the woods or on the heath, where, with a telescope [it was later asserted that Henry used this telescope to spy on courting couples] . . . he would stay peering into the distance by the half-hour.

This is a tribute to his father's lack of what is now called a 'marketing' (or 'Thatcherite') mentality, a dedication to selling and to greed; but in fact Thomas II did well enough by just waiting for people to find him. Much has been made of his 'passiveness', as distinct from his wife's energetic way of dealing with life, thus building Tom up as a boy torn between differing parents. But the conflict between Jemima's undoubted briskness and her husband's more easy-going and relaxed manner was probably, for the most part, a joking one. Writers do not need unhappy childhoods, or for their parents to be at desperate odds, although they do need indignations – and the world outside the family home provided plenty of those, as well as several women and girls for Tom to mourn over and love from afar. Tom could never accept – he even, it might be said, made a grievance out of – Nature's cruelty to herself. But to understand cruelty one needs to know kindliness, and Tom felt kindness in the cottage. Apart from the cruelties inflicted upon people by society and by the law, he always remembered the half-frozen fieldfare at which his father idly threw a stone, 'possibly not meaning to hurt it': 'he [Tom] said he had never forgotten how the body . . . felt in his hand, the memory of it had always haunted him.'

It has been suggested that the boy was 'too ready' to read horror into any situation. But his genius was thus shaped: to draw attention to the human situation, the horror of which perhaps cannot be exaggerated, given the false optimism (especially about war and a now well nigh destroyed environment) which is still generated. His retention of his hypersensitivity, considering his own unhappy lack of a 'tradesman's soul' (an always soothing possession), may have been largely deliberate; and he paid a high price for it. Being rich never meant much to him, because he always *felt* alarmedly poor. After *Tess* he bought plenty of stocks and shares; but he was of the temperament to believe that these might become valueless at any time. As will be seen, he played the Victorian literary market with consummate skill and cunning – something a really 'passive' man could never have done – but he also preserved his integrity. He managed this not only by means of his innate modesty, but also by never allowing himself to fall victim to that indifference to life which is, at best, a sickness and, at worst, a final defeat.

As a boy he sought relief in the joy to be found in music: 'But despite the classics and his general bookishness he loved adventures with the fiddle.' He would accompany his father to supper and bridal festivities, where he would play country-dance tunes on the violin. He wondered why his mother, 'a "progressive" woman', 'did not object to these performances'. His father, he said, 'objected to them strongly'; Thomas II might have found the presence of his young son a hindrance to joining fully in the celebrations, at which lay the opportunity to seduce a woman. Tom suggests his mother's motive for allowing the performances: 'Possibly it was from a feeling that they would help to teach him what life was.' There is no doubt about his capacity for total jollity: he played 'at a homestead where he was stopped by his hostess clutching his bow-arm at the end of a three-quarter-hour's unbroken footing to his notes by twelve tireless couples to the favourite country-dance of "The New-Rigged Ship". The matron had done it lest he should "burst a blood-vessel", fearing the sustained exertion to be too much for a boy of thirteen or fourteen.'

By this age he was, however, accustomed to the five-mile daily walk to Isaac Last's school in Dorchester, which helped to make him strong; with one exception (when he was writing *A Laodicean*), he would enjoy good health throughout his life. The education he received at Last's school was of a Victorian type unknown today: how many contemporary children could extract a cube root without a calculator?; Tom found a 'certain poetry' in the 'rhythm' of the algorithm for it, which he found in the textbook by Walkingame. Last himself was a strict, even fearsome master, once described as furiously chasing pupils round the schoolroom lashing at them with a cane. But he appreciated Tom well enough, and saw in him a bright, well-behaved and promising pupil. He gave him a Latin Testament 'for his progress in the tongue', and another book prize. Indeed, although it has attracted little comment – perhaps because of the mystique that remains attached to public rather than to other schools – Tom's prowess must have been remarkable. He learned his Latin from the 'old Eton grammar', 'Introduction to the Latin Tongue', and from readings in Eutropius and Caesar. He recorded that he was 'rather an idle schoolboy'; but it is more likely that he felt himself to be lazier than he was.

Last was a Congregationalist, and well enough connected with the other Congregationalists in the area to found, in 1853, an Academy, to which Tom proceeded at thirteen, instead of leaving school then, as he might otherwise well have done. (Last's career was ended by bad health; his son, Hardy said, became a 'well-known science-master at South Kensington' – in fact director of the Science Museum.) By staying on at school, Tom was qualifying himself for a profession, and there was no dissension in the Hardy household about finding the fees (extra for the Latin), which were lower than at the Grammar School or at the now declining school in South Street run by the poet William Barnes, whom Tom would soon come to know and love. It seems that his mother and father had by now earmarked the young Henry – called Harry by his family – as successor to the business; that is exactly what he became, after many years of helping his father to run it.

At school, the personal kindliness which was to characterize Tom throughout his life was already evident: he was remembered as always ready to help the other boys to keep up with their work. He was, as he claims, 'popular', and evidently often full of mischief. He took lunch every day in Dorchester with the two spinster sisters of his aunt Maria's husband, James Sparks, and would tease them by flinging his food up in the air and catching it – which did not make him popular with them. Despite these and doubtless other high jinks, he wanted his solitude, and found the attentions of his fellow pupils 'burdensome', for 'he loved being alone'. However, he was sociable enough to help the village girls write letters to their soldier lovers in India. For entertainment he liked best the romances of Dumas *père* and Harrison Ainsworth. His mother thought that it would be unbecoming of Tom to accept money for his fiddling, but on one occasion he could not resist taking up a hatful of pennies in order to buy a copy of *The Boys' Book*, a collection of games and hobbies likely to appeal to any schoolboy.

His taste in reading, although voracious, was not yet unusual, except perhaps for his keenness on the Bible, which he knew as well as, or better than, any Victorian writer; but his thirst for knowledge was insatiable, and he read more than the other boys. He was remembered for the satchel of books that always accompanied him. He started to learn German from the famous *Popular Educator* by John Cassell, whom he justifiably describes as a 'genius in home-education'. He made better progress with the German, as a 1908 translation from Nietzsche shows, than has generally been supposed; and he began French with the 'French governess at the school attended by his sister', and eventually became proficient in it.

Nearly all commentators on Hardy have confidently called him an 'autodidact'. This is rather to underestimate the education he acquired at Last's, which, besides Latin, included 'elementary drawing, advanced arithmetic, geometry and algebra'. One can sympathize with him when he came to read a 1911 thesis on his work, describing him as an 'autodidact'; he protested. The education Tom received was not, it is true, as good for literary purposes as he could have acquired from a public school, at which he would have learned Greek. However, apart from becoming a confirmed bookworm, his purposes were not yet consciously literate. If he ever had any thoughts of being a writer while he was still at school, he does not mention it in the *Life*. He does, however, hint that he did not much want to leave school, in 1856, for he writes that when the question of him going to work in an architect's office arose, he 'had just begun to be interested in French and the Latin classics'. He says that the 'born bookworm' in him was 'alone unchanging' at this point, and it seems that he had dreams of a university education followed by entrance into the Church.

There is a possibility that even at this early age he made some written or even oral enquiry about ordination, and found himself discouraged or even turned away. The secretary of his later years, May O'Rourke, tells a tale, described as emanating from 'an authentic source', that he 'aspired to take Holy Orders but was not accepted by the Salisbury Diocesan Authorities'. This could mean no more than that a tentative first enquiry was snubbed. There are no further details. Any poems written while he was at school, predating 'Domicilium' and expressing religious feelings, were destroyed. But May O'Rourke's notion that he would have allowed such a snub to affect his later, mostly unsympathetic attitude to Christian orthodoxy is unlikely: she was a devout Roman Catholic, easily offended by any irregularity (as was characteristic of him, Tom was protective of her susceptibilities, as she fully and gratefully acknowledged). However, he continued to mark his Bible and prayer book, and became, too, involved in a debate about infant baptism. If there was a slight which aroused resentment, it may have found vent in certain details in *Jude*, in the replies Jude receives when he makes enquiries about entering the University of Oxford.

There is, however, nothing to suggest that at this stage, or until he went to London, he harboured any doubts about his parents' Anglicanism. He was in the habit of considering his personal emotional development, his state of mind and his behaviour, in the light of the scriptures, and did not, for the moment, question their truth. He had hated the confirmation lessons he took from the vicar of Stinsford, the Rev. Arthur Shirley, and remembered with distaste this man's superciliousness for the whole of his life. Florence Hardy told Hardy's bibliographer, the American academic R.L. Purdy, that Tom complained to her, in his old age, of a sermon given in 1856 by Shirley in which he criticized the presumption of the lower orders in seeking to rise through the professions: Tom took it personally, and it seems that it was so meant. However, he kept his dislike to himself, and it was with Shirley's own sons that he taught Sunday School. But Tom's lack of any intense devotion to doctrine itself – unless to the general notion of its correctness, in other words to biblical authority – does not mean that the scriptural words meant nothing to him: he was always a poet, and he always struggled with meaning. After all, as he wrote, he found himself, at the age of about twenty, '*appalled* at the feebleness of the arguments for infant christening' (my italics) in the New Testament. And when, a few years later, he discovered himself to be an 'unbeliever' in the light of all he had read (including Darwin, whose *Origin of the Species* appeared in 1859), this, too, was in a purely intellectual sense. He never would part from what the church service meant to him in emotional terms, and could never contemplate any notion other than that the survival of humanity depended on the survival of religion. However, at this earlier stage of his life much of his emotional satisfaction was derived from playing the fiddle and from the church services. If that is faith, and it is for most young people, then Tom possessed it in full measure.

At this period too, as he described in the *Life*, he was attracted to several girls, whom he adored at a distance in the idealistic manner of adolescents. He was, he says, 'over a week getting over' an attachment to a girl he saw on horseback; he told 'other boys in confidence' about her, and they 'watched for her on his behalf'. This was followed by an attachment even deeper, which occasioned no fewer than four poems ('Transformations'; 'The Passer-By'; 'Louie';

'To Louisa in the Lane'), as well as the mention of her Christian name in the *Life*.

Louisa Harding was one of the twelve children of a well-to-do farmer of Stinsford, for whom his father had done some building work, and Tom seems always to have worshipped her from afar. He had perhaps just then lost interest in a girl from Windsor who annoyed him by 'taking no interest in Herne the Hunter' despite her reading of Ainsworth's *Windsor Castle*, and had got over being despised by a gamekeeper's red-haired daughter called Elizabeth Browne; but his interest in Louisa 'went deeper'. After her death in 1913, at the age of seventy-two, he used often to ponder over her (unmarked) grave in Stinsford churchyard. As a result of one such visit there he wrote 'Transformations', with the beautiful feeling of its final stanza:

> Portion of this yew
> Is a man my grandsire knew,
> Bosomed here at its foot:
> This branch may be his wife,
> A ruddy human life
> Now turned to a green shoot.
>
> These grasses must be made
> Of her who often prayed,
> Last century, for repose;
> And the fair girl long ago
> Whom I often tried to know
> May be entering this rose.
>
> So, they are not underground,
> But as nerves and veins abound
> In the growths of upper air,
> And they feel the sun and rain,
> And the energy again
> That made them what they were!

According to a note inserted into the *Life* by Florence (on the advice of James Barrie), young Tom never said more than 'good evening' to Louisa, and she never uttered a word to him. But despite the lack of encouragement, when he heard that she had been sent to a Weymouth boarding school, 'thither he went Sunday after Sunday, until he discovered the church which [she] attended with her fellow-scholars. But, alas, all that resulted from these efforts was a shy smile from Louisa.' Nevertheless, as he wrote, 'the vision remained'. Louisa never married, and a second cousin described her (long after her death) as 'short and tubby and anything but dignified' with a 'round, jolly face', full of fun, but 'very religiously minded'. She said later, to this same cousin, Ernest Harding, that Tom had been in love with her, but that her parents would not allow her to have anything to do with him on the grounds of his social inferiority. She conceded that she had never spoken to him. Ernest Harding heard from her that although Tom was regarded as 'just a village boy', it was recognized that he was 'an unusual type, and different from the other village children in several ways . . . a quiet, studious child of a retiring disposition'. There is a photograph of Louisa, carrying her school hat, which shows that she was then certainly a pretty girl with an interesting face. Her younger sister Julia, who married a gambler, a lawyer called Green who went to the bad, remembered Tom, too: 'an odd looking boy with a big head. I remember him well and often saw him when I was a young girl – he was a solemn looking little boy.' Louie, as her family called her, lived in Dorchester all her life, but never tried to call on her old admirer when he became famous – nor he on her, although he may well have seen her in the street.

One event the sixteen-year-old Tom witnessed, on 9 August 1856, left a lifelong impression and probably caused him a severe shock. Its effect may have been underrated, even by himself when writing the earlier part of the *Life*, in which he scarcely mentions it except in passing. That it always remained on his mind is evident from a visit he made one day in late 1925 to Racedown, the house which had once been lent rent-free to Wordsworth and his sister by the Pinney family. He went with his wife 'as a pilgrim', and Lady Pinney recollected that he signed the visitors' book, then:

> cleaned the pen on the striped lining of his waistcoat, a thing I remember seeing my father's business friends do. 'It's a very nice pen, my dear,' he said to his wife, 'do use it.' We showed him the rooms the Wordsworths probably used . . . as he was leaving and being hurried home by his careful wife, he turned to me and said, 'Can you find out about Martha Brown? She lived over there' (and he pointed to the west) 'I saw her hanged when I was sixteen'. He was bustled into the car, before there was time for more.

Lady Pinney made enquiries about this murder (carried out by a woman on account of her husband's unfaithfulness), and she passed on the information to him. He replied, on 20 January 1926:

> My sincere thanks for the details . . . about that unhappy woman Martha Brown, whom I am ashamed to say I saw hanged, my only excuse being that I was but a youth, and had to be in town at that time for other reasons . . . I remember what a fine figure she showed against the sky as she hung in the misty rain, and how the tight black silk gown set off her shape as she wheeled half-round and back.

His reaction has the expected sexual component, although his account is unusual in not troubling to disguise it. There is nothing 'unconscious' about the effect on him of the shape of a woman's body: one of the important things about Hardy is that he did not shirk 'unpleasant facts'. No boy of sixteen could have escaped being affected by the ghastly juxtaposition of sex and death, although it cannot have made its fullest impact on him as an adolescent; rather he registered the impression, and then fascinatedly contemplated it at intervals throughout his life. It was not something easily forgettable, and must have contributed to the fate of Tess.

The erotic implications of this experience and young Tom's behaviour with girls make this a convenient point to consider the much canvassed question of the nature of Tom's sexuality. This would not be necessary to discuss, were it not for the fact that Hardy's two previous biographers, Robert Gittings and Michael Millgate, have suggested that he was impotent. Millgate thinks that the idea is 'intriguing', and, though plainly believing in the hypothesis, is too scrupulous to press it, since there is no evidence for it. Gittings pretends to be specific. He begins his discussion with an account of the adolescent Tom at 'the Christian Mummers' rehearsal' at the home, Sparks Corner, of his aunt Maria in Puddletown. He 'started', claims Gittings, 'making violent approaches to his older cousin Rebecca' (born in 1829 and eleven years his senior), and 'was caught'. There 'was a family scene', and Maria is 'said to have shown the door to young Hardy and forbidden him the house. Though this did not last – his early twenties saw him visiting Nat Sparks [younger brother to Rebecca] at Christmas – it was a severe shock to his adolescence.' But no such incident occurred.

Nevertheless the central issue – that one of the mainsprings of the Hardy *oeuvre* is disappointment or frustration owing to some kind of sexual impotence – needs to be examined. Gittings quotes Tom's own declaration in the *Life*: 'His immaturity . . . was greater than is common for his years and it may be mentioned here that a clue to much of his character and action throughout his life is afforded by his lateness of development in virility, while mentally precocious.'

Gittings continues that the difficulty 'in interpreting this "clue" is the term "virility" ':

> Other usage by Hardy seems to confirm that he means the dictionary definition, 'the capacity for sexual intercourse'. In another part of his autobiography, he makes an amount of satisfied play with the fact that he was a founder member of the Rabelais Club, instituted in 1879 by Sir Walter Besant as a 'declaration for virility in literature'. It is clear that the Club equated 'virility' with portrayal of sex in literature, but Hardy, perhaps wishfully, seemed to associate it with sex in life. A subconscious envy of notoriously 'virile' and sexually potent public men remained with him all his life.

Gittings then refers to a biography of Sir Edward Marsh, the editor of *Georgian Poetry*, literary man, translator of La Fontaine, and higher civil servant, who as a child got mumps complicated by German measles and, if only according to Gittings, did not develop sexually. He continues:

> The evidence with Hardy is too fragmentary for any final judgement; yet delayed or imperfect development is quite consistent with sexual curiosity, an attraction to the idea of love without the power to fulfil it. Hardy's continual speculation about almost every woman he meets, and his apparent habit of passing from one to another without conscious volition, suggests such a pattern.
>
> Whether the experience with Rebecca Sparks was really traumatic, or whether in fact there was some more general physical condition, the age of sixteen, up to which Hardy himself said he was 'a child', was in many ways a turning-point.

By the time Gittings comes to this non-event with his cousin Rebecca for the second time, it has been virtually turned into an attempted rape which did not come off owing to the assailant's lack of capacity. But, if so, one wonders what would drive an imperfectly developed or perhaps not-developed-at-all person to such action in the first place. It is not what Edward Marsh would have done, even to the beautiful boys

34

and young men whom his mumps complicated by German measles somehow allowed him to prefer to girls.

The passage from the *Life* in which Hardy offered a 'clue' about himself needs to be looked at in its immediate context. He had just described how, as a young apprentice architect, he used to go out and play his fiddle:

> But young Hardy's physical vigour was now much greater than it had been when he was a child, and it enabled him, like a conjurer at a fair, to keep in the air the three balls of architecture, scholarship [he was reading the Greek and Latin classics between six and eight in the mornings] and dance–fiddling, without ill effects, the fiddling being of course not daily, like the other two.

The sentence quoted by Gittings, with its reference to 'lateness of development in virility' as a clue to his whole life, then follows, and the passage continues: 'He himself said humorously in later times that he was a child until he was sixteen, a youth until he was five-and-twenty, and a young man until he was nearly fifty. Whether this was intrinsic, or owed anything to his having lived in a remote spot in early life, is an open question.'

Is this passage, as Gittings claims, really a 'cluster of hints'? Surely, on the contrary, it is direct and open. In saying that by 'virility' Hardy meant 'the capacity for sexual intercourse', Gittings is using only one, not *the* dictionary definition of virility. The *OED* also gives: 'period of life during which a person of the male sex is in full vigour', and 'manly strength and vigour of action; energy or force of a virile character'. There is no reason to suppose that Hardy did not intend all three meanings, although he certainly seems to have had his puberty in mind. He is telling us (a point missed by Gittings) that he did have a puberty: 'lateness of development' can only imply 'development'. So if Gittings is right, then Hardy was dissembling.

The Rabelais Club, which Gittings then mentions in support of his contention, is described by Hardy in the *Life* in his familiar sardonic manner. At the inaugural dinner, 'Altogether we were as Rabelaisian as it was possible to be in the foggy circumstances, though I succeeded but poorly.' He had, he wrote, been 'pressed to join as being the most virile writer of works of imagination then in London'. This is simply a report of fact, and far from 'making an amount of satisfied play' about it; Hardy maliciously added that Henry James (whose unfulfilled homosexual propensities he would have inferred) had been 'rejected for the lack of that quality'.

Tom, different though he may well have been in some ways, can hardly have differed from other boys in failing to regard the arrival of his puberty as an occasion for immediate sexual intercourse. Few or no boys, on attaining puberty, stride instantly forth to test their new powers. The event is somewhat blurred: there is no 'first period', as there is in girls. If Hardy had broken this rule (which, however comical a notion, is one interpretation of the alleged 'violent approaches' to his cousin), then the fact would surely have become much better known. All that Tom is telling us, as straightforwardly as the times (and Florence and her advisors) would allow, is that he had a late puberty. Gittings' 'very late', for a puberty at sixteen, is a wrong assumption, particularly in relation to the 1850s, although Tom himself *felt* it as late, probably because most of his friends happened to have reached it earlier. But certainly, the phrase he used in the *Life*, 'lateness of development', meant that he had indeed developed, and his late 'youth', a word almost by definition meaning that puberty has been reached, began at sixteen.

What is obvious is that Tom was a hypersensitive boy, well ahead of most others as an observer, and in his grasp of the world and its ways. When puberty, an emotional time, came upon him at sixteen, just as he was going out into the world to earn his living for the first time, he was overwhelmed by it. This experience formed a lifelong outlook; as he indicated, it lay behind much of his future 'character and action'. He remained, sexually, idealistic in the manner of adolescents, rather than just after lustful conquests in the more usual, or overt, manner of young men. Having told us about Julia Augusta Martin in the *Life*, he is careful to record his attraction to the girl he saw on horseback, and he mentions four more girls who similarly attracted him. All that is really unusual about this is the intensity with which he retained his memories of them.

In *The Well-Beloved*, the final version of which is his last novel (he wrote the serial version before *Jude*), he is at pains to reveal his lifelong 'Platonic' (and therefore idealistic) habit of mind; the need to seek the ideal form within the flesh of the woman in which it resides. This does not mean that he was, philosophically, a 'Platonist', but he was well aware of, and interested in, the nature of Plato's philosophy. He had Florence Hardy type out for him, in his old age, this extract from W.J. Courthope's *Life in Poetry*: 'The Greeks had perceived . . . that the first aim of every artist was to imitate an object. It was for this very reason that Plato objected to Art itself as immoral; since he supposed it to be the aim of the poet and painter to copy what was essentially false, as being only an imperfect resemblance of true Being.'

Plato has always been an inspirer of religious thinkers, and Tom would never allow himself to be religious enough, in an intellectual sense, to embrace Plato wholeheartedly. But his emotional habit was doggedly Platonic, in that it recalls Plato's doctrine that material things are no more than copies of immortal and perfect essences (so that poetry and art consisted of copies of copies) which are scarcely accessible to sensual perception. In *The Well-Beloved* Tom shows Jocelyn Pierston (in the serial 'Pearston') seeking for the ideal in three successive women. This will be discussed further in the context of the time he wrote it, but the relevant point here is that Jocelyn seeks for the ideal with an almost desperate irony. The 'ho-ho-ho' of the end of the serial version is authorial, and it is uttered by Hardy because Jocelyn has

> brought into his brain a sudden sense of the grotesqueness of things. His wife was – not Avice but that parchment-covered skull moving about in his room. An irresistible fit of laughter, so violent as to be an agony, seized upon him, and started in him with such momentum that he could not stop it. He laughed and laughed, till he was almost too weak to draw breath.
>
> Marcia [his wife] hobbled up, frightened. 'What's the matter?' she asked; and, turning to a second nurse, 'He is weak – hysterical.'
>
> 'O – no, no! – I – I – it is too droll – this ending to my would-be romantic history!' Ho-ho-ho.

Hardy discovered, and not without irony or self-criticism, that the most perfect essences were to be found in the most youthful bodies. That is in part what the underrated *The Well-Beloved* is about; but the emotional attitude stemmed from what he felt to have been his protracted adolescence. But then Keats and Rimbaud, to mention only two major figures, were both poets of feelings that are essentially adolescent – and the feelings of adolescence are important not only for their intrinsic content (which includes tenderness) but also for what they may adumbrate. To be a 'man' was in Hardy's estimation a rare achievement. Adolescence sees and feels everything freshly and keenly (it is the industrialist, not the poet, who admonishes his son 'not to take it all so seriously'), and a man may retain those qualities throughout his life. Thus, not all the feelings of adolescence need to be or should be transcended. This is another conclusion that might be drawn from Tom's 'clue'.

There is a principle called 'Ockham's Razor', named after the medieval English philosopher William of Ockham, which can be formulated as: 'Entities are not to be multiplied beyond necessity.' To express it differently: 'It is arbitrary and mistaken to postulate the existence of things unless you have to'; or, 'Don't invent new things to drag into your argument unless it demands their introduction'. Applying the excellent principle of Ockham's Razor to Hardy – that we need to explain only what needs explaining – what needs explaining about him? Certainly not Tom's statement that he had a late (only slightly late, in fact) puberty. What else? There is a 'family tradition' that he was 'impotent': a local government clerk in Dorset with Sparks connections will tell you so with a 'nod and a wink', wrote Michael Rabiger in his review of Gittings' book. No one has been able to be specific about this, and other 'traditions' cancel it quite out. Gittings would surely have milked it for all it was worth if there was substance to it, but such vague gossip goes on all the time about anyone well known. The hypothesis must therefore be abandoned.

Tom, at the age of eighty-five, told Edmund Blunden – and Blunden himself said it to this author as he did to others – that 'sexual desire could be a great problem for an old man'. He then mentioned that he had been capable of full sexual intercourse until he was eighty-four. This was not, as Millgate calls it, a 'boast'. It was a confidence.

3

Architect's Office

John Hicks, an easy-going, cheerful and fair-minded man, was an architect and church restorer, previously of Bristol, practising at 39 South Street, Dorchester. Thomas II had worked with him on several jobs, and now in 1856, as the question of a profession for his son arose, had the idea of apprenticing him with Hicks. Whatever dreams Tom, and his mother, may have had about becoming a vicar, he says in the *Life* that although 'he had sometimes, too, wished to enter the Church', 'he cheerfully agreed to go to Mr Hicks's'.

When his abilities were tested on a survey, Hicks approved, and offered to take him on. The usual fee was £100 payable halfway through a three-year term. 'As the father was a ready-money man', Jemima suggested he take £50 for a down payment, 'and to this, Mr Hicks, who was not a ready-money man, agreed'. Tom thoroughly liked him: Hicks knew the Greek that Tom did not know and wanted to know; and his father, a Gloucestershire clergyman, had been 'quite a good classical scholar' (a glamorous thing to Tom just then), who had even given his son a smattering of Hebrew.

It was now that Tom started on a remarkable plan of study. Forced to abandon formal instruction early, he decided to carry on his education himself. In the summers he rose at four, in the winters at five, and would study until eight before leaving for the office. Even there study could, if sporadically, continue. He would come in, often after catching himself 'soliloquizing in Latin' on the way, to a cheerful office where, in between spells of work, vigorous altercations about 'construings' of Latin (and eventually Greek) authors would take place between Hicks, Tom and his fellow pupil and earliest close friend, Henry Robert Bastow.

He cannot have known much Greek at first, and exactly how he began its study is not known, but by 1858 he was working through the *Iliad* (with an interleaved Latin crib): his copy of it is inscribed with that date. Since the young Jude Fawley's knowledge of the *Iliad* is the same as his creator's was (as is known from the passages Tom marked in his copy), no

39

doubt Tom painfully picked up the rudiments from a thirty-year-old, scribbled-upon grammar – like Jude's first Latin grammar. But in his use of his own experience to create Jude, Hardy combined memories from very different periods of time: at sixteen he already knew well enough (through his four years of Latin) that 'the words of the required language' were not 'always to be found latent in the words of the given language'; and Jude's experience of wishing, as 'the little sun-rays continued to stream in through his hat', that he 'had never seen a book . . . that he had never been born' are intensifications and extensions of his own earlier feelings in that circumstance. Tom was soon able to make sense of the *Iliad*, as well as carrying on with Horace, Virgil and Ovid. This is the way of real learning, which must lead to understanding and grasp (similarly, the Italian novelist and translator Elio Vittorini first learned English by working his way through *Robinson Crusoe*). It must have meant much to Tom, with the half-secret excitement in his heart about the worlds of Homer and Virgil, to be able to banter with his master: 'Hicks was ahead of them in Greek, though they could beat him in Latin . . . When cornered and proved wrong he would take shelter behind the excuse that his school-days were longer ago than theirs.' How many first employers are like that?

Bastow, Tom's colleague in these exchanges, had attended what Tom called a 'good school in or near London', and was interested in literature. Whether, like Tom, he was new to Greek, or had already learned some at school, is not clear. He was a nonconformist and, though not lacking a sense of humour, he tended to be grave about his religion. He had himself baptized in 1858, and tried, perhaps rather too hard, to persuade Tom to do likewise.

Paedobaptism was an issue in the nineteenth century that could rouse angry opposition in those who disbelieved in it. Bastow appealed to Tom's reason on two counts: that people should know what they were doing when they undertook to be baptized, and that there was no good New Testament authority for infant baptism. The tradition for it went back only to the third century, and hints for it in the New Testament were not very convincing. A well-armed adversary would soon have driven Tom to the wall, and this adversary was, moreover, one of whom he was fond. Bastow had given him not only a Bible but also a photograph of himself inscribed 'with love' (Bastow would have meant Christian love, with all the decent fervour of that era). Tom always cared greatly about his friends, and carefully considered their feelings. Now, reading such books as Whateley's *Logic*, he was learning to think hard (harder than most undergraduates, who accept their education as a mere *fait accompli*), and, not only that, but to understand the emotional consequences of what he thought. As he describes it, he 'inconsistently determined "to stick to his own side", as he considered the Church to be, at some cost of conscience'. No doubt there was as much fun, and sense of challenge to one of superior education, as seriousness in his own attitude, though not probably in Bastow's. The latter would not long afterwards beseech him, in letters from Tasmania, whence he emigrated, to practise proper religious observance ('don't you let your eye get off Jesus'). Their arguments became so noisy at times that Mrs Hicks would send down a message 'from the drawing-room' to ask them to shut up. So much for Tom's supposedly continuous low spirits!

The famous Hardyan gloom did not – as has so often been asserted – arise from unknown 'terrible circumstances', but from the sensitivity of the nature which God had bestowed upon him. Many young men are as sensitive; few are as gifted or determined. Even the hardship and cruelty he witnessed impinged itself, not upon a 'nature seared by pain' (he saw more of that around him than he ever experienced), but upon one which was already quiveringly vulnerable to all hurt. The Martha Brown hanging, in which stark horror and sex were inextricably mixed, seems to have impressed itself on his nervous system to such a morbid degree that, two years after it, having (presumably) finished his stint of Greek and Latin and got ready for his breakfast before setting out for Hicks' office, he remembered that a man (called Seale) was to be hanged at eight o'clock. He seized the family telescope and rushed up a nearby hill on the heath,

> a quarter of a mile from the house, whence he looked toward the town. The sun behind his back shone straight on the white façade of the gaol, the gallows upon it, and the form of the murderer in white fustian, the executioner and officials in dark clothing and the crowd below being invisible at this distance of nearly three miles. At the moment of his placing the glass to his eye the white figure dropped downwards . . . The whole thing had been so sudden that the glass nearly fell from Hardy's hands. He seemed alone on the heath with the hanged man, and crept home wishing he had not been so curious.

This, he relates, 'was the second and last execution he witnessed', and, as has been seen, even in his old age he would allude to the Martha Brown incident only in passing.

Through Bastow, who had joined the Baptist congregation at Dorchester, Tom got to know the minister, the Rev. Frederick Perkins, and his two 'hard-headed' sons, Alfred and William, 'Scotch youths fresh from Aberdeen University, good classics, who could rattle off the Greek original of any passage in the New Testament'. They did their best to bring Tom to their persuasion, for he bought the newest Griesbach text of the New Testament, which he thus implies that they did not possess, in order 'to confute them'. He also promised them that he would 'give up heathen authors'. How much Greek he really knew by this time (say 1858–60) is hard to say, but he was right in taking Griesbach as his authority, since the original two-volume edition by Johann Jakob Griesbach, of 1775–77, laid the foundation of all future work on the text. That he could hold his own at all against these university students and their formidable father is, even allowing for a little natural exaggeration, remarkable. They caused him to feel, despite the 'High Church principles' to which he clung, 'that he ought to be baptized again as an adult'. That he, still High Church in doctrine, should have considered the matter so deeply is testimony to his innate seriousness.

He pressed on with the Rev. Shirley, who at this time advised him, not unwisely, to read Hooker's *Ecclesiastical Polity*. If he really did read right through this massive and humane work of Anglican theology – and he probably did – he could still discover nothing in it for his immediate purpose; but he discovered the view that the scriptures ought not to be interpreted as a hard and fast set of rules. He wrote that he himself possessed a 'breadth of mind' which his companions lacked. Hooker and his profound work might have helped in this.

The process by which 'the necessity of adult baptism gradually wore out of him' was probably helped when he agreed to meet Bastow and the two Perkins youths at a 'prayer-meeting in the chapel'. He turned up on time, but they, the nonconformists, were late because they were watching Cooke's Circus, which had entered Dorchester that evening. But the man who, as some would have it, 'abnormally' enjoyed hangings, chided himself for merely having wanted to go to the circus: in a note of the mid-1860s he wrote, remembering this incident (but he remembered everything), 'going to the P. meeting . . . having been blaming self for wish to stay away'. Five or six years later he could interpret his behaviour as 'not blameable but great'. To be 'great', in a supremely private sense, i.e. to be virtuous, was his ideal: he was not alluding to himself as a 'great man' in the ordinary sense. He was already an over-conscientious person, who blamed himself for going to hangings and being 'curious'.

In *A Laodicean* he drew on his memories of Bastow and the Perkins family, through whom, he wrote, 'Thomas Hardy first became impressed with the necessity for "plain living and high thinking", which stood him in such good stead in later years'. The good Baptist minister in *A Laodicean* is a drawing, from life, of Frederick Perkins, one of the 'few portraits of actual persons in his novels'.

It seems that Tom never went next door from Hicks' office, to the poet William Barnes' school, over his paedobaptist problems. Perhaps he thought he would receive a dusty answer from Barnes. But he might have got to know another clerical family in Dorchester, the Moules, through Barnes, if he did not do so through Hicks or his own mother. They were to mean far more to him than the Perkins. From them he would draw the closest friend of his life, his true mentor – and one he always generously remembered – Horace Moule. Moreover, this family offered him no doctrinal temptations – if, indeed, the Perkins ever led him to consider nonconformity – for, after Bastow's departure for Tasmania, he soon 'lapsed' again to the Greek 'pagan writings'.

The Rev. Henry Moule had been born in 1801, the son of a Wiltshire solicitor and banker, and took his MA at St John's College, Cambridge, in 1826. When the poet William Barnes became a 'ten years' man' for his Bachelor of Divinity degree at the same college in 1837 – this involved being registered for ten years, spending three full terms in college (he chose two summer terms, 1847 and 1848, and one spring one, 1850), and passing a number of examinations – it was doubtless arranged through Moule. While at Cambridge Moule came under the influence of the pioneer Evangelical Charles Simeon, vicar of Holy Trinity. Handley Carr Glyn Moule, the most famous of Henry Moule's sons, who became Bishop of Durham (1901), would publish a life of Simeon in 1892, twelve years after his father's death.

The Evangelical movement had arisen in the middle of the eighteenth century as a consequence of the generally degraded tone of the Church. It had much in common with Methodism, but the Evangelicals – who included John Newton, author, with William Cowper, of the Olney Hymns – never contemplated separation from the Church of England, although some of them inclined to theological Calvinism. Suspicious of Roman Catholicism, they worked to convert their congregations to a psychologically realistic faith, and they concerned themselves with social reform. In 1768 six of them had been expelled from St Edmund

Hall, Oxford, for 'too much religion'; though by the following century, Evangelicalism had established itself in the public mind as both 'sincere and useful'.

Henry Moule had become vicar of Fordington in 1829 and, as an Evangelical, had often been called a Methodist, and worse, by a section of his parishioners during the first score of years of his incumbency. Fordington, much of it a 'brutal and sour slum', lay between Dorchester and the marshes, and the vicar was unpopular because of his aggressively reforming sermons and his undoubtedly accurate attacks on his parishioners' poor morals. His family became used to being insulted, and were called 'Moule's lambs'. He was, though, respected and appreciated by individuals. Then, following the second outbreak of cholera in Dorchester in 1854, he suddenly became a 'folk hero'. Cholera epidemics raged in London and elsewhere at the same time, and would lead to the setting up of the Metropolitan Board of Works in 1855, presided over by Joseph Bazalgette, pioneer of proper sewerage and the establishment of water-closets in London.

Henry Moule had always known that the behaviour of his slum parishioners was largely the result of the atrocious conditions in which they lived; and throughout the second cholera outbreak he made these conditions perfectly clear. The first outbreak, in 1848–49, had led to the erection of many hovels on waste land belonging to the Duchy of Cornwall, which excused itself from taking any action on the ground that the hovels had been illegally set up. The cholera itself, in London, in Dorchester, and elsewhere, was worse than it need have been because of Home Office neglect, though the first Public Health Act was passed in 1848. Now, in 1854, Moule was able to use the fact that the Duchy was responsible for the bad conditions in Fordington to appeal to the President of the Council, Prince Albert. His appeal gives an incidentally useful picture of the community at the time, one with which Tom must have been well acquainted. On 12 September 1854 he addressed the Prince Consort from the vicarage:

God has, in his providence, again visited this unhappy parish with cholera in its most frightful form . . . I am constrained, by feelings and convictions which I cannot resist, to bring the case . . . fully before your notice. I must write in the few intervals of rest from almost incessant attention to the sick . . .

He went on to lay 'no inconsiderable portion of the blame' on the managers of the estate, who

> when they might have prevented it, allowed such a state of things to grow up, partly, it is true, on a piece of freehold land, but surrounded on all sides by His Royal Highness's property, and inhabited in part by labourers on his estate; and for the twenty-five years of my incumbency the Council has never stretched forth a hand even to alleviate this state of things.

In what amounted to a threat, he told his Royal Highness: 'I shall publish what I write', for 'the Parish of Fordington has long been one of common notoriety'. He provides a 'general sketch' of the locality, which shows some of the conditions Hardy witnessed as a child: 1,100 people were congregated on space 'that can scarcely exceed five acres', 'utterly destitute of the ordinary conveniences of life'. Their 'filth' was cast into an 'open and wretched drain' or into a mill pond from which they 'drew most of their water'.

Despite the observations of Thucydides, who recorded people's fear of catching plague from one another during the epidemic of 430 BC, and of the later ones of Fracastorius, Kircher and Leeuwenhoek, it was not until just nineteen years before Moule wrote his remarkable document that Bassi had shown that muscardine, a disease of silkworms, was caused by a microbe – and suggested that these organisms might be responsible for other ailments in other species. Seven more years were to elapse before Pasteur's famous demonstration; Lister's action on account of it followed even later. So Hardy grew up in an age that was still mostly ignorant of what caused disease. But conscientious men like Moule were abreast of research – he introduced a dry-earth closet in 1860 – and their intuition told them that filth caused disease. He told Prince Albert that on 24 August 1854 he had discovered 'that two women residing in Holloway-row had contracted to work for the convicts', who had been sent from Mill Bank Penitentiary in London, where cholera was raging, to a Dorchester barracks. The bedding and clothes of these convicts were bundled into these women's two cottages, and Moule pointed to a connection – dismissed by others – between this and cholera attacks beginning in nearby cottages.

The Prince replied, through a Colonel Phipps, that he had 'no separate or personal authority in the management' of the Duchy's lands. But Moule, on 21 September, returned vigorously to the attack, urging the

'Consort of the Queen of England', in view of his 'practical vision' and his 'benevolent interest' in the 'physical condition of Her Majesty's subjects', to 'apply his active mind not only to the improvement of the cottages of the working classes, but even to the relief and removal of the evils of sewers and cess-pools'. The spot, he assured him, 'has every year grown worse' – and he attributed this fact largely to 'many of the neighbouring landowners': 232 tenements, he told Albert, were owned by forty-six different proprietors. 'The demand for cottages caused rents to rise', and by 1854 had reached an average of two shillings and twopence halfpenny a week, or more (a sum well beyond labourers' means). It was not uncommon for nine people to sleep in one bedroom, eight feet square in size. Moule quoted a 'poor cottager' as just having asked him, 'Who will build cottages for the poor?'

Such facts would have entered like iron into the soul – to use one of the Hardy family's favourite expressions – of the young Thomas Hardy. The influence of the courageous and humane Moule – who published his letters, and much else besides – would have been reinforced by Jemima, who had known about Moule from at least the days of her service at Stinsford House; she remembered hearing him preach at Dorchester Barracks long before she was married. He would have been a topic of frequent conversation in the Hardy household, and was no doubt compared to the smug Shirley.

One of Henry Moule's sons, Henry Joseph, who also went into the Church, was a gifted amateur watercolourist (some of whose paintings are now in the Dorset Museum). He became Tom's companion, and critic, in watercolour painting during the period of his apprenticeship, which again suggests that Tom early learned to hold his own with people originally more cultivated than himself. Later, in 1903, Henry Joseph would tell Hardy how sad he was at his friend's lack of Christianity; commenting on the ironic poem 'The Impercipient' (in fact more about superficiality of faith in others than Tom's own lack of it), he spoke of 'tears' and of how it went to his 'heart of hearts' that 'my dear old friend (for it can only be T.H. who mourns) should be so craving for assurance of a father'. Tom was also friendly with two more of the Rev. Moule's sons, George and Charles, as well as with his sister Mary's exact contemporary Handley, the future Bishop of Durham. But it was the fourth son, Horatio (known as Horace) Mosley Moule, born in 1832, with whom Tom formed the closest relationship of all.

Although the outlines of his life and death are clear enough, there is much that is unknown about Horace Moule. His character and his fate certainly affected Hardy at a profound level, but there is no reason to suppose that the relationship 'must have had', as has been suggested, 'a sexual component'. Tom knew him intimately from the time he began in Hicks' office. In 1857 Horace, then twenty-five to Tom's seventeen, gave him a copy of Jabez Hogg's *Elements of Experimental and Natural Philosophy*. Hogg was a competent popularizer who had previously written an introduction to the microscope, and the very early gift of this book confirms Tom's lifelong interest in scientific subjects. It was in this period that the two young men saw the most of each other, for Horace was then living at home. He had gone up to Trinity College, Oxford, full of promise – to which many besides Hardy testified – in 1851, and was there until 1854. For some reason he had failed to obtain a degree, although he had been able in that year to transfer to Queen's College, Cambridge. He did not immediately acquire a degree from there, either, partly perhaps because of difficulties with mathematics, which was a compulsory subject. On the other hand, he taught it to various of the many private pupils he took, although not perhaps to as high a level as Cambridge would have expected him to achieve. It is likely, however, that the drinking habits which increasingly bedevilled Horace had begun while he was at Oxford and were the reason for his failure, and that on account of his brilliance and abundant charm, he was given 'another chance' at Cambridge, where his father had powerful connections. He eventually took his BA in 1867, and became MA in the year of his death, 1874. That the university recognized his gifts is evident from the fact that he was awarded the Hulsean Prize in 1858, for the work which he put into his dissertation 'Christian Oratory; An Inquiry into its History during the First Five Centuries'.

He may, potentially, have been the most gifted of all the Moules, and not least because he had a 'dark side' to his nature. Tom remained loyal to the notion that he might have become a major poet, although the few poems he left, while being well accomplished, are in no way outstandingly promising. And his criticism – of which more survives – is intelligent, but no more than that. He seems likely to have been a man whose genius was confined to his conversation. One 'P', an unidentified and ingenuous contributor to *Sunday at Home* magazine in 1915, who had gone to school with Hardy and who knew all the Moules well, wrote after describing his memories of Handley and George Moule:

I really think Horace was the most lovable, as well as the best scholar, of them all! How kind and patient he was when he tried to drive knowledge and understanding into our hard heads! How gentle [sic] and tenderly he dealt with every one, rich or poor, who came and asked his help in any way! How all the women loved his beautiful face, and the men would listen to his counsel when they would to nobody else's, unless it were his father's . . . I am saying what the good Bishop of Durham would himself agree with today, when speaking of Horace, 'This was the noblest Roman of them all'.

This tribute indicates that the habit of treating Horace's extraordinary qualities as little more than a manifestation of Tom's loyalty is a mistake. 'P' was writing of his memories of the now famous and living Hardy, and must have felt deeply about Horace to have bothered to make this high assessment. Personal charm (and an appeal to women) was there in abundance, but something more than that, too.

Horace, like Ben Jonson when he was acting as tutor to the young Walter Raleigh, fell into trouble in Paris. The pupil was Wynne Albert Bankes, who had previously been in the navy. In 1860 Horace went to live in Salisbury with Bankes and another pupil, to teach them Greek, Latin and maths. He had been doing well at home, under his father's roof, but had upset him by buying theologically 'dubious' books such as Mantell's *The Wonders of Geology*. (The perils which the new science of geology held for Christians are best illustrated in Edmund Gosse's classic account, *Father and Son*, of 1907.) Bankes soon became aware of his tutor's drink failing: he was, Bankes reported in his diary, which is now in the Dorset County Record Office, a 'Dipsomaniac, and suffering from D.T.'. Delirium tremens, if it really was that, and not Bankes using the term loosely, is a serious condition for a person of twenty-eight to have reached: it presupposes prolonged bouts of very heavy drinking, and involves alarming hallucinations. Horace was forced to say something about his lapse to his pupil, for Bankes recorded that the drinking started as a result of 'taking opium when reviewing books for Macmillan at Cambridge [Macmillan's headquarters were in Cambridge until 1863] when he worked for 48 or 72 hours at a stretch'.

After making a recovery from the Salisbury bout, Horace accompanied his pupils to France, where he then failed to meet Bankes, as arranged, on 28 July, for the purpose of attending a church service on the following day. By 31 July he had still not turned up. Bankes returned to their base near Paris, where he discovered that Horace 'had ordered a bottle of claret . . . cut his whiskers off & had disappeared' – presumably to dens of ill repute in Paris. Bankes and the other pupil went so far as to make a search of Paris morgues, but Horace turned up safely in Dorchester on 4 August. His father's text for the Sunday service of 5 August, attended by a presumably repentant Horace, and by Tom, was 'All the days of my appointed time will I wait, till my change come'.

Alas, it never did. By 1861 Horace was lecturing on temperance in his own district, but he could not conquer his predisposition. To what extent it went with opium taking, if at all, is not known. It has been suggested by Millgate that his drinking largely originated in his ambisexuality, and that his relationship with Tom 'must have been homosexual': that he eventually made a proposition to Tom, which was turned down. The first speculation, while there is no evidence for it whatsoever, is perfectly possible. On the other hand, it is equally possible that Horace was manic-depressive by temperament, or perhaps just depressive: that, suffering from bouts of suicidal depression, he had recourse to the only 'medicine' then available. But alcohol taken for this purpose, while it acts as a temporary relief, only makes the illness worse, since it is in itself a powerful depressant of the central nervous system.

Concerning Millgate's further speculations of Horace's homosexual relations, although the fact that a man has indulged in heterosexuality is no evidence against his having also indulged in homosexual activity, a story that Florence had from Tom about Horace does make it just that less likely. According to this story, Horace got a Fordington woman (and therefore one of his father's parishioners) pregnant, and she was shipped off to Australia (where, doubtless vindicating Hardy's view of the malign workings of fate, the son she bore was in due time hanged). There is also talk of his engagement to a governess of 'sterling character' who might have been the making of him, but who broke it off because of his drinking. At one time he was employed as a tutor in the household of the egocentric Sir Henry Taylor (who at his dining-table at Sheen wore the robes of an honorary DCL awarded him at Oxford in 1862), civil servant and writer of closet verse dramas, and it may have been there that he encountered her.

Horace's family status, then, was that of Continually Forgiven Brilliant Black Sheep, and, as such, he would have appealed to the dramatic and the unconventional in Tom, for whom he must, if only initially, have been something of a role model. It is, however, a considerable exaggeration to state that, in 1857, he 'took virtual control' of his life. Thomas Hardy, unless he had fallen in love, had expert control of his own life. Horace was a published writer, a skilled classicist, poet, charmer, possible secret father of a bastard, successful teacher and lecturer, open-minded Christian, dark and troubled member of a forthright family earnestly devoted to good works – and, surely, very close confidant indeed. The astoundingly lovely poem, 'An Experience', from *Late Lyrics and Earlier* (1922), certainly seems to be about Horace Moule, whether it is wholly retrospective or a revision of a much earlier draft. Its peculiarities, in particular its expression of a struggle for psychological precision, and the absence from it of conventional praise, are not often encountered outside Hardy in the poetry of the past two centuries. The experience of the title seems, deliberately, to go unstated.

> Wit, weight, or wealth there was not
>   In anything that was said,
>   In anything that was done;
> All was of scope to cause not
>   A triumph, dazzle, or dread
>   To even the subtlest one,
>   My friend,
>   To even the subtlest one.
>
> But there was a new afflation –
>   An aura zephyring round
>   That care infected not:
> It came as a salutation,
>   And, in my sweet astound,
>   I scarcely witted what
>   Might pend,
>   I scarcely witted what.
>
> The hills in samewise to me
>   Spoke, as they grayly gazed,
>   – First hills to speak so yet!
> The thin-edged breezes blew me
>   What I, though cobwebbed, crazed,
>   Was never to forget,
>   My friend,
>   Was never to forget!

This poem surely refers to the earliest days of the friendship with Horace; Tom was, in old age, recollecting the impact which the experienced Horace made upon him when he was very young. The poet seems to say that he was not impressed by certain of the very qualities for which Horace was renowned. The second stanza points to appreciation of elusive qualities: we can only infer that he discovered in Horace an amazing poetic determination unsullied by material concerns – 'afflation' is a word associated with poets and poetry in general. It seems that Tom was so 'astounded' by this afflation, this 'aura zephyring round', that he forgot the very thing which other people would prophesy: the 'bad end'. Equation of landscape with mood is common in Hardy, a part of his technique, and the hills on and below which he and Horace wandered, talking of poetry and Homer and the classics, 'spoke' for the first time under this tutelage. Now the writer is an old man, 'cobwebbed, crazed', but he remembers when his friend made the world come alive for him. It is a breathtakingly beautiful tribute, which can make us, even now, grateful for the existence of Horace Moule.

He was a man whose dramatic nature appealed to Tom's imagination. He was known to sleep with a razor beneath his pillow. Feeling himself also prone to such gestures, or at the least well able to empathize, Tom must always have felt Horace's fate as an awful example, and himself 'played safe': relied on his sense of caution to keep himself out of similar troubles and shames.

On 3 April 1860 he took his sister Mary to begin her teacher-training at the college in Salisbury, where he saw Horace, perhaps for the first time, in the course of an alcoholic collapse. This would have profoundly upset him. When he recorded this Salisbury visit in his prayer book he put a cross by Psalm 119, 9: 'Wherewithal shall a young man cleanse his way: even by <u>ruling himself</u> after thy word' (the underlining is his, and he also underlined, further on in the Psalm, the words '<u>My soul breaketh . . . My soul melteth</u>'). This has been connected with 'darker patches of sexual fantasy', linked up with, by implication, Tom's witnessing of the hanging of a woman. But there is no reason to relate these markings to sex at all. Psalm 119 is about veneration of the law, and the markings more obviously refer to Horace Moule's dark predicament – and, in the second instance, to Tom's own response to it. The line of thought, given that Tom was then still a devout Christian, is typical: the psalm's message is that the 'way' should not be obeyed as mere duty, but because it *is* the truth. It is the psalmist's cry for help. If these markings were prompted by Horace Moule's unhappy experience, then helping him over the succeeding months may have imposed a severe strain on Tom, for he was an intensely conscientious young man, taking his obligations with an unusual seriousness.

Tom cared deeply for Horace Moule, then; but whether his contact with him and his family really 'exacerbated his sense of inferiority', as has been said, may be doubted. That Moule 'incited his ambition for self-improvement' is certain, but then don't most of our friends whom we admire do just that? Horace Moule inspired him, but Tom did not, for long, wish to emulate him. A successful teacher, which Moule by every account was, appeals to his pupils' sense of their own individuality; and Moule brought this out in his younger friend. Tom doubtless felt privileged to be the close personal friend of this eloquent man who could arouse the Dorchester Working Men's Mutual Improvement Society to prolonged applause when he lectured to it, about Oxford, in 1858. But that does not mean that he lacked a strong sense of himself and what he himself had to offer the world. He certainly remained loyal to Moule's memory for the rest of his life, and it has been proposed, by Millgate, that 'such lifelong devotion . . . seems explicable only in terms of a complete surrender to his personal charm'. This seems a strange explanation of close friendship. A commonsense view is that Tom remained grateful to his friend, and thus moved by his memory, for the whole of his life. Moule, memorably, would write to him on 2 July 1863, that 'the grand object of all in *learning to write well* is to gain or generate *something to say*'. Such a statement makes it easier to understand what Tom meant when he indicated, years later, that Horace's 'afflation' was not 'infected' by 'care': by the urge to profit, to impress merely, to be 'someone'. At the beginning of *The Dynasts*, the Pities say:

> We would establish those of kindlier build,
>   In fair Compassion skilled,
> Men of deep art in life-development;
> Watchers and warders of thy varied lands,
> Men surfeited of laying heavy hands
>   Upon the innocent,
> The wild, the fragile, the obscure content
> Among the myriads of thy family.
> Those, too, who love the true, the excellent,
> And make their daily moves a melody . . .

Here Tom would have been thinking of what Moule's insights and aspirations had meant to him, and not of his 'personal charm' or of a 'complete surrender' to it.

One more person important to Tom in these years, and for ever afterwards, was the Dorset poet, teacher and scholar William Barnes, the best known of all local worthies at the time of his apprenticeship. Barnes, born on 22 February 1800 (or possibly 1801) at Rush Hay in Blackmore Vale, was, like Tom, self-educated, and, like Gabriel Oak of *Far From the Madding Crowd*, he acquired 'more sound information' by 'diligent perusal' of a few basic books 'than a man of opportunities has done from a furlong of laden shelves'. He did so well at a dame school at Sturminster Newton (two miles from his home) that a solicitor of the town, Thomas Dashwood, was glad to take him on as a clerk. Dashwood, together with several clergymen, and then his next employer, Combe, another solicitor, of Dorchester, helped him with his further education: Latin, Greek, drawing, music. At twenty he had already published, locally, a collection called *Poetical Pieces*.

Two years earlier he had fallen in love with Julia Myles, whose father, Supervisor of Excise at Dorchester, had natural objections to his sixteen-year-old daughter falling in love with a self-educated poet. But Barnes went to Mere in the adjoining county of Wiltshire to take over a failing school, taught there successfully for four years, and in 1827 was able to marry Julia, whose father was by then won over. With her help he turned his establishment into a boarding school for boys and girls, which they ran together until 1835. But, wrote Barnes, 'I always yearned for Dorset and Dorchester': they set up a new school in Durngate Street (1835–37) and then in South Street. Meanwhile, in 1848, Barnes took Holy Orders. In 1851 his Academy, as it was called, was one of 'the largest, and potentially best-equipped, schools in Dorset for the sons of the middle-classes'. Tom was not sent to it because his parents, hardly 'middle-class', could not afford it – and possibly also because it was by then in decline. In June 1852 Julia, the business brains of the family, died; Barnes was devastated (he wrote in his diary of 'days of horror'). In 1862 he was offered the living of Winterborne Came, just a mile out of Dorchester. In 1861 he had received a Literary Pension of £30 a year from the Queen. He died in October 1886.

A gifted engraver on copper, Barnes knew several languages in addition to the classics: Persian, Welsh, Italian, German. After issuing nine collections of his poems, written in both 'National English' and in the 'Dorset Dialect' – the ones which made him famous and loved by such writers and poets as Tennyson, Patmore, Hopkins, Palgrave and of course Tom – he published the collected *Poems of Rural Life, in the Dorset Dialect* (1879), which Tom reviewed in the *Quarterly*. His daughter Lucy, fancied by Tom in the late 1850s, wrote Barnes' *Life* in

1887. In the selection from his poems which Tom edited for Oxford University Press in 1908, he wrote – and his words are significant for the study of his own poetry:

> Primarily spontaneous, he was academic closely after; and we find him warbling his native wood-notes with a watchful eye on the predetermined score, a far remove from the popular impression of him as the naïf and rude bard who sings only because he must, and who submits the uncouth lines of his page to us without knowing how they come there. Goethe never knew better of his; nor Milton; nor, in their rhymes, Poe; nor, in their whimsical alliterations here and there, Langland and the versifiers of the fourteenth and fifteenth centuries.
>
> In his aim of closeness of phrase to his vision he strained at times the capacities of dialect, and went willingly outside the dramatization of peasant talk. Such a lover of the art of expression was this penman of a dialect that had no literature, that on some occasions he would allow art to overpower spontaneity and to cripple inspiration; though, be it remembered, he never tampered with the dialect itself. His ingenious internal rhymes, his subtle juxtaposition of kindred lippings and vowel-sounds [owed in great part to his close study of Welsh versification], show a fastidiousness in word-selection that is surprising in verse which professes to represent the habitual modes of language among the western peasantry . . . By a felicitous instinct he does at times break into sudden irregularities in the midst of his subtle rhythms, as if feeling rebelled at further drill. There his self-consciousness ends, and his naturalness is saved.

There are no more perfect dialect poems in any language than Barnes' at their best, as in 'Trees Be Company', which adapts the internal rhyming techniques from Welsh poetry, of which Barnes had an extensive knowledge, and which ends:

> When dusky night do nearly hide
> The path along the hedge's zide,
> An' dailight's hwomely sounds be still
> But sounds o' water at the mill;
> Then if noo feäce we long'd to greet
>   Could come to meet our lwonesome treäce:
> Or if noo peäce o' weary veet,
>   However fleet, could reach its pleäce –

ARCHITECT'S OFFICE

> However lwonesome we mid be,
> The trees would still be company.

Apart from poetry, he published *A Philological Grammar* (1854), a remarkable *Song of Solomon* in Dorset dialect (1859), and Dorsetshire grammars and glossaries.

Tom and his first wife Emma would often call on the old man in his last years, and Tom's poem about his death, 'The Last Signal', implies both closeness and true love. It was prompted by the glint of the sun on Barnes' coffin which he glimpsed as he walked across the fields to his funeral, and is subscribed 'Winterborne-Came Path':

> Silently I footed by an uphill road
> That led from my abode to a spot yew-boughed;
> Yellowly the sun sloped low down to westward,
> And dark was the east with cloud.
>
> Then, amid the shadow of that livid sad east,
> Where the light was least, and a gate stood wide,
> Something flashed the fire of the sun that was facing it,
> Like a brief breeze on that side.
>
> Looking hard and harder I knew what it meant –
> The sudden shine sent from the livid east scene;
> It meant the west mirrored by the coffin of my friend there,
> Turning to the road from his green,
>
> To take his last journey forth – he who in his prime
> Trudged so many a time from that gate athwart the land!
> Thus a farewell to me he signalled on his grave-way,
> As with a wave of his hand.

The internal rhymes found in Barnes are reproduced here, in tribute to the old man, as is his own method of recollecting landscape by recreating it.

Another friend, this one a year younger than himself, was Hooper Tolbert, who had been one of Barnes' most promising pupils, and was also taken under the wing of Horace Moule. The son of an ironmonger, he had what Tom called 'an extraordinary facility of languages', did well in the Civil Service Examination, and eventually distinguished himself as a Commissioner in the Bengal Civil Service; he died in

1883 aged only forty-one. Tom wrote his obituary in the *Dorset County Chronicle*, noting, with his usual insistence upon truth, that his genius had been 'receptive' rather than 'productive'. He portrayed him as Oswald Winwood in an uncollected story called 'Destiny and a Blue Cloak' (1874), in which Oswald speaks of sweeping away 'bureaucratic jobbery', as doubtless Tolbert, like many another budding civil servant doomed to failure, did. However, in the story, Oswald cannot explain what he means by 'bureaucratic'. He is cheated of his bride-to-be by an illness which prevents him from keeping an appointment.

It has been suggested that the 'wryness' of 'Destiny and a Blue Cloak' is owed to the fact that Tom recollected himself as having been considered the least promising of Horace Moule's pupils. This is unlikely, despite Tolbert's educational successes. There is no evidence that Horace believed anything of the sort, and it is more probable that he was well able to view his two pupils as distinctly different propositions: one as an exam passer and the other as a writer. At all events, Tom remembered his walks with the two men, and of their having 'biased' him 'further in the direction of books'. He certainly began to write, both poems ('Domicilium' at least, but probably more), and some critical essays. His anonymous and facetious skit, significantly a hoax, about a town clock, appeared in the local newspaper, and was therefore his first appearance in print. He rightly never thought fit to mention it again.

Recollecting these early years, in the *Life*, Tom alludes to what must have seemed at the time a bitter disappointment, which may have provoked a mental crisis. He asked Horace, 'a fine Greek scholar', 'if he ought to go on reading some Greek plays':

> Moule's reluctant opinion was that if Hardy really had (as his father had insisted, and as indeed was reasonable, since he had never as yet earned a farthing in his life) to make an income in some way by architecture in 1862, it would be hardly worth while for him to read Aeschylus or Sophocles in 1859–61. He had secretly wished that Moule would advise him to go on with Greek plays, in spite of the serious damage it might do his architecture; but he felt bound to listen to reason and prudence. So, as much Greek as he had got he had to be content with, the language being almost dropped from that date; for though he did take up one or two of the dramatists again some years after, it was in a fragmentary way only. Nevertheless his substantial knowledge of them was not small.

It seems as if Tom at this time was seriously over-working himself, even neglecting his architectural studies. His parents may have been worried, and Horace Moule may have felt bound to offer such advice as he did. He may have discussed the matter with Tom's father. If Tom had impulsively and dramatically presented Horace with his dilemma, as he probably did, then the latter, being himself already under a cloud, would have felt that he had no alternative but to take the prudent line. He may even have felt that Tom was not really cut out to be a success at Oxford or Cambridge, but rather at authorship – he was a prescient man. Nor would he have wanted the formidable Jemima breathing down his neck as a 'bad influence': the man who caused her son to waste years of training.

It has been suggested that Tom 'resented' Horace's advice; but it is more likely that he was simply unhappy about it. What he wrote was:

> It may be permissible to ponder whether Hardy's career might not have been altogether different if Moule's opinion had been the contrary one, and he had advised going on with Greek plays. The younger man would hardly have resisted the suggestion, so strong was his bias that way. The upshot might have been his abandonment of architecture for a University career . . . But it was not to be, and it was possibly better so.

Whatever the exact cast of his feelings, it was probably Horace Moule's opinion, above all, that started Tom thinking about going to London. If it did appear to him as a slight – and much (admittedly) did – then he soon transcended his feelings. Before he finally left for London, Tom did, however, take a decisive step: he left home, lodging in Dorchester in the week and visiting Bockhampton only at the weekends. Bastow had departed for Tasmania, and 'Hardy's duties grew more exacting', although 'in consideration of his immaturity, the term of his pupillage' had, in 1859, 'been lengthened by between one and two years'. Tom investigated the meaning of 'immaturity' in *A Pair of Blue Eyes*, in the persons of Stephen Smith and Elfride Swancourt. He regarded the state as more like what we would call 'being young'. Now perhaps came a time when he felt that he must assert himself. He was doing his best to struggle against acceptance of the judgement of others. By 1860, anyhow, Tom was earning for the first time, fifteen shillings a week, which must have gone some considerable way towards mollifying his feelings. He was designing houses as well as restoring churches, and getting to know the area which he would turn into the fictional Wessex. Much of the work involved 'renovating' old churches in a manner now generally recognized as vulgar, and that Tom would look back on with dislike. 'Much beautiful ancient Gothic, as well as Jacobean and Georgian work, he was passively involved in destroying . . . a matter for deep regret in later years.'

Then, in early 1862, he made an impulsive gesture whose results cast him into despair – and a desire for new beginnings. He had already approached Horace Moule in an impulsive manner on the subject of his future, almost holding a pistol to his head, and now, persuading himself that he was in love, he proposed marriage to a girl whom he barely knew, and who was, moreover, seven years his senior. She was Mary Waight, the daughter of a printer who had moved his family to Dorchester from Wiltshire some time between her birth and 1862.

The story was first told in 1964 by Constance Oliver, Mary Waight's granddaughter, and is likely to be true. Mary was an assistant at the Mantle showroom, 'the best business in the town', and Tom proposed, or at least declared himself, to her. Her initials, 'M' or 'MW', appear in his Bible, prayer book and copy of Keble's *Christian Year*. There are no other details, except the cryptic remark by Constance Oliver that her grandmother was 'always very generous in every way', whereas Tom, 'although kindly and compassionate', 'was not that way inclined'. But that was the undeserved reputation he had locally, and was simply an echo of gossip to the effect that 'old Tom' (as many called him who did not know him) was 'close'; it can have had nothing to do with the circumstances of Mary Waight's rejection of him. Mary Oliver, as she became in 1865 (but her marriage broke down), kept a signed photograph of Tom, which he must have given to her. She promised it to her granddaughter Winifred, but unfortunately it has now disappeared. When Mary Oliver died in 1910, this granddaughter, Mrs Winifred Turner, stole snowdrops from Max Gate 'as she [Mary] had been so very fond of the snowdrop and knowing that Hardy had been fond of her, I thought Max Gate the most suitable place to gather them'. Tom would doubtless not have minded. The father to Constance and Winifred, a hospital dispenser, apparently knew Hardy, and 'often went', wrote Constance, 'usually of a Sunday morning, to Max Gate'.

What are we to make of this? Millgate is sceptical of the whole story; he believes that a family tradition that Tom proposed to a member of it is slender evidence, especially as the photograph has gone missing. It may well be, too, that Tom only spoke of marriage to Mary, and did not propose it. This perhaps became magnified, in the mind of a disappointed woman whose own husband had left her, with a son to care for, to go to America, into an actual proposition from a man who had since become world famous. But the initials in his Bible, and elsewhere, show that the tale has a sound basis. After all, his departure for London on 'Thursday, April 17, 1862', as he exactly noted in the *Life*, does seem to have been somewhat precipitate. He may well have felt that he had made a fool of himself in the eyes of his neighbours, and did not want to stay in Dorchester to be made fun of. However, in the two and a half years before his departure, he had been in an emotionally volatile state. Although he had become physically strong, he was doing too much: morning study, architectural work, drawing and painting, excitedly discussing literature with Hooper Tolbert and Horace Moule, playing the fiddle late at nights, composing poetry. He was thinking too hard, and was assailed by powerful, unwelcome sexual feelings. His decision to leave was sensible.

4

First Visit to London

Although Tom had stayed in London as a boy, on his way to and from his aunt's at Hatfield, he had never gone back there. He was given reminders of it, on first entering Hicks' office, by the antics of a young clerk, aptly named Fippard, who had whistled quadrille tunes and recounted his London experiences at the Argyll and the Cremorne, both haunts of tarts as well as places of dancing and music. Now, in April 1862, suddenly as it must have seemed, he was in London, alone, armed only with two letters and a little money. One letter was from what he called a 'gushing lady' to an ex-pupil of the famous elder Pugin, Benjamin Ferrey. The other was to John Norton, an architect of Bond Street and an old friend of Hicks. Tom visited Ferrey, who did nothing for him; but Norton, although not in need of an assistant, allowed him to work in his office for a 'nominal remuneration' while he looked around. He found lodgings with a family at 3 Clarence Place, Kilburn, in north-west London, immediately sought out the local church, St Mary's, and, significantly as to his state of mind, became a regular worshipper there.

He was soon lucky in finding a job, although, as he characteristically noted, he 'never forgot' Norton's kindness. Arthur Blomfield, who had opened his offices, at 8 St Martin's Place, six years previously, was in need of a 'young Gothic draughtsman who could restore and design churches and rectory-houses'; the salary was £110 a year, which was good compared to the average earned by an experienced top tradesman, say a glass-worker's, which had reached only £91 by 1867.

Arthur William Blomfield, knighted in 1889 and whose buildings include Sion College Library on the Embankment and Queen's School at Eton, was only eleven years Tom's senior. He was the son of Charles James Blomfield (1786–1856), Bishop of Chester and then of London (1828), who was inconsistent in his churchmanship and given to wavering on certain points such as the Reform Bill, but was a well-reputed classical scholar, and editor of Aeschylus, Euripides and other Greek writers. Arthur, educated at Rugby (for a year or two under Arnold himself), and then, like his father, at Trinity College, Cambridge, was a cultivated man with literary interests. Again Tom was fortunate, and he would remain on excellent terms with Blomfield until the latter's death in 1899.

He has been seen at this time as 'unprepossessing', countrified, and 'sadly lacking in worldly experience and social assurance'. But then so were (and are) almost all other young people in his position. He still had the return-half of his ticket in his pocket. But he rapidly established himself in London, which has been seen as 'quite remarkable'. However, this is only remarkable if one views him as 'sadly' wanting in most qualities. Tom may have been countrified, but he was no country bumpkin, as he has been made out to be by Millgate. He carried with him an iron determination to succeed, and it is clear that those to whom he introduced himself, and who were to be useful to him, liked him. His social accomplishments cannot have been all that poor. And he was qualified in his profession.

He was by no means nothing, then, when he arrived in London, and there is no evidence beyond bland – and partly snobbish – speculation that he did not have some sense of inner security, strengthened no doubt at this time both by the seriousness with which he took his Christianity and by his qualifications. The difficulties Tom experienced through his feelings of inferiority to those better educated than himself have been much exaggerated. More important was his private confidence in his abilities, and his determination to acquire sufficient knowledge to give himself, above all, an understanding of his subjects. The use of allusion in his work, especially in his earlier work, has aroused patronizing comment. But granted that some of his allusions to paintings are self-conscious, and demonstrate a desire to be regarded as an educated man rather than a 'house decorator' (the alleged profession of the author of *Far From the Madding Crowd*), his use of allusions, for the most part, is appropriate, and works as a technical method.

In these first few months in London he fell back on his sister Mary, to whom he confided, and joked, in frequent letters, six of which he kept. Some of these have brief passages scored through: all in the interests of protecting his father from any notion that Tom and Mary thought him a figure of fun, as distinct from having affectionate knowledge of his ways. Mary visited Tom in London in late July or early August 1862, before returning to Salisbury to begin her last year of teacher training. A few days later, on 17 August, he wrote to her in what is his first preserved letter. He began by telling her how he had attended St Mary's on Sunday, saying that the church was 'rather to my taste': 'they sing most of the tunes in the Salisbury hymn book here'. Then he described a visit from Horace Moule, 'the week before last':

> HMM was up . . . We went to a Roman Catholic Chapel on the Thursday evening. It was a very impressive service. The Chapel was built by Pugin [the Jesuit Chapel in Farm Street]. Afterwards we took a cab to Old Hummums, an hotel near Covent Garden where we had supper. He may come and settle permanently in London in a few months, but is not certain yet.

What did the two talk about, and why did they go to this service celebrating the restoration of the Society of Jesus? Since Henry Moule was, as an Evangelical, at least suspicious of Roman Catholicism, and in particular of Jesuits, it seems likely enough that Horace was chafing at the bit, wanting to find out for himself what each aspect of Christianity had to offer.

Thoughts of getting into literary society must have been remote to Tom in 1862, although he excelled in the new company in which he found himself, and did not shrink from expressing himself. He shared rooms with another young architect called Shaw, who read aloud to him from Ruskin, not to his unalloyed pleasure, since it seems (he told Mary) that he was required to make intelligent comment on what he heard. Blomfield's assistants at the time Tom joined him were, he said, 'Tory and churchy'; following the move to 'more commodious and lighter' premises at Adelphi Terrace in February 1863, they used to tease the officials of the Reform League, which had the ground-floor lease at that time. The atmosphere at the office was as merry and as easy-going as it had been at Hicks', but there were many more assistants. Tom certainly learned much more about life from there than he had ever heard of in Dorchester, Fippard notwithstanding. But what was this London of the early 1860s like?

In the first place, lethal though living conditions in Dorchester could be – as Henry Moule's letters to Prince Albert testify – they were as nothing compared to London, although the contrast between town and country could still be seen in the latter, as for example in Kilburn, which was only semi-urban. Diseases caused by filth were rife, although the serious efforts to eliminate them, eventually to pay off, had already begun. Foundations of public health were being laid. Cholera vanished after 1867, and the death rate began to decline; but mortality rates still remained very high during Hardy's decade in London, and infant mortality did not start to fall until 1900. London was a dangerous place in other ways: on 10 March 1863, going to see the 'illuminations on the occasion of the Prince of Wales's marriage', Tom had his waistcoat torn off and ribs crushed at the bottom of Bond Street; six were killed that night, at the Mansion House.

Tom was acutely sensitive to what he saw around him, although he had a sense of humour to temper his pain. He devotes several pages of the *Life* to a description of this London of the 1860s, memories of whose better aspects were always precious to him because, as he said, 'it differed greatly from the London of even a short time after'. It was a very rapidly expanding city, of whose overcrowded slums even such cocky young men as worked at Blomfield's were probably, quite literally, afraid. Society, wrote Dr John Simon in his *Second Sanitary Report to the City of London* (1850), averted her eyes to that 'deadlier presence' than 'pestilence' which stalked the expanding population, 'blighting the moral existence . . . rendering their hearts hopeless, their acts ruffianly and incestuous; and scattering . . . the retributive seeds of increase for crime, turbulence and pauperism'. Tom's young companions, possibly even Blomfield himself – for all that his father had been a leading light, in the East End, to recover the ground the Anglican Church had lost – had little idea what the inside of a slum was like. These unexplored areas lay just behind respectable façades, and their condition was, during this period, getting worse. Almost 60,000 people were displaced by the railways in the thirty years after 1853. Tom did not fail to be aware of the contrast offered between absolute poverty and grandiose opulence.

This was 'the London of Dickens and Thackeray' and the 'ladies talked about by the architects' pupils and other young men into whose society Hardy was thrown were Cora Pearl, "Skittles", Agnes Willoughby, Adah Isaacs Menken and others successively, of whom they professed to know many romantic and *risqué* details but really knew nothing at all'. Of course these well-educated young men talked about everything '*risqué*', about everything to do with sex, and Tom listened.

He must have worked hard for Blomfield, for the latter had no hesitation in proposing him, only six months after he had joined the firm, for membership of the Architectural Association. On 3 November 1862 Tom wrote to Mary to tell her about the 'conversazione' held there on the previous Friday night: 'about 300, or 400 present, including your humble servant', and 'lots of speechifying from learned professors', with which he was unimpressed. He included a tiny humorous drawing of himself wearing the dress-coat that his fellow lodger, the architect Shaw, had lent him for the occasion of the 'conversazione' – and he suggests that he might bring his benefactor down to Dorset: 'It wd. be good fun, he is such a "coddle" [hypochondriac] and wd. enjoy the outing. He wd. be considered a great gun too in our parish.' He also described a visit from his father to London, where they both met an unidentified friend of the family, possibly one of Mary's former classmates, 'Miss A' – in service in the city; Tom had taken them to the 'opera of *Lurline* at Covent Garden'. His father 'went to the top of the Monument (200 feet) "just to pass away the time". He said he shd. not have gone only "she zid a lot of others be gone afore?".' Tom (and Mary) spoke that dialect language to family and local friends, but this passage, out of respect and fear of misunderstanding, is inked over. Tom told Mary, too, to keep copies of the *Saturday Review* which he had sent her, in case he should want them – which showed that he wanted to share them with her, and in particular, no doubt, Horace Moule's regular contributions.

Just after the office move to Adelphi Terrace he wrote to Mary again, on 19 February, and mentioned that he was 'busy getting up a design for a Country Mansion for which a small prize is offered'. That he was awarded the Silver Medal of the Royal Institute of British Architects, for an essay, and the Tite Prize for this design, is testimony to how well he was progressing. It is true that the Institute thought fit to withhold the usual accompanying sum of £10 that went with the essay, owing to certain shortcomings in it; but, even if considerably irritated by this, Tom had the satisfaction of knowing that no entrant had been better.

There are no more surviving letters from him until the end of that year, when, on 19 December, he wrote to Mary again, making some interesting remarks about Oxford and Thackeray. Mary was by then teaching at the National School at Denchurch in Berkshire, only a short distance from Oxford. Although she had received the drawing prize from her college, she must have complained to Tom that she felt divorced from 'art', for he tells her:

I am glad you have been to Oxford again. It must be a jolly place. I shall try to get down there some time or other. You have no right to say you are not connected with art. Everybody is, to a certain extent; the only difference between a profesor [sic] and an amateur being that the former has the (often disagreeable) necessity of making it his means of bread and cheese – and thus often rendering what is a pleasure to other people a 'bore' to himself.

This shows that Tom was already forming distinct ideas of his own, including a few that would not please certain of his future biographers. There is no contempt shown for 'professors', but no conventional awe of them, either. He already recognizes the dangers of the academic life. What follows also displays some independence of mind, and suggests, again, the direction he would later, not at all unaggressively, take:

About Thackeray. You must read something of his. He is considered to be the greatest novelist of the day – looking at novel writing of the highest kind as a perfect and truthful representation of actual life – which is no doubt the proper view to take. Hence, because his novels stand so high as works of Art or Truth, they have anything but an elevating tendency, and on this account are unfitted for young people – from their very truthfulness. People say that it is beyond Mr Thackeray to paint a perfect man or woman – a great fault if novels are intended to instruct, but just the opposite if they are to be considered merely as Pictures. *Vanity Fair* is considered one of his best.

Hardy was plainly implying that novels are best when they are 'merely . . . Pictures', and pointing to the irony that truth is considered bad for the young. More than a decade would pass before he wrote his own farcical variation on the Becky Sharp theme, in his weakest book, *The Hand of Ethelberta*, whose anti-heroine is a kind of philanthropic Becky who sells out – indeed, prostitutes herself to an old man – for money and position. But even in his 1863 letter to Mary he was starting to struggle free from the sort of conventional pseudo-morality which eschews reality, and which can therefore be nothing but ineffective.

Although Tom worked hard, there is nothing to suggest, as Millgate has asserted, that he 'deliberately shunned the more garish aspects of the city's night life, with its teeming crowds, its casual violence, and its open and even aggressive prostitution'. Certainly, he did not write to his sister Mary about such a side of his life – it would be extraordinary had he done so. What is known is that he heard Dickens in 1863, attended Palmerston's funeral in 1865, sang in the office choir, danced at Willis's Rooms, and possibly at the Cremorne and at the Argyll. Had he been an average young Victorian male he would have visited a prostitute or prostitutes, or had an affair with a woman (or women) 'of easy virtue' (they were two a penny, and his office chums would have known where to find them) – but he was hardly average in anything. However, he has struck his readers, if not all his biographers, as sexually experienced, and it is possible that he did obtain his first sexual experience in this way; if so, as a highly sensitive young man, he was likely to be left dissatisfied, and disgusted with himself.

It may have been under the tutelage of Horace Moule, an accomplished musician, that Tom went to hear such famous contemporary singers as Mario, Tietjens, Patti and Parepa, and operas by, among others, Rossini, Verdi and Bellini. He was touched – almost to tears he said – by the collapse of the voice of the singer William Harrison: he thought that his 'courage in struggling on, hoping against hope, might probably cause him to be remembered longer than his greatest success'. This notion always fascinated him, and later he would write: 'I prefer late Wagner, as I prefer late Turner, to early . . . When a man not contented with the grounds of his success goes on alone, and tries to achieve the impossible, then he gets profoundly interesting to me.' He himself did precisely that: tried, as one who regarded fiction writing as inferior to the pursuit of poetry, to achieve the impossible.

The good-humoured banter in the office with his more sophisticated young companions – their regular opening question was 'Any spice in the papers?' – would have taught him about anything that he did not already know. Certainly, for example, he would have learned about the existence of lesbianism, although almost all Hardy critics have assumed he knew nothing of it. Only a few years later he would write the lesbian episode in *Desperate Remedies*, and it is also possible that he could have discussed the subject with Horace Moule. He had yet to make his way as a writer, but he was reading widely and deeply, and talking with sophisticated people all the time.

As he tells us, after some eighteen months of architectural work he became bored. He felt that 'architectural drawing in which the actual designing had no great part was monotonous and mechanical', and, 'having besides little inclination to pushing his way into influential sets which would help him to start a practice of his own' – i.e. he was already not really enthusiastic about architecture as a career, even though it seemed all that was open to him at that time – 'Hardy's tastes reverted to the literary pursuits that he had been compelled to abandon', and 'by as early as 1863 he had recommended to read a good deal, with a growing tendency towards poetry'. The extent of the reading course which Tom now set himself – for such it must have been, given the wide-ranging allusiveness of his fiction – is easy to underestimate. Despite his lack of a university education, by the time of his flowering as a novelist, after *Far From the Madding Crowd*, he had become one of the best read writers of his generation.

He must have talked about his own doubts as to the course he was taking ('forced to consider ways and means') and about his aspirations towards poetry, because someone suggested to him that he might 'combine literature with architecture by becoming an art-critic for the press'. In the *Life*, he writes:

> It is probable that he might easily have carried this out, reviewers with a speciality being then, and possibly now, in demand. His preparations for such a course were, however, quickly abandoned, and by 1865 he had begun to write verses, and by 1866 to send his productions to magazines. That these were rejected by editors, and that he paid such respect to their judgement as scarcely ever to send out a MS twice, was in one feature fortunate for him, since in years long after he was able to examine those poems of which he kept copies, and by the mere change of a few words or the rewriting of a line or two to make them quite worthy of publication. Such of them as are dated in these years were all written in his lodgings at 16 Westbourne Park Villas [whither he had moved from Clarence Place in mid-1863]. He also began turning the Book of Ecclesiastes into Spenserian stanzas, but finding the original unmatchable abandoned the task.

Those who think that Tom's aspirations to be a poet had not hardened into a fierce determination by the time he was twenty-five ought to be convinced by the Spenserian exercise: for any young poet doubtful of his ear, there is no better teacher, or remedy, than Spenser. Tom would, he says, address his office companions on 'poets and poetry' 'on afternoons when there was not much to be done'; one of them remembered him as quiet, gentle, 'rather dreamy', but talkative enough on literary subjects. Even if he kept his inner conflicts and depressions to himself, he was not afraid to put himself forward when he wanted to. He was now, in 1865, writing poetry, and from what he allowed to survive, his genius was already apparent. This genius, however untutored and in need of Spenserian reinforcement, was apparent to him, too. By the mid-1860s, he was coming into a period of acute crisis, not least because he could not formulate the right plan of action for himself. Michael Millgate feels that he participated in the work for Blomfield only so far as he had to, but scrupulously draws attention to the view of Dr C.J.P. Beaty, the leading authority on Hardy as architect, who believes that he was 'more active and creative'. And Tom did indeed do rather better as an architect than Millgate allows, even though, as Millgate emphasizes, his heart was not in it. His drawing was pleasant, and he used both it and his knowledge of architecture as a marvellous adjunct to his literary work, particularly in the manner in which he employed the grotesque in his poetry. In architecture itself, though, he was not original; Max Gate itself is a typical villa of its period. None the less, Tom's competence as an architect was, as Beaty's studies suggest, high.

Although he makes no mention of it in the *Life*, Tom at this critical time was in love. (To have referred to this, for a man of his truthful and candid nature, would have meant going into the kind of detail which he could well manage in fiction and poetry, but which would have been impossible in an official biography 'by' his second wife.) Millgate (following Purdy) discovered that the woman with whom he was involved, for some substantial time at least, was Eliza Nicholls. Before the Millgate biography, it was thought that his acquaintance with a woman referred to his cousin Martha Sparks, who, like her brothers Nathaniel and James, was living in London as a servant. Martha started at Paddington, but then got a better job, as an upper servant, with a family in Kensington; she went to France with them, and learned French. Tom did indeed see something of Martha – it would have been peculiar if he had not, since she was 'family'; he certainly went with her to the International Exhibition in August 1863, and he took in all that she told him about matters 'above stairs'. He may even have 'fancied her' for a time; but it is now quite evident that she was not for long, if ever, the object of his main affections. The statement by her brother Nathaniel that Tom had wanted to marry her (it specifies no time), and that her mother put a stop to the notion, ought to be taken with at least a pinch of salt – not because the Sparkses were untruthful but because, as the years pass, speculations become certainties, particularly when concerning famous people. There is nothing to substantiate the claim (no initials in the Bible or the prayer book or his copy of Keble).

Millgate believes that Tom was 'more or less formally engaged from 1863 until 1867' to Eliza Nicholls. The notion of a formal engagement may be an exaggeration, but the early love poems certainly deal with his experiences with, and of, her. She was the daughter of a Cornish coastguard who had worked at Kimmeridge, on the Dorset coast between Swanage and West Lulworth, where Tom must first have met her. In 1863 her father was living at Findon, a few miles north of Worthing in West Sussex; she was in service as a lady's maid at the house of a barrister who lived near Westbourne Park Villas. Possibly this was a factor in Tom's move there, in mid-1863, from Clarence Place. Millgate has shown that the building in Hardy's drawing opposite the 'She to Him' series of poems in *Wessex Poems* is Clavel Tower, which stands on the cliff-top on the eastern side of Kimmeridge Bay. Eliza left Tom's district some time in late 1863 to nurse another member of the Hoare family, and seems, after this person's death in January 1865, not to have returned there, but to have joined her father at Findon. Tom certainly went to see her on several occasions, and even (according to Millgate) came to prefer her younger sister, Mary Jane, to her.

Millgate convincingly identifies the setting of the poem 'Neutral Tones' with the 'now dried-up pond surrounded by old lime-kilns on the ridge overlooking Tolmare farm, just west of Findon'. It is, however, impossible to reconstruct the course of their affair with any confidence. Millgate uses only the evidence of 'Neutral Tones', which was written after it was over:

> We stood by a pond that winter day,
> And the sun was white, as though chidden of God,
> And a few leaves lay on the starving sod;
>   – They had fallen from an ash, and were gray.
>
> Your eyes on me were as eyes that rove
> Over tedious riddles of years ago;
> And some words played between us to and fro
>   On which lost the more by our love.
>
> The smile on your mouth was the deadest thing
> Alive enough to have strength to die;
> And a grin of bitterness swept thereby
>   Like an ominous bird a-wing . . .
>
> Since then, keen lessons that love deceives,
> And wrings with wrong, have shaped to me
> Your face, and the God-curst sun, and a tree,
>   And a pond edged with grayish leaves.

Later, on 13 July 1876, Tom would write (and think worthy of recording in the *Life*): 'The sudden disappointment of a hope leaves a

scar which the ultimate fulfilment of that hope never entirely removes.'
This does not of course necessarily refer to Eliza Nicholls; there may
well have been other women in his life – of whom he successfully
removed all trace. He was susceptible, and probably willing to interpret
(or misinterpret) every signal he received or thought he received from
women. But his early poems, many (too many, he later thought) of
which he destroyed, confirm that he fell in love.

Before he began to write these poems, Tom set himself the formidable
task of learning how to do so. He bought himself virtually all the English
poets, and also Walker's *Rhyming Dictionary*, to which he made extensive
additions of his own – additions which show his independence of mind.
It is as if he was aware of his destiny, but determined none the less to
prepare himself properly for it. Perhaps, like Kipling after him, he felt
that he had to play the cards he had been dealt, but this was also a matter
of playing the hand well, which in its turn meant playing it for 'truth'
– as he was not frightened to call it. Certainly his feelings should not
be confused with any kind of prophetic grandiosity such as Gittings
attributes to him. Millgate, on the other hand, emphasizes Hardy's 'lack
of self-confidence'. Tom, however, was not an immodest man; he was
a highly conscientious one, who suffered less from self-confidence than
acute anxiety about his capacity to do justice to his own genius. He
worried, too, about his capacity to endure the sufferings inherent in
being a poet: he could not, rightly, envisage his means to do so. This
offers the key to his lifelong, never abandoned, wish to be a poet rather
than a purveyor of fiction.

What he preserved of his early poetry is, with a few exceptions,
supremely confident as youthful poetry – even to the point of its
obscurities, which are, after all, characteristic of his later practice.
Few of the poems are literary exercises, though some are overweighted
with literary diction, mostly derived from Shakespeare, whose works he
bought in a ten-volume edition in 1863. He was also influenced by the
George Meredith of *Modern Love* (1862), but Meredith, too, was much
(too much) influenced by Shakespeare.

If hard evidence is required of Tom's intensive and above all thorough
preparations for a career in literature, then it is provided by one of his
earliest notes – if one may call an elaborately annotated drawing a
note – which is entitled 'Diagram shewing Human Passion, Mind &
Character – Designed by Thos Hardy, 1863'. The scheme is derived
from the writings of the French Utopian socialist François Marie Charles
Fourier, and the design was very probably undertaken when he was still

determined to be a poet, and only a poet. A poet, in his view, was obliged to be well enough versed in the philosophy of his age to be able to express it. He was throughout his life resentful when he felt that his intellectual background was brought into question. This was undoubtedly a consequence of his extreme sensitivity, but it is also indicative of the great difficulties then faced by any writer who lacked a university background. Since all women were subject to this lack, it may well have put him into even stronger sympathy with them.

Fourier (1772–1837), a Lyons businessman and 'bizarre genius' who eventually settled in Paris, is not in the mainstream of sociology, which was in any case virtually founded (and named) by his younger contemporary Comte; but he has had a powerful influence on all thinking of a libertarian strain. It is not surprising that he inspired André Breton, the founder of surrealism, to a long ode. His three main works, published respectively in 1808, 1822 and 1829–30, would have proved too tough for Tom in the original French, since he did not complete his study of that language until 1865; but he read a translation from Fourier by John Reynell Morell, *The Passions of the Human Soul*, published in 1851; this contained annotations, a biography and an introduction. Tom was less likely to have been interested in the details of Fourier's methods of social reform, which involved the division of humanity into *phalanstères* (phalanxes) each of about 1,800 members, than in the reasons underlying them. In his theories Fourier tried to allow for all individual inclinations and 'passions', and to combine them 'scientifically', in the French manner, to produce a Utopia. The organization of the phalanxes encouraged work for passion, rather than for profit: each person would avoid what he did not like, and would perform tasks which fulfilled him.

Fourier's writings and personal influence led to a number of practical experiments, all of which failed or simply, as in America under the inspiration of Josiah Warren, faded away. His scheme worked well on paper, and he did not avoid such burning questions as what to do with lazy and selfish people, and who was to do filthy work, which led to much valuable discussion. Marx disapproved of Fourier because, among other things, while most material goods were commonly owned in his phalanxes, he made provision for some private property – one example of an inequality he believed had to be preserved in order to bring out full human potential. But Marx felt obliged to read him and to answer him; and the anarchisms of Proudhon and Warren were largely evolved through criticism of him.

During the early 1860s Tom was markedly idealistic, for all his tendency towards emotional gloom. He was deeply interested in the reasons for human misery, and therefore in proposals for avoiding them. Fourier had decided that since the creator was benevolent (a proposition with which Tom came to disagree), his human creatures had failed to carry out his plan. The details of this plan he proceeded to supply. It was his account of those passions which had been repressed that intrigued Tom. His painstaking diagram of 1863 – marked 'Fourier' – shows a most remarkable grasp of them, and of their organization. He was fascinated by Fourier's broadly Rousseauist (and proto-Freudian) notion that the passions essential to humanity had been repressed by civilization. When they were released, civilization and the greed attendant upon it would be replaced by harmony – in itself the crowning passion which synthesizes the rest – and self-realization. Tom was also interested in, and shared, Fourier's indignation about man's misuse of his resources: why, asked Fourier, should an apple centuple its value between the time it came off the tree and when it ended up on the table of a fashionable restaurant? Much of the book Tom read dealt with agricultural as well as economic reform.

Fourier divided the universe into four categories: society, animal life, organic life and materiality. He believed that, along with harmony, there were twelve passions: the five senses (individual), ambition, friendship, love, familism or family feeling (group) – and three more under the rubric of 'series', or 'distributive', namely, intrigue, diversification and combination. Tom represents in his diagram, which must have taken him several days to complete, Fourier's notion of life as peaking at the age of nineteen and again at twenty-six, then settling into a sharp decline after forty. He includes, too, Fourier's three 'abstract principles', which are Nature, God and Justice. Nature is passive, and embraces the five senses; God is active and embraces the 'group' feelings; Justice is a neutral or reconciling force which embraces the so-called 'distributive passions'.

Tom thought it worth including in his literary notebooks a brief passage from an article in an 1877 number of the *Fortnightly Review*: 'French thinkers "fall, as regards society & government, into the error against which Bacon warned physical investigators, of supposing in nature a greater simplicity than is found there".' This suggests that he might later have come to distrust Fourier's analysis on the grounds that, like all French thinkers, including Comte, he tended to oversimplify. But he never forgot what he had absorbed from Fourier; this was not his politics, but the psychological system upon which he based them. Indeed, since, unlike the Comtean philosophy – in which Tom also became interested – Fourier's particular system is far from simple, it might be that he would have absolved Fourier from the blanket judgement of the *Fortnightly Review* writer. Tom did not begin his literary notebooks until 1876, the year in which he set out to refine his self-education; yet he had carefully preserved his Fourier diagram from thirteen years earlier, and put it at the very beginning. The gesture is unlikely to have been mere sentiment, because he was still writing about Fourier in a notebook he kept while he was writing *The Trumpet Major* (1880). His view of the creator came to be at variance with Fourier's, but he retained his interest in the 'passions', and in the notion of the conflict between them and the intellect. This is shown in his diagram, dominates *Jude*, and is a main theme of *The Dynasts*.

Exactly when Tom abandoned the idea of making a living out of poetry is unknown. There is no reason to doubt his retrospective assertion that he 'never did much care about publication' of poems. Even in the 1860s he was determined that any gesture he made should have a 'kind of purity' (as Millgate puts it). The 'sense of the truth of poetry, of its supreme place in literature, had awakened itself in me,' Tom wrote. 'At the risk of ruining all my worldly prospects I dabbled in it . . .' In his 'lectures' to his young companions in Blomfield's office he would invariably put the poets first, dismissing even Dickens (whom he admired) as small by comparison. Meanwhile, he received £3.15s. for a fictitious article in *Chambers Journal* (18 March 1865) called 'How I Built Myself a House'; it was a reasonably skilful exercise in Dickensian humour exploiting the sort of banter that went on amongst Blomfield's employees – for whose amusement he originally wrote it. This publication may have encouraged him in the direction of prose, or he may have remembered the cheque from Chambers two years later when he decided to become a novelist. But until 1866 he retained an idea of taking a degree at Cambridge and then of becoming a country parson, while also writing poetry. As he put it:

About this time Hardy nourished a scheme of a highly visionary character. He perceived from the impossibility of getting his verses accepted by magazines that he could not live by poetry, and (rather strangely) thought that architecture and poetry – particularly architecture in London – would not work well together. So he formed the idea of combining poetry and the Church – towards which he had long had a leaning – and wrote to a friend in Cambridge [Moule] for particulars . . . He knew that what money he could not muster himself for keeping terms his father would lend him for a few years, his idea being that of the curacy in a country village. This fell through less because of its difficulty than from a conscientious feeling, after some theological study, that he could hardly take the step with honour while holding the views which on examination he found himself to hold. And so he allowed the curious scheme to drift out of sight, though not till he had begun to practise orthodoxy. For example:

'July 5. Sunday. To Westminster Abbey morning service. Stayed to the Sacrament. A very odd experience, amid a crowd of strangers'.

In a note dated 2 July 1865 in the *Life* he wrote of working 'at J.H. Newman's Apologia . . . A great desire to be convinced by him, because Moule likes him so much.' This has been misread as an over-dependence on Moule, but it implies the opposite: it confirms his great affection for Moule, and proclaims his intellectual independence. When he began his literary notebooks, initially a re-working of the ground he had gone over in the 1860s ('Read again Addison, Macaulay, Newman . . . in a study of style' as he put it in his note of March 1875), he followed the Fourier diagram with quotes from Newman's *Apologia*. One of them, which must have caused him some thought in 1865 on his first reading, is: 'The notion that my calling in life wd require such a sacrifice as celibacy is involved . . . strengthened by a feeling of separation from the visible world.'

Perhaps he equated Newman's feelings with an idea of his own calling as a poet, for if he abandoned architecture for poetry, he could never afford to get married. 'Revulsion', dated 1866, records that 'Out of the night there looms a sense 'twere better/To fail obtaining whom one fails to miss'. And he told the publisher V.H. Collins, late in his life, that the 'bird' in 'Postponement', also 1866, 'is described as not being able to marry for want of money'.

When Cambridge offered him an honorary degree in 1913 his sister Mary reminded him of what he had written to her in 1866, by transcribing this passage:

H.M.M. [Horace Moule] has sent me the Students' Guide to the U. of C. I find on adding up expenses and taking into consideration the time I should have to wait, that my notion is too far fetched to be worth entertaining any longer. To look forward 3 years under any circumstances is dreary enough, but when the end of that time only brings with it commencement of another 3 years (time of residence at C) and that then almost another year will be taken up in getting a title . . . it seems absurd to live on now with such a remote objective in view.

If marriage was one of his worries in such a future, it seems that it was less the practicality of marrying Eliza Nicholls that stopped him than that he simply tired of her. If he was tactless in his determination to be honest about his feelings, and being inexperienced in human affairs he probably was, then he tried to compensate for that, and for his sense of guilt (and perhaps of bewilderment at the way in which desire flows and then ebbs), by speculating on her feelings in the 'She to Him' series of poems, only four of which he preserved. Possibly the affair was never quite as serious for him as it was for her, but it is clear enough from the four surviving poems that he felt guilt at having raised her expectations, which were doubtless much more conventional than his own. 'Neutral Tones' does not seem to refer to any feelings of loss on his part; it implies only that he has had cause (perhaps), by now, to know what deceit does to a lover – has learned it from another whom he loved.

That he considered himself to have been a false lover does not mean that this is how he should be considered, or that he himself, retrospectively, believed in that interpretation. He was interested in achieving psychological truth, but not in leaving clues for biographers.

He was, in this period, in a highly emotional state. He was confronted with evidence of his own genius, and did not know what to do about it. A poem about Horace, dated 1866, called 'A Confession to a Friend in Trouble', but entitled in the manuscript 'To a Friend in Trouble (a confession of selfishness)', is extraordinary for its time. No wonder, one feels, that the unknown editors to whom he sent it, and other poems, were unanimous in their refusal. Published, they would have seemed, in the mid-1860s, odd indeed.

A few years earlier, in 1854, W.E. Aytoun had put paid to the so-called Spasmodic School (the extravagant and 'Gothic' poets, Alexander Smith, P.J. Bailey, Sidney Dobell and others) with his much discussed parody *Firmilian*, which ridiculed the school's violence and deliberate obscurity. The new decade was dominated by Tennyson and, for the more daring, Hardy's own beloved Swinburne. Nothing resembling Tom's sharp, psychologically exact and self-punishing poems appeared during it. Browning had not recovered from the critical disaster of *Sordello*, which had appeared in the year of Hardy's birth, and was still an acquired taste; he was the sort of poet whose *Men and Women* (1855), *Dramatis Personae* (1864) and *The Ring and the Book* (1868) Horace would have carefully read and discussed with his friend, to whom he doubtless read aloud most of his favourites. But those of Hardy's early poems that are known to us do not resemble Browning's or even Swinburne's, let alone Tennyson's (from whom he would be, however, fond of quoting in his novels, especially *A Pair of Blue Eyes*).

Hardy in 'A Confession' had learned most of all from the plain, direct voice of the Shakespeare of the *Sonnets*; and into Victorian poetry he was introducing a new note of absolute sincerity and psychological exactitude, a painstaking clarity. It was an awkward, uncomfortable note in its time, the sort of thing that a more artificial poet could believe beneath him and his rhetorical duties. The average Victorian reader – and editor – might well feel such a 'confession' both morbid and unnecessarily negative. So the poem was in effect suppressed:

> Your troubles shrink not, though I feel them less
> Here, far away, than when I tarried near;
> I even smile old smiles – with listlessness –
> Yet smiles they are, not ghastly mockeries mere.
>
> A thought too strange to house within my brain
> Haunting its outer precincts I discern:
> – *That I will not show zeal again to learn*
> *Your griefs, and, sharing them, renew my pain* . . .
>
> It goes, like murky bird or buccaneer
> That shapes its lawless figure on the main,
> And staunchness tends to banish utterly
> The unseemly instinct that had lodgment here:
> Yet, comrade old, can bitterer knowledge be
> Than that, though banned, such instinct was in me!

Despite its verbal awkwardness, it is an astonishing confession for its time. It remains exemplary for our own. Here is a man who, far from being callous or unheeding (as he has been called), means what he says, and wants only to say what he means. He spurns falsity, searches for genuine compassion, and blames himself for being unable to find it.

Poetry, like religion, is not susceptible to the 'scientific' method, whose proponents usually do not want, for all that, to assert that it is therefore 'untrue'. It is all that the private person has left that is mysterious, and his poem 'Hap' of this period, in which the Doomsters are encountered, demonstrates that Tom already understood this strange quality of poetry, even if he still felt himself lost:

> If but some vengeful god would call to me
> From up the sky, and laugh: 'Thou suffering thing,
> Know that thy sorrow is my ecstasy,
> That thy love's loss is my hate's profiting!'
>
> Then would I bear it, clench myself, and die,
> Steeled by the sense of ire unmerited;
> Half-eased in that a Powerfuller than I
> Had willed and meted me the tears I shed.
>
> But not so. How arrives it joy lies slain,
> And why unblooms the best hope ever sown?
> – Crass Casualty obstructs the sun and rain,
> And dicing Time for gladness casts a moan . . .
> These purblind Doomsters had as readily strown
> Blisses about my pilgrimage as pain.

He wrote in his copy of Reed's *Introduction to English Literature* (bought in 1865) that he felt 'feeble' in the 'presence of a vast concourse of books'. He was, too, practising 'orthodoxy': for one side of him, the emotional, was (and always would be) in need of religious ritual. Yet the picture of 'God' in 'Hap' is already distinctly non-Christian – offensive to the orthodox clergyman of Tom's own time and place. Commentators have been keen to establish that Tom acquired this view of God from Darwin, who, on hearing of Alfred Russell Wallace's work, had hastily abridged and issued his own, as *The Origin of Species*, in 1859. But, while Tom must have been impressed, his notion of an indifferent (i.e. non-benevolent) deity was essentially his own, the result of his temperament, formed around his pre-Darwinian understanding of Aeschylus: 'The world does not despise us; it only neglects us,' he wrote in May 1865, but surely thinking back to the time when he had first studied Aeschylus.

Tom's moments of 'self-reproach' have been described as 'sullen', but they were worth more than that. For example, the sentiment expressed in 'Hap' is not 'resentful'; it is simply the honest record of an 'impression'. He saw that a poet, to do justice to his own calling, has first to understand and accept what kind of human instrument he is: not to strain the odds, as he felt Browning did on occasion, by practising false optimism. An impression for him was an exact moment in the autobiographical record. That is all, which is a great deal.

Aeschylus' words 'Things are as they are, and will be brought to their destined issue' (*Agamemnon*) impinged themselves upon him early. But for the time being the destined issue was confusing, and the more so as the scales fell from his eyes in London, and he realized that he had no intellectual faith in the Christian God as the Church represented him. When he came to look conscientiously at the assumptions that had been formed in him by the circumstances of his childhood, by his mother's faith, by Henry Moule, by Bastow, there was nothing there, no philosophical conviction. However, inner moments revealed a situation that was more complicated (he was to quote Goethe, in Arnold's version, in his literary notes: 'as man must live from within outwards, so the artist must work from within outwards, seeing that make what contortions he will, he can only bring to light his own individuality'). Meanwhile, it was necessary to try to live. No wonder he later wrote to Edmund Gosse, on 30 August 1887, of how often he had 'in bygone years . . . gone to bed wishing never to see daylight again'. This was his version of what has been called 'creative illness'; the 'aloofness' of manner of which he speaks – he was not 'shy in the ordinary sense', he tells us – may have been a part of this.

But for all his natural reticence, he could not live without candour. 'The Fire at Tranter Sweatley's', eventually 'The Bride-Night Fire', his first published poem (*Gentleman's Magazine*, November 1875), besides being a Dorset bawdy tale, has for its forty-first line, 'Her cwold little figure half-naked he views' (and politer variants); but the version Lionel Johnson quotes in his book on Hardy (1894) – 'her cold little buzzoms half-naked he views' – is what he first wrote. For a man supposedly struggling with impotence this is an odd poem to write in his twenty-sixth year.

There was an element, too – a by no means unimportant one – of 'peasant mischief' in Tom. He was of a type, peasant or not, which had been described as 'never so happy as when annoying someone'. That he obtained pleasure from provoking people, provided the cause was good, there is no doubt. The slight poem, 'To a Lady (Offended by a Book of the Writer's)', which he could not resist including in *Wessex Poems*, displays some of the scorn he felt for over-genteel people. His extreme candour in print (not only on matters sexual) has frightened many commentators; no self-respecting gentleman could write on his twenty-fifth birthday (and then quote fifty years later): 'Wondered what woman, if any, I should be thinking about in five years' time.' This remark has been taken to indicate 'a marked deterioration' in his relationship with Eliza Nicholls; but it is the sort of speculation any man, even one madly in love, might make.

Tom's lifelong interest in achieving a sort of drama that might avoid the silliness and superficiality of the 'theatre', which culminated in *The Dynasts*, also began to manifest itself at this early stage. Like Browning and Tennyson, he dreamed of reviving Shakespearian blank verse tragedy, and he even took a walking-on part in a theatrical extravaganza. But he did not make Browning's and Tennyson's (and later Bridges') mistake of actually attempting to write Elizabethan tragedies. This flirtation with the theatre, for which even if he was sometimes entertained by it, he had little but contempt, seems to have been the last episode in what he called his 'visionary' mood. He was missing the country and tired of the town. As he put it:

> Adelphi Terrace . . . faces the river, and in the heat of the summer . . . the stench from the mud at low water increased . . . Whether from the effects of this smell upon a constitution that had grown up in a pure country atmosphere (as he himself supposed), or because he had been accustomed to shut himself up in his room . . . every evening from six to twelve, reading incessantly, instead of getting out for air . . . Hardy's health had become much weakened. He used to say that on sitting down to begin drawing in the morning he had scarcely physical power left to hold the pencil and square . . . his friends in Dorset . . . were shocked at the pallor which sheeted a countenance formerly ruddy with health . . .

Blomfield, who had become fond of him, and had noticed his state, advised him, in July 1867, to go back to the country 'to retain vigour', suggesting that he should return 'at latest' by October. But Hardy 'was beginning to feel that he would rather go into the country altogether'. He noted, too, that he cared 'for life as emotion' rather than as a 'science of climbing'. This suggests that the central idea for his first novel had already formed itself: disgust with the artificiality and superficiality of society life. It was not, as is often supposed, that Tom himself had done badly in London. On the contrary, he was now a valued practitioner of the art he had chosen, and had been able to meet such people as he had felt inclined to meet. But falseness and false manners oppressed him. They were always to do so.

It happened that just then John Hicks was crippled by gout, and needed an assistant 'accustomed to church restoration'. He asked Tom for a recommendation, and Tom recommended himself. Hicks was glad to have him back.

Some of the notes he made during the years 1865–67, which he lists in the *Life* without comment, show how painful he found trying to deal with the feelings with which he would be burdened throughout his life. On a return visit to Hatfield, he noted the 'pied rabbits', 'descendants of those I knew', and regretted that 'the beautiful sunset did not occur in a place of no reminiscences, that I might have enjoyed it without their tinge'. Memory for him always involved involuntary pain; not only did he have the habit of recreating the past by means of the scene he viewed, but also he lamented his irretrievable loss of it. No wonder Proust would pay tribute to him. Tom was thinking, too, of the difficulties involved in realizing his genius: 'A widely appreciative mind mostly fails to achieve a great work from pure far-sightedness . . . The very clearness with which he discerns remote possibilities is, from its nature, scarcely ever consistent with the microscopic vision demanded for tracing the narrow path that leads to them.' He was disturbed by the inhibiting effect that his struggle for a 'wide appreciation', a good all-round education, might have upon his creative faculties. The note seems to point away from poetry, or at least from lyrical poetry, and towards narrative. Another note reads: 'There is no more painful lesson to be learnt by a man of capacious mind than that of excluding general knowledge for particular.' As a poet he was convinced that he required a broad and deep general knowledge – yet now he must dispose his time so as to concentrate on the craft of fiction, something he did not even quite fully believe in.

As he stored his 'books and other belongings' at Westbourne Park Terrace, in preparation for his return to Bockhampton, he must have been pleased with what he had achieved professionally. He was now well practised in architecture. He had made a careful study of art, which he would exploit to the hilt in his fiction (occasionally overdoing it), by going, in his typically methodical way, to look at pictures. During 1865 he had polished up his French by attending classes under Professor Léonce Stièvenard at King's College; although he says that he gave these studies 'but a perfunctory attention', his renderings from French in his literary notebooks are competent. He could not match Moule as a classicist, theologian or historian; he may, though, have already acquired a broader knowledge of English literature, because he absorbed what he read, and he read prodigiously. Possibly no English writer has been more capable of assimilation. The difficulty was, as his note implies, the use that he could make of all this.

5

At Bockhampton and Weymouth

Being back at home soon revived Tom. He was to be badly affected by residence in London, and by the pretensions of many of those who lived there, for the rest of his life. He was not wrong, however, in calculating that a successful writer, and he now intended to be one, would often need to be close to it.

The arrangement he had made with Hicks meant that he could attend the Dorchester office more or less at his own convenience. A few people, as he complained to his wife in his old age, laughed at him because he had accomplished nothing in the five years of his absence – which confirms that he had aroused expectations. He continued to write poetry and to read voraciously, besides doing his architectural drawing. But as well as all that, he wrote, between July 1867 and 16 January 1868, the first draft of his first novel, *The Poor Man and the Lady*, paying only a 'flying' visit in October to Westbourne Park Villas 'to fetch his books and other belongings'. He would never, henceforth, whatever his fears and misgivings, practical and aesthetic, cease to try for a life as a writer.

In turning reluctantly to fiction, he had at last recognized that he would have to subsidize his poetry by writing saleable prose. But even in the composition of his first novel he, at the beginning, interspersed the prose narrative with poems – possibly some of those rejected by editors. Sitting one afternoon in Hicks' office, he made the heading 'The Poor Man and the Lady: A Story with No Plot;/Containing some original verses'. This, he records, 'he plainly did not like, for it was ultimately abridged to *The Poor Man and the Lady;/By the Poor Man.*'

Between mid-January and 9 June 1868 he was engaged in 'copying' (and, certainly, rewriting) his first draft of the novel; printers then, and for many years after, set from the handwritten 'fair copy' of the manuscript. Although it was destined never to be published, and is now lost, Tom believed that this, his first full-length manuscript, was the most original book that he ever wrote, 'for its date', as he told Edward

Clodd, one of his closest friends, in a letter of 5 December 1910. By that time he had given up fiction, and had dispersed too much of the original text into various other works, including in particular the opening of *Under the Greenwood Tree* and 'An Indiscretion in the Life of an Heiress' (a story published in July 1878, but never collected), to consider publishing it. He also told Clodd that it was 'very crude' but 'showed a wonderful insight into female character'.

A summary of the plot was given in the *Sunday Times* of 22 January 1928, after Hardy's death, by Edmund Gosse, who said that the author had outlined it for him. So far as the story can be reconstructed, it is told in the first person by a labourer's son, Will Strong, whose education as an architect is paid for by Mr and Mrs Guy Allancourt, the local squire and his wife. Will falls in love with their daughter, who reciprocates; so he is sent off to London. There, while the affair waxes and wanes, Strong becomes a radical – Tom called the novel 'socialistic' (not 'socialist', as the word has been transcribed).

There is a scene in which a man (unspecified) 'pursues his wife at midnight and *strikes* her' (as publisher Alexander Macmillan would put it, objecting to such a terrible possibility, which he declared, disingenuously, was unlikely); and another in which Strong makes Mrs Allancourt faint and then, pouring water on her face to revive her, causes her rouge to run. Tom wrote of another episode in which Strong, with every circumstantial detail,

> described in the first person his introduction to the kept mistress of an architect . . . the said mistress adding to her lover's income by designing for him the pulpits, altars, reredoses, texts, holy vessels, crucifixes, and other ecclesiastical furniture which were handed on to him by the nominal architects who employed her protector – the lady herself being a dancer at a music-hall when not designing Christian emblems – all told so plausibly as to seem actual proof of the degeneracy of the age.

In what may have been the weakest episode in the book (which, however, he was almost to reproduce in *A Pair of Blue Eyes*), he removed the squire's daughter by killing her off with consumption. It was typical of him that, as an avowedly non-realist novelist, he should have sought medical advice on this point, as well as on another concerning an episode of blindness suffered by Strong on account of excessive study of Greek. He wrote to the brother of his aunt's husband, John Brereton Sharpe, who had once been a physician and was now a vicar in Wales, and received from him an authoritative and friendly reply.

Will Strong, the novel's protagonist, resembles his creator in obvious ways: the name Strong/Hardy; the fact that he is an architect, comes from Dorset but works in London. But he would not have been a psychological self-portrait. Hardy was always clear about this point, in poems as in novels. He did not wish his privacy to be penetrated, and resented simplistic equations being made by reviewers or critics. Many of his main characters tend to be in circumstances which match, in many details, his own. There are, too, certain psychological resemblances. But he never completely identified himself with any one of his characters, and there is neither a complete self-portrait nor an attempt at one in his work.

July 1868 was a difficult month. He had finished putting the manuscript of *The Poor Man and the Lady* into final order, and sent it first to Horace Moule, then in his last months of teaching at Marlborough. Tom recorded a note he made on the first day of the month:

Cures for despair:
To read Wordsworth's 'Resolution and Independence'.
,,   ,,   John Stuart Mill's 'Individuality' (in *Liberty*).
,,   ,,   Carlyle's 'Jean Paul Richter'.

He had made the decision to abandon poetry as a career but he could not quite bear to carry out his intention to the full. He began work on 'a narrative poem on the Battle of the Nile', a modern epic which he never finished but which, he noted in the *Life*, 'shows that the war with Napoleon was even then in his mind a material for poetry of some sort'. When at last he could renounce fiction, he turned straight to the Napoleonic theme: it would find fruition in *The Dynasts*.

On 17 July he wrote, 'Perhaps I can do a volume of poems consisting of the *other side* of common emotions'. He added, 'What that means is not quite clear', as if to emphasize his confusion at the time. By the 'other side' he meant the 'unrecognized' side, the 'shadow' which people do not like to acknowledge. His fiction is full of examples of how people really feel, as distinct from how they would like it to be said they feel. Thus, his lifelong obsession with the male's need for sexual novelty and the effect upon men of the fading of female beauty is as much an insistence upon a universal phenomenon as it is a characteristic peculiar to himself.

Moule, meanwhile, had liked his novel well enough to write him a letter of introduction to Alexander Macmillan, the experienced head of the successful publishing house, Macmillan & Co, founded in 1843. (It was when working such long hours 'reviewing' books for them in his Cambridge days that Moule is said to have taken to drink and drugs.) Moule's letter did not mention the writer's name or age. In his own covering letter when he posted the manuscript to Alexander Macmillan on 25 July, Tom told him that

> the upper classes of society have been induced to read, before any, books in which *they themselves* are painted by a comparative outsider . . . in works of such a kind, unmitigated utterances of strong feelings against the class to which these readers belong, may lead them to throw down a volume in disgust; whilst the very same feelings inserted edgewise so to say; half-concealed beneath ambiguous expressions, or at any rate written as if they were not the chief aims of the book (even though they may be) – become the most attractive remarks of all . . . now a days, discussions on the questions of manners, rising in the world, &c (the main incidents of the novel) have grown to be particularly absorbing . . . as a rule no fiction will considerably interest readers rich or poor unless the passion of love forms a prominent feature in the thread of the story . . . novelty of *position* and *view* in relation to a known subject, is more taking among the readers of light literature than even absolute novelty of subject.
>
> Hence the book took its shape, rightly or wrongly.

The most interesting remark in this letter, which cannily anticipates the criticism the book received from the few who read it, concerns the general reader only enjoying stories which contain strong love interest. No fiction by Hardy lacks a love, or at least a sex, interest – and every one of his novels took the basic form of this first one. Even at this early stage Tom was contriving to be, as well as artistically conscientious, coolly commercial, very practical within his own parameters: he was baiting his book with something to appeal to the high-minded but shrewd Macmillan, an ex-schoolmaster, and publisher of Charles Kingsley's *Westward Ho!* (1855). It did. Macmillan was slightly annoyed by the bitterness of the novel's satire, but he was also amused at the book's youthful venom – and he could recognize a new and unusual talent.

Having sent the manuscript to Macmillan, Tom felt 'free of it', and busied himself with Hicks' commissions and the seventh book of the *Aeneid* 'between whiles'. He was now not so much caught between poetry, prose and a career as a jobbing architect, as contriving a means for living as a writer. 'He feels himself shrink into nothing when contemplating other people's *means* of working. When he looks upon their *ends* he expands with triumph,' he had written of a 'certain man' (obviously himself) a few months earlier in London. This is a reiteration of the customary theme: the assertion of what Millgate astutely calls a 'kind of purity'. Notwithstanding the sense of humour that would see him through his apprenticeship as a writer, Tom was intensely serious. That he was gradually abandoning orthodox Christianity did not mean that he was abandoning the moral seriousness with which he approached it while he had been a believer. His religious feelings he now put into his notion of the high calling of the poet, and doubtless when he contemplated the '*ends*' of most of the writers contemporary to him, he felt them wanting in such seriousness.

The path before him seemed more uncertain than ever. Yet already his scheme, to be as little false to his poetic principles as he could, was fully conscious in him. From the perhaps too daring notion of creating a new form, a hybrid of prose and verse that would not be Menippean, he was turning to the creation of a fiction that would be as truthful as possible, even if by its very form it denied poetry. The 'visionary' nature of poetry, though, continued to haunt him. Such of his notebooks as survive are full of schemes and experiments for ballads both lyrical and narrative, and he was already impressed with Scott's *Marmion*. He has been laughed at for his admiration for this poem, and for writing of himself that 'he preferred Scott the poet to Scott the novelist, and never ceased to regret that the author of the most Homeric poem in the English language – *Marmion* – should later have declined on prose fiction'. It is overlooked that he called *Marmion* 'the most Homeric' rather than 'the best' poem, and that the poetry of Scott, apart from a few anthology pieces, has been unfairly neglected, swallowed up by his achievements in prose. Tom was in any case simply recording his own preference: for poetry over prose, and therefore for poetic narrative over prose narrative. Scott could not have turned back to poetry, even if he had wanted to, or if the muse had not deserted him, because he desperately needed money: he was forced to 'decline on'. That lesson was not lost on Tom.

He waited for his opportunity – for a full quarter of a century – to return to poetry, and this gives his eighteen published works of fiction a unique quality. We may guess that his unpublished nineteenth work, *The Poor Man and the Lady*, also possessed such a quality, possibly to youthful excess.

On 10 August Macmillan replied. As Tom had anticipated, he did object – although not in an unexceptionable manner – to the satire on the upper classes. He feared it was, in part, warranted, but that the 'chastisement . . . would fall harmless from its very excess'. He objected to the 'utter heartlessness of *all* the conversation you give in drawing rooms . . . about the working-classes!'. Nothing, he believed, could justify the 'wholesale blackening of a class but large & intimate knowledge of it'. Speaking of Thackeray's portrayal of the same class, he wrote: 'he meant fair, you *"mean mischief"* '. He thought the book had 'fatal drawbacks', and could not believe that 'any considerable number of human beings – God's creatures – should be so bad without going to utter ruin within a week' (there is surely some indignation in this: the text had stung him). He was finally encouraging: 'If this is your first book I think you ought to go on. May I ask if it is? [many books, like Tom's own first two, appeared anonymously] and – you are not a lady so perhaps you will forgive the question – are you young?' It was a handsome letter, and the report accompanying it was even more so. This report was by John Morley, although Macmillan did not then name him.

John Morley, later Viscount Morley, politician and biographer of Gladstone, at that time notorious amongst some for having written the name of the deity with a small 'g', was two years older than Tom, and was already a leading young liberal agnostic, a Comtean, and a disciple of John Stuart Mill. Tom could hardly have asked for a more sympathetic reader. Later he was to become acquainted with him. Morley thought the book 'very curious and original', with much 'strong and fresh' writing; but it 'hung too loosely together' and often read 'like some clever lad's dream'; if the author was a young man, then he had 'stuff and purpose in him'. But Morley, who was by no means a conventional man by the standards of the day, did not pull his punches: he found in *The Poor Man and the Lady* a 'certain rawness of absurdity that is very displeasing'. The author needed to study 'form and composition', and should avoid 'commonplace' feeling 'turning on the insolence and folly of the rich'. Morley was already putting his finger on a 'displeasing' quality in Hardy that was to repel some of his readers and many of his critics, including his two main biographers. However immature his portrayal of the rich may have been, it had a lively edge of anger – and that made Macmillan and Morley uneasy. If the novel had been safer stuff, Macmillan would probably have taken it.

This mixed response, neither accepting nor rejecting the manuscript, put Tom into acute suspense – so near and yet so far, it seemed – and at one point he made a note about how people 'will laugh in the midst of a misery! Some would soon grow to whistle in Hell.' His reply to Macmillan, now lost, was instant, and while waiting to hear further he sensibly occupied himself in reading, making excursions with Mary (now working at a school at Minterne Magna, but just then on holiday), and doing work for Hicks.

On 10 September, having heard nothing more, he sent Macmillan a remarkably unreserved letter:

> I don't care what happens to the book, so long as something happens. The earlier fancy that *Hamlet* without Hamlet would never do turns to a belief that it would be better than closing the house . . . Would you mind suggesting the sort of story you think I could do best, or any literary work I should do well to go upon?

He may have regretted this appeal, for the manuscript came back for him to improve it. He now worked at *Hamlet* without Hamlet, although to what extent it is impossible to say. He may well have resented it – authors who believe in what they are doing almost invariably do – without necessarily having ill feelings towards Macmillan or his reader. He returned the doctored text to Macmillan in November, and in December went up to London to see him.

'The substance of the interview was that though *The Poor Man and the Lady*, if printed, might create a considerable curiosity, it was a class of book which Macmillan himself could not publish.' This was a matter not of artistic or aesthetic merits, but of commercial suitability: it seems possible that Tom found himself obstinately unable, try as he might, to make enough alterations to satisfy Macmillan.

The publisher's reaction to this first novel anticipates the fate of all his works: offence and even outrage, but acknowledgement of power and ability. That Macmillan gave it so much consideration before deciding that it would harm his image if he published it may be in part because he thought highly of Moule's judgement. Morley had been prompted to remark on 'disgusting' sexual details of the 'violation of a young lady at an evening party, and the subsequent birth of a child', and if 'An

Indiscretion in the Life of an Heiress', the story Hardy based upon it, is anything to go by, then *The Poor Man* must have abounded in the kind of erotic detail which so upset (but also titillated) readers of Hardy's novels. Egbert Mayne, as Will Strong became in the later story, is obsessed with the bosom of Geraldine Allenville (formerly Allancourt) and desires both to 'possess' and to 'exhibit' her. The text has rightly been seen as 'almost an anticipation of pornographic cinema'. But Hardy was less 'abnormal' in all this, for all the majority of critics' representations, than he was a pioneer analyst of male sexuality. He himself called the story a 'sort of patchwork' of its original: a 'pale shadow' of it.

Macmillan gave Tom an introduction to another publisher, Frederick Chapman of Chapman and Hall, whom he thought might publish the novel. Chapman and Hall's authors included Dickens, Trollope, Thackeray, Mrs Gaskell and Charles Kingsley, and when the forty-one-year-old Frederick Chapman had come to the firm in 1864 he had continued with the eminent authors, and with the 'railway' yellowbacks of the late 1850s. But he also introduced some racier writers of lesser calibre – whom Macmillan did not care to consider – such as Ouida. However, Tom noted gloomily on 8 December, his interview with Chapman, whom he had rushed to see, had been 'unfortunate'; it 'brought the year to an unsatisfactory close – so far as it affected Hardy's desire to get into print as the author of a three-volume novel, since he could not do so as a poet without paying for publication'. He still harped on poetry.

He returned to Bockhampton and immersed himself in books again, including the 1868 William Rossetti edition of Walt Whitman, the first English selection, which he had picked up in London. In the new year he was eagerly back there, calling on Macmillan again and meeting Morley for the first time. Morley offered to introduce him to the editor of the *Saturday Review*, which Moule seems never to have done; but he did not take this up. He called upon Chapman again, who pointed Carlyle out to him in his publisher's shop, and who irritated him by what seemed to Tom to be cavalier treatment of the old man in failing to attend to him personally. Chapman, however, told Tom that he would publish *The Poor Man and the Lady* if he would pay him £20 guarantee against loss – then a common arrangement. Tom agreed, and returned to Dorset expecting proofs.

None arrived. After writing to Chapman to enquire, he received a note asking 'if he would call . . . and meet the gentleman who read your manuscript'. He had no idea who this gentleman was, although it so happened that he had been more influenced by him than by any other living writer.

> He went in March, by appointment . . . was shown into a back room . . . and before him, in the dusty and untidy apartment, piled with books and papers, was a handsome man in a frock coat – 'buttoned at the waist, but loose above' . . . his ample dark-brown beard, wavy locks, and somewhat dramatic manner lending him a striking appearance to the younger man's eye, who even then did not know his name.

The august personage began to lecture him upon his manuscript, which he held in his hand, 'in a sonorous voice'. Yes, he told him, the firm would honour its pledge. But he strongly advised the young man against it: if he 'wanted to do anything practical in literature' he ought not to 'nail his colours to the mast . . . so definitely in a first book'. He would be 'attacked on all sides by the conventional reviewers and his future injured'.

The giver of this excellent advice, especially from the 'practical' point of view, was George Meredith. The author of two books of poetry, one of them *Modern Love*, and (at that point) seven novels, Meredith had reason to know about 'conventional reviewers' and their damaging effects on authors, and was less conventional than either Macmillan or Morley, both of whom worked judiciously within the bounds of strict decorum. *The Ordeal of Richard Feverel* (1859), in which he had even written a masturbation scene – either not spotted by reviewers or found impossible for them to mention – had badly damaged his reputation; the novel had been banned by Mudie's Circulating Library, the acme of smug pretentiousness, but important to authors' and publishers' incomes. The *Spectator*, responding to *Modern Love* (1862), had described him as a 'clever man, without literary genius, taste or judgement'. His was, however, a formidable name; he was a regular contributor to the *Fortnightly* and had recently acted as its editor in the place of Morley while the latter was in America.

In a recent private letter, Meredith had told another whom Tom admired, Algernon Charles Swinburne, that he had heard, apropos the latter's new collection of verse, ' "low mutterings" already from the Lion of British prudery', and advised him that he, for one, who loved his verse, 'would ply savagely with a knife amongst the proofs for the sake of your fame'; and because 'I want to see you take the first place, as you may if you wish'. He was now generously trying to give similar advice, albeit to an unknown young man, whose power he had perceived.

Meredith, Tom noted, 'was not taken in by the affected simplicity of the narrative'. What Tom called 'naive realism in circumstantial details', 'pure invention' – he admitted that much of the bland manner of this had been borrowed from Defoe – had taken in Macmillan and Morley, and had genuinely upset them. Tom's record of Meredith's knowingness indicates that he was not innocent of the effects his work had on its readers, contrary to the claim of some critics. But, as will be seen, he would often pose as one puzzled by the effects of his candour: it was a conveniently ironic attitude that seemed to give him, as a supposed country bumpkin who could not really understand London and its sophisticated ways, much satisfaction.

Meredith told him that he could either 'soften the story' – or 'put it away for the present, and concentrate on a new work with a more complicated plot'. In the *Life* Tom said that he could not 'precisely remember' what he then did with the manuscript, that 'he may have sent it to some other publisher'. In fact, although he did not press Chapman to fulfil his promise, he did not take Meredith's advice immediately, but sent it out to two other publishers: first to Smith, Elder, which returned it within a fortnight, and then, after some five weeks' hesitation, on 8 June 1869, to Tinsley Brothers.

Smith, Elder, like Macmillan and Chapman and Hall, was a distinguished house, which had issued, in 1847, the immensely successful *Jane Eyre*. Tinsley Brothers, now run by the elder brother William, Edward having died in 1866, was not in this class, although it had had a phenomenal success with Mrs Braddon's *Lady Audley's Secret* in 1862, and had published much popular fiction since then. In 1865 Meredith had received £400 from them for his novel, *Rhoda Fleming*, although Tinsley was not his regular publisher. The garrulous William Tinsley, a vulgar, easy-going and rather disorganized man whom Tom never took seriously, and of whose manner he made constant fun, characteristically kept him waiting for three months before letting him know, through Moule, that they would publish his manuscript if he would pay them a guarantee against loss. The sum Tinsley demanded is unknown, but it was certainly more than £20, and so Tom was worse off than when he had started: he was now being asked for more money by an inferior publisher. On 14 September 1869 he wrote asking for the return of the manuscript, telling Tinsley that 'the terms on which you wd be willing to publish it . . . are rather beyond me just now'.

Did he now reproach himself for having gone 'too far' in his depiction of the upper classes? For having caused the squire Guy Allancourt to be so mean as to be delighted at getting a tombstone for his daughter designed free by Will Strong? In the *Life*, after mentioning that Meredith had not been deceived by the affected naivety of his satire, he added that 'it was surprising to Hardy to find that, in the opinion of such experienced critics, he had written so aggressive and dangerous a work . . . almost without knowing it, for his mind had been given in the main to poetry and other forms of pure literature'. The 'almost' again indicates irony, a reversion on the part of the memoirist (posing as his own second wife) to his initial strategy of 'surprise' at being considered 'dangerous'.

He set to work on a new novel, this time (he half-complained fifty years later) taking 'Meredith's advice almost too literally' by constructing 'an eminently "sensational" plot'. He had decided to make no mistake this time – but how far was he prepared to compromise? He was more obstinate than anyone has realized. God gives genius, Flaubert had told Louise Colet during the composition of *Madame Bovary*, but has left talent to us. God had given Tom poetic genius, and he already knew it. But, aware of *Madame Bovary* and of its trial, he now had to examine whether he had a genius for the novel as well as for poetry. The latter would depend upon it.

The fears and uncertainties about the reception of *The Poor Man and the Lady* and his future as a writer may have become further complicated in this post-London period by his love life. He successfully destroyed all the evidence, and there are no clear details, but he seems to have had an affair with his cousin Tryphena Sparks and another with a young woman called Cassie (Catherine) Pole; there could have been others. His younger sister Kate, who at this time was still at school in Dorchester, had no revelations to make about Tom's affairs, although quite possibly she did not know about them. (Kate, who lived for a time with her sister Mary at Wantage, would follow in Mary's footsteps and become a teacher – and one a little more easy-going with her pupils, for Mary, although kind, was a stickler for propriety.)

Tom's relationship with Tryphena Sparks has been the subject of much speculation, including the suggestion that he fathered a son, called Randolph, by her in the summer of 1868. There is a Sparks family tradition of his interest in her, and doubtless he associated with his lively young cousin in the summer of his return from London. At some time he gave her a photograph of himself, taken by Bowen and Carpenter, Kilburn, in 1862, and it is said that he undertook to teach her French. It may, or may not, be that they made love – just as he may, or may not, have made love to Martha Sparks in London, to Eliza Nicholls, to Eliza's sister Jane, and to any number of other women of whom we have never heard. There is, however, not only no evidence that he made love to Tryphena, let alone had a son by her, but good reason to suppose that he did not.

Tryphena, born on 20 March 1851, was the youngest child of James and Maria Sparks. She had attended a small school at Athelhampton, about a mile from Puddletown, where she had done well, and become 'monitor'; for 'attention to her duties' she was awarded a book. A silk-worked sampler which she made is still in the possession of her family. It had been decided that she was to become a schoolteacher – one of the chief means for Victorian girls to rise (a little) in society. There was already a pupil-teacher at the Athelhampton school, and late in 1866 she was appointed as a pupil-teacher at the Puddletown school built by John Brymer.

By the mid-1860s Puddletown had come under the sway of Brymer, a vigorous and stern squire who wanted to reform the people of Puddletown in the best paternalist Victorian manner – an attitude which can be assumed to have been more patronizing and less humane than that of, say, the Rev. Henry Moule of Fordington. He had founded the school under the aegis of, to give it its full title, the National Society for Promoting the Education of the Poor in the Principles of the Established Church. By 1866 the school had been divided into a boys' and girls' section, and Tryphena joined the latter, for a reward of ten shillings a year.

Despite the fact that her mother Maria was increasingly ill – she would die in November 1868 – Tryphena did well, except for a weakness in geography. Then abruptly, in January 1868, when she was not yet seventeen, she met trouble. The only details are two entries in the school log, one for 16 January recording 'Reproved pupil-teacher for neglect of duty – parents very angry in consequence – determine to withdraw her a month hence', and the other for 20 January: 'Change of teachers. Frances Dunman being appointed P.T. in T. Sparks' place.' This entry also records that the usual lessons were not given on that day, and that Tryphena was transferred to the boys' section of the school. On 22 January Mrs Collins, the headmistress, 'explained fully to 1st and 2nd classes the 7th commandment'. Whether this (full?) explanation of the sins of adultery had anything to do with Tryphena is not known, nor how unusual such an event was.

After this January 1868 incident, whatever it may have been, at Puddletown school, Tryphena disappears from the record until she turns up at Stockwell Normal College in south London in January 1870. She completed the two-year teacher-training course here, and became the successful headmistress of a Plymouth elementary school for girls until her marriage in 1877 to Charles Gale, a publican, of Topsham, near Exeter. She had four children by him. After the birth of the last, in 1886, she suffered a 'rupture' from which she never properly recovered, and died four years later, in March 1890.

There is no reference, public or private, to any child born to her before she married. But the repeated speculation is that the school incident was connected with her pregnancy by Tom and that she left in order to have the baby in the summer. The conception is thus supposed to have taken place during the previous summer, shortly after Tom came back from London and was building himself up with a bottle of stout a day and walks between Dorchester and Bockhampton – and was busy writing *The Poor Man and the Lady*.

A note in the *Life* has been taken to refer to the pregnant Tryphena's departure: 'In the February following [1868] a memorandum shows that he composed a lyric entitled "A Departure by Train", which has disappeared.' This assumption has no more evidence for it than the other assertion that has been made – that Tryphena did not leave but stayed on as pupil-teacher in the boys' section of Puddletown, then went to a small school at Coryates, a tiny village just west of Dorchester. It is, however, true that in order to qualify for Stockwell College she needed to have completed three years as a pupil-teacher, although those who canvas the case of a Hardy bastard account for Tryphena's acceptance into the College by the fact that a tenth of the entrants had not been pupil-teachers at all.

The argument that Tom fathered a child upon Tryphena is further darkened by the claim that he was not her cousin, but her uncle – she was supposedly the daughter of her 'sister' Rebecca (twenty-one years older) – and that she eventually had another affair with Horace Moule. Maria Sparks, according to another 'tradition', forbade Tom's marriage to Tryphena on the grounds that it would have been incestuous; since marriage between cousins was not forbidden by the Church, the implication is that Maria would have been alarmed by such a match if she were Tryphena's grandmother and Tom her uncle. There is not a shred of evidence for any of this, nor for the existence of a boy called Randolph, Randal or Randy. The assertion is that the boy was looked after by his aunt (grandmother?) Rebecca, who married a Fred Paine, a saddler of Puddletown, in 1872, but left him soon afterwards. Certainly Rebecca lived with Tryphena until her own death in 1875, and certainly she was needlework mistress at Tryphena's Plymouth school.

But there is no trace of a bastard. Mrs Eleanor Bromell (1878–1965), Tryphena's eldest daughter, recollected as an old, and rather confused, lady of eighty-one that when her mother came out of Stockwell College in '1871, & went to Plymouth, Tom gave her a ring. He was "tacking after her" while she was in college, & he in London training to be an architect.' Tryphena was not at Stockwell while Tom was training in London, but Irene Cooper Willis, the co-executor of the Hardy estate and a friend to Florence Hardy, gave some small credence to this story when she confirmed that Florence had told her that the ring Tom eventually gave to his first wife, Emma Gifford, had been intended for a Dorset girl. (Florence, though, enjoyed doing Emma down – and a ring is not necessarily an engagement ring. Perhaps, although not in character, Tom passed out rings regularly; he is supposed to have given a ring to Cassie Pole, too.)

Mrs Bromell owned a photograph album that had belonged to Tryphena and in which was a portrait of a boy. When this portrait was first pointed out to her she remarked that it was 'just a little boy who used to come to see Tryphena'. Later, though, when she was sick in hospital but still in partial possession of her faculties, she said, 'That was the Hardy boy', and 'Everyone knew it was Hardy's boy'. But she could not say who the boy's mother was; nor did she know his name. Still later the photograph was again produced, together with a new one purporting to be of the same person but at a later age (both these pictures have been reproduced in several books and newspapers). There were a few other details, including Mrs Bromell's recollection that the boy was called 'Rantie, R.A.N.T.I.E., Ranty, Randy . . . It *could* be short for Randolph . . . He was a Sparks. He was in Bristol most of the time. That's where he lived.' None of this is, however, relevant to the question of whether this boy was Tom's or Tryphena's son. Mrs Bromell either did not know, or would not say. On the Christmas Day before she died she muttered, 'Hardy loved her but they said she was a *whore* . . . They said she ran around with other men.'

The only other possibly relevant detail concerns two pages of Tryphena's autograph book, which had been presented to her by her

Plymouth pupils upon her retirement and marriage. The pages were decorated with circlets of pressed leaves in the centre of which was written: 'He will be our guide, even unto death'. At the bottom of each page was written, probably in Tryphena's hand, 'Ry/Decr 1873'. Mrs Bromell thought that the leaves had been picked by her brother Charles, born in 1880; but by that time she had become confused.

The inference which has been drawn from these vague and unreliable circumstantial details is all the more unlikely in the light of the poem which Tom published in 1898 in *Wessex Poems*. Called 'Thoughts of Ph – – a', it was subtitled 'At News of Her Death', which he dated 'March 1890'. A full-page drawing accompanied it, depicting a shrouded woman on a sofa – recognizable from the elaborate decorations as that in the dining-room at Max Gate. (In the *Selected Poems* of 1916 he changed the poem's title to 'At News of a Woman's Death', which in the *Collected Poems* becomes 'Thoughts of Phena at News of Her Death'.) This poem identifying Tryphena was open to the scrutiny of his wife, his brother and sisters, and everyone else – including the Sparks family – in Dorchester; and also to the widower, Charles Gale of Topsham, if he had been inclined to read *Wessex Poems*. It seems inconceivable that Tom, by 1898 known as the author of supposedly 'immoral', 'obscene' and outspoken novels, would have published it if Tryphena was the mother of a bastard child by him whom he had successfully concealed for over thirty years.

In the *Life*, which he knew would eventually be published – and which he began twenty years after the poem's first publication – he drew further attention to it, quoting from an entry dated 5 March 1890, which has been, self-explanatorily, doctored:

In the train on the way to London. Wrote the first four or six lines of 'Not a line of her writing have I'. It was a curious instance of sympathetic telepathy. The woman whom I was thinking of – a cousin – was dying at the time, and I quite in ignorance of it. She died six days later [in fact on 17 March]. The remainder of the piece was not written until after her death.

The full poem reads:

Not a line of her writing have I,
  Not a thread of her hair,

No mark of her late time as dame in her dwelling, whereby
    I may picture her there;
    And in vain do I urge my unsight
      To conceive my lost prize
At her close, whom I knew when her dreams were upbrimming
      with light,
    And with laughter her eyes.

    What scenes spread around her last days,
      Sad, shining, or dim?
Did her gifts and compassions enray and enarch her sweet ways
    With an aureate nimb?
    Or did life-light decline from her years,
      And mischances control
Her full day-star; unease, or regret, or forebodings, or fears
    Disennoble her soul?

    Thus I do but the phantom retain
      Of the maiden of yore
As my relic; yet haply the best of her – fined in my brain
    It may be the more
    That no line of her writing have I,
      Not a thread of her hair,
No mark of her late time as dame in her dwelling, whereby
    I may picture her there.

An old and openly identified girl friend with whom the poet had lost touch, or the secret mother of his child? The epithet 'lost prize' surely means 'old girl friend whom I did not marry'. To one of Tom's highly speculative habit, any girl whom he even glimpsed might be speculatively presented as a 'lost prize'. When he was on a trip to Weymouth, with his sister Mary, on 26 April 1868, he recorded (in his 'Poetical Matter' notebook) that on a steamboat to Lulworth Cove he saw a

> woman on the paddle-box steps; all laughter: then part illness & the remainder laughter . . . Saw her for the last time standing on deck as the boat moved off. White feather in hat, brown dress, Dorset dialect, Classic features, short upper lip. A woman I wd. have married offhand, with probably disastrous results.

And this note, so some would have to claim, was written by a man about to become the father of a possibly incestuous bastard by a seventeen-year-old girl from just across the heath a short way from his home.

The note has in any case been misread as an illustration of Hardy's perversity and immaturity. Yet there is nothing pathological (or particularly 'adolescent', as Millgate puts it) about it: any honest young man who wanted to be a poet might have recorded such an impression. In our own times he might well have written 'tried to get off with' instead of 'married'. Tom was recording immediate and spontaneous feelings, without much reference to propriety. Later he added to this note: 'Combine her with the girl from Keinton Mandeville, &c, as "Woman seen".'

The entries in his 'Poetical Matter' notebook simply confirm that Tom was often struck by the women he saw. All of them were 'lost prizes', natural material for a truthful poetry of impressions, fascinating subjects for contemplation for one taken to studying the ways of fate, paths that might have been taken but were not. His note points to his susceptibility to introspective pursuit of the path of sexual attraction into its 'disastrous results' (he wrote this, it should be remembered, before his acquaintance with Emma Gifford, let alone his marriage to her); and it is hardly unique to him.

How far his affair went, if it went any distance at all, with Tryphena in 1867, is impossible to say: to try to show that he went all the way is as futile as to try to demonstrate the opposite – for example, by means of detailing the state of the weather in Dorchester at the time. But in 1890, then again in 1898, and then yet again in 1918 when writing the story of his life, he felt no self-reproach, and was openly making others aware that he had known Tryphena well, and had 'prized' her. It seems unlikely that there was ever even an unofficial engagement. The affair with Eliza Nicholls had been more serious and lasted longer. There has been a suggestion that 'Neutral Tones' was written in 1871 and referred not to Eliza but to Tryphena – yet why put a fake date at the end of it (he added 'Westbourne Park Villas' in Selected Poems) while drawing attention to the actual name of Tryphena Sparks in 1898, in the same volume, Wessex Poems? Tom was a methodical and thorough man. Unless some unimpeachable evidence turns up, in the form of letters or diaries, speculation about his love life before his marriage remains speculation. All that can truthfully be stated is that he was interested in women; the assumption that he had a degree of sexual experience (and a sexual capacity, since that has been challenged by his biographers) is based on the grounds that most if not all highly sexed young Victorians possessed similar experience.

AT BOCKHAMPTON AND WEYMOUTH

John Hicks died in February 1869, and his practice was taken over by a Weymouth architect called G.R. Crickmay. There was much church restoration work outstanding, and in April Crickmay offered some of it to the now experienced Hardy, to be conducted from the Dorchester office. He undertook it, but, as there was 'more than had been anticipated', Crickmay offered him 'three months certain' at the Weymouth office. This period was extended, and Tom did not leave Weymouth until mid-February 1870, by which time he had completed the restoration of the church at Turnworth, near Blandford Forum, where his pleasing designs may still be seen. In Weymouth he lodged at 3 Wooperton Street, near the harbour, where he wrote most of his next novel *Desperate Remedies* (he called Weymouth Creston in the first edition, although it soon became Budmouth) – and a number of poems. His work may not have demanded much of his time, for he also engaged in dancing, listening to the band, and swimming and boating in the harbour: there is a famous (and highly erotic) scene set in a boat out in Weymouth Bay in *Desperate Remedies*.

In a note of 15 June 1869 he comments that the theme of a woman who killed her seducer, only to discover that his wife is her (also seduced) sister, would make a '*Good, tragic ballad*'. This is not evidence that such tragic goings-on characterized his own life at Weymouth; it shows only that he was keenly interested in ballads, which provided a dramatic means of psychological self-projection. Rather more about his state of mind at that time, especially with regard to Tryphena or whatever other girl he was then involved with, is revealed by his poem 'At a Seaside Town in 1869', written 'from an old note', and first published in *Moments of Vision* (1917). It is subtitled 'Young Lover's Reverie'; the first line is 'I went and stood outside myself', meaning (since the fifth line reads 'Then next inside myself I looked'), 'I observed myself', but alluding, too, to the meaning of the word 'ecstasy': 'to stand outside oneself; to be displaced' (from Greek *ex*, out, and *hista'nai*, to stand). The allusion is appropriate: the poem contrasts a dream world, shared with a loved one, with the real world of Weymouth:

> But so it chanced, without myself
>   I had to look,
>   And then I took
> More heed of what I had long forsook:

99

The boats, the sands, the esplanade,
  The laughing crowd;
  Light-hearted, loud
Greetings from some not ill-endowed;

The evening sunlit cliffs, the talk,
  Hailings and halts,
  The keen sea-salts,
The band, the Morgenblätter Waltz.

The self-knowing irony of the line 'Greetings from some not ill-endowed' (like his statement 'I am not always unattracted by other good-looking women, if truth be told'), and the generally painful honesty of the whole poem, point to Tom's desire to tell the essential truth, at whatever expense to his *amour propre* – or misunderstanding by others. The poem ends:

Then rose a time when, as by force,
  Outwardly wooed
  By contacts crude,
Her image in abeyance stood . . .

At last I said: This outside life
  Shall not endure;
  I'll seek the pure
Thought-world, and bask in her allure.

Myself again I crept within,
  Scanned with keen care
  The temple where
She'd shone, but could not find her there.

I sought and sought. But O her soul
  Has not since thrown
  Upon my own
One beam! Yea, she is gone, is gone.

If the substance of this poem was conceived at the time of the 'old note', then Tom was already 'feeling his way' towards a method which would become second nature: that which has been called 'the double show', in which (as in *The Dynasts*, where it is systematic) the drama itself is shown, but is simultaneously watched. The method amounts to an ironic commentary upon ecstasy and upon its likely 'disastrous results'. It points, so far as sexual affairs are concerned, to some dissatisfaction with the marital arrangements made by society.

No biographical inference may be drawn from 'At a Seaside Town', except that it acknowledges that while living in Weymouth he had another falling-out-of-love experience such as is described in 'Neutral Tones'. Could the reason for these experiences be that one or both or more of the women with whom he fell in love failed to satisfy him intellectually? In Hardy, as in most other poets, everything is heightened, so that the mere attractiveness of a woman just glimpsed becomes a discrete experience, which may be speculated upon to its possible conclusion (as in the note about the woman on the steamer who so moved him to desire).

It has been asserted that he sought his mother in all his women, especially Tryphena, but such speculation may be applied to all men – and it may also be rejected. What he did seek was the close sexual companionship of an understanding female soul. He wanted a woman to understand how indignant he felt at the way the world suppressed the truthful and the just; he wanted to share his feelings and consummate them sexually; he could not do with just *impressing* his girls.

When in *Desperate Remedies* Miss Aldclyffe is sadistically taunting Cytherea about her relationship with the young architect Springrove, she accuses her of talking 'unmitigated rubbish'; Cytherea replies, 'it *wasn't* shallowness!' Did he seek a girl who would understand what shallowness was? But none of the women he courted until 1870 had pulled themselves up as he had – not even Tryphena. Yet such women in London society as he had observed seemed remote and false to him. Was that not why, in the first fiction he wrote, he created an aristocratic heroine who *does* love the poor man's son? It was a version of his own relationship with Julia Augusta Martin, who had shown such interest in him. His memories of the rustle of her skirts endowed the experience with erotic overtones. He had not forgotten his London call upon her, in 1862, she who 'had used to take him in her arms . . . But the lady of his dreams – alas!' How he has paid for his candid revelation of how that meeting affected him! And the sudden death of Miss Allancourt in *The Poor Man and the Lady* represents the death of that particular dream, of love with an equal – not love with a 'lady', but love with a woman who had an education of which she had made grateful use.

101

It could be that he wrote the brief 'Her Initials', dated 1869, apropos the experience which prompted 'At a Seaside Town':

> Upon a poet's page I wrote
> Of old two letters of her name;
> Part seemed she of the effulgent thought
> Whence that high singer's rapture came.
> – When now I turn the leaf the same
> Immortal light illumes the lay,
> But from the letters of her name
> The radiance has waned away!

The illustration above this in *Wessex Poems* shows an open book: at the bottom of the second page are his own initials as draughtsman, and in the left margin of the first page there is another pair of initials – which are deliberately made indecipherable, being as near to YZ as to anything. There is no clue as to who the poet is.

Of another two Weymouth poems, 'Her Father' (the manuscript's '1869' was deleted) and 'At Waking', the first contrasts, through a 'cynic ghost', the strength of the poet's love with the more enduring love of a father. But this is a slight poem compared to the other, 'At Waking', which expresses thoughts parallel to those of 'Neutral Tones':

> When night was lifting
> And dawn had crept under its shade,
> Amid cold clouds drifting
> Dead-white as a corpse outlaid,
> With a sudden scare
> I seemed to behold
> My Love in bare
> Hard lines unfold.
>
> Yea, in a moment,
> An insight that would not die
> Killed her old endowment
> Of charm that had capped all nigh,
> Which vanished to none
> Like the gilt of a cloud,
> And showed her but one
> Of the common crowd.

AT BOCKHAMPTON AND WEYMOUTH

She seemed but a sample
Of earth's poor average kind,
Lit up by no ample
Enrichments of mien or mind.
I covered my eyes
As to cover the thought,
And unrecognize
What the morn had taught.

O vision appalling
When the one believed-in thing
Is seen falling, falling,
With all to which hope can cling.
Off: it is not true;
For it cannot be
That the prize I drew
Is a blank to me!

The tenth line, 'An insight that would not die', originally read 'Those words she had written awry', which suggests that this process of scales falling from the eyes was occasioned by the receipt of a letter. The use of the word 'prize' has been taken to indicate that the poem was about Tryphena Sparks; but it hardly matters. Tom crammed intense experiences into a few days, so that it could be about any girl whom he believed he loved until he realized that she was no more than one 'of the common crowd' with whom he could share nothing. She might have been a shop-girl he met at a 'quadrille class in the town': a new assistant at Crickmay's (upon whom he said that he based Springrove in *Desperate Remedies*) 'persuaded' him to go dancing, but he found 'the young ladies of Weymouth heavier on the arm than their London sisters'. A 'great deal of flirtation went on', he said, at the dancing-class, which he described as a 'so-called "class"', being, in fact, a gay gathering for dances and love-making by adepts of both sexes'.

He was clearly being distracted from working on *Desperate Remedies* by frivolous young women, and in February 1870 he returned home 'in order to concentrate more particularly on the MS than he could do in a lively town'. He adds: 'The poem entitled "Dawn After the Dance", and dated "Weymouth, 1869", is supposed, though without proof, to have some bearing on these dances.' The proviso may have fooled the 'author' of the *Life*, Florence Hardy, but is not convincing. In a gay measure, with internal rhymes in the first and third lines of each stanza, the narrator, a young man who has just seen his girl home, confesses his disillusion. It ends:

> Yes; last night we danced I know, Dear, as we did that year
>   ago, Dear,
> When a strange new bond between our days was formed, and felt,
>   and heard;
> Would that dancing were the worst thing from the latest to the
>   first thing
> That the faded year can charge us with; but what avails a word!
>
> That which makes man's love the lighter and the woman's burn no
>   brighter
> Came to pass with us inevitably while slipped the shortening year . . .
> And there stands your father's dwelling with its blind bleak
>   windows telling
> That the vows of man and maid are frail as flimsy gossamere.

When he received a letter from Crickmay, written on 11 February, asking him to 'go into Cornwall to take plans and particulars of a church I am about to build there', he declined, 'the moment being inconvenient'. Instead he completed all but three or four chapters of his novel. Then, when Crickmay pressed him, he agreed to go. He sent the manuscript, still incomplete, to Macmillan on 5 March, and set off for Cornwall on the following Monday.

6

Emma Gifford

Tom had been in scores of churches, and the graveyards attached to them, in the course of his profession. *The Poor Man and the Lady* was, by all accounts of it, full of graveyards; so is *Desperate Remedies*. That death should figure as the background to love was second nature to him. Scene after scene in his work juxtaposes the two. But in 1870 he had never been in a Cornish churchyard; he did not even know Cornwall. Now, rising at 4 a.m. on 7 March, he was on his way there for the first time. He set out 'reluctantly' 'for the remote parish mentioned, in a county he had never entered', on a journey of seeming unimportance – 'yet it turned out to have lifelong consequences for him'.

To reach Launceston he had to take a 'tedious' route from Dorchester (which he had reached from Bockhampton 'by starlight') via Yeovil, Exeter and Plymouth. Then he had another sixteen miles to go by dog-cart, to reach the remote parish of St Juliot (Jilt, as the inhabitants pronounced it), by way of the coastal town of Boscastle, with its tiny harbour. He busied himself with writing in the train; later, when he called at last at the rectory, a piece of blue paper was still sticking out of his pocket – a poem.

It was like entering another world. When a new edition of his only novel with a Cornish setting, *A Pair of Blue Eyes*, was published a quarter of a century later, he wrote of this 'region of dream and mystery'. St Juliot, too, was set in the most romantic – almost preposterously romantic – part of Cornwall. Tintagel, the legendary seat of King Arthur, with all its associations, was only just down the coast. He wrote of his 'dreary but poetical' journey from the viewpoint of Emma Gifford, no doubt remembering what she had told him, in his retrospective poem 'A Man Was Drawing Near to Me': 'On that gray night of mournful drone, /Apart from aught to hear, to see, /I dreamt not that from shires unknown/In gloom, alone, /By Halworthy, /A man was drawing near to me . . .'

The church of St Juliot, which lay, with its adjacent rectory, on a

105

wooded slope, had long been falling into decay, and had been on Hicks' books for at least three years. Hicks himself, not long before his death, had called to inspect it. Tom described it accurately enough in *A Pair of Blue Eyes*, although there he made it lie more open to the sea: 'On the brow of the hill . . . stood the church . . . The lonely edifice was black and bare, cutting up into the sky from the very tip of the hill.' About a mile away was Beeny Cliff and the sea.

What was the thirty-year-old Emma Gifford doing in this remote place? She was the second daughter and fourth child of a solicitor, John Attersoll Gifford, and his wife, also Emma, née Farmer. Gifford, the son of a schoolmaster, had practised as a solicitor in Plymouth and in Bristol; when Emma was born, almost six months after Tom, on 24 November 1840, he was back in Plymouth. By 1855 he seems to have given up the law, either because he was struck off (this was Florence's story, but it is unlikely), or because he retired to live off the income of his widowed mother, who also lived in Plymouth. Gifford had the airs of what in those ultra-class-conscious days was thought of as a gentleman (to be 'retired', even if it meant living off your mother, was preferable in some eyes to practising a profession) and an educated man; but he was given to drink. When his mother died in 1860 it was found that her capital was depleted to an alarming extent – less than £1,000 was available, and that had to be divided. The Giffords fell on harder times. They went to live in rented accommodation near Bodmin, and the girls were at various times sent out as governesses or companions. Just what the Giffords lived on, since John Attersoll – who lived until 1890 – did not take again to the law, is something of a mystery; possibly he did some kind of legal work to augment his 'meagre income'.

Although she attended nothing better than a dame school in Plymouth (run by 'dear refined single ladies of perfect manners'), Emma had tender memories of a genteel life, even if it was rather impoverished, and her father was given to alcoholic outbursts. He had once signed the pledge, and kept to it for a time; but he was given to drinking whenever someone in the family died, and doubtless on other occasions. Emma remembered (with pleasure) an afternoon when, after taking too much wine, he drew the blinds of the sitting-room, got out his Shakespeare folio, and spent some hours declaiming from it. Very little is known of him, but he has been judged not a pleasant man – although if this is a typical memory, there are much worse ways of being drunk.

While acting as a companion, Helen, Emma's older sister, had met the rector of St Juliot, the Rev. Caddell Holder. Born in 1803, the son of a judge in Barbados, and educated at Trinity College, Oxford, he was a relaxed, humorous man. His wife died in 1867, and in the autumn of 1868 he married Helen Gifford – thirty-five years his junior. Emma came to live with her at the rectory: 'my sister required my help, for it was a difficult parish . . .'. But Emma no doubt also needed to escape for a time from a father whom she adored but whose uncertain temper or habits she may have feared.

The rector, at sixty-seven, was in poor health, and subject in particular to painful attacks of gout. The household had long been awaiting 'the architect': 'the whole village was alive about . . . the Church-restoration', wrote Emma in her charming document 'Some Recollections', a substantial part of which Tom printed, with few alterations, in the *Life*. 'The [assistant-architect] of [Crickmay's] office was to come on a certain day . . . it was almost wonderful that a fixed date should at last be given . . . All were delighted.' Emma herself had worked hard towards raising funds for the restoration, with watercolour sketches and economies with the housekeeping. Tom's journey she recollected as 'like a chess-knight's move', as indeed it was. It had included the town of her birth.

Holder had had one of his sudden attacks of gout, and his wife was attending to him, when Tom felt his way along the by now dark rectory drive to the front door, and rang the bell. Emma wrote:

> I had to receive him alone, and felt a curious uneasy embarrassment at receiving anyone, especially so necessary a person as the architect. I was immediately arrested by his familiar appearance, as if I had seen him in a dream – his slightly different accent, his soft voice; also I noted a blue paper sticking out of his pocket. I was explaining who I was . . . when my sister appeared, to my great relief, and he went up to Mr Holder's room with her.

A Pair of Blue Eyes is not a reliable guide to the characters of Emma, Tom (who is 'spread' between Stephen Smith and Horace Knight) or anyone else; but many of the circumstances of its author's past are faithfully mirrored in its pages. Thus:

> 'I am Mr Smith,' said the stranger in a musical voice.
> 'I am Miss Swancourt,' said Elfride.
> Her constraint was over. The great contrast between the reality she beheld before her, and the dark, taciturn, sharp, elderly man of

business who had lurked in her imagination . . . was such a relief that Elfride smiled, almost laughed, in the new-comer's face.

Stephen Smith, who has hitherto been hidden from us by the darkness, was at this time of his life but a youth in appearance [Hardy puts the age of these two characters back by a decade], and not yet a man in years . . .

Before this there is a description of Elfride:

. . . She had lived all her life in retirement – the *monstrari digito* [this echoes the Latin poet Persius, who wrote in his first satire of how the finger is pointed at beauty] of idle men had not flattered her, and at the age of nineteen or twenty she was no further on in social consciousness than an urban young lady of fifteen.

One point in her, however, you did notice: that was her eyes. In them was a sublimation of all of her; it was not necessary to look further: there she lived.

Her eyes were blue: blue as autumn distance – blue as the sea we see between the retreating mouldings of hills and woody slopes on a sunny September morning . . .

Tom fell instantly in love with Emma's artlessness, with her vitality, with her eyes (just as he described them in *A Pair of Blue Eyes*, although they were not as blue), with her almost extreme flurrying naturalness, which was certainly unusual if not (at this point) eccentric. He associated her, as was his wont, with the 'magic' landscape in which she lived:

> When I came back from Lyonnesse
> With magic in my eyes,
> All marked with mute surmise
> My radiance rare and fathomless,
> When I came back from Lyonnesse
> With magic in my eyes!

Emma was attracted by the bookish young man precisely because he was not conventionally 'handsome'. It has been said that he was 'unprepossessing', and that she was 'obliged to make the best of him'; but this is a misreading of the situation, one based on a soap-opera view of sexual attraction. With the directness that was always to characterize her, and which could be as charming and admirable as it could (later) be tactless and disconcerting, she described Tom (in 1911) as he had then been in her perception: seeming 'older than he was' until she studied him by daylight, with yellowish beard and 'shabby greatcoat'. The soap-opera view fails to take account of the 'blue paper' turning out to be 'the MS of a poem', and of what that meant to the young Emma, an accomplished horsewoman who rode about fearlessly, who sang and played the piano, and who read the poets. She might have been impressed by a 'handsome man of business', but she would not have been interested in him and would not have fallen in love with him.

Florence Hardy fostered the story of a conspiracy in the rectory to 'get' Tom as a husband for Emma; but no such conspiracy was necessary. The two fell deeply in love, and remained so for a long time after their marriage in 1874. Indeed, despite the bitter differences which developed between them, they never ceased to love each other. If Tom was tied up with any other woman or women in early 1870, then such evidence as there is shows only his trying to break off such connections. The story of the ring first given to Tryphena, or to another, is inconclusive. The all-out love affair which he remembered so vividly was not an invention of old age, Tryphena Sparks or no Tryphena Sparks. And he not only fell in love with the spirited, strange, 'living' (as he put it) young woman, but also with her enthusiasm for poetry, and for him as a writer. There is little reason to doubt his own words, that his 'wooing' in Cornwall 'ran, in fact, without a hitch from beginning to end, and with encouragement from all parties concerned'. The later discouragement – probably just ill temper, and perhaps drunken ill temper at that – from Emma's father was unpleasant; but it was unimportant, for he finished the above-quoted sentence with: 'any want of smoothness lying on his own side as to the question of ways and means to marriage'. This was cut out by Florence after his death in accordance with her own notion that he had been 'trapped' into marriage.

Thus, even if everyone was pleased by the way in which matters developed between them, there was no special 'plot' for Emma to 'catch' Tom. If the initial love and physical attraction between the couple had started to cool by the time of the marriage four years later (for which there is no evidence), it would be unsurprising: romantic love does cool. This theme recurs in Hardy's fiction, although its emphasis is on what has been called 'deteriorism', that is, the tendency of the loved one to 'decay', to lose beauty and attractiveness. His insistence upon this is indeed harsh and discomforting; he is drawing attention to the habit of men, in general, to be attracted by younger women, and thus to become more sexually interested in them than they are in their middle-aged wives. He is already aware of this, as of love's tendency to fade, in the first of the 'She, to Him' sequences of poems, in which the girl's 'excellencies' have become 'withered'.

The laconic account, in the *Life*, of the three days and four nights he spent at St Juliot in March 1870 shows that the affair ripened rapidly, although by correspondence rather than contact. They would not meet again for five months. His diary for 7 March simply reads, 'Received by young lady in brown (Miss Gifford, the rector's sister-in-law)'. On the next day he did all the work necessary in connection with the purpose of his visit. 'A funeral. Man tolled the bell (which stood inverted on the ground in the neglected transept) by lifting the clapper, and letting it fall on the side.' He took his meals in the rectory, when Emma and he must already have been eyeing each other. In *A Pair of Blue Eyes* he records the sense in which he found her so 'living', so full of vitality. On the Wednesday, his work completed, he was taken to the Tintagel and Penpethy slate quarries 'with a view to the church roofing'. About that visit he wrote the haunting 'Green Slates', remembering 'A form against the slate background there,/Of fairness eye-commanding.'

Forgetting both that beauty is in the eye of the beholder and that a few faded photographs cannot capture the radiance or presence (or anything else) of a once living person, commentators have been grudging about the woman Tom loved most of all: they have judged her by what she became when she was old. There has been a tendency to consider his retrospective poems about Emma without really quite believing in, or considering, the initial spell that she cast upon him: 'her complexion . . . perfect in hue, her figure and movement graceful, and her corn-coloured hair abundant in its coils'. (Florence Hardy cut the additional sentence, 'A lock still in existence shows, even after the fading and deterioration of half a century, that there was no exaggeration in her friends' admiring memories of it.')

On the Thursday morning Emma took him to Beeny Cliff: 'She on horseback'. In the afternoon he walked to Boscastle, Mrs Holder accompanying him 'three-quarters of the way'. He already needed Emma's undivided attention: 'Emma provokingly reading as she walked'. On the last evening they walked in the garden, and then 'music later. . .'. He was enchanted.

EMMA GIFFORD

March 11. Dawn. Adieu. E.L.G. had struck a light six times in her anxiety to call the servants early enough for me. The journey home.

The poem 'At the Word "Farewell" ' relates, he said, to this, or the following (August) visit:

> Even then scale might have been turned
> Against love by a feather,
> – But crimson one cheek of hers burned
> When we came in together.

On the Saturday he charged Crickmay £6.10s.9d. for his expenses, and by 5 April was back in lodgings at Weymouth in order to work on the St Juliot drawings. By then he had started an extensive correspondence with Emma (he destroyed every trace of it), sending her books and, obviously, discussing literature, and his hopes for his own part in it, with her. He was now dwelling much upon his chances as a writer, since that is what Emma most admired in him.

In the months between March and August, when he was mostly in London in connection with the publication of *Desperate Remedies*, absence made their hearts grow increasingly fonder. Tom's chief confidant was Horace Moule, who, having left Marlborough, was also in London at that time, working as a tutor. He told Moule of the 'vague understanding' between them.

Having, he says, 'airily used' Crickmay 'as something of a stop-gap when his . . . literary enterprises hung fire', he left for London on 16 May, but 'sadly', 'for he had left his heart in Cornwall'. He took lodgings in Montpellier Street and did architectural work, rather 'desultorily', for Blomfield, who was always glad to make use of him. It is 'not clear what he was waiting for', he wrote of this time: i.e. he was as confused as he had ever been. He was on the threshold, or so he believed, of a new and exciting intellectual, as well as amorous, relationship, but more caught than ever between architecture and literature. He went to many picture galleries and made notes on certain paintings, such as Gérôme's *Death of Ney*. He was also reading a great deal – something he always did when he was confused – including Comte, the Bible (again) and a book about Islam.

Tom often expressed sorrow that he had been involved in the vulgar exercise of Gothic restoration of English churches, not only because he enjoyed 'picturesque neglect' for its own sake, but also because, as he wrote, he admired 'beautiful ancient Gothic'; he was relieved that he had only been 'passively instrumental' in 'such obliteration'. This may have been why he was so 'much interested' in Russell Brandon, whom he assisted, on and off, for a few weeks in this confused month of May 1870. This architectural author and teacher was devoted to French as distinct from English Gothic. But sympathetic as he was to Brandon's ideas, and to the man himself, Tom could not be so enthusiastic about the scheme for 'unifying railway-fares on the principle of letter-postage', which, his practice having declined, Brandon had devised. Tom felt in an 'awkward dilemma' whether to 'show Brandon its futility, and offend him, or to go against his own conscience by indulging him'.

In this period he wrote the 'Ditty (E.L.G.)' to Emma, a poem which, when he published it in *Wessex Poems* in 1898, she did not by then consider sufficient compensation for other poems to other women, and she complained bitterly. When a critic suggested that it derived from Barnes' 'Maid o' Newton' Tom angrily commented (in the margin of his book) 'Untrue'. It has a somewhat dutiful air, written from the feeling that it was Emma's due from her poet. (He was no doubt recording his deeper feelings in his correspondence with her.) But the sense of the poem is interesting: he records his feelings about her living in isolation from urban ways of 'barter' and selling, but instantly notes that, to all her neighbours and 'fellow-wights',

> Who descry the times as I,
> No such lucid legend tells
> Where she dwells.

The stanzas following are, by his standards, feeble, and suggest that he preserved and published this unimpassioned poem because he did not wish to provoke Emma. He wrote, by his own testimony, no other poems during this period – which has been taken to mean that his passion had cooled, or that he was having an affair with someone else: for example, as has been speculated, with Tryphena Sparks, now at college at Stockwell. Yet if he did not write poetry at this time, then it was, rather, because he was happy, and happiness was not conducive to poetry for Tom except as a recollected state, or as one attainable in a hardly foreseeable future. All that can be said is that 'Ditty (E.L.G.)' may point to some purely cerebral doubts, inasmuch as, in it, he chooses to consider the possibility of never having met Emma. She said in 'Some Recollections' (written after what some have supposed to have been an irretrievable breach) that she found him 'a perfectly new subject of study and delight and he found a "mine" in me he said': this may allude to the 'Mine' of the 'Ditty (E.L.G.)'.

Just as Tom felt love and wonder for Emma, so he felt foreboding: the sense of despondency about marital relationships, a lifelong theme, was already more than merely tentative in him, but his view was not, as has been suggested, 'already overcast with spite'. It was rather that, as a poet – and a poet particularly influenced by Shelley's rebelliousness and by Meredith's disturbing portrait of marriage in his *Modern Love* – Tom felt himself to be out of kilter with orthodox arrangements. That was why he was fascinated by Fourier's proposals, which seemed to him to be more practical, more in keeping with human nature. He did not want, as Shelley so vehemently did, to 'change the world'. He needed all his energies for writing. Nevertheless, he was, at heart, as rebellious and subversive as any poet has been. Nothing in him was then, or ever, agreeable to life as it is normally lived: he preferred, for all of his dutiful forays into society, to place himself firmly outside it. A mankind which made wars, he was finally to state, did not deserve to survive. There is no praise, anywhere in his work, of what society has done. He would, even then, have affirmed what he wrote in his own 'Wessex Heights' (1896):

In the lowlands I have no comrade, not even the lone man's
    friend –
Her who suffereth long and is kind; accepts what he is too weak
    to mend:
Down there they are dubious and askance; there nobody thinks as I,
But mind-chains do not clank where one's neighbour is the sky.

On top of this was his frustration, if not resentment, that he could not do what he wanted to do – devote all his time to poetry – unless he were to become an unmarriageable beggar. As a poet, how could he keep a wife? Have children? He was being forced into a role he did not really want, that of novelist; nor did he want to be an architect. So, while he did not resent Emma herself, a part of him did profoundly resent just that disturbance which provided him with the material for amorous poetry.

On 27 May he went to a church service at St Mary's, Bryanston Square. He put the date by the Epistle of St James, 1,22: 'Be ye doers of the word, and not hearers only.' What did the reader of the positivist Comte mean by this keeping up of his churchgoing habit, even after the loss of his earlier childhood faith? Millgate suggests that he resumed 'his old habit' of churchgoing 'under Emma's influence', but he had attended church services before he met her – he certainly went to church at Stinsford in January 1870, and there is nothing to say that he did not go every Sunday throughout the February that followed. While staying at the St Juliot rectory, it would have been natural to go with her to services taken by his host; he was not posing as a Christian in order to deceive or please her. He continued to attend services with her during their marriage; and he would continue to attend services after she died.

Tom told Florence Hardy, in a letter written just before he married her, that Emma had been an 'Agnostic' – 'had no religious opinion whatever'. But he never repeated this, doubtless feeling that it was not quite true. Although Emma may have said little about it before the marriage, and perhaps thought little about it when she was young, she always assumed the fundamental truth of Christianity. When they first met she probably took it for granted that Tom was a Christian too. Only later did she become militantly Christian, perhaps after the publication of *Jude* (1898) had deeply upset her, and she would object to or lament (depending on her mood) her husband's lack of faith.

Although Tom's lack of intellectual faith in Christianity became clear enough in time (he made sure it did), a man who read Comte *and* the Bible, and attended church services, does not have a simple attitude. Ford Madox Ford tells us, in *Return to Yesterday* (1932), of an occasion comparatively late in his life, while Emma was still alive, and which Gilbert Murray corroborated late in his own life, that he was

> one night at the house of Mr Edward Clodd . . . There were present
> . . . Thomas Hardy, Mr Hilaire Belloc, Mrs Belloc Lowndes, some
> more novelists and Professor Gilbert Murray. Mr Clodd had been one
> of those who, with Huxley, Bradlaugh, Foote the atheist, Ingersoll
> and others, had, in the eighties of the last century, destroyed revealed
> religion. The night was airless. On the black squares that the windows
> made, the lights of solitary fishing-boats hung themselves out. As was
> natural the talk fell on religion.
>
> Thomas Hardy avowed himself a believing communicant of the
> Established Church. Hilaire Belloc, his sister and other novelists were
> papists. Professor Murray had some sort of patent faith of which all
> I can remember is that a black velvet coffin played some part in it.
> Some other form of spiritualism was also represented.

At last, valiant old Mr Clodd threw his hands up above his white hair.

'Was it for this?' he exclaimed tragically, 'that we fought and overcame the priests in the eighties? You would think we had never lived. Here is a collection of the representative thinkers of Great Britain. Every one of them has his form of mumbo-jumbo. The old devils have all come creeping back and brought worse with them!'

In 1892 Tom told the magazine proprietor William Blackwood, apropos a review of *Tess*, that as a child he 'devoutly believed in the devil's pitchfork' because he had been brought up 'according to strict Church principles'. About at least some aspects of such principles he wrote to his rationalist friend Clodd, on 17 January 1897, that theology had arrested 'light and reason for 1,600 years':

> The older one gets, the more deplorable seems the effect of that terrible, dogmatic ecclesiasticism – Christianity so called (but really Paulinism *plus* idolatry) – on morals & true religion: a dogma with which the real teaching of Christ has hardly anything in common.

The phrases 'true religion' and 'real teaching of Christ' are notable here, particularly since he was writing to a man he knew to be a ferocious rationalist and enemy of all religion. The number of years that he calculated is as notable: Clodd would have written 'almost 1900'. There may be a conviction here, but one Tom seldom wished to discuss: that the rot set in, not with Christ, but with the increasingly worldly success of the Church. In a later letter of 27 February 1902, again to Clodd, he discusses the matter in greater depth. He had been reading his old friend's biography of T.H. Huxley, almost a paradigm, for the Victorians, of the agnostic position. Congratulating Clodd, he commented:

> What is forced upon one again, after reading such a life as Huxley's, is the sad fact of the extent to which Theological lumber is still allowed to discredit religion, in spite of such devoted attempts as his to shake it off. If the doctrines of the supernatural were quietly abandoned to-morrow by the Church, & 'reverence & love for an ethical ideal' alone retained, not one in ten thousand would object to the readjustment, while the enormous bulk of thinkers excluded by the old teaching would be brought back into the fold, & our venerable

old churches & cathedrals would become the centres of emotional life that they once were.

Well: what we gain by science is, after all, sadness, as the Preacher saith. The more we know of the laws & nature of the Universe the more ghastly a business we perceive it to be – & the non-necessity of it. As some philosopher says, if nothing at all existed, it would be a completely natural thing; but that the world exists is a fact absolutely logicless & senseless.

This is as inexorably negative on the question of life's being worth living as Tom always liked to be, and even seems linked to his mood when, as a very small boy, he looked through that straw hat. Samuel Beckett, who held the same opinion (as did Sophocles), and who was given to expressing it from time to time, once wrote a work called *I Can't Go On, I'll Go On* – an almost necessary corollary. In about 1908 Tom was taking a cycle ride with an acquaintance, Clive Holland, in the 'sunshine of a beautiful August afternoon'; a blackbird fluttered out of a hedge with a broken wing.

Hardy got off his cycle, and turning after a moment to me a distressed and, indeed, almost agitated face, said 'Will you do something for that poor bird? I cannot.'

I replied 'Certainly, if I can. What is it?'

He replied, almost turning his head away from the wounded bird, 'Kill it'.

Adding 'If you don't – I couldn't – it will be tortured by a cat or stoat'.

I went to the roadside, when I came back to him, he said 'Thank you. Poor thing, poor thing!' . . .

Quite suddenly he looked at me and said 'I am going to ask you a question. Will you answer it honestly?'

'If it can be answered at all, it shall certainly be answered honestly,' I replied.

'Well then,' he said, 'if you had the choice of being born, would you have been?'

In reply I told him that had he asked me the question less abruptly I should probably have answered 'Yes'. But that he had raised great doubt in my mind. Then I asked him 'Would you?'

After a pause the reply came: 'No, surely not'. Followed by several reasons, which were weighty enough as the speaker stated them.

Mood dictates such convictions, and in Tom such a mood was invariably prompted by nature's apparent cruelty. But this view of life not being worth living, as expressed in his letter to Clodd, does not account for the venerable old churches, or the possibility of their becoming 'the centres of emotional life that they once were': what 'emotional life' is there in a 'ghastly world' that ought not to exist and does so only in a 'logicless and senseless' way? Mere ethics cannot account for Tom's own church attendance and the emotional 'life' which he gained from it. He gained emotional life, too, from writing poetry.

He was, as he truthfully told the company that night at Clodd's, a communicating member of the Established Church, and his actions in that respect (attending church services and taking communion throughout his life) must be taken as stronger than his words of rejection of Christian 'supernaturalism' as a matter of intellectual principle. Yet he never rejected supernaturalism at all, despite the struggle of part of him to do so. Without supernaturalism – that mystery which he acknowledged when he said, in introducing *The Dynasts*, that the universe was inexplicable – his poetry is nothing. Clodd was happy in his atheistical agnosticism, and aggressive about priests as 'supernaturalists'; but Tom, although capable of showing them as lustful hypocrites, did not possess any such feelings against them. He refused to be included in a 'Biographical Dictionary of Modern Rationalists' (1920), politely pleading, through Florence, that he was 'an irrationalist rather than a rationalist, on account of his inconsistencies . . . he thinks he could show that no man is a rationalist, and that human actions are not ruled by reason at all in the last resort'. He disliked supernaturalism in himself because it led to pain, instead of to as much indifference as could be mustered. But his rejection of it, being wholly cerebral, was not complete, but rather 'inconsistent'. Had he really thought of churches as ethical temples, then he would not have partaken of the sacraments.

But in 1870 it is enough to note that he attended a church service at St Mary's in Bryanston Square, and that despite himself, or despite what by then were probably hardening intellectual convictions, he responded emotionally to the service. And what is more interesting than his intellectual rejection of Christianity is the complex nature of his emotional life, whether or not he later chose to reject aspects of this in his capacity as a public man forced by earnest people to possess a 'philosophy of life'.

On 15 July 1870 the Franco-Prussian War began, and the following month, on 8 August, he left London to return, as promised, to Cornwall. This three-week visit would afterwards contain many of his most rapturous memories of Emma. He wrote no poems around this time; it was only when he looked back upon his happiness, as irrevocably lost, that he felt impelled to poetry. Nor did the outbreak of the war inspire him, although the famous 'In Time of "The Breaking of Nations" ' was written from notes that he made on 18 August about the quiet pastoral scene he observed – just as the Battle of Gravelotte was being fought. Moule was sending, to him and Emma, his own newspaper comments about the war's course, and Tom wrote in his notebook, 'Quicquid delirant reyes, plectuntur Achivi!'.

During that three weeks, Emma and Tom found themselves fulfilled in each other's eyes. He found her now in 'Summer blue'; he read poetry with her, there was again music, and, most of all, there were trips. On one day they went alone to King Arthur's Castle and were so wrapped up in each other that they 'found themselves locked in, only narrowly escaping being imprisoned for the night by much signalling with their handkerchiefs'. On another occasion, made famous by Tom's sketch of her trying to retrieve it, Emma dropped a picnic tumbler into the rocks of a waterfall in the valley of the little river, the Valency, which wound its way through the valley to Boscastle.

When he returned to Bockhampton at the end of the three weeks nothing had occurred to interrupt the idyll. It has been written that the need to 'recreate again and again the image of the absent beloved . . . led Hardy to project to Emma and to himself, hopes and promises that reality could not in the nature of things fulfil.' But that is a truism. It is easy to equate Tom's emotions about Emma with the lines from the Song of Solomon which he marked 'E.L.G.' on 28 October ('Thy teeth like a flock of sheep . . .'), just after she had told him that she took the 'reserved man' as she did the Bible: 'find out what I am, compare one text with another, & believe the rest, in a lump of simple faith'. It is not so easy to equate this with one of his own Bible markings, of 28 September: 'Do they not err that devise evil?' In fact, however, Tom was just continuing with the re-reading of the Bible which he had begun in the previous May. Those who desire evil could as well be warmongers as anyone else.

Millgate suggests that Emma 'permitted sexual intimacy' that August and then feigned pregnancy in order to force Tom to make a public commitment to marriage. To support this, he cites Arabella's trick on Jude in *Jude the Obscure*, by which she pretends she is pregnant and gets him to marry her. But that trick is far too well known to require the inference that, because Tom used it in a novel, it had actually happened to him. Millgate also cites the poem, 'The Place on the Map'. This first appeared in the *English Review* in 1913, with the subtitle 'A Poor Schoolmaster's Story', and is a dramatic lyric such as Hardy was in the habit of writing, concerning a girl who tells her schoolteacher lover that she is expecting a baby. It may indeed be that Tom and Emma made love; perhaps they could not help themselves. In that case the poem might be based on a recollection of an occasion when Emma told Tom that she believed herself to be pregnant. Such beliefs are as common as they eventually prove to be misguided: anxiety can delay periods. However, even if she did for a short time have such a belief, there is no reason to suppose a blackmailing intention of marriage. This was not in character. The poem ends:

> For the wonder and the wormwood of the whole
> Was that what in realms of reason would have joyed our double soul
>   Wore a torrid tragic light
> Under order-keeping's rigorous control.
>
> So, the map revives her words, the spot, the time,
> And the thing we found we had to face before the next year's prime;
>   The charted coast stares bright,
> And its episode comes back in pantomime.

(For 'order-keeping's rigorous' Hardy originally wrote 'superstition's hideous'.) The dramatic situation apart, the basic assumption here is the radical one that sex should not necessarily be a trigger for marriage. But Hardy's attitude to marriage as an institution was rather more complicated than it is usually supposed to have been, and did not quite coincide with his attitude towards his relationship with Emma, whatever his occasional thoughts about the matter.

In any event Tom returned home to Bockhampton in late August 1870, the love idyll intact, and they continued their correspondence. She encouraged him with his writing, made fair copies of chapters of his novels (not of her own, although she was probably now beginning to write her still unpublished and, alas, inferior story, 'The Maid on the Shore'), discussed them with him intimately, and bade fair to be just the intellectual companion he above all desired. The affair prospered because for most of the time they idealized each other at a distance. It would be four years before they finally married, and reality would not fulfil either's full hopes in the other. But what warm-blooded human person's hopes does reality fulfil? Most of us tend to invent another reality. But not Thomas Hardy.

7

Desperate Remedies

Tom put it on record that he believed *Desperate Remedies* was 'quite below the level of *The Poor Man and the Lady*'. It was, he thought, 'the unfortunate consequence of Meredith's advice to "write a story with a plot"'. *The Poor Man and the Lady* was more satirical, probably in the manner of Thackeray's *Book of Snobs*, than dramatic. But in *Desperate Remedies* he held much of the satire in check, and disciplined himself to write an intricately plotted novel with the aim of attaining publication.

Before setting off for Cornwall in early March 1870 he had sent his new work (of which he had yet to write up the last chapters) to Macmillan. But some time between his return on 12 March and going into lodgings again at Weymouth on 5 April to get on with his St Juliot's work, he received the manuscript back: Macmillan, who had again got John Morley to read it, told him that it had 'decided qualities' but was 'of far too sensational an order for us to publish'. Tom now realized that Macmillan could not be tempted to publish a 'sensation novel' – which is just what he had set himself to write.

The term 'sensation novel' had at that time a special meaning, though it was only in 1919 with W.C. Phillips' book, *Dickens, Reade and Collins: Sensation Novelists*, that the meaning gained whatever precision it may possess. The Oxford philosopher and historian of gnosticism, the 'deep-dyed Tory' Henry Longueville Mansell, provided one of the earliest applications of the word to literature: in 1863 he wrote of 'the cheap publications which supply sensation for the million'. By 'sensation' he meant 'violent emotion', and the word was applied, initially, to describe the 'sensational' effects aimed at by the author. Well before Tom wrote *Desperate Remedies*, the Archbishop of York had preached against sensation fiction as 'one of the abominations of the age'. In its lowest form it resembled the gutter fiction of our own times.

Dickens fathered the genre, but his fiction contains too much else for it to be considered usefully in these terms. Wilkie Collins, however, from whom Dickens learned so much (as Collins learned from him), perfected the genre, with his fantastic, almost mathematical plotting – first in *Basil* (1852) and then, most notably, in *The Woman in White* (1860) and *The Moonstone* (1868). (His *Armadale* of 1866 is almost a paradigm of the genre: its plot is so complicated that at one point there are no fewer than five characters called Alan Armadale.) The prolific Mary Russell Braddon, writing in imitation of Dickens and Collins, and under the pressure of her own unconventional experiences, achieved the biggest hit of all with her bigamy-and-murder novel, *Lady Audley's Secret* (1862). It was published in volume form by William Tinsley, who from his profits built a house at Barnes called Audley Lodge. By the end of the 1860s this kind of fiction was still dominant, and even Trollope in *The Eustace Diamonds* (1872) was influenced by it, as George Eliot had been in her first novel, *Adam Bede* (1859).

In turning to novel-writing after realizing that he could not be a poet and earn a living, Tom put his money, on his second attempt, on this still dominant sensational genre, and it was at Collins' achievement, above that of Mary Braddon (though he came to know and like her), that he looked most closely. The flamboyant Charles Reade, the other leading sensation novelist, was too crude for him. Collins, however, provided a sympathetic model. He was candid; he was an advocate of reform; and he had not yet gone into his decline, during which his writing deteriorated (drug-taking destroyed his powers of visual evocation) and he produced over-polemical novels. He was also admired by the contemporary poet with whom Tom was then in particular sympathy, Swinburne, who had not yet had cause to write:

> What brought good Wilkie's genius nigh to perdition?
> Some demon whispered, 'Wilkie! have a mission'.

Desperate Remedies was modelled mainly on Collins' *Basil* and *The Woman in White*, although there are echoes of *Lady Audley's Secret*; but it also contains much that is uniquely Hardyan. The plot, which is conventional within the genre he chose, concerns the plight of an orphaned and impoverished heroine, Cytherea Graye, who loves a young architect called Edward Springrove. He loves her, but is engaged to Adelaide Hinton, the daughter of a retired newspaper editor. Cytherea falls victim to her mysterious wealthy namesake, Miss Cytherea Aldclyffe, whose maid she becomes, and then to Miss Aldclyffe's steward, Aeneas Manstone. Hardy drops a strong clue as to the real relationship between Miss Aldclyffe and Manston by the names he gives them, both taken from his beloved *Aeneid*. For, although he does not know it, Manston, so named by the widow who adopted him, is the child of Miss Aldclyffe and her cousin, a 'wild young officer' who deserted her and went to India, where he died. The scandalous circumstances prevented Miss Aldclyffe, then Miss Bradleigh (she takes the name Aldclyffe in order to inherit her estate), from marrying the man she loved, the architect Ambrose Graye, who subsequently entered into a loveless marriage of which two children were born, Owen and Cytherea, the latter named after his lost love.

In the first decisively Hardyan touch, the eighteen-year-old Cytherea watches from the town hall as her father slips and falls to his death from a spire on which he and his assistants are working.

> Emotions will attach themselves to scenes that are simultaneous, however foreign in essence these scenes may be – as chemical waters will crystallize on twigs and wires. Even after that time any mental agony brought less vividly to Cytherea's mind the scene from the Town Hall windows than sunlight streaming in shaft-like lines.

As in 'Neutral Tones', the scene is transformed into an arbitrary ('however foreign in essence these scenes may be') symbol for an experience and, therefore, for the meaning of that experience. In the childhood image of the straw hat which Hardy recorded in his autobiography and which remained with him until he died, the life-giving rays of the sun were interrupted by the shadows cast by the straw; the associated thoughts were that he did not wish to grow up, or to possess things, or to have ambitions. He only received the image at all, he wrote, because the lining of the hat had 'disappeared'. In other words, his nature lacked the protective covering that is usual: the pain associated with living was too great, and he felt it so keenly that he had a strong impulse simply to stagnate.

This matching of image to experience, and of landscape to mood and character, would be a major ingredient in all his work, as would the effort to transcend the subjective, or arbitrary, element in it. The original straw hat image gives a clue, too, to the reason why Tom found it so hard to renounce the idea of simply 'being a poet'. Most if not all poets have been content to await visitations from the muse, and Tom felt himself to be so acutely sensitive that he could, at all times, make his response to life in the form of poetry – which is, eventually, just what he did.

123

And here, at the beginning of his first published novel, he presents a key image, the guide to his own method. In attributing the experience to a young woman he seems to identify his imaginative method with a feminine component of himself. In showing a painful event as a vignette he anticipates his practice in *The Dynasts*, in which events on the earth are thus viewed by spirits. And in the sneering and cruel attitudes of some of these spirits there is exactly that element, although on a much larger scale, which was most deplored by Macmillan in *The Poor Man*: 'utter heartlessness'.

After the sudden death of her father, Cytherea is engaged as a maid by Miss Aldclyffe, who also contrives, through tricks, to engage Manston as steward of her estate. She manipulates matters so that Cytherea's affair with Springrove is frustrated, and, when Manston becomes sexually fascinated with the young woman, she furthers his suit, not knowing him to be already married to a Philadelphia actress called Eunice. Cytherea, believing herself deserted by Springrove, and because of her sick brother's poverty, agrees to marry Manston. But Springrove turns up at the ceremony, and, after some suspenseful but melodramatic chasing about by railway, Cytherea, now again in love with him, is saved from the Victorian fate worse than death, which was to be the unwilling (but fascinated) satisfier of villainous lust. In the second part of the book, into which a detective is fashionably introduced, it transpires that Manston killed his wife (by accident) and that he succeeded in passing off a mistress, Anne Seaway, as her. After making a final attempt on Cytherea's virtue ('He lifted her upon the sofa, exclaiming, "Rest here for a while, my frightened little bird!"'), from which she is delivered by Springrove, he is arrested. After revealing all in a written confession, he dies in prison. Miss Aldclyffe also dies, and Edward and Cytherea are free to marry.

Apart from causing an apparition of Miss Aldclyffe to appear to Cytherea at the very moment of her death, Hardy studiously resisted the temptation to indulge himself in Gothic supernaturalism; even of this incident the narrator remarks that she was 'probably dreaming'. The plot is carefully and, especially for a beginner, professionally worked out. The action takes place between 1863 and 1867, and the chapter headings are solely concerned with date and time; almost as if to draw attention to the semi-mathematical task which the author had set himself of inventing a highly manipulative plot. As Morley said of it: 'complex and absolutely impossible, yet . . . worked out with elaborate seriousness and consistency'. It is one of the best imitations of Collins.

More unusual than the plot, though, is the eroticism and, in particular, the lesbian theme. For Miss Aldclyffe falls in love with her victim, the luscious young Cytherea. There is no doubt of this, and no doubt, either, of the author's full awareness of the fact. Morley, knowing very well what was intended, wrote of 'highly extravagant' scenes, and even pinpointed one of them as showing Miss Aldclyffe in bed with her maid. Other erotic scenes in the book are fairly standard from the eighteenth century. The villainous Manston takes on a resemblance to Richardson's Lovelace and to Holcroft's Coke Clifton (in *Anna St Ives*, 1794). He plays to Cytherea an organ – which he has himself constructed – during a thunderstorm. This deeply affects her; but her fascination with him is wholly sexual, for 'his influence over her . . . vanished with the musical chords'. Later, though, she dreams

> that she is being whipped with dry bones suspended on strings, which rattled at every blow like those of a malefactor on a gibbet; that she shifted and shrank and avoided every blow . . . She could not see the face of the executioner for his mask, but the form was like Manston's.

This is standard Gothic sado-masochistic fare, and Manston's sexual fascination is routinely represented, except, perhaps, for the occasion upon which Cytherea, after her clothes have just touched Manston's as he whispers 'Do try to love me', fancies that she hears the shriek of mandrakes being torn up, and feels 'as one in a boat without oars, drifting with closed eyes down a river – she knew not whither'.

More original, and typical of Hardy, is an earlier scene in a boat (with oars) between Springrove and Cytherea. Springrove takes her out on the bay, and the fact of their fragile aloneness on the sea, turning towards and then away from the safety of the shore, is used as a metaphor for their sexual situation. Springrove tells Cytherea that he writes poetry – 'Writing rhymes is a stage people of my sort pass through, as they pass through the stage of shaving for a beard, or thinking they're ill-used, or saying there's nothing in the world worth living for' – and eventually kisses her. This scene is in no way 'extravagant'; on the contrary, it is handled with charm and a knowing delicacy. But it made even Morley nervous. Here was a writer who knew exactly what he was doing – whereas most other Victorian writers, even ones as sophisticated as Browning and the young Henry James (not that Morley could have heard of him yet: *Watch and Ward* would run in the *Atlantic Monthly* in the following year), were ignorant of the sexual tones they set up. The scene also gives the narrator the opportunity to reflect upon his creator's own situation:

> It is a melancholy task for the middle classes, that in proportion as they develop, by the study of poetry and art, their capacity for conjugal love of the highest and purest kind, they limit the possibility of their being able to exercise it – the very act putting out of their power the attainment of means sufficient for marriage. The man who works up a good income has no time to learn love to its solemn extreme; the man who has learnt that has had no time to get rich.

This is putting a very high (and discomforting) value indeed on 'love', treating it as something only to be learned through the study and even practice of poetry and art; it is cruel to 'society'; and it is not an immature observation. It means, in Macmillan's words of *The Poor Man and the Lady*, 'mischief', and would have disturbed the high-minded and intelligent Macmillan and Morley. Were they not 'rich'? But had they *really* not 'had time' to learn 'love to its solemn extreme'? *Desperate Remedies* is full of such authorial asides, some good and some, of course, not so good. Tom first learned the technique from the eighteenth-century novelists, and, above all, from George Eliot – as Horace Moule, with his special knowledge, wrote in his belated notice of the novel for the *Saturday Review*: 'like George Eliot the author delights in running off to *sententiae*'.

Macmillan's reluctance to publish such a novel was not surprising, but Tom later wondered why he had then submitted the manuscript to William Tinsley. In the *Life* he claimed that Tinsley's 'was a firm to which he was a stranger'; perhaps he had forgotten that it had offered to publish *The Poor Man and the Lady* for a deposit. In his old age he could not understand why he had not sent it on to Chapman and Hall, where he could have expected Meredith to take a personal interest. 'Possibly it was from an adventurous feeling that he would like the story to be judged on its own merits . . . possibly from inexperience.' Possibly, too, it was because he was excited: he was more deeply in love than he had ever been before – a man with a soul mate at last.

Tinsley, while stating that there were good reasons for not publishing the book as it stood, and that he was in need of the unwritten chapters (of which he had only a precis) to conclude it, offered to issue it if the author would guarantee £75. Tom did not much like Tinsley, whom he considered to be vulgar, but he did not turn down the offer; he later believed that he had suffered from the 'mistake' of sending the manuscript to Tinsley (and he would in fact later suffer financially in not being able to retrieve the copyright of *Under the Greenwood Tree* from this firm). In the latter part of 1870, however, he set about revising and completing *Desperate Remedies* for publication by Tinsley.

A note he made on 30 June, while in London, shows the cast of his thoughts about it: 'What the world is saying, and what the world is thinking: It is the man who bases his action upon what the world is thinking, no matter what it may be saying, who rises to the top.' He was being as practical as he could, and considering his prospects as a writer and earner. But while he concentrated on producing an acceptable story of the sensational sort, he made use of as much psychological and poetic material as he could, for he was determined to express himself as fully as he could within the limitations of prose.

In making substantial alterations for Tinsley, Tom removed a scene to which Morley had objected as a 'disgusting and absurd outrage', in which Miss Aldclyffe is 'violated at an evening party'. But he did not cut out the scene (about 3,500 words of text), also commented on by Morley, of Miss Aldclyffe in bed with her maid. Even at this precarious stage in his writing career, and already warned by the reaction to *The Poor Man and the Lady*, he felt a need for candour, and could not resist putting in 'daring' scenes. There is nothing 'naive' about the lesbianism in *Desperate Remedies*. The sophisticated verve with which he handles the theme belies the criticism that he was 'blundering in the pre-Freudian darkness' (as though Freud had invented 'sex' and his predecessors knew nothing of it). Indeed the most effective part of *Desperate Remedies*, besides the depiction of comic rustics, lies in the delineation of the lesbian relationship between the two Cythereas.

The Victorians hardly discussed female homosexuality, and Hardy is delicate about it. At the initial interview the two women 'showed off themselves to advantage as they walked forward in the orange light', and each 'showed too in her face that she had been struck with her companion's appearance'. The younger, suffused in the tint of sunlight refracted from crimson curtains and 'crimson-flock' wallpaper, possesses a 'voluptuousness which youth and a single life had not yet allowed to express itself ordinarily', while the elder woman's 'decaying complexion' is 'warmed . . . with much of the youthful richness it plainly had once possessed'. Here is already the voice of an expert, of a fascinated connoisseur of women, of one who had watched their faces when voluptuous and otherwise. It is not knowledge that comes out of books. Miss Aldclyffe, described as of spare but not angular proportions, is about to reject Cytherea as being unsuitably young and too inexperienced, and chokes back a reference to her liking for her 'appearance' as 'offensive to apply' to a 'ladylike girl' (the implication is that she herself has, in a word often used in the novel, *had* unladylike ones). Dismissed, Cytherea Graye turns, 'with as little coquettishness as was compatible with beauty', to leave.

Hardy now interpolates:

> It is not for a man to tell fishers of men how to set out their fascinations so as to bring about the highest possible average of takes within the year: but the action that tugs the hardest of all at an emotional beholder is this sweet method of turning which steals the bosom away and leaves the eyes behind.
>
> Now Miss Aldclyffe herself was no tyro at wheeling. When Cytherea had closed the door upon her she remained for some time in her motionless attitude, listening to the gradually dying sound of the maiden's retreating footsteps. She murmured to herself, 'It is almost worth while to be bored with instructing her in order to have a creature who could glide round my luxurious indolent body in that manner, and look at me in that way – I warrant how light her fingers are upon one's head and neck . . . What a silly modest young thing she is, to go away as suddenly as that!'

And she calls her back. It is notable that even the innocent young Cytherea is not entirely without coquetry in this situation: she is represented as lacking only as much of the quality as is possible for a beautiful young woman. Later the real nature of Miss Aldclyffe's feelings is confirmed when, irascible and confused, she expostulates because she has taken on a maid without references 'all because of her good l-'. The 'l-' is far more eloquent than 'looks' would have been, and demonstrates Hardy's awareness that he was trespassing on dangerous territory. But it was territory both proper to the novel, and irresistible to him: that of female psychology. No doubt he had heard from the women in service whom he had known – Martha Sparks, Eliza Nicholls, others whose names we may not know – tales of the mistress of the house taking their maids to bed with them. He was fully aware, anyway, of the implications. But there is no other scene in Victorian literature to match this one between the two Cythereas. It is as if he had said to himself: very well, I am not allowed to show a master taking advantage of his servant, so I will show a mistress doing so – and I will make that servant just a shade less than innocent in her coquetry!

Cytherea goes to Knapwater House (modelled on Kingston Maurward House), the home of Miss Aldclyffe, and is soon called to attend her: to remove her dress and 'stockings and black boots', and to attire her in 'silk stockings and white shoes'. Miss Aldclyffe, ostensibly because of her new maid's inexperience, falls into a 'smouldering passion . . . lips firmly closed . . . muscles of her body rigid'. This is how a forty-six-year-old sexually excited woman in such a situation would behave. She goes to dinner and returns to her room. At midnight she sounds her bell 'loudly and jerkingly'. Cytherea

> hastened to the room, to find the lady sitting before the dressing-shrine, illuminated on both sides, and looking so queenly . . . that the younger woman felt the awfullest sense of responsibility at her vandalism in having undertaken to demolish so imposing a pile.

Miss Aldclyffe now undresses, half-helped by Cytherea, who sees 'reflected in the glass . . . the fair white surface, and the inimitable combination of curves between throat and bosom which artists adore'. She is told, as she is shown the miniature Miss Aldclyffe wears round her neck – it is of course of her father, whom she recognizes – that 'you win me to make confidences'. Hardy, in recounting a love scene between women which he knew that he could not have got away with between a man and a woman, was perpetrating a degree of chutzpah which has gone unrecognized by those portrayers of him as an impotent voyeur, lacking in self-confidence. His readers would not dare to raise the issue of 'impropriety', but they were discomforted.

At this point the older woman, disturbed by the effect the younger is having upon her, provokes a quarrel; Cytherea, prompted to defy her, and to call her 'ill-tempered, unjust', is dismissed, and announces that she will leave the next day. On returning to her own room, upset and humiliated, 'red and panting', she undresses, 'her mind unconsciously drifting away to the contemplation of her late surprises'.

> To look in the glass for an instant at the reflection of her own magnificent resources in face and bosom, and to mark their attrac-tiveness unadorned, was perhaps but the natural action of a young

woman who had so lately been chidden whilst passing through the harassing experience of decorating an older beauty of Miss Aldclyffe's temper.

Once in bed she cannot sleep for thinking of her persecutor, who haunts 'her mind more persistently than ever'. At two o'clock she hears a 'soft rustle outside her room' (the rustle was significant to Victorian males, and occurs in Trollope). Miss Aldclyffe taps on her door and whispers through the keyhole: 'Cytherea . . . Let me come in, darling.'

> The young woman paused in conflict between judgement and emotion. It was now mistress and maid no longer; woman and woman only. Yes; she must let her come in, poor thing.

To put no finer point upon it, Miss Aldclyffe is in a frenzy of barely controlled lust. As an originally ruined maid, no 'tyro at wheeling' in such a manner as to display her breasts to their best advantage, and a 'wicked old sinner' who subscribes to 'missionary Societies and others of the sort' only because it is 'the code of polite society', she knows all about what has got into her. So does the narrator. Only the younger of the two women is uncertain. Even had Hardy wished to give details of the progress of her lust beyond those various degrees of kiss and entwined hair which he does enumerate, he could not possibly have done so. He would have been rumbled as an underminer of morality, and, worse, depictor of scenes which Queen Victoria did not believe were possible. But he goes as far as he can: as far as to satisfy all but the most reality-shy of commentators on him. She says: 'I want to stay here with you, Cythie', falling into the diminutive just as a seducer might do, 'I came to ask you to come down into my bed, but it is snugger here. But remember that you are mistress in this room, and that I have no business here, and that you may send me away if you choose. Shall I go?' ('"Oh no; you shan't indeed if you don't want to", said Cytherea generously.') If Hardy was indeed ignorant of lesbianism, why should he have inserted that question? Why should the innocent mistress of the servant ask her if she wants her to leave rather than have her in her bed?

Miss Aldclyffe, once in the bed, freeing 'herself from the last remnant of restraint', asks Cythie for a kiss, but the latter's 'passions were not so impetuous as Miss Aldclyffe's', and she is 'discomposed', and does not feel able to 'bring her soul to lips for a moment, try how she would'.

Cythie does give her a 'small kiss', sounding like 'the bursting of a bubble', but Miss Aldclyffe pleads, 'More earnestly than that – come.' 'Why can't you kiss me as I kiss you? Why can't you?'; she 'impressed upon Cytherea's lips a warm motherly salute', confesses her real age, and begins to talk about men.

Miss Aldclyffe here is seen in a sympathetic light, as an unhappy, lonely, temporarily candid and affection-seeking woman. She asks Cytherea if she has ever been kissed by a man, and then begs her to 'try to love me more than you love him – do. I love you more sincerely than any man can. Do, Cythie: don't let any man stand between us. O, I can't bear that!' And she clasps the girl's neck 'again'. The text then becomes explicitly erotic (Tinsley would have grinned and borne this), as the older woman launches into a passionate tirade, clearly implying that she has had previous homosexual experience (after all, she has just engaged Cytherea for her 'good l-'):

> Yes, women are all alike. I thought I had at last found an artless woman who had not been sullied by a man's lips, and who had not practised or been practised upon by the arts which ruin all the truth and sweetness and goodness in us. Find a girl, if you can, whose mouth and ears have not been made a regular highway of by some man or other! Leave the admittedly notorious sports – the drawing-rooms of society – and look in the villages – leave the villages and search in the schools – and you can hardly find a girl whose heart has not been *had* – is not an old thing half worn out by some He or another! who only knew the staleness of the freshest of us! that nine times out of ten the 'first love' they think they are winning from a woman is but the hulk of an old wrecked affection, fitted with new sails and re-used. O Cytherea, can it be that you, too, are like the rest? . . . You are as bad as I – we are all alike; and I – an old fool – have been sipping at your mouth as if it were honey, because I fancied no wasting lover knew the spot. But a minute ago, and you seemed to me like a fresh spring meadow – now you seem a dusty highway.

This is passionate and uniquely bold in polite Victorian fiction. It does not depict, or try to depict, lesbian love itself in an unattractive light – on the contrary – and it remains an achievement in the book which, with the exception of *Ethelberta*, is Hardy's slightest. Cytherea, inexperienced, is impressed and wants to sob. She is also somewhat aroused: Miss Aldclyffe's 'vehement imperious affection was in one sense soothing, but yet it was not of the kind that Cytherea's instincts desired'; she finds it 'too rank and capricious ['sensuous' in the original text] for endurance'. But she allows Miss Aldclyffe, who goes to sleep, to remain in bed with her. In the 'bright penetrating light of morning' the older woman is 'inwardly vexed . . . at the extent to which she had indulged in the womanly luxury of making confidences and giving way to emotions'. The narrator adds that emotions 'would be half-starved if there were no candle-light'.

This careful, accurate and unusual piece of observation, then – together with the small part given over to rustic people, and to Springrove's father (possibly a little reminiscent of Tom's) – amounts to the best of *Desperate Remedies*. It is unlikely that Tom was particularly interested in homosexuality; it was, rather, women to whom he was so susceptible, who fascinated him, and whom he tried to understand.

He later abandoned altogether the techniques of sensation fiction; the genre itself fell into decrepitude during the succeeding decade. But he continued to exploit his knowledge of country people, and to investigate the psychology of women. He would be concerned, also, with the male habit (discovered in himself, too) of making women into objects, into no more than erotic territory. There is little of this tendency to be found in the slightly insipid Springrove: it is emphasized, rather, in Manston, a crude stereotype for Troy and D'Urberville. As for Miss Aldclyffe: although by no means a finished study, she is interesting because through her Hardy gained an opportunity to delineate sexual arousal which, while it is selfish and greedy and based on a mistress–servant relationship, is not of the usual type. He succeeded, too, in giving, in Cytherea, a non-judgemental portrait of budding female narcissism and sado–masochism; and, if less convincingly and more commercially, of healthy instinct in her, too – her final feeling for Springrove.

As he completed *Desperate Remedies* – the last chapters are but the solution to a puzzle and would not have interested him except in a technical sense – he was learning about love from Emma Gifford. It is unlikely that he changed the interestingly passive, although spirited, Cytherea Aldclyffe in the light of the hardly passive Emma, after the idyllic three weeks he spent with her in Cornwall in August; but he sent his script to her and doubtless discussed it and received encouragement in their continuing correspondence. She made a fair copy for him of the by now physically very messy manuscript, and he packed it off to Tinsley before Christmas. But he felt miserable: 'On the margin of his . . . *Hamlet* the following passage is marked . . . "December

15, 1870": Thou wouldst not think how ill all's here about my heart: but 'tis no matter.' This was nervousness: he was going to be exposed to the world at last.

He made clear to himself that *Desperate Remedies* was not all that he personally intended by providing an epigraph from one of his favourite authors, Scott: 'Though an unconnected course of adventure is what most frequently occurs in nature, yet the province of the romance-writer being artificial, there is more required from him than a mere compliance with the simplicity of reality.' He thus announces himself, in prose fiction, as a romance-writer. His very title indicates his ironic state of mind: prose is a desperate remedy for poetry. But he had approached his task as romance-writer conscientiously, and even made use of some of the poems he had been unable to see into print. As he explained in a note to the 1912 edition, the

> reader may discover . . . certain . . . sentiments . . . the same in substance with some in *Wessex Poems* . . . the explanation is that the poems were written beforehand, but as the author could not get them printed, he incontinently used here whatever of their content as being apt for the purpose – after dissolving it into prose, never anticipating at that time that the poems would see the light.

Thus a peroration by Cytherea to her brother Owen about how she will be remembered is an exact paraphrase of a 'She to Him' poem.

In his letter to Tinsley of 20 December he laid out his understanding of the terms of publication: 'if the gross receipts reach the costs of publishing I shall receive the £75 back again . . . Will you be good enough to say if the sum includes advertising to the customary extent, & about how long after my paying the money the book would appear?' Thus began a lifelong habit of carefully looking after his own business affairs. He would occasionally employ agents, but never put his affairs into the hands of one. Tinsley put him right about the arrangement, pointing out that they would share equal profits over and above £75. Tom must have already read Charles Reade's book about authors' rights, *The Eighth Commandment* (1860): 'Thou shalt not steal. Except from authors.'

In January 1871 he paid over the £75, in notes, in person, out of the £123 which was all he had in the world ('Beyond what he might have had from his father'). He corrected the proofs in Bockhampton in February, and on 25 March 1871 *Desperate Remedies* was published, anonymously, in three volumes, at the standard price of 31s.6d. The first reviews, in the *Athenaeum* and the *Morning Post*, were favourable, hailing the anonymous author as 'powerful' and promising to become a writer of novels 'only a little, if at all, inferior to the best of the present generation'. The *Athenaeum* review, of 1 April 1871, noted the skilled plotting, evident in the precise dating of the chapter titles: 'If carefully carried out, as it is in the present book, this gives an air of reality.'

But the *Spectator* review which followed on 22 April strongly disapproved of the book. It was written by John Hutton, brother of the better-known Richard Holt Hutton, editor of the *Spectator*; they were sons of a Unitarian minister, and even the criticism of the latter, although superior, was narrowed by theological considerations. John Hutton was sarcastic at the expense of the anonymous author: 'no assumption of a *nom de plume* which might, at some future time, disgrace his family name', 'no fine characters' in the book, 'no original ones . . . no pictures of Christian virtue', and so forth. He did go on, however, to praise, although patronizingly, the author's 'very happy facility for catching and fixing phases of peasant life', and reproducing the 'tone of thought – if it can be dignified by the name of thought – and the simple humour of the village worthies'; he gave examples of this. The 'nameless author' reminded him of the paintings of Wilkie and Teniers, and 'if we . . . step in silence over the corrupt body of the tale . . . we hope to spur him to better things . . . than these "desperate remedies" . . . for . . . an emaciated purse'.

Hutton was not a perceptive critic. His genuine appreciation of such features in fiction as he felt were proper to it – he made clear that the illegitimacy in *Desperate Remedies* was excluded – was muffled by his view of fiction as a means of 'edification'. Tom never wanted to 'edify' anyone; he believed a dose of reality to be salutary. Hutton would later, after publication of *Under the Greenwood Tree*, write to Tom 'showing some regret for his violence', and Tom 'became acquainted' with him. But the virulence of Hutton's review of his first book, all the more galling after the positive reviews in the *Athenaeum* and the *Morning Post*, had, he wrote, an 'impact' that was 'staggering with good reason'. His immediate feelings were typical of those of a new writer, and typical of Tom's simple candour: 'At the time, he wished he were dead.'

Horace Moule, 'whom Hardy had not consulted on the venture' – he was probably afraid that Moule would advise against Tinsley – wrote a kindly letter telling Tom to ignore the review. In a note to himself, which he reproduced in the *Life*, Tom wrote:

> Strictly, we should resent wrongs, be placid at justice, and grateful for favours. But I know one who is placid at a wrong, and would be grateful for simple justice; while a favour, if he ever gained one, would turn his brain.

This was humorous, since he also wrote of his reaction to the review, 'it does not seem to have worried Hardy much or at any rate for long'. He did not, after all, continue to wish to be dead. But he thought to the end of his life that Hutton's *Spectator* review 'had snuffed out the book'. In fact it merely helped along a common enough process of neglect, and the one truly outstanding episode in the book, the homosexual one, could hardly have been praised in public in any case. In May 1871, as Tom was returning from his third visit to Emma, he saw *Desperate Remedies* offered for 2s. 6d. as a remainder on Exeter station. Horace Moule's favourable and well-judged notice in the *Saturday Review* did not appear until 30 September, by which time it was of little use to Tinsley in advertising the book, which sold only a few more than two hundred copies.

Tom's final verdict on *Desperate Remedies*, that it 'had been concocted in a style which was quite against his natural grain, through too crude interpretation of Mr Meredith's advice', was essentially right, although the novel has its moments, especially the passage between the two Cythereas, and it would in fact do quite well for Tom (it remains in print). He had written it, he said, because 'it seemed necessary to attract public attention at all hazards'. Those hazards were considerable, but he need not have been concerned, for the book attracted little public attention.

8

Under the Greenwood Tree

On 30 October 1870 Tom had entered in his notebook, 'Mother's notion, & also mine: that a figure stands in our van with arm uplifted, to knock us back from any permanent prospect we indulge in as probable.' This has given rise to speculation that Tom, now living at home much of the time, was under his mother's thumb, and that he was beset by a 'feeling of fate' because of the 'maladjusted timing of events'. Yet his remark can be read as a simple variant of the proverb 'Don't count your chickens before they're hatched'. His main worry at this time, reinforced by his mother's cautiousness, was his capacity to earn a living, and the prospects of success for *Desperate Remedies*. He was not yet in a position where he could marry Emma, and his remark, although tending to a pessimistic view of life, perhaps says more about the family caution than his pessimism.

His outlook has been described as 'peasant fatalism', yet it can be seen as natural to anyone, including Greek tragedians who were not peasants. Tom tended to interpret every reverse or temporary failure as 'terrible', not because the events in his life were any more terrible than those of other people, but because of his temperament. Confronted by suffering, he physically winced and shrank before he could even take thought, as he did at the sight of a wounded bird. This was the emotional-instinctive reaction in which his aversion to the notion of existence was rooted. In his conversation with Clive Holland, and on many other occasions, he would not have it, as a general proposition, that life was worth living – but he proved to himself and to us that his life was worth living, by living it and not ending it.

To him, life was an altogether cruel arrangement, an 'unthinking' one, and this one huge 'impression' lies behind the smaller impressions of which he insisted that all his work consisted. It was not a 'philosophy' but an immediate reaction – just as his immediate reaction to the cutting *Spectator* review of *Desperate Remedies* was a wish to be dead. But it did not stop him continuing to live, and to go on writing his next novel.

UNDER THE GREENWOOD TREE

His new work, *Under the Greenwood Tree*, was completed over the first half of 1871, while he was working for Crickmay, lodging at Wooperton Street in Weymouth in the week, and spending his weekends at home, with visits to London and, in May, to Emma. In composing it he turned away from Collins and Mrs Braddon, cutting out the 'coarseness' which reviewers had found in *Desperate Remedies*, and moving towards something altogether more natural to him: rural life, at which they agreed he excelled. In the book's evocative subtitle, 'A Rural Painting of the Dutch School', he meant to indicate his debt to William Barnes' 'rural scenes and humble life'. It also reflects the marathon course of systematized reading and picture-visiting he undertook while in London.

He carved three portions out of *The Poor Man and the Lady* for use in it, all dealing with his first hero's father. He integrated them with great skill: there was no question here of a novel in a fashionable style 'desperately' cobbled together from disparate sources as a 'remedy' for an empty purse. He was as careful with the material he had in hand as he was with money; this was prose fiction, undertaken to make a living, and it could be treated differently from poetry and the more sacred impulses of poetry. *Under the Greenwood Tree* is the first unequivocal triumph of his art over his circumstances, and most agree that it is his most perfectly constructed novel. For someone hardly past thirty, this pastoral novel is an astonishing achievement, a young man's book and almost as supreme in prose as Keats' work is in poetry.

Although Tom's 'education' now made honest communication with his parents, in particular with his mother, more difficult, it was the values of his parents and not those of the city or even of 'enlightenment' which prevail in *Under the Greenwood Tree*. The impulse behind the book in fact represents a reaction against 'education', or at least 'civilization', but its effect is not achieved without some brilliant sleight of hand. *Under the Greenwood Tree* is an apparently light-hearted pastoral, modelled in part on *As You Like It* (from which the novel gained its title) and in part on the folk ways which he knew so intimately. The plot is simple. Dick Dewy, son of the local tranter (carrier), falls in love with the new village schoolmistress, the capricious Fancy Day – a seemingly charming and attractive heroine who embodies the values of 'enlightenment'. Fanny has two other suitors: Shiner, a rich farmer, and the vicar, Maybold. Their advances are resisted and Dick's – despite the objections of Geoffrey Day, Fancy's father – accepted.

The book is a lament for the old order, but with a sting in the tail: its 'romantic' end consists of a future based on a lie. For, just as Geoffrey Day's refusal to accept Dick Dewey as his daughter's suitor is preceded by the killing of a bird by an owl, so the marriage itself is preceded – and surely threatened – by Fancy's decision (no doubt wise enough in practical terms) not to confess to Dick that her vanity had been tempted by Maybold's offer, and that she had shed tears over the matter. For all the delight and harmony which marks the close of the book, the means of redemption have been destroyed – by the beloved herself.

Under the Greenwood Tree is thus a tale of the consequences of the loss of living faith. For Tom, although he too felt impelled to reject, in the light of reason, the supernaturalism inherent in the Christian faith in which he had been brought up, had not dropped, and never would drop, the notion of redemption through love. Hence his frequent use of the term 'loving-kindness', which occasionally becomes, in his coinage, 'lovingkindness'. That notion in itself, although not specifically Christian, is 'supernatural', in the sense that it can never convincingly be accommodated into an atheistic or rational framework.

His nostalgia for the unattainable, for a past which can be recreated in the mind but not in the world, recurs throughout his work. Part of the painful meaning of this process, for him, lay in his yearning for a means of redemption so personally intense, and therefore often erotically supercharged, that it was supernatural. Like many of his contemporaries, he wanted to dispense with the miraculous, but to preserve the ethical element in Christianity. However, he could not conscientiously separate the two, so that his work is pervaded with a sense of the miraculous, either just by a hair's breadth unattained, or tragically defeated. *Under the Greenwood Tree* is the most light-hearted of his novels; only reflection leads to the conclusion that is not light-hearted at all.

In it he avoided the 'mischief' which Macmillan had declared as characterizing *The Poor Man and the Lady*, but he got plenty of unobtrusive 'mischief' into the novel by subsuming it all under the notion of 'peasant sayings'. He knew that reviewers would not take this seriously, while also knowing that rustic conversation, then as now, was quite as 'wise' as that to be encountered at any literary cocktail party. The banter, for example, of Geoffrey Day on the subject of his second wife Jane conceals much 'mischievous' comment on the pseudo-sacred subject of marriage; but the middle-class reader, and his mouthpiece the conventional reviewer (whose attention Hardy urgently required, and at last obtained), could remain comfortably distanced from it, since it relates only to inherently comic rustics.

While he worked on *Under the Greenwood Tree,* Tom was faced by the problem of how he would reconcile the ways of his family with the ways of Emma's. Emma seemed to him fresh, unstuffy and unconventional, but she had had a genteel upbringing, and was already perhaps over-aware of having an uncle who was a canon of Worcester Cathedral, as well as a brother-in-law who had been a 'gentleman-commoner' at Trinity College, Oxford. Some biographers, notably Gittings, have claimed that he tried to conceal his background from her. There is no justification for this; probably he talked as much as he could about it to her, though since she had no direct knowledge of such a background, she may not have understood it. She was much in love with him, and prone to seeing things in the terms in which he wanted her to see them; she had little experience, and believed, with a greater simplicity than he could ever achieve, in the ways of providence. When she wrote, late in life, 'an Unseen Power of great benevolence directs my ways; I have some philosophy, and mysticism', she could equally have been expressing what she believed in 1871. Although she was offering Tom a truly shared life, he saw more than she saw, and he was beginning to be aware of this, even if he sometimes tried to deny it to himself. In Fancy Day there may be, to some extent, Emma Gifford, and *Under the Greenwood Tree* as a whole may reflect his predicament.

He finished the manuscript in July 1871 and, on 7 August, sent it to Macmillan, not to Tinsley; clearly he regarded the latter as no more than a useful stop-gap, and doubtless Moule encouraged him to take this line. Tom's letter to Macmillan was careful and hopeful, and he quoted bits of the favourable reviews of *Desperate Remedies* which Emma had helped him to cull. 'It is entirely a story of rural life, & the attempt has been to draw the characters humorously, without caricature'. This is a reminder of his success in so delicate a task: he had to preserve his real love for his own people, and for the community from which he sprang, and yet show them in a light which they themselves would not be able to understand was funny. Condescension towards the rural characters is minimal, and he was never able, conscientiously, to repeat the idyllic world the novel depicts as background (the foreground is anything but idyllic). Tom concluded his letter by hoping that Macmillan would like the story, but asking in any case for his comments.

The firm replied by requesting full copies of the reviews of *Desperate Remedies* from which he had sent quotations. Tom sent these, mentioning, first, that all the available evidence from the reviews suggested that 'a pastoral story would be the *safest* venture' – he knew his man. He also pointed out that the *Spectator* reviewer contradicted himself, since a 'novel which was good enough to justify two columns of lauded quotation could not possibly be so bad as to warrant its opening remarks'. In mid-September, in the absence of Alexander Macmillan, his son Malcolm (who, in 1889, would suffer the Hardyan fate of being killed, and buried, on Mount Olympus by brigands) strongly hinted that the firm might take it, and enclosed John Morley's report on the manuscript. Morley admired it, advised Tom to read George Sand (which he had already done, on the advice of Moule), and to 'ignore the fooleries of critics' – advice easily given, and virtually impossible for a beginner to take.

On 14 October, when he was again in Cornwall, he wrote a note to Macmillan enquiring about the manuscript, probably because Emma, seeing him depressed, encouraged him to do so. Had Alexander Macmillan really admired the book he ought now to have said so. Instead, he returned the manuscript, and asked that it be resubmitted in the following year. Tom now decided to try the novel out on Tinsley, which he later called 'an unfortunate mistake' – although this was hardly so, given that Macmillan had offered little encouragement and was being decidedly unfair to a gifted young man who needed to get his book into print. Still at St Juliot, Tom wrote on 20 October to Tinsley, offering him either 'a little rural story' (which he pretended was 'nearly finished'), or 'another' work, which he had in fact already begun, and which would become *A Pair of Blue Eyes*.

Tinsley, in his reply of 23 October, prevaricated, telling Tom that if he wrote 'another three-volume work' he would be 'glad to take it', and this time without any prior payment. Like many publishers with little literary taste, Tinsley had a nose for future fame – something the more cautious Macmillan had evidently not intuited. For the time being, then, Tom shoved *Under the Greenwood Tree* into 'a box with his old poems, being quite sick of all such, and began to think of other ways and means'. That, without doubt, meant architecture, for, as he wrote, apropos his and Emma's shared view of the circumstances:

Unlike the case of Browning and Elizabeth Barrett no letters between the couple are extant, to show the fluctuation of their minds on this vital matter. But what happened was that Hardy applied himself to architectural work during the winter of 1871–72 more steadily than he had ever done in his life before, and in the spring of the latter year again set out for London, determined to stifle his constitutional tendency to care for life only as an emotion and not as a scientific game, and fully bent on sticking to the profession which had been the choice of his parents for him rather than his own; but with a faint dream at the back of his mind that he might perhaps write verses as an occasional hobby.

It is likely that his mother was pressing him to this more wholehearted pursuit of architecture. She may have reminded him that, whereas he was much in demand as an architect, his writings were neither successful nor much sought after. She would have been able to soften the blow by telling him that he could write poetry, which was what he really wanted to do, as a sideline; fiction, she may have said, was after all not much different from architecture. However reasonable all this may have been, it was not what Tom wanted to hear. But he wrote off to Emma telling her that he had given up novel-writing in favour of architecture. He received the reply for which he craved, and never forgot his gratitude to her:

> . . . she, with no great opportunity of reasoning on the matter, yet, as Hardy used to think and say – truly or not – with that rapid instinct which serves women in such good stead, and may almost be called preternatural vision, wrote back instantly her desire that he should adhere to authorship, which she felt sure was his true vocation.

Emma had passed a test: she believed in him as a writer, shared in his aspirations, and was ready to make personal sacrifices in order that he might establish himself as one. Her attitude puts out of court the Florence-inspired idea that Emma and her sister contemplated Tom as a 'catch'; if so, she would surely have encouraged her trapped husband-to-be to adhere to the safe choice of salaried architect.

A poem, 'Love the Monopolist', begun in 1871, describes Tom's departure from Launceston station, to which Emma had come to see him off. It is an excellent example of how he could already put himself under the microscope of observation, and thus describe states of mind with extraordinary precision, and it also testifies to his complete absorption in Emma at that time. As the train carries him off he looks hard at the 'airy slim blue form' standing on the platform, and sees her turning to 'greet friends gaily':

> But why remained she not hard gazing
> Till I was out of sight?

'O do not chat with others there,'
I brood. 'They are not I . . .'

The poem ends:

'When I come back uncloak your gloom,
    And let in lovely day;
Then the long dark as of the tomb
    Can well be thrust away
With sweet things I shall have to practise,
    And you will have to say!'

'Love the Monopolist' has been considered 'petulant', and to show, by inference, that Tom was 'hurt' by Emma on that day. Yet the poem is more an ironic and humorous statement about the condition of the romantic lover, as the title and the subtitle, 'Young Lover's Reverie', indicate. The conclusion implies that the state of romantic love is hardly, in certain respects, a perfectly sincere one. It is not that Tom was not in love. He was. But as a poet he could not prevent himself from observing things as they really were.

Despite his assertion that he was determined to stick to architecture, he had not of course given up his hopes of becoming an author: he was trying the familiar, cautious ploy of pretending that he had done so in order to gain some good luck. He calls the years 1872 and 1873 ones of 'unexpectedness'. In accordance with his overt intention to pursue architecture he moved to 1 West Parade, Weymouth, where he did work for Crickmay, much of it on the Weymouth Green Hill estate – sets of villas with decorative turrets, such as Max Gate itself was to have.

From West Parade he wrote on 3 January 1872 to Tinsley, asking about his account for *Desperate Remedies*, and making hints about 'my new MS' (*Under the Greenwood Tree*). On 20 February, having heard nothing, he wrote more pressingly. Two days later Tinsley sent the account. It was 'very intelligible', Tom drily commented: he had lost £15 on the deal. A cheque was promised for 10 March, and on the 13th, while at Bockhampton on his way to London, Tom reminded Tinsley that he had not yet received the money. Ten days later, now at 4 Celbridge Place – not far from Westbourne Park – he acknowledged the cheque, which was for £59.12s.7d., and promised to call on Tinsley very soon. He could thus say to himself that all he was doing was, first, collecting

as much as he could of the £75 he had laid out, and, secondly, trying
to dispose of a manuscript for which he could obtain some more, much
needed money – and which need never be followed by another one.

He had gone to London on a more exacting job than any in which he
had recently been engaged, and which had excellent prospects. Thomas
Roger Smith, Professor at the Royal Institute of British Architects (and
one of the judges of the Tite competition which Tom had won in 1863),
had engaged him to assist in the preparation of designs for new schools
to be submitted to the London School Board, which was holding a public
competition. Tom worked hard at this, as well as doing some drawings
to help Blomfield, for four months; he was simultaneously looking for
a way out.

By chance he ran into Horace Moule in Trafalgar Square. He had not
seen Horace since the previous year, and he told him that he had given
up writing. Horace remonstrated, as he he was supposed to do, and
made the rather peculiar observation – if it was wholly unprompted
– that he should at least keep his hand in: 'supposing anything should
happen to his eyes from the fine architectural drawing . . . he could
dictate a book, article or poem, but not a . . . design'. Tom tells us
that a few days later he became worried by seeing 'floating specks on the
white drawing-paper before him'. He was troubled by discomfort in his
eyes throughout his life; and the fact that he had thought of causing the
protagonist of *The Poor Man and the Lady* to go blind through overwork
suggests that this possibility had caused him anxiety for some time.
Horace Moule may already have been aware of it, and now gave him
the name of a distinguished ophthalmic surgeon, whom Tom consulted
in April. Nothing was amiss; doubtless Tom was easily able to imagine
the specks. He was staking everything on *Under the Greenwood Tree*, but
conscientiously failing to say so.

He recollected that around this time he had a chance meeting with
Tinsley, whose office was near his own: while he was reading an opera
poster in the Strand he felt 'a heavy hand on his shoulder' and heard
Tinsley asking him when he was going to let him have 'another novel'.
Thinking 'of the balance-sheet', Tom, by his own account, 'drily told
him never'.

'Wot, now!' Tinsley asked, 'Haven't you anything written?' Later,
to Tom's announcement that he was going to devote himself to
architecture, Tinsley exclaimed, 'Damned if that isn't what I thought
you was! Well, now, can't you get that story, and show it to me?' When
Tom reminded him that the 'account he had rendered for the other book

was not likely to tempt him to publish a second', Tinsley retorted, "Pon my soul, Mr Hardy, you wouldn't have got another man in London to print it! Oh, be hanged if you would! 'twas a blood-curdling story! Now please try to find that new manuscript and let me see it!'

On 8 April Tom sent it to Tinsley, asking for 'liberal terms' and announcing that he was already getting on with the next story. Tinsley quickly agreed to publish *Under the Greenwood Tree*, this time offering £30 for the copyright. On 22 April Tom accepted this, much though it would cost him financially in later years. His remark that he cared 'nothing about the book' at the time of his acceptance of Tinsley's offer reflects his temporary mood of disillusion with literature as a career, for he wrote:

> Hardy's indifference in selling *Under the Greenwood Tree* for a trifle could not have been because he still had other aims than the literature of fiction, as had been the case the previous winter; for he casually mentioned to Tinsley that he thought of going on with the three-volume novel [*A Pair of Blue Eyes*] before alluded to. Moule's words on keeping a hand on the pen, and the specks in his eyes while drawing, may have influenced him in this harking back.

No doubt, behind his feigned attitude of indifference, he had more faith in *Under the Greenwood Tree* than in his first published work. The new novel appeared in two volumes in early June 1872, again anonymously, but as 'by the author of *Desperate Remedies*'. The prompt *Athenaeum* review of 15 June acknowledged that he had 'worked . . . that vein of his genius which yields the best produce'. Further enthusiastic reviews followed, although Horace Moule's, for the *Saturday Review*, was again long delayed, and did not appear until 30 September.

For Tom, the disgusted turn-away from literature had paid off. There was no hostile review to torment him, and early in July Tinsley asked him for a story for *Tinsley's Magazine*. Writing from Celbridge Place, on 9 July, Tom cautiously replied: 'I have nothing ready I am sorry to say.' He probably did not buy Coppinger's book on copyright and study it half the night, as he claimed (his copy of it is dated a little later); but he may have borrowed it, for he drove a much harder bargain with Tinsley than previously. On 27 July he undertook to provide a serial to run for twelve months, 'about 20 pages', and to give the publisher the right to issue it in three volumes 'for twelve months from the time of its appearance in this form. Afterwards all rights to revert to the author.' In exchange for this he was to receive £200, payable in instalments of £15 per month, plus a final fee of £20.

In what was the beginning of a quarter of a century of faithful professionalism, he got his copy for the first instalment off to Tinsley by 7 August. It is likely that he had to write, or at least very extensively rewrite, whatever he then had of *A Pair of Blue Eyes*, which at first was called 'A Winning Tongue Had He'. 'Apparently without saying anything of his commitment, he informed the genial Professor of Architecture [Smith] that he would take a holiday in August . . . and going home to Westbourne Park wrote between then and midnight a chapter or two.' He was elated, yet very anxious about his ability to fulfil his contract. He drew upon all his present circumstances, including a short voyage, for the detail of his book.

On 7 August he embarked on the *Avoca*, taking the boat from London Bridge to Plymouth and thence to Cornwall, in order to meet Emma. It seems that he had by now written to her suggesting that he might formally ask for her hand in marriage, and had arranged to meet her not at St Juliot but at her parents' home, Kirland House, near Bodmin, to which address he had told Tinsley to send proofs. He pointedly did not go to Bockhampton, thus avoiding any possibility of discussion.

Exactly what happened at Kirland House is unclear, but there was undoubtedly some unpleasantness. According to one item of gossip, Tom was intercepted at Bodmin station by an anxious Emma, who had just discovered that her father was opposed to his suit, so Tom was rushed off to stay at the house of Emma's friends, Captain and Mrs Sargeant. During Tom's visit he did indeed stay a day or two with the Sargeants, but it is unlikely that it was under such initial circumstances. Emma recorded that her father tended to break out into drink on the excuse of any family affair – birth, death or marriage – and she and Tom may have found him in gloomy mood or, more likely, in the aftermath or process of one of his drinking bouts. Tom's scrambled prose account fails to mention any insult he may have received from John Gifford; if the latter had rejected Tom outright as a prospective son-in-law, they would hardly have been able to meet comfortably in later years, as they did. Nor is it likely that Emma would have found any outburst by her father as much of a hitch in the romance so far as it concerned her own feeling for Tom.

Florence Hardy told Clodd in 1913, when she was at the height of her jealousy of the dead Emma, that Gifford had called Tom a 'low-born churl who has presumed to marry into my family'. Although in his cups, John Gifford probably did say something of that kind to Emma – or perhaps to his wife, who then reported it to Emma – it is not likely that he said it to Tom, or that the remark would have anyway caused more than brief anxiety: anyone who knew Gifford would not take such remarks from him seriously. Florence, who liked to be truthful but was driven into unreliability by her misery over Tom's devotion to the memory of Emma, may have had the story from Emma herself – and Emma, unlike Florence, had a sense of humour.

Two poems are connected with this August 1872 visit to Cornwall, but neither offers any evidence to substantiate the claims that have been made that Tom met 'considerable opposition from Emma's family' and that he was 'disingenuous'. The first poem, 'Near Lanivet, 1872', is based, the manuscript says, 'on an old note'; Lanivet is near Kirland House, and the 'stunted handpost' of the poem was identified by Tom, on the endpapers of his friend Hermann Lea's *Thomas Hardy's Wessex*, as being at a place called Reperry Cross. In the poem, Emma, stopping to rest, leans against the post, which 'made her look as one crucified'. The poet cries, 'Don't', but she fails to hear him:

> . . . Loosing thence she said,
>   As she stepped forth ready to go,
> 'I am rested now. – Something strange came into my head;
>   I wish I had not leant so!'
>
> And wordless we moved onward down from the hill
>   In the west cloud's murked obscure,
> And looking back we could see the handpost still
>   In the solitude of the moor.
>
> 'It struck her too,' I thought, for as if afraid
>   She heavily breathed as we trailed;
> Till she said, 'I did not think how 'twould look in the shade,
>   When I leant there like one nailed.'

I, lightly: 'There's nothing in it. For *you*, anyhow!'
  – 'O I know there is not,' said she . . .
'Yet I wonder . . . If no one is bodily crucified now,
  In spirit one may be!'

And we dragged on and on, while we seemed to see
  In the running of Time's far glass
Her crucified, as she had wondered if she might be
  Some day. – Alas, alas!

Other than its setting, there is nothing to relate the poem to the matter of Gifford's attitude to Tom. It implies Emma's future unhappiness, the crucifixion of her spirit, and is in part self-accusatory, leaving open the question of whether Tom felt that he had crucified her. He would later, on 18 January 1918, write to Gosse telling him that 'the scene occurred between us [him and Emma] before our marriage', and shortly afterwards, on 7 February, he told his friend Mrs Henniker that the poem was 'literally true'. To a critic he described the occasion of the poem as 'a strange incident'. But nothing can be gathered from it in connection with what may have taken place at Kirland House.

The second poem related to this August visit is 'I Rose and Went to Rou'tor Town', subtitled 'She, alone'; Rou'tor Town was Tom's name for Bodmin. Like 'Near Lanivet', it appeared in *Moments of Vision*, and is a lament by a maid – for it is a ballad – about 'The evil wrought at Rou'tor Town/On him I'd loved so true'. When the publisher and author Vere Collins asked Tom, in 1920, 'What is "the evil wrought at Rou'tor Town"?', he answered: 'Slander, or something of that sort.' The 'slander' here refers to the poem, not to anything autobiographical, although it has been speculated from Gifford supposedly calling Tom a 'low-born churl' – an insulting rather than slanderous remark – that 'Emma had learnt that Hardy had been involved with other girls . . . The Giffords had many friends . . . in Plymouth, and it is conceivable that, with Tryphena now there, something about her and Hardy had leaked out.' There is, however, nothing to suggest that this was so, nor that there was anything significant to 'leak out' about Tom and Tryphena Sparks.

It has been more plausibly suggested that the mysterious poem 'The Chosen', which refers to a 'Christ-cross stone' that could be the one in 'Near Linvet', 'may give some hint of the stress of the occasion in Cornwall'. The poem (published in *Late Lyrics* in 1926) mentions five women known in the past and a sixth, a 'composite' of them all, who says:

> 'I feel some curse. O, *five* were there?'
> And wanly she swerved, and went away.
> I followed sick: night numbed the air,
> And dark the mournful moorland lay.

There have been attempts by Hardy commentators to equate the five women of the poem with five actual women in his life, just as the sixth is speculated to be Emma and the poem possibly connected with 'stress' during the August visit. But 'The Chosen', Like 'I Rose and Went to Rou'tor Town', is another of his dramatic poems; if it expresses anything autobiographical at all, it could be guilt which Tom felt about Emma after her death – in particular that he had hurt her by the publication of *Wessex Poems* in 1898 – but the number of five women is likely to be arbitrary. As Aristotle in his *Poetics* says of poetic and historical truth: 'It is not the poet's function to describe what actually happened, but the kinds of thing that might happen, that is, that could happen because they are, in the circumstances, either probable or necessary.' Aristotle goes on to say:

> Even if the poet writes about things that have actually happened, that does not make him any less a poet, for there is nothing to prevent some of the things that have happened from being in accordance with the laws of possibility and probability, and thus he will be a poet in writing about them.

Thus Tom was amazed about the poem 'Near Lanivet', because it was something that did come 'literally true': he told Harold Childs, on 11 February 1919, that he had thought 'critics might select (not for its supposed excellence but for the strange incident which produced it, and really happened) . . . "Near Lanivet", but *nobody* did'. This sort of event, which seems to the poet to be in accordance with the laws mentioned by Aristotle, was called by James Joyce an 'epiphany', from the Greek, 'a showing': it sparks off a moment of revelation, 'a sudden spiritual manifestation'. Such moments of realization were recognized by Goethe and many other poets. As in the case of 'Near Lanivet', the incident may be preserved in a 'note', and only afterwards be fully realized as a poem. But the existence of such 'epiphanies', or 'synchronicities', as meaningful to poets and readers, puts into question literal biographical inferences from poems, unsupported by any other explanatory evidence. For poets might simply record what actually happened, as apparently in the case of 'Near Lanivet', or they might very well alter an 'event' to bring it into accordance with the general laws. So, although a spiritual, or internal, state may often be validly inferred from poetry, to infer actual occurrences is a far more dangerous procedure. Shakespeare's plays, for example, may imply that he was a certain kind of man in certain kinds of states of mind and emotion, but they by no means imply anything about the actual events of his life.

Ingenious attempts have also been made to construct a little drama between Tom and Emma, relating to his visit to Kirland House, from the poem called 'The Seven Times', the theme of which is his seven visits to Cornwall. Certainly he made use of his experiences in Cornwall in two or three poems, and in *A Pair of Blue Eyes* he created the character of Parson Swancourt, who rejects Stephen Smith's suit of Elfride on foolishly snobbish grounds. But Tom made molehills into mountains out of his impressions – mountains rich in those 'laws' which Aristotle had explained, even if in a different context, two thousand years ago. When in the *Life* Tom wrote that there was more autobiography to be found in a hundred lines of his poems than in all his novels, he did not mean, as he has been taken to mean, that some of the poems were to be taken literally. He meant that they dealt with states of mind, and were 'literally true' in the Aristotelian sense. Whatever happened with Gifford at Kirland House, there are no further accounts of parental opposition to the intended marriage, which would seem likely if this was as serious as has been made out. Millgate states that Gifford treated his prospective son-in-law 'with open contempt', but that is to accept Florence Hardy's words as fact, and not as supposition.

What is known is that during his August 1872 visit Tom travelled about in Cornwall, spending time at St Juliot and a couple of nights at the Sargeants', and worked on the serial of *A Pair of Blue Eyes* – although in all the excitement he was late with his copy, and had to write to Tinsley from St Juliot on 7 September, promising in future to deliver the instalments (of some ten thousand words each) by the first of the month. Before he left on Tuesday, 10 September, he renounced architecture as a profession. The architect Smith had written to him at St Juliot to tell him that one of Tom's designs for the London School Board had been accepted, and to ask him to return if he so desired. This,

Tom found, 'was now merely provoking', and he told Smith the truth, amicably rejecting the offer.

He returned from Cornwall via Bath, to which he accompanied a friend of Emma's, a Miss D'Arville (who owned a canary which reputedly fainted when shown so much as a picture of a cat). Again, he missed out Bockhampton. It seems that he simply was not ready to tell his parents of his decision – both to give up architecture for writing, and to marry Emma. There was plenty for him to explain: his family had made sacrifices so that he could become an architect, and he had not yet shown that he could make authorship work. His decision, made in the face of a good work offer, had obviously been discussed at St Juliot, but he had avoided discussing it with his parents, or telling them that he intended to marry a woman who was actively encouraging him to abandon architecture.

Because of the eventual estrangement between the Hardys and Emma, there has been an assumption that Jemima was always bitterly opposed to Emma. But Jemima's initial opposition has been exaggerated. Jemina was a formidable woman, likely to disapprove of any marriage made by her children, and particularly the eldest son for whom she had such ambitions; for a mother like her, initial opposition would be much more likely than joyful acceptance. In the circumstances it seems that things went as well as they could have gone, and the fact that some ten years later Tom would build Max Gate for himself and Emma within a few miles of Bockhampton belies the idea that there was a serious estrangement from the start.

The story that Emma made a desperate and 'disastrous' visit to Bockhampton to 'plead' her case comes solely from Florence Hardy, who told it to the poet, and prospective Hardy biographer, Henry Reed, at the end of her life. By then such confused tattle was what she wanted to believe in her relentless, if occasionally conscience-stricken, attempts to poison the very source of the stream which flowed from Tom and Emma's early love. There is no record of a visit by Emma to Bockhampton at this time; Tom does not mention one in the *Life*, and it is as plausible to infer that there was no visit as that there was.

When Tom returned to London after his Cornwall visit he found that he could not get on with his writing there; so at last he went back to Bockhampton, where he continued to live while writing the remainder, and majority, of *A Pair of Blue Eyes*. Going home to live would have been an economical move, avoiding the need to interrupt his writing by taking on architectural work, but the fact that he was able to make this choice suggests that the tension between him and his parents cannot have been very great. Whether he had time to meet Emma at Plymouth, near at hand for both of them, before the end of 1872 is not known, but he made another visit to Cornwall over Christmas and the New Year, probably lasting from 18 December 1872 to 7 January 1873. By then he had received a request that would enable him to make his much wished-for move from Tinsley – who had written to him in October, sending him £10 for the continental rights to *Under the Greenwood Tree*, and mentioning his growing faith in one whom he hoped would become his new author.

9

A Pair of Blue Eyes

Desperate Remedies had been, at best, a botched-up job, since the intricate plot had been no part of Hardy's real intentions. Its two successors are altogether more important, as books in their own right, and within his *oeuvre*. Into *A Pair of Blue Eyes*, despite a pressure to compose hitherto unknown to him, he remained sufficiently astute and tranquil to insert much of what he personally wanted to insert. There is already some excellent 'circumnavigation' of Mrs Grundy, the great bane of Tom's career as a writer of fiction. This novel, which is after all an early work, has been heavily and patronizingly handled by academics, though they are inconsistent in their condemnations, some finding the scenes of social life artificial and others admiring them. Against that, it was loved by Tennyson, Proust, Patmore and many other critically untrained but none the less formidable amateurs. The book contains notable passages, in particular the famous scene of Knight's confrontation with the fossil while he is hanging on the side of the cliff, which automatically gains a place in any anthology of 'great English prose'.

A Pair of Blue Eyes was finished on 14 March 1873. In May it was issued in three volumes – as was then usual, a month or so before the appearance of the last serial instalment – this time with its author's own signature. The printer's copy for the book consisted of the *Tinsley's Magazine* text for the first twenty-eight chapters, which Hardy corrected in proof, plus, for the rest, the manuscript. He continued to revise and improve this text until 1920.

In *A Pair of Blue Eyes*, Hardy wrote in an early preface, he intended to 'show the influence of character on circumstances'. The main characters are the essentially innocent Elfride Swancourt and Stephen Smith, and the more mature, but fatally neurotic, Henry Knight. The young Elfride is content 'to build happiness on any accidental basis that may lie near at hand', and her indecisiveness leads her from Stephen Smith, the unforceful young architect with whom she elopes, only to change her mind at the last moment, to Henry Knight, an older man of letters, an over-rigid and at the same time also passive character – and finally to Lord Luxellian, the widower who marries her, only to lose her five months later through a miscarriage. The 'Gothic', or sensational, element is provided by Mrs Gertrude Jethway, whose son Felix's funeral occurs on the day Stephen Smith first calls at the vicarage (later 'rectory': Hardy disguised St Juliot as a vicarage, just as he protected the St Juliot people by rejecting *Elfride of Lyonnesse* for an alternative title). Mrs Jethway, a premonitory figure whose son's tomb is a symbol of disaster, believes that Felix, who died of consumption – as a tenuously supposed suitor of Emma's may have done – pined away for love of Elfride. She also believes that Elfride encouraged his passion. The revengeful Mrs Jethway is killed when the ruined tower of the church collapses on her (the tower of St Juliot was demolished).

Invention of circumstantial detail in *A Pair of Blue Eyes* is almost non-existent. Hardy drew upon circumstances recently known to him, or actually at hand, and made minimal alterations to them. Just as *Under the Greenwood Tree* is the most exact of the 'Wessex' novels, with the closest geographical resemblances between fictional and real places, so *A Pair of Blue Eyes* most closely reflects his immediate Cornish surroundings. Later his 'Wessex', of which Cornwall is not a true part, became more fictional in character.

The reason why Tom was uninventive of circumstances and locations was that he needed to put all his energy into the creation of his characters, into the central theme of Elfrida's innocence and ignorance of life, and into the parallel which he tried to develop between what he called 'the craze for indiscriminate church-restoration' and the 'three human heads, whose emotions were not without correspondence with these material circumstances'. As he wrote in the preface of 1912, of both the craze for restoration and (by implication) the history of the 'three human heads', 'To restore the grey carcases of a medievalism whose spirit had fled seemed a not less incongruous act than to set about renovating crags themselves.'

Although the novel is mostly light-hearted in tone – enough to make the death of Elfride herself seem 'incongruous' in its context – its tragic message is none the less that redemption (the childhood lesson which he never ceased to try to learn) is impossible, or at least that the author has rejected it as a tenet of intellectual belief: that he had a dark vision of an intractable 'Darwinian' nature, in which redemption from sin is wholly impossible. It is unlikely that he was fully conscious of this at the time, since, as he afterwards wrote, initially 'he had shaped nothing of what the later chapters were to be like', even though he defensively claimed to have 'thought of and written down' the general outline 'long before he knew Emma'. There is no reason to doubt this: he meant that he had long ago sketched some vague general outline for a story in which innocence is destroyed.

The serial begins (after two paragraphs which were dispensed with after the first book edition) with Elfride reading 'a romance'; this suggests that Tom, prompted by Horace Moule, might have read Flaubert's *Madame Bovary* (in the original: there was no translation available then). But this interesting passage was ineffective, and was removed from the book version, never to be reinstated. In his notice for the *Saturday Review*, which appeared on 2 August 1873, Moule remarked that the description of the ten minutes spent by Knight on the cliff recalled 'the intense minuteness and vivid concentration of the most powerful among French writers of fiction'. Which writers did he mean? For the author of the 'unpleasant' *Desperate Remedies*, who had now redeemed himself in the public eye with the pleasant pastoral of *Under the Greenwood Tree*, an admission to the influence of Flaubert would have represented the kiss of death. Nor did he ever mention his name.

While writing the novel, under the unfamiliar pressure of having to meet a deadline, Tom was simultaneously both exploiting and protecting those closest to him: Emma in Elfride, the Rev. Holder in Parson Swancourt (but there is a snide account of Gifford, or at least of Gifford's drunken snobbishness, given in the later manifestations of this character), himself in Stephen Smith and in Henry Knight, and Moule in Knight – and his father and mother, who might well have taken themselves as represented by Smith's parents. He must have explained the Elfride–Emma equation to Emma as a piece of fun; nor did she ever object to the identification, even when foolish people asked her, in later life, why she had 'done' this or that – actions of the book but not of her own. The identification is mostly superficial, and Elfride cannot be taken as an exact portrait, except of Emma's appearance and circumstances and certain of her characteristics. Not every woman would have been so accommodating.

Jemima was anxious about the effect on her reputation, and so Tom hastily claimed that his books could never penetrate into Dorset (though he had, of course, seen one remaindered at Exeter station, farther west). One would give much to know what Jemima said about the character of Elfride when she read the novel, for it is unlikely that she had yet met Emma, notwithstanding Florence's tale to the contrary. Tom's status at Bockhampton was still uncertain, and no doubt he heard much from his mother of that figure in his van, arm uplifted; but he prevailed. His efforts did, however, provoke a sneer from Charles Walter Moule. Giving way to his jealous feelings, and perhaps irritated by his brother Horace's continued support of Tom, Charles, a good man at heart, wrote, on 11 May 1873, a largely well-meaning letter of 'advice'. It reminded Tom of the necessity for literary men to have regular employment to fall back upon, but ended with a catty postscript: 'I trust that I address you rightly on the envelope. I conjectured you wd. prefer the absence of "Esqre" at Upper Bockhampton.' This was a reminder to Tom of his 'origins' and of how being a 'literary man' would affect him socially; it must have stung Tom – and caused Charles Moule some shame when he recollected it.

Tom had long been aware of the anomalies of his social position, and of its complexity, and he deals with it, if obliquely, in *A Pair of Blue Eyes*. At an unobtrusive level he also explores, for his own purposes, the psychological nature of Emma and of his relationship with Horace Moule. Both these relationships, Hardy–Emma and Hardy–Moule (Smith–Elfride and Smith–Knight), seemed to offer examples of proper human feeling transcending class distinctions. How did they really work out? On 24 July 1913, after Emma's sudden death, Tom told George Dewar, then editor of the *Saturday Review*, that while the 'character of the heroine [of *A Pair of Blue Eyes*] is somewhat – indeed, rather largely – that of my late wife . . . of course the adventures, lovers &c, are fictitious entirely . . .' The phrase 'rather largely' is a revealing admission, and the latter claim was true: Emma and Moule never met. This failed hope to bring together the two people, outside his family, whom he loved best was a matter of the deepest regret for Tom. In *A Pair of Blue Eyes* he does bring them together – but not in the wishful manner of a sentimental novelist. The issue is complicated, however, by the fact that, although Knight is primarily modelled upon Moule, Tom also, as he acknowledged, put something of himself into the character. Elfride and Stephen Smith are both ten years younger than Emma and Tom, so that Smith was too young to accommodate Tom's own maturity.

Later, Tom was to compare the atmosphere of the book to that of 'the twilight of a night vision'. He agreed with Coventry Patmore, an admirer who had astutely divined that the book really needed to be written in verse. This was a view which Tom was bound to approve; for he was saying goodbye not only happily to a career as an architect but also, unhappily, to the possibility (as he then saw it) of ever becoming what he really wanted to become: a poet. A poet has imperatives over and above his own hopes and wishes. Because, fortuitously, his narrative clung to what was actually around him or had very recently been so, it took a poetic shape, which accounts for the magic so many have found in the book. Only critics have dismissed it, perhaps because its wild quality, and its enchantment, disturb their sense of decorum. It is a pity that he chose to kill Elfride off, for, although he thus nicely underlined his eschewal of the conventional 'happy ending', he failed to illustrate the destructive force of her passivity. In his previous novel he could suggest to the discerning (amongst whom was D.H. Lawrence) that Dick Dewy was likely to have a bad time of it; here, in a non-pastoral tale, in which he had hardly bothered to develop the character of Lord Luxellian at all, he chose a too easy way out. The poet in him, the lover of that truth which he already saw as tragic, was fast undermining his romantic propensities, but the simple killing off of Elfride (Emma, causer of disturbance in him) does not do justice to the subtlety of the conception. When Stephen and Henry go by train to see Elfride they are, unknowingly, accompanied by her coffin. That is a marvellous Hardyan touch; but it is not enough to acquit the author of a major error of judgement. He had not yet become practised enough in the art of making his purse fatter by supplying the public with romantic fiction which, intended to be detected only by his astuter readers (those who appreciated poetry best of all), questioned the entire romantic project by exposing it as a human tragedy. He did eventually discover a viable version of redemption, but it is not evident in this shimmeringly dark novel: consolation is to be found only in its light surface, and in the impressions given by happy moments – for all that those prove to be doomed. And he could not yet show it, as he would in *The Mayor of Casterbridge* (Elizabeth-Jane's endurance of the emotionally shallow Farfrae on account of his genuine moral excellence), and in *Tess*, by depicting the depth of a woman's sufferings.

There is just one passage in *A Pair of Blue Eyes* to which Emma may have objected, and it was quickly removed. It is the one in the serial (seven paragraphs, only three of which are substantial in length) in which Elfride

> is reading a romance . . . hoping for a kindly ending . . . she was to be disappointed . . . her hero died . . . it was the last time in her life that her emotions were ever moved to any height by circumstances which never transpired . . .

Like Emma Bovary, then, and like the knight from La Mancha long before, Elfride was originally addicted to romances. It is one of the oldest themes in literature, and *A Pair of Blue Eyes*, for all its shortcomings and jejune passages and frequent lightness of tone, has its place as one of those books, romantic in themselves, which question the sentimental origins of romance itself.

Hardy is free of morality (of the kind typified in the attitude of the Huttons) in his analytic judgements of his characters – much more so, for example, than Mrs Gaskell or even George Eliot, who felt more ethically burdened by her eschewal of the Christian faith and her 'irregular' marital position. Yet Eliot's essay-like asides offered him a model. He gives us very rough, inexact approximations of Emma, Moule and himself as victims of romantic illusion; but rather than offer judgement on the resulting characters, he simply sees them as doomed: Elfride to death from grief, Knight to an inability to relate closely to any woman, and Stephen to a permanent sense of loss of his beloved.

If the excellences and achievements of *A Pair of Blue Eyes* outweighed its failings – as some critics now believe – then this was owed to a new confidence Tom felt as he wrote it. For at the beginning of December 1872 he received a request for a serial from Leslie Stephen. Stephen, reviewer for the *Saturday Review* and a well-known and highly respected critic, now felt sufficiently confident in Hardy to ask him if he had any novel in progress that could be considered for the *Cornhill*, of which he was the editor.

Founded in 1860 by George Smith, once the 'boy publisher' of the house of Smith, Elder & Co., the *Cornhill* was the most prestigious and widely read of the fiction-carrying periodicals of its time. Edited first by Thackeray, then by G.H. Lewes (companion and husband in all but name to George Eliot) and now by Stephen, it had a circulation of some fifty thousand and a readership far greater than that. *Tinsley's* was quite popular, but the only serious piece of fiction it ever serialized was Hardy's own current story. The *Cornhill*, by contrast, had published George Eliot (*Romola*, for a fee of little short of £15,000), Trollope, Thackeray himself, Collins, Reade and Mrs Gaskell. In short, there was hardly anyone eminent whose work it did not buy. Now they were asking Thomas Hardy! Stephen had said, too, 'I have no doubt [any agreement] would be satisfactory in a pecuniary point of view.'

Frederick Greenwood, a minor novelist of some merit who had completed both Mrs Gaskell's *Wives and Daughters* and Thackeray's *Denis Duval* with some competence, later claimed to have drawn

Stephen's attention to Hardy. But Stephen's letter to Tom stated that it was from Horace Moule, his *Saturday* colleague, that he had heard that 'he might address him as the author of *Under the Greenwood Tree*', which, although in itself unsuitable (Stephen alleged) for serialization, was 'admirably written'. Tom, deep in the work for *Tinsley's*, told Stephen that he could provide nothing now, but that he was considering a 'succeeding novel' to be called *Far From the Madding Crowd*, concerning 'a young woman farmer, a shepherd and a serjeant of cavalry'. Stephen wrote back that he liked the title and that he would be glad to discuss the projected novel further 'when [Hardy] came to town'. If Stephen was not already aware of *A Pair of Blue Eyes* he soon became so, for he commissioned Walter Besant to write a similar novel for serialization, to follow *Far From the Madding Crowd*.

Moule was now on the way down: his depression and drinking had become worse. Just as Tom's prospects brightened, so his dimmed. He perhaps now had the prospect of marriage, to the governess of sterling character mentioned earlier; but his behaviour was giving both him and his family reason for increasing concern. In an effort to control it, in August 1872 he took a post as Assistant Inspector of Local Government Institutes in East Anglia. That at least meant that he could take rooms in college at Cambridge, and there be watched over by his brothers Charles Walter and Frederick; the latter was not far away at Yaxley in Cambridgeshire, and was used to searching Horace out and rescuing him from the village pubs in which he became drunkenly stranded. A Cambridge doctor was also engaged to keep an eye on him.

Horace was a sensitive man who had inherited and witnessed his father's noble passion for justice for the poor. The conditions in the workhouses he had to visit were still Dickensian, and deeply affected him; also the sense of shame that afflicts alcoholics had increased in him. Its only counter was the prestige conferred by his writing for leading periodicals. And here was his always more cautious and prudent old pupil Tom, eight years his junior, rising in the world. The nature of his family's support seems to have been humane, intelligent and understanding; but by now this made it harder for him to maintain his self-respect. Horace was a poignant case, not of a propensity for alcohol and a weak will, but of severe cyclic depression, interrupted by bursts of abnormally high spirits – which accounted for his ability to charm people, and to excel. The so-called 'manic' aspect of such manic-depressive personalities can be genuinely inspired and inspiring, and capable of great achievement. The word 'afflation' in

Tom's extraordinary poem is an appropriate one for the soaring side
of such personalities, who often make magical and poetic connections
between things; but then they collapse into tragic incoherence.

Tom was careful to divide Henry Knight from Horace Moule in the
eyes of any readers who might know both. Knight has the fellowship
Horace failed to get, and he does not suffer from depression. But he is, as
Moule clearly was despite his contributions to the conservative *Saturday
Review*, something of a radical. There is, too, an enormous amount of
self-insight in this exchange between Emma and Stephen, which points
both to and away from Moule:

> '. . . I shall try to be his intimate friend some day.'
> 'But must you now?'
> 'No; not as much as that . . . You see, it was in this way – he came
> originally from the same place as I, and taught me things; but I am
> not intimate with him. Shan't I be glad when I get richer and better
> known, and hob and nob with him!' Stephen's eyes sparkled.

Tom was more intimate with Horace than this passage – a private joke,
like the relationship as it is depicted throughout the book – suggests; yet
there is a kind of truth in it, too. Tom, as we know, did look forward
to introducing Emma to Horace.

At this point the allegation that the Hardy–Moule relationship 'must
have had a sexual component', 'however unrealized on Hardy's part',
needs to be looked at more closely, as does the further speculation that
Moule himself was a paedophile – for that is what Millgate charges.
The remark about the Hardy–Moule relationship being 'inevitably'
homosexual is hardly worth making in the absence of any intelligible
analysis of its individual nature; this is not given. Millgate's 'must have'
is just the knowing shrug of the sophisticated biographer who knows
his Freud. Thus, every enthusiastic young friendship is 'of course'
homosexual. But such facile Freudianism hardly has the courage of
its convictions. The point worth considering, apropos Tom's own
'unrealized' homosexuality, is whether his fiction contains any special
insights into homosexual relationships. After all, homosexual motiva-
tion is a part of life, and novelists illuminate life. In *Desperate Remedies*
insight into a certain kind of exploitative lesbianism is fully achieved
(but denied by Millgate in the interests of his determination to diminish
Hardy's intelligence). There are two further possibilities: Smith–Knight
in *A Pair of Blue Eyes*, and, more obviously, Henchard–Farfrae in *The*

Mayor of Casterbridge, in which the nature of Henchard's feelings is made explicit. A novelist does not, of course, have to be homosexual in order to discern homosexuality, or vice versa – Henry James' insights into heterosexual relationships would otherwise have little validity. The problem for the Victorian novelist was that he could not be explicit about this, or any other such 'smoking-room' matter, in his work. But in the case of the Henchard–Farfrae relationship Hardy may not even have given any name to its homosexual aspect in the privacy of his own consideration. It is what Freud himself, referring to his own relationship with his erstwhile friend Fliess, called some 'unruly homosexuality': almost an afterthought by a man whose behaviour and habits of thought and feeling were predominantly heterosexual. Apart from that of the Cythereas, there is no physically homosexual relationship in Hardy's work. He was not personally interested in such relationships.

In the Smith–Knight case, though, in which Smith is carefully distanced from Hardy and Knight, the matter of how each stands to the other is crucial. Elfride is at first almost comically jealous of the young Smith's regard for Knight: she is represented as unable to resist the foolishness and pettiness of her vanity, and wilfully dependent upon it. After she has frustrated Smith by refusing to go through with the elopement, thus raising serious doubts in the reader about her reliability, Smith calls on Knight in his chambers to discuss his situation and to obtain advice about his opportunity to go to India. The narrator states that 'Smith was not quite the man Knight would have deliberately chosen as a friend . . . Circumstance, as usual, did it all', and he adds the generalization that our friends are usually the results of 'mere physical juxtaposition long maintained . . . taken into our confidence . . . as a makeshift'. This echoes or anticipates 'The Temporary the All',

> Change and chancefulness in my flowering youthtime,
>   Set me sun by sun near to one unchosen

and indicates Hardy's persistent notion that chance rather than choice determines the human condition. It is his early gloomy intellectual conclusion about life, and it does not diminish his love for the individuals he encounters. This notion that our lives are lived for us by fate is also found in *The Dynasts* and elsewhere.

Smith comes across Elfride's novel *The Court of King Arthur's Castle*, by 'Ernest Field'. Its reviewer, Knight, comments that it is bad, 'written by some girl in her teens'. This is no doubt how Tom expressed his anxieties about the way Horace Moule would judge Emma's intellect; but he did it light-heartedly. Part of Emma's own romance was by now probably already in existence, although unfinished . . . There is no reason to doubt the intensity of Tom's passion for Emma, nor of his loving friendship for Moule; but there is no reason to doubt, either, the extreme severity of his sense of reality. In some men, and Knight is one of them, such reservations inhibit passion. In others, such as Hardy, they do not. He was always confronted by two equally powerful forces in himself.

There is not a trace of homosexuality or ambisexuality in Knight. He feels, the reader learns, that when women are kissed they ought to be observed: 'instead of being charmed by the fascination of their bearing at such a time, we should immediately doubt them if their confusion has any *grace* in it – that awkward bungling was the true charm of the occasion, implying that we are the first who has played such a part with them'. This is unpleasant, but not homosexual; rather, it implies a suspicious and proprietorial attitude, betraying a fear of women as strange, if desirable, objects. Men are supposed to be experienced, but women must remain as objects of exploratory use. This was a characteristic that Hardy had observed in all men, and therefore in himself. Self-critical as always, he does not shirk the issue, and is aware of what today would be called its feminist implication. Indeed, Tom, while he could hardly anticipate women's feminism, did anticipate male feminism. Contemporary women have both applauded his insights as a man who tried, in part successfully, to understand women, and attacked him as one who failed to do so.

Of the kiss itself Knight says, surely provokingly, that a 'woman must have had many kisses before she kisses well'. In his case that means simply, that he, Knight, and no one else, has to train her in his preferences. A woman must not be allowed to develop her own sexuality through her own experiences: she must properly be the object, trained from scratch, of a single man. Knight's ungenerous and, as it turns out, severely neurotic method of judgement indicates that he enjoys consideration of women as objects, not as human beings in their own right, and that in the latter capacity he fears them. Incapable of making an adjustment, he cannot accept Elfride when he considers that she has been in another man's arms; nor is he capable of considering her feelings about *his* past 'experience'.

This kind of obsessive jealousy contains elements of vicarious, voyeuristic enjoyment. Tom did remark that there was something of himself in Knight, but it probably went no further than an exploration of what might happen if certain tendencies he possessed were allowed to develop. He himself saw that when people are in the throes of romantic love ludicrous and irrational egoism could result. He often attributes to Knight feelings of his own, such as when he causes him to inform Elfride, bitterly, that it 'requires a judicious omission of your real thoughts to make a novel popular'. But then he spreads his own *sententiae* – epigrammatic authorial asides, an idea which he acquired from eighteenth-century novelists and from George Eliot – amongst many of his characters, even giving some to the ugly, intelligent Mrs Troyton, who becomes Mrs Swancourt. Only Swancourt is given nothing of consequence to observe. His circumstances are, if vaguely, those of the Rev. Holder, but he resembles him only in his propensity to gout.

It seems rather as though Hardy began by modelling Swancourt on George Eliot's Septimus Brooke in *Middlemarch* (which started to appear in 1871, in instalments), but then used the character – not eventually a good-hearted one, but quite the contrary, for his cruel snobbery is to be the cause of Elfride's death – to express his resentment of Emma's father. Elfride, although immature, is not depicted as foolish: she tartly tells Knight: '. . . there is much littleness in trying to be great. A man must think a good deal of himself, and be conceited enough to believe in himself, before he tries at all.' The man who wrote this is far from the self-obsessed, unconfident, humourless and Bible-marking prophet of the Gittings biography, for in his reply Knight points out that an ambitious man 'may see how little success has to do with merit, and his motive may be his very humility'.

The neurotic Knight, older than the more straightforward Stephen, possesses more authority, and it is through Elfride's sense of this that he displaces Stephen in her affections. The metaphor used is chess, here a game of love-strategy. Elfride allows Stephen to win two games before beating him; Knight shows no such mercy to her, and thus stirs into life her desire to yield herself to one stronger and cleverer than herself, a desire which finally takes precedence over her vanity. But whether Knight really is cleverer, or whether he just has the advantages of culture and greater years, is another matter: 'In truth, the essayist's experience of the nature of young women was far less extensive than his abstract knowledge . . . He could pack them into sentences like a workman, but practically was nowhere.' For all his cold knowledge of the world and its ways, he never loves Elfride in the way that Tom loved

Emma. Thus Hardy early tackles a theme perennially disturbing to many women – their desire to be dominated by men – and one which disturbed and puzzled him. Elfride, though, may be seen as having chosen death rather than bondage. She thus tragically transcends her immature desire. In that respect, however, Hardy failed to develop the character of Lord Luxellian sufficiently.

Emma, whatever she became, was not finally going to be a 'dominated woman', either: she did not decorously follow her husband's celebrated views of life, nor did she become the kind of hostess a great Victorian writer quite 'needed'. However eccentric she was, perhaps we can be grateful to her for showing that much spirit, and for thus trying Hardy's patience and preserving him from complacency. We have heard much more of her than we have of Mrs Gosse, or even of Lady Tennyson. Perhaps the very fact of her not being an ideal Victorian wife and helpmate gave Tom just the unhappiness he required to bring out the best in him.

It seems to have gone unnoticed that the chess episodes between Elfride and Knight, and the entries about them in the latter's notebook, are exceedingly funny. These episodes display both Knight's ignorance of human nature and the indolent superiority, as 'essayist', with which he seeks to disguise this ignorance. What Knight says about Elfride would have been quite risqué had Emma not been in Tom's confidence, and suggests either that he was very confident in their understanding (the more likely) or, just possibly, that he was testing her out. Knight writes:

Aug 7. Girl gets into her teens, and her self-consciousness is born. After a certain interval passed in infantine helplessness, it begins to act. Simple, young and inexperienced at first. Person of observation can tell to a nicety how old this consciousness is by the skill it has acquired in the art necessary to its success – the art of hiding itself. Generally begins career by actions which are popularly termed showing off. Method adopted depends in each case upon the disposition, rank, residence of the young lady attempting it. Town bred girl will utter some moral paradox on fast men or love. Country miss adopts the more material media of taking a ghastly fence, whistling, or making your blood run cold by appearing to risk her neck. (*Mem.* On Endelstowe Tower.) . . .

Knight has just observed Elfride performing her 'giddy feat' on the tower – just the kind of exploit typical of Emma – in the course of which she slipped and almost fell, angering but also disturbing him. The note ends: 'Amplify and correct for paper on Artless Arts'. By depicting Knight in this way Tom was satirizing the sort of cold fish who casually uses other, 'inferior' people for copy – the literary butterfly which he had never wished to be. It causes Knight's essential character to be – far from Tom's notion of Moule – that of a pretentious prig, taking advantage, over Elfride, of his masculine sex and his extra decade.

There is, just after the exchange between him and Elfride on the matter of his notebook entry, a clue to what Tom really meant in the *Life* about developing late, and how he understood the term 'virility'. Elfride says, 'Youths and girls who are men and women before they come of age are nobodies by the time that backward people have shown their full compass.' That has nothing to do with physical development.

The question of homosexuality between Tom and Horace Moule may now be finally disposed of. It has deserved consideration not only because it has been proposed by Hardy's biographer but also because it might explain Tom's lifelong devotion to Moule's memory. But surely the stubbornly obstinate author of the pioneer lesbian passage in *Desperate Remedies* would have insinuated something into the Smith–Knight relationship, had it been homosexual, in *A Pair of Blue Eyes*. One feels that Henry Knight, getting further and further away from Tom or Moule as he develops, becomes increasingly an autonomous portrait of an intellectual, a man whose emotions are fossilized (and one awakened to this fact by being brought face to face with a fossil): a man Tom felt he too could have become, if he dwelt too deeply or jealously upon Emma's past instead of, as he did, simply loving and marrying her whatever the consequences. There is little convincing evidence that Emma had any serious suitor before Tom, and certainly not enough to warrant discussion of the matter at length. But a jealously curious man such as Knight needs no real past: he can soon supply what he so fascinatedly dreads, as Knight does when he imagines Jethway's function in Elfride's life.

When Stephen Smith first discovers that Knight is his rival, he finds the situation singular in 'its form': 'That his rival should be Knight, whom once upon a time he had adored as a man is very rarely adored by another in modern times, and whom he loved now, added deprecation to sorrow, and cynicism to both.' This neither suggests nor precludes homosexuality. When Knight for his part discovers that his 'rival' is Smith, he reflects that he is 'but a boy' to him; it is implied that he is somewhat unhappy about this because it deprives him of his fantasies of her 'contamination': 'an anti-climax of absurdity'. Any homosexuality here is so generalized as to be quite without biographical substance.

The truly tragic figure in this comi-tragedy is Elfride. But she cannot quite carry the weight put on her. She has no passion in her to arouse the reader to tragic emotions. She is still a child when she dies. Her death, like that of a child, is poignant; but even this poignancy is diminished by the grotesquerie – irresistible to Hardy – of her two former suitors' journey in the same train as her coffin.

Despite its deliberately incongruous charm, too many genres are mixed together to allow *A Pair of Blue Eyes* to carry tragic weight. Yet Tom turned this unintegrated mixture of comedy, tragedy, the grotesque, farce and sensationalism, forced upon him by pressure of circumstances, into a genuine piece of experimental writing. A very strong sense of Elfride's victimization at the hands of men – the slightly feeble and colourless Smith; the egocentric and selfish, if serious-minded, Knight; her conceited, cruel, snobbish and bumbling father; even Lord Luxellian, too (undefined as he is) – does come through; and, just like the tragic undertones of *Under the Greenwood Tree* – the simple and straightforward life of Dick Dewy blighted by a woman who rightly thinks him not quite man enough to share her little secret – those of *A Pair of Blue Eyes* become greater in the light of the later fiction, particularly *Tess*.

A Pair of Blue Eyes also has another supremely important function: it represents an action, a piece of behaviour. From the very moment of Tinsley's proposition of a serial for £200 – more than a year's salary as an architect – Tom looks upon himself as a writer once more. He cannot now afford to fail or to look back, and Leslie Stephen's request for another story only reinforces this. Not long before he had chosen to give up writing, in order to test his friends' and fiancée's reaction. Suddenly, commissioned by Tinsley, he renounces architecture with alacrity, even though he is worried that he may have 'done rather a rash thing'. He excitedly writes his first chapters in London, 'in an incredibly quick time', and awaits the proofs at the house of his prospective father-in-law, whom he vainly hopes to impress with them.

Alas, John Gifford is himself a literary man, a declaimer of Shakespeare, and that particular piece of gamesmanship has a bad result (even if it has been exaggerated). Rebuffed, Tom pillories Gifford as Swancourt, in the scene between the latter and Elfride about Stephen Smith's 'social unsuitability'. Later in the novel he castigates him even more severely as a vulgar enthusiast for church restoration, and as insensitive to Elfride's grief; but he does it so that Gifford cannot possibly take exception without drawing attention to his own intoxicated outburst of snobbery and envy.

Tom does not say anything to Emma about this. Perhaps she does not notice it. He is using his work-in-progress in order to please, tease, test and court Emma, who is probably just as well up to the game as Elfride of the novel was up, for all her youth, to the cleverness of Henry Knight's repartee. The central episode of the novel, Knight's predicament on the cliff, is based on an experience of Emma's, when (as she wrote in 'Some Recollections') she 'hung over the "devil's hole" by a tuft of grass'. Knight's suggestion to Elfride that plentiful hair tends to grow thin is assuredly a private joke, especially in view of Emma's own fine head of hair. Sometimes, then, Tom lives a little dangerously in the way he teases Emma. Yet the overwhelming sense is that he is exceedingly confident in her, and in the fact that she understands the extent to which a novelist may have to omit his 'own thoughts' in order to be 'popular' – to make a living. Some six pages of the manuscript of *A Pair of Blue Eyes* is in her hand, from which we may suppose that she was involved in it as soon as the part written in Cornwall was composed, and that she did not seriously object to any of it.

Finally, Tom returns to Bockhampton, braves out whatever his mother (and/or father) has to say about his decisions, and writes the bulk of the book there. The tension between parents and eldest son cannot be very great if he can make this choice, for there are alternatives, although none quite as economical: if he goes to London he will need to interrupt his writing with architectural work, which he plainly wishes to avoid.

However, whatever Tom and his parents say to each other, he knows very well that both they and, more particularly, their neighbours (including ones for whom his father works: people higher up in that now problematical thing, the social order) are going to read *A Pair of Blue Eyes* and that Tom Senior and Jemima are going to be seen as Mr and Mrs Smith, the parents of Stephen. It is a delicate operation, but now he has to go through with it: the story is running in *Tinsley's*. He has committed himself, in his haste, to something based on what looks very like the events of his own life.

His parents cannot be expected to understand the critical niceties of the relationship between characters in novels and their models from real life. So Tom boldly inserts a chapter, XXXVI, not at all necessary to the action, in which Mr and Mrs Smith are suddenly fêted by everyone in St Launce (Launceston), where they have moved from St Juliot, because their architect son Stephen has been mentioned in the newspapers. He is also exceedingly satirical, not of them, but of the people who suddenly pay them court. This seems, to say the least, to have been gratuitous and risky unless he enjoyed an easy relationship with his parents; but to one who had previously been mocked, as was inevitable, in his own district, it must have given satisfaction. It does not suggest that Tom was very frightened of any of his neighbours when it really came to it.

When Stephen Smith sends money to Elfride, the sum is £200: exactly what Tom has just contracted to receive, in instalments, from Tinsley. He still 'means mischief', as Macmillan had once insisted, and as Morley had recognized when he warned Macmillan, of *Desperate Remedies*: 'don't touch it'. Nor can Tom resist the temptation to challenge the status quo from his new, not yet even secure, position as writer.

The most decisive personal use to which Tom put the writing of *A Pair of Blue Eyes* was to exercise the tendency, urged upon him by his culture, to treat women as objects – as either totally obedient or enshrined, but in any case dead, with their vitality, the unexpectedness aroused by their individualities, drained from them. He was able to begin, in Elfride, to make himself see women, his fellow human beings, as they actually were. And he was able to observe the least edifying features of himself in Knight, and to try to purge himself of them. Whatever the shortcomings of *A Pair of Blue Eyes* – it is certainly much more than the mere 'rag-bag of information, ideas, descriptive vignettes, personal experiences' that Millgate pronounces it to be – it is sharp and exact in its depiction of the agreeable literary hack Knight's sexual make-up, as it is in demonstrating how unloved, for herself, Elfride always is, even unto her premature death. Stephen Smith comes nearest to loving her, but is not yet man enough for her: he cannot vie with her intellectually, as symbolically shown when she easily defeats him at chess. As she later tells Knight, her love for him was not 'supported by reverence for his powers'. Smith wants her for young love's sake, and as a '*living*' woman'; she finally responds badly to his self-deprecatory habits, as the narrator tells us. He is too immature to realize her as Elfride, the woman herself, as distinct from the ideal of the beloved who can do no wrong: being human, and not the female stereotype of her disingenuous culture, she *can* do wrong; but he is too lightweight to influence her – as a man may, under happier circumstances, influence a woman. The novel would have been more genuinely tragic if its author could have presented Stephen, upon his return from India, as now more grown up and therefore deprived of a woman he could now love for herself. But Hardy was in too much of a hurry, and when he saw the possibility of improvement, wrote that 'correction by the judgement of later years . . . would have resulted in the disappearance of . . . freshness and spontaneity'.

After Stephen Smith comes Henry Knight, to whose apparent maturity Elfride responds, not able to see it for the smug affectation that it is. It is clear enough that when the young Stephen kisses her, he has kissed before. But Knight, for all his worldly manners, has not kissed a woman before. His nasty and patronizing advice to his young friend (which he forgets having made, but approves of when reminded), to the effect that 'not to kiss nicely' is 'an excellent fault in woman', is the result not of experience but of false cynicism and jealous inability to share sensual pleasure. Unhappy at being disturbed by Elfride's sexuality, he casually disposes of her pretensions by beating her at chess. He is angry at her 'giddy feat' on the Tower. But then she shows true resourcefulness and praticality in rescuing him from his fate as he hangs over the cliff. She does this by divesting herself of her underclothes to weave them into a rope, so that afterwards she has 'nothing between her and the weather but her diaphanous exterior robe'. At that point, we are told,

> it was impossible for two persons to go nearer to a kiss than went Knight and Elfride during those minutes of impulsive embrace in the pelting rain . . . Yet they did not kiss. Knight's peculiarity of nature was such that it would not allow him to take advantage of the unguarded and passionate avowal she had tacitly made.

The sexual implications are obvious. While Elfride loves him, and has been prepared to sacrifice all propriety in order to save his life, he is too inhibited to love her. He is terrified of losing himself in the emotional depths over whose analogue, beneath the aptly named Cliff without a Name – really Beeny Cliff – he has just hung: what he describes as a place where 'nothing but vacancy appears', and where 'the laws of nature appear to be reversed'.

He is immediately grateful to Elfride, of course, and as immediately desirous of her. But soon, in order to make her pay for thus tempting him, he will cruelly needle her about her vanity in the matter of her hair and her interest in her earrings. Yet it was as a result of his own injudicious reaching after his own so proper male appendage, his hat, which hides his balding state, that he was unable to climb to safety.

Even if most readers miss the irony here, we may be sure that Tom did not.

With the inexperienced, loving, innocent good will which characterizes her, and for which she receives no appreciation, Elfride gives him her hand; the result is that she herself slips farther down than she already is, and drops the glass which she brought along in order to view the ship she knew was bringing Stephen: thus she finally gives herself, in spirit, to Knight; but by now they are both in danger of dropping over the abyss – an abyss whose depths she, after all, is more fit than he to plumb. It is thus he who now notes that they must perform their 'feat of getting up the slope *with the precision of machines*' (my italics). He instructs her to clamber up his body; preparing to do so, she reminds him that she had a premonition of such a moment. 'This is not a time for supersition,' he tells her, ever mechanistic in his attitude.

But this is important to her. On Endelstowe Tower, out of sheer high spirits she performed her 'giddy feat', 'without reflecting in the least what she was doing': she walked 'round the parapet . . . quite without battlement or pinnacle'. This is safe when it is naturally done, but the very naturalness of it offends the envious Knight, and his face 'flushes with mingled concern at her rashness'. This is emblematic of the standard Victorian situation between men and women: when later Knight rushes to retrieve his hat, it is not a 'rash' act at all. It is thus his own fussy sense of propriety that causes her to stumble and 'almost' lose her balance, for, as she tells him, she has done it before. And it is Knight's stuffiness that makes her 'sick and pale as a corpse' (the corpse she will all too soon become, as a result of his cruelty). Death is then, as later in the cliff scene that follows, used as the time-honoured metaphor for love-making.

Thus Hardy demonstrates Elfride's sexual instincts as healthy and natural, but Knight's as infected by self-protective impulses posing as protective ones. Not possessing the necessary assurance or experience to tell Knight of his stuffiness, but still disappointed by him, and offended by his confusion of high spirits with 'foolishness', she tells him of her strange sensation that such a moment will recur. Knight's woodenly unintuitive and unimaginative response is: 'God forbid! . . . Think no more of such a foolish fancy.'

Yet Elfride has been right. It is the resourcefulness of the foolish girl that saves him from death. He will not show that mercy to her when she comes to appeal to him, and she will die because of that. He thus kills her spirit.

The nature of the rescue was a *tour de force* of anti-Grundyism, for what Mrs Grundy could object to a girl's stripping herself in order to *save* a man? Hardy was well aware of this. While Elfride is undressing beyond reach of his eyes, the virginal Knight confronts the Tribolite – the fossil on the cliff-face – and time closes up before him 'like a fan': he believes that he is going to fall, and thus 'die'. He thinks of Elfride in a world '*without himself to cherish her*' (my italics). And, in an often misread passage – in which the narrator takes over from Knight – capricious nature is not likened to her (at that very moment making a sensible if highly indelicate sacrifice of her underclothes in exchange for a life), but contrasted with her: as seeming at times 'feline' in her 'tricks'. The action of taking off her clothes has indeed caused the 'blank and helpless agony' to leave her face. When she has rescued him, Elfride is able, generously enough, to reflect that perhaps 'he was only grateful, and did not love her' – which is the exact truth. Knight is, it is true, now propelled towards the possibility of loving her. But he cannot go through with it. In order to protect himself from the givingness involved in love, Knight needs to view a past Elfride exposed to and loved by another man.

Hardly any of this is near to Tom's own literal experience or acts, to his own attitude, to Emma's, or to Horace Moule's. It is indeed autobiographical, but only in the Aristotelian sense explained earlier: as an imaginative exploration of tendencies in himself and in his friends. Just before the rescue scene Stephen Smith spies Knight and Elfride as he scans the coast, from his ship, with his telescope; his not being able to make out who they are is Hardy's symbolic means of distancing himself from them, as of demonstrating the complete exclusion of Smith, who in his turn is watched by the couple through *their* telescope.

Some critics have detected hostility towards women, as well as sexual pessimism, in both *Under the Greenwood Tree* and, more particularly, *A Pair of Blue Eyes*. 'Sexual pessimism', in the sense of being disenchanted by the conventional processes of romantic love, and especially the Victorian model of it: yes. But as regards 'hostility to women', how do such critics explain the young Elfride's poignant words to Knight after he has been perversely tormenting her on the subject of her previous attachments, which lasciviously 'jar' what he calls his 'subtler fancies'?

'Am I such a – mere characterless toy – as to have no attraction in me, apart from – freshness? Haven't I brains? You said – I was clever and ingenious in my thoughts, and – isn't that anything? Have I not some beauty? I think I have a little – and I know I have – yes I do! You have praised my voice, and my manner, and my accomplishments. Yet all these are so much rubbish because I – accidentally saw a man before you!'

In giving these words to Elfride, the author is aware that whereas she is young (nineteen) and confused, and still 'pure' in the sense he later famously used this word of Tess, the elder and supposedly mature Knight, as a lover, is sick: 'perhaps his lifelong constraint towards women . . . was . . . the natural result of instinctive acts so minute as to be undiscernible even by himself'. When Elfride tells him that she had wished him to be 'of a grosser nature' she means, as she explains, 'less delicate', 'less fastidious' – which he instantly misunderstands as 'shallow'. When at last she appeals to him, in his chambers, having run away from her worthless father in order to do so, his love is finally put to the test and found wanting: 'Yet it is wrong for you to stay . . . It is a stain to your good name to run to me like this!' Her capacity to love him has been proved, though. She does not care any more. Later he does repent; but, faced with an emergency, he can never do otherwise than think of what is believed to be proper for a woman. Thus he conceals from himself his own perverse needs.

Elfride is a prototype for Bathsheba, the more complex heroine of *Far From the Madding Crowd*, Hardy's next novel. She is convincing and substantial enough to sum up the matter in one of the most memorable and revealing sentences in all his works: 'It is difficult for a woman to define her feelings in language which is chiefly made by men to express theirs.'

10

Far From the Madding Crowd

When Tom first heard from Leslie Stephen he is unlikely to have sketched out more than a few notes for *Far From the Madding Crowd*, perhaps not yet even including the important character of Boldwood. The novel itself was written at Bockhampton, between the spring of 1873 and July 1874. He did not, as almost all aspiring young authors would have done, rush to make Stephen's acquaintance. He bided his time, and did not call upon him until months later, on 8 December 1873, when arrangements for the serial had already been made. Stephen's first letter to him had been dropped by the children to whom it had been entrusted, and reached him only by the chance that it was 'picked up in the mud of the lane by a labouring man'; it was followed up by a second enquiry, in April 1873, in which Stephen repeated his wish to meet the young author. Although he then got down to some serious work on the book, he still did not take advantage of the invitation when he was at Celbridge Place on 9 June. Instead he sent a few chapters, which Stephen approved but did not immediately accept. Tom took his brother Henry with him to London, and showed him some of the sights. His diary for the month reads, in a part he chose to reproduce:

June 15. Met H.M. Moule at the Golden Cross Hotel. Dined with him at the British Hotel. Moule then left for Ipswich on his duties as Poor Law Inspector . . . *June 20*. By evening train to Cambridge. Stayed in College – Queens' – Went out with H.M.M. after dinner. A magnificent evening: sun over 'the Backs'.

Next morning went with H.M.M. to King's Chapel early. M. opened the great West doors to show the interior vista: we got upon the roof, where we could see Ely Cathedral gleaming in the distant sunlight. A never-to-be-forgotten morning. H.M.M. saw me off for London. His last smile.

This was the last time Tom saw his friend. On 23 May, only a week or two before the final meeting, Horace had written to Tom about *A Pair of Blue Eyes*. His letter has been humourlessly misread – under the common misapprehension about the low degree of the friends' intimacy – as 'mixing warm enthusiasm with cold condescension'. Horace had written:

> You understand the *woman* infinitely better than the *lady*, and how gloriously you have idealized here & there, as far as I have got. Yr slips of taste, every now and then, I ought to say point blank at once, are *Tinsleyean* . . . I long to meet you.

This is the language not of condescension, but of banter between friends, as the joke about Tom's obligation to Tinsley and his vulgar magazine make clear. He and Tom had discussed Tinsley, the niceties of social rank, and much else beside: their friendship had long transcended the social difference between them. That undertones persisted, or that Horace was envious, may well be so; but he knew how to rise above all that. He showed this in the last service he was able to perform: a review (as usual unsigned, but clearly his) of *A Pair of Blue Eyes* in the *Saturday Review* of 2 August 1873.

Horace found in the novel an account of a person's getting over her worst feelings: when Elfride considers Knight's review of her novel, she is intelligent enough to see the justice in it. Horace did not over-praise the book, but supplied a judicious account; above all he saluted the author's promise. He tended to think that Henry Knight was too much of a prig, and the least well-realized character. But he could see the psychological rightness of the Elfride–Knight relationship, and praised Hardy for having escaped from the paraphernalia of the sensation novel: 'he has kept up the interest throughout . . . not only without a single crime or a single villain, but with men of honest heart and high aim' – yet he had achieved 'really tragic power' from his 'simple material'.

Nor did Moule have any delusion about Tom's being a misogynist. He was able to discern Elfride as she essentially is: 'sensitive and conscious, but perfectly simple'. He saw that, although the author's 'general methods' were unlike those of George Eliot, there was one 'decided resemblance': 'Mr Hardy has . . . developed . . . with something of the ruthlessness of George Eliot . . . the power of mere events on certain kinds of character.'

Tom did not read this review until a month after he returned from his travels. For from London and Cambridge he had gone straight to Bath, to meet Emma and her friend of the fainting canary. They journeyed about Bath and Bristol, and made an excursion to Tintern Abbey, 'where we repeated some of Wordsworth's lines thereon'. They also discovered, in a newsagent's shop at Clifton, that the *Spectator*, in the person of John Hutton, had given *A Pair of Blue Eyes* a 'commendatory' notice. On 2 July he was back at Dorchester and got straight on with the new book, which was to bring him to the forefront of Victorian novelists. He needed to be near to the kind of events he was depicting, and he therefore walked to Woodbury Hill Fair – Greenhill Fair in *Far From the Madding Crowd* – on 21 September. Then, on the 24th, he 'was shocked to hear of the tragic death of his friend Horace Moule, from whom he had parted cheerfully . . . in June'.

Moule had been pursuing his duties more or less successfully for just over a year. He had also continued to help young people in Cambridge, if not on a regular basis. His family's understanding of his predicament was enlightened: they regarded his alcoholism as an illness, not as the result of an infirmity of will. In modern terms, he was subject to bouts of psychotic, suicidal, depression, for which there were then no known remedies. He therefore took to alcohol, and, in all probability, regular doses of opium. His brother Charles, in an elegy, later referred to the 'strange disquiet' which 'wore his brain/Till restlessly it seized on rest'. But the part Charles played in Horace's tragic last act, although not his fault, was unfortunate for his own peace of mind, and he always blamed himself. Every 21 September he suffered as he mentally re-enacted the events of that fateful one in 1873.

On 19 September, returning to Cambridge for a holiday after inspecting two institutions, Horace visited his doctor, James Hough, to report alarming symptoms. These suggest that he was suffering from an attack of what is now known as agitated depression, a dangerous state for anyone who has previously expressed a wish to kill himself. It is at just this point that a depressed person can overcome his langour and weakness enough to perform the act of self-destruction; he may even seem more energetic and cheerful.

Hough wired Charles, who was not in Cambridge, and engaged a nurse, who was in attendance from the morning of 20 September, a Saturday. Moule took the usual drink to combat his symptoms, but it did not help: alcohol is in itself a powerful depressant. He managed to struggle through that day. The next morning Charles arrived and the nurse was sent away. The two men had a long and tiring discussion, during which Horace 'explained his fears'. At some stage Horace became excited, but this state was followed by exhaustion. He went to bed, pulled the covers over himself, seized a razor he had secreted beneath his pillow, and cut his throat wide open.

After his brother had gone to bed, Charles, himself exhausted, tried to take his mind off the affair; it was to him a familiar enough situation. He got on with some writing he had to do. As he wrote, he heard a trickling sound. By the time he had traced it to its source it was too late: Horace had lost too much blood. The doctor and nurse were called. Horace was able to mutter, 'Love to my mother. Easy to die'; soon afterwards he did die.

It has been surmised that Horace killed himself because of a fiancée's rejection. This is possible. But there is no evidence of an affair, and Florence never made clear, in her conversations with R.L. Purdy, what Tom had told her about Moule, except that the story of the bastard by a Dorchester girl was true. However, that is likely to have happened much earlier. Horace's suicide was the result of clinical depression.

He had many times previously talked of suicide, but without attempting it. He had been 'perfectly sober' when he went to bed. The coroner's jury brought in a verdict of suicide while temporarily insane – this was usual for people of good family, and meant he could be buried in the Fordington churchyard. Tom went there on 25 September, the eve of the funeral, and drew a sketch of the mound by the side of the freshly dug grave; he would continue to visit Horace's grave for the rest of his life. On that day he also marked, in his *Golden Treasury* which had been a gift from Moule, these lines from Shakespeare:

> Had my friend's Muse grown with this growing age,
> A dearer birth than this his love had brought,
> To march in ranks of better equipage.
> But since he died, and poets better prove,
> Theirs for their style I'll read, his for his love.

He was to remember that Thursday in his retrospective poem 'Before My Friend Arrived'.

Tom also wrote, perhaps in the last years of his life, another, more enigmatic poem about Horace. Called 'Standing by the Mantelpiece', it bears the subtitle 'H.M.M. 1873'; the speaker is Moule himself. The candle motif is a piece of Dorset folklore: if a candle burns one-sidedly, leaving a 'little column of tallow', it is traditionally supposed to forecast a death. Here the speaker regards it as a prophecy of his own death:

> This candle-wax is shaping to a shroud
> To-night. (They call it that, as you may know) –
> By touching it the claimant is avowed,
> And hence I press it with my finger – so.
>
> To-night. To me twice night, that should have been
> The radiance of the midmost tick of noon,
> And close around me wintertime is seen
> That might have shone the veriest day of June!
>
> But since all's lost, and nothing really lies
> Above but shade, and shadier shade below,
> Let me make clear, before one of us dies,
> My mind to yours, just now embittered so.
>
> Since you agreed, unurged and full-advised,
> And let warmth grow without discouragement,
> Why do you bear you now as if surprised,
> When what has come was clearly consequent?
>
> Since you have spoken, and finality
> Closes around, and my last movements loom,
> I say no more: the rest must wait till we
> Are face to face again, yonside the tomb.
>
> And let the candle-wax thus mould a shape
> Whose meaning now, if hid before, you know,
> And how by touch one present claims its drape,
> And that it's I who press my finger – so.

The usual understanding of the poem is that Moule is addressing a woman who has renounced him for some reason, that reason not being made altogether clear in the crucial fourth stanza. Millgate, however, reads it as an address to Hardy himself: Moule, he insists, made a homosexual proposal to him which he repudiated. Since the poem is cryptic, this is a possible reading. But there is nothing to support it: nothing to suggest, for example, that Moule was homosexual. Had he wanted to go to bed with Tom he would have made his wishes clear long before 1873. Could Hardy have brought himself to add the tender note, 'His last smile', to his account of the last meeting? Would he have mentioned Moule in the *Life* at all? If Millgate is right, then the poem suggests that the speaker's death was connected with his interlocutor's refusal of his advances. Is it not more likely, though, that the background to the poem is that Moule got drunk at table, suggested to his fiancée that they go to bed, and that she repudiated him?

The meaning of the poem remains a puzzle, and readers who do not know who 'H.M.M.' is are confronted with an obscurity. All that can be said is that the notion of the speaker's addressing a fiancée who had once accepted him, but then gave him up, strains credulity less than Millgate's interpretation, and that, once assumed, it is straightforward enough. What the fourth stanza seems to imply is: 'You knew what kind of a person I was when you agreed to love me. I told you I had dark tendencies. But now, confronted with extra knowledge of me [drunken behaviour? A proposal? An account of my fathership of a bastard? All three?] which is in fact clearly consequent from what I already told you, you seem surprised.'

Tom wrote yet another poem about Moule, dated 1873 and entitled 'She at His Funeral'. The accompanying drawing in *Wessex Poems* is of Stinsford churchyard, not Fordington, but that is likely to have been intended to put readers off the scent:

> They bear him to his resting-place –
> In slow procession sweeping by;
> I follow at a stranger's space;
> His kindred they, his sweetheart I.
>
> Unchanged my gown of garish dye,
> Though sable-sad is their attire;
> But they stand round with griefless eye,
> Whilst my regret consumes like fire!

This poem imagines, or recalls, the attendance at Horace's funeral of the girl he seduced. Such a girl would have been paid off by the conscientious and humane Moule family; but she would not have been able to approach them at the funeral, and would have viewed it just as this girl does. She, after all, had had a more intimate connection with Horace than even his family had. It seems more than likely, too, that one of Horace's many 'fears', which he expressed to his brother on that terrible last day of his life, included guilt about the way in which he had treated this girl.

Sorrow could not be allowed to interfere with the progress of *Far From the Madding Crowd*. The role of Boldwood in it, however, may have been darkened as a result of the suicide, although there is nothing to connect Boldwood's character with Moule's. Tom kept his sorrow and his shock to himself, but the shattering of this, his closest friendship, affected him for the rest of his life. Until the end of 1873 all his letters are on mourning stationery.

At the end of October, after he had received the first chapters of the new novel, Leslie Stephen asked if Tom thought he could keep up with the printer if the *Cornhill* began to serialize the story in January 1874, which meant it would appear in the third week of the preceding month, as was usual. So it had been accepted; Tom told him that he could manage it. On Plymouth Hoe on New Year's Eve, returning from a Christmas visit to St Juliot, he opened a copy of the *Cornhill* and found the first instalment placed at its front: 'with a striking illustration, the artist being – also to his surprise – not a man but a woman, Miss Helen Paterson'.

In a week or two he read, in the *Spectator* which had once given him so much grief, a note (by R.H. Hutton) to the effect that if the new *Cornhill* story were not by George Eliot, 'then there is a new light among novelists': the 'description of Gabriel Oak is too perfect'; 'the *Cornhill* is giving us a high intellectual treat this time'. Such moments are gratifying for authors; they are also fearful if they have not finished what they have started. Could Tom keep it up? Could he continue to satisfy his severest critic to date? The pressure may have served to keep him from falling into too much depression over Moule, and it is notable that, after attending the funeral on 26 September, he managed to get off the crucial material for which Stephen was then anxiously waiting.

On a short visit to London in early December, he at last entered the lion's den and met the formidable Stephen. He found him good-humoured but caustic, with a dog called Troy. 'That is the name of my wicked soldier-hero,' he exclaimed. 'I don't think my Troy will feel hurt at the coincidence, if yours doesn't,' answered Stephen. At lunch with him on a subsequent day, at which his wife – Thackeray's daughter 'Minna', who was to die in 1875 – and her sister Anne were present, he was able to hold his own. Stephen liked him, and even then did not see in him anything of the quaint, countrified and 'naive' man described by those of his biographers who did not happen to meet him at that time; he was more than glad to see Hardy the following year whenever he was in London. Had he struck Stephen and his circle as an awkward bumpkin, then something of the impression would have survived somewhere, probably in private letters. It is true that Stephen did not ask him for another serial for the *Cornhill* after he had printed *Ethelberta*, and that he refused *The Return of the Native*; but this was because he had become exhausted by Tom's obstinacy over the 'Grundyism' with which he was obsessed, as well as because the *Cornhill* was always particular about whom it asked. Stephen had a large circulation to maintain, which involved pandering to public taste.

After the *Spectator's* flattering mention of the first instalment of *Far From the Madding Crowd* early in the following month, Stephen wrote to Hardy:

> I am glad to congratulate you on the reception of your first number. Besides the gentle *Spectator*, which thinks that you must be George Eliot because you know the names of the stars, several good judges have spoken to me warmly of the Madding Crowd. Morever the *Spectator*, though flighty in its head, has really a good deal of critical feeling. I always like to be praised by it – and indeed by other people! . . . The story comes out very well, I think, and I have no criticism to make.

Tom had so far shown none of *Far From the Madding Crowd* to Emma. This has been taken as indicating two things: that he was frightened of his mother – 'may well have felt awkward about a to-and-fro constant exchange of letters and packages with his fiancée' – and that 'this secretive man did not want to give away too much too soon [about his background] to his middle-class fiancée'. But Hardy's relations with his mother, formidable woman though she was, were nothing like so strained; and he had been exchanging manuscripts by post with Emma since he first met her.

His own simple explanation, although described as a 'schoolboy excuse' in spite of his insertion of it into the *Life*, is more reasonable: 'It can be imagined how delighted Miss Gifford was to receive the first number of the story, whose nature he had kept from her to give her a pleasant surprise, and to find that her desire of a literary course for Hardy was in a fair way of being justified.' And looked at from a practical point of view, how could he make his script available to her? He always needed it at hand to send to Stephen, and it would have been impossibly time-consuming to copy it out solely in order to show it to her.

It is almost a fantasy that Tom deliberately kept anything about his background from Emma; and she would at least have known that the new story was going to reflect, if not give an account of, this background. It was not until much later, under the pressure of Tom's fame and success in London society, that she began to entertain notions of being above him in station – notions which seem to have resembled her father's fancies. Snobbishness of all kinds was endemic in Victorian middle-class society, with its obsessions about ancestry. If Emma held any early views about this snobbery, then it is likely that, as a lively and unconventional young woman, she despised it. There is no indication that she was ever bothered by Tom's social status at the time of their engagement, or that he misrepresented himself to her. So Emma's ignorance of the new book was just a necessity of which Tom made a triumphant virtue as soon as he could present her with its opening in printed form. In his notebook he wrote this entry, dated July 1874:

> E.L.G.'s letter. 'My work, unlike your work of writing, does not occupy my true mind much . . .
> 'Your novel [*Far From the Madding Crowd*] seems sometimes like a child all your own & none of me.'

In other words, as he wrote, the new novel was to be a surprise for her, and she tells him her feelings about it. Her 'work' was helping in the parish: she recognizes and understands his needs.

The publishing house of Smith, Elder owned the *Cornhill*, so Tom could look forward to a better arrangement for his publications in volume form. But cautiously he kept in touch with Tinsley, who, he knew, would not be altogether happy when he saw that the *Cornhill* was carrying the latest Hardy story. Still, even Meredith had fallen back on Tinsley in 1865 when Chapman and Hall had wanted to delay the publication of *Rhoda Fleming*. Tom did not want to get on bad terms with Tinsley. He showed confidence and skill in dealing with both publishers. On 20 November he told Smith, Elder, who wanted to know his terms for *Far From the Madding Crowd*, that

> my ideas on the subject are somewhat undistinct, which is partly owing to the fact that the value of my writing has changed since I made my last agreement for a story. I think that under these circumstances your experience would be a better guide than my judgement . . . The

kind of arrangement I should prefer would be to dispose of the rights to publish for a certain time only . . .

This was shrewd: he was being firm about his new higher value, and yet accommodating and not too greedy. He already realized how important it was not to part with his copyrights, and Tinsley was soon to rub this in by refusing in January 1875 to part with *Under the Greenwood Tree* for less than £300; Tom never got the copyright back. On 29 November he was glad to tell Smith, Elder, who had written to him on the 26th, that £400 for the serial rights alone would be very acceptable. Meanwhile Tinsley, perhaps having heard about the *Cornhill* offer, wrote asking for another story. Tom replied cautiously, on 22 November, telling him 'in confidence' that his next was to appear in the *Cornhill*, so 'that for a few months I shall be fully occupied'. 'But when you want another story . . . I shall be glad to know of it . . .'

However, they did no more business together, and Tom was glad. Tinsley wrote complaining that he ought to have told him about the *Cornhill* arrangement earlier; on 30 November Tom replied that he was 'truly sorry that you consider there was a breach of courtesy'. His additional wish that Tinsley might come to 'see nothing unusual in it', and that it would not 'put an end to the good feeling which has hitherto existed between us' seems to have been accepted, because on 9 December, writing from Celbridge Place while in London to see Leslie Stephen for the first time, he told Tinsley that he could not at present supply him with a new short story, since the current one was only 'one quarter finished'. Then, a few days later, on his return to Bockhampton, still believing that his illustrator was a man, he told Smith, Elder that he had made 'a few correct outlines of smockfrocks, gaiters, sheep-crooks, rick-"staddles" . . . and some other out of the way things that might have to be shown'. He could send these on. But, he added, 'if he is a sensitive man and you think he would rather not be interfered with, I would not do so'.

He did not seriously consider supplying Tinsley with a short story, but quickly agreed, in February 1874, to supply the *New York Times* with one: 'Destiny and a Blue Cloak', a potboiler which he sent off in late September but never reprinted in any of his collections. This was the tale in which he drew, rather hastily, on his memories of Hooper Tolbert. American money was to be an important factor in his decision to take a few months' holiday from writing after he finished *Ethelberta*.

Tom was now in a better position to offer marriage. He could look forward to money coming in for the volume publications of *Far From the Madding Crowd* from Smith, Elder in England and Henry Holt in America, and he had the reasonable expectation of another serial to follow it in the *Cornhill* – and then of the volume rights from that, too. He was able to save much of his *Blue Eyes* money: he was living at home in Dorset, and, a naturally prudent and careful man where money was concerned, had few expenses apart from occasional travel to and from London and St Juliot. He was also acutely sensitive to what his immediate Bockhampton neighbours, let alone Emma, might think about his success or failure.

Leslie Stephen intervened in the writing of the serial version of *Far From the Madding Crowd*, as Tom sent it off to him. It has usually been assumed that his advice, which (naturally enough in the circumstances) Hardy followed, was wholly beneficial to the book and to Hardy's career; Millgate believes, furthermore, that Stephen smuggled in much of this advice under the guise of protecting his proprietors from attacks by Mrs Grundy. Both of these patronizing assumptions, which are at the expense of Hardy's original genius and independence of mind, are questionable.

Hardy admired Stephen, and declared, perhaps more gallantly than truthfully, that his thinking had influenced him more than that of any other contemporary. He must have been touched when Stephen asked him to call on him on 23 March 1875 to witness his renunciation of the holy orders he had taken in 1855 in order to retain a Trinity Hall tutorship won in the previous year. Eight years Tom's senior, and now an agnostic, he had once been, friends claimed, the 'model of a muscular Christian', who 'feared God and could walk a thousand miles in a thousand hours'. Stephen gave occasional sermons while in tenure at Cambridge. He was an almost fanatical mountaineer, and thus retained much of the muscularity if not the Christianity of his active and athletic youth. In the USA he had met all the important Americans of the period, including James Russell Lowell and Abraham Lincoln. When in 1864 he left Cambridge to try his luck in the London literary world he was careful to obtain introductions to the leading personages from his elder brother, the conservative and ferociously anti-democratic James Fitzjames Stephen, whose life he later dutifully wrote. He contributed regularly to the *Fortnightly*, *Fraser's* and the *Saturday Review*. In 1871 he became editor of the *Cornhill*. Later he was editor of, and a notable contributor to, the *Dictionary of National Biography*; his daughter Virginia, later Woolf, complained that she had been crushed by it in the womb. He was, thus, a genuine man of letters, whose *Hours in a Library*, his collected essays on writers and literary subjects, are still worth reading. Knighted in 1901, he was the father, by his second marriage to Julia Prinsep, to Vanessa Bell as well as Virginia Woolf. In Meredith's *The Egoist* he is the introspective Vernon Whitford, 'a Phoebus Apollo turned fasting friar'.

In 1861 Stephen had been the first to climb the Schreckhorn, a 13,386-foot peak in the Bernese Alps, south of Interlaken in Switzerland. In June 1897, when Tom and Emma were on holiday there, Tom 'suddenly' got what he called

> a vivid sense of him, as if his personality informed the mountain – gaunt and difficult, like himself . . . As I lay awake that night, the more I thought of the mountain, the more permeated with him it seemed: I could not help remarking to my wife that I felt as if the Schreckhorn were Stephen in person; and I was moved to begin a sonnet to express the fancy.

He first published the sonnet in 1906, in F.W. Maitland's memoir of Stephen, to which he contributed some reminiscences of him. It is headed 'With thoughts of Leslie Stephen, June 1897':

> Aloof, as if a thing of mood and whim;
> Now that its sparc and desolate figure gleams
> Upon my nearing vision, less it seems
> A looming Alp-height than a guise of him
> Who scaled its horn with ventured life and limb,
> Drawn on by vague imaginings, maybe,
> Of semblance to his personality
> In its quaint glooms, keen lights, and rugged trim.
>
> At his last change, when Life's dull coils unwind,
> Will he, in old love, hitherward escape,
> And the eternal essence of his mind
> Enter this silent adamantine shape,
> And his low voicing haunt its slipping snows
> When dawn that calls the climber dyes them rose?

Virginia Woolf was prompted to tell Hardy on 17 January 1915, when she saw it again in *Satires of Circumstance* (1914), that this 'poem, and the reminiscences you contributed to Professor Maitland's life of him, remain in my mind as incomparably the truest & most imaginative portrait of him in existence'. She understood, for she had inherited her father's manic-depressive personality.

But, as the poem unequivocally states, and as his daughter fully acknowledged, Stephen was a difficult man, who, if he did not care for the company, or was in a bad mood, would sit silent for hours. Early affairs between him and Hardy did not always run as smoothly as even Hardy's genuinely affectionate memories might suggest. Nor need he be over-rated. Despite his seniority in years and his teaching experience at Cambridge he had probably read rather less widely than Hardy, although he was an accomplished mathematician (as he showed when he altered 'parabolic' to 'hyperbolic' in the text of *Far From the Madding Crowd*). He was not, and had never tried to be, a poet or a novelist. His criticism is valuable for its soundness – above all for the guide it gives us to responsible Victorian thinking about literature – rather than for its brilliance. He has been called, and not without reason, 'a book-weighing machine, automatically registering the reactions of the average reasonable gentleman . . .' And that is, after all, what he, as a manic-depressive, desperately tried to be: an average reasonable gentleman, and, against the odds, a capable and valuable one.

Most of his alterations in *Far From the Madding Crowd*, though by no means disastrous, are not improvements. Although he appreciated the book and its author, and gave him the chance he needed, Stephen's interest in his readership outweighed his interest in Hardy's imaginative welfare. It should not be forgotten that he refused *The Return of the Native* on account of its alleged capacity to offend that readership; he was not bold as Meredith, Hardy and, later, George Moore were. But from a practical viewpoint he could have argued that he might have lost his job if he offended the proprietors or, worse, reduced the circulation of their prestigious magazine; also that any injudiciousness might indirectly threaten the future of serial fiction for serious authors, and thus lessen their incomes. Caution was the soundest policy. This can hardly be criticized. After all, this was the age in which Darwin himself, investigating the blush, enquired of artists whether a woman's blush spread all over her body: only they, who had worked with models, could be expected to know.

Hardy's own account of what passed between himself and Stephen on these matters speaks for itself, and has enough edge to it – although without unpleasantness – for him to have been told off for it by his numerous detractors. It first appeared as a part of his account of Stephen for the Maitland volume, but he quoted it in the *Life*, commenting that it afforded a 'humorous illustration of the difficulties of "serial" writing in Victorian days'. Stephen had written warning him that the seduction of Fanny Robin 'must be treated in a "gingerly fashion"', adding that it was owing to 'an excessive prudery of which I am ashamed'. Hardy wrote:

> I wondered what had so suddenly caused, in one who had seemed anything but a prude, the 'excessive prudery' alluded to. But I did not learn till I saw him in April [1874]. Then he told me that an unexpected Grundian cloud, though no bigger than a man's hand as yet, had appeared on our serene horizon. Three respectable ladies and subscribers, representing he knew not how many more, had written to upbraid him for an improper passage in a page of the story which had already been published.
>
> I was struck mute, till I said, 'Well, if you value the opinion of such people, why didn't you think of them beforehand, and strike out the passage?' – 'I ought to have, since it is their opinion, whether I value it or so,' he said with a half groan. 'But it didn't occur to me that there was anything to object to!' I reminded him that though three objectors who disliked the passage, or pretended to, might write their disapproval, three hundred who possibly approved of it would not take the trouble to write, and hence he might have a false impression of the public as a body. 'Yes, I agree. Still, I suppose I ought to have foreseen these gentry, and have omitted it,' he murmured.

This does paint Stephen as excessively nervous of giving offence. Hardy then emphasizes the point:

> . . . when the novel came out in volume-form [November 1874] *The Times* quoted in a commendatory review the very passage that had offended. As soon as I met him, I said, 'You see what *The Times* says about that paragraph; and you cannot say that *The Times* is not respectable.' He was smoking and answered tardily: 'No, I can't say that *The Times* is not respectable.' I then urged that if he had omitted the sentences, as he wished he had done, I should never have taken the trouble to restore them in the reprint, and *The Times* could not have quoted them with approbation. I suppose my manner was slightly triumphant; at any rate, he said, 'I spoke as an editor, not as a man. You have no more consciousness of these things than a child.'

But it was Stephen who was the child in this matter, for, as has been said, he had a 'puritan obsession' with sex, which he attempted to disguise 'by blaming it on the prejudices of the reading public'. He thus told Hardy that he was a 'slave', that he wrote to him as an editor, not a critic, and that 'one is forced to be absurdly particular'. The fact, though, is that he was more absurdly particular than he need have been – and for reasons of his own. But Tom was not taken in. He nevertheless told Stephen, in a letter of 18 or 19 February 1874, that he was

> anxious, to give up any points which may be desirable in a story when read as a whole, for the sake of others which shall please those who read it in numbers. Perhaps I may have higher aims some day, and be a great stickler for the proper artistic balance of the completed work, but for the present circumstances lead me to wish merely to be considered a good hand at a serial.

These 'points' included the obviously Stephen-inspired substitution of 'backs' for 'buttocks' (of sheep), and all this declaration meant, far from representing some kind of 'pathetic' surrender to the superior Stephen, was that for the time being Tom had decided to subjugate his earning to his artistic capacity. There is also some irony here, although no aggression towards the privately as well as publicly obsessed Stephen. As Gittings well says, this passage (quoted by Tom in the *Life* from a letter of which no further details exist) 'should simply be taken as a gambit in his temporary manoeuvres with Stephen, to allay the editor's alarms, and to ensure a profitable sale for the novel elsewhere . . .' Yet it has been seen, too, as indicating an abject utilitarianism! But this assertion, characterized by Gittings as 'hypocritical' (where it was merely prudent), makes nonsense of his own tendentious earlier assertion that Hardy 'wrote at his best under the guidance of a trained but sympathetic mind. He had always needed this, in a pathetic and almost Coleridgean want to supplement his own self-taught judgement'! Under whose 'trained guidance' did Hardy write all the novels after *Ethelberta* – and almost all his poetry?

The extent of Stephen's influence – benign, formative, or otherwise – over *Far From the Madding Crowd* was undoubtedly useful but has been exaggerated. The exact extent of his interventions is not known, because the available correspondence between him and Hardy is incomplete. Many improvements were made by the author himself. But those made by Stephen are by no means all 'perfectly right' or 'important and positive'. To say, as Millgate does, that he 'used the Grundyan threat as a tactful cover for criticism of a more aesthetically significant kind' is to strain the evidence. It puts too much emphasis on the positive effects of his suggestions, and ignores his sexual puritanism – which Hardy recognized, but had to go along with, although not without protest, as shown by his story about the passage subsequently praised by *The Times*.

This passage is worth quoting as an example of Hardy's first maturity. Jan Coggan, Bathsheba Everdene's master-shearer, is speaking:

> 'Well, now, you'd hardly believe it, but that man – our Miss Everdene's father – was one of the ficklest husbands alive, after a while. Understand, 'a didn't want to be fickle, but he couldn't help it. The poor feller were faithful and true enough to her in his wish, but his heart would rove, do what he would. He spoke to me in real tribulation about it once. "Coggan," he said, "I could never wish for a handsomer woman than I've got, but feeling she's ticketed as my lawful wife, I can't help my wicked heart wandering, do what I will." But at last I believe he cured it by making her take off her wedding-ring and calling her by her maiden name as they sat together after the shop was shut, and so 'a would get to fancy she was only his sweetheart, and not married to him at all. And as soon as he could thoroughly fancy he was doing wrong and committing the seventh 'a got to like her as well as ever, and they lived on a perfect picture of mutel love.'

That is Hardy at his best: comic, wise, and restrained in his representation of Coggan's speech – though not exact to the life, it is perfect on the page. It is owed neither to Stephen nor even to Moule, and it negates the bizarre suggestion that in 'some senses he learned his job as a novelist from the editor'. What does this passage represent if not his 'job as a novelist'? It is entirely his own, and such a voice had not been heard in English literature since Shakespeare.

What Stephen actually did, as Simon Gatrell has demonstrated in *Hardy the Creator* (1988), was use the excuse of narrative considerations to cover bowdlerization. He was genuinely offended by Hardy's persistent eroticism, but there was nothing he could say about it which would not implicate him in the Grundyism of which he pretended to be ashamed.

The general direction of his criticism is indicated by his groaning suggestion, on 13 April 1874, that Tom might well dispose of Fanny's baby – is this 'necessary at all', he asked. But such a change would have been disastrous; even he admitted that it would have been 'injurious', but wistfully pursued the point: 'I am rather necessarily anxious to be on the safe side, and should somehow be glad to omit the baby.' What offended him was that the passage offered no censure, of any kind, of the terrible crime of illegitimacy. He did succeed in making Hardy excise one of the most moving pages of the book: the description of the baby itself, whose cheeks and hands had, for the watching Bathsheba, 'the soft convexity of mushrooms on a dewy morning' – mother and child 'both had stood on the threshold of a new stage of existence'.

Stephen's personal feelings closely resembled those of his friend Morley, who had found even *Under the Greenwood Tree* offensive, and had forever been anxious, as Macmillan's reader, to save the firm from embarrassment. It must not be thought that positivism or agnosticism precluded puritanism in the Victorian age – or that Hardy, so far as he was able, was not wholeheartedly opposed to it.

Thus Stephen, in spite of himself, began to slice out the candour from Hardy's writing. Not one of the other changes known to have been demanded by Stephen, and carried out by the never wholly acquiescent Hardy, was unequivocally to the book's advantage. The most substantial involved cuts to what is now Chapter XXIII, to do with the sheep-shearing supper. Much good material is lost, although the magazine if not the volume reader might have felt that the cut passage slowed up the narrative pace; more to the point is that Stephen was able to get rid of some 'embarrassing' or 'unhealthy' sentences, such as a clear indication that Jan Coggan wanted to make love to his wife – that a wife could have a twinkle in her eye, moreover, was at best a smoking-room matter for the likes of Stephen and Morley. Gatrell, a bibliographer and the leading expert on Hardy's texts, feels that there is 'a perfectly respectable case for restoring the original readings to an edited text' of *Far From the Madding Crowd*, even though in the 1877 edition Hardy himself did not go very far towards restoring what he had written, and thus of removing Stephen's woeful presence. On the other hand it may be argued, and has been by James Gibson in his edition, that Hardy made a virtue out of a necessity.

Gatrell draws attention to a more unpleasant alteration made by Stephen, and one which distorts the characterization. Gabriel Oak's humane and decent attitude towards the murderer Boldwood reads: 'Gabriel's anxiety was so great that he paced up and down, pausing at every turn and straining his ear for a sound'. This becomes, in the serial text, nasty and moralistic: 'Gabriel's anxiety was so great that Boldwood might be saved, even though in his conscience he felt that he ought to die; for there had been qualities in the farmer which Oak loved.' That is not, as Gatrell says, in Oak's character at all.

Thus it cannot be argued that Stephen improved this novel, let alone that he master-minded it and gave his author the opportunity he needed to work under the supervision of a 'trained' mind. *Far From the Madding Crowd* has, among other things, all the merits of a novel written by a mind quite deliberately untrained in the too gentlemanly (and inhumane) niceties of the nineteenth century. It was written in the very place in which it was set, which, as Hardy told Stephen, was of great advantage to him. Its comparative maturity is the result of his own work, of the experience he had by now gained in novel-writing; naturally, though, at the same time he felt himself fortunate to be working for a man whose taste and intelligence were so great by comparison with the other editors of the fiction-carrying periodicals. He took notice of suggestions, and kept to himself his own opinion of Stephen's view of him – as a 'child' where the amount of sexual detail to be allowed in serial fiction was concerned; and of course he learned *something* from Stephen. But that does not imply that he did not feel himself to be in charge of his own novel.

All the time that this work was going on at Bockhampton in the first months of 1874 Hardy was contemplating marriage to Emma. That he was every now and then thinking about the wisdom of this step goes without saying. But was he seriously alarmed, as Millgate suggests? He must have been conscious of the difference between Emma's way of talking about literature and that of Stephen's highly sophisticated circle. But this, surely, would have disturbed only a man who did not know his own direction in life. There is every indication, however, that Tom now knew what direction he wanted to take, and that he was already taking it: a career as an author, and marriage to Emma Gifford. Far too much has been made of his feelings, expressed to Gosse in 1906, during the last decade of his marriage to Emma, for Helen Paterson, his illustrator for *Far From the Madding Crowd*. His poem 'The Opportunity' – a rather slight, if not actually 'inept' (as it has been called), one by his own standards – which he wrote about her was published just after her death (in 1926), in *Late Lyrics and Earlier* of the same year. Yet it closely echoes a letter which he wrote to Gosse in 1906: the 'Forty springs back' is there simply to disguise the fact that he wrote the poem in his wife's lifetime, although he may well have extensively revised it between then and its publication:

> Forty springs back, I recall,
>   We met at this phase of the Maytime:
> We might have clung close through all,
>   But we parted when died that daytime.
>
> We parted with smallest regret;
>   Perhaps should have cared but slightly,
> Just then, if we never had met:
>   Strange, strange that we lived so lightly!
>
> Had we mused a little space
>   At that critical date in the Maytime,
> One life had been ours, one place,
>   Perhaps, till our long cold claytime.
>
> – This is a bitter thing
>   For thee, O man: what ails it?
> The tide of chance may bring
>   Its offer; but nought avails it!

This is a characteristically speculative poem, above all retrospective, which states that he and Helen Paterson did *not* care for each other at the time they met in 1874. They might have done, 'had they mused a little space'. (Her marriage to William Allingham, the poet and editor, which took place around the same time as Tom's to Emma, is not known to have been in the least unhappy.) The poem could well have been about any woman, but Tom needed real memories to prompt him to such musings, and memories of Helen Paterson served. He wrote to Gosse on 25 July 1906, in answer to an enquiry:

The illustrator of *Far From the Madding Crowd* began as a charming young lady, Miss Helen Paterson, & ended as a married woman, – charms unknown – wife of Allingham the poet. I have never set eyes on her since she was the former & I met her & corresponded with her about the pictures to the story. She was the best illustrator I ever had. She & I were married about the same time in the progress in our mutual work, but not to each other, which I fear rather spoils the information. Though I have never thought of her for the last 20 years your enquiry makes me feel 'quite romantical' about her (as they say here) & as she is a London artist, well known as Mrs A, you might hunt her up, & tell me what she looks like as an elderly widow woman. [Allingham had died in 1889.] If you do, please give her my kind regards; but you must not add that those two almost simultaneous weddings would have been one but for a stupid blunder of God Almighty.

This letter, like the poem, pays scant attention to the existence of William Allingham or to any feelings he might have entertained in the matter, and so ought not to be taken too seriously. It is just an enquiry by a friend prompting a characteristic but slight poem on a bad day. In that July, Hardy must have been in an exasperated mood. It is no part of this biography to suggest that his marriage was a completely happy one: only that the real difficulties came later than is usually supposed, and that when they did come they were more considerably mitigated by affection and companionship than is usually supposed. The good-hearted Gosse, like Clodd and a few others such as Hermann Lea, knew of Emma's eccentricities and of her jealousy of Tom's fame, and of the depressions into which her behaviour could cast him. Picture Tom, at a time when she had been infuriating him, receiving a letter from his old friend asking about the illustrator of *Far From the Madding Crowd*. He has not, as he says, even thought about her since about 1886 (he had asked for her as illustrator to later novels, but discovered that she had given up book-illustration altogether). Now he is reminded, not of how he loved her, but of how much he liked her, and of how attractive she was. This leads him to a rumination on the nature of fate, and he writes the first draft of 'The Opportunity', but conceals it from Emma.

This is no evidence that his feelings towards Emma had cooled by 1874; rather the contrary. Read biographically, and in the light of facts that it does not itself supply, it means that he is in a bad mood about his situation (perhaps Emma had just then been out in Dorchester, distributing anti-Catholic pamphlets), and that he ought to have noticed someone else more particularly than he did just prior to his marriage. Thus, it is wrong to ascribe to him feelings 'of a different order' from those he had for Leslie Stephen's then sister-in-law, Miss Thackeray, later Mrs Ritchie, for Helen Paterson in 1874: as Hardy specifically says, he did *not*, and nor did she, muse 'a little space/At that critical date'. Nor is there any justification for the assertion that he was 'immediately attracted', and so 'exploited their *Cornhill* association as a basis for further meetings and correspondence': as Tom himself wrote a little later, on 7 February 1878, to Arthur Hopkins, younger brother of the poet Gerard Manley Hopkins, and the illustrator of *The Return of the Native*, '. . . it is more satisfactory when artist & author are in correspondence . . . writer & illustrator of a story can hardly ever be in thorough accord unless they live in constant communication during its progress . . .'. He was simply being professional, for the illustrations were important to the success of fiction in this period. And what man would not prefer an attractive and intelligent woman to another man as his illustrator? Millgate, in his eagerness to prove that Tom's marriage was a disaster from first to last, has again strained the facts.

Far From the Madding Crowd is the first book which shows Hardy writing at the top of his powers, and the first in which he was able, with full success, to function as a poet as well as a novelist. Coventry Patmore put his finger on a weakness in *A Pair of Blue Eyes* when he lamented that it had not been written in verse. Patmore sensed, in its irresolution, its author's reluctance to commit himself to the business of fiction-writing in an age distinguished for its lack of candour. *Far From the Madding Crowd* functions almost perfectly as a novel, but a novel which would be nothing without its poetic foundation. Indeed, Hardy and Emily Brontë were the nineteenth century's only genuinely poetic novelists.

George Eliot brought the prose novel to its height with *Middlemarch*, and in this realistic work achieved many more things than Hardy achieved, or, indeed, tried to achieve. She was not, like him, a reluctant novelist, and her prolific poetry is, with one or two minor exceptions, poor. Her long dramatic poem *The Spanish Gipsy* (1868), while interesting in the context of her fiction and her exemplary life, is linguistically dead. But Hardy followed the poetic example set by Emily Brontë in *Wuthering Heights*. George Meredith, too, would have preferred to be a poet, and was more gifted in that sphere than George Eliot.

Far From the Madding Crowd contains far fewer of those sometimes over-literary or over-cultured comparisons which, although usually apt and effective, and not out of place in a young man's work, could soon have become monotonous in an older one's. That advance was Hardy's, not Leslie Stephen's, decision – unless, of course, Stephen had warned him of the danger of the habit in a letter that is now lost. But that is highly unlikely: Moule had written of this habit in his first review of Hardy, and must subsequently have elaborated upon his criticism.

The rural dialogue is more perfectly judged than any comparable innovation in English fiction of its time. It would have plenty of imitators, from Kipling to Algernon Gissing – the novelist brother of the better-known George – and beyond. The Irish and cockney of Kipling did not come near to it in effectiveness; Kipling's humour is forced by comparison, and the actual speech is wildly innacurate, whereas Hardy's is as true to nature as it can be. Tinsley, somewhat angry at being robbed of Hardy's work by Smith, Elder and the *Cornhill*, wrote to him on 5 January 1875, after Smith, Elder's two-volume edition had appeared:

> I hope you will not think me impertinent but how you could have made such mistakes *in art* in a work so brim full of genius as '*The Madding Crowd*' is one of the things I cannot understand. I think your genius truer than Dickenses [sic] ever was, but you want a monitor more than the great Novelist ever did. Apologising for being so plain spoken . . .

Tinsley, the shrewd son of a Hertfordshire gamekeeper, knew nothing about art, and what he meant by 'mistakes *in art*' is therefore obscure. He may have been reading the review of the book which had appeared in the *Spectator* a few days earlier, on 19 December 1874. Yet again it was by a Hutton: this time R.H. He began by praising the novel which he had already been responsible for ascribing to George Eliot: original, amusing, fresh, 'the nearest equivalent to actual experience which a great many of us are ever likely to boast of'. But he then went on, with a miserable literal-mindedness, to miss the point heroically. His objection was that Hardy had introduced 'a satiric vein belonging' to his own 'mental plane into the language of a class far removed from it'. But no one, Hardy least of all, has ever supposed that Dorset rustics talk exactly as he makes them talk.

What Hardy – originally one of them, and to a certain extent always so – does when he enriches his countrymen's talk is to articulate their souls. He can do it because – as, again, one of them – he never patronizes them: he can thus give them the wisdom they possess but do not, with their limited vocabulary, habitually articulate. It is hardly a fault in the novel, for example, that they occasionally make use of a subjunctive of whose function they are entirely ignorant. It would only matter if Hardy were engaged in the exercise of trying to reproduce their speech exactly. But even a playwright who takes down people's conversations in pubs, buses or elsewhere has to make alterations if the work is to be successful on the stage. *That* is art. Hutton tried to denigrate Hardy's achievement by comparison to Dickens' Mrs Gamp:

> Mrs Gamp is an impossible though most amusing impersonation of the monthly nurse. But Mrs Gamp makes no claim to any shrewdness beyond the shrewdness of the most profound selfishness; for the rest, she is only a delightful and impossible concentration of the essence of all conceivable monthly-nurse experiences. But these [Hardy's] poor men are quizzical critics, inaccurate divines, keen-eyed men of the world, who talk a semi-profane, semi-Biblical dialect full of veins of humour which have passed into it from a different sphere.

Hutton then went on to compare Hardy, disparagingly, to George Eliot. He made a mistake, Hutton asserted, which George Eliot 'never makes': he confused his own ideas with those of his dramatic figures. The religiose Joseph Poorgrass says:

> 'I've been drinky this month already, and I did not go to church a-Sunday, and I dropped a curse or two yesterday; so I don't want to go too far from my safety. Your next world is your next world, and not to be squandered lightly.'

Poor earnest Hutton, who italicized the latter sentence, complained that it was 'quite out of plane with the rest of the speech, and much more in the style of cynical culture'. This is wrong. It isn't quite *Hardy's* 'cynicism' that is being expressed there; it is Poorgrass's spirit given its full due. His are the words which end the novel, and he is, after all, a good, kind man – something that is never unimportant in Hardy:

> 'I wish him joy o' her [Oak of Bathsheba]; though I were once or twice saying to-day with holy Hosea, in my scripture manner, which is my second nature, "Ephraim is joined to idols: let him alone." But since 'tis as 'tis, why, it might have been worse, and I feel my thanks accordingly.'

Let us laugh, but not too much: he means what he says, and such generous meanings are rare, and as much needed in our own as in Hardy's world.

FAR FROM THE MADDING CROWD

In his review Hutton was exposing his own Anglican piety, not Hardy's ineptitude. What would life and humour be without such utterances as Poorgrass's? None of the speech, as it happens, is 'real'. Hardy was never a realist, although that term was not much understood in English magazine criticism at the time. What Hardy writes is what a man like Poorgrass would have said had he been able to say it, and he is only following Shakespeare (unmentioned by Hutton in the review) in inventing this character as an articulate if unconscious comic poet. Hutton might just as well have written that Hardy was superior, at rustic dialogue, to George Eliot (as he was, knowing it at first hand), or at least that he had greatly improved on her attempts at it.

Hardy's rustic speech is just one more example of the Aristotelian exercise of reducing the facts of life, which too often seem mundane or meaningless, to their essence. A religiose rustic would indeed have tried to say exactly what Poorgrass says, but his speech would have been halting and obscure as it fell from his lips. Poorgrass cannot possibly be seen, if he is to be seen truthfully, to more exquisite advantage than through the utterances given to him by his creator: the butt of his own people, he is given to speak everything in his heart. He is no longer an idiot.

As for Hutton: his head was sound enough, but his heart and his humour had become distorted by his years of theology training at Manchester New College, where he would have learned to patronize the poor and ignorant, and to put value on the tedious tracts with which they were assailed by various not so well-meaning parsons. Thus he singles out for particular censure Coggan's remark about such tracts, 'I've consumed a good many in the course of a long and rather shady life': how could a mere peasant be humorous at the expense of an improving parson? Hutton could, it is true, praise the scene in which Troy displays his skill at swordsmanship, and thus bewitches Bathsheba; but he would not have done so had he been sensitive to its erotic overtones – overtones which are quite spoiled by explanation of them: in this book Hardy begins to achieve that level of writing where critical exegesis had better simply point to the text or keep its peace. He ended his notice of the book generously, for he was a generous man when his piety could allow it; but he admonished the author for being too 'preposterously clever' and 'original': 'he ought to be accommodating himself', he concluded, 'to the monotonous habits of a world which is built on usage'. What advice to give to a poet!

Far From the Madding Crowd may be read in many ways. Essentially it is the tale of a courtship interrupted by irresistibly injudicious behaviour on the part of the courted one, Bathsheba Everdene. This capable and spirited woman farmer is led astray, first, by her reckless capriciousness in jokingly sending a valentine saying 'Marry Me' to her unstable neighbour Boldwood, and, secondly, through sexual fascination with a military rascal, Sergeant Troy, who is too irresponsible to act even on the small impulses of love which he feels – and which are in any case for poor Fanny Robin, who dies as a result of his treatment of her. But it is significant that an utterly careless fate plays a part in that, too: his decent impulse is frustrated when she fails, by an error, to turn up to marry him. Although Hardy may have planned the book as a tragedy, the apparently 'happy ending' he gave to it in the circumstances is artistically well justified: Bathsheba's 'tragic flaw', a finely and subtly observed mixture of vanity and impulsiveness, is not at all evil, as that of a later character, the powerful Michael Henchard of *The Mayor of Casterbridge*, is. Bathsheba is punished for her carelessness and disregard of the feelings of others, but her good nature finally triumphs: she learns, in words which probably reflect Hardy's own ideals, that:

> pretty words and warm expressions [are] probably unnecessary between . . . tried friends. Theirs was that substantial affection which arises (if any arises at all) when the two who are thrown together begin first by knowing the rougher sides of each other's character, and not the best till further on, the romance growing up in the interstices of a mass of hard prosaic reality. This good-fellowship – *camaraderie* – usually occurring through similarity of pursuits, is unfortunately seldom superadded to love between the sexes, because men and woman associate, not in their labours, but in their pleasures merely. Where, however, happy circumstance permits its development, the compounded feeling proves itself to be the only love which is strong as death – that love which many waters cannot quench, nor the floods drown, beside which the passion usually called by the name is evanescent as steam.

This, incidentally, is followed – after the intervention of the fifty-seventh chapter heading – with these words, ascribed to Bathsheba: 'The most private, secret, plainest wedding that it is possible to have.' What could have put that in the author's head? It seems unlikely that he did not have his own wedding, which was to be of that very nature, in mind.

The courtship of Bathsheba Everdene by Gabriel Oak, her true friend as well as lover, a man as responsible and loyal as the more exciting Troy is not, is interrupted, then, by means of Bathsheba's, rather than Oak's, shortcomings. She is unlucky with Boldwood. Because of characteristics in him that could hardly have been known to her, her provocative and high-spirited joke – a cruel trick, even if not intended as such – brings her considerably more violence than it deserved. With Troy she yields to her sexual preference, for which she cannot be 'blamed' except in the false language of puritan morality – it is not as if she continues to make the same mistake. The reader of the story for the story's sake, who knows Troy's character better than she does, is cleverly put into suspense as to whether the loyal and protective Oak will succeed in marrying her. Their love story, without which Hardy knew he could not appeal to his audience, is skilfully introduced. Bathsheba saves Oak's life, and from that moment the reader is kept wondering how much she actually does care for him.

But the book, although it does end happily, carries tragic overtones and undertones. It shows tragedy averted where later novels show the opposite. It would have been tragic if such a girl as Bathsheba had married Boldwood, since this obsessive man, 'a hotbed of tropic intensity', would have made her unhappy: there was no 'mass of hard prosaic reality' in him, whereas there is plenty in Oak (as there was in the poet Hardy), who will satisfy her even if he cannot excite her as Troy did. Joseph Poorgrass's thanks will thus be justified.

One of the harshest lessons of the book is that we had better not make marriages while we are romantically excited. For the sake of the lower end of his market Hardy mitigates the harshness as much as he can, and even casts it in a form to please his puritanical, Grundyan readers ('mass of hard prosaic reality'). He does not labour the terrible sense of disappointment in the acceptance of the fact that sexual passion is 'as evanescent as steam'.

Troy is an unscrupulous sexual adventurer, ready to move from woman to woman; he is as ready to ruin his wife's reputation as he is as a farmer to use fraudulent methods to get a quick profit; fate, a misunderstanding, is seen to frustrate his single decent impulse. His character attracts this kind of fate. He trades upon evanescence. Had he married Fanny he would have left her. Thus, when he plants the flowers on her grave, they are washed away: this trick of weather emphasizes the frailty and essentially transitory nature of his feelings. His name suggests romance and adventure – but romance mythical and distant from reality. He is, like Manston of *Desperate Remedies*, a variation on the stock Victorian villain; but he is more originally presented than Manston.

Boldwood is apparently worthier, but the equally egoistic nature of his obsession is symbolized by his contemplation of Bathsheba's valentine 'by a beaming fire of aged logs', and, later, tucked into the looking-glass in his bedroom. This valentine in effect sends him mad – it is, after all, his madness that eventually saves him from the gallows for the murder of Troy. It intrudes into a house whose 'atmosphere was that of a Puritan Sunday lasting all the week': once Boldwood has been sexually disturbed he cannot return to his normal, lonely, 'repressed' means of existence. The large red seal reading 'MARRY ME' becomes 'as a blot of blood on the retina of his eye'. As he lies in bed he imagines the changing mouth of the unknown woman as she wrote out his name and address; when he rises the dawn seems like a sunset, the sun 'visible burnt rayless', the moon 'wasting', 'dull and greenish-yellow'. There is, so far as close relationships with others are concerned, no sane substance in him. All is icy, and his own features he notes as 'wan . . . insubstantial in form . . . eyes . . . wide-spread and vacant'.

But he does not love Bathsheba – he has not, like Oak, been smitten by her beauty. It is usually taken as the narrator's slur on Bathsheba's vanity that it 'was a fatal omission of Boldwood's that he had never once told her that she was beautiful'. But, as Hardy well knew, women possess an essential and innocent beauty beyond any vanity they may have of their mere glamour: properly loved, they must be desperately told, by *their* poets, of this individuality. Boldwood is unconcerned with such details, being suddenly obsessed with, and driven mad by, the idea of his own status in the eyes of this not-long-arrived female neighbour, hitherto a stranger to him. He never noticed her at all – until she seemed to notice him.

At the outset, Bathsheba is fascinated by her own glamour: alone – not knowing that she is observed by Oak – she contemplates it, more curiously than conceitedly, and blushing for what she does. There is no experience here – only innocence and high spirits. However, she has to learn not only that lust is evanescent, but also that she needs a true man to discover her own true beauty – and that this discovery will take place in a more sober setting than that of the excitement provided by bodily contact with the mysterious but shallow Troy. Fate takes a hand in making her the provoker of Boldwood's madness: how could she have known that her prank would have such results? She calls her act 'a wanton thing which no woman with any self-respect should have done', which is as far as she can truthfully go. And she makes up for the careless piece of spirited mischief by being ready, at a later stage, to marry Boldwood, whom she does not love.

There is no equivalent in English for the German term *Bildungsroman* ('formation-novel', 'development-novel', 'education-novel'): the novel, often autobiographical (as in the case of *Jane Eyre*), that deals with the development or spiritual education of its protagonist. Hardy, a thoroughgoingly poetic novelist, did not write in this genre; but it rubbed off on him. He had read and studied Bulwer-Lytton (*Ernest Maltravers*, 1837, and its sequel *Alice*, 1838) and Charlotte Brontë. The female characters in his more important novels who are not physically destroyed, as Eustacia and Tess are, are inevitably shown as maturing into a degree of educated disenchantment with a masculinized world. Even in his slightest novel, *Desperate Remedies*, the elder Cytherea, who has been ill used by a man, is melodramatically seen as being forced into a cynical, man–hating lesbianism. In *Under the Greenwood Tree* Fancy Day is seen as having to settle for a man with whom she cannot share 'the rougher side' of her own nature, a man to whom she dare not confide her greatest secret.

Even when writing for a mass audience, as he had to, Tom does not stint his sense of reality. In *A Pair of Blue Eyes*, written in a period of uncertainty and doubt when he was alternately assailed by fears of failure and buoyed by fits of confidence, he can only show a woman's life cut off. He does not really know what to do with Elfride, and has not yet found means to describe her 'education' in the sense of his own use of the *Bildungsroman*. In the next, much more assured, novel, Bathsheba is fully educated – and she is, with the exception of Tamsin in *The Return of the Native*, the luckiest of all Hardy's major undestroyed heroines. She is the luckiest (Poorgrass's 'it might have been worse' is the luckiest anyone is going to get out of Hardy) because, although it is clear that she is never going to be as excited by Oak as she was by Troy, she can truly value what she does get.

The final partners obtained by Elizabeth-Jane of *The Mayor of Casterbridge* and by Grace Melbury of *The Woodlanders* are dire indeed by the side of Oak: the commercial, too correct, unprofound Farfrae, and the feckless Fitzpiers (distinctly worse than his Scottish predecessor). By the time of the final novel, *Jude the Obscure*, the 'education' of the undestroyed female, Sue, is shown as worse than destruction itself: Hardy leaves us in no doubt of this, in his terrible depiction of her giving herself to the schoolmaster who so repels her. Bathsheba, then, is the most fortunate of all Hardy's women; Oak is the nicest and steadiest, if by no means the deepest or most interesting, of his men.

Or *is* he so 'nice'? At least one good feminist critic, Rosemarie Morgan (*Women and Sexuality in the Novels of Thomas Hardy*, 1988), insists that he is as damaging to Bathsheba as Troy is: 'Hardy has a different perception of Oak from the picture that is handed down to us by critics.' Morgan sees Gabriel as 'stealing Bathsheba's freedom' by 'spying' on her; and as being intent, as part of the 'cash-nexus', on reducing and subduing her. She also presents Oak as a parsimonious profit-seeker, with 'all the makings of a successful businessman'. His 'sense of his own manhood, his sexuality, is so closely linked to his mercantile mentality that in the moment of costing his lover's ricks he also evaluates her worth as a woman. Or rather, he devalues her to enhance his chivalric sense of acting in a worthy cause.' Morgan also cites the scene in which Boldwood draws Bathsheba away while Oak is shearing a sheep, so that he allows his blade to slip:

> In endeavouring to continue his shearing at the same time that he watched Bathsheba's manner, he snipped the sheep in the groin. The animal plunged; Bathsheba instantly gazed towards it, and saw the blood. 'O, Gabriel!' she exclaimed, with severe remonstrance, 'you who are so strict with the other men – see what you are doing yourself!'

Morgan is surely right to see this incident as aesthetically encapsulating the situation between Gabriel and Bathsheba, as she is surely right to insist upon the subtly subversive nature of the novel as a whole. After all, it is true that Gabriel wants to do to Bathsheba just what Troy has done, and Boldwood wants to do. It is useful to be made aware of just how subtly Hardy undercuts himself – or, rather, undercuts the text that he is giving to the general public. He wrote (in the *Life*), unequivocally and truthfully, of how, while he 'cared little . . . for mere popularity . . . as little as he did for large payments', he none the less, 'he would quote, "to keep base life afoot" – had to consider popularity'.

What he never quite admitted, because it might have damaged his sales and brought 'base life' uncomfortably close, was that almost from the beginning he had determined to provide, alongside the popular text, a subtext in keeping with what he described as 'true and genuine substance on which to build a career as a writer with a real literary message'. Morgan does show, too, how Hardy pretended to give the mass of his middle-class, urban public a text that was in general accordance with its prejudices. Notwithstanding the fact that this public contained more women than men, these prejudices were, as Morgan rightly puts it, 'patriarchal'. A few critics did catch a whiff of the subversiveness; the *Observer*, for instance, deplored the fact that Oak was not 'sufficiently manly to refuse to have anything more to say to such an incorrigible hussy' (incorrigible because in her first encounter with Troy she fails to observe 'modesty and reserve' – in other words she is excited by bodily contact with the opposite sex). But the main readership was hoodwinked by the author into thinking that this was a pastoral idyll, a 'romance of the Golden Age'.

Another critic, Richard Carpenter (*Thomas Hardy*, 1964), may seem to take a similar male view of Bathsheba:

> Although Hardy allows us the questionable sop to our feelings of a marriage with Oak . . . the novel does not really end 'happily'. The vibrant and proud girl we see at the beginning has been as thoroughly destroyed as Troy and Boldwood . . . in subduing her to a mature and knowledgeable adult, Hardy has subdued our enjoyment of her as a character.

But this turns out to be developed from a different attitude towards Bathsheba, whom Carpenter sees as a wilful baggage hampered by vanity: Hardy was not aware of it, Carpenter thinks, but really he is simply portraying a woman who, like other proud women, 'desires to be dominated by a sexually aggressive man; and, until that desire has been chastened, she cannot make a wife for Oak, who is essentially a passive lover . . .' In so writing, Carpenter perpetuates the Victorian tradition of seeing Bathsheba as an 'Eternal Eve' whose 'wilfulness has reaped its ultimate reward in the death of one man and spiritual destruction of another'. He then goes on to claim that all Hardy's novels carry the 'implicit moral judgement' that 'rebels against either the common sense of society or the inscrutable nature of the universe have their choice only of destruction or reform'.

There can be no doubt as to which of these two readings is preferable. Carpenter's is Victorian and male-centred in seeking to excuse Boldwood's insanity by blaming it upon feminine 'wilfulness' (a mature or even merely sane man could have forgiven Bathsheba and seen her joke for what it was – a misjudgement). Morgan, however, goes with the spirit of the book. Besides, what can Carpenter mean by writing that our 'enjoyment' of Bathsheba is 'subdued' because she is 'subdued', if in fact she is demonstrating an 'implicit moral judgement'? Either Hardy is a moralist, or he is not. And he is not. Carpenter the reader wants both to 'enjoy' Bathsheba sexually and to judge her as a vain agent of evil. It is the old story, well endorsed by elderly judges in rape cases, of men blaming the madnesses into which they are driven by their desire for women on women's 'wicked' desirability. But, confused by misogynism though Carpenter's reading is, there may yet be some excuse for his writing, of Oak, that he has an 'essential strength of character': he is worthy of gaining Bathsheba's 'substantial affection'.

Although she is the subtler and more perceptive critic, Morgan does rather strain the sense of the text in the interests of the subtext, which is less of an exposure of Oak's character in particular than a critique of Victorian patriarchal society in general. Morgan is all for indulging Bathsheba as a victim, to the extent of alluding too cursorily to her youthful faults – after all, she does begin by being vain and over-impulsive. But Morgan makes no such allowance for Gabriel's faults, and her unfriendly judgement of his character, for all its accuracy, is closer to a Marxist analysis than a human appraisal. Oak does after all love Bathsheba, and he sticks to her. Carpenter falls into the crude error of supposing that, because Gabriel is 'passive' in his approaches to Bathsheba, he is going to be passive as a lover – once he gets her. Morgan falls into the error, less crude, of attributing all his actions to desire for profit and need to subdue, whereas in fact that aspect of his behaviour is inevitable given that he wants to survive at all.

In *Far From the Madding Crowd* Hardy splits himself into three characters, plus a composite fourth which is the rustic chorus. This arrangement was not in the least systematic or worked out, for he had his *Cornhill* deadlines to meet. But what is happening is obvious. Perhaps there is a fifth character, too, although this had better be called a voice, since it plays no part in the action. As Morgan has pointed out, there is a narrator who hoodwinks the reader into believing that he is (from this book onwards) 'Thomas Hardy', a respectable middle-class person with 'correct' views. The 'good hand at a serial' thus establishes himself with the respectable reader. But it is a two-edged voice. Morgan tellingly quotes from an early passage, describing Gabriel's feelings for Bathsheba:

Love, being an extremely exacting usurer (a sense of exorbitant profit, spiritually, by an exchange of hearts, being at the bottom of pure passions, as that of exorbitant profit, bodily or materially, is at the bottom of those of lower atmosphere), every morning Oak's feelings were as sensitive as the money-market in calculations upon his chances.

These chosen metaphors, based on usury – they involve pornographic notions of 'spending' which Morgan does not mention – are undeniable pointers to what she calls Gabriel's 'cash-nexus consciousness'. But she is still too hard on him. She ignores the virtues which are concomitant with these male characteristics. For in creating Gabriel, Hardy was looking at himself as the loyal and reliable provider. To keep base life afoot it is necessary to have, or at least to understand, cash-nexus consciousness. Carpenter and other critics rightly think that the ending of this novel is less happy than it seems – seemed, they could have added, to the consumer as distinct from the common reader.

These critics, however, leave dangling the question of just how Bathsheba, or any other woman, can remain vibrant, as she is at the beginning of the book, and still be fulfilled. So the ending really is comparatively happy by Hardy's standards: she gets the best bargain that an ultimately non-tragic female figure can expect. Oak is a decent man who will look after her in marriage as he did before it. Any reading which suggested that, once having got hold of Bathsheba's money and property, he will change in his behaviour towards her, would be perverse. Morgan's strictures upon his character seem in reality to be strictures upon a social situation. Hardy was at that time carefully considering his future financial position, and that, together with his own parsimonious inclinations – learned in a hard-pressed household – are reflected in Oak.

Thus the book displays Tom's concern with his own problem in the terms in which he was bound to see it at that time: poet or what else? It neither resolves, nor tries to resolve, this problem: it simply reflects it. Troy, whose very name is redolent of poetry and romance, may lack a cash-nexus consciousness – he is a variation on the Victorian stage-villain, although, technically, not quite a criminal – but his irresponsibility is no substitute for anything. The aspect of himself which Tom reveals in Troy is that of the sexual adventurer he would have had to be had he decided to turn 'bohemian' poet, either unable to marry for lack of money, or a ruthless adventurer, as Shelley was in a certain sense. That this is incidental, that it casts no light on the usefulness, or uselessness, of poets (Troy is by no means representative of poets), and hardly relevant to the artistic success or otherwise of *Far From the Madding Crowd*, does not mean that it is not the case.

In Boldwood Hardy begins to survey himself in the capacity of a man over-excited by the attentions, or imagined attentions, of a woman. He was prone to these reactions, although not to the point of madness. The characteristic was to emerge in his behaviour towards Florence Henniker (and perhaps some other women, although to a lesser degree), some twenty years later. Finally the rustic chorus, as it might be called, which supplies commentary, represents the author's poetic voice, apparently quaint and irrational and merely deliciously comic, but wiser than the fiction reader, as distinct from the aware poetry reader, could ever believe possible.

Thus Hardy, in his first full-bloodedly commercial venture, preserved the part of himself he most wanted to exercise: the poet. It must have come as a private blow to him when, soon afterwards, Stephen firmly and uninterestedly rejected a plan for a series of 'tragic ballads . . . an Iliad of Europe from 1789'. This is the germ of *The Dynasts*. Stephen was to ask for a poem by Hardy to be read to him on the last day of his life, almost thirty years later. But the author of the poetry had to persist through thick and thin to turn the exasperated admiration of critics into such a truly heartfelt appreciation as that.

11

Marriage

Tom and Emma were married at St Peter's Church, Elgin Avenue, Paddington (closed by the Bishop of London in 1971, and later rebuilt), on Thursday, 17 September 1874. Emma later noted the weather as having had 'a soft, sunny luminousness; just as it should be'. This too infamous marriage was much less disastrous than has been claimed. Since Emma's reminiscences were not seen by her husband until after her death, it is unlikely that she would have omitted any details about her parents' objections, had there been any. It has been stated that the choice of a church only four years old was 'inauspicious'. In fact it was unavoidable because St Peter's served as the parish church for Chippenham Road, near Westbourne Park, where Emma had been staying in London with her younger brother, Walter, in order to establish the necessary residential qualification. Would Walter have risked a row with his father if the latter had seriously objected? Tom had been staying at his old lodgings at 4 Celbridge Place. They were married by Emma's paternal uncle – as Tom, not without some sly amusement, expressed it in the announcement he wrote for his home paper, the *Dorset County Chronicle*, the 'Rev. E.H. Gifford, D.D., hon. canon of Worcester'. The two witnesses were Walter Gifford and the daughter of Hardy's landlady. Walter also gave the bride away. The absence of anyone from the Hardy family, or of Emma's parents, and of her sister and her husband, need not suggest that there was any hostility towards the marriage, and is hardly 'astonishing'. However, it is unlikely that Jemima would have attended her son's marriage to *any* woman.

Emma, it seems, had quarrelled with her sister quite recently, while still living at the rectory. The details, however, are scant, based on Florence's malicious gossip to Purdy, and on the memorial tablet in St Juliot Church which gives Emma's residence there as ending in 1873; the latter is a mere error. The only potential evidence of 'hostility' is the absence of both sets of parents. The journey, though, was a long one for all concerned, and the French honeymoon was more conveniently undertaken from London than from Cornwall or Bockhampton. It may be that both Emma and Tom had rows with their respective parents about the wisdom of the step they were undertaking, but, if that was the case, it would be foolish to make anything out of it: such things happen every day, and are usually rapidly forgotten. Canon Gifford's genial letters agreeing to officiate mention no objections. And if Emma's father really did object beyond a drunken remark, then he was not doing so three weeks later. On 6 October, when the couple arrived at the rooms at St David's Villa in Hook Road, Surbiton, Surrey, which they discovered and rented on the day after their return from France, they found him playing in the garden with Annie, the daughter of a cousin of Emma's, and a large dog. They must have been very quick indeed to inform him of where they could be found. Everything suggests complete friendliness, and even calls into question Florence's tale of the 'base churl'.

Nor is there a hint of any quarrel with Tom's parents. None of his London friends attended, nor did his sister Mary. Thus it must be supposed that he told his family that he was having a 'quiet wedding' because he and Emma wanted it that way, and because it would save unnecessary expense. Such wishes are not infrequent. Some have remarked on the special significance of Mary's absence, since she and Tom were so close. But that in itself may well explain no more than that only the legally essential people were asked: Mary might very well have been upset despite herself (as Dorothy Wordsworth was on a similar occasion), and Tom, knowing this, may have tactfully arranged things just as he did for that very reason.

After the wedding the couple went immediately to the Palace Hotel, Queensway, where they spent the night. The next morning they went to Brighton, where they stayed for three nights at D. Morton's Family and Commercial Hotel, near the station. They enjoyed the aquarium, the pier and the Pavilion, and on Monday, 21 September, the day they sailed for Dieppe, Tom bathed, despite the roughness of the sea. On arrival in France they took the train to Rouen, arriving there after dark. On the Friday, Tom had written in pencil to his brother Henry from Brighton:

> I write a line to tell you all at home that the wedding took place yesterday, & that we are got as far as this on our way to Normandy & Paris. There were only Emma & I, & her brother, my landlady's daughter signed the book as one witness.
>
> I am going to Paris for materials for my next story. Shall return

the beginning of October – & shall call at once at 4 Celbridge Place to see if there is any letter.

We sent an advertisement of the marriage to the *Dorset Chronicle* – Try to see it.

There is a postscript: 'Thanks for your good wishes'. Nothing in this note implies a quarrel with anyone, and the first sentence rather to the contrary. The second sentence implies that the absence of family had already been arranged and allowed for. It is exactly the kind of brief letter that any man might write to his brother under such circumstances. Alas, being Hardy, he has taken his full share of criticism for it, this criticism being based largely, it would seem, on the omission of intimate sexual details such as 'Defloration occurred in railway carriage *à la* Maupassant's *Bel Ami* – yr famous brother' and other such boons to biographers.

There is no good reason to suppose that Emma and Tom were not deeply in love, nor that they did not thoroughly enjoy their honeymoon. A lack of closeness in the early years of the marriage would make the retrospective poems to Emma very hard to account for. But most have felt differently, one even taking Emma's 'failure to conceive' on the honeymoon itself as evidence of a sexual disaster. Another critic represents Tom as already worriedly pondering upon the 'difference' between Emma and other literary women, such as Helen Paterson and Miss Thackeray, whom he has just met. They were London literati, whereas Emma came from a rectory in Cornwall; but there are no reasons, other than wishful ones, to suppose that she was particularly awkward and unsophisticated, and she was certainly well read. The undoubted eccentricities of her middle age have in some critics' minds been transferred to her youthful self. Millgate writes:

> Given Emma's failure to respond physically to her husband, and the diminished enthusiasm for the marriage he had himself demonstrated over the past several months, it is difficult even to guess at the kind of personal and sexual relationship the couple managed to establish during their honeymoon. Her undiminished girlishness (she was now nearing thirty-four) scarcely seems propitious – nor, for that matter, does the fact that Hardy had a cold.

This is extraordinary – not least for the remark about the cold. Tom was, after all, well enough to take a swim at Brighton. The 'undiminished girlishness' is almost as obscure. This is a perverse interpretation of the high spirits Tom had long observed in Emma, and an odd view of the retrospective poems he wrote about her when she was young. Could he really have fooled himself to that extent?

As for the 'givens' of Millgate's opening sentence, neither is remotely acceptable. Tom had made no such 'demonstration' of cooler feelings. The 'difficult even to guess at', too, is grossly overstated: there is nothing to suggest that Tom and Emma failed to establish other than a normal sexual relationship. Had it been otherwise, there would have been at least a hint of this in the later poems about Emma; but she does not appear in them as in any way sexually peculiar, and nor does the writer of them. Such a view also sits peculiarly with the same writer's suggestion that Emma trapped and held Tom to a promise of marriage by feigning a pregnancy four years before their wedding!

Emma wrote a charming, inconsequential diary of her honeymoon days in Rouen and Paris, illustrated with happy little drawings of things that interested her. The *Life* passes it over in two sentences: a 'short visit to the continent', whose 'first . . . days' were 'spent at Rouen'. That is all. This 'silence' has been explained as the result of embarrassment 'in view of the later fortunes of the marriage'. But is it 'silence', and is it in any way curious? If it is, then could it be because of 'sexual difficulties'? 'But many factors,' explains Denys Kay Robinson darkly in his *The First Mrs Hardy* (1979), 'can prevent sexual accord. The poem "Honeymoon Time at an Inn" gives a possible hint of something amiss at Rouen.' At this point, he also brings in the detail of Ruskin's having believed his wife to be deformed on account of her pubic hair. Must we assume that Tom, writing a book for publication under his second wife's name immediately after his death, and intended to forestall other biographers, first considered giving the intimate details – such as his exact reaction to Emma's pubic hair – of his first honeymoon in it, but then rejected the idea on account of the 'difficulties' he had experienced? That is not a serious question.

'Honeymoon Time at an Inn', first published in *Moments of Vision*, is a dramatic poem about a pier-glass crashing off the wall while two sleepless 'souls opprest' lie in their room. There is nothing in it to suggest Rouen, or Morton's at Brighton, or, indeed, to suggest that it is based on a specific personal experience. It must have been written during or after *The Dynasts* because it features comments by the Spirits of Pity and Irony, to which Tom knew his readers would by then be used. Kenneth Phelps, though, in *The Wormwood Cup* (1975), having made the unusual concession that there can 'be little doubt that Hardy . . . wanted to consummate the union', claims that the poem 'carries a hint of early marital maladjustment', and quotes the first two stanzas:

> At the shiver of morning, a little before the false dawn,
>> The moon was at the window-square,
>> Deedily brooding in deformed decay –
>> The curve hewn off her cheek as by an adze;
> At the shiver of morning a little before the false dawn
>> So the moon looked in there.
>
> Her speechless eyeing reached across the chamber,
>> Where lay two souls opprest,
>> One a white lady sighing, 'Why am I sad!'
>> To him who sighed back, 'Sad, my Love, am I!'
> And speechlessly the old moon conned the chamber,
>> And these two reft of rest.

Phelps comments, 'The moon's phase, between full and last quarter, with "a curve hewn off her cheek as by an adze", coincided with the date of the Hardys' stay at Rouen. In this phase, the moon is at its zenith in the small hours.' If one must be so painfully literal, the moon on 21 September 1874 was not between full and last quarter – it was approaching full; and it had in any case long sunk below any 'window-square' in Rouen by the time of the 'false dawn'. Nor are the difficulties being experienced by the couple in the poem specifically sexual: indeed, they 'fit', the last line of the poem declares, 'all mortal mould'. So much for that. To say, with Kay-Robinson, that there 'may be allusions to sexual difficulty in other poems, too darkly wrapped for anyone to have yet interpreted them', is to say nothing. Alas, there is evidence in Tom's work of knowledge of sexual fulfilment – and we must ask where he obtained it.

The couple were in Hook Road, Surbiton, for almost six months, and in that time Tom made only one entry in his notebook: 'Long Ditton. Snow on Graves. A superfluous piece of cynicism in Nature.' The nature of Nature was the subject of a huge debate in the Victorian period, with Carlyle, Tennyson, T.H. Huxley and George Meredith some of the leading participants. Far from reflecting this, Tom's comment is simply one of those characteristic 'impressions' which he found unavoidable at even the best of times. And times now were at their best: he was

– although for a month or two after the publication of *Far From the Madding Crowd* in volume form on 23 November he did not quite realize it – becoming famous.

Tom had interested serious readers so much that *The Hand of Ethelberta* is the only contemporary novel, Edmund Blunden noted, on Matthew Arnold's 1876 reading list. Tom wrote:

> Its author's unawareness of the extent of its popularity may have been partly owing to the reviews which, in spite of a general approval, were for the most part leavened with minor belittlements in the manner beloved of Victorian critics, and possibly later ones, though there were a few generous exceptions.

This remark, which has been much criticized as demonstrating the extent of his morbid and unnecessary sensitivities, has at least the merit of being exactly true – as was his observation that such strictures were 'really the irritation of dullards at his freshness'. Regular reviewers of books, men who for the most part could not themselves write books (although Hutton at least did write in 1862 *The Relative Value of Studies and Accomplishments in the Education of Women* – and the women loved it), were, after all, 'dullards'. But Tom's comprehension of his extraordinary success with the reading public grew when he and Emma kept seeing, on their train journeys between Surbiton and London, 'ladies carrying about copies of it with Mudie's label on the covers'. He had done better with the book, financially, than he could have hoped, for it appeared as a serial in no fewer than three separate American periodicals, and a new impression of the book version (with a few corrections) was needed by mid-January 1875.

On 2 December 1874, the last instalment of *Far From the Madding Crowd* having appeared, Stephen asked Tom if he could write a new novel, instalments to begin the following April. But Tom was by now exhausted and uncertain, even confused, as to what kind of work to attempt, and so persuaded his editor to agree to July 1875 as a starting date. This pressure for a new work, while obviously welcome, urged Tom into what he called, in the *Life*,

> the unfortunate course of hurrying forward a further production before he was aware of what there had been of value in his previous one: before learning, that is, not only what had attracted the public, but what was of true and genuine substance.

Such an openly admitted distinction between what pleases and what is 'of true and genuine substance' is almost unique amongst nineteenth-century writers, and there was no disingenuousness in Tom's retrospective recollection of the dilemma he felt in early 1875. He perceived it more lucidly than any other writer of his time, though it was hardly something that he could air in public. It was, however, not only his desire to preserve his integrity, to honour the 'true and genuine', that impelled him into the production of the least effective of all his books. He was also too worried, flying in the face of what he later called 'wise counsel', by the 'fooleries of critics'. That he was sensitive to their remarks is certainly true. But the responses of critics, foolish or not, have a close relationship to commercial success or failure. Unfavourable reviews do not always kill sales, but they can do so – and it always seems, to a writer, that they will.

He had been toying with the idea of succeeding *Far From the Madding Crowd* with what later became *The Woodlanders*, but made what he eventually saw as a misjudgement, 'a plunge in a new and untried direction':

> He was aware of the pecuniary value of a reputation for a speciality; and as above stated the acquisition of something like a regular income had become important. Yet he had not the slightest intention of writing for ever about sheepfarming, as the reading public was apparently expecting him to do, and as, in fact, they presently resented his not doing. Hence, to the consternation of his editors and publishers, in March he sent up as a response to their request the beginning of a tale called *The Hand of Ethelberta – A Comedy in Chapters*, which had nothing in common with anything he had written before.

In *The Hand of Ethelberta* he tried to write a satirical comedy of manners; but although comedy was natural to him, the novel of manners in the Jane Austen or Henry James sense, the necessary basis for such a work, was beyond his genius. *The Hand of Ethelberta* is interesting as a part of the Hardy *oeuvre*, and is also an amusing novel in its own right (it has never gone out of print); but by his own standards it is a failed experiment, and, although he made more initial money out of it (£1,250) than out of *Far From the Madding Crowd*, Leslie Stephen, and Smith of Smith, Elder & Co., were not unreasonably disappointed as soon as they saw the opening chapters.

The problem with *Ethelberta* is that its mixture of poetry, romance, farce and satire on society fails to cohere. Tom tried, quite consciously, to subtract from it all his gloom about the puniness of human beings against their cosmic situation – and in doing so discovered that he could not be wholly effective. His genius was at a low ebb, and since he had to provide something for his importunate publishers, and to swell his by no means yet fat enough purse, he could only try to rescue it. He did so through his sense of humour, and by recourse to Thackeray's *The Book of Snobs* and *Vanity Fair*, since Ethelberta is clearly a modified Becky Sharp and Mountclere a pallid Steyne.

Despite these strictures, *The Hand of Ethelberta* is not negligible and contains a few fine passages. The case that can be made out for it is a formidable one, as Millgate – for all that he has missed its point – has shown in his defence of it. The novel is of great interest and intellectual adroitness, but it fails in the reading: it does not grip. As Hardy knew full well, the 'serious popular' novel had, paradoxically, to possess the readability of the junk novel. And the main reason for *Ethelberta*'s failure to hold the attention is the absence of his 'fifth voice' – his rustic chorus. True, there are a few observations made by rustics, and they are telling; but Hardy was conducting an experiment of trying to do without this device. He wrote the first few chapters at Hook Road, but on 22 March he and Emma moved back to London – to Newton Road, near to his old Westbourne Grove haunts. On 27 February he had written to Smith, Elder & Co.:

> I beg leave to trouble you on a question which has lately been present to my mind: that I should like to make, if you conveniently can do so, some definite terms with you for the publication of my next story . . . of which a rough draft of the first part has been submitted to you, & which I am now revising . . . I . . . find a difficulty in applying myself thoroughly to the story whilst there is any uncertainty about it . . . it would be greatly to the advantage of the tale if we could get this cause of distraction cleared out of the way . . .

That, contrary to the usual assessment of Tom as a timid and unconfident man, is tactful but firm. Nearer to the time of the move he told Smith that he and Emma 'were coming to Town on account of Ethelberta, some London scenes occurring in her chequered career which I want to do as vigorously as possible'. These scenes done, he and Emma left London for Bournemouth in July. They soon found

West End Cottage, in Swanage. In his nine months there he almost finished the book, sending the final chapters to Smith from 7 St Peter Street, Yeovil, in mid-March of the following year. These were rooms which he and Emma took between February and July 1876 'to facilitate their search for a little dwelling', which they eventually discovered in Sturminster Newton. *Ethelberta* ran in the *Cornhill*, with illustrations by George du Maurier, from July 1875 to May 1876, and was published in two volumes in early April 1876.

The Hand of Ethelberta, a 'somewhat frivolous narrative' as Tom called it when introducing the 1895 edition, is about the rise in society of an astute young woman, the daughter of a dignified country butler, R. Chickerel (the name of a Dorset village). Her mother and her nine brothers and sisters are all – with the exception of Picotee, who, like Tom's own sisters, is a teacher – in varying degrees, 'servants'. After having been a pupil-teacher, Ethelberta becomes a governess in the house of a nobleman called Sir Ralph Petherwin. She has jilted Christopher Julian, a musician, in order to marry Sir Ralph's son, who dies soon after the wedding. The widowed Lady Petherwin takes up her daughter-in-law and provides her with an expensive 'finishing' education in Bonn.

But on the death of her mother-in-law Ethelberta has to support herself and her family: she has been cut off because she made the mistake of publishing a volume of poems (*Metres by E*), which scandalized Lady Petherwin. In the London house of the Petherwins she now maintains herself – secretly surrounded by members of her family – as a 'Professed Story-teller'. Courted by several ridiculous gentlemen, but also by her old lover the impoverished Christopher Julian, with whom she is in fact in love, she finally settles for an old roué, Lord Mountclere. She 'reforms' him, and, as a sop to the reader who prefers true love to be fulfilled, Christopher is given to her sister Picotee.

There is much satire – not on the whole quite as effective as the author would have liked, recalling what we can reasonably assume was contained in the lost *The Poor Man and the Lady* – on the pretentiousness of the aristocracy. One of Ethelberta's absurd suitors is Alfred Neigh, some of whose characteristics unquestionably resemble – and this was daring on Tom's part – Leslie Stephen's: the large red beard, his preoccupied measuring of it with his fingers, the egotism, and, above all, what Gittings (who first noticed this resemblance) calls the 'false self-depreciation'. This, he notes, matches what Stephen's daughter Virginia Woolf observed about him when she wrote of him

as Ramsay in *To the Lighthouse*: 'talking nonsense . . . was a disguise
. . . the refuge of a man afraid to own his real feelings, who could
not say, This is what I like – this is what I am.' But the pretentious
Neigh, son of a horse-knacker, is in no way a complete portrait of
Stephen, and we must assume that Tom was mischievously getting
even on account of his Grundyism. Hardy's sense of humour has been
persistently under-estimated; but it is only perfunctorily at its best in
this book.

Tom asked Smith for the return of the manuscript and subsequently
destroyed it; a fragment that turned up 1918 he also destroyed. All that
survives is the serial proof. Those who like to attribute Hardy's success
as a novelist to Leslie Stephen, against common sense, have adduced the
corrections in the proof as further evidence of this process. But these
corrections are for the most part either trivial or destructive. In one
famous scene in a churchyard, Neigh forces an embrace on Ethelberta,
who is wearing a rose 'on her bosom'. He is then made to look absurd on
being discovered by the painter Ladywell, another of her suitors, with
its petals on his coat. Stephen made Tom change this, on the ludicrous
grounds that he did not 'quite like the suggestion of the very close
embrace in the London churchyard'. So in the finished version Ethelberta
'idly' offers Neigh some of the petals 'that had shed themselves in her
hand', which he puts into his pocket-book. This is surely Grundyism
driven mad by what was possibly, as Stephen himself admitted to his
much tried contributor, 'hypercritical' and 'over-particular' anxiety.

There was more trouble of this tiresome sort, which reflects not undue
candour on Tom's part but the nature of Stephen's own unhealthy obsessions. One of the points of Lady Petherwin's objections to Ethelberta's
volume of poems is that they are 'amorous'. The latter originally told
her uncomprehending mother-in-law, with an ironic precision, that it
'would be difficult to show that because I have written so-called amorous
and gay verse, I feel amorous and gay'. Stephen's extraordinary response
was that he doubted if a 'lady . . . ought to call herself or her writings
amorous'. He wanted to substitute 'sentimental' for 'amorous', but
Tom, who must have by now been privately nauseated by Stephen's
prurience, rejected this; he was then forced to use 'tender', which hardly
restored his intention but was at least nearer to it. No doubt Tom, for all
his liking and respect for Stephen, regarded these and earlier unnecessary
absurdities as '*neigh*ings': saying *nay* to decent openness. But he neither
wanted nor in any case could paint a complete portrait of Stephen, whose
company he always valued despite his rudenesses, as he eventually wrote

to Virginia Woolf on 20 January 1915: 'I used to suffer gladly his grim & severe criticisms of my contributions & his long silences, for the sake of sitting with him.'

It has often been pointed out that Ethelberta is the most 'masculine' of Hardy's heroines: while her attractiveness to men is fully implied, there is little actual description of it. This is not so for earlier or later heroines. The reason for this omission in *Ethelberta* has usually been overlooked: in this book Hardy was examining his own new situation in the person not of a man, but of a woman. Gittings, to his credit, has noted this, but in the course of a tortuous and inconclusive argument attributes it to 'deviousness'. This is as foolish as it is ignoble: why would so 'devious' a man have bothered to bring up matters of social attitudes towards origins, at such a crucial stage in his career, if he was so pathologically nervous of them? On the contrary, he was highly amused by them, and in *Ethelberta* he determined to expose the falsity and stupidity inherent in them.

But why the rise of a woman instead of – as in *The Poor Man and the Lady*, which he was here still obstinately trying to rewrite, although inverting the theme – a man? The answer does not lie in a wish to conceal anything. Now that he had almost 'arrived', he would not have tried anything at all along the lines of *Ethelberta* had he wished to conceal any specific nervousness, as distinct from normal sensitivity, on the subject of his origins. Nor, Latin then being commonly understood, would he have attached to it the epigraph '*Vitae post-scenia celant*' ('People hide the back-scenes of their lives') from Lucretius. His senses of mischief and humour, as so often, have been under-estimated. He took a miscalculated risk. That he still had his original unpublished first novel firmly in mind is shown by the fact that, discussing both books late in life, he believed them to have been 'ahead of their time'.

Ethelberta is a woman because Tom was interested in feminity and because he recognized – at least intuitively – that the creative part of a man is strongly feminine. He was also trying his hand at a pure comedy, and if his main character were a woman a comedy could be worked out more easily. The contrast between town and country in *Ethelberta*, to the detriment of the former, has always been noted by critics: he wanted to express, in the strongest possible form, his dislike of the town and town life. In the *Life* he explained his unequivocal attitude at this time:

One reflection about himself at this date made Hardy uneasy. He perceived that he was 'up against' the position of having to carry on his life not as an emotion, but as a scientific game; that he was committed by circumstances to novel-writing as a regular trade, as much as he had formerly been to architecture; and that hence he would, he deemed, have to look for material in manners – in ordinary social and fashionable life as other novelists did. Yet he took no interest in manners, but in the substance of life only. So far what he had written had not been novels at all, as usually understood – that is pictures of modern customs and observances – and might not long sustain the interest of the circulating-library subscriber who cared mainly for these things. On the other hand, to go about to dinners and clubs and crushes as a business was not much to his mind. Yet that was necessary meat and drink to the popular author. Not that he was unsociable, but events and long habit had accustomed him to solitary living. So it was also with his wife . . .

There is no reason to doubt the truth of that last remark. He went on to tell of how Stephen's sister-in-law Miss Thackeray (later Mrs Ritchie) made him nervous by telling him: 'Certainly: a novelist must necessarily like society', and then of how Patmore had remarked that *A Pair of Blue Eyes* ought to have been in verse. This confirms his conviction that he was not, by nature, a regular novelist – or, at the least, not a natural writer of fiction as it was then generally understood by critics. It also explains the mistaken (though necessary) experiment of *Ethelberta*, the least poetic of his novels.

He does not, it should be noted, condemn the novel of manners, and he must have known very well that Jane Austen – and, later, Henry James in his own way – and of course George Eliot, from whom he naturally wanted to distance himself, could bring out the 'substance of life' by means of their observations of manners. But even when he is writing the *Life*, at around the age of eighty, he cannot actually condemn his novels as unimportant to him: his income still largely depended upon the sale of every one of them. They were all in print then, and remain so.

So he goes as near to the essential truth as he dares in the face of what he elsewhere called the 'conventional public'. He showed little private respect for this conventional public, who might just as happily read trash such as *The Sorrows of Satan* by Marie Corelli as his own work; but he also knew, from his knowledge of the 'still, small voice' within himself, that within each individual 'conventional' reader there was also such a still, small voice – if only it could be reached.

During the twenty-five years of his fiction-writing life he moved as near to poetry as he dared, from the 'prosing' of a poem in *Desperate Remedies* to the essentially comic *The Well-Beloved*. Then, when at last he published his poems in volume form, in 1898, he immediately ventured upon *The Dynasts*. *Ethelberta* is, in conception and execution, the sole exception to this process. But even here there are a few scenes which could only have come from the hand of a poet: Ethelberta's viewing of the hawk failing to catch the experienced duck, which encapsulates her own future sacrifice of her womanhood in the interests of survival in a world of male predators; and, most notably, the visit to Neigh's Farnfield estate, and the tortured horses seen there (Chapter XXV).

But, even as he writes an attempted comedy of manners, Hardy is unobtrusively telling his initiated reader, and himself, that he will never make the sacrifice Ethelberta has made. Although it fails to come off because the wit is not sharp enough, it is a clever novel – more ingenious than most would allow of the supposedly non-intellectual Hardy. It demonstrates that he was, among other things, a considerable intellectual, as Robin Gilmour has properly insisted in his useful study, *The Novel in the Victorian Age* (1986).

Tom wrote of how, realizing that he must commit himself to fiction, he made a study of prose style at this time: he says that he reread Addison, Macaulay, Newman, Sterne, Defoe, Lamb, Gibbon, Burke – and '*Times* Leaders &c'. But he must also have looked again at Ben Jonson and perhaps at Middleton and other authors of Jacobean city comedies: their influence is very apparent in *Ethelberta*, in which every character is satirically presented as a type rather than as a rounded individual. Thus Christopher Julian, the man of integrity in the book, who really needed to be presented in the round, is peculiarly feeble and lacking in energy for a Hardy hero.

For all his presentation of *Ethelberta* as a comedy, its plot could easily have been made the stuff of tragedy: an intelligent and vital woman sacrifices love for the sake of money, which is needed to keep her family together. Perhaps the book is psychologically insubstantial just for this reason: that its author deliberately refused to see as tragic what by temperament he regarded as a tragic matter.

Hand, besides conveniently being the maiden name of Hardy's mother, to whose story-telling capacities he knew he owed so much, is a pun: Ethelberta's writing hand helps to add to her attractions, but her desire to do something substantial is finally prostituted and turns into the hand in marriage (to an old roué) which she offers in exchange for security. The supreme irony in the book is revealed in its ending.

Christopher, the man of integrity, considers himself a bad catch even for Picotee: 'A marriage with me will hardly be considered well.' But the 'frightened' Picotee points out that Ethelberta has already extorted from the 'toddling' Mountclere a promise of £500 upon her marriage, and says: 'Berta will never let us come to want.' So although Ethelberta renounces this man she loves, her cynical arrangement will provide for him. In that sense Hardy-as-Christopher in the book is foil to Hardy-as-Ethelberta: the poor melancholy artist of integrity, and the woman who sells out. It was Tom's way of saying, at least to himself, that as popular novelist he would continue to subsidize himself, by hook or by crook, as poet. He finally thought of the book as 'frivolous' and improbable, as did some of its more discerning reviewers, because its very subject – the corruption of a poet and a woman – could not but seem tragic to him, and he had been too light-hearted about it. But by his contrast of the London and West Country scenes he managed to point towards the creation of a whole geographical area, Wessex, which he had begun in *Far From the Madding Crowd*. George Eliot, to whom he always felt too close for comfort, now borrowed the term 'Wessex' in *Daniel Deronda*.

After *Ethelberta* Hardy was to take the longest rest from writing that he had yet taken. Only then would he be ready to write the full-bloodedly tragic novel he knew he had in him.

12

The Sturminster Idyll

Tom now took what has been called a 'sabbatical'. On 4 November 1875 he had told William Minto, the editor of the *Examiner*, who had solicited a new novel from him for serialization:

> My intention is to suspend my writing – for domestic reasons chiefly – for a longer time than usual after finishing *Ethelberta*, which I am sorry to say is not nearly done yet. This throws the date of a new story a long way into the future . . .

And on 5 March 1876, writing from his temporary accommodation in Yeovil to ask George Smith if he would issue *Far From the Madding Crowd* or *A Pair of Blue Eyes* in cheap editions, he added: 'My reason . . . is that I do not wish to attempt any more original writing of any length for a few months, until I can learn the best line to take for the future . . .'

He could afford to take a few months off, and he needed to recharge his batteries. The considerable effort that the artificial *Ethelberta* cost him had run them down. He realized already that this was, for him, the wrong direction. *Ethelberta* had been nearer to hack work than anything he had previously written, although he seems to have enjoyed life well enough at Swanage, where their landlord was an 'invalided captain of smacks and ketches' (he figures as Captain Flower in *Ethelberta*) with a penchant for 'strange stories of his sea-farings'.

At the end of June 1875 Tom and Emma left Newton Road for a couple of days to try to find a house. They looked at properties in Childe-Okeford and Shaftesbury, where they found nothing suitable, as well as Blandford and Wimborne. All these were not within too easy reach of Bockhampton – Jemima was a formidable woman, and Emma would have been justified in not wanting to live too near. But, before they had even discovered the Swanage cottage, she wrote to Jemima to suggest a meeting at Bournemouth. Jemima promptly sent back a message, through Tom's sister Kate, to the effect that she thanked her, but was too busy – reasonable enough, since the journey was a difficult one. Some have seen 'disapproval' in this, but the note is unexceptionable and humorous – the couple are not to drown themselves at Bournemouth – and without any significance in itself. Jemima, not very friendly to anyone outside her immediate circle, was making an effort. In September there was a successful meeting with Mary and Kate, who came to Swanage for two weeks.

Tom felt Jemima's standoffishness keenly. She had been difficult since her 'brain fever', which had occurred when he was about ten, and, while he could deal with her, he must have seen how much harder it was for Emma. When Edmund Blunden knew Tom in the 1920s he heard how Jemima had 'treated him like a child' even when he was a famous man; that may have been so only in her old age, or it may have begun much earlier. It is not, however, unusual for mothers to behave like this, especially as they grow older. Emma herself had a difficult father, and would have understood.

If we are to believe Tom's poem 'We Sat at the Window', with its date of 'Bournemouth, 1875', first published in *Moments of Vision* (1917), the couple felt gloomy on St Swithin's Day (15 July) while they were waiting in their hotel or rooms (it is not known where they stayed for the three days they were there) to take the steamer across Poole Bay to Swanage, in the so-called 'Isle' of Purbeck. A great deal has been made of this, as though a serious quarrel were implied – proving that the marriage was already souring. The difficulty with such a view is that this poem, like the rest of those about Emma, is retrospective, so that it is impossible to infer much from it, and even less to discover how Tom actually felt on St Swithin's Day 1875. He is writing perhaps forty years later, in the light of all that passed afterwards. For Millgate to say that he and Emma quarrelled 'for reasons doubtless connected with Kate's letter' (containing the message from Jemima) is little short of absurd – as well as over-literal – especially since 'We Sat at the Window' contains no hint of anything to do with either's family, or, indeed, even of a quarrel:

> We sat at the window looking out,
> And the rain came down like silken strings
> That Swithin's day. Each gutter and spout
> Babbled unchecked in the busy way
>   Of witless things:
> Nothing to read, nothing to see
> Seemed in that room for her and me

THE STURMINSTER IDYLL

On Swithin's day.

We were irked by the scene, by our own selves; yes,
For I did not know, nor did she infer
How much there was to read and guess
By her in me, and to see and crown
   By me in her.
Wasted were two souls in their prime,
And great was the waste, that July time
   When the rain came down.

The manuscript of this poem reads, instead of 'by our own selves, 'by each other', which shows that Tom refined his meaning. It is no use arguing, as J. O. Bailey does, that the 'nature of the scene is made more explicit' by this earlier reading: poets correct their poems until they express their meaning as exactly as possible. There is, of course, the implication that, since it rained on Swithin's Day, it will rain for forty more – thus that there will be unhappiness (rainy gloom) in the marriage, which indeed there eventually was. But of the alleged 'angry quarrel' they had, there is no trace here.

The first stanza says that they were both bored, and had nothing to read or to look at except rain. Far from quarrelling, they were in complete agreement about being in a 'bad mood'. They had not been, Tom finally decided in making his emendation, irked with each other, but with themselves. From his memories of that day watching the rain, Tom now, in the second and closing stanza, generalizes: not only the scene annoyed them, but also their own selves. Then comes the characteristically tragic dénouement, based, just as characteristically, on a 'moment of vision', a remembrance not of a quarrel but of a wet afternoon when both were cross and had made little effort to speak.

The poem may not even have much to do with Tom's own marriage, since it is typical of him to regard such a scene as symbolic of the situation of all husbands and wives: that they do not understand and prize each other until it is too late. That became his own situation, as he felt it had been after Emma's death; but as we already know this, and as he had already published poems telling us so, this particular poem tells us nothing biographically useful. Bailey's remark that it expresses an 'early realisation that he had nothing to say to Emma, and she had nothing to say to him' is a grotesque misreading: since Bailey himself concedes that the poem is retrospective, how can it represent an 'early' realization? As for 'nothing to say' to each other: the second stanza states the exact opposite. It is the tragic *not* reading and guessing and inferring and crowning what was – and is stated to have been – there to be read and guessed and inferred and crowned that is the reason for the 'waste'. The poem thus confirms that there were feelings to be shared.

There was nothing unusually fraught about the marriage at this period; rather the contrary. While Tom laboured at *Ethelberta*, Emma worked at her own story, 'The Maid on the Shore', which is no better, but certainly no worse, than thousands like it in magazines of the time. She was still trying to get this work published – through Florence Dugdale – in the last years of her life. Tom's attitude to it is not known, but was probably one of embarrassment. It has been claimed that it is to his 'discredit' that, since he later helped other women with their literary efforts (the Florences, Henniker and Dugdale, in particular), 'he never acknowledged Emma's help [with his own work] by offering her the smallest literary assistance'. But the women he did help were young, and he wanted to have affairs with them; he had already got Emma.

Tom continued to rise in the world of letters. He had been asked to join with other writers of account in calling upon Disraeli, then prime minister, in March 1875, to urge an improvement of the copyright laws. While in London he saw a good deal of Stephen and met such fellow authors as R.D. Blackmore, whose *Lorna Doone* (1869) he admired when he read it five years after it had first appeared. He took the trouble to write to Blackmore to tell him so. Unfortunately Blackmore, although polite, did not approve of Hardy's work, on account of his own attachment to Mrs Grundy; he must also have been jealous of Tom's greater success. So they never became the friends they might have been. In old age Tom would tell Samuel Chew, a well-intentioned American biographer, that he had 'never read' *Lorna Doone*, although he may only have meant that he had not read it before writing *Far From the Madding Crowd*. He was always sensitive to the faintest suggestion that he had been influenced by anyone; when he had, he liked to be the first to say so. In the case of George Eliot, obvious though the influence is, he never admitted to it; he regarded her as a great thinker, although by no means a 'born storyteller'.

By 3 April 1876, when *Ethelberta* appeared in volume form, Tom and Emma had moved from Swanage to lodgings at 7 St Peter Street, Yeovil. In May they spent two weeks in London, at a lodging near Oxford Circus; then on the 29th they set out for a tour of the Rhine Valley, which ended with a few days in Belgium including a tour of the battlefield of Waterloo. Emma again kept a breathless diary of their progress, recording that she was tired on the day of the Waterloo tour, and that Tom 'was cross about it'. Bizarre attempts have been made, on the sole basis of this trivial entry, to infer that the marriage was already on the rocks ('at least a hint here that . . . he was finding Emma something less than the ideal companion'). But what husband or wife is always an 'ideal' companion?

Tom's opinion of the accuracy of the press was strengthened by the discrepancy between what they saw in Antwerp, from where they returned, and London press reports of it. Placards announcing 'RIOTS IN ANTWERP' greeted their arrival in London; all they had seen was 'a brass band parading the streets with about a dozen workmen walking quietly behind'.

Soon after they returned to Yeovil they discovered a suitable house in Sturminster Newton, a pleasant market town near Blandford Forum and a little less than twenty miles from Dorchester. They moved there, to 'a pretty cottage overlooking the Dorset Stour – called "Riverside Villa"', on 3 July, 'hastily furnishing it in part by going to Bristol and buying £100 worth of mid-Victorian furniture in two hours'. They looked out upon a meadow, beyond which the river, split into two at that point by a small island, resembled a lake. 'It was their first house and, though small, probably that in which they spent their happiest days,' Tom recollected. The qualifying 'probably' refers to other happy days spent in other houses – but ones not as uninterruptedly happy. Here they were near to where William Barnes, always dear to Tom, had grown up. They made many friends, among whom were Robert Young (1811–1908), 'Rabin Hill', a dialect poet directly inspired by Barnes, and Mrs Emma Dashwood, the daughter-in-law of Thomas Henry Dashwood, the solicitor who had given Barnes his first job and who acted as Barnes' legal advisor in his Sturminster property deals for many years after that.

The poems that Tom wrote about the year and a half in Sturminster make his and Emma's happiness there evident, as do some of the notes he made. He called it 'the Sturminster Newton idyll', and later wrote into his notebook, after that entry, 'Our happiest time'. The poems, of which he mentions 'Overlooking the River Stour', 'The Musical Box' and 'On Sturminster Foot-Bridge', are retrospective, and therefore coloured with regret, and have thus been morbidly misread as proving Hardy's neglect of Emma.

They were both anxious about what sort of novel Tom should write next, but were both of one mind – that mind being concentrated on the success of Tom's career. Nor need we suppose that Emma was any less concerned about Tom's artistic integrity than she had been when she gave up the notion of conventional security for the satisfaction of being married to a writer and poet. This was the kind of pleasure they experienced, according to a note Tom made at the time:

> Rowed on the Stour in the evening, the sun setting up the river. Just afterwards a faint exhalation visible on the surface of the water as we stirred it with the oars. A fishy smell from the numerous eels and other fish beneath. Mowers salute us. Rowed amongst the water lilies to gather them. Their long ropy stems.
>
> Passing the island drove out a flock of swallows from the bushes and sedge, which had gone there to roost. Gathered meadow–sweet. Rowed with difficulty through the weeds, the rushes on the border standing like palisades against the bright sky . . . A cloud in the sky like a huge quill-pen.

Another indication of their closeness was Emma's cooperation in the compilation of the so-called literary notebooks – labelled 'Literary Notes' – now meticulously edited and annotated by Lennart Björk (2 volumes, 1985). This collection of transcriptions and cuttings from newspapers and periodicals displays what Björk rightly calls Tom's 'conscious preparations for his craft', and he undertook the task as a substitute for beginning another novel. The reviews of *Ethelberta* did not please him, and in his irritation he may have failed to note the general respect in which he was now held. Both his income and his integrity, he now felt, might be at stake. While admitting that the novel had been received in 'a friendly spirit', he grumbled about remarks that its plot was 'impossible', and was offended by the charge that he did not understand 'society'. 'Had this clever satire been discovered to come from the hands of a man about town, its author would have been proclaimed as worthy of a place beside Congreve and Sheridan,' he complained. He knew in his heart, as he acknowledged in his 1912 preface, that *Ethelberta* did not show him at full strength.

Despite his personal liking for Leslie Stephen, privately he had mixed feelings. It was not just the question of the censorship he had endured. In the spring of 1876 Hardy wrote to him (the letter is lost) to obtain advice about what critics to read. Stephen replied on 16 May, sensibly recommending 'none', but then added:

I should advise . . . Shakespeare, Goethe, Scott, &c, &c, who give ideas and don't prescribe rules . . . If I were in the vein, I think I should exhort you above all to read George Sand, whose country stories seem to me perfect, and have a certain affinity to yours . . .

Stephen was often condescending and thoughtless. Had Tom not carefully read all these writers, including George Sand, to whom he had just been compared in the *Saturday Review* – and had not Henry Holt, his main American publisher, sent him translations of three Sand novels as far back as 1873? Was his supposed lack of learning, he may have contemplated bitterly, considered to be so obvious? He knew much of Sand's work intimately. By June that year, determined to meet Stephen on his own ground, he was rereading at least one of Holt's Sand novels, *Mauprat*. He copied seven passages from it, all expressing notions – such as that 'a single moment can sometimes overthrow in passionate natures the labours of many months' – with which he agreed.

The 'Literary Notes' process, however, while it cannot be precisely dated, goes back to the short period at Yeovil; the endeavour was not prompted by Stephen. Apart from a few entries at the beginning, which were inserted (the first is the diagram based on Fourier), and a single first one in his own hand, the next 228 are in Emma's hand. In other words, as Björk suggests, he demonstrated 'how he wanted the material copied', and then left her to it. We need not suppose that Emma's transcriptions were made without interest in the material, nor that they did not discuss what she copied, nor that her comments were not on a level with his. Much later she would look bitterly back upon this work, which she continued sporadically for many years, as 'contributing to his novels'. But so it was. Almost every one of the allusions in *The Return of the Native* may be traced to these transcriptions. So she had already helped him with his novels, even if she had not written any part of them.

For the rest of 1876 Tom remained free from the labours of writing, although he may have embarked on *The Return of the Native* just before the year end. His own recollection, however, was that he began it in early 1877. This false start, as it turned out, involved him in much urgent, drastic and anxious revision.

It was not Tom's sole concern in 1875–77 to please the public; he also needed to maintain his integrity, to say what he had to say – 'popular' or not – without, however, too much *displeasing* the public. It is as if his artistic triumph came about by some miraculous accident. It is true that he was determined to try to please; he was equally determined to have his own way. His rescue operation on *The Return of the Native* was one of his shrewdest 'peasant moves': although he was more or less forced to take this measure, he may have improved the novel – and where he felt he did not (the sentimental marriage of Venn to Thomasin), he managed, at least by the 1912 edition, to draw his readers' attention to the flaw.

The early drafts differed considerably from the serial and book editions. The names of four characters were different: Wildeve was Toogood, Granfer and Christian Cantle were the more (bearing in mind Christian's androgyny) suggestive Candle, Eustacia was Avice, and Yeobright was Brittan. With an economy typical of him Hardy used two of these names in future works: Toogood in *Life's Little Ironies* and Avice in *The Well-Beloved*. As Simon Gatrell has shown in his introduction to the photofacsimile of the manuscript (1986), the early version was a very different novel. Gatrell has been able to infer much from Tom's habit of using the reverse of sheets of paper on which he had made false starts for the fair copy. Probably the first chapter, featuring only Egdon Heath, was more or less the same. But the final version has been much altered.

First (to give all the characters their familiar names), Wildeve and Thomasin have lived together as man and wife for at least a week, she in the belief that they have been properly married. In an early draft Mrs Yeobright says to her niece (originally her daughter): 'you were away a week with him'. How Hardy stage-managed this is unknown, but it was much to his, if not to his editors', liking as demonstrative of social hypocrisy. Wildeve was not an innkeeper, nor an ex-engineer; originally an older man, he had once practised herbal medicine in the Egdon district, and was called a 'white witch' and 'Conjuror'; Fairways, at least, called him a 'quack', although this could have been facetious rather than pejorative. Probably, in this earlier version, Thomasin and Wildeve do not get married at all: having been taken to bed by him by deceit, she refuses him. All this suggests both a different personality and a more prominent role for Thomasin.

The role of Diggory Venn in the original conception is, again, unknown: but he was not a reddleman, and therefore could hardly have been the apparently 'Mephistophelean visitant' of the final version. He may have had no romantic interest in Thomasin. Clym was to have worked in Budmouth (Weymouth) rather than in Paris, and Eustacia was a native of Egdon. The published version was subjected to a process Gatrell describes as 'gentrification': characters who were once superior 'by the force of their peculiarities' were now raised by social status. Finally, the once influential notion that Hardy originally planned to invest the figure of Eustacia with 'Satanic' and 'diabolical' qualities has now been laid to rest – she was, Gatrell convincingly shows, no more 'Satanic' in the earlier than in the later version.

It is impossible to say how satisfied Hardy was with his early draft; nor to know exactly what he sent to Leslie Stephen, and then others, in February 1877. He asked George Smith of Smith, Elder, kindly to 'bestow a spare half hour upon it', and to tell him if he thought it 'a kind of story likely to create a demand in the market'. Hardy was by then under considerable financial pressure and needed to estimate his earnings over the next couple of years. He even wrote for advice to that master of the extraction of money from publishers and magazine editors, Anthony Trollope. Anxiously he asked Smith for an 'idea of the time when the new [one-volume] edition [of *Ethelberta*] is to appear' (it was in the following May). He had received excellent terms for this novel from the *Cornhill*, but was to be disappointed with those for the new work.

Stephen did not accept what he had been sent. His letter must have been very discouraging, for on 13 February Tom wrote to *Blackwood's*. This periodical had lost much of its circulation to the *Cornhill* after 1860, but it was still prestigious and could afford to pay well. Tom candidly asked John Blackwood 'when a vacancy for a serial story is likely to occur': he had one, he told him, 'dealing with country life, somewhat of the nature of "Far From the Madding Crowd"', although he had not yet enough of it 'to be worth sending'. Blackwood responded favourably, as Tom had hoped, and on 12 April he sent him 'the first fifteen chapters'. In his covering letter he added, anticipating the kind of genteel naggings he had so often received from Stephen, that he would grant Blackwood 'the liberty' of deleting 'any word or reflection not in harmony with the general tone of the magazine' – he did not think he would find anything, though, because 'before beginning it I had resolved to write with a partial view to *Blackwood*'. But Blackwood politely declined the manuscript: the magazine was fully booked up, he said – and in any case he found that there was 'hardly anything like what is called Novel interest'. He had been put off by the opening.

Stephen predictably, as Tom recalled a quarter of a century later, complained that the relations between Eustacia, Wildeve and Thomasin might develop into something 'dangerous' for a family magazine. He therefore wanted to see the whole before he would make a decision; 'This I never sent him; and the matter fell through.' Tom could no longer afford to wait until he had finished the book to reach a deal with someone.

George Bently of *Temple Bar*, the successful London rival of the *Cornhill* (it had published Trollope and Charles Reade), was the next to see it. He promptly turned it down, for reasons unknown. Tom was now probably quite alarmed and turned to *Belgravia*, a magazine founded by the indefatigable Irish publisher John Maxwell, and edited by his wife, Mary Elizabeth Braddon – with whom he had lived from 1860 to 1874, when his first wife died in an insane asylum. Tom eventually met the gifted Mary Braddon in 1879, and much liked her. Once an actress, she was the author of at least seventy-eight works of fiction and nine plays, written between 1854, when she was seventeen, and her death in 1915. She is most famous for the capable and well-written sensation novel, *Lady Audley's Secret* (1862), published by Tinsley.

Miss Braddon's novel *The Doctor's Wife* owed much to Flaubert's *Madame Bovary* – indeed, it is essentially an English adaptation of it – and, while Hardy must have read *Bovary*, he had also, undoubtedly, read her novel, too. It is thus likely that she was particularly pleased by the manuscript of *The Return of the Native*, with its own affinities to these works, when she received it from him. But she could pay Tom only £240 for the twelve instalments of his book, even if he could later sell the serial rights in America, and the volume rights as well. Smith, Elder published the book in three volumes on 4 November 1878; Henry Holt did so in America the following month.

The reviewer in the *Athenaeum* for 23 November 1878 did not like the idea of the novel, and was not perceptive about it, except in one respect. The 'gratification' of the characters' 'passion', he grudgingly conceded, was not 'carried to the point which would place the book on the "Index" of respectable households'. This at least was a satisfactory response to Tom's own reluctant and financially motivated intention of keeping within the bounds prescribed by editors. The reviewer went on to write, suspiciously (he had already mentioned the 'vagaries of some recent novelists, mostly those of the fairer sex' – and among these he probably meant the until recently adulterous Miss Braddon, rather than the even more recently adulterous 'Mrs Lewes'):

. . . it is clear that Eustacia Vye belongs essentially to the class of which Madame Bovary is the type; and it is impossible not to regret, since this is a type which English opinion will not allow to depict its completeness, that Mr Hardy should have wasted his powers in giving what after all is an imperfect and to some extent misleading view of it.

Quite what a 'complete' view of this type would have constituted he does not make clear; but it was Hardy's intention to depict, in *The Return of the Native*, if not exactly 'the Bovary type', then a woman who was of what 'English opinion' would have called 'the adulterous class'. That is to say, he wanted to depict a woman who would have no qualms about committing adultery. He was both fascinated and repelled by the pious hypocrisy of the Victorians, and was determined to upset it – but within its own irritatingly narrow boundaries, boundaries not only rigorously observed but actually reinforced even by such as Stephen, for all his disclaimers and his enlightenment in other respects. Thus Thomasin, not even the more passionate and rebellious Eustacia Vye, says to her aunt: 'Why don't people judge me by my acts?' Hardy knew very well that judging people by their acts would hardly suit a public which, for the most part, judged people by what they said and preached and did not mean, rather than by what they did, which might have been inconvenient. He kept making the point.

The particular strengths of *The Return of the Native*, which outweigh the weaknesses, are in the psychological portraits of Eustacia Vye and Clym Yeobright and his mother; and in the use of the rustic chorus, now nearer than ever to gaining the effect – learned from Greek tragedy – that Hardy wanted. The depiction of Egdon Heath – still, for all its fame, a marvellous example of the transforming powers of the imagination – is a more obvious triumph. It is the factor that confirmed the reviewers' respect for Hardy. The novel's weaknesses lie in its too sketchy depictions of Thomasin, Wildeve and Diggory Venn – weaknesses which may have been forced upon Tom by his need to keep his name off the dreaded '"Index" of respectable households', the visible proof of which was to be banned by the circulating libraries. It is interesting that in the *Life* Tom quotes Mrs Proctor's 'amusing criticism . . . in a letter', to this effect:

Poor Eustacia. I so fully understand her longing for the Beautiful. *I* love the Common; but still one may wish for something else. I rejoice that Venn . . . is happy. A man is never cured when he loves a stupid woman [Thomasin]. Beauty fades, and intelligence and wit grow irritating; but your dear Dulness is always the same.

He probably did not agree with this view of Thomasin as 'stupid' (the 'man' who is 'uncured' is presumably Wildeve), but perhaps he appreciated 'old Mrs Proctor's' full-blooded refusal to condemn Eustacia. For he had succeeded in preserving what had always been most important to him: Eustacia's natural freedom from the prevailing morality. In this sense she differs from Emma Bovary, who fails to understand that this sort of freedom is what she yearns for, and who is less intelligent than Eustacia.

Since the book is deliberately cast within the bounds of respectability Eustacia is presented with a certain irony, some of it quite complex, as when the narrator tells us that 'at times she was not altogether unlovable'. But while Hardy might present her in a respectable frame, and tell his illustrator, Arthur Hopkins, that she is 'wayward and erring', he intends no exercise in morality with her, but rather one in character. She is the most sharply delineated person in his fiction to date, with Clym Yeobright following closely behind.

The proper adjective to apply to Eustacia is 'antinomian', and the unmistakable influence on Hardy in *The Return of the Native* is Emily Brontë's *Wuthering Heights* (1847), the only thoroughgoingly antinomian English novel of the nineteenth century outside pornography. 'Antinomian' was initially a general name for the notion that Christians were, by grace, freed from observation of moral laws. But it should not be taken as meaning 'immoral'. The word acquired that sense because opponents of St Paul, and then of certain gnostic sects, charged them with immorality: Paul because he preferred laws 'written in the heart' to the strict Mosaic Law, and then the more hard-line gnostics because they believed that spirit and matter were opposed, and thus held that physical actions were of little importance.

The history of this word is relevant to Hardy's work. The spirit of antinomianism, as exemplified in *Wuthering Heights*, is neither opposed to, nor supportive of, morality; but it does question its bases, and is therefore opposed to conventional, heartless morality. It is at least indifferent to this, because it finds it irrelevant. The key is provided by Paul's phrase: 'written in the heart'. Hardy's indignation was always directed at false or by-the-book morality, which he considered less morality than cruelty. This is why he has

Thomasin ask why people would not judge her by her acts, rather than by her alleged breaking of some social custom. Acts are in the heart, while observation of regulations is in the head. The distinction is hardly unfamiliar, but then Hardy was one of the keenest, most persistent and, indeed, earliest explorers of what can be termed real morality. When he makes Clym, at the end of *The Return of the Native*, become a 'preacher and lecturer on morally unimpeachable subjects' he is thus being ironic, and is alluding to his own fate as a writer of morally unimpeachable (in other words, saleable) serial fiction. That, unlike the exhausted and half-blinded Clym, was exactly what Tom did *not* plan for himself.

Eustacia impresses us most by the wilfulness of her dedication to the fulfilment of her nineteen-year-old notion of all-consuming passion, by her single-minded amorality, and – most of all – by the degree of her insight into herself. She is by no means *im*moral, in any sense: her will to power involves no deliberate scheme of harm to anyone else. Indeed, it is evident that she will 'give herself', as she puts it, to any man who loves her enough to interest her. She was originally to have come from Egdon, but Hardy, with cynical amusement, turned her into a half-Corfiote: thus, he felt, any feelings of outrage which her existence might arouse would be mitigated. She is represented as being educated as well as any girl of her sort could then have been, and Clym sees no obstacle to her becoming a teacher and helping him in his project. But she is, after all, only an adolescent, a person without experience; a queen of night, but no goddess – she is only the 'raw material for a Divinity'. Such raw material gets no chance to fulfil itself in its social context, no chance to become the goddess it might. Once her extreme youthfulness has been allowed for, the tragedy of her fate is highlighted. Her grandfather is right when he says that her head is full of 'romantic rubbish'. None the less, Rosemarie Morgan's reading of her character is justified:

> It is part of Hardy's purpose . . . to expose the anger and frustration suffered by the intelligent mind and energetic body restricted to an unvarying, unchallenging, isolated existence. Thomasin's domestic world, with all its conventional trappings, throws Eustacia's into relief by contrast; the estranged solitary woman belongs to no circumscribed world, least of all Thomasin's, in the sense of settling in it, becoming habituated to it or wishing to remain in it.

This may be a little unfair on Thomasin (not every woman wants or needs outwardly to defy the conventions), and Morgan does not much discuss Eustacia's immaturity or sheer adolescent silliness – in believing, for example, that Paris will ultimately be different for her. Perhaps Morgan simply takes this for granted: in pointing out that she 'longs for exquisite pain, sublime erotic anguish' she does, after all, comment that Eustacia's 'spirits *begin* at the very idea. It is a challenging, not a tame lover that she needs.' But Eustacia does not acquire such a lover, and is conscious of it: a man who might have matched her and thus helped her, with her keen understanding of herself and her sound sense of what romantic love really is, to achieve maturity. Doomed by her environment, she kills herself by jumping into a weir, the turbulent centre of the heath which she so hates and yet so resembles. Hardy makes more than merely social points; but he does, as Morgan insists, incidentally make those, too.

The narration emphasizes the paradox of Eustacia's relationship to the heath. Clym, by contrast, loves it ('Take all the varying hates felt by Eustacia Vye towards the heath, and translate them into loves, and you have the heart of Clym'), but is almost its temperamental opposite. For Hardy Eustacia probably had a kind of magnificence – as her counterpart, the heath itself, had for him. Like it, she is all of a piece: uncluttered by inconsistencies, true to her gloomy and imperious type. She might well have grown up and, in place of fulfilled passion, have yearned to do some great good in the world. After all, it was Hardy himself who wrote ironically in March 1888, in 'The Profitable Reading of Fiction':

The aim [of fiction] should be the exercise of a generous imaginativeness, which shall find in a tale not only all that was put there by the author, put he it never so awkwardly, but which shall find there what was never inserted by him, never foreseen, never contemplated. Sometimes these additions which are woven around a work of fiction by the intensive power of the reader's own imagination are the finest parts of the scenery.

It is not altogether necessary to this tonic purpose that the stories chosen should be 'of most disastrous chances, of moving accidents by fear and flood.' As stated above, the aim should be contrast. Directly the circumstances begin to resemble those of the reader, a personal connection, an interest other than an imaginative one, is set up, which results in an intellectual stir that is not in the present case to be desired. It sets his serious thoughts at work, and he does not want them stimulated just now; he wants to dream.

THE STURMINSTER IDYLL

Although the character of Eustacia is not autobiographical, she resembles her creator in certain vital respects. She shares his gloom, his strong tendency to react to bad impressions. She has 'an abiding sense of the murkiness of human life'. She has insight into her own immaturity, which goes quite beyond Clym's idealism: 'Yes, I fear we are cooling . . . And how madly we loved two months ago! . . . Yes, 'tis too true!' She did tell him, she reminds him, that she would be 'a serious matter' on his hands; she is his wife and the sharer of, not simply his fate, but his '*doom*'. She does not 'attempt untruths', and has frankly warned him that she lacks 'good wifely qualities'. It is men's desire for Eustacia that puts her into the position of *femme fatale*, about which role she is never less than candid or self-aware. Her aspirations are selfish in ordinary terms, yet are never made to look absurd. She puts down the last farthing for them, even in her self-willed end. It is her dedication to what Morgan calls 'serial monogamy' that turns her into a victim, and the reader who brings his or her 'own imagination' to bear upon her story, as it is told here, is certain at least to question the enshrined Victorian view of marriage.

All this was as near as Hardy, besieged as he then was by the false values of his society, could come to questioning them. He wrote: 'Literature is the written expression of revolt against accepted things', and he did not mean merely 'politically accepted things'. Some of the complexities, though, he could not yet resolve, although the paradox of Eustacia's hatred of what best symbolizes her, the heath, and her intended destruction at the ignorant and malevolent hands of one of its natives, Susan Nunsuch, is clear enough. The heath is above all gloomy, and Eustacia, true to type, gloomily hates the gloom that makes her gloomy. 'But perhaps it is not wholly because of you that I get gloomy,' she tells Wildeve, 'it is in my nature to feel like that. It was born in my blood, I suppose.' Wildeve responds, rather ridiculously, 'Hypochondriasis'; and she replies, 'Or else it was coming into this wild heath. I was happy enough at Budmouth.' The point is that when she came to the heath she came into herself, and she does not enjoy her fate: she as nearly makes a direct acknowledgement of her basic type as a person can. What Hardy is saying is that it is the type in us, our essence, that has to live out its fate. Eustacia does not mask her true individuality, and so, when she quarrels with her lovers, Wildeve and Clym, teeters towards that universal human habit of self-denial, but then edges conscientiously away from it in the interests of truthful declaration. At first she pretends to Wildeve that she has not lit the

5 November bonfire to summon him, but then she owns up. And with Clym it is thus:

'You are my husband. Does that not content you?'

'Not unless you are my wife without regret.'

'I cannot answer you. I remember saying that I should be a serious matter on your hands.'

'Yes, I saw that.'

'Then you were too quick to see! No true lover would have seen any such thing; you are too severe on me, Clym – I don't like your speaking so at all.'

'Well, I married you in spite of it, and don't regret doing so. How cold you seem this afternoon! and yet I used to think there never was a warmer heart than yours.'

She goes on to complain that he can sing, and reproaches him for it: he might have restrained himself out of pity for her own misery (he did not even know that she could hear him singing – a ludicrous air about how sad it is to leave one's loved one at dawn, from a French comic opera – as he worked at his furze-cutting)! Thus she demonstrates the haughty and exasperating unreasonableness which Hardy was to depict again in that most terrible of all his characters, Sue Bridehead. Some believe that they can discern Emma in these women. But it is a part of Tom himself: that intractable subjectivity, that fearful egoism which seems to be an ineluctable part of the 'integrity of the writer' – and which seems to destroy him as a human being, just as Susan Nunsuch, even more primitive creature of the heath, in her savage ignorance, intends to destroy Eustacia. Yet in their directness such types are perhaps only being honest. Are others, more tactful and sensitive, really less selfish? Or do they pursue equally selfish ends in a more devious manner? Of course, only an abiding sense of 'the murkiness of human life' can find the courage to ask such questions . . . And it is the courage of a perpetually self-questioning person – assuredly, alas, a kind of egoist.

It is here that more careful delineation of both Wildeve and Venn, the reddleman, would have helped Hardy to make his meaning clearer. Wildeve was originally conceived as a more interesting character than he is in the final version. There is little hint of what he originally was, or how far Hardy got in his conception of him. All that now remains of this conception is the 'sensitivity' to which he lays claim – 'the double insult', he complains of Mrs Yeobright's forbidding of the banns, 'to a man unlucky enough to be cursed with sensitiveness, and blue demons, and Heaven knows what'. Otherwise – and even that may be no more than self-pity – he is simply another rather unsatisfactory version of the Hardyan 'villain', one of the line which begins in Manston of *Desperate Remedies*, continues (more robustly) in Troy, and culminates in Alec D'Urberville. There is little that is interesting about him. But had he been the ex-herbalist and white witch of the first conception, there might have been more to him.

Venn is a more complex case. Hardy made up as best he could for his lapse by inserting, in the 1912 edition, the following footnote:

> The writer may state here that the original conception of the story did not design a marriage between Thomasin and Venn. He was to have retained his isolated and weird character to the last, and to have disappeared mysteriously from the heath, nobody knowing whither – Thomasin remaining a widow. But certain circumstances of serial publication led to a change of interest.
>
> Readers can therefore choose between the endings, and those with an austere artistic code can assume the more consistent conclusion to be the true one.

This note was written long after Tom had finished with fiction; but it undoubtedly accords with his earliest intentions. It has aroused the extreme ire of Millgate, who complains that the ending as it was given *is* consistent (did not Lord David Cecil, he complains, pronounce that the marriage 'meets the claims of probability'?), and that therefore 'the phrasing seems extremely unfortunate. The obvious implication is that the "unhappy ending", with no marriage between Thomasin and the reddleman, is the "more consistent" and hence the "true one".' So Millgate, the academic, denies the misguided peasant his own after-thought, on his own novel: 'The present ending . . . conforms to the quiet and characteristically "Shakespearean" pattern which Hardy had already adopted in *Far From the Madding Crowd* . . . it has, in short, a "rightness" of its own which Hardy's intrusive footnote disturbs.'

This is revealing. There is nothing technically wrong with Millgate's irritated condemnation of the 1912 footnote: as Tom himself conceded, the reader's own imagination is often the finest part of the scenery (he did add that some readers want, not to be stimulated, but to dream). Such an opinion is not surprising in a critic who objects to Hardy's deliberate pointing up of the incompatibility between Clym's capacities and his 'native' environment as jarring 'credulity' and promoting *'continuous unease* [my italics]': for such a critic what Hardy himself called a 'true exhibition of man' is too impolite and incorrect. I doubt if it was Miss Braddon's intervention which caused Tom to change his mind about Venn: he is alluding, in his 1912 note, to his own determination to supply a 'happy ending' for those of his readers who, like Millgate today, did not wish to be stimulated to any unease about the possible shortcomings of the world: for those who could not share Tom's own 'austere artistic code'.

He was worried about money. On 25 June 1876 he had made a note which anticipated the difficulties with his new book: 'The irritating necessity of conforming to rules which in themselves have no virtue'. After he had read a few of the uncomprehending reviews, he wrote on 28 November 1878: 'Woke before it was light. Felt that I had not enough staying power to hold my own in the world.' He felt just then, in the face of familiar accusations – for instance, that his rustic characters did not speak as rustics spoke – that he might just as well have written *The Return of the Native* as he had originally wished – that he had botched it. Yet, conforming to the rules without virtue, he had tried as hard as he could not to.

He had been able to do a little better with Venn than he had with the colourless stock seducer Wildeve. The gambling scene by the light of glow-worms – so impeccably possible, so wildly improbable – is justly celebrated: although too isolated within its context, it remains one of the most stupendous, and best loved, scenes in English fiction. But Venn is an unrealized character, and the received view of him, as, in Millgate's words, 'the man of courage and good sense who [lies] hidden beneath the grotesque reddleman exterior', simply cannot hold water – except for the dreamer who rejoices in his final abandonment of this unrespectable exterior for the life of a good and happily married bourgeois and, as Thomasin says of him, 'man of money'.

As so often, Rosemarie Morgan blazes a new trail on this subject. In her view, Venn is a 'creeping and crawling' spy, unperturbed 'by his own intrusiveness' but nevertheless seeking 'to perturb'; he is insulting;

[he] does not operate as a benign regulating force. Perpetually meddling and failing to get his facts right, he is also responsible for passing Clym's inheritance into the wrong hands . . . There is no genuine attempt, on Hardy's part, to conceal the unnaturalness of Venn's transformation.

I am not sure that this was Hardy's own view, which was more confused: in this, Venn's 'Mephistophelean' and 'mysterious' qualities figured rather wistfully as he considered 'certain circumstances of serial publication'. More to the point, it is a view justified by as careful reading of the text as anyone may like to make. Venn was originally a half-supernatural protector of the interests, possibly, of a different Thomasin – the Thomasin who had 'lived in sin' (if without knowing it) with Wildeve for at least a week. He is, as he stands, an ambiguous figure. Perhaps his transition from reddleman – grotesque certainly, but also, and more importantly, poetic in his mysteriousness – to respectable burgher, man of money and dairyman, is Hardy's ironic way of alluding to himself: would-be poet turned 'respectable' purveyor of fiction safe enough for inclusion on Mudie's financially all-important list. He tells Thomasin: 'Yes, I am given up body and soul to the making of money nowadays. Money is all my dream.' The words have a very personal ring, and so does their irony. He is not what he seems, and nor is Thomas Hardy. But Tom is finding it hard to hold his own in such a world. Poor Venn would like to be better, therefore, than Morgan will allow him to be.

With Clym Yeobright, however, Hardy succeeded. To a remarkable extent he holds the novel together. He is not, as has been asserted, a devastatingly critical self-portrait. In depicting him, Hardy was testing out his own circumstances. To a certain degree he is even exactly what his creator had avoided becoming. He is thus relevant to, but not at all representative of, Hardy himself. By this time Tom had gained in self-confidence. Where he lacked confidence, as yet, was in 'holding his own' in the world of letters on his own artistic terms. He was able to distance himself from Clym, and thus to create an autonomous character. The ending, the marriage between Venn and Thomasin, nicely handled though this is in terms of popular fiction, would be wholly sentimental and out of place were it not for the majestic closing paragraph about Clym and its magnificent final sentence. Here his rescue of the book is literal.

> Yeobright had, in fact, found his vocation in the career of an itinerant open-air preacher on morally unimpeachable subjects; and from this day he laboured incessantly in that office, speaking not only in simple language on Rainbarrow and in the hamlets round, but in a more cultivated strain elsewhere – from the steps and porticoes of town-halls, from market-crosses, from conduits, on esplanades and

on wharves, from the parapets of bridges, in barns and outhouses, and all other such places in the neighbouring Wessex towns and villages. He left alone creeds and systems of philosophy, finding enough and more than enough to occupy his tongue in the opinions and actions common to all good men. Some believed him, and some believed not; some said that his words were commonplace, others complained of his want of theological doctrine; while others again remarked that it was well enough for a man to take to preaching who could not see to do anything else. But everywhere he was kindly received, for the story of his life had become generally known.

Clym is portrayed as helplessly in the grip of his mother, and Hardy anticipates Freud by comparing him directly with Oedipus. After he has learned some of the truth about his mother's death from Johnny Nunsuch, and when he leaves the 'little dwelling', the 'pupils' of his study-wrecked eyes are 'vaguely lit with an icy shine . . . his mouth had passed into the phase more or less imaginatively rendered in studies of Oedipus'. Tom was now rendering Clym as a man stuck in a phase through which he had himself passed, just as he had to all intents and purposes passed through the phase of active or hopeful positivism – what George Eliot called 'meliorism', something to which any public person who needed to be thought of as half-decent had, perforce, to subscribe. Ideas to the effect that there was little hope for humanity were scarcely expressible until the 1920s. The narrator grants that he was 'ahead of his time', but calls him 'unfortunate': 'the rural world [Susan Nunsuch, the enemy of witchcraft who is so ignorant that she herself practises it?] was not ripe for him'. Clym is Tom as he might have been had he not been gifted with a creative imagination: a preacher and idealist who has lost his Christian faith and turns therefore to new 'ethical systems'. Naturally, he has been presented by Hardy as wholly unworthy of Eustacia – hardly a sexual being at all, in fact, in the light of how he looks upon Thomasin as prospective wife.

Tom told Cockerell that he had portrayed his mother in Mrs Yeobright; but Cockerell seems sometimes to have been unreliable. However Tom had no good reason to make this up, and it would have been very hard for him to present the interfering mother of Clym – not to speak of the tyrant who forbade the banns announcing her niece's wedding – without having his mother in mind. It is not a flattering portrait, and one wonders just what he said about it to Jemima, who must have read the book; the implication is that he was on very easy terms with her, and could handle her rather better, perhaps, than most sons can their mothers. If his biographers have not always seen it in that way, it is because they find it hard to stomach the idea of a 'peasant' Hardy well able to look after himself. But it is not an attempt at a complete portrayal, or else Mrs Yeobright would have been a teller of strange tales and possess a sense of humour. Once again, Tom took from life what he needed for his novel and left the rest unused.

He often settled his accounts in a wry and humorous manner rather than a spiteful one: for example, when in February 1879 Leslie Stephen told him that he would like to see more of *The Trumpet-Major* before he made a decision about it for the *Cornhill*, he remarked that he liked to see such historical figures as George III 'just round the corner' rather than 'in full-front', as they were depicted in *Vanity Fair*. Tom instantly put George III 'full-front' in *The Trumpet-Major*. This was not only 'teasing' Stephen, but gently reprimanding him for putting *Vanity Fair* on a pedestal. In the same way, in creating Mrs Yeobright, Tom made some comment about his mother's possessiveness. And, since Mrs Yeobright turns out to be 'right', he may have been alluding to her shrewdness as well – if not to the motivations for it. He could love someone while still seeing their faults.

The reviews of *The Return of the Native* cannot have pleased him. W.E. Henley, just then setting out as a reviewer, found it less good than *A Pair of Blue Eyes*, and its 'sadness' 'unnecessary and uncalled for'. The *Saturday Review* attacked Hardy for being 'clever' where he should have been merely 'entertaining' (*Middlemarch* was inferior to *Adam Bede* for this anonymous reviewer): 'the primary object of a story is to amuse'. No wonder Tom was depressed. The anonymous *Spectator* reviewer – the evidence points to R.H. Hutton – did recognize that the author was a 'fine poet'; but he objected, predictably enough, to his outlook, which was simply not conventional enough – for poor Hutton, even to amuse was not enough: the novelist must instruct, and not be allowed to depict such 'pure, unalloyed misery' as that of Clym.

But all the reviews took him seriously enough to condemn his tragic view of life as well as his dangerous tendency to depict women as fully human. Hardy had been the subject of a long and enthusiastic piece by Léon Boucher in the *Revue des deux mondes* in November 1875. It took four years for anyone in England to dare to make a full and comprehensive survey of his work, but on October 1879, in the *New Quarterly*, at last it appeared – and it opened by acknowledging that the publication of *Far From the Madding Crowd* had 'brought a new sensation to the novel-reading world'. Naturally, it accused Hardy of failing to create 'thoroughly responsible' women ('creatures'), but it acknowledged the glow-worm scene as 'a masterpiece of fantastic power'.

When he began to survey the reviews of *The Return of the Native* he had been back in London for over six months, a move which he never ceased to regard as a mistake. Life with Emma at Sturminster Newton had retained its charm and intimacy. Their first Christmas, that of 1876, had been spent at Bockhampton, and biographers' efforts to discover any friction have failed. Just before this visit they received Emma's two brothers, Willie and Walter, one of whom made the fatuously urban – and probably sneering – remark that a 'strange bird on the lawn was an event'. For Tom and Emma, of course, a strange bird *was* an event, and one would certainly have called out the other had they had the luck to see it. Tom then went alone to London for a few days, where he heard Gladstone and Trollope speak at St James's Hall. At Bockhampton he noted that his father told tales of his youth, when the 'hobby-horse was still a Christmas amusement'.

On 30 May 1877 he noted that he sometimes 'looked upon all things in inanimate Nature as pensive mutes'. And on 3 June he made a shrewd and practical observation, although not likely to endear him to regular critics: 'The world often feels certain works of genius to be great, without knowing why: hence it may be that particular poets and novelists may have had the wrong quality in them noticed and applauded as that which made them great.' In the same month he was considering 'a grand drama, based on the wars with Napoleon, or some one campaign'. This line of thought was to lead to *The Trumpet-Major* and then to *The Dynasts*.

In June 1877, while struggling with *The Return of the Native*, he recorded the exploits of their servant Jane, 'whom we liked very much'. Tom saw her outside with a man, who was in the outhouse: 'Before I had thought what to do E. had run downstairs, and met her, and ordered her to bed.' Neither Tom nor Emma would have sacked her, but they had her parents to whom to account. They had found that the bolts of the back door had been oiled, and that her lover had 'often stayed in the house'. At about four or five she vanished: 'About one o'clock went to her father's cottage . . . where we thought she had gone. Found them poorer than I expected . . . he seemed to read the bad news in my face. She had not been home.'

Later, in August, they heard that Jane was to have a baby. It was in connection with this news that Tom made the famous and poignant remark: 'Yet never a sign of one is there for us.' The clear implication, which ought to have given the lie to all the ghoulish and footling speculation about his impotence, is that of a still happy marriage disappointed by Emma's failure to conceive. There is no doubt that this failure – and no one can say whose 'fault' that was – contributed to the later 'troubles' between them. The time at Sturminster really was their 'happiest'. But Tom, in his difficulties with editors, continued to confide in Emma, and had her full understanding.

13

Tooting and The Trumpet-Major

U pper Tooting in south-west London in the 1870s was not the rather seedy place that it has since become, and when Tom told a friend that 'for such utter rustics as ourselves' it 'seemed town enough to begin with' he was alluding to the fact that it had not yet been built up. But it was already getting ugly, and The Larches, 1 Arundel Terrace, Trinity Road, Upper Tooting, near Wandsworth Common, to which he and Emma moved on 22 March 1878, was about as nondescript as it could be. A move from their delightful Sturminster dwelling to this dreary, inconvenient end-of-terrace house was, they agreed, a complete aesthetic disaster. More furniture had to be bought, to furnish the three storeys. Tom's note for 22 March reads: 'Our house is the south-east corner one where Brodrick Road crosses Trinity Road . . . the side door being in Brodrick Road.' It is now simply 172 Trinity Road.

Tom's retrospective poem about a pair of lovers he saw one drizzly evening, 'Beyond the Last Lamp', subtitled 'Near Tooting Common', perhaps evokes the atmosphere that the entire district had for him. It begins

> While rain, with eve in partnership,
> Descended darkly, drip, drip, drip . . .

In his own memory Tooting was a place of illness and pain, where, as he put it in the *Life*, both he and Emma felt that 'there had past away a glory from the earth' and 'their troubles began'. So why did they make the mistake of moving to Tooting at all?

It has been suggested that the initiative came from Emma, who felt that Riverside Villa was unhealthy and yearned to play 'the successful author's wife' in London. But that is unreliable. Nor need we believe Florence's tale that Tom was embarrassed because in speaking to some neighbour Emma had exaggerated her part in his writing. What Tom himself wrote is this:

TOOTING AND THE TRUMPET-MAJOR

Despite the pleasure of life at Sturminster Newton Hardy had decided that the practical side of his vocation as novelist demanded that he should have his headquarters in or near London. The wisdom of his decision, considering the nature of his writing, he afterwards questioned.

The mistake was joint: the artificiality of London life made Tom ill, and it deprived Emma of the country and rural social life she enjoyed.

Nor need we suppose that things began to go openly wrong right away at The Larches. Tom was writing more than thirty years after the event, and was able to trace the origin of the difficulties back to that time. In the *Life* he gives a clue, for, albeit with great subtlety, he directly associates the 'troubles' with his poem 'A January Night – 1879': 'The poem . . . in *Moments of Vision* [1917] relates to an incident of the New Year . . . which occurred here at Tooting, where they seemed to begin to feel that "there had past away a glory from the earth" . . .' The poem itself, one of his most mysterious and grotesque, is brief:

> The rain smites more and more,
> The east wind snarls and sneezes;
> Through the joints of the quivering door
>   The water wheezes.
>
> The tip of each ivy-shoot
> Writhes on its neighbour's face;
> There is some hid dread afoot
>   That we cannot trace.
>
> Is the spirit astray
> Of the man at the house below
> Whose coffin they took in to-day?
>   We do not know.

This 'moment of vision' formed itself in Tom's memory as an omen, no doubt unrecognized as such at the time. The picture, as Dennis Taylor suggests in *Hardy's Poetry 1866–1928* (1981), is one of a 'visionary no longer able to sort out his world'; but, dated 1879 though it may be, it is explicitly retrospective. It was written when Hardy was old and lonely and in full realization that he had moved from a vivifying to an uncomprehending woman – one to whom he could never find much

243

convincing poetry to write. The great and justly famous poems of retrospection about Emma are, indeed, about an image within Tom's memory; equally, they acknowledge the dynamics exercised by Emma herself. They do not unjustly immortalize her. The 'meaning' of the poem, taken in isolation, is no more than that a disturbing ghost – presaging death – seemed to be abroad; read as a note of biography, it is legitimate to infer that, if only in his memory, this incident presaged the end of their 'glory' and the coffin of their hopes. It is worth recalling the Wordsworth stanza from which the quotation comes, for it is made in the same sentence as the one referring to 'A January Night':

> The Rainbow comes and goes,
> And lovely is the Rose;
> The Moon doth with delight
> Look round her when the heavens are bare;
> Waters on a starry night
> Are beautiful and fair;
> The sunshine is a glorious birth;
> But yet I know, where'er I go,
> That there hath passt away a glory from the earth.

This, if it is relevant, surely implies that the actual 'troubles' – misunderstandings leading to partial estrangement – did not begin just then. The experience recorded is, specifically, a joint one, as is evident from the final line: '*We* do not know'.

Millgate quotes a passage from a notebook Hardy titled 'Poetical Matter' which, as he admits ('it seems fair to say'), shows that life at Tooting had its quieter side. Tom speaks of candlelight on Emma's hair: 'Light shines through the loose hair about her temples, & reaches the skin as sunlight through a brake.'

Once in London, Hardy was obliged to leave Emma alone more frequently. In June 1878, for instance, he was elected, at the instigation of a new friend, Charles Kegan Paul, to the Savile Club – just the place to make useful literary connections. There is no suggestion that he did not take her with him whenever he could; for example, he used to take her regularly to the nearby Alexander Macmillans.

The following portrait of Tom at this time is surely prejudicial and false: 'small features disguised by a large, soft beard, he walked the streets observing men and women, especially the latter . . . *a confirmed eavesdropper and voyeur* . . .' (my italics). Presumably Robert Gittings, in whose biography the passage occurs, had evidence to support these assertions. His footnotes reveal that this 'evidence' consists of an 1882 caricature (not a photograph) of Hardy in a theatre in which, Gittings writes, 'Hardy is seen hiding his face behind his hand'. In fact Hardy is not hiding his face but merely covering his ear. Gittings' other 'source' is an account made by Hardy himself. On one occasion (he tells us), he overheard a (funny) conversation in a bookshop in Holywell Street, which he reproduces. As for his 'voyeurism': alas, there is no 'confirmation' of that.

'By degrees', Tom 'fell', Millgate writes, 'into the line of a London man again.' He now began to associate, 'cordially', with 'second- and third-rate metropolitan littérateurs', while smart London society – comprising such as the 'infinitely adaptable' Gosse or the novelist Walter Besant – did not agree with him. As we have seen, Tom himself came to question his judgement in having chosen to 'fall into the line' of being a 'London man' again. But the mistake cannot have been quite so evident to Tom or Emma back in 1878. He did gain certain advantages from his three years in London, not the least of them being greater experience in dealing with editors and publishers, and easy access to the British Museum reading-room.

Thus he now began to share the company of people like his publisher George Smith, Edmund Gosse, Alexander Macmillan, W.H. Pollock, William Minto, editor of the *Examiner*, and even Henry Irving, whom he saw at the Lyceum in a pot-pourri of celebrated scenes, including one from *Richard III*, and then in his dressing-room afterwards, 'naked to the waist' while he drank champagne from tumblers. He noticed that Irving 'forgetting his part, still kept up one shoulder' – as Richard III – while playing 'Jingle'.

From 31 August to 9 September 1878 Tom was back in Dorset, partly in connection with research for his new historical novel, *The Trumpet-Major*. He had intended to be away for 'about three weeks', as he stated in a letter of 27 August to George Bentley of the firm of Richard Bentley, and editor of *Temple Bar*, but he returned early in order to be with Emma. While there, he called on the now aged William Barnes at Came Rectory, and dined with his lifelong friends the Reginald Bosworth Smiths at West Stafford Rectory. Four days after his return, on 13 September, he wrote a genial letter to his brother Henry:

I reached home safely, & the next day we went to see the wreck of the 'Princess Alice'. A man rowed me and several others round the steamer – & we splintered off some pieces, one of which I send to you. I will try to send the *Illustrated News* containing a view of the accident.

Tell mother she must make up her mind to come while the fine weather lasts. I will meet her at Clapham Junction.

It is always assumed that Jemima did not make this journey, but there is no reason to suppose that she did not – nor that mutual visits while they had been living in Sturminster Newton were not more numerous than Tom's bare record suggests.

Among the most important of his new friends, and someone whom he now often met, was the Rev. Charles Kegan Paul (1828–1902), who founded a publishing firm of that name which eventually became Routledge and Kegan Paul. Unlike the vast majority of his London friends, including Gosse, Kegan Paul really understood and appreciated Hardy; he was perhaps the first man of letters who did. Vicar of Sturminster Marshall near Wimborne in east Dorset from 1862 until 1874, he went to London as a literary editor and advisor to the publishing firm which later became his own. He co-edited the *New Quarterly Magazine* from 1873 to 1880 and wrote, among other books, *Biographical Sketches* (1883) and *Memories* (1899), an interesting volume of reminiscences in which Hardy figures. He was converted to Roman Catholicism towards the end of his life.

Kegan Paul must have commissioned (although it is clear that he did not write) the first full evaluation of Hardy's work, which appeared in the *New Quarterly* in 1879; but before that he had himself written an anonymous shorter survey of Hardy's work, in Minto's radical *Examiner* (founded by John and Leigh Hunt) on 15 July 1876. Entitled 'The Wessex Labourer', it spoke sound good sense about both Hardy and Barnes, and defended the former against those critics who accused him of making his peasants too intelligent. Kegan Paul had two advantages: he was a less stuffy sort of Christian than the Huttons, and he knew the Dorset people at first hand. Tom was grateful, as always when he met unprejudiced good sense, but it was only in April 1876 that he discovered the author. Kegan Paul wrote to him, in connection with a one-volume edition of *A Pair of Blue Eyes* which his firm was publishing, suggesting friendship. In April 1881 he wrote yet another article on Hardy, by far the most intelligent general survey that had yet appeared, and on 18 April Tom wrote an appreciative letter. Kegan Paul had spoken of him as coming from 'a race of labouring men' and being exceedingly proud of it.

If I have never yet written a good novel your essay should stimulate me to produce one without delay . . . nothing tends to draw out a writer's best work like the consciousness of a kindly feeling in his critics: & the worst work I have ever done has been written under the influence of stupidly adverse criticism – not just criticism of the adverse sort, which of course does good when deserved, as it often has been in my case.

What an exhaustive acquaintance with English fiction your article directly reveals in the writer. And when I remember your reading in other literatures is proportionately wide I cannot help wondering how you can have found time in your life to do so many things. I have nothing to say against the few personal remarks you make, as I fancy you expected I should, though I have an opinion that the less people know of a writer's antecedents (till he is dead) the better. By the way I can tell you (privately) what you may be interested in knowing clearly – that my father is one of the last of the old 'master-masons' left – anywhere in England, I should think – the modern 'builders and contractors' having obliterated them . . . my direct ancestors have all been masters, with a set of journeymen masons under them: though they have never risen above this level, they have *never* sunk below it – i.e. they have never been journeymen themselves.

This demonstrates that Tom was, as he liked to claim, 'ahead of his time' in that he could foresee an era in which sexual reality could be discussed freely in order to explore the truth of things, and in which a writer could express his own visionary outlook without being accused of 'pessimism'. After all, he had a bad time with the majority of reviewers, who in effect acknowledged his poetic power and his gift for comedy but resisted whatever he had to say. Kegan Paul's approach shows how positively Tom could react to 'kindly', or good-willed, criticism. Tom was thus over-sensitive only to '*stupidly* adverse' criticism; his modern critics ought to have recognized this more readily, and been more generous in their assessment of his intelligence and the quality of his intellect. In any case, being self-critical, he certainly disliked himself for reacting as he did to reviewers' stupidity, instead of consoling himself with what they had to allow: his persistence in the face of their incomprehension, and his high status. Modern critics' reluctance to accept this status except grudgingly signifies an unhappily similar type of resistance. In writing to Kegan Paul of his 'worst work' he was thinking, mainly, of *Ethelberta*: his too hasty wish to assert himself as capable of writing really well about London society, in which milieu, although he could well see its artificiality, he was never quite at his best.

Newly arrived in Upper Tooting, he was still concerned about money. During his final month at Sturminster Newton he had had to write to Harper & Brothers in America, who were publishing *The Return of the Native* in their *New Monthly* (he was gradually shifting away from Holt): '. . . in my previous experience . . . it has been [the] custom to remit, at the time of publication, the amount due for the portion of the story issued'. He was anxiously arranging, too, for Tauchnitz editions of previous novels to appear. On 14 June he wrote to Chatto and Windus: 'I have not received your customary letter with enclosure . . .'

On 1 February 1879 he had to go again to Bockhampton. His father had written to him the previous 31 December to tell him that Jemima was ill, and probably another member of the family, perhaps Henry, wrote a few weeks later to say that she had not yet got better. Tom was glad of the opportunity, for he was now well on his way with *The Trumpet-Major* and needed, as he always liked to do when writing a novel, to visit some of the scenes of its action. When he arrived at Dorchester station he found Henry awaiting him in a wagonette drawn by his father's horse, Bob, whose 'behind-part was a mere grey Arabic arch; his foreparts invisible': it was cold and windy, and rain was falling on the snow. A day or two later he went to Weymouth and Portland. Most of the rest of his notes about this visit, which he evidently enjoyed, describe various tales of the past – some gruesome – which his father told him. Tom was now more interested than ever because his book-in-progress was set in the Napoleonic wars, about which he learned most from his grandmother; the poem to her, 'One We Knew', contains this stanza concerning Napoleon Bonaparte:

> Of how his threats woke warlike preparations
>   Along the southern strand,
> And how each night brought tremors and trepidations
>   Lest morning should see him land.

He was back in Tooting within a fortnight, probably to resume work, or research, on *The Trumpet-Major*. It is not known when he began or finished this novel, though serialization ran from January to December 1880. It was a new venture for him since he went back in time further than ever before: to be precise, seventy-four years.

In early March he got influenza, which kept him 'from crossing the threshold' and even interfered with his correspondence. About this time Walter Besant, novelist, Cambridge French scholar and former teacher of mathematics, wrote to ask him whether he would, as 'the author of the most original the most virile and most humorous of all modern novels', join a Rabelais Club which he was proposing to found. Besant was a doughty champion of authors' rights, and in 1884 founded the Society of Authors. Tom, who thought he looked like a 'West-of-England sailor' caught up in 'silent pantomimic laughter', knew him quite well until his death in 1901. Besant founded the Rabelais Club ostensibly to study the works of that author, but in reality to bring together the best, and not the most inhibited, raconteurs in contemporary letters. The very name would have been a provocation to many, who regarded Rabelais as a French pornographer and exponent of lavatorial humour. Tom, aware that Besant's first book had been about French literature, admitted to the extent of his own familiarity with Rabelais in his reply of 17 March 1879:

> I am gratified by your asking me, & I am quite willing to join such good company. But I ought to tell you that I shall be a mere dummy, & that I could not pass a very satisfactory examination in the works of the author whose name you have chosen. I like the principles of the club immensely. Unfortunately the name of Rabelais has been so ill used as to make it misleading to many – but you & the others know best.

The Club's inaugural dinner was held in December in the 'cheerless' Tavistock Hotel. The *Life* contains a perfectly judged account of it – Tom apparently thought it a rather trivial affair – followed by a crack at Henry James. He reports that James was 'rejected . . . after a discussion' for membership, owing to his lack of virility. It seems certain that Tom had already traced the authorship of James' distinctly unpleasant and somewhat contorted (unsigned) review of *Far From the Madding Crowd* in the American *Nation* of 24 December 1874, in which he wrote of 'cleverness which is only cleverness' and drubbed the author for exceeding a length which he very soon himself exceeded in *Roderick Hudson*.

Tom could see James' virtues very well, and he read his novels all his life, giving them judicious praise as well as criticizing them. He called him a 'real man of letters'. But for James, Hardy and his style were the object of an unrelenting dislike, which culminated in his envious

249

remarks to Robert Louis Stevenson about *Tess*, which he described as 'vile'; but Tom did not read their exchange of letters on this subject until after James' death, when he angrily described the pair as the 'Polonius and Osric' of literature, and as 'two virtuous females'. But he welcomed the award of the Order of Merit to James in 1916, and was warm about it privately.

The jokes made about him demonstrate that Hardy had discerned James' unfulfilled homosexuality. This was doubtless canvassed in the 'discussion' Tom records, and Millgate's glum remark to the effect that his 'statement' is 'apparently inaccurate' rather misses the point; but Millgate finds the entire Rabelais Club affair 'rather disturbing'. Tom may, too, have been half-unwittingly responsible for sustaining a well-known *canard* about James. In 1880 he had begun to make regular visits to the eccentric and regal old Mrs Procter in her flat in Queen Anne's Mansions. Once, he thought, she had been a 'handsome coquette', into whose 'withered' visage, as an old lady, a 'momentary archness' would sometimes creep. Certainly she had known almost everybody of importance, including Wordsworth (whose character she disliked), Keats, Leigh Hunt and Charles Lamb. She much pleased Tom by liking Emma – he says that she was not so generous to all women ('far from it!') – and, as he implies, this was a main reason for his seeing more of her. Henry James also took delight in her company, and on 24 March 1880 she told Tom that he had offered her marriage. 'Can it be so?' he asked in the *Life*. However, as Tom knew, Henry James' 'proposals' to her were simply a joke they shared.

Leslie Stephen was not enthusiastic enough about whatever portion of *The Trumpet-Major* Tom sent him. Although he liked Hardy, Stephen was probably not yet ready for another exhausting battle over the proprieties with a man who was such a 'child' in those matters. Later he did tell Tom he was sorry he had not been given the chance to publish it, and said he liked the novel except that he thought the heroine had married the wrong man (they usually do, replied Tom, to which Stephen rejoined: 'Not in magazines'); but he had been initially too suspicious, and perhaps was writing in this vein safely after the event.

Once again Tom had the worrying business of finding a suitable serial outlet. In May he tried *Macmillan's Magazine*, and in June *Blackwood's* ('above all things,' he told John Blackwood, 'a cheerful story, without views or opinions, & is intended to wind up happily'). But both ventures proved unsuccessful – editors could not compromise their circulations by publishing such risky material, and there were plenty of safe story-tellers around who could fill their pages.

Unlike many other authors, such as Dickens and George Eliot, Tom was not in the habit of making a systematic series of notes for his novels; the sole exception is the so-called 'Trumpet-Major Notebook', which has been ably edited and annotated by Richard Taylor in *The Notebooks of Thomas Hardy* (1978). Tom had been in the British Museum on several occasions in 1878, and was often back there in the spring and autumn of 1879. Emma came with him, and it is apparent that while they were at Tooting she continued to be his keen collaborator – more than merely a helpful copyist. As a result of his painstaking research the novel is alive with authentic detail. He was not content just to study in the Museum, either; not only did he visit the scenes and talk to those who remembered the events of which he wrote, but on several occasions he went to Chelsea Barracks to consult old soldiers who had taken part in the campaigns. That work later served him well for *The Dynasts*.

'In the latter half of August Hardy paid a visit to his parents in Dorset and a week later Mrs Hardy joined him there,' says the *Life*. This means that Emma stayed at Bockhampton, before they both, as Tom tells us, took lodgings at Weymouth. Tom was still assiduously collecting *Trumpet-Major* material, and the couple seem to have got on so well with Jemima on this occasion that the latter joined them at Weymouth to drive to 'Portland, Upwey, etc.'. Emma already had a pleasant relationship with both of Jemima's daughters, conducted apart from her husband.

In *Satires of Circumstance* Hardy published a poem called 'She Charged Me':

> She charged me with having said this and that
> To another woman long years before,
> In the very parlour where we sat, –
>
> Sat on a night when the endless pour
> Of rain on the roof and the road below
> Bent the spring of the spirit more and more . . .
>
> – So charged she me; and the Cupid's bow
> Of her mouth was hard, and her eyes, and her face,
> And her white forefinger lifted slow.
>
> Had she done it gently, or shown a trace
> That not too curiously would she view
> A folly flown ere her reign had place,

A kiss might have closed it. But I knew
From the fall of each word, and the pause between,
That the curtain would drop upon us two
Ere long, in our play of slave and queen.

This has proved altogether too much for those who believe that Tom had a protracted affair with Tryphena Sparks, and that he and Emma had drifted apart by 1879. The 'scene of the poem is Weymouth', asserts Gittings, and the occasion is Emma's discovery of the affair ten years later – in the same room! There is nothing, however, to suggest that the scene of the poem is Weymouth – it may just be one of Hardy's dramatic lyrics. Or, more likely, it does refer to a specific occasion now impossible to identify. In any case, the 'charge' is not that the speaker has 'had an affair', but merely that he has 'said this and that': in other words, been attracted to another woman. If the parlour was at Max Gate, then the poem may allude to an occasion upon which Emma (with good reason) may have suspected that Tom had been attracted by a female visitor such as Mrs Florence Henniker. But the poem offers nothing in the way of fact.

Tom was relieved when, after failing with the *Cornhill*, *Macmillan's* and *Blackwood's*, and quite possibly other magazines too, he was able to write on 1 August that it would be a 'great pleasure' to meet Dr Macleod – and, indeed, to have lunch at the Savile. Dr Donald Macleod was the editor of *Good Words*: 'Good Words are Worth Much and Cost Little' was its motto, and in 1861 it had become the only magazine that ever won the approval of the Society for Purity in Literature. Tom was at once on dangerous ground, even though *The Trumpet-Major* is his 'purest' book. Nor was this quite such a descent in the market as might appear: *Good Words*, although not the force it had once been, was still popular, and featuring in it for a year did Tom no harm. In 1866 it had published Charles Kingsley's *Hereward the Wake*. The financial arrangements are unknown, but were satisfactory, and probably an improvement on those offered by *Belgravia*.

The Rev. Dr Donald Macleod (1831–1911) was the eldest son of the Rev. Norman Macleod (1812–72), chaplain to Queen Victoria, editor of *Good Words* from its inception, minister (and hero) of the Church of Scotland, zealous missionary, evangelical journalist and author of instructive novels. He had refused to publish Trollope's *Rachel Ray* because it contained a scene of dancing. His son had taken over as editor of *Good Words* on his death. Tom evidently did meet him for lunch, and must have been highly amused by his good-natured piety. He already knew what to expect, for Macleod had written to him on 20 June:

> We are anxious that all our stories should be in harmony with the spirit of the Magazine – free at once from *Goody-goodyism* and from anything – direct or indirect – which a healthy *Parson* like myself would not care to read to his bairns at the fireside. Let us have as much humour (oh that we had more!) and character – as much manly bracing fresh air – as much honest love-making and stirring incidents as you like – avoiding everything likely to offend the susceptibilities of honestly religious & domestic souls.
>
> Do forgive this homily! But we have had such bothers in the past in consequence of a want of clear understanding beforehand on matters like this that I think it is best to be frank.
>
> You will not, I hope, for a moment imagine that the statement of such views implies any possible doubt as to your sympathies being in perfect harmony with the lines laid down – It is all the other way!

But the good Scot's muscular ecstasy was scarcely justified: the 'harmony' was not quite 'perfect'. However, Tom decided to appear to conform. He wrote to Macleod telling him: 'Should you on looking over the MS. as we go on discover any passage out of keeping with the general tone of the magazine, be kind enough to tell me frankly and I will do anything to get it right.'

The manuscript of *The Trumpet-Major* (309 leaves, one of which is in Emma's hand) shows that Macleod quite often used his blue pencil. All Tom could remember about it, when a clergyman named Sydney Smith who was writing a biography of Macleod asked him for details in July 1925, was that 'he asked me to make a lover's meeting, which I had fixed for a Sunday afternoon, take place on a Saturday, & that swearing should be avoided – in both which requests I readily acquiesced, as I restored my own reading when the novel came out as a book' (which it did on 26 October 1880, from Smith, Elder). It has been said that 'Hardy's memory was . . . slightly at fault' because the meeting actually takes place on a Monday – but what he was recording was what Macleod asked him, not the half-humorous alteration he actually made. As Gatrell has shown, he teased Macleod in other ways, and must have been amused to have this passage (quoted by Gatrell) so easily passed – all that happened was that the 'healthy *Parson*' changed 'swearing' to 'profane noises':

The office was next to All Saints' Church, and the afternoon services at this church being of a dry and metaphysical nature at that date, it was by a special providence that the waggon-office was placed next to the ancient fabric, so that whenever the Sunday waggon was late, which it always was in hot weather, in cold weather, in wet weather, and in weather of almost any other sort, the rattle, dismounting, and swearing outside completely drowned the parson's voice within, and sustained the flagging interest of the congregation at precisely the right moment. No sooner did the charity children begin to writhe on their benches and adult snores grow audible than the waggon arrived.

Gatrell comments that Macleod allowed this to pass because 'it was not his church that was being ridiculed' – and so he must have thought, but the mention of 'special providence', and other details, suggest a Church of Scotland ambience. As well as amusing himself at Macleod's expense (as in the episode of the terribly swearing parrot), Hardy failed to be deterred from his usual analysis of the nature of erotic desire. Indeed, at one level the book is about just that. John Loveday desires Anne, but cannot excite her by being as forward as she requires him to be: the folk around him see it – 'Why don't he clipse her to his side, like a man?' – but he cannot. Anne feels the yeoman's lustful gaze 'travelling over her from his position behind, creeping over her shoulders, up to her head, and across her arms and hands'. She knowingly deals with his unwelcome ardour, and so his 'sword' breaks as he tries to 'rip . . . open' the joints of the window shutters.

The Trumpet-Major represented, for Tom, a sincere effort not to be gloomy. It may even have been an experiment, following the essentially tragic *Return of the Native*, in happy romance. And it is, primarily, a lyrical love story. But, quite apart from the famous ending, when John Loveday, defeated in love, is sent off to die in faraway Spain, it contains much melancholy. However, like most of Tom's melancholy about the state of the world, this is never gratuitous: he could not write about war and pretend that war was not tragic. Thus he insists upon counterpointing the magnificence of the royal review with the tragedy of the future of the men who comprise it:

the gorgeous centre-piece . . . how entirely they have all passed and gone! – lying scattered about the world as military and other dust, some at Talavera, Albuera, Salamanca, Vittoria, Toulouse and

Waterloo; some in home churchyards; and a few small handfuls in royal vaults.

Then there is the strongly implied fact that, after the first flush has worn off, Bob Loveday is not going to make the kind of loyal companion to Anne Garland that his elder brother would have done; as well as the sad fate of the latter, a man who lives his life by the standard of considering others. Anne, a character in the line of Bathsheba Everdene, although with her own individuality, is seen as genuinely lovable, a woman of essential integrity; but her choice of husband, of the irresponsible Bob over the considerate John, although made out of love, is at least as sad as the trumpet-major's fate, even if it cannot actually be seen as tragic. The choice is deliberately made by Hardy in order to be perverse, because he knows that desire itself is perverse when confronted by psychologically unrealistic social requirements. Of course, in a Fourierian world of decent polyandry Anne could have enjoyed Bob physically and chosen to live with the more reliable John; but neither Macleod nor his subscribers were even aware of such horrors, and certainly, if mistakenly, would not have been able to equate them with such 'honest love making' for which Macleod and his bairns had asked his author.

Even though Hardy was opposed to realism in its sense of 'transcriptive of reality', this is his most conventionally realistic – or 'least unrealistic' – novel, chiefly because of the amount of sheer historical detail it encompasses. The opening words of the 1895 preface are:

> The present tale is founded more largely on testimony – oral and written – than any other in this series. The external incidents which direct its course are mostly an unexaggerated reproduction of the recollections of old persons well known to the author in childhood, but now long dead, who were eye-witnesses of those scenes. If wholly transcribed their recollections would have filled a volume thrice the length of *The Trumpet-Major*.

Although it used to be fashionable to deprecate it, *The Trumpet-Major* is a *tour de force*, if a light-hearted one. There is much research in it, based on books, army regulations, hearsay and the like; most novelists would have allowed this huge accumulation of detail to weigh too heavily, as Charles Reade did. Hardy brings it to life. More to the point, he is historically very accurate, whilst carefully eschewing historical analysis:

255

he probably agreed with the oft-expressed notion that it is historians, and no one else, who make 'history'.

The Trumpet-Major is a remarkable historical reconstruction, because it concentrates upon only a few square miles of England and gives the most convincing picture ever drawn of just what the Napoleonic threat meant to those most immediately involved. No historian has equalled it; nor can it be called the kind of history that is made by historians. It has been said that in this novel Hardy 'ultimately creates an effect which is the reverse of historical'. That frigid judgement misses the point: he did not see 'history' as most professional historians see it. He homed in with his imaginative microscope and recorded the impact of specific events on his characters, and the sharpness of his focus is unerring.

If, however, *The Trumpet-Major* is only a minor novel within the canon, this is because psychological consequences are not followed to their conclusion. For all that, the judgement that if 'it had appeared anonymously and without Wessex place-names, few would have suspected that it was written by the author of *The Return of the Native*' is bizarre. Being historical, it served as a basis for his project, now taking on increasing momentum, of transforming Dorset and its immediate environs into the 'Wessex' which we so readily associate with his name. The slight geographical shift of Sutton Poyntz to 'Overcombe' is typical of this imaginative process. Hardy's own touch in this matter, as everywhere else, is perfectly apparent. On the whole readers enjoy *The Trumpet-Major*, so that the tendency of critics to dismiss it as inferior has hardly damaged it; but the same cannot be said of the unjustly denigrated *A Laodicean*, perhaps the most 'major' of all Hardy's 'minor novels'.

14

A Laodicean

On 1 February 1880, as the serialization of *The Trumpet-Major* in *Good Words* was starting, Tom saw a man 'skating by himself on the pond by the Trinity-Church Schools at Upper Tooting, near his own house'. He was 'moved to note down' that it was

> a warm evening for the date, and there has been a thaw for two or three days, so that the birds sing cheerfully . . . What can the sentiments of that man be, to enjoy *ice* at such a time? The mental jar must overcome physical enjoyment in any well-regulated mind. He skates round the edge, it being unsafe to go into the middle, and he seems to sigh as he puts up with a limitation resulting from blessed promise.

He was 'moved' to make this note because he saw something of his own predicament in this man of badly 'regulated mind'. The 'ice' is the inevitable discomfort of creative integrity, the middle of the pond the 'blessed promise' of necessary but unreachable candour. What indeed could such a man's 'sentiments' be? As for the unusual warmth for the season, and the cheerful singing of the birds, they were the feedback Tom was already receiving about the success of his new serial. For *The Trumpet-Major*, both as serial and in October 1880 as book, was from the start a success with readers and reviewers. They saw Mr Hardy's new story as altogether more cheerful and less disturbing than *The Return of the Native*. Even the *Athenaeum* of 20 November 1880, while it predictably whined about his 'habit of putting into the mouths of illiterate rustics idioms which we can scarcely believe to be theirs', and compared him unfavourably to the author of *Lorna Doone*, thought that John Loveday was his 'best character' yet.

But still Tom did not feel financially secure, as his remark in the following autumn, when he became seriously ill, makes abundantly clear: he had, he then wrote, made 'but a poor provision for his wife in the event of his own decease'. In this February, while pleased by the reception of the new serial, he was upset because a scheme to dramatize *Far From the Madding Crowd* was going badly awry. He had tried his own hand at it, and cannot have felt that he had done the job well. He despised the popular theatre for just the reason that he despised London society: it was false and pretentious. None the less, the theatre was a means of getting relatively easy money for work already done. But nothing is known about this attempt except that it was judged unfit for the theatre by those who understood the genre better than he.

'Soon after he finished it [his own dramatization]', writes R.L. Purdy in his Hardy bibliography, J. Comyns Carr and his wife 'proposed a dramatization of their own'. By the beginning of 1881 Tom would already have discussed the matter with Carr, an experienced drama critic and adapter, and would have learned that Boldwood would have to be dispensed with, to give way to Fanny Robin's half-mad gipsy brother. All that is known about the affair is derived from a 'single, imperfect' but printed copy in the Lord Chamberlain's Office, called *The Mistress of the Farm*. This is the Carr version, which he submitted to Hare and Kendal, joint managers of the St James's Theatre, in the summer of 1880. They accepted it for production, but then, because a popular actress named Mrs Kendal did not like it, rejected it the following November. The unfortunate sequel was that Mrs Kendal gave the plot to the successful playwright Arthur Wing Pinero, whose *The Squire*, a free adaptation of *Far From the Madding Crowd*, hit the boards on 29 December 1881. Later Pinero admitted to Carr that he had been given the plot by Mrs Kendal, but denied, unconvincingly, that he knew anything of the novel. Hardy himself sent a letter of protest to the *Daily News* early in 1882. To a drama critic, W. Moy Thomas, he wrote on 30 December 1881:

> In your notice of 'The Squire' . . . you remark that though the author of that play is under obligations to my novel . . . the dramatic & narrative methods of presenting a story are so widely different that the dramatist might well afford to own his obligations to the novel. Now you probably write thus in ignorance of the fact that 'Far From the Madding Crowd' exists also as a play – that the play was submitted to the management of the St James's Theatre, was actually put in rehearsal by them, & then rejected.
>
> Some time ago I was induced to dramatize the story, which I did alone & unassisted . . . Some time after this Mr Comyns Carr asked if I had ever thought of dramatizing the story, when I sent him the

play as I had written it. He modified it in places, to suit modern stage carpentry &c, & offered it to the St James's . . . I leave you to draw your own inferences.

He remained on good terms with Carr, but the contempt expressed in the phrase 'modern stage carpentry &c' is evident.

Taking advantage of the row that had been generated by *The Squire* Carr hastily revised his version, which opened in Liverpool in February 1882. It was transferred to the Globe in London, where it ran until July, simultaneously with *The Squire*, which outlasted it by only a week. Tom, however, felt disgruntled throughout. The true key to his feelings is contained in an irritated note written on the MS of the performing version: 'I should much prefer keeping as near to the book as possible.'

Ever since he had reluctantly decided to write *The Hand of Ethelberta* instead, the scheme which finally materialized as *The Woodlanders*, his own favourite of his novels, had been looming at the back of his mind. But how, so miserably away from his sources, could he write it in London? So he put the *Woodlanders* project off yet again, and started thinking about the third and last of what he would call his 'novels of ingenuity', *A Laodicean* – its two predecessors being *Desperate Remedies* and *Ethelberta*.

He did not feel that he could write a truly Wessex novel while in London, and, although this one is set mainly in Wessex (though at Dunster and Taunton in Somerset, not in Dorset), the place is only a formal presence. By August he had written the first three instalments, comprising thirteen chapters. It is not likely that he had made a start on it by February – he had work on his play to do, in collaboration with Carr, as well as commissioned short stories to write. By April, though, he had, for it was then that he opened negotiations with Harper's for its serialization in the new European edition of their magazine. This was something of a financial triumph: they offered him £1,200, at £100 an instalment. By June he could tell the illustrator, George du Maurier, that he would be able to call upon him at short notice with 'the MS. [of the first number] in his hand'.

He was now moving in the most exalted circles of literary London, largely through his acquaintance with Mrs Procter and his membership of the Savile. Tom socialized with Tennyson; the former Richard Monkton Milnes, Lord Houghton – not only the father of the woman, Florence Henniker, with whom he would fall in love in the 1890s, but also the biographer of Keats and an assiduous collector of pornography; the sculptor Thomas Woolner; Matthew Arnold; Browning; and his illustrator for *Ethelberta* and now *A Laodicean*, George du Maurier.

In July R.R. Bowker of Harper Bros called on him at home in connection with the new serial, and found Emma 'agreeable and youngish . . . immensely interested in her husband's work'. Bowker unquestionably took the two as a functioning couple, and noted how Tom called upon Emma to provide detailed information about the incidents and characters in his 'own stories' which he had forgotten. He was, thought Bowker, 'entirely unaffected and direct'.

This, by one who was there at the time, contrasts with the account of Gittings: Emma was 'nearly forty', and had by now 'run to fat, her figure to dumpiness'; Tom's attentions were roving elsewhere. Doubtless they were, if only in a fairly disinterested manner; most men's do. Gittings' attempt to substantiate his 'findings' is as comic as it is unscrupulous. He gives a footnote referring to the San Francisco sensation novelist Gertrude Atherton's *Adventures of a Novelist* (1932) to 'support' his authoritative animadversions on Emma's figure; but Atherton, in any case an unreliable and silly woman, was then only twenty-two, and did not even glancingly meet Emma until the latter was well past fifty.

Tom was enjoying the company of other writers, and was well able to like them for themselves, if not always for their books – about which he soon learned to remain as non-committal as possible. But he tried to be sincere, and sometimes could be. Thus, writing to the poet Frederick Locker (later Locker-Lampson), to whom he had sent *Far From the Madding Crowd*, he could honestly say that he enjoyed his (mostly) light and unpretentious poems, and that Locker's appreciation of *Far From the Madding Crowd* had meant more to him than 'all the printed criticisms put together'.

But despite the pleasure he gained from all these meetings, his heart remained in Dorset. It must have been just about now that he and Emma recognized their mistake in coming to live in a city at all. Tom's own emotions were painfully jolted back to his youth by sad news on 3 February: the death of the Rev. Henry Moule, at the age of seventy-nine. Not a day or two before, he told Henry's youngest son Handley in a letter of 11 February, he had been discussing his father with Matthew Arnold, who

> talked a good deal about him to me: he was greatly struck with an
> imperfect description I gave him (from what I have heard my father

say) of the state of Fordington 50 years ago, & its state after the vicar had brought his energies to bear . . . for a few years. His words 'energy is genius' express your father very happily.

By 20 April, at the latest, he and Emma had decided that they wanted to live in their own house, not in London but in Dorset. Some have insisted that this project, which was not to be properly fulfilled for another five years, was Tom's own, and the cause of much dissension with Emma. But this is the product of wishful thinking. It is no part of this biography to suggest that Tom and Emma did not eventually have their difficulties; nor to suggest that other married couples do not (and often of a similar type); nor that Emma did not have her own understandable point of view; nor to be clever after the event, and suggest that the marriage was doomed and 'unsuitable' from the start. There is nothing to suggest that Emma did not fully agree with Tom about where they should live.

On 20 April he wrote to his brother Henry, now almost thirty and increasingly active in running the family business with efficiency: 'I have heard from young lawyer Lock about the plot of ground we want to get in Dorchester. He has written to the Duchy of Cornwall . . . I should be glad if you would talk it over and let me know . . .' The 'we' here refers unequivocally to himself *and* Emma, and there is no reason to doubt that he had confided to her how badly he was feeling in London, despite the fact that the serial was going so well. In late March or early April he noted down a 'Hint for Reviewers – adapted from Carlyle': 'Observe what is true, not what is false; what is to be loved and held fast; not what is to be contemned, and derided, and sportfully cast out-of-doors.' His mood is evident, and the more so from an impression of 19 May which he described:

. . . a night on which he could not sleep, partly on account of an eerie feeling which sometimes haunted him, a horror at lying down in close proximity to 'a monster whose body had four million heads and eight million eyes':

In upper back bedroom at daybreak: just past three. A golden light behind the horizon; within it are the Four Millions. The roofs are damp gray: the streets are still filled with night as with a dark stagnant flood whose surface brims to the tops of the houses. Above the air is light. A fire or two glares within the mass. Behind are the Highgate Hills. On the Crystal palace hills in the other direction a lamp is still

261

burning in the daylight. The lamps are also still flickering in the street, and one policeman walks down as if it were noon.

This passage records one of Tom's earliest apprehensions of the masses as a single if many-headed 'monster': in the country he could deal with it, but in town it oppressed him. He was to recollect it when he came to write *The Dynasts*. By the time that was finished Unanimisme had been invented in France, and Jules Romains (the pseudonym of Louis Farigoule) would soon be writing his novel *Mort de quelqu'un* (1911), which is about this 'monster'; but he and his colleagues saw it positively, as 'communal life'. Did Tom ever discuss this novel with his lazy young acquaintance Desmond MacCarthy, who, with Sydney Waterlow, translated it, as *Death of a Nobody*, in 1914? There was always enormous interest in – and sympathy for – Hardy in France. Emile Zola had already explored the 'monster' in such novels as *Pot Bouille* of (1882), with a disgust and yet also with a true and delighted zest; to Tom it was more simply nightmarish. Yet he was the English writer *par excellence* who discerned that there really was such a single life of the masses, and he would demonstrate its existence in *The Dynasts*.

He went to the Derby 'alone' on 26 May, and in June and July 'dined at clubs etc.'. Then, at the end of July, he and Emma decided to go again to the continent. Tom's story of what they experienced at Le Havre suggests that they were still in the habit of thinking and feeling as one unit – and that they were both in a highly nervous and apprehensive state:

> The hotel they chose was . . . old and gloomy in the extreme when they got inside. Mrs Hardy fancied that the landlord's look was sinister; also the landlady's; and the waiters' manner seemed queer. Their room was hung with heavy dark velvet, and when the chambermaid came, and they talked to her, she sighed continually and spoke in a foreboding voice; as if she knew what was going to happen to them, and was on their side, but could do nothing. The floor of the bedroom was painted a bloody red, as if struggles had taken place there. When they were left to themselves Hardy suddenly remembered that he had told the friendly stranger with whom he had travelled on the coach from Etretat, and who had recommended the inn, that he carried his money with him in bank notes to save the trouble of circular notes. He had known it was a thing one should never do; yet he had done it.

They then began to search the room, found a small door behind the curtains of one of their beds, and on opening it there was inside revealed a closet of lumber, which had at its innermost recess another door, leading they knew not whither. With their luggage they barricaded the closet door, so jamming their trunks and portmanteau between the door and the nearest bedstead that it was impossible to open the closet. They lay down and waited, keeping the light burning for a long time. Nothing happened, and they slept soundly at last, and awoke to a bright sunny morning.

On 5 August they went on to Trouville and then to Honfleur, where they saw a Christ, a little reminiscent of Tom's own vision of Emma crucified in Cornwall – except that this one seemed to 'writhe and cry in the twilight: "Yes, Yes! I agree that this travesty of me and my doctrines should totter and overturn in this ghastly world!"' – from which 'strange and ghastly scene' they 'hastened on'.

Tom attributed the severe illness which struck him down in October 1880 to having spent too long swimming at Etretat; it may well have been a contributory factor. In addition, he might have picked up an infection from drinking French water, such as later killed Arnold Bennett.

On his return from France he sent off the final proofs for the volume edition of *The Trumpet-Major* to Smith, Elder and then travelled to Dorset. First he must have gone to Weymouth, for reasons entirely unknown: his letter to the likeable American Bowker, enclosing the first part of *A Laodicean* for the European *Harper's*, is dated 'Sept 10' from there; he added in a postscript that the Upper Tooting address was 'safest' as he was 'moving about'. In the *Life* he speaks only of himself going down to Dorset; and since a letter from Bowker of 13 September was posted on to him from Tooting to Bockhampton, where he had arrived by the 16th, it may be assumed that Emma was not with him. However, if someone else forwarded the letter for him, by arrangement, then indeed he might have taken her. It is otherwise hard to say just what he was doing in Weymouth, or why he wanted to go there. Lock, the lawyer with whom he had been in touch, was based at Dorchester. So it is not certain that Emma was not with him; she may even have joined him at his parents' house.

The talk amongst the family at Bockhampton was about property disposal in the past, for in the *Life* he recounts Jemima's tale about how her maternal grandfather, William, allowed a cunning solicitor from Bere Regis to obtain three-quarters of his property by artfully playing upon his anxieties. The matter of the plot of land which Tom now wanted to buy must, necessarily, also have been discussed. It is, however, unreasonable to assume that Tom and Emma's decision to buy a house near Dorchester represented 'a radical shift of direction on Hardy's part', which led to 'a corresponding shift in the balance of power as between Emma and Jemima', and that 'Jemima's victory constituted for Emma a corresponding defeat, one which she never forgave and from which she never recovered'. This is, again, putting amateur Freudianism in the place of the unknown. Tom had recently told his brother Henry that he and Emma ('we') wanted to purchase land near Dorchester. Whether Emma was present at this discussion or not, there is no evidence for 'a family conclave . . . from which Emma was absent' at which a 'decision was made and confirmed'. There is no reason to suppose that a 'decision' about anything at all was taken on this particular occasion. As we know from Tom's earlier letter to Henry, the main decision, to obtain a plot of land, had already been taken.

On 16 October they both went off to Cambridge, where he was entertained by three of the surviving Moule brothers. By the 18th or 19th he was feeling 'an indescribable physical weariness . . . but he kept going'. He fancied he saw Wordsworth's ghost in King's College Chapel, 'lingering and wandering on somewhere alone in the fan-traceried vaulting'. He was also fascinated by the 'weird shapes' of the candles there as they burned down: they made, he noted, the 'most fantastic shapes' he ever saw. Memories of Horace, and his last meeting with him, haunted him.

By 23 October, when they returned to Tooting, Tom was feeling so unwell that he called in a doctor who lived opposite. He was told that he had an internal haemorrhage – there was blood in his urine – and that he must not get up. This doctor called daily. Emma, 'in her distress', rushed to tell the Alexander Macmillans of her husband's illness. They immediately sent their own doctor, who confirmed the original diagnosis.

Tom was in great pain, and the treatment, although prescribed in good faith and according to the practices of the time, seems to have been calculated to prolong it. In order to avoid a 'dangerous operation' (presumably to remove a stone in the urinary tract, certainly a live-or-die affair in 1880) he was 'compelled to lie on an inclined plane with the lower part of his body higher than his head'; in other words, blocks were inserted at the foot of his bed. He was always to be subject to 'inflammation of the bladder', but it seems likely that he expelled the stone, which itself may have been caused by an infection.

Tom's emotions and instincts had long been out of balance with his mind, his well-being diminished by London and by the 'monster'; the severity of the illness, at least, was of psychosomatic origin. He meditated a great deal during his enforced idleness, and must have recollected how soon he had become well when, thirteen years earlier, ill health had forced him to leave London for Bockhampton. Now, trapped in his bed and afraid for his life, he would not return to Dorset: he chose the care of his wife rather than that of his mother.

This care was heroic. Not only did Emma nurse him and bring him his meals, but she also made it possible for him to go on with *A Laodicean* – work which, if not continued instantly, would 'ruin the new venture of the publishers' and give him a name for unreliability. Most writers would have given up. But Tom had an enterprising and loyal wife who could – and did – help him.

By May 1881, he dictating and she 'working bravely at writing and nursing', they had produced 'a rough draft'. It was an extraordinary achievement, and it is inconceivable that Emma did not greatly aid him in the actual writing of the book. How should she ever forget such a service – or fail to exaggerate her part in it after things became difficult between them? And how should he fail to be embarrassed when she became tactless and awkward about it? It is difficult to conceive that she did not at certain points make suggestions which he, in pain and fear of death as he was (and says so), was glad to take up. The task of dictating such an ironic, subtle and sexually suggestive novel to an unsympathetic person would have been impossible and, to a sick man, irritating beyond words. Tom recollected, in a letter to Gosse written on 30 December 1917, long after Emma was dead: 'I well remember that illness at Upper Tooting which brought you to my bedside. What a time of it I had – six months! Yes: I did dictate "A Laodicean" through it. It was an awful job.'

Tom told hardly anyone of the real extent of his illness, and deliberately kept its seriousness from Bowker, with whom he was dealing over the magazine publication. He told him on 15 November that a cold he had caught had 'left a troublesome local irritation behind': it did not, he assured him, affect his writing, but on the contrary gave him 'more leisure' for it. Solely out of consideration for the feelings of his family, and not because, as Millgate contends, he 'dreaded the tensions that might be consequent upon their arrival at his bedside', he kept them similarly in the dark. Relations between Tom's two sisters and Emma were at this time particularly good; it was not until they all got older that things began to sour. For concealing the seriousness of his illness Tom has been accused of 'very Hardyan . . . qualifications and half-truths'. In the circumstances, this judgement seems astonishing: after all, his livelihood was affected. Nor, of course, did he utter any 'half-truths' to Bowker: he really was working, and so what he said was entirely true.

A Laodicean is Hardy's most sheerly intellectual novel. This is why it remains a relatively minor work. In 1888 Hardy observed that if you 'look beneath the surface of any farce you see a tragedy' but that 'if you blind yourself to the deeper issues of a tragedy you see a farce'. *A Laodicean* does not function on a high level of emotion, but nor is it pastoral in the manner of *Under the Greenwood Tree*. It is something of a farce, but one with tragic undertones – the fate of Charlotte, for instance, is tragic at least by implication.

In plot it is a return to the sensation novel, with a morally ambiguous character (Captain de Stancy) and two villains, one of whom (Abner Power) is introduced at an uncomfortably late stage. *A Laodicean* does not much resemble his other novels – there is little rustic dialogue in it, although the 'cynical' reflections upon marriage that are put into the mouth of Dairyman Jinks are telling – and that is perhaps one reason why critics have dismissed it as 'a fairly disastrous failure' and a 'potboiler of the worst sort'. It is clearly not 'disastrous', or it would surely have gone out of print in the hundred or so years since its publication. To be fair, survival is not a sure test of merit; but the 'worst sort' of potboilers, even those by authors of a generally high standard such as Trollope and Thackeray, do not always survive, either.

A Laodicean is a truly feminist novel, in which sympathy is never withheld from the mysterious heroine, Paula Power, a woman so called (with characteristic irony) because, although she has power in the conventional sense – property and money – she is power*less* because she is not a man. She specifically alludes to this when she explains to Mrs Goodman why she could not 'ease the mind' of her lover George Somerset's father with news of his son: 'I am continually hampered in such generosity . . . by the circumstance of being a woman.' She is unable to be herself because custom will not allow her to express her physical passion for a man. She is, on the contrary, obliged to 'conceal' it.

A Laodicean is also primarily a comic novel. Hardy's humour, especially when not expressed through the sayings of rustics, is still disconcerting to prudes. Thus the scene in which the drunken de Stancy spies on Paula Power doing gymnastics in skin-tight roseate clothing can still upset a few over-earnest or inhibited readers. Richard Carpenter, although he allows for its humour, even admits to 'distress' when he recalls this scene in a bad 'mood'. Gittings states, as an established fact, that de Stancy is, in this scene at least, 'certainly typical of Hardy himself' – but some may make a different guess, especially as Tom found it funny, particularly at the expense of the sanctimonious prigs amongst his readers. It is only fair to Hardy to add that the real peeper at women is not the one who acknowledges the voyeuristic impulses within himself; he is more likely to be the one who too easily and confidently accuses others of the habit. The famous witch-finder, Matthew Hopkins, turned out to have belonged to a coven.

It is obvious, though, why the novel is so under-rated: its plotting is preposterous. But this plotting is quite deliberately typical of the 'worst kind of potboiler' of its time, and simultaneously more adept. Hardy, despite his illness and consequent need to draw upon material easily to hand – his recent travels on the continent, his architectural experience, his reading – brought off a *tour de force*: *A Laodicean*, far from being 'cynical' in the worst sense, is a parody of the contemporary sensation novel, just then running out of steam. Its humour and psychological shrewdness transcend the popular genre. As the young Havelock Ellis wrote, in his remarkable assessment of Hardy in the *Westminster Review* of April 1883, 'If *A Laodicean* can scarcely become one of its writer's most popular stories, it yet marks distinctly the continuous development and the versatility of his genius.' Tom wrote to Ellis on 29 April in warm appreciation:

> As to certain conditions & peculiarities that you notice in the stories, I may mention that many are the result of temporary accidents connected with the time of their production, rather than of deliberate choice. By-the-by, I think that in speaking of men of the Wilhelm Meister & Daniel Deronda class as being my favourite heroes, you are only saying in another way that these men are the modern man – the type to which the great mass of educated modern men of ordinary capacity are assimilating more or less.

George Somerset of *A Laodicean* is such a 'modern man', although Hardy may – with himself modestly in mind – have endowed him with rather more than 'ordinary capacities'. He is apparently an outstandingly gifted architect.

There are additional reasons why *A Laodicean* may have been underrated. Its main theme is erotic. The title means, in a religious context, 'lukewarmness', after the people of Laodicea accused by the author of the Book of Revelations. In Hardy's hands it ironically refers, first and foremost, to the nature of the enigmatic Paula Power's sexuality. Only secondarily does it refer to her difficulties in choosing between old and new, and in any case the old and the new themselves ultimately refer to her sexuality, if only to emphasize that this is never old or new, even though ways of regarding it may change – thus the narrator wryly comments at one point that human nature will always be 'romantic'.

The novel plays about with, but does not try in any way to resolve (except sexually, by the marriage of George Somerset and Paula Power), the conflict between Matthew Arnold's polarized concepts of 'Hellenism' and 'Hebraism', notions with which Hardy must have been familiar from his reading of *Culture and Anarchy* (1869). Arnold's 'Hellene', throughout history, has been governed by spontaneity, his 'Hebraist' by strictness of conscience. The one is vibrant with life, the other moralistic and obedient. Hardy had also read other works by Arnold, and specifically refers to one of these, the essay 'Pagan and Medieval Religious Sentiment' in *Essays in Criticism*: at the end of the book Somerset quotes, to Paula, the phrase 'imaginative reason' – which is not too far from what Keats meant by the 'true voice of feeling' – as by a 'finished writer'.

But Hardy did not even try to take sides: he minded only what Joseph Conrad was later ironically to call his 'business' – in other words he obeyed only the dictates of his own imaginative reason. Thus, while he set out the problems of past versus present in somewhat Arnoldian terms, he set the comi-tragedy of sex above even those. He was not trying to be a 'thinker' here, and can therefore be acquitted of the oft-made charge that in this book he 'lacks coherence'. In spite of his respect for Arnold (whom he did not altogether like) and evident love of his best poems such as 'Dover Beach', he believed that the whole Arnoldian panoply lacked coherence and was artificial. If in his plot he is parodying the by now clapped-out sensation novel, then in his allusions he is laughing at Arnold's, and others', too pale casts of thought. The allusion of his title is a joke: for Paula is 'Laodicean' only as a defence against the violence of her passion, which is anything but lukewarm – and this violence is clearly revealed in her frantic pursuit of George Somerset when she imagines herself to have lost him. The last mention of the word 'Laodicean' is a silent one; she whispers it in George's ear, because it has become a sexual joke between them: he has by then experienced her 'Laodiceanism' in bed, and well knows it to conceal 'enthusiasm'.

> 'I suppose I am . . . something or other that's in Revelations, neither cold nor hot. But of course that's a sub-species – I may be a lukewarm anything. What I really am, as far as I know, is one of that body to whom lukewarmth is not an accident but a provisional necessity, till they see a little more clearly.' She had crossed over to his side, and pulling his head towards her whispered a name in his ear.
> 'Why, Mr Woodwell said you were that too! You carry your beliefs very comfortably. I shall be glad when enthusiasm is come again.'

Arnold's Hellene-Hebraist contrast, one of the many dichotomies which have been invented to explain the history of culture (romantic–classical; naive–sentimental; Dionysian–Apollonian), permeates *A Laodicean*, and might even be said to constitute its universe of discourse. But there is no commitment to it. In a later notebook entry, that of 7 October 1888, Hardy wrote:

> The besetting sin of modern literature is its insincerity. Half its utterances are qualified, even contradicted, by an aside, and this particularly in morals and religion. When dogma has to be balanced on its feet by such hair-splitting as the late Mr M. Arnold's it must be in a very bad way.

The 'aside' here is no less than the truth that is well known but remains unstated; for example, the truth that there were double standards applied to men and women. *A Laodicean*, in its light way, set out to undermine and even mock these double standards. For all Paula Power's portentous intellectual indecisions are brought to naught by her sexual needs (woman's sexual needs were an 'aside' to the Victorians, for whom she was 'too pure' to be 'troubled by' them), and she is even obliged to drop the Victorian woman's habit of 'concealment' in order to get what she wants. But, with her 'modern' money, and with Somerset's understanding, she is able to do this. Charlotte de Stancy is an impoverished aristocrat – in the Arnoldian scheme a person who possesses superficial sweetness and light but who is too much concerned with the maintenance of ancient privileges; in this ironized Hardyan version, however, a person who is simply a victim. The unfortunate Charlotte, also in love with George Somerset, is obliged (by no less than the self-effacing sweetness and light of her true nature, her 'tender affectionateness which might almost be called yearning') to become an Anglican nun. A careful reading of the novel can even suggest that Hardy is deliberately playing with mocking images of 'sweetness' and 'light': the windows of the hideous Baptist chapel, for example, *shine* 'like a good deed in a naughty world', and there are many other such references.

The true concerns of *A Laodicean* are those of an interrupted courtship and Paula Power's struggle to avoid the consequences of her sexual preference; the latter provides the reason for the interruption. Thus, when Somerset first comes upon her through the chapel window, she is standing before a pool, just about to be baptized by the minister. Somerset cannot even see her face, but his imagination, 'stimulated by this beginning', sets about 'filling in the meagre outline with most attractive details'. However, Paula cannot go through with her baptism. As her confidante Charlotte later explains to Somerset, 'the water looked so cold and dark and fearful . . . that she could not do it to save her life'. She led, Somerset discerned at the moment when she contemplated her imminent total immersion, 'a clandestine, stealthy inner life which had very little to do with her outward one'. But she is not yet ready to immerse herself into this sexual turmoil – is anxious, indeed, to conceal it from everyone, especially from herself. As she later tells the good minister Woodwell (modelled on Perkins, the Baptist minister whom Tom had known well from Dorchester) when he confronts her, she does not absolutely refuse, but declines to attend the Baptist Church 'for the present'. Somerset draws her attention to himself by vanquishing Woodwell in an argument on the question of infant and adult baptism, but then tells her that he was not altogether sincere. Her own silent commentary on the argument, as it proceeds, is the mobility of her breasts.

Critics have taken too seriously Paula's interest in medievalism versus modernism, and thus, looking in vain for a deeper comment upon the conflict between the two, have pronounced the novel lacking. In fact her apparent devotion to the conflict merely conceals her real interests, which are more personal. Her real problem is: how can she contain her warm, ardent and thus self-disturbing sexuality? At first she does it by an intense, unconsciously lesbian, friendship with Charlotte de Stancy, to which Hardy loses no opportunity to draw attention. Thus the landlord of the inn at Sleeping-Green tells Somerset: 'they be more like lovers than maid and maid'. But after she has encountered Somerset her mind is nearly made up, and all she can do is to feign a non-sexual 'Laodiceanism' in order to put off the day of what she sees as her surrender. Victorian *mores*, of course, did not see it as 'surrender' at all.

Yet Paula's behaviour to Somerset is continuously and deliberately provocative, a test of his character; even when she forbids him to touch her, her bosom rises and falls 'somewhat more than usual'. Since she must eventually meet his passion, she is for the time being determined to discipline it until it has been trained to her taste, so that at the end of the novel, when she is candidly in pursuit of him – and temporarily devastated, when she thinks she has lost him – she can tell Mrs Goodman that she knows 'every fibre of his character'. However, she adds that he knows only 'a *good many* fibres' (my italics) of her own . . . She rightly feels that she has been rendered power*less* by her interest in and sexual desire for him; but she is determined to retain as much as possible of her original power. She still wishes, as she tells Somerset in the famous last words of the novel, that her castle had not been burned and that he was a de Stancy. We may be sure that, in order to keep him, she will conceal from him at least a few of the 'fibres' of her own character.

A Laodicean discerns, as no other contemporary novel by a man does (except some of Wilkie Collins' work), the way an emancipated and morally scrupulous woman might feel about her sexual susceptibilities. Captain de Stancy does at first seem to offer a way out. Paula neither loves nor desires him, but marriage to him would at least satisfy ambition of a cerebral sort. However, she will not agree to this until Somerset has been represented to her as a drunken gambler, and therefore as a hopeless prospect. It is also significant that, when apparently appealed to for money by Somerset – represented by Dare as destitute after losing at the tables – she instantly supplies it. She only agrees to marry de Stancy because she believes she has lost the love of her life.

The details of Paula's final pursuit are as comic as the names of Somerset's assistants, Cockton, Knowles and Bowles, whom she encounters in the course of it. Paula admits to her aunt that she 'likes' George Somerset 'as desperately as a woman can care for any man'. Lest the nature of her interest in him be misunderstood, Hardy puts in clues: in the old quarter of Lisieux, when trying to find him, she sees carvings of 'satyrs' and even of 'a man undressing' (a typically mischievous Hardyan touch that slipped by Mudie's censors). When she

catches up with him she insists upon immediate marriage: 'in matrimony
. . . you should be slow to decide, but quick to execute'.

As for the rest of the novel, it is only fair to agree with its detractors
that the stage business of the villains Dare and Abner Power, apart from
furthering the necessary plot, has little real connection with the major
themes. That is why *A Laodicean* is a minor novel. But Hardy does keep
to his own rule, that characters should be consistent and not improbable.
He would never, even in what were potboilers by his own standards,
change characters for the sake of the happy endings demanded by the
lower end of his market. He had come perilously near to this in *The
Return of the Native*, when the reddleman had to marry Thomasin –
but he put that right in his footnote of 1912; he was not going to do
it again here. Paula gets her man and Somerset gets his woman – but
it is a well-trained Somerset, who is informed, in the final words of
the book, that he is not up to scratch in every respect. The fire that
destroys the castle is, symbolically, the fire of physical passion putting
an end to other pretensions; but Paula regrets her losses and is never
going to pretend that she does not.

The younger de Stancy is interesting and, if in a minor key, impeccably done. His resolution not to succumb to drink, and through it to
indiscriminate lust – and the manner in which he is nevertheless pursued
by the fruits of this lust in the form of his demonic son and nemesis,
Dare – foreshadows the fate of a far more powerful character, Michael
Henchard of *The Mayor of Casterbridge*. Abner Power hardly fits except
to further the plot. He is Hardy's only attempt at a nihilist, but nothing
like as full-blooded a one as Conrad was to present in *The Secret Agent*.
He has been, after all, only the amoral agent of nihilists.

William Dare is more interesting than either of these two. In *The
Return of the Native* Hardy had not done what he wanted with Diggory
Venn: to present him perhaps as some kind of beneficent but nevertheless
'Mephistophelean' figure who vanishes as mysteriously as he arrives.
Dare is a wholly ambiguous figure, and really does vanish into thin air
after burning down the castle. His malignity has no motive, unless this is
simply greed: he cares nothing about his father, and furthers his project
to marry Paula Power only so that he can get his hands on the resultant
cash in order to put his supposedly infallible gambling system to the test.
But he displays little passion about even this. His best delight is to cause
the maximum amount of unpleasantness. He is, he says, unmoved by
women, although he well understands his father's weaknesses on this
score. He can get drunk – and does so with Havill – but is more vigilant

than a normal drunk would be, and thus catches Havill before he can fully decipher the words tattooed on his chest. He cannot be more than twenty-one or -two at the most, but is seen by various people as being of various ages, most often as a boy.

Hardy had again been reading, or at least remembering, Wilkie Collins, another novelist who may today be called, like him, 'feminist'. He may even have had in mind a novel almost as systematically anti-Grundyan as his own: *The Law and the Lady* (1875). Collins' powers had been weakened by his addiction to laudanum; but his reputation was still high, his books widely read. He died in 1889, and in the following year it was proposed to erect a memorial to him in St Paul's Cathedral. The Dean and Chapter refused – and would have refused more decisively had they had details of Collins' private life, in which he refused marriage but behaved impeccably to his two mistresses and his three children by one of them.

When Tom heard of this refusal, he told a correspondent on 13 March 1890 that he was 'surprised' by it. *The Law and the Lady* was one of Collins' 'marriage' novels, in which he explored power within marriage and woman's role in the struggle for it. The novel introduces one of the most outrageous characters in Victorian fiction, Miserrimus Dexter, who, although without legs and confined to a wheelchair, walks on his hands at night to spy on others. Dexter is sexually menacing; but the asexual and almost hermaphroditic William Dare is like him in some of the mischief he creates. Dexter, for example, destroys a suicide note so that someone will be accused of murder.

Collins, then, seems a more likely source for Dare than Poe or Hawthorne, or even Goethe, all of whom have been suggested: Hardy seldom discussed at any length those to whom he felt most indebted, and that applies to Collins (who does not figure in the *Life*); but he was clearly a man after Hardy's own heart. Not only were Collins' novels the evident first model for *Desperate Remedies*, but Tom felt an affinity with him because of his ability to treat women as individuals, and because of his abiding interest in the miseries caused by marriage.

A Laodicean suffers when discussed in too earnest terms; it is too funny to be the weak novel that it has almost universally been said to be. Given that most of it was written under the shadow of a life-threatening illness, it is all the more remarkable for its lightness of touch. It is not known when the poem 'A Wasted Illness', one of Tom's most powerful and moving, was written, or even whether immediate thoughts of this illness prompted it. But his experiences of 1880–81 form its substance. Once the profound feelings behind it are recognized it is possible to see how much gaiety and good humour co-existed, in Hardy, with the too celebrated gloom:

> Through vaults of pain,
> Enribbed and wrought with groins of ghastliness,
> I passed, and garish spectres moved my brain
>   To dire distress.
>
> And hammerings,
> And quakes, and shoots, and stifling hotness, blent
> With webby waxing things and waning things
>   As on I went.
>
> 'Where lies the end
> To this foul way?' I asked with weakening breath.
> Thereon I saw a door extend –
>   The door to Death.
>
> It loomed more clear:
> 'At last!' I cried. 'The all-delivering door!'
> And then, I knew not how, it grew less near
>   Than theretofore.
>
> And back slid I
> Along the galleries by which I came,
> And tediously the day returned, and sky,
>   And life – the same.
>
> And all was well:
> Old circumstance resumed its former show,
> And on my head the dews of comfort fell
>   As ere my woe.
>
> I roam anew,
> Scarce conscious of my late distress . . . And yet
> Those backward steps to strength I cannot view
>   Without regret.
>
> For that dire train
> Of waxing shapes and waning, passed before,
> And those grim chambers, must be ranged again
>   To reach that door.

A LAODICEAN

Even as it celebrates the 'dews of comfort', this poem simultaneously recognizes the inevitable fact of death, and the reluctance of human beings to face it unless they have been through such an experience. One 'dew of comfort' was the delight he had in being able to finish in pencil, by May 1881, the draft of *A Laodicean*, that gesture of fun against pain and the threat of oblivion.

15

Wimborne and Two on a Tower

For all his insistence that the human circumstance had something wrong and unjust about it, an almost fatal illness failed to dampen Tom's essentially good humour. Nor had the kind of gloom that characterizes *Tess* and *Jude* set in. The good humour came, mainly, from the decision to get out of London and from his sense of gratitude to Emma for enabling him to carry out his obligations to the European *Harper's*. Even in January 1881 he had been gaining confidence, and gaily noted that when one was confined to bed the 'skin gets fair: corns take their leave . . . Keys get rusty; watch dim, boots mildewed . . . children seen through the window are grown taller'.

Only twelve days before making that entry in his notebook (31 January), he had sent a note to Bowker inviting the American to call upon him on 'any afternoon that is convenient to you'. As he was still confined to bed, this gives the lie to Millgate's assertion that he had been deceitful to Bowker. Tom had been anxious to demonstrate that work on his novel really was going on. On 15 February he wrote to Bowker again, to say that 'ill or well I shall be glad to see you'. Meanwhile he had noted the passing of both George Eliot and Carlyle 'into nescience' . . . while I have been lying in here', and confirmed his non-political stance ('Conservatism is not estimable in itself, or Radicalism'). His friend the mathematician George Greenhill called on 21 February, and they had some fun when he explained the principles of flight to Emma, in the course of which he proposed to transform her into a 'flying person'. By 27 March Tom had sufficient energy to plan a 'Homeric Ballad' about Napoleon, which notion, he says, was 'superseded' by another idea:

> Mode for a Historical drama. Action mostly automatic, reflex movement, etc. Not the result of what is called *motive*, although always ostensibly so, even to the actors' own consciousness. Apply an enlargement of these theories to, say, 'The Hundred Days'!

He added that this note was 'apparently, Hardy's first written idea of a philosophic scheme or framework as the larger feature of *The Dynasts*, enclosing the historic scenes'.

By 6 April the only reason he was not going out was the east wind; but by the 18th he told Kegan Paul that he was going out for an hour a day '& am getting on nicely'. He must have been further reassured by his consultation on 3 May with the eminent surgeon Sir Henry Thompson, recommended to him by Kegan Paul. Evidently Thompson, one of whose specialities was the removal of gall, kidney and bladder stones, could not find anything amiss. The question of whether Tom's sexual capability was affected by this illness has, naturally enough, been raised. Obviously intercourse would have been ruled out while he was bleeding, and perhaps while he was confined to bed. But the bleeding could not have lasted long. It has been suggested that 'he may have found the act of intercourse so liable to bring on a painful attack as to amount to a form of impotence'; but the writer of those words cannot have experienced a stone himself, since sufferers are obliged to abstain only for the brief periods when the urinary tract is inflamed. Otherwise nature proves strong enough to overcome the fear of further inflammation – which seldom materializes.

On 20 April Tom wrote to his landlord to give his notice. He was still resting for most of the time, and therefore still meditating. On 9 May, in trying to 'reconcile a scientific view of life with the emotional and spiritual, so that they may not be interdestructive', he came to the following conclusion:

General Principles. Law has produced in man a child who cannot but constantly reproach its parent for doing much and yet not all, and constantly say to such parent that it would have been better never to have begun doing than to have *over*done so indecisively; that is, than to have created so far beyond all apparent first intention (on the emotional side), without mending matters by a second intent and execution, to eliminate the evils of the blunder of overdoing. The emotions have no place in a world of defect, and it is a cruel injustice that they should have developed in it.

If Law itself had consciousness, how the aspect of its creatures would terrify it, fill it with remorse!

This was to be the theme of his next novel, in which mere 'emotion' was to be put at the mercy of 'scientific' nature, and to be dwarfed by it. His acute sense of justice, which went around with him as an unshakeable conviction, was outraged at the co-existence of defect, by which he meant cruelty, and the capacity to be wounded by it.

One sunny May morning he went to Wandsworth Common, where, all alone, he 'repeated out loud to himself' these lines from Gray's 'Ode on the Pleasure Arising from Vicissitude':

> See the wretch, that long has tost
>   On the thorny bed of Pain,
> At length repair his vigour lost,
>   And breathe and walk again:
> The meanest flowret of the vale,
> The simplest note that swells the gale,
> The common Sun, the air, and skies,
> To him are opening Paradise.

Thus he really was thankful for his recovery. But he could not, like so many before and after him, reconcile the notion of a good God and an evil world.

Towards the end of May he and Emma left London for Dorset, where they searched for an agreeable house: they had

> concluded that it would be better to make London a place of sojourn for a few months only in each year, and establish their home in the county, both for reasons of health and mental inspiration, Hardy finding, or thinking that he found, that residence in a city tended to force mechanical and ordinary productions from his pen, concerning ordinary society-life and habits.

The night of 25 June they spent, for the first time, at Lanherne, a pleasant detached house which they had found in The Avenue at Wimborne Minster in east Dorset, near Bournemouth. This was not the part of the county to which Tom was most used, or loved best, but he took care to explore the area in the two years he spent there. On that day, too, they saw from their small conservatory the 'new comet', Tebbutt's, which was expected to appear again in the fourth millennium. Hardy, always a keen amateur astronomer, must have been delighted. At the new house Emma had a proper garden, always a matter of importance to her; when they moved in it was already stocked with plenty of fruit and 'all sorts of old-fashioned flowers'.

A drawing by Hardy of his birthplace at Bockhampton in Dorset.

Hardy at nineteen.

William Barnes, Hardy's true mentor.

Emma Gifford in 1870.

Hardy's house in Trinity Road, Tooting, photographed in 1944.

Perhaps the most eloquent of all the photographs taken of Hardy.

Max Gate in 1919.

A reconstruction of Hardy's study, housed in the museum at Dorchester.

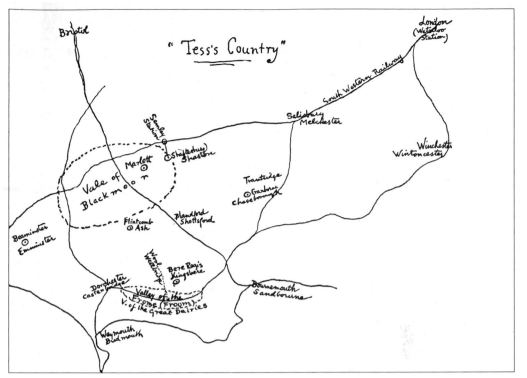

Hardy's own map of Tess' country, reproduced in *Harper's* in 1925.

A key scene from *Tess*, drawn by Hubert Herkomer for the *Graphic*, 1891.

Hardy as perceived by Spy, 1892.

Within a day or two of their arrival Tom was writing on 29 June to his cousin John Antell, a local poet, on the subject of the tombstone of his father, of the same name, who had died three years previously and had been married to Hardy's aunt Mary Hand. This was the alcoholic cobbler whose unhappy attempts to educate himself made a small contribution to the character of Jude Fawley. Since Tom is supposed to have ignored his relatives at Puddletown, it is as well to note that John is addressed by his Christian name and that the letter ends 'kind regards to all'. He told Antell that he had come down 'for the air', which was 'considered necessary' to his 'complete restoration'. There was never any assumption that they would stay at Wimborne; it seems that even then they were waiting to go ahead to build in Dorchester.

Wimborne is much larger than Sturminster Newton – so it was perhaps a deliberate choice to avoid too great a contrast in social life after London; Tom did not want to become a recluse. That year he and Emma got to know the Scottish baronet, landowner and romance writer Sir George Douglas; his brother Robert was at Wimborne studying land agency, and Emma had allowed him the use of some stables at the bottom of her garden. Douglas was a poor novelist, whose romances and verse probably found publishers because he was a baronet rather than because he had any merit. But Emma seems to have liked him, and his wife; they remained leading acquaintances, and Douglas proved a reliable friend. He was, however, a little pompous – and canny and pawky with it. Behind Emma's back he mentioned that Tom gave a deference to her views which he thought they did not deserve – but he was no judge, and he had not contributed to *A Laodicean*.

On Tom's side there was some reserve: as Millgate has noted, he could hardly conceal his contempt for Douglas' literary productions, and (although this is more controversial) he seems to have used Douglas himself as a model for some aspects of the character of Donald Farfrae in *The Mayor of Casterbridge*. Unlike Farfrae, though, Douglas did possess a Scottish home, Springwood Park, near Kelso, where he lived for some of his time. Before meeting Tom he had addressed a sonnet to him, as the author of *Far From the Madding Crowd*, beginning 'Yours is the empire of an Arcady/More precious than the dreamland of the Greek'.

There were other friends too, closer to home, such as the retired judge Tindal-Atkinson, who 'took care that they should not mope if dinners and his and his daughter's music could prevent it'. Tom joined the local Shakespeare Reading Society, and made amiable fun of it in the *Life*. Alas, he was noted as a poor, expressionless reader of the parts assigned to him. He was also, by late October 1881, offering to do all he could to help the Society for the Protection of Ancient Buildings 'in the matter of the Minster' which is Wimborne's most famous feature.

In August and early September he and Emma made a short tour of Scotland, where they met an old guide who told them that he remembered Sir Walter Scott. On his return Tom corrected the proofs for the volume version of *A Laodicean*, which was brought out by Sampson, Low, the publishers of the European *Harper's*. It was not a success. But this time he did not complain about the poor reviews. He must have been amused by the one in the *Athenaeum*, however, which remarked that the gymnastic episode 'will displease many readers' (this reviewer gave the game away by comparing it to the story of Gyges, whose wife was finally naked, rather than merely in skin-tight clothing), and added that, while Mr Hardy was not 'in the least degree a fleshly writer', he nevertheless had a 'way of insisting on the physical attractions of a woman which, if imitated by weaker writers, may prove offensive'. In other words, the pornographers whose works were no doubt familiar to this reviewer might well study Hardy's novels with a view to improving upon their own. As to what was 'offensive' about the physical attractions of a woman, we may be sure that Tom did not know.

Despite his uncomplaining stance, Tom cannot have been pleased by the review attacking *A Laodicean* in *Harper's*, which had, after all, published it. He was, therefore, doubly interested when in late September he was approached by Thomas Bailey Aldrich (1836–1907), the editor of the *Atlantic Monthly*, which sold in London as well as in America. Aldrich was in certain respects one of the most suitable editors Tom ever had. He was by no means the intellectual equivalent of Leslie Stephen, but he did understand something that Stephen did not – the difficulties facing conscientious writers of fiction. By 13 January 1882 Tom had come to terms with Aldrich for a novel of eight instalments, to begin in the May number. The sum he received seems to be unknown, but it is not likely to have been much less than £800 for the serial rights alone.

Resident in Boston, Aldrich had only recently taken over the *Atlantic Monthly* from William Dean Howells. For the next decade he was to prove a stickler for 'Boston-plated' propriety. Although he and his printers did not bowdlerize *Two on a Tower* to any great extent, he did complain that Hardy, asked for a 'family story', had replied with a 'story in the family way'. Few readers were not deeply offended, just as Tom had intended. It was not his way to attack people's foolish hypocrisies in a direct manner: he preferred the oblique approach. When accused, he then pretended to be 'as a child', and mocked their orthodoxy in his ironically outraged defences of his own 'respectability'.

When Tom signed up with Aldrich his mind had long been at work on the new book. It may even have been planned during his illness, and therefore before *A Laodicean* was finished. In July he had jotted down some notes on fiction, thinking perhaps of *A Laodicean*, of 'mechanical productions' in general, and of the book to come:

> The writer's problem is, how to strike the balance between the uncommon and the ordinary so as on the one hand to give interest, on the other to give reality.
>
> In working out this problem, human nature must never be made abnormal, which is introducing incredibility. The uncommonness must be in the events, not in the characters; and the writer's art lies in shaping that uncommonness while disguising its unlikelihood, if it be unlikely.

But his efforts to disguise the sexual elements in his novels, even if his readers only pretended that these were 'uncommon', were doomed to a naughtily deliberate failure. In *Two on a Tower*, a title he did not much like but had decided on before he started writing, and so stuck to, he continued to give offence to Mrs Grundy and even to less thoughtful adherents of the Established Church, who did not believe that any of its functionaries could ever be funny. He was determined to feature a child born out of wedlock, to mock, at least implicitly, any ideas of wedlock as being sacrosanct, to portray a pompous, lustful and hypocritical bishop, and to comment upon many social arrangements the wisdom of which he questioned.

Two on a Tower was in trouble almost before it left the press. For most modern critics it has remained in trouble. But it is a delightful book, rather more energetic than *A Laodicean*, and once again light-hearted in spirit until near the end. It makes no attempt to conduct itself on a high emotional plane, and is, for the most part, 'farce as tragedy': Hardy, perhaps trying to escape from the gloominess of his own 'philosophy', felt able to experiment by treating tragic themes in a light manner. To take too earnest a view of this novel, as of its predecessor, is unfairly to diminish it; to read it as if Hardy intended anything more than 'probability of character' is to misread it. It is slyly funny up to its thirty-ninth chapter (there are forty-one), and this still upsets its modern detractors, one of whom grimly says that it 'seems impossible . . . to feel confidence in the soundness of the morality' in it. This critic is horrified because Tom, in a preface answering those who had accused him of 'immorality', remarked that the offensive and deceived Bishop Helmsdale of Melchester (Salisbury) was 'every inch a gentleman': this playful remark is 'not sufficient to dispel the brutal irony,' laments Millgate – 'the position he adopts seems scarcely defensible'. If anything is clearly satirical, then surely it is this mock-conventional defence, designed to force his adversaries into silence by making it necessary for them to commit too specific indelicacies in order to sustain their attack.

Tom was by now writing short stories for both American and British magazines; it was for this reason – and because of a short visit to London with Emma in December 1881 – that he could not get down to work on *Two on a Tower* before January 1882. Story-writing always represented an interruption to whatever novel he might have on hand, but it was profitable. How seriously he took these stories is hard to say; at first he probably regarded them as potboilers, but in time he was to write five or six of the best tales in the language.

He had been pleased to rescue what he had not already used from *The Poor Man and the Lady* and print it in the *New Quarterly Magazine* in July 1878, and as five instalments in *Harper's Weekly* entitled 'An Indiscretion in the Life of an Heiress'. Since then requests had steadily increased. A long time earlier he had written 'Destiny and a Blue Cloak', a trivial tale which he never reprinted, and then, more recently, 'The Thieves Who Couldn't Help Sneezing' for a children's Christmas annual in 1877. Just before doing 'An Indiscretion' he had written 'The Impulsive Lady of Croome Castle', for Robert Buchanan's short-lived weekly *Light*, about (significantly) a marriage made by the heroine's ambitious father – as 'The Duchess of Hamptonshire', this story later formed part of his collection *A Group of Noble Dames*. Tom's first substantial story, 'The Distracted Young Preacher', had appeared in the *New Quarterly* and *Harper's* in 1878. Now, before getting down to *Two on a Tower*, he had two more commissioned stories to complete.

He had completely knuckled down to the business of being a journeyman novelist. It was nearer to poetry than practising as an architect. He could not see his way to becoming a poet and nothing else; he had failed to follow up on the success of *Far From the Madding Crowd*, and reviewers were as hostile to his cast of mind as the majority of his modern critics have been. He dreamed of making an epic success with what was to become *The Dynasts*; but meanwhile it was essential for him to continue as a novelist. The notion of creating 'Wessex', that area of imagination formed upon geographical reality, was still forming in him. This was perhaps his and Emma's main motive in making excursions into the countryside surrounding Wimborne. Some of these were undertaken in the company of members of his family (for Emma's relations with his sisters remained good), and some alone or with friends. *Two on a Tower* is more firmly and consciously set in Wessex than is *A Laodicean*: he now had its countryside all around him.

His increasingly conscious concern with the conception of 'Wessex' – which should never be confused with either the old kingdom or even with specific south-western English counties – is made further evident by the plan to write a book about Wessex in collaboration with Henry Joseph Moule, eldest brother of Horace and the watercolour mentor of his childhood. The gifted Moule was to supply the illustrations and designs, and Tom the text. The idea was Emma's, which strongly suggests that, as one who could both draw and write, at that time she lacked personal ambition. But she did start to compile a directory of the real Wessex names and their equivalents or near-equivalents in her husband's fiction. The projected book was never written, because Tom felt that it would not make enough money; nor was it a project that an author in his position could risk, since the fictional Wessex was going to be even more firmly his own than it already was.

Two on a Tower has a number of sources: its author's reading, his experience and his journeys into the countryside. Those who cannot appreciate its humour, or the manner in which sexual reality keeps rudely breaking in upon its not so innocent text, accuse it of being artificial and excessively 'got up'. But it is accomplished enough to suggest that this is not the case: that the love-astronomy theme does, for most of the time, find organic life in the language. Tom himself said, in a letter to Gosse of 4 December 1882 which accompanied a copy (in three volumes, from Sampson, Low once again), that he had wanted 'to make science, not the mere padding of a romance, but the actual vehicle of romance'. The 'execution', he admitted, had been 'hurried, & far from what I intended – but it could not be avoided'. In the 1883 one-volume edition he gratefully took up a suggestion made by Gosse, who always liked this book, to preface it with the epigraph from Crashaw's 'Love's Astrology'.

What Tom meant about unavoidable hurry was that, because the manuscript had to be sent to Boston, he had to send a duplicate (presumably carbon) copy, after the first, in case the latter should go astray – and that all this flurried and flustered him. The details are complicated and unresolved, but Gatrell has made it clear that the text as it exists is badly in need of re-editing. Emma helped him, and some twenty-eight out of 350 pages of the known manuscript are, in whole or part, in her hand. (Tom may even have made three copies, bearing in mind the one he would need for the volume publication; but no trace of a third copy has been found. However, since Swithin writes his paper on variable stars in triplicate, and sends it off to three people, it is reasonable to infer that Tom did the same with his story of Swithin.) As he confirmed on 21 January 1883 to Gosse, after receiving praise from him on the 18th:

> You are too generous when you only see slightness in the work. The truth is that, though the plan of the story was carefully thought out, the actual writing [this was finished by September 1882] was lamentably hurried – having been produced month by month, & the MS. dispatched to America, where it was printed without my seeing the proofs.

Though well aware that the novel was 'slight', he was still irritated. He had told Aldrich that he would trust him with the proofs, but, since Aldrich was for part of the time in Europe, correction (on occasion not being correction at all, but misreadings of his script) was sometimes done by the compositors. The copy for the volume edition he in fact provided from the printed serials, except that he did not have the last two numbers of the *Atlantic Monthly* to hand when he was preparing it: he then had recourse, either to the hypothetical third copy, or, more likely, to a duplicate of the copy for the seventh and eighth instalments which he had made specially for that purpose. The whole affair cost him a good deal of worry and frustration at the time, and may have caused the actual writing to be full of hidden satirical messages for the benefit of the enlightened.

Two on a Tower is markedly original along the lines that Hardy had suggested to Gosse, and in the manner of its exploitation of the ancient poetic equation between beauty and the stars – although the suggestion that it may have been sparked off by a brief passage from George Eliot's *The Mill on the Floss* is plausible. Maggie Tulliver humorously speculates, on the subject of the astronomer in the *Eton*

College Grammar who hated women, 'I suppose it's all astronomers: because, you know, they live up in high towers, and if the women came there, they might talk and hinder them from looking at the stars.' But the immediate and topical event which caught his poetic attention was the possibility of drawing symbolic capital from the transit of Venus (Goddess of Love) across the face of the sun which was due in December 1882, when the book would be out in volume form. Such transits of Mercury are relatively common, but those of Venus rare: there had been one in December 1874, and there will be no more until 2008 and 2012.

For *Two on a Tower*, which reveals the extent of his knowledge of astronomy, Tom had read Alfred Proctor's *Essays in Astronomy* (1874) and its successor *The Poetry of Astronomy* (1881). Both these were good books for their time, and made excellent supplements to his earlier study. In November or December 1881 he visited Greenwich Observatory – only by representing himself, to the Astronomer Royal, as one anxious to 'ascertain if it would be possible for him to adapt an old tower, built in the West of England for other objects, to the requirements of a telescope'.

It may well be that certain modern critics' relative ignorance of astronomy has misled them about Tom's own knowledge, which has been called 'painfully obvious' and 'off the peg'. He meditated on the subject constantly, as two poems ('In Vision I Roamed' and 'At a Lunar Eclipse' – perhaps that of 31 March, otherwise the one of 24 September 1866) demonstrate. But if you are too prosaic to be awed by the immensity of the universe and the comparative puniness of human beings, you cannot appreciate the writings of someone who was. That awe, although comically treated, is a serious ingredient in this farce-as-tragedy. This sense of immensity Swithin, though still youthfully over-enthusiastic, points out to Viviette at their second encounter, when she asks him what 'monsters' are in the sky:

> . . . Immensities. Until a person has thought out the stars and their interspaces, he has hardly learned that there are things much more terrible than monsters of shape, namely, monsters of magnitude without known shape. Such monsters are the voids and waste places of the sky . . . These are deep wells for the human mind to let itself down into . . .

In the novel, the tower itself is an Italianate one standing a few miles south of Wimborne (Hardy's Warborne) in Charborough Park, built in 1761. But, confusingly, he set this in a landscape to be found at Milbourne St Andrew, a village between Blandford and Dorchester nearer to his preferred territory, where there is a small obelisk. He visited the tower, but did not visit Charborough House – in the book Welland House, Lady Constantine's residence.

Hardy's 1895 preface opens with a famous paragraph:

> This slightly-built romance was the outcome of a wish to set the emotional history of two infinitesimal lives against the stupendous background of the stellar universe, and to impart to readers the sentiment that of these contrasting magnitudes the smaller might be the greater to them as men.

This, as bitterly ironic (even sarcastic) at the expense of human egocentricity as at the relentlessness of the universe, and reflecting Hardy's recent thoughts about its cruelty, sets the essentially comic tone: let us, it implies (in the light of what follows) experiment with laughter at the tragedy of a self-sacrificing and voluptuous woman. Thus the last sentence: 'The Bishop was avenged.' This has been much derided, and even more deplored. The dismayed Millgate, who speaks of the 'questionable morality' of Lady Constantine, asks: 'is it proper?'. But these critics fail to understand that what Hardy meant was not so much that the Bishop himself was avenged, as that crass lust posing as spirituality, pomposity, cruel arrogance and fine hypocrisy are avenged, by Viviette's death, over an unselfish love that can only cruelly be called 'improper'. Such patriarchal moralizers lack Hardy's own sense of the unjust penalty that a Victorian woman paid for any indulgence, even merely verbal, of her natural inclinations.

While he continued, in successive editions, to clarify the fact that Viviette's child is conceived *after* she is aware of the invalidity of her marriage – her desire therefore decently overriding her sense of bureaucratic propriety – Hardy wrote in the 1895 preface that he had observed 'scrupulous propriety' and that there 'is scarcely a single caress in the book outside legal matrimony'. Nothing could more clearly imply his contempt for the sort of ungenerous 'morality' which attaches importance to such matters, especially in an age when men expected their sons, as Dickens admitted, to frequent brothels. It 'maintains literal scrupulosity', Millgate declares; but he adds, despairingly, in a sentence worthy of the Bishop himself, 'it seems scarcely an adequate acknowledgement of the fact that the all-important caress during which

Swithin's son is conceived occurs precisely at a moment when the marriage is known to be invalid'. Comment is superfluous . . .

Hardy was well acquainted with the language of Shakespeare and other Elizabethan and Jacobean dramatists, and well aware, as were some Victorian critics, of its sexual allusions and obscenity. The implications of 'Th'expense of spirit in a waste of shame' did not elude him. He even made a note about an incident at one of the Shakespeare readings he was attending while writing *Two on a Tower*: 'The General reads with gingerly caution, telling me privately that he had blurted out one of Shakespeare's improprieties last time before he was aware, and is in fear and trembling lest he may do it again.' The language of the novel is far more circumspect than anything of Shakespeare's – there could be no 'large and spacious' Wills in those days – but it is as loaded with sexual allusion as it could possibly be: more so, owing to its author's restored spirits, than *A Laodicean*.

Two on a Tower has a simple plot. Lady Viviette has been unhappily married to Sir Blount, who has deserted her for the pleasures of big-game hunting in Africa. The twenty-year-old, orphaned Swithin St Cleeve, son of a peasant mother and a parson who foresook the Church for farming (Swithin is thus half a 'gentleman'), has but one interest: astronomy. This interest is so intense that he has failed to awaken to his own sexuality: 'the natural result of inexperience combined with devotion to a hobby'. In the disused tower on Sir Blount's estate, near which he lives with his grandmother, he has set up a small observatory. Just as George Somerset was a gifted architect, so is Swithin a gifted astronomer: his creator credits him with drawing, despite his extreme youth, the same inferences about variable stars as the American astronomer E.C. Pickering made in 1880, and published in a paper of 1881.

Viviette discovers the young 'Adonis-astronomer' in her tower, and, being sexually frustrated and lonely, falls in love with him – though reluctantly, and against her best intentions. The nature of Sir Blount's 'ill usage' of her is something that the narrative does its best to emphasize: she is terrified when Swithin puts on clothes which have belonged to him, and it is not too much to assume that she has known great unhappiness, and a complete lack of love or affection from her husband. She buys Swithin a large telescope, with which he makes his researches into the nature of variable stars. But on his return from posting off his paper, he collects his copy of the astronomical periodical in which Pickering published his work, and the shock causes him to collapse in the rain and become so ill that his life is despaired of. In her distress Viviette reveals her love for him; however it is not that (of which he remains entirely unaware) but the announcement of the imminent arrival of a comet which causes him to rise like a phoenix from the ashes of himself. The comet anticipates his sudden access to his sexuality and the opportunities it presents. He 'comes out of it' (as she had previously requested, although not quite realizing what she was saying) when he overhears the village people, with their down-to-earth candour, speculating about her feelings for him.

A report of Sir Blount's death in Africa seems to free Viviette from the need for her false scruples, by which the narrative demonstrates her to have been entrapped. Under Swithin's now fervid persuasions (her eyes will be his stars in the future) she secretly marries him. She agrees with the narrator that her passion for Swithin has reduced him from a good astronomer to a commonplace innamorato, but she cannot, despite her ten years' seniority, resist him. She is, however, aware of her weakness in not wishing the marriage to be generally known because of her position in the 'county', and deplores it.

Meanwhile, love and desire make Swithin 'subtle', and he learns to dissemble. But the promise of a legacy of £600 a year from an uncle, on the condition that he does not marry before the age of twenty-five, cannot deter him from going ahead – and saying nothing to Viviette about it. Hardy has some fun with the uncle's misogynistic posthumous letter, which contains many Victorian-style animadversions upon women. However, it is worth recalling that Viviette is described as 'either lover or *dévote*' (devout or pious), and that this is passed over almost affectionately by the narrator:

> she vibrated so gracefully between these two conditions that nobody who knew the circumstances could have condemned her inconsistencies . . . it was, after all, but Convention's palpitating attempt to preserve the comfort of her creature's conscience in the trying quandary to which the conditions of sex had given rise.

Was Emma Hardy even now beginning to show at least certain tendencies towards 'piety', towards the kind of orthodoxy which Tom – for all his admitted 'churchiness' and outward observation of the conventions – could only condemn? And was he, at least for the time being, disposed to excuse this lapse, as he would have seen it, by explaining it in terms of the cruel restrictions imposed by society (whose arrangements he was satirizing in this very novel) upon her sex? The split between them, which came decisively in the next decade, must have had some beginning; but at Wimborne it can be assumed that they were still sleeping together, so that he would not have felt too frustrated. The novel contains discussion of Viviette's piety and apparently orthodox social attitudes, suggesting that Emma's direction in these respects was worrying him, or at least that, in tracing Viviette's thoughts as she seeks to release Swithin from his marriage to her, he was labouring to understand – sympathetically – the roots of Emma's increasingly theological outlook.

No sooner have the couple been married than Hardy introduces his 'villain', Louis Glanville, Viviette's elder brother, already disliked by her as casual, 'vexatious and indolent'. Louis – more unpleasant and unscrupulous than villainous – has already caused the marriage to take place early, by announcing his arrival by letter. In ignorance of her state, he wishes her to make a marriage to the Bishop, solely so that he might benefit.

The degree of Viviette's outward subservience to this selfish brother is deliberately made painful to read; her deference to Bishop Helmsdale's office, on the contrary, is presented without comment – although she admits to Swithin that he has deficiencies of character. The Bishop does propose marriage ('my earnest hope is that a mind comprehensive as yours will perceive the immense power for good that you might exercise in the position in which a union with me would place you'), and she refuses him.

Just as she has done so, report of the real circumstances of her husband's death come through: it had occurred, as the plot demands, after her marriage to Swithin, which is thus invalidated. The details of Sir Blount's demise are farcical: having himself committed bigamy by marrying a native princess according to 'the rites of the tribe', he took to drinking deeper than ever, and shot himself in a fit of depression. Swithin deems himself ready to legalize the marriage immediately; but, now learning that he can enjoy his annuity of £600 if he does not, Viviette has scruples about his future. Feeling that he is but a boy whom she has kidnapped for her own amorous reasons, she decides to sacrifice her own happiness for the sake of his future. But at their last meeting she yields to her passion for him, and a child is conceived. She tries to catch up with Swithin, but he has left.

Now follows what offended and still offends: the deceit of the Bishop. This is arranged, even to the Bishop's call upon her with the renewal of his proposal, by the cynical Louis. She considers it in the following terms:

> Hitherto there had seemed to her dismayed mind. unenlightened as to any course save one of honesty, no possible achievement of *both* her desires – the saving of Swithin and the saving of herself. But behold, here was a way! A tempter had shown it to her. It involved a great wrong, which to her had quite obscured its feasibility. But she perceived now that it was indeed a way. Convention was forcing her hand at this game; and to what will not convention compel her weaker victims, in extremes?

Viviette, wanting to redress the wrong to which she feels she has subjected Swithin, wishes to do him good. At the same time she wishes to preserve her own good name (and, it should not be forgotten, the future good name of her as yet unborn child). As Hardy has taken the immense trouble to engineer it, the only 'wrong' that she has done in the entire course of her affair with Swithin is to have yielded to him, once, when she knew that she was not married to him. And she did that after being perfectly used to making love with him as one married to him.

Only the most uncharitable critic would blame her for this, since it is a matter of ill luck and false report. Yet one modern critic is so insensitive that he can happily remark upon her 'questionable morality'! No wonder Tom was concerned at the lack of charity in human social arrangements. He was not attacking the customs themselves, but the cruel manner in which they were interpreted. 'I have done a desperate thing,' Viviette explains to Swithin in a letter. 'Yet for myself I could do no better . . . I was not alone concerned. What woman has a right to blight a coming life to preserve her personal integrity?'

'Surely,' commented the *Saturday Review*, 'we have not spoken a whit too harshly in calling this a most repellent incident, which the author was extremely ill advised to include in the scheme of his plot.' Henry Quilter in the *Spectator* objected to the 'mingling of passion, religion, and false self-sacrifice' in Viviette's feelings for Swithin: 'very near to the repulsive . . . objectionable without truth'. But Tom had been deliberately 'ill-advised', not only because he enjoyed – perhaps over-perversely for one who, after all, preferred a quiet life – provoking ugly displays of Helmsdale-like outbursts of morality, but also because he hoped that someone might comment upon the cruelty of convention in its forcing of a woman into a repulsive marriage and into deceit! In fact, her second (or third) marriage does prove, in the report of the kindly village parson, Torkingham, to have been little better than the first: the Bishop had been 'arrogant' and wanting in 'temperate discretion', he tells Swithin upon his return from the Cape.

Apart from many appreciative letters which Tom told Gosse he had received – they included one from Kegan Paul applauding what he, a parson, saw as the delicious joke against the Bishop – Havelock Ellis, almost alone among reviewers, could appreciate Viviette; but even he said that he preferred Proctor for astronomy, and did not think the book important. Ellis, however, was to become the pioneer English sexologist of his time, was to have his *Psychology of Sex* banned and maligned, and was to enjoy – and describe – being pissed on by the American poetess Hilda Doolittle. It is intriguing to conjecture quite what Tom would have made of this now celebrated episode. Would he have pronounced it 'a most repellent incident'? I doubt it. I think he would have said that there is no accounting for taste.

The last two chapters of *Two on a Tower*, by contrast to most of what precedes them, are poignant. Swithin, 'too literal, direct and uncompromising in nature to understand such a woman as Lady Constantine', gradually forgets her, even though he remains loyal to her in his intentions and has genuinely tender feelings for her in her predicament. When he hears, through a newspaper, that his son has been born, and again when he hears of the death of the Bishop at the age of fifty-four, he has got beyond passion. Women, as he slowly completes his astronomical work at the Cape, become 'no more to him than the inhabitants of Jupiter', although he is occasionally tormented by 'the ghostly finger of limitless vacancy' in the southern skies. When he gets home he sees Viviette, and at once realizes that he loves her no longer. She seems like an old woman to him (although she is but thirty-five); while he has turned into a 'scientist', and there is now 'something in' his 'inexorably simple logic which partakes of the cruelty of [the] natural laws' which he studies. Yet he determines to marry her, to act with 'loving-kindness' towards her: he kisses her, and tells her so.

Hardy now reverses the plot of the most famous of the 'novels of sentiment' of the previous century, Henry Mackenzie's enormously popular *The Man of Feeling* (1771), in which the hero, Harley, falls dead when he learns that his love is returned: Viviette's heart gives way from joy, and she dies. It is made evident that Swithin's future lies with his contemporary, the village organist Tabitha Lark, who has always been attracted by him: she will, she tells him, be glad to act as 'amanuensis' for him in the enormous task of rearranging and recopying the 'voluminous notes' he has amassed in the course of his 'great undertaking'.

Although *Two on a Tower* cannot fairly be criticized for the injustice to which its plot draws attention, it may certainly be found wanting. The descent into poignancy is too abrupt: the tragic weight of this descent can hardly be borne by its generally comical, even farcical, structure. Viviette could have been a truly tragic figure; and it is evident, from *Tess* and elsewhere, that Hardy was fully capable of giving her more substance. The reader is intrigued, too, by the perhaps equally tragic transformation of the young Adonis–astronomer into a mere scientist whose sexual needs are going to be somewhat mechanically served by an 'amanuensis'. Yet Swithin's change from ecstatic boy to hard-faced Darwinian lacks psychological substance. Tom sent off the last instalment to Aldrich in mid-September 1882: he was in a hurry to take a trip to France, and, as Millgate rightly says of at least this portion of the novel, did not give it his 'full creative attention'. It begins to falter soon after the point at which Viviette and Swithin are 'married'. The finely bawdy subtext ceases too hastily, and, although he knew that only one in a thousand of his readers could follow it, Tom was struggling after that point: this exercise had buoyed him up and satisfied his sense of fun. Doubtless he was celebrating his own newly found enjoyment of a lovemaking which had been impossible or difficult for several months.

T.R. Wright, in his *Hardy and the Erotic* (1989), might be thought merely tiresome when he describes the landscape of *Two on a Tower* as 'sexually symbolic . . . dominated by a "tower in the form of a classical column" which "rises to a considerable height" over its surrounding firs'. But Hardy himself, in this instance, was wholly conscious of what he was doing – even if the snook he was cocking at the Grundyans and their earnest successors was private to himself (was Emma in on it?).

The main joke is Swithin's slow arousal – an old enough theme in literature. John Bayley has drawn attention to the manner in which even the couple's first night of marriage is given an extra 'erotic charge' by the way in which the following chapter opens: 'When Lady Constantine awoke the next morning Swithin was nowhere to be seen.' She is not, of course, 'Lady Constantine' any more – but Hardy thus 'contrives to make marriage seem more shocking, or more romantic, than living in sin'.

Hardy's well-hidden *doubles ententes* are to be found, however, almost from the beginning of the book. If as modern readers we think that he was too gleeful in carrying out this exercise, we must bear in mind the force of his response to the bawdiness of Elizabethan and Jacobean language, particularly to that of *Measure for Measure*, to which he refers twice in the text – and, of course, to the absurd nature and extent of Victorian prudery. Viviette is bored and sexually frustrated, but in Hardy's day the attribution of such feelings as lust, to a woman in particular, were entirely *verboten*, so her tower, as she strolls around it, is presented as an 'aspiring piece of masonry, erected as the most conspicuous and ineffaceable reminder of a man that could be thought of' – it is a memorial to one of Sir Blount's ancestors. She comes upon the flaxen-haired Adonis, and the narrator comments:

> He was a youth who might properly be characterized by a word the judicious chronicler would not readily use in such a connexion, preferring to reserve it for raising images of the opposite sex. Whether because no deep felicity is likely to arise from the condition, or from any other reason, to say in these days that a youth is beautiful is not to award him that amount of credit which the expression would have carried with it had he lived in the times of the Classical Dictionary. So much, indeed, is the reverse the case that the assertion creates an awkwardness in saying anything more about him.

No wonder Gosse, a covert homosexual, enjoyed this novel! Tom was writing only some three years before Henry Labourchere tabled his infamous Amendment, or 'Blackmailers' Charter', which made homosexuality illegal: this is his ironic comment on the atmosphere which enabled the 'viper' (as Prince Albert called him, although not in that connection) to get it through the Commons. Oscar Wilde, and many others, thus found 'no deep felicity' from their attribution of beauty to young men . . .

Throughout the novel Hardy counterpointed the cold astronomical imagery, representing 'nature's cruel laws', with the hotness of the lovers' desires: thus he hoped to make his point that the emotions have no place in 'a world of defect'. So Swithin is looking through his telescope at the 'catastrophe' of a 'cyclone in the sun' when Viviette first meets him, this cyclone being a metaphor for her own sexual susceptibility.

There is more of this kind of bawdry, culminating in the scene when he shows her the new telescope (of whose usual angle Hardy was undoubtedly aware) which she has bought for him. The wood cabin which is to be the scene of all their lovemaking, and in which their child is conceived, is described as being 'not unlike a bathing-machine without wheels' – the bathing-machine being a place where women undress. Since the new telescope, a 'magnificent object', is mounted upon an equatorial, the dome of the tower runs 'on the [iron] balls with a rumble like thunder'. Viviette tells Swithin that he must 'accept it all' as a present for his forthcoming birthday: 'The possession of these apparatus would only compromise me.' Her appropriation (as she comes in time to feel that it has been) of the 'apparatus' does indeed 'compromise' her! 'Already they are reputed to be yours, and they must be made yours.' 'I wish I could do something for you!' expostulates the youth, still completely unaware of Viviette's state of mind, although her voice has just 'lost some firmness'.

> '. . . I shall never marry'.
> 'Why not?'
> 'A beloved science is enough wife for me – combined, perhaps, with a little warm friendship with one of kindred pursuits.'
> 'Who is the friend of kindred pursuits?'
> 'Yourself I should like it to be.'
> 'You would have to become a woman before I could be that, publicly; or I a man,' she replied, with dry melancholy.
> 'Why I a woman, or you a man, dear Lady Constantine?'
> 'I cannot explain. No; you must keep your fame and your science all to yourself, and I must keep – my troubles.'
> Swithin, to divert her from melancholy – not knowing that in the expression of her melancholy thus and now she found much pleasure, – changed the subject by asking if they should take some observations.
> 'Yes, the scenery is well hung tonight,' she said, looking out upon the heavens.

The expression 'well hung' (still current as 'sexually well endowed') occurs in Egan's 1823 edition of Grose's *Dictionary of the Vulgar Tongue*, with which Tom, as one of the most famous living masters of dialect, would have been familiar. He hardly means us to believe that Viviette would have known it (unless the loathsome Sir Blount had told it to her, while drunkenly pointing at his grossly expanded member; perhaps this was the occasion, referred to in the text, when he put her out of the house after she had refused his horrible attentions); what Tom is doing here is having some fun at the expense of those whom he regarded as his enemies, but who believed him to be a misguided rather than a 'fleshly' writer. Swithin keeps a silence of ten minutes, while he studies the skies through his new 'magnificent instrument'. She lays her hand upon his arm, and he interrupts himself with an 'almost painful' effort. "'Do come out of it," she coaxed, with a softness in her voice which any man but the unpractised Swithin would have felt to be exquisite. "I feel that I have been so foolish as to put in your hands an instrument to effect my own annihilation."' This is exactly what 'the instrument' does.

As he wrote these words, Emma had some months to go before she would reach her forty-second birthday, on 24 November 1882. In 1856 Jemima Hardy had, at the age of forty-three, given birth to Tom's sister, Kate. Did Tom and Emma still hope that, relaxed and on an excursion to Paris where they would try to live like natives, in an apartment and not in a hotel (hotels put many women off lovemaking), she might conceive just such 'a lovely little fellow' as Tom had described in *Two on a Tower*?

16

Dorchester

There was to be no full-length book for over three years. But when *The Mayor of Casterbridge* came – it began serialization in the *Graphic* on 2 January 1886, and was published by Smith, Elder in two volumes on 10 May of that year – it was, arguably, the best novel Hardy had yet written. It was a long time in gestation, and the work was constantly interrupted until he eventually finished it in April 1885.

In his own words, 'he seems to have done little in the French capital', apart from buying, with Emma, 'groceries and vegetables, dining at restaurants, and catching bad colds owing to the uncertain weather'. They took a 'little *appartement* of two bedrooms and a sitting room, near the left bank of the Seine', and stayed there for 'some weeks'. During all those weeks – the main purpose of which, as I have suggested, may have been for Emma to conceive a child – Tom made 'only one memorandum', which, although a generalization in itself, could be connected with such a purpose without undue strain:

> Since I discovered, several years ago, that I was living in a world where nothing bears out in practice what it promises incipiently, I have troubled myself very little about theories . . . Where develop-ment according to perfect reason is limited to the narrow region of pure mathematics, I am content with tentativeness from day to day.

Whether they ever consulted anyone, even a doctor, about their difficulties is unknown. They were in any case to be disappointed, and the effects of this disappointment upon their marriage, and upon Emma's well-being, have been under-estimated. The much-aired notion that Tom was 'responsible' for Emma's failure to conceive, in the sense that he was in some way impotent, has no more merit than any other random suggestion that any childless man is impotent. This does not mean that Emma, as she grew older and increasingly embittered by her childlessness, did not begin, irrationally and unconsciously, to

296

blame him for it. If they did obtain advice, it would have consisted of instructions to do exactly what they intelligently did: relax, go away on holiday together, keep away from whatever irritated them. Tom says that they kept 'away from English and American tourists, roved about the city . . . studying the pictures' – acted, in other words, as casually as they could, and enjoyed each other's company rather than anyone else's.

On their return Emma heard of the death of her agreeable brother-in-law, the Rev. Cadell Holder. Tom, who had liked him, devoted two pages of the *Life* to reminiscences of him. (From these pages, Florence excised a sizeable paragraph relating an anecdote which she or her advisors thought indelicate, since it concerned pregnancy.) Tom's words imply that they may, although retrospectively, have regarded Holder's death, together with the failure of their mission to France, as another milestone marking the decline of their relationship: 'they realized that the scene of the fairest romance of their lives, in the picturesque land of Lyonnesse, would have no more kinship with them'. When in London on 24 June 1883, just before they left Wimborne to live in Dorchester, he had noted that Lady Duff-Gordon was 'emphatically in the family way', perhaps indicating that this desirable condition had recently been on his mind (Florence, as might have been expected, cut this from the *Life*).

As early as March 1882 they had decided to leave their temporary accommodation at Wimborne. On the 21st Tom had written to the Land Steward of the Earl of Ilchester asking about the price of a 'freehold plot' on his land at Stinsford Hill. In December he told Gosse that the Wimborne house was 'rather too near the Stour level for health'. Even before setting out for Paris ('playing truant') in October 1882 they had taken a 'small circular tour of the adjoining counties'. This little journey was the occasion on which they met an old man, at Lyme, who had reversed his trousers 'because the knees had worn through'.

During 1883, learning to milk the market, Tom was busy with short stories. On 15 January he told the by now well-established authors' agent A.P. Watt that he was 'unable to make an engagement for another story this year'. 'The Three Strangers', one of his best, appeared in *Longman's* and *Harper's* for March 1883. In February he sent off the long story 'The Romantic Adventures of a Milkmaid' to the *Graphic*, where it appeared in the special twice-yearly supplement that summer. Thus began a nine-year association with the *Graphic*: only *The Woodlanders*, in this period, did not first appear in its pages. Despite all the precautions taken by Harper's, the American publisher of 'The Romantic Adventures of a Milkmaid', Tom had to endure its frequent pirating there: he was eventually forced to improve his copyright position, collecting it in *A Changed Man*, although he thought little of it – 'written only with a view of fleeting life in a periodical'.

It has been called his most deliberately unrealistic piece of prose fiction. Yet even here he juxtaposed elements of the fairy story (Margery Tucker, the milkmaid of the title, has her wish to attend a ball granted by a mysterious and decidedly Gothic baron) with careful rural realism. Though slight, it is a thoroughly professional piece of work, such as he could hardly have brought off five years earlier; it is also, with its fantastic plot, mostly hinging on the vagaries of fate, quite an effective joke at the expense of the expectations of the more conventional readers of the *Graphic*. Tom patterned the plot so as not to offend Arthur Locker, its editor: he gave it a happy ending, in which the Byronic Baron von Xanten overcomes his worst desires, to carry Margery off away from her lime-burner lover. But in a typically provocative note of 1927 he stated that, in his original conception, the girl did disappear for ever – aboard the Baron's yacht. All he mischievously did in successive revisions, however, was to make Margery's susceptibility to the Baron more explicit. In one way this story anticipates *The Mayor of Casterbridge*: Margery marries Jim in the full knowledge that, for her, he is only second best as a lover. That is exactly what Elizabeth Jane does when she marries Farfrae.

So Hardy might be seen, at this point, as marking time. But an anecdote rightly reported by Millgate as 'worth recording' suggests otherwise. A cook in their service at Wimborne is said to have described to her new employers 'how Hardy would spend much time in the kitchen, smiling at the servants and encouraging them to talk, and then disappear into his study . . . and write for the rest of the day, ignoring even mealtimes'. He was thinking a good deal, in particular about his political stance and as novelist of Wessex.

The previous year the novelist Mrs Oliphant had invited him to contribute a 'sketch or series of sketches', as he put it to her in his letter of 22 July 1882, about the 'labouring poor of this my native county'. He had, he told her, often thought of taking them 'seriously', and had once gone 'so far as to write out a list of headings for sections of the subject'. But, he continued, he was 'so hopelessly behindhand with the less substantial productions that editors demand of me' that he had no leisure for the work – 'much as I should like it for a change'.

He felt impelled, though, to express himself on the subject after subsequent pressure from Charles J. Longman: an article entitled 'The Dorsetshire Labourer' appeared in *Longman's* in July 1883. It displays, above all, Tom's quietly realistic attitude towards his fictional subjects. Always averse to aligning himself with political parties, he preferred to comment on affairs from the doctrinally, if not morally, neutral position of the person who judges matters on their merits. But the National Agricultural Labourers' Union leader Joseph Arch – regarded by many as a dangerous and dishonest agitator after the unsuccessful Suffolk strike of 1874 – had succeeded for a time in increasing agricultural wages, and even the Liberal Party had just committed itself to extending the franchise to rural workers. Tom knew that whatever he said might be taken amiss not only by the many critics generally hostile to his candour, but also by those whom he regarded as friends, with whom he had no desire to discuss politics. Far from wishing to be 'a prophet and leader of his generation', as Gittings suggests, he wanted to lead a quiet life. Few 'prophets' and 'leaders' have been as reticent in their expression of direct opinion on specific topical events. But he was dedicated to the truth as he saw it, because he had an elevated notion of the poet's calling. Writing to John Morley on 25 July 1883, just after 'The Dorsetshire Labourer' had appeared, he said that although he was 'a Liberal', he had 'endeavoured to describe the state of things without political bias'.

In 'The Dorsetshire Labourer' Hardy sticks as far as possible to his own business. His tone is only moderately ironic; the text is never 'condescending' towards its subject, as it has been called – though without a single example being given. Doubtless recalling the occasion upon which Leslie Stephen had tactlessly suggested that he might like to write sketches about 'Hodge', he begins by attacking this absurd peasant stereotype. He had in mind, too, Richard Jefferies' recent and much discussed book, *Hodge and his Masters*. In the *Life* he recalls meeting Jefferies in 1880, its year of publication. He refers to him as 'a modest young man then getting into notice, as a writer, through having published his first book, entitled *The Gamekeeper at Home*'. That book, subtitled 'Sketches of Natural History and Rural Life', had appeared in 1878, and was in fact by no means Jefferies' first book, but it is true that *The Gamekeeper* brought him to public notice. Tom appreciated his powers of observation, for Jefferies had grown up on a farm and, as well as being a visionary in his fiction, he wrote with a fine unsentimental accuracy about the Wiltshire scene which he knew best.

The gently ironic tone of 'The Dorsetshire Labourer' as a whole, and its main preoccupation, are exemplified in the following paragraph:

The pleasures enjoyed by the Dorset labourer may be far from the pleasures of the highest kind desirable for him. They may be pleasures of the wrong shade. And the inevitable glooms of a straitened hard-working life occasionally enwrap him from such pleasures as he has; and in times of special storm and stress the 'Complaint of Piers the Ploughman' is still echoed in his heart. But even Piers had his flights of merriment and humour; and ploughmen as a rule do not give sufficient thought to the morrow to be miserable when not in physical pain. Drudgery in the slums and alleys of a city, too long pursued, and accompanied as it too often is by indifferent health, may induce a mood of despondency which is well-nigh permanent; but the same degree of drudgery in the fields results at worst in a mood of painless passivity. A pure atmosphere and a pastoral environment are a very appreciable portion of the sustenance which tends to produce the sound mind and body, and thus much sustenance is, at least, the labourer's birthright.

In such sentences as the first one quoted above, Hardy is being critical of the kind of minds which, in their turn, objected to him as being of an 'immoral' tendency. When country people's pleasures are depicted in the novels, they are depicted with gusto, and with no sense that they are in any way 'undesirable' or of 'the wrong shade'.

The expression of Hardy's feelings about life in town as distinct from country is scarcely unexpected. But it cannot be assumed that, because he deplored town life, he thought that the process of urbanization could be reversed. Men of later generations than his have also deplored it. Claude Lévi-Strauss has written of the manner in which urban life attracts evil consequences: he speaks of the 'outbreaks of stupidity, hatred and credulousness which social groups secrete like pus when they begin to be short of space'. Hardy would most probably have agreed. But Lévi-Strauss has not advocated that this dreadful process 'should be' reversed: like Hardy, he knows that only some grand natural disaster could check it, if perhaps never the selfishness and greed that cause it.

It is not a question of Hardy's being 'progressive': he was only cautious about expressing his pastoralism and his pessimism. His general view is echoed in a note of 26 April 1883, written when he was thinking specifically of the Dorset workers: 'Rural low life may reveal coarseness of considerable leaven; but that libidinousness which makes the scum of cities so noxious is not usually there.' He did not want people in towns and cities to be unhappy, but saw that they must be. Thus he is realistic in his general assessment of the labourer's lot. He points out that the 'regular farmer's labourers' are better off than the 'unattached labourers', who are 'out of sight of patronage; and to be out of sight is to be out of mind when misfortune arises, and pride or sensitiveness leads them to conceal their privations'.

'The Dorsetshire Labourer' goes on to criticize the presumptions of those who 'look down upon' a class 'from the Olympian heights of society'. Such people equate squalor with 'the misery of the labouring classes'. Throughout the essay the emphasis is upon the facts rather than upon any polemic about them. Joseph Arch is discreetly praised as a 'humourist', but for what he achieved rather than for his motives or his political views. Hardy, who had heard him speak, casually refers to him as 'that agitator' – probably with a few of his angrier friends in mind. His 'bias', as it would be called by some, is evident: he deplores the shift to the towns, and finds it 'poignant'. The terrible results of it – as depicted in the world of Mixen Lane in *The Mayor of Casterbridge* – he saves for fiction, and even there he is content to leave his own 'impressions' to his reader's judgement. And in any case, readers might ask, where is it better to be unhappy – in Mixen Lane or in the countryside? Those who have found the undoubted 'impartialities' of 'The Dorsetshire Labourer' too 'strenuous' have failed to discern two important factors: Hardy's distaste for over-simplified polemic, and his irony. The latter is apparent in such sentences as

> . . . the reflection is forced upon everyone who thinks of the matter, that if a farmer can afford to pay thirty per cent more wages in times of agricultural depression than he paid in times of agricultural prosperity, and yet live, and keep a carriage, while the landlord still thrives on the reduced rent which has resulted, the labourer must have been greatly wronged in those prosperous times. That the maximum of wage has been reached for the present is, however, pretty clear; and indeed it should be added that on several farms the labourers have submitted to a slight reduction during the past year, under stress of representations which have appeared reasonable.

It is the words 'stress' and 'appeared' that offer the key to Hardy's 'impartiality', which he surely did not have to work too 'strenuously' to achieve.

He ends with two paragraphs which are more evidently emotionally charged than the rest of the piece. The first explains that villages used to contain, 'in addition to the agricultural inhabitants, an interesting and better-informed class . . . who had remained in the houses where they were born for no especial reason beyond an instinct of association with the spot'. They were the 'liviers', life-holders, whose cottages – originally built, as the house of Bockhampton had been, at their own expense – were now being pulled down by all but a few philanthropic landlords as soon as they 'fell in'. So (and this is the bitter heart of the matter): 'The occupants who formed the backbone of the village life have to seek refuge in the boroughs.'

Hardy has little time for the 'statisticians' who speak of the 'tendency of the rural population towards the large towns'. It is rather, he thinks, in an emotional image that would be quite alien to a statistician, 'the tendency of water to flow uphill when forced'. It is inconceivable that Hardy believed that the pulling down of cottages was the only cause of the drift towards the towns, but it was a cause that he had himself seen, and it moved his common sense as well as his sense of justice. In so far as history is largely a story of a few power- or money-greedy people manipulating the majorities, and then of such majorities occasionally overthrowing their masters, only to see new and equally manipulative élites immediately arising in their place, then his words on the subject of the exiled cottagers have some point:

> The system is much to be deplored, for every one of these banished people imbibes a sworn enmity to the existing order of things, and not a few of them, far from being merely honest radicals, degenerate into Anarchists, waiters on chance, to whom danger to the State, the town – nay, the street they live in, is a welcomed opportunity.

Then, in the final paragraph, he beats the moralists over the head with their own weapon:

> A reason frequently advanced for dismissing these families from the villages where they have lived for centuries is that it is done in the interests of morality; and it is quite true that some of the 'liviers' (as these half-independent villagers used to be called) were not always shining examples of churchgoing, temperance, and quiet walking. But a natural tendency to evil, which develops to unlawful action when excited by contact with others like minded, would often have remained latent amid the simple isolated experiences of a village life. The cause of morality cannot be served by compelling a population

hitherto evenly distributed over the country to concentrate in a few towns, with the inevitable results of overcrowding and want of regular employment. But the question of the Dorset cottager here merges in that of all the houseless and landless poor, and the vast topic of the Rights of Man, to consider which is beyond the scope of a merely descriptive article.

Quite how Hardy felt about the 'Anarchists' with whom, with perfect reason, he now threatened his critics, is not clear. It would be absurd to depict him as a man who wanted the boat to be rocked by riots or revolution. But, as would be witnessed by his reaction to the sinking of the unsinkable *Titanic* in 1912, he was not without a streak of inner nihilism – of satisfaction that not all of man's more grandiose projects are safe from the vagaries of the nature which he ignores or pretends he can master. And, even if Fourier was not exactly an anarchist, he had inspired and would continue to inspire many who were. Fourier, too, was a man of peace, a fact which Tom undoubtedly appreciated. He had not long since stuck his famous Fourier-derived diagram into the front of the scrapbook of which he intended to make systematic future use. There is no reason to suppose that he did not still prefer such a scheme as Fourier's to any of those he saw around him. Meanwhile, what he really thinks about the 'Rights of Man' he leaves safely open. His continuing interest in what Fourier had to say, if not agreement with him, is confirmed by the so-called 'Trumpet-Major Notebook', into which he copied details from Hugh Doherty's introduction to the Rev. Morell's 1851 translation of Fourier's *The Passions of the Human Soul*.

Some have considered Hardy first and foremost as a writer in lament for the tragic passing of the old rural ways: the regretful recorder of the yielding of the old instinctive type of farmer to the new scientific and commercial one. This view became influential as a result of the late Douglas Brown's sensitive book *Thomas Hardy* (1954), to which he added a study of *The Mayor of Casterbridge* in 1962. Brown's books, though excellent, are limited by his thesis, which is less subtle than his discussions of individual poems and novels.

While he did lay his finger on a certain general temperamental preference in Hardy for the emotional over the scientific, there is no evidence of the latter's wishing seriously to exercise this preference in 'The Dorsetshire Labourer'. As I remarked earlier, I do not believe that this was because Hardy was intellectually 'progressive'; on the contrary, I think he was convinced, throughout his life, that things on the whole were getting worse, not better. But his own 'impressions' (of, for example, life in towns), together with his own personal preferences (for example, for Henchard over Farfrae in *The Mayor*), were not allowed to affect his view of details, some of which he believed showed improvements in individuals' lives, while others did not. These details he took upon their merits. Thus, he is at some pains to point out that what seems 'squalid' to a fine philanthropic lady may not be squalid at all in terms of happiness. In short, he was not prepared to reject improvements for the sake of his own preferences. For reasons that are obvious, this refusal is at its most evident in his few, and usually more or less reluctant, public statements, such as those made in the course of 'The Dorsetshire Labourer'. But such objectivity also adds a substantial dimension to his fiction, for all that his real interest was in poetry.

In 1883 *the Mayor of Casterbridge* was hardly, if at all, conceived. As late as March 1884, when he and Emma were safely in their new house at 7, Shire-Hall Lane (this was, before being demolished to make way for a laboratory, renamed Glyde Path Road) in Dorchester, he wrote a note, which he quotes in the *Life*:

> March. Write a novel entitled 'Time against Two', in which the antagonism of the parents of a Romeo and Juliet *does* succeed in separating the couple and stamping out their love, – alas, a more probable development than the other! (The idea is briefly used in *The Well-Beloved*). [Hardy's own brackets.]

It cannot be inferred from this that *The Mayor* was not in his mind, especially as he had just come to live in Dorchester, where it is set; but he may not, even by then, have had any very clear idea of its plot. At some time in 1883 (the entry is undated) he even thought of writing 'the Autobiography of a Card Table'. The removal to Dorchester was motivated by overwhelming creative needs. By the end of June 1883 he had not worked or tried to work on a full-length novel for well over a year. He was tired of the reviewers' uncomprehending hostility (and had complained about their reception of *Two on a Tower* to several of his correspondents). Also, however much the three successors to *The Return of the Native* may deserve defending, and however much they have been misunderstood and under-rated by those critics who are more in sympathy with Victorian reviewers' notions of morality than with Tom's own predicament as a poet forced to write fiction for his living,

it would be foolish to pretend that any of the three can be compared to
The Mayor of Casterbridge – or even, for that matter, to the lesser but still
powerful *The Return of the Native*. He needed to return to the scenes of
his youth in order to achieve the substantial new novel he planned.

What did Emma feel about the move? If what I have suggested is true
– that they went to Paris, away from hotels and tourists, in order to have
a last try for a child – they must both have realized by the end of 1882 that
this project was probably now irrevocably doomed. And she attached
this final disappointment to that move to Dorchester, into the maw of
his family. This failure to conceive, which was a sort of doom to her,
left Tom, however disappointed, with his own 'children': his works. It
left Emma with nothing beyond the social life of a distinguished author's
wife. That by no means cancelled out the generally grudging status
accorded to the Victorian middle-class wife, who was admired upon
her pedestal of moral superiority only so long as she remained there
silently.

Large clouds of moral wind have been dutifully passed, by commentators in puritanical or other difficulties, on the subject of who was 'to
blame' for the severe problems encountered by the Hardys later in their
marriage. The word 'blame', with due apportioning of it, crops up in
every biography. But maybe it is advisable not to 'blame' anyone – and
rather to understand how each felt. Emma's feelings are as humanly
important as are Tom's works; but they are less well known, and for
at least that reason have been largely ignored, or even cast aside as,
literally, the ravings of a madwoman.

It may seem strange for Emma's lost private feelings to be equated in
importance with Hardy's extant works. The reason lies in the nature of
poetry. Hardy's own recognition of this 'human importance' of Emma's
(and anyone else's) feelings is desperately apparent in the poetry he wrote
about her after she had died. The feelings, and by implication their
importance, became his chief poetic subject; such feelings were for him
the very stuff of poetry. Emma thus triumphed, posthumously, in at last
becoming the muse she had not quite always been in life. For the final
subject of any literature that is worth regarding as truly 'living' (what
Tom called Emma) is that everyone's feelings are equally 'important'.
The assumption is built into the charity which lies at the heart of all
creation.

It is always assumed that Emma had special notions, which are for
some reason presented as being high-flown, pretentious or silly, about
her social status as an 'author's wife'. But she *was* an author's wife,

305

and presumably had feelings about it, especially as she was still actively helping him with his work (four of the pages of the hurriedly written 'The Romantic Adventures of a Milkmaid' are in her hand, and so is much else: for example, over one hundred pages of *The Woodlanders*). There is no record from those days of her later social awkwardness, although Gosse told his wife in July 1883 that she was 'garrulous' and 'middle aged' (he did not add that he, too, was middle-aged); he recognized, though, that she 'meant to be very kind'. The value of this last intention – so intimately connected with Tom's own concept of loving-kindness – has, alas, been under-estimated in favour of less charitable judgements.

Her discontent, at this time on account of her childlessness, was only just starting to show itself. There is no evidence of her ever having shown any special pretentiousness about the status of author's wife; the decision to spend so much regular time in London was quite as much Tom's as her own. But she had no child, and she now knew that she was to have no child; and all the attention was going towards her husband. She sensed what all authors' wives sense: a lack of real interest in her. Gosse was an exception because, whatever he might say about her privately, he always paid attention to her. This is why Tom invited him to the new Dorchester house soon after they had moved in. Nor is there, from this period, evidence of any aggressiveness in Emma's Christianity. No record has been found of any objection to *Two on a Tower* on religious grounds: yet that was the main burden of the disapproving reviewers' song, as it is now of Millgate's complaint. This is Tom's own account of the move:

> In this month of June the Hardys removed from Wimborne to Dorchester, which town and its neighbourhood, though they did not foresee it, was to be their country quarters for the remainder of their lives. But several months of each spring and summer were to be spent in London during the ensuing twenty years, and occasionally spells abroad. This removal to the county-town, and later to a spot a little outside it, was a step they often regretted having taken; but the bracing air brought them health and renewed vigour, and in the long run it proved not ill-advised.

There is an air, unusual in the *Life*, of ambiguity or muddle here, as well as the half-truth of the phrase 'though they did not foresee it'.

In the months before the move to Dorchester Tom spent as much time as he could, in Dorset and Paris, in Emma's company. During May and June 1883 they were, 'on and off', in London together, 'seeing pictures, plays, and friends'. He lunched with Lord Houghton, father of his future beloved Florence (then twenty-eight, a year into her marriage to the army officer Arthur Henniker-Major), met Browning again twice, and, for the first time, at the Savile with Gosse, W.D. Howells. Tom noted that Houghton had 'the manner of a man who means to see things properly done in his own house'. Much has been made of this socializing, but its chief value was the opportunity it offered for quiet observation. If society patronized countrymen, some countrymen could take shrewd 'impressions' of it. Tom's view of London social life is apparent in early novels, was not a feature of his middle period, but then resurfaced strongly (and perhaps unexpectedly) in *The Well-Beloved*. That in 1883 he still felt more satirically than otherwise about high society is shown by the passage in 'The Romantic Adventures of a Milkmaid' in which the hostess of the ball to which Baron von Xanten takes Margery is described: 'the wife of a peer of the realm, the daughter of a marquis, has five Christian names; and hardly ever speaks to commoners, except for political purposes'.

Although he did not publish his famous poem 'He Abjures Love' until 1909, in *Time's Laughingstocks*, he did then take the trouble to date it 1883. It was much admired by the classical scholar Gilbert Murray for its specifically Horatian qualities – 'severity and clearness of form, and the fine stinging rhythm', he told the author – and by others for its 'gauntness' and stoicism. It has occasionally been read as a renunciation of Emma, which it is not, and it has been been attacked – extraordinarily, since that is one of its subjects – as 'lacking a detached philosophical attitude to the inherently tragic and insoluble problems of life'. But it is not, by Hardy's standards anyway, a particularly 'personal' poem; it does not allude to any particular woman or women. It is indicative of an intention to move out of a 'romantic' phase into a newer one which is, however, already seen to be too generalized and 'philosophical' to work. It echoes what Hardy had long ago realized, and had been thinking about only recently when he made the Baron tell Margery Tucker, in 'The Romantic Adventures of a Milkmaid': 'You must remember that marriage is a life contract, in which the general compatibility of temper and worldly position is of more importance than fleeting passion, which never long survives.' The irony is implicit, since the splendid and so carefully justified intentions of the first lines are, in effect, negated by the last:

At last I put off love,
    For twice ten years
The daysman of my thought,
    And hope, and doing;
Being ashamed thereof,
    And faint of fears
And desolations, wrought
    In his pursuing,

Since first in youthtime those
    Disquietings
That heart-enslavement brings
    To hale and hoary,
Became my housefellows,
    And, fool and blind,
I turned from kith and kind
    To give him glory.

But – after love what comes?
    A scene that lours,
A few sad vacant hours,
    And then, the Curtain.

It should be evident, then, that, in view of the louring scene and those sad vacant hours, few are likely to be able to resist the pleasures, dubious though they may be, of love. Thus the ability to, 'at length'

                              sound
            Clear views and certain

is not of much use against the need to relieve the vacancy before the end, or 'Curtain'. Thus the poem is in essence an expression of an emotion that most of its readers have known: 'I will never fall in love again!' With the sting in its tail that they have also known . . . The 'great solemnity' with which it was composed is not 'earnestness', as it has been called, but a self-parodic recollection of the solemnity of such moods. To take seriously the idea of its actually being a confident abjuration of love by a man who was in that sad habit is to take Hardy as a simpleton. He knew what had happened since he wrote it, and yet he published it twenty-six years later. It had nothing to do with Emma, because, after all, as any sophisticated reader knows, and as the Baron said, 'fleeting passion' does not long survive, and marriage is another matter.

However, 'He Abjures Love', because it grimly contrasts the good sense of giving up the 'fatuous fires' of love with the emptiness of renouncing such delusions, may fairly be read as confirmation of Hardy's wish to abandon the form of the romance. He did later describe it, in a letter written to Alfred Noyes on 19 December 1920, as a 'love poem' – but meant, by that, 'poem about love'; he then added, aware that it had been 'counted against him', that lovers are 'chartered irresponsibles'. It is significant that in *The Woodlanders* he returned, if not to romance, then at least to a sour (as well as beautiful) love story. *The Mayor of Casterbridge*, though, is a tale of fate and power, almost lacking in any romantic interest. Elizabeth-Jane sacrifices romantic love in settling for the well-behaved commercialist Farfrae. Thus 'He Abjures Love' perfectly reflects its author's creative development. However, there is embodied within it the notion of turning from 'kith and kind' to give glory to love: since it was written almost concurrently with his decision to return to his birthplace and the close proximity of his own 'kith and kind', this must be taken to demonstrate his consciousness of what he was doing.

On the last day of 1883 Tom planted Austrian pines in order to screen the new house, to be called Max Gate after the name of the nearby tollgate, Mack's Gate, from the high winds and, eventually, from the road itself – to give newspapermen and tourists the erroneous impression that Hardy was a savage recluse, as distinct from one who merely liked privacy. But he could hardly then foresee the huge fame that the 'scandals' over *Tess*, and then *Jude*, would bring him.

Within a day or two of moving into the dark house in Shire-Hall Lane, of which it was said that 'he have but one window, and she do look into Gaol Lane', Tom wrote to old William Barnes, who was now at Winterborne Came, two or three miles out of Dorchester. He asked him if 'Mr Edmund Gosse, one of your reviewers, & a most accomplished man' might shake hands with him; the invitation to Gosse was tied up with this plan, since he added that Gosse would be abroad in August. On 16 July he wrote:

Poet Barnes has just called on me – & says that it would give him real pleasure to see you . . . My wife wishes me to tell you that she will be delighted if you can arrive here by any train next Saturday – & stay as long into next week as you can afford time to do

. . . We are sufficiently settled into our new house to make you tolerably comfortable, & you will under the circumstances dispense with apple-pie order I am sure.

On Saturday the 21st July he met him at Dorchester station. On the following day they walked over the fields to Winterborne Came:

> To Winterborne Came Church with Gosse, to hear and see the poet Barnes. Stayed for sermon. Barnes, knowing we should be on the watch for a prepared sermon, addressed it entirely to his own flock, almost pointedly excluding us. Afterwards walked to the rectory and looked at his pictures.

It has been asserted that Emma was already feeling severe distress, and that Tom, wittingly or unwittingly, rode roughshod over this. Thus Denys Kay-Robinson, in his book about her:

> His inability to see how little the site [of the ongoing Max Gate] would please Emma, his probable efforts to keep her away from his family while he was arranging the building work, his desertion of her to visit the Channel Islands, his insensitive excursion to Eggesford and behaviour when he got there, the fatalism and despair evinced in *The Mayor*, the rejection of love expressed in 'He Abjures Love' – all these must have spelled for Emma a fading of the pleasant *rapport* gracing Tooting and Wimborne that the ritual activities in London did little to counter.
>
> If she had charged him with his growing neglect as she seems to have charged him at Weymouth with the concealment of his engagement to Tryphena, it might have launched a first-class quarrel . . .

This, admittedly, resembles speculative journalistic 'investigation' rather than serious or psychological analysis; but it is sadly illustrative. (After all, as I have already shown, it is highly unlikely that Emma ever did charge her husband with 'growing neglect . . . at Weymouth', and it is only a very vague supposition that he was ever 'engaged' to Tryphena.) Once a *canard* has been established, it can quickly become a serious assumption. Thus a brief visit to the Channel Islands becomes 'desertion', and the tone of a novel a 'fading of pleasant *rapport*'. It is more likely that Emma, if she then saw 'He Abjures Love', understood it perfectly well.

As to her alleged dislike of the site on which Max Gate was to be built, and Tom's again alleged efforts to 'keep her away while he was arranging the building work', these are both unwarranted assumptions. They have been made because of the existence of a number of Emma's letters of general complaint to friends, including, in particular, Rebekah Owen and Alfred Pretor. As we shall see, these letters have been misunderstood and taken far too seriously. In addition, they all belong to a much later date: nothing in them relates to this period, and they contain no complaints about either the site or the house that was eventually built upon it.

Few loyal devotees of Hardy have tried, however, to pretend that Max Gate was anything but gloomy. In the words of his secretary May O'Rourke, it was 'the solidification in brick of Hardy's intermittent mood of helplessness at the ugliness in life', and 'strangely inappropriate' as a 'dwelling of a poet'. Not unusual for its time, it resembles those Victorian 'villas' at Poole upon which Hardy worked earlier in his career. His failure to design something less conventional could as well be put down to the influence of Hardy & Son of Bockhampton, Builders, who were about to construct it, as to the fact that he had his living to earn and was thus too busy to pay it as much attention as he might have done. It might, too, be put down to the preferences of Emma herself. Kay-Robinson says that Tom was an ordinary Victorian husband who took scant heed of his wife. That hardly squares with what is known of him, or with the poems he wrote after his wife died. It is unlikely that Emma made objections either to the site or to the house, which was larger and better appointed than any other she had lived in. An undated letter to her from Kate, which seems to belong to 1882, says: '*Success to the building scheme*!!!' Would Kate have written thus to someone who had no heart for it?

The Hardys were paying out a great deal of money for their project: the land alone, at £450, was very expensive for those times, and, while it is not known what Hardy & Son were paid for the building, Tom would surely never have asked them to do the job at cost, which they could not have afforded. There was a family tradition that he paid £1,000, but this has been dismissed as too high. It might, though, represent an instance of Tom's generosity towards his family.

Against this view of the matter a passage from the *Life*, to which Kay-Robinson does not allude, might be quoted. It refers to the 'insensitive' 1885 visit to Eggesford:

Lady P[ortsmouth] . . . wants us to come to Devonshire and live near them. She says they would find a house for us. Cannot think why we live in benighted Dorset. Em would go willingly, as it is her native county; but, alas, my house at Dorchester is nearly finished.

This might or might not indicate that the Hardys (but not just Tom) were having second thoughts about Dorset at this stage of the proceedings, just before the move into Max Gate; but it confirms the view that they were still sharing their decisions. And it is Lady Portsmouth, not Tom, who cannot think why they live in 'benighted Dorset' – it could even be that the last sentence, too, summarizes the excuses Tom made to her, rather than what he thought or knew. But the remarks, made at the time, are not those of a man who rules his wife with a rod of Victorian iron. Since he did not think that Dorset was benighted, and was its premier novelist, it is even likely that he is drawing quiet attention to the sort of tactless inanities that he had to endure. Such a remark was almost tantamount to asking Trollope if he agreed that church affairs made a boring subject for fiction. But Lady Portsmouth, who had three Christian names (Evelina Alicia Juliana), if not quite the 'five' of the hostess of the ball in 'The Romantic Adventures of a Milkmaid', had captured Tom's heart when he and Emma first met her in the summer of 1884:

During this summer they became acquainted with Lord and Lady Portsmouth and their daughters . . . Lady Portsmouth . . . a woman of large social experience who afterwards proved to be the kindest and firmest of friends till her death, told Hardy that Ethelberta . . . who had been pronounced an impossible person by the reviewers, and the social manners unreal, had attracted her immensely because of her reality and naturalness, acting precisely as such women did or would act under such circumstances; and that the society scenes were just as society was, which was not the case with other novels.

It was on this occasion that Evelina, a daughter of the Duke of Carnarvon, issued the 'long-standing invitation' to her home at Eggesford, near Chumleigh in mid-Devon. Tom took it up in March 1885. Emma said she was ill and could not come, and so on the 13th he wrote to her (the first extant letter from him to her):

My dearest Em,
I arrived at Eggesford Station a little after 4, & found there Ld P's

brougham waiting to take me up to the house, so there was no trouble at all. The scenery here is lovely & the house very handsome – not an enormous one – but telling on account of its position, which is on a hill in the park. I have had tea with Lady P & the ladies – the only members of the family at home – Lord P not having returned from hunting yet (6 p.m.) The young ladies are very attentive, & interested in what I tell them. Lady P charges them to take care of me – & goes away to her parish people &c – altogether a delightful household. There are ladies here too, visiting – but of course I have had only a glimpse as yet. They sympathise with you – & Lady P says you *must* come when you are well. I am now in the library writing this. I shd say that a married daughter, Lady Rosamund Christie, I think she is, who is here, strikes me as a particularly sensible woman. If Lady P's orders are to be carried out my room will be like a furnace – she is so particularly anxious that I shd not take cold &c. The drawing room is lined with oak panels from a monastery. When I arrived the schoolchildren were practising singing in the hall, for Sunday in church. In haste (as you will believe)
Yours ever
Tom.

That he wrote the letter at all shows him to have been a normally, if not fanatically, attentive husband; yet it has been thoughtlessly seized upon to 'prove' all kinds of insubstantial nonsense. He does not, even Halliday in his generally sensible and helpful *Thomas Hardy* (1972) grimly observes, 'add that he hopes she already feels better, nor does he send his love'! (Emma might not have been ill, but simply not have wished to go.) The letter is interesting for two reasons: it demonstrates that so far all was well between him and Emma, and it makes no comment on the Duke's unpleasant habit of hunting helpless animals, something which Tom was later to oppose bitterly. In this Emma anticipated, and influenced, him. He was always full of admiration for her promptness and courage in opposing cruel or thoughtless behaviour to animals. Millgate, quoting Tom's description of the women at Eggesford as 'extraordinarily sensitive' – a description written almost ten years after Emma's death – speaks of his 'somewhat insensitive expression of delight in his letter home'. His 'emotional susceptibility was as naive and adolescent as it had ever been . . . It is possible to perceive in the circumstances of the Eggesford visit . . . ominous signs of those difficulties within his own marriage which were to cause grief . . .'

Possible, but inadvisable. The description of Lady Rosamund Christie as 'a particularly *sensible* woman' might be taken to imply surprise, since he and Emma had discussed what they felt to be the frequent inanity of the titled classes. He had not, after all, shrunk from giving this view in his fiction. The accusation of 'insensitivity' might stem from a notion that it must inevitably be the husband's part to be insincerely 'sensitive' in giving accounts of his impressions to his wife: you must not tell a lady with whom you are under contract that you like other ladies, as she might take it that you lusted after them. This in itself implies a more Victorian view of women than Tom himself took. Perhaps he was writing as he felt, to one he trusted and who trusted him, and was in his intimate confidence. After all, in a letter to Emma of 16 May 1885 he first wrote 'the Portsmouth bevy', only on second thoughts substituting 'the Portsmouth sisters'. Indeed, this letter is more significant than the first. It begins, not 'My dearest Em', but 'My dear(est) Emmie', which, for a man of Tom's natural reticence, is effusive, putting special emphasis, as it does, on the dear*est*. He is just up in London, a few days before she arrives, for the last visit there before moving into Max Gate. He has been at Lady Carnarvon's the night before. The Portsmouth sisters were also present.

> You were much enquired for . . . all expressing sorrow that you could not come . . . There were more people – rather more – present than the other Friday, but more of a mixed kind – not quite so select. Among others there was Mrs Oliphant – to whom I was introduced. I don't care a bit for her – & you lose nothing by not knowing her. She is propriety and primness incarnate. Robert Browning was there . . . Also Mrs Jeune the irrepressible. She was very cool – I think because you have not called – & I could not get her to tell why. However a little delay will do her no harm.

Tom liked Lord Portsmouth, 'a farmer-like man' with a 'broad Devon accent', even though he hunted. He took Tom walking in the park, as well as putting his library at his disposal. He also showed him 'a bridge over which bastards were thrown and drowned, even down to quite recent times'.

Far from cutting themselves off from society, Tom and Emma made as much effort as work permitted to establish themselves socially in Dorchester. It is not known how often or under what circumstances he, or they, visited, or were visited by, Tom's relatives; there is no reason to suppose anything untoward. Any quarrels or coolings off came later, and, if the jealous Mrs Yeobright really is a part-portrait of Jemima, then it is clear how they came about. But, because of Tom's recognition of that difficult and clannish aspect of his mother's nature, and of the fact that the resemblance between Mrs Yeobright and Jemima would have been discerned by Emma, and have been fully discussed, there is every reason to suppose that it was well understood that she was indeed peculiar, and somewhat of a trial, in that respect.

Meanwhile, their local friends the Bosworth Smiths soon came to visit them from nearby, and Tom became involved in the affairs of the Museum, of which Horace Moule's brother, Henry James Moule, was now curator. On 24 August 1883, within two months of their arrival, Tom was writing to his old acquaintance, Walter Pollock, author, lawyer and sub-editor (later editor) of the *Saturday Review*, about the 'really valuable & curious' *Records of the Town of Weymouth*, which had just been published by a local firm. To a request for an article from Percy Bunting, editor of the *Contemporary Review*, he was cautious. Bunting, having just read him on the Dorsetshire Labourer, wanted his views on how he might vote. Tom, saying he had no time at the moment, but vaguely promising to consider the matter later, told Bunting, perhaps a trifle devastatingly as well as truthfully: 'Just now there seems very little to say about them as voters – the franchise being a subject to which the labourers as a body have (as far as I see) given no thought at all.' He was happy enough to tell Morley that he was a Liberal, but not to declare himself publicly.

On 18 October he was trying to use his literary influence to attract the author Bret Harte, then US Consul in Glasgow, to talk to the Dorchester Lecture Society. Harte had long ago lost his brief but high American popularity as satirical parodist and spinner of regional yarns, but was still sought after by English magazine editors. Tom suggested that, as the Society had little money, Harte might like to make a tour of 'Weymouth, Exeter, &c', at its expense, rather than charge a fee: 'I may say that my wife will be happy to see you here, & we can offer you a bed, if plain accommodation will suffice.' But although he met Harte at a dinner in London in 1886, there is no record of the latter's having accepted the invitation. That it was made, however, demonstrates the efforts that both Hardys were making to be good neighbours and to serve their town's interests. Whether he heard, or took up an invitation to meet, Oscar Wilde, who lectured the Society on 'The House Beautiful' in September, is not known; but in any case he did meet Wilde, also in

1886 in London – if not before. Characteristically, he never commented, as Henry James (pejoratively of Wilde), did, on Wilde's 1895 trial.

Despite the fact that his recent fiction had not been well received, at least by reviewers, around this time Hardy seems to have developed a new confidence that he could survive as an independent thinker. It is reflected in the novel he started to write early in 1884, perhaps soon after he returned from a visit to London in January. On the 23rd he told Mrs Isabelle Oppenheim, the daughter of the painter W.P. Frith, with whom he was friendly, that he and Emma 'had run up almost entirely to see the Winter Exhibitions'. He says in the *Life* that he saw 'Henry James, Gosse, and [Hamo] Thorneycroft [the sculptor of whom Gosse was enamoured]'. He also met the artist, Alma-Tadema, who 'was much excited' by the 'Roman remains he [Hardy] was finding on the site of his proposed house', 'as he was painting . . . a picture expressing the art of that date'. The notes made at this time, such as this one from 'March or April', are not those of a man anxious to be thought of as 'progressive', but rather those of a poet seeking his own bent: 'Every error under the sun seems to arise from thinking you are right yourself because you *are* yourself, and other people wrong because they are not you.'

Such observations can scarcely be popular among men who really do feel themselves to be 'right', but not so, they think, because those who are opposed to them are 'not them'. The emphasis is upon the discovery of a process by which truth and wisdom are actually achieved. But these doubts about what is 'right' did not prevent him, in April, from accepting the post of Justice of the Peace for Dorchester, a duty which he took seriously even though his attendance on the bench proved erratic. Possibly he took it up because of Jemima, or, more likely, because he felt that when young he had been ridiculed as over-ambitious by various citizens of Dorchester and Bockhampton.

On 3 June 1884, the day after his forty-fourth birthday, he watered 'the thirsty earth at Max Gate', and then indulged what he calls his 'craze' in those years for circuses, of which Emma may not have approved. Entering one in Fordington Field, he noted 'the damp orbits of the spectators' eyes' gleaming in the rays of the artificial light, and the 'sub-expression' of the clowns, under their paint, of 'good-humoured pain'.

Shortly afterwards they went up to London, where Tom met Matthew Arnold for the second time, and liked him 'better now than he did at their first meeting'; he was also struck by the 'nebulous gaze' of Henry James, of whom he seems to have seen a good deal. This was also the occasion of the invitation by Lord and Lady Portsmouth. While in London he received a circular letter from a Detroit medical journalist, Dr Hugo Erichsen, who was compiling a work to be called *Methods of Authors* (it was published in the following year). He enjoyed his laconic reply, written from the Savile on 26 July:

> Mr Thomas Hardy begs to state . . . that (1) he prefers night for working; but finds daytime advisable as a rule; that (2) he follows no plan as to outline; that (3) he uses no stimulant unless tea can be considered as such; that (4) his habit is to remove his boots or slippers as a preliminary to work; that (5) he has no definite hours for writing; that (6) he only occasionally works against his will.

On 14 August he witnessed *Othello* performed by strolling players at Dorchester, in the market-field:

> Othello is played by the proprietor, and his speeches can be heard as far as to the town-pump. Emilia wears the earrings I saw her wearing when buying the family vegetables this morning. The tragedy goes on successfully, till the audience laughs at the beginning of the murder scene. Othello stops, and turning, says sternly to them after an awful pause: 'Is this the Nineteenth Century?' The conscience-stricken audience feel the justice of the reproof, and preserve an abashed silence as he resumes.

By this time Tom was writing *The Mayor of Casterbridge*, 'off and on'; he also agreed with *Macmillan's Magazine*, 'no time being fixed', to supply them – for £600 – with the twelve-part serial that became *The Woodlanders*. The *Macmillan's* approach came from John Morley (late of Macmillan) who, as editor of the *Fortnightly Review*, had never, perhaps mindful of his earlier experiences, asked him for anything. But Morley left the paper after only a very short time, after which Tom had to deal with the Macmillans themselves, and with the bowdlerizing editor Mowbray Morris. Possibly Morley did not like Morris, and so thought he would leave him with an insoluble problem . . . On 20 October Tom made a note which expresses his agreement with, but does not mention, the Tolstoyan view of history: 'are not [events and tendencies] in the main the outcome of *passivity* – acted upon by unconscious propensity?' None of those – chiefly Barrie and Cockerell – who oversaw, or advised upon, the publication of 'Florence's' *Life* spotted that Tom accidentally put back the general election of 23 November 1885 by one year: he quoted from letters written to him just after it, from Professor E.S. Beesly, a leading positivist, editor of the *Positivist Review* from 1893 and author of *Comte as Moral Type* (1885), who had stood unsuccessfully for Westminster; from John Morley, who as a Liberal MP (1883) was vociferously involved in it; and from Leslie Stephen ('like Hardy himself, quite outside politics'), referring to a book he had just published, which must have been *The Life of Henry Fawcett* (1885).

It is interesting that, although Tom's practical interest in positivism as a movement (he had read the works of Auguste Comte, its founder, in 1865) began as early as the 1880s, he never joined it. His friendship with the leader of the English positivists, Frederic Harrison, dates from this period. That Emma had by this time turned as avidly Christian as she later was is made the more unlikely by the fact that she was quite happy to attend, with Tom, a lecture-course by Harrison – to whom Tom wrote on 17 June 1885: 'I have much missed the lectures since their close. We liked the last one best – by "we" I mean my wife & I.' An absolutely committed Christian would not have bothered, would even have been repelled by, the idea of lectures directed at those who had lost their faith in the supernatural. Nor, had Emma been disgusted, would Tom have bothered to tell a lie about it to Harrison. Furthermore, while still living at Tooting, she had herself been invited in April 1881, by the wife of their Dorchester friend Benjamin Lock, to a 'presentation' – a 'Positivist baptism' – at Newton Hall, the positivist headquarters. It has been suggested that only etiquette prompted the invitation to her rather than to Tom, but this is unconvincing: it may be taken to mean that Emma at this time – for all her the tendency to piety which Tom may even earlier have intuited – was at the very least tolerant of positivism. Tom himself had made an undated note towards the end of 1880, while he still lay ill:

> If Comte had introduced Christ among the worthies in his calendar it would have made Positivism tolerable to thousands who, from position, family connection, or early education, now decry what in their heart of hearts they hold to contain the germs of a true system. It would have enabled them to modulate gently into the new religion by deceiving themselves with the sophistry that they still continued one-quarter Christians, or one-eighth, or one twentieth, as the case may be: This as a matter of *policy*, without which no religion succeeds in making way.

This is quite as objective, even 'cynical', as it is sympathetic, and illustrates, above all, Tom's determination to keep away from all sects or political or ethical groups. But to Morley, an avowed atheist for whom Comte was second only to John Stuart Mill, he wrote less sceptically on 20 November, just three days before the 1885 election.

> I have sometimes had a dream that the church, instead of being disendowed, could be made to modulate by degrees (say as the present incumbents die out) into an undogmatic, non-theological establishment for the promotion of that virtuous living on which all honest men are agreed – leaving to voluntary bodies the organization of whatever societies they may think best for teaching their various forms of doctrinal religion.
>
> I was to have met you at Mr F. Harrisons one day last summer but much to my regret I could not be there.

These words have been criticized as expressing an 'excessively optimistic hope of ethical regeneration', as if the idea were Hardy's own invention. But it almost exactly echoes the Comtean dream, and not at all the Hardyan one: he was preaching to the converted, and deliberately so. Perhaps he was grateful to Morley for the *Woodlanders* commission. Tom, unusually, was simply seeking to please. But his absence from Harrison's on the occasion he specifies may be regarded as opportunistic, for he had nothing more to hope for from Morley, who would not now be dealing with the manuscript.

Always the first to admit to his 'inconsistencies', Tom used that word on 18 February 1920 when dictating to Florence a letter to the rationalist Joseph McCabe, who wished to include him in his *Biographical Dictionary of Modern Rationalists*. He took the trouble to include this in the *Life*, so it must have represented as much as he wanted to say on the subject outside his imaginative work:

> [Hardy] says he thinks he is rather an irrationalist than a rationalist, on account of his inconsistencies. He has, in fact, declared as much in prefaces . . . where he explains his views as being mere impressions that frequently change. Moreover, he thinks he could show that no man is a rationalist, and that human actions are not ruled by reason at all in the last resort.

When McCabe's book appeared, his rationalist friend, the banker

Clodd, wrote raging at his omission from it. But Tom was not going to be categorized. So far as the public was concerned, he wanted to appear nearer to the quasi-rationalist than to the Christian position; but never to be labelled.

The novel he was now in the process of finishing was not concerned with sexual relations, but even so he would be troubled by censorship. Arthur Locker and W.J. Thomas, respectively editor and proprietor-publisher of the *Graphic*, badly wanted a Hardy story to grace their pages; but, knowing that he was 'dangerous', they made sure that they would have plenty of time to slice out whatever might offend them or their readership.

17

The Mayor of Casterbridge

W hile Tom was reading proofs of the complete edition of his works, published in 1912, he told his friend Clement Shorter on 8 October that he did not expect to get to London much that year because of the work involved. He added:

> I wish that half the volumes were consigned to oblivion instead of being reprinted – I mean those novels written in the past on conventional lines for magazine editors – 'to keep base life afoot'. However, there they are, unfortunately.

But which 'half' did he mean? It would be unreasonable to expect him to have specified, to Shorter of all people. The author who wants his work to go on selling must leave others to be specific on such matters. One thing, however, is certain: he did not consider *The Mayor of Casterbridge* to be one of the potboilers. Thus he regretfully recollected in the *Life* that 'it was a story which Hardy fancied he had damaged more recklessly as an artistic whole, in the interest of the newspaper in which it appeared serially, than perhaps any other of his novels . . .'. Yet he prepared for it more thoroughly than for any other novel. In the spring of 1884, within a few weeks of starting work, he started to read the files of the *Dorsetshire County Chronicle*. By now he had a historical novel in mind.

There is a marked difference between his arrangements with the *Graphic* and all the other magazines for which he supplied serials. By the time *Macmillan's* received the end of *The Woodlanders*, for instance, the first chapters had, as was customary, already started to appear. But everything for the *Graphic* was sent to them well in advance. It may be that this was a *Graphic* house rule – or perhaps the magazine made it a special requirement for Thomas Hardy alone. If his previous work had offended the atheist Morley ('do not touch it') and sorely tried the freethinking Stephen ('a child in such matters'), as well as agonized the reviewers, then the notion of dealing with copy from him would have given such men as Locker and Thomas, of the *Graphic*, apoplexy. They had the healthy morality of their readers to look after. Yet these same readers enjoyed reading stories by Thomas Hardy, who, having originated in the countryside, did not understand the gentlemanly need to avoid candour. What better plan could there be, therefore, than to tell him that plenty of time was required in order to arrange for effective illustrations?

The bowdlerization of *The Mayor of Casterbridge* is a complicated story, described in detail in Gatrell's *Hardy the Creator*. It was not disastrous to the novel, except that the necessity to bow to an over-polite convention made Tom feel constrained, and the more constrained he felt the more annoyed he felt. Lucetta, Henchard's long-term mistress, had to be married to him in the serial version; and a score or so of swear-words were excised from the English text (*Harper's*, in which it appeared in America, was less fussy). On one occasion Tom made his own sharp comment on the emendation which Locker forced upon him. In the police-court scene the constable, Stubberd, dutifully abbreviates all the curses in making his report (this in itself amounted to a commentary on public habits). Henchard interrupts him impatiently: 'Come – we don't want to hear any more of them cust d's.' The *Graphic* made Tom cut out the 'cust'. So, obediently cutting it out, he gave additional words to Henchard: 'Say the word out like a man, and don't be so modest, Stubberd: or else leave it alone.'

However, the enforced bowdlerizations hardly mattered, for Tom had chosen a spectacular way of tackling unmentionable truths: he began with a wife-sale. What man had not at some time wished to be rid of the encumbrance of wife and children in order to assert his independence or, at least, his inclinations? But what man would admit to such impulses? In this way Tom tapped deeply and offensively into the unconsciousness of his Victorian reader. Reading an item about just such a sale in the *Dorsetshire County Chronicle* shaped for him the novel of Dorchester to which he was already committed.

He was attempting to write not a realistic novel, but a mythopoeic one. Yet he searched assiduously, not for probabilities, which did not interest him – 'it is not improbabilities of incident but improbabilities of character that matter' he wrote on 6 January 1886, the day that serial publication began – but for strict possibilities: for a number of plausible facts which he could weave into an archetypal tale – a tale in which each personage acts true to character. Thus, the anonymous reviewer writing in the *Saturday Review* on 29 May 1886 missed the point in saying that the novel was 'too improbable', and was wrong in asserting that the opening scene was 'impossible to believe'. 'My art,' Tom wrote two days after serialization began, 'is to intensify the expression of things . . . so that the heart and inner meaning is made vividly visible.' This desire to follow a character to its external destiny did not arise from a 'fundamental puritanism', as has been charged, but from his poet's need to express the truth.

At the same time, he was now shrewdly and deliberately capitalizing on the 'Wessex' he had half-accidentally created. At this point, as Millgate has admirably demonstrated in his two books about Hardy, Wessex became for the first time a conscious entity. Dorchester (Casterbridge), after all, is the hub and centre of his Wessex, although his Wessex is by no means what the Wessex of a historian of Dorset (and parts of Somerset and Hampshire) would have been. His Wessex is a complex perception – what he would have called a series of impressions – of Dorset and some of the adjacent countryside.

The Mayor is Hardy's most tightly and economically plotted novel. It shows nothing of the real intricacies or careful credibilities of plotting seen in George Eliot or Henry James; yet its weaknesses in that respect are incidental. Michael Henchard gets drunk and sells his wife and daughter to a sailor at Weydon-Priors Fair. In her ignorance, his wife, Susan, believes this arrangement to be legally binding and goes off with Newson, the sailor. Next morning Henchard is ashamed of what he has done, and so vows – in a church, being of a 'fetishistic' rather than Christian nature – to abstain from liquor for twenty-one years, the number of years he has lived. But he cannot find Susan or his child Elizabeth Jane.

Eighteen or nineteen years pass. The third chapter begins with Susan and her daughter coming to Casterbridge, Newson having apparently been lost at sea, in search of Henchard. Susan does not tell her daughter of the wife-selling incident, simply referring to Henchard as a 'relative'. Henchard, now the most powerful man in Casterbridge and 'quite a principal man in the country round besides', is its mayor and leading corn factor. But a bad harvest has threatened his prospects: his grain is poor. He forms a strong friendship with a young Scot, Donald Farfrae, who, on his way to America, has left him a note suggesting a means of improving the grain. Henchard takes him into his business as manager. Meanwhile, he remarries Susan. His carelessness in business leads him into increasing trouble, and gradually, but without any unscrupulousness, Farfrae begins to take control. Henchard resents Farfrae's acumen, and eventually drives him into going into business for himself. Soon he has taken Henchard's place as the leading corn factor of Casterbridge, and is even elected mayor – so Hardy's title refers to him, too.

Henchard's former mistress, the vain Lucetta Templeman, now a rich heiress, turns up in Casterbridge in pursuit of her former lover. Susan dies, and soon afterwards Henchard accidentally discovers that the young woman called Elizabeth-Jane is not his daughter after all, but Newson's; his own daughter died. His love for this new Elizabeth-Jane turns into an intense, although temporary, hatred. He is driven into bankruptcy by a combination of his own impulsiveness and Farfrae's successful methods, and is also robbed of Lucetta, whom Farfrae courts and marries.

When Henchard so impulsively appointed Farfrae to be his manager he had already 'as good as engaged' the unattractive Joshua Jopp. Subsequently he dismissed Jopp's claim too callously, giving hardly an explanation, thus making an enemy of him. Now Jopp discovers old letters between Lucetta and Henchard, and can have his revenge. The people of the lower end of the town, informed by Jopp, organize a 'skimmington-ride': the effigies of any so-called guilty couple are ridden through the streets on a donkey to a deafening din (an event for which Hardy had abundant precedent as recently as 1884). The pregnant Lucetta, unhappily more susceptible to 'moral' ignominy than to anything else, dies of a miscarriage caused by the sight of the 'skimmity-ride' passing her house.

Things go from bad to worse for Henchard, though he has at least made his peace with Elizabeth-Jane, and now lives with her, as his daughter. He is happy running a little shop; but his contentment does not last long. Newson, not drowned at all, turns up in Casterbridge for news. Henchard, living for the moment, and knowing that he will be discovered, tells him that Elizabeth-Jane is dead. She is meanwhile courted by Farfrae, and agrees to marry him. When Newson turns up, she repudiates Henchard. He returns to his first job, as a hay-trusser, disappears, and then dies, like Lear, on the heath, with only the fool, Abel Whittle, to attend him.

The Mayor of Casterbridge is not poetry, because it is in prose, and prose made saleable to a conventional magazine at that: until 1895 Tom still had to be 'a good hand at a serial', despite what it cost him in time lost to poetry. But it is pre-eminently the novel of a poet, and is also a poetic novel: poetic in a sense that, say, the kindly and worldly-wise Barchester series, or the exquisite *Portrait of a Lady*, or even the majestic

Middlemarch, are not. It was the first major poetic novel in English since *Wuthering Heights*, and it remains one of the peaks of English fiction. The tragic stature of Henchard, which eludes few readers, could not have been achieved outside a poetic framework. *The Mayor* is good enough to have recalled *Lear* to many, and not just because of a few superficial (and deliberate) resemblances. Ironically, when Tom wrote his dramatic verse epic *The Dynasts*, his historical subject denied him the opportunity to write verse of the kind of poetic majesty with which his fictitious subject, in *The Mayor*, could have provided him.

What Hardy does is to transform a person, Henchard, who is by any reasonable standards a thoroughly bad man, into a tragic hero. Simultaneously for the majority of readers he somehow justly robs Farfrae of his apparent virtue. If the love interest is circumscribed in *The Mayor*, as it is always said to be, it is solely because Farfrae's romantic impulses, towards Lucetta and then towards Elizabeth-Jane, cannot carry weight or interest. Readers ought to dislike Henchard wholeheartedly, and applaud Farfrae's excellent, just and principled behaviour; yet few do. However, Hardy does not cheat: this, we feel, is rightly judged. Thus Ian Gregor writes in *The Great Web* (1974) – deservedly still one of the standard critical texts on Hardy's major fiction: 'Clearly, it would be absurd to read the novel in such a way as to make it an indictment of Henchard and a vindication of Farfrae.' What must be resolved is *why* it would be so clearly 'absurd' to read the novel in that way. For, as Gregor reminds us in his account of Henchard's shortcomings, Douglas Brown's famous reading just will not do. He summarizes Brown pertinently:

> *The Mayor of Casterbridge*, then, is the tale of the struggle between the native countryman and the alien invader; of the defeat of dull courage and traditional attitudes by insight, craft and the vicissitudes of nature; and of the persistence through that defeat of some deep layer of vitality in the country protagonist . . . *The Mayor of Casterbridge* turns on the situation that led to the repeal of the Corn Laws. The consequences of the repeal to Victorian agricultural life are the centre of this book, provide the impulse that makes it what it is.

But, as Gregor points out, Hardy's preface to *The Mayor* makes it clear that the emphasis is not on the repeal of the Corn Laws, but rather on the uncertain harvests which preceded it. Brown certainly put his finger on the mysterious fact that Henchard is in some way the superior of Farfrae;

but the exact manner in which he is superior is, while central to the book, enigmatic. It was poetry which was needed to demonstrate this, and it was poetry which Hardy had. Brown fell prey to the temptation to explain this mysterious superiority in terms of agricultural economics. But the novel is not about agricultural economics – that is only the background. Had Hardy been a lesser novelist, he might have written a work which did make some such simplistic comparison between Henchard and Farfrae. Doubtless he felt a superficial sympathy for Henchard's rough and ready methods as distinct from Farfrae's more meticulous ones (although his conduct of his own financial affairs seems to have resembled Farfrae's more than Henchard's). Gregor comments: 'Far from presenting an innocent agrarian economy undermined by new grasping business methods, Hardy shows in Henchard (if we really want to talk in these terms) the last of the old profiteers, existing by courtesy of a closed system of economic protection.'

In essence, therefore, we do not, as Gregor implies, want to talk in economic terms when trying to explain our sympathy with Henchard. Indeed, we ought first, as Gregor does, to put the counter-case: for Farfrae as hero and Henchard as villain. After all, might not Henchard's appeal have been brought about by sheer romantic sleight of hand? Might not he just be more impressive than the charming but lightweight Farfrae? Might not the novel be a subtle illustration of how rhetoric and presence carry a false and misleading power? However, as Gregor unequivocally pronounces, such a reading really is 'absurd': the counter-case clearly does not hold. But *why* exactly?

Henchard not only gets drunk in order to rid himself of his wife and child for the sake of ambition, but he is, in Gregor's words, 'tetchy, grasping, superstitious, and indifferent to any consequences beyond the immediate present'. The morning after, ashamed of what he has done, he puts the blame on Susan: 'Seize her, why didn't she know better than bring me into this disgrace!' he roars. He does then make and keep his oath to abstain from drink for a 'year for every year that I have lived', and he does set about trying to trace his wife and child. But 'a certain shyness of revealing his conduct prevented Michael Henchard from following up the investigation with the loud hue-and-cry such a pursuit demanded to render it effectual'. His effort is vitiated by his inability to give any 'explanation of the circumstances under which he lost her'. All this arises from feelings of shame: what would others think of him if they knew? The oath can be interpreted in the same way: what will others think of him if he keeps getting drunk? There is no regret.

When he has done all that he can manage, and failed, he sets off for Casterbridge, 'a district which he had had for some time in his mind'. Had he succeeded in his lukewarm enterprise of tracing Susan and the child, he would not have risen in the world – or at least, not in Casterbridge. It is clear enough that, having succeeded in ridding himself of the perceived encumbrance, he is going to carry out an old ambition: to make good, to gain power, in a particular place. Impulse, we may be sure – and hot irresistible sexual impulse at that – got him into marriage, and just as hot irresistible impulse has got him out of it.

Did Tom feel that he, too, had in some way 'sold', sacrificed, his own wife in moving to Dorchester, in order to fulfil *his* destiny? This is quite incidental to the novel, but impossible to ignore in the context of his biography. It does not imply that Emma was complaining about living in Dorchester at the time – doubts and misgivings about the move were, so far as Tom says anything about them, shared. Indeed, it rather implies the contrary: it is not likely that he would have touched upon such a theme had Emma constantly complained. But it does suggest a dark premonition on Tom's part that, by coming to live in the only place in which he felt he could fulfil himself creatively, his birthplace, he was sacrificing Emma and his love for her – and hers for him. That same intuition had already seen her against a signpost, looking as if crucified. If 'Near Lanivet' truly represents a foreboding that he had during their courtship – and there is every reason to suppose that it does – then he might have looked, gloomily, at each of his moves as the driving of yet another nail in the cross upon which Emma had, from the outset, been affixed.

When we first see Henchard as the Mayor of Casterbridge, nineteen years after his drunken sale of Susan, he is at his apogee. But circumstances have already sown the seeds of his downfall. A bad harvest has made his wheat poor and 'growed' (starting to sprout in the ear before being gathered): the resulting bread is described as 'unprincipled' by one of the townspeople. As the leader of this community, now 'strong' in his bearing and in his will in keeping his oath, where he had once felt himself weak, Henchard is by no means prepossessing; nor is Hardy's emphasis on this any accident. Henchard is no longer a self-degraded young hay-trusser. He is now, it must be admitted, even less attractive than he was then, no longer having the excuse of youth and inexperience. The reader sees him first as a nameless corn factor responsible for 'unprincipled bread'; just afterwards, admittedly through the medium of Susan's meekness (although that has point, too), he is seen directly: a man with a terrible laugh (one 'not encouraging to strangers'), 'pitiless' towards 'weakness', yielding 'ungrudging admiration' to 'greatness and strength', whose 'personal goodness . . . *if he had any*' (my italics) would be 'fitful', 'occasional', 'oppressive'. Subsequently his life is destroyed by the peculiar intensity of emotion with which he makes his crucial decisions. He is never swayed by calculation (which may imply meanness of spirit, but may just as easily indicate sober consideration of the feelings of others). His most self-destructive moves inevitably arise from his unbridled passion.

The ideal tragic character for the Greeks, whom Hardy had studied, was not – in Aristotle's words – a man 'pre-eminently virtuous and just', but one whose downfall is brought about by some flaw or error in himself: *hamartia*. Richard Carpenter describes Henchard's flaw as consisting of 'self-destructiveness'. This is not far off the mark; unfortunately, it is just far enough off to be misleading. The exhausted Henchard's impulse to destroy all trace of himself is the quality which finally gives him grace: he destroys the periphery of his being, whose 'luck' is in and then out on the wheel of fortune, in order to retain its essence, in which lies recognition of the need to renounce the material personality. He writes his famous will, directing that Elizabeth-Jane should not be told of his death, nor be made to 'grieve on account' of him, '& that

> I be not bury'd in consecrated ground.
> & that no sexton be asked to toll the bell.
> & that nobody is wished to see my dead body.
> & that no murners walk behind me at my funeral.
> & that no flours be planted on my grave.
> & that no man remember me.'

But of all the characters, only Elizabeth-Jane recognizes this:

What Henchard had written in the anguish of his dying was respected as far as practicable by Elizabeth-Jane, though less from a sense of the sacredness of last words, as such, than from her independent knowledge that the man who wrote them *meant what he said*. She knew the directions to be a piece of the same stuff that his whole life was made of, and hence were not to be tampered with to give herself a mournful pleasure, or her husband credit for large-heartedness. [My italics.]

This careful and crucial report of Elizabeth-Jane's attitude puts a special emphasis on Henchard's last gesture, for it is through her sensibility that the reader sees most of the action of the novel. Strict in her assessments, she denies herself the luxury of conventional grief, and, in keeping with the spirit of Henchard's final self-denial, will not allow her husband to gain *credit* (the word is used advisedly) for a large-heartedness that he does not possess. The hint of Farfrae's lack is faint but, in the context, unmistakable.

An exactly similar impulse is found in Tess Durbeyfield, as Hardy made clear in the last stanza of the poem 'Tess's Lament':

> It wears me out to think of it,
>   To think of it;
> I cannot bear my fate as writ,
>   I'd have my life unbe;
> Would turn my memory to a blot,
> Make every relic of me rot,
> My doings be as they were not,
>   And gone all trace of me!

The notion of self-destruction (or, more exactly, of destruction of an inessential part of the self) is not a familiar one, especially in the context of ordinary Western thinking. Those average, non-philosophical or non-theological Victorians (most of Hardy's readers) who believed that they would go to heaven, owing to their correct conduct, thought of themselves as doing so *in propriis personis*. It is pertinent, therefore, to raise the question of Hardy's connection with the German philosopher Arthur Schopenhauer (1788–1860). Much has been written about this association, although mostly in relation to *The Dynasts*.

There seems to be little actual debt beyond Hardy's intellectual formulation of the 'Will' in *The Dynasts*; what he really did owe to his reading of Schopenhauer was a crystallization of his own thinking. It is interesting in this respect that he had a great liking for Schopenhauer's own favourite author, the seventeenth-century Spanish moralist Baltasar Gracian. Tom transcribed many of Gracian's writings into his literary notebooks in 1877, and made abundant use of them in *A Laodicean*.

In his own chief work, *Die Welt als Wille und Vorstellung* (1819), some paragraphs of which he considered to have been dictated by the Holy Ghost (even though he believed this to be an illusion), Schopenhauer regarded the world as the product of 'Blind Will'. Will is the master, and even intellect – let alone sexual appetite, what is called love, and all the other desires – is the slave: the intellect is the 'tool' of this Blind Will. There is thus a partial affinity between the thinking of the two men, which led Hardy to acknowledge, in the 1922 'Apology' to his *Late Lyrics and Earlier*, that Schopenhauer and Einstein, among others, had 'his respect' (if not agreement).

In 1885, however, Tom was probably acquainted with Schopenhauer only through writings in periodicals and through a book by a psychologist, James Sully, called *Pessimism: A History and Criticism* (1877). He probably also read Helen Zimmern's *Schopenhauer: His Life and Philosophy* (1876); he certainly transcribed a quotation, mentioning Schopenhauer, from an article by her on the poet Lenau in the *Cornhill* for October 1881. Schopenhauer's chief work appeared in an English translation in three volumes, *The World as Will and Idea*, between 1883 and 1886; but it is unlikely that Hardy read the work until a few years later. However, a caveat should be added: Hardy was always nervous of admitting what could be taken as his sources, and annoyed when they were pointed out to him; he therefore could have read or skimmed the work as it appeared, despite a later disclaimer to the effect that he used to read Darwin and others more than Schopenhauer.

Schopenhauer began to be discussed in intellectual circles when he published a collection of aphoristic essays in 1851, in the wake of the failure of the 1848 revolutions. To many of those who, like Hardy, did not automatically equate technological advance with human progress, the 'pessimism' of these essays seemed to amount to a valid philosophy; but, long before the advent of his popularity, Schopenhauer himself had thoroughly and joyfully absorbed every negative trend in his own life and in his disillusioned age. That Hardy recognized the zealous extremeness of Schopenhauer's negativity is suggested by the narrator's comment on old Clare in *Tess*: 'His creed of determinism was such that it amounted almost to a vice, and quite amounted, on its negative side, to a renunciative philosophy which had cousinship with that of Schopenhauer and Leopardi.' But he did transcribe the following maxim of Schopenhauer's, culled from Sully's *Pessimism*, into his literary notebooks – and possibly did so, in that age of obligatory optimism, with some relish of his own: 'Study to acquire an accurate & connected view of the utter despicability of mankind in general.'

The philosophical status of the world was never really Hardy's concern: it was enough for him that it did not merely seem to hurt. But Schopenhauer, surprising though it may seem, did preach compassion as the prime consolation for the suffering which is the inevitable lot of the individual who does not comprehend that happiness is illusory, and that the absolute and irrational Blind Will (not to be confused with God, who does not exist) constantly deceives and tricks humanity. Moreover – and this is relevant to *The Mayor of Casterbridge* – Schopenhauer was profoundly influenced in his thinking by the ancient Sanskrit texts known as the Upanishads and by the Buddhist idea of nirvana: dissolution and extinction of the individual will in order to bring peace and release from the eternal cycle of human suffering.

By 1885 Hardy could have picked up this much from Helen Zimmern's book. This continued interest is demonstrated by the fact that in 1888 he copied part of an article about Buddhism by the Bishop of Colombo from the July issue of *The Nineteenth Century*; it contained a sentence which Hardy abbreviated thus: 'Nirvana is the state in wh. there is not left any capacity to suffer.' He was, of course, in the habit of paying special attention to whatever he committed to his literary notebooks, and *Tess* includes an echo of what he had read in the Bishop's article about the doctrines of reincarnation and of karma – a payment for past actions, which can end only when nirvana is attained. But he had already encountered the concept of nirvana in Zimmern's *Schopenhauer*, and it had chimed in with his own thinking – rather, perhaps, than actually influenced it. He was thus led to Henchard's last gesture: this is, after all, most appropriately seen as an insistent dissolution of his individual will. So Hardy was already beginning to think about the philosophical arguments of *The Dynasts*, as well as of its historical details. But there is more to it than that.

There are clusters of selves, both 'bad' and 'good', in the Hardyan light of 'loving-kindness' (almost identical with Schopenhauer's *Mitleid*, compassion), in every human being. We call a cruel man who is also devoted to good works a hypocrite. However (to take a hypothetical example), we should be more accurate if we described the founder of a soup-kitchen, a doer of good works, who is also a ruthless tyrant and usurer, to be 'good' in the former activity, and 'bad' in the latter: neither is a whole person. Each is a single self, or a cluster of selves, contained in one person. Henry Thoreau, a writer whom Hardy seems to have liked although he seldom mentioned him, opened his memorable early poem 'Sic Vita' thus:

> I am a parcel of vain strivings tied
> By a chance bond together,
> Dangling this way and that, their links

Were made so loose and wide,
Methinks,
For milder weather.

Hardy would have liked a later stanza in this poem:

And here I bloom for a short hour unseen,
Drinking my juices up,
With no root in the land
To keep my branches green,
But stand
In a bare cup.

He demonstrated his own awareness of this in a note of 2 January 1888: 'Different purposes, different men. Those in the city for money-making are not the same men as they were when at home the previous evening. Nor are these the same as when they were lying awake in the small hours.'

And in another, of 4 December 1890, he said: 'I am more than ever convinced that persons are successively various persons, according as each successive strand in their characters is brought uppermost by circumstances.'

Such selves or clusters of selves tend to be ignorant of each other. Hardy's 'villains' – Aeneas Manston, Sergeant Troy, Alec Durberville – can all be convincingly analysed along such lines; so can the other characters upon whom he bestows depth. But the 'real person' of whom we hear so much in life and in literature (the person Troy cannot become, but perhaps Giles Winterbourne or Tess – and even Henchard – can), who is she or he? He is no more than a glimpse of the person who is able to develop his type – the essential self with which he was born – to 'live out his fate' voluntarily, and therefore learn to interpret actuality as it is, objectively, and with no trace of fantasy. Developed, this would be a single and coherent person.

Henchard is no Winterbourne, no hero. He is in certain respects, in his rash and compulsive need to follow out his desire of the moment, even nearer to a villain. But he never intends harm – indeed, he fears doing harm, and, whenever he gets round to thinking about his actions, wants to right such wrongs as he sees he has done; nor does he ever enjoy his evil, as do Manston, Troy and, in particular, William Dare of *A Laodicean*. He tries, as he says when he is tempted to 'communicate to

Farfrae the fact that his betrothed was . . . legally, nobody's child: how would that correct and leading townsman receive the information?', to recognize 'visitations' of the devil, and to keep them at bay.

So why is it that most readers identify with Michael Henchard, most wretched of sinners, seller of his wife, drunkard and liar, rather than with the upright young Scot, Donald Farfrae, who is 'right' all along in his actions, or seems to be so by conventional standards? Is it not because of some quality essentially inner in its nature – some kind of internally bred power or authority? Why is Henchard tragic, and Farfrae lightweight by comparison? A wholly 'rational' reading of *The Mayor* would be one in which Farfrae is the hero who deals nobly with a mentor who turns out to be a bad lot. Such a novel could be written; but that particular Farfrae could not be found in it. The reading is a shallow one. Henchard's hell is beyond Farfrae's scope – it is that of the man who sees his fate through, even to its tragic last act. In the very moment of his wish to become nothing, to attain to the realm of complete oblivion or nirvana, he becomes a real person and reaches a sort of unity – terribly damaging though his actions have been to so many others. 'Each man is the novelist of himself,' wrote the Spanish philosopher Ortega; 'he can be an original novelist or a plagiarist, but he cannot escape the choice.' This is the inescapable poetry of *The Mayor of Casterbridge*.

Thus Hardy found the Bishop of Colombo's account of Buddhist belief in reincarnation from the 1888 article worth transcribing. He gave it a delicate twist – took out of it the notion of rebirth, but subtly retained the essence, the sense of burden, and the melancholy beauty of the original, in Tess's heart-rending outburst to Angel, in a passage that comes as near to poetry as prose can possibly come:

> 'Sometimes I feel I don't want to know anything more about [history] than I know already . . . Because what's the use of learning that I am one of a long row only – finding out that there is set down in some old book somebody just like me, and to know that I shall only act her part; making me sad, that's all. The best is not to remember that your nature and your past doings have been just like thousands' and thousands', and that your coming life and doings'll be like thousands' and thousands' . . . I shouldn't mind learning why – why the sun do shine on the just and unjust alike . . . But that's what books will not tell me.'

But Tess is 'pure' (as Tom insisted, in the provocative subtitle, *A*

Pure Woman, that he gave to the novel), an absolute victim; Henchard is anything but pure in that sense. The more we *think* about him, the more repelled we may fairly be. Yet the more we *feel* about him, the more we can sympathize with his anguish. That anguish, and his attitude to his fate, is something deeper than anything Farfrae could ever feel. Henchard, then, is, for all his failings, or even because of them, a 'man of character', as the full title tells us: *The Life and Death of the Mayor of Casterbridge: A Story of a Man of Character*. But what exactly does Hardy mean by 'character' – and does it in any case have any connection with the following oft-quoted passage, in which the narrator discusses the reasons for Farfrae's success?

> But most probably luck had little to do with it. Character is Fate, said Novalis, and Farfrae's character was just the reverse of Henchard's, who might be described as Faust has been described – as a vehement gloomy being who had quitted the ways of vulgar men, without light to guide him on a better way.

This packs in two direct allusions and another hidden one: from the German romantic lyric poet Novalis' novel *Heinrich von Ofterdingen*; from Carlyle's 'Goethe's Helena', about *Faust*; and (the hidden one) from George Eliot's *The Mill on the Floss*. It is inconceivable that Hardy ever read the original (1802) or the translation (1842) of the Novalis work, in which the quoted remark means, in its context, something different from what we should ordinarily understand by it. He lifted the allusion, already well known, straight from George Eliot, probably because it reminded him of the saying attributed to Heraclitus, 'Man's character is his daimon' (that is, personal destiny).

Lennart Björk, in one of the annotations to his edition of the *Literary Notebooks*, says that this allusion to Novalis is

> not primarily of a pessimistic nature . . . In fact, it is often taken as an affirmation on Hardy's part that man is not a mere plaything of the gods. While this impression may be true enough as far as the fate of Henchard is concerned, it does not seem equally valid for the rest of Hardy's *dramatis personae*. In *The Dynasts* sceptical overtones are added to the very words of Novalis: 'if character indeed be fate' ([2], vi.vi).

There is a misunderstanding (if not necessarily on Björk's part): the narrator's remark that 'character is fate' does not imply that Hardy himself is affirming that men are not, after all, mere playthings of the gods. The statement cannot be taken to imply either pessimism or optimism about the human situation, unless it is to be understood as meaning that 'a strong will, what is called "character", can turn adversity into good fortune, so we are not mere playthings of the gods'.

But Henchard, not Farfrae, is the 'man of character' of the title – and he, whether he brings much of his bad luck on himself or not, is never fortunate, but, rather, domineering. Nor does 'character' in *The Mayor* mean what it would be required to mean in that interpretation. The thrust of the subtitle, 'a man of character', is, as so often in Hardy, bitterly ironic. The destroyed Henchard carries more weight than Farfrae, is more worthy of sympathy, because he is capable of mythical status. Faust is not just more interesting than an ordinary corn factor. Farfrae has not quit the way of 'vulgar men', and could not be a Faust, or, as such, have to pay his due to the devil – thus, ultimately, to understand of what that due consists. This is the sense in which Farfrae's 'character' is the 'reverse' of Henchard's: it is the latter's archetypal weight that he lacks. Farfrae's appealing little songs of the home which 'he loved so well as never to have revisited' are as nothing compared with Henchard's determination to expunge all traces of himself from the earth.

If Hardy pays no attention to Farfrae's inner life, he is justified: there is none. He has principles, he has charm, but nothing in him is deep; whereas, although Henchard is devoid of both qualities, he attains a noble level of being even in the act of forfeiting that being. He is described as 'self-alienated'; Farfrae does not possess the capacity to alienate himself from himself. If we transform 'character is fate' into the old notion that 'the quality of a human being attracts the events of his life', then we have Henchard. Despite himself, and his inarticulacy, he is impelled to pursue his fate to its bitter end. When he understands that he has failed, that he does not deserve to exist, he wants to destroy himself. Unlike Cain in Genesis, he says, he will bear his punishment. This comes at the end of his life; but it is remorse of a sublimity undreamed of by the merely principled commercialist Farfrae. Henchard's terrible conscientiousness in the matter of his fate is in his bones. In his dealings Farfrae is correct. Henchard is rough and ready, exasperating and wicked in his carelessness, even 'terrible'; but he is ultimately, when he sees the truth of the matter, good-willed, just as he had carelessly been when he gave Whittle's mother real coal when she was in need – something that Farfrae would have been careful not to notice unless he could have had credit out of it. Henchard can be led into seeing the truth of matters.

When Hardy was not observing, or writing imaginatively – his intellect and emotion fused in the never easily attained act of creation – he was forced into thought. His persistent habit of sitting down at his desk to work was undertaken in the desperate hope that he would be able to write. Often, though, as he testified, he could not. Then he was an uneasy man whose emotionally religious heart was divided from his agnostic head: a victim of metaphysics, a sitting duck for the *poète manqué* McTaggart's good-willed, over-elaborate, ingenious and fantastic scheme as ultimately laid out in his famous *The Nature of Existence* (1921–27). Tom's intellect stood bravely aloof from inventing, yet could not help yearning for, a 'proof' of the existence of a universe that was ultimately benign: in other words, his thinking wished to achieve that valid fusion with his emotions, that 'true voice of feeling', which he could only experience in creation. Thus the unwilling thinker Hardy, the man caught between poems, was deeply attracted by McTaggart's unique system when, as a layman, he learned of it from articles in the philosophical periodical *Mind* and then from McTaggart's book *Some Dogmas of Religion* (1908).

Meanwhile, in 1885 he put more thought into *The Mayor* than he had put into any other novel, for all that it is a deeply emotional book; it may be regarded as the main precursor to *The Dynasts*, with Henchard as a kind of rehearsal for Napoleon. But Napoleon, as a dynast with millions rather than a few his victims, is hardly a sympathetic figure.

There is, of course, more to the novel than just this aspect, which, represents a groping for the meaning of life rather than any implied solution. But it is its most important aspect. Such gropings are often more genuinely religious than strictly orthodox observations. Henchard is no Christian, is even less Christian than his creator; but he does recognize, in his 'fetichism', that a church is a holy place: he has a sense of the holy. This is not mere superstition (although Henchard is superstitious, too), because he intends to keep the oath, and does keep it, thus investing his 'fetichism' with true meaning. We may feel that Hardy denied his own sense of the holy by disowning it as 'superstitious', by being interested in positivism and such nominally atheistic metaphysical schemes as McTaggart's, by trying to combine the irrational with the purely rational. So indeed he was inclined to do in his interludes of public thinking. But on the other hand he had steeped himself in Greek drama, which is hardly atheistic – and, above all, he himself went to church.

Some evidence of what Henchard meant to Tom is provided by the origin of his name, first brought to light by Peter Casagrande and Charles Lock ('The Name "Henchard"' in *Thomas Hardy Society Review*, 1, 1978). 'Henchard' is a combination of 'Trenchard' and 'Henning'. Tom had known both these Dorchester names since serving as Hicks' apprentice in his twenties. The powerful old Trenchard family had a Dorset branch, the back of whose town house, known as Trenchard Mansion, had faced into Shire-Hall Lane. It was pulled down in about 1848, so Tom would have remembered this sacrilegious act. He mentioned the house in his speech accepting the freedom of Dorchester in November 1910, and it is the subject of his poem 'A Man'.

This branch of the Trenchards had their estate at Wolfeton Manor on the outskirts of Charminster, a village two miles from Dorchester. Around 1800 Wolfeton was bought by James Henning, and he (or another member of the family) also lived at the old Trenchard Mansion until it was pulled down. Furthermore, a James Lewis Henning became Mayor of Dorchester in 1840. It cannot now be established that he was a member of the same family that lived at the Mansion, but it seems likely enough. So it may be that, as Casagrande suggests, 'the name "Henchard" combines the name of a fallen house with the name of a former mayor of Dorchester'; his conclusion is that 'Hardy fused the human with the architectural, a man with a mansion, in a peculiarly significant way'.

He goes on to compare Henchard with 'H. of M.', the subject of 'A Man (In Memory of H. of M.)'. This poem is set in Casterbridge in Elizabethan times, and concerns a humble stonemason who refuses to demolish the 'noble pile/Wrought with pilaster, bay and balustrade' which 'smiled the long street down for near a mile', and who therefore 'wandered workless' until he died:

> None sought his church-yard place;
> His name, his rugged face, were soon forgot.
>
> The stones of that fair hall lie far and wide,
> And but a few recall its ancient mould;
> Yet when I pass the spot I long to hold

As truth what fancy saith:
'His protest lives where deathless things abide!'

Although he died long before 1848, but equally did not live in
Elizabethan times, this is Tom's one (deliberately concealed) tribute
to his maternal grandfather, George *H*and of *M*elbury. By a happy
coincidence these initials are also those of Horace Moule, the friend who
perhaps agreed with Tom that the demolition of Trenchard Mansion was
an act of sacrilege. And it has been generally agreed that Hardy may have
found a model for Henchard in what he had been told – and it must have
been a great deal – about Jemima's mysterious father.

But it is unwise to try to connect too closely with Henchard the
'H. of M.' of the rather lightly written if fervent poem. Casagrande
thinks that Henchard might originally have been conceived by Hardy
as an itinerant stonemason who sold his wife and children and turned
himself into Casterbridge's leading builder: like the grain that he cannot
make right, the 'analogous phenomena' of the crumbling buildings of
Casterbridge cannot be 'made right'. But this is somewhat far-fetched,
because Trenchard Mansion still ought not to have been demolished,
and that is the point of the poem about it.

However, Casagrande's emphasis on the general theme that 'underlying all illusions of restoration is a tragic reality' – that the past must
be ineluctably destroyed – is right enough; and, more to the point, it is
also true that 'Henchard can for a time conceal the truth of the past and
repress the urgings of his nature in order to be a "new" man as mayor
and merchant, but because his character cannot change he is always, in
his essence, what he was at Weydon-Priors.'

Since he fails to be a 'new man' and cannot discover himself as
tradesman or dignitary, I believe Henchard determines to suffer the
fate of being what he actually is, and by his death and final repentance
– which is realized in his self-humiliation and determination to bear
his punishment – transforms himself into his very essence. He is
inarticulate and incapable of self-knowledge, and can only face the
evil of his errors when they explode in his face: those explosions,
however, are what he believes to be the 'sinister intelligence bent
on punishing him'. Without some equivalent to the notion of karma,
which does have parallels in such Christian thinking as Hardy would
have been familiar with, the novel makes little sense. Karma here,
though, is enacted not in many successive incarnations, but within a
single life.

Millgate is right in his assertion that Henchard is Hardy's 'most remarkable exercise in characterization . . . richly and sympathetically imagined'. But, misled by his hypothesis that Hardy was an inadequate bumpkin, he adds that Henchard possesses 'those qualities of ambition, authority, vigour, violence, and sexual aggressiveness which Hardy knew to be most lacking in himself – though he had a "source" for at least some of them in his maternal grandfather George Hand'. Although Hand had been dead for eighteen years when Tom was born, it is likely that Henchard does embody, for his creator, his impression of Jemima's recollections of her father, who may have been similar to the Henchard first glimpsed by Elizabeth-Jane and Susan when they arrive in Dorchester: a somewhat 'terrible' man. But it is a bizarre *non sequitur* even to suggest that a writer of Hardy's stature was lacking in determination. That Hardy 'backed into' fame is not a tenable view. He enjoyed his fame less, perhaps, than many who achieved equal repute; but it was an inevitable corollary of his exercise of his creative power, and he knew and felt that power.

Tom himself in no way outwardly resembled Henchard, but he had as much authority (*pace* Millgate), vigour ('violence' is not a 'quality'), and 'sexual aggressiveness' as anyone else. He did not exhibit these attributes overtly. 'It was perhaps psychically necessary for Hardy that so virile a fig-ure should suffer so catastrophic a fall'! Alas, *The Mayor* amounts to much more than a simple-minded compensation for Tom's alleged inferiority feelings. The power of his novels could hardly have emanated from anyone other than himself; nor does it need to be mediated by professors.

However, Millgate is right to detect, as others have done, that Henchard is representative of 'an ancient, deep-rooted, peculiarly English quality of life that never could be replaced or revived'. Nostalgia for the past is keen in Hardy, who could see where it had been improved upon as well as where it had not. This is therefore incidental to the book's main themes, of redemption through obliteration of self (Henchard), and through acceptance of an inevitably disappointing reality (Elizabeth-Jane). Millgate thinks that Elizabeth-Jane might be based on Eliza Nicholls, to (or about) whom, as he has demonstrated beyond reasonable doubt, 'Neutral Tones' was written. This interesting suggestion is undermined by the fact of Elizabeth's second name, which is that of the person Millgate describes as Eliza's 'treacherous sister'. However, insufficient evidence is offered that Mary Jane Nicholls actually was 'treacherous', and it remains a somewhat melodramatic assumption on Millgate's part – although it does give him the opportunity of accusing Hardy of 'ungraciousness'. We are in debt to Millgate for providing us with a credible alternative to Tryphena Sparks as the most important influence in Tom's early life. The affair with Eliza Nicholls is better documented, but only relatively so. Prudy talked to Eliza's niece, Mrs Sarah Headley, in 1955, and then passed on what he had heard to Millgate. It is not quite clear from Millgate's biography exactly what Mrs Headley did tell Purdy. Millgate gives an account of the affair based, mainly, on 'Neutral Tones' and the 'She to Him' poems. He is right that these poems do refer to Eliza, but his inference that Tom jilted her and then turned seriously to her sister Jane does not follow: it is known that he destroyed many of the poems of the 1860s. This was presumably Mrs Headley's belief, but it might have been based on a misunderstanding or, indeed, a bitter series of them.

Insufficient evident exists to make a useful guess about whom Elizabeth-Jane was based upon – if upon anyone. Tom might just as well have been thinking of Emma, or his beloved sister Mary, as of Eliza or Mary Jane Nicholls. For Elizabeth-Jane as a character convinces the reader less by her forcefulness of personality than by the cast of her mind, and she was in all probability, therefore, invented by him, even if a real woman or two casually provided him with a model. She is not high-spirited, like Bathsheba, Paula Power or Emma; but nor is she pious and conventional, which Eliza may have been. However, it must be added that the persona of the 'She to Him' poems, for all that there are now only four of them, does in certain ways fit in with her character, and that this character is reminiscent of Cytherea in *Desperate Remedies*.

The Mayor of Casterbridge is superior to and a more widely read work than *The Dynasts*, though it is not on the same grand scale. But it was by means of the latter that Tom, after trying out two collections of poetry on the public, was able to assert himself as a major poet. It is ironic that there is not much actual poetry in *The Dynasts*: most of it is, and deliberately so, verse. It is also ironic that so few reviewers really warmed to *The Dynasts*, or to the philosophy behind it; yet Hardy stubbornly succeeded in forcing it on the public at his own valuation rather than on theirs. Its status is now that of a 'great' but largely unread work – though not through any lack of vigour, virility and ambition on its author's part.

The Mayor is a study, in the form of fiction, for this historical work, which by the time he wrote the novel was looming very large in Tom's mind. Its chief purpose is to illustrate that the pattern which is innate in character must become that character's history: that character is, indeed, fate, but that fate can be lived through and endured. When we leave the prospering Farfrae his life seems to have little significance; when we leave Henchard, dead in his hut on the heath, he has endured his own worst.

18

The Woodlanders and Max Gate

On 17 April 1885 Hardy wrote the last page of *The Mayor of Casterbridge* at 7, Shire-Hall Lane. He and Emma then went up to London, which they would continue to do, for about three months every year, until almost the end of Emma's life. On this occasion they were there until the end of June, on the 29th of which Tom had to go back to Dorchester – perhaps unexpectedly early, for he had spoken of being in London until 'the end of July' – to superintend the removal of furniture to their new house. Emma had preceded him. What were their motives, separate or joint, for deciding to make this annual pilgrimage, during which they took either flats or rooms? Much has been alleged about Tom's snobbishness and enjoyment of high society. Much has been alleged, too, about Emma's excessive notions of the social homage which she believed to be her due as the wife a famous author. But both speculations are groundless and in themselves painfully snobbish.

The annual London pilgrimage was well established before Tom reached the apogee of his fame. As George Moore, who kept himself well informed, jealously told his publisher T. Fisher Unwin on 9 January 1906, 'Hardy's books . . . did not begin to sell really well until the complete edition came out' (in the Osgood, McIlvaine collected edition of 1896). It was the scandal over *Tess* that first put Hardy into the truly popular reckoning; before it, publishers would have hesitated to consider such an edition. Until then, to London society, he was no more than the very well-known, but not quite famous, author of *Far From the Madding Crowd*. Only to the local people was the situation rather different: Tom was the native who had made good, now returned. As such he and his wife were already subject to every kind of gossip.

The annual London visit was part and parcel of the decision to build Max Gate and take up residence there. There is nothing to suggest that Tom and Emma were not in full agreement. It is not known what illness, if any, had prevented Emma from going to Eggesford in March 1885; at any rate, it could not have been long. It is perhaps noteworthy that, for an alleged high flier, she did not care to struggle harder to overcome this illness. As for Tom's own alleged snobbery: he never changed his mind about the nature of London, or its high society, and, as he got older, grew more unwell while he was there. He had grave trouble with trying to write *The Woodlanders* (then still called *Fitzpiers at Hintock*) in London, and told Robert Louis Stevenson in a letter of 7 June 1885, 'I have some writing to do whilst in town, & *can't* touch it: it is becoming quite a nightmare.' But he decided that he could not afford to become a recluse, and that he would need an annual rest from his rigorous schedule. He spent most of each day in his study above the drawing-room, and did not allow his success to change his way of living.

Tom did not like London any more then than he ever had, or was going to, and in the *Life* quotes this note he made about it:

> May 28th. Waiting at the Marble Arch while Em called a little way further on to enquire after ——'s [unidentified, but it was almost certainly Emma's brother Walter] children . . . This hum of the wheel – the roar of London! What is it composed of? Hurry, speech, laughter, moans, cries of little children. The people in this tragedy laugh, sing, smoke, toss off wines, etc, make love to girls in drawing-rooms and areas; and yet are playing their parts in the tragedy just the same. Some wear jewels and feathers, some wear rags. All are caged birds; the only difference lies in the size of the cage. This too is part of the tragedy . . . At last E. returned, telling me that the children were ill – that little L[illian?]—— looked quite different, and when asked 'Don't you know me?' said, 'Not now; but I used to know you once.' How pathetic it all is!

On this visit, he was 'reading philosophy at the British Museum'. Was he reading Schopenhauer's *The World as Will and Idea*, all but the last volume of which was now available in translation? That his mind was on the *The Dynasts* rather than on the next novel is suggested by notes about his attendance at a 'crush', probably at Lady Carnarvon's, a few days before the announcement of the death of General Gordon on 26 January that year in Khartoum. 'It must have been his experiences at these nominally social but really political parties,' he wrote in the *Life*, 'that gave rise to the following note':

> History is rather a stream than a tree. There is nothing organic in its shape, nothing systematic in its development. It flows on like a

thunderstorm-rill by a road-side; now a straw turns it this way, now a tiny barrier of sand that. The offhand decision of some commonplace mind in high office at a critical moment influences the course of events for a hundred years. Consider the evenings held at Lord C——'s, and the intensely average conversation on politics held there by average men who two or three weeks later were members of the Cabinet. A row of shopkeepers in Oxford Street taken just as they came would conduct the affairs of the nation as ably as these.

Thus, judging by the bulk of effect, it becomes impossible to estimate the intrinsic value of ideas, acts, material things: we are forced to appraise them by the curves of their career. There were more beautiful women in Greece than Helen; but what of them?

What Ruskin says as to the cause of the want of imagination in works of the present age is probably true – that it is the flippant sarcasm of the time. 'Men dare not open their hearts to us if we are to broil them on a thorn fire'.

There is not, as yet, a single report of Emma's inability to hold her own socially; all that came later. But, despite her forgetfulness, she was never an incompetent hostess. Nevertheless it may be taken for granted that she was never socially smooth, and always inclined to the eccentric. Would Tom have respected her any the less for that? Or did he prefer conventional women? Both he and Emma were regarded by the fashionable French artist J.E. Blanche as 'dowdy', Blanche wrote in his *Mes Modelès* (1928). But where the society portraitist saw him as 'pathetic', others, more interested in literature and in art, saw him as impressive. The American novelist W.H. Howells, when he met him in 1884, had been able to appreciate his shyness because he valued his writings. London society was no more enlightened as a whole than were the woodlanders and farm labourers around the semi-fictitious villages of Tom's prose – only better informed about matters of no consequence, reminding us of the Austrian polymath Karl Kraus's remark about 'quality' journalists: 'To know nothing, and *be able to express it!*'

The house into which the Hardys moved on 29 June was designed by Tom in favour of convenience and comfort rather than appearance. His builder father – now getting on and badly troubled by rheumatism – is supposed to have said that not even for the thousand pounds he had been paid for the job would he ever repeat it. This does not suggest, however, that there was more fuss than might have ensued between any father and son. Neither does it suggest that there was not heavy pressure on Tom himself. He needed to be in Dorchester, and he could not have asked anyone else to build a house for him there; if the proceedings were fraught, then they would have been so for anyone. Disputes with his father and possibly with his brother Henry account for the majority of the interruptions he noted as having dogged the writing of *The Mayor*.

Max Gate is not 'badly built', as it has been called. It is solidly built; by today's standards exceptionally so. It was not impressive, and was not obviously the house of a former architect; this is because it was intentionally designed to be quite 'ordinary', and unpretentious: a residence for people who needed privacy, but who did not wish to appear too grand in the eyes of their neighbours. It was also designed to let in the maximum light, even to the extent of making the windows asymmetrical. It is therefore puzzling that Tom did not allow his screen of trees to be thinned from time to time; but he insisted that this would 'wound' them. F.E. Halliday is surprised that Hardy, 'architect, neighbour of Portland and lover of stone, could have designed such a house': the 'cheerless, red-brick Victorian villa, with meaningless turret, fancy projections and windows of uncertain size' is 'something of a mystery' to him. But it is a mystery only to those who assume that Hardy planned Max Gate as an expression of his poetic genius, rather than as a modest residence typical of its time, which would fit in unostentatiously with its surroundings. Even Halliday admits that the 'inside was better, though conventional: an entrance hall, dining-room to the left, drawing-room to the right'. The unhappiness that was to be associated with Max Gate grew over the years, especially after 1893–94, but it probably had more to do with its furnishings and atmosphere than with the building itself.

Nevertheless Tom was not feeling elated as he moved in. All decisive moves filled him with dread: the figure in the van was always waiting to strike him down. The *Life* is reticent, as it always is, on intimate personal details. He does record a fit of despondency, however, between November and the end of the year, when he made a now famous note from which perhaps too much has been inferred:

This evening, the end of the old year 1885 finds me sadder than many previous New Year's eves have done. Whether building this house at Max Gate was a wise expenditure of energy is one doubt, which, if resolved in the negative, is depressing enough. And there are others. But:

'This is the chief thing: Be not perturbed; for all things are according to the nature of the universal.' [Marcus Aurelius.]

These words confirm that he was troubled by the consequences of his coming to live in Dorchester. It is not the first time that he recorded such doubts. But the note cannot be taken as implying that there was yet anything seriously wrong with his marriage. It is true that W.R. Rutland, in his *Thomas Hardy* (1938), made a faint hint that he had found evidence of an affair, or friendship, with an unhappily married woman, but there is no further detail or confirmation from another source. Is the tenderness implicit in 'Everything Comes' (*Moments of Vision*) altogether retrospective? On the contrary, it seems honestly to recollect the intentions of 1885:

'The house is bleak and cold
　　Built so new for me!
All the winds upon the wold
　　Search it through for me;
No screening trees abound,
And the curious eyes around,
　　Keep on view for me.'

'My Love, I am planting trees
　　As a screen for you
Both from winds, and eyes that tease
　　And peer in for you.
Only wait until they have grown,
No such bower will be known
　　As I mean for you.'

'Then I will bear it, Love,
　　And will wait,' she said.
– So, with years, there grew a grove.
　　'Skill how great!' she said.
'As you wished, Dear?' – 'Yes, I see!
But – I'm dying; and for me
　　'Tis too late,' she said.

The phrase 'eyes that tease/And peer in' suggest that Emma, too, valued her privacy, and that Tom fully appreciated this.

The depression as Christmas approached may be explained more simply. First, he was apprehensive about the reception of *The Mayor*: he could no more grow used to unjust, stupid or Grundyist handling of his books than he could to restraining himself by failing to annoy such reviewers. But in this latest work, apart from its shocking beginning, he had managed to refrain from too much verbal teasing. His general apprehensiveness was aggravated by the fact that he now had to write another book. His inclinations were all towards his grand project of *The Dynasts*, but owing to his financial circumstances he knew that he could not yet attempt it. He had just spent a considerable sum on the house, and he needed a success, – or, better, two. He may have assumed, too, that he would have the excessively Grundyist John Morley to deal with at *Macmillan's*, which had commissioned the new novel. But he knew in any case that Mowbray Morris, Morley's successor, was even more conservative in matters of taste. When on 17 November he began serious work on *The Woodlanders*, he finally settled upon the plot he had shelved just before starting *Ethelberta*. He wanted to get his 'mind made up on the details', but simultaneously experienced a 'fit of depression, as if enveloped in a leaden cloud.' On 21 December he wrote dejectedly:

> The Hypocrisy of things. Nature is an Arch-dissembler. A child is deceived completely: the older members of society more or less according to their penetration; though even they seldom get to realize that *nothing* is as it appears.

Only nine days earlier he had noted 'Experience *unteaches* – what at first one thinks to be the rule in events.'

From where, if not from within, was the disturbance coming? It has been easy for commentators to assume that it must have been from Emma. But there is more than a hint, even in the *Life*, that it was his mother's behaviour that was giving him cause for concern.

On 17 October he had called on William Barnes at Came, which both he and Emma would often do until his death in the following year. In the course of talk about ancient Dorset families Barnes had told him a story about Louis Napoleon, the Emperor's nephew, who, during his exile from France, had been friendly with the Damer family who lived at Winterborne Came. While walking in town with Colonel Damer Louis Napoleon had, 'for a freak', slipped his walking-stick between the legs of Barnes' usher and nearly made him fall. This usher was called Hann, and Tom remarked in the note of this visit to Barnes, from which he quotes in the *Life*, that his 'people seem to have been of my mother's stock'. He continues:

> Hann was peppery, like all of that pedigree, my maternal line included, and almost before Barnes knew what was happening had pulled off his coat, thrown it on Barnes, and was challenging Louis Napoleon to fight. The later apologised profusely, said it was quite an accident, and laughed the affair off . . .

This note suggests that Tom, when quoting it, remembered how intransigent and interfering Jemima had been at the time when her famous son had built his own house and returned to his place of birth. Who knows how much she had poked her nose into the details of the design and the subsequent building? It would have fallen to Tom to fight for his wife's preferences in the house which was being built by his father but for his wife to dwell in. Jemima was the kind of person who is loved and revered within a family, but not much liked outside it. Both Mary and Kate, now teaching in Dorchester and living there from about 1888 in a house purchased for them by Tom (another drain on his expenditure), often came to Max Gate in the early days, as did the Sparks cousins from Puddletown; Jemima and Thomas senior also came there. The walk from Max Gate to Bockhampton takes about fifty minutes, and, while Tom took it every Sunday until his mother's death in 1904, she could hardly be expected to take it often in the reverse direction. In 1885 she was already seventy-two and well set in her ways; and the rheumatism-disabled Thomas senior was to die in 1892. When Tom and Emma first moved into Max Gate, then, things were more or less normal except for difficulties in dealing with the 'peppery' Jemima. But even this has to be inferred, as no substantial details exist outside that most unreliable of sources when uncorroborated: 'family tradition'.

During August Robert Louis Stevenson, his American wife Fanny – ten years older than he, and Emma's exact contemporary – her son Lloyd Osbourne by her unhappy first marriage, and an unspecified cousin all called at Max Gate. Stevenson, a perpetually sick man, was living at Bournemouth, where he had been visited on many occasions in the early summer by Henry James, there to see his invalid sister Alice. James had no more thought of calling upon Tom than Tom would have desired it. About this occasion Fanny, although she maintained a correspondence with Emma during the following winter, made a number of derogatory remarks. Tom says no more than this:

Almost the first visitor at their new house was R.L. Stevenson, till then a stranger to Hardy, who wrote . . . to announce his coming, adding characteristically: 'I could have got an introduction, but my acquaintance with your mind is already of old date . . . If you should be busy or unwilling, the irregularity of my approach leaves you the safer retreat.' He arrived two days afterwards . . . They were on their way to Dartmoor, the air of which Stevenson had learnt would be good for his complaint. But, alas, he never reached Dartmoor, falling ill at Exeter and being detained there until he was well enough to go home again.

Many years later, Hardy told May O'Rourke that Stevenson arrived wearing a sealskin cloak with a bunch of daffodils pinned to it – but where did he obtain daffodils in August? Perhaps it was some other yellow flower.

Stevenson left no record of his own impressions; but Fanny took a dislike. To Sidney Colvin she simply said that 'we saw Hardy's wife – but here one naturally drops a veil. What very strange marriages literary men seem to make' (many had felt, and do feel, that Stevenson's marriage to her was 'strange'). To her friend Dorothy Norton-Williams she generously confided:

> He is small, *very* pale, and scholarly looking, and at first sight painfully shy . . . His wife, he is lately married [the Hardys had been married for eleven years], is *very* plain, quite underbred, and most tedious . . . one remembers him as a most pathetic figure . . .

She also wrote to her mother-in-law: 'Did I tell you that we saw Hardy the novelist . . .? A pale, gentle, frightened little man, that one felt an instinctive tenderness for, with a wife – ugly is no word for it! – who said "Whatever shall we do?" I had never heard a human being say it before.'

Most of this is just chatter. Emma was by no means ugly in the sense that George Eliot was ugly (it was Henry James who said that she looked like a horse), and no one but Fanny Stevenson ever said that she was. As for the question, 'Whatever shall we do?', Fanny's objection to it is idiosyncratic, and casts doubt on the validity of her impressions. While not forgetting her courage in support of Stevenson, we should also not forget her possibly bad judgement: on bad, even possibly Grundyist, grounds she made him burn in the Bournemouth grate the first draft of *Dr Jekyll and Mr Hyde*. Gittings, reasonably enough in the face of this acidic evaluation, quoted from Alice James' animadversions on Fanny (and might have quoted from Henry's own), 'an appendage to a hand-organ' of 'such egotism and so naked!', and spoke of pots and kettles. But such insults have nothing to do with the matter: they have more to do with the universal habit of literary people to be mindlessly bitchy about one another except to their faces.

Millgate's prim belief that Fanny 'sharply perceived' the 'difficulties in the marriage' – held because it fits in with the Florence-inspired, and male-centred, thesis, first filtered through Purdy, that Emma failed to be a suitable helpmate to her genius-husband – is even less convincing. Significantly, he does not quote from the letter describing Emma's utterance of the innocent remark, 'Whatever shall we do?', which casts doubt on the soundness, let alone the sharpness, of Fanny's perceptions. As if realizing his error, and because he is always scrupulous, Millgate does add that these perceptions were perhaps more unkind than 'the circumstances then justified' – almost as if a proper male literary life must be surrounded by obedient female worship and never be interrupted by unseemly exhibitions of individualism, and also as if Fanny had been no less than that epitome of excellent judgement, a male academic critic. But Fanny's odd outbursts cannot be dignified by the word 'perceptions'. If a casual observer believes a marriage already more than a decade old is recent, then his or her judgement of its state can hardly be of value.

Stevenson remained unaffected by this silliness, and wrote to Tom in June 1886 to praise *The Mayor of Casterbridge* and to suggest a dramatization of it, which came to nothing. That the two men got on well together is suggested by Tom's confidence to Stevenson about the difficulty of working in London. Gosse's later letter to Tom telling him that Stevenson had packed up *The Woodlanders* to take with him to America may, however, be taken with a pinch of salt. Gosse meant altogether too well, and liked to inform his friends that even their enemies really admired them: he told Tom that Henry James admired *Tess* just as the latter was jealously denouncing it in a letter to Stevenson as 'vile'!

As late as 1891 his friend Sir George Douglas was pontificating about how over-seriously, in his view, Tom took Emma's criticisms of his novels, saying that he regarded the couple as 'well-assorted' and 'happily married', and even noting Tom's 'chivalrous attitude'; so the degree of their differences at this date has possibly been greatly exaggerated, even invented, by some. The tone of Millgate's judgement, that Tom's letters of mid-April 1891, from London, where he was alone, to Emma, 'are quite long and detailed, and perhaps sufficiently affectionate for a husband to write home to the wife to whom he has been married for sixteen years', requires no comment, except that it perfectly suits the patriarchal context in which its author is so happy. Tom was given to writing passionate letters at night – which is known because he suggested that they ought to wait until morning to be posted – when, of course, they would not be. What is more interesting, and needs no exercise of marriage guidance style judgement, is when his written salutation to Emma became more distant. In April 1894 she was still 'My Dearest Em'. A year later she was only 'My Dear Em'. Later still she was just 'Dear E'. It was, of course, Mrs Florence Henniker, or Tom's regard for her, that caused the first real trouble. But did Emma precipitate him into that affair, or did he simply find himself stricken?

But before the advent of Florence Henniker, and even during the time of Tom's intense friendship with her, he and Emma could share pleasure in their animals. There seem to have been four cats, including one called Kiddleywinkempoops-Trot, and a labrador bitch called Moss, who would usually accompany Tom on his walks. Delight in animals is a means of communication, and a means of conveying feelings of love, especially when verbal means have started to break down. The importance of these Hardy animals cannot be over-estimated; unfortunately, those who have little interest in animals do not appreciate this point. Early in the new century Emma had planks laid between certain pieces of furniture for the convenience of the cats – and, although Tom must already have been irritated by some of Emma's ways, he would hardly have reacted against that; it may even have been undertaken jointly. Unhappily the Max Gate cats tended to wander on the nearby railway line and some of them lost their lives, small but important to Tom and Emma. Thus we owe the most moving elegy for a domestic pet ever written, 'Last Words to a Dumb Friend', to the fate of Snowdove, 'purrer of the spotless hue', in October 1904. The feeling in this poem is apt demonstration of the part played by animals in Tom's emotional life.

Could the following entry in his diary, quoted in the *Life*, have been prompted by the nature of his relationship with Emma? On 3 January (1904) he had made the note about his art being 'to intensify the expression of things'; three days later he wrote:

Misapprehension. The shrinking soul thinks its weak place is going to be laid bare, and shows its thought by a suddenly clipped manner. The other shrinking soul thinks the clipped manner of the first to be the result of its own weakness in some way, not of its strength, and shows its fear also by its constrained air! So they withdraw from each other and misunderstand.

This keenly sensitive observation of situations sufficiently commonplace is remarkable. It has never, however, been suggested that Emma herself, although not articulate to the degree her husband achieved, was possessed of a similar sensitivity. She was only a woman, and so such a fact would not much matter to the biographer anxious only to establish the paramount genius of his subject. Yet this subject, to be able to achieve genius – or, more precisely, the insight of poetry – must be more troubled by such things: notice them even more keenly than he notices hedgehogs crossing the lawn. And the lines of communication must still have been fairly open: there are nearly five hundred manuscript pages for *The Woodlanders*, of which about one-fifth is copied in Emma's hand. There is no evidence of Emma's participation in the writing (and none against it), but there must have been plenty of discussion.

Meanwhile, back in 1885–86 there was *The Woodlanders* to finish. Tom knew that he had to work hard if he were to keep up his commitments and earn his £600 (about £135,000 by today's standards) for the serial rights. He was initially reluctant to work on it, however much he was eventually going to prefer it to his other novels '*as a story*' and because of his fondness for its setting. It would have suited his peace of mind to get it done as quickly as possible, since the first of the twelve instalments was due out in *Macmillan's* (and *Harper's Bazaar*, since the *Atlantic* had refused it) by May 1886. But he did not finish it until 4 February 1887, thus having it run ahead of his invention; when he did so he recorded that, although he had thought he would 'feel glad', he was not 'particularly, – though relieved'. While still struggling with it, he wrote under the date of 4 March 1885:

> Novel-writing as an art cannot go backward. Having reached the analytic stage it must transcend it by going still further in the same direction. Why not by rendering it as visible essences, spectres, &c. the abstract thoughts of the analytic school?

This notion was approximately carried out, not in a novel, but through the much more appropriate medium of poetry, in the supernatural framework of *The Dynasts* as also in smaller poems. And a further note of the same date enlarges the same idea:

> The human race to be shown as one great network or tissue, which quivers in every part when one point is shaken, like a spider's web if touched. Abstract realisms to be in the form of Spirits, Spectral figures, &c.
>
> The Realities to be the true realities of life, hitherto called abstractions. The old material realities to be placed behind the former, as shadowy accessories.

So he and Emma shortly hurried up, as he tells us, to rooms in Bloomsbury 'to have the Reading Room of the Museum at hand'. They were in London for four months in all, until the end of July, and Tom describes himself in the *Life* as 'quite resigned to novel-writing as a trade, which he had never wanted to carry on as such. He now went about the business mechanically.' But he was not so 'resigned' that he could carry on with *The Woodlanders* while he was in town: it became 'quite a nightmare', as he doubtless again told Stevenson when he met him for the second and last time at Sidney Colvin's in July. This also implies that, quite apart from his wish to devote himself to poetry and *The Dynasts*, he deprecated the limitations put upon him as a storyteller by the various false proprieties which he had to observe if money was to be made. He thus agreed with the sentiments of a letter written to him at this time by the then aspiring novelist George Gissing, from which he quotes: 'the misery of it [novel-writing] is that, writing for English people one may not be thorough: reticences and superficialities have so often to fill places where one is willing to put in honest work'.

The reviews of *The Mayor*, while respectful as always, did little justice to it, and were indeed beset with just the false attitudes mentioned by Gissing. Tom was not happy with them. He can hardly have been happy, either, about Smith, Elder's reluctance to put it out in volume form: their witless reader had told them that 'lack of gentry among the characters makes it uninteresting'. R.H. Hutton wrote in the *Spectator* of 5 June 1886, concerning the passage about Henchard which ends 'He had no wish to make an arena a second time of a world that had become a mere painted scene for him':

> To our minds, these very pagan reflections are as much out of place as they are intrinsically false. The natural and true reflection would have

been that Michael Henchard, after his tragic career of passionate sin, bitter penitence, and rude reparation, having been brought to a better and humbler mind than that which had for the most part pervaded his life, the chief end of that life had been achieved, and that it mattered little in comparison whether he should or should not turn the wisdom he had acquired to the purpose of hewing out for himself a wiser and soberer career.

Such moralistic missing of the point from not unintelligent minds could only have sickened Tom, as it had already sickened the young Gissing. Tom was not satisfied, and told the consoling Kegan Paul on 1 June 1886 that he fully recognized that the *Saturday Review*'s reference to the setting as a 'remote region – which we are unable to localize' was malicious:

I am not disposed to think of the review as entirely the product of stupidity. That there should be no mistake about the locality I told the editor the real name of the town: so the paragraph about not recognising it is meant as a civil snub, I suppose.

I have not, however, expected any great praise of the book; I know its faults too well.

Impressions gathered from his reading of the philosophers, including Hegel, in the British Museum, and related reflections on the form that *The Dynasts* might take, are not absent from the new novel, although he may not have fully realized this. During May, while he was struggling with the way the rest of *The Woodlanders* would develop, he wrote:

Reading in the British Museum. Have been thinking over the dictum of Hegel – that the real is the rational and the rational the real – that real pain is compatible with a formal pleasure – that the idea is all, etc. But it doesn't help much. These venerable philosphers seem to start wrong; they cannot get away from a prepossession that the world must somehow have been made to be a comfortable place for man. If I remember it was Comte who said that metaphysics was a mere sorry attempt to reconcile theology and physics.

But idealism as such – the notion that everything is mental – did not much appeal to, or interest, him. He found Hegel's idealist rival Schopenhauer more congenial only because his view of the world was a fundamentally gloomy one – and, no doubt, because he was more interesting as a writer, and did not think of the development of the state as embodying the final perfection of man. All this reading did no more than confirm his notion of a Will indifferently *unfulfilling itself in human affairs. Thus, early in the novel, speaking of the woodlands, he writes in a famous passage:

> Here, as everywhere, the Unfulfilled Intention, which makes life what it is, was as obvious as it could be among the depraved crowds of a city slum. The leaf was deformed, the curve was crippled, the taper was interrupted; the lichen ate the vigour of the stalk, and the ivy slowly strangled to death the promising sapling.

How Tom understood Hegel it is impossible to say, more especially in the light of the fact that so many professional philosophers have understood him so differently. On 13 March 1904 he was to tell Henry Newbolt, to whom he was grateful for sensible criticism, that he agreed with him that the word 'Will' in *The Dynasts* 'is not quite accurately used'. But, he continued,

> the difficulty was to find another, fit for poetry, which would express an idea as yet novel in poetry – that condition of energy between attentive & inattentive effort which the scientific call 'reflex', 'instinctive', 'involuntary', action; 'unconscious formative activity', &c. 'Urgence' occurred to me, and I think I used it once, but it seemed scarcely naturalized enough. Just as the Original Cause did not (apparently) foresee the pitch of intelligence to which humanity would arrive in the course of the ages, & therefore did not prepare a world adequate to it, so the makers of language did not foresee the uses to which poor poets would wish to put words, & stinted the supply.

This, besides demonstrating how calm and sensible Tom could be when confronted by reasonable, unprejudiced criticism, suggests that Hegel may have left his mark on his mind. Reading Hegel, or about Hegel, may also have helped him to form the character of Edred Fitzpiers, perhaps the most interesting of all Hardy's variations on his Mephistophelean-visitant type. Fitzpiers is not really a villain, but he is thoroughly odious.

Jean Brooks in her *Thomas Hardy: The Poetic Structure* (1971) put her finger on another potent connection with his current thinking:

The woodlanders are involved closely in the battle of natural selection that links all species in a mystery of suffering. Trees, woodland creatures, and human beings alike sound the dominant note of pain at the disharmony of natural things interrelated in 'one great network or tissue which quivers in every part when one point is shaken, like a spider's web when touched' . . . a disharmony made poignant so often by the human character given through imagery to vegetation.

She then quotes the famous passage about the Unfulfilled Intention. And she is surely right in her claim that the 'plot is a metaphor of the Unfulfilled Intention that pervades the natural world with manifestations of frustrated desire'. Millgate has astutely pointed out, too, that Marty South may be said in one sense to resemble the 'Spirits of *The Dynasts* – perhaps, since she suffers'; he could have added, more specifically, the Spirit of the Pities. The concept of the great web appears in a description of Marty and Giles working together: 'And yet their lonely courses formed no detached design at all, but were part of the pattern in the great web of human doings then weaving in both hemispheres from the White Sea to Cape Horn.'

It seems improbable that Jean-Paul Sartre ever read *The Woodlanders*, but, if he did, he would have discovered it to be analogous, in respect of plot, to his own play *Huis Clos* (sometimes entitled, in translation, *Vicious Circle*). This is set in a hell in which a man loves a woman who loves another woman who loves the man, and so on round and round. Hardy presents a similarly vicious circle, although it is not as resolutely or neatly closed; the hell in which it is set is far more pleasantly adorned, too, and has a comic personage in the obsessed George Melbury. The village girl Marty South loves the apple and cider dealer Giles Winterborne who loves the daughter of the timber factor, Grace Melbury, who is drawn to Edred Fitzpiers, a doctor and romantic metaphysician reputed (if only by the humblest characters) to be 'in league with the devil' (as Wildeve was to have been in *The Return of the Native*), who amorously experiments with a 'hoydenish' village lass, Suke Damson, with Grace herself (whom he marries), and then with the 'foreigner', Felice Charmond, an unhappy, wealthy and vain woman of easy virtue who owns much of the local property, which she has no interest in properly administering – indeed, she hates her estate to the point of malicious boredom.

The various settings of the novel have always proved hard to pinpoint precisely, and this was deliberate. The area is unequivocally Melbury Osmund, the place in which Jemima Hardy was born and grew up. Tom told Gosse in letters of 31 March and 5 April 1887 that Great Hintock 'had more of *Melbury Osmund* in it than of Minterne [Magna]', and that Little Hintock, upon which the novel is centred, was a 'hamlet anywhere within 2 miles of the former' – which means, in effect, a real hamlet called Hermitage. As Tom wrote in 1912, in an addition to the introduction, when he and a companion (probably Hermann Lea) went on their bicycles to look for 'Little Hintock' itself they could not find it at Hermitage. It was in Tom's mind. As Lea wrote in his *Thomas Hardy's Wessex* (1913), the 'descriptions in the book would seem to be chosen from one or other of [Hermitage, Middlemarsh, Minterne, Melbury] without much attempt at exact localization'.

The Woodlanders is the first novel to make it clear that the countryside of Hardy's Wessex is not a real place but an inventive picture drawing upon its creator's memories of a real place. It has, in the Aristotelian sense, a greater reality than the tourist's 'Wessex'. *The Mayor* had dealt almost, although not quite exclusively, with the town of Casterbridge. As Hardy said (or, rather, made sure that his excellent and intelligent friend Lea said):

> . . . the descriptions given in the novels and poems must be regarded in their totality as imaginative places. The exact Wessex of the books exists nowhere outside them, as Mr Hardy himself indeed has hinted. Thus, instead of declaring *Casterbridge* to be Dorchester, we dare say only that the presentment is undoubtedly founded on salient traits in the real town.

This is almost the last word on the matter. The 'topographer' is, Lea added, in 'a dangerous position, since there is an undoubted tendency to fall into the error of confusing the ideal with the actual'.

But *The Woodlanders* is not, like *The Mayor*, a historical novel. It is set, so far as may reasonably be inferred (attempts to date it exactly have always fallen down, as Hardy intended), in the second half of the 1870s. But the precise dating matters even less than it does in *The Mayor* because, as Lea pointed out, the region in which it is set was 'inhabited by simple-minded people', and 'many old-fashioned ideas and superstitions' still lingered there. These people, who form a more substantial chorus than that of *The Mayor*, are not so much 'simple-minded' as lacking in information. They are literal and shrewd.

Mrs Charmond and Fitzpiers are strangers in a remote area not much intruded upon by such as they.

The plot, having lingered for twelve years in Hardy's mind, partakes of the sensational – especially so for a mature and major novel. But the characterization, like that of *The Mayor*, shows a marked advance on that of the minor novels. Nor is there any real wickedness or madness, *à la* Dare or Boldwood, in *The Woodlanders*. Richard Carpenter alludes to a 'scrupulous (sometimes almost ridiculous) observation of the proprieties in the narration', but this judgement seems confused. Perhaps he has missed Hardy's ironies or, possibly, the violent attack on those proprieties that Hardy made, if only incidentally, when he caused Giles' death by his own 'ridiculous' observation of them. There is no reason to suppose that his highly ironic 1895 introduction, with its careful distinction between 'heart' and 'head', was in any way an afterthought:

> In the present novel, as in one or two others of this series which involve the question of matrimonial divergence, the immortal puzzle – given the man and woman, how to find a basis for their sexual relation – is left where it stood; and it is tacitly assumed for the purposes of the story that no doubt of the depravity of the erratic heart who feels some second person to be better suited to his or her tastes than the one with whom he has contracted to live, enters the head of the reader or writer for a moment.

His views on marriage had not been formed by his personal experiences, and no doubt if he and Emma ever discussed Fourier they agreed that the Frenchman's sensible views about it were superior to current social practices. But Mrs Henniker had not then intervened.

Ian Gregor, in his discussion of this novel, quotes the above sentence up to 'left where it stood' and then calls it 'singularly graceless . . . odd in tone as well as substance, as if Hardy wishes to draw attention to an issue which might escape the reader's attention and then felt absolved from pursuing it'. But that judgement is odd in itself, since the end of the sentence, which he does not quote, fully explains the deliberate 'gracelessness' and 'oddness'. Tom felt that the Victorian novelist's inability to discuss the truth about 'sexual' relations was more than merely 'graceless', and was therefore deliberately graceless about it. What he means is that the sexual relations *must* be left as they stand in an unjust and hypocritical society. He did not feel 'absolved from pursuing it' but *forced* from doing so: he could not do his work, which involved the pursuit, not of what he believed to be the truth, nor of what he wanted to be the truth, but the truth itself, in the form of a novel that would be acceptable to readers. 'Finding a basis for sexual relationships,' says Gregor, rather innocently and complacently, 'is more likely to bring twentieth-century writers to mind . . .' But none of these, despite the current easier climate in that respect, has possessed Hardy's power.

He endured the usual bowdlerizations from Mowbray Morris and Frederick Macmillan. Morris begged him to tone down the Fitzpiers–Suke Damson relationship: 'human frailty' must be 'construed mild' for the sake of the 'pious Scottish souls' who read the story. (It is notable how all these Grundyist editors, including Stephen, apologized, and put the onus on the simplicity of their readers: no conspiracy has been more open than the Grundyism of the Victorians.) Although by this time Tom knew full well that he would have to do this toning-down in the serial versions of any piece of fiction he liked to write, he could never quite resign himself to it. Unlike George Moore, he steered clear of antagonizing the circulating libraries; but in his own way he was as resolute an opponent of their false morality, and one perhaps even more irritating to the literary establishment, in that he worked, with a greater degree of irony than most (even now) accord to him, inside the enemy lines. His inner fury and frustration, though, were prompted not by people's holding of sincerely moral views, whether he agreed with them or not, but by their general refusal to 'tell it as it is' – by just such animadversions as the persistent ones of R.H. Hutton and other even less perceptive reviewers, all victims of the fallacy that 'is' must always be 'ought' in literature.

The Woodlanders may be seen as a new and more tragic treatment of the theme of *Far From the Madding Crowd* – as a novel in which the comic is subordinate to the tragic. Giles Winterborne, doubtless embodying some of the qualities Tom saw in his father, although by no means modelled upon him, resembles Farmer Oak. But he does not marry his love; he dies young and unhappy, instead, and the reader protests – and is supposed to protest – that no man ought to suffer so much. Fitzpiers is a subtilized, refined, intellectual Troy – as William Wallace pointed out in the *Academy* of 9 April 1887. Grace is, fatally for her happiness, a better-educated Bathsheba, a natural woodlander hoisted up by her father into something that makes her susceptible to the fascinating but false values of Fitzpiers. The plotting is not tight, as in *The Mayor*, the 'superiority' of the pastoral over the urban is asserted discreetly, and as no more than the author's personal 'impression' or preference, not as a programmatic 'philosophy of life'. Only the plight of the *livier*, the lifeholder, seen in the predicament of Giles Winterborne when he is dispossessed of his property, is at all pressed upon the reader; but even this is done with tact and discretion. Tom's father was a *livier*.

The book arose in part as the result of Tom's musing over his new position. He was a well-off semi-suburbanite within hailing distance of remote childhood haunts, an inhabitant not only of the artificial urban world, but also of a remoter pastoral one – yet spying, as an urban sophisticate famous for his rustic comedy (presenting local friends as comic fodder for learned London worthies), on his own family and people, and feeling, like the speaker in Norman Cameron's 'Public-House Confidence', that he must never

> let the rumour get across
> Of how I am no use at all to either,
> And draw the pay of both for doing neither.

He loves the pastoral world best, but sees that it, too, is victim 'as everywhere' of the Unfulfilled Intention, 'which makes life what it is'. But he was not now, and never would be, the man of the newspaper legend whose pessimism became a byword. He had his sad and angry moments, which he concealed beneath a taciturn and pale aspect; but, like any pessimist worth the name, and like Schopenhauer himself, he got much enjoyment out of being what he really was:

> Let me enjoy the earth no less
> Because the all-enacting Might
> That fashioned forth its loveliness
> Had other aims than my delight.
>
> About my path there flits a Fair,
> Who throws me not a word or sign;
> I'll charm me with her ignoring air,
> And laud the lips not meant for mine.
>
> From manuscripts of moving song
> Inspired by scenes and dreams unknown
> I'll pour out raptures that belong
> To others, as they were my own.

THE WOODLANDERS AND MAX GATE

> And some day hence, towards Paradise
> And all its blest – if such should be –
> I will lift glad, afar-off eyes,
> Though it contain no place for me.

The Woodlanders, then, is a transitional novel that explores its author's newly found position in the world. If there is no hero or heroine to dominate it – with the exception of Marty South – this is because Tom was feeling in no mood to identify with any part of himself. Thus Giles is more loyal and worthy than resolute, and Fitzpiers, although not evil, seems more disgusting than Troy only because he lacks his panache. But this hardly matters, and may even be regarded as an interesting new development. It does tend, however, to undermine Hardy's ill-considered aside about Little Hintock:

> It was one of those sequestered spots outside the gates of the world where may usually be found more meditation than action, and more listlessness than meditation; where reasoning proceeds on narrow premises, and results in inferences wildly imaginative; yet where, from time to time, dramas of a grandeur and unity truly Sophoclean are enacted in the real, by virtue of the concentrated passions and closely-knit interdependence of the lives herein.

This novel, after all, having no very robust characters, is less Sophoclean than its immediate predecessor. But it is genuinely experimental precisely for that reason, since an author who can create strong personalities if he wishes to do so here eschews that option.

The story – described by the appalled reviewer in the successful society weekly the *World*, edited by the flamboyant bohemian Edmund Yates, as one 'of vulgar intrigue, and nothing more' – is soon outlined. The initial, and fatal, act has been performed, in all innocence – although by no means without self-interest – by the timber factor George Melbury. He is now married to his second wife, Lucy, in an 'arrangement – for it was little more' that had 'worked well enough'. Being 'of the sort called self-made', and anxious to appear as 'a well-informed man', Melbury has given Grace, his only daughter by his first marriage, for whom he has an overwhelming but touching fondness, an expensive education. The obsessive nature of his concern is aptly illustrated by these words he addresses to her when she has just observed that the Melburys have been in Little Hintock for as long as the formerly grand Fitzpiers family were at Oakbury Fitzpiers.

> 'O yes – as yeomen, copyholders, and such like. But think how much better this will be for 'ee. You'll be living a high, perusing life, such as has now become natural to you; and though the doctor's practice is small here he'll no doubt go to a dashing town when he's got his hand in, and keep a stylish carriage, and you'll be brought to know a good many ladies of excellent society. If you should ever meet me then, Grace, you can drive past me, looking the other way. I shouldn't expect you to speak to me, or wish such a thing – unless it happened to be in some lonely private place where 'twouldn't lower 'ee at all. Don't think such men as neighbour Giles your equal. He and I shall be good friends enough, but he's not for the like of you. He's lived our rough and homely life here, and his wife's life must be rough and homely likewise.'

Returning from finishing school, she has become socially and intellectually superior to her betrothed, Little Hintock's apple-tree man and cidermaker Giles Winterborne, who still loves her. As an adolescent she had wanted his kisses more than he dared to give them. But now she is dubious about him, although she could have been drawn back to him had he been more resolute. Giles suffers financial reverses when he is dispossessed of his cottages, in part because he has annoyed the owner, and Melbury is therefore glad, though decently uneasy, to break the engagement in favour of his daughter's marriage to the learned and handsome Fitzpiers. But in doing so, he is aware that he has missed the opportunity to redress an old deceit: he had behaved badly to Giles' father when he robbed him of the woman who became Grace's mother. The attractive widow Felice Charmond, owner of much of Little Hintock, soon steals Fitzpiers from his wife, and Giles and Grace think they might find happiness through the new divorce law of 1878. But this hope proves illusory.

Throughout, Marty South loves Giles silently and hopelessly. She has decided to sell her beautiful hair, nature's one real gift to her, to the pretentious Barber Percomb (a 'Perruquier to the aristocracy' who also runs a back-street shop for the ordinary folk) for two sovereigns, for the use of Felice Charmond. This is because she has discovered that Giles loves Grace, and also because she needs money to support her sick father, who dies in the course of the story. Fitzpiers returns, and Grace flees for refuge to Giles' cottage in the woods. Though already sick, Giles sleeps out of doors so as not to seem to offend Grace's virtue; this kills him. Mrs Charmond is then shot by a former lover from South Carolina, while Marty is left to mourn Giles, and Grace to her ultimately unhappy marriage to Fitzpiers ('She's got him quite tame,' observes Mr Upjohn. 'But how long 'twill last I can't say.' We know that it will not be long before Fitzpiers' eye roves again.) Respectability, however, has been preserved – and at the mere cost of one life and several people's happiness.

The Woodlanders was a success, and the reviews, despite the usual moral carping, were the best Tom had received for many years. It was William Wallace, Whyte Professor of Moral Philosophy at Oxford, who gave the novel its most perceptive notice. In the *Academy*, a literary review which ran from 1869 until 1915, Wallace wrote that it was Hardy's 'best and most powerful work' since *Far From the Madding Crowd*; but it would, he added, be regarded as his most unpleasant book

not only by the ordinary clients of Mr Mudie, who feel dissatisfied unless Virtue passes a Coercion Bill directed against Vice at the end of the third volume, but even by those of Mr Hardy's own admirers who complain, as Mr Morley complains of Emerson, that he is never 'shocked and driven into himself by the "immoral thoughtlessness" of men', that 'the courses of nature and the prodigious injustices of men in society, affect him with neither horror nor awe'. In recent fiction, even in recent French fiction, there has figured no more exasperating scoundrel than Edred Fitzpiers, who yet . . . figures as the repentant, or, at all events, the returned prodigal . . . In *The Woodlanders* [Hardy] gives us the Unfulfilled Intention of the actual world . . . Even *Far From the Madding Crowd* does not contain more passages worthy of quotation than *The Woodlanders* – passages in which Mr Hardy permits his readers, though not himself, to turn from the tragedy of the Unfulfilled Intention, in order to enjoy the pensive contentment of a Coleridgean sabbath of the soul.

As the author of a life of Schopenhauer to be published in 1890, and upon which he may already have been at work, the discriminating Wallace well understood the nature of Hardy's pessimism and his intention in making Marty South 'sublime' by the end of the book, when she mourns Giles Winterborne. He recognized, too, that Tom's own 'sabbath of the soul' could never be otherwise than a sabbath of mourning over the creator's lack of foresight. When he took the gamble of giving up prose for, first, epic drama, and then poetry, he could express these ideas altogether more delicately than he could in the novel. *The Dynasts* itself offers no more than a reasonably well elaborated philosophical framework within which can be read the infinitely more subtle poems.

One of the most precious of all brief appraisals of Hardy's achievement as a novelist occurs in Proust's *A la Recherche du temps perdu*. The narrator is explaining to Albertine that 'the great men of letters have never created more than a single work, or rather have never done more than refract through various media an identical beauty which they bring into the world'. Then:

> I returned to Thomas Hardy. 'Do you remember the stonemasons in *Jude the Obscure*, and in *The Well-Beloved* the blocks of stone which the father hews out of the island coming in boats to be piled up in the son's work-shop where they are turned into statues; and in *A Pair of Blue Eyes* the parallelism of the tombs, and also the parallel line of the boat and the nearby railway coaches containing the lovers and the dead woman; and the parallel between *The Well-Beloved*, where the man loves three women, and *A Pair of Blue Eyes*, where the woman loves three men, and in short all those novels which can be superimposed on one another like the houses piled up vertically on the rocky soil of the island. . . .'

Inspired by Proust and by the ideas of Georges Poulet, who viewed literature primarily as the expression of a state of mind, the American critic Joseph Hillis Miller wrote *Thomas Hardy: Distance and Desire* (1970), which, like Gregor's *The Great Web*, is one of the few books on its subject to have attained almost classic status in that it has stimulated the most illuminating discussions. Miller's reading of Hardy's poetry and fiction may be said to elaborate Proust's, and, although Proust does not mention *The Woodlanders*, Miller finds this novel particularly evocative of Hardy's most essential concerns. Gregor agrees, and, echoing the English mistranslation of Proust's title (*A la Recherche du temps perdu*: *In Search of* – not simply 'remembrance of' – *Lost Time*), writes: 'Recollection, the remembrance of things past, a concern to render a consciousness increasingly susceptible to the tensions of the present, these elements give the peculiar colour to *The Woodlanders*.' And he aptly quotes part of a note Hardy made just a month before he finished the book:

I don't want to see landscapes, i.e., scenic paintings of them, because I don't want to see the original realities – as optical effects, that is. I want to see the deeper reality underlying the scenic. . . . The simply 'natural' is interesting no longer. The much decried, mad, late-Turner rendering is now necessary to create my interest. The exact truth as to material fact ceases to be of importance in art – it is a student's style – the style of a period when the mind is serene and unawakened to the tragical mysteries of life; when it does not bring anything to the object that coalesces with and translates the qualities that are already there – half hidden, it may be – and the two united are depicted as the All.

Tom found Turner a congenial figure, and, in the creative solitude forced upon him by uncomprehending reviews, found that he could identify with him. Not long after completing *The Woodlanders* he went on 8 January 1989 to the Royal Academy, where he noted:

Turner's watercolours: each is a landscape *plus* a man's soul. . . . What he paints chiefly is *light modified by objects*. He first recognises the impossibility of really reproducing on canvas all that is in a landscape; then gives for that which cannot be reproduced a something else which shall have upon the spectator an approximative effect to that of the real. He said, in his maddest and greatest days: 'What pictorial drug can I dose man with, which shall affect his eyes somewhat in the manner of this reality which I cannot carry to him?' – and set to make such strange mixtures as he was tending towards in 'Rain, Steam and Speed'. . . . Hence, one may say, Art is the secret of how to produce by a false thing the effect of a true. . . .

He might have been speaking of Cézanne. And on 25 March 1886 he had transcribed into his notebook a sentence from a *Times* leader of the previous day, underlining the phrase 'more than': 'That *more than* mathematical accuracy by which a great painter reveals the subtle depths of character'. Björk rightly relates this to his interest in Turner, whose paintings, after all, had been described in 1816 as 'pictures of nothing, and very like'.

Tom, like other gloomy-minded people, probably enjoyed his gloom, and therefore he probably also enjoyed the drudgery of writing pseudo-respectable novels for a magazine public when what he actually wanted to do was write poetry. But novel-writing gave him less pleasure except when he was actively engaged in it, and the difficulty with which he got down to the task of sending off the instalments of *The Woodlanders* has already been described. Yet, for all that he was just then so preoccupied with philosophy and with planning his epic drama, the reluctant novel is by no means sicklied o'er with the pale cast of thought. On the contrary: in it he satirizes his own over-cerebral state of mind. Here is the first glimpse of Fitzpiers:

'Was he really made for higher things, do you think? Is he clever?'

'Well, no. How can he be clever? He may be able to jine up a broken man or woman after a fashion, and put his finger upon an ache if you tell him nearly where 'tis; but these young men – they should live to my time of life, and then they'd see how clever they were at five-and-twenty! And yet he's a projick [prodigy], a real projick, and says the oddest of rozums [oddities]. "Ah, Grammer," he said at another time, "let me tell you that Everything is Nothing. There's only Me and Not Me in the whole world." And he told me that no man's hands could help what they did, any more than the hands of a clock. . . . Yes, he's a man of strange meditations, and his eyes seem to see as far as the north star.'

This humourously encapsulates Tom's own situation: he needs to be practical, and write this novel, just as a doctor has to 'jine up' his patients when they report their symptoms; but he is getting lost in abstract speculation, as well as in poeticization. He needs to please his audience with another *Far From the Madding Crowd*, but finds himself distracted from the task because it requires narrative prose-writing. He is now settled in Dorchester, whether he likes it or not. He has just completed a novel whose chief theme, apart from the creation of the great tragic personality required for the purpose, explores the old notion of 'character as fate'. It has not had the critical due that he would have appreciated. Is this owing to his own weakness of invention, he wonders, or is it because critics fail to understand – because the world does not wish to understand?

Because it seizes his imagination, he will shortly note, as he reads his acquaintance the anecdotal painter William Frith's *My Autobiography* (1888): '*Scene*. Turner crouching over a morsel of fire in his gaunt

paperless gallery . . . with dreadful cold – refusing to sell the pictures.'
Will the world ever allow itself to listen to what he, Thomas Hardy,
has to say? Why is he not, as later he will confess he desired to be, an
architect in some small town? How can he manage a transition from
prose to poetry?

His intuition, his mother's behaviour, and much else, tell him that he
has sown the seeds of trouble in making his recent decision. Yet he tries
to be stoical after the practical manner of Marcus Aurelius. No doubt he
asks himself: 'Would things have turned out differently if events had been
otherwise than they were, given my own character, Emma's character,
Jemima's character?' And his mind falls again upon this now irrevocable,
and therefore more immediately threatening, choice.

He knows that he could never have succeeded in London – where
he finds going on with *The Woodlanders* a 'nightmare' – even in
turning out more minor comedies. He knows that he will be more
than ever dependent upon his family's reminiscences, especially those
of his mother, for the detail and the feel of his fiction. But, here
in Dorchester, is he not a fraud, the country boy transformed into
sophisticated city-dweller – now only an artificial countryman, mocking
his most loved ones? What does the true rural life mean, and can it be
preserved in any way? Above all, can he himself recapture it? He needs
therefore not simply the 'remembrance' of that past of his own which
had been genuinely rural: like Proust, he has to *search* for it.

Despite what may well have been a conscious determination simply to
press on with a pastoral romance in the same vein as his greatest success,
and to do his best with the plot he had shelved years earlier, Tom set to
working out his own problems in this new novel. Not since *A Pair of
Blue Eyes* had he written a novel so personal to himself, although in
that instance he intended to employ the book itself to try to solve them.
Coventry Patmore, sensing the presence of a poet, had felt that the novel
would have been even better in poetic form. *The Woodlanders* is as poetic,
in this sense, as *A Pair of Blue Eyes* or *The Mayor of Casterbridge* had been.
But it is poetic in a different manner.

The Mayor is high tragedy, with little of Hardy's usual humour in it.
It is poetic because true tragedy demands poetry, and cannot be attained
without it. Hardy was one of the least ambitious or flamboyant of those
people universally (if in his own case somewhat reluctantly) regarded as
'great writers'; artistically, however, he was one of the most consciously
ambitious. *The Mayor* wants to give the tale it tells the status of such
legends or myths as those of Oedipus, Saul or Lear.

But *The Woodlanders* seeks the status of a different sort of myth, in which the individual plays a smaller part. Myth has been called 'metaphysics in its primary and purest form'; it was towards myth that his readings at the British Museum, in less pure forms of metaphysics, drove him. Thus, the mythology of *The Woodlanders* partakes more of the nature of folklore or fairy-tale; it resembles a soured *Midsummer Night's Dream* rather than a *Lear* or an *Othello*. Nature is paramount in it, and it is therefore appropriate that the characters should not be dominant. They are presented as a part of nature, subject to the same 'law' of the Unfulfilled Intention.

Marty's father John South, for instance, who has worked with trees for the whole of his life, has watched the elm outside his house grow from a sapling; now its life is his life, and if it is destroyed then he too will be destroyed. Marty tells Fitzpiers: 'He says that it is exactly his own age, that it has got human sense, and sprouted up when he was born on purpose to rule him, and keep him as its slave.' The trees, too, do feel pain, and will eventually be felled; but they will feel far less pain than the people, whose intelligence, Tom already believed, was developed to a pitch far too keen to be able to exist in a world so 'inadequate' to contain sensitivity. But the so-called rationalist Hardy cannot resist arranging his narrative so that South does indeed die when Fitzpiers, his doctor, insists that the tree must be felled if he is to live.

In 1883, well before the publication of *The Mayor* or *The Woodlanders*, Havelock Ellis, in his long *Westminster Review* essay on Hardy's work, took special notice of his devotion to trees. 'Mr Hardy is never more reverent, more exact, than when he is speaking of forest trees.' Ellis related this to 'lingering echoes of the old tree-worship', and to 'Nature-worship' in general. *The Woodlanders* is Hardy's 'tree-novel', and, in the deliberate absence of strong or resolute characters, the trees themselves, with their sobbing and sighing, dominate it. They are always present, and so, too, is the awareness that they are all eventually to be felled. No wonder this poet of the woods could not later bear his own Max Gate trees to be felled or even pruned for fear of giving them pain! Writing of these woodlands, and of the almost religious power they had for him, brought out the poet in Hardy. The world of the woods is so closed that Fitzpiers, even though his family comes from Oakbury Fitzpiers (that is, Oakford Fitzpaine, only a few miles east of Melbury), is utterly foreign to it, even if the woodlanders pay him deference because of the connection.

Coventry Patmore, himself a poet, was even more attuned than the young Ellis to the poetic in Hardy; so, too, in 1886, was Patmore's then unknown friend Gerard Manley Hopkins (brother of Hardy's illustrator). Like Hardy, Hopkins was a transitional poet, writing in Victorian times and even in a Victorian manner, but already anticipating the future. He could sense the poetry in Hardy's novels, and in a letter of 28 October 1886 to Robert Bridges cited scenes from *The Return of the Native*, *Far From the Madding Crowd* and *The Mayor of Casterbridge* to support his point that 'the amount of gift and genius which goes into novels in the English literature of this generation is perhaps not much inferior to what made the Elizabethan drama'. Hopkins was not to live to read the poet Hardy in bulk, but his judgement was astute. What might he have written had he known of what was to come?

Much of the substance of *The Woodlanders*, if not its sheer delight and poignancy as a story, Hardy expressed in a poem called 'In a Wood'. He wrote the first draft in 1887, then revised it in 1896 and published this version with the subtitle 'See *The Woodlanders*'; in the first edition of his *Collected Poems* this subtitle was misleadingly changed, probably by a proofreader, to 'From *The Woodlanders*'. The poem tells us something important about the element of struggle in Hardy's development:

> Pale beech and pine so blue,
>   Set in one clay,
> Bough to bough cannot you
>   Live out your day?
> When the rains skim and skip,
> Why mar sweet comradeship,
> Blighting with poison-drip
>   Neighbourly spray?
>
> Heart-halt and spirit-lame,
>   City-opprest,
> Into this wood I came
>   As to a nest;
> Dreaming that sylvan peace
> Offered the harrowed ease –
> Nature a soft release
>   From men's unrest.
>
> But, having entered in,
>   Great growths and small
> Show them to men akin –

369

Combatants all!
Sycamore shoulders oak,
Bines the slim sapling yoke,
Ivy-spun halters choke
    Elms stout and tall.

Touches from ash, O wych,
    Sting you like scorn!
You, too, brave hollies, twitch
    Sidelong from thorn.
Even the rank poplars bear
Lothly a rival's air,
Cankering in black despair
    If overborne.

Since, then, no grace I find
    Taught me of trees,
Turn I back to my kind,
    Worthy as these.
There at least smiles abound,
There discourse trills around,
There, now and then, are found,
    Life-loyalties.

It has an analogue in the passage about the Unfulfilled Intention, quoted earlier; it also bears signs of Tom's recent heavy reading in metaphysics at the British Museum – and of his attempts to modify the pessimism of which he was so widely accused. For it denies, or tries to deny, the truth of what he really finds in human beings' treatment of one another, which he was finally to affirm in the late poem 'We Are Getting to the End' and elsewhere. That denies the 'evolutionary meliorism' which he dutifully attempts to suggest in *The Dynasts*, which he adumbrates in this poem, and which he felt obliged to disseminate. Schopenhauer's *Parerga and Paralipomena*, the essays he published in 1851 (though not translated into English until after *The Woodlanders* had been written), contains some grim words which summarize what Tom felt in 1886 and 1887 and until the end of his life:

Right in itself is powerless; in nature it is might that rules. To enlist might on the side of right, so that by means of it right may rule, is the problem of statesmanship. And it is indeed a hard problem, as will be obvious if we remember that almost every human breast is the seat of an egoism which has no limits, and is usually associated with an accumulated store of hatred and malice; so that at the very start feelings of enmity largely prevail over those of friendship.

The words about universal egoism, although more remorseless, recall 'She to Him II', the poem Hardy 'prosed' and put into the mouth of Cytherea in *Desperate Remedies*. Ellis alludes to this passage, and remarks that in the '"Parerga" there is, indeed, a short passage [he did not mean the one quoted above – but there is an abundance of such utterances] of which Cytherea's cry is but a paraphrase'. The early 'Confession to a Friend in Trouble' is an honest declaration of a similar egoism – but one that few would care to make, either then or now. Hardy never believed otherwise of the human condition.

His invention (as he believed it to be) of an Imminent Will becoming gradually more conscious of itself was, thus, although entirely sincere, only a philosophical experiment. His true hope, when he could become no more than the poet he wished to be, lay in a different direction. When the darkling thrush sang on 31 December 1900 he could not, in all truthfulness, admit to more than a blessed hope of which he was unaware. But he left hope in the dogged honesty of his own equally dogged search for it.

The Woodlanders itself, though, is in general gloomier than, say, *The Dynasts* is intended to be. Its hope, like the hope in Hardy's poetry, lies in the lyrical and affirming beauty of its last passage – the fact that even this world can produce something of that order. There is some incidental comedy in the sayings of the rustics – and in George Melbury's absurd hopes for his daughter – as well as the usual wisdom, but it is hard to see what critics mean when they speak of it even as a 'tragi-comedy'. The burden that Grace, as irresolute in her way as the man she finally comes to love, must now carry is a heavy one indeed, for her husband Edred Fitzpiers is not only contemptible but, clearly, as incapable of self-control as of self-knowledge. 'It's a forlorn hope for her!' mutters her repentant father. What we are left with is not a convincing notion of Fitzpiers having learned from bitter experience, but rather a snapshot of a man in a habitual phase: that of 'repentance'. Moralizing reviewers were not fooled, and complained of it. If Tom sentimentalizes his ending in order to please his serial and other readers, or such reviewers as Hutton, then he does so in a manner that satirizes their tastes. (If only, Hutton moaned in the *Spectator*, Mr Hardy would 'give us a little more of human piety'.) Marty's life – something, the reader soon learns, which she never valued much – is to be one of loss and miserable servitude.

So the poem 'In a Wood' gives rather a false view of the book to which it explicitly refers, since the latter emphasizes in almost every respect that the life of human beings does, indeed, resemble the Darwinian one of the trees. True, in Giles and Marty we do see a limited example of 'life-loyalties'; but both are defeated – Giles by the observation of an unnatural respectability which leads to his death, and Marty by loss of everything that she has held dear. And fate denies them the togetherness which would have made them happier. *The Woodlanders*, then, is not a comi-tragedy or a tragi-comedy, but a tragedy relieved by comedy – and in that sense, if only in that sense, 'In a Wood' is true to Tom's beliefs.

The drift of this Darwinian novel demands that its characters be weak or foolish, or caught in the meshes of romantic love: that they merge into nature so ineluctably as to suffer the consequences of it. In *The Mayor of Casterbridge* Henchard had tried to rise above nature, only to accept it in the end. The characters in *The Woodlanders*, rooted like the trees, make little effort to evade their destruction. The snobbish weakling Fitzpiers is sexually stimulated only by the presence of whoever coincides with his Idea (a theme Hardy was to explore further in *The Well-Beloved*), and, described as a man at one phase in the first sign of the zodiac, and at another in the second, and so on, has little lasting interest in any consequences. Grace is fascinated by him, at the same time dreading the effect he has upon her – but is too weak even to insist on the marriage in the Little Hintock church which she wants. She gets it only at the expense of ignoring what she has seen with her own eyes: Suke Damson coming out of his house in the early morning. Grace does not want to question his glib lie. Giles Winterborne cannot rescue her, as she plainly desires to be rescued, by enforcing his suit and his prior right to her. After all, he impresses himself upon her only as a man 'who hardly appertained to her existence at all'. She gains some spirit and robust sarcasm only when she has fully understood Fitzpiers' treacherous nature. Felice Charmond is solely dependent upon the satisfaction of her vanity. No one profits or can be happy. The way for *Tess* was clear, and it did not even take the experience of falling in love to set Hardy resolutely upon that path.

19

Marking Time

On 14 March 1887, the day before Macmillan published *The Woodlanders* in volume form, Tom and Emma fled England for Italy. Although he was now regularly insisting to himself, to the extent of distinctly remembering it thirty years later, that his novel-writing was 'mechanical', he none the less wished to avoid the unpleasant impact of poor reviews. However, expecting them as a matter of course, he wanted to come upon them in one piece rather than in a steady and inexorable trickle. This seemed the best way of mitigating the known effect upon his nervous system. The Italian trip had been planned for a long time, perhaps with this unpleasantness partly in mind. He had not felt elated when he finished *The Woodlanders* – only 'relieved'. Perhaps he was still feeling sad about the death of Barnes the previous October.

Tom had been on closer terms with Barnes than with any other fellow writer since Horace Moule. He had always been determined to extend his own range beyond the boundaries of Dorset, but to keep Dorset, as the only place he knew really well, at the heart of the enterprise. He realized that, as well as being fond of Barnes, he had found in him a master, if only a limited one; he shared this recognition with Emma. On the day following Barnes' death he wrote to Gosse: 'I promised to let you know if such an event occurs, but I did not think it would be quite so soon. My wife was almost the last person – if not the very last – outside his family, whom he was able to converse with.'

Within a few days he had written an obituary for the *Athenaeum*, which appeared on 16 October. But his deepest personal feelings about what he owed to the man, as kindred spirit as well as master, were reserved for a poem, 'The Last Signal'. He was anxious that he might be too close to his subject to be able to assess him within the context of English poetry as a whole, although he need not have worried: he remains the best commentator upon a poet and scholar who, because of his eccentricity, has attracted little criticism. Coventry Patmore had written perceptively on him in the *Fortnightly*, and in the course of doing so, mentioned Hardy's fiction favourably. Tom wrote to him on 11 November 1887:

> I should have written you before now a line of thanks for the good feeling which prompted your word about me there as a novelist. It is what I might have deserved if my novels had been exact transcripts of their original irradiated conception, before any attempt at working out that glorious dream had been made – and the impossibility of getting it on paper had been brought home to me.
>
> Your criticism of Barnes's work was most instructive. I have lived much too long within his atmosphere to see his productions in their due perspective, as you see them.

He added that he thought it 'extremely difficult' to convey a notion of 'Barnes's quality as a poet by selections'; eventually he was to be pressed into becoming the first person to attempt this difficult task.

Lucy Baxter, Barnes' daughter and eventual biographer, had long since settled in Florence with her husband. Once one of the many apples of Tom's schoolboy eye, she was soon to guide him and Emma around her adopted city. On 13 December 1887 he wrote to her:

> I quite agree with your friends in thinking that you are the born biographer of Mr Barnes. . . . I have been trying to think over the conversations I used to have with your father. Unfortunately for their use to the public – this is quite between ourselves – our talk was almost invariably of a personal character – people we had known, & other such details, intensely interesting to us as we talked, but which would have no attraction for outsiders, even if it could be made intelligible.

This letter shows how essentially private the relationship with Barnes was. There is a hint, if no more, that they talked together in Dorset dialect – an intriguing notion. At least there was nothing formal about the friendship, for all that Tom was some forty years younger than Barnes. But Tom made it clear that he was going to disclose nothing intimate, even to Lucy. In his *Athenaeum* piece he had this to say of the Dorset dialect, and of Barnes' studies in it:

> Born so long ago . . . it is no wonder that Barnes became a complete repertory of forgotten manners, words and sentiments, a store which

afterwards he turned to such good use in his writings on ancient British and Anglo-Saxon speech, customs and folklore; above all, in the systematic study of his native dialect, as a result of which he has shown the world that far from being, as popularly supposed, a corruption of correct English, it is a distinct branch of Teutonic speech, regular in declension and conjugation, and richer in many classes of words than any other tongue known to him.

Tom's own use of Wessex words was less philological and more literary than Barnes', who could be pedantic. Tom recognized from the outset that it was useless to transcribe, word-for-word, what people say: 'On the page, the liveliest dialogue taken down word for word seems flat, complicated, heavy . . . To reproduce the effect of spontaneous spoken life on the page, you have to bend language in every way – in its rhythm and cadence, in its word,' wrote the French author Louis Ferdinand Céline, who used Parisian dialect. Tom understood this, and so did Barnes at his best.

For himself, Tom had no 'reservations' at all about Barnes, as has been suggested, nor did he find him 'evasive'; but he felt bound to point out his limitations to his *Athenaeum* audience, few of whom were country people. So he pointed out that the dialect poems took their inspiration from Barnes' native Vale of Blackmore, 'where the fields are never brown and the springs never dry'. This was, almost exactly, the setting of *The Woodlanders*, then nearly completed. He never, Tom continued, 'assumed the high conventional style', as Burns and Béranger and 'other poets of the people' had done:

he entirely leaves alone ambition, pride, despair, defiance, and other of the grander passions which move mankind great and small. His rustics are, as a rule, happy people, and very seldom feel the sting of the rest of modern mankind – the disproportion between the desire for serenity and the power of obtaining it. One naturally thinks of Crabbe in this connexion; but though they touch at points, Crabbe goes much further than Barnes in questioning the justice of circumstance. Their pathos, after all, is the attribute upon which the poems must depend for their endurance; and the incidents which embody it are those of everyday cottage life, tinged throughout with that 'light that never was' [this phrase is from Wordsworth's 'Elegaic Stanzas Suggested by a Picture of Peele Castle . . .'], which the emotional art of the lyrist can project upon the commonest things. It is impossible to prophesy, but surely much English literature will be forgotten when 'Woak Hill' is still read for its intense pathos, 'Blackmore Maidens' for its blitheness, and 'In the Spring' for its Arcadian ecstasy.

So much for Tom's 'reservations' (they should be called exactitudes) and 'evasiveness'. As Harold Orel has written, Barnes was not only 'the hero' of Hardy's youth, but 'indeed of his entire life'. Sam Hynes, in an essay in the *South Atlantic Quarterly* (Winter 1959), thought that, Shakespeare apart, only the influence of Barnes was apparent in Hardy's poetry: 'and the direction of his influence is the direction taken by English poetry in the transitional period between High Victorianism and the twentieth century'. Hynes has forgotten about the early influence of Meredith; but his remark is shrewd, and not an exaggeration. As to what Tom owed both to Barnes' *A Grammar and Glossary of the Dorset Dialect, with the History, Outspreadings and Bearings of South-Western English* (1864), published when he was twenty-four, and to his many and close discussions with him, this is quite incalculable. Barnes' *Poems of Rural Life, in the Dorset Dialect* was the only book Tom ever reviewed (for the October 1879 issue of the *New Quarterly*), and that he did unsigned. No doubt he was able to complete his obituary notice of him so quickly because he reproduced in it most of this review. But he ended the latter:

> Though not averse to social intercourse, his friendships extended over but a small area of society. But those who, like the present writer, knew him well and long, entertained for him a warm affection; while casual visitors from afar were speedily won to kindly regard by the simplicity of his character, his forbearance, and the charming spurts of youthful ardour which would burst out as rays even in his latest hours.

These words go as far as possible in their indication that such private friendships cannot be publicly described. And they contain, too, a prefiguring of what Tom himself said towards the end of his own even longer life: that he would like to have been a more obscure man. He admired Barnes for his lack of ambition, as well as for the degree of 'pathos' he could achieve without touching on the grander passions.

Yet the two men differed considerably. Barnes was a sturdy and wholesome Christian, whereas Tom, for all his religious impulses and lifelong churchgoing, can scarcely be thus described. Tom was not bothered about linguistic purity and would not have troubled to call an omnibus a 'folk-wain', as Barnes quaintly did. Yet without him, he could not have written as he did. For Tom he represented the past of remote 'pastoral recesses' such as the Hintock of *The Woodlanders*. Now this past seemed even more inaccessible. His death sent Tom into contemplation, and, if he had any specific person in mind as he wrote the immortal closing words of his own favourite among his novels, it must surely have been Barnes.

As he looked forward to his visit to Italy he was struck by the mechanical nature of too much of the urban existence with which he, as distinct from the strictly local Barnes, had chosen to deal:

> You may regard a throng of people as containing a certain small minority who have sensible souls; these . . . being what is worth observing. So you divide them into the mentally unquickened, mechanical, soulless; and the living, throbbing, suffering, vital. In other words, into souls and machines, ether and clay.
>
> I was thinking a night or two ago that people are somnambulists – that the material is not the real – only the visible, the real being invisible optically. That is because we are in a somnambulistic hallucination that we think the real to be what we see as real.

He was under no illusions as to the nature of the society for whose edification he, unlike Barnes, had decided to interpret pastoral remoteness; but in them none the less he sought such 'sensible souls' as his words could quicken into life. Not so long afterwards, back in London again in March 1888, he wrote of the 'fiendish precision or mechanism of town-life', and of how this 'made it intolerable to the sick and infirm'.

The Italian trip went well, although it began badly: as they proceeded to Turin by way of Aix-les-Bains a snowstorm seemed to dog their progress. After Turin, Genoa and Pisa they finally reached Florence, where Lucy Baxter met them and took them to lodgings she had obtained for them at the Villa Trollope, which had once belonged to the Trollope family; Anthony's novelist elder brother, Thomas Adolphus, had lived there with his mother, and Anthony himself had written *Doctor Thorne* there in the late 1850s. Emma's interests were concentrated more on cats than on scenes of historical interest, but she accompanied Tom on most occasions. Her diary discourses affectionately upon the demerits of the short-haired nature of the Italian cats: '*No* lovely cats in Italy as in

France'. Later, when they got to Rome, she found the churches there 'full of trash'. Tom fell asleep in the Sala delle Muse of the Vatican, 'the weariness being the effect of the deadly fatiguing size of St Peter's':

I sat in the Muses' Hall at the mid of the day,
And it seemed to grow still, and the people to pass away,
And the chiselled shapes to combine in a haze of sun,
Till beside a Carrara column there gleamed forth One.

She looked not this nor that of those beings divine,
But each and the whole – an essence of all the Nine;
With tentative foot she neared to my halting-place,
A pensive smile on her sweet, small, marvellous face.

'Regarded so long, we render thee sad?' said she.
'Not you,' sighed I, 'but my own inconstancy!
I worship each and each; in the morning one,
And then, alas! another at sink of sun.

'Today my soul clasps Form; but where is my troth
Of yesternight with Tune: can one cleave to both?'
– 'Be not perturbed,' said she. 'Though apart in fame,
As I and my sisters are one, those, too, are the same.'

– 'But my love goes further – to Story, and Dance, and Hymn,
The lover of all in a sun-sweep is fool to whim –
Is swayed like a river-weed as the ripples run!'
– 'Nay, wooer, thou sway'st not. These are but phases of one;

'And that one is I; and I am projected from thee,
One that out of thy brain and heart thou causest to be –
Extern to thee nothing. Grieve not, nor thyself becall,
Woo where thou wilt; and rejoice thou canst love at all!'

This, written long after the event, is not one of Hardy's best poems; but it is a key one. He alluded to it again in the *Life*, when he came to deal with the occasionally mean and foolish reception of *Wessex Poems*, in which he included it and some other of the travel poems occasioned by this journey. Reviews had attacked him for suddenly attempting (as they saw it) a new form of expression, after producing prose for years. He wrote:

Probably few literary critics discern the solidarity of all the arts.

Curiously enough Hardy himself dwelt on it in a poem that seems to have been little understood. It is called 'Rome: The Vatican: Sale della Muse'; in which a sort of composite Muse addresses him . . .

He then quoted the passage '"Be not perturbed . . . one"', the first phrase of which he had himself quoted on the last day of 1885 from Marcus Aurelius, and which he requoted in *Tess*, Chapter 39. But what the poem relates to above all is the paradox underlying all Hardy's poetry: that he found a pattern in diversity. In 1909, not long after William James' 1908 Oxford lectures, collected as *A Pluralistic Universe*, were published by Longman in Great Britain, he quoted the following passage from it:

We live forward, we understand backward . . . The line of least resistance, then, as it seems to me, both in theology & in philosophy, is to accept, along with the superhuman consciousness, the notion that it is not all-embracing, the notion, in other words, that there is a God, but that he is finite either in power, or in knowledge, or in both at once.

This notion of a limited God, implicit in gnosticism and familiar from Hardy's *Dynasts*, has been taken up by the media in the late twentieth century, albeit in a wildly over-simplified form, as a popular interpretation of the formulations of modern physics. Dennis Taylor recalls the remark in the *Life* about the 'somnambulistic hallucination' in which we live, and then aptly quotes the conclusion of the James passage that Hardy copied: 'concepts, being so many views taken after the fact, are retrospective and post mortem'. For Tom the tragedy was that the brain was the last to 'understand' the body's situation: to grasp the whole. In 1890 he noted, of a 'staid, worn, weak man' seen at the railway station at Dorchester, that his 'back . . . legs . . . face, were longing to be out of the world. His brain was not longing to be, because, like the brain of most people, it was the last part of his body to realize a situation.'

When Florence was preparing the *Life* for publication she was in a panic of anxiety lest anything good about Emma should seem to be recorded there. Excited by her excision of the fact that the sculptor Woolner had given to Emma (and not to Tom) a landscape attributed to Bonington which subsequently hung in their drawing-room, she confidently cut out a further substantial passage, four pages later, telling of how Emma, through her typically impulsive behaviour and 'usual courage', saved Tom from being robbed by three ruffians of a picture he had bought. For good measure she also cut a reference to Emma's having got what Hardy called 'an attack of malaria' by lingering 'for a long time in the underground dens of the Coliseum' (the connection between malaria and mosquitoes then being unknown).

In Rome, too, Tom was struck by the tired and artificial nature of modern Christianity. The monk who showed him and Emma the hole in which St Peter's Cross is supposed to have stood in the Church of San Pietro in Montorio, and whose actions implied that it had been there 'ever since the apostle's crucifixion', he thought, 'was a man of cynical humour who gave him an indescribably funny glance from the tail of his eye as if to say: "you see well enough what an imposture it all is!"' He wondered if perhaps there was not something in his own appearance which made such people 'think me a humorist also'. Despite that remark, however, commentators have on the whole mistakenly chosen to regard him as a pessimist with no entry to the world of humour. Pointedly and provocatively, he wrote that he preferred the pagan to the Christian in Rome, and, 'of the latter . . . churches in which he could detect temples from ancient temples'.

While in Rome, he corresponded with various people, including old Mrs Procter and Gosse, to whom he thoughtfully sent violets picked from Keats' grave. When they returned to Florence he was relieved, and 'found the scenery soothing after the gauntness of Rome'. But he found Venice most pleasurable, despite bad weather, and rejected Ruskin's description of St Mark's: 'conventional ecstasy, exaggeration – shall I say humbug?'

After Milan and a visit to the French Crown Jewels while passing through Paris, they were back in London at the end of April – just in time for Tom to attend the annual dinner of the Royal Academy on the 30th. They remained in London, in lodgings at 5 Campden Hill Road in Kensington, until the end of July.

He found the reviews of *The Woodlanders* less uniformly depressing than he had probably been expecting, and the Wallace review of 9 April, with its withering references to Mudie and Grundyism, must have been particularly cheering. But the general incomprehension, despite the clear indications in the text that Fitzpiers had not and would not 'reform', must have been discouraging. This was especially so when it came from such hands as that of Coventry Patmore, who had written in the *St James's Gazette* that 'Grace Melbury [forfeits the reader's sympathy] altogether when she marries Fitzpiers . . . the whole interest of the story is spoilt by our being expected to believe in that incredible event, the abiding repentance and amendment of a flippant profligate.' That was to read the book against the text in the interests of propriety, or, worse, to read it carelessly, or not at all, and would have been galling for any serious novelist. Tom was also, doubtless, annoyed by the more telling thrust with which Patmore concluded his notice:

> Why such a master of language should, in his latest work, have repeatedly indulged in such hateful modern slang as 'emotional' and 'phenomenal' (in the sense of 'extraordinary' instead of 'apparent'), and in the equally detestable lingo of the drawing-room 'scientist', seems quite inexplicable.

But, and despite (or because of) R.H. Hutton's finding of 'serious fault' with Hardy's 'moral standard' in the *Spectator*, Mudie was continuing to buy the book, and on 6 May Tom was glad to tell Frederick Macmillan that the seven shilling royalty he proposed on each copy of the three-volume edition (and one-sixth on the forthcoming single volume edition) was 'quite satisfactory'.

By 30 August he had returned to Max Gate and was writing to Gosse about a statue to be erected in memory of Barnes, a letter which suggests that he was in an unusually cheerful state of mind. He says that he is sorry not to have seen Stevenson since his departure for Colorado (allegedly with *The Woodlanders* in his bag), and that he imagines he was in 'the same high-spirited ardent mood we are accustomed to look upon as his natural state, irrespective of circumstances'. Then followed the famous and oft-quoted passage about his having, in the past, gone to bed 'not wishing to see daylight again'. But he added:

> This blackest state of mind was however several years ago – & seldom recurs now. One day I was saying to myself 'Why art thou so heavy, O my soul, & why art thou so disquieted within me?' I could not help answering 'because you eat that pastry after a long walk & would not profit by experience' . . .

All in all, he was feeling pleased – particularly, no doubt, because *The Woodlanders* looked like doing well financially. He would have recalled the reluctance of Smith, Elder to issue *The Mayor of Casterbridge* as a volume at all, as well as their reader's fatuous comment. There was, too, his agreement of late June to give Tillotson & Sons Newspaper

Fiction Bureau the serial rights to his next novel in exchange for the satisfying sum of one thousand guineas – equivalent today to a good deal more than £25,000.

William Tillotson, of Bolton in Lancashire, was the proprietor of many newspapers in the north of England including the *Bolton Weekly Journal*. In 1873 he had founded this now highly successful agency, which was clever enough to negotiate terms for authors with its own newspapers as well as with other provincial ones. They would print and distribute the serials they had acquired, to whomever they could persuade to buy them. Tillotson, a decent man by Tom's own account written later to his widow, made a fortune and his authors did well, if (as is only proper) less well than he. Tom contracted to provide the first four instalments by the end of June 1889, and then to provide each succeeding instalment weekly until the end. But he eventually got Tillotson's to agree to a three-month delay, so that when he began serious work on the book in September 1888 he had a year to think about it.

As Millgate writes, 'it was well for [Hardy's] peace of mind that he could not foresee the vicissitudes through which the book would pass', since the book was *Tess*. That is true enough: he cannot then have stopped to calculate just what his candour would cost him in frustration. And yet, did not an obstinate part of him foresee these vicissitudes perfectly well? He was ever provocative, not to speak of his determination to challenge the prevailing morality; his angry temperament was by no means above paying back public stupidity with further furious assaults upon it, such as are implied in the defiant description of Tess as 'a pure woman'.

But there is more than that to be said about his earliest conceptions of *Tess*. It was over four years before he could publish it, and in that time he put out two volumes of short stories. On a personal level, these years were perhaps Tom's happiest and most high-spirited. He had been able to re-establish himself as a novelist with *The Woodlanders*, was as satisfied with his marriage as any sensible person has a right to be, and had arranged his life into an acceptable pattern. But *Tess*, published at the end of that period, was the darkest of all his novels so far. Did its darkness grow out of events in his own life, or out of tragic convictions which he had always held? It seems that the latter were responsible, since the affair with Florence Henniker, and the resulting strain between him and Emma, did not begin until after it had been published – and Tom had become an even more famous, or infamous, man than he already was.

He truly enjoyed being a London social man and distinguished author only when he could discover 'sensible souls', which he doubtless encountered in equal proportions amongst rich and poor, aristocratic and plebeian. He knew that there were no laws to determine which people are nice or nasty, intelligent or silly, shrewd or stupid; he could enjoy the company of the simple-minded old huntsman Portsmouth as much as that (a little later in his life) of the more socially humble Hermann Lea. But those who, like Lea, enjoyed his confidence and were close friends did not get into the *Life* as much as the acquaintances like Portsmouth. That is because the *Life* is as non-personal a book as Tom could make it. Lea is in fact not mentioned there at all – perhaps almost a sign of his closeness to Tom. He was, after all, at his easiest with such men. What place could they have in so non-intimate a record?

Thus, doing the social round was for the most part a bore, but no more of a bore than much else in life. He dutifully kept notes – a common Victorian practice, as homage to method and 'science', as Millgate observes – and as dutifully made use of them for what he called 'novel padding', as some repayment to himself for the effort involved. Of course he threw away the more critical of these when he came to go through his papers towards the end of his life, and of course he must have doctored many others. But it is unlikely that he altered much more than was absolutely necessary.

A few of the observations he made in that summer of 1887 were to find their way into those substantial parts of *The Well-Beloved* that are satirical of society. On 14 June he found one of the Portsmouths' apparently inexhaustible supply of daughters to have 'Round luminous enquiring eyes'; these are transferred to Lady Nicola Pine-Avon in the novel. But since Florence's own eyes had been regarded as special by Tom, she chopped out that reference. The notes he made during this visit, or those that he preserved, are nearly all critical. He was to include them in the *Life*, though, because he knew that readers liked references to titled people. A wholly humorous one records the 'forty-seventh birthday of Thomas the Unworthy', and this is followed by brief accounts of meetings with the indefatigable Mrs Procter, Browning, Arnold, Lady Jeune, and the 'very jolly-looking' Queen Victoria, just in the process of recapturing the allegiance of her subjects on the occasion of her Golden Jubilee, which Tom and Emma witnessed from the Savile Club. On 25 June he records tersely that at a concert he saw 'Souls outside Bodies'. His and Emma's time was passed 'gaily enough', but the inescapable general impression is one of 'a thoughtless world of chit-chat and pleasure'. When he and Emma went to a lunch given by the Stanley family, the latter indulged themselves in an 'exciting family dispute . . . at which they took no notice of the guests at all'.

But, as Tom wrote, his own thoughts were 'running on other subjects'. At this point in the *Life* there occurs an ironic apology for the cynical plethora of jottings upon society, and a concealed (and wholly deniable) comment on the quality of his second wife's, 'the author's', intellect:

(It must always be borne in mind that these memoranda on people and things were made by him [Hardy] only as personal opinions for private consideration, which he meant to destroy, and not for publication; an issue which has come about by his having been asked when he was old if he would object to their being printed, as there was no harm in them, and his saying passively that he did not mind.)

That sums up his true view of the *Life*, Florence's project, of which she was, as he recognized (though not unkindly), incapable, and which he, the subject, therefore had to carry out anonymously for her – and at the same time give away as little as possible of the real events of this *Life*. The comic side of it could hardly have escaped him.

Meanwhile, in July 1887, he recorded what kind of impression all the bustle and 'progress' in London society made upon him, commenting that all the sadness in the world arose from its 'on-going – *i.e.* the "becoming"': 'If the world stood still at a felicitous moment there would be no sadness in it'; this observation of 14 July is immediately followed by one made back at Max Gate, in August, to the effect that country children brought up in 'solitary' places are 'imaginative, dreamy, and credulous of vague mysteries'. He was himself simultaneously 'credulous of vague mysteries', and a near positivist.

As the summer passed into autumn he wrote a series of short stories, including one of his finest, 'The Withered Arm'; but in the intervals he was thinking perhaps mainly of the shape of the epic he planned, noting that he would have to follow Coleridge 'in holding that a long poem should not attempt to be poetical all through'. Doubtless he was dreading the necessity to get on with the novel, which Tillotson had accepted without even asking for an outline.

On 11 December he made an oddly antinomian, even Byronic, note, which he reproduced in the *Life* without any explanation of what had prompted it: 'Those who invent vices indulge in them with more judgement and restraint than those who imitate vices invented by others.' One is bound to wonder just what kind of vice he was contemplating. Since the remark occurs in the context of discussion of *The Dynasts* it is possible that he was thinking of Napoleon and the 'vice' of conquest; but then Napoleon hardly invented that vice. Perhaps on the other hand he was thinking of Jemima and her bossiness and the difficulties into which this led him with Emma.

Clearly he remembered that the time had been one of comparative happiness and ease, and reproduced a note made on the last day of the year remarking that it had been 'fairly friendly' to him: it had shown him the South of France and Italy, given him new acquaintances, and 'enabled me to hold my own in fiction, whatever that may be worth, by the completion of *The Woodlanders*'. His reading, as always, had been extensive:

> Books read or looked at this year:
> Milton, Dante, Calderon, Goethe.
> Homer, Virgil, Molière, Scott.
> The Cid, Nibelungen, Crusoe, Don Quixote.
> Aristophanes, Theocritus, Boccaccio.
> Canterbury Tales, Shakespeare's Sonnets, Lycidas.
> Malory, Vicar of Wakefield, Ode to West Wind,
>   Ode to Grecian Urn.
> Christabel, Wye above Tintern.
> Chapman's Iliad, Lord Derby's ditto, Worsley's Odyssey.

A note, clearly addressed to himself for further reference in times of stress, made on 5 January 1888, reads:

> Be rather curious than anxious about your own career; for whatever result may accrue to its intellectual and social value, it will make little difference to your personal well-being. A naturalist's interest in the hatching of a queer egg or germ is the utmost introspective consideration you should allow yourself.

This shows that he was trying to cultivate the kind of objective thinking that he felt necessary to the practice of poetry. Such cultivation of a bird's eye view of himself has puzzled those commentators who are used to authors' complete belief in their own fame. What it means is not, as has been suggested, that he felt good about himself, but that he was determined to retain a still small solitary voice within himself that would always be independent. On 24 January he thus reflected that he was 'neither Tory nor Radical'. He then seems to have coined the odd word 'intrinsicalist' (not acknowledged in the OED or its more recent supplement) in order to describe his position. He was, he explained, opposed to all 'privilege derived from accident of any kind', and therefore 'equally opposed to aristocratic privilege and democratic privilege'. He would not countenance 'the taxing of the worthy to help those masses . . . who will not help themselves when they might etc'. 'Opportunity should be equal for all, but those who will not avail themselves of it should be cared for merely.'

In late February he received a communication from the worthy theologian the Rev. A.B. Grosart, editor of the Fuller and Chertsey Worthies Libraries, of Spenser, and of poets such as Herbert and Samuel Daniel. Grosart, worried by the conflict between science and religion, was innocent enough to address him and a few dozen others on the question of how the 'horrors of human and animal life, particularly parasitic' could be reconciled 'with the absolute goodness and non-limitation of God'. This was perhaps waving a red rag to the intellectual bull in Tom, who was just convincing himself of the limitations and unfairness of God, although not of his non-existence. He was unusually scathing in his reply:

> Mr Hardy regrets that he is unable to suggest any hypothesis which would reconcile the existence of such evils as Dr Grosart describes with the idea of omnipotent goodness. Perhaps Dr Grosart might be helped to a provisional view of the universe by the recently published Life of Darwin [presumably the *Life and Letters* of 1887, but possibly a *Life* by George Thomas Bettany], and the works of Herbert Spencer and other agnostics.

Soon afterwards he discovered that Leslie Stephen had also received a copy of this complex questionnaire. Stephen had been equally, although more characteristically, unkind in his reply, informing Grosart that it was his business as a theologian to explain the difficulty, and not vice versa.

In March 1888 Tom returned to London, at first without Emma, in order to read in the British Museum. 'Souls,' he perceived, 'are gliding about here in a sort of dream . . . dissolution . . . gnawing at them all, slightly hampered by renovations'. He found his acquaintances 'abraded', balding, their flesh disappearing 'by degrees'. Almost certainly he was thinking about his financial future in connection with the risky project for which he was so assiduously reading up. Back in January he had written to Sampson Low, the publisher of his novels in their cheap single-volume format, asking them to use the 'words "Wessex novels" at the head of the list': 'I was the first to use [it] in fiction . . . and it would be a pity for us to lose the right to it for want of asserting it.' He was also shrewdly calculating the amounts he could obtain for stories: *Blackwood's* paid him £24 (more than £500 in today's money) for 'The Withered Arm', and he was able to extract more than that from other periodicals. *Wessex Tales*, the title of the Macmillan publication, in May, of five of his stories ('The Three Strangers', 'The Withered Arm', 'Fellow Townsmen', 'Interlopers at the Knap' and 'The Distracted Preacher'), was intended to consolidate his position as the original Wessex writer, and thus as its 'inventor', which of course he was. He had proposed the volume to Macmillan in February, and received a royalty of one-sixth the published price of twelve shillings, with £50 in advance. He would follow this up with another collection, *A Group of Noble Dames*, in 1891 – and experience more of the usual trouble with the *Graphic* on the way to book publication.

In September of the previous year Tom had been asked by a New York paper, the *Forum*, to write an article called 'The Profitable Reading of Fiction' for a fee of forty guineas. He was cautious in his reply, and probably did not welcome the labour of undertaking it. On the other hand, he did want to say a few words about fiction, if only in reply to some of his more idiotic critics. He told Lorettus S. Metcalf, the editor, that he could not do the article at present, having 'promised as much MS as I can safely undertake'; but he asked him to leave the matter open. In fact he had written the piece well before he went to London, for it appeared in the March 1888 issue of *Forum*.

Plainly the writing of this sort of prose gave Tom trouble, and although 'The Profitable Reading of Fiction' is by no means without its fitful ironies, many of them (he must have felt) almost private, the first three paragraphs, in particular, are laboured and commonplace. But within a page or two he has warmed to his theme. The first sentences in which irony takes over come just after he has explained that, in reading for the sake of health, for the relief of 'spiritual fatigue', 'it may be asserted' that 'there is to be found refreshment, if not restoration, in some antithetical realm of ideas which lies waiting in the pages of romance':

In reading for such hygienic purposes it is, of course, of the first consequence that the reader be not too critical . . . his author should be swallowed whole, like any other alterative pill. He should be believed in slavishly, implicitly . . . let him never be doubted for a moment.

He then inserts remarks that anticipate modern 'reader-response' criticism, or at least its gist:

The aim should be the exercise of a generous imaginativeness, which shall find in a tale not only all that was put there by the author . . . but which shall find there what was never inserted by him, never foreseen, never contemplated. Sometimes these additions which are woven around a work of fiction by the intensive power of the reader's own imagination are the finest parts of the scenery.

How seriously he meant this is uncertain, since, to any but the most theory-bound or aggressively deconstructionist reader, there must be some kind of limit to what is 'inserted'. The personal ripples that are spread must come from the stone that has been cast by the author: there must be harmony between total intention and response. That the topic was unwittingly entered upon here is suggested by subsequent sarcastic sentences describing the 'invalid' in the course of his reading:

Directly the circumstances [of the book] begin to resemble those of the reader, an interest other than an imaginative one is set up . . . It sets his serious thoughts at work, and he does not want them stimulated; he wants to dream.

Tom is here being obliquely nasty about a certain type of reader, the most prevalent, to whose attentions to his texts he owes his livelihood. But this initial discussion may very well be taken, just as Pinion takes it in his *Hardy Companion*, not as a blow at *most* readers, but, rather, as a sympathetic consideration of just the sort of reader whom almost everyone imagines he or she is not. One of the most important assertions in the essay is that the best fiction appeals not to 'logical reason' but to 'emotional reason'. That Tom defined this distinction between the intellect of the mind and that of the heart is notable, for, psychologically, such a distinction does exist: under the term 'emotional reason' may be subsumed, for example, symbolic systems. The main argument is Aristotelian, although Tom does not refer to Aristotle: 'It must always be borne in mind, despite the claims of realism, that the best fiction, like the highest artistic expression in other modes, is more true, so to put it, than history or nature can be.' He then makes a statement which few of his reviewers – even Gosse in the last analysis, when it came to *Jude* – could accept, or, perhaps, even properly consider:

It may seem something of a paradox to assert that the novels which most conduce to moral profit are likely to be among those written without a moral purpose. But the truth of the statement may be realized if we consider that the didactic novel is so generally devoid of *vraisemblance* as to teach nothing but the impossibility of tampering with natural truth to advance dogmatic opinions. Those, on the other hand, which impress the reader with the inevitableness of character and environment in working out destiny, whether that destiny be just or unjust, enviable or cruel, must have a sound effect, if not what is called a good effect, upon a healthy mind.

He went on to pretend that the effect of good novels on 'weak' minds was 'not our duty to consider too closely' – after all, he was always busy provoking such minds, even if only in the interests of what he felt he must do to be truthful to his own convictions.

The short essay entitled 'Candour in English Fiction', which he wrote soon afterwards for a symposium in the *New Review* in January 1890, adds a little more and asks what response Shakespeare would have received if he had sent up *Hamlet* 'in narrative form' to the 'editor of a London magazine': 'One can imagine the answer that young William would get for his mad supposition of . . . fitness from any one of the gentlemen who so correctly conduct that branch of the periodical Press.' He goes on to point out that, were Sophocles' *Oedipus*, or Goethe's *Faust*, or a number of other classics, to be presented as 'new fiction', then they would be 'excluded from circulation'. But it is not necessary to dwell on his arguments in this essay, beyond noting that it may have acted as a second nail in the coffin of Mudie's respectability – his enemy George Moore's 1885 essay 'Literature at Nurse' having been the first. Those arguments are familiar enough, as is the declaration with which the essay ends: '. . . the position of man and woman in nature, and the position of belief in the minds of man and woman – things which everybody is thinking but nobody is saying – might be taken up and treated frankly'.

This article, which was much stronger in its condemnation of

Grundyism than others by Mrs Lynn Linton and Walter Besant (who felt that 'free love' was best left to the French), reflected the frustrations of sixteen years, as well as immediate troubles with the serialization of *Tess*. But meanwhile, Tom's full awareness of the situation as presented in 'The Profitable Reading of Fiction' did not prevent him in the following July from sending to the *Graphic*, in just the form he wanted them, the stories which would make up the volume *A Group of Noble Dames*.

The publication of these stories in volume form in May 1891, before *Tess*, marks the beginning of a six-year association between Hardy and Osgood, McIlvaine, a new firm which, although autonomous, also represented Harper's in Great Britain. John Ripley Osgood had been Harper's representative in London from 1886. He and Clarence McIlvaine, a Harper's employee, set up their business in 1890–91, at the time of the passing of the International Copyright Bill. Osgood, the more energetic and enterprising of the two, died in 1892; but the firm continued until 1898, after which Harper took it over – thus both *Wessex Poems* and *Poems of the Past and the Present* were published by 'Harper & Brothers, London and New York'.

Not much is known about Hardy's reasons for turning to them, and temporarily away from Macmillan, but the main ones must have been, first, that it was convenient for him to deal with almost the same publisher in London and in New York, and, secondly, that Osgood projected a collected edition. After *Tess* had made him so famous, that is just what he got between April 1895 and September 1896. It could not have been issued much earlier because Sampson Low's ownership of the rights to eight of the novels, which they issued in their cheap one-volume editions, did not expire until 1894. *Harper's Weekly*, as the events concerning *A Group of Noble Dames* were to show, was also far more accommodating, and less nervous, than the *Graphic*. Much of what the *Graphic* insisted on taking out appeared in *Harper's*.

Tom might have thought, in April 1889, that he had just pulled off a profitable little piece of business. Arthur Locker, the editor of the *Graphic*, in which *The Mayor of Casterbridge* had been serialized, was pressing him for fiction. Eventually Locker was to come to the rescue of the serial *Tess*. On 7 February 1889 Tom told him that, although he hoped to write again for the paper 'some day', just now he could not. But in letters of 28 March and 1 April he offered him a story of the same length as 'The Romantic Adventures of a Milkmaid', for £125 ('to include the *Graphic* right only'). And he did supply them, in the following year, with a text of this 'short novel', *A Group of Noble Dames*, which he had meanwhile sold to *Harper's Weekly*. This is his description of it, sent on 7 March 1890, for Harper's consideration:

> I may say that it is to be a Tale of Tales – a series of linked stories – of a somewhat different kind from the mass of my work of late, excepting The First Countess of Wessex, which comes near it in character. The scenes, which are numerous, will be laid in the old mansions and castles hereabouts: the characters are to be proportionally numerous, & to be exclusively persons of title of the last century (names disguised, but incidents approximating to fact). Like the Wessex-Folk stories, these may be divided easily into parts. The whole Tale of Tales will consist of 30,000 words. There is, of course, much more incident in a scheme of tales of this kind than in a single story of the same length . . .

Simon Gatrell has convincingly suggested, in his and Juliet Grindle's Clarendon edition of *Tess* (1983) and elsewhere, that Tom set out deliberately to provoke his editors. He seems continually to have put off beginning *Tess*, and probably did so until he was in London later in the summer of 1888. But when he did start it, he was determined to make it a challenge to the prevailing hypocrisies. That he thus so substantially added to his fame was simply an added irony, although not necessarily one that he never anticipated.

Gissing, when he stayed at Max Gate in September 1895, perceived that 'he had a great deal of coarseness in his nature'. He ascribed this to his 'humble origins'. As his friend H.G. Wells observed, Gissing was crippled by an 'inherited gentility' and could appreciate Hardy even less well than he could appreciate anyone else. Appreciation was not his strong suit and the visit was not a success. But by genteel standards, and by those of the aristocracy with whom he hobnobbed in London, Tom could indeed have been seen as excessively coarse – had he been inclined to display that side of his nature when he was with them. But he was never so inclined, and his abstemious habits helped him: he did not 'forget himself'. But it was all something of an act. He saved what was no more than a countryman's directness of utterance for such men as his friend Hermann Lea – and before that, no doubt, William Barnes. Emma's notorious animadversions upon him in the destroyed 'What I Think of My Husband' (if this existed), exaggerated though its contents must have been by the excessively genteel Florence, are probably mostly concerned with this. It is likely, too, that his so-called 'coarseness' began to assert itself as his self-confidence about being able to 'hold his own' increased, and as he was able to mix with people of his own kind, who shared his 'humble origins'.

He had not, then, started on *Tess* when he thought up the *Noble Dames* project. But when agreement was finally reached with Locker, in November 1889, the troubles with *Tess* had already begun. Gatrell, who in his *Hardy the Creator* has established the course of events as precisely as they ever can be established, comments that 'whatever Hardy may have expected in the way of trouble' over the story 'Squire Petrick's Lady', 'he cannot have imagined that the response', by Locker, 'would be so destructive'. He had finally agreed to supply the *Graphic* with the serial for their special Christmas number of 1890, and sent in the material on 9 May that year. Whether this remained unread and was sent straight to the printer by the *Graphic*, or whether it simply lay in a drawer, nothing was heard until the following month. Tom recalled that on 23 June he

> called on Arthur Locker [editor] at the *Graphic* office in answer to his letter. He says he does not object to the stories . . . but the Directors do. Here's a pretty job! Must smooth down these Directors somehow I suppose.

But Gatrell and others have shown that this must be a misrecollection, if only one of trivial import, since Arthur Locker's son William wrote the following letter on 25 June:

> I have now read 'A Group of Noble Dames' and am sorry to say that in the main I agree with our Directors' opinion. In the matter of tone they seem to me to be too much in keeping with the supposed circumstances of their narration – in other words to be very suitable and entirely harmless to the robust minds of the Club smoking-room; but not at all suitable for the more delicate imaginations of young girls.

The chief objection was, apparently, that all the stories in one way or another dealt with the atrocious subject of childbirth. Locker thought that four of the tales could be easily modified, but 'Squire Petrick's Lady' and 'Lady Mottisfont' were 'hopeless'. Clearly, he and those on whose behalf he was writing were seriously offended, and believed that Tom had done them a genuinely bad turn:

MARKING TIME

Frankly, do you think it advisable to put into the hands of the Young Person stories, one of which turns on the hysterical confession by a wife of an imaginary adultery, and the other upon the manner in which a husband foists upon his wife the offspring of a former illicit connection? . . . Now, what do you propose to do? Will you write us an entirely fresh story, or will you take the 'Noble Dames' and alter them to suit our taste . . .?

The history of the dispute is complicated, particularly in the matter of whether Hardy or the editors altered certain passages. What is indisputable is that, instead of writing a new story in the place of 'Squire Petrick's Lady', Tom changed it out of all recognition. There are angry notes on the manuscript, such as 'N.B. The above lines were deleted against the author's wish, by compulsion of Mrs Grundy . . .' and so forth. Had the editors cut up really rough it could have been financially awkward for him, so he went much further in their direction than he really wanted. On 24 July he wrote from the Savile Club to Emma, who was at Max Gate, telling her, 'I think it is all right with the *Graphic*.' It is fair to infer from this that she was fully in sympathy with him.

It was not all right, though, or not quite, because one of the directors had read the old unrevised proofs instead of the ones incorporating the revisions. On 30 July Tom told Arthur Locker what had happened, and asked him if he could now 'presume . . . the question settled'. And so it was; but, as Gatrell points out, the

> kinds of change forced upon Hardy . . . reveal the extent to which the stories . . . dramatize the dynastic sense of the ruling class, and rejoice in showing the twists by which the desire for an acceptable heir is thwarted or perverted.

A Group of Noble Dames is in a certain sense, if not an important one, the most provocative Hardy novel of all: it is, to employ Gissing's later term, coarse, and perhaps challengingly so. It consists of countryman's tales, and not only the *Graphic* complained: in our own day, so does an again 'disturbed' Millgate, who describes the stories as 'at best undistinguished, at worst distasteful'; while T.S. Eliot found 'Barbara of the House of Grebe' written 'solely to provide a satisfaction for some morbid emotion'. To urbanized and genteel minds, and to those middle-class people described by Tom in an interview with a parson-journalist for the

Pall Mall magazine in 1892 as 'strained, calculating, unromantic', it was intended to seem like that. The writing is perfunctory and sometimes careless, and the stories are 'coarse' by comparison with much of the rest of Tom's work. It would be perverse to find the collection truly 'distinguished', and he can hardly have attached great importance to it, except as a useful money-maker; but it is not so much 'distasteful' as annoying to most of his readers, whose interest is, however, beguiled by his capacity to tell a tale.

All in all, it has been an under-rated volume, whose entertainment value conceals much sharp comment and artistry. After all, it is only 'undistinguished' within the context of Hardy's own fiction. In it Tom drew on local history, perhaps at times recklessly. One tale which only ever appeared in an American newspaper, 'The Doctor's Legend', may have been left out because it would have given offence to a local family. He stressed in his 1896 preface that its roots were in those 'pedigrees and supplementary material' to be found in 'the pages of county histories', and his main source was undoubtedly John Hutchins' *The History and Antiquities of the County of Dorset*, of which he possessed the latest, four-volume edition of 1861–73, updated by W. Shipp and J. W. Hodson. But, as Pinion suggests in his *Hardy Companion*, 'he took risks', and there may have been repercussions which have largely been dissipated by time – and, doubtless, by the affected families' wish to keep what they felt to be their skeletons safely within their cupboards. The Earl of Ilchester, Lord Lieutenant of Dorset, was annoyed at what he took to be calumnies against his forebears, and on 21 December 1905, in a letter to Florence Henniker, Tom alluded to this when he told her of his death ('The one who was angry with me'). From that time onwards all Tom's prose was to go directly against the conventions of his time and place, and was to provoke friends, supporters and future critics.

20

A Roving Eye

On 28 April 1888, while in London lodgings with Emma, who had recently joined him, the theme of *Jude the Obscure* came to him: 'A short story of a young man – "who could not go to Oxford". – His struggles and ultimate failure. Suicide.' In the *Life* he is quick to deny the absurd autobiographical inferences that had already been made in abundance. Adding that this notion was 'probably' the germ of *Jude*, he wrote: 'There is something [in this] the world ought to be shown, and I am the one to show it to them – though I was not altogether hindered going, at least to Cambridge, and could have gone up easily at five-and-twenty.'

The urge that 'the world' *ought* to be shown something was, in this time of creative self-confidence, paramount in Tom's mind. Even *A Group of Noble Dames*, when completed as a sort of 'short novel', would 'show' how class and convention undermined humanity, and would reflect its simultaneity with *Tess* by its concern with the fate of women, shown, as Kristin Brady writes in her study *The Short Stories of Thomas Hardy* (1982), to be damaged as human beings by 'the injurious effect upon them of the clash between convention and sexual passion'. *Jude*, written during and after the Henniker affair, and in the initial but painful stage of his first estrangement from Emma, is less the result of these two personal traumas than of his poetic and imaginative conviction. The worst conventions were, for him, ill-willed transgressions of the 'loving-kindness' which he always sought – but in which, like everyone else, he found himself wanting.

Tess, as he contemplated her creation, would become the victimized symbol of this sort of transgression. Yet, as he told Elliot Felkin in 1919, 'in one's heart of hearts one did not of course *really* think one's heroine was as good and pure as all that, but then one was making out a case for her before the world'. The key words in this sentence are 'think' and 'before the world'. He meant that he *felt* this about Tess, even though he had to persuade his reader willingly to expend a little thought – and that, just as in *Jude*, he had something to 'tell the world'.

There was no single 'real' Tess, much though an original for her has been sought, especially in view of his repeated insistence that her 'position', as he put it to his publisher Osgood, was 'based on fact'. His statement in his letter of 29 October 1891 to his old friend the painter Thomas Macquoid, written while *Tess* was being serialized in the *Graphic*, to the effect that he had not been able 'to put on paper all that she is, or was, to me', has seemed to some to point to a single fleshly original, a real and therefore mysterious woman (even, for some, a Tryphena Sparks!). Others have believed that she was his grandmother, Mary Head – and, indeed, certain details do seem to have been suggested by the latter's life.

The essential Tess is, however, the externalization of a quality which lay at the depths of his own being, and is compounded of features he appreciated, both sensually and otherwise, in many women. When, as a very old man, he became enchanted by the beautiful Gertrude Bugler, who first played Tess in his own dramatization of the novel, he saw her as Tess's apotheosis, 'the very incarnation' of her. He even claimed that her mother Augusta, once a dairymaid on Kingston Maurward estate, had been the original inspiration for his character. But then so were a number of other woman – anyone, indeed, who struck Tom as in some way lovely. Thus, when on 23 July 1889 he sat next to Agatha Thorneycraft, wife of the sculptor Hamo, he found her 'lips . . . roses full of snow', and eventually added her to the list of beauties who 'were' Tess.

Included in this plethora of original Tesses, then, one might fairly speculate, was Emma as she had been when he first courted her. And since, when she suddenly died, he wrote the famous love poems to her, it may be claimed that she was the true archetype – inasmuch as there was one at all. The book is so defiant – it calls a 'murderess' a 'pure woman' – that he needed some means of defence against the outrage he knew he would provoke by so antinomian a gesture. What better than a refuge in 'fact'? But there was no single fact behind Tess: only that almost infinite tissue of exact facts so usual in Hardy's fiction, and so necessary to him in his defence of it.

On 28 May 1888 he and Emma went abroad again, this time to Paris. They noticed on their arrival 'as they always did "the sour smell of a foreign city"'. Tom was shown around the Archives Nationales, which he found more interesting than he had expected. He was alone, and felt that much closer to 'those corridors of white boxes, each containing one year's shady documents of a past monarchy'.

When they returned to London in mid-June they rented lodgings at 5 Upper Phillimore Place, in Kensington, and Tom almost immediately became ill with what, in a letter to Anne Ritchie (the former Miss Thackeray), he called 'one of the worst colds in the head I have had for years'. In the *Life* he calls it a 'rheumatic attack'. His illnesses when in London would become increasingly worse as the years wore on; yet he was probably right, Emma's needs apart, to make the sacrifice of going there each year – otherwise he would have become too much of a recluse. The Dorchester gentry never welcomed or liked him, which, along with his work, limited his social life at home. He wrote, some time in July, about 'the value of life':

> I have attempted many modes of finding it. For my part, if there is any way of getting a melancholy satisfaction out of life it lies in dying, so to speak, before one is out of the flesh; by which I mean putting on the manners of ghosts, wandering in their haunts, and taking their views of surrounding things. To think of life passing away is a sadness; to think of it as past is at least tolerable.

The attainment of this sort of objectivity, even indifference, too, was something that the world 'ought to know'. He saw it as the only possible counter to the pain which the suffering in the world caused him. The very writing of *Tess*, full of acute suffering as it is, represented an objectification of the process of it and a relief from it. Some have believed that the amount of suffering in the book implied 'personal suffering during these years'. But Tom's greatest personal suffering was to come just after he had completed it. Existence, the very act of recollecting an irretrievable past, was, for him, acute suffering in itself.

Back at Max Gate by 17 July 1888 – probably because a portion of his drawing-room ceiling had fallen down – he felt impelled to lash out at R.H. Hutton. He informed him that 'I published "The Woodlanders" & the *Spectator* objected to that story. I publish "Wessex Tales" which are unobjectionable, & the *Spectator* takes no notice of them at all.' Hutton replied on the following day, complaining that Hardy was being 'a little unreasonable'. But the letter had the desired effect: Hutton rushed a favourable review of *Wessex Tales* into the 28 July number.

Within a few days of this expostulation he had finished the story

'The Melancholy Hussar', which was widely printed in periodicals and newspapers, by courtesy of the Tillotson Bureau (to whom he later sold it), before it appeared in *Life's Little Ironies*. Subsequently Tom transferred it from that volume back into later editions of *Wessex Tales*, as being more appropriate there.

By 1 August he was at work on one of his very best stories, 'A Tragedy of Two Ambitions', and plainly enjoying it. 'I am at present up to the elbows in a cold-blooded murder,' he told Gosse. This comment, incidentally, casts light on his own uncompromising attitude to the moral status of the action of two brothers who fail to rescue their drunken father when he falls into a weir. Brady writes that the story 'treats ambition with both censure and compassion', but might rather have said that, while quite unambiguous in its refusal to treat murder as anything but murder, it does not withhold sympathy on that account.

Although its ending is tragic, up to that point 'A Tragedy of Two Ambitions' is a half-comic treatment of the theme which would be taken up more substantially in *Jude*: unfulfilled ambition. Joshua Halborough is contrasted with his less ambitious, and more sincere, brother Cornelius, who may be taken as a faint adumbration of Jude. The conception of their sister, Rosa – for all that she is a minor character in the drama – demonstrates the degree to which the notion of woman-as-victim was possessing his mind in these weeks before he began *Tess* in earnest.

The opening establishes the situation: Joshua and Cornelius are 'plodding away at the Greek Testament, immersed in a chapter of the idiomatic and difficult Epistle to the Hebrews'. Their fourteen-year-old sister wants them to play with her. Their father, 'in the light drab clothes of an old-fashioned country tradesman', once a 'thriving master-machinist', a millwright, reels home and has to be put in the straw-shed to sleep it off. Now an embarrassment to both sons, he has already got through the £900 their mother left them to go through 'one of the universities'. Joshua says:

> It drives me mad when I think of it . . . here we work in our own bungling way, and the utmost we can hope for is a term of years as national schoolmasters, and possible admission to a Theological college, and ordination as despised licentiates.

But Joshua's 'anger' is reflected 'as simple sadness' in his brother's face; he replies, 'with feeble consolation', that they can preach the Gospel as well 'without a hood on our surplices as with one'.

'Preach the Gospel – true . . . But we can't rise!' replies the elder.

Joshua's lack of interest in the Gospel for itself is several times emphasized. He tells Cornelius not to 'think lightly of the Church': there are 'torrents of infidelity to be stemmed'; a man of 'limited human sympathies', he has persuaded himself that 'it was ardour for Christianity which spurred him on, and not pride of place'. The victims of his snobbery are Cornelius – drawn into murder by his impotence to resist the force of Joshua's mean ambitiousness – his father, and, last but not least, his sister Rosa. Her chance of marriage to a widower, in fact a dreary and calculating one, is threatened by the advent of old Halborough; it is on that occasion that the brothers allow him to drown. But, because they know they are guilty of murder (Cornelius, notably, more keenly), the tale ends with hints of the suicide of him at least, and consequently of Rosa's ruin.

The story contains two richly comic episodes: the old reprobate, a shameless blackmailer, but with some energetic humour and crafty knowledge of his sons' prissy and snobbish earnestness, is seen confronting, first Joshua at his theological college with a new 'wife' he has acquired, and then both his sons just as they are rejoicing over the coup of getting Rosa 'respectably' married. This latter episode is transformed into tragedy when the young men are revealed as having been so stripped of their humanity by ambition that they can allow their own father to drown. They are lovelessly lacking in humour, and have lost all sense of truly human values. They are unmoved by his state, although he is their father; they care only for the threat he poses to them. Nor, all too evidently, do they care for Rosa except as a cipher who can help them to 'rise'. The theme of the story is not only the distorting effect of social inequality, but also the equally distorting effect of coldness ('limited human possibilities') on the capacity to love.

Tom made a particularly fine revision to this story before its appearance in *Life's Little Ironies*. After the drowning Joshua sees his father's walking-stick on the bank, and, 'hastily picking it up', sticks it 'into the mud among the sedge'. As a brilliant afterthought, for the final episode of the story, which takes place six months later, just after Joshua, rather 'than let in a stranger', has said the burial service over the 'unknown' drowned body of his father, he sees that the hidden stick has taken root as a 'straight little silver poplar'. This ties together the biblical symbolism that runs through the story, and points to Joshua's failure to '*endure* the cross, *despising* the shame,' as Cornelius reminds him when he says, 'Ah, we read our *Hebrews* to little account, Jos!' Aaron's rod, which burst into miraculous almond blossom because it symbolized God's choice of the House of Levi to assist the Jewish priests, is mentioned in Hebrews; but the sprouting poplar belongs only to Joshua's father, and thus mocks him. In translating from Hebrews the brothers would also have come across the admonition to purge their conscience from, as the Authorized Version has it, 'dead works to serve the living God'. Joshua has earlier wept 'hot tears' at his predicament and written to his brother:

> For a successful painter, sculptor, musician, author, who takes society by storm, it is no drawback, it is sometimes even a romantic recommendation, to hail from outcasts and profligates. But for clergymen of the Church of England! Cornelius, it is fatal! To succeed in the Church, people must believe in you, first of all, as a gentleman, secondly as a man of means, thirdly as a scholar, fourthly as a preacher, fifthly, perhaps, as a Christian – but always first as a gentleman, with all their heart and soul and strength. The essence of Christianity is humility, and by the help of God I would have brazened it out. But this terrible vagabondage and disreputable connection! If he does not accept my terms and leave the country, it will extinguish us and kill me. For how can we live, and relinquish our high aim, and bring down our dear sister Rosa to the level of a gypsy's stepdaughter?

The convoluted irony here spares nothing and nobody: not Joshua in his lack of humility, nor society, nor the state of the Church within it. Sincere Christianity, however, is nowhere mocked. It never is in Hardy. Despite his scepticism, he was a communicating Christian for the whole of his life, and so might be said to have felt in emotional need of the sacraments even while failing to believe in them intellectually.

The last tale he wrote before settling down to work on what was to become *Tess* was 'The First Countess of Wessex', another of the *Dames* group, and one which was much altered before finally appearing in volume form as it was originally conceived. A 'Christmas story', it went first into *Harper's*, but not until December 1889. He said nothing about his progress on the *Tess* manuscript to Sir George Douglas, when the latter sent him copies of some of the poems which he would include in his *Poems of a Country Gentleman* of nine years later. But he did display his sly sense of humour, which is so often missed. As always, he kept entirely to himself his reservations about the poems' quality:

> I have been looking into the poems . . . & have lighted upon some very happy lines: one couplet, for instance, strikes a genuinely pathetic note – that of the bird
>
> > 'Singing – uncared for and unheard –
> > A song that's all too hard for me!'
>
> Without venturing to express my opinion as to ultimate results I feel that verse is your more natural form of utterance. It sometimes occurs to me that it is better to fail in poetry than to succeed in prose . . . Poetry has certainly not had its day. You must remember that the Muses have occasionally to 'draw back for a spring' . . . & they may have been doing so lately.
>
> Your contemplated title is an *excellent* one: it ought almost to sell the book . . .

This comment manages to be precise without being in the least unkind, since the verdict that the poems as a whole were 'pathetic' (which they were), and written while the Muses had drawn back, is far too cleverly wrapped up. But this is not malicious: all it demonstrates is Tom's desire to stay as close to the truth of his feelings as he could without upsetting anyone.

Progress on *Tess*, whose heroine was for some time named Sue, must have been slow. The book was first called 'The Body and Soul of Sue', then 'Too Late, Beloved!'; *Tess of the d'Urbervilles*, the final choice, was more apt because it was more cool in contrast to the story's passion. It was written from a complex of emotions, the most basic of which was Tom's fundamental love-hate for fiction, complicated as that was by the impossibility of writing it as he wished. He would soon be fifty, and his eye was beginning to rove – although at this stage it was nothing more than his eye. All kinds of details about the women who moved him when he met them, or whom he remembered, were now filling his mind and memory. Although it is a mistake to think that he made specific comment on the character of any single real individual in *Tess*, it is true that many characteristics of many individuals went into it – and none more, perhaps, than those of Horace Moule into the person of Angel Clare. That must not be taken to mean, though, that Angel is a portrait of Horace Moule. No attention needs to be given to the 'family tradition' – Sparks family gossip – that Tess represented Kate Hardy, who is supposed to have had an illegitimate child. This tale is based – with the usual mixture of malice and silliness – on her deathbed ramblings in 1940 about one of her pupils whom she temporarily lost, but who became, for the fourth or fifth person who heard of it, a 'lost daughter'.

The notion of the decline of 'aristocratic' blood was common at the end of the nineteenth century: it was one of the official tenets of the naturalistic movement in France. Thus on 30 September 1888, just about ready to start work on *Tess*, Tom noted:

> In the afternoon by train to Evershot. Walked to Woolcombe, a property owned by a – I think the senior – branch of the Hardys . . . The decline and fall of the Hardys much in evidence hereabout. An instance: Becky S.'s mother's sister married one of the Hardys of this branch, who was considered to have demeaned himself by marriage . . . This particular couple had an enormous lot of children. I remember when young seeing the man – tall and thin – walking beside a horse and common spring trap, and my mother pointing him out to me and saying he represented what was once a leading branch of the family. So we go down, down, down.

This is an important element in his feeling and thinking, especially in the light of such very late poems as 'Family Portraits'. Surely Tom did believe in the decline of great families, and surely he did believe, like his contemporary Emile Zola, in 'tainted blood' and in the passing down through families of sinister hereditary diseases. There is even an undocumented tale that he believed himself to be the victim of one of these diseases. Surely, too, and with perfect good faith, he believed in the legend of the once aristocratic Hardys with which his mother would have regaled him. In every rural district at that time tales were told, based on little more than resemblances of name, of great families brought down. The precise facts of the ancestry were as hard to trace as those of Hardy's have been – and that has not been for want of trying.

Too much emphasis may be put upon such matters, though, if we ignore the humour with which Tom regarded his own susceptibility to them – the reader's first impression of Durbeyfield's sense of fallen grandeur is that it is funny. However, Tom did share the Victorian fascination with genealogy, as his copy of *Hutchin's* clearly shows. In common with many others he enjoyed investigating family trees. His own attempt to provide himself with one, although unscientific by modern standards, demonstrates enjoyment and curiosity rather than snobbishness. After all, he had become one of the most distinguished men of his age, and was interested in any alleged reasons as to why this was so.

Cockerell asserted that Tom told him, in 1920, that he would like to have called his book *Tess of the Hardys* if it had not seemed 'too personal'. But at the novel's centre is no single woman, ancestor or otherwise; its focal point is a sense of innocence malevolently destroyed. Tom was in love with his creation, and at that time she was no single woman. The very first name he gave her was, after all, Love (after that it was Sis, then Sue, then Rose Mary). Despite cerebral reservations, she would represent for Tom innocence personified, one of the non-'artificial' and 'enfranchized' people whose existence is implied in the notebook entry he made on 21 September just as he was starting on the manuscript, in which he observed that the 'literary productions' of 'rigidly correct' men of 'rigidly good family . . . mostly treat of social conventions . . . the artificial forms of living – as if they were cardinal facts of life'. This note arises from the same feeling that prompted another entry, of 15 March 1890: irritated by the artificiality of the 'most beautiful women' at a crush that he and Emma attended, he exclaimed, 'But these women! If put into rough wrappers in a turnip-field, where would their beauty be?' That is indeed the 'coarse' comment of a countryman, and suggests that 'coarseness' is by no means always a merely negative quality.

It was at just this time that Tom's eye began to rove. Far too much has been made of this by prudes, hypocrites and over-solemn commentators: after all, it is the most natural thing in the world. But it cannot be ignored because of that. Eventually that excitable eye was to fall upon Florence Henniker, who was to excite his lust, his love – and finally, if only temporarily, a fierce involuntary resentment, which he would express in the story 'An Imaginative Woman' and less directly in *Jude*. Tom was able to acknowledge and deal with his feelings for Florence Henniker and, more efficiently, for her predecessor, Rosamund Tomson – so there is no question of his being more 'adolescent' than any other man; if anything he was less so. If this were not the case, then the famous poem 'I Look Into My Glass' would be simply the adolescent outpourings of an unfortunate male. Alas, the neo-Victorian concept of the mature man as serene and untroubled by romantic emotion is false. It is surprising that Yeats, who in his old age was truly indiscreet in sexual matters, is never referred to as adolescent.

Tom's interest in the beautiful Mrs Tomson, a minor but by no means technically incapable poetaster and landscape painter who would in 1896 be divorced by her husband, another landscape painter, and who would die in 1911 at the age of fifty, was in any case slight. However, Mrs Tomson – later Mrs Marriott Watson – was opportunistic and provocative, anticipating the more formidable Florence Henniker. Tom early gave up his interest in her, as he reminded Mrs Henniker on 16 July 1893:

> I am writing too much as the mentor. . . . I will . . . trust to imagination only for an enfranchised woman. I thought I had found one some years ago – (I told you of her) – and it is somewhat singular that she contributes some of the best pieces to the volume of *ballades* you send. Her desire, however, was to use your correspondent as a means of gratifying her vanity by exhibiting him as her admirer, the discovery of which promptly ended the relationship, with considerable disgust on his side.

This, as we shall see later, was as much a sort of dire warning to Mrs Henniker as a recollection; but in any case Tom forgave Rosamund Tomson. In his old age he wrote a typically generous poem in memory of her, called 'An Old Likeness', with the subtitle 'Recalling R.T.'. In the manuscript it was called 'The Old Portrait'. Once she had sent him (and Emma) photographs of herself, and he must have kept them. The stark, almost analytical honesty of the opening is notable – after all, an aged man is admitting to the rather mawkish act of kissing an old picture:

> Who would have thought
> That, not having missed her
> Talk, tears, laughter
> In absence, or sought
> To recall for so long
> Her gamut of song;
> Or ever to waft her
> Signal of aught
> That she, fancy-fanned,
> Would well understand,

A ROVING EYE

I should have kissed her
Picture when scanned
Yawning years after!

Now the old portrait takes him 'by storm/Here in this blight-time!'
and

I took its feinting
As real, and kissed it,
As if I had wist it
Herself of old.

The attachment he almost formed for her was based on his genuine search for an enlightened ('enfranchised', as he called it) woman. In the early summer of 1889 she sent him her poems, *The Bird-Bride*, signed as by Graham R. Tomson. He may or may not have known that the author was a woman, but, by his own contrivance, he sat next to her at an Authors' Society dinner on 3 July, and by 5 September was writing to thank her for sending him her *Selections from the Greek Anthology*. He invited her and her husband to stay, and added:

No: wild horses shall not drag it out of me – that estimate of a poetess's works which came to my ears – till I see her. If you go back to town this month I hope you will not stay there, but get away again to be braced up for the winter. Upwey would be an excellent place for late Autumn, as it has a genial air if not wet.

But, to do her justice, she did not or could not then rise to this mild and playful bait, and on 6 October he returned to the attack:

We are greatly disappointed that you are not able to include Dorset in your programme. . . . No, I cannot come to Sussex either: but then my conscience does not prick me in saying my negative as yours ought to prick you in saying yours; for, you see – I had never raised anyone's hopes.

This banter, reinforced by a reference to lovers sharing a single umbrella ('which makes all the difference'), was, however, completely 'harmless'. Tom just liked pretty women, and in particular he liked them when they could turn a pretty verse, which Mrs Tomson just about

405

could. His yearning for an intellectual *and* sexual companion was still tucked away at the back of his mind, finding its chief outlet in the creation of Tess. Nor did the friendship with Mrs Tomson deepen, despite a subsequent visit to Max Gate with her husband. In November he refused to contribute a piece of fiction to a 'painter's weekly' which she was thinking of producing. After the end of 1891 – when he did not dare send her *Tess*, just published, and so sent *A Group of Noble Dames* instead – he seems to have ceased to write to her at all. But in 1895 he was quite annoyed when an article signed 'Graham R. Tomson', making false allegations about the manner in which he had acquired Max Gate, appeared in the *New York Independent*. It asserted that he had only got the land through the personal intervention of the Prince of Wales, proprietor of the Duchy of Cornwall, and therefore its owner. George Herriot, an official in the Duchy's London office, wrote to him to question the story, and to his denial of it he added on 10 January:

A woman is at the bottom of it, of course! I have reason to know that the writer of the account is a London lady, pretty, & well known in society (The signature is not I believe her real name). Why she should have written it I cannot say – except that it was not to please me; for such gossip annoys me greatly even when true.

There is no evidence that this little affair, if it can be called that, meant much to Tom, or that it made Emma feel threatened. There are elements of Mrs Tomson in Nichola Pine-Avon of *The Well-Beloved*, but nothing that suggests embitterment. Certainly, though, his interest in her marks the beginning of a pattern, since his letters to her reveal that in his fiftieth year he was becoming rather more of a deliberate lady's man. This may have irritated Emma, or filled her with apprehension; but if it did, there is no sign of it, and the conclusion must be that Tom continued to treat her with his usual consideration. Conjectures that Emma was at that time seriously disturbed about her husband's eye for other women, though occasionally made with great confidence, are without foundation.

Emma certainly contributed to the writing of *Tess*, and it must be supposed that she fully shared Tom's views about its essential virtue. As late as January 1892 she wrote to the *Spectator* to explain that the current meaning of the word 'whorage', as used in it, did not imply the 'idea of its root meaning'. A portion of manuscript for the serial version of the tenth and eleventh chapters is in her hand. Obviously Tom put no restraint upon her collaboration: on the contrary, he turned to her for help in the silly but financially necessary task he now had before him. In the *Life* he wrote:

> Hardy spent a good deal of the time in August and in the autumn [1891] correcting *Tess of the d'Urbervilles* for its volume form, which process consisted in restoring to their places the passages and chapters of the Original MS that had been omitted from the serial publication.

That is how Florence published the passage. She deleted the sentence, 'That Tess should put on the jewels was Mrs Hardy's suggestion', just as she had deleted a slightly earlier passage referring to Emma as 'being rather well-dressed'. This is important evidence both of Florence Hardy's determination to expunge Emma from the record so far as she could, as well as of Emma's willingness at that time to help with, and therefore fully discuss, Tom's fiction.

Tom never forgot or forgave the nature of the world for what he described in the *Life* as 'a novel's dismemberment'. Given the singular beauty of that novel, readers should be in full agreement with him: the nature of the Grundyism that conspired against its appearance is indeed mean and malicious. Yet those who protested were sincere. Such a clash between Tom's values and the world's was, after all, inevitable. It is only surprising that a man who could fight the world so openly as he deliberately did should have been thought of as so insecure and lacking in confidence. But, as he himself had noted on 21 August 1888, society 'consists of Characters and No-characters – nine at least of the latter to one of the former'.

Back in London at the beginning of 1889, he again rhapsodized so much over Turner – 'each is a landscape plus a man's soul' – that we must suppose that the famously successful and oft-noted equation of landscape and emotion in *Tess* was the result of a conscious decision to try to emulate Turner in reverse. For instance, after Tess has re-encountered Alec in his guise as preacher, and has been repelled by his newly awakened lust for her, the ploughing up of the land in preparation for the spring sowing, in anticipation of what ought to be a thing of joy and newness, is perceived as 'joyless monotony'. Again, when Tess's situation at the farm at Flintcombe Ash has become almost impossible, and she is caught in Alec's trap, the figure of the 'engine-man' is introduced: a hellish spectre, a stranger to the fields, yet inevitable. And when the re-paganized Alec lusts after her as she labours in the fields it is in the shadow of the phallic giant of Cerne Abbas ('Abbot's Kernel').

Discouraged by the dense fog in London, he and Emma were soon back at Max Gate. A painter, Alfred Parsons, was to stay there for a few days to do the illustrations for 'The First Countess of Wessex' for *Harper's*. Clearly Tom liked Parsons, who told him that he lived in London because he could mix with intellectual people and allow them to do their thinking for him – Tom added that he thought this would be disastrous to his brush. Parsons, or a part of him, appears as the painter Alfred Somers in *The Well-Beloved*.

The early months of that year were taken up with work on *Tess*. In the spring he replied to a letter of 9 April from John Addington Symonds, who was living at Davos in Switzerland, praising *The Return of the Native*. Tom had met Symonds, and now expressed his sympathy with his writings, telling him that he had for a long time read his essays as 'correctives' to those of Matthew Arnold ('in need of the counterpoise that some of yours afford'). The letter is interesting because of what it says about how Tom, now in the midst of *Tess*, felt about the pessimism with which he was so often charged. He told Symonds, possibly in complete ignorance of the reasons for his own pessimism (he was a married homosexual) – but possibly not – that he got 'smart raps from critics who appear to think that to call me a pessimist & a pagan is to say all that is necessary for my condemnation'. He continued:

The tragical conditions of life imperfectly denoted in *The Return of the Native* & some other stories of mine I am less & less able to keep out of my work. I often begin a story with the intention of making it brighter and gayer than usual; but the question of conscience soon comes in; & it does not seem right, even in novels, to wilfully belie one's own views. All comedy is tragedy, if you only look deep enough into it. A question which used to trouble me was whether we ought to write sad stories, considering how much sadness there is in the world already. But of late I have come to the conclusion that, the first step towards cure of, or even release from, any disease being to understand it, the study of tragedy in fiction may possibly here & there be the means of showing how to escape the worst forms of it, at least, in real life.

He ended the letter by promising to send Symonds a copy of *The Woodlanders*, even though he thought it 'a failure towards the end'.

Even now the false ending forced upon him rankled, for all that he had made his non-acceptance of it clear enough, at last to more perceptive readers, in his first non-serial text. Later that year, when the possibility of dramatizing the novel came up, he insisted that the fact of Fitzpiers' lack of repentance be further emphasized. On 7 August 1889 he wrote to one of those concerned: 'In the story the reunited lovers are supposed to live *un*happily! . . . how that would seem on the stage I am at a loss to say. Still anything would be better than the old old style.' But this adaptation, although completed, was never produced.

In February, probably still struggling with *Tess* and, surely, by now, with anticipations of the trouble it would cause him, he read Plato's *Cratylus*. Its spirit he seems to have understood, since he made this comment:

> A very good way of looking at things would be to regard everything as having an actual or false name, and an intrinsic or true name, to ascertain which all endeavour should be made. . . . The fact is that nearly all things are falsely, or rather inadequately, named.

One may fancy that Tom, without being particularly philosophical, regarded poetry as a means of 'ascertainment'.

In late April he and Emma went to London, first staying at the West Central Hotel and then renting 'two furnished floors in Monmouth Road [it was at No. 20], Bayswater'. During a shorter visit earlier that mouth he had made a note: 'London. Four million forlorn hopes!'; now the city made its usual impression upon him. On the 20th April he called upon his friend the painter Lawrence Alma-Tadema, 'like a school-boy, with untidy hair . . . I like this phase of him better than his man-of-the-world phase'. Alma-Tadema introduced him to Hippolyte Taine, of whom he wrote on 1 June to his near-neighbour Mary Sheridan – the American wife of a descendant of the playwright, who lived at Frampton Court near Dorchester:

> a most interesting man – M. Taine, the French critic and historian. Probably you know him. He told me that one of the first English books he read was Spenser's 'Fairy Queen' – every word of it: & I was obliged to confess that, in common with so many English, I had never read it quite through.

In the same letter he mentioned how impressed he had been with the paintings of Monet, and of how 'you could almost feel the heat of the sun' in his pictures. On 29 May, to the amazement of some commentators, he remarked on yet another girl he had encountered, this time on an omnibus:

> That girl . . . had one of those faces of marvellous beauty which are seen casually in the streets but never among one's friends. It was perfect in its softened classicality – a Greek face translated into English. Moreover she was fair, and her hair pale chestnut. Where do these women come from? Who marries them? Who knows them?

On 24 June Tom, still sympathetically interested in Gissing, whose *The Nether World* was just then making a fine profit for his publishers Smith, Elder, but nothing for him (he had an initial £150 for the copyright, and that was all), wrote inviting him to Monmouth Road. In fact, the meeting could not have taken place: Gissing was at Wakefield in Yorkshire from May until August, while his London flat was being repainted. It was at about this time, or possibly just before, that Tom met Gissing's friend Edward Clodd, a wealthy banker and aggressively rationalistic popular author. They were to remain close for the rest of their lives: Clodd, Hardy's exact contemporary and a friend to George Meredith, outlived him by two years. This sociable and genial man would provide Tom with a welcome refuge at his home at Aldeburgh in Suffolk when things became difficult between him and Emma – it was also a place where he could take his mistress, Florence Dugdale.

A letter of 10 July to an American author, Mrs Louise Chandler Moulton, shows that he was still undecided about the title of *Tess*, upon which he had probably done a little work in London. She had sent him her book of stories called *Miss Gyre from Boston*, and he replied: 'The titles . . . look tempting. I wish you would think of one for poor me – for I have not yet absolutely hit it off.' On the following day he was proposing to Tillotson & Son that the novel be called 'The Body and Soul of Sue'. But, back at Max Gate on 7 August, writing to Osgood about the *Harper's Bazaar* publication, he had decided upon 'Too Late, Beloved!'. He worked hard at *Tess* throughout August, only pausing to give icy encouragement to a local man, W.G. Lockett, who solicited his approval of an article called 'Love and Literature', which he had published in *Arts Monthly: The Official Organ of the Arts Society*: '. . . decidedly promising. The society seems to be fostering excellent preparatory literary work . . . though I am unable to become a susbscriber just now I shall be glad to hear of its well-doing.' Splendidly, he was more interested in, and devoted more space to replying to, an enquiry about a song beginning:

> King Arthur he had three sons
> Big rogues as ever did swing,
> He had three sons by whores
> And he kicked them all three out of doors. . . .

Then, on 9 September, off went the portion of 'Too Late, Beloved!', as it still was, to Tillotson's: 'equal to about one-half, I think'. For a week or two he had grounds for thinking that he might have got away with, as he put it, 'truth to fact', that 'crime in literature'. For John Brimelow, W.F. Tillotson's successor and sharer of his Congregationalist and Sunday School views, had sent the manuscript straight to the printer. Tom's enormities were not seen until proofs came back towards the end of the month. Immediately Tillotson's wrote demanding that he make changes. He refused; the firm offered to pay for what they had received; again he refused, and the agreement was cancelled. It was an honourable transaction on both sides. The exact nature of the manuscript he sent to Tillotson's is unknown, since he destroyed it. In the *Life* there is nothing about this episode, and a note of 13 October merely refers to the fact that three wooden-legged men used to do a dance at Broadmayne – which is doubtless how he felt about the minds of the publishers of popular serial matter, although he must have appreciated Brimclow's plain dealing. He does, however, record that he tried the story on *Murray's* and then on *Macmillan's* (neither of course could accept it), and so he

adopted a plan till then, it is believed, unprecedented in the annals of fiction. This was not to offer the novel intact to the third editor [Locker of the *Graphic*] on his list . . . but to send it up with some chapters or parts of chapters cut out, and instead of destroying those to publish them, or much of them, elsewhere . . . as episodic adventures of anonymous personages . . . till they could be put back in their places at the printing of the whole in volume form . . . Hardy carried out this unceremonious concession to conventionality with cynical amusement, knowing the novel was moral enough and to spare. But the work was sheer drudgery. . . . He resolved to get away from the supply of family fiction to magazines as soon as he conveniently could do so.

411

Tom has attracted remarkably little sympathy for his predicament, doubtless because it has been felt that he had got himself into it and because, as Millgate puts it, 'he protests too much'. No family magazine could willingly have printed *Tess* as it stood. Today we have made progress in that direction, and so he deserves the credit of having been a pioneer. Besides, he really did not protest much – he was just temperamentally over-sensitive about fundamental injustice from fools or knaves; so much the worse for those modern fools or knaves who cannot see this. Far too much has been made of his rather mild degree of annoyance. It is hard to sympathize with the cowardly, lustful and disingenuous Mowbray Morris, the editor of *Macmillan's*, who had published the serial *Woodlanders* and who wrote to Tom on 25 November:

> I cannot think there should be any theological offence in [your manuscript] . . . there is nothing that can in reason be called irreverent, for poor Tess was in very sober earnestness [in the baptism].
>
> But there are other things which might give offence, &, as I must frankly own to think, not altogether unreasonably. . . . It is obvious from the first page what is to be Tess's fate at Trantridge; it is apparently obvious to the mother, who does not seem to mind. . . . You use the word *succulent* more than once to describe the general appearance of conditions of the Frome Valley. Perhaps I might say that the general impression left on me by reading your story . . . is one of rather too much succulence. . . .

Morris tried to pretend that he was solely concerned with 'fitness' for the magazine; but, as Millgate has noted, he was profoundly upset by the book's sexuality. He pretended that his objection to the word 'venust' to describe Tess was etymological; in fact he was, quite literally, afraid for his own morals. In April 1892 Morris, hiding beneath the skirts of anonymity, showed his true colours in the *Quarterly Review* where he discussed *Tess*: 'It is indisputably open to Mr Hardy to call his heroine a pure woman; but he has no less certainly offered many inducements to his readers to refuse her the name.' His review criticized the 'hole-in-corner' method of publication, and made fun of the novel, not incapably, but wholly insensitively, causing Tom to make his famous note: '. . . smart and amusing . . . but it is easy to be smart and amusing if a man will forgo veracity and sincerity . . . Well, if this sort of thing continues no more novel-writing for me. A man must be a fool to deliberately stand up to be shot at.' Yet he must have known that, even while never himself forgoing truth or sincerity, he had, in the person of Tess, flung every pious hypocrite's lust back into his face.

At least Tillotson & Son, in accordance with their nonconformist principles, had been straightforward about the matter. To make things right they had immediately solicited a story from Tom; soon they received 'The Melancholy Hussar', which they marketed with great success. And in due time they would serialize the first version of *The Well-Beloved*. There had been no attempt at any dressing down from them. Small wonder, then, that Tom thought Morris and his kind odious and insincere; that is why he wanted to be free of such people. Ultimately he took a financial risk to be so, although his chief motive was to devote himself to poetry. And, ironically, it was the success of *Tess* as a book, and the fortuitous passing of the Copyright Act in America, that made this step possible.

It is interesting that Morris, who not only attacked *Tess* in the *Quarterly*, but also 'Candour in English Fiction' in *Macmillan's*, should have objected to Hardy as coarse: *Tess* was, he believed, 'a coarse and disagreeable story' told in a 'coarse and disagreeable manner'. The effect on polite editors of Tom's capacity for being 'disagreeably' straightforward in a countryman's manner, a faculty he could amusedly conceal when in high society, cannot be over-estimated.

It is doubtful whether Tom was 'genuinely incapable of anticipating the effect of his writings on readers less "advanced" than himself,' as Millgate patronizingly asserts. His sarcasm may occasionally have been ineffective, and he was cunning and evasive in his dealings with editors and objectors; but this does not need to be equated with over-earnestness or with any real 'disingenuousness'. One has to counter disingenuousness with disingenuousness unless one is a revolutionary, and Tom needed to avoid becoming the latter for many good reasons.

Our interpretation of his attitude must depend upon the degree of our own commitment to truth and to humour. What about the title of the midnight baptism episode, printed as a detached piece in the *Fortnightly* in May 1891: 'The Midnight Baptism: A Study in Christianity'? After all, just how wholesome were the tactics of the opposition? Millgate, Purdy and others of Victorian kidney have been stiffly grieved that Tom spoke of *Jude* as 'a tale that could not offend the most fastidious maiden', and of *The Well-Beloved* as a book that could 'be circulated freely in schools and families – nay in nurseries'. Others will smile.

However, Millgate's charge that 'he was not prepared to forgo the financial rewards of the serial, to step outside the current system of publishing fiction and cast himself specifically in the role of a revolutionary' is justified. He did, too, seek to persuade his editors that the 'stories envisaged would not actually transgress . . . the unwritten conventions' – and then proceed to offend them. All that is true. But then, why should not a poet and novelist of his stature, with something like *Tess* in his heart, treat those pious editors just as a peasant might treat the gentlemanly but greedy urban buyer of a field or barn?

Millgate speaks of Tom's 'naivety' in such matters, just as he imagines that so uneducated a man could never have been aware of the existence of lesbianism, a nicety confined to university men. He finds it 'scarcely credible' that Tom 'should not have known the trouble he was likely to provoke' – but, of course, he knew it perfectly well. That is the secret, although it hardly ought to be a secret. Millgate solemnly goes on: 'he was capable of acknowledging . . . that his critics, if misguided, were not entirely to be blamed', and quotes a letter to Cockerell of 1912 in which Tom wrote: 'When *Jude* comes out at the end of this month in the new series, and you read the Preface and Postscript you will say to yourself (as I did when I passed the proof for press) "How very natural, and even commendable, it is for old-fashioned cautious people to shy at a man who could write that!"' But why will these critics not indeed 'shy' at him, and confine themselves to less disturbing, less teasing and inferior writers?

Tom himself recorded that the 'cynical' treatment was a 'complete success'; 'the mutilated novel was accepted by . . . the *Graphic*' and appeared there between 4 July and 26 December 1891. The restored text was published by Osgood, McIlvaine in November 1891 – as usual, about a month before the last instalment had appeared – and prefaced by the following 'explanatory note':

> The main portion of the following story appeared – with slight modifications – in the *Graphic* newspaper . . . I will just add that the story is sent out in all sincerity of purpose, as an attempt to give artistic form to a true sequence of things; and in respect of the book's opinions and sentiments, I would ask any too genteel reader, who cannot endure to have said what everybody nowadays thinks and feels, to remember a well-worn sentence of St Jerome's: If an offence come out of the truth, better is it that the offence come than that the truth be concealed.

Is this really protesting 'too much'? Or is the writing of *Tess* of rather more account than notorious and long since demolished Victorian disingenuities?

The process was more difficult than Tom wanted to admit. As soon as he had concluded his arrangements with the *Graphic*, he seems to have postponed his work on the novel yet again. Probably he would have preferred to have been as 'coarse' – this is to say, straightforward, and anything else unconventional – in it as he needed to be; but that was impossible. He was in negotiation with Arthur Locker before either *Murray's* or *Macmillan's* had actually declined the novel; but there was nothing wrong in this, because, had one of these unexpectedly accepted it, he could have given a completely new serial novel to the *Graphic*, in all probability *The Well-Beloved*, but possibly *Jude*. He was temporarily able to abandon work on *Tess* because Locker finally gave him until the end of September for delivery of half of it. This gave him some six extra months to make his 'cynical . . . dismemberment'. But, as we have seen, these months involved more attacks on his impropriety and his tasteless dwelling upon such rare events as childbirth in *Life's Little Ironies*. He managed to obtain from Locker the sum of £590 for *Tess*, and reserved his own right to sell it to *Harper's*, which he did. It is notable that he always remained on courteous terms with Locker, as he did with Tillotson & Son.

At the end of January he noted that, since he had been looking for 'God 50 years' (he was now a few months short of his fiftieth birthday), he thought that he would have discovered him 'if he exists'. He added: 'As an external personality of course – the only true meaning of the word'. Such a provocative note hardly amounts to a theological treatise, and is perhaps chiefly interesting as recording that, after all, he *had* been looking for God, as well as denouncing him (if he existed) for insensitivity.

He went up to London for a few days in March, and then again, this time with Emma, in May, just after he had sent in the *Dames* material two months before it was due. He told Osgood on 18 May that neither of them was 'very well', and thought of returning to the country and then coming up again after Whitsun; nevertheless they remained in London until the beginning of August. There they indulged in their 'customary round of picture-viewing, luncheons, calls, dinners, and receptions'. Once again people seemed to him to act mechanically, 'like somnambulists . . . moving about under enchantment'. At a service in St George's, Hanover Square, he found the electric light and the 'old theology' incongruous, the sermon irrelevant to modern life. Going to the Criterion for supper after the service, he suddenly found himself, on the second floor, to be amongst men in evening clothes, 'ringed and studded', and women in low-bosomed dresses, 'their glazed and lamp-blacked eyes wandering'. He went downstairs to the grill-room and ate there instead. He heard a man say: 'When one is half drunk London seems a wonderfully enjoyable place . . .' The fact of London's millions seemed to press upon him, and, coming back from seeing Henry Irving in *The Bells*, he noted: 'The 4,000,000 suggest their existence now, when one sees the brilliancy about Piccadilly Circus at this hour, and notices the kiln-dried features around.' Also in May he met, at Gosse's, first, Caroline Balestier, who was to become Kipling's wife, and then Kipling himself. He had read Kipling's tales and poems carefully, and with approval, and now enjoyed hearing their author telling of 'curious details in Indian life'. They remained on good terms, but eventually he became disgusted with Kipling's vulgar imperialism and, no doubt, with his violent anti-Semitism. Tom was one of the very few writers of his time and place who never made a hostile remark about other races.

During June he went a great deal to the Savile Club, and, on the 2nd, celebrated his fiftieth birthday. He visited many music-halls, observing the women as 'seldom well-formed physically', and commented that the 'morality' of actors and actresses cannot be judged 'by the standard as that of people who lead slower lives'. He thought, sarcastically, that either theatres should be 'put down . . . altogether because of their effect on the performers' or that the performers should be forgiven 'as irresponsibles'. He met the explorer Stanley but was not impressed by him: he was disdainful and wore a look which implied that he would soon be a resentful man. The Bishop of Ripon, also at the dinner at which Stanley made a conceited speech, had a 'nice face' whose 'ingenuous archness' suggested to Tom that 'he would be quite willing to let supernaturalism down easy, if he could'. He also spent periods of time at police courts, 'being still compelled to get novel padding'.

He had promised a favourite actress named Ada Rehan, whom he described as an American twenty years his junior and a personal friend, 'a kindly natured, winning woman with really a heart', that he would write some verses for a charity sponsored by their friend Mary Jeune: her Holiday Fund for Children. These verses were not intended to be poetry, and he did not even attend the ceremony at which Ada Rehan delivered them; he had finished them at the Savile while she awaited delivery of them. He was therefore annoyed when a newspaper condemned them as poor stuff. In the *Life* he implies that this commission was the reason why he could not accompany Emma to her father's deathbed, whither she was now summoned. What is most likely, however, is that both Emma and he felt that he might not be welcome at so delicate a time. Emma's mother died in the following year, and doubtless needed much support now. Although it is assumed that Tom never saw Gifford again after the latter's visit to Surbiton years earlier, this may not be true. He may have come to Max Gate, and may have met Tom in London; there is every 'normal' reason to suppose that he did, and little to suppose that he did not. Why should Tom record such a meeting in the *Life*, whose readers would in any case have assumed (if they thought about it at all) that occasional meetings took place?

The couple were back together at Max Gate by early August. They had now been married for more than sixteen years, and their relationship was frayed at the edges. Whose are not, after sixteen years? But the picture given by some of Hardy's biographers, of Emma almost desperate with anxiety over what is far too often presented as her husband's womanizing and their marriage on the rocks, is quite unjustified. Nor may it be so easily supposed, as it generally is, that within a year Emma had started to keep her so-called 'black diaries', allegedly chock-full of bitter remarks about her husband. Even if they existed (and they probably did, if not to the extent and degree of venom that Florence Hardy liked to imagine), there is no guarantee that they were started in 1891. Emma had written diaries of her travels, and no doubt she began and then dropped many more similar records. She might have started one in 1891 – but did it have anything at all about her husband in it? Gosse, who visited for a few days in September 1890, never dropped a hint that anything was seriously wrong at this stage. Nor has anyone else – except Florence, who managed to convince Purdy, an inexperienced bachelor, and no psychologist, of the truth of her account. She, though, was at that time an eleven-year-old schoolgirl.

Emma was still 'My dearest Em' on 24 July, when Tom wrote to her at Compton Giffard in Devon – where her father, having moved from Cornwall some years before, had died. He told her about Mrs Rehan and the contretemps with the newspaper (he had, as so often, allowed himself to become far too concerned with the idiocies of the press), and about the current difficulties with the *Graphic* because someone 'had read the 1st proofs in mistake for the second' – but then added the single sentence: 'I told Mrs J [Jeune] briefly, of your father's death – & she was very sympathetic.' These words demonstrate that there was still much between them that did not need to be put in writing and that Emma, like Tom, was a private person.

At the end of August, anticipating the heavy task before him, he took Henry to Paris for a few days, 'solely,' he assures us in the *Life* 'on his brother's account'. He took him to the Moulin Rouge and to most of the other sights. On the railway journey back to Le Havre they sat in a carriage with a married couple: the husband seemed to study his wife, 'a good-natured amative creature by her voice; and her heavy moist lips', and wonder why he had married her and why she married him. Tom was now procrastinating, 'visiting and entertaining neighbours', and was in fact late with the cynically bowdlerized manuscript he had promised to the *Graphic*. It had been due at the end of September, but he was unable to send it off until 8 October. The most demanding task, of course, still lay ahead: that of restoring the dismembered novel.

The work may have been put back a little by the death of their much-loved retriever, Moss. These matters were always of great importance to both Tom and Emma, and Tom even recorded the fact, briefly, in the *Life*. He gave a fuller account in an affectionate letter to Gosse – who had been with them, with his wife, for five nights two weeks earlier – of 25 September:

> We are quite in grief today. Our poor dog Moss died this morning, and we have buried her under the trees by the lawn. It was singular that your last photo included her. That happens to be the only portrait of any sort that was taken of her: so if you can let us have it when developed (even if not a good picture in itself) we should be glad. You see there was a fate at work in your securing Moss though you missed Kidleywinkempoops-Trot.

Gosse, who genuinely enjoyed being obliging and considerate, hurried to send the photograph, and on 5 October Tom replied thanking him, and added the postscript: 'The wife says I must tell you that she greatly values the photograph & thinks it such a fortunate chance that you secured Moss.'

When Tom went up to London alone for a week on Wednesday, 3 December he sent Emma no fewer than four letters, all of which are affectionate – the last of them, dated 10 December, begins, 'My dearest Emmie'. No doubt distress at the death of the affectionate Moss, deepened because it was the result of a beating from a tramp, brought them particularly close for a time; but such a renewed affection did not arise from any serious breach, or, indeed, from any breach at all. The tone of these letters, like that of a similar batch sent in 1891, quite precludes the notion that there was anything painfully wrong with the relationship at this time.

By the time he made this visit, which was in part to see the Jeunes, then living in Wimpole Street, he had long managed to make up for his week's lapse in delivery of the mutilated *Tess*: the rest, after hard work throughout October, went off a week early. This no doubt gave him some satisfaction since he must have felt humiliated by the *Graphic*, not only in the matter of the *Dames* but also by their further unspecified objections to details of the mutilated *Tess*. If he had wished to demonstrate how small minds can ruin a masterpiece, then he did so with the serial *Tess*. But relations between him and the *Graphic* remained polite and in December he was a guest at what he described to Emma on 5 December as 'an *enormous* affair': a dinner marking the *Graphic*'s twenty-first anniversary and honouring its founder, William Luson Thomas.

Nevertheless there was an undercurrent of dislike on both sides. Thomas himself felt threatened by his popular author's needless ventures into truthful territory; and there are Tom's own angry (though entirely private) notes on the script of the *Dames*. In February 1891 there was almost a row about his slightly late delivery the previous autumn: on the 13th he had to write to Locker protesting that 'the charge the directors bring against me of "having delivered the MS so much later than was agreed on" is not quite accurate'. But he agreed to pay his 'fair share' of the costs of the typewriting they claimed had been involved in preparation of the text – and, no doubt ashamed, they did not charge him.

On his second day in London, 4 December, Tom was moved to note what, as he says, had by now become a conviction: 'I am more than ever convinced that persons are successively various persons, according as each special strand in their characters is brought uppermost by circumstances.' It is an extraordinary and unconventional insight, and, since this was not the first time he chose to make it in the *Life*, might well be taken to explain his own characters.

By now he certainly knew Edward Clodd, because he refers to him in the *Life* for the first time – a reference which shows that he was well aware of the unsubtle Clodd's severe limitations. He had put to him the question of why the superstitions of a 'remote Asiatic' and a 'Dorset labourer' were similar. Clodd answered, with all the superior certainty of the crude rationalist, that 'the attitude of man at corresponding levels of culture, before like phenomena, is pretty much the same, your Dorset

419

peasants representing the persistence of the barbaric idea which confuses persons and things, and founds wild generalizations on the slenderest analogies'. Commenting on this as 'excellently neat', Tom added acidly, in parentheses: '(This "barbaric idea which confuses persons and things" is, by the way, also common to the highest educational genius – that of the poet.)'

Back at Max Gate, Christmas Day found him thinking about resuming the writing of poetry: 'new horizons seemed to appear, and worrying pettinesses to disappear'. On the last day of the year he stood outside his door just before midnight, 'confronted by the toneless white of the snow spread in front, against which stood the row of pines breathing out: "Tis no better with us than with the rest of creation, you see!"' And, he noted, perhaps in anticipation of the famous poem 'The Oxen' of 1915, that he could not hear the church bells. But, it must always be remembered, he was listening for them, hoping that it might be so. The notion of his being a rationalistic simple-ton, in the mould of Clodd, is unacceptable. For such as Clodd there was never any 'blessed hope', only dull reductionist certainty.

The next year, until the November publication of *Tess* in its proper form, by Osgood McIlvaine, was taken up with its restoration and with the writing of stories. In January he found himself alone in London again. His one extant letter to Emma, of Saturday, 24 January, is exceptionally affectionate. He has telegraphed to say that he would not be back until Monday, and hopes that she received it, 'otherwise you may be alarmed'. He has, he tells her, paid a dressmaker's bill for her.

In March he took her with him, on a similarly brief visit. In April he was back again on a longer visit from which there are four extant letters to Emma. Of these Millgate remarks:

> These letters . . . are quite long and detailed, and perhaps sufficiently affectionate for a husband to write home to the wife to whom he has been married for sixteen years and with whom he expects to be reunited within a week or two at most. On the other hand, Hardy was still on friendly terms with Mrs Tomson at the time and it is of course conceivable that the very length and specificity of the letters, and their stress on the dullness of London, were deliberately designed as a smokescreen for other activities it was better Emma should not know about.

It is perfectly feasible that Tom had a mistress, or was in the habit of visiting a select brothel, in London. Later, when he really did have a mistress there, Florence Dugdale, he did set up a smokescreen. But Millgate, who believes Emma not to have been the genius's helpmate nor the qualified critic essential to highly rated authors, perhaps works too hard at his thesis. Here is the letter of 11 April:

> My dearest Em:
>   I have received your letter. Nothing has happened here, except that I have called on Osgood; the book [the *Dames*] is coming out about the first week in May. The weather is so bad here – a cold east wind, with now & then a drizzle, that I am glad you are not in town for your own sake, though not for mine, everything being so dull. A certain lack of energy I feel may be owing to my having hitherto kept to milk & water as a beverage in alternation to tea. I went to the Gaiety theatre last night – some of the burlesque was funny – some of it stupid. 'The bogie man' which I went to hear, is not much. 'That's how you mesmerize him,' another song in the piece [*Carmen Up to Date*] is funnier. I have written two pages of MS & shall recover energy no doubt next week. I am at the *annexe* of the hotel – a comfortable room – except that the street is noisy at night – all the single rooms are in front. I am going to try Mr Herriot's [the Duchy of Cornwall man, also a friend] plan of wool in the ears tonight. I have slept however pretty well – & have had no dyspepsia at all. I lunched with Besant [the novelist] yesterday here; we met by accident. I should not go to the 'At home,' unless you wish to. Next week I shall look about more – & write again.

And he signed himself off 'Ever your affecte husbd Tom'.
    Can we really infer from this that Tom was indulging in 'activities it was better that Emma should not know about'? There is certainly nothing here to suggest any liaison with a specific woman, least of all Mrs Tomson. The letter does tell us that Tom had been feeling listless after a bout of indigestion, for which he had been taking milk and water. It is hardly fair to suspect that his 'stress' on the dullness of London is a smokescreen.
    In his next letter, written two days later, he says that the weather is bad, that he has 'little zest for London, and cannot get up any interest in theatres and entertainments', and that he has lunched with Kipling. He also makes a joke about their friend, the poet Agnes Mary Frances Robinson, now Mme Darmesteter, author of six collections of

poetry and of *Poésies, traduites de l'anglais* (1887): 'She looks rather more matronly than formerly – though one rather wonders what reason there is for her doing so, her husband being so small.' Gittings tried to suggest possible 'activities' between Tom and the former Mary Robinson, but the remark to Emma about her matronliness surely precludes this. The joke does, though, imply an intimate understanding between Tom and Emma, who certainly shared her husband's sense of humour – which not all his critics do.

In the third letter, dated 16 April and answering one of Emma's, he tells her that he has not yet been able to find suitable accommodation for them: 'I think we must settle down in a quiet lodging, where I can work, for I am quite indifferent to society at present.' This deserves to be regarded as a gentle way of announcing that he will have to work harder, and do less gallivanting, than was usual for them in their London visits – rather than as a subterfuge to conceal some *amour*. He added: '& I am engrossed in the matter of a story which shall have its scene in London – I am going out looking about on that account now'. This story was 'The Son's Veto,' containing the odious Randolph.

The letter also contains evidence discomforting to those who wish to present Emma as already cut off from the Hardy family: 'Will you ask the gardener before you come when & how he wishes to be paid? I think we might make Polly Antell our agent for paying him.' Polly was Tom's Puddletown cousin, the daughter of John Antell the angry shoemaker, who had died in 1878, and sister of the local poet, also John. Polly and her mother Mary were in charge of Max Gate for the whole of Tom and Emma's absence that year. Mary and Kate, both now teaching in Dorchester, were living in the house Tom had bought for them in Dorchester. There is nothing to suggest that, at least in the very early 1890s, any limitation apart from Tom's need to work was put on visits by anyone to anyone else's house. Gittings claimed that Tom was embarrassed by his brother and sisters, and particularly by their country accents, but the suggestion has no merit. Henry would have been bored by literary people; Mary and, to a lesser extent, Kate, were shy, and would not have put themselves forward. But in any case it is not known how often Tom called on his sisters, or vice versa. People who are entertaining do not usually have their siblings regularly in attendance, whether they live in the same town or not.

In the last of these letters, shortly after which Emma joined him and they found lodgings at 12 Mandeville Place, off Manchester Square, he has lunched with Kipling again, this time in company with his father,

Lockwood Kipling. Tom was doubtless dreading doing the social round yet again, while Emma probably rather enjoyed it – as it is reasonable that she should.

George Douglas's well-known comment on Emma runs as follows:

> She belonged essentially to that class of women, gifted with spirit and the power of deciding for herself [he might have said 'emancipated'], which had attracted Hardy in his early manhood. She had the makings of a Bathsheba, with restricted opportunities.

This last sentence Millgate calls 'enigmatic'; in fact it can tell us little beyond that she was spirited. But at least Douglas, a fair man, who knew the Hardys as a couple almost as well as anybody, recognized Emma's vitality and liveliness. As to his disapproval of Tom's deference towards her: that, no doubt, was the voice of the Victorian patriarch. The poet Mabel Robinson, also quoted by the eager Millgate, spoke of the inconsequentiality of Emma's conversation, but she was hardly alone in that. The notion that she was 'unhinged' came from Florence; but Robinson denied that interpretation. Millgate's judgement that Tom gave her copying tasks merely to pacify her, and not because he valued her contribution, is unfair. That he did not 'urgently want the job done' is to fly in the face of the evidence: she had saved the day with *A Laodicean*, and she helped with the necessary mutilation of *Tess*. The whole midnight baptism piece, done for Frank Harris's *Fortnightly*, is in her hand. Another of his observations, based again on Mabel Robinson, that Emma's golden hair had 'faded drab' since the Tooting years, is as peculiarly offensive as it is revealing of his own mentality.

The Hardys were not yet truly well off. Tom noted their 'inability to afford a London house or flat all the year round'. But that state would only last another few months: Tess became a best-seller, and he could recoup all his American royalties because of the passing of the Copyright Act. The resulting prosperity would free Tom of pressing financial anxiety, but it would make things harder for Emma. Tom's family, but in particular Kate, became nervous that a 'foreigner' – that is, not a Hardy – would 'get' his money. Neither Mary nor Kate had a husband to worry about, nor children, and so they devoted themselves more and more to 'family'. Their attitude put Emma into a difficult position – she was now eyed with jealousy since she was acquiring money and new fame which, given her status as a Hardy by marriage only, she did not deserve. In view of the circumstances of the two sisters, this was as inevitable as it was narrow. There is certainly a cooling-off of relationships after the publication of *Tess*. Before it, though, things remained as cordial as ever, and Mary (more silent than Kate, and quite possibly more sympathetic) visited them at Mandeville Place.

Meanwhile Tom had still to 'restore' *Tess*, and he probably needed the quiet lodgings in London that year in order to think about it. In April, now joined by Emma, and just after yet another lunch with Kipling at the Savile, he fancied that if he were a painter he would 'paint a picture of a room as viewed by a mouse from a chink under the skirting'. His friend Joshua Fitch took him round two training colleges for schoolmistresses, the second of which was the institution attended by Tryphena Sparks. He observed, of the young women at Whitelands:

> Their belief in circumstances, in convention, in the rightness of things, which you know to be not only wrong but damnably wrong, makes the heart ache, even when they are waspish and hard. . . . There is much that is pathetic about these young girls, and I wouldn't have missed the visit for anything.

Under pressure from the Gladstonian Liberal Robert Pearce Edgcumbe, whom he respected, Tom agreed to vote for him at a forthcoming by-election (which Edgcumbe lost). Nevertheless he warned him on 21 April him that he did 'not take any active part in politics', adding two days later that 'the pursuit of what people are pleased to call Art so as to win unbiassed attention to it as such, absolutely forbids political action'. Such a mess had been made by all parties over the Irish question, he went on, that he could not support any approach. By 8 May, writing to console Edgcumbe on losing, he could sport the address of the Athenaeum Club, to which, after a campaign on his behalf, he had at last been elected.

Then, in August, it was back to Max Gate and work on the real *Tess*. In September he and Emma visited Sir George Douglas. In November the editor of the *Bookman*, Robertson Nicoll, wrote to ask him how, and whether, 'national recognition' should be given to men of letters. He replied:

> I daresay it would be very interesting that literature should be honoured by the state. But I don't see how it could be satisfactorily done. The highest flights of the pen are mostly the excursions and

revelations of souls unreconciled to life, while the natural tendency of a government would be to encourage acquiescence in life as it is.

And so, with that not quite patriotic thought, as well as with the approach of his delivery from financial problems, the day for the publication of *Tess* approached. At almost the same time, according to his own account, the *Graphic* begged him to provide more decorous means of transport for Tess and the three dairymaids across a flooded lane. Could not they be taken over in a wheelbarrow? 'This was accordingly done.'

21

Tess of the d'Urbervilles

The publication of the real *Tess* instantly increased Hardy's reputation. This was in large part owing to what he called its 'scandalous notoriety', which, although emanating from 'a certain small section of the public and the press', led salacious individuals to want to read it. He wrote that this was 'quite inexplicable to the writer himself' (originally he wrote: 'to any fair judge and to the writer himself'). Of course it was not 'quite inexplicable' to him, or to any fair judge; but irony was the best means of defending himself. He had set out to write not pornography, but the opposite. It was evident that this was the author who remained 'unreconciled to life'; but critics, and unsalacious readers too, recognized the power of the book. A few dissenting voices such as Mowbray Morris (in the *Quarterly*) apart, he had won a considerable victory. For *Tess* is his most passionate book, and nowhere is it more passionate than in the subtitle angrily added at the last moment: 'A Pure Woman Faithfully Presented'. After the passage in the *Life* ending 'inexplicable to the writer himself', Florence omitted the following:

> The sub-title of the book, added as a casual afterthought, seemed to be especially exasperating. It would have been amusing if it had not revealed such antagonism at the back of it, bearing evidence, as Hardy used to say, 'Of that absolute want of principle in the reviewer which gives one a start of fear as to a possible crime he may commit against one's person, such as a stab or shot in a dark lane for righteousness' sake.' Such critics, however, 'who, differing from an author of a work purely artistic, in sociological views, politics or theology, cunningly disguise that illegitimate reason for antagonism by attacking his work on a point of art itself', were not numerous or effectual in this case. And, as has been implied, they were overpowered by the dumb current of opinion.

It was true. Mrs Oliphant, reviewing it in *Blackwood's*, admitted at the outset that she 'privately' preferred fiction about 'cleanly lives' and 'honest sentiment', and remarked that she had never been able 'to get over a certain expedient of grotesque and indecent dishonesty' in *Two on a Tower*. But then, comparing it to Mrs Ward's *David Grieve*, which she had just discussed, she exclaimed: 'But with all this, what a living, breathing scene, what a scent and fragrance of the actual, what solid bodies, what real existence . . .!' She conceded, too, that Tess was 'of an extraordinarily elevated and noble kind', an 'exceptional creature'. She took Hardy to task for his 'anti-religion', but did not in her heart object to the 'defiant blazon of a Pure Woman, notwithstanding the early stain'. What she did not quite understand, or perhaps what her kind of Christianity could not allow her to understand, was that Hardy was not protesting, throughout *Tess*, against religion, so much as against a too easy, as well as only pseudo-religious optimism.

For some of the negative impressions he created in the minds of such reviewers he was this time, however, responsible. He did not object to Mrs Oliphant's criticism: it was fairly stated, and exhibited true, if conventional, feeling – rather than the kind of hypocritical cant with which Angel Clare is so unnaturally imbued that, while he is not surprised that Tess can forgive him for his own past surrender to lust, he cannot forgive her for something far less 'culpable', namely her seduction by Alec. That false morality conceals his disappointment that she is not the virgin of his dreams.

Angel is accurately summed up by a whispering milkmaid: 'too much taken up wi' his own thoughts to notice girls'. Real girls, that is. This is why he is so moved by Tess when he first registers her at breakfast at Crick's: she suggests to him a time when thought had not made things 'gray'. But he is unable to do justice to that side of himself, and in this respect is a subtler presentation of Knight in *A Pair of Blue Eyes*.

Of Morris's effort to criticize him in the *Quarterly* Tom wrote, in a passage suppressed from the *Life*:

Such reviews as *The Quarterly* are a dilemma for the literary man. There is the self reproach on the one hand of being conventional enough to be praised by them, and the possible pecuniary loss of being abused by them on the other.

But he comforted himself with the thought that not to be attacked by papers like *The Quarterly* was not to show any literary *esprit* whatever.

Commentary upon *Tess* which concentrates on its exact sources and then tries to use these to make biographical inferences is interesting when not too wildly speculative. It is doomed to failure, though, because the tiny reality represented by each of the hundreds of facts of which it is made is transcended by the whole. The vast majority of facts have undergone metamorphosis. It is true that Tom told a friend he had not been able 'to put on paper all that [Tess] is, or was, to me'; but he also told George Douglas (who seems to have taken the book literally, as a semi–fictional account of a real woman) that 'I too, lost my heart to her as I went on with her history.'

Two examples from thousands will illustrate the relationship between literal fact and Hardy's various texts, be they poetry, drama or fiction. In the 1920s he told his secretary May O'Rourke, who had lived in the Moules' house, the Old Vicarage at Fordington, that in *The Dynasts* he had 'placed the Vicar, the Reverend Mr Palmer, leaning against the post of his garden door as he waited to observe the ceremony' of the burning of Napoleon's effigy. Tom admitted 'cheerfully' to her that 'no view of Fordington Green was possible from the site'. Since this kind of thing happens all the time in Hardy, it is clearly unwise to draw exact biographical inferences from his work. Lois Deacon and Terry Coleman's ingenious book *Providence and Mr Hardy*, really a speculative novel of what, just possibly, might have been, offers the prime example of that hazardous process. Here Tom's mother Jemima gives birth to an illegitimate daughter, who was brought up by Maria Sparks as her own daughter, Rebecca – making Tryphena his half-sister!

Tom tells us in the *Life* that he based the milkmaid Marian, who takes to drink, on a girl he knew when he was fifteen years old:

> . . . as a pupil in his class he had a dairymaid four years older than himself, who afterwards appeared in *Tess of the d'Urbervilles* as Marian – one of the few portraits from life in his works. This pink and plump damsel had a marvellous power of memorizing whole chapters in the Bible, and would repeat to him by heart in class, to his boredom, the long gospels before Easter without missing a word, and with evident delight in her facility; though she was by no means a model of virtue in her love-affairs.

Thus, although Marian was suggested by a memory of this girl, the drunkenness, and other details, were of his own invention, like the range of vision of the Rev. Mr Palmer. Each fact is slightly altered.

Tess is based on a commonplace that was treated by the Victorians with varying degrees of sententious disingenuousness: the ruined maid. Alec initially appears as the conventional Victorian villain; later, after his conversion and relapse, he develops into a more individual character. Since he declares, against Tess's protestations, that if there is no God then all is permissible, we may even see in him an attempt, if a half-hearted one, to explore this Dostoievskian theme. But even as a mere stage villain, suitably hissed at by the reader (and in the dramatizations of the novel he actually was hissed), he is sufficient foil to Tess to display her special qualities. He is not, however, one of Hardy's greatest successes as a character.

What is different about Tess as Victorian victim is the genuineness of what Tom called her 'purity'. The claim, thus starkly and provocatively made, runs against the grain of Victorianism; it would not have been made had it not done so. As he wrote in the preface to the fifth edition, his critics ignored 'the meaning of the word in Nature'. This was a unique gesture from a man determined not to be an overt rebel. The word was chosen, no doubt – inasmuch as it did not just leap into his agitated mind – because it offended the strictly Victorian sense of it. This sense was unnatural, corrupt and *impure*, and laid absurd burdens on the female sex by putting women on such a high pedestal that they were divested of not only their femininity but also their humanness. That, equally precisely, is Angel Clare's failing: he does not possess the robustness to transcend his susceptibility to double standards. When he does transcend it, it is too late, and in any case he is reduced to what he really, mentally, always was – a wreck. At best, the harp ironically awarded to him was 'second-hand', its notes 'thin'. As Tom again wrote, people associated 'purity' with its 'artificial and derivative meaning', the one that had 'resulted to it from the ordinances of civilization'.

Not so extremist doctors such as the reforming sexologist Dr Acton would say of upper-class women that they 'were not much troubled by sexual desire'; and the vast majority, against their own instincts and feelings, were obliged to play up to this nonsense. It is even possible, because of the hints in the narrative about Clare's lack of sexual robustness, that the news of Tess's 'lapse' comes to him as something of a relief. He does not really have it in him to love completely, as distinct from having the sexual fling with a 'loose woman' to which he confesses, in a physical act. Even when he watches 'the red interior of her mouth', which seems 'like a snake's', Tess is no more than an idea to him, and, although he does not realize it, a threatening one. He has not renounced the pseudo-Christianity of his upbrining: she is Eve in the Garden of Eden, *and* the snake. On the subject of the word 'purity' Tom wrote to his friend Roden Noel on 17 May 1892:

> As if it mattered a straw whether I have, or have not, put too liberal a construction on the word 'pure'. Reading over the story after it was finished, the conviction was thrust upon me, without any straining or wish for it on my own part – rather, indeed, with some surprise – that the heroine was essentially pure – purer than many a so-called unsullied virgin: therefore I called her so. That was my impression of her – nothing more. But the parochial British understanding knocks itself against this word like a humblebee against a wall, not seeing that 'paradoxical morality' may have a very great deal to say for itself, especially in a work of fiction.
>
> Then the literalists who are willing to concede something, say 'She was not pure *at the end*'. Well – even granting it, was Mary Queen of Scots beautiful during the later years of her life? But she is called the beautiful Q. of Scots. One might easily argue on in this fashion, if it were worth while.

By contrast to Angel's distorted feelings, which even lead him, in his sleep, to place the 'sullied' Tess in a grave, as 'dead', Tess herself is a natural young woman with feelings unspoiled by pseudo-religious abstractions – and quite as naturally intelligent as anyone else in the story. But, denied the full education her intelligence deserves, she is, as Tom carefully demonstrates, lacking in information. When she reaches Emminister (Beaminster) after her long walk from Flintcombe Ash, she sees Angel's two brothers walking back from church, and hears them talking, so that she is dissuaded from calling at the vicarage; Mercy Chant walks just behind them. The educated Mercy, by deliberate contrast to Tess, is, although 'interesting', both '*guindée*' (prim) and 'a trifle prudish'. Tom implies that education or civilization robs women of their naturalness. Thus Mercy reveals her lack of charity when confronted by Tess's boots, which she has concealed in the hedge to await her return journey. They are discovered by one of Clare's 'starched and ironed' brothers, and Mercy declares: 'Some imposter who wished to come into the town barefoot, and so excite our sympathies.' Tom is obstinately at it again, doing what had so disturbed Macmillan when he read *The Poor Man and the Lady*: demonstrating the supercilious and unfeeling nature of the privileged classes.

But not all of them, as Tom again conscientiously points out, share this heedlessness. The narrator tells us, specifically, that Tess's greatest misfortune was brought about by a 'feminine lack of courage' in that she estimated her 'father-in-law through his sons'. She would have been 'a fairly choice sort of lost person for their love'. To be an object of charity rather than valued for yourself is bad; but it is not worse than the fate she actually endures. Angel's nature, though, is unhappily divided between a charity in his parents that is, after all, natural, for all that it seeks a socially acceptable outlet, and the artificial haughtiness of his brothers. Even when he finally accepts Tess, it is rather as a 'fairly choice sort of lost person' than as a woman loved for herself – for all that his remorse is great.

Contrast Tess's own judgement of her seducer, Alec, when she discovers him operating as a fiery preacher. She immediately discerns that he is just the same man as he ever was: 'riotousness was envangelized to-day into the splendour of pious rhetoric'; but she 'would admit the ungenerous sentiment no longer'. The result is inevitable:

> As soon as she could reflect it appalled her, this change in their relative platforms. He who had wrought her undoing was now on the side of the Spirit, while she remained unregenerate. And, as in the legend, it had resulted that her Cyprian image had suddenly appeared on his altar, whereby the fire of the priest had been wellnigh extinguished.

It could be objected that, in this as in other passages of *Tess*, Hardy's narration is confused. At exactly what point, it could be asked, does this description shift from a record of Tess's thinking to an omniscient voice providing the reader with information about the superficiality of Alec's conversion ('Such flashes as you feel, Alec, I fear don't last' she tells him)? However, there is no shift: the voice reflects her lightning intuition. She has seen his face change, she has understood the force of her 'ungenerous sentiment', and she knows in a flash how he still is. Thus, as she walks away from him, 'her back seemed to be endowed with a sensitiveness to ocular beams'. The lustful nature of these 'ocular beams' is unmistakable. Tom, always in mind of Mrs Grundy, delighted in making such implications.

The world can only confuse Tess's simplicity and the purity of her sexual impulse: 'in inhabiting the fleshly tabernacle with which nature had endowed her she was somehow doing wrong'. When the 'converted' Alec asks her to marry him, it is not simply because he wants her: as he tells her, he wants to be 'a self-respecting man'. Frustrated, he even exclaims, when she tells him that she loves another (it is natural to her to speak first of love, rather than of the mere formality of marriage, the contract robbed of all its meaning by false morality): 'Has not a sense of what is morally right and proper any weight with you?' So we see exposed, in the male, the gross transformation of selfish desire into 'duty', with all its implications. It is from such distortions of true feeling that the less gross Angel is unable to save Tess; her 'purity' is this true feeling preserved within her. It leads her to declare to Alex, when he protests at Farmer Groby's bullying behaviour towards her: '*He's* not in love with me!' Later, when he tells her that he has abandoned his preaching, it is 'as a woman' that she is 'appalled'. Never, even when she is in the thick of the persecutions she is made to endure, is her lack of learning allowed, by her creator, to impair the purity of her judgement.

There is a connection between the episode at the desolate place called Cross-in-Hand (actually Crossy Hand) and Tom's poem 'At Lanivet'. In that poem he recalls his impression that he saw Emma as a woman crucified. Here Alec makes Tess swear, on this 'thing of ill-omen', a pagan monument (to the torture of a 'malefactor' who was hanged by his hand from a post), that she will 'never tempt' him (thus shifting the 'blame' for lust from male to female). Since *Tess* is written from a feminine part of Tom, there is no doubt that the guilty image of this impression, of somehow forcing Emma to pain by his own grossness and lack of awareness of her femininity, was still with him. Alec remarks to Tess of 'the pleasure of having a good slap at yourself': the key to Alec is the pleasure he can extract from whatever it is he does or thinks or wants; the less superficial Tom took little pleasure in such mental exercises as 'having a good slap' at himself.

Tess represents his own feminine sensibility having a slap at the disingenuous maleness within him. If he really did tell Cockerell that he would have called the novel *Tess of the Hardys* had that not been 'too personal', then this is what he meant. While he wrote *Tess* I doubt if he had in his mind more than memories of Emma as a young woman, but the sort of emotion he was now tapping was none the less identical to the emotion he tapped when he wrote his poems about Emma after her sudden death. His experience of Emma remained, for him, the paradigm of romantic experience. Therefore, inasmuch as the narrative voice is not the feminine part of himself, Tess actually is Emma to a greater degree than she is any other woman. Even in his love for Mrs Henniker he was trying to transform her into a young woman again. But that could hardly

432

be a consolation to Emma. The woman in his fiction who contains no elements of Emma is, I suggest, the Sue Bridehead of his final and savage prose blast at the 'intolerable antilogy of making figments feel'. The agony in *Jude*, felt by all its readers to the point of protest, comes quite as much from Tom's sense of himself as Phillotson finally having his way with Sue as it comes from anything else. But where Tess kills Alec for his role, Sue, with an intense perversity, forces herself to submit.

Tom's use of plot was at its most adept in *The Mayor of Casterbridge*, which remains his most aesthetically satisfying novel. If *Tess* is more powerful and more passionate, and if Tom was more emotionally identified with its protagonist, this is because its victim of fate is a woman rather than a man. The plot of *Tess*, on the other hand, is a melodramatic patchwork which any contemporary popular novelist might have used; it is Tom's handling of the plot that is outstanding. The insistence upon Tess's 'purity' that found its way into a subtitle pervades the whole novel, and quite overrides its inconsistencies. Indeed, *Tess* is often quite a careless book, as might well be expected from a man exasperated at having to write novels when what he really wanted was to write poetry. But the mere 'impression', which Tom told Noel he had got, of his creation's purity was an exceedingly powerful one. He needed her to be executed, because throughout the book she is seen as the feminine rural victim of male lust or misplaced idealism, and of male industrialization. In the threshing scene, no one could fail to discern the terrible engine, with its faeces of straw and its intrusion on the old, natural ways, as being anything but malignantly male. Yet Tom's quite evident hatred of it, too, is only an 'impression'. He knew all too well that the times demanded such horrors, so he adds a caveat to that effect. He knew, too, that the world was run by men in the interests of 'progress'.

The book is a highly emotional one, quite different from the sort then being written by such as Henry James, who, so jealous of Tom that he referred to him as 'the good little Thomas Hardy', was led to pronounce it 'chock-full of faults and falsity' – the former, yes, certainly; the latter, no. But the language of James' novels, even when it veers towards the poetic, eschews the rhythms of poetry. He did not fully understand poetry: only enough to fear it. He wrote novels far more aesthetically satisfying than any of Tom's, but they were only novels: they did not illuminate a whole panoply of poetry and poetic effort carried out under the guise of fiction. One can see why he so resented Tom, and one can sympathize. And *Tess* is more than a 'poetic novel': it is the novel of one who is a poet or not a writer at all.

Nothing is more emotional in *Tess* than her execution, not described, but ordered by men (she has killed a man), and carried out by a man, a vengeful surrogate for Alec. But not all readers realized how essential it was to Tom's scheme. Jerome K. Jerome, the editor, critic and author of *Three Men in a Boat*, good-naturedly commented in his magazine *To-Day*, apropos a lenient sentence given to a man who had stabbed his wife, that the 'last part of "Tess" will have to be rewritten, which many would welcome'. All he meant, and Tom knew it, was that he and other readers believed her execution to be excessive – that Tom had won them over to the notion of her purity. Andrew Lang, in a review written in 1892, had already questioned its probability. Lang did not approve of Tom's work, and Tom did not like Lang: 'I believe it was Andrew Lang who put about the idea that she would not have been hanged. But a curious thing is that a Home Secretary informed me that he would have seen no reason to interfere with her sentence.'

But Lang and Jerome had got hold of the wrong end of the stick: Tess was a *woman* who had stabbed her *husband*. Then, as now, in the eyes of most judges, there is one law for men who kill their wives, and quite another for women who kill their husbands.

In the scheme of *Tess*, in any case, femininity had to be seen as brutally trampled underfoot by intractable laws. The real point was that the authorities would not have gone after a *man* where a woman could be taken and destroyed. After all, the reader of good heart receives the information of Alec's death as being an *execution* and the killing of Tess as *murder*. It is not really quite as simple as that, and of course Tom knew it; but that is how most of us, on an emotional plane, first take it.

Tess has not pleased everyone, but more than ample notice has been taken of it, only because it is so powerful that those who dislike it feel bound to diminish it – as philosophy, or as theology, or as realism, or even as symbolism. In his discussion of the novel in *Tess of the d'Urbervilles* (1987) Terence Wright divides the different critical approaches as follows: 'social', 'character', 'ideas', 'formal or structural', and the pragmatic approach which he calls 'genetic', and which may be understood as bibliographical – the study of the actual layers of composition so far as their details are available. Even if many approaches are inevitably composites of these, the scheme is a convenient and sensible one.

The social approach attracts mainly Marxist critics such as Arnold Kettle or Raymond Williams, for the good reason that the narrator of *Tess*, who is so close to the author himself, is clearly critical of existing social conditions – for all that he is no Marxist himself. This is evident in such a work as George Wotton's *Thomas Hardy: Towards a Materialist Criticism* (1985), in which the tragedy of Tess is seen as part of a historical process. Wotton sees most of the non-Marxist interpretations of Tess's (and Sue Bridehead's) characters as duplicitous: 'the Thomas Hardy who exists in the discourses and material practices which form the apparatus of the ruling class is the construction of an ideological discourse which maintains the deep social divisions in our society'. There are 'no neutral positions' and 'every reading of Thomas Hardy is an act of political commitment'. Wotton is also, apparently, anxious to rescue Hardy from the still prevalent critical notion that he viewed woman as non-intellectual, a primitive child-bearer, representative of the untamed forces of nature – and he analyses to great effect the writings of some modern critics who, however unwittingly, are shown to take the view. But he does not explain his own view of Hardy clearly enough; rather, he complains about the critical de-emphasis of the 'workfolk'. But Tom was not a Marxist any more than he was a Christian, and, even if, following current fashion, the text of *Tess* is viewed without reference to him, neither Marxism nor orthodox Christianity can be found in it. What the reader does find, towards its end, is that Tess has reached an intellectual view of existence not far away from the one her creator thought he had reached: '"Why, you can have the religion of loving-kindness and purity at least, if you can't have – what do you call it – dogma." [the passage originally read "if you can't have more"]'. The many considerations raised by such passages are not germane to Marxist discussion, and the 'social' approach, valuable as it is, is therefore not wholly adequate.

An illuminating 'character' approach is to be found in Roy Morrell's *Thomas Hardy: The Will and the Way* (1965), one of the best of the general books. Whereas so many critics take the novel to be simply deterministic, and Tess as crushed by an implacable fate – the victim of 'bad luck' – Morrell takes a 'character is fate' approach. If Tess, he writes, 'could bring herself to write the letter of confession, she could have made sure that Angel received it; if she could endure hardships and humiliations at Flintcombe Ash, she could have risked a snub from Angel's father . . .'

There is more, as Morrell has no difficulty in demonstrating, that Tess could have done to avoid her fate. Yet, right as he is in insisting upon this, the accident that befell her letter of confession to Angel – pushing it beneath the mat, instead of on top as she intended – is a device that Tom valued as truly demonstrative of the way human existence actually is. Just at the most crucial moments in people's lives, small things seem to turn against them: 'chance' malevolently emphasizes their chief defects. Tess is afraid of how Angel will react, as she has every intuitive reason to be. She is always triumphantly and innocently herself, but is passive and lacks the strength to assert herself. Therefore her letter is 'lost', is interrupted in its progress; it obeys, not her courage in writing it, but rather her weakness in fearing the effect it will have. Tess *wants* to enjoy her passivity and trust that things will come right, that Angel's bad feelings will be overcome by better ones: despite people's scruples, therefore, fate, 'chance', assists their primary, unrealistic desires. 'The incident of the misplaced letter she had jumped at as if it prevented a confession; but she knew in her conscience that it need not; there was still time.'

Thus the intensely poetic question arises, and is posed in *Tess*: are fate, chance and 'accident' what they seem to be? Do they arise from defects of character? Is there a means of escaping their malignity? Morrell comes near to this mysterious and ambiguous area of enquiry when he reminds us that Hardy was concerned with the notion of 'survival' (which, however, he called 'happiness') in Darwinian terms: he thought as if 'every species is a "pessimist", toning up the effectiveness of its defences by "imagining" its enemies to be even more vigilant and voracious than they are'. It is as well to read the mature novel *Tess* in the light of the definition of 'wisdom' offered in the immature *Desperate Remedies*: a 'steady handling of any means to bring about any end necessary to happiness'. Hardy the author, and Tom the man, are both temperamentally like a tortoise threatened by a cat pacing about it: they peep from their shell vigilantly, ready to withdraw with the utmost rapidity, whether they perceive good or ill fortune, friendliness or enmity. The apparently hard carapace can serve, they think, as protection; but, unlike that of the tortoise, this carapace is combed with myriad fine and quivering nerves, each one of which has a horrified curiosity about being alive at all.

The mishaps that befall Tess, like the portents that attend her, while they mysteriously reflect passivity and even obstinacy, are ambiguous. The still small voice within her, which will at last assert itself as her scream, voiceless or otherwise, as the knife is plunged into the heart of a male, is also protesting: 'Why *should* I need to justify myself in this unjust scheme of things?' Only one quality in the book is not ambiguous, and this is Tess's own purity of being: her determination, perfectly innocent, to fulfil herself as a woman by loving, trusting and giving herself to a man. That can be called 'passivity'. But there is at least a hint in the book, announced boldly enough in the subtitle as her purity, that it is a profound form of femininity – not a helpless thing at all, but a yin in contrast to a yang.

The murder of Alex – which *is* a murder, as the reader finally has to accept – is Tess's final surrender: she is forced at last to indulge herself in a male act, sanctified by millennia as the last resort of 'politics', of killing. The female is thus murdered within her. After the death of her baby Hardy begins a new chapter:

'By experience,' says Roger Ascham, 'we find out a short way by a long wandering.' Not seldom that long wandering unfits us for further travel, and of what use is our experience to us then? Tess Durbeyfield's experience was of this incapacitating kind. At last she had learned what to do; but who would now accept her doing?

Who indeed?

Morrell, although not an irritable or nagging or petty moralist, does ultimately take up a moral position. He views Hardy as a compassionate and profound moralist indicating how the possession of a sounder character could have saved Tess from her fate. The deterministic interpretation, he thinks, is not supported by this passage, which occurs in the part of the story concerned with Tess's sojourn at Talbothays. Clare has just thought to himself how 'fluty' the voice of the new milkmaid (Tess) is. She is in conversation with the others:

'I don't know about ghosts,' she was saying; 'but I do know that our souls can be made to go outside our bodies when we are alive.'

The dairyman turned to her with his mouth full, his eyes charged with serious enquiry, and his great knife and fork (breakfasts were breakfasts here) planted erect on the table, like the beginning of a gallows.

'What – really now? And is it so, maidy?' he said.

'A very easy way to feel 'em go,' continued Tess, 'is to lie on the grass at night and look straight up at some big bright star; and, by fixing your mind upon it, you will soon find that you are hundreds and hundreds o' miles away from your body, which you don't seem to want at all.'

For the dairyman this is nonsense: he has travelled under the stars often enough, but never felt his soul 'rise so much as an inch above' his shirt-collar. But Angel is touched to the quick:

'What a fresh and virginal daughter of Nature [in early draft the feebler and less revealing 'what a genuine daughter of nature'] that milkmaid is!' he said to himself.

He seemed to discern in her something that was familiar, something which carried him back into a joyous and unforeseeing past, before the necessity of taking thought had made the heavens gray.

There can be few lovelier passages in all fiction. But the dairyman Crick's 'great knife and fork', planted *erect on the table* (resembling a gross penis determined to plunder, to 'eat', Tess) are 'like the beginning of a gallows', and thus anticipate Tess's own end: she dies of the lack, in her world, of the poetry of which, for her creator, she is the embodiment. It is Crick's knife and fork, the weapons of his need for a large breakfast and no nonsense of the spirit, that are shaped as a gallows: he is prosaic, and can respond only negatively to Tess's poetry. Morrell misses this, and quarrels too much with the view of another critic, John Holloway, that this comparison 'is incandescent . . . does more than any volume of generalities to fix in us Hardy's sense of the unalterable sequence of things'. Morrell replies:

This won't do. It is Holloway, not Hardy, who is trying to 'fix in us' this sense . . . and he asks us to accept the interpretation (which is, to say the least, unproven) not instead of a 'volume of generalities' but instead of Hardy's novel . . . the whole rhythm and tension of our interest is controlled by the reprieves, the rallies, the second chances; by our sense of what might, even at a late stage, be done to prevent the disaster.

Holloway is indeed wrong in inferring that this passage has anything at all to do with determinism, with the notion that things will happen whatever human beings may do to prevent them; but Morrell's indignation will not do, either, for it denies the gallows image any significance – in a novel about a woman who ends on the gallows! To view Tess's 'weakness' as the sole reason for her downfall is not enough: of what does such 'weakness' consist unless of the kind of poetry she utters when she describes gazing at the star and not wanting her body 'at all'? That is the poignant question. Crick is a kind enough man, but he is prosaic, and he cannot 'prevent the disaster'. Alec is cruel and coarse, despite his better impulses and his not always unattractive frankness; far from preventing it, he is its main cause. Angel is finer, but he, too, causes the disaster: his dreams are not of real people. After that passage, if not before it, we, like Hardy, are in love with Tess. Alas, a novel whose readers love its heroine cannot operate along accepted critical lines! Yet Charles Darwin himself (quoted by Gregor at the beginning of his excellent discussion of this novel) wrote in his *Autobiography*: 'A novel, according to my taste, does not come into the first class, unless it contains some person whom one can thoroughly love, and if it be a pretty woman so much the better.'

Tess could indeed have avoided her fate. She could have told Angel of her 'lapse' when she first felt impelled to do so. But that would have been calculating, and therefore a breaking of faith. She lives in the impossible golden age, before thought made 'the heavens gray': the novel as a whole is a triumph of unreason, a wild challenge to reason itself, haunted by that 'joyous and unforeseeing past' of which Angel suddenly obtains a clue – from Tess. This is the girl who wants to give her baby 'a Christian burial'. But the vicar, although one who struggled for ten years 'to graft technical belief on actual scepticism', cannot agree. So she exclaims: 'Then I don't like you! . . . and I'll never come to your church no more! . . . Don't for God's sake speak as saint to sinner, but as you yourself to me myself – poor me!' She has nothing of his education, but she sees straight through him, and remains intelligently real while he simply feels cornered. Nor is he a bad or even a supercilious man. Thus it is throughout the course of the book with Tess and all the others. None of them can outdo the vicar's own 'Don't talk so rashly' – as if that came anywhere near her own sublime simplicity. Morrell is entitled to his view that she deserves sympathy and yet is morally reprehensible; but, uncensorious as he is, this is out of tune not only with Hardy's own feelings but also with his text.

Tom is always at pains, often subtly so, to demonstrate Tess's intelligent search for understanding (rather than mere knowledge). Gatrell points out one particularly striking instance which may be inferred from his revisions. Tom first wrote that Tess was 'somewhat vexed with her mother for giving her so many little sisters and brothers'; this became 'she felt quite Malthusian towards their mother'; but in

1895, although it meant work for the printer, he substituted 'she felt quite a Malthusian'. As Gatrell remarks, this 'subtly increase[s] the strength of the inference that Tess herself might know what it is to be a Malthusian'.

This is more or less the view expressed by Irving Howe in *Thomas Hardy* (1966). Terence Wright is sympathetic to it, but feels that it is 'extreme': it invites the danger of 'losing the individual in her virtues', and it is 'intensely "affective"'. Howe feels Tess as 'a static representative of a cluster of human virtues'. But this word 'static', like 'weakness and passivity', begs the question: Tess would not be 'static' when she came to make love to Angel, which she is never, of course, able to do; and she is not 'static' when, frustrated at last, she plunges the knife into Alec's heart. The question raised by the novel is this: what would woman be if she were released from male oppression and allowed to be herself? It is as much of a mystery to Hardy as it is to the reader – perhaps to most female readers, too – but at least he can show us Tess. And at least Howe's interpretation is true to the narrator's heightened, 'intensely affective' vision of her. Another critic, Benjamin Sankey, remarks in *The Major Novels of Thomas Hardy* (1965) that although Tess represents 'the best that human nature has to offer . . . she cannot be exonerated'. This draws useful attention to one of the paradoxes underlying the novel: one cannot, after all, condone murder, even of Alec. One also feels bound to add that Sankey need not worry, for Tess is by no means exonerated.

What Wright calls the 'ideas' approach might perhaps better be called the 'philosophical'. Since Tom was not a philosopher but a poet, this approach cannot be 'intensely affective'; and yet *Tess* is just that, whatever moral lessons critics might fairly wish to draw from it. The portrait of Tess herself cries out to demonstrate that an unjust scheme of things need not be. But no critic is obliged, because of that, to treat it as an affective work. David De Laura takes the title of his influential article in the *Journal of English Literary History* (September 1967), '"The Ache of Modernism" in Hardy's Later Novels', from a passage in *Tess*:

He [Angel Clare] was surprised to find this young woman . . . shaping . . . sad imaginings. She was expressing in her own native phrases – assisted a little by her Sixth Standard training – feelings which might also have been called those of the age – the ache [Hardy first wrote 'approximating to the spirit', but then replaced it with this masterstroke] of modernism. The perception arrested him less when

440

he reflected that what are called advanced ideas are really in great part but the latest fashion in definition – a more accurate expression, by words ending in *logy* and *ism*, of sensations which men and women have vaguely grasped for centuries.

The really important feature of this passage, so far as the novel is concerned, is the emphasis upon the high quality of Tess's mind despite her lack of education. De Laura argues, though, that in *Tess* Hardy was intentionally expressing these ideas, and, specifically, making a critique of Arnold's solution to the problem, which was to adopt a position which was 'metaphysically agnostic but emotionally and morally traditional and "Christian"'. He can cite Angel Clare as an example of how high a price men have to pay for this compromise between old and new. De Laura then rather overplays what he takes to be Hardy's attacks on Christianity, citing the remark about the agnostic, 'technically believing' vicar and his feelings about Tess's 'home-baptism': 'Having the natural feelings of a tradesman at finding that a job he should have been called in for had been unskilfully botched by his customers amongst themselves . . .' This is neither 'sneering' nor 'crude' (these are Terence Wright's epithets), though, since the vicar's agnosticism is carefully set up: Hardy was simply drawing sharp attention to the undoubted fact that many Victorian vicars did not believe in the dogma of Christianity. Nowhere (as Wright, discussing De Laura, is at pains to point out) does Hardy satirize sincere Christianity.

The truth is that *Tess* is set against just the background De Laura defines, but that this background is not its primary theme – and its author is not at especial pains to make an attack on his own 'neo-Christianity' (attending church for emotional reasons but disbelieving in dogma for intellectual ones: the author's own practice). Hardy sees that modernism does have an ache, and makes sure that this ache is registered, but he does not see it as fundamental to Tess's tragedy, which is that she is a defeated woman in a world of men. In that respect he could have set it in the late eighteenth century instead of the late nineteenth: neither the social nor the philosophico-religious changes of that time cause the tragedy, nor does what we can interpret as Tess's 'weakness'. They are incidental to it. The one possible exception lies in Tess's quiet acceptance of Angel's disbelief at the very end of the book:

'. . . Tell me now, Angel, do you think we shall meet again after we are dead? I want to know.'

He kissed her to avoid a reply at such a time.

'O, Angel – I fear that means no!' said she, with a suppressed sob. 'And I wanted to see you again – so much, so much! What – not even you and I, Angel, who love each other so well?'

There is more than just an ache here, but the passage points only to Tess's trusting nature – and to Angel's incapacity, not unlike the diminished musical powers of his 'second-hand' harp, to give some kind of answer. That is not to suggest that he is anything other than scrupulous, or that he ought to have lied. But he is an inadequate lover – not what Tess has deserved, and no angel to her. There are things he might have said, and the proof of that lies in our reading these words on the page over a century after they were first written – the words of a man in love with Tess, as we must be (unless, as moralists, we spurn her). That is the strange force of the novel. De Laura's interpretation puts too much emphasis on Angel, who is by no means the hero.

A delicate ambiguity does hang over the passage, though, for Angel's silence at the 'critical question at the critical time' is compared to a similar one on the part of 'a greater than himself' (Christ's silence before his accusers, Matthew 26, 62–3; 27, 12–14). Just why is such a comparison made? Why should the agnostic Clare be compared to the alleged Son of God, 'greater' than him? It could suggest Christ as the supreme ethical teacher – a view that Hardy accepted. But is that all? There is not only the blessed hope, of which we are unaware, and for which Hardy can hardly be said to make no allowance. There are also other hints, such as the lines from the poem on his mother's death: here the affirming student of MacTaggart (the avowed atheist who disproved the existence of time, and postulated immortality for human beings) writes that Jemima is 'prisoner in the cell/Of Time no more'. How long, he asks in 'Before Life and After', shall it be before 'nescience shall be reaffirmed/How long, how long?' In 'God's Education' it is 'Time' that God bids 'throw . . . carelessly away' the 'sweets' of the beloved, and therefore of Tess:

> Said I: 'We call that cruelty –
>   We, your poor mortal kind.'
> He mused. 'The thought is new to me.
> Forsooth, though I men's master be,
>   Theirs is the teaching mind!'

Could Tess 'teach God to feel'? Under any kind of orthodox or unmystical Christianity, certainly not. But in some of the gnostic systems which the early Church was so anxious to destroy, 'God' is a malign demiurge artificially created by wisdom's lapse. Behind this God lies something more complex and mysterious. That Tess's own beliefs concerned Tom, and that they were more profound than Angel's well-educated ones, is amply evident: Tess thus answers her brother Abraham's question about whether the stars are 'worlds . . . like ours': 'I don't know, but I think so. They sometimes seem to be like the apples on our stubbard-tree [early codling-apple tree]. Most of them splendid and sound – a few blighted.' And she goes on to tell him, even though she has not yet suffered a single mishap beyond her parents' shortcomings, that we live in a blighted part of the universe. That, too, is a gnostic notion, and one which is built into Tess from the start. It transcends the question of the dogmas and creeds which Tess herself – and her creator – distrusted. In the poem 'God-Forgotten', the 'Lord Most High' tells a messenger from earth sent 'to win/Some answer to their cry' that he has forgotten that he created the earth, but that

> 'Of its own act the threads were snapt whereby
>   Its plaints had reached mine ear.
>
> 'It used to ask for gifts of good,
>   Till came its severance, self-entailed,
> When sudden silence on that side ensued,
>   And has till now prevailed.
>
> 'All other orbs have kept in touch;
>   Their voicings reach me speedily:
> Thy people took upon them overmuch
>   In sundering them from me!
>
> 'And it is strange – though sad enough –
>   Earth's race should think that one whose call
> Frames, daily, shining spheres of flawless stuff
>   Must heed their tainted ball! . . .
>
> 'But sayest it is by pangs distraught,
>   And strife, and silent suffering? –
> Sore grieved am I that injury should be wrought
>   Even on so poor a thing!

'Thou shouldst have learnt that *Not to Mend*
For Me could mean but *Not to Know*:
Hence, Messengers! and straightway put an end
To what men undergo.' . . .

Homing at dawn, I thought to see
One of the Messengers standing by.
– Oh, childish thought! . . . Yet often it comes to me
When trouble hovers nigh.

The idea of the 'other orbs' might seem mere rhetoric; but it persists too much to be just that – most features in Hardy's poetry, including rhetorical embellishments, are worth careful attention: the poem is more 'metaphysical' than its 'old-fashioned' appearance and recourse to archaisms immediately suggests. Immortality, in any case, as MacTaggart's fantastic but rigorous theorizings suggest, is not even necessarily a matter involving the existence of a God or a creator. Hardy's own 'His Immortality' says that it is the 'finer part' of a person, giving life to 'those bereft'; but that definition does not preclude others. In 'A Dream Question' the 'Lord' asks that he be 'saved' from those 'friends' who declare that he rages against those who call him cruel: he does not care what his creatures say!

'Why things are thus, whoso derides,
May well remain my secret still . . .
A fourth dimension, say the guides,
To matter is conceivable.
Think some such mystery resides
Within the ethic of my will.'

Tom was agnostic so far as public declarations were concerned; but as a poet he was nearer to a gnostic.

Wright's two final categories, 'formal or structural' and 'genetic', valuable though they are, need not concern a biographer. A moderately formalist approach is taken by Ian Gregor, who writes as illuminatingly on *Tess* as he does on the rest of the major novels. He insists, and rightly insists, on the ambiguities underlying it. He singles out, for example, the ambiguity of Tess's relationship with Alec, who is her 'creator and destroyer', and the exact nature of whose violation of her – rape or seduction? – must therefore remain open. In *The Language of*

Fiction (1966), on the other hand, David Lodge finds the Hardy of *Tess* wanting: he is a poor writer, Lodge asserts, because he is hopelessly confused between several points of view. The following is bad writing because, Lodge claims, no country girl could possibly think like it:

> It just crossed her mind, too, that he might have a faint recollection of his tender vagary, and was disinclined to allude to it from a conviction that she would take amatory advantage of the opportunity ['amatory . . . opportunity' was changed from 'advantage of the undoubted opportunity'] it gave her of appealing to him anew not to go.

This paragraph occurs just after the sleep-walking scene, before Angel packs up and leaves Tess. Its apparent awkwardness is certainly not without precedent in Hardy. But I think I can defend it. In the first place, while confusing at first reading, it becomes clear at the second or third reading. Many of Hardy's sentences need reading over – and, while some of them are undoubtedly clumsy, others are seeking to express complex matters. Here he was dealing with a delicate and subtle matter, especially to his over-polite general audience.

Tess, we know, is exceedingly scrupulous. It is one of her chief virtues, and it is convincingly put across. The exact meaning, here, is something that the Victorian censor would not have liked. The 'tender vagary' referred to is the interlude during which Angel kissed Tess and then placed her in a coffin. Tess has interpreted it as 'tender', although its real significance has been that she is dead to him, since she is revealed as no longer the virgin of his somewhat asexual dreams. She is thinking of the kisses, and is therefore anxious to avoid 'seducing' him from his intention. How else could Hardy have conveyed Tess's extreme delicacy and subtlety of apprehension? Lodge may be guilty of just the assumption which Hardy is challenging throughout: that 'mere country girls' who have only been through the Sixth Standard of schooling are not as subtle and delicate as the fine ladies of society. In any case, Lodge is applying the standards set by Jamesian fiction to a technique quite alien to them.

Wright's discussion of the 'genetic' criticism is mostly concentrated upon J.T. Laird's empirical study of 1975, *The Shaping of Tess of the d'Urbervilles*, in which the author traces its composition from manuscript through to the very last revisions. This bibliographical work, though not criticism in the usual sense, gives invaluable information. Gatrell, more sympathetic than Laird towards Hardy, has emphasized further details, such as an improvement made during 1892: originally he had written of the girls at Trantridge, 'marriage was the rule before means here'. But because this resembled, as Gatrell puts it, the 'generalized sententious comment of the superficial moralist', in 1892 he substituted 'a field-man's wages being as high at twenty-one as at forty, marriage was early here . . . [an] informed and concerned perception'. Laird's reconstruction shows, above all, how Hardy's Tess further exercised her grip on his imagination, and how he altered his text to reinforce his sense of her purity. He also demonstrates that Hardy remained genuinely uncertain about the character of Angel Clare – and, to a lesser extent, about that of Alec, whose behaviour towards Tess finally suggests rape rather than seduction. *Tess* is, admittedly, as novels of its stature go, a careless one: as a poet, its author could force himself to no easy conclusions. One can see how right Henry James was, from his own point of view, to condemn it. If a shifting or uncertain point of view is a fault, then *Tess* is flawed. Wright makes the point that 'we never completely understand human beings in life, either'. Therefore it must be left to the reader to judge whether this is a 'vital irresolution' or a 'considerable artistic flaw'. What is certain, though, is that very few novels indeed lend themselves to such fine judgements at all – they are simply not worth the trouble. In this one, Angel is real enough, and his failure is convincing enough, to make us want to know why he was at fault. However, De Laura's 'ache of modernism', while relevant to Angel Clare's intellectual circumstances – but it should be remembered that he, unlike his two brothers, did not go to a university – is not sufficient to account for his behaviour. Hardy at first described him as having, in Tess's eyes, both 'a purity of mind' and a 'slight coldness of nature'; then he substituted a 'chivalrous sense of duty'; then he put 'what she deemed the self-controlling sense of duty'; the final version read: 'by what she deemed, rightly or wrongly, the self-controlling sense of duty'. Wright thinks that this indicates that 'Hardy has doubts about what kind of young man Clare was'. But it may not: despite the 'rightly or wrongly', it may indicate only that his difficulties lay in correctly presenting Tess's understanding of him. Hardy was in any case barred by Mrs Grundy from being as fully explicit about Clare's sexuality as he would have liked. As I have suggested, his previous experience may have made him afraid of it altogether.

The most celebrated criticism derives from Lionel Johnson's early book on Hardy, and his objections to *Tess* must be taken seriously. They lie in the inconsistent presentation of 'Nature'. Hardy's answer, expressed in a letter of 16 November 1894 to Douglas, seems to have been that Johnson was 'too pedantic'. 'What is this "Nature", of which or of whom, Mr Hardy speaks?' asked Johnson. 'Is it a conscious power? or a convenient name for a whole mass of physical facts?' It is true that the concept of 'Nature' remains unworked out, in intellectual terms, throughout *Tess*. At one time it is presented in its Rousseauist sense – the thing in contrast to the terrible threshing-engine – but then, at another, as destructive and unheeding. But is it perhaps 'too pedantic' to bring to bear, upon a poetic novel, the standards of thoroughly worked out Jamesian novels?

Hardy finds that the natural is beautiful, whatever else it is; throughout he presents Tess as beautiful and in harmony with all nature's non-human aspects. Instead of comparing his methods, then, to such as those of Henry James, perhaps we should recall the words of the Czech-German poet Rainer Maria Rilke at the beginning of the first of his Duino Elegies, written not so long after *Tess* itself: '*Denn das Schöne ist nichts/als des Schrecklichen Anfang, den wir noch grade ertragen,/und wir bewundern es so, weil as gelassen verschmäht,/uns zu zerstören*' [For the beautiful is nothing but the first apprehension of the terrible, which we are still just able to endure, and we admire it because it serenely disdains to destroy us]? The beautiful does eventually destroy Tess, but that – it could be said – is because she invites it to do so, having become convinced that her femininity cannot find its counterpart. Her act in killing Alec is, indeed, *unnatural* in just those terms. This is often true of Hardy's confusions: that they are the confusions of us all, and that resolutions of them attempted by other thinkers have tended to favour intellect over emotion, and thus to be incomplete. Nor is pastoral nature too 'pedantically' to be confused with its instigator: the ineffable and unknown intelligence which made something where there was nothing.

Finally, there is the much vexed question of the 'quotation' from Aeschylus at the end. Hardy wrote:

Justice was done, and the President of the Immortals, in Aeschylean phrase, had ended his sport with Tess [originally; 'Time, the Archsatirist, had had his joke out with Tess']. And the D'Urberville knights and dames slept on in their tombs unknowing. The two speechless gazers spent themselves down to earth, as if in prayer, and remained thus a long time, absolutely motionless: the flag continued to wave silently. As soon as they had strength they arose, joined hands again, and went on.

And in the *Life* he commented:

> . . . the first five words were, as Hardy often explained to his reviewers, but a literal translation of Aesc, *Prom* 169 . . . . The classical sense in which he had used them is best shown by quoting a reply to some unknown critic [Andrew Lang, in the February 1892 issue of the *New Review*, in the course of a facetious article, had asked: 'If there be a God, who can seriously think of Him as a malicious fiend?'] who had said in an article:
>
> 'Hardy postulates an all-powerful being endowed with the baser human passions, who turns everything to evil and rejoices in the mischief he has wrought'; another critic taking up the tale by adding: 'To him evil is not so much a mystery, a problem, as the wilful malice of his god.'
>
> Hardy's reply was written down but (it is believed), as in so many cases with him, never posted; though I am able to give it from the rough draft:
>
> As I need hardly inform any thinking reader, I do not hold, and never have held, the ludicrous opinions here assumed to be mine – which are really, or approximately, those of the primitive believer in his man-shaped tribal god. And in seeking to ascertain how any exponent of English literature could have supposed that I held them I find that the writer of the estimate has harked back to a passage in a novel of mine, printed many years ago, in which the forces opposed to the heroine were allegorized as a personality (a method not unusual in prose or poetry) by the use of a venerable trope. . . . Under this species of criticism if an author were to say 'Aeolus maliciously tugged at her garments and tore her hair in his wrath', the sapient critic would no doubt announce that author's evil creed to be that the wind is 'a powerful being endowed with the baser passions', etc., etc.

What these and other critics said was, indeed, 'ludicrous', although their understanding of the spirit of what Hardy meant is perhaps not quite so unforgivable as he likes to make out. Hardy does mean his conclusion to be, as Gregor claims, a 'multiple' one – but that first sentence obtrudes, and originally he meant it to do so. The word 'sport' (originally 'joke') does, after all, suggest malicious or at least careless pleasure. His translation is, as he claims, 'literal' – or literal enough to satisfy most people, although it could be claimed that 'Lord of the Blessed Ones' is more accurate than 'President of the Immortals': the last word refers to gods, of whom Prometheus was one, and of whom Zeus was the despotic ruler (rather than a relatively benign 'president'). But the more 'pedantically' correct phrase would have introduced confusion where none was needed. Emotionally, Hardy did see the odds as stacked against the 'happiness' of the feminine or sensitive person – that, in Rilke's poetic terms, it is in the beautiful that the terrible begins. But he was justified in objecting to being categorized as the preacher of a creed which defined the president of the immortals as being actually malicious.

As Gregor writes, the correct reading must be to take the final paragraph altogether, rather than any of its four sentences in isolation. The first reflects Tess's own feeling that the world is 'blighted'; the second states the present's independence of the past; the third is, unequivocally, a statement of hope – and even carries within it a semblance of prayer; the fourth implies nothing less than resolution. Angel is, of course, accompanied by 'Liza-Lu, Tess's sister, 'a tall budding creature – half girl, half woman – a spiritualized image of Tess, slighter than she, but with the same beautiful eyes'. This brief characterization of 'Liza-Lu is careful and deliberate: dare we therefore believe that, in her, a humbled Angel will find his redemption – that he has learned something from his experience, and in particular from his rejection of Tess, an action which is really at the crux of the book? At least Hardy does not put him out there alone.

22

Throbbings of Noontide

The notoriety of *Tess* made Tom feign shyness of presenting copies of it, especially to women. One of the chief of those whom he called the book's 'supporters' was Lord Salisbury, whom he had met and who was then still prime minister. Salisbury's eventual successor, A.J. Balfour, agreed: he allowed his unmarried sister to be taken in to a dinner at the Jeunes' by Tom in May 1892. Tom liked her 'frank, sensible, womanly way of talking', and told her 'plainly' that he did not want 'to get into hot water with her' by giving her a copy. Her response, 'Now don't I really look old enough to read any novel with safety by this time!' pleased him, and he added, rather cryptically, 'Some of the best women don't marry – perhaps wisely.'

It was no longer a question of Thomas Hardy gaining an entry into society: everyone in society now wanted to meet Thomas Hardy. Tales of his lack of self-confidence are based on the reports of people like the French painter Blanche, who mistook his boredom with them for diffidence. He saw, as usual, a good deal of Gosse. He may have felt closer, though, to Roden Noel, whom he had met in 1887 at Mary Robinson's. Roden Berkeley Wriothesley Noel, fourth son of Lord Gainsborough, an 'aristocratic socialist', was a poet, travel writer, critic and friend to Tennyson. Sadly, he died suddenly at Mainz, at the age of fifty-nine, in May 1894.

Tom's friendship with John Addington Symonds, whom he respected as an emancipated spirit, and the fact that he seems to have sought out Noel as a friend worth cultivating, raise a question: just how much did he know about the homosexual underworld of his time, and how sympathetic was he to it? Tom was one of the most reticent of literary men about people or politics, but he was inwardly conscientious. Thus, although the name of Oscar Wilde is mentioned in the *Life*, it is not in connection with his trial in 1895. Tom's discretion made him the opposite of another friend of Symonds', Gosse, who was on the fringe of the homosexual and paedophilic underworld and was as indiscreet as he dared to be. The outraged student of a universe in which people were impelled to feel passions they had better have done without could hardly have been uninterested in those whose natures inclined them towards their own sex – unless Millgate is right, and such notions were altogether beyond such a country simpleton, *sans* Freud or a Cambridge education to boot. Yet Tom displayed great interest in everything Noel had to say, as a letter to him of 3 April 1892 demonstrates. Noel, author of *A Philosophy of Immortality* (1882) as well as of a *Life* (1887) of Byron, had written to him praising *Tess*. Tom replied, with evident sincerity, that 'So far from being bored by your ideas . . . I was deeply interested, & they started me off on a mental journey into the infinite – whatever that may be.' He continued:

I hope you will not mind my owning to a mistrust of metaphysic. My shyness arises from my consciousness of its paternity – that it is a sort of bastard, begotten of science upon theology – or, in another form, a halfway house between Deism & Materialism. It ultimately comes to this – such and such things *may* be. But they will ever be improbable: & since infinitely other things may also be, with equal probability, why select any one bundle of suppositions in preference to another? I prefer to relegate such thoughts to the domain of fancy, & to recognise them as pure imagination.

He went on to tell Noel that he found Spinoza's notion of 'all matter' being 'mind-stuff' 'a very attractive idea this, to me'. Then:

What you, & so many more, have called Pessimism, is, after all, to be regarded as such only in respect to a fancy-standard. Pessimism is used arbitrarily of such views, say, as mine: but it is really only a relative term. Suppose the conditions of existence on this earth to change to such a degree that normal life becomes pervaded by a sensation equivalent to what we now call pain, & the pains of that period to be what we now call tortures, our present pessimism will be optimism to these unhappy souls.
    I, too, believe in Byron – though less in what he says, than in what he struggles to say, yet cannot. He was a clumsy fellow – but I, for one, am always willing to meet him halfway.

Symonds, who was profoundly tortured by the nature of his own

451

sexuality, confided the following observations to his secret *Memoirs*, given to the London Library on the death of his executor in 1926 and not published until 1984. Writing of the period round about 1875, he said that Noel

> had done and [was] in the habit of doing what I had now begun to desire . . . [He] was married, deeply attached to his wife, a poet of high soaring fancies, a philosopher of burning nebulous ideas. He justified passion to his own eyes and preached it to others in an esoteric quasi-Manichean mysticism. He was vain of his physical beauty, which was splendid at that epoch; and his tastes tended to voluptuousness. The attraction of the male governed him through his vanity and this voluptuousness. He loved to be admired. He enjoyed in indolent sultana fashion the contact of masculine desire, the *attouchements* of excited organisms, the luxurious embracements of nakedness. Strange to say, the indulgence of these tastes did not disturb his mental equilibrium. Both as poet and thinker, he remained vigorous and grew in comprehension. Finally, I think, he outlived, absorbed, and clarified by religious mysticism the grossness of his passions. But for me the conversation of this remarkable man was nothing less than poisonous – a pleasant poison, it is true . . . [he] remained superior in being sensitive to the attractions of the female.

Tom, let us remember, was a friend of Gosse – who was in on these secrets, and who as chairman of the London Library Committee in 1926 oversaw the acceptance of the Symonds *Memoirs* – and the subtle pioneer depicter of subterranean lesbian passion in his first published novel. To what extent, if at all, was he aware of this aspect of Noel?

There was still no visible rift between Tom and Emma, and in the *Life* he mentions that many 'of the details . . . concerning his adventures at dinner parties' in London which he (writing as 'Florence Hardy', the 'author') did not 'think worth recording' were 'obtained from diaries kept by' Emma. At this juncture Emma seems to have attracted only minuscule attention on the grounds of her eccentricity. There is every reason to suppose that she was fully behind her husband over the matter of the 'morality' of *Tess*, and nothing to suggest that she was not. It was the affair, if it can be called that, with Mrs Henniker that put – to use a favourite phrase of Tom and his sisters – the iron into her soul, followed as it was by publication of *Jude* which she may have connected with this. She never really recovered from the blow, although she may in the meantime have become ill.

According to Florence, writing to Clodd after Emma's death, from 1891 she started keeping diaries which contained passages critical of her husband; but, since these diaries were destroyed by Tom, we have only Florence's word for that. It seems unlikely that the criticisms began in earnest before 1893 or 1894. We do not know that Florence read them: she never claimed to have done so. We cannot even be certain that they existed.

When Raymond Blathwayt, a literary journalist, wrote in January 1892 to request an interview, Tom asked Emma to write out a note of agreement including train times – he merely signed it. Blathwayt may even have stayed the night at Max Gate. Emma was present throughout the interview, which appeared in the magazine *Black and White* in the following August. Allowing for normal journalistic deference, and Blathwayt's heavily florid style, this is one of the less unrevealing newspaper accounts of Hardy – largely, no doubt, because it was conducted comparatively early in his career as a 'celebrity' and before he had learned to distrust the press. Blathwayt wrote, in part:

[Thomas Hardy] is regarded by the public at large as a hermit ever brooding in the far-off seclusion of a west country village. A fond delusion . . . His wife, some few years younger than himself, is so particularly bright, so thoroughly *au courant du jour*, so evidently a citizen of the wide world, that the, at first unmistakable, reminiscence that there is in her of Anglican ecclesiasticism is curiously puzzling and inexplicable to the stranger, until the information is vouchsafed that she is intimately and closely connected with what the late Lord Shaftesbury would term 'the higher order of the clergy' . . . Mrs Hardy's clever little water-colours go far to prove the verisimilitude of her husband's delightful fictions . . .

Millgate, as ever out to diminish Emma, believes this to be 'deliberately ironic'; but, while it is true that Emma did like to dilate upon her relationship to the Archdeacon, this reads more like conventional journalistic praise. Blathwayt was, after all, talking to a master of irony – and could a man capable of writing in that style be capable of irony anyway? His 'some few years younger than himself' is just conventional gallantry, and makes any attempt at irony all the more unlikely. Nor is there irony in his record of Emma's remarking that Hardy had received many letters, while *Tess* was being serialized, 'begging him to end his story brightly'. Tom protested to Blathwayt that Tess's 'innate purity remained intact to the very last . . . I regarded her then as being in the hands of circumstances, not morally responsible, a mere corpse drifting with the current to her end'. He added, as a polite rejoinder to Blathwayt's idiotic comment to the effect that 'Nature . . . remorselessly . . . exacts a purity in women which she does not demand from man . . . you have shown this truth in *Tess* I think': 'Exactly . . . I draw no inferences, I don't even feel them.' Angel Clare, 'a subtle, poetical man', was, he told Blathwayt, 'cruel, but not intentionally so. It was the fault of his fastidious temperament.'

Tom was even more pleased with the sales of *Tess* than with the reviews supporting it: by the end of 1892 they amounted to over twenty thousand. That alone, serialization and America apart, meant some £5,000 to him. He was therefore now a wealthy man, or knew that he soon would be, and made arrangements accordingly. On 20 January 1892 he asked Clodd (by profession a banker) what he thought of City of London Electric Company shares, which had been recommended to him. Clodd found them sound, so Tom bought some for himself and (exercising his so famous meanness) some for his sister Kate. He knew by then, as he told Gosse on the same day, that Osgood was 'reprinting frantically'. Tom also bought a house for letting – 51 High West Street, in Dorchester – as an investment; and began to make investments through a broking firm called Foster & Braithwaite.

Tom had been so violently criticized for his attitude to reviews that it is worth considering the matter in connection with *Tess*. His extreme sensitivity is not in question; what is in question, though, is exactly what he was sensitive to. From some accounts it was to any kind of criticism, just or unjust. But careful examination of his extant letters of the time demonstrates that he was angered only by unintelligent criticism, or criticism distorted by pseudo-moral considerations. The review printed in the *Saturday Review* on 16 January 1892, stating that *Tess* had 'no gleam of sunshine anywhere . . . except for some hours spent with cows', and that 'Mr Hardy did well to make [Tess] pay the full penalty', was, as he told Walter Besant in an angry letter the following day, 'an absolute misrepresentation'. His comment that the piece had been devised 'with almost fiendish ingenuity' was, while exaggerated, a normal enough immediate reaction to an insult, as was his dramatic suggestion that he should resign from the Savile Club because every time he went there he met with 'a number of S. Reviewers, one of whom is probably my libeller'.

Besant would not give him what he really wanted, the name of the writer of the piece; instead, he diplomatically (and hastily) replied that Tom was unlikely to meet that reviewer, since the Savile did not admit women. On 18 January, still nettled, Tom wrote to Gosse: 'Have you any idea of the writer . . .? I ask because what he has done has never before come within my experience'; and he lists his objections, all of which are cogent, for the piece really was frivolously offensive and unprincipled by any standards – it included the deliberate use of an obvious misprint in order to accuse Hardy of bad grammar.

On the 20th he was still angry, reiterating his objections in a letter to Clodd, with whom he and Besant had recently been staying at Aldeburgh in Suffolk. More interestingly, in acknowledging Clodd's 'generous, yet incisive' criticism of *Tess*, he remarked: 'What you say: "The motive – as a constant – is everything; the deed – as a passing accident – nothing," contains the whole gist of the story, & might stand as its motto, so well have you put it.'

Gosse had replied by return to his earlier letter of complaint, saying that he, too, thought the review must be by a woman. Unfortunately he also lied, claiming that Henry James had praised the novel to him. This seems unlikely in view of what James wrote to Stevenson about it ('vile . . . The pretence of "sexuality" is only equalled by the absence of it'). Tom replied on 20 January:

> I hardly think the writer [in the *Saturday Review*] can be a woman – the sex having caught on with enthusiasm, as I gather from numerous communications from mothers . . . and from women of society who say my courage has done the whole sex a service (!). Surely, then, it must be a man. My mind flew to G.S. There is some evidence of the work of two pens in it – a woman's may have been one; the curious vamped-up wit . . . by the other.

'G.S.' was George Saintsbury, then on the staff of the *Saturday Review* and later a professor at Edinburgh University. Since Saintsbury later confessed to Florence that he had written it, and even expressed the hope that Hardy had forgiven him for it, one can only say that the piece was unworthy of him. In his useful *Short History of English Literature*, of 1911, he was able to escape making comment on *Tess* because Hardy was still living, and thus beyond the scope he had set himself. But it is not true that Tom was so permanently incensed that 'his hostility . . . towards Saintsbury never abated', as Millgate states. As Richard Taylor claims in his edition of the *Personal Notebooks*, Saintsbury's opinions were often quoted by Tom, in various notebooks, 'with implicit approval'. Florence, not a subtle woman, remarked to Purdy, in 1933, of Saintsbury's 'hope': 'little he knew!' But Tom was not prevented by fury from making a careful study of Saintsbury's *History of English Prosody* (1906), or from approvingly writing out a passage from Saintsbury's appreciation of Swinburne in the *Bookman* in 1909.

To Clodd on 4 February Tom commented on the review which annoyed him most of all: Andrew Lang's in the *New Review*. He pointed out, by no means inaccurately, that Lang 'had a hollow place where his heart ought to be'; later, in his preface to the fifth edition, he appropriately alluded to

a gentleman who turned Christian for half-an-hour the better to express his grief that a disrespectful phrase about the Immortals should have been used . . . I can assure this great critic that to exclaim illogically against the gods, singular or plural, is not such an original sin of mine as he seems to imagine. True, it may have some local originality; though if Shakespeare were an authority on history, which perhaps he is not, I could show that the sin was introduced into Wessex as early as the Heptarchy itself. Says Glo'ster in *Lear*, otherwise Ina, king of that country:

As flies to wanton boys are we to the gods,
They kill us for their sport.

When Lang read this he replied in a gossip column that he wrote for *Longman's Magazine* called 'At the Sign of the Ship'. Deliberately missing the point, he wrote that 'nobody in his senses now believes in a wicked malignant President of the Immortals', and went on to express his too obviously envious dissent from the prevailing opinion that *Tess* was a masterpiece. In the process he commented that 'one hears the same opinion from a great classical scholar . . . and from a Scot living his life out in a remote savage island, which, by the way, is *not* Samoa' – an odd allusion to Stevenson.

Tom did not reply to this item, feeling that he had got the best of the exchange. Lang knew many people with whom Tom was friendly, including Gosse, Colvin, Barrie and George Douglas. Immensely prolific, he was, among other things, a well-known failed novelist and poet; he was most successful as an editor. Swinburne's guardian Theodore Watts (from 1897, Watts-Dunton) said, after his death: 'I never knew a man of genius who did not loathe Lang', and Gosse himself, who did not care to be openly nasty, compared him to an angora cat which unsheathed its claws too rapidly when affronted. His malice was legendary; and in a letter to Gosse, Tom's old enemy Henry James criticized him for cultivating 'the puerile imagination and the fourth-rate opinion'. But he was an influential literary journalist, and it is hard to see how Tom could have ignored his hostile comments. The term he used of Lang, 'great critic', was cruel and pointed, but hardly undeserved in view of his malice, which was notorious – he was a man easier to appreciate at a distance than at hand. Yet once again, when Lang wrote something that interested him, Tom wrote it out – an item about ballads from 'At the Sign of the Ship', which appeared in 1900.

Quite apart from the impact made by *Tess*, and the resulting higher income and higher attention paid to him, 1892 was an eventful year for Tom. Some time in early March he shaved off his beard in recognition of all this; he never grew it again. To take the least important, although not least irritating, event first: the terrible Rebekah Owen, with her most pleasant sister, the self-effacing and silent Catharine, in tow, now descended upon the Hardys. Rebekah Owen was a rich American, sporadically bright (but hardly intelligent), persistent, idle, treacherous and without sensitivity. She became a parasite upon Tom, whose works she knew practically by heart, and she repaid the genuine kindness and loyalty of Emma with flighty, jealous, inaccurate and evil-minded denigration by letter and through spoken gossip. Once she had established herself as a friend of the couple, through flourishing an introduction from a publishing director, she attached herself like a limpet. She had formed various 'Hardy Societies' on both sides of the Atlantic, and so Tom endured her with fairly good humour, but left first Emma and later Florence to deal with the irrepressible flow of by no means ingenuous nonsense that emanated from her. All that she reported as fact – such as that Emma disliked *The Hand of Ethelberta* because 'it had too much about servants in it' – is unreliable, because it is all mischievously selective, distorted by the rancour that was natural to her. It is fortunate that she was incapable of writing a book, or she would have written one on Hardy and done even more harm. Tom's real opinion of her is expressed in the poem 'To a Lady', inspired by her disapproval of *Jude*.

This was the year, too, in which the *Illustrated London News* serialized the story upon which he had been working since the previous year, *The Pursuit of the Well-Beloved* – perhaps the most under-rated of all the novels of his maturity. It was based upon an idea he had had in his mind for many years. In one sense at least, it was his last work of fiction: in its revision for volume publication (1897) it is almost a different book. As Gatrell has written, his 'alterations were so extensive that they give rise to the question of whether in making them he was revising the story or was turning it into another story'.

The usual visit to London this year was interrupted by news of the worsening of Thomas Hardy Senior's already serious illness. Tom recorded that on 27 April he 'went upstairs for the last time'. Subsequently he had gone to London in late May for the funeral of his publisher Osgood, and Emma had joined him shortly afterwards. But on Tuesday the 31st he told Gosse that he had 'just received alarming news of the illness of a near relative', and that he would be leaving London by the following Friday. He was considerably upset, because he told Roden Noel, in a letter written from the Savile Club on that Friday morning, that 'for myself I feel quite unable to write or read'.

But his father lingered on, and occasionally rallied, though little hope was held out. Tom rushed up to London again for a few days at the end of June. By 14 July he was telling John Lane, publisher-to-be of Lionel Johnson's 1894 book on his work, that he could only leave Max Gate for a 'few hours at a time . . . it being a case of illness which detains me, which I fear may end fatally'; he was being pressed to pose for the artist William Strang for a portrait to be used in the Johnson book. Tom had been visiting Bockhampton regularly, although the old man – now eighty – 'could not bear the sound of voices'. He was not present at the death, since his brother Henry had told him that their father was 'no worse'; but he died quietly six days later, leaving Jemima (Hardy later declared) devastated and alienated from her surroundings.

For Emma as well as Tom this marked an epoch, for the old man, although confined to the house as an invalid in his last years, must have acted as a good-humoured mediator between his rather ferocious wife and the interloper. Tom wrote 'T.H. (Sen.)' at the top of the famous Ode 22 (1st Book) in his copy of Horace, with perhaps not only the first lines, but the whole poem, in mind: he who is 'pure of life and devoid of wickedness' does not require the darts of the Moor nor poisoned arrows to counter adversity – but that is because he is in love: did not a wolf flee from me, lately (says Horace), while I was unarmed, because I was singing of my Lalage? Given Tom's father's early reputation, this is not inappropriate. He had quoted his own version of the first two lines of the poem in *Tess*: 'The man of upright life, from frailties free/Stands not in need of Moorish spear or bow'. His own poem in tribute to his father, 'On One Who Lived and Died Where He Was Born', which takes one or two unforgivable liberties with dates (Bailey complains that he was eighty years and five months, not eighty, when he climbed upstairs for the last time!), ends:

> Wise child of November!
>   From birth to blanched hairs
> Descending, ascending,
>   Wealth-wantless, those stairs;
>   Who saw quick in time
>   As a vain pantomime
> Life's tending, its ending,
>   The worth of its fame.
> Wise child of November,
> Descending, ascending
>   Those stairs!

Emma and he did not spend any more time together in London in 1892, and on 4 August Tom wrote to his friend, the American journalist Louise Chandler Moulton, a publisher's wife, that he feared he had 'not set foot in London . . . & I fear I may not do so just yet. My wife & I have just lost a near relative: & we have gone nowhere.' It was not long after that, in early September, that Rebekah Owen descended upon them. He was in melancholy mood, as well he might have been as he counted the cost of wide fame, and told George Douglas on 8 October that he 'had passed through many glooms such as I hope you will never see; & I cannot say they were ever the result of material surroundings'. He added: 'I was in London very little last season – owing to the illness of my dear father . . . ' Perhaps he was feeling sad for another reason, too: because on 17 September Stinsford House had burnt down. He and Emma were driving past it in a carriage, on their way home from Dorchester. He left the carriage and ran across the fields; by a coincidence he met his sister Mary, who had been laying flowers on their father's grave, 'on which the firelight now flickered'.

A journey to London, and thence to Fawley in Berkshire, birthplace of his father's mother, failed to cheer him up. He saw his new publishers about their plans for the collected edition, which pleased him; but the visit to Fawley, possibly made with *Jude* in mind, seems to have helped to put him into the gloomy frame of mind implied in the letter to Douglas. 'Although I am alive with the living I can see only the dead here, and am scarcely conscious of the happy children at play,' he wrote in a note about Fawley.

He was soon back at Max Gate, but then heard that Tennyson had died on 6 October. On the 12th he attended the funeral, but found it inadequate compared to the one he had attended some three months earlier: 'At Tennyson's funeral in Westminster Abbey. The music was sweet and impressive, but as a funeral the scene was less penetrating than a plain country interment would have been.'

In the *Academy* in February the poet William Watson had applauded *Tess*, but in the course of his review made some severe strictures, which included a wish that such phrases as 'his former pulsating flexuous domesticity' had been absent. Tom remained on good terms with him, since he was not offended at what he took to be fair criticism. On the day of Tennyson's funeral he lunched with him, Gosse, Austin Dobson and Theodore Watts. He wrote to Emma:

> My dearest Em:
>   I have attended Tennysons [sic] funeral – & find I cannot get back very well tonight – so I will wait till to-morrow – returning about the usual time . . . George Meredith was there – also Henry James, Huxley, &c. I will tell you more when I come.

This was signed 'Yours always'.

There is no evidence for Millgate's glib suggestion that Tom 'had of course been for some time engaged in an active search for someone to fall in love with'. What active search? Had Millgate written that he had perhaps been visiting high-class brothels quite frequently, or simply that he was susceptible to women younger than himself who were good-looking, then we should feel more persuaded. But he is always far too keen to write Emma off. Tom was certainly in a unique situation, especially for an untutored genius – ignorant of homosexuality, over-sensitive to criticism, sexually impotent, perpetually adolescent, lacking in self-confidence, and possessed of an ageing wife and a propensity for young girls! Even a well-hung (to borrow the phrase from *Two on a Tower*) professor might have failed to cope.

Nor does the famous entry of 18 October, intimately connected with the more famous poem 'I Look into My Glass', 'strongly' imply a 'recent rebuff from a younger woman – possibly Rosamund Tomson'. There is no evidence of the presence in his life at this time of Rosamund Tomson, to whom Tom's last known letter had been written in December 1891. Probably he had already become disillusioned by her – and not by any rebuff he received from her, but by her opportunism, which he would not have regarded as 'emancipated'. His note of 18 October reads:

> Hurt my tooth at breakfast-time. I look in the glass. Am conscious of the humiliating sorriness of my earthly tabernacle, and of the sad fact that the best of parents could do not better for me . . . Why should a man's mind have been thrown into such close, sad, sensational, inexplicable relations with such a precarious object as his own body?

Most would read this as expressing one of those universal insights for which we value Thomas Hardy, rather than any sense of inferiority brought on by a particular 'rebuff'. Its melancholy was the result of recent blows: the death of his father; the fire at Stinsford, which had seemed to destroy all the memories of his youth, just as his father had been destroyed by time; the departure of that poetic fixture, Tennyson; and the visit to Fawley. The poem is one of his most moving:

> I look into my glass,
> And view my wasting skin,
> And say, 'Would God it came to pass
> My heart had shrunk as thin!'
>
> For then, I, undistrest
> By hearts grown cold to me,
> Could lonely wait my endless rest
> With equanimity.
>
> But Time, to make me grieve,
> Part steals, lets part abide;
> And shakes this fragile frame at eve
> With throbbings of noontide.

So powerfully do the majority of Hardy's critics resist this as a poem making a universal statement about how both men and women feel

461

about ageing that they invent all kinds of special occasions for it, all more or less subtly derogatory of its author. Bailey is sure that Tom felt especially bad about his own features, and Millgate, unable to imagine any man's general feeling of dissatisfaction with so splendid a thing as even his fifty-two-year-old body (male, after all), invents a specific sexual rebuff. The sixth line of the poem is usually connected with Tom's awareness of Emma's specific hostility, but its sense, surely, is that human beings do not often feel romantic love for older, wrinkled specimens. The poem may quite as well be read in a woman's as in a man's voice, although the latter, too, runs against the grain of the Victorian sensibility, which held – even in the teeth of the evidence – that women were the spotless receptacles of masculine impurity, themselves 'untroubled' by sexual feelings.

That 'emancipation' for Tom, however susceptible he may have been to beautiful women, often transcended sexual boundaries is shown in a letter of 16 October 1892 to the playwright, critic and translator of Ibsen (of whom Tom approved) William Archer:

> I am glad the *Tess* reached you. I have been so drawn to your writings by their accord with my views that I have often thought of testifying to that agreement by sending a book: but I have hitherto been deterred by a fear lest you might have the same volume to review.

He similarly addressed many of those with whom he felt instinctively in sympathy, as people immune from contemporary hypocrisies. But he longed, too, for such a communion with a woman – and was at the same time aware that, although to this point he had certainly had one with his wife, certain 'throbbings' could too easily direct him elsewhere. To say that he was 'of course' actively searching for a woman to fall in love with is to ignore how desperately he wished to avoid that eventuality. Similarly afflicted 'adolescents', even ones deeply influenced by Hardy, such as Robert Graves, have described the feeling:

> Pity the man who finds a rebel heart
> Under the breastbone drumming
> Which reason warns him he should drown
> In midnight wastes of sea.

One may recollect what Jocelyn Pierston tells the painter Somers in the 1897 version of *The Well-Beloved*:

'. . . And let me tell you that her [the elusive well-beloved] from each to each individual has been anything but a pleasure for me – certainly not a wanton game of my instigation . . . I have been absolutely miserable when I have looked in a face for her I used to see there, and could see her no more.'

'You ought not to marry,' repeated Somers.

Meanwhile Emma was 'socially ambitious' enough to ask that an account of her by a journalist called Dolman should not be accompanied by a picture. Tom told Dolman on 24 November 1892, 'Mrs Hardy requests me to tell you that on consideration she prefers that no photograph of herself should be published.' The piece finally appeared in the *Ladies' Home Journal* in May 1895 – with a photograph, doubtless obtained surreptitiously.

So the first year of Hardy's world-wide fame came to an end. Over Christmas he was busy with one of the best of his stories, 'The Fiddler of the Reels', which he sent off to Scribners on 13 January 1893: they had requested it for the Chicago World Fair number of their magazine, *Scribner's*, where it duly appeared in May 1893. For sheer professionalism, it is perhaps the most accomplished piece of prose he ever wrote.

The central character, a Paganini-like violinist, embodies Tom's conviction that, in the modern world, the irrational, and its pull, remain unchanged. Car'line Aspent has been under the spell of Mop Ollamoor, the wizard violinist, from the time she first heard him, and refuses her suitor Ned Hipcroft on this account. Ned therefore goes to work in London, where, in 1851, the Great Exhibition opened. At this time Car'line writes offering to marry him, and he accepts. She turns up with a child, Carry, clearly Ollamore's. But he marries her, and soon afterwards takes her to the Exhibition, at which she thinks she sees Ollamoor in a mirror (here Tom alludes to the belief – in fact correct – that the demonic appears in reflected forms).

Later, when work becomes scarce in London, Ned takes his wife and her daughter back to Casterbridge, and, while he is enquiring about work there, she and the child walk to Stickleford (Tincleton), where they rest in an inn. There, about to burst into tune, is Mop and his violin. Car'line is impelled to dance, and does so until she drops. When Ned arrives he finds that Ollamoor has gone, taking his child with him. He searches for him everywhere, including London, where he has heard reports of him. Eventually he discovers that he has apparently emigrated to America, where, an old man, he still fiddles while Carry, now forty-four, dances to his music.

The music motif was prominent because of the recent death of Thomas Hardy Senior, whose musical services to his church Tom had been at pains to emphasize in the leaflet he prepared for his memorial service at Stinsford. He also laid out before himself in this story, as he so often did, the two sides of his own nature: the good and kindly Ned, who is lacking in sexual energy ('his was a nature not greatly dependent upon the ministrations of the other sex for its comforts'), and the 'foreign', 'oily', fiendish and sexually charismatic Ollamore, the irresponsible wanderer that every man wants to be, the maker of music, the one of 'ecstatic temperament' (as Tom defined himself). The main intention of the story, written specifically for Americans attending the Chicago World Fair, was to present a vision of a man who had played at the Great Exhibition, and was now repeating this performance in Chicago more than forty years later. Thus Hardy was saying, in his inimitable way: 'Beware! However modern you think you may be over there in the New World, you will never be safe from the irrational.'

In April, thinking of animadversions upon his style and awkwardness, and of his pending career as a full-time poet, he noted that 'a clever thrush, and a stupid nightingale, sing very much alike'. This cautious man was about to become as 'stupid' as he ever was in his life. The name of the woman concerned came up in his correspondence almost four months before he met her and was swept off his feet.

On 29 January he had the duty of writing to Lord Houghton to thank him for a copy of his *Stray Verses*. His response was characteristic of his privately humorous side. He knew that the recipient, son of the 1st Lord Houghton, whom Tom had known, would never, however much he desired to, ask the question: 'And what did you think after you returned from your walk – *did* the wind allow you?'

I have received from your publisher a most welcome copy of 'Stray Verses'. Many thanks for the same, & your kind remembrance of me. I have just read a few of the pieces (& I think I like the more serious of them rather the better) & I am putting the book in my pocket to continue on a walk, if the wind will let me. I wish I had a new book of my own to send back.

He ended: 'I hope Mrs Henniker's novel "Sold Out". But these are bad times for large editions, the publishers say.'

THROBBINGS OF NOONTIDE

Mrs Florence Henniker, the present Lord Houghton's sister, was married to the ferociously moustached Arthur Henry Henniker-Major of the Coldstream Guards. But that is only the polite half of the story. The other half is that she too was unhappy, although she had no dislike of her military husband (who began as a lieutenant and ended as a major-general), philistine though he was – and, as it happened, an impoverished one, too, for he was the youngest son of the 4th Lord Henniker. Outwardly devoted to him, and determined to remain so, whatever her inner feelings, she was nevertheless unable to talk to him about the things that most mattered to her. As an undoubtedly enlightened woman, this caused her some frustration. In those days it was always a woman's duty to suppress such neuroticisms, or at least to conceal them – and she did. But the inference is unavoidable. Her father, Monckton Milnes, besides possessing the finest and fullest collection of pornography in England, the joy of Swinburne, had been a literary man and an enlightened one: poet, classicist, biographer of – and editor of the first decent edition of – Keats, reforming MP (slavery, the rights of women), friend to Tennyson, Hallam and Thackeray, helper of Swinburne, advocate of Blake and Shelley. He is Vavasour in Disraeli's *Tancred*, and of him Carlyle said that there was only one post for which he was fit: 'the office of perpetual president of the Heaven and Hell Amalgamation Society'. An eclectic man, he was once a Tractarian, praised by Newman; later he came under the spell of Islam while travelling in the East.

Florence was childless, and it was only in her fiction that she expressed her desire – a weak counterpart of Tom's need for a close cross-sex relationship, a union of enlightened minds – for something different. In her novels she specialized in unhappy marriages against a high society background. She had even acquired a name for being too keen on matters involving old men's interest in young girls (Tom was fifteen years her senior). She did not find it difficult, with her connections, to practise as a successful journalist; she became President of the Society of Women Journalists in 1896. The money she earned from her writing came in useful to her household. Association with the up-and-still-coming Thomas Hardy could do her no harm, especially if he invited a collaboration in a fictional enterprise – and, alas, that is just what he very soon did.

What she lacked in beauty Florence Henniker made up for in presence, a striking handsomeness, social grace, what was called in those days 'dash' (the conventional, and Tom, mistaking her sense of fun and mild flirtatiousness for defiance, called her 'fast'), and a moderate but spirited intelligence. She made competent translations from German, French and Spanish poetry, of which she had an excellent knowledge, and she was well travelled. Florence lived the life which most interested her entirely on paper – and, alas for Tom, she was determined to keep it that way. Above all, from his point of view, she loved animals (although not to the extent that she objected to her husband's later naming of his unfortunate and innocent French bulldogs as Milner and Empire) and hated cruelty to them. She genuinely appreciated the terrible bird-shooting scene in *Tess*.

However her own novels, stories and plays have sunk without trace, and deservedly so. This is not to belittle her: she knew how to please and even faintly titillate a society audience, and had already done so in three novels by the time Tom came across her. The novel he alludes to in his letter to her brother is her third, *Bid Me Goodbye*, a not unHardyan affair with a tragic ending. Indeed, her fiction abounds in Hardyisms of every sort – as did that of so many others. Tom was doubtless pleased to discover such a trenchant woman so determinedly under the spell of his fiction, but can hardly have failed to recognize that she lacked the talent of even a Rhoda Broughton or a Mary Cholmondeley, Victorian authors of bestsellers which can still be read with some pleasure today. Alas, her books are pretty conventional, and Tom may have hoped that by collaborating with her on the short story 'The Spectre of the Real' he would be able to bring out the unconventional best in her. He would later upbraid her for her conventionality; but it was to get him nowhere. Fortunately it all led, ultimately, to many years of cheerful and pleasant friendship.

If the 2nd Lord Houghton's wife had not died prematurely, then Tom would not have met Mrs Henniker when he did. Houghton was Lord-Lieutenant of Ireland, and when both Hardys visited him in Dublin in May 1893 his sister was acting as hostess for him at the Viceregal Lodge, an institution which Tom himself amusedly called, in his diary, a 'little court'. He had been up to London for a week during March. A day or two after he returned, on Monday the 20th, he received a letter from W.M. Colles, an agent who acted for the Authors' Syndicate, asking him for a story. On 26 March he had answered:

> I adopt your suggestion to ask £100, for world rights in a story of 6000 words – this being in fact exactly on the scale of payment I am receiving from another English periodical. Simultaneous publication

everywhere, & once only, is understood. But I hope they don't want the story just yet? as I have nothing ready or thought of.

Florence Henniker was to provide him with something to 'think of' when he came to write that story. It was to be published as 'An Imaginative Woman' in the *Pall Mall*, although not until 1897.

By mid-April he was back in London, this time with Emma. As a reflection of their newly found financial status they took an entire house, 70 Hamilton Terrace, to which they brought up their own servants from Max Gate. Writing to Colles from there on the 14th Tom finalized the arrangements for the story, adding, in a world-weary postscript, 'Quite a proper story of course'.

On 18 May he and Emma left 'Euston by 9 o'clock morning train . . . for Llandudno, *en route* for Dublin'. The retrospective poem 'Alike and Unlike' (in manuscript the words 'She speaks', under the title, are crossed out) is closely related, by its subtitle 'Great Orme's Head', to this entry, which continues: 'After arrival at Llandudno drove round Great Orme's Head. Magnificent deep purple-grey mountains, the fine colour being on account of an approaching storm.' There was another storm approaching, and this poem may have been occasioned by Tom's reading of this entry in his diary as he prepared the *Life*. It was first published in *Human Shows* (1925):

> We watched the selfsame scene on that long drive,
> Saw the magnificent purples, as one eye,
> Of those near mountains; saw the storm arrive;
> Laid up the sight in memory, you and I,
> As if for joint recallings by and by.
>
> But our eye-records, like in hue and line,
> Had superimposed on them, that very day,
> Gravings on your side deep, but slight on mine! –
> Tending to sever us thence alway;
> Mine commonplace; yours tragic, gruesome, gray.

Is it ironic that so private a man as Hardy, who (if very properly) desired above all to keep the intimate details of his life away from the prying eyes of biographers, should have written so many poems that are rescued from comparative obscurity only by facts that we ought not, by his own severe intentions, to know? For example, the many readers of

Human Shows could not have known about the two words cancelled in the manuscript of 'Alike and Unlike', or about an as yet unpublished diary entry, let alone about the passion for Florence Henniker which was going to sever the Hardys' precious joint memory of places 'alway'. Judging from, say, Bailey's comments on this poem, which treat it as so much biographical data, we might answer the question in the affirmative. But what does the text, taken alone, tell us?

We may infer that there are two watchers of the mountains and arriving storm, who are taking the drive, and even – without too much faculty-stretching – that they are man and woman, probably a married couple. But perhaps, after all, they are a father and daughter, or a mother and son, or even, if it comes to it, a father and son, and so on. Why not? Two people who have been close enough to share such moments in the face of nature: there is no clue as to which is the speaker. Yet the poem does well enough on its own. The situation is universalized. The facts necessary to understanding are given. And what it tells us (read, first, as a bare text) adds, if not crucially then still usefully, to our biographical understanding. For the subject of the poem is not sexual love or desire, but friendship.

The two people, says one of them, viewed the scene in perfect accord; only the 'as if', in the opening stanza, hints that something will trouble their joint memory of it. On 1 July 1892, ten months before this recalled incident, Tom had noted in his diary:

> We don't always remember as we should that in getting at the truth, we get only at the true nature of the impression that an object, etc., produces on us, the true thing in itself being still, as Kant shows, beyond our knowledge.

The poem does not disturb this convinced Kantianism, but does suggest that, for people close enough, 'the true nature of' impressions may be shared. We are, once more, near to Rilke's allied sense of the beautiful, as the 'first apprehension of the terrible': the mountains are beautiful, yet a storm is nothing if it is not 'terrible', and here it heightens the beauty of the scene – this is implicit in the text, in the phrase 'magnificent purples', so that we do not have to fall back on the diary entry. The second stanza fulfils the promise contained in the first's foreboding phrase 'as if': defines the nature of the difficulty as lying in the contrast between the 'gravings' 'superimposed' on the impressions, 'eye-records', of the two people. The speaker's were 'commonplace', but the other's were 'tragic, gruesome, gray'. 'Gravings' are 'burials' (of joint recallings) as well as 'engravings of lines': they represent the subjective states of mind of the watchers, their expectations and assumptions, the 'lines' their minds carved, or 'superimposed', on the thing-in-itself that is 'beyond knowledge'. 'Alike and Unlike' is characteristic of Hardy in its combination of clumsiness and extreme psychological precision. Yet clumsiness is hardly a fault in him, for one is usually put in mind of the glib dangers of elegance.

Biographically the poem confirms that it was the Henniker affair, rather than *Jude*, which 'severed', or *tended* to sever (the modification should be noted) the understanding between Tom and Emma. The words 'tragic' and (especially) 'gruesome' are strong ones to be applied, retrospectively, by Tom to his mood and expectations of 18 May 1893 (19 May being the crucial date of the meeting with Florence Henniker). The poem immediately following this one in *Human Shows* must surely point to Tom's again retrospective view of how the affair had ended, and may also offer a biographical clue to the nature of Florence Henniker's behaviour towards him. It is a short poem, called 'The Thing Unplanned':

> The white winter sun struck its stroke on the bridge,
>   The meadow-rills rippled and gleamed
> As I left the thatched post-office, just by the ridge,
> And dropped in my pocket her long tender letter,
> With: 'This must be snapped! it is more than it seemed;
>   And now is the opportune time!'
>
> But against what I willed worked the surging sublime
>   Of the thing that I did – the thing better!

Once again, the situation is sufficiently generalized: 'the thing unplanned' is not defined overtly, nor is 'the thing better', but we may fairly take it that they are identical, and that therefore the action the speaker of the poem did take was 'unplanned'. He was going to sever his connection from the author of the 'long tender letter', but instead took another, unplanned action. This clearly implies that he did *not* sever the connection, so that we are left with two alternatives: either he continued the affair, or he turned it into friendship – and everything favours the latter conclusion, if only because the first six lines posit a situation in which the 'tenderness' between the speaker and the woman has to be 'snapped', and for the usual reasons. Now the post office at Bockhampton (paradigmatic to him of all post offices) was in a thatched house, and Tom would have needed to cross a bridge to reach it, and, as Bailey claims, 'the water-meadows are filled with rills during the winter rains'. So perhaps, as Kenneth Phelps suggests in his little essay *Annotations by Hardy in His Bibles and Prayer-Book* (1966), he really did receive, *post restante*, a letter from Florence Henniker which was, or so he thought, 'long and tender'. Against this interpretation there is no evidence that she ever made any advances to him (as distinct from being coquettish), epistolary or otherwise.

Tom did not want to suppress what he wrote about Florence Henniker when he came to write the *Life*:

> [May] 19. Went on to Holyhead and Kingstown. Met on board John Morley, the Chief Secretary . . . Were awaited at Dublin by conveyance from the Viceregal Lodge as promised, this invitation being one renewed from last year, when I was obliged to postpone my visit on account of my father's death. We were received by Mrs Arthur Henniker, the Lord-Lieutenant's sister. A charming, *intuitive* woman apparently. Lord Houghton . . . came in shortly after.

The italicized word is striking; what Tom meant by it then, and what he meant by it as he recalled it for the *Life*, is that she seemed sympathetic, understanding and, above all, 'emancipated'. But the word is qualified by 'apparently'. Was that word a retrospective addition? Since he is quite free with his allusions to Florence in the *Life* we should be none the wiser about his feelings if some of his letters to her had not come to light. These show that his interest in other women, often represented as seriously predatory, was seldom more than openly flirtatious.

None the less, it is impossible to be certain about what exactly happened between Mrs Henniker and Tom. However, the opinion that he fell in love with her 'without much encouragement on her part', while tenable, is unlikely; he usually required encouragement. Nor does Millgate's view that Tom's use of the word '*intuitive*' suggests that he entertained 'a strong element of wishfulness in [his] early attitudes to her, an assumption of a sexual as well as intellectual responsiveness which may simply not have existed', take us far. It only does so if we wish to repress our own predilections in the interests of some grimly donnish delusion of 'maturity', which patronizes the 'perpetual adolescent' and author of so many regrettably immature love poems. As for the 'element of male predatoriness', whatever that means – he was a man, and it is surprising to find a quasi-advocate of his impotence drawing attention to so disagreeable a possibility. Tom was excited by Florence Henniker, and especially, no doubt, by her vivacious playing of the zither at a well-attended dinner in Dublin on 22 May.

There is some indication that Florence led Tom on. When the Hardys returned to Holyhead at the end of the month she was with them – and so was another woman. For some reason the following sentence is missing from the *Life* as it was originally published: 'Found on board General Milman and Miss Milman, Sir Eyre Shaw, Mrs Henniker and others.' Just why did Mrs Henniker decide to take that particular boat back to England? We are bound to ask whether it was mere coincidence – or whether she '*intuitively*' scented literary and even personal advantage in being a companion to the now famous Thomas Hardy and therefore informed her brother that she must instantly depart. It would have been a venal decision. However, sandwiched between the account of the Irish visit and the return to London there is another passage omitted from the *Life*:

> The chief significance of Hardy's visit to Dublin was his meeting there with Mrs Arthur Henniker (Florence Henniker) who became afterwards one of his closest and most valued friends, remaining so until her death many years after. As befitted the daughter of Monckton Milnes (Lord Houghton) she had a love of the best in literature, and was herself a writer of novels and short stories, none of which, unfortunately, ever received the recognition which, in Hardy's opinion, they undoubtedly deserved. Some of his best short poems were inspired by her, and the only time he ever wrote in collaboration was with her in a short story, 'The Spectre of the Real'.

That is equivalent to stating that he had been in love with her.

So far as the literary value of Mrs Henniker's work is concerned, Tom is by now in a minority of one. Indeed, the other female companion on that little voyage back to Holyhead was more accomplished and more intelligent. She was Lena (abbreviated from Angelena) Milman, daughter of the Keeper of the Tower of London. There is a certain irony in the fact that just then Tom became associated not only with Lena Milman but also with yet another woman close to the fellow writer whom he disliked most of all, doubtless because of his crass and persistent denigration of *Tess*: George Moore. Pearl Craigie, 'that

471

brilliant woman' whom he met on 8 June, wrote under the pseudonym of John Oliver Hobbes, and had been Moore's lover (which Lena Milman had not). There are, perhaps, elements of both women in Moore's cruel and brilliant portrait, 'Mildred Lawson', in *Celibates*, but it is more likely that he is thinking of Pearl Craigie. Lena Milman, a translator of such Russian writers as Tolstoy and Turgenev, was helpful to Moore as a critic, wrote for the *Yellow Book* (on, for example, her friend Henry James, who thought her a 'charming girl') and played the violin. She was also the author of poems and at least one outstanding short story, 'Marcel: An Hotel Child' (*Yellow Book*, January 1897), of which Moore told her: 'Your story is charming, much better than Mrs Craigie or Mrs Henniker could do.' Mrs Henniker had herself been on good terms with Moore, but there may have been a coolness between them after she failed to send him a copy of her novel *Foiled* (1892).

Moore's quarrel with Tom, initiated by Moore, caused needless grief to both men. It was a pity, because they had certain things in common, especially a hatred of Mrs Grundy, and Moore was a good (if now a neglected) writer; however, Tom had nothing in him of Moore's sheer silliness, nor was he as affected. In Moore's eyes the reception of *Esther Waters* (1894), his first bookshop success, and a late one, was clouded by too frequent comparison with *Tess*. But in private conversation he had been attacking *Tess* before that, almost to the point of tedium, ever since it was published. He parodied Tess's confession to Clare in *Esther Waters*, and again in the 1895 revision of his novel *Vain Fortune* (1890). Moore seems to have been obsessed with Tom's novel. The quarrel was exacerbated by Edmund Gosse, who, at least as close to Moore as to Tom, cattily informed Moore that Hardy wanted to avoid him.

The climax of the unseemly affair came thirty years later, in 1924, with the publication of Moore's *Conversations in Ebury Street*. Some of these 'conversations' purport to be with John Freeman, an insurance man who was also a poetaster of some small account at the time. Like Charles Morgan, Freeman used to hang around Moore in his old age – others similarly represented in the book are Gosse himself, and Tom's friends Walter de la Mare and Harley Granville Barker. Freeman is represented as a feed – sometimes an argumentative one – to Moore's increasingly and deliberately preposterous opinions, such as that Landor is 'above Shakespeare'. Freeman says that Hardy's poetry is better than his prose, but that in both 'he has helped the ordinary man to realise pessimism as a theory of life'. This sets Moore going. Hardy has written the worst prose ever. There follows an attack on the description of the washing away of Troy's flowers on Fanny Robin's grave, and then a longer one on *Tess*. The woods and fields Hardy writes of are never 'before our eyes'. Moore scores a few points, but as a whole the onslaught is too obviously the result of jealousy (Moore ought to have appreciated *Tess* just as Tom ought to have appreciated the tender *Esther Waters*). It includes this passage:

> *Freeman* Like Pilate, I ask you: What is truth? Your judgment is at variance with opinions that proceed from the highest to the lowest. Everybody believes –
> *Moore* The entire Press believes, and would shed the last drop of its ink in defence of the literary opinions of the many.
> *Freeman* You would then set aside the literary opinions of the many? Even that of your friend, Mr Edmund Gosse, who salutes Mr Hardy as *the poet who is, without dispute, the head of the literary profession, and so I believe the first of living men of letters in the world?*
> *Moore* Mr Gosse speaks out of his lights, and I speak out of mine, and I do not think that anything would be gained by my decrying his as a false light and mine as a true. A great deal of what I am saying, Mr Freeman, will appear in print as soon as Mr Hardy steps on board Charon's boat.

Any reader in doubt about Moore's intention to be abusive need only turn to the passage comparing Hardy to the playwright Henry Arthur Jones. Freeman quotes Oscar Wilde's three rules to dramatists: the first rule was not to write like Jones, and the second and third were the same. He then asks Moore if he would adopt Wilde's formula, were he called upon to give advice to novelists. Moore replies:

> The two men [Jones and Hardy] are curiously alike, and the physical likeness is as striking as the mental. William Archer once asked me if I had ever seen Mr Hardy. I said that I hadn't, and he answered: Well, you'd be surprised at the likeness, the physical likeness: same height, same build, same type of face, same complexion. And it so happened that a few days afterwards Mr Hardy was pointed out to me going round the pictures with his wife, and I said: Archer is right; the two men are very like each other.

Plainly Moore was out to embarrass as many people who knew and respected Tom as he could, and he would have been well advised to

473

omit from his book all but a straightforward expression of his dislike of him.

Tom was understandably irritated that such friends of his as Granville Barker, de la Mare and Gosse had lent themselves to being included in the book as feeds for Moore's hurt vanity. He referred to them in a letter on 9 April 1924 to John Middleton Murry, who had defended his reputation against Moore's onslaughts in the *Adelphi*, as Moore's 'disciples': 'What a disgrace for them. They must be a timid lot, not to protest, & remind me of performing dogs in a show, obeying their master with fear & trembling lest they shd get the hot iron behind the scenes.'

Meanwhile in December 1893 Moore, with *Esther Waters* not yet quite published, was having to assure the long-suffering Lena Milman that 'Of course I will not speak of Hardy's book if you do not wish it'. She had been reading the proofs of *Esther*, and had become weary of his obsessive insults about her new friend, who had, meanwhile, taken the trouble to write to her several times and who respected her as yet another 'emancipated' woman. On 17 July, having met her and enjoyed her conversation on several occasions, he wrote to her about Herbert Spencer's *First Principles*: 'Whether the theories are true or false, their effect upon the imagination is unquestionable, and I think beneficial.' He added, reassuringly, that the literary rank of Sir Thomas Browne's *Urn Burial*, into which he had been looking, was 'immeasurably higher than Spencer's'. On 4 September he sent her a photograph of himself, which she had asked for, and asked for hers in return. He repeated this request on the 18th, adding that no photographer 'is likely to do justice to you', and again on 9 November. In the latter he told her that he wondered how well *Tess* had been translated into Russian (it had just appeared, serially, in a Russian magazine), and remarked, evidently not yet put off the name for ever, 'I feel rather jealous of George M.!' By Christmas she had sent him the portrait, which he found a 'very pretty one . . . But much is absent – much that I like to recall in you – which will make it quite necessary that I should see the original sometimes.'

These letters to her have been seen as 'mildly flirtatious', but, as that phrase carries an implication of 'predatory', 'pleasantly gallant' would have been more accurate: he genuinely liked and appreciated her, and, understanding the pleasure to be gained from his esteem, wanted to compliment her. He saw no reason why he should not be on close terms with intellectual women. In the *Life* he mentions having gone with her and Emma to Barrie's play *Walker, London*, and 'going behind the scenes with Barrie'. Lena Milman, who died in 1914, was lively and pretty; but she did not lead him on. I do not think that Tom ever seriously dreamed of actually conducting 'affairs' with any of the women to whom he wrote, and I therefore think, although there can be no proof in such circumstances, that Mrs Henniker did lead him on – although it is necessary to allow for his extreme excitability in these matters. One side of him, though, watched the other pursuing her. By the end of July he could confide this note to his diary, one significant enough to quote in the *Life*: 'I often think that women, even those who consider themselves experienced in sexual strategy, do not know how to manage an *honest* man.' Evidently the duly flattered (and ambitious) Mrs Henniker was not 'managing' Thomas Hardy very well, and was going to have to agree to a meeting – surely secret from all? – with him on 8 August, so that she could put her position to him.

23

Florence Henniker

A spate of letters to Florence followed the meeting in Ireland. Tom told Lord Houghton in his thank you letter of 31 May that Emma and he 'had not forgotten the romantic atmosphere which surrounded us' on that occasion. He also thanked him for a further gift, which may have been his *Gleanings from Béranger* (1889), a privately printed volume of versions from Pierre Jean de Béranger: 'I . . . am struck with your many felicitous turns of phrase.'

Not all the letters to Florence are extant, and a crucial one of 3 August is certainly missing (destroyed, with others, by Florence herself); all hers to him, of this crucial period, were also destroyed. Any student of nineteenth-century affairs notices how much faster the post was in those days. Tom had already received a note from Mrs Henniker when he wrote to her on Saturday, 3 June, from 70 Hamilton Terrace:

> I am glad to get your note, as I was beginning to wonder if you would soon be here [she had taken a house at Southsea, to be near her husband, then stationed at Portsmouth]. I will see about Ibsen immediately . . . I have already obtained the books [some of his own works which she had requested from him] – & should have sent them on to you, but that I want to ask you something first . . . I have nothing to do from next Monday till Wednesday that is of any consequence. But I have a dreadful confession to make. In a weak moment I have accepted an invitation to lunch, to meet
>
> John Oliver Hobbes!
>
> She is very pretty, they say; but on my honour that had nothing to do with it – purely literary reasons only.

This last was certainly contrived to make her a little jealous, for Mrs Craigie was both more accomplished, and a literary star of greater magnitude, than herself. Like Lena Milman, she had collaborated with

Moore or would do so in the future. In her case it led to a bitter quarrel, in the course of which Moore behaved preposterously – alas, it was his wont.

Tom had probably met her before, because in the *Life* he modified his account of the lunch on 8 June: '. . . he met for the first time (*it is believed*) that brilliant woman Mrs Craigie . . . [my italics]'. Pearl Mary-Teresa (this hybrid was acquired after her conversion to the Roman Catholic faith in 1892) Craigie (née Richards), well-heeled owing to the profits from Carter's Little Liver Pills and other patent medicines, was American but came to England in her infancy. At the age of nineteen she married a banker, Reginald Craigie. After bearing him a son and leaving him, both in 1890, she declared to her friends that he was an unfaithful and syphilitic drunkard who had infected both her and her child. She may thus have felt that she had better claims to the fictional theme of the awful marriage than Mrs Henniker, who also used it, but was happier with the enormous but uninfected moustaches of her warrior spouse. Pearl Craigie was divorced from her husband, after painful proceedings, in 1895. There is no way of telling whether Tom had read Craigie's novel *Some Emotions and a Moral*, about unhappy marriage, suicide and infidelity; as he was interested in women, he probably did. It was the hit of 1891, and gave her notoriety. She wrote more successful bohemian novels and plays before she died of heart failure in 1906 at the age of thirty-eight. Her books have failed to survive, but were not incapable. The effect they had on the majority of her readers is summed up in a foolish verse written when she was at the height of fashion:

> John Oliver Hobbes, with your spasms and throbs,
>   How does your novel grow?
> With cynical sneers at young Love and his tears,
>   And epigrams all in a row.

Pearl Craigie's cynicism was eventually modified by her mystical and Newman-influenced Catholicism. Hardy's influence upon her fiction is negligible: her chief model was Meredith. She was Mrs Henniker's predecessor as President of the Society of Women Journalists, and was later a member of the Anti-Suffrage League. Tom admired her, especially her conversation. When William Archer published *Real Conversations* in 1904, including 'conversations' with Hardy and Mrs Craigie, Tom commented, in a letter of 11 February 1904 to Archer, 'Mrs C's talk is, I think, the best, as would be natural, she being such an amusing companion.' But it is unlikely that, as has been woodenly suggested, her sensational and scarcely readable novel *The Gods, Some Mortals and Lord Wickenham*, serialized in the *Pall Mall Budget* in 1895, provided him with a plot source, namely the 'marriage-trap', for *Jude*. That is rather an old 'plot'.

We know, then, from this very first (extant) letter to Mrs Henniker that she had already written to him asking him for copies of his books. We know, too, that she had sent him a book (for which he thanked her); probably it was one of her own, perhaps *Sir George* (1891) or *Foiled* (1892). If it was the latter, then how much would he have appreciated this passage (quoted by K.G. Wilson in his article in the *Thomas Hardy Year Book*, 6, as an illustration of her belief in 'traditional values')?

> If the dead lovers whose hearts had been so cruelly wrung many a year agone in this same quiet room could have looked down upon these other two – the friend of one, the child of both – with arms entwined, and happy eyes and lips that met, they might perhaps have seen in them a symbol of forgiveness and peace, of the mercy held out at last to all who have suffered, and wept, and sinned.

If Tom did read this passage (there are plenty more like it, even in such late works as *Second Fiddle* of 1912), and felt that it reflected conventional beliefs, then he soon hoped to cure her of such *'petty'* folly. He still believed her to be faithful to Shelley in her heart, and therefore thoroughly susceptible to such a cure. It was always the potential in Florence Henniker that he was chasing.

By the following Wednesday, 7 June, he had seen her again briefly, for he confesses to having been 'very absent-minded not to hand over the photograph'. He also tells her that he has been to an architectural bookshop and bought 'the handbook that will suit you'. He continues:

> I can post it on, or keep it to make use of in the lesson which I shall have great pleasure in giving. Westminster Abbey, St Saviour's Southwark, and St Bartholomew's Smithfield, contain excellent features for study. I want you to be able to walk into a church and pronounce upon its date at a glance . . . Oral instruction . . . is, of course, a much more rapid and effectual method than from books, and you must not think it will be any trouble to me.

He ends by telling her that upon his return to Hamilton Terrace after the book purchase he had found 'the author of The Heavenly Twins' sitting waiting for him. Sarah Grand, whose real name was Frances McFall, née Clarke, Mrs Henniker's junior by a year, was yet another successful author. Her novel *The Heavenly Twins* had just taken London by storm on account of its sensational plot and its (for those days) vivid description of syphilis. She had published it at her own expense in Manchester in 1892, after George Meredith had turned it down for Chapman and Hall; now, under Heinemann's imprint, it was selling in thousands, and had to be reprinted six times in that year. Tom did not think much of it, although Mrs McFall (Mr McFall, a widowed army surgeon almost a quarter of a century older than his second wife, whom he married when she was only sixteen, is portrayed in Grand's *The Beth Book*, 1897, as a tyrannical old man of disgusting predilections) was another beauty whose enticing photograph adorned her publications. Her male readers could thus the more satisfyingly contemplate the nameless ways in which she, as a spotless young virgin, had been ill used by the hideous old surgeon from whom she had separated herself. Tom was interested enough in *The Heavenly Twins*, however, to copy from it a passage which he abridged and dated 'May 1893'.

> '"We are long past the time when there was only one incident of interest in a woman's life, & that was its love affair . . . It is stupid to narrow it [life] down to the indulgence of one particular set of emotions . . . to swamp every faculty by constant cultivation of the animal instincts."'

He must have taken the literary notebooks up to London with him; but did he add this item immediately after his Irish visit, during which he met Florence Henniker – or had he already done it before he left? At all events, he was well aware that Mrs Henniker would realize that she had potential rivals, and ones who could also be given oral lessons, if only in architecture, by the ex-architect author of *Tess*. Later, after he had given up hope of being anything more than a friend to her, he told her on 16 September:

> If you mean to make the world listen to you, you must say now what they will all be thinking & saying five & twenty years hence: & if you do that you must offend your conventional friends. 'Sarah Grand', who has not, to my mind, such a sympathetic & intuitive knowledge of human nature as you, has yet an immense advantage over you in

this respect – in the fact of having decided to offend her friends (so she told me) – & now that they are all alienated she can write boldly, & get listened to.

But Florence was not made of that kind of stuff, nor does her fiction show any superiority to Sarah Grand's on that account.

Ibsen, in translations by Gosse, William Archer and others, was just then the playwright whom enlightened and 'emancipated' people had to see. Tom was an eager defender of him. He had already seen *Hedda Gabler* and *Rosmersholm* earlier in that week ending 10 June; on the 8th he apparently lunched with Pearl Craigie and went to yet another Ibsen play, *The Master Builder*, in the company of Mrs Henniker and her sister and brother-in-law, Sir Gerald Fitzgerald. Tom seems to have contrived to get Florence alone at, or perhaps just after, the play: in his letter of 10 June, written in the Athenaeum while bishops ('lords spiritual') snored around him, he wrote, as a postscript:

I am afraid my chronicle is mere 'frivel', or a great part of it: but having made a serious business of un-serious things I must follow on for the present, to redress by any possible means the one-sidedness I spoke of, of which I am still keenly conscious.

I sincerely hope to number you all my life among the most valued of my friends.

In the *Life* he reports Mrs Henniker as having been 'so excited by the play as not to be able to sleep all night'. Was she excited only by the play? What had he said to her? What did he mean by 'one-sidedness'? She had in some way reproached him – but for what exactly, and with how much sincerity? His note at the end of that month suggests that he had been *honest*, and that she, as a society-trained strategist (this was not necessarily pejorative, and, after all, his novels show that he knew all about that kind of thing), had not 'managed' him very successfully. Did he want to make her his mistress? If the poem 'The Thing Unplanned' does refer to her then he could not, initially, have desired only what he later called a 'spiritual union'. 'One-sidedness' must be equated with the later Ibsenite word he used in letters to her 'trollish': sexually desirous.

Tom's own little one-acter *The Three Wayfarers*, done at James Barrie's suggestion from his story 'The Three Strangers', had been running all that week, with three other short works, at Terry's Theatre. Mrs Henniker did not get to see it before it had to close after only a few performances. If Tom was disappointed, he did not show it. He had already called it, to her, 'my little scrap of a play'. There is no extant letter to her between 10 and 20 June, though he probably wrote several. The tone of the 20 June letter, again written from the Athenaeum, suggests that she may have forgiven his 'one-sidedness'. He boldly proposed a rendezvous for the following Saturday, 24 June, '1/4 past ten, Sloane Square Station, shall we say? – if no earlier day'. The time was to be devoted to instruction in architecture. Another sentence reads: 'Well – perhaps you are right about the story of the two people spiritually united – as far as the man is concerned.' There may have been some real story, something she was working on and wanted advice about; more likely the letter is coded, so that her husband could read it without being made anxious. Henniker was resolutely unimaginative, and even Ibsen would have been a mystery to him.

On 29 June he wrote again, telling her that he had been reading *Foiled*, which he found 'really . . . clever' and better, as 'a transcript from human nature', than *The Heavenly Twins*. 'If I were ever to consult any woman on a point in my own novels I should let that woman be yourself – my belief in your sympathy and insight being strong, and increasing'. This would not have pleased Emma, had she read it; she must by now have guessed which way the wind was blowing. Since she had done so much for Tom – not least come to his rescue when he fell ill at the beginning of *A Laodicean* – her unhappiness is as understandable as his excitement.

But he continued, despite his promise, to be 'one-sided' towards Florence, and continued with this rather risky paragraph (he was to obtain from her, in due course, many photographs of herself brilliantly, if not quite excessively, *décolletée*):

> After the theatre we met . . . a great many vain people we knew . . . A well known woman in society, who is one of those despicable creatures a flirt, said to me when I was talking to her: 'Don't look at me so!' I said, 'Why? – because you feel I can see *too much of you?*' (she was excessively *décolletée*). 'Good heavens!' said she. 'I am not coming to pieces, am I?' and clutching her bodice she was quite overcome. When next I met her she said bitterly: 'You have spoilt my evening: and it was too cruel of you!' However I don't think it was, for she deserved it.

Tom, who could be wise even while he was being foolish, knew that a reproach to someone is best – and, paradoxically, most clearly –

conveyed by oblique means. A direct accusation risks putting a person on the defensive, whereas a parabolic reproach carries no such implications, and can only be 'taken personally' in the internal sense required for it to be effective. Here he is – if she can take it that way – warning Florence not to be 'despicable' or flirtatious, not to offer him the promise of her breasts; and he is, simultaneously, reproaching her for having done so. This is not to say that he did not, in his fifty-three-year-old excitement, exaggerate whatever signals she really was putting out to him. Probably the signals were confused. She was not excessively conventional, but conventional she certainly was: there is nothing to indicate otherwise. So she must have been both flattered and afraid: flattered by the attentions of a leading novelist whose work she genuinely admired (and was, to a reasonable degree, capable of appreciating), but afraid for her secure and socially – if not spiritually – satisfying marriage, and for her reputation. She may even have reciprocated his feelings for her, but drawn back from expression of them. Tom was, after all, the author of books which had scandalized many readers – and there was really no guarantee that he might not turn out to be 'scandalous' in his sexual behaviour. This may have tempted her, and even made her ready to think about risking serious indiscretion. But indiscretion to what degree? The pressure exerted upon her by Tom, for all his apologies, was mounting, and his tone seems to have been confident throughout; but it is still hard to judge how much encouragement she really gave him, or how much he 'deliberately misunderstood'.

On 30 June he wrote suggesting that he escort her by underground train from Sloane Square to Portland Road, on their way to visit his friend Mrs Moulton on the following Tuesday, 4 July: 'it will be no trouble'. Evidently Florence had asked him to write 'the true names of the places' in her copy of Tess, and he agreed, adding that the idea 'is a very pleasing one'. He had not done it for anyone else, but 'you may not think it any objection in the future that you will possess the only copy thus marked'. He was glad that she was coming to town again so soon; his own engagements were 'getting less'.

She agreed to the meeting he had proposed, as a means (of course) of getting her to himself, and on Sunday, 2 July he wrote, 'I have received your card, and shall be much pleased to conduct you through the pestilential vapours of the Underground to Mrs Moulton's: your sister [Mrs Fitzgerald] may be sure you will be in safe hands.' With her card she had sent him three sets of her translations: one each from German, French and Spanish. He inserted them into the second volume of his literary notebooks, adding to each of them, in pencil, the date 'June 30, 1893'; there they remained until after his death. They were on ruled stationery, and may or may not have been executed especially for the occasion. The German poem 'An Autumn Lyric' is from Lebrecht Drêves, an obscure romantic (except that he was favoured by Eichendorff). The other two poems are better known: 'From the Spanish of G. Becquer' and Gautier's 'Affinity'. Gustavo Adolfo Bécquer (1836–70) was the pre-eminent Spanish poet of his time, and his single volume, *Rimas*, on the theme of a failed love affair, offered the point of departure for the modern poetry of his country. Florence's choice showed both good taste and knowledge.

This sending of poems, if translated ones, really did amount to a signal, and one which she may shortly afterwards have regretted sending. The German verses end:

> The love & the weeping; – the rapture & sorrow,
> Are they but dreams that come never again?
> What will be left when the day knows no morrow?
> Darling, we sigh, but we question in vain.

> Though the perfumes be shed, & the rose-leaves be blighted,
> The new year must come, & the new roses blow,
> And lovers will kiss, & their vows shall be plighted
> On the green of our graves, while we slumber below.

This is a theme that Tom himself frequently touched upon, but we must remember that Florence Henniker knew him '*intuitively*' at that time, and not as a poet at all.

The Bécquer poem (from *Rimas*, xxx) is shorter:

> We were together, – her eyes were wet,
> But her pride was strong, & no tears would fall;
> And *I* would not tell her I loved her yet,
> And yearned to forgive her all!

> So, now that our lives are forever apart,
> *She* thinks – 'Oh! had I but wept that day!'
> And *I* ask in vain of my lonely heart –
> 'Ah! why did I turn away?'

No wonder he was excited.

The Gautier consists of eleven quatrains, translated from '*Affinités secrètes: madrigal panthéiste*' (Tom may have known the French title since he was familiar with some of Gautier), and is concerned with the souls of two lovers, imprisoned in blocks of stone. It begins:

> Yet each, by a strange metamorphosis
> Is born anew in some fairer form;
> And the rose may live in red lips that kiss, –
> And marble in limbs that are white and warm!

and ends:

> So my heart, that within me burns & glows,
> Would read *your* heart, – ask you whether
> You were pearl, or marble, or dove, or rose
> In that fairer world, when we were together.

Whatever Florence meant by sending him these – and it cannot just have been to demonstrate her talent for translation – he was set on fire by the promise of red lips, and even more by the notion of white, warm limbs released, by his passion, from their marble form. 'What beautiful translations those are! I like the two verses from the Spanish best,' he replied in his letter of 2 July. And he was going to escort her through the pestilential vapours within forty-eight hours! What happened on that journey? Certainly he would have talked of those poems. And the one he told her that he preferred, the Bécquer, surely provided him, as Wilson was the first to suggest, with the occasion of one of his most famous and cryptic poems, 'Had You Wept' (*Satires of Circumstance*). Many theories, some bizarre, have been put forward about this poem. However, the Bécquer-Henniker poem is its source:

> Had you wept; had you but neared me with a hazed uncertain ray,
> Dewy as the face of the dawn, in your large and luminous eye,
> Then would have come back all the joys the tidings had slain
>   that day,
> And a new beginning, a fresh fair heaven, have smoothed the things
>   awry.
> But you were less feebly human, and no passionate need for
>   clinging

FLORENCE HENNIKER

Possessed your soul to overthrow reserve when I came near;
Ay, though you suffer as much as I from storms the hours are
   bringing
Upon your heart and mine, I never see you shed a tear.

The deep strong woman is weakest, the weak one is the strong;
The weapon of all weapons best for winning, you have not
   used;
Have you never been able, or would you not, through the evil
   times and long?
Has not the gift been given you, or such gift have you refused?
When I bade me not absolve you on that evening or the morrow,
Why did you not make war on me with those who weep like rain?
You felt too much, so gained no balm for all your torrid
   sorrow,
And hence our deep division, and our dark undying pain.

Although he believes the poem has no 'biographical significance at
all', Wilson thinks it is addressed to Florence Henniker. But it is not. It
was written after Emma's death, she is the addressee, and the subject is
his affair, or attempted affair, with their friend. At some time – probably
after his journey to Winchester with Florence on 8 August 1893, at
which point he gave up hope of gaining more than friendship from
her – he must have told her about the state of his feelings. This is
made all the more likely by the fact that he told Rebekah Owen
about this meeting quite soon after it took place – and he certainly
was not so poor a student of human nature as to do that if he wanted
it kept secret.

   Looking back at this event twenty or so years later, as he writes the
poem, he sees that Emma's frozen and 'strong' response to his confession
prevented the 'new beginning' that they might have had. It is being far
too literal to claim that the poem cannot be to Emma because her
eyes were not 'large and luminous', whereas Florence Dugdale/Hardy's
were. The latter is true; but anyone's 'eye' can seem 'large and luminous'
under certain circumstances. That would be a careless reading of a poem
whose addressee precisely does *not* require to have that large-seeming,
luminous eye which is the prelude to tears: the sense is, '*if* you had
come near to me with your eye luminous with a tear – but you
didn't'.

   The poem explores the paradox of weakness and strength in women, and in addition defines Emma as one who found it hard to cast off her reserve and show her feelings, yet as one who 'felt too much'. It is thus a tribute, declaring, 'you refused to stoop to emotional blackmail' – although that is a banal way, beside the poem, of saying it.

Soon after Tom had made the visit to Mrs Moulton in company with Florence Henniker, he and Emma returned to Max Gate, on about 11 or 12 July; but he was back in London, staying with the Jeunes in Harley Street, from the 19th until the 27th. He did not see Florence while he was there, but did manage to visit her at her temporary home, in Southsea, on his way up. He was not yet ready to write the *Pall Mall* story, he told the agent W.M. Colles on 13 July: 'not until after next week'. But he did not in fact write it until early September, and by then he had something to write it about.

'An Imaginative Woman' is not 'about' Florence Henniker, but it is deeply influenced by the circumstances of his encounter with her – so much so that he had to say, in the *Life*: '*December*. Found and touched up a story called "An Imaginative Woman".' He did not 'find' it at all – and it is such a good example of his grim humour that he probably felt a little guilty about it, even though he had not spared himself in it any more than he had spared poor Florence.

On the same day that he wrote to Colles, he also wrote to Florence. He tried to tempt her up to London, to a dinner, dangling Lena Milman as a possible substitute, and then added: 'I would give Ada Rehan [American actress appearing in London], Miss Milman, Lady G. Little, her sister, Mrs S. Wortley, or any other of that ilk, lessons in architecture at astonishingly low fees, to fill up the time.' Subsequently she playfully begged him not to do this. Then:

> You seem quite like an old friend to me, and I only hope that Time will bear out the seeming. Indeed, but for an adverse stroke of fate, you would be – a friend of 13 years standing [he alludes to her father's invitation to him to Fryston, which he could not accept owing to his long illness] . . . I am afraid I am lapsing into a morbid mood; and my whole letter is very inadequate to the occasion, and to what should be written to such a valued correspondent.

By return she sent him Gleeson White's *Ballades* and *Rondeaus*, which contained twelve poems by Rosamund Tomson. This led to further warning remarks, in his letter of 16 July. He had last met her on the afternoon of the day he left London for Max Gate, although he had already told her that he was 'glad' he had called. Any discouragement, then, is more likely to have been contained in her letter of reply to his of 13 July. There is a hint of reproach in his third paragraph:

> As to my beginning to write again Heaven only knows when I shall do it. – I feel much more inclined to fly off to foreign scenes or plunge into wild dissipation. Next week in London may bring some change of mood. And though at Lady J's dinner I may be able to fill your place at table with some new female acquaintance she will certainly not remove my disappointment at your absence.
>
> I will religiously obey orders about the architectural lessons. You shall hold the copyright in them. Is not that promise very handsome of me?

That implies: 'So you will not even leave your dreary husband to get up to dinner with me which you easily could.' But what follows is more serious and direct:

> I too have been reading 'Epipsychidion' – indeed by mutual influence we must have been reading it simultaneously. I had a regret in reading it at thinking that one who is pre-eminently the child of the Shelleyan tradition – whom one would have expected to be an ardent disciple of his school and views – should have allowed herself to be enfeebled to a belief in ritual ecclesiasticism. My impression is that you do not know your own views. You feel the need of emotional expression of some sort, and being surrounded by the conventional society form of such expression you have mechanically adopted it. Is this the daughter of the man who went from Cambridge to Oxford on the now historic errand! [Monckton-Milnes, as one of the so-called Apostles, and as a representative of the Cambridge Union, went with Hallam to the Oxford Union, in December 1829, to argue that Shelley was a superior poet to Byron – it was actually not all that 'historic' an errand, though known about.] Depend upon it there are other values [thus the Millgate-Purdy edition of the letters, but is it not more likely to be 'valves', as it has also been read?] for feelings than the ordinances of Mother Church – my Mother Church no less than yours.

Now the gloves were off. Immediately following is the paragraph about trusting, in the future, to his imagination 'for an enfranchised woman', occasioned by Rosamund Tomson's pieces in the *Ballades* volume she had sent to him. But evidently he had not really given up; or perhaps her reply to this letter gave him new hope – and did so deliberately.

Epipsychidion is a poem describing Shelley's lifelong pursuit of the image of the beloved, of Eternal Beauty, and contains outspoken and unequivocal praise of free love (called by him 'True Love'), together with an attack on conventional marriage. Tom was indeed putting his cards on the table, especially since Florence, too, had just been reading the poem. Its theme is echoed in the novel he had just serialized, but had not yet put into volume form. Shelley wrote:

> In many mortal forms I rashly sought
> The shadow of that idol of my thought.
> And some were fair – but beauty dies away:
> Others were wise – but honeyed words betray:
> And One was true – oh! why not true to me?

On the following day he wrote to Lena Milman about Herbert Spencer, perhaps thinking as he did so that she was more worthy. But by the next day, 18 July, he had faith in Florence once again: she had invited him to lunch on his way up to London!

> This is rather a happy thought, of my coming to see you, since I shall be so near. My thanks for your kind invitation to lunch with you and your cousins; but it will be more convenient to myself to call afterwards, and as you are going out early I will be there at 2. I afterwards continue my journey to London.

This visit took more trouble than Tom would admit to, but Florence was his life-blood just then; his refusal of the lunch invitation both saved his face a little and got him out of a boring hour and a half chattering to Florence's probably non-Shelleyan, and certainly non-free-loving, cousins. He added in his postcript:

> What I meant about your unfaithfulness to the Shelley cult referred not to any lack of poetic emotion, but to your view of things: e.g. you are quite out of harmony with this line of his in Epipsychidion:
> 'The sightless tyrants of our fate'
> which beautifully expresses one's consciousness of blind circumstances beating upon one, without any feeling, or against.

Clearly she had been thrusting Anglican correctitudes at him, and it had irritated him. Possibly, too, and despite an air of conventionality, she really believed in these. Perhaps, fired by the Bécquer verses and other encouragements, he was holding the Shelleyan gun at her head; perhaps she pleaded an affection for Emma, of whom she had seen much in Ireland. Perhaps she had told Tom, or hinted, that she would like to become his lover but could not do so. This is the most likely: it best fits Tom's reactions. I think it certain, however, that they never were lovers, and that, indeed, the relationship never did proceed in the direction Tom desired – even to a kiss.

Meanwhile, he kept up his attack. It is not known what transpired between them when he called upon her at Southsea, but he wrote to her from the Jeunes' house in Harley Street on 20 July, giving as his excuse that it was too wet to do anything else. Since Shelley had failed, he was now planning to send her something even more shocking, Swinburne's *Poems and Ballads*: he was going to hunt them up as soon as it stopped raining. Her father had been of great help to Swinburne, and she must have read this most famous of his volumes. But that did not deter him. Evidently he had taken with him to Southsea a book which he had lent her, and she had lent him one in turn: 'Please keep the volume I lent you, say for a month or two, marking or annotating anything, and I will do the same in yours: we can then restore each to each . . . ' Unfortunately it is not known what these volumes were, but perhaps his loan was connected with his hope for her enlightenment: 'I cannot help wishing you were free from certain retrograde superstitions: and I believe you will be some day, and none the less happy for the emancipation.' Was it Spencer's *First Principles*? Probably not: Tom would have realized that, however valuably effective on the imagination Spencer could be – as he affirmed to Miss Milman – he lacked a concomitantly amorous power. The book she gave him was almost certainly the *Poetical Works* of Dante Gabriel Rossetti, newly edited by his tax-man brother, William.

Tom's letter of 24 July to Emma, also from Harley Street, says that he is 'feeling very tired'; he is 'doing next to nothing'; had he not promised to dine on the 26th with Sir Henry Thompson, the eminent surgeon whom he had consulted after his serious illness of 1880–81, he would 'have returned this morning'. He tells her of the goings-on at the Jeunes, and of his attendance with them at a 'farewell performance' by the actor Sir Henry Irving.

On 30 July, after his return, he and Emma entertained to lunch their neighbour from Radipole in Dorset, Mrs Richard Eliot (her husband was a lawyer, JP and reader of Tom's books), and were intrigued by her story of twins who had different birthdays, one having been born on 31 May between eleven and twelve and the next on 1 June between midnight and one.

On 8 August, having written a letter on the 3rd which apparently caused offence and was therefore destroyed, he slipped away to meet Florence Henniker at Eastleigh, a station near Southampton which was on his usual route from Dorchester South to Waterloo. They intended to visit Winchester together. Whether he told Emma that he was going to do so is not known; in all probability, in accordance with his honesty, he did so, although it is unlikely that at this point he added that he was in love with Florence and had written a day or two earlier to tell her so – later in the year, on 6 October, he declared that 'letters have grown trollish again of late'. Doubtless that one of 3 August had been the most trollish of all. Two days after writing it he had copied into his literary notebooks these lines from Dante Gabriel Rossetti's poem 'Spheral Change', though without observing the stanza break, and mistranscribing one word and a few insignificant details of punctuation:

> Oh dearest, while we lived and died
>   A living death in every day,
> Some hours we still were side by side,
>   When where I was you too might stay
>   And rest and need not go away.
> O nearest, furthest! can there be
>   At length some hard-earned heart-won home,
> Where – exile changed to [original has 'for'] sanctuary –
>   Our lot may fill indeed its sum
> And you may wait, and I may come.

The preceding stanza reads:

> If only one might speak! – the one
>   Who never waits 'til I come near;
> But always seated all alone
>   As listening to the sunken air,
>   Is gone before I come to her.

It is not known when the arrangements for the Winchester visit were made; was the excuse the architecture of the cathedral there? But it always remained fresh in Tom's memory, as confirmed by the fact that some years after his death, Florence Hardy talked to Henry Reed about it, and even told him that, when the two went into the George Inn in Winchester to have lunch, and Mrs Henniker wanted to wash her hands, a servant showed them into a bedroom, believing they were married. This incident would have added a pleasant touch to their story, especially for a student of life's little ironies. In the railway carriage on the way to Winchester (a journey of fifteen minutes at the outside), Florence Henniker made her feelings, or at least her decision, clear to him. Perhaps, like Jocelyn Pierston in *The Well-Beloved* when he is travelling up to London with Marcia Bencombe, the 'guard looked in, thought they were lovers, and did not show other travellers into that compartment', and, perhaps too, like Jocelyn, Tom 'dreaded intrusion'.

He resented what she had to tell him on that brief trip (or perhaps it was when they were returning, *after* clasping hands at the high altar in the cathedral – but Tom's wording suggests otherwise), for on 17 August, after returning from a visit he had made with Emma to their friends the Milnes-Gaskells at Wenlock Abbey, he told her so. After a brief description of the Wenlock trip, he wrote:

> You allude to the letter of Aug 3. If I shd never write to you again as in that letter you must remember that it was written *before* you expressed your views – 'morbid!' indeed! *petty* rather – in the railway carriage when we met at Eastleigh. But I'm always your friend.

This is cryptic, and we should not pretend to understand exactly what it means. However, I take it that, originally, Florence Henniker had led him on to expect not an elopement but what would then have been called a discreet liaison – a physical relationship. The implications of the word 'trollish' were, after all, known to both of them, and used by Tom in due time – as though his state of sexual desire for her had been declared and was well understood by both. The sentence 'I am always your *friend*' substantiates this: 'friend' as distinct from 'lover'. The sense of 'If I shd never write to you again as in that letter . . .' is 'Since I have been forbidden . . .'. Once again, Tom was simply being honest. True, it is hard to imagine his being so direct in private social intercourse, because he was so reticent in public; but there is in fact every reason to suppose that he was direct when he did not feel

491

overlooked. Reports of his social reticence tend to come from strangers: callers, journalists, tourists. Not Graves, Sassoon, T.E. Lawrence nor Blunden (who knew him particularly well, and to whom he responded with great warmth) thought him in the least reticent, and Blunden 'knew he was a real countryman' when he urinated as he walked, without stopping what he was saying or adjusting his stride. Fancy if Mrs Oliphant had known that! Nor could he have been exactly reticent, even by his own account, with Pearl Craigie. He took a two-hour walk with her while he and Emma were the guests of the Jeunes at their country house, during which 'she explained to him her reasons for joining the Roman Catholic Church, a step which had vexed him somewhat. Apparently he did not consider her reasons satisfactory, but their friendship remained unbroken.'

Tom's reference to morbidity, if this is what it seems to be – an allusion to something that Mrs Henniker herself said about her reasons for resisting him? – is a little puzzling. But such a remark as 'I am sorry to seem morbid, but my religious convictions . . .' would have been a reasonable get-out in those days. You might assail a lady, but not her religious convictions. More likely, she may not have been a sexually responsive woman, and for all we know may have married Henniker-Major in 1882 because he had promised to make few 'demands' upon her, or even because he really preferred officers or slim young drummers. Who knows? Tom was shortly to represent her as possessing a very peculiar sexual make-up when he took her as his part-model for Sue Bridehead. What Tom called 'petty' in her is anyone's guess, but one thing is certain: he would not have described religious or moral scruples in such a manner had he believed them to be genuine. The best guess as to what he meant could doubtless be summed up in some such words as 'too conventional to be a true Shelleyan'.

Their progress on that day is known, if Rebekah Owen and Clodd are to be trusted on the matter of what he told them. After lunch at the George they attended Evensong in the cathedral. For the first time for almost exactly twenty years Tom commemorated this fact in his prayer book. The last time he had marked anything in it had been when he went to church with Emma on 8 September 1872. Then, at St Juliot, he had read the lesson (Jeremiah 36: the story of the burning rolls). He then marked the Gospel for the day, Matthew 6, 24: 'No man can serve two masters: for either he will hate the one, and love the other; or else he will hold to the one, and despise the other. Ye cannot serve God and mammon.' By Psalm 41 ('Blessed is he that considereth the poor . . .')

he had written 'Day 8, St. Juliot, Sept. '72'. Now, or soon afterwards, he wrote beneath that note, 'Aug 8, 1893, Winchester'. After the service he and Florence walked out to the spot where Angel Clare and 'Liza-Lu saw the black flag raised as a signal of male vengeance upon Tess for killing that most precious thing: one of their own. In 1896 he told Clodd, a confidant in such matters, that he had clasped hands with Florence before the high altar; Clodd wrote this up in his diary.

It might have been at this meeting that Tom offered her the definite chance of becoming his literary collaborator: the matter was first raised in the letter of 20 July: 'I will think over the scheme of our collaborating in the talked of story . . . ' By 6 September he was returning her own stories to her, with 'scribblings for amendments on their pages', and pointing out that 'the simple & sole fault' of one called 'His Excellency' was 'its conventional conclusion'. He was not going to allow her to get away with any more 'conventionality', at least not of a purely literary kind! But the matter of what eventually became the indifferent story 'The Spectre of the Real' (at first mischievously referred to, by him, as 'The Desire') does not arise in his letters again until 10 September, when he sent her his modification of 'the "Desire" sketch'. It finally appeared in Jerome K. Jerome's magazine *To-Day* in November 1894. It is essentially his work, but unfortunately subdued by those touches of hers which he tactfully allowed in. Millgate's verdict on its literary value cannot be bettered: it was, he says, 'compromised not so much by Mrs Henniker's participation as by Hardy's attempt to give that participation a greater substance than the circumstances really allowed'. There is no reason, human nature being what it is, to suggest that Tom did not communicate his difficulties in this collaboration to Emma, who might after all have wished her own writings to remain quite independent of her famous husband's name. When these were published, they certainly showed less literary accomplishment than Mrs Henniker's – but they were infinitely more interesting.

He was now able to thank Florence for the present she planned to send him, the nature of which may well have considerably annoyed him (or, of course, simply tickled his sense of humour):

What a thoughtful present you tell me of! Oddly enough I am badly off in inkstands. But really I have done nothing to deserve it. The pleasure however, will lie in thinking that it gave you pleasure to get it for me. Certainly the next big story [*Jude*] shall be written from its contents.

He could not resist a further good-humoured jab at her, playing on the apt title of Jones' play:

> Henry Arthur Jones is going to read a new play next week, called 'The Tempter' (a good title) . . .
> You may be thankful to hear that the *one-sidedness* I used to remind you of is disappearing from the situation. But you will always be among the most valued of my friends, as I hope always to remain one at least of the rank & file of yours.

The conclusion of the final sentence hints at Mrs Henniker's undoubted preference for social life over literature, or at least the theories of Shelley. But he was genuinely grateful for the inscribed silver inkstand ('T.H. from F.H. 1893'), and used it for the rest of his life. For he really was determined to will, or at the very least sublimate, the surging sublime, and do the 'thing better' – and, indeed he quickly got down to work on the new novel, in which her sexuality would be depicted as Sue Bridehead's. He thanked her in a short letter of 13 September; but by the 15th, encouraged by a letter from her, he was in sterner (and bawdier) mood:

> I wrote this with ink from your pretty present; & have already jotted down a few notes for the next long story – which I hope may be big as well as long.
> Since you are nice, & a *little* candid in your last, I will be *quite* so, & tell you that I was a trifle chilled by your letters from Dublin [it is not clear when those were written, but Mrs Henniker was very frequently there] & your first from Crewe [Crewe Hall, in Cheshire, the seat of her uncle, Lord Crewe], & much regretted having sent the effusive ones to which they were in answer, especially as you read parts of them aloud. Feeling that something was influencing you adversely, & destroying the charm of your letters & personality, I lost confidence in you somewhat. I know, of course, that there is nothing in my epistles which it matters in the least about all the world knowing, but I have always a feeling that such publicity destroys the pleasure of a friendly correspondence.

He then went on to add the somewhat odd paragraph: 'I thought you might know that Capt. Henniker [her husband] & I had corresponded.'

FLORENCE HENNIKER

What they could have corresponded about remains problematical, but it would not have been about his new, long and, he hoped, big novel.

It had been insensitive and disloyal of Florence Henniker to read his letters aloud, to her family and friends. Did she do it in order, simultaneously, to show off and to persuade herself that she had not been coquettish with him? He remained devoted to her until her death, and she must have been a pleasantly mannered woman – yet one wonders, too, whether he did not have his reservations about her, and whether those reservations were always wholly private. One of the poems associated with her, and said to have resulted from her failure to turn up at an appointment they had made at the British Museum, is 'A Broken Appointment'.

> You did not come,
> And marching Time drew on, and wore me numb. –
> Yet less for loss of your dear presence there
> Than that I thus found lacking in your make
> That high compassion which can overbear
> Reluctance for pure lovingkindness' sake
> Grieved I, when, as the hope-hour stroked its sum,
> You did not come.
>
> You love not me,
> And love alone can lend you loyalty;
> – I know, and knew it. But, unto the store
> Of human deeds divine in all but name,
> Was it not worth a little hour or more
> To add yet this: Once you, a woman, came
> To soothe a time-torn man; even though it be
> You love not me.

This is not an attack on someone for failing to keep an appointment, for which there might have been any number of good reasons. It is an appraisal of character prompted by that failure, which is seen as unhappily characteristic. The triviality is deliberately counterpointed by the high stateliness of the lines themselves, which underlines the grave typicality of the incident: here is one who was much loved, and who finally failed the test. And it may be that Florence Henniker was, for all her charm, poise, good humour and indignation against cruelty to animals, both cold and hard, with an added touch of the coquette –

and therefore a profound disappointment to a man who had determined that his love should not alter when it alteration found. Were we to judge her work, not by its literary values, but by the amount of heart in it, then we might well find it deficient – and deficient exactly for the reason that grieved Tom, for its lapses into the conventional and for its superficiality.

He stayed loyal to her throughout the rest of her life. When her husband went to South Africa as commander of the 2nd battalion of the Coldstream Guards Tom wrote specially to him ('I have long thought you the most perfect type of the practical soldier that I know'), even though he vigorously opposed the Boer War. Later he sympathized with her when she was widowed. He took the trouble to arrange that the agent A. P. Watt, with whom he had occasional dealings, should handle her literary affairs to their best advantage. He seems to have been able to enjoy the best of her, too. But he always regretted what he saw as the foolish and unrealistic social arrangements which had forbidden his conducting a full physical liaison with her. He may, too, have continued to believe that the opportunity to love, in the fullest sense, might have awakened and released her from the bonds of convention and hypocrisy in which she was imprisoned.

In Tom's letters to her for the rest of 1893 – after that they became more occasional – the intensity of his interest in her peters out only gradually. If he felt it tactless and insensitive of her to continue to send him 'beautiful large photographs' of herself, then he did not say so, but thanked her effusively for them, as on 6 October: 'I prize them all highly, though they represent only the outward form of my most charming friend!' His criticism of her style of life, and his view of what it would do for her creative aspirations, is maintained, if at a low ebb: '. . . perhaps you are so engrossed with millionaire sportsmen that you take small thought of a mere scribbler who would not kill a fly!' This letter continues:

> I did not at all *mean* my last note to be unkind, & am sorry that it seemed so, & hurt you about the MS. The fact is that letters have grown trollish again of late; therefore I propose to drop the subjects we drifted into, which we can explain when we meet. Never would I give *you* pain!

The final sentence there certainly implies that she had given *him* pain. But he also recognized how drastic his 'Shelleyan' attitudes must have seemed. Most people in those days made a bow to Shelley, and then forgot about his extremist proposals. Not so Tom, although he was well aware of their shortcomings. He ended his letter: 'So far from my not forgiving you anything, & not feeling as friendly as ever, I can say that if we are not to be the *thorough* friends in future that we hitherto have been, life will have lost a very very great attraction . . . '

Apart from a few remarks such as 'I would say I much wish to see you again if I thought you wished to see me' (22 October), the letters from this time become affectionate, and concentrate on helping her with her writing, which he may have come to see in a different light. Almost the last truly felt passage came at the end of the year, in a letter of 18 December, when he may have been philosophically reviewing, to himself, the happenings of the previous year:

Of course I shall *never* dislike you, unless you do what you cannot do – turn out to be a totally different woman from what I know you to be. I won't have you say that there is little good in you. One great gain from that *last* meeting [earlier that month, in London] is that it revived in my consciousness certain nice & dear features in your character which I had half forgotten, through their being of that ethereal intangible sort which letters cannot convey. If you have only *one* good quality, a good *heart*, you are good enough for me.

But a letter to her of 15 January 1894, the last known one of that batch, significantly mentions the development of the character of Sue Bridehead just before delivering the final, sad verdict:

I am creeping on a little with the long story, & am beginning to get interested in my heroine as she takes shape & reality: though she is very nebulous at present . . .
I have been thinking that the sort of friend one wants most is a friend with whom mutual confessions can be made of weaknesses without fear of reproach or contempt. Do you want such a one for yourself? – I wonder if I shall ever find one?

And that, politeness and true regard and superficial friendship apart, was the virtual end of that.

Not many of Tom's poems – six or so out of almost a thousand known ones – can with any degree of certainty be associated with

Florence Henniker. The chief ones, apart from those already mentioned, are 'At an Inn', 'The Division', 'A Thunderstorm in Town', 'The Month's Calendar' and 'In Death Divided'. They tell us nothing more, although 'At an Inn' tends to confirm that the people at the George did take them as married, as he told Florence Hardy — and he himself certainly told Hermann Lea that the poem was actually written there (but this seems highly unlikely, unless it was tossed off while Florence was 'washing her hands'):

> When we as strangers sought
>   Their catering care,
> Veiled smiles bespoke their thought
>   Of what we were.
> They warmed as they opined
>   Us more than friends —
> That we had all resigned
>   For love's dear ends.

They even wish that 'bliss like theirs/Would flush our day!'; but

> . . . we were left alone
>   As Love's own pair;
> Yet never the love-light shone
>   Between us there!
> But that which chilled the breath
>   Of afternoon,
> And palsied unto death
>   The pane-fly's tune.

Love 'lingered numb':

> As we seemed we were not
>   That day afar,
> And now we seem not what
>   We aching are.
> O severing sea and land,
>   O laws of men,
> Ere death, once let us stand
>   As we stood then!

Pointedly, on 15 February 1899, telling Florence that he had received a request to set the poem to music, he wrote: 'You have never noticed that one, by the way.' If she had not, then this was because its last stanza might have suggested to a reader that she, a respectable married woman, might be 'aching' under the effect of some illicit emotion – she was just not that sort, and it was Tom's great loss.

'The Division', dated '1893' but not published until *Time's Laughing-stocks* (1909), underlines the keenness with which he deplored what he saw as Mrs Henniker's imprisonment in the meshes of conventionality, and may even imply that she actually confessed to him that she did not 'love' her husband:

> Rain on the windows, creaking doors,
>   With blasts that besom the green,
> And I am here, and you are there,
>   And a hundred miles between!
>
> O were it but the weather, Dear,
>   O were it but the miles
> That summed up all our severance,
>   There might be room for smiles.
>
> But that thwart thing betwixt us twain,
>   Which nothing cleaves or clears,
> Is more than distance, Dear, or rain,
>   And longer than the years!

On 14 September Tom had told Colles that he had 'the P.M.M. [*Pall Mall Magazine*] story . . . ready. Are you in town, & shall it be sent to you?' 'An Imaginative Woman' is one of the few unequivocal masterpieces of comi-tragedy among his short stories. It is one of his final comments on the conventional and sentimental fiction which, to a certain extent, he had had to pretend to write over the past quarter of a century, in order to gain a living in a world which dutifully and respectfully read poetry but without adhering to any of its principles. As I have said, the story is not 'about' Mrs Henniker in a literal sense; yet it contains comment upon her situation – if she had been able to make use of it. I doubt, however, that she was able to do so.

The plot has its roots in Flaubert, and Mrs Ella Marchmill's 'imagi-nativeness' (Tom had initially entitled it 'A Woman of Imagination', and his change is instructive) is of the Bovary type. She is married unhappily to a brutal and commonplace man, whose business is 'that of a gunmaker in a thriving city', and whose 'soul was in that business always'. The setting is Solentsea, which is none other, in the Hardyan scheme, than Southsea – temporary home of the Hennikers. As if to distance himself from any notion that Ella Marchmill (Florence's full married name was Florence *Ellen* Hungerford Henniker-Major) could be taken to be a representation of Mrs Henniker, his narrator caused her to shrink 'humanely . . . from detailed knowledge of her husband's trade whenever she reflected that everything he manufactured had for its purpose the destruction of life' but to hope also that 'some, at least, of his weapons were sooner or later used for the extermination of horrid vermin and animals almost as cruel to their inferiors in species as human beings were to theirs'. It was pretty in women to entertain such emotions, always provided they were not acted upon; but Florence Henniker, as a lover of animals, would probably not have wanted her husband's guns used to kill any animals, even horrid vermin. Nor is William Marchmill, of course, an exact portrait of Henniker, whom Tom then hardly knew, if at all. However, the fact remained that however 'refined' he might be, he could not give his wife either the sort of companionship or the kind of conversation that she desired. Like his analogue, he was probably 'supremely satisfied with a condition of sublunary things which made weapons a necessity'. No Shelleyan, in fact. Had she admitted as much to Tom? These two witheringly ironic paragraphs might have given Florence, had she been at all sensitive, or imaginative in the non-Bovaryist sense her lover thought desirable, pause for considerable reflection:

She had never antecedently regarded this occupation of his as any objection to having him for a husband. Indeed, the necessity of getting life-leased at all cost, a cardinal virtue which all good mothers teach, kept her from thinking of it all till she had closed with William, had passed the honeymoon, and reached the reflecting stage. Then, like a person who has stumbled upon some object in the dark, she wondered what she had got; mentally walked round it, estimated it; whether it were rare or common; contained gold, silver, or lead; were a clog or a pedestal, everything to her or nothing.

She came to some vague conclusions, and since then had kept her heart alive by pitying her proprietor's obtuseness and want of refinement, pitying herself, and letting off her delicate and ethereal emotions in imaginative occupations, day-dreams, and night-sighs, which would perhaps not have disturbed William, if he had known of them.

The melancholy and solitude-loving young poet with whom Ella Marchmill becomes enamoured without ever actually meeting him is given, in the published version, the name of Robert Trewe (= True). But in the manuscript he has the name Crewe: Florence's maiden name was Crewe, and it was from her uncle's residence, Crewe Hall, that Tom had received a chilly letter. His afterthought gave him the happy idea of retaining the resemblance but adding the significant homonym. Trewe is a quite deliberately humorous and satirical portrait of certain aspects of himself.

The young poet gives up his rooms at the house in Solentsea for the sake of the Marchmills and their children, and the landlady's purse, and goes to a house at a 'lonely spot' on the Isle of Wight. The landlady tells Ella that he 'is a poet – yes, really a poet – and he has a little income of his own, which is enough to write verses on, but not enough for cutting a figure, even if he cared to'. Ella is intrigued:

> Herself the only daughter of a struggling man of letters [ironic for Lord Houghton], she had during the last year or two taken to writing poems, in an endeavour to find a congenial channel in which to let flow her painfully embayed emotions . . . These poems, subscribed with a masculine pseudonym ['John Ivy'], had appeared in various obscure magazines, and in two cases in rather prominent ones. In the second of the latter the page which bore her effusion at the bottom, in smallish print, bore at the top, in large print, a few verses on the same subject by this very man, Robert Trewe.

Trewe's verse is different from that of his contemporaries: 'impassioned rather than ingenious, luxuriant rather than finished'. He is a pessimist, whose feelings sometimes outrun his 'artistic speed'. He is, reports the landlady, Mrs Hooper, often 'out of spirits . . . Odd in some things.' There is even a poem written on the wallpaper, most of which he has tried to rub out. He has written a 'mournful ballad on "Severed Lives"'(see, in this connection, Tom's 'The Division' and 'In Death Divided'). All this further fascinates poor Mrs Marchmill, who continues to try to imitate his work, and weeps because she cannot succeed. Earlier, when Trewe collected his poems, she had a volume of her own published, in like imitation, but it had fallen dead in a fortnight

– her husband paid the printer's bill along with the doctor's for delivering her third baby. Just as she is in the process of feeling some of her former 'afflatus' returning, her children discover Trewe's mackintosh, in a cupboard; this she secretly puts on, 'with the waterproof cap belonging to it'. '"The mantle of Elijah!' she said. "Would it might inspire me to rival him, glorious genius that he is!"'

When Ella asks Mrs Hooper for a photograph of Trewe she tells him that there is one in the frame in her room (usually Trewe's room):

> 'No; the Royal Duke and Duchess are in that.'
> 'Yes, so they are; but he's behind them. He belongs rightly to that frame, which I bought on purpose; but as he went away he said: "Cover me up from those strangers that are coming, for God's sake. I don't want them staring at me, and I am sure they won't want me staring at them." So I slipped in the Duke and Duchess temporarily in front of him, as they had no frame, and Royalties are more suitable for letting furnished than a private young man . . . '

As 'an adept' in 'subtle luxuriousness of fancy' Ella titillates herself with the thought of the photograph, leaving it covered and 'reserving the inspection till she could be alone, and a more romantic sea and stars outside'. This Bovary gets rids 'of superfluous garments' (a typically Hardyan touch), reads some of her poet's 'tenderest utterances', and only then takes out the photograph:

> The poet wore a luxuriant black moustache and imperial, and a slouched hat which shaded the forehead. The large dark eyes . . . showed an unlimited capacity for misery; they looked out from beneath well-shaped brows as if they were reading the universe in the microcosm of the confronter's face, and were not altogether overjoyed at what the spectacle portended.

The imagery of the erotic fantasy in which she now indulges herself is derived, as Kristin Brady noted, from lines 737–51 of Shelley's *Prometheus Unbound*. Two lines are actually quoted:

> Forms more real than living man,
> Nurslings of immortality . . .

Her husband, whom she had not expected back that night from a sailing trip, unexpectedly returns, and, with supreme irony, a fourth child is conceived. In the morning Marchmill awakens, wondering what it is 'that has been crackling under me so': it is Trewe's photograph, which she hastily slipped under the pillow when he arrived, and which she now manages to explain away.

When she has returned home she writes to Trewe, as 'John Ivy', to express her admiration for him. He replies briefly and courteously: he will look out for Mr Ivy's productions in the future. She begins to send him her verses, 'which he very kindly accepted, although he did not say he sedulously read them, nor did he send her any of his own in return'. Then she learns that Trewe is in Wales with the landscape painter brother of 'the editor of the most important newspaper in the city', whom her own husband is entertaining. Immediately she writes to this brother, asking him to stay and to bring his companion: 'Ella was blithe and buoyant . . . her beloved though as yet unseen was coming . . . ' But when the painter arrives, he is alone: 'Trewe is a curious fellow . . . He said he'd come; then he said he couldn't.' Then comes some further description of Trewe, this time not through the eyes of the commonplace landlady, but through those of the landscape painter. They will inevitably remind the reader of Thomas Hardy.

> He's a very good fellow, and a warm friend, but a little uncertain and gloomy sometimes: he thinks too much of things. His poetry is rather too erotic and passionate, you know, for some tastes; and he has just come in for a terrible slating from the *Review* that was published yesterday; he saw a copy of it at the station by accident . . . O, it is not worth thinking of; just one of those articles written to order, to please the narrow-minded set of subscribers upon whom the circulation depends. But he's upset by it. He says it is the misrepresentation that hurts him so; that, though he can stand a fair attack, he can't stand lies that he's powerless to refute and stop from spreading. That's just Trewe's weak point. He lives so much by himself that these things affect him more than they would if he were in the bustle of fashionable or commercial life . . .

Then Ella reads in her newspaper that Trewe, 'one of our rising lyrists', has shot himself. He had 'recently attracted the attention of a much wider pubic than had hitherto known him' by the publication of his new volume of verse, 'mostly of an impassioned kind, entitled "Lyrics to a Woman Unknown"'; apparently the adverse notice in the *Review* was the cause of his suicide. He left a letter, addressed to a friend, stating:

> Perhaps had I been blessed with a mother, or a sister, or a female friend of another sort, I might have thought it worth while to continue my present existence. I have long dreamt of such an unattainable creature, as you know; and she, this undiscoverable, elusive one, inspired my last volume; the imaginary woman alone, for, in spite of what has been said in some quarters, there is no real woman behind the title.

This 'shook' Ella 'to pieces'; had she met him, 'she would have suffered shame and scorn, and died, for him!' She obtains a lock of his hair from Mrs Hooper, the landlady at Solentsea, and is caught sobbing over it by her husband. In order to give some substance to her pathetic fantasy she makes no attempt to allay his suspicions, and, exclaiming to himself, 'What sly animals women are!', he 'placidly dismissed the matter'. But when she rushes off from her Midlands home to Trewe's funeral at Solentsea he follows her, and discovers her crouching by the newly made grave in the middle of the night:

> 'Ella, how silly this is . . . Running away from home – I never heard of such a thing! Of course I am not jealous of this unfortunate man; but it is too ridiculous that you, a married woman with three children and a fourth coming, should go losing your head like this over a dead lover! . . . I hope it did not go far between you and him, for your own sake.'
> 'Don't insult me, Will.'

On her death-bed she does begin to try to explain to him:

> 'Will, I want to confess to you the entire circumstances . . . I thought you had been unkind; that you had neglected me; that you weren't up to my intellectual level, while he was, and far above it. I wanted a fuller appreciator, perhaps, rather than another lover – '

But she collapses, and in any case Marchmill is not interested. Two years later, when he is about to marry for the second time, and wishes to destroy old papers, he comes across the lock of hair:

Marchmill looked long and musingly at the hair and portrait, for something struck him. Fetching the little boy who had been the death of his mother . . . he took him on his knee, held the lock of hair against the child's head, and set up the photograph . . . By a known but inexplicable trick of nature there were undoubtedly strong traces of resemblance . . .

'I'm damned if I didn't think so!' murmured Marchmill. 'Then she *did* play me false . . . Let me see: the dates – the second week in August . . . the third week in May . . . Yes . . . yes. Get away, your poor little brat! You are nothing to me!'

This story offers an unequivocal example of how Tom could be funny about himself and his circumstances. He caricatures himself as Trewe, and he satirizes the state of emotion he has been in (and to a certain extent still is in) over Mrs Henniker; he also manages to see her in a new and more prosaic light. The conventional story would have fulfilled the sentimental promise of Ella's obsession with Trewe, but Tom inverts this, and incidentally demonstrates the uselessness of basing realistic expectations on dreams – yet, as he also demonstrates, such day-dreaming can kill, especially when no one really cares in the least about anyone else, but only about their own fantasies, or, in the case of Marchmill, crude physical requirements. Despite what he wrote to Florence in his final truly personal letter to her, of 15 January 1894, about wishing for a friend in whom to confide without fear of reproach, he knew that even this notion, different from the wish for a lover of the same ilk, was scarcely possible. He never found such a friend, and certainly did not do so in his second Florence, his second wife. Perhaps those who came closest were such as Hermann Lea and possibly his brother Henry and sister Mary, non-literary and non-society people whom he could trust and whose opinions he did not need to fear. He might now have turned to Emma, as many men gratefully do when the passionate and overheated affairs of their middle age fail. That she must have been hurt by his attentions to Florence Henniker, and to Florence Henniker's literary career, goes without saying. It is impossible that she could not have been. Yet there is no sign that she could not find it in herself to forgive him, as so many wives have done before and after her.

Jude was, he told Gosse on 10 November 1895: 'really sent out to those into whose souls the iron has entered, and has entered deeply at some time of their lives'. More elaborately, he told Florence Henniker, on the same date: 'The tragedy is really addressed to those into whose souls the iron of adversity has deeply entered at some time in their lives, & can hardly be congenial to self-indulgent persons of ease & affluence.' Just how and why did this book, which he was now working on, put an unwelcome iron into Emma's soul? Or did she, despite a conscious determination inspired by her new sense of Christianity to forgive and forget the Henniker affair, unknowingly allow it to affect her response to *Jude*, and to see in it something that was not there – or was not meant to be there? He had succeeded in doing the 'sublime', the 'thing unplanned', with regard to Florence Henniker, and had succeeded in doing it, perhaps, quite quickly. But when he turned back to Emma he found a changed woman.

24

Jude the Obscure

When Tillotson's turned down *Tess* they had no wish to alienate their author, and were happy to market 'The Melancholy Hussar' and, later, to arrange for the publication of *The Pursuit of the Well-Beloved* in the *Illustrated London News*. Tom's last serious gesture in the direction of prose was to rewrite this, as *The Well-Beloved*, for volume publication in 1897. *Jude* he took more seriously. Indeed, in certain ways he took it, written as it was from the contents of Florence Henniker's inkwell, more seriously, more emotionally, than any other novel he wrote. Yet this could hardly be inferred from what he wrote about it to Florence on 1 December 1893: 'I am not sure that I feel so keen about the, alas, unwritten long story as I should do. I feel more inclined just now to write short ones.' In other words, it was almost too much for him, especially since he would have to go through the wearisome routine of bowdlerization for the serial, and then rewriting for the volume publication. The publication of *Life's Little Ironies* at the end of January 1894 made the writing of short stories seem a more satisfactory means of existence for a poet.

As he got into the book, though, he began to 'warm up', as he had told Mrs Henniker he thought he would – and especially, no doubt, to the figure of Sue Bridehead who, for all that he did have living models for her, grew under his eyes. There is a faint hint of such a type in one or two of his heroines, even in Bathsheba Everdene, and more certainly in Paula Power; but none of these had been epicene, and Sue represents an innovation in his fiction, especially in the peculiar cast of her sexuality – a cast which has led many readers, women no less than men, to become exasperated with her wilfulness. As early as 22 October 1893 Tom had asked Mrs Henniker for advice upon what he should call her. Eventually she was called Susanna Florence Mary Bridehead; he would not have insisted upon this formidable list if each name, for one reason or another, had not been significant to him. The middle two are easy: 'Florence' is for Florence Henniker, and 'Mary' for his beloved sister (whose unhappy experiences at a teacher training college he drew upon). Unfortunately (as it turned out), Tom wrote in his preface to the first edition of *Jude*:

> The scheme was jotted down in 1890, from notes made in 1887 and onwards, some of the circumstances being suggested by the death of a woman in the former year. The scenes were revisited in October, 1892; the narrative was written in outline in 1892 and the spring of 1893, and at full length, as it now appears, from August 1893, onwards into the next year.

Unfortunately, I say, because this has encouraged those who believe that Tryphena Sparks played a paramount part in Tom's physical and emotional life to feel assured that Sue Bridehead is mostly based upon her. Readers will by now be aware that I take the view of Millgate rather than that of Gittings: that Tryphena's passage through Tom's life was fairly, if not absolutely, unimportant. What, after all, is a 'lost prize' in the existence of such a potent nostalgist as Thomas Hardy, especially when we consider that this one came from his almost native Puddletown? Had she been all-important in his life, and the chief model for Sue, he would hardly have drawn attention to her existence in the preface to a novel which he knew was about to be widely read. In so doing he would be laying himself open to questions which he would not wish to answer. The teachers' college in *Jude* is, moreover, based not on Stockwell but on the one in Salisbury attended by his sisters.

Millgate's suggestion as to the identity of this woman who died in 1890 and whose 'circumstances' suggested *Jude* is at least as plausible – even if it, too, is a shot in the dark. It might, after all, have been one of any number of unknown women whose fate caught Tom's imagination: one of ten thousand news items in that year. However, on 23 December 1890 an intelligent and enigmatic twenty-four-year-old woman called Mary Eleanor Pearcey, also known as Mary Wheeler, was hanged for allegedly luring Phoebe Hogg and her child to her house in Hampstead, and there murdering both of them with a chopper, on the previous 24 October; she maintained her innocence and may, in fact, have been innocent. The affair was much discussed, and Tom mentioned to Emma, in a letter of 3 December 1890, that everyone was talking about the verdict in London. The police alleged that Mrs Pearcey was the lover of Frank Hogg, the murdered woman's husband, who had a key to her house. What may have affected Tom, who was affected by such matters in any case (as we know from *Tess*, and from his much later poem about the judicial murder of Mrs Thompson), was the fact that Mary Pearcey's feelings for Frank Hogg were said by *The Times* to have been comradely rather than sexual. Millgate's suggestion is given rather more force by the fact that a newspaper – in fact the *News of the World* – wrongly reported that Mary Pearcey's father had been executed for murder.

Other features of the background of *Jude* are more obvious: his grandmother Mary Head, who had come from Fawley in Berkshire (the surname finally given to Jude, after others had been rejected); the personalities of the angry shoemaker, John Antell, and George Hand, the first his uncle by marriage and the second his maternal grandfather. Millgate gives an undated entry from the 'Poetical Matter' notebook, in the possession of R.L. Purdy: 'Poem. "The man who had no friend" – Auto. by J.Antell Sen. cf. "The Two Leaders." Swin.' Presumably the projected poem, apparently never written, was to tell the story of John Antell's decline into violence and drink owing to his inability to fulfil his aspirations. The second of the two stanzas of Swinburne's 'Two Leaders' runs:

> With all our hearts we praise you whom ye hate,
>   High souls that hate us; for our hopes are higher,
>   And higher than yours the goal of our desire,
> Though high your ends be as your hearts are great.
> Your world of Gods and kings, of shrine and state,
>   Was of the night when hope and fear stood nigher,
>   Wherein men walked by light of stars and fire
> Till man by day stood equal with his fate.
> Honour not hate we give you, love not fear,
>   Last prophets of past kind, who fill the dome
> Of great dead Gods with wrath and wail, nor hear
>   Time's word and man's: 'Go honoured hence, go home,
> Night's childless children; here your hour is done;
> Pass with the stars, and leave us with the sun.'

The first stanza speaks of the 'fierce juggling of the priests' loud mart' and the 'blind hard foul rout whose shameless shows/Mock the sweet heaven whose secret no man knows/With prayers and curses and the soothsayer's art'. Grandfather George Hand's life, though the man himself had been unknown to Tom, was perhaps even more dramatic an instance of disappointment and defiance. He may have formed a crucial element in that 'hereditary curse' within his family of whose existence Tom was convinced, but about which he remained largely silent except in certain cryptic poems such as the terrifying late one called 'Family Portraits', which ends:

> I have grieved ever since: to have balked future pain,
> My blood's tendance foreknown,
> Had been triumph. Nights long stretched awake I have lain
> Perplexed in endeavours to balk future pain
> By uncovering the drift of their drama. In vain,
> Though therein lay my own.

The poetic effectiveness of this does not depend on any morbid and dogmatic Victorian view of heredity, even though Tom may have been convinced of it. (He was, though, well up with current thinking in genetics, and read August Weisemann's *Essays upon Heredity* – which was influential in the refutation of Lamarckianism, and argued that the 'germ cell' ran independently of environmental circumstances – when it was published in 1891.) The poem can be read simply as a comment on the effects of heredity, even if it was inspired by a dark notion of 'tainted blood'. The idea in *Jude*, which Hardy seems to have believed (to Gosse, on 10 November 1895, he wrote: 'bad marriages, owing in the main to a doom or curse of hereditary temperament peculiar to the family of the parties') – that the love of Jude and Sue Bridehead is doomed because they are cousins and share tainted blood – now seems old-fashioned. But since it operates throughout the book as an assumption, it need not cause its modern readers any unhappy suspension of disbelief. The notion that some kind of curse – like, and yet horribly unlike, a musical or other gift – can run in a family is unscientific only in the sense that it cannot be refuted; but it is a potent one. Nor is the idea of the existence of unknown ancestors, working out a mysterious and perhaps sinister pattern, unscientific: it is simply a part of a gloomy speculative process carried out in the minds of those susceptible to it. In *The Well-Beloved* Jocelyn Pierston discovers that Ann Avice suffers from the same 'idiosyncrasy' as himself; and in 1897 he makes this reflection: 'The startling parallel . . . meant probably that there had been some remote ancestor common to both families, from whom the trait had latently descended and recrudesced.' Such speculations came naturally to Tom, increasingly so as he grew older.

JUDE THE OBSCURE

Heredity exists, and, pattern or no pattern, some people regard it in a morbid light. Weisemann's insistence that the 'immortal germ plasm' could under no circumstances be influenced by any experiences of the 'soma', the mortal individual, might even have put some more iron into Tom's soul: he might have interpreted it as meaning that in no way can people escape their fates. Further lines from 'Family Portraits' read:

> They set about acting some drama, obscure,
>   The woman and he,
> With puppet-like movements of mute strange allure;
> Yea, set about acting some drama, obscure,
> Till I saw 'twas their own lifetime's tragic amour,
>   Whose course begot me;
>
> Yea – a mystery, ancestral, long hid from my reach
>   In the perished years past,
> That had mounted to dark doings each against each
> In those ancestors' days, and long hid from my reach;
> Which their restless enghostings, it seemed, were to teach
>   Me in full, at this last . . .

In December 1893 he agreed to allow Harper's, who were very closely associated with his British publishers, to handle the serial rights of *Jude*. It ran in *Harper's New Monthly* from December 1894 to November 1895. On the first instalment the serialized version was entitled *The Simpletons* (in other words, people who believed, despite their own flaws and the nature of the world, that they could live a natural life in private); but someone pointed out that Charles Reade, although dead for a decade, had in 1873 published a novel called *A Simpleton: A Story of the Day* which had previously been serialized not only in *London Society* but also, in America, in *Harper's* itself. Tom was therefore forced to change the title to *Hearts Insurgent*, under which the last eleven instalments ran. His rather better second thought, *The Recalcitrants*, arrived too late for the printer. But the poem of that title, written probably at the same time, although not published until it appeared in *Satires of Circumstance*, casts clear light upon his feelings about the marriage theme, if not upon any practical proposals – apart from the greater ease of divorce in which, in common with many others, he believed. It begins:

511

Let us off and search, and find a place
Where yours and mine can be natural lives,
Where no one comes who dissects and dives
And proclaims that ours is a curious case,
Which its touch of romance can scarcely grace.

You would think it strange at first, but then
Everything has been strange in its time . . .

He could not then have had the course of *Jude* clear in his head, because on 7 April, according to his own record, he wrote 'to Harper's asking to be allowed to cancel the agreement to supply a serial story to *Harper's Magazine*'. Henry Harper, whom he knew 'very well', later reported that Tom told him he felt the story was carrying him into 'unexpected fields' and that he could not predict its 'future trend'. In the event he had to promise that he would make whatever alterations the Americans felt might be needed, and of course, many were – although the editor of *Harper's* for once seemed to mean it when he acknowledged that he was embarrassed to make such requests for his 'family magazine'. Tom could easily sympathize with such difficulties, and without rancour. What disgusted him was the salacious hypocrisy of such men as Mowbray Morris. Although the book was being written out so that it could conveniently be restored to its original form, Tom did in fact retain a few of the required bowdlerizations. It was the general situation that he disliked, not the specific instance. But *Hearts Insurgent* is, as has often been remarked, a quite ludicrous travesty of what we know as *Jude*; it is thus of interest only to such bibliographers as Gatrell, who has extensively analysed it in *Hardy the Creator*, and who has made many subtle points in the process, most of them pointing to Tom's capacity for improving his texts.

But when he first set out to write this novel, and before it got hold of him, he had become tired of fiction-writing and was planning simply to do his best on two general themes which particularly concerned him: marriage and education. The serial version of *The Well-Beloved* had been a very careless performance which, when he came to collect it in the uniform edition, he had to put right in the interests of his reputation.

Jude as it turned out, though, is not primarily about marriage and education, although the state of both and attitudes to them in Victorian England play an important part in its background. Ultimately it is about two people who love each other but who cannot live together happily, and as such it is a psychological study of each. As he told Gosse on 10 November 1895: '. . . the plot is almost geometrically constructed – I ought not to say *constructed*, for, beyond a certain point, the characters necessitated it, & I simply let it come'. That remark reveals the process which led him to write to *Harper's* to release them from their contract, and indicates the point at which the story took its hold upon him.

The name finally fixed on for the hero, at first called Jack England and then successively Head, Hopson and Stancombe, suggests not only Judas Iscariot but also Jude, an obscure brother of Jesus, whom Tom would have taken to be the author of the Epistle of Jude, the brief penultimate book of the New Testament. There is nothing much specific, aside from the 'blackness of darkness', about the latter association, and even the former only hints at the notion of betrayal – of the spirit by the flesh, no doubt (at a deeper level, Jude's sense that he is favoured like God's son is shown to be false). Sue's first full name, Susanna, is equally vague in its connotations: the Hebrew word for lily, it is most immediately reminiscent of the Apocrypha tale of Susanna and the Elders, one of the earliest of the world's great short stories. There is an ironic reference, Susanna being the name of the woman who most famously 'resisted temptation', to Sue Bridehead's sexual fastidiousness – and to her final, unnatural but 'legal' and 'Christian' submission to Phillotson, whose righteous lusts are deliberately made, by the novelist, to resemble the evil impulses of the voyeuristic elders. Florence Henniker must have turned away Tom's sexual proposition, whether he hinted at it or made it plain, with 'religious' pleadings; this is his comment, representing not any 'revenge' on her (as has been claimed) but just what he feels. It has in any case just the right sexual connotations to lead naturally forward to 'Bridehead'. By combining 'bride' with 'maidenhead' (also the name of a place, not far from Fawley in Berkshire – and Bridehead is a Dorset place name) it brilliantly compresses Sue's ultimate fate (to submit, with hysterical righteousness, to the 'legal' attentions of a man who physically repels her) and her inclinations (to be a coquette who shrinks from fulfilling the physical expectations she needs to arouse). As Millgate puts it: 'the "bride" in Sue is fatally inhibited by the "head"'.

Tom's denial in the *Life* that there is 'a scrap of personal detail' in *Jude* has been described as 'typically devious'. But is it really? Or is it, rather, that the approach of commentators is in itself distorted by assumptions about Tom's character – an assumption based upon the notions that authors owe some debt to those who will come to criticize them, and that Tom was not just a private man but an exceedingly devious one? I have taken some pains to show that he was no more devious than anyone else would have been in his circumstances. It is of course impossible that any novel could fail to contain some 'scrap of personal detail', but Tom knew that, and was protesting at the idea, taken up eagerly in the late nineteenth-century equivalents of today's gutter press, that *Jude* was an autobiography. 'He underwent', he wrote, 'the strange experience of beholding a sinister lay figure of himself', constructed by those with 'nice minds' but 'nasty ideas'. Novels and poems are autobiographical, but seldom literally so: they are records of the patterns of inner, not outer, life. Tom remarked of some of the reviews of *Jude* that

> Tragedy may be created by an opposing environment either of things in the universe, or human institutions. If the former be the means exhibited and deplored, the writer is regarded as impious; if the latter, as subversive and dangerous; when all the while he may never have questioned the necessity or urged the non-necessity of either.

One is reminded, too, of the narrator's remark about Pierston (in the 1892 serial *Well-Beloved*, and retained): 'It was in his weaknesses as a citizen and national-unit that his strength lay as an artist . . . ' *Jude* is more of a universal tragedy than a pointer even to specific characteristics of its writer. In view of the fact that any novelist is bound, in creating his characters, to depend upon his knowledge of and interest in specific individuals, there is no need to question his remarks in the *Life*:

> When they [he and Emma] got back to Dorchester that December [from London] Hardy had plenty of time to read the reviews of *Jude* that had continued to pour out. Some paragraphists knowingly assured the public that the book was an honest autobiography, and Hardy did not take the trouble to deny it till twenty years later, when he wrote to an inquirer with whom the superstition still lingered that no book he had ever written contained less of his own life, which of course had been known to his friends from the beginning. Some of the incidents were real in so far as that he had heard of them, or come in contact with them when they were occurring to people he knew: but no more. It is interesting to mention that on his way to school he did once meet with a youth like Jude who drove the bread-cart of a widow, a baker, like Mrs Fawley, and carried on his studies at the same time, to the serious risk of other drivers in the lanes; which youth asked him to lend him his Latin grammar. But Hardy

lost sight of this featful student, and never knew if he profited by his plan.

There is nothing disingenuous, furtive or devious about that. His own experiences as a child had been wholly unlike Jude's. His consideration of going to Cambridge did not in the least resemble Jude's determination to go to Oxford. And, although a few random facts of Horace Moule's help to Tom may possibly have been inserted into the novel, Phillotson can hardly be made out as an attempted representation of Horace. However, elements in Moule – his susceptibility to alcohol and possibly to unfortunate liaisons with girls of a class beneath him – if not Moule himself, must have gone into the character of Jude.

As for Sue, her creation is neither more nor less bound to Tom's own experience than is any other novelist's for any of his characters, major or minor. The hypothesis that he in any way resembled Jude must have been peculiarly irritating, for all that he tried, as he wrote, to see 'the ludicrous side of it all'. He had never, after all, been a stonemason, nor addicted to drink, nor trapped into a marriage by a false declaration of pregnancy. But it may be that this 'ludicrous side of it all' had its effect upon Emma, above such vulgarity as she certainly was.

Tom was a working popular novelist, anxious to continue as such only so long as he needed the money that novels brought in. Plot was less important to him than it has been to his critics, but he did not take it too lightly, and that of *Jude* is almost as good as he ever achieved. Any reader of any biography of Hardy will have read *Jude*, if not all his other novels, and it is no more necessary to outline its plot than it is that of *Tess*. Its most important feature is that it lacks what Millgate calls 'weak links', and approximates most closely to Sophoclean drama. Technically, it was most powerfully influenced by the scheme of Sophocles' *Oedipus Tyrannus*, a play he studied in Buckley's prose translation and, we may be certain, in the original as well. *Jude* is, as Millgate claims, 'like a solidly constructed play'.

But *Jude* is 'terrible' in its effect upon the reader; it is one of those novels that, like *The Brothers Karamazov*, is upsetting to read. Many of these 'shocking' novels were written in Europe at the turn of the century, as a result of naturalist influence. One typical example, out of hundreds now forgotten, is *Cintas rojas* (1916), *Red Ribbons*, by 'Pármeno' (José López Pinillos), in which in the course of an afternoon the protagonist kills eight people simply in order to purchase a ticket to a bullfight. But neither *Red Ribbons* nor most of the novels like it were terrible in the sense that *Jude* is terrible, for all that the fiction of these years abounded in such incidents. When in 1942 the eventually Nobel-winning novelist Camilo José Cela wrote *La familia de Pascual Duarte*, reviving just that earlier tradition, timid Spanish critics invented the term *tremendista* to describe the impact. In *Jude*, an early example of this 'tremendously disturbing' genre by any standards, the incident of Father Time's hanging of himself and the other children was certainly *tremendista*, and as a result odium was heaped upon the author. But this sort of overwhelming, shocking scene or incident was usually indulged in for sensationalist effect: the contexts seldom justified the indulgence.

The question is, did Tom overdo it in *Jude*? He is almost always at his best when just falling short of going right over the top – like his unhappy poet Robert Trewe of 'An Imaginative Woman': 'rather too erotic and passionate, you know, for some tastes'. Did he rise up too far, and so fall over, in *Jude*?

Edmund Gosse, although he sincerely admired the book in part, clearly thought that Tom had done just that – and so to some extent, if only in his capacity as a 'safe', polite, establishment man, he was resentful. It must be remembered that Gosse did not become the librarian of the House of Lords for nothing, nor did such younger writers as Virginia Woolf or Robert Graves despise him as a smarmy hypocrite for no reason. Tom believed in loyalty, and had almost too fervently supported Gosse when in 1885 he was viciously attacked (not without good reason) by Churton Collins over his *From Shakespeare to Pope* lectures, which were deficient in scholarship. He knew that Gosse knew that he had overlooked the justice at the heart of Collins' unnecessarily cruel attack. But it was quite beyond Gosse to repay the favour in the present circumstances: he had to be a trimmer in order to rise still further as a 'literary man', as distinct from the writer he could have been (as *Father and Son* demonstrates) had he chosen to face himself. Later, in the summer of 1909, he had some now unknown grievance against Tom and wrote to him about it – his letter is lost, probably destroyed. Tom soothed him, told him that he had not said whatever he was supposed to have said, then added what we should otherwise not have known:

> I am reminded by this that the only time you made me really angry was when you said to my face at the lunch-table at the Savile that *Jude* was the most indecent novel ever written. But that was long ago, & I had nearly forgotten it.

We may be fairly sure that everything Gosse said was supposed to be accompanied with a wink and possibly a vinous nod, and even that it was uttered before an audience of stuffed shirts. Nevertheless it cannot have been easy for a man like Tom to endure it in front of these fellow clubmen, towards whose opinions – as is known from the letter he wrote to Besant pretending to ask if he thought Tom ought to resign over a hostile review of *Tess* – he felt as much sensitivity as contempt. 'Indecent', even then, was a pretty annoying word, especially in a place like the Savile, when *Jude* was being called 'pornographic' in certain quarters. Although it has always been assumed that the incident occurred soon after November 1895, the date of publication of *Jude*, it could have been later. However, there is no letter to Gosse extant between March 1896 and March 1897, so the *faux pas* was probably committed within two or three months of publication, while the book was at the centre of heated discussion.

Tom was in any case initially grateful to Gosse, who, anxious to please, whatever his own reservations, wrote two reviews of the book, the first for the *St James's Gazette* in November 1895, and then another amplified one for the new and short-lived magazine *Cosmopolis* in the following January. Before considering what Gosse said, it is worth looking at William Dean Howells' review. This was admittedly for *Harper's*; but he was reviewing the volume and not the serial, and, while he himself has occasionally been accused, largely unfairly, of a degree of mealy-mouthedness, he was an infinitely superior critic to Gosse, as well as an undoubtedly gifted novelist – a man who needed to square himself with Mark Twain as well as with his own close friend Henry James. Howells, writing for the very audience for whose too nice tastes the editor of *Harper's* had apologized to Tom, and himself an experienced editor of the *Atlantic*, took an unmistakably different view from Gosse's, for all his polite phraseology:

> I allow that there are many displeasing things in the book, and few pleasing [here follow allusions to Arabella's 'dimple-making', the pig-sticking, the boy suicide and homicide, 'Sue's wilful self-surrender to Phillotson'] . . . these and other incidents are revolting. They make us shiver with horror and grovel with shame, but we know that they are deeply founded in the condition, if not in the nature of humanity. There are besides these abhorrent facts certain accusations against some accepted formalities of civilisation, which I suppose some readers will find hardly less shocking. But I think it is very

well for us to ask from time to time the reasons of things, and to satisfy ourselves, if we can, what the reasons are . . . I find myself defending the book on the ethical side when I meant chiefly to praise it for what seems to me its artistic excellence . . .

This is carefully worded, but amounts to a defence of all that Tom had done, including what many others were just then describing as 'gratuitously impossible' excesses. One particularly notable phrase is 'grovel with shame', which implies, as it is meant to imply, that Howells believed that Tom had made a valid point about the human condition and had not really strained it. The reader of Howells' review could, of course, if he or she so wished, understand the words differently and take it that the book was offensive.

Mrs Oliphant, whom Tom had recently visited at Windsor, chose to pretend that this 'nauseous tragedy' was a deliberate crusade against marriage ('an assault on the stronghold of marriage . . . now beleaguered on every side'), and that, as Richard le Gallienne put it in defending Tom in the *Idler*, he had catered for 'unclean appetites'. Le Gallienne referred to Oliphant's piece as 'pitiful spleen' and as 'either very malignant or very mistaken'. But in the *National Review*, the Italian scholar A.J. Butler agreed with Mrs Oliphant, and thought that men and women (with the exception of the 'utterly abandoned') would 'hurry over' its pages 'with shuddering disgust'. Tom did, in fact, get as many good reviews as bad ones, and it is often asserted, notably by Millgate, that he was unreasonable in his reactions: 'Hardy at bay – seized by a blind, sullen, unforgiving, peasant anger – is not an attractive spectacle . . . he did not consider long or deeply the justice or appropriateness of his own first self-defensive lunges . . . did not forget or forgive those who wounded him . . . ' Obviously, too, Millgate feels that Tom was a trifle unkind in never quite forgiving Gosse for what he concedes was a 'brutal' remark.

He fails, I think, to understand his subject: over the Churton Collins attack Tom had given Gosse lavish personal support, and he expected the same now that he himself was under attack as 'Hardy the Degenerate', author of 'Jude the Obscene': he was simply surprised to discover what, by his standards, Gosse was made of. Yet clearly he did 'forgive' him, just as he could see the virtues of George Saintsbury long after the latter's silly attack on *Tess*. Millgate's sympathy with Gosse's critical position over *Jude* has misled him.

The truth is that Tom's anger at having the ashes of his book sent to him in a parcel from America, at being branded as an advocate of free love and immorality, and at (as he subsequently discovered) having his book banned from Smith's lending library at the behest of a foolish bishop (commended for his self-reported act of burning *Jude* in the fire by poor, jealous, ailing and once excellent Mrs Oliphant) was just as anyone else's would have been. Millgate says that Mrs Oliphant was 'perfectly justified in discussing *Jude* within an "anti-marriage" context'; but that really is 'disingenuous': we need only read her review to discover what sort of performance it was, as le Gallienne recognized. Such sweet reason as Millgate propounds has no existence in reality. To state that Tom's letters in response to all this high-sounding and in itself disgusting nonsense were 'anguished' is, again, to exaggerate. They were ironic in that they humorously hoist the complainers on the petard of their own earnest morality, as when he pointed out that the now dead Bishop How, who claimed to have burned his copy of *Jude*, 'would have found [in Tom] a man whose personal conduct, views of morality, and of the vital facts of religion, hardly differed from his own'. Millgate comments:

> What is remarkable about this passage is not so much that Hardy, surely no lover of the episcopate and least of all of the 'miserable second class prelate' [as he had very properly and truthfully called How, as any student of Victorian Christianity will tell you] in question, should have imagined that he and the Bishop might have profited from knowing each other, but that he should have felt the necessity, in such a context, not merely of defending his work but of protesting his personal virtue and morality.

This grim comment entirely misses Tom's casual and wholly humorous point – that he was as 'blameless' in his conduct as the good bishop. Millgate takes all this far more seriously than Tom ever did, despite the fact that as a man who enjoyed society it was hardly useful to him to be attacked by a bishop of the Established Church: the smoking-room had its stories about bishops all right, but complete openness was not a possible remedy. Tom did not, of course, think that anyone would have profited from a friendship between him and How – and, as for his not liking the 'episcopate', what about his sincere love and admiration for Perkins, Kegan Paul, Barnes and all the Moules? Tom admired men for what they did and not for what they said.

But Millgate writes beautifully on *Tess*, which moves him quite as much as it moves all those sound in heart, and well on *Jude*, from whose power he cannot, even though he seems to agree with Gosse, really escape. Having been driven into extreme and justified irritation by the antics of Mrs Grundy, Tom was not going to allow the real *Jude* to be destroyed by outcries of false morality: it is not peculiar if a man defends himself even in a bad cause, and the author of *Jude* surely had good cause, especially on the score of morality. What is most grotesque, for all that we are used to the peculiar nature of Victorian sexual morality, is the nature of the fuss that was made.

I suspect that Millgate did not wish to offend Purdy, who handed over to him all the material he had gathered in the course of a lifetime: Purdy was a sound scholar and collector, but incapable of psychological insight into sexual matters (emotionally, he probably tended to agree with the reviewers: sex was a closed book to him), far too reliant on Florence Hardy and her suburban view of her husband, and short on critical acumen. Had he not been at least vaguely aware of his own shortcomings, he would have written the biography himself – and we must admire him for deciding not to do so.

Gosse, meanwhile, was equivocal about *Jude*, especially when we compare his notices of the book with le Gallienne's or with the forthright anonymous one in the *Saturday Review*. His *Cosmopolis* piece is an extension of his earlier and shorter one, to which Tom had responded by finding it 'the most discriminating that has yet appeared'. He really was trying to forgive Gosse for his conventionality, the kind of disingenuous conventionality he had finally seen too much of in Florence Henniker: her Church, he had reminded her, was his too. Gosse said in the *St James's Gazette* that the book was 'grimy' – a nasty adjective, if not quite as nasty as 'indecent':

> It is a gloomy, even a grimy story . . . The genius of this author is too widely acknowledged to permit us to question his right to take us into what scenes he pleases; but, of course, we are at liberty to say whether we enjoy them or no. Plainly, we do not enjoy them. We think the fortunes, even of the poorest, are more variegated with pleasures, than Mr Hardy chooses to admit . . . in his new book Mr Hardy concentrates his observation on the sordid and painful side of life and nature. We rise from the perusal of it stunned with a sense of the hollowness of existence.

Millgate believes that the charge brought here against the Hardy of *Jude* 'is perhaps impossible to refute as completely as one would wish'.

But, while charges of 'immorality', hinted at by Gosse, are not tenable, it is a tenable view in respect of the Father Time suicide incident. Tom himself, almost as if to refute Millgate's charges of peasantish sullenness, wrote very warmly to Gosse, and left it to a PS to reply to the unpleasant charge of 'griminess':

> One thing I did not answer. The 'grimy' features of the story go to show the contrast between the ideal life a man wished to lead, & the squalid real life he was fated to lead. The throwing of the pizzle, at the supreme moment of his young dream, is to sharply initiate this contrast. But I must have lamentably failed, as I feel I have, if this requires explanation & is not self-evident. The idea was meant to run all through the novel. It is, in fact, to be discovered in *every*body's life – though it lies less on the surface perhaps than it does in my poor puppet's.

This is true: *every*body's life, including Gosse's, is thus unennobled. Tom was disappointed that Gosse, who could have treated him as he wanted to be treated – 'a friend with whom mutual confessions can be made of weaknesses without fear of reproach or contempt', as he had put it to the suddenly churchy Mrs Henniker – was not putting forward his true feelings but taking refuge in hypocrisy. Gosse felt that his advancement might be threatened if he were now seen to be failing to reproach the great novelist for straying outside the bounds of the smoking-room: this little telling-off would get about, and would in due time be seen as establishing Gosse as a 'safe' man, worthy of the honours which he planned for himself.

In his *Cosmopolis* review he made points which Tom found useful, especially the important one that, although *Jude* had 'appeared . . . at a moment when a sheaf of "purpose" stories on the "marriage question" (as it is called) have just been irritating the nerves of the British Patron', it ought not to be confused with any of these. But he insisted, sure of his brief, that Tom had strained reality, which, for both Gosse and the men he relied upon to advance him, must at all times be revealed to the masses as not all that bad. Thus Gosse referred to the 'unduly exalted' Zola's 'deplorable fiasco of *La Terre*': a truly comic as well as tragic novel, in the course of which a character farts so sharply at a tax-clerk that he imagines he is being shot at, and takes the evasive action that is his proper lot. Gosse was anxious to avoid any important person's gaining the impression that, because he had translated the dangerous (but not unclean) Norwegian Ibsen, he was in any way subversive or in favour of unhealthy and 'unenjoyable' literature. The half-dismissal of Zola, long felt by *The Times* to be the very epitome of impropriety, was in that way useful to him. There are few passages more effective in literature than the famous pig's pizzle incident: as soon as the idealistic and aspiring Jude is confronted with his sexual instincts, he finds himself holding not a prayer book but the penis of a dead pig! But is there more worrying substance in this charge, as Millgate, sympathetically taking it up from Gosse, puts it? 'There does seem to be something gratuitous about Jude's sufferings, the death of Father Time and the other children, the violence of Sue's abnegation and self-flagellation.' He does, however, scrupulously concede that, in view of 'Greek precedents' this violent procedure can 'perhaps be explained, if not entirely justified, in terms of a deliberate determination to leave the reader precisely "stunned with a sense of the hollowness of existence".' It can, however, be fully justified, and for the following reason.

How much a reader can take is, to some extent, a matter of temperament. *Jude* really is painful. But the age, the novel-reading public and, more precisely, their disingenuous and falsely pious spokesmen – those who appealed to the dishonesty inherent in society – deserved to be shaken up. If that could be done without vulgar sensationalism, then it ought to be done – if not for social, then for purely imaginative reasons – reasons which, for Tom, were poetic. It must be recognized that full candour, outside pornography, was not possible: the situation in itself – suppression of truth in the interests of the preservation of convenient lies – provoked irony, and some degree of violence as well as obliquity. There is a sense in which certain of the works of Hardy cannot be edited. In 1903, for example, he toned down the pig's pizzle scene: did he do this out of fear that it would prejudice his sales, or for aesthetic reasons? If for the latter, then we should need to print his latest version – whether we thought he was wrong or right. But if we could find a letter or note which said that he did it for the former reason, then we might be justified in restoring it (this is Gatrell's position, even in his capacity as a bibliographer). It is the fault not of Tom, but of a peculiarity of his age – no worse than ours, and in many ways better, but one which had its share of absurdities. The original passage, in which Jude and Arabella engage in amorous dalliance with the pizzle hanging between them, is comic – and preferable.

Tom was perfectly justified, too, in pretending, with a convolute irony, that he had been worried in case the ending of the book, when

Sue gives herself physically to the by now wholly uncomprehending Phillotson, would be taken to be too 'High-Churchy'. This is what he wrote on 20 November 1895 to Douglas, who, unlike Gosse, had proved loyal, and even wrote a reply to critics on Tom's behalf. Tom's letter said:

> The marriage question was made the vehicle of the tragedy, in one part, but I did not intend to argue it at all on its merits. I feel that a bad marriage is one of the direst things on earth, & one of the cruellest things, but beyond that my opinions on the subject are vague enough.
>
> I fancied that, having made Sue become a Christian, & recant all her 'views' at the end, I shd be deemed High-Churchy in tone: you can imagine my surprise at the *Guardian* saying that everything sacred is brought into contempt, &c. in the novel! Did you see that the *World* nearly fainted away, & the *Pall Mall* went into fits over the story?
>
> I am glad you like Sue. So do I – depressed as I am at the feebleness of my drawing of her.

He ended by saying that he wished Douglas to continue with a book he was then writing, to be called 'The Pleasure Seeker': 'Excellent title!'

Tom knew that the scene of Sue's final surrender to dogma and conventionality was one of the most horrible in the novel, and he was demonstrating just how much the letter could kill the spirit ('the letter killeth' provides the epigraph). We cannot fairly regard this final episode as 'gratuitous', nor, even, solely as an indictment of conventional behaviour: it provides, at the novel's profoundest level, an illustration of the operation of a certain law. This law (in Eastern terms karma) Strindberg stated, in a simple form, in his play *Easter* (1901), in the person of Lindkvist: 'everything comes back'. Creditor of the family of Elis Heyst, Lindkvist finally has mercy because Elis' father was once kind to him. The law operates in reverse for poor Sue: whether or not she has been driven a little crazy by the miseries inflicted upon her, she finds herself, now fanatical, giving in to someone who repels her (and who has earlier informed her that, in obeying the dictates of her own nature, she is 'committing a sin'). Previously she has withheld herself from someone who does not repel her, and, more to the point, played the coquette with him, requiring him to want her but then finding justifications for not giving herself. This is not 'immoral' in her, but it is not, either, as one or two modern feminists have found it, a question simply of her 'right to withhold herself'. That is putting theory before practice. If she had wanted to exercise that undoubted right, then she could have behaved consistently. Certain things are perfectly apparent to her. She tells Jude:

> 'My life has been entirely shaped by what people call a peculiarity in me . . . I have not felt about [men] as most women are taught to feel . . . no man short of a sensual savage – will molest a woman by day or night . . . unless she invited him. Until she says by a look "Come on" he is always afraid to, and if you never say it, or look it, he never comes . . . '

Then she goes on to tell him of her 'friendly intimacy' with the Christminster undergraduate whose death was at least partly caused by her refusal to sleep with him. She does tell Jude that she 'wasn't in love with him', but she also tells him that, knowing what the position was, they had 'shared a sitting-room for fifteen months'. This might have been no more than an unfortunate situation resulting from lack of experience; but it does not tell us what Sue believed was the right procedure in the event that she did love a man, and it leaves open the possibility that, although she upbraids herself for her cruelty, she gained some kind of enjoyment from tormenting the consumptive student. She won't have it, she tells Jude, that she is either 'cold-natured' or 'sexless': 'Some of the most passionately erotic poets have been the most self-contained in their daily lives.' This exchange follows:

> 'Aren't you *really* vexed with me, dear Jude?' she suddenly asked, in a voice of such extraordinary tenderness that it hardly seemed to come from the same woman who had just told her story so lightly. 'I would rather offend anybody than you, I think!'
> 'I don't know whether I am vexed or not. I know I care very much about you!'
> 'I care as much for you as for anybody I ever met.'
> 'You don't care *more*! There, I ought not to say that. Don't answer it!'
> There was another long silence. He felt that she was treating him cruelly, though he could not quite say in what way. Her very helplessness seemed to make her so much stronger than he.

Although Sue rejects the idea that she is 'cold-natured' or 'sexless', at a subtle level she is playing the coquette: when she implies that she wants only companionship from men, she is not being honest. Her later remark on the 'literary enormity' of the synopses of the Song of Solomon 'explaining away the real nature of that rhapsody' pains the studious Jude – and who is to say that a young female cousin who could make such an observation did not hold out some sort of sexual promise in making it – and mean to do just that?

Later her confusions on these matters are made clearer. Jude can hardly be blamed for booking a single room in the hotel at Aldbrickham after she has left Phillotson, yet when she hears of it she tells him, 'But I didn't mean that!' 'Even at this obvious moment for candour Sue could not be quite candid as to the state of that mystery, her heart.' Nowhere in Hardy's fiction is any character so real as Sue Bridehead – and yet this reality lies in her ambiguity and her confusion. As Tom said, he liked her, and he was not in any way trying to make morals out of her complex nature, which he could not help seeing as destructive, at least of men as they are made.

'George Egerton', the pseudonym of Chavelita Clairmonte, perhaps the most naturally gifted of all the 'new woman' novelists, told him that Sue was 'a marvellously true psychological study of a temperament less rare than the ordinary male observer supposes'. She should have known. Born in Australia of Welsh-Irish parentage as Mary Dunne, she was highly experienced and, as well as being more gifted than Florence Henniker, was an unconventional woman who formed the subject of much gossip. She was the author of *Keynotes* (1893), a volume of impressionistic stories which gave her lover, the publisher John Lane, the form for his successful 'new woman' series. She had eloped with a married man, an alcoholic called Higginson, and had then married another quite as unsuitable – ostensibly a Canadian novelist called Egerton Clairmonte. Before that she had, according to the Norwegian writer and dedicatee of *Keynotes*, Knut Hamsun (another 'sullen peasant', a future Nobel Prize winner and eventual Nazi, and, much more certainly and deliberately than Tom, a liar), asked him to marry her. Tom told her on 22 December 1895: 'I have been intending for years to draw Sue, & it is extraordinary that a type of woman, comparatively common and getting commoner, should have escaped fiction so long.'

There might seem to be a bit of confusion here. Did Egerton, and did Tom in answering her, mean Sue to be understood as a 'new woman', or one sexually inhibited, or both? Egerton liked sex, and when young did not exercise her right to withhold herself; I think her observation was made in order to praise Tom's subtlety of depiction of a type that she was not, but that she understood. Tom was even more explicit in a letter to Gosse dated 20 December 1895, when he still had hopes of his general support.

> You are quite right: there is nothing depraved or perverted in Sue's nature. The abnormalism consists in her disproportion: not in inversion, her sexual instinct being healthy as far as it goes, but unusually weak & fastidious; her sensibilities remain painfully alert notwithstanding, (as they do in nature with such women). One point illustrating this I cd not dwell upon: that, though she has children, her intimacies with Jude have never been more than occasional, even while they were living together (I mention that they occupy separate rooms, except towards the end), & one of her reasons for fearing the marriage ceremony is that she fears it wd be breaking faith with Jude to withhold herself at pleasure, or altogether, after it; though while uncontracted she feels at liberty to yield herself as seldom as she chooses. This has tended to keep his passion as hot at the end as at the beginning, & helps to break his heart. He has never really possessed her as freely as he desired.
>
> Sue is a type of woman which has always had an attraction for me – but the difficulty of drawing the type has kept me from attempting it till now.

The phrase 'withhold herself at pleasure' is significant here, for, although Tom does not quite state it – and the narration cannot quite state it, not only because it is in the 'candour-trap' but also because it cannot be certain – she does obtain a kind of perverse sexual gratification from thus withholding herself, and from thus breaking Jude's heart. This is what she means when she tells Jude that sometimes a woman's *'love of being loved'* gets the better of her conscience. On balance, although she does not mind making love when she has decided to do so (she returns his kisses 'in a way she had never done before' when she feels threatened by Arabella), she gets more pleasure from withholding it. It may be that she is angry that she cannot be a man, and is therefore determined to make people who are men pay for it, and so feels guilty at her behaviour, whose motives she fails to understand. It may be, too, that, having proved to herself that she is too capable of orgasm, she is afraid of the loss of identity that it entails: of 'letting go' or of feeling 'possessed'; and that Jude, whose failure is after all one of the flesh, cannot love her quite enough to persuade her otherwise. After the disaster of the suicide of Little Father Time he exclaims to her: 'I seduced you . . . You were a distinct type – a refined creature, intended by Nature to be left intact. But I couldn't leave you alone!' Patricia Ingham, editor of the World's Classics edition (1985), writes of that remark: 'Locked into this most feminist of all Victorian novels is a strange fragment of the orthodoxy exalting female chastity . . . ' That is to miss the point. It is true that according to the patriarchal orthodoxy woman was a spotless creature, scarcely susceptible, in her middle- or upper-class form, to sexual feelings of any kind, while man was a beast to whose sensualities it was her duty to submit for the perpetuation of the race. But this was, like all such popular models, an utterly confused one, due largely to repression of discussion of self-evident truths – such truths as Tom was anxious to ventilate. Jude is speaking of the individual Sue, and of her trying peculiarities. He was only echoing a popular myth.

Sensitive men's experience of this 'type' – if one may be 'anecdotal', and speak as Tom spoke to Gosse – seems to confirm this. They enjoy being coquettish, but are also penitent, and feel themselves to be wicked ('so bad and worthless,' says Sue to Jude, as to deserve the 'full rigour of lecturing'); and yet they are exceptionally lovable, and nowhere less so than in their occasional transparent honesty. If Tom had always been attracted by such women, it would be because they offered him a possibility of understanding real women as distinct from the Victorian stereotype: Sue, as well as behaving unfairly to poor Jude (most women feel that she *is* unfair), is trying to discover her authenticity as a woman, beyond stereotypes. He loves her for that, too. Nothing 'moral' is intended in this attempt at objective character depiction. Nowhere is Sue more frustrating to Jude than in her attitude to his having 'had' (as Tom liked to express it) Arabella, despite his protest that 'she was, after all' his 'legal wife': 'Why are you so gross! *I* jumped out of the window!' – referring to her flight from Phillotson's equally 'legal' advances. Yet: 'It was true that he did not understand her feeling very well. But he did a little; and began to love her none the less.'

When Tom told Gosse that Jude's passion was kept hot by Sue's attitude, he knew that Sue knew it, too: she preferred the hot passion to the satiated passion, and what man is to blame her for that – or for feeling, at the same time, 'unworthy', 'unprincipled' and all the other attributes with which she upbraids herself? Yet one of her faults is her self-pity ('always much affected at a picture of herself as an object of pity'); this reinforces her resistance to the pure and loving pleasure of which she is capable. Patricia Ingham draws attention to the ambivalence of the text on the question of whether Sue ever really feels desire, even for Jude. It might be even better stated in these terms: that she does desire him (as Tom continued to revise the novel until 1912 he came nearer to what he told Gosse about her, showing that she certainly was capable of sexual feeling), but feels that she should not, and is thus inhibited, or inhibits herself, in her expression. Ingham claims that the text can be read both ways: as showing that she felt desire, and that she did not. But the text shows, unequivocally, that she did and does feel desire ('I find I still love him [Jude] – O, grossly! I cannot tell you more', she tells Widow Edlin just before she forces herself to go to Phillotson's bed – nothing could be less equivocal, and it cannot be read otherwise). All that the text tells us to the contrary is that she resists this feeling, or smothers it – thus on one occasion Jude tells her that she is not quite as passionate as he could wish. It is a delicate point in a novel which, for all its elements of *Grand Guignol*, is consistently subtle.

The extreme unhappiness suffered by these two people does not seem so 'gratuitous' when we realize that neither Arabella Donn nor Richard Phillotson, the two main characters, is ever *as* unhappy: the author does what he does in order to demonstrate that happiness is in direct proportion to sensitivity – sensitivity of a peculiar kind, which he is intent upon defining. Arabella has elements of the 'good sort' in her, and her sensuality could be described as healthy by contrast to Sue's neuroticism; but she lacks sensitivity, and is ruthless, irrational and pleasure-seeking. Nor is Phillotson, for all his generous impulses and his suffering, really sensitive: prisoner of false assumptions, he ends by torturing a woman he desires more than he loves (in contrast to Jude, in whom these two feelings are in desperate and tormenting balance). What a corrupt society would describe as 'gratuitousness', operating as a metaphor in a poetic and psychological rather than strictly realistic novel, could be called a necessity in the context of its age. The book is truly 'terrible' only because it is *not* gratuitous.

But this still leaves the Father Time episode. Is that necessary in the sense just defined, or does it strain the fabric of the book? *Jude*, even though it draws attention to poor and unjust social conditions, is not a novel of social protest and is not designed as one. At no point does it imply that its author has any 'political' solutions to offer. Tom did not admire politicians as a class, although he may have liked and even admired some of them as individuals. His criticism of life is at a profounder level than that of practical politics and, had he wished to make a protest about poverty and its effect on children, he would have either thought better of it or written a letter to the press.

The main tragedy of Jude and Sue may indeed be, ultimately, what Mary Jacobus suggests in a fine article, 'Sue the Obscure', *Essays in Criticism* (July 1975): 'No longer sustained by an enduring rural context [they] have nothing to fall back on but their ideas, and one by one these fail them . . . ' There are ideas, or what passes for them, in any age. *Jude* can hardly be prised from its historical setting, but it is not limited by it. If it drew attention to social and other evils – to the manner in which universities denied entrance to worthy members of the lower classes, to the position into which women were driven by being forced to conform to an impossible stereotype, and to the perpetuation of a hypocritical Christianity in whose details few could honestly believe – then it did so because Tom saw his age truthfully, and not because he was full of reformist zeal. For him, reform could come only when the nature of what needed to be reformed had been understood. That, as Conrad would have said, was his 'business': politics would only be for after that business had been fully performed.

Jude may not be a realistic novel in the accepted sense; but it is psychologically realistic. And Tom always liked – indeed, he may be said to have always insisted upon – some precedent for every fact and happening in his novels. Wife-sale is only one famous example. For the suicide of Father Time he had ample precedent, although in his depiction of the event he was, as so often, 'ahead of his time'. Until quite recently it was generally believed that clinical depression in children could not exist. In fact, in the light of recent studies of this unhappy phenomenon, Tom's account of Father Time and his poignant end amounts to a classic study of child depression and suicide a century ahead of its time! In it he displays an astonishing intuition. The suicide is certainly an instance of *tremendismo*, but why should a novelist not pick up on rare events? It is the poetic novelist, who need not strain to achieve outward credibility – what the reader would see if he could have a mere photograph of reality put before him – who is best able to pick up on these rare events, such as wife-selling and child suicide: he can explore them for their full metaphorical potential. But this kind of novelist does well to get his details right. In an extraordinary *tour de force*, prophetic of the psychiatry of a century later, Tom does just that.

Each detail given by the narrator about Little Father Time has been shown, in psychiatric studies undertaken only in the 1980s and 1990s, to be conducive to depression. Handed over to his grandparents in infancy, he is thrown out after growing up with them. Returned to his mother by some friends travelling from Australia, he is treated kindly, but quickly shoved on to his father, whom he does not know. The description of his apathy is clinically exact to the last detail (see Dr Keith Horton's *Suicide and Attempted Suicide Among Children and Adolescents*, 1987).

Not content with that, Hardy adds a poetic dimension to Little Father Time, and makes him a symbol of deprived and oppressed children everywhere. He is just an encumbrance: 'What a view of life he must have, mine or not mine!' exclaims Jude just after he first hears of him. He means so little to anyone that he has not even been baptized, and his kindly elders have explained to him the reason: 'Because, if I died in damnation, 'twould save the cost of a Christian burial.' By the time Sue and Jude take him over, he is too depressed to rally – and there is no evidence that he does so. Tom is exceedingly subtle here: it might be argued that the boy does, at least, become attached to Sue, and that this is a sign of his becoming happier. But, given at last some sign that he is loved and cared for, he now puts to his new mother some of those questions natural to children. 'I ought not to be born, ought I?' he has asked her, and had no answer. Her status in his eyes must not be under-estimated: she is the first woman who has ever cared for or about him. He asks again:

'It would be better to be out o' the world than in it, wouldn't it?'
'It would almost, dear.'

Then, when she tells him that there is another baby on the way, he bursts out: 'I'll never believe you care for me, or father, or any of us any more!' He believes that, in spite of the extreme difficulties which they encounter as a result of there being three children already, she has 'sent for another'. She is too tired to make a proper effort to explain, for which she later (and not altogether wrongly) blames herself. Of course the suicide of Father Time is more than a mere clinical study; but it is important to understand that it is perfectly depicted, and quite beyond the crudity of, say, Parmeno's character who kills eight people to obtain a ticket to a bullfight. The 'advanced man', the doctor called in to attend the case, believes that it is 'the beginning of the coming universal wish not to live'. But that is one of the glosses that Tom puts upon the appalling event. Another, outside the novel, was undoubtedly the poem 'Midnight on the Great Western', only in part a representation of himself, and not only as a child: it is another version of Housman's 'I, a stranger and afraid/In a world I never made', and, perhaps, of John Amner's less well-known, and more overtly Christian, fragment (1615):

> A stranger here, as all my fathers were
> That went before, I wander to and fro;
> From earth to heaven is my pilgrimage,
> A tedious way for flesh and blood to go.
> O thou, that art the way, pity the blind,
> And teach me how I may Thy dwelling find.

For Tom the quest was a similar one, but, as the 'advanced man', the doctor, said of poor Little Father Time, there were by his time 'new views of life'. His poem concentrates upon a scientific instance, caught in a moment of time in a railway carriage, but does not quite cancel the possibility of a way:

> In the third-class seat sat the journeying boy,
>   And the roof-lamp's oily flame
> Played down on his listless form and face,
> Bewrapt past knowing to what he was going,
>   Or whence he came.
>
> In the band of his hat the journeying boy
>   Had a ticket stuck; and a string
> Around his neck bore the key of his box,
> That twinkled gleams of the lamp's sad beams
>   Like a living thing.
>
> What past can be yours, O journeying boy
>   Towards a world unknown,
> Who calmly, as if incurious quite,
> On all at stake, can undertake
>   This plunge alone?
>
> Knows your soul a sphere, O journeying boy,
>   Our rude realms far above,
> Whence with spacious vision you mark and mete
> This region of sin that you find you in,
>   But are not of?

This has no specifically Christian implications, except that the 'sphere . . . Our rude realms far above' would imply, to an average reader of that time, Christian rather than any other belief. *Jude*, though, abounds in Christian parallels. Nor is it so easily dismissed as an agnostic statement (or even, as in the case of Norman Holland: 'Hardy's Symbolic Indictment of Christianity', in *Nineteenth-Century Fiction*, June 1954), as some critics, misled by the intellectual, quasi-positivist position he chose to take up in public, have believed. There is a difference, as Christ himself more than implied on occasion, between Christianity as it is usually practised and as it is utilized in materialistic and other interests (Tom's target), and Christianity itself, anyone's *actual* profession of which ought always to be regarded – whether from a standpoint of belief or unbelief is irrelevant – as an astonishing, even miraculous, thing. Father Time's death itself suggests the crucifixion: 'For the rashness of these parents he had groaned, for their ill-assortment he had quaked, and for the misfortunes of these he had died.' His death-note, '*Done because we are too meny*', may echo the Aramaic words ('Numbered, weighed, [divided'] in Daniel 5, 25: MENE, MENE, TEKEL, [UPHARSIN]', writes Walter Gordon in 'Father Time's Suicide Note' (*Nineteenth-Century Fiction*, December 1967): 'This is the interpretation of the thing: MENE; God hath numbered thy kingdom, and finished it. TEKEL; Thou art weighed in the balances, and art found wanting.' This suggestion is greatly strengthened by the early passage in which Jude is trying to imagine the 'exact point in the glow' of Christminster where Phillotson might be: 'like one of the forms in Nebuchadnezzar's furnace'.

Ian Gregor believes that it would be 'foolish' to deny that the introduction of Father Time is a 'failure'. Yet he calls the suicide the 'most terrible scene in Hardy's fiction – indeed it might reasonably be argued in English fiction'. 'Hardy has set aside the conventions of realism too easily, so that the child seems to have strayed into the novel from another art form, Lady Macduff's son unnervingly encountered on the Great Western.' But Tom intended to set aside those conventions; that 'art form' was poetry; and there was nothing he wanted to do so much as to 'unnerve' his readers. After all, if it really is so terrible, can that be so serious a 'failure' except in the eyes of those who insist that prose works must remain tied into rigid conventions? What he was up against was what he described in his 1912 postscript to the book as the attitude of the 'conflagratory bishop':

We Britons hate ideas, and we are going to live up to that privilege of our native country. Your picture may now show the untrue, or the uncommon, or even be contrary to the canons of art; but it is not the view of life that we who thrive on the conventions can permit to be painted.

To overcome this without indulging in sheer sensationalism Tom needed to have recourse to poetry, and in *Jude*, his last major novel, he moved even nearer to poetry than he had in *Tess*.

In *Hardy's Use of Allusion* (1983), Marlene Springer has shown clearly and definitively how Hardy, by enmeshing the novel in a web of allusion, caused Jude to be both a 'Christ figure' and a man 'betrayed and abandoned by God, society, and himself', who became 'an example of the coming universal wish not to live in a world which no longer offers any stable and humane values' (to quote from the remarks made by the 'advanced doctor' about Little Father Time's suicide). And, as Patricia Ingham suggests, his text, overtly an exposé of Christian values, 'subverts itself: its attack on the Church draws power from the acceptance of a central Christian image. The imaginative attraction of the creed is still felt, just as it was by Hardy himself' – 'the hatred of the Church shows a powerful sense of affinity with its founder'. This was ironic indeed: a society nominally devoted to Christ, fully supported by its Church, inflicts upon its most sensitive members Christ-like suffering. There are no hints in *Jude* of a Christ in any way supernatural. But the book is not the 'symbolic indictment' of Christianity that it has been called; it is an indictment of pseudo-Christian practice. It is as if the question of Christ's status – grand humanist, supernatural phenomenon or both – must be left open until his humane teaching is understood and acted upon. The passion here is hardly secular.

To describe *Jude* as a comedy would be absurd. But Tom's sense of humour is never far beneath its surface. Jude is himself almost a comic figure at the beginning, with his dreams of middle-class distinction. The brutal comedy of the pig-killing scene is only mitigated by its later consequences. It is clearly shown by the narrator that the Christminster which Jude thinks he sees is not the Christminster of any reality: what he actually sees may not even be Christminster at all. Arabella Donn, her name suggesting 'belladonna', his undoing, is in part a comic figure: her earthiness, unscrupulous as it is, always acts as some necessary relief to the *Grand Guignol* aspect. Her ignorant indifference to Jude's aspirations counterpoints the absurd element in them, poignant though they are. Her temporary 'conversion' to nonconformism, completely in character, introduces a sheerly comic element; it sets the highly serious Christianity of the youthful Jude, and that of the repentant, maddened Sue, into grotesque relief.

In his 1912 postscript Tom, having summarized *Jude*'s 'career as a book', remarked: 'the only effect of it on human conduct I could discover [was] its effect on myself – the experience completely curing me of further interest in novel-writing'. This was precise, and ought not to have led to the long-prevalent assumption that he abandoned fiction out of disillusionment. He says only that the experience *completely* cured him: he would now be able to do what, via *The Dynasts*, he really wanted to do: become a full-time poet. The financial success of *Jude*, as of *Tess* before it, and of the collected edition, made this step less unsafe than it would earlier have been. In that sense *Jude* really was his last novel; the drastic revision of *The Well-Beloved* arose from the fact that he needed to add it to the collected edition, and found the serial form too careless to be suitable.

No man could have arranged his exit from fiction more aptly. If any single reason needs to be given for this exit, then it is that poetry, as in *Jude*, was beginning to threaten his effectiveness as a novelist: it was beginning to burst the dams that separate it from prose. He was now finding prose no longer adequate for what he wished to say and was writing more poems; and, as 'Wessex Heights' (1896) and the 'In Tenebris' (1895–96) group show, a time of severe personal trial was in store for him.

25

Dissension at Max Gate

It was in 1895, with the publication of *Jude* in volume form on 1 November (or whenever she read it), that some form of the famous iron finally entered into Emma's soul. She developed a hostility to her husband that had previously been held in abeyance. After all, no one can live with another person, especially a 'genius', for almost twenty years without developing hostility to, or distaste for, some element in him or her, even if it be kept wholly in the unconscious. The genial 'Some Recollections', written so late in her life, shows that this newly overt hostility must have been intermittent, for her recollections display a genuinely charming – and touching – gratitude for her life; but when the hostility did express itself, it was trenchant. It poured itself out, in a haphazard way, in letters to Rebekah Owen. Many other such letters written by the wives of all sorts of men have been destroyed by wiser and kinder recipients, who have recognized them as necessary safety valves. What Emma occasionally said about Tom, to a few people, is not much more than most wives have thought, and many have said . . . But, for all that, the grounds of her discontent need to be noted.

Apart from unhappy poems of whose biographical significance we cannot be certain, and from what he told Clodd and Gosse, briefly and almost enigmatically, years later after Emma's death, the only indication of a rift on Tom's side lies in some of his letters to her. He became terse, and ceased to address himself affectionately at their beginnings or their ends. This is a small matter, and not too much should be made of it; but it was not caused by carelessness. He felt alienated from Emma, and that was the way he expressed it. It might reflect some severe row, or series of rows, between them. Or, equally possibly, it might reflect their inability to have a row. At one point, on 12 May 1900, he signs himself simply 'T.H.'. But the 'Yours affly' returns later. The initial trouble, fuelled by Tom's feeings for Mrs Henniker, silent or otherwise, was over *Jude*.

We have no means of knowing whether Emma read this book as Tom wrote it, or whether she read it as it appeared in *Harper's*, or whether she waited until it appeared in volume form. Perhaps, as seems most likely, she read the volume proofs. But she read it, and it upset her deeply. It may even have caused her to behave hysterically. Perhaps Tom, who knew that he had to make it very strong stuff, was fearful of her likely attitude and suggested that she wait for the volume publication, or at least for the proofs. None of the manuscript is in her hand, and the now forgotten dramatist and translator of Maeterlinck, Alfred Sutro – then a Dorset neighbour – maintained, in his autobiography *Celebrities and Simple Souls*, that she told him that *Jude* was the first of her husband's books which he had not allowed her to read in that form. He reported that Emma said that the book had made 'a difference to them in the County', and that, had she been able to read the manuscript, it would not have appeared in the form it did. Tom kept his eyes on his plate, and said nothing. We can sympathize with both parties: Emma because she of all people had the right to dissent from it if she wished, and Tom because he believed in it implicitly, and was apt to consign those who did not to the category of bigots, prudes and miserable second-class prelates. But Emma was no prude, and may have conceived her antipathy for the book not so much because of her smouldering resentment of Mrs Henniker, but because for the first time she felt cut off from the composition of one of his novels. She had doubtless all along valued these works more highly than he did. If, she felt, Tom could discuss the writing of the book with Mrs Henniker, then why not with her, who knew more about his methods?

While he was writing *Jude*, which involved writing and dismembering it for serial publication simultaneously, life seemed to go on fairly normally once he had got over his passion for Florence Henniker. It is obvious that Emma knew about his attachment and probably about his real wishes in regard to it; whether she commented on this to him is not known. There is no evidence of a quarrel followed by a reconciliation until 1896. But the fuss she made about *Jude* must have been fuelled by the hurt she had experienced: *Jude* became the victim of her feelings about Florence Henniker, or, rather, about Tom's passion for Florence. She may at this time have refused him sexually; if so it might account for the conviction with which he depicts Jude's frustration.

The *Life* states that 'Hardy's entries of his doings were always of a fitful and irregular kind, and now [after the usual visit to London] there occurs a hiatus which cannot be filled.' While staying at 90 Ashley Gardens, which he and Emma occupied from May until July 1895, he had been consulting Forbes Robertson and Mrs Patrick Campbell about a dramatization of *Tess*, with the latter in the name part. Emma preceded him to Max Gate, and on 24 July he wrote to her from the Athenaeum:

> I am going to meet Mr Forbes Robertson at his house to-morrow morning about the play . . . It is not always cheerful to be here now that we have no foothold – & the season seems over. I *live* almost entirely at this club or at the Savile . . . I wish we had a permanent place here – it wd be so much nicer. But I don't see how to afford £200 a year for a flat.

There is not a word about *Jude*. Within a few days of writing that letter, on 4 August, now back at Max Gate, he was telling Florence Henniker that he had been very ill with a 'sudden attack of English cholera' (what we should now call gastric flu): he had been in bed for four days, dosed with 'medicine & iced brandy'. Having just acknowledged on 29 July a copy of Havelock Ellis's pamphlet *Sexual Inversion in Women* (though he did not tell Florence this), his mind was on Sappho, for he ended his letter to her provocatively: 'I have made myself a present of Wharton's *Sappho* – a delightful book. How I love her – how many men have loved her! – more than they have Christ I fear.'

On 17 August he described himself to the artist Winifred Thomson, who had not long before painted a portrait of him, as being 'chained here, to the drudgery of misplaced commas'. He was working extensively on the new (Osgood) edition of his novels and stories, and concentrating particularly on the 'Wessex' application.

A glimpse, if a rather jaundiced one, of Tom at home in the early autumn of 1895 has been provided by George Gissing, whose gloomy and evocative novels Tom favoured. He had last met Gissing, on 13 July 1895, at a dinner, held at the Burford Bridge Hotel near Box Hill in Surrey, of the Omar Khayyám Club, at which George Meredith had been the guest of honour. Clodd, who knew Gissing before he knew Tom, was there, and so was Gosse. Gissing wrote to him on 3 September 1895, telling him of some stories he was writing for Clement Shorter for the *English Illustrated Magazine*, and which he described as 'blotched impressions of miserable, squalid lives. They are not worth much, but such work needs to be done.' Tom replied on 6 September:

> Your welcome letter comes just at a time when I was thinking you

might be disposed to spend a day or two in Dorset. Can you come & stay with us from Friday or Saturday next the 13th or 14th till Monday? It is very quiet & solitary here but if you are not familiar with this part of England it might interest you a little.

Gissing was a sour man, and at that point was going through a desperately difficult period in his second marriage (as wretched as his first had been, to a prostitute who gave both him and a friend a dose of clap – a disaster ended only by her death); but he had nevertheless long ago written to Tom to tell him how much refreshment he got from his work. However, while they had got on well at their short meetings, more prolonged exposure brought out the best in neither.

Tom left no record of his impression, but Gissing, as was his wont, whined. 'On the whole very little pleasure from this visit,' he confided. Tom he found 'a trifle spoiled by success . . . Cannot let himself go in conversation; is uneasy and preoccupied.' It might have been a mistake on Tom's part to invite his publisher, Clarence McIlvaine, at the same time as Gissing, who had every reason to dislike and resent all publishers. McIlvaine would have struck Gissing as paying more deference to Tom than to him, and therefore spoiling his host.

Gissing had visited Meredith at Box Hill a few days earlier, and had angrily noted: 'Dinner poor'. He suffered greatly from poverty, and his novels abound in descriptions of badly fed people: he appreciated a good lunch or dinner, felt annoyed if he did not get it, and resented bad cooking in particular from those who could, by his standards, afford good. His own wife's cooking was non-existent. Tom liked to get on to easy and equal terms with his fellow writers if he could, whereas the smooth Meredith did not at all object to his feet being sat at. On this occasion Tom paid for his attempts at familiarity: Gissing told his friend Bertz that he had liked Meredith, as a 'scholar': 'I feel proud to sit in his room.' Hardy, though, had 'far less vigour and intellectual distinction. Born a peasant, he yet retains much of the peasant's view of life.' He did not note that Meredith had a Portsmouth naval outfitter's view of life – but only because Meredith was so good at concealing his 'origins'. Because Tom did not put on airs, Gissing made the astonishing observation that he seemed not to 'read very much'; 'I grieve to find that he is drawn into merely fashionable society.' He believed, he told Bertz, that Tom did not 'know the names of flowers in his own fields' when he took him for a walk on Egdon Heath. 'A strange unsettlement appears in him; probably the result of his long association with a paltry woman.' He had not taken at all to Emma, who, despite their 'easy circumstances', had also given him a poor dinner: 'cooking of course bad'. She was 'very foolish', 'unrestful and disagreeable in face', 'utterly discontented' and (again) 'extremely silly & discontented'. However, he did notice one other thing about her, something which once again suggests that her interest in social climbing has been grossly exaggerated: she 'talked fretfully of being obliged to see more society than she liked'.

More disagreeably, Gissing reports Emma's having said that it was 'hard to live with people of humble origin' – 'meaning Thomas, of course', he added. Since the habit was noted by others, this is quite important evidence that she had already started to indulge herself in it. However, Gissing may, as the others did, have missed the teasing humour of it – which, and Tom would have agreed, did not much mitigate its offensiveness. But we forget that she had Jemima to contend with. However, she had now started to become a little odd and graceless, at least at home – the worst place in which to get to understand the enigmatic Tom, Gissing thought.

Gissing, as his friend H.G. Wells wrote, was 'an extraordinary blend of a damaged joy-loving human being hampered by inherited gentility': he was more snobbish, and in a more convoluted manner, than Tom ever was. Thus he could say of Tom: 'I perceive that he has a good deal of coarseness in his nature – the coarseness explained by humble origin.' He was here confusing plain behaviour with insensitivity – even with a lack of the gentility with which he was himself so afflicted. Perhaps Tom had relieved himself while they (presumably McIlvaine was also with them) were walking together on Egdon Heath, and in the manner later noted by Blunden, who was not a snob and well understood that it was no more than the unashamed way of a countryman. To attain gentility all poor Tom needed, doubtless, was a dose of clap, preferably from a woman of the lower orders. The gifted Gissing was also, alas, a prude, who as late as 1890 was shocked by the liaison between Hetty and her squire in *Adam Bede*. It is likely that he allowed his envy to show itself too obviously, and that this embarrassed his host and perhaps also his hostess, especially in front of McIlvaine.

His wife Edith, who became unequivocally mad five years afterwards, was just at this time leading him the sort of dance (he called it 'the utmost domestic misery', and was left little time for work) which caused him to project his own problems into other writers' situations. Thus he described Tom's life, too, as 'misery'. It was one of his favourite words. He may not have been in a balanced state of mind: he even reported that Tom 'did a very odd thing at breakfast – jumped up and killed a wasp with the flat of a table-knife!' While this is interesting as a demonstration that the hater of cruelty in nature was not up to tolerating the buzzings of wasps (unless the wasp was tormenting his publisher, an important man in terms of his future), it was ordinary rather than odd – and odd of Gissing to think it odd.

Just ten days before Gissing arrived on his unhappy little visit, Tom met the thirty-two-year-old Agnes Grove, the married daughter of General Pitt-Rivers. As good-looking as Mrs Henniker, she was more talented and spirited. She was also contented with Walter Grove, her intelligent husband, who called her 'my little pepper-pot' – and she really was outspoken as well as assured. Tom danced with her under the trees at an evening country-dance party at Rushmore, her father's estate on the Wiltshire Downs, and got stiff knees for 'some succeeding days': 'It was on the occasion of the annual sports at the Larmer Tree, and a full moon and a clear sky favouring, the dancing on the green was a great success.' The scene was illuminated by 'thousands of Vauxhall lamps'. He may still have been full of his genuine pleasure at this encounter when Gissing arrived, and thus caused the envious younger man to gain the erroneous impression that he talked 'of lords and ladies more than [of] ordinary people'.

Tom liked Agnes Grove, but far too much has been made of it. It is even suggested that he fell in love with and indulged in fantasies about her. There is not a shred of evidence to support this. He was merely fond of her in the socially permissible manner in which an older man may admiringly be of a younger woman. In 1907 Agnes wrote a lively book, *The Social Fetich*, and, significantly, dedicated it to Tom. It is a critique of vulgarities and social pretensions. Tom got on well with Agnes, wrote to her frequently, and helped her with advice on her polemical publications. Without mentioning her, he told Florence, on 11 September, that the Rushmore visit was the 'most romantic time' he had experienced since he met her in Dublin. When Agnes Grove died on 7 December 1926 he published (first in the *Daily Telegraph* for 21 May 1928) 'Concerning Agnes', in which he refers to her as 'that fair woman' with whom he hoped to dance many times:

DISSENSION AT MAX GATE

I could not, though I should wish, have over again
  That old romance,
And sit apart in the shade as we sat then
  After the dance
The while I held her hand, and, to the booms
Of contrabassos, feet still pulsed from the distant rooms.

But whatever Emma had registered about Tom's admiration for young Agnes Grove, if anything at all, she was still anxious to do things with her husband. Inspired by an impromptu visit from the Thorneycrofts, who were on a cycling holiday in the district, she began to learn how to ride a bicycle herself. After a few days Tom joined her.

Emma had not mastered the skill by 1 November, the day of *Jude*'s publication: according to George Douglas, who, having just arrived at Max Gate, was with Tom in his study when he opened a parcel containing a copy, she had just had an accident. This had possibly been caused by apprehension on behalf of both her husband and her own beliefs. We do not know when she read the unexpurgated *Jude*. We know of the furore with which the novel was greeted in the dullest quarters, and of how Tom soon got over the worst of it when he realized that he was not going to be shunned by society. Indeed, he seems not to have been shunned by anyone, since he was not on personal terms with any of his detractors – few of whom in any case would have had the courage to ignore him socially had they run across him.

Probably the single event that upset him most deeply – which, well aware of the nature of the world, he could be said to have called down upon himself – was the unkind apostasy of Gosse, who could hardly have believed in his strictures except as an insurance against losing the esteem of those who could advance him. Or was that event what Tom would have thought of as the apostasy of the much more important Emma, who, far from having been 'uncomprehending' in the past (as she has been called), had helped him and understood his purposes? What was her state of mind during these months? For she did not like *Jude* at all – and she let Tom know it. He for his part interpreted this, as most husbands might, as extreme disloyalty – and as taking the side of his smug and insincere enemies. For his bitterness about the state of the world, an element in which was its refusal to consider *Jude* – or many other more vital matters – on truthful terms, was not one whit mitigated by his relief at finding himself accepted, after all, by his old aristocratic and other society acquaintances.

I have already suggested that Emma was deeply upset over the Florence Henniker affair, and that she had slightly withdrawn herself from Tom because of it. Her reasons are obvious: Florence Henniker was a smart and supposedly more literate woman than herself, already successful as a writer; she was also 'a younger woman'. Emma may even have refused Tom her bed, although we know no details – nor even when she experienced the menopause, usually a difficult time in any woman's mental and physical life. This could have begun in 1880, or even a year or two earlier; equally, it might have been delayed until as late as 1890. Since all our hard knowledge, apart from malevolent inference and irresponsible speculation, of Emma's extreme eccentricity or maladroitness in society dates from about 1895, one might guess at a very late menopause, and a difficult and disturbing one at that. Whether Tom handled this situation sensitively or insensitively we cannot say; the subject was not even discussed by most Victorian couples. There is much more that we do not know about which went on behind the closed doors of Max Gate – unless nothing went on, and it all simmered beneath the surface. The gossip that was collected in the 1960s, from servants and others, relates to the years after 1900.

Emma's antipathy to *Jude* became well known, although there are no precise details concerning the particular nature of her dislike. In a letter dated 19 February 1897 to Rebekah Owen, who had turned up at Dorchester yet again in 1896, she complained of the latter's being what she called a 'Jude*ite*': 'One thing I abhor in authors. It is their blank materialism . . . I do not want T.H. to be hand in glove with Zola. Alas that *you* are a Jude*ite*'. (The Zola reference, however, refers to the possibility that he would write an anti-vivisection book – which he never did – and not to *Jude*.) In fact, as we know, Owen was not really a 'Jude*ite*', and even wrote a verse about the *Pall Mall Gazette*'s characterization of the book as 'Jude the Obscene' – a verse which, incidentally, exactly catches the status of her accomplishments:

> The vex't question of title may now, I submit,
> Be settled at last, with small straining of wit.
> Change two letters only, the u r I mean,
> And you better the sense, for Obscure, read Obscene.

But Owen did apparently apologize to Tom for her attitude, and thus

542

annoyed Emma. Eccentricity of expression apart, the difference between her and her husband was an ordinary enough one: she objected to his pessimism about the future, and believed that 'the thickening clouds of evil advancing' could be countered by Christianity and reform. Presumably she thought that he should lend his name to more good causes. However, he did share in Emma's pro-animal and, later, suffragist activities. Thus they did share a belief in the nature, and the presence, of 'thickening clouds of evil'.

By far the most authoritative comment on the matter of *Jude*, however, has come from Gordon Gifford, Emma's nephew (and the brother of Lilian, who was to become a trial to everyone in the future). He was then at school in Dorchester, and was in and out of Max Gate all the time. In a letter to the *Times Literary Supplement* (1 January 1944), prompted by Lord David Cecil's book on Hardy, he wrote:

> . . . my aunt, who was a very ardent Churchwoman and believer in the virtues and qualities of women in general, strongly objected to this book, and, I think, the outlook of some of the characters depicted therein. I should, however, mention that this was the first of the Hardy novels in which she had not assisted by her counsel, copious notes for reference and mutual discussion.

Gifford, a quiet man who had a good notion of what was going on around him, could not agree, however, that the marriage itself was in a bad state. It was just a question of dissension over *Jude*.

Nor, indeed, was the marriage ever quite as desperate as it has been made out to be: there could be no better witness than Gifford. The late Carl Weber, the American professor who pretended that he knew Florence Hardy when in fact she would never receive him, made a collection of all Emma's alleged 'foolish remarks'; when this list is analysed it is found to contain little of substance, and much more of unreliable tittle-tattle (of which he was inordinately fond). It is Weber who looks foolish.

Most people who met the Hardys unthinkingly expected Emma to be in awe of her genius husband, and were shocked when she showed signs of independence. It broke their set of rules. That her own ideas, while not contemptible (they were directed towards the sudden betterment of the world through Christ, and the abolition of darkness and suffering), were not as interesting as Tom's should not deter us from appreciating that they were hers, that they sprang from her deep kindness and concern, and that she did not consider them ridiculous. Nor would they have been held up as such had her husband not been Thomas Hardy.

Ford Madox Ford's famous account of Tom, related in *Portraits from Life* (1937, in America – published as *Mightier than the Sword* in Britain in the following year), has truth in it – he does not pretend more than he tells. Although Ford, an ironist, liked a good story, and although he embellished some of the best in his repertoire, there was little that he related which did not have a kernel of truth in it. When he indulged himself in fantasy, it was obvious what he was doing; only fools were shocked.

He wrote of how, when he was nineteen and had published his first book (*The Brown Owl*, 1892), he met Tom, who was 'marvellously kind' to him about it, and suggested to him that he might like to drop into Max Gate when he 'was passing'. But then, before he could do so:

a storm burst on the British Museum. The young Garnetts [children of Richard Garnett, keeper of printed books at the British Museum] went about with appalled, amused, incredulous or delighted expressions . . . It began to be whispered by them that Mrs Hardy, a Dean's daughter . . . had taken a step . . . She had been *agonized* . . . she hadn't been able to stand it . . . The reception of *Tess* had been too *horrible* . . . for a Dean's daughter . . . All the Deans in Christendom had been driven to consternation about *Tess*. They had all arisen and menaced Max Gate with their croziers. (I know that Deans do not wear croziers. But that was the effect the young Garnetts produced.)

It came out at last . . . Mrs Hardy had been calling on Dr Garnett as the Dean of Letters of the British Isles and Museum to beg, implore, command, threaten, anathematize her husband until he should be persuaded or coerced into burning the manuscript of his new novel – which was *Jude*. She had written letters, she had called. She had wept; like Niobe she had let down her blond hair . . . The Agnostic and Nihilist young Garnetts rejoiced, the Anglicans were distraught. Doctor Garnett had obdurately refused . . . [all but one of the ellipses are Ford's own]

At last, Ford went on, Hardy replied to a letter he had written to him, again asking him to call. He 'staged a walking-tour', and called. But Hardy was out: 'He had gone, I think, to witness a parade of the militia at Weymouth which I had just left.'

So, instead of listening to Mr Hardy's Wessex folklore, I listened nervously whilst Mrs Hardy in her Junonian blondness of a Dean's daughter read me her own poems over a perfectly appointed tea-table in a room without roses peeping in at the window but properly bechintzed.

I don't know whether it was really a militia parade that he had gone to Weymouth to witness any more than Mrs Hardy was really a Dean's daughter. That was merely the Garnettian slant on the Hardy household. Those lively young people, whose father was really very intimate with the novelist, had projected such an image of the household that I had gone there expecting to find in a low inner room of a long white farmhouse with monthly roses peeping in at the window, the kind elderly gentleman who had held his head on one side and said: 'Ow . . . ow' [which Ford had described his doing when trying to pronounce the title of his book, which he had wrongly thought was ornithological, at their first meeting] . . . And in another room the Dean's daughter would be burning the manuscript of *Jude the Obscure*.

It was all naturally nothing of the sort. Max Gate was not an old, long, thatched farmhouse; it was quite new, of brick, with, as it were, high shoulders. Not a single rose grew on it at that date. And the Dean's daughter was not a Dean's daughter but an Archdeacon's niece . . . And she was not burning *Jude the Obscure*, but read me her own innocuous poems . . .

And immediately on hearing that he was out, my mind had but jumped to the conclusion that he was witnessing a review of militia . . . I suppose because I knew that one of his stories was called *The Trumpet-Major* . . .

This, then, is by no means what Millgate calls it: 'Ford Madox Ford's story of Emma imploring Richard Garnett to stop the publication of *Jude*.' To call it that belittles Ford: the passage is, rather, an amused account of how such stories get about. Ford specifically debunks much of what he says he heard from the young Garnetts, and is clearly sceptical of every detail except what he himself saw and heard.

While more people did read poems aloud in those times, to each other if not at public readings, it must be accorded rather eccentric, if not reprehensible, of Emma to read hers to a young man who had come to talk to the great Thomas Hardy. But Ford, above all a kind as well as a subtle man, does not say that. He just calls the poems 'innocuous' –

which is exactly what they were. Here is a later one, dated 28 March 1910 and entitled 'Poem by Emma Lavinia Hardy' when it was published in the *Dorset County Chronicle*, and 'The Trumpet Call (to the single Daffodil)' in *Alleys*, which she issued at her own expense in December 1911. Differences between the newspaper and the book text show that she took some trouble over it.

> Who has not heard with every bird
>   That stirring trumpet's call
> Of the Daffodil true (not fashioned anew,)
>   Nor felt his heart bound at that magical sound
> Though folded in Winter's pall?
>   Waving, waving, shining, gleaning [misprint for 'gleaming']
> And 'dancing' merrily too;
>   Calling and singing they wake the worlds' dreaming
> With their golden trumpet's call.
> *He* who entranced, memoried that 'dance',
>   Knew only that Daffodils true.
> With laughter shaking, the spring cure for all aching,
>   They sound out their gold trumpets' call –
> 'Comes the Summer with skies clear and blue.'

Many have sneered at this. Tom would have been embarrassed, indeed horrified beyond measure, when it appeared in his local paper and then in *Alleys*. Other similar poems appeared in the *Academy* and the *Sphere*. But no wonder – when he found himself suddenly and poignantly without her, a little over two years later – that, having known her as no one else ever had, he loved the memory of her. Florence Henniker, even the superior Agnes Grove, let alone Florence Dugdale, were all quite unequal to such a heartfelt and sincere lack of sophistication.

Perhaps the truth is that Emma, in an outburst, did write an injudicious letter to Richard Garnett, asking for his advice on how she could prevent Tom from bringing disaster upon himself. Or she may have come across Garnett at a social gathering, or at Gosse's house, or (just possibly, if she had wind of the final form of *Jude* and the 'direction' it was then taking) even at her own house in London in the summer of 1895, and simply asked him for advice – a slight blunder, and as innocuous as her poems. After all, she did tell Sutro, in Tom's presence, that *if* she had read the manuscript, then it would have been emended (which is precisely why she was not allowed to read it). No doubt what she asked Garnett, if anything, was whether he could influence Tom to have second thoughts. Of course there was nothing he could do. He did indeed know Tom well, if not intimately (though it would have looked like that to the young Ford); he was Gosse's close friend, and even wrote a book in collaboration with him. In August 1901 he and his wife were guests at Max Gate, which at least shows that good relations prevailed.

Emma's objections to *Jude* on account of what she took to be its positivism and its pessimism, and perhaps, as well, its slurs on the Church to which she suddenly became devoted, would have distressed Tom. He had just decided to make the best of Florence Henniker's devotion to what he thought were the most unattractive aspects of religion ('Yes – I am rather surprised at your reading any book by J.S. Mill – & still more that you agree with him on anything,' he sarcastically informed her on 3 September 1895 when she told him she had been reading *On the Subjection of Women*; six days later he told her that he did not remember ever reading it himself . . .); *Jude* had been, at least symbolically, burned by a bishop; and Mrs Oliphant had accused him of being against marriage; he had seen the headlines *JUDE THE OBSCENE* and *HARDY THE DEGENERATE*. No one, however determined, could have enjoyed that. He may therefore not have realized what Emma's hostility to *Jude* was really all about. But at the same time it is unlikely that Emma objected to it on account of its 'immorality'. Perhaps she believed that it implied that her husband did not want to be married to her: that, after all, is exactly what critics have wrongly inferred. All Tom had ever really wanted was an affair with Mrs Henniker – 'free love', if you want to put it that way.

Yet Tom's letters to her of this time, apart from that occasional (and not consistent) brusqueness of salutation and farewell already noted, do not suggest much disturbance of the surface of their life together. In October, three weeks before publication, he attended a house party given by George Curzon, the future foreign secretary, at Reigate, and he wrote Emma a brief and affectionate little note telling her that he had travelled with Mrs Craigie. Had Emma been a real prude, or imitator of the nasty section of society, he would hardly have mentioned this. Nor, if things were really bad between them at that point, would he have bothered to write to her at all. After the *Jude* furore had started he wrote on 10 November to Clodd, his enlightened ally, on the subject of marriage. The letter to which it is a reply has not survived, but it seems that Clodd, as was his wont, had taken the novel as a rationalist tract or polemic.

. . . What you say is pertinent & true of the modern views of marriage [as] a survival from the custom of capture & purchase, propped up by a theological superstition.

The story of Jude, however, makes only an objective use of marriage & its superstitions as one, & only one, of the antagonistic forces in the tragedy. You are right in assuming that I have no suggestion or guide to offer. I can only state (most imperfectly, alas!) cases in which natural & human laws create tragic dramas. The philanthropists must do the rest.

Owing, I suppose, to the sheaf of purpose-novels we have had lately on the marriage question, – though written long before them – some of the papers class mine with them – though the case of my people is one of temperamental unfitness for the contract, peculiar to the family of the parties.

He was right to separate himself from the 'new woman' or 'purpose-novels' of the 1890s, since, with the exception of Gissing's *The Odd Women* of 1893 (one of his best novels, and not to be categorized as a 'purpose' one) and, at a lower level, Egerton's *Keynotes*, scarcely any has literary or psychological merit. Even Meredith's own *One of Our Conquerors* (1891) is not of account. It is obvious from his letter to Clodd that he did not consider his own marriage to be relevant to *Jude*; if occasionally he yearned to be free, then he was only doing what three-quarters or more of people, husbands and wives, have done, and still do, privately, since the institution of marriage. Not all of these would assert that they 'meant it'.

As for Emma, she was kindly in intention (and usually in action) above all, and there is no doubt that her letters to the rhino-skinned and deceitful Rebekah Owen – rushed, effusive and sometimes emotional though they may have been – took account, if only unconsciously, of the spoiled American's ignorance of sexual and marital matters, and that they failed to allow for the general level of her intelligence, which was not elevated. Thus, for all the not ill-humoured series of complaints, there is little that is really seriously considered, in their contents, about such questions as marriage and the rights of women. It is possible to tell from them what her own position was on the matter of the so-called 'new woman' novels, although she became a suffragist.

As 'the wife of a genius' Emma was taken on sufferance, and she deserves sympathy on that account. Owen, a malevolent scatterbrain, would agree with anyone if it suited the social instant. We should not judge Emma's intellect by the tone of these kindly letters to Owen, who may have amused her as much as she amused Tom, who himself came to avoid her as much as he decently could. When she first arrived at Dorchester, Owen was a good-looking girl; but there is no indication that Tom ever treated her as having a mind of her own, and he soon tired of her company.

But Owen, who never did a day's work in her life, and lived in what Bailey calls 'petted luxury', is a case apart. She simply used Emma (and afterwards Florence Hardy) to get as close as she could to Tom. It was she who informed the world that when Emma met Florence Henniker for the first time, in Dublin, she was got up like 'Charlie's aunt'. The value of such testimony is obvious enough.

Nor, while we cannot ignore their testimony as we can ignore Owen's, should we judge Emma entirely from what she seemed to be to neighbours and society people in awe of Tom's fame. It would be stupid to deny that there was estrangement between them, but it is not stupid to suggest that its extent has been exaggerated. This exaggeration is partly the result of treating Tom as though he was as unique in life as he was in literature. The difficulties of this marriage were of a kind very often encountered. It is hard to be the wife of a 'great man'. Thus Christine Wood Homer of Athelhampton Hall, the only daughter of a farmer friend, who had known Tom from her schooldays, wrote: 'She could not, and never did, recognise his greatness.' She too reports Emma in the 1900s as showing her paintings, or reading to some visitors 'her latest poem':

> But this was not so with every visitor. Mr Hardy had to like a person before he would enter into any conversation. If Emma Lavinia suspected the visitor had no interest in or friendship for her, but had come only to see Mr Hardy and worship at his shrine, she would not let her husband know he was there, and many a visitor went away without seeing his hero. She, herself, wrote indifferent poems, but they pleased her . . . She would have liked to have received the admiration of the world for talents she believed she possessed, but which were not discernible to anyone else . . . much of the unhappiness in her married life was because she always wanted to be *the great one* . . . It had been a burdensome grief to him that the first Mrs Hardy had not cared for any of his family.

But Christine Wood Homer never met Jemima, or knew of Emma's difficulties.

Emma did, alas, treat Rebekah Owen as someone she could trust, and in her letter to her of 4 March 1902, one of the most vehement she wrote about her husband, and therefore one of the most eagerly quoted, said: 'I can scarcely keep a "mere" cat to say nothing of a "mere man" whom all the world claims, which would not so much matter if his later writings were of a more faithful truthful, & helpful kind.'

Her jealousy increased over the years, and she could never forget *Jude*. 'He should be the last man to disparage marriage! I have been a devoted wife for at least twenty years or more – but the last four or five, alas! Fancy it is our silver wedding this year! The *thorn* is in my side still,' she wrote to Owen on 24 April 1899. But that was after *Wessex Poems*, the publication of which in 1898 caused her more pain than perhaps any other single work. It seems that she rationalized what were straightforward feelings of jealousy, first engendered by Tom's attention to the intellectual qualities of other, less odd (and younger) women, into a fervent oppositional evangelicalism: what she thought and believed increasingly tended to be what he did not, and vice versa. That she was *so* optimistic resulted from his being, or seeming to be, *so* 'pessimistic'. Millgate quotes a splendid example of her extreme optimism from a letter about education which she wrote, obviously in her capacity as 'Mrs Hardy', to the *Daily Chronicle*. But it is worthy of note that Tom preserved a cutting of it – although, according to Millgate, he misdated it 'Sept. 5 1891':

> Eliminate evil, stamp it out at its source. Eradicate selfishness, the rage for power and advancement, the accumulation of wealth by others' woes. Expenses will be moderated, violence utilized, punishment abolished; and through every necessary exercise of brain and body a world will be evolved progressing towards perfection from this present chaos. Lives would be prolonged blissfully, and in one or two generations nearly every person would in some way or other be a *maker of happiness*.

This is naive, characteristically hyperbolic, artless, and peremptorily expressed. Nobody could disagree with a word of the implied diagnosis, except by denying that evil, selfishness or usury existed in the world. Some twenty years or so later, in admittedly more creative vein in 'The

DISSENSION AT MAX GATE

High Delights of Heaven', Emma's style had progressed somewhat, although the prose is still recognizably hers:

> Our capabilities will be increased richly to enjoy everything that will be there that has delighted us on earth; the loveliness of another Eden (this more beautiful than the first) also its tame creatures with higher intelligence – lost pets and martyred ones; not altogether a garden, nor town, nor country, but a splendid city with unending exquisite environments; all who are *there* of the creation no longer travailing and waiting for redemption, the lion and the lamb lying down together, actually as first intended. Pleasures will be in every way exhilarating and in full measure. No vice, lust, evil act, or evil desires of any kind. 'The just made perfect.'

And so it goes on. There is even a passage that, bearing in mind what Emma told Owen about her loathing of authors' 'blank materialism', might well be intended for Tom:

> However, heaven will not be the same for all saved ones. Those who have accepted late – having therefore not delighted in God's service on earth – yet have said in their hearts, and confessed that they believe entirely in the Plan of Salvation, will have happiness made for them of the kind they most like, more material than those who have had life-long communication with God on earth. It cannot be supposed that the variety of human nature will not be satisfied most completely.

The style here is the result of a mood of passionate indignation which has seized the writer. It was not a permanent state of mind, but one that erupted violently at intervals. In content it is orthodox stuff, and is probably peculiar not because it was written in the first place but because it was actually published (in 1912, in *Spaces*). Emma had once been broad-minded, sympathetic to Tom's views (for example, she was at least tolerant of positivism in the 1880s), and appreciative of his work. Nor was she ever driven by orthodoxy for its own sake. Her grudge against him for turning away from her and her advice and help expressed itself in that manner, largely because it was a maintainable position in her time (and would be even today). There seems to be no reason to doubt the journalist Clive Holland's story that when he and Sarah Grand (author of *The Heavenly Twins*) dined with them on

21 March 1903, and discussed religion, Emma sent a note to Holland at his hotel telling him that 'she hoped neither he nor his visitor would regard what her husband said on religious matters as serious, adding the information that he regularly read his Greek testament'! But this was merely quaint, and, as I insist, not intended totally seriously: by then it had become a habitual means of getting at him. T.P. O'Connor claimed that Emma once complained, to his wife, that Tom was 'very vain and very selfish. And these women that he meets in London society only increase these things. They are the poison; I am the antidote.' But she would happily have said this to Tom's face: once again, it ought not to be taken too seriously, and perhaps has been taken so only by humourless men standing on what they do not realize is their own dignity. One can quite easily imagine such a remark being made affectionately, or even in jest.

All this was sporadic, not continuous. Tom was exceedingly sensitive to any slight, real or imagined, and also exceedingly volatile, and such incidents caused him much more suffering than they would have done to most men. He was gentle enough about the matter after she died, mentioning it in letters to Mrs Henniker, Dorothy Allhusen (daughter of Lady Jeune, one of their oldest and closest friends), Clodd and Gosse. To Henniker he wrote on 12 December 1912: 'In spite of the differences between us, which it would be affectation to deny, & certain painful delusions she suffered from at times, my life is now intensely sad to me now without her.' And to Dorothy Allhusen a week or so later, on the 23rd: 'As you know, she was peculiar and difficult in some things, but in others she was so simple & childlike as to be most winning, & I regret her more now than you can think.' There is also a fragment of a letter to Florence Dugdale (as she still was), which she transcribed for Clodd in a letter to him of 13 January 1913. Here Tom refers to his sorting out of her papers, and discovery of diaries with hostile remarks about himself, in which he says 'it was, of course, sheer hallucination in her, poor thing, & not wilfulness . . .'

Some of these phrases – 'delusions', 'sheer hallucination' – have been taken as indications that Emma became clinically mad, or that Tom believed her to be so. There is no support for this view. She was eccentric and odd, but in no way clinically mad. This notion of 'madness' was Florence Hardy's canard, and she doubtless felt ashamed of herself for inventing it. What Tom meant was that Emma made false assumptions; but that is not madness. Millgate quotes Tom's old acquaintance Sir Thomas Clifford Allbutt as having told one of

Florence's sisters that in his 'unofficial opinion' she was 'certifiable'. Allbutt was from 1892 Regius Professor of Medicine at Cambridge, and had been a Commissioner in Lunacy; but this 'opinion', if he really gave it, may be swiftly disposed of. It came to Millgate through Purdy, and therefore from the jealous Florence, who was obsessed with the idea, and even had Tom half-believing it at the height of his grief. She later spoke of Emma's 'tainted stock'. The Dugdales could be vulgar, and Florence's sister Margaret Soundy was incapable of interpreting such a remark, as distinct from holding it up triumphantly like a flag or a tabloid newspaper headline. Purdy himself was convinced of the legend of Emma's insanity: he did not care to understand that there is a distinction between eccentricity, ramblingness and a degree of self-pity and discontent, combined perhaps with premature senility – and clinical insanity. If there were not such a difference, then at least a quarter of the population aged over sixty would be 'certifiable'.

However, let us suppose Allbutt did make some such pronouncement. Even as we have it, reinforced by the prejudices of Florence Hardy, her sister, and the uncomprehending Purdy, it remains 'unofficial'. He did not know Emma well enough to make such a judgement, never having seen her for more than a hour or two at a time, if that. He may have issued a reluctant or conditional judgement on the basis of the wild excited tattle eagerly flung at him, as an 'expert', by the Dugdales, anxious to establish the legend of how wonderful their own relation had been in tending the old genius, by contrast with his mad and horrible first wife. Through those months when she was deceiving Emma – living at Max Gate, working as her secretary and helping her to 'place' her work, and pretending to be devoted to her – Florence never said a word about her being 'mad': not to Clodd or to anyone else in whom at that time she confided. Why not? True madness is a phenomenon sufficiently obvious at close quarters. (Later, she revised her recollections.) Allbutt himself was a distinguished and humane doctor, who invented the clinical thermometer. When young he had run a notably progressive infirmary in Leeds, around which he had shown George Eliot, whom he also consulted about 'his long engagement'. But he was vain, and thoroughly deserved his inevitable knighthood. His claim that he was the original of Lydgate in George Eliot's *Middlemarch* (the novel's most conspicuous human failure) is taken seriously to this day; but, as Gordon S. Haight makes clear in his biography of Eliot, it has no foundation. Nor, despite or perhaps because of his having been a Commissioner in Lunacy, was he any kind of pioneer of psychiatry. Christine Wood

Homer had known Emma much better than Allbutt had. All she would say of Emma, basing her opinion in part on what she had been told by her mother about the younger Emma, was that in old age she became 'an increasing embarrassment' to Tom, and that while 'at first she had only been childish . . . she got steadily worse with advancing age and became very queer and talked curiously'. So does everyone's grandmother. Being 'very queer' included such actions as watching 'the flies on the window panes' and expressing 'enthusiastic delight at the sweet way in which they washed their little faces and stroked their pretty wings'. Christine Wood Homer was a child at the time, and it seemed to her 'very strange behaviour'. But she did not call it mad, and it was not. It was distracted, but may have been done as a misguided attempt to please the child. Nor could Christine Wood Homer say that Emma ever spoke to her family in disparagement of her husband: significantly, she had only 'heard from several people in Dorchester that she spoke unpleasantly about him to them'. Such incidents were probably few and isolated: like Tom, Emma was subject to variations of mood. Her bad ones were quite enough to upset a man of his keen sensitivity, but they did not necessarily last for long. She continued to act as as an efficient hostess until the very end of her life.

Those who canvass the notion of Emma's clinical insanity draw on one more piece of what they consider to be evidence: Tom's poem 'The Interloper'. Entitled 'One Who Ought Not to Be There' in manuscript, it was first published in 1917 in *Moments of Vision*; its motto, 'And I saw the figure and visage of Madness seeking for a home' was added in the *Collected Poems* of 1923. Purdy, inspired by the eager Florence, was confident that it recalled Tom's realization of his wife's 'increasing derangement'.

> There are three folk driving in a quaint old chaise,
> And the cliff-side track looks green and fair;
> I view them talking in quiet glee
> As they drop down towards the puffins' lair
>   By the roughest of ways;
> But another with the three rides on, I see,
>   Whom I like not to be there!
>
> No: it's not anybody you think of. Next
> A dwelling appears by a slow sweet stream
> Where two sit happy and half in the dark:

DISSENSION AT MAX GATE

They read, helped out by a frail-wick'd gleam,
　　Some rhythmic text;
But one sits with them whom they don't mark,
　　One I'm wishing could not be there.

No: not whom you knew and name. And now
I discern gay diners in a mansion-place,
And the guests dropping wit – pert, prim, or choice,
The hostess's tender and laughing face,
　　And the host's bland brow;
But I cannot help hearing a hollow voice,
　　And I'd fain not hear it there.

No: it's not from the stranger you met once. Ah,
Yet a goodlier scene than that succeeds;
People on a lawn – quite a crowd of them. Yes,
And they chatter and ramble as fancy leads;
　　And they say, 'Hurrah!'
To a blithe speech made; save one, mirthless,
　　Who ought not to be there.

Nay: it's not the pale Form your imagings raise,
That waits on us all at a destined time,
It is not the Fourth Figure the Furnace showed;
O that it were such a shape sublime
　　In these latter days!
It is that under which best lives corrode;
　　Would, would it could not be there!

This is a poem about madness, and Tom possibly did believe, at the moment he wrote it, that it was about his wife. When the publisher V.H. Collins called at Max Gate on 27 December 1920 (the result was his unconciously comic *Talks with Thomas Hardy at Max Gate 1920–1922*, of 1928) he asked Tom about it. Collins quoted his colleague at the Oxford University Press, the poet and novelist Charles Williams, as having suggested that the thing 'under which best lives corrode' was 'no definite thing, but a sort of undermining rot which destroys everything'. Tom answered: 'That was a remarkably good guess. He got as near it as one possibly could', re-read the poem over Collins' shoulder, and then added: 'Write down "Insanity"; that is a better word than "Madness". I wonder how I could make it clear.'

But then Florence got Collins alone:

> She told me that [Emma] came from a tainted stock. More than one of her relatives had been in a lunatic asylum. She herself was subject at times to delusions. She would then make the wildest accusations against anyone, including her husband. 'As his secretary I had, of course, experience of these fits. Life with her at such times was almost unbearable. Yet she kept to the end of her life a strange lovableness – a gay, inconsequent, childlike charm.'

Before this Florence had made similar accusations. To Rebekah Owen she wrote on 24 October 1915, with more than a touch of Enfield malice, that Emma's father had been a bankrupt (untrue), that one of her brothers was mad, and that another 'was bringing the whole family into disgrace' (also untrue). It is curious, therefore, that when she was at Max Gate with Emma in 1910, having 'experience of these fits', she did not tell Clodd about them. She was, in fact, lying to Collins.

It is true that insanity, either schizophrenia (then called 'dementia praecox') or what used to be called manic-depressive psychosis (now usually called 'bi-polar' illness or 'affective disorder') does 'run in families'. It is also true that Emma's brother, the civil engineer Richard Ireland Gifford, became mad and was institutionalized. Lilian Gifford, her niece, was wrongly diagnosed as 'paranoid' and spent a year in a mental hospital. But there was no earlier history of 'insanity' in the Gifford family, and it is possible, even likely that, as Gittings suggests, Richard was poisoned by his (recorded) kidney condition: that is how the case would have been looked upon today, just as Gittings claims. The collapse of Lilian Gifford was certainly menopausal, and she fully recovered from it.

'The Interloper' is an intensely dramatic poem, in which a past apparently unvisited by madness, the undermining and destructive rot – the breakdown of reality – is retrospectively seen as having been haunted by the spectre of it. Tom, like so many of his contemporaries, especially Naturalists such as Zola, firmly believed in the notion of 'hereditary taint'. Again and again he insisted that it was a central feature of *Jude*. The news of Richard Ireland Gifford's 'madness', when it came in 1889, must have deeply affected him; probably some of his horror at it went into *Jude*. But he was a poet, apprehending matters of heredity at a high metaphorical level. He was not a psychiatrist any more than his genial acquaintance Allbutt was, and in any case psychiatry was at that time only in its earliest stages of development. Clinicians had already made a distinction between illnesses in which there was disintegration of the personality ('dementia praecox') and affective or hysterical illnesses from which the victims recovered; but that was about all. Whenever he wrote this poem, he was at the height of his grief and remorse over Emma, and obviously veering between moments of self-blame and relief from it. Florence, knowing his susceptibilities, and bitterly jealous, fed him with the idea that Emma had been actually 'insane'. Once he did indeed use the term 'unhinged' of her, to Florence Henniker.

The poem thus came into existence, and it is as fictional in essence as any of his novels: hence his later dithering over exactly what to tell Collins (he did say, 'I knew the family'). As she got older Emma became increasingly scatty, but her sense of reality never broke down, not even on the morning of her death, or on the afternoon before it when she had to force herself, with typical kindliness, to be polite to Rebekah Owen, who had literally forced herself – her sister in tow – into the house, and, as insensitive as ever to others' feelings, refused to leave: Tom said in the *Life* that they had stayed '*very* long', but Florence, anxious to appease her ally, the long-term denigrator of Emma, cut these words. The solicitor Irene Cooper Willis, a friend of Florence Hardy's, was so disturbed by the latter's spiteful accusations that she went through Emma's letters in the Dorchester Museum and specifically stated:

These letters appear to me to dispose of the idea that Mrs Hardy No. 1 was 'mad' – as Mrs Hardy No. 2 so often declared. The truth was, I think, that Miss Dugdale . . . got to know T.H. through the first Mrs Hardy, & evidently, as these letters show, flattered her power of writing, & was grateful for the friendship. When T.H. became very fond of Miss Dugdale, Mrs Hardy No. 1 probably became very jealous & may have shown her jealousy by unusual behaviour . . . This *can* be the only explanation of the madness . . . Apart from one or two 'bees in her bonnet' on cruelty to animals and Romish practices in the Church of England, the whole correspondence . . . goes to disprove the notion.

This not only disposes of the notion that Emma was ever clinically mad, but also exposes the extent of Florence's duplicity: Irene Cooper Willis was her supposed confidante, and yet Florence could never bring herself to confess to her that she had known Tom long before any meeting with Emma in London had been engineered. Willis was a shrewd woman, well versed in literary spite and excess: she was the trusted executrix of 'Vernon Lee' (Violet Paget), the critic and novelist to whom we owe the coinage of the word 'empathy', and she was well known to Tom and Emma as a close friend to the Robinson sisters, Mary and Mabel.

There is nothing exceptional about Emma's letter, now in the Bodleian Library, to Elspeth Grahame of 20 August 1899. Elspeth, already well known to Tom, was a sister of the artist Winifred Thomson, who had painted him in 1895. Their stepfather was father to his long-standing friend Louise Chandler Moulton. In 1899, just after Kenneth Grahame (then author only of *The Golden Age* and *Dream Days*, and ex-contributor to the short-lived *Yellow Book – The Wind in the Willows* came later, in 1908) had been made Secretary of the Bank of England, Elspeth married him. He turned out to be difficult, too much of a natural bachelor. His bride had many friends, but chose to turn to Emma for advice. That in itself indicates a different side to Emma from the one usually represented: Elspeth Grahame was intelligent. Emma wrote:

It is really too 'early days' with you to be benefited by advice from one who has just come to the twenty-fifth year of matrimony. (I knew T.H. in 1870 (April) married Sep. 1874.) You are *both* at present in a 'Benedict' state. (Women can be anything these days.)

Do I know your choice, perhaps I have met him, perhaps not. However it is impossible to give 'directions for all', – besides characters change so greatly with time, and circumstances. I can scarcely think that love proper, and enduring, is in the nature of Man – as a rule – perhaps there is no woman whom 'custom will not stale'. There is ever a desire to give but little in return for our devotion, and affection – their's [sic] being akin to children's, a sort of easy affectionateness, and at fifty a man's feelings too often take a new course altogether. Eastern ideas of matrimony secretly pervade his thoughts, and he wearies of the most perfect, and suitable wife chosen in his earlier life. Of course he gets over it usually somehow, or hides it, or is lucky!

Interference from others is greatly to be feared – members of either family too often are the cause of estrangement. A woman does not object to be ruled by her husband, so much as she does by a relative at his back – a man seldom cares to control such matters when in his power, and lets things glide or throws his balance on the wrong side which is simply a terrible state of affairs, and may affect unfavourably himself in the end.

Keeping separate a good deal is a wise plan in crises – and being both free – and expecting little, neither gratitude, nor attentions, love, nor *justice*, nor anything you may set your heart on. Love interest, adoration, and all that kind of thing is usually a failure – complete – someone comes by and upsets your pail of milk in the end. If he belongs to the public in any way, years of devotion count for nothing. Influence can seldom be retained as years go by, and *hundreds* of wives go through a phase of disillusion, – it is really a pity to have any ideals in the first place. This is gruesome, horrid, you will say – and mayhap Mr Graham [sic] is looking over the bride's shoulder as bridegrooms often do – but you have asked me. Ah some day we may talk further of these matters. There is so much to say – and to compare. Everyone's experience is different – *very*. The Spartan style was wise doubtless.

Yet I must qualify this by saying that occasionally marriage is undoubtedly the happy state (with Christians always if *both* are) which it was intended to be. There must, of necessity, be great purity in the mind of the *man*, joined with magnanimity, and justice, and where, or rather, how often are these qualities to be found combined? Similarity of taste is not to be depended on, though it goes some way, but rivalry, fear, jealousy, steps in often.

A love-match has failed completely over, and over again. Christian philosophy is the only oil certain to work the complication. I see that continually . . .

This, a private letter, is not even eccentric; on the contrary, it is full of excellent observations. Florence Hardy could never have written it: it is beyond her in its directness and absence of received opinion. Tom would have been the last to deny that 'eastern ideas of matrimony' had pervaded his thoughts. Fortunate his previous biographers to have been spared such offensive intrusions! Emma had every right, too, to her comment on 'the nature of Man': at least it spares us of the pretence into which so many otherwise intelligent Victorian women happily entered, that men were not as they are. Emma was capable of self-criticism – after all, it was she, not Tom, who was 'jealous'. She tried to resist her negative feelings. Her sometimes quaint behaviour in no way precludes an inner life characterized by struggle and good intention.

Emma had yet another confidant, a fellow writer to whom she sometimes poured out her literary frustrations. Not all their correspondence is extant, but there is enough to show what sincere trouble they took with each other's works. He was Alfred Pretor, Fellow of St Catharine's, a classical tutor at Cambridge who was as good a friend to Tom as he was to Emma. Pretor, like Mrs Henniker and both the Hardys, had a proper attitude towards animals, and was an active opponent of vivisection. Did Tom know of his past? Gittings remarks that he had been involved in a 'sensational scandal' in his schooldays. That is exactly what he had *not* been involved in: the whole matter had been hushed up, and the only threat to the cover-up had been Pretor himself, with his 'incredible levity and imprudence'. If Tom did know about it, then he would have heard it from that connoisseur of such matters, Gosse. How Pretor would have reacted, had Tom brought up the subject of his friend the classicist John Addington Symonds, is quite a question. Pretor and he had not seen each other since 1859. They would have had a lot to talk about.

Charles John Vaughan (1816–97), yet another Cambridge classicist, was vicar of St Martin's, Leicester, until in 1844 he became headmaster of Harrow. Among his older pupils in the later 1850s were John Addington Symonds and the Dorset-born Alfred Pretor. Between them, these two did for him. Vaughan preached from the school pulpit against the evils of the flesh, and in particular against vice between the boys in his charge (Harrow was at that time more like a paedophilic brothel than a place of education). But he was, as his wife subsequently confessed as she 'flung herself' – a Stanley! – at the feet of Symonds' father, 'subject to' a certain 'weakness' – which, however, she claimed 'had not interfered with his usefulness in the direction of the school at Harrow'. Not everyone agreed with this judgement. In 1859 he was forced to resign, and to decline two bishoprics. Initially he had accepted the second of these offers from a grateful government, but the senior Symonds telegraphed him to warn him off. He was allowed, from 1860, to become the vicar of Doncaster, and, says the *Dictionary of National Biography*, 'for love of the church privately trained ordination candidates in ministerial work, 1861–1897'. Evidently there were certain things that Vaughan just could not do without.

He fell deeply in love with Alfred Pretor, described by Symonds in his *Memoirs* as 'a vain light-headed and corrupt lad, without intellectual or moral foundation'. Symonds' 'own inclinations' prevented him 'from utterly condemning Vaughan', except for his taste: 'I regarded Pretor as a physically and emotionally inferior being.' But Pretor, through vanity (according to Symonds), handed him Vaughan's 'enthusiastic letters'. Symonds now remembered how once, when 'reading Greek iambics' with him, Vaughan had started 'softly to stroke my right leg from the knee to the thigh': 'I never liked the man; he did not possess the intellectual qualities I admired.' A few months later he was up at Oxford; after much agonizing he informed his father, who wrote to Vaughan with his terms: resignation for silence.

Whatever this may have done to Pretor, he behaved with tact and kindness towards Emma. His dog, Judy, had dictated her memoirs to him, and he dedicated these to her in 1898, followed by a second batch from the same animal in 1905. When *Wessex Poems* was published in 1898 Emma was distraught, and wrote in her usual style to Rebekah Owen, who must have two-facedly egged her on: 'Of recent poetry perhaps you admire "The Ivy Wife". Of course my wonder is great at any admiration for it, and *some* others in the same collection'. Although 'The Ivy Wife' *may* not have been written with Emma in mind, it was tactless of Tom to include it; nor was the rather trivial 'Ditty', dedicated to her, sufficient to appease her. She wrote complainingly to Pretor, who told her: 'T. has said again & again to me little casual things that are absolute proofs that all his reminiscences are little fancies evoked from the days of his youth & absolutely without bearing on the real happiness of his life.'

He also told her, with the best of intentions, that it was a satisfaction in itself to be the woman behind a great man! However, he did add: 'I *do* wish T.H. wd. dedicate a book to you.' T.H. apparently never felt disposed to make this gesture; but then he was not in the habit of dedicating more than individual poems to anyone.

The year 1896 is full of contradictory indications, some of which may suggest that Emma kept her complaints to herself apart from occasional outbursts. The basic trouble, whether Tom had chosen to be 'honest' or not, was, of course, the affair with Mrs Henniker, which found its chief outlet in protests about *Jude*. Thanking Douglas on 5 January for his *Bookman* article 'On some critics of *Jude the Obscure*', he told him that he and Emma had had a 'quiet Christmas and New Year' and added:

> The truth is that an author's means shd be judged by the light of his aim & end. If I say to a lady 'I have met a naked woman' & no more, it is indecent. But if that is only a part of what I say, & I add, 'she was mad with sorrow', there has been no indecency. And so with telling the ruin & defeat of a man's spiritual aims.

Two days later, to Grant Allen, author of *The Woman Who Did* (1895), the most notorious of the 'new woman' novels, he indulged himself in an unkind swipe at Mrs Oliphant, who had in fact had to be prolific, after she was widowed early, in order to finance her sons' Eton education:

> Talk of shamelessness: that a woman who purely for money's sake has for the last 30 years flooded the magazines & starved out scores of better workers, should try to write down rival novelists whose books sell better than her own, caps all the shamelessness of Arabella, to my mind.

Two other letters, to Archer and Gosse, also protest about the reception of *Jude* (these private responses to such hostile criticisms, however, are in no way unusual amongst authors). The letter to Gosse repeats the 'naked woman' example, except that Tom replaces the word 'indelicate' with 'indecent', which he presumably wished to avoid in the disenchanting circumstances of Gosse having used the term to describe *Jude*. Do these manifold demonstrations of irritation signify arguments with Emma on the question? Together they entertained Mrs Patrick Campbell, who was staying at the King's Arms in Dorchester, on several occasions at Max Gate. Mrs Campbell, who really wanted to play Tess but never did, said in a letter to a friend that she had been improvising steps to tunes played by Tom on his violin; she did not mention any awkwardness of atmosphere owing to Emma.

By 2 February Tom was in London, and his letter to Emma of that date is genial, beginning 'My dear Em' and ending 'Yours affectly'. It contained this intriguing passage:

> I then called on the Hennikers. The Major (who is really a very good fellow) was very amusing – describing the only time ever he studied poetry: when he was getting engaged to Mrs H. – at which time he bought a copy of Byron, & read him manfully through. He then got married, & has never read any since.

He also here mentions having met 'Violet? Hunt'. She had been the lover of his acquaintance Walter Pollock, the poet, novelist and parodist of Rider Haggard, and would be the lover of the young Somerset Maugham. Later Violet Hunt became the self-styled 'Mrs Hueffer', and even forged a cheque on poor Ford's already depleted bank account after he had returned from war service – but not to herself. In her *I Have This to Say: The Story of My Flurried Years* (1926), she reported a dream that

Tom had related to her: 'I am pursued, and I am rising like an angel up
into heaven, out of the hands of my earthly pursuers. . . . I am agitated
and hampered, as I suppose an angel would not be, by – a paucity of
underlinen.'

He took the trouble to write to Emma again on the following day.
Once more the letter is friendly. He told her that he had got over 'the
most fearful depression', and that it was

> very cold, & raw, but not very foggy. I don't think you could stand
> it here just now. If I take a house *soon*, you must promise to come
> straight up into it, & not to go out of doors while this sort of
> weather lasts.
>
> I have seen the loveliest 'Byke' for myself – wd suit me admirably
> – 'The Rover Cob'. It is £20! I can't tell if I ought to have it.

He did buy it, perhaps from Tilley of Dorchester, who gave both
him and Emma lessons in cycle-riding. While all this demonstrates
beyond doubt that they were both making a serious effort to settle
their differences, especially by means of their 'Bykes', it does not mean
that they were being more than temporarily successful. Emma did have
a point about *Jude*, if only a social one, which Tom acknowledged much
later, when he opened Chapter XXIII of the *Life* thus:

> Hardy found that the newspaper comments on *Jude the Obscure*
> were producing phenomena amongst his country friends which
> were extensive and peculiar, they having a pathetic reverence for
> press opinions. However, on returning to London in the spring he
> discovered somewhat to his surprise that people there seemed not to
> be at all concerned . . .

Were we in the moralizing business we should no doubt wish to defend
Tom for his insistence on writing *Jude* as nearly as he could in accordance
with his conscience. But we can sympathize with Emma, too, for any
askance looks (it probably amounted to little more than that, although
there are no further details of the 'extensive and peculiar' 'phenomena')
she was receiving on account of her marriage to the beast and degenerate
who dealt in pigs' penises. All that she went through made her ill with
one of the most 'psychosomatic' and least well understood of all known
diseases – and an exceedingly unpleasant one at the best of times. It was

to plague her for the rest of her life, and, undoubtedly, to cause her much misery: aided by a proprietary opium mixture, she kept this misery to herself and has received little credit for her discretion. The first hint of it comes in a letter from Tom to Florence Henniker, written from Max Gate on 11 February. He was sending her a copy of the *Saturday Review* which contained a favourable notice of *Jude*. It was unsigned, but, as he later discovered, written by the young H. G. Wells, who had been much moved by it. The review began with a sentence that read to him – and reads to us – like a draught of fresh air: 'It is doubtful . . . whether for many years any book has received quite so foolish a reception . . .'

'I don't suppose you will care to read a word in favour of poor Jude,' he wearily said of this to Florence Henniker. He was at this time much concerned with the dramatization he had made of *Tess*, which was finally produced in New York on 2 March 1897, after Lorimer Stoddard had made extensive alterations, with the American actress Minnie Maddern Fiske in the name part. In the course of telling Florence all about the difficulties of getting his own script to America he mentioned that he was returning to London on the next Monday, 17 February, 'if all is well': 'Em was going there with me – but she is unwell, I am sorry to say, so perhaps I shall go alone.'

Then, on the same day, to Mary Jeune, with whom they had planned to stay, he wrote: 'I fear Em will not be able to accompany me . . . owing to this eczema which troubles her – It is however, apparently going off.' By the following Sunday, the 16th, when he wrote to Lady Jeune to confirm his arrival on the morrow, Emma had left Max Gate: 'she has been obliged to go to Brighton for a change'. On the afternoon of the 19th, having on the previous evening attended a masked ball and found it the 'most amusing experience that I have lately had', as he told Emma in a letter written to Brighton from the Savile on that morning, he returned to Max Gate. The only clue to the nature of the illness is from his letter: 'Lady J. says it *may* be shingles that you have had, as that goes in a circle round the body.'

But it is unlikely to have been shingles. Emma later had trouble with breathlessness, exhaustion and eczema of the scalp. From what we know of her symptoms, she is most likely to have suffered from some form of dermatitis, perhaps atopic, which is liable to flare up – and cause severe breathing difficulties – under emotional stress. Little was known of allergies until 1905, but an allergy was no doubt also involved. There was an allergy, alas, to all the attention now regularly received by her husband, and to the discourteous manner in which the growing number of journalists ignored her, and showed no knowledge of or even interest in her contributions to his success. The so-called fainting-fit that she had on 30 May 1906 ('my heart seemed to stop'), of which Tom included her description in the *Life*, is entirely consonant with such a condition. If she made every effort to suppress feelings which, as an increasingly serious Christian, she felt unworthy, such as jealousy of Agnes Grove and Florence Henniker, both of whom Tom was just then helping with their publications, this would have aggravated her wretched illness.

But by early April she and Tom were able to take up residence again at 16 Pelham Crescent in South Kensington, where they had been in 1894. By Monday the 20th Tom was himself unwell, as happened so often when he was in London, and had only just got up from bed: he asked Lady Jeune for the name of a doctor, should the rheumatism from which he was suffering, caused by a 'chill', get worse. Five days later he wrote to the artist Winifred Thomson: 'It must have been my astral body that people have seen all over London, for I have been confined to the house, unwell, for nearly a fortnight . . .' Then Emma fell prey to 'severe bronchitis', and they both went off to a boarding-house at 12 Oriental Place, in Brighton, for a 'few days' change of air'. While he was there he received a request to stand as Lord Rector for the University of Glasgow, against the wily statesman Joseph Chamberlain, on the grounds that the latter was 'not a man of letters'. He refused.

Tom did not really feel better until he made a flying visit to the 'dry air' of Max Gate at the end of May, he told Mrs Henniker on 1 June. Notwithstanding, he and Emma frequently entertained in a 'form then in vogue, one very convenient for literary persons, of having afternoon parties', from 16 Pelham Crescent. 'Possibly soured' by the Bishop of Wakefield's comic intervention into his morals, Tom wrote, when his birthday came round: 'Every man's birthday is a first of April for him; and he who lives to be fifty and won't own it is a rogue or a fool, hypocrite or simpleton.'

One thing is certain: the eight-week trip that he and Emma undertook, from August to October, was a reconciliatory one. They attended the wedding of Lady Jeune's daughter Dorothy Stanley to Henry Allhusen, went home, packed, and on 12 August were off to the Midlands. During the few days at Max Gate Tom called in on his rapidly ageing mother, whose face, he thought, 'looked smaller'. They went to Malvern, Worcester, Warwick and then for a whole week to Stratford-on-Avon, where they did the Shakespeare rounds. After this, on the way to Dover, they visited Reading. It is interesting that Emma did not object to this roundabout route: Reading was the scene of the youth of Tom's paternal grandmother, as well as the Aldbrickham of *Jude*. He had started to re-read *Lear* at Stratford, and finished it at Dover, whereupon, on 6 September, he made the following note:

> The grand scale of the tragedy, scenically, strikes one, and also the large scheme of the plot. The play rises from and after the beginning of the third act, and Lear's dignity with it. Shakespeare did not quite reach his intention in the King's character, and the splitting of the tragic interest between him and Gloucester does not, to my mind, enhance its intensity, although commentators assert that it does.

His mind was on his own planned epic play, and the extreme difficulties with which, in an age devoid of even half-successful verse tragedy, his attempt would present him. His confidence in himself must have been enormous. He was going to succeed where Browning and Tennyson had failed, and yet avoid the snare of the theatre at the same time! He would borrow for it the 'cinematic' technique of *Lear*, and, in particular, *Antony and Cleopatra*. Like every other poet, when things were going well he could feel himself to be the equal of Shakespeare. The difference is that he sometimes almost was, although not in *The Dynasts*.

Tom did not take his 'Byke', but Emma, who was suffering from lameness on top of her other troubles, did take hers – a green affair jokingly named 'The Grasshopper'. It caused many problems, none of which seem to have been taken with less than good humour. Tom wrote, 'Mrs Hardy, having brought her bicycle with her, was knocked off it by a young man learning to ride, and was laid up by the accident.' In fact she badly injured her shoulder. But Florence Hardy took her angry scissors to that too caring reminiscence. They had to stay in Dover for more than a week in order for Emma to recover fully. During that time, they must have read Matthew Arnold's 'Dover Beach' together, for Tom wrote by its title, in the copy he had brought with him on the trip, 'TH/ELH September 1896'. Emma would normally not have been in sympathy with the pessimistic sentiments of this poem, and it could be inferred that on this occasion she was prepared to acknowledge that it was moving, or at least that it afforded an acceptable presentation of her husband's attitude. No doubt both registered the beautiful final lines, never too familiar not to quote:

Ah, love, let us be true
To one another! for the world, which seems
To lie before us like a land of dreams,
So various, so beautiful, so new,
Hath really neither joy, nor love, nor light,
Nor certitude, nor peace, nor help for pain;
And we are here as on a darkling plain
Swept with confused alarms of struggle and flight,
Where ignorant armies clash by night.

The Grasshopper caused more trouble when they got it across the Channel to Ostend: in Belgium, where they travelled about extensively, 'it kept getting lost' and at Liège 'really did seem gone'. They gave up, but were then approached by an official, 'who took them with a mysterious manner to a storeroom . . . and with a leer said, to Hardy's dismay: "*Le véloze!*"'

While in Brussels they stayed, 'for association's sake' – and in accordance with their intention of trying to recapture their past – at the hotel they had used 'twenty years before', the Hôtel de la Poste, but found it much run down since then. Tom wrote in his notebook:

Europe in Throes.
Three Parts. Five Acts each.
Characters: Burke, Pitt, Napoleon, George III, Wellington . . .
and many others

Then, on 2 October, he walked, 'alone', along the English line at Waterloo: 'Shepherds with their flocks and dogs, men ploughing, two cats, and myself, the only living creatures on the field'. On their way back to England, in early October, they found the hotels and shops 'boarded up . . . Mrs Hardy being the single woman bicyclist where there had been so many'.

All this long holiday tells us is that Tom and Emma were trying to come back together, despite their differences. How much they discussed these differences, or how much they irritated each other, is not known. Tom's letter to Mrs Henniker from Liège of 24 September, beginning 'My dear little friend', warns her that if she 'shd write' to 'put *Mr*' (it is impossible to say what this indicates: probably it has something to do with the hotel's postal arrangements), and for the most part speaks as though he were journeying in Belgium alone. He here wishes that he could 'go through with you some of the churches &c, that I have seen'.

> The 'Grasshopper' (bicycle) which has accompanied us, has been the source of extraordinary alarms, (& expenses! –) It disappears unexpectedly on the railway journeys, & turns up again just as unexpectedly – its discoverer exclaiming 'V'la le *veloze* de Madame!'

His concluding 'rather saddening' reflection that, because he had not been in Belgium for twenty years, he asks himself 'why am I here again, & not underground!' cannot be used as evidence of a melancholy mood with regard to Emma: it was the sad way he felt intermittently throughout his life. He was just as amused and wryly pleased by the droll fact that there was 'a man staying at this hotel just like Ld Salisbury'.

While they were staying in Brussels, at the Hôtel de la Poste in the Fossé aux Loups, Tom received, sent on to him from Max Gate, a letter which he regarded as important in his Wessex scheme – which he shrewdly saw as being of great extra value to the purse of a man about to abandon prose fiction. Bertram Windle, an educated hack who later wrote *The Wessex of Thomas Hardy* (1902), wanted his help in preparing a new edition of the much used *Murray's Handbook for Residents and Travellers in Wilts and Dorset*. He told Windle that the information he would give him might 'perhaps relieve me of the many letters I receive on the subject'. Later he was to enter into a more thoroughgoing collaboration with his close personal friend Hermann Lea. He told Windle on 28 September that he would soon be back in England, '& will then answer any questions'. He added a postscript: 'On second thoughts I send a few rudimentary notes.' There follows a fairly long list – a very long one for anyone to send off while on holiday. These notes are almost all in Emma's hand, and include references to *Jude*, although Tom added three more of his own in this connection. It is likely, therefore, that it was she who wanted to send some information to Windle immediately. Nor was she, at that moment, averse to mentioning *Jude*, since the note 'Shaftesbury (vide ante)/The "Shaston" in which Phillotson renounces Sue in "Jude the Obscure"' is in her hand. Therefore she was probably in sympathetic agreement with his plans.

That Tom was often unhappy about his marriage is undoubted. But, so far as life must be considered as a philosophical (or just general) proposition, he was unhappy about that, too; no one is surprised to learn that in his 1901 'conversation' with William Archer (whom he trusted) he affirmed that he agreed with Sophocles that 'not to be born is best'. In the circumstances 'pessimist' cannot be too inappropriate a word to describe him, although it cannot cover the case in a world in which optimism is an increasingly surreal duty. But that was his *Weltanschauung*: his 'world-philosophy', not to be confused with his permanent emotional state. Those who seek to show that it was the result of the special unhappiness of his marriage are misguided, unwise and too literal in their approach.

26

Poetry at Last

W ithin a few days of returning to Max Gate, on 17 October, Tom made a crucial note to which he gave pride of place in the *Life*. He sees out 1896 with it:

Poetry. Perhaps I can express more fully in verse ideas and emotions which run counter to the inert crystallized opinion – hard as a rock – which the vast body of men have vested interests in supporting. To cry out in a passionate poem that (for instance) the Supreme Mover or Movers, the Prime Force or Forces, must be either limited in power, unknowing, or cruel – which is obvious enough, and has been for centuries – will cause them merely a shake of the head; but to put it in argumentative prose will make them sneer, or foam, and set all the literary contortionists jumping upon me, a harmless agnostic, as if I were a clamorous atheist, which in their crass illiteracy they seem to think is the same thing . . . If Galileo had said in verse that the world moved, the Inquisition might have let him alone.

Like all poets, Thomas Hardy wrote because he was impelled to by forces which he could not fully explain – not because he wanted to justify his agnosticism or any other system. What he had on his mind as he wrote this note was *The Dynasts*, preparatory work for which was soon well under way, although it took until 1904 before he could publish the first section. At this point, nearing sixty, he had published only a handful of poems and was known solely as a novelist. When he had sent out his poems to magazines in the 1860s he had received only snubs. Despite his newly found financial status, with *Tess* and *Jude* and the earlier novels in the Osgood uniform edition selling like hot cakes, in setting himself up as a poet he was taking a prodigious risk in terms of literary status. He only had to prepare *The Well-Beloved* for volume publication, and then he could be finished with prose fiction for good. (There were to be just two more fairly lightweight short stories, 'A Changed Man' and

'Enter a Dragoon'.) Notwithstanding the equally prodigious challenge of successfully producing a verse drama in an age in which none had been produced, *The Dynasts* was a vital statement of his 'philosophical' position and, for him, the bridge between fiction and poetry. The long planned poetry collection, carefully entitled *Wessex Poems* – this title was decided by 4 February 1897 at the latest – in order to cash in on the Wessex scheme laid by the novels, was as important; but he did not mind taking Tolstoy on in the meanwhile. He did not, in *The Dynasts*, equal Tolstoy; but he did not disgrace himself.

Poetry had always been imperative. Now it became particularly so because, according to his own dating, he had within the past twelve months written four of the most powerful poems of his entire output: the most sustained work that he had yet attempted. These are the three poems comprising the group collectively entitled 'In Tenebris', and 'Wessex Heights', which he may already have been writing or trying to write in that very October (it is dated December 1896 in the manuscript, but just 1896 in the printed version). He did not feel up to including the grim 'In Tenebris' until his second collection, of 1901, and 'Wessex Heights', owing to its autobiographical elements, he held back until *Satires of Circumstance*, published just after Emma's death.

These poems, among his best, are better called tragic than pessimistic; they could not be called joyful. The idea that the state of his marriage was chiefly responsible for them, however, is wrong. Their gloom is wholly endemic to Tom's temperament: they reflect his inner and not his outer life, and he would have written them whatever his circumstances. Tom had a keen sense of real, external misery – hardship, lack of employment, the pains of war, the status of women, the agonies caused by the demands of convention, the tricks and lies of bankers, munition-makers (for whom he had a particular dislike) and politicians. But he did not claim that his own life had known much of that. One of the last things he ever wrote in his own hand, in pencil on the front of an envelope addressed to him (it is postmarked 'Pa/Nov 14 – / – /1927'), is one of the most revealing. Clearly he had intended to use it in the *Life*, but fell into what was to be his last illness. Florence could not have seen its importance. It reads, under the heading '*H's altruism*' (he underlined it himself):

It must not be forgotten that H's own life & experiences had been smoother & happier than many – perhaps than the majority. It was his habit, or *strange* power of putting himself in the place of those who endured sufferings from which he himself had been in the main free, or subject to at but brief times. This altruism was so constant with him as to cause a complaint among his readers that he did not say 'all's well with the world' because all was well with him. It should really have caused commendation.

It has often been observed that the *Life* is really an extraordinarily modest book, and an extraordinary feat under the circumstances. This is so particularly because, in ghosting it for a wife mainly ignorant of literature, but aspiring to it, he could have put in more praise for himself than he actually did. But that note, if not immodest, can hardly be described as modest. And, since modesty (rare amongst writers) was a necessary keynote in his life and doings, there must have been a special reason for him to risk testing his usual rule. Then, as 1927 closed, he no longer had anyone to talk to who could understand as Emma, all those years ago, had understood – and had encouraged him to continue with his true ambition even against the odds and her own interests; and he must have felt, or even known intuitively, that the end was near – a matter of weeks. So this needed saying.

In 1920 the positivist Frederick Harrison, a personal friend of long standing, had written in the *Fortnightly Review*, in a review of the 1919 *Collected Poems*, that his 'monotony of gloom, with all its poetry, is not social, not human, not true'. This, patently *un*true, and selective, had upset him, and so he recalled it in the 'Apology' to *Late Lyrics and Earlier* (1922). He probably recalled it again now, and remembered how the wooden Gosse had affected to complain, when he read the 'Apology', that only Tom failed to appreciate the 'reverence' in which he was now held ('. . . friends can not turn cold/This season as of old/For him with none'). For Gosse and his like, unless they are temporarily jerked out of their complacency by some kind of shock, as Gosse was when he wrote *Father and Son*, 'reverence' is what writers seek; they do not really seek truth. (One of the sarcastic sayings of Nietzsche with which Tom would certainly have agreed, if he read it, is: 'Good writers have two things in common; they prefer to be understood rather than admired; and they do not write for knowing and acute readers'.)

To such as Gosse truth must finally be disposable, in the interests of state and of self-advancement. Such critics cannot understand the nature of the annoyance that Tom displayed in that bitter 'Apology'. It was not on account of any feeling that his own prestige was threatened: on the contrary, he deprecated the 'vested interests' which prevented people from reaching, not agreement, but understanding.

Tom, although by nature hypersensitive, would be criticized far less often for his 'over-sensitivity' if this were recognized. There is vanity and egoism in poets as in everyone else, as he would have been the first to concede; but poetry itself is not an expression of vanity and egoism. That is one of the differences between Hardy and Yeats, who has seemed to so many critics to have been more sophisticated and 'modern' and 'important'. There is poetry in Yeats, but also much more vanity and egoism. This is why so many readers have ultimately turned back to Hardy.

One of Tom's last poems – when fame can scarcely have mattered to him in any case – was 'A Private Man on Public Men'. It is not mentioned by Gittings or Millgate, and Bailey, made acutely unhappy by it, assures us that the title is 'misleading': Hardy was 'apologising' (to professors?) for 'an attitude he adopted in his later years'! The title is not, of course, misleading, and the poem means exactly what it says. It was printed in the *Daily Telegraph* just after Tom's death, and then in the posthumous *Winter Words*:

> When my contemporaries were driving
> Their coach through Life with strain and striving,
> And raking riches into heaps,
> And ably pleading in the Courts
> With smart rejoinders and retorts,
> Or where the Senate nightly keeps
> Its vigils, till their fames were fanned
> By rumour's tongue throughout the land,
> I lived in quiet, screened, unknown,
> Pondering upon some stick or stone,
> Or news of some rare book or bird
> Latterly bought, or seen, or heard,
> Not wishing ever to set eyes on
> The surging crowd beyond the horizon,
> Tasting years of moderate gladness
> Mellowed by sundry days of sadness,
> Shut from the noise of the world without,
> Hearing but dimly its rush and rout,
> Unenvying those amid its roar,
> Little endowed, not wanting more.

Bailey's bizarre and puzzled interpretation – 'he sought no office';

'his biography is full of his enjoyment [sic] of society' – is instructive. Tom did not write for those with orthodox minds, who believe that poetry is like football: just something at which to achieve skill and, by that, fame. 'A Private Man on Public Men' is not a profound poem, and would hardly be noticed at all were it not for its context. But he meant every word of it. It reflects exactly what Gertrude Bugler, the straightforward young woman and outstanding amateur actress whose chance on the London stage as Tess was almost killed by Florence Hardy's violent jealousy, said of him in his old age:

> A great deal has been said and written both during his lifetime, and since his death, of the sad philosophy and pessimistic attitude to life of Thomas Hardy, but to us he was not the grim, cynical man often pictured, and if he sometimes emphasised the darker side of life, he never forgot the sunshine of laughter. I can still hear him laugh . . .

When we read 'In Tenebris' and 'Wessex Heights' we should therefore bear in mind the final note about what he called his 'altruism'. This note was written in much the same frame of mind as 'A Private Man on Public Men' – one from which he was seldom far. The kind of anguished poetry of 'In Tenebris' and 'Wessex Heights' is written in periods of great gloom and depression; but such moods do not persist (hence Tom's phrase, 'but brief times'), and in any case – provided they do not arise from clinical depression, as, say, Gerard Manley Hopkins' so-called 'terrible sonnets' clearly do – are the result of internal rather than external attitudes. It is when external events – for example, in the mid-1890s, Florence Henniker's rejection of him, the frustrations caused by Mrs Grundy, Emma's and his own ageing, the disappointments caused by the stupidities and insensitivities of such erstwhile friends as Gosse – seem to mirror internal patterns that the poetic conscience is stirred. Commentators such as Bailey feel that Tom, despite the attacks on *Tess* and *Jude*, never had it so good. He was now famous and rich; he had not lost any valued friends; he moved in high society and, according to them, 'enjoyed' this; why should he feel so miserable unless he really were – as Gittings portrays him – a vain, mean and selfish egoist? But one who was essentially a vain and selfish egoist could never have written what he wrote . . . And if we read, with care, what he did write, including these four key poems, we find that it was not his fame or reputation that troubled him, but the nature of his life. The opening 'In Tenebris' poem is candidly about moments of despair that are universal, and must have been felt by any sensitive man or woman at the onset of middle age:

> Wintertime nighs;
> But my bereavement-pain
> It cannot bring again:
> Twice no one dies.

This opening stanza is grim and miserable in mood; but it also sounds a note of consolation. Too often the gloominess of general atmosphere in Tom's poetry distracts the reader from what he is actually saying.

The two poems following this describe progressively more personal instances of despair. Such moments are, after all, well known enough to have been enshrined in the psalms, three epigraphs from which (from the Vulgate version) preface the 'In Tenebris' group respectively: the Authorized Version has: 'My heart is smitten, and withered like grass'; 'I looked on my right hand, and beheld, but there was no man that would know me . . . no man cared for my soul'; 'Woe is me that I sojourn in Mesech, that I dwell in the tents of Kedar! My soul hath long dwelt with him that hateth peace.'

Tom's first title for the group, 'De Profundis' ('From the Depths'), is perhaps more expressive of their universality than his second thought. These depths are everyone's depths. The convolutedly ironic second poem is more original and disturbing than the first, which, so far as content is concerned, is a fairly conventional expression of the kind of gloom which everyone, at some time or another, must feel. But its last word, 'unhope', is interesting as being an early example of those many absolute negatives which Tom coined, and which are frequently encountered in gnostic and cabalistic writings. This is not to put Tom forward as an actual student of gnosticism: he was not. However, without going into technical or scholarly detail, the gnostic attitude has persisted since thinking began, and Tom is an example of one who intuited it. He was specifically interested in Manichaeism, a gnostic movement whose prophet, Mani, combined elements of 'Zoroastrianism' (properly, 'Mazdaism'), Christianity and Buddhism. He asked William Archer, in his 1901 'conversation' with him:

> Do you know Hartmann's philosophy of the Unconscious? It sug-
> gested to me what seems almost a workable theory of the great
> problem of the origin of evil – though this, of course, is not

Hartmann's own theory – namely, that there may be a consciousness, infinitely far off, at the other end of the chain of phenomena, always striving to express itself, and always baffled and blundering, just as the spirits seem to be.

W.A. Is not that simply the old Manichaean heresy with matter playing the part of the evil principle – Satan, Ahriman, whatever you choose to call it?

Mr Hardy. John Stuart Mill somewhere [it is in *Three Essays on Religion*, 1874, always a strong influence upon him] expresses surprise that Manichaeism was not more widely accepted. But is not all religion in essence Manichaean? Does it not postulate a struggle between a principle of good and an independent, if not equally powerful, principle of evil?

Of course it does not. But in this prose conversation, with Archer acting as feed, Tom could not really come to the point. In some of his poems, though, he did – and without too much need for irritable searching into the history of religion. The coinage, or use, of those absolutely negative terms such as 'unhope' is more immediately reminiscent of cabalistic than of strictly gnostic writings; but not much was known about either in his day, except by intuition. From his general reading, Tom probably understood the term Manichaean as one used by enlightenment thinkers to scoff at and score points off orthodoxy. Gibbon, in the notorious fifteenth chapter of *The Decline and Fall of the Roman Empire*, had jokingly and provocatively referred to the gnostics as the 'most polite, the most learned, and the most wealthy of the Christian name'; Voltaire introduced the wandering scholar Martin into *Candide* as a 'Manichaean' who says, significantly in terms of the Hardyan cosmology: 'I cannot speculate in any other manner: I believe that God has abandoned this globe, or rather this globule, to some maleficent being.' He may also have known Voltaire's brief story '*Songe de Platon*' ('Plato's Dream'), in which the world is created by an incompetent demiurge. Certainly he concluded 'The Respectable Burgher' with the lines:

> All churchgoing will I forswear,
> And sit on Sundays in my chair,
> And read that moderate man Voltaire.

Tom's own thinking about creation in its most poetic form – creation being a subject which all human beings make their own, and are not inferior to anyone else when they dwell upon it with true wonder – resembles the ponderings to be found in the Cabala. But this question will be taken up again, when we come to the poems roughly contemporary with *The Dynasts*, and to *The Dynasts* – that first and last attempt to put forth a complete 'philosophy of life' – itself. It is significant that in this conversation with Archer, as elsewhere, Tom carefully avoided making any atheistic pronouncement. That is why he was so perpetually irritated by G.K. Chesterton, who asserted that he 'tried to say (at the same time) that God did not exist, and that He ought to be ashamed of existing'. This was witty, but palpably untrue and unjust, and a serious challenge to a thoughtful man who would never have dreamed, as a conscientious poet and seeker after truth, of being so foolish as to state that God did not exist.

It is in the two final poems of the 'In Tenebris' group that Tom's poetic thinking began to develop. This is distinct from the more conscious 'philosophy of life' after which his epic project obliged him to strive: interesting, but not as interesting as his poetry, which was always ongoing, always 'becoming', never final. We will never have an exact chronology of the poems, and it is clear that many were developed from older jottings, or were re-worked from uncompleted early drafts; but the old-fashioned idea that this poetry shows no development is not tenable. There is an obvious development in the successive volumes by which Tom chose to present them to his readers – who were more important to him than the professional critics, whom he only ever really appreciated when they made intelligent or suggestive remarks. Because of what he called his 'altruism', in that last note, he was concerned less with the sense of personal insult than with what he saw as the justice, or otherwise, of what was being said.

The second 'In Tenebris' poem, 'When the clouds' swoln bosoms echo back the shouts of the many and strong', reflects an intellectual crisis, and a painful religious perplexity, quite as much as it reflects anything personal. Critics who relate it too closely to the reception of *Jude* miss the point. Tom's response to the criticism of his 'pessimism' in that book was intense, but it was not naive: he had expected such criticism, and well knew what he would experience as a result of being true to his own 'impressions'. What better strategy could he have chosen but that of indignation at his critics' disingenuousness or stupidity?

Who now can say that these 'impressions', as he called them, were 'wrong'? Only those who do not much care for poetry. Two wars, the second of which was quite the worst known to mankind, were to come within his own lifetime – not to speak of what came after his death. No amount of that 'reverence' from the public, so valued by such as Gosse, could assuage his bitterness about the human situation. What particularly aroused his indignation and irony were what he had called 'vested interests': the arrangement by which society pretended that 'All's well with us: ruers have nought to rue!' It prompted this final, contortedly ironic stanza:

> Let him in whose ears the low-voiced Best is killed by the
>   clash of the First,
> Who holds that if way to the Better there be, it exacts a full look at
>   the Worst,
> Who feels that delight is a delicate growth cramped by crookedness,
>   custom and fear,
> Get him up and be gone as one shaped awry; he disturbs the
>   order here.

It has been rightly said that response to much of Tom's poetry, and to this poem in particular, depends upon temperament. A reader of conformist temperament, who really does believe that the world is on the whole a good place, and that we live in an excellent part of the universe, can hardly admire this, although he might appreciate its power. Those who really love Hardy do not, however, see his attitude to the world as a peculiarity: they agree with what he says about it. Many Victorians admired the equally rebellious Shelley, although many also expressed rather arch reservations about him; Tom, although he sought quietism in a way that Shelley neither did nor could, never held such reservations. His 'pessimistic' cast of thought, his temperament quite apart, was based upon his conviction that not all was right with the world. Was he mistaken? Some rich or powerful Victorians could doubtless be forgiven for believing that he was. But can we? And was he not, as he always believed, ahead of his time?

The third 'In Tenebris' poem, 'There have been times when I well might have passed and the ending have come', moves into an area of more personal experience, explicitly recalling his mother ('she who upheld me'), who was then still living. It records a mood of regret that his reading, or his impulse to read and learn – and therefore, by plain implication, his tendency to question Christianity and to speculate theologically, to retreat into a necessary scepticism –

gave him a 'numbing' knowledge of the world as a 'welter of futile doing'. It should not, however, be understood as a kind of permanent autobiographical statement: 'I perpetually regret that I did not remain a countryman.' Instead, it truthfully records a mood which often came upon him. He always remained consistent in his view, or conviction, that the world had not been created with human happiness in mind; but his moods changed, so that he could write poems like 'Let Me Enjoy' as well. *The Dynasts* explores and tries to consolidate some kind of a conscious philosophy of life. Certain poems that follow it, however, are more ambiguous, and have often been misread as wholly positivist declarations of disbelief in the supernatural. They came, in fact, from an advanced scepticism. Examples include 'A Plaint to Man' (in manuscript entitled 'The Plaint of a Puppet') and 'God's Funeral', intellectually ambitious poems upon which he worked between 1908 and 1910, after he had published the last part of *The Dynasts*. In 'A Plaint to Man' the invention of God by man is described by God, and then,

> . . . now that I dwindle day by day
> Beneath the deicide eyes of seers
> In a light that will not let me stay,
>
> And tomorrow the whole of me disappears,
> The truth should be told, and the fact be faced
> That had best been faced in earlier years:
>
> The fact of life with dependence placed
> On the human heart's resource alone,
> In brotherhood bonded close and graced
>
> With loving-kindness fully blown,
> And visioned help unsought, unknown.

'God's Funeral' is a comparatively long, and more extensively worked, companion poem to 'A Plaint'. But, although born from the same perhaps fruitless impulse to reach a tenable theological (or atheological) position, it is slightly different. In 'A Plaint' it is suggested that 'loving-kindness' itself, without recourse to the kind of specifically anthropomorphic God who is speaking the lines, should have prevailed from the beginning. The question of what relationship, if any, loving-kindness might have to a creator, or to a strictly *non*-anthropomorphic God, is left entirely open. The poem must be read as an exhortation to act from inner conscience, and not from an artificial God; it does not state that a real God, if there is one, is artificial. If there is a God, then he could only be discerned from spontaneous acts of loving-kindness. Thus the anthropomorphic God, the speaker, is divorced from loving-kindness.

In 'God's Funeral', a poem Hardy knew would be found provocative by the conventionally minded, a 'slowly-stepping train' of people is seen bearing the dead God across a mournful plain. Originally, when it appeared in the *Fortnightly*, it had a subtitle: 'An Allegorical Conception of the Present State of Theology'. This dead God varies according to those who worshipped him: 'At first seemed man-like, and anon to change/To an amorphous cloud of marvellous size,/At times endowed with wings of glorious range'. However, possessed by 'phantasmal variousness', 'throughout all it symboled none the less/Potency vast and loving-kindness strong.' The God whose funeral it is, then, is not separated from loving-kindness here. Later, however, one of the 'sick thoughts' of the mourners is that what they had created they had then mistakenly believed to be *their* creator.

But, although full of ingenious lines and stanzas, these two poems do not show Tom quite at his best: poetic language is too much at the service of thought. There is a confusion in every religiously susceptible person's mind when he or she *thinks* about God, or the concept of God. In prose or recorded conversation, and occasionally in 'philosophical' poems, Tom tended to abandon his emotional approach; then he allowed his confusion to show. In various letters he lamented the 'arrest of light and reason by theology', and claimed that dogma had departed from 'the real teaching of Christ'. He asserted that the 'element of the supernatural' ought to be 'quietly abandoned', and thought that the churches and cathedrals would thus become 'the centres of emotional life they once were'. But this was to Clodd, who was a straightforward, and unsubtle, rationalist. To Frédérick Lefèvre in 1925, however, he pleaded for 'the religious spirit': 'I dream of an alliance between religions freed from dogmas. The religion which ought to be preserved . . . would be created by poetry . . . Poetry, pure literature, and religion are the visible points of the most authentic mental and emotional life.' The nature of 'poetry' is here left open, except that Tom connects it closely with the kind of religion which he believes must be preserved 'if the world is not to perish'. This is positivist-influenced, but not positivist. He can never quite bring himself to plead for an atheist, or secular, religion. And, of course, he remained a churchgoer, and affirmed that emotionally he needed to be so.

One potentially interesting question may be dealt with here, before returning to 'Wessex Heights' and to a time when Tom was not quite ready to try to philosophize in verse. The notion of the 'death of God' will inevitably raise thoughts of Nietzsche – and Tom is known to have read English translations of the German philosopher, and to have been interested in him. Alexander Tille's attempted version of *Also Sprach Zarathustra* appeared as early as 1896, and there were articles pro and con in English periodicals from that time. Tom's friends Arthur Symons and Havelock Ellis were prominent defenders. Tom himself was well aware of Nietzsche by 1902, and mentions him pejoratively in a letter of that year, quoted in the *Life*. Apart from telling the American Ernest Brennecke Jr, in 1913, that 'with many of his sayings I have always heartily agreed', Tom is known only as his relentless opponent. It has even been plausibly suggested that Tom was one of the major influences in the lowering of the English estimation of Nietzsche, which had been much raised by the series of translations of his complete works of 1909–11, edited by Oscar Levy (who himself, though described by a good Hardy critic, Dennis Taylor, as 'the great Nietzsche translator', translated none of them). He wrote in a letter to the *Manchester Guardian* (7 October 1914) that Nietzsche had 'demoralized' his country, that he was a megalomaniac and 'not truly a philosopher at all'. In a private letter of 26 September 1914 to Cockerell, who had lent him John Adam Cramb's crudely pro-German *Germany and England* (1914), he spoke of Nietzsche and others 'insanely' regarding life 'as a thing improvable by force to immaculate gloriousness'; 'it is a bit rough on Kant, Schopenhauer, &c, to be swept into one net of condemnation with Nietzsche, &c . . . the truth is that in ethics Kant, Schopr &c are nearer to Christianity than they are to Nsche'. A passage in the *Life*, on the occasion of the seventieth anniversary of Nietzsche's birth in 1844, prompted further similar musings and suggests that Tom had looked through the Levy *Collected Works*.

The difficulty lies in the fact that almost all these translations which Tom read, especially Thomas Common's *Zarathustra*, are often highly inaccurate ('cosmological' for 'cosmopolitan', for example, or 'more German' for 'more clear') and stylistically barbaric: they give no idea of Nietzsche's own often playful as well as horrisonous style. Therefore Tom, through no fault of his own, largely misunderstood Nietzsche, and was probably unaware of his dislike of German militarism (pointed out in the course of the extensive *Guardian* correspondence by the conductor Thomas Beecham, among others) or even of his hatred of anti-semitism. There are in fact many affinities between them – not least their shared antinomianism, as shrill in the case of Nietzsche as it was muted in the case of Hardy – as Oscar Levy himself noted in an article in *Outlook* in 1928; but, he wrongly added, 'Hardy has the *horror fati*, Nietzsche proclaims the *amor fati*' – Nietzsche's term for the apotheosis of joy of the person who leads a creative life. If only Tom could have had the advantage of later translations, and the chance to consider Nietzsche away from the German war-mongering with which he was unfairly associated.

The fear of invasion by Germany, after the Franco-Prussian War of 1870, had remained high, and Tom, as one already deeply read in early nineteenth-century English and French history, was not immune to it. Nor was he spared from the misinterpretation of Nietzsche as an apostle of the Teutonic 'superman', much aided by the pseudo-biblical versions of his works then current (and by the exploitation of him as a nationalist by his demonic sister, the widow of an anti-semitic and proto-fascist thief, the distorter and sometimes forger of her brother's works, and a future Nazi). Yet there is even less reason to doubt Brennecke's report, for this passage (given in Common's 1910 version, from what he called *The Joyful Wisdom, Die Fröhliche Wissenschaft*, 1882 – now often translated as *The Gay Science*) must surely have played its part in the gestation of 'God's Funeral': 'Do we not hear the voice of the grave-diggers who are burying God? Do we not smell the divine putrefaction? – for even Gods putrefy.' There is more that is just as pertinent, and it is unlikely that Tom would have picked up the notion of the 'death of God' from his (no doubt mercifully) restricted reading of Hegel, although Hegel does mention the notion.

But in December 1896, as he finished 'Wessex Heights', he was not ready to philosophize; he would do that in *The Dynasts*. 'Wessex Heights', when taken out of its geographical and biographical context, is extremely moving. It possesses a certain kind of partial obscurity peculiar to Tom. This kind of obscurity – it is important to recognize it as only partial, pertaining only to details rather than to the poem as a whole – became a deliberate part of his poetic technique. What was mysterious in part reveals its universal meaning through the whole: a holographic blur comes into focus only when the entire poem has been registered in the mind. Many critics, 'weird detectives', haunting the author like the ghosts that were so natural in his outlook, have treated 'Wessex Heights' as a kind of crossword puzzle – as an autobiographical code to be unscrambled for their own use. We have even seen the good Quaker Lois Deacon pick over it for details of her Randy, Tom's fictitious son

POETRY AT LAST

by Tryphena Sparks: he is, for her, the ghost in the railway carriage!
The heights mentioned are at the corners of Wessex.

There are some heights in Wessex, shaped as if by a kindly hand
For thinking, dreaming, dying on, and at crises when I stand,
Say, on Ingpen Beacon eastward, or on Wylls-Neck westwardly,
I seem where I was before my birth, and after death may be.

In the lowlands I have no comrade, not even the lone man's friend –
Her who suffereth long and is kind; accepts what he is too weak
    to mend:
Down there they are dubious and askance; there nobody thinks as I,
But mind-chains do not clank where one's next neighbour is the sky.

In the towns I am tracked by phantoms having weird detective
    ways –
Shadows of beings who fellowed with myself of earlier days:
They hang about at places, and they say harsh heavy things –
Men with a wintry sneer, and women with tart disparagings.

Down there I seem to be false to myself, my simple self that was,
And is not now, and I see him watching, wondering what crass
    cause
Can have merged him into such a strange continuator as this,
Who yet has something in common with himself, my chrysalis.

I cannot go to the great gray Plain; there's a figure against the
    moon,
Nobody sees it but I, and it makes my breast beat out of tune;
I cannot go to the tall-spired town, being barred by the forms now
    passed
For everybody but me, in whose long vision they stand there fast.

There's a ghost at Yell'ham Bottom chiding loud at the fall of the
    night,
There's a ghost in Froom-side Vale, thin-lipped and vague, in a
    shroud of white,
There is one in the railway train whenever I do not want it near,
I see its profile against the pane, saying what I would not hear.

As for one rare fair woman, I am now but a thought of hers,
I enter her mind and another thought succeeds me that she prefers;
Yet my love for her in its fulness she herself even did not know;

Well, time cures hearts of tenderness, and now I can let her go.

So I am found on Ingpen Beacon, or on Wylls-Neck to the west,
Or else on homely Bulbarrow, or little Pilsdon Crest,
Where men have never cared to haunt, nor women have walked
   with me,
And ghosts then keep their distance; and I know some liberty.

The poem almost revels in cryptic references; but it cannot be said to indulge itself in them: the very vagueness of personal detail, the natural reticence (implying: 'this is so close to the bone that I cannot speak of it openly'), about what are self-evidently painful circumstances, contributes to the effect, and gives it universality. For painful circumstances are what, at some time or other, temperament apart, characterize everyone's inner emotional life. The writer of the poem knows that when, eventually, he publishes it (if his bid to be a poet comes off in public terms) it is going to be signed with a name famous amongst some and infamous amongst others: Thomas Hardy. He is already the subject of public curiosity; journalists come to interview him and ask him astonishingly foolish questions; he is 'news', and especially so to 'the world', that absolutely conventional abstraction which nonetheless intrudes so unpleasantly upon everyone. Some people who live locally 'know' that his books contain 'unpleasant' incidents and that his private life is equally 'unpleasant'. One such man, a John Shepherd who had known and admired Barnes, 'knew' this, and pronounced wisely upon the matter, declaring that Tom 'repelled him'; but he could not give a single example of his repulsiveness . . . So this author knows that he is not always liked or admired locally. He writes in this poem about himself as he is, but does not wish to be. That is one key to 'Wessex Heights'. Everything on the lowlands, including his own success, alienating him from his former self, is at odds with poetry. Yet poetry could be over-idealized: its practice does not lead automatically to virtue. The third and fourth stanzas are quite specific about this: characteristically precise about the essence of the situation – but not the specific personal details, which are dramatized. Thus, in the dramatic poem's topographical scheme, 'the tall-spired town' must be Salisbury, but nothing biographical may be inferred from this – and a few months later Tom indeed was in Salisbury, and particularly pleased and happy to be there. He wrote in the *Life*, referring to that visit, that it was a 'place in which he was never tired of sojourning, partly from personal associations' and partly because of its 'graceful cathedral'.

Unfortunately Florence Hardy wrote to Alda, Lady Hoare (the Hoares, Sir Henry and his wife Alda who owned the estate at Stourhead in Wiltshire, later given to the National Trust, first became friends of the Hardys not long before Emma's death), about this poem on 6 December 1914):

> When I read 'Wessex Heights' it wrung my heart. It made me miserable to think that he had ever suffered so much. It was written . . . before I knew him, but the four people mentioned are actual women. One was dead & three living when it was written – now only one is living. [Three days later she added more] 'Wessex Heights' will *always* wring my heart, for I know when it was written, a little while after the publication of 'Jude', when he was so cruelly treated.

This has been taken (for example by Bailey) as having the imprimatur of Tom himself: 'When Hardy's reticence is considered, one may suppose that he asked Florence not to reveal the women's names even to an intimate friend'! This rather implies that Tom said something of this kind to Florence: 'Reveal the unhappiness to Lady Hoare, but none of the names!'

It is, however, more likely that he had no idea that Florence had written to Lady Hoare about the poem: he had, after all, no idea of what she had written or was going to write to Clodd, to Owen or, later, to Cockerell about him and his feelings for Emma. And Florence alone was responsible for creating the myth of the absolute unhappiness, as distinct from the difficulties and pains, of her husband's first marriage. These two letters were written only a few days after the publication on 17 November 1914 of *Satires of Circumstance*, in which the section entitled 'Poems of 1912–1913' concerned not his new wife of ten months, but his older, more important, but dead one. Florence was a woman who could not help complaining, even though conscious of what she always felt was her unworthiness ('I am not lovable', she told Rebekah Owen of all people). The second Mrs Hardy was now beginning to regret her 'catch' of the great but rather too set in his ways old genius. She also, in her outrush of jealousy and disappointment, exclaimed to Lady Hoare:

> It seems to me that I am an utter failure if my husband can publish such a *sad sad* book. He tells me he has written *no* despondent poem for the last eighteen months [this gives a good idea of the level on which he preferred to keep his conversations with her about poetry],

& yet I cannot get rid of the feeling that the man who wrote some of those poems is utterly weary of life – & cares for nothing in this world. If I had been a different sort of woman, & better fitted to be his wife – would he, I wonder, have published that volume?

He would have published the book whoever had been his wife. Florence had, completely understandably, desired the book to be filled with thrilling love lyrics about her, but had to make do with 'After the Visit', which, though a handsome tribute, ended, surely rather despondently:

> Through the dark corridors
> Your walk was so soundless I did not know
> Your form from a phantom's of long ago
> Said to pass on the ancient floors,
>
> Till you drew from the shade,
> And I saw the large luminous living eyes
> Regard me in fixed inquiring-wise
> As those of a soul that weighed,
>
> Scarce consciously,
> The eternal question of what Life was,
> And why we were there, and by whose strange laws
> That which mattered most could not be.

It was all quite beyond her – including the 'scarce consciously' – and it is instructive to compare her complaints to those of Emma, declared by the admirers of Florence as literary critic to be 'uncomprehending' and 'certifiable'. The former's were semi-abusive, angry, jealous and derived from grievance (largely justified) over Tom's neglect and failure to acknowledge her. Florence's were quite as jealous, far more generalized, far less sharply intelligent, far more commonplace, and far more reminiscent of bourgeois Enfield values: she seems to be declaring that 'he has married *me*, his first true helpmate, and yet he is still so *sad*'. They also contained an admixture of her temperamental and perpetual self-blame, her feeling that she was not doing her duty properly. She based her life upon what she understood as her duty, and always felt that she fell just short of it. Sometimes she did not.

But the man she had married was in quite a different league: she could not connect her native gloom with poetic gloom. 'Wessex Heights' was grist to her mill – that Tom had been shamefully treated, first and mainly by Emma, who had not worshipped his genius and had wanted an existence on her own account, and then, but only secondarily, by a world as yet uninstructed by his Order of Merit. This bore no relevance to the fact of her husband's temperament. For in 'Wessex Heights' the personal references are quite deliberately shadowy.

The 'lowlands' (life as it is lived and must be lived) throw the essential loneliness and independence of the poet, and of poetry, into as sharp relief as the heights themselves stand against the skies. As Hermann Lea observed, and as *The Dynasts* by its nature demonstrates, Tom loved panoramas: to be on heights from which he could observe extensive areas. 'Wessex Heights' is, yes, about the pains that life brings; but it closes with an affirmation of the consolations of poetry, the writer or reader of which is on a height above pettier pains, however agonizing these may be. The 'liberty' it grants, as Shelley would have agreed, is the liberty that only the search for truth (in the Hardyan sense of it) can grant. On 27 June of the year following the completion of 'Wessex Heights', Tom was with Emma in Lausanne in Switzerland. He sat until midnight in Edward Gibbon's old garden there, and wrote the poem 'Lausanne', which ends with one of the most magnificent poetic paraphrases of prose ever made. Milton wrote in *The Doctrine and Discipline of Divorce*, as Tom gives it in a footnote in the *Life*.

> Truth is as impossible to be soiled by any outward touch, as the sunbeam; though this ill hap wait on her nativity, that she never comes into this world, but like a bastard, to the ignominy of him that brought her forth; till Time, the midwife rather than the mother of truth, have washed and salted the infant and declared her legitimate.

This became (in the only two lines in all poetry which successfully rhyme 'world' and 'hurled'):

> 'How fares the Truth now? – Ill?
> – Do pens but slily further her advance?
> May one not speed her but in phrase askance?
> Do scribes aver the Comic to be Reverend still?
>
> 'Still rule those minds on earth
> At whom sage Milton's wormwood words were hurled:
> *"Truth like a bastard comes into the world*
> *Never without ill-fame to him who gives her birth"*?'

587

There is no sign that Florence ever understood this area of thinking – or, rather, feeling. Emma, at least in her youth, did – and was able to encourage her lover to adhere to it; he may sometimes have forgotten this during her life, but he certainly remembered it after her death.

Basing himself upon Florence's literal interpretation of 'Wessex Heights' as the complaint of an at last fully acknowledged genius against shameful treatment, rather than as a poem about poetry, Bailey identifies the 'four women' (and no doubt Tom did give her some such explanation, if only in order to satisfy her curiosity). These he lists as Emma ('no comrade, no friend, without charity, and without tolerance'), Jemima (the figure against the moon), Tryphena Sparks (the ghost at Yell'ham Bottom because, allegedly, they had a quarrel in the dale below Yellowham Hill!) and Mrs Henniker (the rare fair woman). All this is plausible, but not definitive – because it is dramatized, altered, and, last but not least, supposed to be non-definitive. The Tryphena Sparks identification is the least persuasive: it might just as easily have been Eliza or Jane Nicholls, or a score of other women of whom we have never heard. More to the point in that connection, surely, is a fact of which Tom was well aware: that there was, in Hermann Lea's words, a 'Wild Man o' Yall'm' who fathered all the 'love-children' of the surrounding locality. This does not suggest any specific love acts in that locality, but is, rather, a dramatization of various guilts about sexual acts, making reference to local folklore. One could even interpret the 'rare fair woman' stanza as being about Emma, and, although I think that would be biographically far-fetched, it is poetically appropriate: these identities do not matter. Bailey rushes in where angels might be unwise to tread, and interprets the difficult second stanza as being about Emma: 'the lines present a tangle of elliptical phrases in apposition with "the lone man's friend"'. He notes the biblical allusion in the phrase 'Her who suffereth long and is kind' (I Corinthians 13, 4): 'Charity suffereth long, and is kind; charity envieth not; charity vaunteth not itself, is not puffed up.'

Poetry that comes out of books, or from knowledge gained only in the intellect, is unconvincing and fails to last. It needs to come from experience, and if it is about suffering – which much poetry is, and which 'Wessex Heights' undoubtedly is – then it cannot be written by one who has not suffered. But in Tom's case it is almost always dramatized, and the facts of the experience behind it are rearranged. There is no doubt, biographically, that Emma believed Tom was paying less attention to her in favour of other and younger women, and that he took her reaction to be disloyalty in the matter of *Jude*. No doubt, too, when he wrote the phrase 'one rare fair woman' he did have Florence Henniker immediately in mind. In the second (9 December) of her letters to Lady Hoare, that of 9 December, Florence Hardy wrote that

> in 'Wessex heights' there is one 'rare fair woman' of whom he says 'Now I can let her go'. *She* has always been a sincere & affectionate friend to him, staunch & unalterable – & I am glad to say that she is my friend too. There was never any idea of letting her go – for he, too, is true & faithful to his friends but the *poet* wrote that.

This is reasonable if inane comment, except for the italicized '*She*' – a swipe at Emma. It shows Florence at the height of her critical powers – unless she got it straight from the horse's mouth by foolishly asking Tom why he had *not* let Mrs Henniker go! But does it matter, or add to the meaning of the poem? What matters is that Tom convinces us that he has indeed had personal experiences, some of which were sinister, like the ghost in the train who says unwelcome things which he doesn't want to hear. This vision in particular, of the ghost in the passing train whose profile may be seen accusing as it passes by, is metaphorical, compressing several now irrecoverable personal impressions into one.

Bailey claims that the second stanza is specifically about Emma because of the use of the pronoun 'Her'. It is worth quoting his argument, because this poem is crucial not only as one of Tom's most moving but also as an example of the poetic procedures of his maturity. When he resumed the habit of poem-writing he found, to his 'consternation', an 'awkwardness in getting back to an easy expression in numbers . . . but that soon wore off' – it had by 1896 worn right off, and his decision was made. Bailey writes:

> The second stanza as a whole, using the terms 'they' and 'nobody', seems to refer to people of all kinds in the lowlands who are intolerant of Hardy's ideas, but the word 'Her' suggests that the first two lines refer to the first of the four actual women mentioned by Florence Hardy [according to Bailey, who is probably right so far as Florence is concerned, this was Emma] . . .

But 'Wessex Heights' is not a cryptic autobiographical record dealing with the persecution of the writer: it is about unhappiness in life, and

589

about the contrasting purity achieved by poetry which transcends, as the heights tower over, the 'ordinary' and unhappy world of the lowlands; the implication is that such purity is not attainable in the lowlands, and therefore not attainable by anyone in 'life'. The word 'Her' simply acknowledges the feminine nature of charity: it cannot refer to charity *and* Emma – who does not in fact come into it at all, and is not suggested by it.

The last line of the first stanza has told us that the writer 'seems', when on the heights, to have achieved some kind of immortality and purity: he is where he was before birth and where he 'may' be after death; he is consoled at 'crises' because he is 'above' them; he is not false to his early self any more. In the lowlands there is no one who understands: not even charity, the lonely man's friend, who would accept his failure to achieve purity of vision and thus the objectivity conferred by a panoramic viewpoint. The heights free him from that mechanical ('clank') thinking which sicklies things o'er (he was familiar with, and well understood, this quotation from *Hamlet*); they unfetter his heart (and he can thus 'know some liberty'). The thinking here is explicitly religious in his own sense, as expressed to Lefèvre: 'The religion which ought to be preserved . . . would be created by poetry . . . Poetry, pure literature, and religion are the visible points of the most authentic mental and emotional life.'

'Wessex Heights' may also be read as a farewell to prose, to novel-writing as a trade, to compromise. What it is above all, though, is a declaration of independence: the former man of the world states his other-worldly terms. Little more – apart from the deaths of animals (many cats tragically lost to the railway that ran near Max Gate, and, alas, the great and 'unflinching' Wessex, who would have wished to survive Tom, but failed by two years to do so), of his mother, the surreptitious taking of a mistress, and then the sudden and devastating disappearance of Emma, an emotionally disappointing second marriage to the mistress, and the death of his beloved sister Mary – was to 'happen' in his life from that time onwards. All those things were deeply felt, but they were not unusual things. Yet his life would go on for more than thirty years. He did not then expect it to. But for as long as he went on he would pit himself against the values, or non-values, of the lowlands people, and achieve as much as the 'strange continuator' could manage, by remembering its 'chrysalis'. He would write for others who felt as he did when on the heights which nature's kindly hand seemed to shape. His admission of falsity to his 'simple self that was' acquits him of arrogance or self-pity. One might reasonably put the theme of the poem thus: it expresses a determination to withdraw from 'involvement in the contamination that destroys clarity of vision' (words used by James Robinson in introducing *The Nag Hammadi Library in English*, 1988 – the gnostic texts found in a cave in Egypt just after the Second World War). And of course, *pace* Millgate, the matter of society's actually suppressing truth and explicitness in the interests of fear, and from other and worse motives, is a much more moral matter (as Thomas Hardy would often insist) than any official morality: it bodes ill for the health of such a society.

That Gosse could shuffle through snaps of pretty boys while mourning Browning, and indulge perfectly decent feelings of love, lust or both for Hamo Thornycroft, and then have his fellow clubmen (those whose admiration he required for the sake of his career) register his disapproval of *Jude* really was a shocking and, above, all, disappointing matter to his friend. Had Tom told him that he had been sad as well as angry about it, he might have been even more accurate. But Gosse's condemnation of *Jude*, whether in or out of drink, justifies the cruel verdict of Virginia Woolf, one of those who really loved Hardy: Gosse, she wrote, was a 'crafty, wordly, prim, astute little beast . . . a mean skunk'.

One other poem undoubtedly of this period, 'Between Us Now' – its *terminus ad quem* is 1901, when it appeared in *Poems of the Past and the Present* – is more straightforward, and, although readily understandable, may fairly be described as personal. It is directed to Emma, and, as we know, Tom made no effort to prevent her seeing it.

Between us now and here –
  Two thrown together
Who are not wont to wear
  Life's flushest feather –
Who see the scenes slide past,
The daytimes dimming fast,
Let there be truth at last,
  Even if despair.

So thoroughly and long
  Have you now known me,
So real in faith and strong
  Have I now shown me,
That nothing needs disguise

Further in any wise,
Or asks or justifies
    A guarded tongue.

Face unto face, then, say,
    Eyes my own meeting,
Is your heart far away,
    Or with mine beating?
When false things are brought low,
And swift things have grown slow,
Feigning like froth shall go,
    Faith be for aye.

These lines express emotions that might well be addressed by almost any husband to his wife after some twenty-five years of marriage. The poem may suggest to some that he had, as I have tentatively suggested, been more open to Emma about his feelings for other women than most allow, and that she was more discreet about particulars, for example to the egregious Owen, than she seemed to be. Her complaints to Owen, and others, are invariably generalized: almost as if they might have been based on readily acknowledged feelings on the part of her husband. Later, so far as Florence Dugdale was concerned, Tom would certainly not be open about his feelings or, especially, his doings. But by 1907, when he met Florence, Emma's habits of mind, even if expressed in sporadic outbursts rather than continuously, had become set: she had finally failed to suppress them, which she may well have tried hard to do. The poem is strangely prophetic of those written after Emma's death, when the 'truth' about what she had been to him became immediately evident.

Tom knew of his own failings, and tried to understand them. His understanding that everyone has such failings is far surer, and more generous, than is that of those moralists from the lowlands who now dance upon his grave. Another saying of Nietzsche's with which he would have 'heartily agreed', in that connection, and which Robert Gittings and other detractors would have done well to try to grasp, is this: 'It says nothing against the ripeness of a spirit that it has a few worms.'

If we are not to think of Tom in such terms as ripeness (and its consequent worms), then we had better not think of him at all. He cannot be accommodated to conventional systems, and, although by no means as mentally brilliant or overtly antagonistic to the status quo, is in his own quieter way quite as subversive as his lifelong hero Shelley. Here is Nietzsche again: 'The worst readers are those who behave like plundering troops: they take away a few things they can use, dirty and confound the remainder, and revile the whole.' The 'marks of the good writer', on the contrary, are two, and are worth repeating: good writers 'prefer to be understood rather than admired; and they do not write for knowing and over-acute readers'. This is why Tom appreciated the companionship of Hermann Lea, whom he might well have refused to rate below even any modern, better educated, 'knowing and over-acute' critic. As Lea himself wrote, there was a 'grand simplicity' about him. The majority of his contemporaries, including most of those who knew him, missed it. The recognition came from younger men, in the last days of his life: from such as T.E. Lawrence, Robert Graves and Walter de la Mare. In our own times, this simplicity, and the fundamental modesty that must go with it, have often been dismissed: he is seen as the kind of man who was so unsure of himself and his place in the universe that he had to keep 'literary notes', a naive and unsophisticated bumpkin whom, however, the universities are now drawing up into their kindly care. But neither this nor the putting of his head on a postage stamp is going to clear creation of his charges against it.

27

The Well-Beloved

The Well-Beloved, Tom's recasting of the serial of 1892, appeared on 16 March 1897. It was his last novel, and, although persistently undervalued as what he called it, a farce with a tragic aspect, it is a squib by the side of *Jude the Obscure*. His career in fiction thus ended with a sardonic whimper, rather than with the big bang of *Jude*.

Had he not troubled to revise this book, it might have proved an exception: a book by him that has not remained in print. But no original book he published has ever gone out of print. He is one of the best sellers of his time, and when Macmillan had the rights to his works he outsold Kipling, whose rights they also owned. When Hardy's work came out of copyright in 1978, *The Well-Beloved* continued to sell and was taken up by other publishers. This is what he must have had in mind when he decided that the originally too scrappy serial needed an extensive overhaul before it could be added to the collected edition; he made further improvements for the 1912 Macmillan edition.

In the serial version the cynical ending had been authorial. It could hardly have been other than distressing to any but a youthful wife. In its amused savagery, it is unique in Victorian fiction. That savagery had not been directed at Emma, since *The Well-Beloved* is not about the disappointments of companionship but about the state of romantic love; however, he modified it for her sake, as well as for the book's. Such savagery might have been acceptable in a short story whose theme was the contrast between beauty and age, and its effect on a man; it was hardly appropriate for a novel about to see a new and hopefully permanent existence in volume form. Again, it is one thing to express a contempt for the serial audience in the serial itself – another to do so in a volume read by more discerning people. He more or less admitted, in his Preface, that he had departed from his usual custom:

> As for the story itself, it may be worth while to remark that, differing from all or most others of the series in that the interest aimed at is of

an ideal or subjective nature, and frankly imaginative, verisimilitude in the sequence of events has been subordinated to the said aim.

At 'about this time' he wrote a poem, 'The Well-Beloved' (in *Poems of the Past and Present*, 1901), and stated that the theme was 'the theory of the transmigration of the beloved, who only exists in the lover, from material woman to material woman – as exemplified also by Proust many years later'. The most immediate inspiration is Shelley, and in particular the Shelley of 'Epipsychidion', a phrase from which, 'One shape of many names', serves as the epigraph to the novel. The poem is spoken by the lover, who idealizes his beloved, of Kingsbere (Bere Regis), thus:

> – 'O faultless is her dainty form,
>   And luminous her mind;
> She is the God–created norm
>   Of perfect womankind!'

But the 'Shape' itself appears:

> She, proudly, thinning in the gloom:
>   'Though, since troth-plight began,
> I have ever stood as bride to groom,
>   I wed no mortal man!'

When the speaker meets his actual bride her 'look was pinched and thin,/As if her soul had shrunk and died,/And left a waste within.'

The novel, though, is only ostensibly on this theme of the 'Platonic Idea' which, in connection with it, Tom hardly took seriously. But he had to pretend to. *The Well-Beloved* is really a comic exploration of the physical nature of what some have called the 'disease' of romantic love. It has an obvious sexual sub-text, and this was immediately, although with the usual disingenuousness, recognized by certain appalled reviewers. This sexual sub-text is underlined by the frequent allusion to the 'Island Custom' of pre-nuptial union.

The character Jocelyn is, as he claimed, 'innocent and moral' in finding this custom 'a bygone barbarism'; but he is not 'innocent' in living with Marcia in London. Tom's obstinacy in this matter of offending moralists suggests that by this time he actually thrived on baiting them. He could not have failed to anticipate adverse reactions from the usual quarters, such as the *World*; he was particularly venomous about this reviewer. But in fact the *World* was almost the only place in which he was met with real vehemence – and this may have disappointed him: despite himself, he liked to flush out the enemy in force. He had meant what he said in 'Wessex Heights', and, within a month of completing it, told Mrs Henniker (on 24 January 1897) that

> I have been thinking that of all men dead whom I should like to meet in the Elysian fields I would choose Shelley, not only for his unearthly, weird, wild appearance & genius but for his genuineness, earnestness, & enthusiasms on behalf of the oppressed.

Shelley was the most aggressive rebel of all the English poets – not excluding Byron, who was more of a showman, and avoided earnestness. When the book, with its epigraph by Shelley, came out and the reviews appeared he commented to the same correspondent on 31 March:

> . . . my poor little innocent book *The Well-Beloved* has had a horrid stab delivered it in one quarter, *The World*, which is as unaccountable as it is base. You will imagine how it amazed me when one of my reasons for letting the story be reprinted was that it cd not by any possibility offend Mrs or Mr Grundy, or their Young Persons, even though it cd be called unreal & impossible for a man to have such an artistic craze for the Ideal in woman as the hero has. It is truly the unexpected that happens.

He added a criticism of Zola which he often repeated: Mrs Henniker was mistaken, he told her, in believing he admired Zola. 'It is just what I don't do. I think him no artist, & too material.' The 'animal side' of human nature, he felt, or said he felt, 'should never be dwelt on except as a contrast or foil to its spiritual side'. (He always had reservations about Zola, and at the time of his death remarked that, although he had been a truth-seeker, he had not been an 'artist': he had, instead, discovered his 'vocation' in his staunch defence of Dreyfus against the French Establishment.)

His defence of *The Well-Beloved*, to Mrs Henniker, more or less repeated what he wrote on the same day to Gosse, who had tried to make up for his *Jude* lapse with a favourable review. He told Gosse that he had been on a walk with a Cambridge don (this was Charles Moule) 'of 40 years experience of every kind of young man': he had read it through twice, 'without the least sense of anything but its obvious meaning, or want of meaning'. Acknowledging a rather formal letter of thanks for the book from Swinburne, he wrote: 'I have been much surprised, and even grieved, by a ferocious review attributing an immoral quality to the tale.' He and Swinburne were indeed ones to grieve over such charges.

The story may be briefly told. Jocelyn Pierston (in the serial 'Pearston', but 'Pierston' is nearer to the pun, *Pierre* = Stone, appropriate to his profession), who becomes a famous sculptor, is the son of a purveyor of Portland stone. Like his creator, he uses what is ordinary and commercial in his father's life (the Wessex ways) to make art (and money). He comes from the so-called Isle of Slingers, in other words Portland Bill, just off Weymouth. He tries to pursue the 'migratory, elusive idealization he called his Love' through three generations of Portland women: Avice Caro, her daughter, and her granddaughter. He is interrupted in his initial project, however: being about to marry Avice Caro (who does not wish to observe 'Island Custom'), he meets Marcia Bencomb and, caught in a storm, goes off to a hotel with her. It is, significantly, Marcia's steaming clothing, drying out after the rainstorm, which persuades him that his Love is taking a new shape. They go to London, arrange to marry, live together, but then part. Jocelyn courts, with vicissitudes, Avice's daughter and granddaughter; but he ends up by marrying the aged Marcia.

Though there is nothing 'immoral' about *The Well-Beloved*, it is provocative to those immoral enough to oppose candour; he must have known this. It is not enough to suggest that he was naive. He was teasing his tormentors, and the future critics of his 'morality'. In a letter of protest to the *Academy* he asserted that Jocelyn Pierston was 'an innocent and moral man throughout'; he did so in the full knowledge that, although there was in fact nothing immoral about it, Victorian *mores* simply did not allow unmarried people to cohabit in a hotel – as Jocelyn and Marcia Bencomb do in London at the beginning of the book (and, as the author is careful to point out in his final revision, without consequences). He knew, too, that to draw candid attention to the action of time and its effects upon sexual attractiveness was neither popular nor tactful. As he had surmised, to do it in a poem was a different matter, and 'Amabel', placed at the beginning of *Wessex Poems*, makes it seem commonplace enough because it is about death rather than directly about diminishing powers of sexual attractiveness. One anonymous reviewer, in the *Athenaeum* of 10 April 1897, rumbled him, and was not tricked into believing that the Platonic theme was, in this novel, taken with any great seriousness. Surely this review was by a woman?

> He has imagined a temperament which we believe to be that of the great majority of male human beings – nay, of male beings of every species . . . not instinct – or temperament if you like to call it so – but hard reason, aided in certain cases by the policeman, alone can persuade the normal man to monogamy. It is all very well to talk about the pursuit of the 'Well-Beloved', to sublimate the elementary instinct into a fantasy of a 'Beloved One' who does not usually 'care to remain in one corporeal nook or shell for any great length of time, however he [the pursuer] may wish her to do so'; our forefathers were quite familiar with the idea, but they called it being off with the old love before you were on with the new. But conscious as most people must be of possibilities of this kind in themselves, 'it is', as Mr Hardy's hero says, 'a sort of thing one doesn't like to talk of', and, indeed, it has usually exhausted itself before a man reaches the age when he finds out that after all people are for the most part built very similarly, and therefore does not mind talking of anything . . . Where Mr Hardy's hero differs from the mass of mankind is not, therefore, as he himself supposes, in the fact that his 'Beloved' has had many incarnations. His practical painter friend hits the real peculiarity when he says, 'Essentially, all men are fickle, like you; but not with such perceptiveness.'

When she (or he) added, however, that 'of the physical side of passion, [Pierston] knows as little as any man so susceptible can do', one is left floundering a little. After all, the attraction of Marcia Bencomb for Jocelyn was physical, and it had physical consequences, although she did not become pregnant. The question of Jocelyn's physical propensities is left unresolved, and the *Athenaeum*'s reviewer leaves it open, too: only as physical as such a man can be! And how much is that? Tom told Gosse on 31 March 1897, and always protested, that

> The attack [in the *World*] must have been dictated by personal malignity, since nobody could honestly read such ideas into a book containing repeated demonstrations & statements that the Visionary hero's craze for the Ideal woman was innocent.

It was then that he added that he had the walk with the experienced

The dreary monument to Hardy in Dorchester: most of the townspeople had disliked him.

PLEASE DO NOT WALK ON THE GRASS

Hardy in his garden in 1927, a few weeks before his death.

The unhappy and always ailing Florence Emily Hardy.

Hardy in 1911, the year of Emma's death.

Emma photographed for the *Tatler* in 1904.

Caricature of Hardy drawn by Max Beerbohm for the *Pall Mall* magazine, 1902.

Hardy in 1894, around the time he was in pursuit of Florence Henniker.

Mrs Florence Henniker in 1909.

A famous scene from *Jude* drawn by W. Hatherall for the serialized version in
Harper's, 1895.

Another scene from *Jude* visualized by Hatherall.

Cambridge don. It is only necessary to repeat once more that in the revised story Jocelyn does go to bed with Marcia. He was quite obviously, therefore, not 'innocent' in the sense in which Tom was insisting to Gosse that he was. His feelings towards those women who were inhabited by his beloved were therefore not innocent either – not innocent, that is to say, in the absurd and unrealistic Victorian sense. How, after all, could the author of so many erotic books have seriously believed in such a concept of 'innocence'?

In the face of this it is hardly to be wondered at that some have assumed Tom to be either highly disingenuous in a sly and unnecessary manner, or simply foolishly naive. In fact, I am quite sure, it is an instance in which his sense of humour and irony got the better of him, largely owing, no doubt, to the disillusion he experienced over *Jude*, where the case was clear cut. He meant what he said in 'Wessex Heights'; but he would need time to adjust to his circumstances. Probably he had not expected the *World* attack, silly though it was, to be quite so virulent. We must remember that Gosse, if not really a close friend in the sense of the sort of confidant of whom he had spoken to Florence Henniker, was one of his closest literary friends. The public charge of 'indecency' made him (as he confessed so many years later) angry. Who among literary friends could he trust, if he could not trust Gosse?

Emma, if perhaps usually friendly and accommodating, was now in the habit of directing occasional but devastating tirades at him: his domestic circumstances had become more uncertain. The long holiday with her may not, in the long run, have led to any improvement in their home life – or only to a temporary one. The breakdown might have been in part his own fault, but it was now irremediable. How could he talk over serious and confidential matters with people like Rebekah Owen (who had herself objected to *Jude* on old-maidish grounds)? He had lost Florence Henniker in the deep sense that he had had to 'let her go': she was not what he had hoped she might become. He needed some kind of secret relationship with a woman; he was not completely clear about whether it should be sexual or non-sexual. Most men are not – until they recognize that they want it to be the former.

He told Swinburne, and declared elsewhere, that he thought his Jocelyn Pierston was a 'fanciful exhibition of the artistic nature, & has, I think, some little foundation in fact'. And Jocelyn never actually renounces an interest in the physical: indeed, it could be said that he likes his women younger than himself! (What older man, as Tom was well and mischievously aware in writing the book, does not?) Agnes Grove, although witty, satirical and amusing, was not at all what he was looking for. He never entertained the kind of feelings for her that he had briefly entertained for Florence Henniker – and, once upon a time, and more intensely, for Emma. It is no wonder, in this confused if defiant state of mind, that his remarks about his last novel read oddly.

This is the appropriate, as well as the chronologically almost correct, point to bring in one of Tom's close non-literary friends about whom we know most. For something that Hermann Lea wrote about his character illuminates his puzzling behaviour over *The Well-Beloved*.

Tom's non-literary friends eventually included, as well as Charles and Henry J. Moule – brothers of his never-to-be-replaced comrade Horace – his Dorchester solicitor H.O. Lock and his son Arthur, the Wood Homers of Athelhampton, of whom we have already heard, and other local people such as the banker Thornton. He enjoyed their non-literary but by no means philistine company, and, if he ever did allow what sounded like political opinions to pass his lips, it would have been to them that he confided. As Hardy the degenerate, he naturally had a healthy horror of being 'revealed', in society, as a strong partisan of any 'position'. He knew that this was tantamount to crude misrepresentation. He was content to be known as a man of liberal sentiment (and, much later, as a non-partisan sympathizer with some of the aims of the Labour Party), who openly supported all action against cruelty to animals, in particular hunting and inhumane slaughtering methods. His barber from 1907, W.G. Mills (he kept Tom's hair in a box and eventually sold what was left of its contents – he had given away some locks to Tom's admirers – to his interviewer, J. Stevens Cox, in April 1963 for an undisclosed sum), observed that although he 'could sometimes be induced to talk of the weather or local matters' he would never discuss either 'politics' or 'his books'. He lived in the full glare of publicity for almost forty years, but he was never less than afraid of it and its possible effect upon his poetic independence.

Hermann Lea, son of an English father and a German mother, was born at Thorpe-le-Soken in Essex in February 1869, and was thus Tom's junior by nearly thirty years. Not many of the salient details of his long life (he died at Linwood in the New Forest in 1952) have been recorded; but he was an unusual and, his nephew Alfred Scudamore noted, 'strange' man. His father was perhaps equally strange. A regular officer, he retired from the army and went to New Zealand as a missionary. After translating some of the Bible into Maori, he died at the early age of forty-five. His son, who left some tantalizingly fragmentary notes towards a life of Hardy which he wanted to write but never could get round to executing, went at the age of eighteen or nineteen to Wood Homer's farm at Athelhampton to 'learn farming'.

He had already become attached to the work of Thomas Hardy: in 1886, while waiting at Tunbridge Wells station for a train to take him to a farm, he had bought a copy of *Far From the Madding Crowd*. Lea was not an accomplished writer, and freely admitted it; but throughout his life he tried to remedy this. Such writing as he did – articles on country matters and folklore, a few stories, his guides to Wessex – though not quite as articulate as he would have liked it to be, has the inevitable charm of honesty and lack of artifice. In 1904, when he wrote a story based on true events and failed to place it with a magazine, Tom told him on 21 April:

> The reason why it has been declined by magazines is, I should almost certainly say, its unconventional ending, & this brings you face to face with a question which nobody could decide but yourself: whether you will write what you choose, & be denied magazine publication, or write the artificial magazine story & be accepted.

It is obvious why, for all his lack of skill, Tom liked Lea: he was a man as independent as himself, and he chose not to write artificially. When he writes, 'Ten years of fitful vicissitude piled themselves over my head', the reader at least knows, from the context and the writer if not from the sentence alone, that they really were years of fitful vicissitude. He had been a vegetarian from an early age, at one time refusing to wear leather shoes – and when he saw anyone being cruel to an animal, he would intervene physically. Bearded, of small stature but with a 'magnetic personality' and 'courtly manner', he had 'strong emotions'. Once, to keep 'women with squabbling children' out of a railway carriage, he pretended to be an ape. He enjoyed his unconventionality and his queer humour. This latter was described by his nephew as being strongly 'Rabelaisian' in cast, a feature which certainly pleased his 'coarse' friend Hardy.

Of his youthful railway station purchase Lea wrote:

> I grew deeply interested in the book, though not from the farming point of view, but because of the philosophy it contained. Notes made on the fly-leaf referred to twenty-one passages, all of which had struck me as fitting in with my own scheme of things, and which shed light

on many obscurities of my youthful mind. Often in the days to come I referred to the wisdom-words between its covers.

Here was a real reader, who loved the book for better than mere literary reasons. Tom's observations about life struck a chord in him, as they did and do in so many others. However, despite Wood Homer's acquaintance with Hardy, Lea was not to meet him for another ten years. But he enquired about him in the district (Athelhampton is only a mile or two from Puddletown). He talked to some who had been at school with Tom at Bockhampton, one of whom told him that he had been 'somehow different from the rest of us boys, kind of dreaming, seeming to prefer to be by himself'. Above all Lea, who did less farming at Athelhampton Hall than horse-riding, tennis-playing and dog-keeping (he had twenty dogs), took to photography, and went about Dorset taking pictures of various locations from Tom's fiction, which he was all the time avidly studying. He became a prominent member of the Dorset Photographic Club, and through this met the secretary, the Rev. Thomas Perkins, who was the vicar of Turnworth and a friend of Tom's. Together he and Perkins planned to bring out an edition of Hardy's novels with photographs. But this project was dropped, and instead they decided to publish sets of picture postcards, six in each set, through the Oxford printing firm of George Bryan & Co. Some time in 1898 Perkins, whom Tom was at pains to state that he trusted, took Lea along to lunch to meet Tom, and a close friendship developed: 'From that day,' wrote Lea, 'Hardy took an active part in our venture, and many were the excursions we made together . . . He was exceedingly helpful in identifying some of the less obvious spots . . .'

Lea, the twice married but childless inventor of a humane rabbit trap, was a jack-of-most-trades: bee-keeper, pioneer of cycling and motoring, builder, gardener, mechanic, water-diviner (he found water for many villagers at no charge), and owner of, among other dogs, an Irish terrier which smoked cigarettes. He was, in the latter-day terminology of Claude Lévi-Strauss, a *bricoleur*, an improviser, a man of infinite resource who worked with anything immediately to hand. The comparative success of *A Handbook to the Wessex Country of Thomas Hardy's Novels and Poems* (1905) led to the better-known and more comprehensive *Thomas Hardy's Wessex* (1913). Tom was at first lukewarm about the idea, but gradually warmed to Lea as he came to realize that the man understood him. For some years Lea lived at Var Trees, Clyffe, near the tiny village of Tincleton, a mile or two to the south-east of Puddletown, in a house which he helped to build. Tom tried to help him name it, suggesting Hurst Firs, and rejecting Var Ridge only because it would not tell 'something of where it is'; Var Trees was Lea's compromise.

Then, in 1913, Lea moved into Tom's birthplace, where he remained until 1921 when he left Dorset for Hampshire. The place had fallen vacant when Henry left it to move into his own house at Talbothays, and, although Lea is modest about the matter, it confirms that Tom trusted him as absolutely as he trusted any man, since he could successfully have opposed the tenancy. Lea got the first refusal from the owner, a Major Balfour, but went to Tom and 'asked him what he thought of the idea'. '"No," he said, "I do not know anyone I would rather see there than you, for I feel you will respect the associations of the place, and leave things as they are."' Which he always did. What is most striking about their relationship, though, is the amount they saw of each other – and the opportunities Lea had to observe both Emma, and later Florence Hardy, at close quarters. But he gave little away, despite the fact that, as is evident from the hints he gives, Tom confided much to him. Tom did eventually make a habit of visiting Lea at the cottage, but at the outset not for some years, because, Lea tantalizingly wrote, 'the associations of the place were to him not entirely of the best':

a visit here was not without sadness to him, as he freely admitted to me more than once. It was but natural that sight of the old scenes should awaken memories of the long past, and that, moreover, as usual in life, pain should predominate.

From 1898 onwards Tom got into the habit of accompanying Lea, on foot or by bicycle, on photographic and other expeditions. Emma often came with them. By 1900 Lea had acquired his first car, a red Oldsmobile, steered by a tiller, with a huge fly wheel and a dangerous kick start. It was probably in this vehicle that he drove Emma to Bardolf, the house that Wood Homer had bought after leaving Athelhampton. Together with Mrs Wood Homer and Lilian Gifford they then went, some on bicycles, to visit Bulbarrow. Tom became excited when he examined the landscape with glasses, and Lea realized that he was drawn in particular to such 'high view-points': they visited many more together over the years. On the drive back to Max Gate Emma talked freely to him about Cornwall, *A Pair of Blue Eyes* and 'horses and riding'. After this expedition he took Tom, or Tom and Emma, or Tom and Florence, on hundreds of trips in a later car, a Hupmobile (in 1915 alone, when petrol was in short supply during the First World War, they took fifteen trips). No man saw more of Tom than Lea, at least until 1921; but even then they did not lose touch, and there was no more welcome visitor to Max Gate.

Lea knew more about Tom than most men. That is why he could never complete his projected biography of him. It is notable that he never tried to cash in on his knowledge after his friend's death, although he could have made a great deal of money simply by putting himself forward. However, he was not a journalist: he was loyal to the notion of friendship, and had other and better things to do. The Hardy collector E.N. Sanders, who bequeathed most of his items to the Dorset Museum, became a friend in later life, but Lea did not vouchsafe any confidences to him. He wrote:

> Though reserved on the question of his own writings, Mr Hardy responded at once to certain questions of mine and launched out on many details regarding his work, his methods, his aspirations and his achievements, as we rode slowly homewards in the cool of the evenings. It was always amazingly interesting to me to get him to speak in this unreserved manner, and he occasionally at those times gave me confidences which remain confidences still, and will to the day, too, when I pass to the otherwhere.

Of a specific incident he wrote:

> One evening in particular is indelibly written on my mind. It was April 8th, 1911, and I talked over with him a matter which was causing me considerable trouble and worry. Hardy was ever a good listener, and his comments and advice – all of which in later years I found to have been extraordinarily sound, and on some points verging on the prophetic – wonderfully relieved my mind. At the end of our discussion he told me of certain incidents in his own past life, drawing parallels between my position then, and his own of years ago, and pointing out where he had made certain mistakes which led to results such as his advice now sought to guard me from.

Here we see Tom as we seldom see him, but as he often was. When he read 'Florence Hardy's' *Life* Lea wrote to Sanders:

> The reading does not bring back to me the man I knew – I think I

may say pretty intimately – for nearly thirty years . . . What I miss most is a certain simplicity which, to me, always seemed an integral part of Hardy's make-up – his whole-hearted interest in the little things of life.

Sanders may not have known who the author of all but the last chapters of the *Life* was. But Lea was probably in on the secret (work on the book was begun while he was still at Higher Bockhampton) and, bound by his word, added as if in explanation: 'But I recognise that in all probability this side of him would have little appeal to the bulk of his readers . . .'

He did not give his opinion of either the first or second Mrs Hardy. On 12 January 1947 he told Sanders:

Emma I knew well. She once took me up to the top of the house (Max Gate) and showed me a lot of wooden boxes in which she said her unpublished poems were stored. She also told me once that she had inspired *Tess*! I knew her brother and his wife and their son and daughter [Gordon and Lilian Gifford] and stayed with them in the same house once upon a time. I also knew, pretty intimately, Florence's two sisters. Florence once asked me, when she was going to marry Thomas, whether I thought they could have a child safely – because of his age.

Had Lea lived on to a point at which he would have thought it decent to divulge hitherto private and confidential facts to a biographer indisposed to treat Hardy as a great writer *manqué*, many misconceptions might have been corrected. But such was not to be. Evelyn Hardy dedicated her biography, the fullest to date when it appeared in 1954, to David Cecil, and does not seem to have consulted Lea. He is not even in her index.

In 1943, Cecil published a critical book on Hardy which Sanders sent to Lea. Lea praised its generally good intentions, but pointed out that Cecil knew nothing about country life, and had no intimate knowledge of Hardy. He wrote:

Now Hardy had a very definite way of conversing with the various people with whom he came in contact. With literary people the conversations were literary: with more humble folk (such as myself) he would discuss country matters with intimate knowledge; mentioning details of minuteness which one would not have credited him with noticing: with 'ordinary' people he would discuss ordinary everyday matters.

After reading some of the book again he commented that Cecil was 'essentially conventional, orthodox, and largely deficient in humour'. This is true, and greatly to the point, and brings me back to what is perhaps the most important of all Lea's observations of Tom, and one to which many of his critics – if not his readers – will object with great indignation. For the modest Lea was much more 'literary', in Tom's sense of the word, than he thought, and Tom found it easier to talk to him than he did to the many literary journalists who came to his house in awed search of him. Lea respected him, but was not in conventional awe of him: he was no literary journalist, but a man in his own right. What he was at some pains to point out, and what few others ever did point out, thinking perhaps that it would be unsuitable to a grand old man of letters, casts more light upon his apparent attitude to *The Well-Beloved* – one case in which, as I have suggested, he did go a little over the top. Lea wondered if a man constituted as Cecil was

> could hope to understand either a man or his writings who was so diametrically opposite. Hardy possessed a sense of humour both subtle and whimsical: I never knew him to be conventional about any subject – except perhaps 'with his tongue in his cheek' – and he was certainly not orthodox. See what I mean?

This could be put down to the impertinence of an ignoramus, a non-professor trespassing on hallowed ground; perhaps it was. But Tom would have agreed with it, and with Lea's final comment on Cecil: that even if a 'reliable critic' cannot fairly be expected to know 'everything about something' he should 'at least know something about everything'. He added that he was expressing no more than his own opinion. And in an earlier letter to Sanders, of 8 June 1940, he had more to say of Tom's humour:

> You see . . . my own intercourse with Hardy was a fairly intimate one, and I always felt that he was not on 'on guard' when rambling about with me or talking to me. I think he knew that anything he said was not for publication, and as he often touched on matters distinctly intimate I feel quite certain that he regarded me as a person to whom

he could speak his thoughts in the confidence that they would not be passed on to others. Then, too, we both seemed to know instinctively when the other spoke words to be taken seriously or otherwise. Do you see what I mean? Often he would tell me of something he had said to someone else and would add: 'I really believe he thought I meant it' – or words to that effect. He often added that so-and-so appeared to lack entirely a sense of humour . . . This sense of humour which I have been insisting on was one which enabled T.H. to thoroughly enjoy a joke against himself . . . I often felt that he had much the same feeling of 'apartness' from life which I have myself – almost as though I did not belong to the human family at all! Does this read a bit mad? Sorry!

He also wrote, not in a letter, but on 14 November 1918 while he was still living at Tom's birthplace: 'Perhaps few people who did not know Mr Hardy intimately suspected the vast fund of humour which filled him. This was always cropping out . . .' Tom himself wrote a passage in the *Life* on this same subject. It is not one that has been given much attention, but it is all-important:

> Hardy had a born sense of humour, even a too keen sense occasionally: but his poetry was sometimes placed by editors in the hands of reviewers deficient in that quality. Even if they were accustomed to Dickensian humour they were not to Swiftian [Hardy once suggested that the children of poor families should be used as 'sport' by huntsmen]. Hence it unfortunately happened that verses of a satirical, dry, caustic, or farcical cast were regarded by them with the utmost seriousness.

Lea's letter probably did read a bit 'mad' to Sanders; but Tom himself did have just that sense of 'apartness' mentioned in it. However, he was less puzzled by it than Lea. He was, though, increasingly careful not to let on about it to those who, like Gosse, could never quite understand it. After all, if the good Gosse – one of the best of Tom's 'literary friends' – was a poet *manqué*, why was he so? Because he lacked this sense of apartness. The poem 'Wessex Heights' cannot be understood without reference to this state of mind. Thus – and this is vital – it was easier for Tom to talk to Lea; though not well versed in literature as Gosse undoubtedly (and often appreciatively and usefully) was, Lea was both a reader of literature and a thinker on his own account; he well understood what he so discerningly called 'apartness'. Such a feeling of apartness is not to be misunderstood as one of superiority, although it is often angrily treated as though it were. In many people it dies even before adulthood is reached, to give way to a conformity deeply and enviously resentful of all 'differentness' and 'apartness' – although ready enough to pay lip-service to its existence in the safely dead. The 'freedom' referred to in 'Wessex Heights', and gratefully received by its readers, is gained by escape, if only temporary, from the lowlands of the poem. That Lea understood it in Tom is clear from his few basic sentences, already quoted, about what he had learned of his schooldays. In reality it is not a voluntary feeling at all, nor, though rare in adults, is it peculiar to 'literary men'. It takes many forms, but Lea's brief definition of it can hardly be bettered, provided always that by his 'human family' we understand the world at large, as distinct from the world within. Here is one reason why Tom later insisted upon the genius of Charlotte Mew, whose 'Fame' begins:

> Sometimes in the over-heated house, but not for long,
>   Smirking and speaking rather loud,
>   I see myself among the crowd,
> Where no one fits the singer to his song,
> Or sifts the unpainted from the painted faces
> Of the people who are always on my stair;
> They were not with me when I walked in heavenly places . . .

From this feeling of 'apartness' springs the dislike of convention that everyone noticed in Lea. It forms the key to his honesty and to his exemplary failure to achieve his own literary aspirations by resorting to artificiality. But he appreciated Tom's privately teasing ways, including to such as Gosse, let alone to real literary pretenders. When Tom called *The Well-Beloved* his 'innocent little book' he scarcely knew if these people believed him or not. His intentions were not unkind. But he was certainly joking, or, in more modern parlance, 'sending them up'.

28

A Malignant God?

Much emphasis – perhaps a little too much – has been put upon how 'separate' Tom became from Emma. They did not share their days as they had done, but a writer cannot – even if he wants to – write poetry and epic drama with assistance. He started working in earnest on *The Dynasts* in 1901; before that he was thinking about it, reading for it, and at the same time gathering together the material for two books, *Wessex Poems* and *Poems of the Past and the Present*. After he published the third and final part of the drama in 1908 he did no more – except sit in his study, contemplating poetry, and writing it when he could. No major poet has so single-mindedly sat, in such a manner, for so long a period: twenty years. During the last seven years of his life he did not even go to London, and for the preceding five or six years he became increasingly reclusive. But most men of that age are forced into that way of life. His second marriage was not, I think, even as successful as one of his non-sanguinary temperament might have hoped, although he bore no grudge. Nor was it Florence Dugdale's fault. As he said of Emma, 'she was so *living*'. Florence, for all her good intentions, was of almost the opposite persuasion: so *dead*.

In 1897, he and Emma were seeing much of each other. They still went to London together. They would continue the habit of reading to each other in the evenings until her sudden death. There remained much agreement between them: about certain of the books they read together, about the status of women, about that cruelty to animals which both realized was symptomatic of mankind's liking for settling disputes by means of war, about war itself. In the end, as he told the poet Siegfried Sassoon (*Siegfried's Journey 1916–1920*, 1946), Tom came to believe that wars were caused by 'supernatural agencies' over which mankind as a whole had no control.

Emma's supposed faults and shortcomings have been well aired by many from Florence Dugdale onward. Her excellent qualities, however, have not received more than the most grudging recognition – except, and the fact may be significant, from Tom himself. He was never heard to criticize her. Accounts of her were almost, if not quite exclusively, given by unkind, foolish or fatuous people ranging from the spoiled Owen to the waspish portrait painter Blanche; and they were always delivered in the context of her husband, whom people assumed that she ought to worship. In many ways she was an ideal wife for a writer, having never been an 'easy' one, by any means. Would Tom have written all the poems of 1896–1912, let alone those after her death, if she had been easy, worshipful and no trouble to him? 'Between Us Now' does contain more than a hint that he felt that she had 'turned against him' – 'Is your heart far away, Or with mine beating?' – a feeling to which Tom was by temperament bitterly susceptible, and one which she failed to quell. But such a man was quick to imagine, as well as to register, slights; and such a man would have been unhappy, in that way, with any woman. The problem was not really Emma: it was the human condition. To a degree he had mocked himself, as Jocelyn Pierston, in his tragic farce *The Well-Beloved*. He could not be satisfied, or even imagine himself to be satisfied, with any state for long. Now a full-time poet at last, he was only really at home with what was wrong with the universe. The Emma who tormented him from time to time was his true muse, and therefore to an extent his own wilful creation. But as an individual woman she did her job well.

There was now, in the spring of 1897, a measure of harmony between them. On 27 April he told Florence Henniker that he and Emma 'were in doubt about a house in London this season'. In May, he wrote to his sister Kate from the Midland Temperance Hotel in Guildford Street that they were still in doubt about 'staying in London'. He asked her to send on letters from Max Gate, which means that she was looking after things there. Then, as he puts it in the *Life* in one of those typically clumsy – and so extraordinarily expressive – Hardyan sentences, they 'adopted the plan of living some way out, and going up and down every few days, the place they made their temporary centre being Basingstoke'. Thus Tom conveyed the essential boredom of the whole enterprise. We can gather that this summer in London was not an exciting one, for in the 'middle of July they started for Switzerland, thus entirely escaping the racket of the coming Diamond Jubilee, and the discomfort it would bring upon people like them who had no residence of their own in London'. At Basingstoke they were in lodgings called Dinmont House; but not for long. They returned to Max Gate on 2 or 3 June before they left on the 16th for Neuchâtel via Southampton, Le Havre, Paris and Dijon. There were fewer people in Switzerland than usual, because of the attractions of the Jubilee in London on 20 June; on that day, from Berne, he wrote to George Douglas that they were 'in a fair way of accomplishing the unprecedented Alpine feat of journeying from one end of the country to the other' without seeing a mountain – but the weather improved, and they were able to have a comprehensive trip and return to England by early July.

This was just the time of his abandonment of prose fiction, about which he was eventually quite eloquent in the *Life*:

> It was not as if he had been a writer of novels proper . . . stories of modern artificial life and manners showing a certain smartness of treatment. He had mostly aimed at keeping his narratives close to natural life, and as near to poetry in their subject as the conditions would allow, and had often regretted that those conditions would not let him keep them nearer still . . . It was now with a sense of great comfort that he felt he might leave off further chronicles of that sort.

He still worried about the decision. Financial security, after all, hung on the success or otherwise of the uniform edition and its various paperback, European and 'colonial' offshoots. In point of fact, from the time when Macmillan took it over from Osgood early in the twentieth century, this edition went from strength to strength. Now both *Tess* and *Jude* were selling well. But, for all he knew, sales might suddenly flounder, leaving him with the necessity of adding to his fiction when he had nothing more to add except *The Dynasts* and then poetry. Emma, too, may have worried, on both commercial and personal grounds. We have seen how, while in Belgium, she was eager to add to information for a guidebook. That, as a reader of some of the poems in manuscript, she may not have been altogether happy otherwise is suggested by her outbursts over *Wessex Poems* and then over its successor, *Poems of the Past and the Present*. On 4 March 1902 she begged Owen not to read 'or at least accept, as anything but fiction some of the poems'; she added that they were 'Written "to *please*" . . . others! or himself – but not ME, far otherwise'.

This reticent man, then, reluctantly depended on keeping his name before the public. This necessity offers an explanation for one of his few public acts that seem out of character; it is described by Millgate as an 'odd piece of officiousness'. An Englishman mysteriously disappeared at Zermatt, along, as Tom put it in the *Life*, 'the very path he had been following'. He exhausted himself when, having put Emma on a pony and sending her on with a guide, he carefully searched the track for a clue – and then, as he again put it, wrote 'a brief letter to *The Times* to say there was no sign of foul play anywhere on the road'. This action demonstrates a characteristic that he tried not to advertise: proneness to nervous over-excitement. Usually this was expressed over certain women he encountered who excited him; more often than not, such attacks passed off as quickly as they had arrived. He would not have succumbed to the impulse for self-publicity – usually carefully restrained – which led him to write to *The Times* had he not been in a state of semi-collapse. He may have felt a little ashamed or even chagrined about his letter for, from the bed to which a doctor sent him in the Grand Hôtel de la Paix in Geneva, on 3 July he wrote a long letter to Florence Henniker but without mentioning what he had been up to, or the letter to *The Times* – which she might be expected to have seen. It had suddenly become very hot, 'like a melon-frame', and he only told Florence that at Zermatt he had seen 'the exact spot where the tragedy occurred on the Matterhorn in wh. Whymper was the only Englishman saved'. He had just written to Clodd (28 June), at whose house he had heard the mountaineer George Whymper himself tell the tale, to tell him where he now was. All he told Florence was that he felt 'pulled down a little, Em being in excellent health and vigour'. He also wrote:

> Not only is it untrue that I have a novel ready, but also that I have changed my style, am in doubt about a title, &c, &c. Indeed I have not given a single thought to novels of my own or other people since I finished the corrections of the W.B.
>
> I wonder if I ever told you that the plot of the story was suggested to me by the remark of a sculptor that he had often pursued a beautiful ear, nose, chin, &c, about London in omnibuses & on foot?

When they returned some improvements were still being carried out at Max Gate: on 3 August they set out on a nine-day tour of the surrounding Wessex countryside, taking in Wells, Frome, Longleat and Salisbury, where they stayed for a few days at the Crown Hotel. Kate Hardy was still looking after things at Max Gate, and on the 7th he wrote asking her to join them for a day there. He cannot, therefore, have been nervous about relations between her and Emma. He would not have risked spoiling a few days in a place he loved.

A MALIGNANT GOD?

On 10 August they went to Stonehenge, of which he remarked: 'The misfortune of ruins – to be beheld nearly always at noonday by visitors, and not at twilight'. On the same day they attended Evensong at the Cathedral, and Tom especially noticed the beauty of the lesson, 'beautifully read by the old Canon'. This lesson was from Jeremiah 6 and he quotes:

> The day goeth away . . . the shadows of the evening are stretched out . . . I set watchmen over you, saying, Hearken to the sound of the trumpet. But they said, We will not hearken. Therefore hear, ye nations . . . To what purpose cometh there to me incense from Sheba, and the sweet cane from a far country? Your burnt offerings are not acceptable, nor your sacrifices sweet unto me.

He recollected this in the *Life*, and marked his Bible: 'To what purpose . . . sweet unto me?' – verse 20 of Chapter 6 – is underlined, and there is a marginal note reading 'Salisbury Cathedral with E. Aug 1897'. Nor is that all. They attended Evensong on the next day, too, and against Psalm 59, 'Deliver me from mine enemies, O my God: defend me from them that rise up against me', he wrote again, 'Salisbury Cathedral with E. Aug 11, 1897'.

These and many other attendances at church services with Emma – who accompanied him on a series of tours of the cathedrals within cycling distance of Dorchester in the next year or two – suggest that he was simultaneously trying his hardest to be at one with her in her religious feelings, and trying to be truthful: to achieve, with her, the honesty he craves in the poem 'Between Us Now'. She must have tried, too: on his fifty-ninth birthday she gave him a Bible, inscribed: 'T. Hardy from E.L.H. June 2, 1899. At Wynnstay Gardens, Kensington'. Into this new Bible, by Chapter 6 of Jeremiah, he wrote: 'Salisbury Cathedral, E.L.H. and T.H. Aug 1897'; the fourth verse, 'Woe unto us! for the day goeth away, for the shadows of the evening are stretched out,' is specially marked. This suggests some attempt at understanding or accommodation. But there are no more such marginal notes or markings in this Bible, only a few references to texts pencilled in on a blank leaf at the end. The poem 'The Impercipient', which appears towards the end of *Wessex Poems* (and therefore certainly known to Emma when she gave him the Bible, possibly to see in the new century), was originally entitled 'The Agnostic'; the subtitle is 'At a Cathedral Service', and the accompanying drawing is of the nave of Salisbury Cathedral.

That with this bright believing band
   I have no claim to be,
That faiths by which my comrades stand
   Seem fantasies to me,
And mirage-mists their Shining Land,
   Is a strange destiny.

Emma may not have been so aggressive towards Tom about his failure of orthodox belief as towards what she took to be his public undermining of the faith. She shared the feelings of the Rev. H.J. Moule, who wrote to him on 16 June 1903: 'But "The Impercipient"! Of that there is no more to be said than that I can hardly write – I could not speak – without tears. It goes to my heart of hearts that my dear old friend (for it can only be T.H. that mourns) should be so craving for the assistance of a Father.' Many might have been annoyed by that kind of remark, although Tom probably was not. The poem is not without irony:

Since heart of mine knows not that ease
   Which they know; since it be
That He who breathes All's Well to these
   Breathes no All's-Well to me,
My lack might move their sympathies
   And Christian charity!

As it stands, it is hardly a personal poem:

Yet I would bear my shortcomings
   With meet tranquillity,
But for the charge that blessed things
   I'd liefer not have be.
O, doth a bird deprived of wings
   Go earth-bound wilfully!

When he came to print it, he omitted the following stanza:

But ah, they love me not, although
   I treat them tenderly,
And while I bear with them they go
   To no such lengths with me,

A MALIGNANT GOD?

> Because – to match their sight I show
> An incapacity.

The poem ends abruptly: a row of dots, and then

> ~~Enough. As yet disquiet clings~~
> About us. Rest shall we.

This is hardly an improvement on the manuscript's

> Enough. As yet confusion clings
> About us. We shall see.

Tom, then, did resent what he sometimes took to be Emma's lack of charity towards his failure to believe in the supernatural elements of Christianity. But he found it hard to be direct about it, as his removal of the 'love me not' stanza indicates. 'God-Forgotten', written only a year or two later, is more purely philosophical:

> I towered far, and lo! I stood within
>   The presence of the Lord Most High,
> Sent thither by the sons of Earth, to win
>   Some answer to their cry.
>
> – 'The Earth, sayest thou? The Human race?
>   By Me created? Sad its lot?
> Nay: I have no remembrance of such place:
>   Such world I fashioned not.'
>
> – 'O Lord, forgive me when I say
>   Thou spakest the word that made it all.' –
> 'The Earth of men – let me bethink me . . . Yea!
>   I dimly do recall
>
> 'Some tiny sphere I built long back
>   (Mid millions of such shapes of mine)
> So named . . . It perished, surely – not a wrack
>   Remaining, or a sign?
>
> 'It lost my interest from the first,
>   My aims therefor succeeding ill;

Haply it died of doing as it durst?' –
  'Lord, it existeth still.' –

'Dark, then, its life! For not a cry
  Of aught it bears do I now hear;
Of its own act the threads were snapt whereby
  Its plaints had reached mine ear.

'It used to ask for gifts of good,
  Till came its severance, self-entailed,
When sudden silence on that side ensued,
  And has till now prevailed.

'All other orbs have kept in touch;
  Their voicings reach me speedily:
Thy people took upon them overmuch
  In sundering them from me!

'And it is strange – though sad enough –
  Earth's race should think that one whose call
Frames, daily, shining spheres of flawless stuff
  Must heed their tainted ball! . . .

'But sayest it is by pangs distraught,
  And strife, and silent suffering? –
Sore grieved am I that injury should be wrought
  Even on so poor a thing!

'Thou shouldst have learnt that *Not to Mend*
  For Me could mean but *Not to Know*:
Hence, Messengers! and straightway put an end
  To what men undergo.' . . .

Homing at dawn, I thought to see
  One of the Messengers standing by.
– Oh, childish thought! . . . Yet often it comes to me
  When trouble hovers nigh.

This, if not of his best poems, is better than 'The Impercipient', which is flawed by its abrupt and feeble ending. It is almost as if Tom had felt his real subject to be Emma's 'unfair' attitude towards his beliefs, or lack of them, but had preferred not to pursue it – and so cancelled out all traces when he came to print it. Yet 'God-Forgotten' is not an agnostic poem, nor was Tom a true agnostic. As first coined by T.H.

Huxley (according to R.H. Hutton, at a private meeting in 1869 of James Knowles' new Metaphysical Society, of which Gladstone and the future Cardinal Manning, as well as Leslie Stephen and Hutton himself, were members), the term agnosticism, besides acting as a useful separation of lack of belief from unbelief (atheism), implied reliance upon materialistic evidence: nothing outside the materialistic was knowable.

If, though, one had to classify Tom only as an intellectual, then it would have to be as an agnostic, especially in the general sense that the word soon acquired, of 'any sceptic'. But, although more intellectual than he is given credit for being, he was not primarily an intellectual – he was a poet: a man to whom feeling is as real as reason. 'God-Forgotten' is actually more theological than agnostic, since it does not express the pain of unknowingness – something that Tom did express occasionally in conversation. For example he once remarked to Hermann Lea, of a quatrain by William Watson (misremembered by Lea, not him) – 'And Ah! to know while with friends I sit/And while the purple joy is passed about/Whether 'tis ampler day, Divinelier lit,/Or Darkest night without' – 'That is just the point. If we but knew!' But such unconsidered conversational doubts are casual by comparison to poems.

'God-Forgotten', like the three poems which follow it in *Poems of the Past and the Present*, 'The Bedridden Peasant', 'By the Earth's Corpse' and 'Mute Opinion', is written within the philosophical scheme that was to form the framework of *The Dynasts*. The place of human beings in the universe is here particularized – and emphasized – as a peculiarly bad one, precisely as gnosticism represents it to be. There are other flawless 'balls', but ours is 'tainted'. 'The Lord Most High', the Creator, is represented as having forgotten our earth. But whose is the responsibility? Here this is ambiguously answered. On the one hand 'It lost my interest from the first'; on the other, 'Of its own act the threads were snapt whereby/Its plaints had reached mine ear.' Yet it is clear from the context that the Creator's 'aims' did not include suffering. However, whether God's interest was lost because the earth fulfilled his aims badly is left ambiguous. The only possible inference in the face of these propositions is that something went badly wrong – which is the central tenet of ancient as of contemporary gnosticism.

In the thinking of Marcion, the heretical shipowner from Sinope in Pontus who settled in Rome in about AD 144, and who published the first canon of Christian writings (now lost, it consisted of the ten epistles of St Paul and an edited St Luke's Gospel), the Jewish God of the Old Testament is rejected. Marcion rejected the mythological cast of thought of the gnostics proper, for he made faith and not knowledge the means of redemption; but his thinking certainly coincides with (and was undoubtedly influenced by) theirs on many points, and after his death almost all the considerable support he had gained was absorbed into Manichaeism.

This system is particularly interesting in the light of what Tom was groping for in the last half of his life. Although there is no direct evidence that he had ever read anything about Marcion, he did make a note at some time between April and August 1900. He was in London with Emma in June and July, and must have made it in the British Museum Reading Room while studying the works of the Carthaginian heresiologist Tertullian: 'Heretical notions of God. Tertullian (De Testimonio Animae, c.ii) speaks of some who believe in a non-active & passionless God.' This makes it likely, if not certain, that Tom had read, or at least perused, the main source of our knowledge of Marcion: Tertullian's Five Books against Marcion, which had been translated in 1868 by P. Holmes. He could have culled the De Testimonio Animae quotation from several sources: from Hort's Six Lectures on the Ante-Nicene Fathers (1897), or, most likely, from the volumes devoted to Tertullian in the Ante-Nicene Christian Library: Holmes' Against Marcion was one of these, but there were three further volumes. The extent to which Marcionism played a part in the formation of the orthodox creed which Tom so decisively rejected is disputed; that it was a crucially important one is not.

Although Marcion advocated a strict morality (for the sake of 'metaphysical alignment'), he was antinomian in the sense that, like Tom, he believed in Christianity as a Gospel of Love (loving-kindness?) to the 'absolute exclusion of Law' – which meant, for him, the Law of the Old Testament. The 'just' Jehovah of the Old Testament was a malevolent demiurge; Christ's purpose was to deliver mankind from this Creator God (demiurge means 'craftsman') whose 'right' to his 'property' Marcion, strangely and almost paradoxically, conceded. What he would not concede was that 'justice' and 'goodness' could co-exist in a single god – mainly, no doubt, because he could not equate the cruelty inherent even in justice with absolute love. More to the point here, the Father, the True God, is an Alien God: there is absolutely no connection between him and those he chooses, out of a pure and inexplicable goodness, to save. Worldly events are not changed by the salvation that Christ brings about: the saved Marcionite – and this is significant in the light of such final poems of Tom's as 'We Are Getting to the End' – simply leaves the created world to destroy itself, and distances himself from it as much as possible until he dies.

There is more in Marcion that is pertinent to the philosophical subtleties of Tom's poetry. In his theology Marcion opposed his two gods – the demiurge, the false one, and the alien, the true one. Tertullian speaks of Marcion's scorn of the corporeal world of Jehovah as 'known', petty, inconsistent – and as resembling his horrible creation, man. This, although viewed in his case through a humorous lens, is very much the world of Hardy, full of 'satires of circumstance' and 'little ironies'. The alien, the true god, is a stranger, unknown, hidden, different, not perceivable – and 'new': he is, says Tertullian, 'naturally unknown and never except in the Gospel revealed'.

This powerful and for a time successful heresy made the orthodox Christians hysterically anxious. The great heresiologists raged against it. In their orthodox scheme the Old Testament was concordant with the New, and their single God embodied within himself both justice (Jehovah) and mercy (Christ), creating a tension which gave their religion a new and unique force. But the Marcionite scheme in one form or the other, including the gnostic, has persisted throughout history. We are once again in that world of apartness and differentness which Lea mentioned. And, if we grant that poets are gifted with an intuition of the matters which most trouble human beings in their inexplicable journey from the cradle to the grave, then we are in that world in some of Tom's more difficult poems – in the relatively obscure, personal ones as much as the overtly philosophical ones.

This gnostic type of thinking has persisted for many reasons, chiefly perhaps because it is not a peculiarity of any particular time, or a quirk of history. After all, the Christian orthodoxy established by the early Fathers of the Church, at the Council of Nicea, in AD 325, is a reaction to it. As a converted Christian, the former Manichaean Augustine struggled above all to insist upon the notion of God as all-good and all-seeing. But the vision of a malign God must persist in a world beset by evil and misfortune. And, whether 'true' or not, the Marcionite and gnostic view of the created world is of a truly dreadful place, a place of which that haunting late poem by Tom, 'Family Portraits', must remind us. A twentieth-century gnostic vainly tried to draw attention to what he called the 'terror of the situation'. Tom would have understood at least that.

For the Marcionite this horrible created world may be abandoned only by faith; for the gnostic, by knowledge. 'Good works', though certainly to be preferred, are irrelevant. Gnostic ascetism is not espoused for the sake of virtue: if a gnostic abstains from eating more than he needs in order to survive, he does so in order to condemn and abominate what the demiurge, in his malice, created. The case of sexual intercourse is similar: Mani specifically taught that the reproductive urge exists only as an elaborate trick by demons, by which further souls will continue to be imprisoned in the world. By all kinds of abstinence from his own creations the demiurge was, in any case, 'vexed': he ought so to be vexed. Consolation in this terrible world is nothing that can be understood in terms of the senses: the other world, of salvation, is not even definable (thus, in Tom's poem 'He Resolves to Say No More', 'none shall gather what I hide!'). In Marcion's system – not quite as scarifying as that of some of the gnostics – the Christ of a Luke whose text is purged of all Old Testament references offers a state of grace freely and for no definable reason: a blessed hope indeed, but one of which we are and must be wholly unaware. It could be argued that Marcion was something of a prophet, at least so far as his picture of the known world is concerned: this represents nothing so much as the totally accidental and meaningless world of certain modern physicists, untrained and uninterested in theology or philosophy – but none the less, alas, the admired 'engineers' of our planet. Tom's 'religiousness' consists largely of his struggle to resist this notion of meaninglessness, and – like Dostoievsky – to reject a concomitant humanism without a foundation in the human heart.

Tom was of course no thoroughgoing or self-conscious 'gnostic'. However, these two gnostic worlds, the loveless known and the loving-kind unknown, are concepts towards which he was groping in his poetry. His thinking was more influenced by his reading of Schopenhauer and other philosophers than by his much less intense investigations of Tertullian and the history of the early Church; but what he read in the latter sounded a chord. He took what his critics called his 'pessimism' with the utmost seriousness, and, although he disliked the unjust accusation of wishing for evil, he clung to it.

What else in fact was he clinging to but an old gnostic habit of thought? It is better, he would always insist whether in a cheerful mood or otherwise, not to be born. Such an idea might seem ludicrous – unless viewed in the light of this ancient style of thought about creation. Therefore, in a term used by a puzzled reviewer of his *Poems of the Past and the Present*, he often appears to be 'half-articulate'. However, as we have seen in 'Wessex Heights', once the framework of the poem has been established, he gains his desired effects. He inhabits an area of emotion that is hardly articulated in anyone. It is one which professional critics of poetry are always trying (vainly) to define and even to limit. From the publication of *Wessex Poems* his poetry was therefore unclassifiable by 'professionals'; yet it made its impact because all his readers of good faith knew that he was trying to express something; that he was, almost desperately, the opposite of pretentious or rhetorical.

For a long time it has been conceded that one of his main philosophical themes (it was really a speculation, ultimately quelled by disillusionment) is that of a God-Creator, a cosmic intelligence, getting to and ultimately reaching consciousness. It was a view which he believed to be original to himself, he told a correspondent. The only parallels in Jewish or Christian theology to this idea of a flawed or limited God are to be found in gnosticism and in Jewish cabalism, with which it has close connections. At the age of twenty-seven Tom had written: 'Had the teachings of experience grown cumulatively with the age of the world we should have been ere now as great as God.' At sixty he speculated: 'there may be a consciousness, infinitely far off, at the other end of the chain of phenomena, always striving to express itself, and always baffled and blundering'.

On 30 June 1899 Charles Hooper, the Secretary of the Rationalist Press Association, invited him, along with Leslie Stephen and others, to become an Honorary Associate. On 2 July he replied that although he was 'interested' he felt that it

> would naturally compose itself rather of writers on philosophy, science, & history, than of writers of imaginative works, whose effect depends largely on detachment. By belonging to a philosophic association they place themselves in this difficulty, that they are mis-read as propagandist when they mean to be simply artistic & delineative. While thanking you for this proposal I will therefore decline associateship for the present.

Shortly afterwards he was prompted to this reflection, which he quotes as written in a letter, but 'apparently not sent':

> My own interest lies largely in non-rationalistic subjects, since non-rationality seems, so far as one can perceive, to be the principle of the universe. By which I do not mean foolishness, but rather a principle for which there is no exact name, lying at the indifference point between rationality and irrationality.

Could anything be more expressive of the strangeness of the gnostic's world than that final sentence?

F.R. Leavis called Hardy's cosmology 'poor stuff'; his label has stuck. But viewed in the light of 'ordinary' – that is, non-'expert', non-orthodox – speculation about creation, it is far from poor stuff – and it accounts for Hardy's continuing popularity amongst readers. The notion that it is poor stuff derives from an assumption that the only non-poor sort of speculation about the nature of human existence is 'professional'. In that sense Tom is indeed, like the unorthodox Marcion and the gnostics themselves, an 'amateur'. But he was an amateur who was well able to understand the thinking of professionals; and he remained amateur only by choice. The poet, like his reader, is eminently an amateur, and not one who would wish to associate himself with either rationalists or non-rationalists:

> I traversed a dominion
> Whose spokesmen spake out strong
> Their purpose and opinion
> Through pulpit, press, and song.
> I scarce had means to note there
> A large-eyed few, and dumb,
> Who thought not as those thought there
> That stirred the heat and hum.
>
> When, grown a Shade, beholding
> That land in lifetime trode,
> To learn if its unfolding
> Fulfilled its clamoured code,
> I saw, in web unbroken,
> In history outwrought
> Not as the loud had spoken,
> But as the mute had thought.

Thus runs 'Mute Opinion', a tribute to the Leas and other 'ordinary' men of this world; and to his readers, learned or otherwise, who could apprehend his style of speculation by making reference to their own.

Tom's Creator-God becoming conscious of himself, at least a fervent hope while he struggled with *The Dynasts*, is none other than the gnostics' demiurge in another guise: he is the unwitting inventor of human misery who yet might become conscious of that utter stranger to the known universe, his rival. On 5 February 1898 Tom proposed to himself to 'Write a prayer, or hymn, to One not Omnipotent, but hampered; striving for our good, but unable to achieve it except occasionally'. He added later, in a parenthesis:

> This idea of a limited God of goodness, often dwelt on by Hardy, was expounded ably and at length in MacTaggart's *Some Dogmas of Religion* several years later, and led to a friendship which ended only with the latter's death.

'God-Forgotten', then, is not an agnostic or rationalistic poem. It never seriously occurred to Tom that the universe or universes could have come into existence by their own accord; nor, however, could he pretend to 'know' the nature of the creator. The speaker of the poem is an obverse of Christ, who was sent to earth by a Father: he, though, by contrast, is 'Sent thither by the sons of Earth to win/Some answer to their cry'. God tells him that he lost interest in the human race because it did not fulfil his aims (or did not 'do anything about it': this is not clear). It is usually held that the lines beginning 'Hence, Messengers' imply that the God of the poem will annihilate his creation because, for him, not to mend (its ways) means not to know or understand; but this is, again, ambiguous – it does not happen in the poem. Nothing at all seems to happen. Rather, the speaker returns to earth at dawn, hoping to see a messenger (to annihilate or to help?). He tells himself that this is a 'childish thought', yet finds he still has it when he (or the world, or both) is facing trouble (suffering).

These last two stanzas can have a number of meanings, most of which may be entertained simultaneously. The kind of God who had already forgotten the earth, because it was beyond redemption, might discover that it was already so well on its way to destroying itself that there was no point in sending a messenger to do that work. The absence of such a messenger could imply that everything that has happened up to that point has been a dream: there is no knowable creator, or at least no creator who could have a hand in earthly affairs, and it is 'childish' – if irresistible in face of trouble – to suppose that there is. This would match what Tom says (in the *Life*) that he told a Dr Arnaldo Cervesato on 20 June 1901: that an 'Idealism of fancy' might be developed 'as an imaginative solace in the lack of any substantial solace to be found in life'. Or perhaps the speaker can only recognize the messenger, real though he might be, when trouble threatens. And so on. We are, in this poem as in most of Tom's speculative or philosophical poems, back in a pre-Nicean mode of thinking: in a time before canons became fixed, before there were any orthodoxies. Tom always tended to take things on their merits rather than on their reputations, good or bad, and the part of the *Life* which deals with this transitional period abounds in wry remarks about assumptions which have not been properly and independently examined. He always fiercely insisted that a man could go on adding to his work until he dropped dead. In this connection he made a significant note about Verdi, a man with whom he had numerous affinities, and whose name came into his mind while he was considering some of the lesser critics' antipathy to his 'turning poet' at sixty:

> It may be observed that in the art-history of the century there was an example staring them in the face of a similar modulation from one style into another by a great artist. Verdi was the instance, 'that amazing old man' as he was called. Someone of insight wrote concerning him: 'From the ashes of his early popularity, from *Il Trovatore* and its kind, there arose a sudden sort of phoenix-Verdi. Had he died at Mozart's death-age he would now be practically unknown.' And another: 'With long life enough Verdi might have done almost anything; but the trouble with him was that he had only just arrived at maturity at the age of threescore and ten or thereabouts, so that to complete his life he ought to have lived a hundred and fifty years.'

In January 1899 he wrote that no man's poetry could be truly judged until 'its last line is written'. 'What is the last line? The death of the poet.' And for Tom, for all that so much of his poetry is about death and its inevitability, actual death did come as a mere interruption to his writing of poetry. He had little idea that the illness that took him in the December of 1927 was to be his last: he was too wrapped up in contemplating the next poem. Meanwhile, now, as the old century drew to a close, he was in a process of re-educating himself. He spent much time reading.

However, the philosophical poems of the turn of the century, though superior to anything being written at that time by even the better living poets – with the sole exception of Housman – are not his best, any more than *The Dynasts* – with the exception of lines or scenes here and there – is representative of his poetic genius at its most supreme. His finest poems are more emotionally based, written in a denser, more powerful and more ambiguous language. But they could come about only as a result of all the intellectual work – the reading, thinking and technical effort – which went into the philosophical poems.

Most of the best poetry, the really strange poems such as 'In Front of the Landscape' (opening *Satires of Circumstance*), those at the level achieved in 'Wessex Heights', or even above it, came after the first two collections. There are of course exceptions, such as 'The Darkling Thrush', one of the most inspired lyrics in the English language and a song of hope from the depths of an extreme and extraordinarily honest scepticism. It is a startling affirmation from a man who would take absolutely nothing on trust, and it is difficult not to see it as a welcome to the aged thrush's song of a knowledge, or faith in, something wholly alien to humanity. Nor does this seem so far-fetched when we recognize that both the Christian and the non-Christian speculations of people at the beginning of our era are no more than historically individualized reflections of universal habits of human thought.

I am aware that a more usual reading of Tom's philosophy is to pay attention to his so-called 'evolutionary meliorism'. But even J.O. Bailey, who has paid most attention to this aspect of his secular thinking, admits that he gave up his 'belief' in it. In reality, although Tom did feel that it was important to have hope against convictions, he was never imaginatively convinced of this 'meliorism'. It was a prose concept. In inventing a God who was slowly 'improving' or becoming conscious of his creation's sufferings – as suggested in the poem which closes *Poems of the Past and of the Present*, 'To the Unknown God' – he was experimenting with hope. As he became older and increasingly wrapped up in poetry he moved towards profounder, and only apparently similar, apprehensions.

29

Wessex Poems

Emma and Tom did not have their bicycles with them in Salisbury; but their cycling was continuing quite intensively – as this currently fashionable pastime was in the country as a whole – and must have provided solace to both in their disagreements, difficulties and reconciliations. In September Emma injured her ankle when she crashed the 'Grasshopper' into a heap of stones. Because she was laid up with it, Tom was unable to have the recently appointed editor of the *Morning Post*, James Nicol Dunn, to stay. This accident is eagerly, though revealingly, blamed by Millgate on Emma's 'impetuosity'. There is no full account of it by a witness. Everyone, including Gosse, who later bruised himself badly while cycling in company with Tom, and Tom himself (in Bristol) had nasty accidents: the bikes, although better by that time, were still not all that safe. There were many mishaps in such centres of perfect learning as the great university town of Cambridge: even august and unimpetuous professors were known to part company with their machines in an undignified manner. Anyhow, whether or not in acquiring her injury Emma once again demonstrated her unfitness to be the wife of a national genius, her badly bruised and painful ankle and foot, which troubled her for many months afterwards, obliged Tom to invite Dunn and his companions to tea only. Alas, it could be made difficult for him if he should offend such people. He became an adept at treating them with the utmost courtesy, making as few statements of opinion as possible to them, and adroitly cutting down their trespass on his time. Some years later Wessex, a large wire-haired terrier of impeccable pedigree, would act, as Tom described it on his grave, as the 'staunch' and 'unflinching' symbol of his attitude towards the external world – but for the politeness he would substitute unseemly nips.

On 25 January 1899 Tom wrote, cryptically: 'A principle of conduct: acquiescence, but recognition'. Richard Taylor sensibly comments: 'A suggestion of stoicism: perhaps the artist's necessary "recognition" in submitting to the demands (and criticism) of his public while recognising that it is the nature of his position which requires this'; he goes on to point out that the reviews of *Wessex Poems* were appearing just at this time. The note deals with Tom's sense of responsibility towards his enlightened readers and probably, too, towards his unenlightened ones. It could mean, though: 'An author with a public ought to be conscientious about the latter's susceptibilities, and even to seem to acquiesce in them, but always recognise the truth.' Or it might mean: 'Accept criticism with grace but insist upon recognition as a poet.' But Tom never really 'submitted' to anything, whatever appearance he gave. He was courteous to such as Dunn, and continued to try to explain to them why he wrote as he did. Another entry – linked, but made later in 1899 – on the subject of the pessimism with which he was so often charged, reads:

1899 later. Pessimism. Was there ever any great poetry which was not pessimistic? . . .
   'All creation groaneth,' &c.
   'Man that is born of women,' &c.
   'Man dieth and wasteth away,' &c.
   'I go hence like the shadow that departeth' &c (& other Psalms).
   Is that pessimism, & if not, why not? The answer would probably be because a remedy is offered. Well, the answer tarries long.

Taylor suggests that this entry was prompted by Emma's birthday gift of a Bible on 2 June. This seems likely. It arose, perhaps, from a quarrel, or discussion, about his 'pessimism' and its effects on others. She has just given him a Bible to help cure his pessimism, and so he upbraids her from its text. But if the entry really did arise from this symbolic gift, a book which throughout his life he valued above almost all others, then it does at least demonstrate that Tom took Emma's arguments with the utmost seriousness – and thus that she could be cogent, reasonable, and not merely exasperatingly eccentric. Poetry had captured his wholehearted attention once again, after many years. He was behaving more absent-mindedly and abstractedly than ever before. It could even be granted that he might frequently have been a pain in the neck, especially when challenged in his pessimism. To our advantage, no doubt; but to his wife's day-to-day advantage? Emma possessed a sense of humour which went along with her vitality and gaiety; but whether even these at their most flexible could always withstand his Swiftian ironies and acidly expressed indignations is another matter. His obstinacy served him, and us, in good stead; as a factor in his childless household it may have been less attractive. Poetry such as Tom's is not made without cost to others, as he himself came to recognize after Emma's death.

Their childlessness had for some years been mitigated by long visits to Max Gate from Emma's nephew and niece. Since the mid-nineties they had seen so much of Gordon and Lilian, the son and daughter of the post office official Walter Gifford, that by this time they had half-adopted them. When the impoverished Walter died in 1904 they took responsibility for Gordon and Lilian's welfare. Tom had already arranged for Gordon to study architecture with the firm of Arthur Blomfield, his old employer and, until his death in 1899, his good friend. It has been supposed that the apprenticeship had its difficult side; but there is no evidence to support the conjecture, and Gordon went on to become a competent architect with the London County Council.

Tom had always liked Lilian, and in the 1880s used to make drawings to amuse her. Although she eventually gave considerable trouble to both Emma and then to Florence Hardy (but *all* the Giffords troubled Florence), Tom is not known ever to have criticized her – but then he was scant with both blame and praise, which is what makes those personal opinions that he did state so interesting and significant.

He enjoyed taking the young people out and about in Dorset and in London; often Emma came, too. Their presence for long periods at Max Gate did not lead to much adverse comment or criticism. Tom was known to his friends as conscientious, kindly and not at all awkward or bored with young children; several of the latter, such as Gosse's daughter Sylvia and, later, Middleton Murry's daughter, remembered him as such.

For the rest of the year 1897 – and, indeed, of the century and just beyond it – Tom was busy at poetry, even writing nonsense words to various highly complex prosodic patterns in order to get his hand in once more. There has been no more persistent experimentalist: the gap of several years between the completion of *The Well-Beloved* and the beginning of *The Dynasts* was no idle one for him. For all his modesty, he never seems seriously to have doubted that *The Dynasts* would be a major work; what he always did doubt was whether he could do justice to the genius he knew he possessed. 'Poetry is but emotion put into measure,' he wrote at just this time. 'The emotion must come by nature, but the measure can be acquired by art.' He would always apologize for not doing as well as he might have done: it is a chief feature of his comments to his friends. Of these years he wrote afterwards: 'His personal ambition, which had always been weak, dwindled to nothing, and for some years after 1895 or 1896 he requested that no record of his life should be made.'

From this time onwards, with some obvious exceptions such as his conduct of an affair with Florence Dugdale, what Tom read and thought and wrote becomes more interesting than what he did. He was reluctant to be represented except by his actual creative work, as his retrospective account, as well as wryly modifying its 'author's' mental capacities, confirms: 'it becomes difficult to ascertain what mainly occupied his mind, or what his social doings were'. His life conformed more or less to the pattern established in the late 1890s: seasonal visits to London and sometimes to the houses, there and in the country, of such friends as the Jeunes, work at Max Gate – and the new craze of cycling, which shortly after the turn of the century he admitted, cheerfully, to be 'vulgar'. Although he continued to suffer, especially when in London, from neuralgia of the face and teeth, rheumatism, occasional flare-ups of the old bladder trouble, colds, and, from 1899, a weeping and prickly eye from which 'he was seldom entirely free', he was as strong as a horse, and the exercise of cycling suited him and continued to do so for many years. He said modestly that he never exceeded forty or fifty miles a day, but 'kept vigorously going within the limit'. Here he exhibited what had always been one of his greatest assets: moderation and the observation of a wise economy. He did not smoke, and drank little – although he liked cider and wine, and would, for the rest of his life, stop off occasionally at the Antelope in Dorchester for a beer. He recollected of these years that he 'possibly thought it wise to economize, seeing that he had sacrificed the chance of making a much larger income by not producing more novels'. He has been called hypochondriacal, but was no more so than any other sensitive person ravaged by the physical troubles of age: he never invented or imagined illnesses, even if, as he drew near to completing the first part of *The Dynasts*, he had fears of dying. These fears were not hypochondriacal, though: they shared, rather, the feeling so famously expressed by Keats: 'When I have fears that I may cease to be . . .' Freedom to express himself in the manner in which he had always wanted to express himself could hardly have been without such fears.

The continuance for many years of the annual London visit is often put down to Emma's desire to shine in society as one better born than her husband. It is held that she forced him to do what he did not really want to do. In fact he forced himself – to an extent, they forced themselves. Emma wrote to Owen, at one point, of not wishing to endure society. She was more concerned with her cats, and Millgate quotes a touching sentence from one of her newspaper articles about them: 'Always give a cat free ingress and egress and attend to his voice, remembering that he has no language but a cry.'

The London visits, then, although they invariably caused Tom to feel unwell, were always undertaken by mutual agreement, in order not to become too reclusive, to see certain friends they genuinely liked (the Jeunes in particular), and to know (if not to love) their own times. Tom's objections to the state of things in the world have not sat well with his critics, who find existence more tolerable. Emma agreed well enough with his diagnosis, but differed in her view of the solution. As her own writings show, she relied on mystical transformations more than he could – outside his poetry. These writings are fairly inept, but 'Some Recollections' is exceptional. It does not possess the 'literary skill' which has been attributed to it, but rather the opposite: it is totally without artifice, and thus possesses something beyond literary skill. It is likely to have been a generous gesture of forgiveness – 'loving-kind' or Christian, according to how we prefer to look at it: it reads like that. It must be remembered that the description of the other material she allegedly left, as full of 'hatred & abuse', was made by Florence Hardy, and at the time when she was feeling most jealous of and angry at Emma. We do not know that she read it, only that whatever it really was had a severe impact upon Tom. However, *anything* that may be interpreted as critical is felt most deeply just after a person has died. No doubt, too, much of it was true.

In the summer of 1900 Emma was certainly not incompetent to receive a host of distinguished visitors, none of whom left animadversions upon her, or even, Gissing-like, upon her cook. It seems as though everyone in the world whom they (rather than just Tom) knew well descended upon them with bicycles. During July, August and September, in addition to regular guests such as Gordon and Lilian (who stayed on into 1901) and the Thorneycrofts, they had Clodd, A.E. Housman and Arthur Symons down on the same weekend (this was in early August). Tom and Emma had planned this, together, three weeks earlier. On 13 July Tom wrote to Clodd asking him for Saturday, 4 August ('it will be a great pleasure both to my wife & myself to see you'), and similarly to Arthur Symons (whom he invited to 'our cottage here' – an odd, humorous and perhaps wistful way of describing Max Gate). The invitation to Housman (whom he had met on the previous 18 June) has not survived, but was probably written on the same day.

The mixture of guests at that weekend is an intriguing one: Clodd the rationalist, Symons the member – along with Yeats, Lionel Johnson and (spasmodically) the ill-fated John Davidson – of the Rhymers' Club, and the unique and lonely Housman, whose plight one may be sure that Tom had appreciatively and sympathetically spotted from the poems of *A Shropshire Lad*. As for Symons, Tom really liked some of his poems, and not only told him so but went so far as to repeat his praise in a letter to Florence Henniker.

Earlier that summer Tom had been suffering from extreme lassitude. Emma had not at first felt well enough to come to London, partly on account of her injured ankle; Tom therefore went up for a few days alone in May. One of the important things he did was to call on the Blomfields, essentially on Emma's behalf, to see how her nephew Gordon was getting on. He had fairly good news – 'he sticks to a piece of work till he has tackled it' – which he reported to her on 14 May. Within a day or two, having what he called, in a further note to Emma, 'toothache, headache &c', he returned to Max Gate. By that time Emma was better, and preceded him to London. She had by now joined a women's club, the Alexandra, where she could stay. It was, Tom told the artist Winifred Thomson on 19 June, 'the first [season] for years in which we have not taken a house or a flat'. They were both back by July, and he did not recover his energy until the following month: he told Florence Henniker on 29 July that he had 'no energy of late to write anything'.

In October news came of the severe illness of Emma's sister, Helen Holder, now living in the Hampshire town of Lee-on-the-Solent, where she had spent her widowhood. Emma at once dropped everything to nurse her and try to put some order into her finances. Tom was left alone with Lilian, who was unwell and therefore useless to him as a housekeeper. Not all the letters he wrote to Emma in Lee-on-the-Solent are extant; the surviving ones show acute concern for her emotional and physical state – and the fact that he was missing her badly. Her absence plunged Tom into fresh gloom, and when on 22 October he wrote to Florence Henniker he offered her the question, whether, if one could ask the forty thousand slaughtered in the Boer War 'if they wish to wake up again' 'would they say Yes, do you think?' But he did not mention Emma's errand of mercy, and apologized for writing 'like that'. Then his thoughts ran back to unhappy things, and he told Florence that he did not care enough for the 'British stage to care to write for it', despite a new request from Mrs Patrick Campbell. As to the collection which would be *Poems of the Past and the Present*:

> If I print them [the poems] I know exactly what will be said about them: 'You hold opinions which we don't hold: therefore shut up.' Not that there are any opinions in the verses; but the English reviewers go behind the book & review the man.

Critics – by whom he here meant reviewers – had, he added, paralysed the English novel.

Expenses – there would have been some incurred by Emma's absence – caused him once again to worry about his future. How was he to know that his books would still be in print after a century? He ended his letter to Mrs Henniker by observing that the poems of T.E. Brown, which he had just been reading, were spoiled by his having been a parson – and then added that his beloved Barnes, too, had written 'parsonically'. Whenever things seemed to turn against him, he somewhat playfully took it out on parsons; one is reminded of his remark to Hermann Lea that their mutual friend the Rev. Thomas Perkins was a pretty decent man *in spite of being a parson*.

On the next day he wrote poignantly to Emma, already missing her:

> Everything is stagnant here, & there is nothing to tell . . . I hope that you get good advice . . . on the re-arrangement of your sister's affairs . . . I hope you will not break down, but you must be careful. Lilian has had to stay in for some days with a slight cold. But it has gone off, & we bicycled yesterday to the Upwey wishing well . . .

Fortunately Emma had left strict instructions about some of the cats, particularly about Tip, Croppy and Marky, the first two of which continued to fight. He could not, he told Emma on 6 November, get them 'to agree anyhow', and he was having to keep Tip in his study for most of the time. He told her that he had neuralgia in the teeth ('not serious') and that he was 'dreadfully afraid' that she would 'break down': he could not see 'why you shd have so much to do'. Lilian was 'longing' for her to come back, 'less, I tell her, from a wish to see you than from a desire to escape her penal servitude here'. He ended: 'L. says you mean that you are coming back *this* week; but I do not think so.' Millgate says that this letter contains a 'strong' hint that he wanted her back at Max Gate, although 'he did not specifically insist' on it. However, in thus displaying his usual sympathy with the Victorian hierarchy, Millgate is scarcely allowing for Tom's own nature, which, no doubt reprehensibly, never 'insisted' upon anything in regard to his wife: he was well aware that she knew best about when to come back, and was being affectionate and sympathetic, and showing that he missed her. She did come briefly back to Max Gate on two occasions (Lee-on-the-Solent was not far, and especially not in those days, when the railways provided a service), but was present when her sister died in early December.

Unfortunately for Tom, in mid-November Rebekah Owen chose to pounce. He did his best to dissuade her with a terse note written on the 9th, in which he told her that Emma had been away 'with a sick relative, which will account for her silence. She is rather broken down.' This had no effect, and, with her sister in tow, she came to Dorchester and proceeded to make every effort to assert herself. Tom was undoubtedly amused by this monster's extraordinary selfishness and heedlessness; but he badly needed Emma to help him to manage her. In addition to all her other sins, it is obvious that Owen liked to fantasize, in her childish way, that the great author was in love with her: she jealously ran Emma down to all the Hardys' friends in Dorchester, begged for cycle rides, signatures and evenings at Max Gate, and thought of Lilian (whom, in a bizarre and perhaps slightly mad turn of phrase, she described as a 'chaperone') as preventing Tom from flinging his arms around her and begging for deliverance from Emma. Later in her visit, during one of Emma's quick visits back to Max Gate, she complained that it 'was so rude in Mrs H' not to invite her more often.

Yet by New Year's Eve the generous Emma was confiding in her yet again, in a letter written when Owen had, mercifully, returned home to the Lake District. Owen must have had an attraction or charm of some kind to be accepted at all by the Hardys – or by anyone else. But her virtues died with her in 1939. The degree of her hypocrisy towards Emma, whom she once spitefully described as 'in virginal white muslin & blue ribbons, with fat feet in baby-slippers & open-work stockings posing before her tea-visitors', was extreme. Yet it reveals such jealousy of Emma that one is led to suspect that both the Hardys, and some of their friends, simply felt sorry for her, and perhaps took the attitude that, considering how unfortunate she was, she was not really so bad.

Tom was never a man who reached hardened conclusions about

really important things – only that it would have been better not to have been born and that the universe was unfair. His eternal scepticism is part and parcel of his belief that writers and composers and artists could go on until they were physically stopped in their tracks. He was always learning. Inasmuch as everyone, however sceptical, is bound to entertain surmises about the unknown, even his own 'Unknown God', of the concluding poem in *Poems of the Past and the Present*, resembles him in this:

> Long have I framed weak phantasies of Thee,
> O Willer masked and dumb!
> Who makest Life become, –
> As though by labouring all unknowingly,
> Like one whom reveries numb.

This God, although unknown – the reference is to Acts 17, 23 – is in the process of learning and becoming aware. The poet, who resulted from that 'making' process, is descrying him (or it, or her – it is various in Hardy) by a similar process, doggedly and until death. The God did not make life 'become' in the past: he *is* making it, in an eternal present which, therefore, only time can end. As Bailey wrote, the last two stanzas of this poem present the 'meliorism' of the After-Scene of *The Dynasts*. The second stanza questions the extent of this deity's consciousness. Then,

> Perhaps Thy ancient rote-restricted ways
> Thy ripening rule transcends;
> That listless effort tends
> To grow percipient with advance of days,
> And with percipience mends.

> For, in unwonted purlieus, far and nigh,
> At whiles or short or long,
> May be discerned a wrong
> Dying as of self-slaughter; whereat I
> Would raise my voice in song.

This is so hedged about with qualifications that it hardly amounts to a 'belief' in 'meliorism'. Once again, there is a failure of language, a descent almost into prose, as the poem progresses to its end. A few years later, in such poems as 'The Convergence of the Twain', language would not thus fail; and the message, so far as any conventional notions of the betterment of the world were concerned, would be bleaker. For the time being, in these two first collections, sensitive to the 'charge that blessed things' he'd 'liefer not have be' (made, we may be sure, by Emma), Tom was trying to restrain his wilder flights of language: what he expressed in them may have shocked even him – writer of the 'In Tenebris' sequence – by its apparently nihilistic import. In *Poems of the Past and the Present*, he probably comes nearest to how he really felt, to how nature was leading him to write, in the solemn poem 'I Have Lived With Shades'. This is the first of the three concluding poems of the volume (of which 'The Unknown God' is the last) that are given the general title 'Retrospect'. There is less striving, here, to suppress the immediately inexplicable elements, and there is a reliance on the supernatural which was so natural to him, and which, as an intellectual, he resisted so fiercely:

> I have lived with Shades so long,
> And talked with them so oft,
> Since forth from cot and croft
> I went mankind among,
>> That sometimes they
>> In their dim style
>> Will pause awhile
>> To hear my say;
>
> And take me by the hand,
> And lead me through their rooms
> In the To-Be, where Dooms
> Half-wove and shapeless stand:
>> And show from there
>> The dwindled dust
>> And rot and rust
>> Of things that were.
>
> 'Now turn,' they said to me
> One day: 'Look whence we came,
> And signify his name
> Who gazes thence at thee.' –
>> – 'Nor name nor race

Know I, or can,'
I said, 'Of man
So commonplace.

'He moves me not at all;
I note no ray or jot
Of rareness in his lot,
Or star exceptional.
   Into the dim
   Dead throngs around
   He'll sink, nor sound
   Be left of him.'

'Yet,' said they, 'his frail speech,
Hath accents pitched like thine –
Thy mould and his define
A likeness each to each –
   But go! Deep pain
   Alas, would be
   His name to thee,
   And told in vain!'

Here the poet is only as clear as he can be about his meaning. He cannot conscientiously work it out further, and the emotional bewilderment leaks into the language, as it does, but more formidably, in 'Family Portraits'. The 'Shades' are not only his memories of real people, living and dead, but also the characters in his novels to whom he thought he gave life; now they have taken on life of their own. In this mood, which takes him often, he exists amongst ghosts, who, in turn, give him life: he is real only in their sinister attention. They are presented as wiser than himself. They show him when the future will have become the past. Presumably the 'Dooms' that stand 'half-wove and shapeless' represent nameless catastrophes: the life of the world does not appear to promise much, and it could hardly be argued that the world is here presented as anything but an awful place. What the Shades bid him behold is his own future self, itself looking at him as he is looking at it now. What he sees is chillingly null and 'commonplace'. Even if read as the comment of a novelist upon those characters he believed he had omnisciently created, this is a difficult poem. It goes beyond that, though, consisting at heart of a self-accusation of solipsism. Or the figure he is asked to survey by the Shades, in fact himself, may be that of the poet who has failed to achieve the necessary 'greatness' of character which was always so important to him, and by which he certainly meant virtue.

He did not achieve acceptance as a poet with *Wessex Poems*; for that he had to wait until late 1901 and the publication of his second collection. But, all things considered, he accomplished the transition from novelist to poet with great speed – and this despite some of the responses to *Wessex Poems*, which were quite remarkably hostile, even for an age less delicate than our own – in which, alas, purveyors of verse are terrified to criticize one another for fear they may themselves in turn be criticized. George Meredith wondered, privately, why Tom should have taken to verse – but he may have been aware that his own *Odes in Contribution to the Song of French History* (1898) hardly offered serious competition. Some of the remarks in the periodicals are reminiscent of John Hutton's ill-tempered and supercilious outburst against *Desperate Remedies* in the *Spectator*: the *Saturday Review* wondered why Hardy had not burned the poems in case they fell into the hands of an 'indiscreet literary executor', and alluded to 'the most amazing balderdash that ever found its way into a book of verse'. There were one or two other similar attempts at ridicule. This can only be further evidence, if such were needed, of the hatred for Tom felt by the orthodox and their friends.

At a more serious level, the general reaction to the first book is summed up in the puzzlement expressed by the civil servant E.K. Chambers – who became a valuable scholar of Shakespeare and the English stage, but who never, as his biography of Coleridge demonstrates, really understood post-Elizabethan poetry – in a review in the *Athenaeum*. Chambers acknowledged at the outset that Tom's thirty (actually thirty-one) drawings and designs showed 'a real sense of the decorative values of architectural outline and nocturnal landscape'. It was, however, difficult for him 'to say the proper word' about the poems. He found the rhythms of some of the 'trifling' ones 'wooden', their diction 'needlessly inflated'. But he praised the seriousness of the collection as a whole, and did not attack the 'uncompromising pessimism' as a fault. Modern poetry, he thought, could ill afford to dispense with such an achievement; but he added, uneasily, that the achievement itself was 'of a very narrow range'.

Tom exhibited little interest in the bad reviews: he had expected them. In all his letters to friends about the forthcoming volume he affected an extreme indifference, famously telling Gosse, for example:

Well, the poems were lying about, & I did not know what to do with

637

them. Considering that the Britisher resents a change of utterance, instrument, even of note, I do not expect a particularly gracious reception of them. It is difficult to let people who think I have made a fresh start know that to indulge in rhymes was my original weakness, & the prose only an afterthought. Besides, in the full tide of a fashion which seems to view poetry as the art of saying nothing with mellifluous preciosity, the principle of regarding form as second to content is not likely to be popular.

He then added an over-handsome compliment to Gosse about his own poems, perhaps worried that he would review *Wessex Poems* and indulge himself in the sort of reservations he had expressed in his handling of *Jude*. Gosse did not review the book; but when in March 1899 he had to write an unsigned leading article in *Literature* on 'Form in Poetry' he hung it around Tom's collection, and without causing offence.

Tom himself was most interested in the review by Lionel Johnson, whose own poetry he had evidently spotted as above the poor level of its time. Yet Johnson, although the only critic instantly to recognize Tom's special qualities as a poet, had not been wholly uncritical. Writing in the *Outlook* of 28 January 1898, he complained at what he took to be the uniform grimness of the volume (despite a slightly bowdlerized version of 'The Fire at Tranter Sweatley's' being included), and felt it was unlucky for Wessex to be labelled as so gloomy a place. Tom wrote to him on 9 February:

> I write an over late line or two to tell you that I did not miss reading your kind review of *Wessex Poems* in *The Outlook*. For one who can write such verse as yours to take the trouble to examine & appreciate mine struck me as being a generosity I do not often meet with.
>
> I have learnt by the publication of this volume what an appalling lack of insight into, or rather feeling for poetry of any sort prevails among reviewers outside a limited circle. They praise by guess, & condemn at hazard, till one feels that there is no opinion to appeal to. I was struck with this on observing some criticisms of your poems, as I am again now.
>
> You are right about the title being hard upon Wessex. But the word was used in my inability to think of any other convenient one.

He could not write to Gosse – no poet – in quite that way, although he knew him so much better than he knew Johnson. The complete lack of protest, in this letter from one poet to another, and without the reassurance necessary to poets *manqués*, is notable.

The greater success of *Poems of the Past and the Present* with the reviewers and the general public was in part fortuitous. It was connected with an event of which Tom eventually took literary advantage, even though he would have preferred that it had never happened. Nor of course did he manufacture the poems with which the volume opened – a group of eleven 'War Poems' – in order to find favour with the public. But these did, although without a shred of affectation, strike a popular chord. Indeed, why, when Alfred Austin died in 1913, the pallid if super-competent technician Robert Bridges was appointed to succeed him as Poet Laureate is still something of a mystery. But it was a good thing: since the death of Tennyson these appointees have ranged from the resolutely minor to the ludicrous. Gosse later said that Tom had secretly coveted the laureateship; but this was just the more ambitious Gosse's opinion. He was, after all, to refuse a knighthood from Asquith before he received the Order of Merit in 1910.

Tom was always unequivocally against the fighting of the Boer War; but he was not against those who fought in it. One of these was Major (later Major-General) Henniker, whom he genuinely admired as a fine example of a soldier ('the most perfect type of the practical soldier that I know,' he told him in a letter dated 19 October 1899, seeing him off on his voyage to South Africa). It was scarcely to be expected that he should go about loudly preaching against the war when so many of the sons and husbands of his personal friends were involved in it. Yet Henniker (one of whose dogs, of course, was called Milner, after the villain who started the conflict) had not been in Africa two months before Tom was writing to Florence on 19 December that 'This Imperial idea is, I fear, leading us into strange waters.' He also told her, perceptively, that he thought the British generals were 'deficient in strategic instincts'. He rightly believed that the war would take three years rather than three months. He had told her two months earlier, on 11 October, that he had been disappointed in a militaristic sonnet published by Swinburne in *The Times* – and even before that, on 17 September, that he presumed 'this unfortunate war with the Boers' would come. On 5 November he wrote to George Gissing congratulating him on having attacked Swinburne in the *Review of the Week* for his militarism: this came 'as the right word at the right moment,' he told him. Considering his personal loyalty to Swinburne, whom he could only excuse by thinking that he had dashed off the poem 'in a hurry', this note to Gissing gives evidence of his passionately anti-war, and anti-imperialistic, feelings.

The war poems, which are the first of the century in that unhappy genre, are, however, like *The Dynasts*, in part the result of his interest in war itself. As he told Florence Henniker on 25 February 1900:

> I take a keen pleasure in war strategy and tactics, following it as if it were a game of chess; but all the while I am obliged to blind myself to the human side of the matter: directly I think of that, the romance looks somewhat tawdry, & worse. I do not, of course, refer to this particular war, & the precise shade of blame or otherwise which attaches to us. I met a religious man on Friday (by the way, he is son of the old parson [Henry Moule] whose portrait I partially drew in Angel Clare's father), & I said, We the civilized world have given Christianity a fair trial for nearly 2000 years, & it has not yet taught countries the rudimentary virtue of keeping peace: so why not throw it over, & try, say Buddhism? (I may have said the same thing to you.) It shocked him, for he could only see the unchristianity of Kruger.

There is nothing contradictory in this, and, as he told the same correspondent later, not one of the war poems is jingoistic. What he thought of Rudyard Kipling's performance he did not record until later; he must have felt disappointed, because not long previously he had cycled about Dorset with him, helping Kipling look for a house to buy.

Only one poem preceded the war group, and this was the 'Reverie' called 'V.R. 1819–1901'. Much later, writing on 20 April 1921 to Lytton Strachey to thank him for the gift of a copy of his *Queen Victoria*, published that year, he said:

> I was deeply interested . . . notwithstanding that your subject was a most uninteresting woman . . . Perhaps I should not to be quite so absolute as to hold that she was uninteresting all through, since during the 20 years of her married life she was certainly more attractive.
>
> I often wished you could have had a more adequate & complicated woman to handle . . . However, Victoria was a good queen, well suited to her time and circumstances, in which perhaps a smarter woman would have been disastrous.

The poem shows that he had no personal feeling for the Queen (he said that when he wrote it he had a bad headache); certainly it is not the performance of a man intent on becoming laureate – it more or less ruled him out.

That he was deeply concerned with the question of nature's cruel violence, even to itself, is evident from many of the poems in *Poems of the Past and the Present*, and nowhere more so than in the sonnet 'The Sleep-Worker':

When wilt thou wake, O Mother, wake and see –
As one who, held in trance, has laboured long
By vacant rote and prepossession strong –
The coils that thou hast wrought unwittingly;

Wherein have place, unrealized by thee,
Fair growths, foul cankers, right enmeshed with wrong,
Strange orchestras of victim-shriek and song,
And curious blends of ache and ecstasy? –

Should that morn come, and show thy opened eyes
All that Life's palpitating tissues feel,
How wilt thou bear thyself in thy surprise? –

Wilt thou destroy, in one wild shock of shame,
Thy whole high heaving firmamental frame,
Or patiently adjust, amend, and heal?

Here no distinction is made between nature and the Immanent Will, except that the latter is always 'It', whereas this is feminized. Bailey does not know whether she is 'the Shade of the Earth or the Immanent Will'. However, he recalls that Von Hartmann suggested that if the Will were made conscious, It would 'relieve pain by . . . annihilation of the world'.

The war poems are unequivocally anti-war. Tom had watched the departure of the troops from Southampton on the afternoon of 20 October 1899, expecting to see Henniker. But the major did not leave until early the next morning, so Tom despatched Gordon Gifford on a bicycle with the letter. He wrote, in the poems, on the embarkation of the troops; but the best of them is 'Drummer Hodge' – originally entitled, when it first appeared in *Literature* in December 1899, 'The Dead Drummer'. It must have been read by all the 1914–18 war poets, including Rupert Brooke, who unconsciously lifted from it his comparatively specious (if not insincere) 'The Soldier' ('Yet portion of that unknown plain/Will Hodge for ever be' deteriorates into the more jingoistic 'some corner of a foreign field/That is forever England'). More important, the bitterness and indignation embedded in the poem helped to inspire superior poets such as Sassoon and Owen. These poets (though Owen did not live to appreciate Hardy, and did so only through the use that Sassoon and Graves made of him) reacted more readily to Hardy's plain statement of fact

> Yet portion of that unknown plain
>   Will Hodge for ever be;
> His homely Northern breast and brain
>   Grow to some Southern tree,
> And strange-eyed constellations reign
>   His stars eternally

than to Brooke's sentimental patriotism, of which Charles Sorley, one of the earliest victims of the war, was the first to complain. All this is now commonplace, and has been for some fifty years. Yet Millgate can write that Tom's poem 'anticipates' Brooke's! This, unless it is a deliberate attempt to rehabilitate the complacency of Edwardian poetry, indicates an astonishingly crass view, for all that the innocent Brooke – whose slight but charming talents lay elsewhere – never had a chance to see the trenches, or the worst that war could do. We do not know how he would have reacted; but it seems unlikely that he had sufficient poetic resource to have done so meaningfully. Whoever cares to link Tom to this nationalistic tradition in English poetry understands him poorly indeed.

The use of the name 'Hodge' reveals the attitude of the war clerks and 'patriots' towards their victims in its true colours: the poem begins with his being tipped, coffinless, like rubbish, a mere country yokel, into a pit. To the war machine he is the 'pitiable dummy known as Hodge' of *Tess*. I think, too, that Bailey is right when he maintains that an 'archetypal feeling runs through the poem that the soul must wander lost forever when the body lies in an "unknown plain" under "strange-eyed constellations"'. The sense of the terrible and casual insult done to a human being, for no good reason, is made all the more poignant because of the lyrical restraint with which it is presented: this 'anticipates' (but then Tom anticipated almost everything of importance in the twentieth century, and probably beyond it, in one way or another), not at all the superficially moving metrical prose of Brooke's 'Soldier', but that poetic reaction to Brooke's attitude which is so important to English poetry. Sassoon, at the time when he was recovering from war wounds, and defying the authorities by tempting them to court-martial him, told Wilfred Owen that he admired Hardy above all the other poets (Owen alas, with his usual sad petulance of judgement, found him 'potatoey'). When Tom later welcomed Sassoon to Max Gate he knew his war history full well.

Tom, as already mentioned, was careful to give out as few opinions as possible of a political or polemic kind. He knew what the result would be; and in any case he believed what he wrote in August 1901, in the preface to *Poems of the Past and the Present*:

> Of the subject-matter of this volume – even that which is in other than narrative form – much is dramatic or impersonative even where not explicitly so. Moreover, that portion which may be regarded as individual comprises a series of feelings and fancies written down in widely differing moods and circumstances, and at various dates. It will probably be found, therefore, to possess little cohesion of thought or harmony of colouring. I do not greatly regret this. Unadjusted impressions have their value, and the road to a true philosophy of life seems to lie in humbly recording diverse readings of its phenomena as they are forced upon us by chance and change.

He therefore confined himself to animal welfare, and tried, for all his wholly justified passion on the subject, to be moderate even in that. Thus, when in 1923 he was asked to become a vice-president of the Animal Defence and Anti-Vivisection League, he replied, or intended to reply – this is a pencilled draft of November of that year, probably for his secretary May O'Rourke:

> Shd be delighted, if it does not commit me to absolute anti-vivisection . . . May be cases in wh. a very small amount of suffering, such as a human being wd submit to, may lead to enlightenment on some point of great value in relieving the suffering both of men & of the animals themselves. So I don't know what to say. Pps you cd suggest – Say title. 'Animal defence and Controlled Vivn Soc' or 'A Defence Soc.' alone, & I wd join.

There could be nothing more reasonable, and it should be noted that Tom did not ask that any more violence be directed against animals than a human being might be asked to endure. Like many others, such as Elgar at a distance, and Robert Graves on the spot in 1915, he was horrified by the ill-treatment accorded to horses in war, and wrote of it often, particularly to Florence Henniker.

Millgate's scarifying remark that from a 'late-twentieth-century standpoint Hardy's especial concern with the sufferings of animals tends to seem mildly eccentric and beside the main point' displays a strange lack of understanding of his subject, who was certainly, as his war poems demonstrate, not unconcerned with human suffering, and who clearly saw that a humanity which cannot treat its animals properly cannot treat itself properly, either. Those who use horses as the war machine used them in 1899 will all the more 'naturally' use the village trash, Hodge, in the same manner. It is humanity which is – and more than 'mildly' – eccentric: it is perverse in its violation of its stewardship of the animals, just as Tom so 'pessimistically' charged. Was Leonardo da Vinci 'mildly eccentric and beside the main point' when he wrote: 'The day will come when men such as I will look upon the murder of animals as we now look upon the murder of men'? What of

Yea, the coneys are scared by the thud of hoofs,
And their white scuts flash at their vanishing heels,
And swallows abandon the hamlet-roofs.

The mole's tunnelled chambers are crushed by wheels,
The lark's eggs scattered, their owners fled;
And the hedgehog's household the sapper unseals.

The snail draws in at the terrible tread,
But in vain; he is crushed by the felloe-rim;
The worm asks what can be overhead,

And wriggles deep from a scene so grim,
And guesses him safe; for he does not know
What a foul red rain will be soaking him!

Beaten about by the heel and toe
Are butterflies, sick of the day's long rheum,
To die of a worse than the weather-foe.

Trodden and bruised to a miry tomb
Are ears that have greened but will never be gold,
And flowers in the bud that will never bloom.

Mildly eccentric? Beside the main point? The prophet Mohammed is said to have once cut off a piece of his garment rather than disturb a sleeping cat, and made an important point in so doing.

Tom's more sensitive readers are, in the main, in agreement with his so-called 'eccentricity'. Exiguous conformism offers no useful way into the heart of his work. But, apart from running the perpetual risk of being patronized as eccentric – which perhaps he could afford – he was on safer grounds in the public expression of his love for animals than he ever could be in the making of political pronouncements. When asked for his views on capital punishment he carefully avoided giving them, contenting himself with uttering his belief that it was the most powerful of all deterrents; the question of society's right to use it, however, he refused to discuss. By contrast, on a cycle tour in 1906 with an American visitor, Professor William Lyon Phelps, he declared that hunting was 'wicked' (the puzzled Phelps particularly remembered his use of this word). He was, again, being truthful rather than 'eccentric'. As so often, he was ahead of his time – and, apparently, ahead of ours too, if critics can still make remarks of that sort.

Politics, and even literary likes and dislikes, were different and more dangerous topics of discussion, and, apart from not worrying too much about his (even so, private) expression of contempt for the crazily egotistic popular novelist Hall Caine, who had attended Rossetti in his last unhappy years, Tom was exceedingly circumspect. He was both conscientious and carefully gracious to those strangers who sent him their works, and sometimes, as in the cases of George Douglas (whom he liked as a man) and Alfred Austin, ironic in so subtle a manner that he could never be reproached. He liked to be kind if he could, and only when wounded would he strike back. Apart from being clear in his liking for Shelley and a few other poets of the past he was circumspect about his literary tastes, usually choosing politeness over close or specific criticism. Sometimes he would tell an author that he had liked some passage in a particular work, or pick out one poem or another (as with Gosse, whom he comforted by over-praising); he was seldom unequivocal (unless in the case of women upon whom he had his romantic eye). Thus, while he approved of the social intentions of Grant Allen in his feminist novel *The Woman Who Did*, it is far from clear that he regarded it as a successful work of art (which, unhappily, it is not).

He could parry, with unabashed humour, the journalist or professor eager for a quote from the great man. Thus he astonished Phelps, who wanted to tap him for a few quotable opinions on contemporaries, when he told him, in answer to a casual enquiry as to whether he owned the dozens of cats who entered the room at teatime: 'Oh, dear, no. Some of them are [ours], and some are cats who come regularly to have tea, and some are still other cats, not invited by us, but who seem to find out about this time of day that tea will be going.' Phelps got little out of him.

In a letter to Florence Henniker, dated 26 January 1900, Tom wrote: 'I am just interested in – of all authors in the world – Otway the poet. Really his 'Venice Preserved' is a strong play, though nobody reads it now.' He owned a copy of the three-volume 1757 edition of Thomas Otway's works. In *Venice Preserv'd*, Pierre's answer to Jaffeir's question as to 'how that damn'd Quality/Call'd Honesty, got footing in the World' has the stamp of the sort of humorous and convoluted irony which Tom was soon to update and to make his own:

> Why, pow'rfull Villainy first set it up
> For its own ease and safety: Honest men
> Are the soft easy Cushions on which Knaves
> Repose and fatten: Were all mankind Villains,
> They'd starve each other; Lawyers wou'd want practice,
> Cut-Throats Rewards: Each man would kill his Brother
> Himself, none would be paid or hang'd for Murder:
> Honesty was a Cheat invented first
> To bind the Hands of bold deserving Rogues,
> That Fools and Cowards might sit safe in Power,
> And lord it uncontroul'd above their Betters.

Just after this Pierre expresses, exactly, the Hardyan ironic ethos: he tells Jaffeir that, although he pays his debts and is loyal to his friends, he is still a villain

> To see the suffring's of my fellow Creatures,
> And own my self a Man: To see our Senators
> Cheat the deluded people with a shew
> Of Liberty, which yet they n'er must taste of;
> They say, by them our hands are free from Fetters,
> Yet whom they please they lay in basest bonds;
> Bring whom they please to Infamy and Sorrow;
> Drive us like Wracks down the rough Tide of Power,
> Whilst no hold's left to save us from Destruction;

WESSEX POEMS

All that bear this are Villains; and I one,
Not to rouse up at the great Call of Nature,
And check the Growth of these domestic spoilers,
That make us slaves.

This rousing speech, with its crossing of the tones of Shakespeare and John Marston, its deliberate reversion to pre-Restoration modes – and with its own poetry behind the bombast, too – aptly delineates the satirical, anti-establishment habit of mind which Tom enjoyed in the Jacobeans. For it is, despite its Restoration date, Jacobean in spirit. Of nineteenth-century poets both Beddoes and Darley had been susceptible to it, and so had Swinburne, who did such sterling work in the rehabilitation of the Jacobeans; but Tom felt it more deeply, for all his public reticence and suspicion of 'revolutionary' impulses to rock – or sink – the boat. This subversiveness (which is what he meant by his so-called 'intrinsicalism'), the kind of thing splendidly rampant in the Jacobean city comedies and in the plays of Thomas Middleton, is only one side of Tom. There are also caution, reserve and love of tradition. In his poems, he twisted traditional forms into many new and often grotesque shapes; but he never abused them. However, in so far as his subversive irony had roots in his reading as well as in himself, those roots are in the Jacobeans and in those after them who, like Otway, tried to continue that line of feeling.

Poems of the Past and the Present was welcomed as *Wessex Poems* had not been. Most of the war poems had appeared in prominent periodicals and newspapers, and even those reviewers hostile to Tom recognized that their battle against him was lost. Thus the *Saturday Review*, in its issue of November 1901, remained critical but had to drop its insulting tone. The anonymous reviewer granted the author a 'melancholy sincerity' as well as a marked originality, though he believed that he danced 'in hobnails' and was 'inharmonious'. It would take some years before the main body of critics and even readers could begin to value Tom for his 'inharmoniousness', and to realize that, unlike most contemporary poets, he really had something to say, and *meant it*. It was perceptive of this reviewer to acknowledge that Tom could 'always force words to say exactly what he wants them to say', and then to add: 'but their subjection is never quite willing, they seem to have a spite against him because he is stronger than they'. One does not say this of a poet for whose powers one has no respect, and it is well enough said, for all that no poet, not even Shakespeare, can ever really be 'stronger than

647

words' – he can only pretend to be. Yet the phrase does point to a special quality in Tom's poetry – of doggedness, of determination not to be defeated by his inevitable weakness in that he was, ultimately, the servant of words.

T.H. Warren, who in 1911 would be elected Professor of Poetry at Oxford, reviewed the book in the *Spectator*. He did not like it, and was disturbed by what he called Tom's 'coarseness' – 'he permits himself a Swiftian turn such as was pardonable, or at least not surprising, in Swift two centuries ago, but which we do not expect, and which ought not to be sprung upon us in a book by an English writer of repute'. When one remembers that Warren was no less than President of Magdalen College, Oxford, one begins to understand just what Tom was up against, and why he worried about his income drying up, his visits to London, and his possible meetings with professors. He had no need to be paranoid. But even Warren, insistent that Tom's genius lay in fiction, reluctantly allowed the poems some 'fineness', while doubting whether in fact they were poetry at all: 'Mr Hardy is barely a poet.' His command of vocabulary was 'wonderful', but 'almost too great'! Warren, interestingly, was also upset because the Boer War had not stirred the author to 'enthusiasm' and because his loyalty to the 'great and good' Queen was 'strangely expressed'. Yet he felt forced to accord this new poet some respect – an indication of the status that Tom had by now achieved.

This status was almost certainly due to a combination of two factors: the appearance of the Boer War poems in the national press, and the liking felt for the book as a whole by that elusive person, the common reader. A thousand copies were printed; soon another five hundred were demanded. Yet he had not compromised himself a whit. The war poems, as he told Mrs Henniker, did not have any of the 'Jingo or Imperial' about them. Indeed, he had stuck to his own point of view throughout. 'A Christmas Ghost-Story', written for Christmas Eve and therefore thus dated, appeared in the *Westminster Gazette* on 23 December as follows:

> South of the Line, inland from far Durban,
> A mouldering soldier lies – your countryman.
> Awry and doubled up are his gray bones,
> And on the breeze his puzzled phantom moans
> Nightly to clear Canopus: 'I would know
> By whom and when the All-Earth-gladdening Law
> Of Peace, brought in by that Man Crucified,
> Was ruled to be inept, and set aside?'

On Christmas Day the *Daily Chronicle* published an editorial attacking this poem as pacifist. Tom replied good-humouredly, dissociating himself from any notion that he wanted to persuade British soldiers to cowardice (the *Daily Chronicle*'s belief was that soldiers ought to want to die); but when he published the poem in volume form he added these four lines (continuing the question begun with 'I would know'):

> 'And what of logic or of truth appears
> In tacking "Anno Domini" to the years?
> Near twenty-hundred liveried thus have hied,
> But tarries yet the Cause for which He died.'

The tone of this poem, as it now stands, makes even more obvious the source of Sassoon's similar tone just fifteen years later.

This supposedly shy and unconfident bumpkin, though guilty of Swiftian excess – and never repentant of it – now succeeded in imposing himself on the public as a poet; and, despite his 'pathetic' lack of a university education, he was now being hailed by an Oxford scholar, Warren, who disliked him, as being himself a 'scholar, and of good pedigree', and, again, as an 'accomplished scholar, and that not only in English' (this was on account of the 'imitations' of Heine and others in *Poems of the Past and of the Present*). After that he would take on the reviewers yet again: he would tackle the drama! The reception of the first part of *The Dynasts* was by no means good, and even threw him into temporary dejection. But he prevailed, and it was that which, above all else, got him his Order of Merit.

30

The Dynasts

Tom took more than five years to write *The Dynasts*, after beginning to draft it in earnest in June 1902. He had been contemplating it in one form or another since the age of eight, when he discovered his grandfather's illustrated periodicals in a cupboard at about the same time that he made his first visit to London. In its final form the epic combined his sense of local and national history with his philosophical outlook. He published the work in three separate parts in 1904, 1906 and 1908; the first complete edition appeared in 1910.

Tom's external circumstances did not much change until towards the end of this period, when in 1905 he met, and then gradually became aware of, Florence Dugdale; his conception of the work never changed. He was eventually sorry that he had published the first part separately; but in that way he did effectively rule out even the possibility of making fundamental changes. These years were perhaps the most unhappy of his life; and he is reported by many of those who met him to have looked ill during much of the time. The estrangement from Emma, while never absolute, or uninterrupted, or 'desperate' (as it has been called), continued. Her general ill health, which eventually forced her to cut down on her London visits, did not improve her temper or her tact. Her outbursts became more frequent. On a few occasions she upbraided him like a child in front of guests. Tom felt these attacks upon him keenly – unfortunately, more keenly than her periodic revivals of the old affection as exemplified in 'Some Recollections'. The meeting with Florence Dugdale improved his situation in one respect; in another, though, it made it worse, since he felt oppressed with a guilt which he probably never fully confided to anyone, and about which he could not be specific in the poems written to Emma after her death. There was the added difficulty (in my speculation) that Florence never allowed herself to become his wholehearted mistress, and therefore blew hot and cold until Emma suddenly died. It was not her fault, but Florence could not be what he really wanted: a new and young Emma. Nor was she a strong or interesting enough character to present herself as a new and different woman.

Although all fully achieved poetry is, in the most important sense, 'equal', there is still a useful distinction to be drawn between the 'minor' and the 'major'. Among the features of a major poetry is that it develops – the poet argues with himself. Thus, in Housman, there is no development: he is, therefore, a minor, though an exquisite poet. There is development in Tom's poetry; but is *The Dynasts* to be considered as part and parcel of that development, or is it separate, a continuation of his fiction-writing under the guise of closet-drama, with the prose turned into a monotonously regular blank verse? Such a passage as this – selected at random from many just as typical – would hardly suggest major anything, let alone major poetry:

> Your majesty, I now must needs suggest,
> Pursuant to conclusions reached this morn,
> That since the front and flower of all our force
> Is seen receding to the Basamberg,
> These walls no longer yield safe shade for you,
> Or facile outlook . . .

Torn from its context, it is hardly better than passages from the unreadable 'tragedies', such as *Nero*, of the eventual Poet Laureate (1913–30) Robert Bridges. This kind of stuff, practised with great theatrical success for a few years by Stephen Phillips, is probably less a reflection upon its various authors than of the degraded taste of a culturally exhausted age. It may also account for the exaggerated reputation of George Bernard Shaw, whose plays were so much better than almost anyone else's of his times. Tom disliked the theatre of his time so much that he finally stopped trying for London dramatizations of his novels and stories, and put his faith in local productions.

Yet, whatever we may think of *The Dynasts* – and it is thoroughly admired by only a few – it is curiously hard to dismiss as 'minor', let alone as a total failure. And this is so despite various facts that would seem to militate against such a view. Many of Tom's admirers have still not read it, for instance, and the majority of his critics, even the sympathetic ones, continue to ignore it. It is not really playable, in its entirety, on the stage (it is not, of course, supposed to be). Nor has it ever had a truly triumphant performance on radio (it has been broadcast five times: in 1933, 1940, 1943, 1951 – by far the best – and 1967), for which it might have been designed, or in adapted form on the stage (Granville Barker's production of 1914–15 was successful, but in no way a triumph – and was in any case disapproved of by Tom as not being a true representation of his intentions). Although eminently cinematic, *The Dynasts* has not yet been turned into a film, and the chances of this happening recede yearly, as the art of the cinema continues to decline. And finally, it cannot be said to contain much of its author's best poetry.

Nevertheless it *is* a major work: the most successful – not even least unsuccessful – long prose poem, or (as Tom properly called it) dramatic epic, of the twentieth century in any language. The many resentful attacks that have been made upon it turn out to resemble nothing so much as the failed Napoleonic intrusion into Russia which forms a part of the story it tells: whatever part of it one critic tries to knock down, another one comes along and sets it up again. The blank verse is far less monotonous when not quoted out of context; Tom deliberately stuck to Coleridge's dictum: that a long poem cannot be poetic all the time. Critics often complain that he should have used prose; but his metric prose, or verse, is more effective than prose could have been. Also, the considerable amount of prose that it does contain is superior in quality to the verse; yet it would not seem so if the work were all in prose . . .

Countless epics of the same size and scope have been written, but most have remained unpublished. In his *Some Contemporary Poets* of 1920, a hasty but useful little book in which Hardy is treated as paramount, Harold Monro referred to 'Rowbotham, self-styled "the modern Homer"' as one whose work he would have liked to consider if only he had had more space at his disposal. I could never find any trace of this Rowbotham, who must either have been an enthusiastic but perpetually rejected contributor to Monro's various magazines and anthologies – or, more likely, was invented by him, as a joking reference to the thousands of authors who do write, and try persistently to publish, such epics. At all events, to me and some others who have edited poetry for magazines or anthologies, authors of this type have always been known, collectively, as 'Rowbotham'. One of them, by a supreme irony, was (as Gittings discovered) none other than Tom's eldest brother-in-law, Richard Ireland Gifford, who was engaged (according to a record in the Warneford Hospital in Oxford, to which he was confined) in writing a 'poem describing the battle of Waterloo', which was obviously intended to be epic. This hospital report is dated 1900, and one can only suppose that Emma, or someone else in the Gifford family informed by Emma (Walter Gifford?), told Richard of Tom's planned epic, and that he immediately set out to rival it. It does not survive, and in all probability did not run to more than a few lines.

This story does suggest that the children of John Attersoll Gifford shared a streak of literary pretension, inculcated by him into them in childhood; and that what he most resented in Tom in the early 1870s was the fact that he was trying to become a writer. Walter, the father of Gordon and Lilian, is said to have been 'supercilious', and may, too, have had an air of superiority and a conviction that he could, if he wished, equal his brother-in-law's achievement. The Giffords, including Emma, felt that they must hold their own, somehow, against the eventually successful Thomas Hardy. When Emma believed that he had 'turned against her' by writing *Jude* outside her sphere of influence, she may have reverted all too easily to John Attersoll Gifford's ideas about her young fiancé. Although candid and notably unmoralistic about his drinking, she refers to him as an accomplished literary man.

The only real rival to *The Dynasts*, though, since Browning's *The Ring and the Book* (1869) and Tennyson's *Idylls of the King* (1891 in its complete and final form), is Charles Doughty's immense *The Dawn in Britain* (1906). Bridges' *The Testament of Beauty*, which appeared in the year after Tom's death, was a short-lived middlebrow success which has since sunk almost without trace: Doughty, and for that matter Bridges and perhaps even Rowbotham, essayed the straightforward long poem. *The Dynasts*, on the other hand, although an epic, is an idiosyncratic hybrid: a mixture of blank verse, song, stage direction, prose and dumb-show. That it is majestically *poetic* there can be no doubt; it is also an eminently readable history of the Napoleonic campaigns in the period 1805–15, with special emphasis on the part played by the English in the defeat of the vainglorious Corsican. After it has been read for sheer enjoyment, as an accurate and skilful piece of patriotic history, it may be appreciated at other, profounder levels. But it is this immediate appeal, to the pleasure in a good story which is shared by us all, which sustains the work.

The plan, to represent Napoleon's exploits with particular reference to their impact on England in 'three parts, nineteen acts, and one-hundred and thirty scenes [actually there are 131]', according to the title page, is 'potentially ridiculous'. Yet no one has ever been able to back this up in reality. The strength of Hardy's structure lies in the restraint he exercises, and in his consideration for his reader's intelligence: readers are asked in the preface to treat it as a 'mental performance' and to complete the action themselves – to 'fill in the junctions required to combine the scenes into an artistic unity'. It is the critics who, if only in the course of their legitimate work, have picked it to pieces, analysing its supposed deficiencies. But the majority are agreed that the whole is greater than its parts. We do not and cannot hear from the ordinary reader: one of the definitions of that elusive person is that we do not hear, in a critical way, from her and him. The ordinary reader's message is the keeping of books in print; and, over almost a century, *The Dynasts* has done well for the sort of work it is. It is not just a curious feature on one of the many paths which branch off from the mainstream of English literature; it is part of that mainstream.

Harold Orel, who has written one of the most useful books on it (*Thomas Hardy's Epic-Drama: A Study of 'The Dynasts'*, 1963), as well as editing the best edition (1978), believes that it is above all a 'patriotic' work. It is only a patriotic work, however, at the primary level – vital though that is. At that level, with cunning artistry, *The Dynasts* imitates the way in which the events of great wars – victories, individual heroic deeds, acts of courage and so on – themselves affect the public. It thus shares the nature of Shakespeare's *Henry V*. But that merely offers the way into it. Tom himself, it will be recalled, wrote in his letter to Florence Henniker about his attitude to the Boer War:

> I take a keen pleasure in war strategy and tactics, following it as if it were a game of chess; but all the while I am obliged to blind myself to the human side of the matter: directly I think of that, the romance looks somewhat tawdry, & worse.

A few months before writing that letter he had noted that, despite his hatred of war as 'old and barbarous', 'few persons are more martial than I, or like better to write of war in prose and rhyme'. By the end of 1900 he had come to the conclusion that the war resembled 'a snow storm in one respect: it is grand and romantic at the first, but dreary and tedious in its disappearance'. The heart of his creative procedure, in individual poems and in his epic, became increasingly pragmatic: rejecting what he *ought* to feel and think as irrelevant, he examined (and afterwards assessed and analysed) what he *did* think and feel.

By the time, approximately two years later, that he took up his pen to begin actual work, he felt ready to come to terms with this apparent paradox by combining his 'pleasure' with his acute sense of the 'human side'. Just as his own attention was reluctantly held by war, so he would hold his readers' by his story-telling art; then, their attention captured, he would remove the scales from his own eyes, and thus from theirs too: he would no longer suffer to be 'blind'. Now too mature and dedicated to honesty to try to stifle or disown the 'pleasure', he would accept it and enlist its aid: he would make it a first step in as vehement a denunciation of violence as he could manage. Yet, even with his scheme fully prepared, he still did not know how it was going to work out. He knew that he was going to tell a story, and he knew what the story was. He knew how he was going to present it. He was aware of the general nature of the philosophical rubric under which he would tell it, too. Had he been one jot or tittle more 'prepared', the work would inevitably have lost its energy. But he judged it just right: now he had to find the words.

When the first part appeared in 1904 one of its bewildered and resentful reviewers complained of its 'hard Pyrrhonism'. He spoke more truthfully than he was aware. It is commonplace, through quite justified, to compare the philosophy in *The Dynasts* to that of Schopenhauer and to Eduard von Hartmann's popular elaborations of it; but scepticism (more or less a synonym of Pyrrhonism) is less frequently cited as an influence. It is significant that in just these years Tom should have singled out Thomas Otway for praise: radical scepticism is one of the chief components of his language, and one of Otway's erstwhile patrons was John Wilmot, Earl of Rochester, one of the foremost Pyrrhonists of the time.

Tom knew about Pyrrho: some three or four years before he began writing *The Dynasts* he copied from Eduard Zeller's *The Stoics, Epicureans and Sceptics* (1870, later revised) the following short passage:

> Pyrrho's teaching may be summed up in the three following statements: (1) We can know nothing about the nature of things. (2) Hence the right attitude towards them is to withhold judgement. (3) The necessary result of suspending judgement is imperturbability.

He chose to write down this passage because he had always been interested in the third statement; it is evident from other notes that he carefully absorbed the whole of Zeller's still instructive book.

The early Pyrrhonists liked to quote Socrates' dictum 'All that I know is that I know nothing', which they believed gave support to their negative theory of knowledge. Tom had long been concerned with the notion of *ataraxia*, 'imperturbability', as is evident from his frequent citation of the Stoic Marcus Aurelius on the subject: from reading Zeller's book he may for the first time have become aware of a new approach to it. However, he already knew, as a poet if not as a philosopher engaged in a battle with dogma, that such imperturbability was unattainable, owing to (as his Spirit of the Pities says at 1, IV, v) the Immanent Will's 'intolerable antilogy' in 'making figments feel', which was always the ground of his most indignant emotive protest against existence. In *The Dynasts* he set out to try to resolve the paradox: to attain and explore, from his personal point of view, a degree of imperturbability, a kind of creative *ataraxia*, by achieving the suspension of judgement recommended by the sceptics.

Just after returning to London from France in June 1888 Tom had met his old friend Lady Ritchie, the former Miss Thackeray, who had told him that the value she put on life lay 'largely in the fact that she has children': 'She says,' he wrote in the *Life*, 'that when she calls on L. Stephen and his [second] wife she feels like a ghost, who arouses sad feelings in the person visited.' This set him to thinking, and a day or two later he wrote, 'whimsically':

I have attempted many modes [of finding 'imperturbability']. For my part, if there is any way of getting a melancholy satisfaction out of life it lies in dying, so to speak, before one is out of the flesh; by which I mean putting on the manners of ghosts, wandering in their haunts, and taking their views of surrounding things. To think of life as passing away is a sadness; to think of it as past is at least tolerable. Hence even when I enter into a room to pay a simple morning call I have unconsciously the habit of regarding the scene as if I were a spectre not solid enough to influence my environment; only fit to behold and say, as another spectre said: 'Peace be unto you!'

This, as well as casting some light on why Emma might on occasion have found Tom difficult to live with ('putting on the manners of ghosts', an excellent description, self-supplied, of the remoteness of manner which had always characterized him), shows how he was seeking some sort of 'imperturbability' even before he had reached his fiftieth year. A decade and more later he was seeking it more specifically: as the ghostly and therefore 'objective' author of an epic. As Susan Dean writes in her outstandingly imaginative and sympathetic book, *Hardy's Poetic Vision in 'The Dynasts'* (1977), this helps us to complete our explanation of the Overworld Spirits [of the Pities, and so on, in *The Dynasts*] by connecting them, finally, to the truths that [Hardy's] anatomizing perspective [in *The Dynasts*] has revealed to us. Life is insubstantial; flesh is spectral; meaning is phantasmal; the course of action cannot be changed or even grasped by one's understanding. Therefore the mind that would view the scene of human life must climb to an Overworld, must distance itself willingly even as it is distanced unwillingly, and remember that it is as restricted by life as though it were in its body but effectively out of it.

Tom's own scepticism, of which this ghostly procedure is no more than a variation, was as much directed against dogmatism and its bad consequences as it was the result of his reasoning. The most enduring influence upon his intellectual attitude was that of the eighteenth-century Scottish philosopher David Hume, whom he noted as one of his mentors in his letter to Helen Garwood, author of the dissertation 'Thomas Hardy, an Illustration of the Philosophy of Schopenhauer' (1911). Hume cannot be called 'a sceptic', but he was a man of extremely sceptical temper who did not hesitate to employ sceptical arguments. One of the most important and influential arguments in Hume's *Treatise* is to the effect that, although it is innate in human beings to hold beliefs about the external world, these beliefs have no status: all we can examine is the psychology of them. Thus, in a sense, Hume's name is written all over the 'philosophy' in Tom, and provides an excellent example of the benign influence that a professional philosopher can exercise (through himself and his heirs) over a poet, whose business it is, after all, to examine subjective psychological phenomena. Tom's disinclination to make moral pronouncements, especially of a dogmatic kind, must have owed much to, or found comforting confirmation in, Hume's famous and ironic statement – which in any case should be quoted in relation to the general attitude he cultivated, above all in his consideration of the exact form which *The Dynasts* should take:

In every system of morality, which I have hitherto met with, I have always remark'd, that the author proceeds for some time in the ordinary way of reasoning . . . when of a sudden I am surpris'd to find, that instead of the usual copulations of propositions, *is*, and *is not*, I meet with no proposition that is not connected with an *ought* or an *ought not*. This change is imperceptible, but is, however, of the last consequence. For as this *ought* or *ought not*, expresses some new

657

relation or affirmation, 'tis necessary that it shou'd be observ'd and explain'd; and at the same time that a reason should be given, for what seems altogether inconceivable, how this new relation can be a deduction from others, which are entirely different from it.

This is a better statement of what G.E. Moore – the Cambridge philosopher whom Tom met in the course of his visits to Cambridge, and whose *Principia Ethica* he read in 1915 – put forward in 1903 as the 'naturalistic fallacy'. It, and Moore's proposal (which, curiously, did not cite it), has meant a great deal in technical terms to professional philosophers, only some of whom regard it as a fallacy at all; to Tom it meant a relatively simple anti-dogmatic distinction between *is* and *ought*, a distinction which runs, if only by indignant implication, throughout all his work. Thus, if one were to choose a handful of epigraphs from other writers with which to preface *The Dynasts* in its entirety, Hume's elegant and ironic words would have to be among them.

Tom chose the Napoleonic story as the basis for his epic because it had been familiar to him from childhood: people from his own family had been involved in it, and so had many more whom he had known. He made it his business to talk with Chelsea pensioners over a number of years, to traverse the battlefield of Waterloo twice, to go to Milan Cathedral, and to read books of every kind on the subject. Only a few, historians included, could have read more. He was, after all, an astonishingly well-read man. A calculatedly pedestrian truthfulness to the facts, which he tried hard and with success to observe, gave him the secure basis necessary to his enterprise. One of the most common arguments against the success of *The Dynasts* has been that Tom failed to make the best of his 'stirring' material (this opinion is put forward most notably in Walter F. Wright's book *The Shaping of 'The Dynasts': A Study in Thomas Hardy*, 1967). But, as Susan Dean has shown, the 'thin' treatment was essential to his intention: to present what he called 'the diorama of a dream': 'model', as she well puts it, 'of the human mind'. In Dean's interpretation, Hardy proposed to enact two things simultaneously: the historical events and the watching of those events. The work is completed, though, by the reader himself, who must bring his or her imagination to bear upon the whole.

Eventually, in order to put his plan into execution, Tom had to begin to write: he would have lost energy and inspiration had he not finally surrendered to his creative impulse, to the process of actual composition. However, Tom, as a post–romantic who retained a belief in inspiration (and who knew that creativity was as unknowable as his own Will), held his lyrical and dramatic impulses in remarkable check. Hence the comparative 'thinness' of the language. He worked with great cunnning, carefully calculating the effect he wanted to produce. If some wish to call this 'peasant cunning', then the term does at least distinguish it from academic cunning, with which it has little in common, for it is unlearned but wise (like a 'peasant saying'), untutored but shrewd. Tom was in fact an intellectual, although of an unusual sort: a man deliberately untutored, but not at all incapable or unlearned. When he was operating at a creative level, however, he liked to rely on poetic faculties, which always transcend critical prescriptions. He has here remained far ahead of all his critics, many of whom enjoy presenting him as a kind of half-articulate but gifted oaf. Some of these critics, as we have seen, complain that *The Dynasts* lacks the fire of what they would call a 'great patriotic poem'. Others, like Millgate, agreeing with its first bewildered reviewers, think of it as 'grandiose'.

He did not want to write a great patriotic poem, or anything grandiose. There is no such thing, he well knew, as a 'great' patriotic poem: great poetry, which he equated with what he thought of as 'greatness of character' – the practice of virtue and of the precepts of Christ (for whom he always had reverence, whatever his views of the Christian religion) – must go beyond what is usually thought of as patriotism, which is well redefined by *The Dynasts*. While he was working on it he wrote a key phrase in one of his notebooks: 'Patriotism, if aggressive & at the expense of other countries, is a vice: if in sympathy with them, a virtue.' In other words, love of country is not love of country if it lacks an understanding appreciation of other countries. If it lacks that quality, it is not properly human. The official British attitude towards the Boers, and then towards Germany in 1914, was anything but 'sympathetic' (the opposite also applies): those whom he called war-adepts did not want understanding of or sympathy with the enemy. In *The Dynasts*, in order to achieve his effect, he chose to work on feelings common to almost everyone. What he wanted was to expose the true nature of nationalism and war, just as, on a smaller scale, he had exposed the attitude of the 'war-adepts' in a single lyric, 'Drummer Hodge'. Never mind, then, if the patriotism to which he initially appealed was pure patriotism (free of egoism) or not. No dishonesty was involved: the deeds of Nelson, Wellington and others are genuinely stirring – and the more so when the reader had questioned the true nature of his own devotion to them. More important in *The Dynasts* than even their bravery is the brutality and pointlessness of war, and the selfishness of the participants. England is not excluded, although the English are seen as necessarily defending themselves against a terrible threat.

This brings us to the comparison which stares us in the face: Tolstoy's *War and Peace*. Curiously, it has not often been thoroughly made, possibly because most people find Tolstoy's view of history discomforting since it takes from individuals all the power they may think they have to influence events – it is, as Tolstoy himself called it, 'fatalist'. (A notable exception to this lack of thoroughness is Emma Clifford's '"War and Peace" and "The Dynasts"', *Modern Philology*, August 1956.) Tom admired Tolstoy, read and perceptively commented on *What Is Art?* when it appeared in English in Aylmer Maude's translation in 1899 ('a suggestive book, in which there are a good many true things, & many more that hover round the truth but just miss it'), and had read *War and Peace* in its 1889 English version by the American Nathan P. Dole – his copy of it, containing his markings of the passages about Napoleon which he wanted to dramatize, is still in existence.

Tolstoy's view of history is close to Tom's though not identical, and it must have influenced Tom's own formulation. The best statement of that view is still the one made by Tolstoy himself, which appears in the epilogue ('Part Two') of *War and Peace*, and also at the end of Book III, I, i. I quote – with ellipses – from Rosemary Edmonds' 1978 translation:

. . . History, that is, the unconscious. universal, swarm-life [other translators have 'hive-life'] of mankind, uses every moment of the life of kings for its own purpose.

Though Napoleon . . . in 1812, was more convinced than ever that to shed or not to shed the blood of his peoples . . . depended entirely on his will, he had never been more in the grip of those inevitable laws which compelled him, while to himself he seemed to be acting on his own volition, to perform for the world in general – for history – what was destined to be accomplished.

The people of the west moved eastwards to slay their fellow-men. And, by the law of coincidence of causes, thousands of minute causes fitted together and co-ordinated to produce that movement and that war . . .

Why does an apple fall when it is ripe? Is it brought down by the force of gravity? Is it because its stalk withers? Because it is dried by the sun, because it grows too heavy, or the wind shakes it, or because the boy standing under the tree wants to eat it?

None of these is the cause. They only make up the combination of conditions under which every living process of organic nature fulfils itself. And the botanist who finds that the apple falls because the cellular tissue decays, and so forth, is just as right and just as wrong as the child who stands under the tree and says the apple fell because he wanted to eat it and prayed for it to fall. In the same way the historian who declares that Napoleon went to Moscow because he wanted to, and perished [i.e. was defeated] because Alexander desired his destruction, will be just as right and wrong as the man who says that a mass weighing thousands of tons, tottering and undermined, fell in consequence of the last blow of the pickaxe wielded by the last navvy. In historical events great men – so-called – are but labels serving to give a name to the event, and like labels they have the least possible connection with the event itself.

Every action of theirs, that seems to them an act of their own free-will, is in the historical sense not free at all but is bound up with the whole course of history and preordained from all eternity.

Compare this insight with some of the fragmentary material Tom collected together in the notebook now called 'Memoranda II', as 'old notes written before "The Dynasts"', on 29 May 1922 (this later went into the *Life*):

We – the people-Humanity – a collective personality – (Thus 'we' could be engaged in the battle of Hohenlinden, say, & in the battle of Waterloo
– Dwell with genial human [sic] on 'our' getting into a rage for 'we' knew not what.
The intelligence of this collective personality Humanity is pervasive, ubiquitous, like that of God. Hence, e.g., on the one hand we could hear the roar of the cannon, discern the rush of the battalions, on the other hear the voice of a man protesting, &c.
Tit: 'Self-slaughter': divided agst. ourselves'
   Now these three (or 3,000) whirling through space at the rate of 40 miles a second – (God's view).
'Some of our family who' (the we of one nation speaking of the 'we' of another)
– A battle, army as somnambulists – not knowing what it is for –

– 'We' were called Artillery' &c' 'We were so under the spell of habit that' (drill)

After outlining a poem on the subject of God's omniscience but lack of omnipotence (the words used, astonishingly gnostic in their intuition, are: 'limitations, difficulties &c from being only able to work by Law'), and another on the 'difference between what things are & what they ought to be (stated as by a god to the gods – i.e. as god's story)', he adds:

> We will now ask the reader to turn eastward with us . . . at what the contingent of us out there were doing.
>   Poem. A spectral force seen acting in a man (e.g. Napoleon) & he acting under it – a pathetic sight, this compulsion.

One is reminded, by this notion of Napoleon as 'a pathetic sight', of Tolstoy's daring and deliberately provocative description, in Part 2 of *War and Peace*, of both Tsar Alexander and Napoleon as 'weak' individuals. We think of such men as Alexander the Great, Genghis Khan, Napoleon and Hitler as being anything but weak – and yet, regarded as the puppets of the Will, that is exactly what they are. This is why, in Bailey's wooden words, 'Hardy omitted much of the praiseworthy in his characterization of Napoleon, the emperor's love for order and his dreams of a united Europe.' This kind of schoolmasterly weighing up of pros and cons is irrelevant – and doubtless Tom would have rejoined, to Bailey, that both the love of order and the dream of a united Europe were wholly conditional on the premises that Napoleon, or his descendants, should maintain the beloved order, and that the united Europe should be dominated by France. What might have been 'praiseworthy' has been rendered worthless: the man who made laws so as to create order subsequently causes the miserable deaths of tens of thousands of his subjects by creating the disorder of war. Tom's portrait of the Corsican is, for obvious reasons, less hostile, softer, than Tolstoy's; but it is just as negative and 'pathetic'. However, he resists the temptation to present him as a 'wicked man': he is, rather, a man in the grip of a force that he cannot understand. In that respect Tom could almost be providing deliberate confirmation of Tolstoy's view of him. When we first encounter him, as he is crowned in Milan Cathedral, the Spirit of the Years admonishes the Spirit of the Pities:

THE DYNASTS

Thou reasonest ever thuswise – even as if
A self-formed force had urged his loud career.

There then follows this exchange:

SPIRIT SINISTER

Do not the prelate's accents falter thin,
His lips with inheld laughter grow deformed,
While blessing one whose aim is but to win
The golden seat that other bums have warmed?

SPIRIT OF THE YEARS

Soft, jester; scorn not puppetry so skilled,
Even made to feel by one men call the Dame.

SHADE OF THE EARTH

Yea; that they feel, and puppetry remain,
Is an owned flaw in her consistency
Men love to dub Dame Nature – that lay-shape
They use to hang phenomena upon –
Whose deftest mothering in fairest spheres
Is girt about by terms inexorable!

The language here, especially as exemplified in the six lines ending the quotation, and often elsewhere in *The Dynasts*, seems extraordinarily complex and 'awkward' – until we recognize that what Tom is labouring to say is almost unsayable. (I am not sure that it is possible to make sense of the above speech, made by the Shade of the Earth, except by inferring the presence of some grammatical construction: for example, for 'in her consistency/Men love to dub', we might read 'in the consistency of that which men love to dub . . .') Thus the manner in which Tom comes out with what he is struggling to say is, after all, not so inappropriate, even if it is occasionally hard or even impossible to follow, for 'awkwardness' characterizes the 'impossible' material itself: if, as Barker Fairley claimed in an article printed in Tom's lifetime ('Notes on the Form of *The Dynasts*', PMLA 34, September 1919), he is struggling to make the 'implicit explicit', then he may even have chosen the *only* appropriately honest means of expression – in preference to the sort of false and rhetorical polish he might have achieved by giving in to an impulse merely to please an audience.

One of the reasons Tom was so genuinely down on his old persona as a fiction-writer was because, by his standards as a poet, he had pleased his audience far too much: he had resorted to bowdlerization for the serialized novels, and had been forced to conceive each successive book in terms of how it would go down with the public. The trouble he encountered over *Tess* and *Jude*, in both of which his own artistic needs clearly surpassed his need to produce best-sellers, became too great, and so he abandoned the form altogether. His meaning in his poems, too – and not always in inferior poems, for 'Wessex Heights' offers an excellent example – is similarly difficult to grasp, and is a legitimate part of the poems themselves. What he is trying to say is well worth fumbling for and puzzling after, because the process can be nothing but illuminating in a mind of such depth, such concentration and, above all, such honesty. *The Dynasts*, being, as Susan Dean so convincingly demonstrates, a model of a mind at work – of the individual reader's, as of the author's – is his fullest illustration of the process. It represents how an individual's mind attempts to grasp a historical episode, and shows how it fails to do so.

Despite a few errors and misinterpretations of fact, *The Dynasts* is still by far the most comprehensive account and explanation of Napoleon. This is not to decry the histories, of which he made the fullest use: it is only to say that Tom's work acts as a comment upon how history is made and what its real nature is. This is perhaps its most important feature: it amounts to an astute and full phenomenological study of how a substantial episode in history was understood by one majestic mind. This is to say, Tom's method was based upon a scrupulous investigation of his own consciousness, in so far as it impinged upon the story of Napoleon and upon the formation of his conscious philosophy. That is one of the reasons why the 'fire' and 'stirringness' which would have been required of a merely patriotic, and shallower, epic are lacking: such fire comes largely from the unconscious mind, and Tom was not here concerned with that area of extreme 'inspiration'. Here he did away with inspiration as much as he dared, retaining only that modicum of it which he knew was indispensable.

Like the Austrian philosopher Edmund Husserl, the pioneer of phenomenology, Tom hoped by this means to investigate not the process of introspection, but the establishment of such 'essences' or meanings as are common to all minds. Although Tom had probably not heard of either Husserl or his chief predecessor in his enterprise, the ex-Roman Catholic priest Franz Brentano, such investigations were 'in the air'. Tom transferred his intuitions to the realm of imaginative literature. At the end of the Fore-Scene, in which we meet the various Spirits, the 'General Chorus of Intelligences' speaks, to aerial music:

> We'll close up Time, as a bird its van,
> We'll traverse Space, as spirits can,
> Link pulses severed by leagues and years,
> Bring cradles into touch with biers;
> So that the far-off Consequence appears
> Prompt at the heel of foregone Cause –
> The PRIME, that willed ere wareness was,
> Whose Brain perchance is Space, whose Thought its laws,
> Which we as threads and streams discern,
> We may but muse on, never learn.

This imagery of the brain, as Dean shows, recurs throughout. Some may feel unconvinced by her interpretation of the whole work, based as it is upon Tom's one use of the word diorama ('And their great Confederacy dissolves like the diorama of a dream'). But, as she declares, whether

> or not Hardy was thinking of the diorama when he gave form to the vision of his poem is not important . . . All we need to do is to show that the figure offers a clear scheme and useful terms for envisioning what is at work in *The Dynasts* . . . perhaps the diorama is accidental and unconscious . . . if the thing that is at work is not a diorama, it is very like one.

That is exactly what she shows.

The diorama, invented by Daguerre and Bouton, was first exhibited in London in 1823, and Dean is right in her claims that most Victorians would have been familiar with it. As she demonstrates, it is often used by them (such as by George Eliot in *Middlemarch*, and by various newspapers) without recourse to explanation. A diorama

> is an optical exhibit, housed in a cubicle with a viewing frame on the front. As on a conventional stage, there are stage borders and wings leading to an opaque backcloth. The diorama achieves an additional dimension of depth by placing a series of translucent veils between the fore-frame and the back-cloth. When coloured lights positioned

above are played upon and through these veils, they create vivid optical illusions in which apparently solid views disappear into one another and then reappear at will.

I am not fully convinced that Tom was 'enjoying a silent, allusive joke between himself and the knowing reader'; but the diorama does prove, as Dean claims, to be a convenient and valid way of viewing the text. Many have seen it, reasonably, as conceived in cinematic terms; but the metaphor of the diorama has an appropriate touch of Victorian quaintness and ingenuity which that of the cinema lacks. The metaphor serves Dean well in her study, which remains closer to the text than any other. Many who have previously rejected the work as worthy, but too flawed or too awkward, have been persuaded otherwise by Dean, and have returned to it with new pleasure and understanding.

Another influence upon Tom in *The Dynasts* was Edmund Burke's *A Philosophical Enquiry into the Origin of Our Ideas of the Sublime and Beautiful* (1757, revised and amplified 1759). He did not mention Burke often, but it is clear that he regarded him as a great stylist and took careful note of his later political writings. He was interested in him, it seems from a transcription he made from an article by Morley, as a man who had been frightened by revolutionary violence into a conservative attitude. Two things attracted him in the work on the sublime and the beautiful, whether he fully realized it or not: the young Burke's refusal to consider conventional morality as of much importance in a study of the sublime; and his insistence upon the way in which, in their response to the grand and the terrible (which most impinged upon the architect Tom in its grotesque aspect, with which he had become so familiar in churches), the sublime and the beautiful appealed to nobility of spirit (equivalent to Tom's 'greatness of character'). 'To make anything very terrible,' Burke wrote, 'obscurity seems in general to be necessary . . . The mind is hurried out of itself, by a crowd of great and confused images.' And, as Harold Orel points out, Tom found confirmation in Burke for the effectiveness of his habit of looking down on events: Burke actually states that looking down from a precipice is more striking than looking upwards at something of equal height. Orel is surely right to claim that he 'took the thought as a guide to the writing of dozens of descriptions' throughout *The Dynasts*.

We have seen how struck Tom was with the notion that human beings consist of different selves, or (as I have suggested) clusters of selves, one or another of which is foremost at any given time. An example he gives is that of the money-maker in the city and the money-maker at home: these are, he asserts, different men. I have already quoted the two relevant notes, from 1889 and 1890. There is also the late poem 'So Various', from *Winter Words*, the last collection. This is not one of the great poems, being linguistically rather flat; but it is a charming, modest and interesting one, and it demonstrates Tom's lifelong interest in the concept. Bailey, despite the fact that he, too, quotes one of the relevant notes, thinks it centres on 'Hardy's long-continued tussle with reviewers', on the grounds that he once told Shorter, on 8 August 1907, that

> I endeavour to profit from the opinions of those wonderful youths & maidens, my reviewers, & am laying to heart a few infallible truths taught by them: e.g., – that T.H.'s verse is his only claim to notice. That T.H.'s prose is his only real work . . .

and so on, joking about the various things said about him. But the poem is not about that at all, and cannot be: whereas the reviewers' opinions about him (against some of these he wrote such remarks as 'lies' and 'invention') were fictions, the various selves in 'So Various' are real. The poem begins:

You may have met a man – quite young –
A brisk-eyed youth, and highly strung:
   One whose desires
   And inner fires
   Moved him as wires.

And you may have met one stiff and old,
If not in years; of manner cold;
   Who seemed as stone,
   And never had known
   Of mirth or moan.

And there may have crossed your path a lover,
In whose clear depths you could discover
   A staunch, robust,
   And tender trust,
   Through storm and gust.

After ten more stanzas presenting differing Hardys, it concludes:

Now . . . All these specimens of man,
So various in their pith and plan,
   Curious to say
   Were *one* man. Yea,
   I was all they.

This tendency to split up such entities is relevant to *The Dynasts*, in which, in his Otherworld personages, Tom deliberately splits up various mental components (of himself as of others), each of which may be seen to be a part of himself and a persona in his work. The 'author' or part-author of 'The Convergence of the Twain' is, for example, the product of the Spirits Sinister and Ironic. Only the Will itself does not speak, because it is 'insentient', and because, no doubt, of Its 'limitations, difficulties &c from being only able to work by Law'. The energy of 'It', the First Cause and 'PRIME', underlies every process. Tom borrowed the term Will (*Wille*), from Schopenhauer (he did not think it 'perfectly fitted the idea to be conveyed', but could find no better – and he rejected 'Impulse'), but, although more influenced by the truculent Danziger than he probably cared to admit, in view of his own alleged 'pessimism', and particularly by the notion of the Will's irrational, blind, pointlessly striving nature, he may also have been independently influenced, as Schopenhauer himself was, by Goethe's *Faust*. Again, Schopenhauer made a point of atheism, whereas Tom did not wish to be associated with it. Schopenhauer's view that in reality we are all one, and only in one sense phenomenally distinct, did, however, affect *The Dynasts*.

'Hardy's' Will operates above all in a mechanical and blind manner; it is not aware of itself; its 'fibrils, veins,/Will-Tissues, nerves, and pulses' are 'like the lobule of a Brain/Evolving always that it wots not of'. The process resembles, too, that of composition: the author-god is never absolutely clear how his novel or poem or epic will work out: a statement can become modified, or turn into its opposite, without his even being, at first, aware of it. There are all sorts of parallels of this kind in *The Dynasts*, and the creative process is not the least of them. Of the 'theory' underlying *The Dynasts*, he wrote to Edward Wright on his sixty-eighth birthday – before he had finished the third part – that it seemed to him

to settle the question of Free-will v. Necessity. The will of a man is, according to it, neither wholly free nor wholly unfree. When swayed by the Universal Will (which he mostly must be as a subservient part of it) he is not individually free; but whenever it happens that all the rest of the Great Will is in equilibrium the minute portion called one person's will is free, just as a performer's fingers are free to go on playing the pianoforte of themselves when he talks or thinks of something else and the head does not rule them.

He reiterated this in a letter to Caleb Saleeby of 21 December 1914:

there is a proportion of the total will in each part of the whole, & each part has therefore, in strictness, *some* freedom, which would, in fact, be operative as such whenever the remaining great mass of will in the universe shd happen to be in equilibrium.

Tom was thus a determinist. But he never even tried to ignore, or to evade, people's 'intuition' of being free. *The Dynasts* does not in fact make any philosophical contribution to the much vexed determinism–freewill problem; that would be asking too much. Of the three positions, and the various versions of each of these – determinism, libertarianism and compatibilism – he can only be said to have veered towards the first. The above observation is neither determinist nor compatibilist: it is psychological. All Tom allows is that the Will works through the intellect. But the approach to the Will taken in *The Dynasts* is not in fact philosophical at all, even if it is influenced by the writings of philosophers: it is nearer to the theological, and once again nearest of all to gnostic or cabalistic speculation. For here we have an unknowable Will, a Prime Mover, an Absolute, emanating waves of energy throughout the universe. In some versions of gnosticism this energy deteriorates in quality as it descends. Finally it becomes grossly material, and ends in Nothing, which immediately turns again, by an inexplicable process, into its ineffably refined opposite. Tom's note about the Will's 'limitations, difficulties &c from being only able to work by Law' offers a firm clue as to how he really thought of It.

What does he mean? It seems that he is denying not only 'sentience' to 'God' but also absolute power. For Christianity in general, and in particular for early Christians such as St Augustine, any 'limitation' on the absoluteness of God is the rankest heresy. But in many of the 'heretical' speculations God was alienated from himself and in other ways 'limited' by 'laws' which he (or It) had made. When at the death

669

of Nelson the Pities quote Sophocles, '*who dubbed the Will "the Gods"*' and who accused these Gods of burdening the time '*with mournfulness for us,/And for themselves with shame*', Years responds: '*Blame not!*':

> *In that immense unweeting Mind is shown*
> *One far above forethinking; processive,*
> *Rapt, superconscious; a Clairvoyancy*
> *That knows not what It knows, yet works therewith. –*
> *The cognizance ye mourn, Life's doom to feel,*
> *If I report it meetly, came unmeant,*
> *Emerging with blind gropes from impercipience*
> *By listless sequence – luckless, tragic Chance,*
> *In your more human tongue.*

To which Pities replies, with an awkwardness that, somehow, also turns into its opposite:

> *And hence unneeded*
> *In the economy of Vitality,*
> *Which might have ever kept a sealed cognition*
> *As doth the Will itself.*

To which the Chorus of the Years rejoins:

> *Nay, nay, nay;*
> *Your hasty judgements stay,*
> *Until the topmost cyme*
> *Have crowned the last entablature of Time.*
> *O heap not blame on that in-brooding Will;*
> *O pause, till all things all their days fulfil.*

Whatever It is, this Will is not, as Tom had suggested or conjectured in his note, 'omnipotent', even though It may be 'omniscient'. Certain critics have suggested that the Spirits, or some of them, have the function of helping It to become omnipotently compassionate. But that is a misreading. These Spirits are not more than mental representations, mere commentators; they do not cause the suicide of Villeneuve, who would have performed the deed without intervention; they cause nothing and change nothing, and are each an attitude: ironic, nihilistic, sad and sorry, and so forth. Tom told Clodd on 22 March 1904, after completing the first part, that he had been 'somewhat indifferent' to any 'inconsistencies' concerning them, in any case: '. . . they are not supposed to be more than the best human intelligences of their time in a sort of quint-essential [sic] form. I speak of the "Years". The "Pities" are, of course, merely Humanity, with all its weaknesses.'

When, on the evening of 15 September 1907, sometime before 11.30 at night, Tom completed *The Dynasts*, he seems to have had that notion clearly before him as he wrote, or passed as fit, the final version of its last words:

> *But – a stirring thrills the air*
> *Like to sounds of joyance there*
> *That the rages*
> *Of the ages*
> *Shall be cancelled, and deliverance offered from the darts that were,*
> *Consciousness the Will informing, till It fashion all things fair!*

After the First World War he said at least twice, and probably more often, that he would not now have written that. Tom's respected friend H.W. Nevinson, who had long been alert to his extreme sensitivity, quoted, in his *Last Changes, Last Chances* (1928), a letter to *The Times* written by Professor Albert Cock a day or two after Tom's death:

> In your leading article on Thomas Hardy you 'read into the sublime last chorus of "The Dynasts" some fugitive hope'. It is doubtful whether the poet himself had that fugitive hope. In 1922 I had a conversation with him at Max Gate, and I happened to refer to the very passage quoted by you from the last chorus. I expressed my gratitude to him for the note of deliverance offered there. He shook his head and said, 'I should not write that now.' 'Why not?' I asked in great surprise. Thomas Hardy replied, 'The Treaty of Versailles'.

But a careful reading of the final scene of *The Dynasts* reveals that it was presented, even in 1907, as only a hope. It suggests, too, that, since the fatal Versailles Treaty was man-made, only the changed behaviour of men and women could lead – or could have led – to the fulfilment of such a hope. The inference is inescapable: Tom, like Nevinson and others, saw that the treaty offered a blueprint for further upheaval, and that it opened the way for yet other 'men of destiny', such as Mussolini and, above all, Hitler. This is akin, although by no means identical to, the theological notion of a God (or Will – whatever one likes to call it) who waits to be 'completed' by man, which cannot fulfil its potentialities *until* it is so completed. It is bound to this by its own 'Law'. A paradox is thus set up. To an orthodox Christian this paradox is both preposterous and non-existent. But it is second nature to a cabalist or a gnostic to consider it – and, because that kind of thinking persists even in a world devoted to suppressing it, it haunts all our own humbler speculations. Thus the cabalist Isaac Luria (1532–74) made great play with the notion of *tsimtsum* ('contraction', in Hebrew): God (or the Will, or the Absolute) 'contracted himself' to make way for the 'world', which was just as Tom and other 'pessimists' described it, but was none the less permeated by the faintest traces of a perfume, as is a vial which has been emptied of its precious contents. Luria was concerned, among other things, with accounting for the presence of evil in the world, and with the avoidance of pantheism. Tom would have been interested in this, had he known about it; but all I claim is that in *The Dynasts* we are in this area of speculation, rather than in a purely philosophical one.

When at the beginning of 1915 Caleb Saleeby sent him the English version of the French philosopher Henri Bergson's main work, *Creative Evolution*, Tom was interested and read it right through carefully. He included a draft of his reply in the *Life*. Unfortunately he did not refer to the doctrine of the *élan vital*, which Saleeby had thought akin to his own, but confined himself to expressing his refusal to share Bergson's optimism: 'I would gladly believe them [Bergson's ideas] but . . . he does not adduce any proofs whatever.' Presumably therefore he rejected one of Bergson's key assertions, to the effect that 'the whole universe is a clash and conflict of two opposite motions: life, which climbs upwards, and matter, which falls downwards'. On the other hand, he may not have grasped it fully. It was in fact this idea which gave Bergson's speculations something in common with contemporary gnostic thinking, and with the postulation of 'negentropy', a force, just like the *élan vital* (Shaw's 'life-force' was a vulgarization of this), which was opposed to 'entropy', seen by many as the 'heat-death of the universe' – in other words, that the universe was 'running down', or descending into total disorder. Tom did tell Caleeby, however, that he had always *wanted* to be a Bergsonian: 'But I fear that his philosophy is . . . only our old friend Dualism in a new suit of clothes.' He had always insisted that *The Dynasts* was 'monist', although in that assertion he was getting into matters more technical than he could happily handle. For his hope, although viewed through dark spectacles, rather than the rosy-coloured ones worn by the good Bergson, is a kind of ghostly equivalent of Bergson's *élan vital*. The Will might be an equivalent of Bergson's other, and negative force, matter, which for him was mechanism, flowing downwards. He pays grudging tribute to the *élan vital* when he ends his letter to Saleeby with words that have become famous:

> You must not think me a hard-headed rationalist for all this. Half my time (particularly when I write verse) I 'believe' – in the modern use of the word – not only in the things Bergson does, but in spectres, mysterious voices, intuitions, omens, dreams, haunted places, &c, &c. But then, I do not believe in these in the old sense of belief any more for that; & in arguing against Bergsonism I have of course meant belief in its old sense when I aver myself incredulous.

This, from a poet, was a big admission, for no one was less likely to have suggested that poetry was a useless activity. He was simply erring on the side of the rational, as was his nervous wont. For, if he had been forced to defend poetry as a human activity, he would have had to argue that there *was* value in such beliefs as Bergson's 'in the modern use of the word', and that would have led him, inevitably, into Bergson's irrational and intuitive world. The point is, which do we value more? Is it the philosopher Hardy, writing to Saleeby, or the poet Hardy who believed in the 'unprovable' thing which Bergson (not a philosopher in the Anglo-Saxon sense, but rather a French romantic trained in philosophy, and one who, as it happens, had begun as an adherent of Herbert Spencer) made the subject of his writings?

The truth is that philosophy in the tradition of Hume and Kant was only one of the two poles which generated Tom's work; the other was the wildly romantic and irrational one which he admitted to Saleeby. He loved the precision of Hume; and Hume's ironic expatiations upon the philosophies of Bergson and McTaggart, had they been possible, would have been delightful and instructive.

But if Henri Bergson drew from Tom at least as much appreciation as he could express to Saleeby, then McTaggart drew more, and directly to himself: the latter was infinitely more rigorous. He is so rigorous that he has had to be ignored rather than disposed of. Tom told Cockerell on 16 February 1925 that he had been surprised that more attention had not been paid to McTaggart's death, a sure sign of his importance to him as a thinker. On 23 May 1906 he had informed McTaggart, in connection with *Some Dogmas of Religion*, published that year, that his vague 'philosophical basis' for *The Dynasts* had been 'not far from what you suggest by your negative conclusions'. Again, on 22 August 1908, Tom told him that he was in agreement with his view of time, which was that it did not exist, or not in the form that people generally think of it as existing (McTaggart did criticize the Irish for their bad time-keeping.)

On 10 June 1923, just after the death of Florence Henniker, he wrote: 'Relativity. That things and events always were, are, and will be (*e.g.* Emma, Mother and Father are living still in the past).' That note has at least as much in common with the philosophy of McTaggart as it does with Einstein's theories, which he mentioned to McTaggart in one of his letters. It was not a mere fanciful observation, but rather one that arose from his realization that time was not at all the simple linear concept that most people imagine it to be. McTaggart, it must be remembered, was the philosopher who combined a kind of atheism with a belief in the immortality of the soul; he is the exponent of the thesis that reality consists of a society of minds (and their contents) in close inter-relation.

It is perhaps surprising that books on *The Dynasts* tend to ignore McTaggart's influence upon it, especially in view of what Tom wrote to him. Susan Dean takes Tom's point about belief when writing poetry, and 'belief in its old sense', although her interpretation is more rationalistic than mine. Whereas I see Tom as a religious man over-frustrated (in his prose statements) by his intellectual and rational faculties, and therefore as one whose poetry should be searched for its religious insights, she tends to see him as, or does not wish to represent him as other than, aesthetically aware: using his ghosts and intuitions and the rest 'imaginatively, as part of his conscious interest in the strange and subtle gropings of the mind'. Had she taken account of the influence of McTaggart (whom she does not mention), however, and in particular of his notion of time, she might have been able to see more in Tom than ordinary rationalism.

McTaggart appealed to Tom because he succeeded in applying a brilliantly rigorous (as well as ingenious) methodology to his 'proof' of something which, to the ordinary mind, was totally 'irrational': that time did not exist, and that, even more startlingly, 'it is reasonable to believe, and unreasonable to disbelieve, that all substances are spiritual'. Furthermore, according to his Cambridge friend Goldsworthy Lowes Dickinson, who edited a book on him in 1931, McTaggart (who was much loved by everyone with whom he came into contact) did admit to a 'private' religious 'inspiration': an 'emotion', which he derived from Plato, Spinoza and Hegel, 'resting on the conviction of a harmony between ourselves and the universe at large'. Hardy the poet might well also have laid claim to a 'private' religious inspiration: the world of his poetry. That he did not do so, out of his respect for philosophical scepticism and for his semi-rationalist stance in the world, is neither here nor there. Any conviction against the philosophico-scientific odds, such as atheism or theism or Christianity or 'gnosticism', or a harmony between ourselves and the universe, is at least as 'religious' as it is 'rational'. And it is worth noting that the never less than astonishing McTaggart defended – as Tom did – the Church of England.

But the man whose job it was to write poetry and 'believe' while he was pursuing this activity, which he did not regard as an idle waste of time, is less on the side of rationalism than such rationalists as, say, Tom's friends Clodd and Frederic Harrison. He would never become a positivist, or willingly appear in a directory of rationalists, and told Clodd on 22 March 1904 that he had not thought that 'the *Dynasts* would suit your scientific mind, or shall I say the scientific side of your mind'.

I fully accept Susan Dean's contention, and demonstration, that the subject of *The Dynasts* is the human mind. Tom's only model, in deference to the inevitable subjectivity of such an exercise, could be his own mind. But I agree with her, too, that he achieved what he wanted to achieve: a discovery of much that is common to the workings of all minds. I think, though, that he transcended philosophy and, indeed, mere rationality, which cannot account for so much that passes in the world: the work amounts to more than it set out to demonstrate.

The first reviews were undistinguished. Nor, of course, to do them justice, did even the better-disposed reviewers have the whole work laid out before them. On 29 January 1904 an unsigned piece appeared in the *Times Literary Supplement*; it was by a frivolous theatre critic, Arthur Bingham Walkley, who objected to the unusual form and tried to make fun of the work by suggesting that it should be presented as a puppet-show. Tom knew who had written the review (he made his peace with him, though, and told William Archer in 1904 that, on the only occasion he had met Walkley, he 'rather liked him') and wrote two fierce replies, on 5 February and 19 February. Privately he observed that Walkley's objections were really based on the British Philistine's '*odium theologicum*'. This critic's objections, though, were less likely to have stemmed from theological feelings than from journalistic irritation at Tom's technical boldness and originality: he had put himself into an awkward position by denying the viability of the closet-drama form at all. That meant that plays by Shelley and Byron, not to speak of Fulke Greville (whom Tom did not cite), were also off the orthodox path and to be rejected. The gist of Walkley's criticism was that plays were not to be read. The contest was essentially one between an intelligent but stage-struck newspaper writer floundering out of his depth, and a serious writer – as Max Beerbohm's almost contemporaneous review, with its tacit understanding of the huge task that Tom had set himself, incidentally demonstrates. Tom remained acutely aware of the deficiencies of *The Dynasts*, but also of the fact that he could have gone on tinkering with such a massive work for ever. A letter of 13 March 1904 is important because it contains a plain statement of how he felt about the universe; it was addressed to Henry Newbolt, a man whose critical intelligence was usually ahead of his poetic achievement. Thanking him for his notice in the March number of the *Monthly Review*, Tom said that he was grateful for the right approach he had taken. Other critics had

> mostly contented themselves with picking out bad lines, which any child could do, there being myriads of them. Just as the Original Cause did not (apparently) foresee the pitch of intelligence to which humanity would arrive in the course of the ages, & therefore did not prepare a world adequate to it, so the makers of language did not foresee the uses to which poor poets would wish to put words, & stinted the supply. Your generous remarks make me feel that you have met me halfway: 'Pieced out my imperfections with your thoughts' [this is from the Prologue to *Henry V*] . . .

Max Beerbohm's notice in the 30 January number of the *Saturday Review* was wiser and more generous than Walkley's. He had a bit of fun at Tom's expense, but only after he had pointed out that it was easy 'to ridicule such a work': 'One regrets that the Immanent Will put him to the trouble of writing it. "Wot's the good of anythink? Wy, nothink" was the refrain of a popular coster-song some years ago, and Mr Hardy has set it ringing in our ears again.' But soon, he conceded, this impression passes: 'And, even as in the stage-directions of *The Dynasts* we see specks becoming mountain-tops, so do we begin to realize that we have been reading a really great book. An imperfect book, as I have said – inevitably imperfect.' He went on to claim that the work would have been better in prose, but

> when every reservation has been made, *The Dynasts* is still a great book. It is absolutely new in that it is the first modern work of dramatic fiction in which freewill is denied to the characters . . . Mr Hardy's puppets are infinitesimal – mere 'electrons', shifted hither and thither, for no reason, by some impalpable agency. Yet they are exciting. Free-will is not necessary to human interest. Belief in it is, however, necessary to human life. Cries Mr Hardy's Spirit of the Pities
>
> > This tale of Will
> > And Life's impulsion by Incognizance
> > I cannot take.

Nor can I. But I can take and treasure, with all gratitude, the book in which that tale is told so finely.

Tom met Beerbohm, with Yeats and others, at Gosse's house early in the following May, and one might guess that he was far from annoyed, for this review must have been one of the few which encouraged him to continue even in the face of the uncritical adulation of such as Gosse, or the wilful uncomprehendingness of Walkley. He had not changed his mind about the literary situation, which he had described to Arthur Symons on 19 May 1902, just before getting down to serious work. He seems to have been unusually fond of Symons, whose now neglected poems he appreciated. He told him then that his 'growing sense that there is nobody to address, no public that knows', was taking away his 'zest for production. The few who do know,' he added, 'are submerged in a mass of imbecilities.' None the less, he now proposed to go on writing for those who did 'know'. And by the time that the third part of *The Dynasts* appeared, in 1908, he had won almost all the critics round: the autodidactic bumpkin had silenced them!

31

Deceit

Tom 'did not make many private memoranda' on the reviews of *The Dynasts*. One he did make, and recorded, noted that he had 'thrown back [his] chance of acceptance in poetry by many years'. The Walkleys of this world, he thought, were really saying: 'This is not the view of life that we people who thrive on conventions can permit to be painted.' Despite Millgate's defence of Walkley as an 'acute' critic who scored a critical victory over a 'grandiose' Hardy, this was a fair appraisal. Had he 'constructed a world of fairies', he thought, he would have fared better with the reviewers, but 'having chosen a scheme which may or may not be a valid one, but is presumably much nearer reality than the fancy of a world ordered by fairies would be, they straightway lift their brows'.

He felt depressed as he sent off to Clodd a letter of 22 March – the same one in which he had gently pointed out that he recognized that *The Dynasts* was not really quite 'rationalistic' enough for its recipient's taste. Many had died, including Horace Moule's eldest brother, the antiquary H.J. Moule, 'an old friend,' he told Clodd, 'of 47 years standing . . . whose opinions differed almost entirely from my own on most subjects' and yet who was 'good and sincere' despite having 'old-fashioned views of the Evangelical school'. Leslie Stephen, too, had died; Meredith had been seriously ill. 'They are thinning out ahead of us.' Within a few days, on Sunday, 3 April 1904, the redoubtable Jemima also died. She never lost her faculties, and had, Tom told Arthur Moule on 20 March that year, 'told me, as well as she could in her feeble voice, of her first sight of your father (about the year 1830 . . .) . . . "a fine, noble-looking young man" . . .' She had sent up flowers from Bockhampton to the funeral. But, he added, he did not expect her to get well. His mind had been, he explained in the *Life*, 'drawn away from the perils of attempting to express his age in poetry by a noticeable change in his mother's state of health'.

She had been a woman with an extraordinary store of local memories, reaching back to the days when the ancient ballads were everywhere heard . . . and her good taste in literature was expressed by the books she selected for her children in circumstances in which opportunities for selection were not numerous. The portraits of her which appeared in the *Sphere*, the *Gentlewoman*, the *Book Monthly*, and other papers – the best being a painting by her daughter Mary – show a face of dignity and judgement.

The remark about Jemima's circumstances give the lie to much-canvassed notions that Tom was ashamed of his origins. When his local detractors spread a rumour of his 'meanness' in 'forcing her' to stay at Bockhampton, and it appeared in the *Daily Chronicle*, he was able to arrange a denial. It had, of course, been by her own wish.

How Emma felt about Jemima's death is impossible to say. The old lady had muttered more and more about her dislike as she got older, and probably bored everyone who was forced to listen; but the rift between Kate and Emma had undoubtedly widened. Jemima's feelings were well known, and it seems that Emma did not attend her funeral – she is not reported in the local newspapers as having done so. Indeed, it might have seemed a little odd if she had. Probably she sent out a diplomatic message to the effect that she was ill. She had kept her own specific opinions of Jemima, if not of the old lady's influence on Tom, strictly to herself; but Jemima had hardly been discreet. It is likely that Emma felt ashamed of her feelings of relief, and prayed. There is no reason to presume that she was stupid, and it has seldom been pointed out that she had an entirely unfrivolous inner, and for her Christian, life which may have been less confused and rambling than her writings and actions occasionally were.

'After the Last Breath' is a characteristic Hardyan elegy for Jemima, ending

> We see by littles now the deft achievement
> Whereby she has escaped the Wrongers all,
> In view of which our momentary bereavement
> Outshapes but small.

No doubt he wrote the associated poem 'In Childbed' at about the same time – it appears immediately after it in *Time's Laughingstocks*. A mother tells her daughter, who is in childbed, that her pride in her

'fond exploit but shapes for tears
New thoroughfares in sad humanity.

'Yet as you dream, so dreamt I
When Life stretched forth its morning ray to me;
Other views for by and by!' . . .
Such strange things did mother say to me.

It seemed astonishing to Tom's contemporaries that, successful and famous as he now was, he could take so grim a view, and think of himself and others as doomed to inevitable pain. But, as he was to insist several times to Florence Dugdale, and to cause her to reiterate in her journalism about him, this did not mean that he was himself always full of gloom. Nor was he gloomy when he was with people he liked, although we know that he was, for at least half his time 'at home', wrapped up in contemplation. Besides, what should we make of a poet who changed his basic view of life because he became successful and financially secure? The financial security meant less to him that it might have done – it came just too late for him ever to get used to it, or really to believe in it. His habit of mind remained that of the penurious writer who had desperately to try to repeat the success of *Far From the Madding Crowd*. He saw it all dissolving away in front of his eyes, perhaps reduced or destroyed by some terrible act of war: the figure in the van with its arm raised. Yet he was generous to his family in spite of it – to Lilian, to Gordon, to their father Walter, to his widow, and to his brother and sisters – and only, possibly, not terribly generous to Emma. But she never complained. With Florence it was different, because she had a legacy, although not a large one. However, Tom was parsimonious by habit, and it has not been sensible of critics to labour the point too much. There are worse, and more interesting, faults. Extravagance is not a key to 'greatness of character', and parsimony of itself could not rob a character of greatness. No man or woman thought of as 'great', whether as writer or as person, ever seemed 'great' to those who immediately surrounded them. Great people do not have little habits, do not brush their teeth or go to the bathroom or have fantasies or complain of colds, earache or neuralgia. 'Greatness of character' does not exist until long after death has occurred, and posterity has had the chance to judge the person when such little accidentals have dropped away. Now, for some of us, Tom seems like his own paternal grandmother, to whom, on 20 May 1902, he wrote 'One We Knew':

DECEIT

She told how they used to form for the country dances –
   'The Triumph', 'The New-rigged Ship' –
To the light of the guttering wax in the panelled manses,
   And in cots to the blink of a dip.

She spoke of the wild 'pousetting' and 'allemanding'
   On carpet, on oak, and on sod;
And the two long rows of ladies and gentlemen standing,
   And the figures the couples trod.

She showed us the spot where the maypole was yearly planted,
   And where the bandsmen stood
While breeched and kerchiefed partners whirled, and panted
   To choose each other for good.

She told of that far-back day when they learnt astounded
   Of the death of the King of France:
Of the Terror; and then of Bonaparte's unbounded
   Ambition and arrogance.

Of how his threats woke warlike preparations
   Along the southern strand,
And how each night brought tremors and trepidations
   Lest morning should see him land.

She said she had often heard the gibbet creaking
   As it swayed in the lightning flash,
Had caught from the neighbouring town a small child's shrieking
   At the cart-tail under the lash . . .

With cap-framed face and long gaze into the embers –
   We seated around her knees –
She would dwell on such dead themes, not as one who remembers,
   But rather as one who sees.

She seemed one left behind of a band gone distant
   So far that no tongue could hail:
Past things retold were to her as things existent,
   Things present but as a tale.

As a girl of eighteen in 1800, Mary Head had known poverty and hardship as an orphan in Fawley, of which 'her memories were so

681

poignant that she never cared to return to the place'. Must we know how often she washed, or counted whatever pennies she had, or annoyed her husband, Tom's grandfather, in order to appreciate her grandson's tribute to her? Yet Tom could write that sort of poem, could make us feel for others, in such simple terms, in a peculiarly poignant manner. It is poignant because he indulges in no false or sentimental praise: rather, he tells us exactly how people were, and in so telling us implies the warmth they generated. We are entitled to feel grateful towards him, as a man, for preserving these qualities, for defying convention, for not writing poetry that was supposed to attract attention to himself rather than to what it said. Is this more important than being mean with tips to the man who bagged his hair after he had cut it off?

He was full of regrets, most of which he kept to himself. He had known for some time that his mother was close to her end, and was thus thinking of time and some of its crueller effects, perhaps of his mother's opposition to his marriage thirty years earlier, of her obstinate and continued opposition to Emma thereafter, and of much else pertinent to his life. He would have been asking himself if Jemima had been 'right'; whose 'fault' was it in any case? We do not have many details of how this problem was handled by Tom and Emma; but we know that it was a problem. They were not simple questions, and he could not supply simple or straightforward answers. So he wrote (or completed an old draft of) a longish narrative poem, 'The Revisitation', which appeared in the *Fortnightly* – with an earlier title, 'Time's Laughingstocks: A Summer Romance' – in the following August, and which opens the collection *Time's Laughingstocks* of 1909. It appears to have no connection with the happenings in his own life. He offered it to the *Nineteenth Century* (which did not publish it) just six days before his mother died.

The poem is ambitious, and, as Dennis Taylor writes, 'ungainly' – but ungainly in that successful manner which Tom was beginning to make his own. Ezra Pound, always far more generous to Tom than Eliot, acknowledged that passages in it looked forward to 'the great poems of 1912–13'. It is, in part, one of the earlier 'great poems', although there are rhythmical faults (some of the longer lines simply do not work), owing to his experimentation, and the whole is not fully resolved.

The setting is in the country he knew best: Dorchester and its environs. A 'war-worn' soldier quartered by chance at the barracks in Dorchester looks twenty years back to an old romance:

DECEIT

　　As I lay awake at night-time
In an ancient country barrack known to ancient cannoneers,
And recalled the hopes that heralded each seeming brave and bright
　　　time
　　Of my primal purple years.

Twenty years earlier the soldier had had a love affair with a farmer's
daughter, Agnette. Now he rises and takes a long-remembered route
to their old trysting-place, a sarsen stone. There Agnette materializes,
not as a ghost, but as a real woman walking the land she has by now
inherited from her father. Together they recapture the past. Then, in
the morning, the soldier awakes by Agnette's side, and sees that

　　Time's transforming chisel
Had been tooling night and day for twenty years, and tooled too
　　　well,
In its rendering of crease where curve was, where was raven,
　　　grizzle –
　　Pits, where peonies once did dwell.

Agnette tells him that, indeed, she is 'old':

　　'Yes: that movement was a warning
Of the worth of man's devotion! – Yes, Sir, I am *old*,' said she,
'And the thing which should increase love turns it quickly into
　　　scorning –
　　And your new-won heart from me!'

He leaves, 'like to one who had watched a crime'. The poem ends:

　　Did I not return, then, ever? –
Did we meet again? – mend all? – Alas, what greyhead perseveres! –
Soon I got the Route elsewither. – Since that hour I have seen
　　　her never:
　　Love is lame at fifty years.

　　The chief fault of the poem, apart from its occasional rhythmical
failures, is that, at thirty-five stanzas, it is too long. Tom should
have been more economical. Taylor thinks it was written partly

for self-indulgent and sentimental reasons, that there is 'too much grotesque plotting' in it, and that 'there are too many reveries'. The last stricture is right; the first two are more dubious. 'The Revisitation' can hardly be regarded as 'sentimental' in any sense, although one of its sub-themes might be said to be the transitory sentimentality which leads older men to imagine that they can revivify old romances; it may be excessive, but not sentimentally so. It has been suggested that it is a fantasy about Tryphena Sparks, but, if it is about anybody, then it is much more obviously about its author's situation with Emma: a relentlessly self-critical and honest description, disguised or dramatized into a narrative, of an unpleasant fact of culture. Tom was well aware that women entertained desires for men younger than themselves, but that contemporary culture discouraged them to the point that it would not acknowledge them. When Florence Dugdale recited the final line to him he protested that it was 'not true'; but she was almost forty years his junior, still enticing to him – and he had not been thinking of her, or anyone of her age, when he wrote the line. Agnette's bitter words to her wandering soldier are unanswerable. Tom had been right to assume that he could make such discomforting statements in the form of poetry, and narrative poetry at that. It was simply not in his nature to turn a blind eye to his desires, or to repress his knowledge of them. Yet he was now looking for a younger woman, and soon, within a year, he would meet one. Millgate speaks of 'the reticences of a lifetime' as inhibiting him from fulfilling these desires; but he misreads his subject – there is no evidence that Tom was ever sexually reticent.

Millgate also claims that Jemima's death led to, not a breach between Tom and Emma, but, on the contrary, a greater degree of 'kindliness' and tolerance between them. In this I am sure that he is right. There is certainly much evidence, which he sensitively cites, of their shared pleasure in their cats. At one point a visitor noticed – he could hardly have failed to do so – that boards were laid between pieces of furniture, so that these cats could move more easily between them. Kitsea, a white cat, was (or became) Tom's 'study cat', but mixed with the others on occasion. Others, of various eras, were called Peachblossom, Snowdove, Marco (or Marky, short for 'the Marquise', an 'aloof and perverse' cat, much loved for her superiority) and Comfy. Although by 1908 there were only three of them, as Tom jokingly told his French translator Madeleine Rolland (sister of Romain Rolland), they were 'very exacting' and 'too much indulged'. These cats had kittens, and during the first weeks of the latter's lives Tom had to go around in stockinged feet in case he should tread on them. This pleasure in cats was perhaps the most precious of Tom and Emma's communications – and it was important. When Snowdove met his death on the railway track in October 1904, a bad year for deaths, Tom wrote one of the most heart-rending elegies for an animal ever written, 'Last Words to a Dumb Friend'. Here he displayed no sentimentality whatever, and, indeed, made the avoidance of it a part of his theme. Yet the poem is unashamed in its use of clichés which would have disfigured it in the hands of anyone else. Readers would perhaps call it a minor poem because it is 'only about a cat', and cats are less 'important' than people; yet it is so perfectly about a cat and our common ways of regarding cats that one wonders whether it really is so minor. Its basis is that it so exactly records the immediate response to the death of an innocent and pleasing creature:

> Pet was never mourned as you,
> Purrer of the spotless hue,
> Plumy tail, and wistful gaze
> While you humoured our queer ways,
> Or outshrilled your morning call
> Up the stairs and through the hall –
> Foot suspended in its fall –
> While, expectant, you would stand
> Arched, to meet the stroking hand;
> Till your way you chose to wend
> Yonder, to your tragic end.

> Never another pet for me!
> Let your place all vacant be;
> Better blankness day by day
> Than companion torn away.
> Better bid his memory fade,
> Better blot each mark he made,
> Selfishly escape distress
> By contrived forgetfulness,
> Than preserve his prints to make
> Every morn and eve an ache.

> From the chair whereon he sat
> Sweep his fur, nor wince thereat;
> Rake his little pathways out
> Mid the bushes roundabout;

Smooth away his talons' mark
From the claw-torn pine-tree bark,
Where he climbed as dusk embrowned,
Waiting us who loitered round.

Strange it is this speechless thing,
Subject to our mastering,
Subject for his life and food
To our gift, and time, and mood;
Timid pensioner of us Powers,
His existence ruled by ours,
Should – by crossing at a breath
Into safe and shielded death,
By the merely taking hence
Of his insignificance –
Loom as largened to the sense,
Shape as part, above man's will,
Of the Imperturbable.

As a prisoner, flight debarred,
Exercising in a yard,
Still retain I, troubled, shaken,
Mean estate, by him forsaken;
And this home, which scarcely took
Impress from his little look,
By his faring to the Dim
Grows all eloquent of him.

Housemate, I can think you still
Bounding to the window-sill,
Over which I vaguely see
Your small mound beneath the tree,
Showing in the autumn shade
That you moulder where you played.

Not long before that, on 2 March, he had written to a clergyman who had written to him concerning 'sport', that he had not been able to say which is 'qualitatively, the most cruel'. He just thought that sports which involved witnessing the sufferings and deaths of weaker creatures provided 'one of the many convincing proofs that we have not yet emerged from barbarism'. And, he added, with Swiftian mirth:

In the present state of affairs there would appear to be no reason why the children, say, of overcrowded families should not be used for sporting purposes. There would be no difference in principle: moreover these children would often escape lives intrinsically less happy than those of wild birds & animals.

'Last Words to a Dumb Friend' easily persuades us that Tom was no mere injustice-collector. Confronted with the painful death of his cat, the injustice-collector tends to blame someone for its death: he seeks revenge in his grief, and inveighs against injustice. Tom sees such a death as it is, which is why the poem is so exact and perfect. There is thus no attack upon the demons who terrify and torment animals for their casual pleasure. Nor has the poem gone unnoticed by readers. There is really nothing that a critic can say about it, beyond asking a challenger of its importance to point out where it is sentimental, or psychologically inexact. It may be that a critic could accuse (say) 'Purrer of the spotless hue' of being a suburban cliché, typical to a suburban versifier – but perhaps that is exactly why it works so well and so movingly.

To what extent was this cat-haunted comparative peace between Tom and Emma disturbed by the advent of Florence Dugdale? Just when did Emma learn of Florence's existence, and of her husband's liaison with her? Apart from one possible but not proven allusion to her – the famous and entirely humorous outburst of May 1908 to Rebekah Owen, to the effect that 'My Eminent partner will have a softening of brain if he goes on as he does & the rest of the world does' – she never made any complaint on this score, and, when in 1910 she came to employ Florence at Max Gate as secretary-companion, she was consistently nice to her. Emma often flew and mocked at Tom in her last years, but Florence, even in the bitterest of her misrecollections, could not charge her with rudeness to herself.

It is not even certain when Tom first met Florence Dugdale: she gave so many versions of the event, even to her own sisters, that it is impossible to know for sure. One of her stories (told after Mrs Henniker's death in 1923) was that she had known Florence Henniker in 1904, and called upon Tom and Emma in her company in 1905. But she did not in fact get to know Mrs Henniker until much later, at the end of 1910, well after the beginning of her intimacy with Tom, which began to develop in 1906 and deepened throughout the succeeding years. All her own stories put the meeting early rather than late, for an obvious reason: in 1910 she was staying, as Emma's friend, companion and helper, at Max Gate for long periods, and during that time she was Tom's lover (whether or not his mistress) and the recipient of certain published love poems. She knew very well that, if it could be shown that she had known Tom intimately for at least four years before 1910, had gone on numerous trips with him, had entertained him at a London flat borrowed from a friend, and had spent many periods with him as Clodd's guest at Aldeburgh, then she could be exposed as a deceitful and treacherous woman. She lied because she had something to hide, and she lied unskilfully and carelessly. As time went on, and in 1912 she was accused of having been the mistress of a distinguished man who had bequeathed a large sum of money to her, her versions of the meeting with Emma doubtless went further and further backwards in time. She ended with a tale in which she approached Emma Hardy at her (and Florence's) London literary club, the Lyceum, and asked her if she might send flowers to her husband on his birthday. That was a foolish (and certainly untrue) story, even though she did once send flowers to him. But it was important to her to establish, if possible, that she had met Emma first. For, as the more or less impoverished daughter of an Enfield headmaster who had made her living as a 'companion' as well as by teaching and journalism, she was vulnerable to the malicious criticism of those who regarded themselves as her superiors, and to poisonous London literary gossip.

Let us go forward to an incident early in the period between January 1928 and her lonely and painful death from cancer of the anus in October 1937. Florence was then the most distinguished literary widow in the world, a woman in declining health, but still regarded as her husband's 'biographer' and still talking to a few scholars, mostly Americans, about certain cloudy events in his life. Thus we may understand what she felt herself to be up against, and what her chief fears may have been.

In 1930 Hardy was high in popular estimation. In that year W. Somerset Maugham, who had barely met him or either of his wives, published his genial comic novel *Cakes and Ale*. It contained a wickedly accurate portrait of the novelist Hugh Walpole, whom Maugham did know very well. Tom himself had met him at Gosse's house just before the outbreak of the First World War. Maugham did not later deny that he had mercilessly satirized Walpole (who remained devastated by the all too accurate caricature for the rest of his life). The famous novelist Edward ('Ted') Driffield, around whose character and two marriages the comedy is built up, is based in part on the figure that Tom cut as a celebrated old author to the public ('humble origins', international fame, writer of a 'scandalous novel', second marriage to his 'typist'). But it is not based very much more on Tom the man than it is on H.G. Wells (who, like Driffield in the novel, was a known womanizer) or on Joseph Conrad (who, again like Driffield, was an ex-seaman). Maugham later told a friend that he had got certain specific ideas for a treatment of the British great old man of letters syndrome from the public fuss over Tom's death; and we know that he picked up a few more details from Stephen Tennant, the lover of Siegfried Sassoon who had been a frequent visitor to Max Gate. There is no reason to doubt the essential truth of what Maugham himself later wrote (except in the matter of memory of the name, possibly omitted to spare the children of the man he had known in his childhood):

> In point of fact I founded Edward Driffield on an obscure writer who settled with his wife and children in the small town of Whitstable . . . I do not remember his name. I don't think that he ever amounted to anything and he must be long since dead. He was the first author I ever met . . . It was a shock to me when one day he vanished from the town leaving his debts unpaid.

Cakes and Ale contains many caricatures of writers and critics, but the only actual character portraits in it are of Walpole and of Maugham's cheerfully promiscuous old girlfriend Sue Jones – daughter of Tom's acquaintance the playwright Henry Arthur Jones – upon whom he gratefully based Rosie Driffield, the great writer Driffield's first wife. Rosie has no relationship whatever to Emma Hardy. But Maugham, himself ambisexual, carefully omitted from *Cakes and Ale* any hints of Walpole's homosexuality. Just after the novel appeared, Walpole, remonstrating to an amused Virginia Woolf and others about Maugham's calumny, said he knew very well that Maugham had done things for which he might have been 'jugged' (indeed, they both might have been imprisoned for what they had 'done' in those intolerant days); but he had no reason to complain on that particular score. The two had moved through the same homosexual underworld, but Maugham had not even hinted at its existence.

The prosody of the name Jasper Griffin exactly echoes that of the name Stephen Phillips, but, apart from the fact that the unfortunate Phillips 'tippled' and was suddenly taken up as a poet (1898) and then just as abruptly dropped (1906), there is no further resemblance. The Colvins,

Gosse and other literary characters all too capable of pretentiousness are also caricatured: what Maugham was satirizing was the hollowness of the London literary scene. Gosse, alas, although certain his personal qualities put him into a different category, was, as a public figure, eminently deserving of satire. Unlike Walpole, though, he had been dead for two years. Apart from his wish to pay tribute to Sue Jones, Maugham wanted to target public attitudes and the tendency amongst men like Walpole and Gosse to pander to them (Gosse actually left a 'tribute' to Tom on a gramophone record: a dreadful affair rightly never played).

Alroy Kear (Walpole) agrees to write an 'official' life of the dead Driffield at the invitation of his not very bright second wife, Amy. Unfortunately from Florence's point of view, Maugham had picked up a few personal details about her from Tennant and from newspaper reports; and, although he not been intent upon hurting her, and knew little about her personal life or characteristics, he mortified her to a greater and more long-lasting extent than he had devastated Walpole, who after all then had his health, his readers and his enormous royalties. Florence did indeed somewhat resemble the stock figure of 'the great author's wife'. She was thus certain that Amy Driffield really was supposed to be her to the very life. It was understandable that she should have felt that Maugham had acquired even more information about her than he actually had. Perhaps he or someone else would write yet another novel about her famous dead husband, this time accusing his second wife of treachery to his first! That would have been all too true, and she knew it. She felt that she had become the laughing-stock of the literary world. Naturally, she wildly protested to all her own friends and advisors. Florence told Sassoon (who, like the literary executor Sydney Cockerell, was already rapidly getting fed up with her) that the whole affair had made her want to shake her 'fists against the sky, or shriek aloud in rage'. That was how she had often felt within herself; in this case she had good reason. It was not only unfair: it had not been intended. Maugham had no reason to know that the Amy Driffield, the minor figurehead he had created – hardly even a substantial character in the novel – fitted the real Florence quite so well.

So she cannot be blamed for putting up one of her friends to write a novel called *Gin and Bitters*, which was published by Farrar Straus in America in March 1931. Signed 'A. Riposte', it was by Evelyn May Mordaunt (c. 1877–1942), known professionally as 'Elinor Mordaunt'. She was a woman who felt perpetually ill used by life, and who had written novels, some of them hopefully imitative of Hardy, with such titles as *While There's Life*. Her feeble *roman-à-clef*, which contained an attempted portrait of Maugham as 'Leverson Hurle', was issued in England by Martin Secker in October 1931 as *Full Circle* (an echo of the title of Maugham's successful play *The Circle*). Maugham took out an injunction against it on the advice of his publisher, Charles Evans of Heinemann, and of his legal brother Frederick, and it was withdrawn without opposition. Hugh Walpole – called 'Polehue' in the novel – fearful that he would be taken as the author of so poor and spiteful a work, supported Maugham in this action, describing *Gin and Bitters* as 'nauseating' and 'a foul attack'. It was wretched beyond words.

It is likely that Florence read things into *Cakes and Ale* that were not even there, for she did have one very embarrassing secret. She had been a party, however unwilling, to deceiving Emma; not only that, but she had managed to deceive her future husband, as well, by becoming confused and pouring out indiscretions about him, as well as about Emma, to Clodd. When during the First World War Clodd announced that he was working on his memoirs, both she and Tom became alarmed. But she was most particularly worried: would he quote from her private letters to him, about which even Tom did not know? She was a genuinely dutiful woman, and her difficulties, for one so timid and essentially unsophisticated, had been immense. It is easily understandable. But would the London literary world, in which she did not feel easy, have understood? She seems to have wanted to marry both Siegfried Sassoon and Sir James Barrie, and thus to have alienated them both. Our hearts go out to her in her constitutional unhappiness and loneliness; but we need not, for all that, find her an attractive character. Seen over a day, she could make herself delightfully helpful. Seen over longer periods of time, she could become cloying and treacherous. She did not really quite understand sincerity, and did not feel herself capable of it in her poor circumstances, which she always bitterly resented.

Florence Emily Dugdale was born on 12 January 1879, and was thus thirty-nine years younger than Tom. Named after Florence Nightingale, she was the second of five daughters of a schoolmaster who, since his twenty-second year, had been headmaster of St Andrew's School for Boys in Enfield, Middlesex. He was a trenchant man, insensitive, facetious (before caning a boy he would say, in a threatening voice, 'I am not the father-in-law of Sir Thomas Hardy for nothing'), strongly Christian in principle, and therefore a keen delight to his superiors.

His wife, an ex-governess after whom Florence took, was sometimes almost an invalid, but did not die young; she was – as perhaps any but a woman of real spirit would have been under the semi-benign rule of the staunch Tory Edward Dugdale, founder of the Enfield Independent Building Society – somewhat of a cipher, taking what little colour she had from her surroundings. But she was kind. Florence resembled her in this, but had, too, a quietly independent streak, which enabled her to wrench herself free of the orthodox Christianity of her father. That was entirely by her own decision: she could not see any truth in the gospel story; it was too consolatory for her, in any case. She had seen some fearsome parsons in the Enfield educational establishment, and she came to dislike clergymen. All this made her, for Tom, refreshingly different. She was none the less conventional, not at all the emancipated woman whom he had hoped and failed to find in Florence Henniker. He never did find such a woman for himself – except Emma, in 1870. And that was what he was looking for throughout the rest of his life.

Florence's health was almost spectacularly poor, and seriously jeopardized her chances of a career. Like her mother, she suffered from a variety of ailments; sometimes she could not teach because she lost her voice; worst of all, she suffered from what were then described as 'mental depressions'. Tom never loved her as he had loved Emma, but he was deeply attracted to her gentleness, her modest love of literature and her air of quiet hopelessness. She probably did not get much affection from her father – the manner of his affection was authoritarian; he related everything, in a commonplace way, to the sound practice of what he believed to be Christian doctrine. Her mother may have been, in private, too much of a quiet 'martyr' to give her much affection, either. She was, after all, one of five, and not even the eldest. But she did not have a bad childhood, and her parents were not bad people. Bustle, loudness, passion, her brisk father: all these frightened her. She most enjoyed ministering, and ministering charmingly and affectionately, to those for whom she could genuinely feel sorry. Thus it was that she first conceived her feelings for the great author Thomas Hardy, whose poetry was so unhappy and who had had so many *sorrows*. When for a while she came close to his wife, Emma, she felt, as she told Clodd, 'so *intensely*' (her italics) sorry for her – indeed, sorry for them both: Tom, she told him, had been a trifle unjust to Emma, although she did not specify exactly how. Alas, Tom would have told her that Emma 'did not understand' him: in certain respects it was perfectly true. But did she, Florence, understand him any better? The answer is that she did not – she did not understand him at all. All she knew was that he was a 'great man' who must be protected and consoled.

So Florence drifted in and out of relationships, and even got herself into trouble when a man for whom she had felt intensely *sorry*, and whose mistress she may have been on a few occasions (or perhaps she just 'relieved' him: she thought of herself as lacking in sexual feeling), left her in 1912 the then considerable sum of £2,000 – say £50,000 or even more in today's money. Left alone, she would feel systematically sorry for herself; as Mrs Hardy she would occasionally go into the kitchen at Max Gate and 'have a good cry'. She could well tolerate animals, and it was she who introduced the legendary dog Wessex into Max Gate. At first the old man objected to this intrusion. An eavesdropping maid reported that Tom told Florence there were two things she had introduced into his house which he did not like: one was Wessex and the other was the noisy child of a cook, Mrs Stanley, an unpleasant woman brought from Enfield.

From her early years Florence Dugdale was determined to be a writer; but she studied to become a teacher. Like Tom's sisters, and like Tryphena Sparks, she was at first a pupil teacher. But when she gained admission to a training college she was refused: her constant throat infections marked her as unsuitable. She carried on, choosing to obtain her qualification through an Acting Teacher's Certificate, a hard grind which required attendance at a day training college as well as teaching duties. These latter she performed at her father's own school. But she was twenty-seven before she gained her certificate – and her health was so bad that she soon had to give up the profession, owing, it seems, to over-frequent absences. There is no question of her having been a hypochondriac or a malingerer: she really suffered from her throat throughout her life, and was a frail woman who easily became exhausted. She hated teaching, often describing it as drudgery, and may well have had her life made a misery by an inability to keep her rough little male charges in good order. However, Gittings, who with his wife Jo Manton wrote a short and often highly speculative biography of her, *The Second Mrs Hardy* (1979), did find, from some former pupils or those who had known them, evidence that some of them had liked her as a teacher, and that she was good at her job if given the chance. She was lacking in humour, and understood it only through observing its workings in other people, whom she would then sometimes imitate in that respect.

Alfred Hyatt is not in the *Cambridge Bibliography of English Literature*;

but there is no reason why he should be excluded. His anthologies are as good as, and sometimes better than, the work of many of the minor critics who happen to be included. It was through this unfortunate and kindly Enfield journalist that Florence became interested in, perhaps even adoring of, Thomas Hardy. On the few occasions when the adoring younger woman has actually married the great elderly author of her dreams, a feeling of sorrow for his plight is usually present. Alas, Florence was not to make Tom particularly happy after his marriage to her; but she did give him solace during part of the six years up to Emma's death; and she did, too, see him through his old age without too much inefficiency. But she was not the kind of woman to whom poets write poems, and there are surprisingly few to or about her. 'After the Visit' is the most poignant: it first appeared in the *Spectator* on 15 August 1910 – but, of course, without the dedication to 'FED'. Presumably Emma Hardy never saw the *Spectator* – and, hardly presumably, Florence much desired to see a printed poem by Tom about her – she rushed it to Clodd before it had even appeared. She was never happy at Max Gate, before or after her marriage. Tom had once valued her 'mute ministrations' to him, and this would have especially pleased her: it was what she did best.

But the first person for whom Florence could really feel sorry, and thus love in her way of loving, was Alfred Hyatt, and, as she told Rebekah Owen in a moment of truthfulness and perhaps the sort of despair to which she was so often driven, she always thought of him as the only man she had ever really loved. But she put it in reverse: 'the only person who ever loved me' (this was in December 1914, just eleven months into her marriage with the now seventy-four-year-old Tom); she repeated the sentence, demonstrating that she had it self-pityingly by heart, in a letter to Lady Hoare (six years later). She added that she would gladly have died for Hyatt. There is no reason to doubt it. They would indeed have made a happy couple dying for each other: both undemanding, humble, in love with their idea of literature, and not wholly untalented. But it could not be. Hyatt, although only ten years older than Florence, was already an invalid: in addition to an appalling stammer, which made him seem a feeble personality, he had contracted tuberculosis and was thus marked out for an early death. He led a life of quiet courage, publishing his own books, and was worthy of Florence's lifelong feelings about him. Gittings' and Manton's appreciation of his sad life, and of his literary taste, is sensitive and appropriate. He was a poet who dressed up in a cloak and broad-brimmed hat in imitation of Tennyson, and there can be little doubt that he fell in love with Florence – whom he had known since she was a girl – when, around the turn of the century, she started to write on her own account. It is usually assumed, wrongly, that it was Tom who introduced Florence Dugdale into the literary world. But it was Hyatt who helped Florence, the only Dugdale ever to show a serious interest in literature, to get her work published first in local newspapers. The happiest times in her life were undoubtedly those spent discussing poetry and prose, and learning about it, with and from Hyatt.

Hyatt knew some influential people by correspondence, and, although Florence was never a stickler for hard work, she was good at asking for favours. She was never a 'fine critic', as Tom so extravagantly called her; but she owed her first appreciation of poetry to Hyatt. All her own literary work – journalism, stories and verses for children, school readers, a few tales for adults (two of them substantially by Tom) – was resolutely minor but never much less than competent.

Florence may have helped Hyatt, in 1905, with his 1906 selection, *The Pocket Thomas Hardy*; according to the busybody Carl Weber, always a dubious source, she said that this was her introduction to Tom. This may be true, since it was in 1905 that she first made a beeline for the poet. That he, on his part, showed the first signs of a more than passing interest we know for sure.

Florence had always wanted to be a 'writer', and, as the first decade of the century passed by, could feel that she was one. Gittings believed that she was 'Angela' of Clement Shorter's *Sphere*, but there is no evidence of this, although she may have contributed a few pieces to the 'Angela' column – a general interest affair which was almost certainly composite in any case. But she did write short book reviews – summaries, really – for the *Sphere*, the *Mail* and some other papers. She was also on the staff of the *Standard* for some months in 1910.

She complained of the life that journalism caused her to lead; but then she complained about everything except what she had once had, but could never have again, including her marriage to Tom. 'Her' chief publications, apart from the *Life* which bore her name, were two stories, each of which appeared in the *Cornhill* (in 1907 and 1911); each bears heavy traces of Tom's own hand. Gittings feels that this was achieved at a high cost to 'personal integrity', presumably to Florence's for pretending to be sole author and to Tom's for ghosting it. I do not think we need be so harsh unless we are actually setting out, with forensic determination, to collect evidence against them. But we are not in a court of law. Tom wanted – and was occasionally 'having', as he liked to say – Florence; the glow of being a writer for the *Cornhill* delighted and encouraged her; and they could both plead that it was 'really' by her. Tom, a strict mentor, probably made sure that she attended to the stories as fully as she was capable. What harm was done?

It is not possible to trace the exact details of Florence's life after she left teaching in 1908. She got what scrappy work as a journalist Tom (and probably Hyatt, too) could obtain for her by way of introductions to men like Shorter, she wrote her little books, she lived at home in Enfield for much of the time. She was employed by the *Standard*. But she may also have gone off as temporary companion, perhaps to literary people if she could find them, of whom we have never heard. If the post, or unofficial arrangement as it usually seems to have been, involved living in or near London, then this meant bed and board, getting away from Enfield and her guilt-inducing father's presence, and the opportunity to attend to at least some journalism there. She was a fairly good manager of money. None of this is 'pathetic' (one of Gittings' favourite adjectives), since it shows some independence of character, and an essentially modest and humble devotion to literature, on the part of an easily exhausted woman who often had to look after her mother when she was depressed and could not be left alone.

One can imagine the attitude of the almost muscular Christian Edward Dugdale towards such 'weakness'; he was not best pleased, either, by Florence's frequent absences from the school of which he was headmaster. But, if not 'pathetic', it is a little sad. There were thousands of similar literary aspirants in London at that time, and while the humble and honest ones were kept in the background, the slicker and less sincere often gained the limelight for a few years. George Gissing's *New Grub Street*, which deals with a period only a little earlier in time, gives an incomparably accurate picture of the drabness and misery of lower London literary life, and of the pretentiousness of the half-successful. Perhaps modesty was a feature in Florence that appealed to Tom. Certainly, with her pallor and misery, she might have come from the pages of one of Gissing's finely drab novels.

How Florence actually did meet Tom is banal enough, and makes one wonder why she bothered to make up so many precautionary tales. Neither Tom nor Emma necessarily knew, at the end of each day, who had called at Max Gate. Tom would often tell servants to say that he was out. Emma would meet others – such as Ford – who wanted to see Tom, but then 'receive' them as an author in her own right, and as the inspirer and (possibly) writer of certain of his novels. They would often be sent off without having seen Tom at all, by a forgetful hostess who believed she had satisfied their curiosity. It must be remembered that these callers were already myriad, and that many of them were not right in the head. On one later occasion a servant found an Indian praying in the porch, saying he had come one thousand miles to see 'the master'. But he did not get in. In any case, it would simply not have been possible to receive all the callers.

And so when, between 10 August 1905 and the end of that year, Florence called on Hardy for an interview, Emma may have known nothing about it. Florence had written to ask if she might call, and he replied on 10 August. Plainly he either did not know her from Eve, or had met her glancingly at some 'crush' at which he had said he would consider her request if she would not use the meeting as copy (which most did, after they had promised not to); or she had used someone's name to introduce herself:

Dear Madame:

As you are not going to print anything about your visit I shall be happy to be at home to you some afternoon during this month, if you will send a post card a day or two before you are coming.
Yours truly,
T. Hardy.

This situation had changed radically by the following January. It seems clear that she did come during August, and was then asked again – and that in all probability she had already been out on at least one walk with Tom, and had talked about the beauty of the flowers. On 2 January 1906 he wrote:

Dear Miss Dugdale:

I must thank you for the box of sweet flowers that you sent me. They are at this moment in water on the table, & look little the worse for their journey.

I do not think you stayed at all too long, & hope you will come again some other time.
Yours sincerely,
Thomas Hardy.

Florence must have been excited at thus attracting Tom's attention;

she would soon become frightened, too. For he was himself excited – as was his wont when confronted by good-looking young women. The very 'sweetness' of the flowers proves it. He was eventually more importunate to Florence Dugdale than he had been to Florence Henniker more than a decade earlier. But there was not necessarily anything sly or opportunistic about her gesture: she did love flowers (Hyatt, passionately devoted to gardens, had taught her much about them) and she did want Thomas Hardy to accept them.

There is nothing in extant correspondence until 11 May, when Tom agrees with George Macmillan to 'let Mr Hyatt publish the little book of extracts' (later he referred to the selection as being 'superficial'). He was with Emma in a flat in Hyde Park Mansions from April until 17 July. In those months he and Florence must have met once or twice, for Tom gave her an inscribed copy of the pocket edition of *Wessex Poems* and *Poems of the Past and the Present* and, shortly afterwards, a copy of Edward FitzGerald's *Rubaiyat*. He was still working on *The Dynasts* and therefore often in the British Museum Reading Room. Her application for a reader's ticket, in order to 'verify certain facts' for Mr Hardy, was not made until November 1906. She began going there on his behalf in early December. Some of what he wanted verified did not actually need verifying, as she long afterwards acknowledged. Later, terrified of being thought of as a mere researcher and typist (which she had been), she made a point of saying – especially to a Mrs Dorothy Meech, whom she engaged to do some typing work after Tom's death – that this research had been unpaid. But it is obvious that he paid at least her expenses, just as he punctiliously paid those of his friend Hermann Lea, who, never having found Tom mean, emphasized the fact.

The romance was slow to start; it must have proceeded seriously from the early summer, and the gifts of the inscribed books. By 23 March 1907 Tom was writing to her even more tenderly – 'you are not to go & search in the British Museum for me if you are not *quite* well'. To be solicitous about health was one of his habits towards such women as he favoured. He was by now advising her about her stories, about what fees to ask from publishers; and he was telling her about the beautiful spring weather. What Emma knew of this, if anything, is unknown. If she suspected anything, then she kept her own counsel. But Florence was not deterred from seeking other work. She is said to have taken a holiday as a companion in December 1906; no details have been given. However, at some time, or perhaps on several short occasions, she went to Dublin. One of her friends in Enfield was the Irish writer Katharine

DECEIT

Tynan (1861–1931), who had married a barrister called H.A. Hinkson. Tynan had been a close friend to Yeats, played an important part in the Irish Revival, and in her early career was thought of as one of the most promising poets in Ireland. She had, moreover, referred to herself in 1894 as a 'true-blue Hardy person'. From 1893 until 1911 she lived in Enfield with her husband. She was a well-known and highly prolific journalist who knew everybody, including, probably, Tom himself. It is clear, too, from an affectionate inscription in one of her poetry collections of 1911, that she was fond of Florence and was on familiar terms with her. She also knew, and tried to help, Alfred Hyatt. As her autobiographies (beginning with *Twenty-Five Years* of 1913) show, she was a kind and intelligent woman, who only went out of favour in Ireland because she took up a pro-British position after her return in 1911. As well as poetry she wrote over a hundred exceedingly indifferent novels, which harmed her reputation as a poet.

Amongst the countless people whom Katharine Tynan knew were the Stoker brothers: Bram (Abraham), the author of *Dracula* and several other less successful works, and secretary to the actor Henry Irving; and Thornley, from 1910 Sir Thornley, a leading Dublin surgeon. The Stokers' mother, a woman of almost demonic energy, was a great spendthrift who had kept her family perpetually on the verge of bankruptcy.

For a time Florence was a sort of assistant companion to Lady Stoker, who died in November 1910 in a nursing home to which she had finally had to be removed. Her illness had been kept a closely guarded secret: Thornley Stoker, determined to keep her at home, engaged a 'secretary', really a capable nurse, called Miss Betty Webb, to look after her. Florence was, or had been (she was in Dublin over the Christmas holiday of 1906–7), Betty Webb's assistant, and, according to what Gittings and Manton were able to discover from a descendant of the family, a conscientious one. She must have been, because Stoker gave her not only a typewriter for her literary and journalistic works, but also, later, an expensive amethyst ring. Her tenure of this post must either have been of short duration or sporadic: between 1908 and 1910 she was more often in England, and at one time actually on the *Standard* staff. Thornley Stoker died in 1912.

His bequest of £5,000 to Betty Webb is understandable; the £2,000 to Florence is harder to explain – harder than anyone has been prepared to allow. Stoker was well known as a kind and medically enlightened – but also, as the Irish poet and physician Oliver St John Gogarty said, 'troubled' – man; Florence must have impressed him deeply. Bram's side of the family were convinced that she had been Thornley's mistress – and she may very well have, at the least, shown him sexual consideration. I mean, not to be too mock-delicate about the matter, that she may have masturbated the old man. Florence most certainly was the sort of woman who would prefer this to intercourse – the sort who is initially sexually aroused only when she can see herself as 'helping' or 'relieving' a man. Rather too much has been made of her sexual prudishness: for example, of her disapproval of the novels of May Sinclair on the grounds of their 'sex mania'! Not having an original mind, she tended, like her mother, to take on the colour of her surroundings: her disapproval of Sinclair was based on what she had heard from polite literary and pseudo-literary acquaintances.

Such verdicts were often passed on May Sinclair, who had cycled about Dorset with Tom, was also a friend of Emma's, and was well worthy of Florence's jealousy as a successful serious novelist. Similarly, Florence's savage attacks on Roman Catholics in 1910 simply reflected the prejudices or opinions of the friends to whom she expressed them: Asquith, she told Emma, was in league with the Romanists. She had picked this up from Dublin talk: Thornley Stoker and his friends did not like Asquith's arrangements for Ireland, and she knew that Emma would agree. She was herself not a Christian at all. Her expressed notion that Tom had an affection for her like a father's for a daughter was wishful thinking, or simply decorous: had he not been courting her sexually when he protested that his own line, 'Love is lame at fifty years' was 'not true, not true'? She was no fifty-year-old Agnette: she was still a young girl, and that is what he meant. She lacked the style and the expensive clothing of such friends of Tom's as Florence Henniker and Agnes Grove, but most judge her as considerably more attractive than either.

Certainly in the famous photograph of her on Aldeburgh beach, with Tom, she looks desirable – and he looks so unusually relaxed as to seem to have had his own desire fulfilled not a half an hour before the beach photographer took the little lid off the lens of his camera. To be aroused, or perhaps just to act sexually without being herself much aroused, Florence had to feel that she was performing what she conceived of as not only a duty, but a grave one. She was always lacking in humour, and tended to take everything literally and at face value. It was partly her lack of humour that made the *Cakes and Ale* episode so desperate for her.

DECEIT

The sexual plight of Thornley Stoker, charming, 'troubled', ageing, distinguished, a 'wise doctor' and therefore able to pronounce on what 'men need', could well have attracted Florence into compassionate duty. She had undoubtedly been instructed in this by her mother, who had to deal with the attentions of her strictly Christian husband. Many women of the governess and similar class were thus attracted, and seldom by men as scrupulous or decent as Stoker. One feels, after all, suspended from official morality when acting under instructions from a doctor, especially one whose wife is raving in another part of the house, as the schizophrenic Emily Stoker was. If Florence did thus respond – and there is no strong evidence for it – then it would have been an act far more 'moral' than the 'immorality' socially implied by it. It is certainly nothing of which she *should* have been ashamed; but she *would* have been ashamed: she did not have the capacity for candour, and always, from early 1914, felt under the threat of invasion by an excited Tom whom she had not married, she would have felt, for *that*.

Florence may never have been consciously calculating, but she managed to do enough to attract towards herself circumstances in which she could be labelled as calculating – if anyone found her out. Her business was calculation, and we should remember just what the prospects then were for women in her position not very fond of physical sexuality and yet not lesbian, either. It is obvious that the myth of Emma's 'madness', which she developed and fostered, was clumsily modelled upon the last years of Emily Stoker. At the time when Florence actually knew Emma, and was indiscreetly writing to Clodd about her experiences at Max Gate, there is not a single word that could be construed as suggesting that she thought of her in any way as similar to Stoker's wife, or as in any way 'mad'.

Florence, then, was not quite a consciously determined schemer; her poor self-confidence and passivity, however, did lead her into sometimes treacherous or disingenuous patterns of behaviour. Genteel people without resources, in any case, develop a sixth sense about what may be of advantage to them. They have to.

Since the year 1908 was the one in which Tom's relationship with Florence developed into something to which Emma could have had quite unequivocal objections, it may be that Florence fled to the job in Dublin in order to escape from an increasingly embarrassing and guilt-inducing situation. She could not and did not anticipate Emma's death at the age of seventy, and so could not play a waiting game even had she felt so disposed. Gittings and Manton confidently treat the

Dublin episode as formative in Florence's life. But there is no evidence to substantiate this supposition – only the fact that Florence, ever anxious to magnify her 'connections', referred gratefully to the Stokers in a few letters, written long after their deaths, to Owen and others. It really is more likely that when Sir Thornley made his will he remembered this young woman with vivid gratitude, and therefore suitably rewarded her for her sexual kindness – short-lived though it had been – to him.

Millgate suggests that Tom, fretting at the 'restrictions' imposed upon him by the law, really wanted to divorce Emma, but 'could not invalidate one of the decisive acts of his life'. Stern and solemn as ever, he does, though, believe that it is at least 'understandable' that Tom, nearing seventy, should have 'indulged a little the vanity of knowing that younger women – younger, handsomer, cleverer than Emma – still valued his friendship', and quotes the famous remark made in a letter to Mrs Kenneth Grahame about his attention being distracted on the tops of omnibuses by girls in fluffy blouses! This is quaint, and made so, I suspect, by Millgate's sheer disbelief – despite there not being an iota of evidence to the contrary – in what could be called Tom's 'normal sexuality'. Such matters cannot, I submit, be dismissed as either eccentric or beside the main point, even by someone who regards plain statements of sexual fact, in candid discussions with adults, as 'boasting'. Just as Tom had once put hopeful pressure on Florence Henniker for a Shelleyan romance (the airy Shelley had no disdain for the physical), not altogether knowing where it would lead him, so now, not altogether knowing where it would lead him, he started to put sexual pressure on Florence Dugdale.

The gift of the volume of his poetry of June 1907 had merely been inscribed 'To Miss Florence Dugdale with the author's kind regards'. This correctness was not because she told him that she would like to be able to show it to her father and, no doubt, to Hyatt: the affair had not proceeded far by then. He had, it is true, written in a letter to her of 4 April, from Hyde Park Mansions, that (untruthfully, no doubt) he would be

> hunting up something at the South Kensington Museum, on Saturday after next I believe, & as that is a day on which you can be away from school you might be able to join me there, in the search. I will look for you in the architectural gallery at 4 – say by the Trajan column – but do not come if it is wet, as you have had such a bad cold this winter. I am, of course, assuming that you

have *quite* got over it, & can come out with impunity in this cold atmosphere.

But this was perhaps his first positive move. It was followed up by more substantial ones, including writing to Macmillan and others on her behalf, and, of course, working on the *Cornhill* story, 'Apotheosis of the Minx'. In addition, he was meeting her as often as he could; that would have meant evenings and weekends. His hopes of getting her to write as herself, with a sense of self-candour, were still not dead – she had an idea for a 'psychological novel' – and this was important to him. Quite soon he was to have confirmation that she was not as gifted as he had idealistically hoped. He had similarly failed, years before, with the more talented Florence Henniker, and so, on 29 September, he rather went for the latter's new novel, *Our Fatal Shadows*. Many of his letters to Mrs Henniker, from the time when he decided to do the right thing and continue as her loyal friend, had contained sarcastic and admonitory passages; whether or not they were over her head is another matter. She had disappointed him by sticking to second-rate writing for conventional reasons. On one occasion, when she was proposing to publish a collection of stories, he had acidly suggested that she add a few more the following winter since it was quantity that people liked. Now he commented on *Fatal Shadows*:

> In point of workmanship it shows I think a great advance upon your previous novels, & it is, in truth, a really literary production by a facile pen, which cannot be said of many novels nowadays. It is absolutely convincing – nothing in it *made up* to produce a melodramatic effect (my taste was depraved enough to make me wish there had been towards the end, to confess the truth; but please excuse me, it was late at night, when one can swallow anything.) It is quite Trollopian, indeed, in its limitation within certain strict lines of naturalness . . . Of course *I* should not have kept her respectable, & made a nice, decorous, dull woman of her at the end, but shd have let her go to the d—— for the man, my theory being that an exceptional career alone justifies a history (i.e. novel) being written about a person. But gentle F.H. naturally had not the heart to do that. The only thing I don't care much about is her marrying the Duke's son – whom she did not love; an action quite as immoral, from my point of view, & more so even, than running off with a married man whom she did love would have been. But convention rules still in these things of course.

703

How his mind was then working, or rather what he dreamed of, is quite obvious. And, forgetting for once to be polite and not unkind, he added, with more than mild sarcasm: 'There is really no reason why you should not go on writing scores of popular novels & making a fortune beyond the dreams of avarice, as poor Walter Besant used to say.'

The completion of *The Dynasts* – hardly a work by which he could be accused of seeking to please anyone who did not, as he had put it to Symons, 'know' – on 15 September made him bolder than was his wont, even to his favourite women. He was excited, and therefore still confident that, under his tutelage, he might develop Florence Dugdale into a truthful writer. When the impulsive and spirited Lady Grove sent him an early copy of her *The Social Fetich* he found it 'prettily bound' and 'entertaining'; but, although it was dedicated to him, he sternly added in his letter to her of 3 December:

> I am not going to agree to your always frittering yourself away on these whimsical subjects. You can do much more solid work, & no doubt you will as you get older. People, however, will buy light literature when they won't buy that of a more weighty kind!
>
> The portrait is, of course, very charming, & the objection I urged against a portrait in a book of grave essays does not apply to one of this sort.

Poor Lady Grove. In the previous August this 'little pepper-pot' had received a sharp letter from Emma, who had seen the proofs of *The Social Fetich*, in which there are some cogent criticisms of her use of language: 'You may think me hypercritical perhaps but I love words, & pounce upon sentences by early habit having to search for error & misprints.' Perhaps Emma and Tom had agreed between them that Lady Grove's book, although amusing, was rather pointlessly snobbish and did not do full justice to her capacities. On the other hand, Tom had helped Lady Grove with her writings and was not apparently doing anything with Emma's, and the book was dedicated to him. All the more reason, then, for Emma to let her know who was who. Lady Grove's frequent presence that summer at Hyde Park Mansions may have been a trifle overpowering: she was hardly lacking in self-confidence. However, the fact that there are so few adverse comments on Emma as hostess in those busy months in London, and again in 1910, suggests that she was far more efficient at the job than she has ever been given credit for.

There was extensive and probably expensive work on Max Gate

during that autumn, almost all in Emma's interests: her attic room was enlarged, and a new window put into it. She went off to Calais in September, apparently unable to endure the inconvenience any longer; she did not return until 22 October. Tom wrote affectionately to her from Max Gate, giving her a running commentary on the progress of the work. The chief problem was that the new plaster in her room would not dry.

Tom ended the year by correcting the proofs for *Dynasts III*. On New Year's Eve he wrote again to Florence Henniker, signing himself off 'Your affecte & rather gloomy friend'. He told her that both the *Fortnightly* and the *Nation* had refused his ballad 'A Trampwoman's Tragedy' (he had had no problem with it in America) on the grounds that their magazines were 'read in families': 'Yet people complain that the authors of England have no strength like those of Elizabethan days. If they had it they could not show it!' Reacting to the recent award of the Nobel Prize for Literature to Kipling, probably the General's favourite author, he commented that it was 'odd to associate him with peace'.

In January the still neglected Irish novelist and critic Forrest Reid wrote him a letter of appreciation, now unfortunately lost. Knowing quality of mind when he encountered it, Tom took the trouble to reply at some length, ending his letter, dated the 24th, with the exquisite and truly friendly and complimentary observation that

> One of the experiences of writers of books which has to be set against the pains & penalties such people bring upon themselves by floating spiritually into the lives of persons they have never seen, is that of being made welcome there.

Tom rarely permitted himself to perform critical tasks of any kind, but when in January 1907 Walter Raleigh of the Oxford University Press asked him to make a selection from the poems of William Barnes he could not but be interested. He had put him off then on account of having to complete *The Dynasts*, but when the request was renewed in a letter of 26 January 1908 he quickly replied on the 29th, saying that he would undertake the commission, and adding:

> Several of Barnes's good lyrics have an unfortunate stanza or two of a prose didactic nature that drag the poem as a whole down to a lower level than it would reach without them, Barnes, like Wordsworth, having had little power of self-criticism. Would it be permissible to

curtail a poem occasionally, so as to be able to include it? There are enough to make 100 without such, however, if you think that readers would object to such omissions.

Raleigh gave him *carte blanche* to do what he liked, and the result, *Select Poems of William Barnes*, was published in the following November; while a monstrosity from some points of view of modern scholarship, it remains the best introduction to Barnes' poetry – at the least it has formed the aesthetic basis of the later and more accurate editions, the best selection being that of the poet Robert Nye. It proved to be a tedious task, owing to difficulties of copyright and to the fact that Barnes' son had been prompted to produce his own selection for a rival publisher, Routledge. Tom was in certain cases disallowed from publishing the poet's own revised and often improved versions of his work. But he had finished the bulk of the task by March, and was able to add a few previously unpublished poems: this 'act of piety' (as he himself described it) gave him much satisfaction. His only objection to the production was that it had not been possible to get his (still invaluable) glosses in the margin instead of at the bottom of the page.

He was gaining satisfaction, too, from local presentations of dramatizations of some of his novels. After a successful production of episodes from *Far From the Madding Crowd* in the autumn of 1907, the pharmacist A.H. Evans, father of the actor Maurice Evans and of Evelyn Evans, who for many years looked after the Hardy birthplace, dramatized *The Trumpet-Major*. He knew that these productions, to which newspapers in search of copy sent reporters, were rough and unsophisticated, but he enjoyed them for that very reason: they did not have the air of the London theatre, whose smartness and commercialism he detested. However, he took time to get used to the idea: when *The Trumpet-Major* was produced in November 1908 he pleaded influenza (which was true) and sent Emma in his place. On later occasions, and there were many, he participated more warmly – although often missing first nights owing to constitutional fear of disaster and humiliation. In fact he was always made excited by these ventures, and it is interesting that Harold Child of *The Times*, who knew him well, wrote, on the top of one of the letters he received from him on the subject, that he did not want to get him 'excited'. That is the other side of Tom: much of his rather too famous 'melancholy' was the result of repenting previous 'excitement': love, lust, hope, idealistic feelings. So far as poetry is the result of 'emotion recollected in tranquillity' – and the definition still has much to recommend it – then Tom's tranquillity was of a decidedly melancholy cast. We need to look more closely into what is recollected, whatever conclusions may be made, to see the other and happier side of him.

There are no extant letters of 1908 to Florence Dugdale. After Tom's own famous bonfires of personal material, Florence had ones of her own, after his death. She was then in a difficult position: on the one hand she wanted it to be known that she had been dearer than his life to him (as he had put it in 'On the Departure Platform'); on the other, she greatly feared being exposed as an ex-adulteress, or, at the very least, as the betrayer of the friendship of Emma. Of the various Hardy researchers on the rampage in her lifetime, she trusted the quiet and courteous American academic R.L. Purdy most of all. Unlike Carl Weber, who was a boorish vulgarian in comparison, he was an admirably discreet bachelor. He did not, for instance, reveal Tom's authorship of all but a scrap of the *Life* until Florence had been dead three years, and then only in an obscure New York lecture; and, like Millgate – with whom he collaborated on the magisterial edition of the *Letters* – he was not, as a writer and bibliographer, much interested in, and certainly was not enthusiastic about, sexual matters. Florence did recognize the poet Henry Reed as being an altogether more sophisticated and critically inclined person, a young man of the world by contrast with the American bibliographer and collector, who never attempted criticism; but he did not turn up until much later, by which time she was a sick woman who could not be pressed, tactfully or otherwise. Thus she protected herself from enquiry, and was able to keep the world in the dark about how her romance with Tom had progressed in the last years of Emma's life. This was her undoubted privilege; but no one, now, can be harmed or outraged by such boldness of discussion as, with good reason, she feared.

As I have suggested, by the beginning of 1908 Florence was simultaneously flattered, genuinely moved by, and afraid of Tom's attentions. She taught at her father's school until April, when she was granted three months' leave of absence. Gittings and Manton found no evidence of her returning to teaching, 'even for a day', after that. Tom may have started to become disillusioned with her literary as distinct from journalistic (and physical) abilities, although two more Hardyan stories, signed by her, did appear in the *Pall Mall* and the *Cornhill*, but not until 1909 and 1911 respectively. He could not get away from Max Gate much in the early part of the year, partly owing to pressure of work and partly owing to Emma's severe illness. On 5 March he wrote to Gosse that 'It was a wonder your letter did not find me just going to London. But Emma has been in bed with bronchitis for nearly a week, & the house is rather disorganized, so I have put off going.' And on 11 March he sent a letter to Arthur Symons, telling him that 'partly' on account of the illness 'we have not the courage to think of taking a flat or house in town this year'. He also told Symons, who on 4 March had written him a long letter of appreciation about *The Dynasts*, that there it was: 'some pages done carefully, others galloped over, & now staring me accusingly in the face. I wonder if I shall ever be able to revise them.'

There is always the unlikely possibility that Emma, who after all knew her husband and his amorous habits better than anyone, knew all about the attachment, and that her bronchitis was in part strategic – even, possibly, 'to save him from himself'. We may be sure, in any case, that Tom was aching to get away and meet Florence – and that, when he did succeed in getting to town for a few days, on 26 March, he was able to do so. During the days between the letter to Gosse and the 26th he had an opportunity to vent his frustrations. A.G. Gardiner, editor of the *Daily News*, had published on 14 March in his own paper a leading article called 'Thomas Hardy: A Character Study'. On the 17th Tom wrote to tell him that, although he felt flattered by the 'good things you said', it had 'occurred to him in passing that' his statement

concerning a person of whose life you know next to nothing, that his 'pilgrimage has been downward, ever downward (!), the shadows of the prison house closed around him' [the man is still living!] 'There is no return to the cheerful day . . . The journey has ended in despair,' etc, etc, was rather ridiculous, & showed an apparent lack of humour in the writer. I regarded it all as well meant, & should never have thought any more about it if it had not happened that acquaintances & friends of mine are protesting against this estimate as preposterous & an utter misrepresentation of character.

And he concluded by asking Gardiner, who had attacked his pessimism on an earlier occasion, to alter the piece when he reprinted it (which he did), or not to reprint it at all.

Gardiner's reply has not survived, but he must have tried to stick up for himself a little. Tom, now back in good humour, perhaps because the 26th was by this time only a week away, replied on the 19th with apologetic modesty, in a letter which surely gives the lie to those who maintain that his objections to criticism were freakishly abnormal. He told Gardiner that he was so used to being mishandled in the press that he had become case-hardened to it, and read all criticism of himself 'as if it concerned a third person'. He assured him that the accusations of lack of humour and ridiculousness had not been directed at his 'personal self, of course':

> 'Pessimism' – as the optimists nickname what is really only a reasoned view of effects & probable causes, deduced from facts unflinchingly observed – leads to a mental quietude that tends rather upwards than downwards, I consider. As for professional optimists, one is always sceptical about them: they wear too much the strained look of the smile on a skull.
>
> So far as my experience goes, conclusions about the universe do not affect the spirits, which are a result of temperament . . . But I am preaching a sermon at you . . . I truly would thank you for your kind sense of my being worth an article at all.

On the same day, he incautiously told his publisher Macmillan something that he would not have liked his detractors to know about. He believed that a proposed German translation of *The Dynasts* might help British sales because the reading public were 'like sheep, & when they discover that foreigners think it worth while to translate a book, & are discussing it in their press, they feel that they, too, ought to read it'.

It is obvious that he did meet Florence during this March visit, doubtless more than once. Now that work on *The Dynasts* had ceased, he had to find some excuse to maintain contact with her. Most probably it was then that he suggested she become, so far as was practicable, his 'secretary'. He did not refer to her as that until the following year, by which time she was also, to Clodd, his 'amanuensis'. Was it this proposal that gave her the courage to abandon teaching – or not to struggle any longer against its gradual abandonment of her? Sixteen months later, whether technically Tom's mistress or not, she was inextricably tied to him.

32

Emma's Death

Tom and Emma took no London flat in 1909, so he travelled up and down as often as he could manage it, usually staying at the West Central Hotel in Southampton Row. For most of that year, far from being at Ely House in Dublin, the residence of Thornley Stoker, Florence Dugdale was working as a reporter for the *Standard* in London. Mostly she commuted between her parents' house in Enfield and the office; but she had an aunt in London, and could stay at her professional women's club, the Lyceum. Tom also made several visits to see Clodd at Strafford House at Aldeburgh in Suffolk, and took one or two tours. Emma had never been in the habit of accompanying him to Aldeburgh, and she disapproved of Clodd – though just about within the bounds of politeness – for his rationalist writings and presumed bad influence upon her husband and upon churchgoers in general. She would write to him and upbraid him for the opinions expressed in his books. As a frequent guest to Max Gate, he took it in good part. He was a man of the world, separated from his own wife, and certainly the one amongst all his literary friends whom Tom could safely choose as a confidant. Victorian male moralists did not sacrifice their 'needs' for long, and Clodd was not even one of those; in 1914 he emulated his friend and made a second marriage to a much younger woman. Tom was to be deeply grateful to him in the year 1909.

The Dynasts behind him, he had little to do except gather up the poems for his third collection, *Time's Laughingstocks*. He was also, probably quite furiously, adding to its contents. For a time the plan with Macmillan had been for a book, uniform with a complete *Dynasts* in two volumes, that collected the contents of *Wessex Poems* and *Poems of the Past and the Present*. But this was shelved until 1919, when the first *Collected Poems* was issued. In 1909 Tom badly wanted to publish his new poems. He now felt that he could, with tact, control his publications, and, more important, his life: he began to try to compensate for the long period during which he had been constrained by the need to compromise, to supply novels for a market. In acknowledging on 16 January 1909 a long review of *The Dynasts* by Henry Newbolt in the *Quarterly*, he observed:

> Happily one can afford to dismiss the fear of writing ones [sic] self out, which we used to hear so much of. No man ever writes himself out if he goes on living as he lived when he began to write. It is the other thing, the social consequence of his first works, that does the mischief, – if he lets it.

The degree to which, at this time of liberation, he wished to commit himself to a life of what he saw as poetic virtue has been underestimated, perhaps not even recognized. Yet one of the themes of his autobiography, as may be seen from those notes written throughout his life which it so painstakingly reproduces, is the pursuit of virtue. Thus his attempt to have an affair with Florence Dugdale, not a notably virtuous undertaking, was something of a thorn in his side. It was not a thorn which he was at all anxious to pull out. Like St Augustine, if with somewhat different aims, he wanted to be virtuous, but not yet. Besides, he probably held more radical views of marriage than he had ever dared to express, even though of course he never contemplated leaving Emma. His main overt complaint was against the stringent divorce laws: when marriage became a misery, he always maintained, it should be easy to end it. But in a skittish letter to Shorter of May 1909 he was perhaps a little more extreme:

> . . . I do not object to the coming of woman-suffrage – for a reason you evidently have never thought of. As soon as women have the vote & can take care of themselves men will be able to strike out honestly right & left in a way they cannot do while women are their dependants, without showing unchivalrous meanness. The result will be that all superstitious institutions will be knocked down or rationalized – theologies, marriage, wealth-worship, labour-worship, hypocritical optimism, & so on. Also some that women will join in putting down: blood-sport, slaughter-house inhumanities, the present blackguard treatment of animals generally, &c, &c. End of my sermon.

Meanwhile women, if only in the form of Emma and Florence

Dugdale, were giving him different sorts of trouble, the one painful, the other with its component of guilty pleasure. Despite Emma's attacks on his lack of religious faith, he was not prevented from writing on 21 April to his friend, the gentle musician and man of letters Reymond Abbott, that he wished he could have been at the Tenebrae services which Abbott had attended in London during the week before Easter. These were special forms of Matins and Lauds held in the last three days of Holy Week: one candle was extinguished at the end of each psalm, until only the darkness of the crucifixion remained. By 1 May, though, Tenebrae or no Tenebrae, he was so thoroughly worn down by Emma's behaviour that he allowed himself his first written complaint against her. Clodd invited him for the usual happy Whitsun gathering, and, in a fit of angry depression, he replied:

> I should so much like to join you at Aldeburgh at Whitsuntide, & feel it so very kind of you to ask me, that I am tempted to promise that I will do so. The only scruple I have about it lies in my domestic circumstances which, between ourselves, make it embarrassing for me to return hospitalities received, so that I hesitate nowadays to accept many. However I will throw that consideration to the winds in the present case, & aim to be with you. Let me know the train you go down by [from his London home in Tufnell Park] & the day.

The presumably very fierce row that prompted this unusual outburst is likely to have started from Tom's mention of Clodd's invitation. Clodd's aggressive and over-confident rationalism, irritating to many (as both English and American reviews of his books testify), must have acted as a constant provocation to Emma. While there is no doubt that her behaviour at home was now sometimes so eccentric and stormy as to be intolerable by any standards, it may have partly resulted from great suffering: her knowledge of Tom's 'excited' state of mind over Florence Dugdale or some woman whose name she did not know. She may have decided upon a virtuous plan of action, but failed to carry it right through. In June the previous year Rebekah Owen, much to the distress of her sister, had become a Roman Catholic, and Emma could not control her stream of violent reproaches, some of them rather magnificent – if she would only read the Bible now forbidden her, Emma suggested, she would escape 'Satan's guile'; and she conjured up a picture of Owen's relatives being tortured by the Inquisition.

It is odd that no one has yet suggested that she might have been the victim of premature senility, perhaps of the syndrome named after the German Alzheimer's description of it in 1906. The Alzheimer hypothesis fits the facts far better than the madness hypothesis, at least as the latter has (rather amateurishly) been presented. Tom in any case felt himself in no position to tell her to stop anything.

The early months of the year were punctuated by only a few brief visits to London. Tom must have met Florence, but she may well have been holding him at arm's length. He had a problem. Where could he safely meet her? What work could he now give her? There was none except whatever he could invent. Now, in his gloom, with a row looming over the Strafford House visit, he was reading Henry Handel Richardson's (the Australian-born Anglo-Irish Ethel Richardson) novel *Maurice Guest* of 1908. Richardson was later to write two masterpieces, *The Getting of Wisdom* and the trilogy *The Fortunes of Richard Mahoney*; but this first novel – 'Freudian' and 'amoral' – already displayed the promise which she was later to fulfil. Set in Leipzig, and containing a portrait of the young Richard Strauss, it is one of the first novels in English to present an unambiguously homosexual character. Tom did not miss its quality, which was nearer to that of Virginia Woolf than it was to that of Mrs Henniker or any other woman novelist active in 1908. Mrs Henniker had objected to its 'bad characters', and on 24 May Tom gently and obliquely reproached her for her chatterbox foolishness:

I, also, read that novel 'Maurice Guest', the author having sent me a copy. Yes the characters are rather a bad lot, but the woman is well done (utterly unattractive to me personally: – there are scores of them about; but attractive as a drawing, because of its accuracy).

How discouraging it must have been for him to find that a woman whom he had once believed to be emancipated and intelligent was criticizing fiction not on the grounds that its psychology was deficient, but because its characters were not sufficiently conventional for her taste, now further depraved by her adventures in high society. But this did not prevent him from expressing to her his opinion about the respective merits of Swinburne and Meredith, both of whom had recently died: the former he thought the greater writer, 'though he is much the smaller thinker'. He was not, he told Mrs Henniker, surprised that she had got stuck in Meredith's *The Egoist*. Here he put his finger upon something that has always proved hard for critics to explain:

Meredith's failure to be read as widely as his gifts suggest he ought to have been.

> Why he was so perverse as to infringe the first rules of narrative art I cannot tell, when what he had to say was of the very highest, & what he discerned in life was more than almost any novelist had discerned before. A child could almost have told him that to indulge in psychological analysis of the most ingenious kind in the crisis of an emotional scene is fatal – high emotion demanding simplicity of expression above all things, – yet this was what Meredith constantly did. Wordsworth knew better: & so I believe Meredith did, only he would not practise what he knew because he was so exasperated by bad criticism.

The next day, 25 May, Tom was considering making a sacrifice for Emma's sake by not going to Aldeburgh. He told Clodd that he was still hoping 'to keep faith' but was at present in bed 'with a violent influenza' which had come on two days before, on his return from London after the service at Westminster Abbey for Meredith. He had not mentioned any illness to Mrs Henniker, and had previously told Gosse that he did not think it was going to amount to anything much. But then, at least so far as Clodd was concerned, it turned into a full-blown 'true & genuine London influenza'. He finally decided not to go, and, having wired Clodd, wrote to him wistfully on 29 May: 'I . . . pictured the trip: the bustle at Liverpool Street, the lively conversation in the carriage . . . the jolly dinner after . . . But, as the poet says, O the difference to me!' He ended by telling him that he was still 'husky and sniffy' and had to keep indoors 'till dry-eyed'. He may have felt guilty about the possibly fictional severity of this influenza, because in the *Life* he speaks of it as having only 'nearly passed off' by the beginning of July. Clodd, however, well understanding his difficulties, immediately issued a new invitation, so that on 21 June Tom was able to write to him: 'since you so kindly renew your invitation I am tempted . . . I will arrange to go by the 5 o'clock train from Liverpool Street . . . July 2, as you suggest.' This visit he did make, and spent the weekend with Ford Madox Ford, Violet Hunt, Gilbert Murray, and others.

This visit was to have further consequences, for on 5 July, according to Clodd's diary, on the train back to London he had a long talk with him about his situation. He confessed that his relations with Emma were strained, and in some way managed to introduce the subject of Florence

Dugdale, whom he described as his 'amanuensis'. Tom put himself at the mercy of his friend's understanding, and fortunately Clodd took the hint. Before a few more days had passed, on the evening of Wednesday, 14 July, he was able to be of service.

During the interim Tom, who had first arrived in London on the evening of 1 July on his way to Aldeburgh, remained there, at the West Central; nor did he return to Max Gate until the evening of Saturday, 17 July. He must have been seeing a great deal of Florence, and she must have been at the height of her apprehensions about his intentions. He was not slow to declare either himself or his Shelleyan principles, as fleshly as they were ethereal. Meanwhile there was the matter relating to the evening of the 14th to deal with.

Baron Frédéric D'Erlanger, son of German and American parents, was born in Paris in 1868. He studied music in Paris, and later became a naturalized English citizen. A banker by profession, he was a financial supporter of Covent Garden Opera House until his death in 1943. He had excellent connections, and was able to obtain the services of Luigi Illica (librettist or part-librettist of *La Bohème* and many other famous operas) as his collaborator in an Italian libretto adapting *Tess*. As Tom wryly put it in the *Life*, he was to 'Italianize' it so much as to render it scarcely recognizable. The result was first presented at Naples in 1906, and was successful enough there for Covent Garden to take it on for a season in 1909, as a vehicle for one of the most celebrated sopranos of her time, the thirty-one-year-old Czech Ema Kittl, who then sang under the name of Emmy Destinn. She had sung Butterfly to Caruso's Pinkerton at Covent Garden in 1905; in 1910 she created Minnie in Puccini's *Girl of the Golden West*. When Tom saw her sing Tess on 14 July, in the presence of a Queen shortly to be widowed, and other notables to whom D'Erlanger had easy access, he was amused by her portliness – not an unusual feature of operatic sopranos – but seems to have found her performance excellent: 'Destinn's voice suited the title-character admirably; her appearance less so.' It 'was a great success in a crowded house', and was repeated several times in the following weeks; but there has not to my knowledge been any revival or even studio performance. It is interesting that Destinn, who later changed her singing name to Destinova, herself wrote poetry and novels, and so must have been interested in singing a role whose ultimate origin lay, not in the usual romantic potboiler, but in a novel of quality.

Emma made the journey to London to witness this historic event. To oblige Tom, Clodd had agreed to take Florence Dugdale, but had

715

to leave a little early with her in order to catch his train from Victoria to Tufnell Park. Or that was what, saving face to himself, he told his diary. Suppose he should come face to face with Emma and Tom as the audience threaded its way out of the opera house? What could he say? 'This is *my* new amanuensis?' No, better to catch the train . . . This would seem to suggest that the sixty-nine-year-old Emma had not yet had the pleasure of seeing Tom's thirty-year-old amanuensis in her young and attractive flesh. She herself had once been Tom's actual amanuensis, for *A Laodicean* and doubtless for much else.

Tom had been in London for at least a few days during June, since he wrote three letters from the Athenaeum. In the two most important of these, dated 9 and 11 June, he tried to avoid being made President of the Society of Authors in succession to Meredith. The grounds he cited were that for 'personal & unavoidable' reasons he could not guarantee to take an active part in its affairs; he suggested Lord Morley as an alternative. In the next letter he pleaded that he could not guarantee, either, not 'to kick over the traces again'. His moral teaching, he told the poet and novelist Maurice Hewlett, who had written to him on behalf of the Council, was not of 'the correct & accepted pattern', as Tennyson's and Meredith's had been (or so he asserted, rather surprisingly, of the latter). He would continue to 'exhibit,' he almost angrily continued, 'what I feel ought to be exhibited . . . to show that what we call immorality, irreligion &c are often true morality, true religion, &c, quite freely to the end'. (Thus would he have defended Florence's sexual kindliness to Thornley Stoker, had she ever dared to speak of it to him.) This letter was written in the interests of his pursuit of what I have called virtue. He was anything but a casual man. But the Society was not going to have any of this, and the Presidency was eventually forced upon him. The quality of his resistance to the proposal reveals, of course, his state of mind and emotion at just that point of time: although excited and not quite in control of himself, he knew very well that he wanted to embark upon an affair with a woman forty years younger than his wife. This quick visit to London had been made with a view to meeting her yet again. Can we doubt it?

Soon, after a day or two back at Max Gate, it was July, and he was at Aldeburgh confiding to Clodd. Then he was hanging about in London, at the West Central, confusedly or otherwise, awaiting the *Tess* performance. He was vague about its date to Emma, but could not have been thus on 5 July to Clodd, to whom he wrote on the 13th:

EMMA'S DEATH

I have seen my young friend Miss Florence Dugdale, & she is pleased with the programme you kindly shaped out for taking her to the Opera to-morrow night. She will be at the Lyceum Club (128 Piccadilly) waiting for you at 7 o'clock to call for her, & take her somewhere for a light dinner (this bright idea of yours she highly appreciates) – & then on to Covent Garden. If it should be a wet evening please make her wrap up as she is very delicate. I am sorry to put you to the trouble of donning evening clothes, by the way; it is doubly troublesome this weather.

I will call round upon you in your seats between the acts if I possibly can, & at the end of the performance. If I cannot, all you will have to do is to put her into a cab. Should you feel any uncertainty about getting the last train to your place, send me a wire here [the Athenaeum], & I am almost sure to be able to secure a room for you at my hotel. Being the first performance it *may* be a little after 11.10. But I don't know.

The performance did run late, and, as we have seen, the adroit Clodd wisely chose to make a hasty exit rather than face 'the end of the performance' and a drink with his old friend before retiring to a room in his hotel. He took Florence to the Gaiety Restaurant, and she stayed, not with an aunt who might ask her questions which she did not feel inclined to answer, but at the Lyceum. A fellow member was Mrs Emma Hardy.

In his letter to Emma written on 9 July, only four days before the one to Clodd quoted above, when he had been seeing Florence Dugdale on (we may fairly guess) most days, he was much vaguer about the date of the forthcoming operatic version of *Tess*. Here was a man who was intending, just as soon as possible, to deceive his wife, but trying to act as if he were doing nothing of the kind. He intensely disliked himself for it, but he liked the timid and delicate Florence Dugdale with even greater intensity. The novelist had been better at this kind of intrigue (with which he had occasionally enjoyed shocking his audience) than the man, who had once raced off to Winchester without really knowing whether he wanted to elope with the wife of a military man or not. What would he have said, fifteen years back, had that other Florence flung herself into his arms in the empty railway carriage and said, with Shelleyan passion: 'Let's go to Paris! I'm packed! To hell with tomorrow!'? But there was no military man in the offing now, only a headmaster of stern Christian principles and, luckily, Clodd.

Tom was an honest man caught up in affairs in which he was no expert. But the immorality here was not too easily going to transform itself into any kind of morality which he could recognize or of which he could inform Hewlett and the nation. (Thinking of the nation, and his fames, he must already have anticipated Asquith's offer of a knighthood, made in the following November, and rehearsed his decline of it.) It was not until 7 September that he sent up the full contents of *Time's Laughingstocks* to Frederick Macmillan. Was it at about this time that, recollecting a tender passage with Florence in some half deserted museum behind such a column as Trajan's at Kensington, or on a moonlit park bench, perhaps even one in an Enfield to which he had accompanied her on her dreary train, he wrote 'The Sigh'? Or was it written a little later?

> Little head against my shoulder,
> Shy at first, then somewhat bolder,
>   And up-eyed;
> Till she, with a timid quaver,
> Yielded to the kiss I gave her;
>   But, she sighed.
>
> That there mingled with her feeling
> Some sad thought she was concealing
>   It implied.
> – Not that she had ceased to love me,
> None on earth she set above me;
>   But she sighed.
>
> She could not disguise a passion,
> Dread, or doubt, in weakest fashion
>   If she tried:
> Nothing seemed to hold us sundered,
> Hearts were victors; so I wondered
>   Why she sighed.
>
> Afterwards I knew her throughly,
> And she loved me staunchly, truly,
>   Till she died;
> But she never made confession
> Why, at that first sweet concession,
>   She had sighed.

EMMA'S DEATH

It was in our May, remember;
And though now I near November,
    And abide
Till my appointed change, unfretting,
Sometimes I sit half regretting
    That she sighed.

This could be a recollection of Emma, but is more likely to be related to his experience of Florence, who might have sighed for Hyatt, or just out of the self-pity from which she habitually suffered. The poem, within its brief compass, seems to condense the whole experience: such are the illusions of love, which changes rapidly.

We can either moralize at Tom, or sympathize with him, as now he writes to Emma to try to convince her of how vague he is about the *Tess* performance, and of how much he wants to come home – indeed, a part of him did. Already on 1 July he had told her how 'tired' he was, and how he did not wish to stay in town to go to 'that dinner' (his excuse for staying after returning from Aldeburgh): he would, he explained, have come straight home on the 5th had it not been for that. But Friday morning, 9 July found him still in London:

I have just got your note, & the bundle of letters. I did not remember that I said definitely that I would return Wednesday [7 July], which will show you what a confusion I am in . . . Before you get this you will see from the *Times*, &c, that the Opera is coming on next *Wednesday* eveng. Baron d'Erlanger [sic] . . . writes simultaneously to say the same thing, & asks what stalls I require. I can only think of two – one for you if you come, & one for myself. The fact is I don't know how many I am expected to ask for . . . I think I cannot decently ask for more [who procured the two for Clodd is unclear].

The question now is, will you come? The hotel is so crowded that if you came there we shd be obliged to have a front room, where the din is terrific, & having given up my little back one I shd not get it again . . . You cd of course come up for that one evening, though it wd be a fag . . . If you feel absolutely disinclined to undergo the fatigue of coming you will no doubt be able to hear the Opera later . . . I was thinking of returning tomorrow if this had not happened.

But Emma did choose to come, and he was back at Max Gate on 17 July. On the 22nd he wrote to Clodd, acting on a hint made by the latter on 5 July, during their delicate and no doubt coded discussion about his situation:

> I left London last Saturday, & have not been in the best of health & spirits since, though I am rapidly picking up.
>
> Your kindly opinion of my young friend & assistant pleases me much (& her, too, whom I told of it). I have known her for several years, & am very anxious about her health and welfare; & am determined to get her away to the seaside if I can, or she will break down quite. Your timely hint that I might bring her to Aldeburgh is really charming. After a few days there I could send or bring her to Weymouth.
>
> What date would be quite convenient? Would Bank holiday-week suit, or would you prefer a later time? . . . If you will fix a date I will suggest it to her, & should it suit (as it is almost sure to) you could write directly to her, or through me.
>
> If we do come there will be such a clicking of the typewriter as never was in your house before (she is not really what is called 'a typist', but as she learns anything she has learned that, though as I told you she writes original things, is a splendid proof-reader, & a fine critic, her taste in poetry being unerring – only doing my typewriting as a fancy).

In view of Clodd's generosity, Tom did not need to pretend to him about the true nature of the relationship, although later, on 11 August 1910, he was calling her 'my little cousin' (Dugdale having originally been a Dorset man), and, to the novelist Netta Syrett (yet another ex-mistress of Somerset Maugham's), his and her families had 'known each other for centuries'. Clodd must have well understood that he could not or would not admit to anything more than a 'father and daughter' interest. Tom always played his cards as closely as he could to his chest, but what he was absolutely obliged to do openly, he liked to do openly – his concealments and tricks were, after all, no more than ironic mockeries of those conventions which he despised. He hoped posterity would understand; but on the whole, its spokesmen have refused to do so. On this occasion, though, he just could not act openly towards Emma about what he was doing, or wanted to do, with Florence Dugdale. He was thus doubly grateful to Clodd for not pressing him into further disclosures. Nor, alas, could he yet be at all sure what the young woman herself thought. He carefully asked Clodd to send her the invitation – it must come from Clodd, not him – and he counted on his friend to word it as though he, Clodd, wanted to see her as much as Tom did: 'Tom will be here if he can', he wanted him to say, or something to that effect. Miss Dugdale was certainly not quite ready to come away alone with Mr, almost Sir, Thomas Hardy, author of *The Dynasts*. He was thus relying on Clodd, who indeed acted as a good friend to him, not only to be discreet to Emma, but also to help in the manipulation of his little cousin and amanuensis. Alas for morality. We can but hope that the moralists have not had childhood mumps, and, with the mad Lear, admonish them thus: 'Thou, Rascall Beadle, hold thy bloody hand: why dost thou lash that Whore? Strip thy own back, thou hotly lusts to use her in that kind, for which thou whip'st her.'

On the 25th, as Tom waited for Friday, 30 July, the appointed day, to arrive, one who was to become something of a bugbear to him turned up again in his life: the unfortunate Frank Hedgcock, who, although he did not die until 1954 when he was in his late seventies, was never regarded as an authority on Hardy. He had first written in 1907. Now Tom had to write to Gosse that he was sorry that he had been 'bothered by one of these "thesis" writers on my account . . . Like you, I cannot see how details of one's personal history, when certain books were read, &c, can be required for any legitimate criticism.' Tom was annoyed at Hedgcock's not unreasonable insistence that Schopenhauer had influenced his work: he believed, he told Gosse, that he was 'more modern' than that. Hedgcock, who published his thesis, *Thomas Hardy: penseur et artiste*, in 1911 in French – it was for the University of Paris – always irritated him beyond measure, although he did receive him at Max Gate in the summer of 1910. No one has bothered to translate his work – Tom successfully opposed it and was enraged at its opening biographical chapter, which he savagely annotated with such remarks as 'This is not literary criticism, but impertinent personality & untrue.' Only the American Ernest Brennecke's 'biography', *The Life of Thomas Hardy* (1925), annoyed him more.

On 28 July disappointment struck: he heard, somehow, from Florence that she was too unwell to travel. His friend Hermann Lea, whom he trusted implicitly, might conceivably have acted as a go-between. Another, perhaps more likely, candidate is his brother Henry, who later in that year accompanied Tom and Florence on a tour of cathedrals. In whatever manner he received this news, he seems to have walked from Max Gate up to the Dorset County Museum, obtained a piece of its notepaper, struck through the letterhead, and – presumably sitting in its reading-room rather than in his study at Max Gate – written to Clodd. (There was no point in this piece of subterfuge, if subterfuge it was, and it must be put down to his generally confused and guilty frame of mind concerning Florence. Millgate and Purdy in the *Letters* attribute the use of the Museum letterhead to 'discretion rather than economy', but discretion in the interests of what or whom?) He was sorry, he told Clodd, to have heard that his 'young friend' was 'so unwell' that she could not join him to travel to Aldeburgh on Friday. However, he added, she would 'probably be well enough to come next week'. Should he wait till next week before coming, and bring her then, or should he leave on the following Friday just as they had arranged? 'I need hardly say that I like visiting you with or without others, but I should like you to decide this . . . Please wire to let me know.' Clodd wired him to come: he could stay at Strafford House and await Florence's arrival there.

But Tom remained at Max Gate until the following Friday. One must suppose that, if he was expecting a wire, he could get hold of it without Emma's being aware. As for the timid Florence's illness: colds and sore throats had long been a way of life for her, and it is not too much to suggest that she had been using them for some years as a means of manipulating and annoying people, but most particularly her father, who disapproved of 'weakness'. She may well, true to her type, have got back at him by means of them: by making him angry and unhappy. This particular 'unwellness' therefore enabled her to put off what was not only an exciting but also an evil and frightening day. Florence, unlike Tom, could seldom be entirely happy: she was always full of reservations about everything.

On the following Wednesday, 4 August, hurriedly misdating his letter 4 July, Tom wrote again to Clodd:

My thanks for your kind idea last week that I should go down . . . then, & stay on. You received my telegram that I thought I had better wait . . . I have heard from our friend this morning, who says that she is now practically well & can go next week if you are good enough to have her. It will be an excellent restorative after this little ailment . . . A letter from you direct to her suggesting the day will be best for fixing her. I want to get down to that coast again especially if this glimpse of fine weather should continue.

Once again the invitation had to come from Clodd. He and Florence did, at last, travel up to Aldeburgh, with Clodd, from Liverpool Street on the afternoon of Friday, 13 August.

The days until the 13th were fraught for Tom. He wondered if Florence was going to be 'well' enough to go to Strafford House after all. Much of this anxiety – was she going to agree to an affair? was he going to, as he had once put it, 'have her'? – had crept into poems he was now writing, especially those in the section called 'More Love Lyrics'. He began to send the contents of *Time's Laughingstocks* to Macmillan on 29 August, and had completed the task by 7 September. It is possibly significant that he left it until after the Aldeburgh visit. Many of the self-styled 'love lyrics' deal with themes of the withdrawal of the beloved. Even the very title of 'On the Departure Platform' is redolent of it: she who is more than his life to him is seen in the poem as vanishing; the notion that 'nought happens twice thus' is based not only on his own Heraclitan cast of feeling, but also on the recognition of a quality in Florence's personality, an essential unhappiness and notion that nothing can ever turn out well. '1867' was no doubt originally written to Eliza Nicholls or to another girl friend of that year; in resurrecting (and perhaps working over) such old poems, Tom seems to have been deliberately laying out the pattern of his most recent, and current, amorous history. Thus the 1866 sonnet 'Her Definition' was appropriate as a record of what he was experiencing now, as he lay awake all night excited by thoughts of Florence Dugdale; so was the 1893 poem to Florence Henniker, 'The Division', now here printed for the first time. 'In a Cathedral City', another poem in the older style, is also likely to be about Florence Dugdale, who had not then visited it: it links her to a place of great significance for him. 'I Say, "I'll Seek Her' might very well have been written on one of the occasions, numerous for all we know, when Florence was too 'unwell' to meet with his plans:

> I say, 'I'll seek her side
>   Ere hindrance interposes;'
>   But eve in midnight closes,
> And here I still abide.

It ends:

> 'Far cockcrows echo shrill,
>   The shadows are abating,

723

> And I am waiting, waiting;
> But O, you tarry still!'

She was frightened of her father and of his sternly Christian opinions, so that 'Her Father', dated 'Weymouth 1869' in the manuscript, fitted in well with his apprehensive mood. Another Weymouth 1869 poem (described by one critic as expressing 'physiological or biological depletion . . . following the marital act'! – whatever 'marital act' could he have meant? Paying over the housekeeping money?) was at least not extraneous to the general theme: for Tom a kiss was as potent for such moments of disillusionment as 'the act'. Thereafter the sequence becomes concerned with considerations of Emma, his older love, and perhaps culminates in 'In the Night She Came', when he tests her lack of sexual attractiveness for him: the young woman comes to her lover, the speaker, in the night, 'Toothless, and wan, and old,/With leaden concaves round her eyes,/And wrinkles manifold':

> I tremblingly exclaimed to her,
> 'O wherefore do you ghost me thus!
> I have said that dull defacing Time
>   Will bring no dreads to us.'
> 'And is that true of *you*' she cried
>   In a voice of troubled tune.
> I faltered: 'Well . . . I did not think
>   You would test me quite so soon!'

and so

> when next day I paid
> My due caress, we seemed to be
> Divided by some shade.

The phrase 'My due caress' by now carries – if only in biographical terms – a weight of terrible meaning: 'my responsibility for you'; 'the sacrifice I ought to make for you if love is not to alter now that it has alteration found'. The situation, for a man so self-driven towards poetic purity, was indeed an insuperable one. By way of making amends it would lead him to a not greatly desired second marriage.

The holiday at Aldeburgh lasted more than a week, during which Florence was introduced to such friends as William Archer and to

Clodd's married daughter Edith Graham: Clodd did not, as Gittings and Manton state, invite them 'alone'. It was important that he should not. For Tom, this relationship had to seem public and respectable, even if it was not, and even if it had to be kept from Emma. On the afternoon of Monday, 16 August he, Clodd and Florence were sailing in their host's boat. The boatman misjudged the tide and they got trapped by it: they had to fly a flag of distress so that a punt was attracted to their rescue. Tom was anxious to keep the story out of the London papers. At the end of the week it was reported in a local paper headlined: 'EMINENT AUTHORS ON THE MUD'. But it did not get taken up by the London press, although Clodd could not resist teasing Tom about it: 'PERILOUS POSITION OF ENGLAND'S GREATEST NOVELIST', he quipped, 'RESCUE OF THE ILLUSTRIOUS BY BRAVE BOATMEN OF ALDEBURGH'.

Millgate writes:

> Although the friendship between Hardy and Florence Dugdale was now deep and intimate, it is questionable whether it was, or became, actively sexual. Hardy would scarcely have been so anxious to accompany Florence to Clodd's if he had been conducting the sort of liaison for which his solitary visits to London would have provided much readier opportunities. There was undoubtedly a strong sexual element in Hardy's attraction to Florence . . . But it seems doubtful whether she, with her strong ties to a warm and thoroughly conventional home background, was quite the liberated woman he had been searching for . . . and it is perhaps significant that she confessed, many years later, to an inability to 'enter into' the love-making described in Marie Stopes's novel *Love's Creation*: 'a lack of real feeling on my part I suppose'. Nor would it have been easy for Hardy, at the age of sixty-nine, to have overcome the reticences of a lifetime.

To this paragraph, I think, one might fairly add, apropos of sexual and psychological matters and in particular 'reticences', the famous quotation from Pope's *Essay on Criticism*:

> A *little Learning* is a dang'rous Thing;
> Drink deep, or taste not the *Pierian* Spring:
> There *shallow Draughts* intoxicate the Brain . . .

I am not of course impugning Millgate's prowess; only his conclusions.

He later feels able, on the basis of the above 'argument', to assert that since 'the relationship did not involve him in technical "infidelities" to Emma it seemed exasperating that it should have to be conducted with such discretion'. It seemed 'ridiculous' to Hardy, he continues, that he should not be able to make more use of Florence's 'secretarial skills . . . on a more regular basis'.

It is, however, infidelities that matter to a wife: she is perhaps interested less in what has happened than in the present state of her husband's feelings towards another – in what he wants to and may do in the future, rather than in what he may have done. Besides, Tom had no need of Florence's secretarial skills for the writing of poetry, and she herself did not like the 'drudgery'. He had already told Clodd that she was not really a typist – that doing his typewriting was 'a fancy'. The secretarial work was always a cover to conceal the true nature of the relationship, and, as we have seen, Tom made it clear that he looked upon her not as a secretary but as a writer. That *was* 'disingenuous'; but there was nothing else he could do.

Biographically, Millgate's argument is not unimportant. That Tom would not have wanted to take Florence to Clodd's if they were having (or were about to have) sexual relations does not follow. In London he was known. A man of sixty-nine would not have wanted (as he might have wanted, and enjoyed, forty years back) to have sexual relations in some park or on some heath. He could not take Florence up to his little back room at the West Central, to be observed (and perhaps even blackmailed – he had not been a novelist for nothing) by some sly porter or boots who knew that the famous novelist's elderly wife was sometimes a guest. Nor could he run the risk of being recognized at any other hotel at which he booked in Florence as his wife. He could not climb in through the window of Florence's room at either Enfield or her aunt's; least of all could he thus enter her room at the Lyceum, where his work was actually the subject of lectures from time to time . . . A kiss and cuddle was one thing; full-blooded love-making was entirely another. Later, in 1911, in a letter to Clodd, she deprecated his casual notion of renting a flat for the season in Finsbury Park – but, since he would have been hoping that Emma would not be there, we can see why he was then interested in such a dingy district: not many, there, would recognize the great novelist and pessimist, or care if he had a mistress visiting him or not.

There was, by contrast, some opportunity for discreet love-making at the house of an understanding and tolerant host. Surely Millgate knows that? Clodd let Clement Shorter into the secret in his letters: in one of them he told him, 'Hardy and the Lady are enjoying themselves.' This was code for: 'are sleeping together'. For 'the Lady', to these two friends and admirers of George Meredith, meant the Lady of the sequence *Modern Love*, still notoriously 'modern' in the middle-class estimation of 1909. Tom may have been more timid in his practice of adultery, but we may be sure that he endorsed 'sonnet' XXV of Meredith's sequence quite as wholeheartedly as they did, and similar sentiments were expressed by him, in his own manner, on scores of occasions:

> You like not that French novel? Tell me why.
> You think it quite unnatural. Let us see.
> The actors are, it seems, the usual three:
> Husband, and wife, and lover. She – but fie!
> In England we'll not hear of it. Edmond,
> The lover, her devout chagrin doth share;
> Blanc-mange and absinthe are his penitent fare,
> Till his pale aspect makes her over-fond:
> So, to preclude fresh sin, he tries rosbif.
> Meantime the husband is no more abused:
> Auguste forgives her ere the tear is used.
> Then hangeth all on one tremendous IF: –
> *If* she will choose between them. She does choose;
> And takes her husband, like a proper wife.
> Unnatural? My dear, these things are life:
> And life, some think, is worthy of the Muse.

I have already made it clear that, unlike other biographers, I believe Florence Dugdale and Tom were lovers (Millgate believes that not even their marriage was consummated). They became so at Strafford House at the time of her first visit there. I do not think, however, that at Strafford House it went as far as full intercourse. That would first have happened in April 1910, when Florence was able to borrow for a few weeks a flat, in a block near Baker Street, from a friend who went abroad. She received a number of people there, including some of her own family; but that did not prevent her also receiving Tom, who stood small risk of being recognized as, no doubt well muffled against the usual London sore throat, he entered the anonymous block and climbed the stairs. He was in London during that April, searching for a flat. At Strafford House I do not think it went further than masturbation, or, as Florence would have thought of it, 'relief': just, in fact, the activity which gave her the most intense pleasure she could experience from any sexual activity. For I do not believe in Tom's 'reticences' any more than I believe in the more obviously hilarious nonsense about the invented mumps. True, there is no more actual evidence for my supposition than there is for Millgate's. But then there seldom is in such cases. It is hard, no doubt, for people to visualize this respectable and timorous woman yielding, in the house on the Suffolk coast, to Tom's exhortations. But it is difficult to visualize any sexual activity, especially on the part of those with whom one is hardly, or not at all, acquainted. Yet such activity is, Millgate will perhaps reluctantly concede, nothing like as rare as it ought to be.

Millgate's view must be based, at least in part, on his theory of Tom's impotence. That theory is based on his childlessness – there is nothing else to support it. My view is based on ordinary expectations; on Tom's own declaration (made – to my own personal knowledge – to Edmund Blunden, in the course of a conversation about age and its effects on sexual potency) that he had been capable of full sexual intercourse until the age of eighty-four (that is, until 1924); and on the knowledge of sexual matters displayed in his writings – knowledge which has not struck many as deficient (an example is Jude's physical longing for Sue). The eroticism of the novels, now widely accepted and the subject of at least one book, *Hardy and the Erotic*, is not likely to have been the result of mere sexual curiosity or of that voyeurism which Gittings tried suspiciously hard to show was exclusive to Hardy. As for the statement to Blunden, this is altogether too much for the fastidious Millgate, who regards it as a 'boast'. None the less, scrupulous as ever, he does gloomily concede at one point that it is 'at least worth considering'. This demonstrates his true opinion of his subject, or at least his fervent hope for him: Tom was an impotent liar who boastfully misled a younger fellow poet as to his sexual prowess. But that hardly matches his other view of Tom as an over-sensitive, prickly, reticent and unconfident autodidact, out of tune with his times, who possessed incidental literary gifts and who wrote one great novel, *Tess*, and a few good untutored poems.

Millgate's other arguments in favour of the 'no sex with Florence' hypothesis may be disposed of more briefly. Her ties to her conventional family were not really particularly 'strong', and they were certainly not 'warm' because her father was not a warm man; in any case women do not need to be 'liberated' or unconventional to be led into adultery, especially by very famous men. The awful daring of a moment's surrender may be unconventional but it is not uncommon, and there is no reason to suppose that Tom, once on the job, was not an astute seducer. That was a burden which his virtue had to bear – but what is virtue without something to bear? As for Marie Stopes' *Love's Creation*: this is a notoriously mawkish and embarrassing novel, and Florence, who had at least a modicum of taste, was merely being polite in telling her that she could not enjoy the love passages.

However, it is not my own intention to suggest that Florence enjoyed sexual intercourse, or that she eagerly became Tom's mistress. She was, I have speculated, the type of woman who regarded sex as a 'duty': she preferred giving 'relief', which was far less strenuous and alarming and gave her the opportunity to provide the comfort and consolation she most enjoyed having within her power. It was her way of loving. Just before she married Tom, when they were toying with the notion of having a child, she asked Hermann Lea if this would be 'safe', 'because of his age'. She was terrified of the prospect. But would she have asked at all if she had not been having, or at least was not expecting to have, sexual relations with him?

On 30 August the grateful Tom wrote to Clodd: 'Would you like a first edition of *The Hand of Ethelberta*, with all Du Maurier's illustrations?' This was accepted, and Clodd's daughter Edith Graham was sent, a few days later, *A Pair of Blue Eyes* as a 'memento of my visit'. A letter of the same month to Florence begins, significantly, not 'My Dear Miss Dugdale' (as the most recent extant one had) but 'Dear F'. Clearly Tom believed that there was now a full understanding between them. Part of this understanding was based upon an agreement that he would help her to push herself forward as a writer, for he was trying to help her with a newspaper sketch about Nelson, and had written a (now lost) covering letter recommending it: 'The sketch reads remarkably well. If you feel you do not like my supposed improvements, rub them out; though I *advise* you to recopy the story as it now stands.' But if she sent it then, the newspapers declined it. It did not appear until a year later, in the *Daily Chronicle*, to an employee of which Tom then had to write, on 20 September 1910, a letter which ended, almost threateningly: 'If you & the Editor tell me that the *Daily Chronicle* do not want literature I have, of course, no answer to make.' But the Nelson sketch was not 'literature', and he knew very well that it was not literature: once married to Florence, Tom discouraged any more writing from her until, understanding at last what she wanted, he was forced to a bizarre compromise. She must have complained, and complained persistently: in 1917 they conceived the idea of a 'biography' of himself, from none other than her hand.

From the following 30 October until 2 November he was once again at Strafford House – and once again with Florence. (For that Clodd received, on 3 December, a copy of *Time's Laughingstocks* fresh from the press and a case of burgundy – the only known occasion upon which Tom sent anyone wine.) Before this second visit and after visiting Chichester Cathedral with Florence, at the end of September and beginning of October, Tom met his brother in London and they all three took a tour of northern cathedrals, including Edinburgh and York. What kind of 'chaperon' was Henry? One as absent as often as possible, one may guess. Here was Tom's closest confidant of all – and one of whom Florence was always fond. One one occasion she compared him to Giles Winterbourne, and no doubt she was prompted in this by a hint thrown out by Giles' creator.

It does not really matter whether Florence was 'technically' Tom's mistress or not. They were having an affair in any case, and she became his 'dearest F'. In the summer of 1910, therefore, they were guilty of an elaborate and even extreme deception of Emma; yet by the autumn Florence was suddenly on close and affectionate terms with her. She became the fulsome praiser of Emma's literary work, and an active agent for it, while living for long periods at Max Gate as her – not Tom's – secretary-assistant and companion.

Yet perhaps 'guilty' is an inappropriate word to describe Tom and Florence in this context. We are dealing here not with 'bad' people deliberately and cynically 'nasty' or in sophisticated pursuit of criminal pleasures, but with people who were 'ordinary' in the sense that they not only wished to be seen as virtuous but also actually wished to be virtuous. Tom rightly deprecated hypocrisy and false morality; but he never advocated deceit as a virtue. And Florence's sense of duty, far less de-conventionalized than Tom's, was one of the main driving forces of her life. These, then, were decent people who had got themselves into a bad way – chiefly with themselves. They felt bad about what they were doing and Florence, in particular, who was never the woman Emma had once been, was forced into a confused and feeble equivocation of attitude that is as understandable as it is unattractive. It is easy to hand out judgements, and to see it all in the light of conventional morality. If we do that, then certainly Florence Dugdale was guilty of slyness, hypocrisy and callous deception of a half-senile old lady. She was quite out of her depth, and, although Tom was much affected by her melancholy, its negative and protesting, even whining, side dragged him down, too. He came to have some reservations about her before he married her; left to himself, he would not, I think, have asked her to marry him. However, that is simply a description of the way these two guilty people felt: the one vastly wise but unsophisticated in the ways of sexual deceit, the other weak, unhappy, passive and perpetually undecided.

Florence and Tom went together to Clodd's at Easter in 1910, and they also visited the Isle of Wight, where they stood at Swinburne's grave. Of this occasion the *Life* says:

> In March, being at Ventnor, Hardy visited Swinburne's grave at Bonchurch, and composed the poem entitled 'A Singer Asleep'. It is remembered by a friend who accompanied him on this expedition how that windy March day had a poetry of its own, how primroses clustered in the hedges, and noisy rooks wheeled in the air over the little churchyard. Hardy gathered a spray of ivy and laid it on the grave of that brother-poet of whom he never spoke save in words of admiration and affection.

The poem, which combines full-blown lyricism – and a certain degree of deliberately high rhetoric – with extreme bitterness, arose from a mixture of emotions. They encompassed memories of how much the poems of the rebellious young Swinburne had meant to him when he was a young man, indignation at the stuffy opposition to him – and the presence of Florence at his side, as, apparently, he then and there wrote some of the first draft. (When Harrison, who by now had taken over the *English Review* from Ford, wrote to him for a poem, he replied: 'All I can lay hands on is a half-finished monody on Swinburne, which I am completing'.) The image of Swinburne's 'garland of red roses' falling about 'the hood of some smug nun' in 'Victoria's formal middle time' points to his defiant and sexually awakened mood.

'In . . . April,' the *Life* informs us, 'he was looking for a flat again in London, and found one at Blomfield Court, Maida Vale, which he and his wife and servants entered in May.' This was while Florence luxuriated in the little borrowed flat near Baker Street, where she was visited by Tom. Gittings and Manton, rather comically in the circumstances, mention that Florence often invited to the flat her married sister Mrs Ethel Richardson, with her little son of six. She wrote, in a reminiscent piece published in a college magazine, that 'there were occasional meetings with T.H. when he was in London'. But Gittings and Manton then add: '. . . she would hardly have taken her little boy to meet him unless Hardy's friendship with Florence had appeared perfectly proper to the Dugdales'. Naturally, it did appear perfectly proper to the Dugdales! It would appear perfectly *improper*, too, to all the Dugdales, and certainly to Gittings and Millgate, if, after marriage, Florence had refused the now State- and Church-licensed demands of her old husband, even if Mrs Dugdale might have added, to the famous advice that had been given to Queen Victoria: 'think of England – and of the Order of Merit!' For Tom was admitted into that Order in June 1910 – and when he received it on 19 July he was accompanied, not by his wife, but by his secretary and amanuensis, who had been sent to Buckingham Palace by her (and by his sisters) to make sure that he did not fail in the formalities, which nevertheless he firmly (and no doubt with secret delight) believed he had.

Blomfield Court was the last of the seasonal London residences that Emma and Tom were to take; however, there is not the remotest possibility that either Tom or Florence was aware of this. There was an element of opportunism in Florence's behaviour, even though she 'backed into it' rather in the manner that her later admired acquaintance T.E. Lawrence 'backed into the limelight'; but it did not amount to any anticipation of, or even conscious wish for, Emma's death. Doubtless there were flashes of hope instantly dismissed as guilty beyond words. These are familiar to everyone except the few who are adept at totally repressing them. It was, however, at the Blomfield Terrace flat that Florence suddenly found herself the close friend and great admirer of Emma.

Her various stories of how it happened are hardly worth repeating, but one actually believed in Dorchester was that she first met the Hardys at Wareham and that Emma took a fancy to her and so invited her to spend a fortnight at Max Gate. This was not true; but doubtless she and Emma did spend an afternoon at Wareham.

Although she was no longer on the staff of the *Standard*, Florence was able – aided and abetted by Tom – to persuade the paper that, as his 'secretary', she was in a position to supply them with the finest celebration of his seventieth birthday on offer in the market. It appeared on his birthday, 2 June 1910, and was in essence his own account of himself, written up with his usual sardonic humour as 'just what they would want' – and indeed it was, for they were 'much pleased' with it. He allowed Florence to believe it was her own work; but it is obviously master-minded by its subject. At almost exactly the same time Florence received an invitation to attend one of Emma's own afternoon gatherings in Maida Vale. Tom made sure, as Millgate rightly points out, that a number of other 'literary women' were present. They included Lady Grove and May Sinclair, of whom he seems to have been genuinely fond and to whom he wrote several letters of invitation to Max Gate – although he was just then busy introducing into his circle as many such women as he could to minimize Florence's prominence.

It has been said that Emma became spontaneously fond of her – and that is true, if it is added that she received considerable help from Florence herself, a naturally ingratiating woman who now set out to be especially so. Unthinkingly, and performing the actions which most satisfied her – helping those for whom she felt sorry – Florence flatteringly fluttered around her, thus simultaneously expiating her guilt. Yet, in discussing the writing of an article she was now working on – at the grateful Tom's suggestion – to celebrate Clodd's seventieth birthday, again for the *Standard*, she told Clodd that, while she believed Tom to be 'a great writer', she did not think he was 'a great man'. This illustrates how naturally double-dealing came to her: at heart she was committed to nothing but, if in the nicest possible way, her own self-advancement. Any notion that such a remark involved disloyalty to her lover was quite beyond her. Tom had been agitating her with his advances, and such women do not like being agitated. Besides, she still liked poor Hyatt best. Her verdict is of course meaningless except to those who wish, not to explain Hardy, but to deduct moral points from him.

Either Emma knew all about Tom's attachment for Florence, and reacted in that 'Christian' (but why should I put the quotation marks around the word?) and kindly manner which would have been appropriate to her character; or, more likely, being the kind and compassionate person that she was – but now incipiently wayward and senile – she gladly fell for it hook, line and sinker. By July Florence was at Max Gate working as Emma's trusted assistant.

What was the extent of Tom's complicity in all this? He cannot have been pleased about Florence's new tenderness towards Emma – when at last he registered it. In the battle of the sexes, if there is such a thing, he had been dealt a severe blow: his mistress had joined up with his wife! The mistress could not be aware of how, one day not so long in the future, she would come to hate the wife's memory! I do not think Tom had planned for Florence to come and join the household in Dorset; he merely wished to gain more and easier access to her – such access as he already had to Lady Grove, May Sinclair and other women younger than himself, married or otherwise. And towards that purpose he wished to introduce her to a circle known to Emma. He succeeded beyond his wildest fears! By July this little mouse of a person was in a position of great power. She had got herself into it by a combination of hypocrisy, lack of the kind of fibre which gives a person genuine loyalty, and luck. But her hypocrisy arose from feebleness of conviction. She had a genuine appreciation of such literature as she could understand; but other motives in her were far stronger. And, no matter how lucky she might seem to be in others' eyes, her fate was always something for her to complain about.

When Emma left Blomfield Terrace that summer for Dorset, Tom stayed on. He could not see how things were going to develop. On Friday, 15 July he sent her a letter suggesting that, if the cough with which she had been troubled was not better, she should spend 'a few days by the sea-side': 'But I would not go very far, & certainly would not come back to London.' If she came back to London, his tentative plans for staying on there with Florence would be stymied. He described how he was getting on in the flat emptied of her:

> If I can get off on Tuesday afternoon I think I will run down to the sea somewhere for a day or two before coming home . . . Henry sends a post card saying he *saw* Rolls the aviator killed at Bournemouth! Put 'O.M.' *only*, on the envelope after my name.

On the following Monday, in a further letter to Emma, he noted that he proposed to return on the Wednesday, which he did. He seems to have failed to persuade Florence to join him at the seaside. But he now mentioned her to Emma for the first time in writing: 'Miss Dugdale is coming this afternoon, if she can or to morrow, to see that I am all right, & to put things straight preparatory to my leaving & to write some letters.' His meaning is a little uneasily expressed. Miss Dugdale had been asked to keep an eye on him and the flat by Emma, and, by the former's sleight of hand, Emma was now her devoted friend.

It is not known how Tom reacted to Florence's volte-face. Certainly such astonishing and effective duplicity could only have been practised by a person capable of turning her gaze away from her own motives. We do know that, whether or not Florence was already Tom's mistress, he wished to draw her more and more tightly into the web of his affections. We know, too, what he really thought about the 'sanctity of the marriage vows'. Such women as Florence do not enjoy being sexually disturbed, even by OMs. They are flattered, but they want – even need – to keep their distance: if they commit themselves, then they might have to surrender altogether to their powerful sense of duty. By attaching herself to Emma and moaning about Tom in letters to Clodd, she could retain her attraction for Hardy but edge away from his urgent spiritual and physical attentions. What chance would he now have of being close to her under his own wife's roof, and she his wife's warmest critic, agent and now even her virulent anti-Catholic co-religionist! Max Gate, far from being a dangerous place, was the best of all Florence's avenues of escape: it left her with all options open.

33

A Usual Mistake

In the concluding months of 1910, Florence established herself as Emma's indispensable guest at Max Gate. To Tom, as well, she was apparently indispensable as a 'handyman', as he jokingly described her to Clodd in a letter of 15 November 1910, when she had just turned up with her typewriter.

Emma had almost two years of life left to her. She suffered from breathlessness, coughing, lameness and other ailments of old age – and possibly, as I have suggested, from brief bouts of dementia. But she still had energy, and continued to make visits and even did some cycling. Her book *Spaces* consisted of four prose poems, 'High Delights of Heaven', 'Acceptors or Non-Acceptors' (of this piece Florence Dugdale had written, to Emma: 'I am just burning with anxiety to know the fate of [it]), 'The New Element of Fire' and 'Retrospect'. Published privately by Longmans of Dorchester in April 1912, this work has been said to contain signs of 'mild religious mania'. But although an artistic failure, which Charles Moule (to whom she sent it) had tried to persuade her to postpone on the grounds that the world was not yet ready for it, it contains no sign whatsoever of mania. Its contents, especially for one who had loved the woman who, in her old age, wrote it, are moving – even the inadequacy of expression is, in its way, moving. We can see why Tom said of her that she was so 'living'. But he was embarrassed by the presence of *Spaces* on the counters of some of the Dorchester shops; perhaps he secretly bought up all the copies and burned them. But how did he feel about it a few months later, when Emma was suddenly taken from him? His response must then in no way have resembled that of his biographers, who have judged it, not by the standards of his private feelings, but, ludicrously, by those he publicly set as a writer.

Florence, now ensconced at Max Gate except for quite brief periods in London or at Enfield, began to write to Clodd regularly. Being by nature all things to all men and women, and having little character of her own, she effortlessly took on his colour. He was genial, teasing, a little mocking, loyal, not truly sensitive, seeing the funny side of the world unless driven to dogmatic indignation by what he saw as the absurdities of superstition-religion. He was a connoisseur of literary people, and knew many; he was also, after his limited fashion, enlightened and well disposed; but he understood little of what literature, and in particular poetry, was about. His reaction at the news of Emma's death was that it would be a great relief to his friend. His response in his diary to the death of his own estranged first wife was that he was glad to find himself a widower.

In her letters to Clodd, Florence began to poke fun at Tom and Emma – especially at Tom for his parsimony and even for that apparent absent-mindedness which was necessary for him as a writer. Clodd did not think him 'a great man' (whatever that meant to Clodd), and so she did not, either. When she met him by chance in London in early 1911 she was able to relay intimate Max Gate gossip about the difficulties between these two people who had been so good to her, to whom she had so eagerly attached herself, and whom she had flattered so fulsomely to their faces ('the highest forms of literature,' she had consolingly told not Tom, but Emma, 'seem rarely to have any great commercial value'). When her first week's visit was over Tom had written the poem 'After the Visit', speaking of her 'mute ministrations' 'Beyond a man's sayings sweet', and published it in the *Spectator* almost immediately. How 'sweet' would he have thought it of Florence to have passed on to Clodd a copy of it, even before it appeared, describing it as written in tribute to herself? The Max Gate situation, she officiously told Clodd in 1910, 'wore an air of comedy'. Tom luxuriated 'in misery'. She felt '*intensely*' sorry for Emma; indeed, she felt sorry for them both. This did not prevent her from inveigling Tom, the comic hypochondriac whose depression should not be taken 'too seriously', into writing the story 'Blue Jimmy the Horse-Stealer' to help enhance her literary reputation: it appeared under her name in the *Cornhill* for February 1911. It was in late September that he wrote the sharp letter to Milne of the *Daily Chronicle* about her Nelson piece. She seems never to have slackened her resolve to get Tom to further her literary cause. But even by then he must have been disappointed that she still showed no sign of writing anything 'serious' of her own. She did, however, continue with her children's books – but these were mere hack-work to which he himself contributed the best bits. And did he know that she was thinking, or said she was thinking, of collaborating on a novel with Emma? He did not for the time being consider the implications of her friendship with Emma, because she aroused him sexually. Of that, she must have been well aware. Yet she could tell Clodd: 'Mrs Hardy is good to me beyond words.'

When Kitsey, his favourite cat, died in early November, he was broken-hearted. On 19 December he told Mrs Henniker, simply: 'Yes: the poor cat was such a loss. She was "the study cat", & used to sleep on my writing table on any clean sheets of paper, & be much with me.' 'In the face of such a calamity, I cannot', Florence gratuitously told Clodd, 'write and sympathize with T.H. upon the death of Kitsey.' The calamity? Sir Thornley had had a 'crushing blow. His wife, Lady Stoker, died last night.' Even here she could not bear to omit Emily Stoker's only very recently acquired title, of which Lady Stoker herself can have known nothing. As for Tom, he did not know Lady Stoker; nor did he know Sir Thornley. Florence exaggerated her own importance in order to impress Clodd: Lady Stoker was her 'dear, dear friend', and Sir Thornley was her 'good and kind friend in Dublin'. Although she could not help her confusion, it is hardly surprising that the Stoker family eventually regarded her as a pious hypocrite, the 'woman who got the Stoker money'. But Tom was not to register this fully for some years. Then he was obliged to fling her the gift of the *Life* to keep her from what was undoubtedly a long litany of complaint and cleverly directed reproach.

On 8 November she told Clodd:

Mr T.H. has been in the depths of despair at the death of a pet cat. 'Providence,' he wrote, 'has dealt me an entirely gratuitous & unlooked-for blow' . . . he is also finding a melancholy pleasure in writing an appropriate inscription for 'Kitsey's' headstone, so that Providence has not done all the harm it intended this time.

There is a nasty tone about this: it does not make affectionate fun of him. And she thus, and instantly, reported to Clodd, Tom's intimate letter – surely all too obviously intended for her own eyes only – for what she hoped would be his laughs. When, a day or two later, on 14 November, the trusted 'handyman' turned up at Max Gate, she found him at work on 'The Roman Gravemounds' (then 'By the Roman Earthworks' and later, in the *Fortnightly* where it was published in the following year, 'Among the Roman Gravemounds'). On the 16th she rushed to pen and paper to regale Clodd with yet more facetious tattle:

I went into Mr Hardy's study yesterday & found him working at a pathetic little poem describing the melancholy burial of the white cat. I looked over his shoulder and read this line: 'That little white cat was his only friend'. That was too much even for my sweet temper, & I romped about the study exclaiming: 'This is hideous ingratitude.' But the culprit seemed highly delighted with himself, & said, smilingly, that he was not exactly writing about himself but about some imaginary man in a similar situation.

This is the 'pathetic little poem':

> By Rome's dim relics there walks a man,
> Eyes bent; and he carries a basket and spade;
> I guess what impels him to scrape and scan;
> Yea, his dreams of that Empire long decayed.
>
> 'Vast was Rome,' he must muse, 'in the world's regard,
> Vast it looms there still, vast it will ever be;'
> And he stoops to dig and unmine some shard
> Left by those who are held in such memory.
>
> But no; in his basket, see, he has bought
> A little white furred thing, stiff of limb,
> Whose life never won from the world a thought;
> It is this, and not Rome, that is moving him.
>
> And to make it a grave he has come to the spot,
> And he delves in the ancient dead's long home;
> Their fames, their achievements, the man knows not;
> The furred thing is all to him – nothing Rome!
>
> 'Here say you that Caesar's warriors lie? –
> But my little white cat was my only friend!
> Could she but live, might the record die
> Of Caesar his legions, his aims, his end!'
>
> Well, Rome's long rule is oft and again
> A theme for the sages of history,
> And the small furred life was worth no one's pen;
> Yet its mourner's mood has a charm for me.

Had he then explained to Florence that he had chosen the Roman example as an apt parallel to his own fame, she would doubtless have replied how wonderful it was to be famous, and how much the nation honoured him.

Meanwhile (in an undated letter, but written about this time in 1910) she told Emma: 'I cannot find words sufficient to thank you for your great kindness . . . The days I spend at Max Gate are all so happy that I sometimes fear I shall be spoiled for the sterner realities of life.' But those sterner realities were going to play into her hands sooner than she believed possible.

Exactly how life was conducted under the Max Gate roof in those months is not possible to say. Florence could with good reason frustrate any desires Tom might wish to put into effect, and she was in any case busy pretending to market Emma's work. She typed out the ancient 'The Maid on the Shore' and tried to sell it, only venturing to make vague criticisms about its datedness in certain respects ('I do quite *honestly* admire it,' she told Emma). Did she tell Tom that she really must humour his wife, or did she carry on with the flattery regardless, relying on his infatuation with her? Tom, knowing nothing about her letters to Clodd, himself wrote on 11 August:

> I have seen my little cousin F. for a brief while. As you say, a change will do her a world of good. She has to get home by the 7th for a wedding on the 8th (the Thursday after Sept 2) & is coming down here a day or two later. So that I don't think fortnightly tickets [between London and Aldeburgh] will be necessary; but that perhaps may be left open.

He and Florence were at Aldeburgh from 2 September until the 6th; there they met the armchair anthropologist James Frazer of *Golden Bough* fame, and, once again, the classical historian J.B. Bury and his wife. On 4 October he wrote again to Clodd, asking him down for the weekend of the 14th; but he was ill and was unable to come then, or on another date Tom offered him. Did he fight shy of the whole set-up?

While Tom was having his portrait done by William Strang (who had painted him seventeen years earlier, in 1893) over the weekend of 23–26 September, he prevailed upon him to do a portrait of Florence. When he received it he wrote to Strang on 5 October:

> The portrait . . . is charming. But what am I to give you for it? I was

meaning a mere outline that would have taken you five minutes, & here is this beautiful sketch, with its touch of idealism deftly thrown over a strictly honest likeness.

Florence had become the pet of the household, just as (apparently) she had become the pet of the Stoker household. Tom's pet, certainly, too: on the day before Strang arrived she and he had gone to Maiden Castle: a bunch of dried flowers with the date on it – noted by Purdy – memorializes the occasion. By December she had become the pet, too, of Mrs Florence Henniker, to whom Tom had hopefully sent her. In his 19 December letter to her about Kitsey he wrote:

Miss Dugdale mentioned to me that she had been with you. It was a great enjoyment for her. *Nobody* but you does kind things like that, & I am sincerely grateful to you. I am so glad you like her: she quite loves you – indeed you have no idea what a charm you have for her. Her literary judgement is very sound.

But pet or not, she was determined not to go to France with Emma, who in November 1910 was planning a trip there in order, she said, to do her husband good – by leaving him to fend for himself. Quite possibly Florence feared for her own health; equally possibly she was egged on by Tom, who may have dreamed of some scheme by which she might 'look after him' during Emma's absence. She pleaded that her father had forbidden her to go, on account of the cold weather. There was also the question of Sir Thornley Stoker: meetings between these two – in London or even briefly in Dublin – cannot be ruled out. She destroyed all Stoker's letters to her; hers to him have not come to light. Doubtless she told him to destroy them, as she later begged Owen (who of course did not). After all, Stoker not only left her a large sum of money, but also gave her – at some time unknown, but perhaps at the end of 1910, since his effects were then being sold up – an antique ring of great value. It is just possible that Florence was playing him along as she was playing Tom along: she had no idea that his days were numbered. She had two trump cards: her 'sweetness', which she had cultivated by careful study, and her undoubted beauty, which did not turn into dowdiness until a year or two later, after her marriage. That she concentrated upon the notion of herself as sweet, helpful and fragile we may be sure. However, the genuine sense of duty, the scrupulosity, always ran parallel to the sweetness; therefore guilt could never be far away except in relatively brief moments of intoxication with what she thought of as her social successes.

Tom obtained more satisfaction from the freedom of the Borough of Dorchester, awarded to him at a ceremony on 16 November 1910, than he ever did from the OM. He may have known that he was not popular locally, and that the honour had not been easy for his few friends to arrange; but he was still determined to enjoy it – largely, no doubt, because he remembered how he had been mocked by certain people while still an unknown young man. He managed a speech of acceptance, in the presence of the whole of his surviving family and of Emma and Florence; but the experience hardened him against further public speaking unless it was unavoidable. In the *Life* he wrote:

> After the presentation – which was witnessed by Mrs Hardy, by Mr (afterwards Sir Henry) Newbolt, by the writer of this memoir, and by other friends, the Dorchester Dramatic Society gave for the first time, at the hand of their own dramatist [A.H. Evans, the pharmacist], an adaptation of *Under the Greenwood Tree* entitled *The Mellstock Quire* – the second title of the novel – Hardy himself doing no more than supply the original carols formerly sung by the Quire of the parish outshadowed by the name 'Mellstock' – the village of Stinsford, a mile from the town.

He enjoyed this performance, and took an increasing interest in all similar future events. One of them was, much later, to be the indirect cause of Florence's greatest agony of jealousy.

He was much less interested in the project of one F. Outwin Saxelby of Handsworth, which provoked this icy letter written on 26 December:

> My reply . . . has been withheld owing to my inability to perceive how the work you contemplate can be satisfactorily carried out . . . Before you proceed I should wish to have a letter from Messrs Routledge authorizing you to perform the work.

The work which the wretched Saxelby had in mind, and did carry out, was *A Thomas Hardy Dictionary* (1911). He promptly sent Tom the required material, and received this even more icy reply dated 4 January:

> To make matters clear before you proceed, you will quite understand

that there is no wish on my part that such a book should be prepared. I have no objection to your publishing it – that is all; so that I could not consent to any statement being made that it is authorized by me.

Tom may have been in an ill humour just then: according to Florence, but only according to her, he had had a fearful quarrel with Emma on Christmas Day. When, according to this not unlikely tale, he wanted to take Florence to see Mary and Kate, Emma claimed that they would poison Florence's mind against her. No doubt, by this time, they would have done. Only Henry, it seems, now had easy access to Emma.

His hostile attitude towards Saxelby may have arisen, too, from his regard and friendship for Hermann Lea. It is significant that he quoted to Saxelby Lea's *Handbook* as an authority on the matter of his attitude towards identifications of real places with ones mentioned in his work. On 22 February 1911 he sent a card to Lea specifically asking him to call. Was this the genesis of Lea's more thorough work of 1913? By early 1912 he was the tenant, with Tom's blessing, of the Bockhampton cottage. And when Saxelby, 'slogging down the busless Dorset lanes disgustedly' (as a foolish poet has put it), had completed his task and sent Tom the proofs, he received this reply dated 9 September 1911:

> . . . I could not possibly give them [the proofs] an exhaustive examination, but I have drawn your attention to a few statements that caught my eye in turning them over.
>
> The words added to the preface are indispensable . . . By inserting them the awkward necessity I might otherwise be under of publicly disavowing any authorization of the book, will be avoided. In the interests of the book I advise you to omit the deleted words of the dedication.

Saxelby did add Tom's 'indispensable' words: 'It is to be clearly understood that Mr Hardy has not authorized this book, and can accept no responsibility for its production.' But, gallantly, he retained his dedication (actually, 'inscription'), and the 'by permission' – presumably the words Tom wished him to delete – remained. Two days later Tom was writing cordially to Lea about a photograph 'for the book' – that is, the book he trusted by the man he trusted. Much later, on 9 January 1926, writing to Sir Frederick Macmillan who had asked him if he would agree to a new and revised edition of the Saxelby book, he said:

I have looked up 'The Thomas Hardy Dictionary' by F.O. Saxelby that you mention . . . It is, I think, rather a useless book, being a compilation of commonplace ingenuity . . . In addition to this it tells the supposed real places concealed by the fictitious names, which is merely an overlapping of Mr Lea's book.

He thought that if another publisher took it up there would be no difficulty: 'I should have a free hand in asserting it to be incomplete, ill-proportioned, erroneous, or what not.' A little later he told an interested party that Saxelby, along with another, was a mere guesser and was 'wrong'. Only Lea's book, he declared, had his approval. And thus Saxelby vanishes, along with Hedgcock, as one of the most rejected of all those who tried to write on Hardy. Only the terrible Brennecke was to come.

For almost two years Tom had to meet Florence away from Max Gate. Why, then, did she not return there until Emma's death? She may have decided that, if she returned, she might herself become directly involved in some new row. Or she may have decided that she could go no further with this deceit. Perhaps Tom himself decided that it was taking matters too far. Perhaps she had not liked her experience during her November visit, when Emma had jokingly asked her if she did not think that Tom looked a good deal like Crippen, the American dentist and notorious killer of his wife. She, too, Emma felt, might end up buried in the cellar. Florence, whose sense of humour was not well developed, related this to Clodd with an air of dismayed solemnity which demonstrates how far out of her depth she was at Max Gate.

Most likely of all, though, Florence made a compact with Tom – one that she could have made if she had been his mistress and thus in a position of strength. She could hardly threaten him with exposure. Nor would she have thought of that: as well as exposing herself, it was too like plain blackmail. What I think she told him, while no doubt she 'romped around' (that had been a phrase a little too revealing, in the letter to Clodd: it implied an intimacy beyond friendship), was that she could no longer live under his roof (as his mistress), but that she would continue the relationship if, and only if, he did more to help her with her writing. She would have represented herself like this: what chance do I have, as your mistress, now fatally compromised, to do anything for myself unless you help me to establish myself?

We do not know enough of the nature of their intimacies to be able to say exactly *how* she brought this off; but that was the dilemma which she put before him. Perhaps she did not make it sound like an ultimatum, but instead cajoled him into this course of action. She had not reckoned on the mediocrity, though, of her own literary performance: that she would have to get beyond the kinds of journalism and hack-writing for children in which she was presently engaged. So far as is known, he had not helped her to obtain the commission from Hodder and Stoughton for two books, *The Book of Baby Beasts* (1911) and *The Book of Baby Birds* (1912), picture books with detachable texts (partly by him). But that was not what she wanted. She wanted to be a 'famous writer'.

Having disposed, for the second time, of the indefatigable Saxelby on 4 January 1911; and having refused, again for the second time, to compose anything in honour of the accession of King George V (whose coronation, despite an invitation from the Earl Marshal, he also refused to attend – by reason of 'unavoidable circumstances', which he was able to anticipate on 2 March for an event of 22 June), Tom could turn his attention to what was occupying his mind most of all. But Saxelby was still rankling in his mind (he even mentioned him, bitterly, in the *Life*): for in writing to her (as his 'dearest F.') on 11 January for her thirty-second birthday on the following day, he added to his gift of a lamp, doubtless already given at Christmas in anticipation of the birthday, a copy of Lea's little 1905 *Handbook*: 'It is the best of the several published.' He was in London soon after that, at the end of January, perhaps on her literary behalf. He had tried to get her to do real and personal work on the 'Blue Jimmy' story, now out, and told Reginald Smith, editor of the *Cornhill*, that she had taken trouble to verify the facts in the British Museum.

His reward, of which he had no knowledge, was that his dearest F. wrote to Clodd on 2 February 1911 as usual: to mock her helper. She may have been at the height of her excitement with the Henniker establishment, and thus particularly heedless. Tom had a 'sore throat and it's my fault, because I make him talk in the London streets and then the germs attack him. He was taking germ-killers the whole time too.' This is, again, not the language of affection.

When she was not at Enfield, Florence was revelling in the company of Mrs Henniker. She later gushed about how she had used the Henniker household 'as a hotel practically whenever I liked . . . as if it were my home, almost'. She had the privilege of taking the French bulldogs Milner and Empire for walks in the park and typing Mrs Henniker's stories (not so easy this, for she resented hard work and tried to fight shy of it).

Tom's letter of 11 January to Florence mentions a project:

> I am not sure whether you did wisely or not in telling the editor what
> the idea of the book was: you may depend upon it now that if you
> don't carry it out somebody else will. I have repeatedly mentioned
> schemes & abandoned them, & found them used by others.
>
> However, you must try it. I have been hunting for my notes, but
> have not time to write them out this evening. I find that though my
> first thought was that 'she' (the country) should be the teller – i.e., a
> person in the singular, I subsequently modified it to 'we' (the people)
> as being more workable.

The 'notes' referred to here must be those (already quoted) as copied out
ten years later, in 1921. It seems, therefore, that the latest project he had
thought up for her had something to do with *The Dynasts*: an exposition
of it, master-minded by its author? One may be sure that, whatever it
was, most of the hard work would have to come from Tom. It did not
materialize. There is, it may be observed, a certain briskness (born of
weariness?) in his 'However, you must try it.' By now she was much
engaged with Mrs Henniker and her household.

Florence would at first work on projects with enthusiasm, but had
little staying power: energetic excitement too soon gave way to melancholy, depression and exhaustion. What excited her most was the company of the titled people to whom Tom, and then Mrs Henniker, introduced her: the reason, no doubt, for the inclusion of so many lists of them
in 'her' *Life* of her husband, which she was persuaded to curtail after his
death by Cockerell and Sir James Barrie – as if he had included them.

During 1911, despite not coming to Max Gate, she met Tom many
times. Apart from frequent occasions in London, and going to Clodd's
together twice, she went with him on no fewer than three 'tours' –
of cathedrals in April, of the Lake District in June, and of the West
Country in December. On each occasion they were accompanied by
others. In June they had not only Henry Hardy and Florence's sister
Constance (five years her junior, and another teacher) with them, but
also the facetious headmaster of St Andrew's National School for Boys,
Enfield. It may have been his presence, at least in part, that inspired Tom
to note, of the dungeons in Carlisle Castle, that 'evil men out of the evil
treasure of their hearts have brought forth evil things'. Constance told
Purdy that Tom was then (she was twenty-seven) trying to make a
match between her and Henry (who was sixty); but it is more likely

that he made a few jocular remarks which were taken with the usual Dugdalian solemnity.

Edward Dugdale had undoubtedly been persuaded to be there by Florence, anxious to reassure him that there was nothing but respectability between her and her famous friend. Throughout that year and the next she was doing all she could to interpose such barriers between herself and Tom. The rather Shelleyan poem 'To Meet, or Otherwise' appeared in Clement Shorter's *Sphere* on 20 December 1913, just a few weeks before Tom married Florence, and is often supposed to have been written that year – and in any case after Emma's death. But, as Millgate, too, suggests, it seems rather to have been prompted by the circumstances of 1911 or 1912:

> Whether to sally and see thee, girl of my dreams,
> > Or whether to stay
> And see thee not! How vast the difference seems
> > Of Yea from Nay
> Just now. Yet this same sun will slant its beams
> > At no far day
> On our two mounds, and then what will the difference weigh!
>
> Yet I will see thee, maiden dear, and make
> > The most I can
> Of what remains to us amid this brake
> > Cimmerian
> Through which we grope, and from whose thorns we ache,
> > While still we scan
> Round our frail faltering progress for some path or plan.
>
> By briefest meeting something sure is won;
> > It will have been:
> Nor God nor Demon can undo the done,
> > Unsight the seen,
> Make muted music be as unbegun,
> > Though things terrene
> Groan in their bondage till oblivion supervene.
>
> So, to the one long-sweeping symphony
> > From times remote
> Till now, of human tenderness, shall we
> > Supply one note,

Small and untraced, yet that will ever be
   Somewhere afloat
Amid the spheres, as part of sick Life's antidote.

This poem could not have existed without the example of Shelley and
Keats; but it has the authentic Hardyan note. It transcends its occasion,
but nevertheless surely presupposes not only that there is some officially
moral, 'world-imposed' reason why the couple should not meet, but also
that there is a valid reason why they should not do so. That is why it
seems to belong to a period when such a bar was in place. If Florence
Dugdale was anxious above all things to avoid scandalous imputations,
Tom, too, was concerned with his own deceit. He may have believed
that such prohibitions ought not to exist, but he knew that they did,
and he knew that his deception of Emma involved pettinesses of a sort
he detested. That Tom was deeply depressed, and felt himself to be
living in a 'brake Cimmerian' (the Cimmeril, referred to in the *Odyssey*,
were doomed to live 'where the sun never shone'), is evident. Emma
had by this time become unpredictable in her behaviour, and perhaps
too quickly forgot that she had ever made her wilder outbursts. Perhaps
we need not take too seriously such Florence- and town gossip-inspired
tattle as that she threatened his life and that he had to call for his
brother's help, or that she called the police and that he was subsequently
given a 'dressing-down', for infidelity, by the chief constable; these are
exaggerations, and the latter one is comic. Yet Emma was also just then
writing 'Some Recollections' . . .

   Tom buried himself as much as he could in a new project. In October
1910 Macmillan had received a request from a Boston publisher,
Hinkley, for a so-called edition de luxe of his complete works, of
which he was to sign five hundred copies printed on Japanese paper.
That fell through, but developed into the Macmillan Wessex Edition
of 1912–13, for which he wrote a new general preface, updated the
individual prefaces, and gave all his texts their last radical (although
not in all cases their absolutely last) revision. He himself drew the map
of Wessex, and it was Hermann Lea who was credited as the supplier of
the frontispiece photographs. He was thus able to get into his study with
a good excuse, should that be needed – and he did in fact become very
interested in revising his novels, which he thought 'immature' by the side
of his newer work. Through the work involved in the preparation of this
edition he managed to involve Florence in some typing and, possibly,
proof-reading.

Forced to labour, despite ill health and exhaustion, as a teacher until she was twenty-seven, Florence yearned for a life of ease amongst titled and famous people, as well as fame as a novelist in her own right. The two desires were hardly reconcilable. Tom was by now not altogether happy with her tastes, and, in writing on 17 March 1911 to Mrs Henniker, observed that

> Miss Dugdale has written this week, & tells me that she went to the play with you, & much liked going. My taste for the theatre is, I fear, weakening, which hers is certainly not . . . I am very lonely and dull down here, & wish I could be more in London; but I always get influenza or a putrid throat if I go.

He meant the London theatre. In the same year he looked forward to a Dorchester amateur production of a short play, *The Three Wayfarers*, based upon his 'Three Strangers' story, presented together with the Evans' adaptation of his 'Distracted Preacher'.

In March he was irritable and fretting. On the 22nd, having returned from a trip to Bristol Cathedral and Bath Abbey, he replied in these terms to the Rev. R. Grosvenor Bartelot's request for money for an extension of the church of Fordington St George, which he had always opposed: 'Frankly, I have no money for church building; &, still more frankly, I don't care about altering the excellent proportions of the old church.'

Having returned from his trips to Aldeburgh and the cathedrals of Lichfield, Worcester, Hereford and Birmingham, he told Clodd that *they* (the 'sisters', Constance and Florence, and Henry) had 'enjoyed the brief tour greatly'. Florence's sisters, who knew nothing of and cared nothing for literature, were to remain somewhat of an irritation to him – but one of them, Eva, a trained nurse, would be at his side when he died. 'However,' he added to Clodd, 'I never had a more cheerful time at Aldeburgh.' The company on the little tour had doubtless annoyed him. It may be that Mrs Henniker was now receiving some of the barbs that might more reasonably have been directed at Florence Dugdale. But she had been getting them, whether she recognized them or not, for years. He wrote to her on 3 May telling her that he had to be in London during the week of the 15th to the 22nd for a Foreign Office function which Emma wanted to attend, 'so I suppose I must', and then went on:

> . . . In your last very charming letter (you *can* write them when you

choose) you say you wd like to see those poems which appeared in
the F. Revw called 'Satires of Circumstance'. Perhaps you have met
with them by this time, but if not I have a copy here & will send it
on your letting me know. You will remember, I am sure, that being
satires they are rather brutal. I express no feeling or opinion myself
at all. They are from notes I made some twenty years ago, & found
were more fit for verse than prose.

He had already told her, in March, that he did not 'dare' send her a
copy of them: 'I *know* you won't like them . . . We have drifted so far
apart in our views of late years.' That feeling was an old one: they had
started to 'drift apart' in the railway carriage on the way to Winchester.
This was his only way of expressing his feelings about Florence Dugdale,
at that moment no doubt excitedly sharing her new aristocratic friend's
safer opinions. If the line about the white cat had inspired her to romp
about and protest, then what could she have thought of those fifteen
pieces? Whether he truly worked them from earlier 'notes' or not, 'At
Tea', the first, assuredly re-enacts a moment in 1910 at Max Gate,
although it cunningly makes the wife 'young':

> The kettle descants in a cosy drone,
> And the young wife looks in her husband's face,
> And then at her guest's, and shows in her own
> Her sense that she fills an envied place;
> And the visiting lady is all abloom,
> And says there was never so sweet a room.
>
> And the happy young housewife does not know
> That the woman beside her was first his choice,
> Till the fates ordained it could not be so . . .
> Betraying nothing in look or voice
> The guest sits smiling and sips her tea,
> And he throws her a stray glance yearningly.

The second of the 'Satires', 'In Church', may satirize both Tom and
Florence in their pious pretences towards each other. But self-knowledge
did him no more good than it does anyone in such circumstances: he
remained besotted. He went to London by himself in late May, and
must have seen as much of Florence as she would allow. He wrote to
Emma on the 20th emphasizing how much he wanted to be at home:

I think of returning . . . I was coming sooner, as I am beginning to feel fatigued . . . I must stay over . . . It is cold and wintry . . . I should not be able to stand the knocking about the streets – which one cannot avoid doing – if I did not eat more than I do at home. I try to do this.

He could not even find the energy to call on Mrs Henniker, and was, evidently, acutely miserable. The tedious June trip to the Lakes, with Constance and Edward Dugdale, may not have improved his temper. Whatever letters he sent to Florence Dugdale at this time have long been cast into oblivion: there is nothing extant until a postcard of 6 September, which demonstrates that she did some work on the Wessex Edition. In it Tom adds, plaintively: 'You may like to know that the indisposition is passing away.' His interest in his health has been much mocked by his biographers, as it also was – if only behind his back, and more mildly – by Florence; but he was, after all, over seventy, and he especially felt his age in London. Clodd continued to invite him to Strafford House, and his breaks there were always refreshing; yet he had no clear understanding with Florence, since he had to write to Clodd on 3 October:

Your inquiry whether I am going to see you at Aldeburgh before 1912 has set me thinking. If I come at all, I think it had better be before the weather turns into complete winter, & whilst it is only half-way, as at present.

Would Saturday to Monday, the 21st or 28th of this month, suit for my run down to you, with my young friend? If so, would you mind sending her a line suggesting it? Two or three days of your air does pick her up so.

Sincere thanks for your unceasing hospitality.

And he tacked on to the end Florence's address 'for the next ten days or so': 'Grosvenor House, Esplanade, Weymouth'. She had already spent some days at Worthing, in West Sussex, with Emma; now she was at Weymouth 'for a week or two's change', Tom told Mrs Henniker, also on 3 September – and he 'ran down' that afternoon to see how she 'was getting on'. But she would not even look in at Max Gate.

At this time his life was made easier in the respect of the disposition of his manuscripts. In 1908 Sydney Cockerell, once William Morris' secretary, had been made director of the Fitzwilliam Museum in Cambridge. He remained there until 1937, and died in 1962 at the age of ninety-five. An insensitive man, of enormous *chutzpah* – but not dishonest – he was brilliant at insinuating himself into authors' good graces and getting their personal papers from them. He was astonishingly, sometimes terrifyingly, overbearing. He wrote to Tom and asked him if, although he had not read his works, he could have the manuscripts of some of them for the Fitzwilliam! Then he called at Max Gate on 29 September and more or less ordered Tom to distribute his manuscripts according to his own scheme. For some reason Tom valued him so much that he made him one of his executors. His letters of 5 and 11 October 1911 hand over to Cockerell the entire disposition of his literary effects – he threw in for good measure his lines on Swinburne's death: would 'this short MS', he asked, 'be any good?' However, it may be seen at Putney Public Library in London and so for that and for much else we do have reason to be grateful to Cockerell.

In early December Tom and Florence took a short trip to Bath and Gloucester, in which they were accompanied by Mary or Kate – probably the latter, since Mary's health had begun to decline. When a little later he came to send Florence his greetings for Christmas and the New Year he added: '"Ye have been called unto liberty" – Gal. V.13'. This passage reads, starting at verse 12: 'I would they were even cut off which trouble you. For, brethren, ye have been called unto liberty; only *use* not liberty for an occasion to the flesh, but by love serve one another.' This, surely, means that 'they' had decided not to sleep together, and that Tom had now reconciled himself to the fact; if verse 12 was too 'coarse' for Florence, it certainly was not for the always bawdy Tom. Alternatively, it could mean that they *had* slept together on the trip, in which case it is a joke – but Florence in that case would hardly have been a suitable recipient of the card. She lost no time in giving a chatty and full report to Clodd of this trip. She was unhappy: her friend Hyatt had just died on 9 December, after a sudden attack of bleeding. She told Clodd all about Hyatt's death, and may also have told Tom – but if she did, then that letter is missing. It is more likely that she kept her feelings for Hyatt from him. In a complaining letter of December 1914 to Rebekah Owen she said that she would have given the rest of her life to be able to spend just one hour with Hyatt.

There are only one or two accounts of Emma in her last days. It is clear that, although she was often ailing, her death came out of the blue and was quite unexpected by the family doctor, Gowring. Her pain she controlled by the use of a popular and exceedingly potent sedative of the time, *Liquor opii sedativus*, a mixture of sherry, pure alcohol and opium.

She was able to order this at her pleasure, and there is no way of knowing how much of it she may have secretly imbibed. She could have obtained it at various chemists in Worthing, Weymouth and elsewhere, as well as Dorchester. Like many before and after her, she was terrified of surgery and preferred to allay her pain rather than submit to it.

Her behaviour had by now become so eccentric that when a highly unlikely pair, Henry Newbolt (agonized by toothache until relieved by laudanum) and W.B. Yeats, came down to Max Gate on Tom's seventy-second birthday to present him with the Gold Medal of the Royal Society of Literature, he had to ask her to leave while the ceremony was in progress: 'the audience was quite properly limited' he later recorded. What Yeats felt about the two cats who sat on the dinner table by Emma he never recorded: throughout the meal she regaled him with details of their lives and habits, while Tom talked to Newbolt about architecture.

In early September they entertained Gosse and the author of 'Land of Hope and Glory', A.C. Benson, a depressive Cambridge man who became Master of Magdalene in 1915. He was the brother to R.H., a Catholic convert, and E.F. the novelist. A.C. kept an enormous and highly readable diary, full of malice and acute but limited observation. Too much has therefore been made of his entry about this visit: for hatred and pathological fear of women was one of his chief features, and so he expounds upon the pitiable state of Emma and the run-down condition of Max Gate. But all he really tells us is that Emma was by now a rambling and inconsequential old lady – and that, perhaps, her husband's more tactless guests often brought out the worst in her. If one were sufficiently malicious, one could compile an equally poisonous account of any visit to any old couple.

The low point of 1912 was Emma's sudden death. The high point, at least for us, was Tom's speedy, almost miraculous, response to the loss of the *Titanic*, with fifteen hundred lives, on 15 April. The White Star owners had been so arrogant in their belief that their ship was unsinkable that they had not bothered to provide sufficient lifeboats. That attitude, reflecting the hubris of an over-complacent world soon to be plunged into a war of unprecedented savagery, was a perfect subject for Tom, who did not look in a sanguine spirit upon the notion of 'human progress' and deplored those who so foolishly did. The poem was finished just over a week after the disaster, on the 24th, and was first printed in the programme of the Dramatic and Operatic Matinée in Aid of the Titanic Disaster Fund, given at Covent Garden on 14 May, for which event it had been commissioned. Millgate, appreciating its stately magnificence, writes that it demonstrates that Tom could have been 'an outstanding poet laureate'. That, though, is just what he could never have been, and Millgate does recognize this when he concedes that he would never have been 'deemed sufficiently "safe"'. He could not have written the poem to order, as he did, if the nature of the disaster had not so closely confirmed his own ways of thinking and feeling. The poem which describes the event it celebrates – it does not mourn it – as 'august' is quite unsuitable for a 'tragic national occasion'. It has more than a shade of nihilism, an edge of satisfaction that truth has struck at complacency and arrogant criminal neglect, that the rich and opulent do not always escape suffering. The poem as a whole transcends its element of nihilism, but could not have been completed without the energy that the nihilism supplied.

It is about the *Titanic* disaster, and not, specifically, about Thomas and Emma Hardy, as has been suggested. But it is also about marriage (or companionship and friendship between man the iceberg and woman the ship) and the part that sexuality plays in these. Tom's own sexual experience, and his experience of marriage, contributed to it; but it remains a religious and philosophical poem rather than a personal one. It demonstrates the manner in which public events must relate to private ones in our experience of them; but the private experiences are, here, too generalized to have any precise autobiographical bearing. Tom counterpoints the vanity of women (as he had long ago portrayed it at the beginning of *Far From the Madding Crowd*) with the icy indifference of the male when he is not sexually aroused. If we take the sunken ship as a woman, then over her mirrors 'The sea-worm crawls – grotesque, slimed, dull, indifferent'.

> Well: while was fashioning
>   This creature of cleaving wing,
> The Imminent Will that stirs and urges everything
>
>   Prepared a sinister mate
>   For her – so gaily great –
> A Shape of Ice, for the time far and dissociate.
>
>   And as the smart ship grew
>   In stature, grace and hue,
> In shadowy silent distance grew the Iceberg too.

Alien they seemed to be:
No mortal eye could see
The intimate welding of their later history,

Or sign that they were bent
By paths coincident
On being anon twin halves of one august event,

Till the Spinner of the Years
Said 'Now!' And each one hears
And consummation comes, and jars two hemispheres.

The sexuality of the language is inescapable, and the final 'disaster' is none other than consummation. Thus the poem is 'metaphysical' in a manner almost unrecognized at the time. (Tom's friend and admirer H.J. Grierson published his edition of John Donne in 1912, but his influential anthology of the metaphysical poets did not appear until 1921. Tom had read his metaphysicals elsewhere.)

If any individual woman was in Tom's mind as he actually wrote – but that is highly unlikely – then it would have been Florence Dugdale, young like the new ship, and still sexually attractive to him. One might say that the poem partakes, if only in an autobiographical sense, of an intuition that his romance with Florence Dugdale was going to lead to no good: for, difficult though she would be to please, was he not going to be, as an old and often distracted man, somewhat of an 'iceberg' to her, as he had been to Emma? That affinity between them at which he had hinted in 'After the Visit' in the spring of 1910 was an affinity based in common melancholy, and little else, as they would discover to their cost in the bleak years of their life together: she as nurse-typist-complainer and guardian, and he as lonely, increasingly isolated and distracted writer of poems.

In her last year of life Emma was still active, mostly on account of good works – not all evangelical. Her kindnesses to children and to poorer people are usually forgotten in the interests of calling her 'pathetic' – as if all human creatures when they become old, whether prematurely or not, were not 'pathetic', and as if, too, that were really the right compassionate word. Perhaps in the end only Tom himself did not forget her special qualities. The matter is simpler than the grim diagnoses of the biographers suggest: Emma became a rather scatty old lady who may have been in the early stages of Alzheimer's disease. Tom, on the other hand, was not, as Millgate suddenly claims, 'too rigid in his judgements' of her: he had to look at what she had become, and put up with both that and with his guilt about Florence. Sometimes the gardener, called Trevis, wheeled Emma in a bath chair to church at Fordington; at other times she took (even now) to her bicycle or walked. Her distribution of Protestant pamphlets increased with her age, and she really did hope, if vaguely, that they would do some good.

Florence was still working, on and off, for Mrs Henniker (whose husband, having been kicked by an ungrateful horse, died on 6 February 1912). She had a 'beautiful nature', Mrs Henniker told Tom, who misguidedly replied that he agreed: he felt, indeed, he said, that Florence's own health depended upon the health of those around her. Having so whole-heartedly endorsed Emma's hatred of popery, even to the extent of asserting that Asquith was in league with the Pope, Florence now suddenly thought of entering the Roman Catholic Church. She was unhappy: she could see no future with Tom, and Hyatt (undoubtedly the one love of her life) was gone. There would be no more talks, no more commiserations. She seems to have found a priest through the Shorters, and he seems to have helped her; he failed, or perhaps did not even try, to convert her. There is no doubt that, her sadness at the death of Hyatt apart, the affair with Tom lay heavily upon her own conscience. She was quite seriously alienated from him during part of 1912, and wanted to escape his influence (which was not in favour of the Roman Catholic Church as an institution, as Pearl Craigie had well understood). Much later he would become intensely exasperated when she tried Christian Science.

Relief for her must have come (although she did complain) when in July she 'got the Stoker money'. In those days £2,000 of capital meant a sort of independence. She was a generous woman, though, and almost immediately directed part of the income from the money to putting her youngest sister through a domestic science college. Gittings and Manton also discovered, through a former pupil, that she spent some money in taking rest cures at places on the Sussex coast. It is surely significant that she did not come to Weymouth before November.

At the beginning of 1912 Tom had expressed the hope, to his old and valued friend Dorothy Allhusen, that he would be in London 'oftener' that year than he had been in 1911. It was not to be; in fact he travelled less. In February he did not wish to be at Devizes in Wiltshire to judge 'a Town-criers' contest, but was polite in turning down the Mayor's invitation. There was only one visit to Aldeburgh that year, in May. Refusing an invitation on 3 March, he wrote to Clodd: 'I should much like to go to Aldeburgh again at Easter, as you so kindly want me to, but I fear I cannot. However perhaps I can go a little later when you run down for a day or two. Yes, the chances are diminishing.' By the last sentence Tom must have been implying that it was now harder for him to get away – and, no doubt, that, since Florence's time was now divided between Mrs Henniker and Enfield, she too was not available (or willing?) for meetings. However, a little later he managed to persuade her, and from the 10th until the 13th of May they did stay at Strafford House with Clodd; fellow guests were Shorter and his wife Dora Sigerson. In early July Tom went to London in order to give his eyes a rest (he told Hermann Lea, who was in the final stages of *Thomas Hardy's Wessex*), and from there made a day visit to Felixstowe, from which he sent a picture postcard to Kate.

He had taken refuge in the job of revising his novels, the last of which was now seventeen years behind him; it made him, as many remarks in letters of the time confirm, more than ever certain that his vocation was poetry and, moreover, always had been poetry. But the fiction was important as a source of income, and the 1s.6d. he obtained from each 7s.6d. volume of the Wessex Edition would have to serve him as his main income for the rest of his life. He never treated cash in hand (now in fact considerable) as quite real, believing that it could all be wiped out at a stroke by catastrophe; he was also anxious to see that his family would be looked after. Anecdotes of his meanness are more than offset by factual details of his generosity towards even obscure members of his family. When he took the coals off a too blazing fire – a tale based upon a single instance observed by a servant, and much bandied about by his detractors – he was thinking, not of what coal cost, but of the waste: he had been brought up in that way. His tips to local tradesmen were small, and took no account of inflation; but he had little reason to like the people of Dorchester. He was honoured within his own Wessex, but not in Dorchester, where he was regarded as 'immoral' and 'irreligious'. Inevitably his servants' accounts of him, later assiduously collected, partake not only of their own observations but also of the nature of his reputation: famous but disliked. When they are sifted, they show him as being no more than a man distracted by his work from what was going on around him; this they could not understand.

On 10 November he replied to a letter from a journalist called James Douglas, pertaining to a matter close to his own heart. George Gissing's friend Morley Roberts had just published his novel *The Private Life of Henry Maitland*, a mixture of fact and fiction about Gissing which led to his being ostracized by Gissing's friends such as Clodd. Douglas had worked himself up into a state of indignation, and wanted this 'degradation of the English novel into a scandalous chronicle of private affairs' to be 'tried' in an 'academic court'. Tom, who allowed a modified and shortened version of his letter to be printed, was upset by the implications, but tried to be balanced:

> The point at issue seems to be: Does such a book as 'The Private Life of Henry Maitland' injure the dead man's memory? In this case I feel that it may possibly do so. But to set against this is the fact (as I understand) that Gissing authorized, or half authorized, the book. Who is to tell?

However, he ended his letter with a postscript making his own position clearer: 'Of course I am leaving untouched the question whether, even if every word be truth, truth shd be presented (unauthorized) by so stealthy a means. It has a sneaking look.' He had himself partly in mind when he wrote 'The power of telling lies about people through that channel ['fiction'] after they are dead, by stirring in a few truths, is a horror to contemplate.' He thought it worth while to reproduce this in the *Life*, but did not give Roberts (who died in 1942) the satisfaction of mentioning his work or its subject.

But Tom would soon have his attention distracted from the dead Gissing's affairs, and from what was about to be perhaps the greatest pleasure of the year (Florence Dugdale having played so deliberately inconspicuous a part in it): the local presentation of a revival of Evans' 1908 dramatization of *The Trumpet-Major*, always a favourite with him. He wrote to Clodd on 19 November enclosing a 'stall' for the London performance: 'The play is, of course, of a very local cast, but picturesque.' Florence Dugdale was herself in Weymouth waiting to see it.

What then happened is best told by Tom himself, since none of his details is wrong. Gittings' account of the same events – which for a time, until corrected by Millgate, had wide currency – to the effect that Hardy '*pretended*' (my italics) that Emma's death had been 'sudden and unexpected', is vituperative rubbish, as is his verdict that the 'terrible conclusion is that Hardy shut his eyes to his wife's state, and tried to shut the eyes of others after her death'. He scarcely bothered to offer serious evidence for these statements, beyond comically scant reference to a 1917 *Manual of Nursing*. Tom's 'horror' had been in the anticipation of a fictional account of his life with some truth mixed in with it. He hardly anticipated a non-fictional account of his life with some fiction mixed in, or he might well have repeated what Baron Lyndhurst said on learning that he had not yet been included in Lord Campbell's *Lives of the Lord Chancellors*: 'Campbell has added another terror to death.'

Tom was not less attentive to Emma than he had hitherto been during what turned out to be her last months. Having had to endure a popular farce, *Bunty Pulls the Strings*, in London with Lady St Helier, with whom he had stayed briefly in June, he went to see it again at the Pavilion Theatre, Weymouth, for the sake of Emma and Lilian Gifford. Lilian would not have been a guest at Max Gate had Emma shown signs of serious illness. True, Lilian did leave before her time was up, but that was because she made herself insufferable – not an uncommon occurrence. Emma and he shared a fondness for Lilian: perhaps they felt that her deficiencies of personality were compensated for by her being, with her brother, all they had of 'family'. She had lived with them for long periods in previous years, and they had grown used to her.

He tells in the *Life* of how he returned to Max Gate in July just in time to attend Emma's last garden party on the 16th. She was then, as he wrote, 'in her customary health and vigour'. There is no doubt that this, from evidence entirely external, appeared to be true. A high proportion of deaths are, in fact, unexpected. However, Tom is nothing if not scrupulous in his record:

> . . . she was noticed to be weaker later on in the autumn, though not ill, and complained of her heart at times. Strangely enough, she one day suddenly sat down to the piano and played a long series of her favourite old tunes, saying at the end that she would never play any more. The poem called 'The Last Performance' approximately describes this incident.

The poem, following a suggestion first made by Weber, has always been interpreted as recording an attempt on Emma's part, which her husband ignored, to attract his attention by playing him the songs she had played him during their courtship. However, this is a misreading, unless we are to interpret poems simply to fit in with preconceived theories.

> 'I am playing my oldest tunes,' declared she,
>   'All the oldest tunes I know, –
> Those I learned ever so long ago.'

– Why she should think just then she'd play them
    Silence cloaks like snow.

When I returned from the town at nightfall
    Notes continued to pour
As when I had left two hours before:
'It's the very last time,' she said in closing;
    'From now on I play no more.'

A few morns onward found her fading,
    And, as her life outflew,
I thought of her playing her tunes right through;
And I felt she had known of what was coming,
    And wondered how she knew.

Had he really pretended to everyone that he had not been aware of what was coming, when in fact he was well aware of it, then this poem would have been a diabolical piece of disingenuousness: a slick stealing of poetical copy from a tragedy which he had daily expected. It can read like such a piece of deliberate hypocrisy, though, only to a sick and envious mind. Moreover, there is nothing in it to suggest that he ignored Emma's playing over of her old songs, or that she played them to attract his attention. It is more likely that he was touched.

Following upon this description is the one of Emma's death:

She went out up to the 22nd November, when, though it was a damp, dark afternoon, she motored to pay a visit six miles off. The next day she was distinctly unwell, and the day after that was her birthday [her seventy-second], when she seemed depressed. On the 25th two ladies called; and though she consulted with her husband whether or not to go downstairs to see them, and he suggested that she should not in her weak state, she did go down. The strain obliged her to retire immediately they left. She never went downstairs again.

Thus the version of the *Life* issued by Florence Hardy. But she altered what Tom had written, as a sop to a friend of whom she was (and with every good reason, although she never realized it) afraid because she had sent her indiscreet letters (she even wrote: 'I *entreat* you to burn every scrap of my writing'). What Tom actually wrote was this: 'Unfortunately they stayed a *very* long time, and the strain . . .'

Readers will have no difficulty in recognizing the chief offender: it was, of course, Rebekah Owen, in Dorchester ostensibly to see the play, but really to sit at the feet of her idol, the imagined Romeo to her Juliet. After acknowledging (to both: 'Dear Misses Owen') the wreath they had sent, Tom never wrote to Rebekah again. In 1915 he was asked to supply a reference for her to American Express, with which she wished to open an account. Apparently she had not consulted him beforehand. He wrote back without enthusiasm:

> I am able to inform you that I have known Miss Rebekah Owen for many years. She and her late sister were introduced to me by a publisher more than twenty years ago as American ladies who desired to make my acquaintance; and they came to live in Dorchester till twelve or fifteen years ago, when they went to the north of England. While here many local people became friendly with them in addition to myself & they were always known as amiable & interesting ladies.
>
> I do not, of course, know anything of Miss Owen's business affairs, but I have always imagined them to be of ordinary stability.

This is frigid, even for a man used to writing letters in a formal and reticent style. Tom also took another opportunity to snub Owen (whose sister was released from her by death in 1914) when he refused to autograph a copy of *Moments of Vision* in February 1918, and left Florence to explain it to her. It is true that he returned, unsigned, almost all the books thus sent to him; but he had usually signed them for Owen. Now, remembering her behaviour two days before Emma's death, and also perhaps her coy reaction to *Jude*, he at last did the right thing. Although in the preface to *The Mayor of Casterbridge*, he called her, by implication, a good judge from across the Atlantic, he none the less did not mention her name. She had, it must be remembered, formed a club for Hardy enthusiasts: one does not easily bite the hand that feeds one's sales. In October 1915, writing to an acquaintance called Charles Rumbold, then serving in the army, he significantly recalled that he and another had been 'the last guests that my late wife entertained', which showed that he did not count Owen as a guest at all.

Rebekah Owen arrived at Max Gate unannounced on 25 November and immediately and imperiously demanded to see Tom. Tom advised Emma, as he reported, not to see them as she felt so unwell. Emma was, it must be remembered, taking her opium mixture, probably at this point in order to control severe back pains. Out of kindness of heart, she made her way downstairs. Owen herself recalled that she actually wept a little and expressed fear of being 'cut up' if she should see the doctor. She would not leave, but ordered Emma to summon Tom from his study. Clearly Tom, having the Wessex Edition to get on with (he was, after all, a writer whose 'office' was in his home, and was absorbed by the work he had to do), and not believing anything to be seriously wrong with Emma, had begged to be spared the ordeal of a conversation with Rebekah: Emma resisted her suggestion. Whereupon Owen herself ordered the maid to fetch Tom. According to her, he was polite and affable; but he would have had to be downright insulting to have made any impression upon such a person. At last she and her sister left.

> The next day she agreed to see a doctor, who did not think her seriously ill, but weak from want of nourishment through indigestion. In the evening she assented quite willingly to Hardy's suggestion that he should go to a rehearsal in Dorchester . . . that he had promised to attend. When he got back at eleven o'clock all the house was in bed and he did not disturb her.
>
> The next morning the maid [this was the fourteen-year-old Dolly Gale] told him in answer to his enquiry that when she had as usual entered Mrs Hardy's room a little earlier she had said that she was better, and would probably get up earlier on, but that now she seemed worse. Hastening to her he was shocked to find her much worse, lying with her eyes closed and unconscious. The doctor came quite quickly, but before he arrived her breathing softened and ceased.

If anyone, at that late stage, was to blame at all for Emma's death, then it was Dr Gowring for failing to recognize the seriousness of the situation, and for not informing Tom in case he wanted another opinion. But doctors cannot always make the right diagnoses, and the tale that Emma would not allow him to examine her, probably true, would have made it hard for him in the case of a patient whom he hardly knew. Furthermore, Emma could have (some would say should have) consulted him when her serious symptoms began to manifest themselves; instead, she deliberately kept them to herself. She is not known to have consulted any doctor. Dolly Gale, recently engaged as her personal maid, gave an account of the events fifty-one years later, when she was Mrs Alice Harvey. This need not be treated as gospel, although she remembered as best she could at such a distance in time.

A USUAL MISTAKE

According to her, she had been sent by a severely distressed Emma to fetch Tom, and had some difficulty in getting him to recognize the seriousness of what she had to tell him. As anyone might when confronted with alarming news, he looked at her and told her that her collar was crooked. He expanded a little on the essentially truthful account he gave in the *Life* when he told Mary Sheridan, whom Emma had liked for her 'loyalty' (as Tom now told her), that he had

> had no suspicion that there was anything precarious in her constitution, & reproach myself now for a lack of insight, which, if I had had it, might have enabled me to prolong her life a little by assiduous attention, & insistence on her taking more rest. However, that will never be known.

This is straightforward, and exactly expresses the immediate feelings that any spouse caught up in similar circumstances would have: 'Could I have done more?' He repeated this in many of his replies to letters of condolence from close friends, adding in most cases that, as he put it to Florence Henniker, he still could not help expecting to see her in the garden with her trowel in her hand, 'the cat trotting faithfully behind her'. His letter to Mrs Henniker repeats the information given in the *Life*, and suggests that Mrs Harvey (Dolly Gale, the maid) slightly misremembered the train of events on the morning of 27 November 1912. He, after all, had better reason to remember them exactly, whereas she had been no more than a frightened child:

> Emma's death was absolutely unexpected by me, the doctor, & everybody, though not sudden, strictly speaking. She was quite well a week before, & (as I fancy) in an unlucky moment determined to motor to some friends about 6 miles off [these were the Wood Homers]. During the night following she had a bad attack of indigestion, which I attributed to the jolting of the car. She was never well from that time, though she came down to tea with some callers on the Monday evening before her death on Wednesday morning. I was with her when she passed away. Half an hour earlier she had told the servant that she felt better. Then her bell rang violently, & when we went up she was gasping. In five minutes all was over.

He went on to praise her '*courage*' in the cause of animals, 'surpassing that of any other woman I have ever known'. He also mentioned his feelings of self-reproach that he had not guessed that 'some internal mischief' had been at work. Such feelings were, of course, inevitable. They are, in such circumstances, universal. Florence Hardy's later tale that just at this juncture Tom and Emma were on the verge of a final quarrel, and that Tom was about to leave her, may be put down to a combination of paranoia and wishful thinking – certainly Mrs Harvey would have recalled something about such a quarrel, had it been in progress.

What *was* 'at work' cannot now be fully known. Dr Gowring gave as the cause of her death 'heart failure from some internal perforation': 'impacted gallstones'. Such stones can form without causing symptoms at all; when there are symptoms, and when they at last become apparent, they are to this day frequently confused with just that 'indigestion' which had been observed by both the doctor and her husband. The stones are insoluble deposits formed from the bile, and occasionally may leave the gall bladder and migrate to the bile ducts – this might have happened in Emma's case. There was, at least, nothing peculiar about such a death at such a time, and suggestions that she could not possibly have suppressed her agony for at least a year previously are based on fictitious notions of medicine, and take no account of the opium she was taking. This was exactly what everyone (until Gittings' inventions) said it was: a sudden death. Had Gowring called a specialist on the evening of 26 November, when he saw her, and had she had her gall bladder immediately removed, she might have survived; but it is more certain that she would not.

Tom was devastated. But, because so many people – Florence Dugdale, Rebekah Owen and her sister, and others – had come so far to see *The Trumpet-Major*, the performance could not be cancelled. Her death was announced from the stage.

Many years earlier she had fancied that she would like to be buried at Plymouth, her native place; but on going there to the funeral of her father she found that during a 'restoration' the family vault in Charles Churchyard, though it was not full, had been broken into, if not removed altogether, either to alter the entrance to the church, or to erect steps; and on coming back she told her husband that this had quite destroyed her wish to be taken there, since she could not lie near her parents.

There was one nook, indeed, which in some respects was pre-eminently the place where she might have lain – the graveyard of St Juliot, Cornwall – whose dilapidated old church had been the cause of their meeting, and in whose precincts the early scenes of their romance had a brief being. But circumstances ordered otherwise. Hardy did not favour the thought of her being carried to that lonely coast unless he could be carried thither likewise in due time; and on this point all was uncertain. The funeral was accordingly at Stinsford, a mile from Dorchester and Max Gate, where Hardys had been buried for many years.

She was buried alongside her old enemy Jemima, and Mary Hardy did not – perhaps for that reason, but perhaps because she was unwell or upset – attend the ceremony. Nor did Gosse, Clodd or any other of her old friends. Nor, although Emma had stood in as something like a mother to him, did Gordon Gifford attend. His sister, maladroit as ever, turned up after the service was over. The card on Tom's wreath read: 'From her Lonely Husband, with the Old Affection.'

At the moment of Emma's death, Florence Dugdale had been in the train on her way to Weymouth, Tom told Florence Henniker on 17 December, '& on her arrival at Weymouth, where she was going to stay for the sea air, was met by my telegram'. She had come immediately, but went back after a day or two. Kate, too, although Tom did not mention it, was at Max Gate. This death was a relief for everyone, no doubt; but not for him. Now Lilian Gifford, too, was with him 'attending to the house affairs,' and 'Florence Dugdale has also come to help me with the proofs . . . which happen to be in full swing'.

The servants disapproved of her presence. In fact, although it has been overlooked, Tom was now about to make a mistake. Perhaps it was not, given his age and inevitable withdrawal into himself and into his own past, too serious a mistake. It had its advantages. But Max Gate was to become a place of almost unrelenting misery because of it. At the end of her life Emma wrote a little poem about wishing again to be a dancing child. Tom may not have loved the efficiency of the verses, but he did love and ever remember the vivacity of the woman who wrote them: her joyful love of nature even when in great pain. Her successor 'appreciated nature' and animals, but had little energy to express her feelings, which were almost excessively conventional. She could never have danced dangerously and flirtatiously on a wall, as Elfride had done in *A Pair of Blue Eyes*. She wanted to become known as the primary inspiration of a great poet. But that was an impossible dream: she could not fill the role.

Eventually Tom would regard Walt Whitman, at least in matters of technique, as the 'original sinner'. He would assert that Whitman wrote in free verse because he could do no better. But he might well have said with him, in December 1912:

> Enough! Enough! Enough!
> Somehow I have been stunn'd. Stand back!
> Give me a little time beyond my cuff'd head, slumbers, dreams, gaping,
> I discover myself on the verge of a usual mistake.

There was no one to hold him back, nor would he in any case – now free, if unhappily free – have allowed anyone to hold him back. Florence Dugdale soon moved in to take charge.

34

Too Late, Farewell

Florence had long since learned to use her illnesses, her 'delicateness', to her own advantage, but her sense of duty ultimately over-rode everything else. She may have been peculiarly short-sighted in her diagnoses of circumstances, but she did care for the well-being of those around her: she wanted them to be happy. She admitted to Owen that she was given to 'profuse grumbling'. It is right, too, to claim that once she had had her grumble her immediate grievance was dissolved. The trouble was that almost immediately it was so dissolved, she would start grumbling again. Like most of those trapped by a strong sense of obligation which they feel they are inadequate to fulfil, she resented those towards whom she felt dutiful. She was able to express her resentment, during 1913 and then after her marriage, in letters to Clodd, to Alda, Lady Hoare, to Owen, and to Cockerell.

When Clodd was writing his memoirs she seems to have become hysterically anxious about her own indiscretions (which might already, had Shorter been a more ruthless man, have caused serious difficulties for both her and Tom), and to have sent him a half-threatening letter promising that, if he were indiscreet, she would get her husband 'to write to the papers'! She was to display just this kind of doom-ridden hysteria when confronted with Tom's fondness for Gertrude Bugler. But Tom, in his own extant letters to Clodd, never mentioned this, and it seems that their friendship was uninterrupted. Florence's more intelligent correspondents learned not to take her wailing too seriously. Cockerell, who treated her and most other people with scant respect, was not exactly wrong when he called her 'an inferior woman with a suburban mind': that indeed is what she was when in literary waters. But her despair and melancholy, her sense of doom and sadness were not so much 'inferior' as innate, and Tom was fond of her for her hopeless vulnerability.

It was not only the recipients of her letters – people at a safe distance from her, with their own lives to lead – who had to try to deal with her grievances. There were long gaps of time between these complaints. And in those long gaps it was Tom who received the full force of her resentments: of him and his late time of life; of the lonely circumstances of Max Gate; of her disappointed dreams; of what she called the 'dreary middle age' into which she felt she had moved immediately upon the death of Emma (she was then thirty-two). That so sensitive a man should not eventually have become aware of her perpetual discontent is not credible. One has only to look at her photograph to gauge the effect she must have had on those who shared the same roof. She usually looks the picture of misery, and could scarcely ever raise a smile. Florence was in awe of her husband's reputation, and preserved her strongest sense of duty in its behalf: she was the guardian of the flame, the great man's protector. Even as a conventional person she did not perform her duties as well as she might have done: a long string of indiscreet complaints, however much regretted later, is no part of the life of 'the servant of a genius'. That is certainly how she wanted to see herself, and how she was seen at the time of her death.

Tom was making an extensive trawl of his past. Florence saw that in early December 1912, when she returned to Max Gate; she saw it as clearly as she saw his advancing age, his ways becoming increasingly set, his strict habits of work, his country ways so unlike those of the lower middle-class Enfield to which she was used. She learned to hate the name Gifford, in which she had the support of Tom's sisters (Henry was more phlegmatic, but may have shared their feelings); but she also learned to hate what she was bound to regard as the peasant clannishness of the Hardys themselves – against which she would also, later, complain. In 1913 all three had left the Bockhampton cottage – which Lea then took over and rented from its landlord – and went to live with Henry in the nearby house at West Stafford, Talbothays, which Tom had designed and he had built.

Most of all, though, Florence hated the dead Emma Hardy, whom she could discern (as could Tom himself, which was doubtless why he tolerated her) in the supercilious, idle, sharp-tongued and perpetually immature Lilian. This niece made snide and in themselves ill-bred remarks about Florence's origins, and praised her aunt as the inspirer of Thomas Hardy. She called Tom her 'Daddy-Uncle', and kept him amused and even charmed; he thought of her more as a grown-up child than as an adult. She may have had her eye on the money which he would leave. In the circumstances, though, who could truthfully have been unable to put that completely out of mind? The two sisters, Kate

– who, although lively, was not without malice or acquisitiveness – in particular, were passionate about its not being allowed to go outside the Hardy family.

Yet despite all this, and a year of coping with the most difficult aspects of it, and of wailing about it to Clodd, Florence married Tom in February 1914. She did it for a complex of reasons: she did not love him, but had sometimes seen to his sexual needs, which she called a 'responsibility'; she was never so happy, as she admitted more than once, than when she had someone to look after; and she might yet, as Mrs Thomas Hardy, achieve immortality as a writer herself. That last dream existed vaguely in the background, but she would not forget it. Taking her colour from that of her correspondent, she wrote in November 1916 to the married Sydney Cockerell – whose definition of marriage was that it provided a woman with the opportunity to express devotion – that she had married Tom 'that I might have the right to express my devotion and to endeavour to add to his comfort and happiness'. But Thomas Hardy was worthy of something less official than that. She has been described as having given him 'sacrificial devotion', which was undoubted. But he could have had that, and with less complaint, from a paid housekeeper or even from his sister Kate.

In December, confronted with the openly hostile presence of Lilian, Florence went back to her family at Enfield. By Christmas, however, she was back at Max Gate, and typing some letters for Tom in reply to the hundreds he had received. But to Emma's first cousin Florence Yolland he wrote, in his own handwriting, of Lilian's being there 'keeping house for me in my solitude'; Lilian was certainly still there over Christmas and for some time afterwards.

Florence eventually settled in as housekeeper, to the scandalized disapproval of both the Max Gate servants and Dorchester – they were all certain that she was Tom's mistress, and some even claimed to know it. Florence kept up a running commentary in letters to Clodd, letters which, as always, she kept from Tom. By only 16 January 1913 she was groaning that life at Max Gate was '*lonely* beyond words'. Why, then, had she consented to come? Tom was a working writer who could not and would not give up his time for anyone. She told Clodd that she knew she ought not to talk to him as she was writing. She had, it seems, no one to talk to: only those, like Kate, with whom she could pick over specific, anti-Gifford, grievances.

Was Tom now so distracted by thoughts of Emma that he had no time for her? This is not likely; and in fact she would change her mind, even in the same paragraph, in her letters to Clodd: Tom was now all right, had regained his youth (this, however, was Kate's verdict), was laughing again, was in a bad state. She was incapable of reporting matters as they really were, and possessed no stability of outlook. At night Tom sat up reading not only 'Some Recollections' but also Emma's animadversions upon him in a series of private diaries she had been keeping – and would no doubt have destroyed herself had she had the opportunity – from some undetermined time in the 1890s. Occasionally he would read Florence little bits from them. Her reactions were superficial and lacked balance: she was concerned with how Tom's moods affected her own immediate emotional convenience. She does not seem to have been shown the diaries, and only ever half-implied that she had actually read them. The notion of their having been consistently 'diabolical' therefore originated not with Tom but with her. She reported them as such because she was jealous of the intense attention he gave to them, and because she heard one or two vituperative passages from them – expressions of rage such as any wife might have made, but perhaps not written down. Grief over Emma was very bad for him, she insisted, not even recognizing that, in his state of shock, he, like anyone else, needed time to work his feelings out. Was she not planning to marry him? Could he not *instantly* devote himself to her, now that he was finally free of the woman who, not long ago, she had been so fulsomely praising? She was over-reacting, hysterically, to what was then a perfectly natural period of mourning at a sudden death.

That she gave Tom some kind of sexual comfort at this time, when he needed it, is likely – the town gossips and the servants were for once probably right. But if she did, then he was not allowed to forget it. When she went away for a few days at the end of January, on the 29th he wrote her a 'three-page letter' containing something about the diaries; instantly, on the 30th, she informed Clodd. From Tom's letter she quoted the following:

> . . . I am getting through E's papers . . . It was, of course, sheer hallucination in her, poor thing, & not wilfulness . . . If I get you here again won't I clutch you tight: you shall stay till spring. I felt very sad & lonely yesterday; not quite so much today.

Of Tom's letter itself there is no trace, so what this extract tells us is hardly valuable since it was torn from its context, which might have shown Emma in too good a light and Florence as too compromised.

She had already learned to hate Emma, in which she had drawn support from Kate and the others – probably mainly from Kate, who could be spiteful and who, without Mary's gifts in painting and music, was not Tom's own favourite.

Florence's state of mind is understandable – too easily understandable for her to emerge as other than essentially commonplace. If she could not understand Tom's own state of mind (a perfectly normal one of passionate mourning, since Emma had been dead for only a few weeks), if she was even now beginning her campaign of hatred and libel of the 'mad' Emma (only a year or so earlier, according to her, the badly treated wife of the not-great-as-a-man Hardy), then how could she ever have learned to understand him, or his value to others in his ability to draw, from his own experience, poetry to which everyone could respond? The pity that she expressed for him was of a proprietorial nature. Having little judgement of her own, she drew recklessly upon whatever opinions she could find to hand that would justify her immediate emotions – and the Hardy clan, if not Tom himself, was of course to hand. She worked them up and they worked her up. Kate, at least, wanted to preserve his money and keep it in the Hardy family; Florence wanted his hand in marriage and the privilege of doting upon him and caring for him as a woman might dote, publicly, upon an aged and venerable father. He was a 'child' with whom things had 'somehow gone wrong', she eventually told Lady Hoare.

Yet what did she say to Tom himself? She must have alternated between humouring him and, in her own inimitable way, threatening him. She knew that he needed her comforting presence. The fragment of his letter which she transcribed to Clodd says '*if* I get you here again . . .' The phrase 'of course, sheer hallucination' (by which he meant 'imagination') may reflect her own influence. She may already have been able to persuade him that the Gifford family was 'tainted' – he was susceptible, and half-believed his own family to be 'cursed'.

There is little evidence that she succeeded in wholly persuading him that Emma had been technically mad: he made use of the idea in a few highly dramatic poems, and that is all. The first detailed letter he wrote about Emma to anyone outside his own immediate circle was the one to Florence Henniker of 17 December, already referred to, which described the manner of her death. In it he wrote: 'In spite of the differences between us, which it would be affectation to deny, & certain painful delusions she suffered from at times, my life is now intensely sad to me now without her.' This acknowledges that 'at times' she imagined

771

things: perhaps such things as that Kate had stolen a pair of her earrings (one of the tales current after her death). But if Emma had long intuited elements of envy and spite in Kate, how wrong was she?

It might fairly be inferred that when Florence again departed for Enfield, and then for Mrs Henniker's house at Southwold, she was trying to consider her position while she was away from Max Gate – even that she had left precisely so that she could be away from the old man. On 1 February, the day after she had, unknown to him, given her latest report on him to Clodd, he himself wrote to Clodd:

> As you were truly informed, I have been quite inert for the last two months, though I have been invited to stay with several kind friends – among whom I include yourself not as the least.
>
> However, next week I hope to make a slight move . . . Miss Gifford is staying here with me still – attending to household management . . . Certainly you must come . . . I will remind you when I get back from Plymouth or wherever I go.
>
> I don't know when I shall be able to see Aldburgh [sic] again: sometimes I think never. I am glad to hear that Miss Dugdale looked well & bright. She had influenza when she wrote last.

Clodd had seen Florence at Enfield on 29 January: he gave a lecture there (on no less a subject than 'The Origins of Right and Wrong'), arranged by her. There is a touch of acid wistfulness about Tom's reference to her in the above letter: once again, as in the extract from his own 29 January letter which she had rushed off to Clodd, he seems entirely uncertain, and not quite happy to trust to her descriptions of herself as 'ill'. The implication is that she had not been too unwell to attend Clodd's lecture. For himself, Clodd referred to Emma with total contempt.

But Florence was back, in charge again, by the time Tom made his pilgrimage to St Juliot in early March. He had determined to be there by the 7th, the anniversary of his first visit. And Lilian was still at Max Gate. Yet Florence, who had servants in the house and Mary, Kate, and Henry nearby, was so melodramatic about her 'loneliness' that she told Clodd she kept a loaded revolver in her bedroom. Does not this imply an enormous fuss, made to Tom, about 'being left'? 'All I hope is that I may not, for the rest of his life, have to sit and listen humbly to an account of her virtues and graces,' she lamented. She was hardly giving Tom a chance: Emma had been dead for just three months. Clodd's and doubtless her own wish that this death would be seen by Tom as a 'happy release' was not being fulfilled.

But might she not have been angry and jealous for two precise reasons, both relating to the allegedly 'diabolical diaries'? First, she had not been allowed to read them; she never actually quoted a single word from them. Secondly, when she had heard about the nature of parts of them, she had hoped that Tom would quickly and finally turn against both Emma and the memory of her but instead they had appeared only to increase his affection. And from that arises the question: may not her own shortcomings, her superficiality, ambitions and lack of 'life', have been in part responsible for the 'obsession', if that really is the right word, which he later developed about his dead wife? A more robust and less conventional woman might have made all the difference.

In one of her many further reports to Clodd during 1913 she mentioned that Tom had suggested she go into permanent half-mourning as a sign of devotion to Emma: was there not, she wailed, 'something in the air of Max Gate that makes us all a little crazy?' That would indeed have been preposterous, had Tom been serious. But we see everything that happened at Max Gate at this time only through the filter of her own volatility. It is more likely that, in the face of her continual moaning, Tom yielded to an ironic impulse and made the suggestion in that spirit. One is reminded of what Hermann Lea said: 'Often he would tell me of something he had said to someone else and would add: "I really believe he thought I meant it" . . . He often added that so-and-so appeared to lack entirely any sense of humour.' Florence was aware of the existence of a humorous side of things, and could even occasionally enter into it; but this was continually overwhelmed by a sharp sense of self-pity – even a pity for a self which was inadequate, lacking in humour and warmth, and so on. Too often commentators officiously ignore the fact that the run-down Max Gate was the house which Tom chose to inhabit, that the grief he felt for Emma was his grief, and that the poetry which they choose to admire arose from these and all his other circumstances – rather than from the inspirations of *Ideal Home* magazine or the self-pity of Florence Dugdale, whose lamentations were, alas, as platitudinous as her devotion.

Tom wrote to her from the Wellington Hotel at Boscastle, where he was staying with Henry, whom he had chosen to accompany him. It has been suggested that Henry 'was an uncongenial companion, in one sense, given his bluff commonsensicality and hearty dislike of Emma'; but this may be assuming too much. Tom was always close to his brother, about whom little is known apart from his bluffly commonsense manner; whether he had disliked Emma or not – and perhaps he had remained wisely indifferent – he might, even though only a 'peasant', have been capable of giving able, sensitive and glad support to his brother. Such sensitivities are not limited to those with cultured backgrounds and higher degrees.

Tom gratified Florence by telling her that he wondered why on earth he had come to Cornwall: 'The visit has been a very painful one to me, & I have said a dozen times I wish I had not come. What possessed me to do it!' Had she looked more deeply, she might have been less gratified: why indeed had it been so painful? She had sent him off reluctantly; but with a careful reminder of her own bad cough:

> Looking back it has seemed such a cruel thing that events which began so auspiciously should have turned out as they did. And now suppose that something shd happen to you physically, as it did to her mentally! I dare not think of it, & am sure you will not run any risk if you can help it.

In a postscript he added that he hoped Lilian – by whom Florence presumably pretended to be charmed – was about the house 'as usual', and a remark to the effect that Emma had, when at St Juliot, been an 'Agnostic'.

Tom was living in the past of Emma's young adulthood. As soon as he returned he devoted himself to the details of the inscription he had designed for her tomb in Stinsford churchyard. He had already arranged for a memorial tablet to her, also designed by him, to be placed on the wall of the church at St Juliot. Since Gordon Gifford went to check on it later in the year, it must be supposed that he had had an excellent reason for his earlier absence from his aunt's funeral. According to Florence, the only item which he ever expressed an interest in acquiring from the Hardy estate was Max Gate, because he claimed that his aunt had promised it to him. He did not get it.

Tom went to see Clodd at Strafford House from 25 to 28 April; Florence did not come, since, she told Clodd on the 20th, she thought that he and Tom could talk more freely alone (which Clodd arranged that they should be). She certainly did not confide to Clodd any hopes or schemes for marriage she may have been harbouring; but she regarded him, if only in a somewhat scatterbrained manner, as her ally. Tom had seen her at Southwold, at Mrs Henniker's house, which he visited immediately before he went on to Aldeburgh. Despite what she had told Clodd on the 20th, three days later Florence told Tom that she would follow him to Strafford House on Saturday the 26th. She then changed her mind, and he wrote to her from Aldeburgh making arrangements for them to meet, on the following Tuesday, for the return journey to London. It seems that she had at last agreed to come back to Max Gate permanently, for she is now his 'dearest girl', and he has read a letter which she had given him to deliver to Clodd: 'I *did* read the letter though you said I was not to. Naughty girl, to be so independent. But I will leave that for the present.' And at Aldeburgh, according to Clodd's diary, he did talk extensively. But the problem is that Clodd himself believed his friend's dedication to Emma's memory to be absurd – he may even have been acting as Florence's mouthpiece. He thought that Tom was in some kind of pathological or half-unhinged state. That estimation is, again, all very well. But are all the poems that Tom wrote about Emma also unhinged? Or do they offer the most precise and passionate analysis of the process of a marriage, and of mourning at its end, that is known to us? And do they not contain intimations of a remarkable woman, an ultimately effective muse?

Tom told Clodd that Emma had latterly believed she was being followed when she was not, and – here Clodd echoed Florence in appealing to Tom's sense of the macabre – he spoke of a taint of madness in her family. But what did Clodd omit? He listened to what he wanted to listen to. He had not liked Emma, genuinely wished to spare Tom from further distress over her, and was not a sensitive or subtle man. He was a civilized and humane rationalist banker, with all the implied limitations. But clearly Tom was concerned at this time with the change that had occurred in Emma in the course of her sixties, and he dramatized it. Fate had ordained it that way. It should also be recognized that Emma was the wife of a very famous man, and may therefore have had better cause than ordinary people for feeling that she really was being followed.

In the absence of epistolary evidence commentators have always wondered exactly what was going on between Florence and Tom. For some weeks he had been composing some of the most justly celebrated and best-loved lyrics in the world, all to the memory of his dead wife. Whether or not Florence only got to know about those poems the following year, when they appeared in *Satires of Circumstance* (the fact that she did not complain of them suggests that he held them back: *Satires of Circumstance* caused her to explode with jealous rage), his attention to Emma's memory already provoked anger in her. The poems' fervent sincerity – indeed, naked honesty – is not in question, and is a major element in their appeal. Whoever faced his own failings towards a companion with more precise relentlessness?

But how did the living Florence Dugdale appear to Tom in the light of these memories of Emma? It is impossible to say for certain, but I do not think he had any serious or long-term difficulty in separating the living Florence from the dead Emma. Nor can I really understand the accusations that he treated Florence without any consideration for her feelings: that he 'had no thought to spare for Florence's feelings'. On the contrary: what little direct evidence we have (for instance, 'won't I clutch you tight . . .') suggests the exact opposite. We know that her complaints were constitutional, and would have continued even had she been created queen of the realm and world's chief novelist: discontent was her *raison d'être*. She knew him, or ought to have known him, as a dedicated poet always ruminating, and always liable to be completely wrapped up in his work; she knew him to be in mourning for his only recently dead wife. She also knew him to be itching for her presence, and as the writer of tender letters to *her*, too. But that was not enough, because nothing was ever enough.

The matter is by no means simple: we have no knowledge of what passed between them, or of how their arrangements and agreements developed and changed as the days, weeks and months went by. Had there been no sexual exchange she would have had rather less power over him, since she would have had to stake everything on his eventual possession of her. But had there been some sexual exchange – the most likely situation – she could have used that as a basis for his indebtedness to her (in those days, for a woman, giving up her virtue was giving up all). Certainly a letter from her to Marie Stopes of 5 September 1923 makes it certain, *pace* Millgate's mildly eccentric determination to avoid one of the main points of most marriages, that they had had at least what he would call conjugal relations:

> I find on talking to him that the idea of my having a child at his age fills him with horror . . . He said he would have welcomed a child when we married first, ten years ago, but now it would kill him with anxiety to have to father one. However, I shall make use of your kind advice with regard to the alkaline douche, as I think it may be beneficial to health.

Robinson (who, more sensible than Millgate in this respect, does not try to deny what I have called natural expectations) thinks this means that sexual intercourse had ceased owing to Tom's fear of begetting a child. Since he told Blunden that he *had been* capable of it until the age of eighty-four, he might have meant to the beginning of his eighty-fourth year (that is, the year beginning 2 June 1923), which gives credence to Florence's remarks to Marie Stopes. Telling the truth was always an important part of Florence's sense of duty – if only when that was operating. She frequently deviated from it, but only under the influence of hysterical depression, when she exaggerated her suspicions. After these lapses she would be overwhelmed by the bitterest sense of self-recrimination, and beg her correspondent to burn what she had written. There are many examples of this behaviour, even in extant letters. In this instance, though, she was certainly telling the truth – and no one talks of 'welcoming' a child if there is no physiological basis for it.

The only detail that is virtually certain is that the idea of marriage was discussed during April 1913; therefore the agreement or 'compact' (there still exists a poignant bunch of dried flowers dated 16 April) may have been endorsed at Mrs Henniker's house at Southwold. This may have prompted Tom to pour forth comparatively negative views of Emma at Clodd's immediately after his visit there: perhaps such negative views were some sort of 'condition'. His letter to Florence from Strafford House spoke of leaving 'for the moment' the matter of her 'independence'. What did he think she would take that to mean? But he did not tell Clodd of any agreement. Had Florence, always a double-dealer, sworn him to secrecy? Mrs Henniker herself was certainly surprised at the marriage. However, it seems that some kind of agreement was made at that time, because Florence came to Max Gate and stayed there until her marriage: in the face of Lilian Gifford, and, worse, in that of the unpleasant local disapproval of her own 'immoral' presence. She would not have done so had she not been assured that she would end up as the mistress of Max Gate. Her sensitivity to being made the subject of scandal was always notorious – and was understandable enough in a prudish daughter of Enfield who had not an ounce of subversion in her. Had she not herself, in one of those typical little outbursts of almost enthusiastically resentful disloyalty, once told the literary society in Enfield that Thomas Hardy's 'loftiest motives' in *Jude the Obscure* had nevertheless been 'ill-judged'? She had told Clodd at the end of January how unpleasant the local comment would be; now she was prepared to endure it. Yet she knew that the presence of 'chaperones' (including Lilian, a year her junior!) would not silence people's tongues; nor did it. Tom himself has been said to be very concerned, too – and he must have been to a certain extent; but most of his concern was directed towards satisfying her sense of respectability. For him it was a matter of convenience (there were the Hardy Players to consider, and he was still on the bench); for her it was a matter of wishing to be his wife in title, and as soon as possible. For while he wanted her presence (no doubt, given Victorian 'morals', he was selfish and casual in this) he may not have been so anxious about marriage: the 'proposal' may have consisted much more of pressure exerted by her than of declaration by him on his bent knees.

The year 1913 otherwise proceeded quietly. Tom went twice to Cambridge, first in June to receive a D. Litt, and then again in November to be installed as an Honorary Fellow of Magdalene. He had to curtail his walking owing to varicose veins, which were then believed to be more life-threatening than they normally are today. He was cycling until he was eighty-two, so they must have cleared up. Although Clodd (and through him Shorter) knew all about Florence's presence at Max Gate – and indeed knew more than Tom was aware, owing to Florence's running commentary on most of his private affairs – he kept her existence from Gosse and other old friends. When he called on Gosse on his way back from Cambridge in June he seems to have said nothing about Florence. Emma's cook, Jane Riggs, had declared it her opinion that Florence, unlike Emma, was not 'a lady' (others said this of her, too, perhaps because she so desperately wanted to be one) and there were always problems with food for guests. Gissing, another in love with his own discontent, would have revelled in describing them. But Tom and she together managed to entertain Cockerell and the artist William Strang in June, and then, in July, Clodd, Shorter and his poet wife Dora Sigerson. The latter invitation was a damage limitation exercise and an ordeal for Florence, who must have worried that Shorter might accidentally give away her Roman Catholic adventure, or Clodd her wild indiscretions. On the other hand, she would have taken comfort from the presence of Dora Sigerson, a mutual friend of Katharine Tynan's. But the visit went off well; Clodd (tipped off by Florence) went away understanding that a marriage would soon take place, and Tom wrote warmly to Dora on 17 July:

I must send just a line for your very sweet nice letter. I shall tell my brother & sisters when I see them that you & Mr Shorter much enjoyed your visit to Talbothays & making their acquaintance. I hope you will go there, & come here, again. Their meeting you was quite an event, as they have known of your poetry for years.

At just this time Gosse, acting in his capacity as the old pussy well armed with sleek and shiny *Schadenfreude*, felt obliged to comment on the appointment of Robert Bridges to the laureateship. Referring to the previous incumbent, Alfred Austin, as a 'slack poetaster' (one of the mildest of the many epithets applied to this unfortunate and diminutive man) he told Tom that both he and Austin Dobson (a skilled but very minor poet well known to Tom) must have been candidates. Tom did not fall for this bait, replying on 18 July:

> . . . 'God's Funeral' [in the MS dedicated to Gosse] would have been enough to damn me for the Laureateship, even if I had tried for or thought of it, which of course I did not. Fancy Nonconformity on the one hand, & Oxford on the other, pouring out their vials on poor Mr Asquith for such an enormity! Swinburne told me that he read in some paper: 'Swinburne planteth, & Hardy watereth; & Satan giveth the increase' [he was always very proud of this; the reference has never been traced].
> Bridges is, on the whole, a very good, & what is more, a safe man.

Gosse later spitefully told Rupert Brooke in a letter that in fact Tom had hoped for the appointment and been disappointed; but that was clearly untrue, and perhaps prompted by pique that his old friend had so skilfully parried his letter by failing to denounce Bridges except by subtle implication.

Florence and he also entertained Keats' biographer Sidney Colvin for a weekend in July; Tom had known him for more than a quarter of a century. Colvin came to Max Gate by design, for on 20 July he wrote to Sir Edward Elgar:

> I am at Hardy's, and this is a line to say that my embassy is successful, in so far as I find the old man not only willing but *keen* to co-operate [sic] in an opera with you (there's a rotten kind of a pun come without my meaning it). – In a first afternoon's chat . . . three possible alternatives shape themselves in his mind . . .

These he enumerated: something based on *The Trumpet-Major*, or on *The Return of the Native*, or, finally, on *The Dynasts*. 'He is delighted at the idea, and convinced, as we all are, that the combination, if it could come off, would have a huge effect.' Elgar himself wrote to Tom on 22 July, and he replied on the 28th:

> It will be a pleasure if we can do something together. I daresay Colvin told you that a first consideration which occurred to me was whether it should be a production in the grand style based on 'The Dynasts', or a romantic or tragic Wessex opera based on one of my best known stories.

He suggested *A Pair of Blue Eyes*, mentioning that Patmore and Tennyson had been 'attracted' by it. Alas, after writing back on 31 July saying that he would read some of Tom's books from a musical point of view, Elgar dropped the matter. A collaboration would have had a 'huge effect' – a far greater one than did the D'Erlanger *Tess*. As it is, Tom is best celebrated in music by Holst's symphonic poem *Egdon Heath* – and by many settings of his poems, the most evocative of all these being those by Gerald Finzi, with Britten's not too far behind.

All these guests, and the production of the Hardy play by the Dorchester Debating and Dramatic Society that year, mitigates the picture that has been painted of Tom himself being fearful of the effect of Florence's presence – or, indeed, of 1913 being a 'searing' year for her. His house was always open to Lea, his friend the garage proprietor T.H. Tilley (a member of the Dramatic society who was a gifted comic actor) and, so far as can be ascertained, to anyone else who had a legitimate claim on his time. Tilley sent him Evans' adaptation of *The Woodlanders* in early August. On the 4th Tom asked him to call at Max Gate 'at any time'. It seems as if a not negligible part of the pressure that Florence was exerting upon him, as the price of her devotion and no doubt other more intimate matters, was that of her 'compromised position'. He put in a new conservatory that autumn and was, Florence told Clodd, pleased about it. So was she.

Now he began to think of his next volume of poems. To Maurice Macmillan he wrote on 6 August: '. . . I find that enough poems to fill a volume are lying in my drawer ready for the press at some indefinite date.' Macmillan was in the process of issuing *A Changed Man*, to him a ragbag collection of short stories, hitherto uncollected, which he was 'not anxious to issue . . . at all'. He was worrying, too, about the effect that the projected volume of poems would have. He had not had a wife unequivocally delighted at any volume of his poems; nor was he about to get one.

Purdy discovered, and Millgate relates, that Eliza Bright Nicholls, who had never married and who still kept Tom's ring and portrait, called at Max Gate some time in 1913. According to Purdy's informant (Eliza's niece Mrs Sarah Headley), she came to offer herself as a second wife, but was met with the announcement that he was going to marry Florence Dugdale.

Whenever Eliza called, and it might have been at about this time, Tom made sure to receive her. There was one thing, however, that he was not going to do. Thus his reply of 9 August to one H.A. Huxtable, town clerk of Weymouth, perhaps read a trifle humorously to him if to no one else:

> I should much like to accept the . . . invitation to meet 300 Canadian teachers at the Pavilion, some of whom are doubtless my readers. But I am sorry to say that the strain and stress of one thing and another of late have rendered me [and so on] . . .

He was soon expecting the company of both Constance and Eva Dugdale, and this, with the necessity to make a speech, was too much. On 16 August *The Times* reported him ill, but only because, he told Rider Haggard in a letter dated the 20th, he had expressed himself carelessly, thinking his words would be 'private only'.

Perhaps the first hint that he was not 'getting over' his mourning for Emma comes in this letter to Haggard: he found it, he said, 'strange' that the 'loss becomes more apparent & grievous after a few months have passed' than it seemed at first. Was this 'obsession' inevitable, or might a more spirited woman than Florence have inspired him to acceptance of his loss, if not to a spate of new love poems? For he was to write few more poems to Florence – but many more to Emma. Was Florence's enchantment beginning to die away? Was the price she was exacting for services rendered too high? He was in any case thinking of Emma on 22 August, just as the visit of the Dugdale sisters loomed: he wrote to the rector of St Juliot on that day, offering to help pay for a new screen, and it

> interested me very much to learn from you that some of your parish remember my late wife when she lived there as Miss Gifford. They

may perhaps recall her golden curls & rosy colour as she rode about, for she was very attractive at that time. If they mention any incident in connection with her I shall be glad to know it.

The old Emma appealed to him so much more than his dreary new companion. August had been a busy month, for at the beginning of it, as the *Life* retails, he was in Blandford for a couple of days

> with Mr John Lane searching about for facts and scenes that might illustrate the life of Alfred Stevens, the sculptor, whose best-known work is the Wellington monument in St Paul's, and who was born and grew up in this town . . . The house of his birth was discovered, but not much material seems to have been gained.

But Lane never undertook the projected biography, possibly feeling that he could not add substantially to the biographical study of 1881 by William Armstrong.

One wonders how Florence reacted to the following paragraph in 'her' *Life* when she came to type it – and whether it was to make amends for her negligence that she introduced into the household the magnificent and humorous dog Wessex (a literary critic who very properly admonished Galsworthy by chewing his trousers to pieces). The puppy Wessex – a fox terrier like Edward VII's famous Caesar – arrived at Max Gate, at any rate, in August.

> The autumn glided on with its trivial incidents. In the muddle of Hardy's unmistressed housekeeping animal pets of his late wife died, strayed, or were killed, much to Hardy's distress . . . and in the middle of November the Dorchester amateurs' version of *The Woodlanders*, adapted by themselves [A.H. Evans], was performed . . . but Hardy was not present on the occasion.

His absence seems to have been the result of a bad cold while in Cambridge receiving his Fellowship. But he had gone to some of the rehearsals, as recalled by the actress who played Marty South:

> During one rehearsal I plucked up courage to ask him how I should say a certain line of Marty South's beautiful and haunting lament . . . but he would give me no help and said I must speak them just as I felt them. So, I did.

782

'No-one,' wrote the adapter-producer's daughter, Evelyn Evans, 'who heard Gertrude Bugler, then in her teens [she was seventeen], utter these moving words will ever forget the tears shed by the audience.'

Gertrude Bugler went on to record how, soon afterwards, Mrs Hardy (as Florence had by then become) asked her if she had ever thought of taking up acting as a career: her husband believed that she had some talent, but that it would need training. She did not follow up this idea at the time, and can hardly have guessed that, when invited to do so, it would be this same concerned Mrs Hardy who would stab a spoke decisively in her wheel. Nor can Florence herself have guessed that this spirited young woman would cause her greater grief and hysteria than had even the ghost of Emma. But Tom, a man used to noticing such girls, had already registered her beauty – and perhaps, too, her 'livingness'. On 10 December he told Clodd, who had attended the London performance at the Cripplegate Institute two days earlier, that the company was to perform the play again at Weymouth, and that he might have a chance to see it then; he added that Marty was played by 'the pretty daughter of a baker here'.

On 13 November, 'liquid-eyed' with his 'clergyman's cold', he wrote to his old friend Frederic Harrison: 'As for your not being a literary man, I must argue that out with you when I see you.' He would not have been so eagerly complimentary had he been able to anticipate what Harrison would say about him in the *Fortnightly* in 1920, after which he regarded their friendship as at an end. But for now, having just read Harrison's *The Positive Evolution of Religion*, he was genial and confiding:

> What a *full* man you are. But you are a trifle hard upon the Dissenters to my hurried seeming. Their horn of the revelation dilemma is not so bad as the Roman Catholic one. They did go half way across the stream towards truth & reasonableness. Why they halted there – in the middle of the plank – & why they have never moved from that utterly illogical position for erecting an edifice upon I am too ignorant to be aware.
>
> But some of the things done & left undone by the R.C's – However I'll go no further this evening.

Then, significantly in view of his quiet and tentative drift back to a more positive attitude towards his own early faith – the letter was, after all, to a leading positivist – he added a postscript: 'I was, as you may know, brought up as an orthodox English churchman.' He, at least, had been giving consideration to the inner reasons for Emma's Christian beliefs, and had been doing so initially, no doubt, by means of tenderly remembering his own.

As the year drew to its close, Tom was in what he called on 14 November to Mrs Humphry Ward, who had sent him a copy of her novel *The Coryston Family*, 'a chronic muddle that appears like busi-ness'. Florence had not managed to impose any real order on the Max Gate household, unlike her supposedly 'certifiable' predecessor. Tom was, apparently, unreasonable on one point: Lilian Gifford. She was Emma's niece, he had known her as a very young child and still thought of her as one, he was thoroughly used to her presence – and he himself did not have to deal with her more capricious manifestations. She knew how to get round him without upsetting him, and she knew just how and when to needle Florence with remarks about her lack of class and breeding. Worst of all, she superciliously refused to do any work in the house. In one of her regular lamentations, Florence mentioned a fearful row that Lilian had provoked while her own sister Constance was staying at Max Gate. She may have exaggerated, as was her wont, but Tom, her Daddy-Uncle, had failed to notice the effect this niece was having on the people around her. He never seems to have been quite charmed enough by her to allude to her in a poem; in the last analysis, perhaps, he tolerated her only for the sake of Emma's memory. When she later fell ill and had to be confined to an institution for a time it was, typically, a guilty Florence (if at his behest) who visited her and who arranged for her conditional release. It is plain that Lilian had no place in any self-respecting household. A defence of her behaviour at Max Gate would be impossible.

But in mid-November matters had not yet quite come to a head, and Florence was reading Tom such tales as 'Oh, Whistle, and I'll Come to You, My Lad', from *Ghost-Stories of an Antiquary* by M.R. James, the new Cambridge Vice-Chancellor. The volume had been sent to him by A.E. Housman, whom he had just met. 'I was agreeably sensible of their eeriness, even though the precaution was taken of keeping them at a safe distance from bed-time,' Tom told Housman on 15 November. There is more evidence from this month, too, of his interest in church matters: he wrote letters to Handley Moule, now the Bishop of Durham, and to his friend Reymond Abbott. Moule had sent him his *Memories of a Vicarage*, about his childhood in Fordington, and Tom now acknowledged it with a poem ('The Abbey Mason') 'on the origin of the "Perpendicular" style'. To Abbott he wrote:

I have not yet tested your revised version of the psalm-tune, but my niece, who is staying here, shall try it over. I had a saddening experience of another old tune when I was at Plymouth . . . Mrs Hardy as a child lived near the Hoe, & used to listen as she lay in her cot to the chimes of St Andrews Church playing the 'Old 113th' at night-time. It was also a familiar tune to my father. When I listened for it I found it was no longer played. I daresay you know it: it is in Hymns A. and M.

Had Tom been a businessman, or what he called a 'munitions-maker' and 'war-adept', then those closest to him might no doubt have pronounced him over-morbid in his new habit of harking back to the past. But he was a poet, and this was the stuff of his poetry. When, in *The Wound and the Bow*, Edmund Wilson fruitfully compared the imaginative writer to Philoctetes, the owner of a magic bow who had a stinking wound, he drew attention to the fallacy of believing that the advantages of the bow could be enjoyed without enduring the stinking presence of Philoctetes himself. Florence did not understand the nature of the magic inherent in the bow, but she certainly subscribed to that fallacy. Besides, was Philoctetes really being quite as loathsome and stinking, in this particular instance, as all that?

It is almost always assumed that Tom 'proposed marriage' to Florence Dugdale. I think, however, that, with an absent-mindedness no doubt highly convenient to his sense of well-being, he 'proposed' that she simply stay on at Max Gate as his dearest girl; she, on the other hand, made marriage the price for staying on. It must all have been, of course, infinitely more subtle than that. Nor did she ask Tom for anything unreasonable. But she did decide to stay on; she did know better than anyone else what the situation at Max Gate really was; and therefore she knew very well what she was getting into. He was going on as he had always gone on, but missing Emma and the management she had exerted over the household. That had not, and never would be, replaced. It was not Florence's fault, and it was not his. I do not think, either, that he would much have minded having her there as his mistress, provided that appearances could be preserved and he could represent her as his secretary-housekeeper. Could they take away his OM? Hardly. Although there was a part of him that cared for his standing, there was another that was amused by the load of polite and formal rubbish that was involved. In this he differed from his second wife.

A handwritten letter of 21 December to Florence Henniker – really his best friend now, for all their past differences – shows his state of mind a few days before Christmas 1913, and just a few weeks away from his marriage. She had not long before retreated to what she called her pleasant little cottage at Shoreham in Kent.

> I had reserved my reply to your last kind letter till to-day, in order to make it a Christmas greeting, & now I have a double impulse to write, having received the picture-card & words on it this morning. It seems, so far as I can judge, a very pretty place . . .
> The new Christmas does not exhilarate me much. But of course I cannot expect it to. The worst of a sad event in middle life & beyond is that one does not recover from the shock as in earlier years; so I simply say to myself of this Christmas, 'Yet another!'
> . . . The half page of [Shorter's] *The Sphere*, which I enclose as a sort of Xmas card, gives a few verses I was asked for by the editor, but a periodical is a chilling place for poems: the mood induced by a newspaper is just the wrong one, & puts them out of tune.

The poem in question was 'To Meet, or Otherwise', and one may well imagine Florence Dugdale, to whom he would certainly have shown it, urging for its prominent publication in a 'periodical', or newspaper. Is the above short paragraph a coded message to himself to the effect that the nature of Florence's ambitions, which included newspaper announcements, was 'chilling' to him?

He had not long before subscribed to *Poetry and Drama*, Harold Monro's new magazine, and had humorously told Gosse on 5 October that 'it seemed to be written by queer young men whose wrongnesses are interesting'. Now he commented upon it again to Florence Henniker. Probably he was thinking of the editor's 'manifesto' in which he exhorted his followers to forget 'God, Heaven, hell, Personal Immortality' and to 'lift the eyes from a sentimental contemplation of the past [and] always *live*, in the future of the earth'.

> Do you ever see a quarterly magazine called 'Poetry & Drama'. It is written by a group of young men whose idea of verse is that nobody has ever known how to write it in the whole history of literature till they came along to show the trick to the world; so it is amusing reading, which I think you would like.
> A young lady came this week to photograph me in colour . . . The

specimens she showed me were extraordinary in their reality. But I am getting tired of it all. My niece & Miss Dugdale are here ministering to my wants: I don't know what I should do without them, & I am sorry to say that just now Florence has a bad cold. I want her to stay in bed, but cannot get her to. I do not see many people . . .

One thing more: did you see my letter in the *Times* about performing animals? . . . what I object to most are performances *with* animals – in which they are passive . . . Every spectator can see that the wretched creature is in the greatest misery, & I believe that a great many are 'used' in these tricks – that is, tortured to death.

I wonder when I shall see you. Not very soon I suppose; and you have many interests outside my life.

The last sentence sounds a little wistful, and as though he valued Mrs Henniker's intellectual company over that of Lilian and Florence, whom he could not get to *stay in bed*. It does not sound, either, as though he himself was in any great hurry to seal what Florence called, in a report of New Year's Day to Clodd, the 'compact' which she believed they had made.

But she was determined that he should, and after a Christmas that may have been marred by more ill behaviour from Lilian, she made it clear to Tom either that she would not marry him, or that she would not stay at Max Gate, unless Lilian were sent away. To Clodd she wrote:

If the niece is to remain here as one of the family, then I will not enter into that compact of which I spoke to you last summer. This must be decided in a week, and if it is settled that she stays, I return to my own home and stay there.

This smacks of an ultimatum. The upshot was that Lilian was dismissed, and, as a person whom her Daddy-Uncle well knew was virtually unemployable for any length of time, received both a larger annuity (her current £13 was raised to £52) and some shares which she later cashed in for ones of more dubious value. She got more than Florence knew until the time of Tom's death, upon which she received even more. But then Tom must have made it quite clear to Florence that, apart from a housekeeping allowance, she was not to be privy to his financial affairs, which he had always conducted with the ferocious assiduity of a literary agent. That was a Victorian habit from which he never showed much sign of becoming emancipated. She told Owen, of all people, that she had asked him for a marriage settlement, but 'it seemed to annoy [him], so I desisted'. Later, in 1915, Florence grumbled profusely about his alleged stinginess, but she had had fair warning of it – if indeed she ever asked him properly for a settlement, and was not later exaggerating the seriousness of her request. It may therefore be said that she should either have persisted, or refused to go through with it.

But the truth is that she wanted desperately to marry him and acquire the title of Mrs Thomas Hardy, and only the presence of the impossible Lilian seemed to her to act as an obstacle to her wish. Lilian did return to Max Gate, if only as a temporary visitor, even as early as 1914, and so did Gordon Gifford; Florence was vociferous in her unhappiness over these visits.

If she did not have the support of Kate and Henry, then she soon enlisted it – although we have only her word for it. Their elder brother – they would have reckoned – needed looking after, Kate did not want to do it, and a Dugdale was better, somewhat more efficient, and more easily influenced than a Gifford any day. As she reported to Clodd on 1 January 1914, Kate openly and humorously referred to them, as they were walking together in Stinsford churchyard on the last day of the year, as the most 'dismal critters' that she had ever seen. And Tom, after the hasty marriage, confirmed this view by telling Frederic Harrison that, to the participants, the wedding had 'been of a sober colour enough. That the union of two rather melancholy temperaments may result in cheerfulness, as the junction of two negatives forms a positive, is our modest hope.' But he added, forebodingly from Florence's viewpoint, that although it might seem odd to Harrison, 'the sense of continuity through her having been attached to my late wife is not the least of my satisfaction'. This implies that, apart from consolingly accounting for Emma's late eccentricities by means of rubbing in the fact of her 'madness', of the 'taint' in the family, Florence had by no means allowed Tom to know what she had been saying to other people, notably Kate, about Emma's character. Had he known what she had been writing to Clodd for the past months, the wedding would not have taken place at all, and this might have been better for his happiness; but poetry meant more to him than happiness. The remark to Harrison and others also implies that he had, in whatever form their intimate discourse took, made it clear to Florence herself that he believed she was offering him a 'sense of continuity'.

I think he had been reluctant about getting a move on, or putting his best foot forward. That he was selfish about this there can be no doubt, although he was as busy as ever with his poetry and his contemplation. We have to view the situation in the light of the fact that he really was an old man, and one who was going to need increasing care. He flourished on his own native ground, but soon got unwell and upset when away from it. We cannot judge his behaviour as if he were an eager young man getting married for the first time. He would therefore have been happy to allow matters to drift on – Florence was there, after all. So he dillied, and then dallied, and Florence became increasingly impatient. He dreaded the newspapers, and the attention they would no doubt give to his marriage with a much younger woman; the situation had salacious intimations which such a master of eroticism could hardly miss. She, on the other hand, was looking forward to the newspapers, although she would later protect him fiercely against the incursions of their representatives – the service she performed most efficiently of all.

So at the beginning of February she renewed her assault, utilizing the various means (sexual and otherwise) which she had by now learned. Sad and reproachful looks; being made to feel ill at bedtime by the position into which she had been placed; her lack of 'real feeling' in sexual matters having been sacrificed for the sake of his passion; poor eating; sulking – who knows? There are no existing standards by which she can be 'blamed' for this; but he may have discerned in her a commonplaceness which he had hardly discerned before.

Tom capitulated. A special licence was applied for. It arrived on 6 February, and the wedding took place on the 10th. Why a special licence, unless there had been pressure from her, or perhaps from the Dugdale family at Enfield? The strongly Christian and brisk Edward Dugdale would no doubt have been hotly declaring that, never mind who this Sir Thomas Hardy was, he must now repay his daughter for her devotion. He too could write to the newpapers. Had not she also been fatally 'compromised'? Would that not be a view any Christian person might reasonably take? What future would his daughter have if Sir Thomas did not do his duty, OM or no OM? The necessity of privacy could have had nothing to do with the haste. You can be as discreet with an ordinary licence as you can with a special one – indeed, more so.

May O'Rourke, the secretary who in 1923, at the age of twenty-six, was engaged by Florence for her own sake and on behalf of her husband, published three or four careful pieces about life at Max Gate. She was a scrupulous person, a sincere and truthful as well as devoutly pious Roman Catholic. She wrote and published poetry and had seen (in Ireland, naturally), a leprechaun. Tom, always keenly aware of the susceptibilities of others, pretty girls in particular, protected her from divorced callers and from anything else he deemed unfit for so pious a girl.

Even in her published work about life at Max Gate O'Rourke did not withhold her criticisms of Florence as often tense and jealous, even if she did explain them, and rightly, as largely arising from depression, ill health and an all too justified dread of cancer. In private, though, she went further, making two observations which she always refused to allow to be made public. No mere recipient of town tattle, she knew and had watched Florence over a number of years, had lived in the Old Rectory at Fordington, and had first met Tom in 1918. She had family connections with the Scudamores, relations of Hermann Lea's; she much appreciated Lea, who became her friend, and had stayed with him at the birthplace at Bockhampton. Her information must have come from him, so it is possible that it originated with Tom himself – if Tom ever talked really intimately with anyone outside his own family, it would certainly have been with Lea. He liked, he said, to be alone with him. May O'Rourke maintained that Florence had been determined from the start to marry Tom, 'by fair means or foul'. She also stated that Edward Dugdale had exclaimed, when he heard that the special licence had been sent for: 'She's pulled it off.' It would not have been out of character. Dugdale's influence in all this, especially as a weapon brandished by Florence over the grieving old man, can by no means be discounted.

The wedding was at Enfield – it could hardly be held anywhere near Dorchester – and the utmost secrecy was observed:

> The vicar [he told Clodd on 11 February from Max Gate], who is a friend of Florence's, lent his assistance, & the result was that, though the Church door was wide open, not a soul was present except her father & sister [the youngest, Margaret] & my brother, & the officiators & contracting parties. We came straight back here, & I am going to put over my study door, 'Business as usual during alterations'.

Despite the 'secrecy', twenty-six reporters knocked on Dugdale's door not so much later that morning; and there is little doubt who had tipped them the wink. As to the absence of Tom's sisters, Mary was in ill health, though soon afterwards she wrote to Tom to give him her qualified approval; while Kate might just have baulked at attending the actual wedding. There was no mention of either an engagement or a wedding ring, but it seems unlikely that the latter was not provided – at least for the ceremony.

The wedding was reported in the *Enfield Gazette* on 13 February, in terms of which Tom could hardly have approved but which were plainly inspired by Edward Dugdale, named as having 'long' been 'a member of Mr Hardy's select circle of friends'. Of the groom it was said:

> It is curious that Mr Hardy is credited with the conviction that his poetry is of greater literary value than his prose . . . Perhaps it would be a fairer test if one could ask 'the powers that be' why Mr Hardy received the highest distinction in the land . . . Surely their reply would be prose not poetry.

Of his bride:

> Miss Dugdale had previously followed a literary career, her first effort being a series of articles in this Journal under 'The Children's Corner'. From the beginning her work became more ambitious, and she was a contributor to 'The Standard', 'The Cornhill Magazine', 'The Daily Mail' and other London papers of the first rank . . . It is to be hoped that the promise of youth will be developed by closer association with the greatest of authors, and perhaps the world will be the richer for the simple ten minutes' ceremony in the parish church of Enfield.

The world was indeed in a sense made the richer: Tom was so greatly to regret his folly in encouraging her, and her literary ambitions would become so heavy a burden upon him, that he would have to invent and write 'her' *Life* of him.

Florence had this time not dared to post her usual report to Clodd, and merely added a coy postscript to Tom's letter:

> My dear Mr Clodd:
> Of course I wanted you to know before anybody else, but I was under the strictest orders not to tell anyone. I wrote you a long letter but finally decided to be obedient & not send it.

Florence behaved no worse than any other young woman who has married a famous and venerated old man; but she was out of her depth from the start. She would in due course quarrel with almost everyone, even with Rebekah Owen, to whom – in the extremity of her despair over Gertrude Bugler – she sent a savagely denunciatory letter for which, typically, she immediately apologized. Whether it had any truth in it will never be known – Rebekah, after all, could have done with such home truths as she did not obtain from her confessor. When Beatrix Potter – who lived at Sawrey in the Lake District and became the friend and then executor (her husband was a solicitor) of Owen – came to sort out Florence's letters in 1939 she had to destroy a number of them, on the grounds that they were, as she called them, 'positively libellous'. In all likelihood she thus wisely protected many of Florence's 'libels' of her husband from ever seeing the light of day. Many of her letters were wild and inconsistent in their accusations, and far too much reliance has been placed upon them as evidence of what actually went on at Max Gate; usually she wrote them when she was driven to it by hysterical self-pity. She would quote Tom's conversation, but through the lens of her own dismal outlook. Her letters were unconsidered, dashed off, and without wit or wisdom or perception. Before finally quarrelling with Cockerell after Tom's death, she alternately denounced and praised him to Rebekah Owen. There is no doubt that Cockerell was terrifying when in action, nor that he ignored the sensibilities of everyone except the person upon whom he was concentrating his acquisitive attentions, nor that he openly and officiously took notes of whatever was said that interested him; but Florence's attitude might well have been designed to make him into a maximum threat. She was too timid to stand up to him, too timid to speak to Tom about him, and so could only express herself to a third party.

There is little point in quoting extensively from her letters of complaint, since they all tell the same story: of extreme emotional volatility, mostly tending in the direction of depression and suspicion and, occasionally, of sudden and unreasoning dislike – even of the person to whom she was writing. The letters then became hateful; but these were always instantly apologized for. To previous correspondents she added Lady Hoare, and, later, Louisa Yearsley, the sympathetic wife of the surgeon who operated on her nose in 1915. It is ironic, in the circumstances of her lies about Emma, that, when she was at her most hysterically depressed, Florence was herself quite 'mad' and certainly subject to 'delusions'. As her undoubtedly much tried husband might have said, the fates had planned it that way.

Tom's own attitude to the arrangement, or 'trifling incident' as he called it, he made perfectly clear in various letters dated 11 February. To Cockerell he wrote: 'We thought it the wisest thing to do, seeing what a right hand Florence had become to me, & there is a sort of continuity in it, & not a break, she having known my first wife so well.' To Gosse: 'I was on the point of writing to you . . . after marrying my long friend & secretary Miss Dugdale, till I found that in some unforseen way the trifling incident had got into the London afternoon papers . . .' To Florence Henniker: 'You do like her I am sure, & I want you to like her better still, if you will be so kind – though as you *always* are kind I needn't have said that, & I am sure you will go on liking her.' To Lady Grove: '. . . we thought our affair would be rather humdrum . . . But the fine morning, the quiet old church, &c. were not without romance. There were only 7 present.' And to Lady Hoare he described Florence as 'a literary woman, but not a blue-stocking at all'.

Only Florence Henniker – who knew Florence as the others, with the exception of Clodd, did not – seems, if ever so discreetly from her privileged position, to have slightly demurred. She did, however, write that Florence had 'a beautiful nature – very full of sympathy, and she combines (which is perhaps rare) the quality of enthusiasm with common sense'. That last, alas, was not true: Florence did have sympathy, most especially with any form of suffering, but her enthusiasm was gushing and insincere, and her common sense was in short supply. Tom answered Mrs Henniker carefully on 6 March:

> I rather am surprised that *you* were surprised at the step we have taken – such a course seeming an obvious one to me, being as I was so lonely & helpless. I think I told you in my last letter that I am very glad she knew Emma well, & was liked by her even during her latter years, when her mind was a little unhinged at times, & she showed unreasonable dislikes. I wonder if it will surprise you when I say that according to my own experience a second marriage does not, or need not, obliterate an old affection, though it is generally assumed that the first wife is entirely forgotten in such cases.
>
> . . . Even now I have not answered your question on what people wrote about our marriage. Well: they all say they foresaw it, except one besides yourself – I forget who. Of course, they *might* say so to show their penetration or to claim it. But perhaps they really did.

On 23 March he told Harrison that their honeymoon, 'if it could be called such', was still being taken in bits: 'It will take up about two years to use up the whole moon at the rate at which we go on at present.'

Florence was by now almost ready to resume her litany of complaint, and by June she had done so. She could not manage the servants, the cook was impossible, and she was 'in despair', her soul was 'destroyed'. Her misery continued for the rest of her life, fluctuating not so much with external circumstances as with the ups and downs of her internal health. When Tom wrote to Clodd for financial advice on 11 February 1915, Florence, having written to him (in a lost or destroyed letter the receipt of which, however, he noted in his diary) of her married misery, felt constrained to add a postscript: 'We have been married a year & a day, & *really* & *truly* (I am not joking now) it has been a year of *great* happiness.' She had not 'meant' the miserable letter, and now wanted it dismissed as 'a joke'; but neither did she mean the *really* and *truly*. It was all a question of how she felt at the moment (usually, therefore, miserable), and of how she estimated that people might think she, as Mrs Thomas Hardy, *ought* to feel. It was meaningless. She was directed in her behaviour not so much by inner feeling as by her notions of what the outside world expected. Psychologically without resilience, she remained dominated by her authoritarian father, and to a certain extent she superimposed the image of the feared Enfield schoolmaster on to that of her perhaps more subtle husband.

Yet it must be added, so far as her essential inner nature is concerned, that a kind of 'loving-kindness' did lie at its root. Her repentance at her lapses into weakness and savage denunciations of others was more deeply felt than the denunciations themselves, which were simply the inner rages and frustrations of a feeble and, alas, drab person who knew in her heart that she had plunged far out of her depth. In the nine years left to her after Tom's death, she was, thankfully, able to become herself to a certain extent, and at a level most suitable to her. Despite atrocious health and a series of painful operations for cancer, she used her wealth to work for Dorchester hospitals and for the poor. She was kind to other sick people, and gave them rides in the chauffered car she bought for herself. She had an unfortunate experience with the strange little Sir James Barrie, fantasizing that she might become his wife. When he got wind of her intentions, he made himself scarce. She quarrelled with both Sassoon and Cockerell. She was made acutely unhappy, too, by Maugham's *Cakes and Ale*; but with her public work she was satisfied. Characteristically, she chopped down eighty of the Max Gate trees and filled the conservatory with captive budgerigars – something Tom would have found unbearable. She died there, relieved from her acute pain by drugs, in 1937; in those final years she had complained less, for her husband was dead.

35

War – and More 'Adolescence'

The outbreak of the First World War had a devastating effect on Tom. He had for once failed to foresee it, or, more likely, had put the probability out of his mind while he worked on the contents of *Satires of Circumstance* – and not without some unease about how Florence would receive it. But, as he later declared, his poem 'Channel Firing', written a few months before the outbreak of war, was 'prophetic' and 'to say the least' displayed 'a perception singularly coincident'. There is much in May O'Rourke's assessment of him, bearing in mind that hers was a strictly Roman Catholic temperament. She quoted St Thomas Aquinas in connection with Tom's attitude towards human suffering: 'He is spiritually nailed to the Cross whose mind is crucified through compassion for his neighbour.'

In his letter of 28 June to Gosse he did not mention the storm clouds gathering, seeming to be more nervous about his poems. One may read between the lines, even if Gosse, not appraised of his personal situation, could not:

> I have a watery eye, owing to sitting by an open window. I am also exercised on what to do with some poems. When I am dead & gone I shall be glad – if I can be anything – for them to have been printed, & yet I don't quite like to print them.

By 17 July, having written to Frederick Macmillan to protest that his verse was not to be included in a 'limited edition' (delayed until 1919, when it began to appear as the Mellstock edition), he had made his decision. He told Florence Henniker that he was collecting the poems:

> Some of them I rather shrink from printing – those I wrote just after Emma died, when I looked back at her as she had originally been, & when I felt miserable lest I had not treated her considerately in her later life. However I shall publish them as the only amends I can

make, if it were so. The remainder of the book, & by far the greater part of it, will be poems mostly dramatic or personative – many of which have been printed in magazines, &c. (I have let nobody but you & Florence know as yet that I purpose this.)

We are going on calmly enough here as you guess. She is a very tender companion & is quite satisfied with the quietude of life here. But we flit about a little. Last week-end we spent at Sir Henry Hoare's at Stour-head in Wiltshire . . .

Tom mentions this visit in the *Life* (it brought great delight to Florence):

To Hardy as to ordinary civilians the murder at Serajevo [sic] was a lurid and striking tragedy, but carried no indication that it would much affect English life. On July 28th they were at a quiet little garden party near Dorchester, and still there was no sign of the coming storm.

On 4 August they were lunching at Athelhampton when 'a telegram arrived announcing the rumour to be fact': 'The whole news and what it involved burst on Hardy's mind next morning, for though most people were saying the war would be over by Christmas he felt it might be a matter of years and untold disaster.' He half-echoed this sentiment when he wrote to Macmillan on 10 August, having previously suggested that he might, in view of 'recent events', hold back the manuscript of *Satires of Circumstance* if they thought fit: 'I have sent off . . . the MS . . . as you suggested . . . If you decide to print it, it could, of course be published at any favourable time – say, when people get tired of the war, if they do!'

The suddenness of the event shocked and aged him. He wrote gloomily to his friend Pouncy, assistant editor of a local paper, that he was

afraid that the continuation of 'The Dynasts' into this twentieth century will have to be done by other pens than mine. They will probably not, however, be able to continue it into the twenty first century, all dynasties likely to be finished by that time.

He was almost right in that, and, as usual, ahead of his own over-optimistic time in his view of the future. But, as he told Mrs Henniker, he felt that Great Britain was 'innocent for once'. Asked by the *Daily News* to make any comment he wanted on the war, he declined, on the grounds of 'insufficiency of data':

> While as to general opinions & prophecies, they would be laughed at: e.g., such a highly rational one as that all the Churches in Europe should frankly admit the utter failure of theology, & put their heads together to form a new religion which should have at least some faint connection with morality.

He did write, in the course of the war, a few of what he called (in *Moments of Vision*) 'patriotic' poems, but none can be described as jingoistic. He felt, though, that as the leading older poet he ought to set an example. He collected the 'Poems of War and Patriotism' in *Moments of Vision*. The opening poem, 'Men Who March Away', sets the tone. This had appeared in *The Times* on 9 September, and then as a postscript to *Satires of Circumstance*, from which he reprinted it to head the group in *Moments of Vision*. Significantly from the point of view of his usual poetic intentions, he told Arthur Symons – now happily recovered from the strange bout of madness which had assailed him in Italy in 1908 – that he feared the poem was 'not free from some banalities which it is difficult to keep out of lines which are meant to appeal to the man in the street, & not to "a few friends only"' (that last phrase echoes his earlier 'those who know', also to the much valued Symons).

On 3 September he attended, at Wellington House, a conference of authors concerned with 'the organization of public statements of the strength of the British case' to neutral countries. Arnold Bennett (later satirized by Ford for his pomposity at such meetings) was there, and so was G.K. Chesterton – but Tom did not, in the *Life*, mention the latter. Instead he listed others, such as Wells, Barrie, Newbolt, Arthur Benson (to advise on the hope and the glory) and his Catholic brother, Bridges and Gilbert Murray.

> In recalling it Hardy said that the yellow September sun shone in from the dusty street with a tragic cast upon them as they sat round the large blue table, full of misgivings, yet unforeseeing in all their completeness the tremendous events that were to follow. The same evening Hardy left London – 'the streets hot and sad, and bustling

with soldiers and recruits' – to set about some contribution to the various forms of manifesto that had been discussed.

On 5 September he wrote 'Men Who March Away':

> Is it a purblind prank, O think you,
>   Friend with the musing eye,
>   Who watch us stepping by
>   With doubt and dolorous sigh?
> Can much pondering so hoodwink you!
> Is it a purblind prank, O think you,
>   Friend with the musing eye?

He did not reserve his copyright and it was reprinted in many places, winning, as he claimed, 'an enormous popularity'.

The *Life* goes on to tell of the publication of *Satires of Circumstance*, and to lament the fact that the satires, written 'with a light heart before the war,' 'ill harmonized' with the rest of the book, which, he said, 'contained some of the tenderest and least satirical verse that ever came from his pen'. He did not tell of Florence's reaction to this book, which appeared on 17 November (not in October, as he states). Whatever had held her back until then, the publication let loose the floodgates of lamentation. Not many days afterwards she was telling Owen that Hyatt had been the only man who had ever loved her – and that she was not lovable.

It is hard to see quite what she expected from *Satires*, unless it was public acclaim. Unable to consider the poems in terms of what Tom had achieved in them, she read them, she said, 'with a horrible fascination': they wounded her self-esteem, and she negatively related them to a notion of herself as a kind of national and official muse. She mourned to Lady Hoare:

> I am an utter failure if my husband can publish such a *sad sad* book
> . . . I cannot get rid of the feeling that the man who wrote some of
> those poems is utterly weary of life & cares for nothing in this world.
> If I had been a different sort of woman, & better fitted to be his wife
> – would he, I wonder, have published that volume?

Tom must have been deeply disappointed to receive this reaction, and even more so when he read a 'crudely patriotic' (as Millgate rightly calls it) story, which appeared in the *Sunday Pictorial* for 13 June 1915, called '"Greater Love Hath No Man . . .": The Story of a Village Ne'er-Do-Weel' by 'Mrs Thomas Hardy'. This was possibly more embarrassing than anything ever published by Emma. With this tale Florence had not received, or sought, the assistance of Tom; it shows. It may even have been an attempt to show him what she could do on her own. She had become a temporary victim of the jingoism which she had picked up from the upper-class women whom she was now at last able to meet on equal terms – people who attacked the 'great unwashed' for their slowness in volunteering for immediate death in France, and who might even present educated young men with a white feather if they did not seen sufficiently eager to offer themselves.

Florence's *Pictorial* story, redolent of jingoism of the worst kind, must have repelled Tom. He believed in the necessity of the fight against Germany, and in the general rightness of the British cause, but he eschewed all such jingoism and was critical of it to Mrs Henniker. In the *Life* he remembered his earlier reactions to war-fever: 'When the noisy crew of music-hall Jingoes said exultingly, years earlier, that Germany was as anxious for war as they were themselves, he had felt convinced that they were wrong.' He now refused to hate the Germans, and initially attributed their wickedness to the 'madness' of one man, the Kaiser; by early 1915, rather more accurately, he was pointing the finger of blame at 'the group of oligarchs & munition-makers whose interest is war'. 'The Pity of It', printed in the *Fortnightly* in April 1915, sums up his feelings:

> I walked in loamy Wessex lanes, afar
> From rail-track and from highway, and I heard
> In field and farmstead many an ancient word
> Of local lineage like 'Thu bist', 'Er war',
>
> 'Ich woll', 'Er sholl', and by-talk similar,
> Nigh as they speak who in this month's moon gird
> At England's very loins, thereunto spurred
> By gangs whose glory threats and slaughters are.
>
> There seemed a Heart crying: 'Whosoever they be
> At root and bottom of this, who flung this flame
> Between kin folk kin tongued even as are we,

'Sinister, ugly, lurid, be their fame;
May their familiars grow to shun their name,
And their brood perish everlastingly.'

After years of encouragement, and of allowing Florence to imagine
that he admired and valued her gifts, the scales fell from Tom's eyes: he
recognized that she was a 'literary woman' of a very limited kind. It was
his own fault: he had brought the difficult fact of her still undimmed but
unfulfillable literary ambitions upon himself. But he none the less tried,
vainly as it now seems, to discourage her from original composition after
1914. He did not even like her writing the digests of books she was still
doing for Shorter. Florence was early aware of his antipathy to these and
wrote to Lady Hoare on 26 July 1914 that she knew 'deep within' that
her husband 'rather dislikes my being a scribbling woman'.

Both Gittings and Millgate have put great stress on what they call the
'adolescence' of Tom's old age. In this matter, of Tom's pretending to
himself, and then to certain women who attracted him, that they had
literary gifts, such superior critics might seem to have the argument their
way. Yet 'adolescent' is, after all, a strangely inappropriate adjective to
apply to Tom the poet: his love poetry is hardly reconcilable with the
connotations of that word. True, his excitement over women whose
beauty and high spirits attracted him did lead him, on a number of
occasions, to express an excessive admiration of their work. He was
seldom as enthusiastic about the work of any *man*. But that this
enthusiasm was not wholly opportunistic (no one can deny that it
was sexually opportunistic) is illustrated by his apparently genuine
enthusiasm for the poetry of 'Laurence Hope', the pseudonym of
Violet Nicolson. He met the then thirty-eight-year-old poet in 1903,
and was so struck by her beauty that he believed her to be thirty or
less – a belief which she did not discourage. A year later she poisoned
herself in Madras, on account of the death of her husband, a general of
sixty-two. Hearing of this suicide, Tom wrote at once to Symons on
23 October 1904: 'I trouble you with this intelligence merely because
the moment affords an opening for publishing a critical summary of
her passionate verses by anybody who is acquainted with them, & may
wish to do so.'

He was pleased with Symons' romantic reply, which stated that he was
glad that there were 'still people who can do such things'. Tom wrote
an obituary notice of her in the *Athenaeum*, in which he over-rated her
poetry, and then a preface to Heinemann's publication of her posthumous

volume *Indian Love* (1905), in which he again over-rated her. He was more than merely irritated when the publishers failed to make use of this preface, and on 16 July 1905 wrote William Heinemann the following letter which shows him at the height of his ire:

> Will you kindly return me the MS, of the Preface . . . (which I was particularly pressed to write) & let me know as a mere matter of civility, why you did not print it? – seeing that, though worthless in itself, it would have helped the sale, if the prices paid me for a few lines of fugitive writing be any criterion, & was gratuitously contributed.
>
> Yours truly
Thomas Hardy
>
> To avoid misapprehension I hereby withdraw all right to its publication, in another impression . . . or elsewhere. T.H.

Since Tom had discussed Violet Nicolson's poems enthusiastically with Gosse just before the news of her death, and since they are merely perfervid, it does seem as if he was always much taken, and his judgement adversely affected, when confronted with 'passionate' poetry written by women. There was little of this about in Victorian times: he was responding not, perhaps, to poetry, but to passionate feeling. The least sign of passion or sexual interest from a woman was enough to set him off into the belief that she must be capable of good writing. If it was not yet good, then surely it must become good when she had been educated (by him) out of orthodoxy.

As far as is known there had been no lyrical poetry from Florence Dugdale, but Tom's susceptibility to women's passionate verse tells us that he was susceptible, too, to any indication of a capacity for sexual desire or sexual affection. Thus he was excited at 'Laurence Hope's' love for her general, only two years his own junior.

Would the word 'adolescent' not perhaps be better applied, therefore, to those who have no insight into these susceptibilities, but who cling to more respectable and unreal notions of masculine sexuality? And is Tom's journey into the 'abyss' of his memories, amorous and otherwise, of his now dead wife merely 'adolescent'? Some ungenerous readers might call his critics in this respect stuffy or even 'adolescent' themselves: pompously unwilling to face up to what strikes them as 'unpleasant'.

The element of 'remorse' in the poems about Emma has also been much exaggerated, if only by being isolated from its context. This is no more than the remorse of any suddenly bereaved person, who has not been given the opportunity to say goodbye or to consider the full meaning of a whole married life, and who therefore feels that he has taken things too much for granted. These are not the devious poems of a hypocrite who has spectacularly ill-treated his wife. They tell, in essence, an 'ordinary' story, although they do not tell it in an ordinary manner. If the story itself were not ordinary, then the poems would not possess the appeal they do.

But remorse, regret and self-reproach are none the less a part of the process going on in this initial group of poems about Emma, which he called 'Poems of 1912–13', with its epigraph from the *Aeneid* (IV, 23) '*Veteris vestigia flammae*' ('relics of the old fire'):

> You did not walk with me
> Of late to the hill-top tree
> > By the gated ways,
> > As in earlier days;
> > You were weak and lame,
> > So you never came,
> And I went alone, and I did not mind,
> Not thinking of you as left behind.
>
> I walked up there to-day
> Just in the former way;
> > Surveyed around
> > The familiar ground
> > By myself again:
> > What difference, then?
> Only that underlying sense
> Of the look of a room on returning thence.

Thus 'The Walk'; remorse here of course plays its component part. But it would have been imprecise and dishonest to have omitted it from the record.

There is another, later, poem which aptly describes the nature of the self-examining and self-analytical process that was proceeding in him all the time. Tom deliberately placed it at the end of the volume *Late Lyrics and Earlier*, heading it with a motto from Psalm 119: '*Cogitavi vias meas*' ('I thought on my ways'). This poem relies wholly on New Testament allusions, and its theme is the extent to which its writer had observed charity – that is, of course, his own 'loving-kindness' – in his own life.

> A cry from the green-grained sticks of the fire
>   Made me gaze where it seemed to be:
> 'Twas my own voice talking therefrom to me
> On how I had walked when my sun was higher –
>   My heart in its arrogancy.
>
> '*You held not to whatsoever was true,*'
>   Said my own voice talking to me:
> '*Whatsoever was just you were slack to see;*
> *Kept not things lovely and pure in view,*'
>   Said my own voice talking to me.
>
> '*You slighted her that endureth all,*'
>   Said my own voice talking to me;
> '*Vaunteth not, trusteth hopefully;*
> *That suffereth long and is kind withal,*'
>   Said my own voice talking to me.
>
> '*You taught not that which you set about,*'
>   Said my own voice talking to me;
> '*That the greatest of things is Charity . . .*'
> – And the sticks burnt low, and the fire went out,
>   And my voice ceased talking to me.

The man who wrote this is not reconcilable with a fundamentally mean one, in whom there was 'no largeness of soul'. That was the wrong-headed verdict of Clodd, at Tom's death. But in January 1928 Clodd was a very old man, and his careless remark acts as a guide only to his own lack of appreciation of that very quality which stands out in the poems of Thomas Hardy.

There is, too, the testimony of countless others to the contrary. Nor is it the mindless praise of newspaper admirers of 'great men'. His supporters included Barrie (who thought that Tom was like one of Christ's disciples!); Sassoon; Blunden; Graves (most eloquent about it in his own old age: 'Ah!', he exclaimed to me in a heartfelt manner in the last years of his life, when he said little, 'he was a darling!'); and T.E. Lawrence (Tom was 'so refined into an essence,' he told Graves). What they admired above all else were his simplicity and integrity. This

803

quality is nowhere more apparent than in 'Surview', not a poem that many English poets would have been capable of writing – although the quality is present in the Shakespeare of the *Sonnets*, a powerful initial influence. Not even the poetry of Tom's beloved Shelley contains this element of self-questioning. But it had been present in Tom's poetry from the 1860s, when he began to write it: even, in order to examine the nature of his failings, to the extent of taking on the actual voice of a woman whom he felt he had wronged.

In his poem 'The Choice' W.B. Yeats made a distinction which has since become famous:

> The intellect of man is forced to choose
> Perfection of the life, or of the work.

Tom refused to contemplate such a distinction. It is clear that he did not believe that either his life or his work was perfect, and that he did not believe, moreover, that perfection was even possible in a universe fashioned as ours is. The war finally confirmed him in his belief that, as he put it in the *Life*, 'the never-ending push of the Universe was an unpurposive and irresponsible groping in the direction of the least resistance'.

Something else that Yeats said, though, is relevant here, and in particular to Tom's own gropings – demonstrated by the deepest meaning of his poetry – towards a means of achieving the *most* 'resistance' possible. It is from an unpublished speech of 1907 concerning Lionel Johnson, the poet and critic who had thought it worth his while to devote much time and effort to a substantial study of Thomas Hardy.

I have no sympathy with the mid-Victorian thought to which Tennyson gave his support, that a poet's life concerns nobody but himself. A poet is by the very nature of things a man who lives with entire sincerity, or rather, the better his poetry the more sincere his life. His life is an experiment in living and those that come after have a right to know it. Above all it is necessary that the lyric poet's life should be known, that we should understand that his poetry is no rootless flower but the speech of a man, that it is no little thing to achieve anything in any art, to stand alone perhaps for many years, to go a path no other man has gone, to accept one's own thought when the thought of the world has the authority of the world behind it, . . . to give one's life as well as one's words which are so much nearer to one's soul to the criticism of the world . . . Why should we honour those that die on the field of battle, a man may show as reckless a courage in entering into the abyss of himself.

Tom did not share Tennyson's view, either, for all his desire to protect himself from the press and from journalists. But he was less of a public man than Yeats, and it was the 'few friends only', capable of discernment, whom he wished to allow into his personal circle. He knew, too, that this circle would for the most part comprise readers whom he could not know personally. None the less, Yeats' words might just as well be applied to him as to Johnson, and are in any case more appropriate than attempts to portray him as a particularly mean and deceitful man, or even as an eccentric and impotent autodidact who failed to see the main point. Those who themselves yearn for public attention and acclaim seldom recognize what fame, for an honest man, is actually like.

With his usual deliberation of choice, Tom opened *Satires of Circumstance* with the stately and alliterative 'In Front of the Landscape'; he felt that its seventy-two lines summed up, at least for his 'few friends only', his poetic situation. It was an important poem for him; it is certainly one of his most magnificent – and most magnificently and fruitfully bewildering. Although it has been attacked as 'too vague', so much in it is seen through the fogs of ignorance and misunderstanding that that criticism is neither apt nor useful. In fact it contains images of brilliant and extraordinary precision (for example, of the rills in the grass-flat 'stroked by the light'). These images recall objects made vivid when they are seen in sudden close-up, in a generally foggy context. It is a key poem, very deeply felt, and as specifically autobiographical as any he ever wrote. Therefore I quote it in full (some have read 'drear' for 'dear' at the end of the second line):

Plunging and labouring on a tide of visions,
  Dolorous and dear,
Forward I pushed my way as amid waste waters
  Stretching around,
Through whose eddies there glimmered the customed landscape
  Yonder and near

Blotted to feeble mist. And the coomb and the upland
  Coppice-crowned,
Ancient chalk-pit, milestone, rills in the grass-flat

805

Stroked by the light,
Seemed but a ghost-like gauze, and no substantial
  Meadow or mound.

What were the infinite spectacles featuring foremost
  Under my sight,
Hindering me to discern my paced advancement
  Lengthening to miles;
What were the re-creations killing the daytime
  As by the night?

O they were speechful faces, gazing insistent,
  Some as with smiles,
Some as with slow-born tears that brinily trundled
  Over the wrecked
Cheeks that were fair in their flush-time, ash now with anguish,
  Harrowed by wiles.

Yes, I could see them, feel them, hear them, address them –
  Halo-bedecked –
And, alas, onwards, shaken by fierce unreason,
  Rigid in hate,
Smitten by years-long wryness born of misprision,
  Dreaded, suspect.

Then there would breast me shining sights, sweet seasons
  Further in date;
Instruments of strings with the tenderest passion
  Vibrant, beside
Lamps long extinguished, robes, cheeks, eyes with the earth's crust
  Now corporate.

Also there rose a headland of hoary aspect
  Gnawed by the tide,
Frilled by the nimb of the morning as two friends stood there
  Guilelessly glad –
Wherefore they knew not – touched by the fringe of an ecstasy
  Scantly descried.

Later images too did the day unfurl me,
  Shadowed and sad,
Clay cadavers of those who had shared in the dramas,

WAR – AND MORE 'ADOLESCENCE'

Laid now at ease,
Passions all spent, chiefest the one of the broad brow
  Sepulture-clad.

So did beset me scenes, miscalled of the bygone,
  Over the leaze,
Past the clump, and down to where lay the beheld ones;
  – Yea, as the rhyme
Sung by the sea-swell, so in their pleading dumbness
  Captured me these.

For, their lost revisiting manifestations
  In their live time
Much had I slighted, caring not for their purport,
  Seeing behind
Things more coveted, reckoned the better worth calling
  Sweet, sad, sublime.

Thus do they now show hourly before the intenser
  Stare of the mind
As they were ghosts avenging their slights by my bypast
  Body-borne eyes,
Show, too, with fuller translation than rested upon them
  As living kind.

Hence wag the tongues of the passing people, saying
  In their surmise,
'Ah – whose is this dull form that perambulates, seeing nought
  Round him that looms
Whithersoever his footsteps turn in his farings,
  Save a few tombs?'

Tom was lost in the past: the 're-creations' of his memory were like night to him: killing the daytime, and therefore, by implication, affecting his attitude to his present everyday life. We may see him as in the mood of 'Surview': painfully reappraising his treatment of those who had played parts in the drama of his past. Some have hated him, some have loved him (was he thinking of, amongst others, Eliza Nicholls, who had not so long ago called on him at Max Gate?). The seventh stanza is enigmatic, although no more so than passages in 'Wessex Heights' – and for similar inescapable reasons. The identities of the two friends, apart from the fact that one is likely to have been the writer, are not now determinable, even if the 'hoary headland' seems sinister, and to resemble Portland Bill. But does that matter? Is the poet being too obscure? No, because the psychological situation is, by contrast, made crystal clear.

Two friends stand at morning by a headland feeling innocently, even ecstatically, happy for reasons which they can hardly understand. The 'one of the broad brow' now entombed suggests Horace Moule, because the image connotes a learned and authoritative person. But the vision that the poet is undergoing is, startlingly, '*miscalled* of the bygone': this must mean that the journeying in the past is so real in its effect as to influence the present: to inhibit his behaviour in it. There is thus a suggestion that the poet is forced to re-live his life and its mistakes painfully, under the pleadingly dumb gaze of those now dead – and that he is compelled to do so because he 'slighted' them in 'their live time': failed to notice them in his eagerness to poeticize their emotions (it had then seemed better to call them 'Sweet, sad, sublime'). The quest is thus for a nakedly true poetry, without elaborations or rhetorical frills (and that was eventually fulfilled, notably in 'Surview').

The penultimate stanza, then, records his recognition that the past is indeed, in a certain terrible way, 'miscalled': now the 'ghosts', under a more intensely intellectual consideration, seem to 'avenge' his 'slights' of them: they are, with bitter irony, more real to him as ghosts than they were when in life: 'with fuller translation than rested upon them/As living kind'. And the final stanza demonstrates his awareness, for those who may have doubted it, of how he appeared to others: rapt and contemplative, transforming his past into a future by a process of acute self-critical reappraisal – his past lay before him! It was as if he had read the most famous of all passages in Nietzsche:

What if a demon crept after you one day or night in your loneliest solitude and said to you: 'This life, as you live it now and have lived it, you will have to live again, times without number; and there will be nothing new in it, but every pain and every joy and every thought and sigh and all the unspeakably small and great in your life must return to you, and everything in the same series and sequence – and in the same way this spider and this moonlight among the trees, and in the same way this moment and I myself . . .'

There is every reason to suppose that Tom had indeed read this, for the 'translation' of *Zarathustra* by Thomas Common was available together with an earlier one. As it happens, the essence of it does come across, even in Common's ghastly rendering; but, given the fact of Tom's own creditable attempt in his scrapbook at a translation of a passage from Nietzsche, suggesting that his German was not so poor as is still generally supposed, Tom might even have tackled it in the original. But his concern was perhaps less with the experience of affirming life (as Nietzsche was doing in that much misunderstood passage), than of altering it in some mysterious way by living through it again. Later, though by then truly aged, he would read Einstein and become at least fascinated with notions of time which would make such alterations possible. Despair about the war, and the wisdom of his relationship with Florence, had begun to soften the hard edges of his rationalism, if not of his contempt for the attitudes of the Church.

Tom allowed Granville Barker to go ahead with the patriotic adaptation of *The Dynasts* for the Kingsway Theatre, where it opened on 25 November 1914, just a week after *Satires of Circumstance* appeared. As was his wont, being haunted by fears of outright rejection such as he probably knew Henry James had experienced many years earlier, he pleaded a cold on the first night. He had, however, attended rehearsals. Only when it had played successfully for a few nights would he agree to go up to London to see it. He did not really approve, and told Clodd on the 30th that 'I have had very little to do with the production . . . I am glad for [Granville Barker's] sake that the press has been so appreciative, for it was a courageous & patriotic venture.' To Gosse, who had gone to see it with his wife, he said on 1 December that it had been staged

> mainly for patriotic & practical objects.
> It is, indeed, rather a comical result of the good Barker's abridgement that I am made to appear as orthodox as a church-warden, although he has, as you remark, been most loyal to the text & characterization in the parts selected. He has a wonderfully artistic instinct in drama.

Friends like Gosse apart – and to these he remained loyal in his pronounced opinions, perhaps preferring to think of Gosse as the author of *Father and Son* rather than as a literary manipulator or a poet – Tom was adamant in his view of the taste of the general public. However, he knew very well that amongst that public, although he could not know them personally, were many whom he could count on as his 'few friends only'. Florence once found him muttering, after he had got to know him and had read his war poetry (by far the best of his output), that he wrote 'for people like Siegfried Sassoon'. He would have added De La Mare, Blunden, Graves and some others, had that been a considered remark and not just a private expostulation. He was, after all, in a paradoxical situation: he had long owed his livelihood, and now his riches, to the 'public taste'. He knew that if he put a foot wrong he could lose public support and people might stop buying his books. He took as careful and conscientious note of such matters as he did of hedgehogs crossing his lawn, and deserves credit for it.

The reviews of *Satires of Circumstance* were not perceptive; Lytton Strachey was an exception. In the *New Statesman* he did score some palpable (and not unnecessary) hits by quoting such lines as 'Dear ghost, in the past did you ever find/Me one whom consequence influenced much?' and 'And adumbrates too therewith our unexpected troublous cast'; but Strachey recognized that this clumsiness was 'an essential ingredient in the very essence of his work', and he spoke of how that work had 'the subtle disturbing force of poetry'. Anticipating modern judgement, he compared Hardy to Bridges, then highly regarded:

All the taste, all the scholarship, all the art of the Poet Laureate seem only to end in something that is admirable, perhaps, something that is wonderful, but something that is irremediably remote and cold; while the flat, undistinguished poetry of Mr Hardy has found out the secret of touching our marrow-bones.

He might well have substituted 'deliberately unrhetorical' for 'flat, undistinguished', but he was right none the less. Strachey, for one, was not bothered by the inclusion of the group of poems which gave the collection its title – Tom himself fretted about it, but never changed their position. The sentimentalist, thought Strachey, 'will find very little comfort' in the poems – and he was astute enough to note, admiringly, that what he called the 'gloom' was not 'relieved by a little elegance of diction' (the laboured-for 'beauty' of the pallid Bridges). The volume, as Strachey recognized but did not mention, was in accord with the sombre mood of the times, although it did not reflect its foolish and false patriotism. As a conscientious objector, he would have been the first to have picked up any speciousness.

On 23 December 1914 Tom summed up his own reception of his reception to Florence Henniker, to whom he had asked Macmillan to send a copy. He must have had his wife's unhappy reaction in mind when he wrote this – and, apparently, her ungrateful coolness over the poem to her, written when they were rather better 'acquainted' than he was prepared to admit here:

At first I thought I would not send any copy to any friend owing to the harsh contrasts which the accidents of my life during the past few years had forced into the poems, & which I could not remove, so many of them having been printed in periodicals – those in fact which I liked least. And unfortunately they are the ones the papers have taken most notice of. My own favourites, that include all those in memory of Emma, have been mentioned little. The one to Florence ['After the Visit', which Mrs Henniker had singled out for praise] was written when she was a mere acquaintance: I think she likes it. I am so glad that you like 'When I set out for Lyonnesse'. It is exactly what happened 44 years ago.

Just after Christmas he sent a postcard to Ford about his *Antwerp*, which he had sent to Tom as a Christmas card: 'Many thanks. Verses quite beautiful in their spontaneity.' This, as it happens, is exactly the nature of this charming minor poem. But he seems to have been less impressed with the so-called Georgian poets, and told Gosse on 13 January 1915 that he thought 'the Tibbald's row school of rhymeless youngsters', or rather the newspaper critics 'who follow that school', might be responsible for contemporary ignorance of earlier poetry. He must have just read the first of Edward Marsh's *Georgian Poetry* anthologies (published in December 1912, the second was not to appear until November 1915). But he cannot have read it very carefully, since it contains a poem which he greatly admired, and which he had read to him just before his death: De La Mare's part-rhymed 'The Listeners'. If, however, he could get through T. Sturge Moore's 'A Sicilian Idyll', then he might well have worried about the future of English rhymeless poetry. What he felt was, not that the rhymelessness of poems damned them (there is not much rhyme in Shakespeare's plays), but that many poets failed to make rhymes because they could not.

As we know, Tom still yearned for a child, and Florence – even if terrified at the prospect of bearing one – certainly thought seriously about it. But one did not arrive, for reasons unknown. Tom now therefore fixed upon a suitable 'heir'. Gordon Gifford might have seemed the obvious choice, but Florence – and the fact that he was a Gifford, and therefore not acceptable to Kate or Henry, either – maliciously saw to it that he was not. She had taken a dislike to him because she did not like his sister Lilian, because he had told her that his aunt had wanted him to have Max Gate, and because he had made a marriage of which, in her new wildly snobbish mood, she disapproved. After Tom's death she would have Gifford's skilful wife (the daughter of a stationmaster, she expostulated in 1915, and a waitress to boot) run up dresses for her. She also made the extraordinary suggestion that Gordon had married only in order to avoid military service (the National Service Act became effective, in fact, in February 1916; and in due course Gifford became a despatch rider).

The chosen 'heir', Frank William George, was a cousin twice removed, a young man whom both Tom and Emma had instantly liked when he first called at Max Gate. Since he had worked in a bank in Dorchester (as well as elsewhere) Tom had been well aware of him for many years. Moreover George had refused to accept the lifelong boredom offered by his job, had successfully studied law (with some financial help from Tom), and was called to the bar in 1913. At the outbreak of war he enlisted in the Dorsetshire regiment. On 19 March 1915 Tom wrote to General Sir Evelyn Wood on his behalf:

> A young barrister in whom I am interested, Mr F. W. George, enlisted at the beginning of the war from a sense of duty, and is now applying for a commission in the Dorset regiment. I can say from personal knowledge that he is a most deserving man, who worked his way into the law by his own exertions; cool in judgement; while abandoning a promising position to defend his country shows his character. I think he would make a good officer.

Wood did help, and Frank got his commission. And in five months he was gloriously and obediently dead at Gallipoli. Tom was notably upset at this waste of life – to the extent that his grief and indignation have, with an astonishingly cruel and injudicious coldness, been called, in Millgate, 'factitious' and 'extravagant'. He was, however, keenly and actively affected by the fate of all the young men threatened by immediate death in that war, the true nature of which was becoming increasingly obvious. He and Florence made a point of entertaining soldiers at Max Gate, and of 'assisting in the evenings at the soldiers' tea-room established in the Dorchester Corn Exchange'. Thus he tells George Douglas on 5 April of his fellow-countryman, a Lieutenant

Gillon of the King's Own Scottish Borderers, 'a well-read & most intelligent man', who used to come to Max Gate. This officer, a solicitor in civilian life, survived the war (only to join, alas, the Inland Revenue), lived to the age of seventy-seven, and corresponded with Tom until at least 1925. When Tom heard the news of the less fortunate Frank George's death, he visited his mother, offered whatever help was needed, and did everything he could to lighten the blow. He also wrote 'Before Marching and After', subtitled '*In Memoriam F.W.G.*', which begins:

> Orion swung southward aslant
> Where the starved Egdon pine-trees had thinned,
> The Pleiads aloft seemed to pant
> With the heather that twitched in the wind;
> But he looked on indifferent to sights such as these,
> Unswayed by love, friendship, home joy or home sorrow,
> And wondered to what he would march on the morrow.

There is nothing manufactured either in this poem or in Tom's various other expressions of his distress. A clue as to why the charge of 'factitiousness' has been made may lie in some words he addressed to Cockerell on the matter, on 17 September:

We [he and Florence] went to see & bid goodbye to a brother of the boy who was killed at the Dardanelles last month. He had only 3 days leave after 11 months in France & Flanders. The third brother of the family is in the front line of trenches. All the soldiers one meets have a pathetic hope that 'the war will soon be over': fortunately they do not realize the imbecility of our Ministers or the treachery of sections of the press which try to make political capital out of the country's needs . . .

Such mildly eccentric outbursts still ruffle some sternly patriotic feathers.

In the late April of 1915 Tom and Florence went to London, almost certainly at the latter's behest. The visit soon had to be abandoned because Tom, by now hating every moment of such trips, fell ill with diarrhoea; but they did have time to call on the Gosses. At the beginning of May they were back in London, when they stayed with Lady St Helier (the former Lady Jeune, now widowed) at Portland Place. It was from her that the still socially obsessed Florence claimed that she heard the

813

absurd story of Emma's Archdeacon uncle once having described her, in public, as 'the most horrible woman in the world'. Once again, though, the sudden attacks of unreasoning venom of which Florence was capable had caused her to indulge in some too heavily wishful thinking. Although a few of Emma's detractors have earnestly fallen for the tale, it is too far-fetched and plain silly even to consider, especially in the light of what is known about the Archdeacon's character.

Florence was, by now, grumbling vociferously about the manner in which her seventy-five-year-old husband was treating her: his thoughts dwelt too much in the past, she told Rebekah Owen in July, and he was fast becoming a 'recluse'. This latter claim at least was quite untrue: not only were there almost daily visits to Max Gate by all manner of local people, and Sunday visits to Talbothays, but she herself had made three visits to London (not counting one for the purposes of an operation), and enjoyed many of the much craved for meetings with titled people; Tom was paying Lea to chauffeur them around the countryside, sometimes on quite long journeys, and occasionally to meet yet more people of good family and credentials. She had also been able to spend time in Enfield. Lea recalled that in 1915 they took no fewer than thirty-six motor tours, and in 1916 thirty-two, before he finally gave up his car owing to wartime shortage of petrol. (Gittings unscrupulously translated this into a claim that Tom was too mean to pay the 4½d. a mile for the petrol; in fact he insisted upon paying, as Lea was at careful pains to point out, all expenses incurred.)

Already, then, Tom's wife of less than two years was giving him serious cause for concern. For we cannot imagine that he, as well as Owen and the rest, was not on the receiving end of her manifestations of discontent. She would, true, have kept certain of her grouses from him, being in awe of him on the subject of Emma, for example; she might not have repeated to him, either, her opinion (given to Owen in October 1916) of how 'disgustingly country-people of the servant class talk' but she well knew how and when to grizzle, grouse, sulk and whinge about her 'loneliness', her lack of literary opportunities, and the difficulties of exercising her new ladylike proclivities. She hated herself for what she knew herself to be: a woman, in her own estimation, unsuited to be what she had deliberately chosen to be. The truth is that, although she admired and respected and honoured her husband, she did not really like him and could not appreciate his writings. He was not, in fact, her idea of 'a great man'. Despite her bad health, she was much happier after his death.

WAR – AND MORE 'ADOLESCENCE'

Even in 1915 Florence's health, in the form of nasal catarrh, began to give cause for concern. Eventually, on 26 May, she went into a London clinic to be operated on by Macleod Yearsley, a surgeon who also wrote books. Tom did not join her there only because he was already unwell; he knew that being in London could only make him worse, especially in the wartime atmosphere. He showed great concern for her well-being, and several times offered to come up should she need him. To him, as to his family, an operation was a cause for extreme alarm; nor, as it happens, in those days of unnecessary surgery, did this one do any good. Henry was unable to sleep for anxiety over the affair. Florence remained in the clinic for more than a week, and then arranged to have some extensive dental injections immediately after leaving. This caused Tom some alarm, in case she would not be ready for what he called another operation. He was less careful of his own health: it is known that he stuck to the spectacles he had long ago bought over the counter at the Army and Navy Stores rather than undergo any examination of his watery eyes.

Whatever he may have thought about London, and however he felt when there, they were back again between 13 and 16 July, staying, to the relief of Florence's dislike of country servants' disgusting talk, with Lady St Helier; he told Mrs Henniker on the 10th that they were 'merely lodging there while we attend to prosy London matters'. Florence meanwhile deplored, to Owen, the fact that she had been forced to pay for her operation herself. That was not necessarily true. Tom might have reimbursed her later, or expected to pay: on 31 May, in a letter to her in the clinic, he suggested that she stay for longer, as 'a cold might cause the scarcely healed wound to burst out again': 'I don't at all mind paying the extra days.' Florence was not quite so poor at getting her own way as some commentators have wished to believe from reading her letters. Obsessed with how Tom treated her, they have not stopped to think about how she treated Tom. But as he became older and consequently more frail and more obviously in need of help, she warmed to him a little, and did learn how to manage social gatherings and guests at Max Gate. The shrewdest of those who observed her at work, Virginia Woolf, who did not like her, noticed how docile and 'resigned' she was – and how she had 'learned her part'.

His gloom over the progress of the war deepened even before he heard of Frank George's death. On 25 August he wrote to Galsworthy, thanking him for a copy of *The Freelands* which Florence read aloud to him:

The look of things in Europe is not cheering . . . to an impartial eye. – At least to mine Germany seems slowly attaining her object of mastering the rest of us. But in England one must not look things in the face: yet my experience has been that nothing leads to success like doing so.

To Mrs Henniker, just after hearing of George's death, he wrote that it was quite against his present mood to wish to enter into 'any movement of a spiritual or even ethical nature':

My 'faith in the good that is in humankind' – except in isolated individuals, of whom happily there are many – has been rudely shaken of late . . . The death of a 'cousin' does not seem a very harrowing matter as a rule, but he was such an intimate friend here, & Florence & I both were so attached to him, that his loss will affect our lives largely.

Cockerell sent him *The Daffodil Murderer*, Sassoon's strange parody of Masefield's *The Everlasting Mercy*, issued under the pseudonym of Saul Kain, and he shrewdly observed that it was 'not quite sufficiently burlesque to be understood'. He was yet to read Sassoon's bitter war poems in *The Old Huntsman* (1917), which was dedicated to him, and *Counter Attack* (1918). These owed perhaps more to him than to any other living poet – and Sassoon never again equalled them in poetic intensity. He came to know Sassoon (who was the nephew and ward of his old friend Hamo Thorneycroft) by correspondence in 1916 or 1917, but did not warm to him until later, after he first called at Max Gate in November 1918.

The slight and temporary hardening of feeling against Germany – as originally responsible for the conflict – which Frank George's death had caused in him did not affect his judgement. Although he disliked some aspects of Henry James, he had heard that he was ailing, and was sincerely glad to join in a congratulatory letter from the Authors' Society upon his becoming a naturalized Englishman: 'I can say that nothing would please me better than to do so'. He also added in the postscript to a letter to Redmond Abbott that, while he had not read James' *Notes on Novelists*, 'not caring much for those personages', he always could 'read H.J.'. He also acknowledged that, although James had 'no grain of poetry, or humour, or sponteneity', he was yet a good novelist – and a more readable one than Meredith.

In certain respects the slaughter going on around him seems to have made him even kinder and more considerate, so that he reconsidered an idea for which he had little private enthusiasm: that of A.E. Drinkwater, father of the playwright John Drinkwater, to make *The Dynasts* into a film. He wrote to him on 6 November, telling him that he was sorry to say that he looked upon the project as 'impracticable'; but the very next day, to Macmillan, he said:

> You probably know him [Drinkwater] as the manager who was entrusted with Mr Granville Barker's production, & who had the entire responsibility of it after Mr Barker had gone to America. I have proved him to be a man of integrity, & I should like him to have some little advantage from such a production, if it were done.

And he left the matter open if Macmillan should after all think it practicable. The Turner Film Company, which it seems Drinkwater wished to approach, had already made *Far From the Madding Crowd*, and there had been a film of *Tess* before that. But nothing came of *The Dynasts* project. Short of a spectacular musical by Andrew Lloyd Webber, with someone like Terry Wogan as Napoleon, it seems unlikely, now, that anything ever will.

Then, later in November, there was another blow, not entirely unexpected but nevertheless sudden. Mary Hardy died of emphysema. 'We saw & talked to her the day before her death (24 November], & I did not think it would be so soon,' he told Florence's mother. To Cockerell on 5 December he noted that she had been 'of rather an unusual type'. He added: 'It is a gloomy time, in which the world, having like a spider climbed to a certain height, seems slipping back to where it was long ago.' On the 7th he told Mary Sheridan, a more intimate local friend who may have met Mary, that he missed her very much, and again emphasized his closeness to her: 'she had always been the one with the keenest literary tastes & instincts'. In the *Life* he gave a fuller account of Mary and her peculiarities:

> The hobby of her life had been portrait-painting, and she had shown an aptitude in catching a likeness . . . But she had been doomed to school-teaching, and organ-playing in this or that village church during all her active years, and hence was unable to devote sufficient time to pictorial art till leisure was too late to be effective. Her character was a somewhat unusual one, being remarkably unassertive,

even when she was in the right, and could easily have proved it; so that the point of the following remark about her is manifest:

'*November 29*. Buried her under the yew-tree where the rest of us lie. As Mr Cowley [Vicar of Stinsford] read the words of the psalm "Dixi Custodiam" they reminded me strongly of her nature, particularly when she was young: "I held my tongue and spake nothing: I kept silence, yea, even from good words". That was my poor Mary exactly. She never defended herself; and that not from timidity, but indifference to opinion.'

The opinions of the other Hardys about Tom and his wives had largely in fact been those of Mary's younger sister, Kate; even Henry, who died not long after his brother (Kate lived on until 1940), knew how to keep his own counsel. But Mary herself, more sensitive and intelligent than Kate, had taken the trouble to write to Tom (the letter was in the possession of Purdy) just before he went to Enfield to marry Florence, to the effect that he was 'taking the right step under existing circumstances and I really think you will be happy this time . . . if Florence is loyal, making you comfortable at all times, as we think she will, you are likely to live as long as Mother . . .' Florence did her duty, and did indeed see, despite her lack of skill in household management, that he was kept physically comfortable; his degree of mental comfort is more open to doubt.

To George Douglas' letter of sympathy he replied in much the same terms. In the same letter Douglas asked him when he would start to write his reminiscences. Tom's answer to that was short, sharp and to the point: 'My reminiscences: no, never!' But in a year or so he was to be forced into a drastic reconsideration of that firm and so often reiterated decision.

36

Gertrude Bugler

Mary had left money, but no will. As almost always when money is in question, and when a family is devastated by a death, there were ugly scenes: Kate wanted Mary's money and was not going to allow anyone else to get their hands on it. Henry, who had had a mild stroke at the beginning of the year, was fed up and quarrelsome: his brother upset him by not coming to Talbothays after the funeral. Kate put her greed and suspicion on temporary full display. In a sense it was Tom's money, for what Mary had left amounted almost exactly to what he had generously allowed her. But they all made way for Kate; she got her money and calmed down. (Kate became even more 'nice' when Tom made a will which ensured that not all his money would go to Florence.)

Florence related all this, and other matters repulsive to her, in letters to Rebekah Owen. She wrote, for instance, of the widespread country habit, practised by the Hardys and vainly urged on her by Kate, of kissing corpses; Tom, it must be said, also refused.

Dashing off a letter to Owen a few days after the second anniversary of her marriage, Florence stated that no two years could have been happier (what she believed she ought to be seen as thinking), and that there was much to complain of (her natural state of being). Then, driven into a frantic anxiety lest her long affair with the married Tom should become known, she wrote off angrily and threateningly to Clodd. She said that Tom had urged her to write the letter, but in view of later correspondence this is doubtful. Clodd was not a man to make a fuss, and he had his own new young wife and former secretary, Phyllis *née* Rope, to worry about. But Florence's spate of letters to him abruptly ceased, though Tom continued to write to him in exactly the same old way. The chief recipients of her woes now became Cockerell, who at certain times seemed terrifying to her, while at others he seemed exactly the opposite; Lady Hoare, whom she praised thus: 'There is a broad band of radiance falling across our path – and that is *you!*' and above all the deplorable Rebekah Owen.

It is not clear how much Tom knew of Florence's by now hysterical fear of Clodd, but he, too, had slight cause for worry. Even coded hints by the teasing rationalist in his forthcoming *Memoirs* (which in the event proved innocuous) could have been embarrassing. Further, there was the fact that Clodd had shared all his gossip with Shorter, and Tom must have had more than an inkling of that, although he did not know of the abundant intimate material with which Florence had been steadily feeding Clodd over the years. Tom did not like Shorter, and in particular did not like his habit of acquiring Hardy items and printing them in private editions under the general title of *A Bookman's Hobby*. Cockerell had only recently, and quite properly, warned of such arrangements. Later there would be several small limited editions officially issued by Florence herself, under Cockerell's close supervision.

In mid-March Shorter sent Florence a parcel of books for review for the *Sphere*. This alone was irritating to Tom. Shorter's plan to issue a private edition of a poem he had just published in the *Sphere*, 'The Dead and the Living', was even more annoying. Florence was away at Enfield, where on her own authority she had decided that her father, who was suffering from an ordinary attack of painful 'muscular rheumatism', was 'dangerously ill' and the victim of a 'complete nervous breakdown'. She may have exaggerated his condition in order to stay away longer from Max Gate, from the old husband whom she did not much like, and from his possibly considerable sexual 'demands' which she disliked even more. In June 1924 she hinted at this in a letter to Louisa Yearsley, another young woman with an older husband, when she spoke of 'all sorts of things one cannot write about'. The housekeeping even then was, for her, enough to 'drive anyone into an asylum'.

On 15 March Tom wrote to Shorter, for once hardly politely:

My wife was leaving home for two or three days when your letter & parcel came, & she asked me to acknowledge receipt of them . . . which I gladly do . . .

The verses you speak of are published in America also [in the *World*]; & being hastily written & subject to annihilation, I don't care to have them reprinted in your pet limited edition. Of course, if what you say is true – that anybody may print such an edition of anybody's writings without permission, you must do your worst.

GERTRUDE BUGLER

In a letter of 19 March there is a sinister hint of what was quite soon to follow. Arthur Quiller Couch, historical novelist, critic, anthologist and an old acquaintance from Cambridge and Cornwall, sent them his *On the Art of Writing*, published that year. Tom did not think much of his famous *Oxford Book of English Verse*, but he liked and respected Q (his pseudonym) and wrote him a letter of thanks beginning:

> We are reading aloud in the evenings, with great pleasure, I need not say, the handsome book you have been so kind as to send. (My wife has gone ahead privately with it, & says that now at last she thinks she may become a great writer in spite of me.)

This was not so much of a joke as Q must have taken it to be: there is every reason to suppose that the receipt of this book did re-inspire Florence with the desire to become, if not a 'great' writer, then at least a famous one. But how was she to achieve this ambition? She had finished her last children's book: *A Book of Baby Pets*, with some verses by Tom to Detmold's pictures, was published by Hodder and Stoughton in March 1915. This sort of thing seemed to get her nowhere. Now there were only reviews for the *Sphere* – and they were hardly reviews, more plot summaries; Shorter himself does not seem to have been much impressed by her abilities.

She complained in letters that Tom stayed upstairs in his study and would not come down. That, however, was simply a complaint – and not really a very cogent one – by a writer's wife about the writer's keeping his usual hours: it was surely a good thing that Tom had decided to continue working. Still, and there can be little doubt of it, Florence could not prevent herself from being envious even of his capacities and his fame. After all, there were all those motor trips, there were usually meals (occasionally, if things were going well, he would have his food brought up to him in his study – but if people do not like things of that sort then they should not marry writers), there were the sessions when she read aloud to him, and there were the frequent occasions when they entertained people. He wrote by hand to Cockerell on 8 April: 'I don't like to press you, as you know how dull it is here; but here we are, & perhaps we could invent some business matter to discuss? In fact I can think already of two or three.' Cockerell did come down, on the weekend of 17–19 April. Tom had added a postscript to his invitation: 'My wife is not so strong as she ought to be in this good air, & I can't think why.' A slight puzzlement or boredom with the matter of

Florence's weakness may be inferred: he, at almost seventy-six, was the one who might be expected not to be 'strong'. A week later, awaiting the visit of the man he had in February appointed as co-executor with Florence, he wrote off to G. Herbert Thring of the Authors' Society with a list of questions about the 'copyrights of deceased authors'.

A new project, we may guess, in view of the invitation to Cockerell and the letter to Thring, was already being mooted – and we need have no doubt that it was first mooted, not by Tom, but by Florence – although Cockerell himself had mentioned it as a possibility in December 1915. However, for the time being it hung fire. Florence now had trouble with the mastoid bone of her left ear (it may, conceivably, have resulted from the recent nasal operation), and at the end of April went up to London to consult Yearsley. She thus missed a call from George Bernard Shaw, his wife, and the classicist J.B. Bury and his wife, Jane – and much argument between the women about the Easter Rising, which had no 'terrible beauty' (as Yeats put it) for Tom, who had little patience with the Irish, and even wished that Gladstone had never raised the question in the first place.

He now tried to soothe Shorter, who was still smarting from his letter of 15 March. After inviting him to stay at Max Gate on his way down to Devon, Tom told him that he would explain why he believed that he was 'getting off the track in these private printings'. He was more conciliatory in tone to the (Irish) Shorters than he usually was on this subject: 'Poor Ireland . . . her people are too imaginative to be able to govern themselves, always seeing snakes where there are none.' Neither Shorter nor Nevinson was able to persuade him to sign a petition, in July, for the reprieve of Sir Roger Casement, who had been sentenced to death for trying to land arms from a German submarine for the use of the Irish: he told Shorter that had it been 'simply a question of mercy to one man, which would end there, the case would be different'. Alas, he added, it was not. Nevinson, understandably, was shocked and distressed by this refusal. Nor was it typical of Tom. He did, however, plead to Shorter that he had 'no special knowledge' of the case.

Although his regard for Granville Barker never waned, he was more pleased by the local presentation of excerpts from *The Dynasts*, called *Wessex Scenes from The Dynasts*, which embraced episodes of 'a local character only': 'Though more limited in scope . . . it was picturesque and effective as performed by the local actors . . . and was well appreciated by the London press.' Into *Wessex Scenes from The Dynasts* he wrote a special part for the beautiful Gertrude Bugler; but he was not the only one who had registered her beauty and charm. In time Florence, after the Bugler affair of 1924–25 had almost driven her out of her mind, would put an end to these local performances.

The play was presented in Weymouth in June, then in London, and finally in Dorchester in December – all the proceeds went to the Red Cross. He worked hard to add relevant and topical scenes, and became quite overwrought about it, although Florence's complaints to Owen about the extent of his concern are, as usual, exaggerated; possibly, too, they arose from her dislike of seeing him – or anyone else – in a state of thorough enjoyment. Florence, who had declared that the townspeople – to whom these Hardy plays above all belonged – 'infected' their own town, Dorchester, told Owen in January 1916 that the 'times when these hateful plays are being performed' were 'so unsatisfactory'. They made her feel jealous and unwanted: she would see Tom locked in his study with someone like the lowly garage-owner Tilley, discussing something she knew nothing about, and would feel helpless.

Florence preferred the glittering West End productions to which Louisa Yearsley – and, earlier, Florence Henniker – had taken her. In 1917 in London she would break down into tears at Barrie's *Dear Brutus*: just as, curiously, Carrie Kipling did, muttering that the sentimental old theatrical wizard 'oughtn't to have done it'. Tom, it is clear from one or two remarks he made, quite liked Barrie but had no time for his skilful but shallow and sentimental plays for adults.

Mary's death and the subsequent family quarrelling had made Tom tetchy. He may just at this time have been repelled by Kate, who had no artistic interests: he did not go to Talbothays for some time after the funeral. Made angry by Florence's propensity for gossip and gush, he told her not to inform Kate who had and had not called at Max Gate. He even (according to her) refused to autograph her own first editions of his work. Had he known of the letters Florence was sending he would have been horrified. When he told her at the beginning of her marriage to '*keep off*' people (which she later divulged) he was not expressing any peculiar reclusiveness of his own, but rather appealing to her not to indulge herself in the sort of vulgar and injudicious gossip to which she was so impulsively prone. Little reliance may be placed on many of her reports: she rushed to whatever was at hand, regardless of its context, in order to express her resentment. Thus she exclaimed that she had wanted to make Max Gate into the kind of place to which she could welcome people she liked: in fact a haven, with herself as gracious hostess, to titled and well-known people as well as to her own family. But that cannot have been any part of her 'compact' with a seventy-three-year-old working writer.

Then, at the end of August, the spectre of the project again raised its head, ugly or otherwise. Frederick W. Slater of Harper Brothers made an enquiry, which Tom answered thus:

> The reference in 'The Sphere' [Shorter's paper, for which Florence was still doing plot digests] to a Bibliography which Mrs Hardy is said to be compiling & of which you inquire particulars, seems to be based on a remark of hers concerning some erroneous bibliographies recently published [by Henry Danielson: *The First Editions of Thomas Hardy and Their Values*, 1916; A.P. Webb: *A Bibliography of the Works of Thomas Hardy*, 1916 – but see below], to the effect that she hopes, or would like, to make a correct bibliography of my works some day.

Tom is not known ever to have mentioned Webb's book. It now seems old-fashioned and amateurish in its presentation, but it is not particularly inaccurate. He made no other complaints about it. As for Danielson: on 27 July he had written to him, saying: 'I am greatly obliged to you for sending me this beautifully bound & printed copy of the bibliography you have compiled'; he had told Cockerell in February that he had been struck with Danielson's 'thoroughness'.

No, in the letter to Slater of Harper's he was seeking some means of excusing Florence for her characteristic failure to keep her mouth shut – or even for jumping the gun – to Shorter. Florence was grateful to Shorter even while she feared his propensity to gossip; Tom did not like him. On 28 August 1917 she told Owen: 'I have a tremendous job in hand – literary.' A bibliography is not a 'tremendous job'; it was, even then, rather a technical one; it would certainly have been beyond her powers and knowledge. But a *biography* . . . That is what she had been too excitedly going on about to Shorter. She may not have understood the difference.

Now she was pressing Tom hard. It is not conceivable that he himself had changed his mind about his 'reminiscences': his impulse was still: 'never!' No reason has ever been advanced to suggest that he had changed his mind since 1910. Then he had told H.M. Alden, the editor of *Harper's Magazine*, that 'it is absolutely unlikely that I shall ever change my present intention not to produce my reminiscences to the world'. No one will ever know how the idea came about, or even when he started serious work on it.

My contention, in brief outline, is as follows. In 1916 Florence – taking advantage of a casual suggestion by Cockerell – began to press Tom to allow her to write his biography from the voluminous notes and memoranda still in his possession. He was extremely reluctant, but she prevailed. She was able to point out that biographies would inevitably appear, that Hedgcock's book had already done so – look how he had hated that! – and that these new ones would, equally inevitably, contain impertinent errors, slights and the rest. (When Brennecke's 'biography', far more impertinent and silly than Hedgcock's, arrived in April 1925, it was to provoke a further crisis.) He eventually agreed: her argument, after all, was a good one. Had she been even faintly competent, all might have been well for her own side of the project. But this turned out to be an unrealizable dream. She had, I think, been making his life a misery by her importuning; perhaps she was even refusing him sexually.

So she began work. But it soon became evident to them both that she was as much out of her depth here as she was in her marriage. What she had called a 'tremendous . . . literary' task – and how potent that word 'literary' was for her, despite her inability to comprehend it – she had taken on with great enthusiasm. However, it quickly proved far too much. Getting children's books written, especially with the help of her husband, was one thing; compiling a biography from this mass of notes was quite another. She did not even possess the necessary literary background. And so he, trying to make some sort of purse from a sow's ear, intervened with words to this effect: 'All right, *I'll* write it, but *you* can have the credit. Publish it when I'm dead. We'll make it very objective in style.' It would have been a process reached through perhaps weeks and months of misery and complaint: 'I am unworthy of you, oh, if I were a suitable woman for you, I am not lovable, I cannot even perform this task, if only I could respond *properly* to your passion, but I lack real feeling, and I cannot even manage the servants . . .' Unfortunately her gushes of misery were not balanced by bouts of intelligent consideration. She leaped mindlessly from one impression to the next: complaint, denunciation, shame, remorse, back to complaint . . . And so it went on in an everlasting circle, punctuated only by letters of complaint or denunciation, medical consultations, operations and courses of injections, and new resolutions quickly broken. So Tom, always obstinately ready to make the best out of a bad situation, at last resigned himself to the inevitable. Once he had done so, however, he came to enjoy cynically presenting himself as through the eyes of a somewhat officious third party.

Gittings explains all this as Tom's own cunning idea, and as a literary deception undertaken to hoodwink the public. But Millgate, more scrupulous and far better informed, while he refrains from moral inference, does write: 'There seems . . . no reason to doubt the insistence of the Prefatory Note to *Early Life* that it was at Florence's "strong request" that the project was launched, although the original idea may have been Cockerell's.' I need only add that, on one of Cockerell's frequent visits, it would have been easy enough for Florence to drop a hint about the desirability of a definitive biography. He despised her literary capacities, but was not above using her for his own purposes (which, it should always be remembered, were eminently sensible and, despite his occasional ferocity, impeccably correct) – he resembled a terrible but necessary machine and would instantly have seen the sense in such a proposal. Tom, left to himself, would never have left a 'record' of any kind.

In early September 1916 he and Florence went together to Cornwall, first to Launceston to see Kate Gifford, Emma's cousin, and then on to Tintagel and St Juliot. Florence, as usual, acquiesced, but two or three days before they left complained in private to Lady Hoare that she had 'to blind' herself 'to the past'. At this point she was at the height of her jealousy of Emma's memory. Later she seems to have contained it, and, interestingly, the dying down of her allusions to Emma coincides with the period taken up with 'her' work on the 'biography'. Tom wrote to Cockerell:

> . . . We went to Cornwall – & saw the tablet at St Juliot, Boscastle; & thence to Tintagel. Alas, I fear your hopes of a poem on Iseult – the English, or British, Helen – will be disappointed. I visited the place 44 years ago with an Iseult of my own, & of course she was mixed in the vision of the other. The hotel-crowd rather jarred: but the situation of the hotel is unrivalled.

Florence had indiscreetly jumped the gun yet again, in a letter to Cockerell. Seven years later Tom did publish the strange and muffled play *The Famous History of the Queen of Cornwall*, and stated that the idea had formed in his mind on that visit. But no writer enjoys having such confidences broadcast. Furthermore, at a certain level the *Queen* does deal with Tom's own problem of his 'two wives'.

Of the visit he preserved a note in the *Life*, doubtless hoping that the offending cleric would still be living, by the time of its publication a canon or even bishop – and that he would be gleefully informed by his 'friends' of what had been said about his ecclesiastical behaviour by the famous writer:

> To Tintagel Church. We sat down in a seat bordering the passage to the transept, but the vicar appalled us by coming to us in his surplice and saying we were in the way of the choir, who would have to pass there. He banished us to the back of the transept. However, when he began his sermon we walked out. He thought it was done to be even with him, and looked his indignation; but it was really because we could not see the nave lengthwise, which my wife, Emma, had sketched in watercolours when she was a young woman before it was 'restored', so that I was interested in noting the changes, as also was F., who was familiar with the sketch. It was saddening enough, though doubtless only a chance, that we were inhospitably received in a church so much visited and appreciated by one we had both known so well.

One may doubt if 'F.' was really so appalled, interested and so forth – but she did tell Cockerell that she had never seen her husband so angry. As the Cornish visit demonstrates, Florence had by no means succeeded in banishing the Giffords from Tom's mind. On the same day that he wrote to Cockerell, 20 September, he wrote cordially to Gordon Gifford telling him that he had now seen Emma's memorial tablet and asking him to tell Lilian, adding that he would send her a photograph if she wanted one. The letter is not typewritten and no good wishes from Florence were sent on – which was honest because there was only hatred.

After the Cornish visit he was in an angry and depressed mood, telling Quiller Couch on 22 October that

> As to any other kind of writing interesting me . . . I sometimes wonder if it is not beneath the dignity of literature to attempt to please longer a world which is capable of atrocities as these days have brought, & think it ought to hold its peace for ever.

This anticipates one of his final poems, 'We Are Getting to the End'. But he forgave Q for an earlier 'slight' in terms of such candour that they give the lie to those who have exaggerated the degree of his antipathy to 'bad reviews': they show that he was more humorously aware of his own sensitivities than are most writers. Long ago, in 1896, Q had written that he preferred Moore's *Esther Waters* to *Tess*. He now, rather foolishly, apologized, but without specifying. Tom replied:

> I cannot remember now [but he could, as his half-punctuated parenthetic afterthought shows] what criticism of yours it was that I thought wrong – something you wrote in your salad days when you were more dogmatic than you probably are now. It was when I was interested in novels, which I have not been for the last 20 years and more. However, whatever it was it did not much hurt my feelings. I simply said to myself, 'He be d—d: I know better.' (At least I feel sure I said that, just because that's what the victim always says.)

A visit during this autumn to German prisoners at a camp in Dorchester, and to a hospital for English wounded, filled him with his usual indignation. The 'conjunction led him to say':

> At the German prisoners' camp . . . were many sufferers. One Prussian, in much pain, died whilst I was with him – to my great relief, and his own. Men lie helpless here from wounds; in the hospital a hundred yards off other men, English, lie helpless from wounds – each scene of suffering caused by the other!
>
> These German prisoners seem to think that we are fighting to exterminate Germany, and though it has been said that, so far from it, we are fighting to save what is best in Germany, Cabinet ministers do not . . . speak this out clearly enough.

He saw to it that the camp was supplied with German translations of his own books, and later employed some of the men in clearing space for potatoes at Max Gate. He rather deprecated the fact that they received only 1d. of the 6d. an hour which he paid them.

In the *Fortnightly* for April 1917 he read a sympathetic article by the editor, W.L. Courtney, about his work, in particular *The Dynasts*. This prompted him to make an important statement, quoted in the *Life*, about his own assessment of himself and his position during these dark days. He never departed from these views.

> Like so many critics, Mr Courtney treats my work of art as if they [sic] were a scientific system of philosophy, although I have repeatedly stated . . . that the views in them are *seemings* . . .
>
> As to his winding up about a God of Mercy, etc. – if I wished to

make a smart retort, which I should really hate doing, I might say that the Good-God theory having, after some thousands of years of trial, produced the most infamous and disgraceful state of Europe – that most Christian continent! – a theory of the Goodless-and-Badless God (as in *The Dynasts*) might perhaps be given a trial with advantage.

Much confusion has arisen and much nonsense has been talked latterly in connection with the word 'atheist'. I believe I have been called one by a journalist who has never read a word of my writings [this sentence, omitted by Florence, refers to Chesterton – he first wrote: 'One writer's almost whole stock-in-trade consists of that word and "blaspheme"'] . . . Fifty meanings attach to the word 'God' nowadays, the only reasonable meaning being the *cause of Things*, whatever that cause may be . . .

He was always irritated by the philosophically illiterate charge of atheism, and so goes on to explain that he has always been 'churchy' and only wants the bishops to drop 'preternatural assumptions' from the liturgy: 'few churchgoers would object to the change for long, and congregations would be trebled in a brief time'. This idea really was 'naive', but it was not disingenuous. At an intellectual, as distinct from a poetic, level, he could never admit that his own self-acknowledged 'churchiness' partook of the miraculous nature of the existence of the *'cause of Things'*. Yet 'The Oxen', written in 1915, states that he would still rather experience the hope of childhood than the doubt of adulthood:

> . . . Yet, I feel,
> If someone said on Christmas Eve,
> 'Come; see the oxen kneel
>
> 'In the lonely barton by yonder coomb
> Our childhood used to know,'
> I should go with him in the gloom,
> Hoping it might be so.

It is significant that in 1919, when at last Tom did see a ghost (which, as he had told Lea, he had always so much wanted to do) it should have been on Christmas Eve. He was putting a sprig of holly on his grandfather's grave in Stinsford churchyard when, suddenly, the old man (whom he had never known) appeared to him in eighteenth-century costume and said: 'A green Christmas.' Tom replied, as one does to ghosts, 'I like a green Christmas.' The old man wandered into the church, but when Tom followed him he found it empty: he had returned to his grave, happy with the apt reply.

Recently, on 31 March 1916, he had told John Galsworthy that he thought life 'would be much more interesting than it is' if there were a purpose to it: 'The mystery of consciousness having appeared in the world when apparently it would have done much better by keeping away is one of the many involved in the whole business.' But he acknowledged that Galsworthy's notion of 'Pity' as a pearl in a diseased oyster was 'very beautiful, and, I think, a very close parallel'.

What he believed in above all, as he told Sassoon in a letter of 18 May 1917 thanking him for 'The Old Huntsman', was 'the sustaining power of poetry': 'I don't know how I should stand the suspense of this evil time if it were not for the sustaining power of poetry.' This did not refer to the distracting effect of his own compositions, but to all that poetry, and being able to be a poet, had meant to him throughout the years – and, let us recollect, 'Half the time (particularly when I write verse) I believe . . . in spectres, mysterious voices, omens, dreams.'

During 1916 Tom stayed at Max Gate; London in wartime was too much for him to bear. He continued to take a gloomy view of the war, and believed either that Germany would exact huge payments from Great Britain for its right to exist, or that the two sides would go on fighting indefinitely. He refused to take part, on the grounds of age, in a trip to the front in France with John Buchan and James Barrie. But Florence refused to make the right inference, that he was now happiest at home, making only short local trips; ignoring his eye condition, she pressured him to make longer journeys. Her illnesses mysteriously became more frequent, and she went to London in May and again in June to consult Yearsley and a quack specialist who recommended a useless and possibly dangerous series of injections of bacteria in order to cure her 'chronic pharyngitis'. She herself was sceptical of their value, and Tom perhaps left her to pay for them – about which she complained vociferously to Owen, together with more execrations of the name Gifford. As on the previous occasion, Tom might well in due time have reimbursed her, or would have done had she asked; but she may have preferred to have the pleasure of her resentment. They went together to stay with Barrie at Adelphi Terrace, and, while she could not persuade him to attend her youngest sister Margaret's Enfield wedding to an airman, Reginald Soundy, in late February – she went with Kate, while he went off to Plymouth 'to gaze, once again, I suppose, at the house where SHE was born' – she did manage to have the couple to stay at Max Gate for their short honeymoon ('ten days' leave for the whole business', Tom told Mrs Henniker). At first he called them, to Cockerell, a 'pair of rather thoughtless young people'; but he eventually accepted Florence's *fait accompli* with good grace and mellowed in his attitude towards them, especially when he considered the current nature of Soundy's life, which was to fly over the lines on most days at the greatest possible danger to himself. Fortunately he survived the war. A later visit to Plymouth and Torquay had to be aborted owing to rain.

A start on the biography was made soon after Margaret and Reginald Soundy left Max Gate. There is a short typescript of notes headed 'Notes of Thomas Hardy's Life by Florence Hardy (1840–1862)'. It can be seen that, after dealing in purely fragmentary form with the first twenty-two years of Tom's life, from material he had dug up for her from notebooks, she gave up. An error of 'End of last week in April 1917' for 'End of last week in April 1862' reveals exactly when she was working on it. So she gave up not long before she went to see Yearsley. On 9 May Tom noted to Margaret Soundy that, having returned from London some four days earlier, she was 'feeling rather tired . . . London always takes so much out of her when she now fags about shopping, &c.' A note of exasperation is detectable. And by 20 May an agreement might well have been reached or have been under negotiation, because, in writing to Mrs Henniker on that day about her own illness and other matters such as the Germans' linguistic kinship with the English (for which he had been castigated by a Tory MP), he stated:

> She [Florence] is hoping to be in London after Whitsuntide, & to call & see you. She still keeps up her reviewing, but will soon drop it; not having quite sufficient spare time with the household to look after, & the garden also, which she has taken upon herself, much to my relief. She sends her love . . .

Tom was now under a hail of irritations from her. She was continually complaining of her health, and was doing expensive shopping in London under the influence of Yearsley's young wife Louisa, whom she had managed to make sorry for her hard lot in life. She may thus have been particularly discontented with 'lonely' Max Gate, and have shown it by sulks, signs and expressions of extreme fatigue and despair over servants. No doubt she was therefore more pressing than ever about the *Life*, at the same time recognizing that its completion was wholly beyond her own competence.

It may have been in 1917 that the undated 'Private Memorandum' came into being. Its first page, up to 'included every one', is in Tom's own handwriting; the remaining four pages are carbon typescript, but corrected in his hand. All the few corrections are on the typescript. I have given the corrections and/or additions in italics, followed by the original wording in roman, placed between slashes. I have quoted up to the top of page four of the whole.

Private Memorandum

Information for Mrs Hardy in the preparation of a biography
As there seems to be no doubt that so-called biographies of myself will be published which are unauthorized & erroneous, one having already appeared [Hedgcock's], it becomes necessary that an authentic volume should at any rate be contemplated by her, & materials gathered by her while there is still time.

The facts to which she has access will form a chronicle more or less complete of my life. They are not enjoined to be included every one in the volume, if any should seem to be indiscreet, belittling, monotonous, trivial, provocative, or in other ways unadvisable; neither are they enjoined to be exclusive of other details that may be deemed necessary. This statement does not apply to the extract from Mrs Emma Hardy's 'Recollections', which being past revision by the writer are to be printed intact [the typescript extract is extant].

The facts here given can be supplemented by the insertion of some more of *my*/Mr Hardy's/ letters of an interpretative kind at their several dates, if wished; or not, if otherwise (as they might be printed separately, though this *is*/was/not desired by *me*/him/. Also by references to newspapers, reviews, and other publications if thought expedient.

It must, however, be remembered, in consulting newspaper 'Interviews' with, and other personal sketches, /of him/ [deleted], or reports of what *I* /he/ may have said, that they were not revised by *my*/himself, and that some were surreptitiously obtained or *imagined*; they must therefore be accepted with considerable reserve. Also that, in respect of other letters than *my* /his/, permission to print such (if any are required) must be obtained from such writers' representatives, *except in the case of extracts that are too brief to be of consequence.*

> The whole book before printing should be put into correct literary form, by an experience writer and scholar. Should Mrs Hardy wish that her name alone should stand on the title page, such a one might possibly be found for her who would do what was required if paid a reasonable fee.

This is is many ways a curious document, and one which makes it abundantly clear that Florence knew that Tom knew that she was not 'an experienced writer and scholar'. But was it written while she was still supposed to be writing the book herself – or was it a deliberate piece of deception, concocted so that Florence could produce it for scholars, should they enquire after Tom's death? Was it the embryo of some kind of intended introduction to a biography?

Tom was anxiously concerned with the book up to a few weeks before his death, when he wrote in the already quoted insertion about his 'altruism'. Although we know very well, chiefly from what Florence admitted to Purdy, that Tom himself wrote it, Florence was somewhat careless: she ought to have, and was expected to, make a clean copy of the entire document from which I have quoted the main part. For the alterations from the third to the first person make it plain that the document was, indeed, produced in order to protect, first, Florence from accusations of forgery (signing and obtaining kudos from a book which she did not write, which is exactly what she did) and, secondly, the posthumous Hardy from accusations of having written his own biography under his wife's name (which, of course, is exactly what he did, too).

What made them agree to practise such a deception? The idea that Florence herself had written the book persisted for many years after Purdy had divulged the truth in a lecture to the Grolier Club in America in April 1940; the *New York Times Book Review* reported it in May. However, when Evelyn Hardy (not, admittedly, a scholar) came to write her biography of Hardy, which was published in 1954, she had not heard of this revelation and alluded to the work as being by Florence. This was all the more peculiar because she had received some personal help from Cockerell, who by that time at least must have known the truth. Indeed, it is not unlikely that he knew it from the outset. It was he who destroyed, just after Tom's death and in accordance with his instructions as executor, the mass of notebooks from which it had been compiled; he spent a whole morning at it. The gardener, Bertie Stevens, does not remember Cockerell, but he described one 'grand clearance':

I was given the task of burning his clothes and bundles of newspapers on a bonfire in the garden. Mrs Hardy stood by the whole time and watched, presumably to ensure that nothing escaped the flames. All was burnt in her presence except a scarf which she gave me for my use. Mrs Hardy herself burnt, on another bonfire, baskets full of the letters and private papers that I had carried down from the study to the garden under her supervision and watchful eye. She would not let me burn these, but insisted upon doing it herself, and after all the papers had been destroyed, she raked the ashes to be sure that not a single scrap or word remained. It was a devil of a clear out. I never knew so much stuff come out of a room or such a burn up. My impression was she did not want any of the letters or papers to be seen by anyone and she was very careful to destroy every trace of them. I had wondered when she was burning them what had been among the papers. Had they not been private I should have had them with the clothes and newspapers on my bonfire. Whether she was destroying them on her own initiative or carrying out the wishes of her dead husband I never knew, and the world will never learn what went up in flames on that 'bonfire day'.

Whether this was a preliminary 'burn up' before Cockerell came to do his bit is not clear. Possibly he stayed in the house, sorting, for most of the time. Other documents, such as Emma's diaries and the manuscripts of the *Life*, had been destroyed by Tom long before his death.

When Florence wrote to Cockerell in September 1917 that her husband intended to 'go on giving me facts about his life. I have got as far as the time he started work in London, but a lot can be filled in. He seems quite enthusiatic now about the idea, and of course I love doing it' she was lying – with her husband's encouragement. He had begun the process of writing his own life in the third person, and the 'author', the voice in which the account is written (apart from the very abundant quotation from his own private writings, which undercuts and almost reprimands the conventional narrative voice at more or less every point), is that of his wife. It is the voice of the author of the respectable and wholly artificial Victorian genre of 'Life and Letters', with its reverence for its subject and its eagerness to purge the life in question of any irregularities – in short, to sanitize it. Tom was thus parodying the voice of his second wife in all the narrative part of his book: was saying what she, the admirer of the OM but not him, would say, had she possessed the capacity to do the orthodox job. Florence was able to tell Cockerell that Tom was 'now quite enthusiastic' because, in truth, she was no longer in charge of writing it: he was keeping her quiet by promising her the eventual credit for it. When in 1930 she reacted so violently to *Cakes and Ale*, it was in part because she felt guilty of what Maugham's novel did not, in fact, accuse her of: putting her own name to a book that her dead husband had written.

Yet there is a sense in which the book was not a fraud at all: Florence did make a few additions and deletions, and she did compile, if in a perfunctory and unprofessional manner, the last two chapters. Above all, the title page reads thus:

THE LIFE OF/THOMAS HARDY/compiled largely/from contemporary notes, letters,/diaries, and biographical memoranda,/as well as from oral information/ in conversations extending/over many years/by/ FLORENCE EMILY HARDY.

The page was thus misleading, but hardly a downright lie. It had come about simply because, when it came to it, Florence was not up to the job.

One may well ask: why did she tell Purdy, or indeed anyone? The answer is that, despite her failings, she preferred the truth, and had a dismayed and disarming manner of telling it in full – provided it was tactfully put to her. This is common to her type, one of whose considerable charms, virtues and attractions is that it cannot, eventually, resist the truth. The deception must have haunted her: the biography, which came out in two volumes, *The Early Years* in 1928 and *The Later Years* in 1930, was respectfully received, and many distinguished people – for example Virginia Woolf – wrote to praise her: 'Nobody', wrote Woolf on 21 July 1932, 'could have given the book the atmosphere and unity that you did.' Nobody, that is to say, except the dead Thomas Hardy.

The details of the actual process of the writing of the book, and of who knew and who guessed at its authorship, are not altogether recoverable. But Florence did give Purdy some important details. By 1919 Tom had completed the manuscript up to 1918. If anyone came into his study he would slip the sheets under his blotting paper and pretend to be working on something else. Then Florence typed up, in triplicate, what he had written. Tom made his corrections on the second carbon, and she transferred these to the first carbon. When he had approved the draft, she would make the necessary changes to the top copy. The corrections were written in a calligraphic hand, in Hardy's case with the expertness of an architect, in Florence's rather less so. As the book passed into corrected typescript, the manuscript was destroyed. It may well have been that Tom, tactfully, always referred to this final script not as final at all, but as something Florence could and would 'work on' when he was dead and she came to publish it.

To a very small extent, of course, that is exactly what happened – and, because of the preservation of the typescripts, the publication of the reconstructed work has been possible. In his edition of the *Personal Notebooks* Richard Taylor prints all the substantial deletions separately from the text. Most of them were made by Florence, often under the influence of Barrie; but a few must have been made by Hardy himself. Florence was solely responsible for all the deletions concerning Emma, which would have much upset her husband. Possibly she obtained instant satisfaction from this; later, according at least to the lawyer Irene Cooper Willis, she became more balanced on the subject. But she did have a largely unconscious streak of spite: Tom's will had referred to the desirability of 'condemnatory action against the caging of wild birds'. After his death, to her delight, colourful budgerigars flew about in the conservatory at Max Gate. His own Tess had been, for him, a trapped or caged bird! Yet she liked animals, and herself found much solace in the dog Wessex, whose ways she defended against his many detractors. Just as shared enjoyment in serving the walking needs of this lively dog provided some means of communication between them, so, long ago, had interest in their cats and in the dog Moss performed the same function between Tom and Emma. But the latter relationship was the more potent because of its length and the sexual charge which had once informed it.

If we leave aside the removal of passages about Emma, the reasons for which require no further comment, then the rest of the cuts may be grouped into three categories: propriety, lists of society people, and attacks on critics. Under the first heading there are only one or two deletions, such as the reminiscences of Caddell Holder, and humorous matters which the solemn Florence felt might be taken amiss (the phrase 'emphatically in the family way' was cast out as vulgar). Barrie was most influential in the case of the second and third categories, although it was Charles Whibley, Macmillan's reader, who first drew attention to the too full society lists. Barrie's main concern was that Hardy might look over-sensitive to footling reviewers. In fact, of course, Tom was extremely sensitive only to unjust or wrong-headed reviewers, and never to fair criticism. When in 1918 he came to reduce his collection of reviews of his books, he destroyed only those which had themselves been foolish. Of course he made some errors of judgement, but what writer does not? The *Life* is all the better for the inclusion of these passages about critics: it thus deals more honestly with a subject about which the vast majority of writers are wholly dishonest – either pretending that they are unaffected by reviews, or that they enjoy criticism; and it shows us the man as he was, regardless of how he ought to be 'made to look'. Barrie himself, though, had long before graduated into a master of evasion. On the matter of the lists of society people: I think these may well have been put in originally as much for Florence's sake as for Tom's, and that in any case their inclusion was made in a sardonic spirit. They are obtrusive enough to give that impression. After all, we know Tom's real attitude to high society *per se*, even if he genuinely liked some members of it. And so by 1920 or thereabouts most of the work had been done, the 'biography' as finished as it could be: the most substantial and interesting ghosting job that Tom had yet done for Florence.

Then, in 1923, an American called Ernest Brennecke called at Max Gate, representing himself at that time, as Tom informed Macmillan on 4 April 1925, as 'a student of German philosophy, and not an interviewer'. When in 1924 he published his *Thomas Hardy's Universe: A Study of a Poet's Mind*, Tom was just about mollified, and even told Brennecke that his sins had been 'venial' by comparison with those of some others. He was annoyed by the references to the influence of Schopenhauer upon his own work, but would still have allowed the matter to pass without protest. But then in the spring of 1925 the American, by no means as 'innocuous' as has been claimed, issued *The Life of Thomas Hardy* under the imprint of the New York firm of Greenberg. In January he had impertinently cabled Tom from America for permission to use, in it, the illustrations from *Wessex Poems*. Tom cabled back: CANNOT PERMIT REPRODUCTION OF ILLUSTRATIONS OR ANYTHING COPYRIGHT. DISAPPROVE OF BIOGRAPHY ALTOGETHER. Macmillan was right behind Tom, but did not think that the book could be withdrawn.

At the beginning of November 1924 Tom had asked his secretary May O'Rourke to write to Brennecke, on his behalf, to tell him that 'he regrets that he cannot authorize anything of the nature of a biography of himself to be published'. But Brennecke, who was working for a newspaper, would not be put off and even sent his work to Fisher Unwin, the firm which had issued his *Thomas Hardy's Universe* in England.

Hardy therefore wrote, on 1 April 1925, to a member of this firm, his remote cousin Christopher Borlase Childs:

> As I am writing I may mention that the American author, whose book entitled 'T.H.'s Universe' you issued in England . . . has now brought out a large biography of me, as if it were an authorized Life. I would caution you in respect of it in case he should ask you to take it up . . . as it is a mass of unwarranted assumptions & errors that are at times ludicrous, & has been published in New York in the face of my protests against such an impertinence.

Fisher Unwin wrapped it up and returned it to Brennecke, which he seems to have thoroughly deserved, since, as Tom told Macmillan on 4 April:

> It is a large volume, announcing itself on the cover as: 'The first biography of England's novelist–poet; a work which will probably always stand as the most authoritative and comprehensive book on the subject. Mr Brennecke records every known fact of Hardy's life . . . This biography is the result of ten years of research and personal contact.'

In the remainder of the letter he is not unjust to Brennecke. The first five chapters, the biographical ones, were 'quite eulogistic' and 'ridiculously incorrect' (he was, for instance, made into a smoker). It would not matter so long as the book appeared only in America. But as a literary work, he scrupulously added, it was 'fairly able'. He mentioned that Brennecke had only been able to publish the miscellany *Life and Art* (which he privately condemned as an '*olla podrida*', Spanish for 'rotten stew', in other words 'nasty hodgepodge') in America because of the copyright laws. Macmillan suggested a public disclaimer, and on 11 April a letter, concocted by himself and Cockerell, appeared in *The Times*.

That, so far as Tom was concerned, was the end of the matter. But Florence, as the 'author' of a now completed, or almost completed, typescript which would be issued as his authorized biography as soon as possible after the death of her husband, was plunged into panic. Brennecke, she felt, had been just about dealt with: Tom was still alive, and with his connections he had managed do it. But what if other and seemingly better qualified, English, writers were to publish new biographies? Would she alone be able to queer their pitch? She may even have suspected Rebekah Owen of planning such a venture, for it was in January 1925 (just when Tom was sending his cable to Brennecke warning him not to attempt a biography) that she wrote her denunciatory letter – the ostensible reason was that she had seen her talking to Gertrude Bugler after a performance of *Tess* – for which she almost immediately apologized. She had only recently undergone an operation, much more serious than any earlier medical treatment, for a cancerous tumour on her neck. And it was in very early February that she was to make a secret call on Gertrude Bugler at her Beaminster home. In that January, as she admitted to Cockerell, she was out of her mind.

Later in the year, as she began to get a little better, she started to worry in case 'her' book was not good enough. She certainly read Brennecke's, and it may well be that she found the critical part of it (all but the first five chapters) desperately intimidating. What did she know of Schopenhauer and Hegel and their alleged influences upon her husband's writings? He himself had conceded to Macmillan that the critical parts of the book were 'fairly able'. How alarming! At this level she was a non-starter. Since this Brennecke had included a long critical section, would not her readers expect one from her, too?

So, in what may well have been a characteristically ambitious plan really to rewrite the book after Tom's death – to turn it into a masterpiece of sensitive critical tribute – she must have reasoned. To what extent she took Tom into her confidence is unknown. But by this time, since he was ageing rapidly and was much wrapped up in himself, he may have been in the increasing habit of preserving a silence towards her.

T.E. Lawrence was now stationed, as Private Shaw of the Tank Corps, at Bovington Camp, Wool, near Max Gate. He was fascinated by poets and poetry, and admired Hardy; so he had written to his intimate friend Robert Graves for an introduction. Graves wrote to Florence, and thus Lawrence turned up for tea, on the afternoon of 29 March 1923, on his Brough motorcycle. Until he went to India he was a regular and welcome visitor to Max Gate: Florence adored him and his good manners, while Tom admired him greatly and made him into one of the closest of his younger friends (the other two were Sassoon and Blunden). On 21 April, a couple of weeks after the Brennecke book had been read at Max Gate, Lawrence was writing circumspectly to the publisher Jonathan Cape in these terms:

A very distinguished person's wife once asked me if I would care to edit or 'ghost' her husband's diary, written quite intimately before he became famous, but showing, very wonderfully, the growth of his mind and the slow accumulation of his knowledge . . . Please keep this entirely to yourself, the existence of the material is not known, even to Macmillan's . . .

Now I believe that Lawrence had been shown a good deal of 'material' (the code-name by which Tom himself used to refer to all the biographical papers and scripts) by Florence: not only the typescript, but also, possibly, some portions of the 'diaries' which had not at that point been destroyed. I think that, partly in anger at her old husband who had so recently wounded her, she passed off to Lawrence what was in fact his composition as her own. I doubt if, at this point, Tom had any knowledge of it, although he must eventually have been informed. On 15 April Lawrence had written to Florence that he would like to see it, although it might take him a long time to come to a conclusion. By 26 August 1925 he had seen it; but on 13 February 1926 he returned it:

I was sorry to send the book back. I had been reading it deliberately, tasting it all over: and I swear that it's a very good thing. There is a strange *individual* taste about the story of those early days. It's very beautiful. Rarely so. If T.H. injures it, a very great harm will be done. He is no judge (in this subject alone!) indeed he should be disqualified from sitting on the bench. Also you have done it.

I was seeing, every page I read, little things which might be done to polish the jewel more excellently. I do hope you will send it me back. I'll tackle it more humbly and honestly.

Why did he so tactfully return it? Was it because he had by then been told the truth about it? Sassoon had recently been approached by Harper Brothers for a biography, and had had to be informed of the prior existence of one when he mentioned the offer at Max Gate. We know what Florence told her own and Tom's friends. What we do not know is what Tom told them, when he was alone with them.

Lawrence wrote again about the matter to Florence, each time with what Richard Taylor calls a note of 'teasing ambivalence'. On 21 June 1926 he referred to the destruction of a part of the manuscript, which suggests that Tom had been rewriting – unless these were old pages which had escaped earlier holocausts.

Other people who might have known or guessed at the truth, apart from Cockerell, were E.M. Forster, Barrie, Sassoon, Graves (through

Lawrence) and even Virginia Woolf, since she said, in the letter of praise of Florence from which I have already quoted a sentence, that she felt honoured that 'it ever crossed your mind to suggest my doing it'. In the end it was Barrie who performed most of the editing, and his letters to Florence show that, while he had guessed who wrote the *Life* (he was not in fact allowed to see it until after Tom's death), he was determined (and quite properly, we may feel) to maintain the myth of Florence's authorship.

I can add only a little to the complex mystery of who knew for certain and who guessed and who was deceived. One of Lawrence's most intimate friends and confidants was Robert Graves, to whom he even divulged intimate secrets about himself which did not become known until some thirty years after his death in a motorcycle accident in 1936. In 1943 and then again in 1944, before Graves knew anything at all about Purdy's revelations in America (I am by no means sure that he ever knew about them), he told me that both Lawrence and Sassoon had told him that the *Life* was really by Tom himself, and not by Florence, because the latter 'had tried but was too stupid – and the old boy wanted to spare her feelings'. Unfortunately I never thought fit to go further into this statement with him until he was too old to remember the details. I would not put too much weight on it, but it does tend to confirm that everyone stuck together to make Florence feel pleased, and that they did not judge her as wicked for trying to continue the deception. Millgate wisely withholds all judgement and finds, as most do, that the arrangement worked well enough for both parties and for posterity.

As to whether Tom ever mentioned anything about Florence's difficult nature to Sassoon or Lawrence, I do not know. Lawrence thought that Tom was not very comfortable with Florence in the company of those who understood literature. Sassoon regarded her as unsuitable for Tom in his old age, and did not at all like her. But my feeling is that Tom kept his difficulties mostly to himself, beyond a few sardonic and coded comments. He was, however, tenderly fond of Florence always, and was attracted by her timidity and by the true humility of her sudden outbursts of honesty and self-deprecation. But he must have been disappointed when he tried to talk to her as he could talk to Blunden, Sassoon and, above all, to Lawrence.

Her behaviour over Gertrude Bugler (who died in 1992 at a very great age) was, in itself, very unwise, immature and unattractive. But it has to be taken in the context of what was almost certainly post-operative depression, as well as in that of her maladroitness in handling her by now aged husband. Characteristically, afterwards she was desperately sorry for what she had done and tried hard to make up for it, although, naturally enough, in private Miss Bugler could never forgive her for it.

Tom had already noticed the beautiful Gertrude, and had written a special part for her for *Wessex Scenes from The Dynasts*. At the end of 1920 she scored yet another success, as Eustacia Vye in the dramatization of *The Return of the Native*. This was played in the drawing room at Max Gate in front of the entire surviving Hardy family, as well as Florence, who conceded that the occasion gave her husband 'intense joy'. They played it as if they were village mummers, and it enchanted him. Florence also made a joke, if it really was a joke, in a letter to Cockerell: 'T.H. has lost his heart to [Miss Bugler] entirely, but as she is soon getting married I don't let that cast me down too much.' When she did get married on 19 September 1921, to a farmer cousin, Ernest Bugler, Tom pasted a newspaper cutting reporting the event into the notebook known as 'Memoranda II' (prepared for the *Life*).

In 1922 she was to have played in the dramatization of *A Desperate Remedy* (from *Desperate Remedies*), but could not do so owing to her pregnancy. Disappointed, Tom asked her to call at Max Gate so that he could give her an inscribed book. She did so, but found Florence suddenly cold and hostile. On 13 June, knowing nothing of Florence's habits, she received a critical and complaining letter rebuking her for having called at Max Gate: it was '"not done" in our station of life'; 'I am regarded and treated as hostess'; Mrs Bugler lacked 'refinement', and was a disappointment.

Not put off by what, if anything, Florence may have said to him, in the following year Tom wrote the leading part of Iseult, in his play *The Famous Tragedy of the Queen of Cornwall*, for Gertrude Bugler. But once again she could not play the part because of pregnancy (she had lost the previous baby). Showing more maturity than the forty-three-year-old woman who had appointed herself her 'rival', she approached Florence and tried to patch up the quarrel; indeed, she believed that she had done so.

Although, unlike Florence, Tom disliked and despised the West End stage, he had always hoped that some great actress such as Mrs Patrick Campbell would play Tess in London. 'Memoranda II' is a kind of diary as well as a guide for the composition of the latter part of the *Life*, and it records his 'intense' interest in what was by every account

Miss Bugler's brilliantly moving portrayal of Tess in the version that Tom had himself made back in the 1890s. He commented sourly in a brief note that its success now made it clear that 'it could probably have made a fortune to a theatre manager' if it had been played at the time that Mrs Campbell, Eleonora Duse, Ellen Terry and even Sarah Bernhardt had shown an interest in it. The diary, having expressed his usual apprehensions and reservations, reads:

Nov. 21. To rehearsal of *Tess* in Corn Ex.
24. J.M. Barrie, & Harold Child came to attend rehearsal. Col Lawrence came & met them at dinner, & all went.
25. Barrie & Child left.
26. Wedy. 1st pefce. of Tess play. Sassoon and E.M. Forster came. Col L met them in theatre. I sat in wings.
27. Cockerell came. Sassoon stayed on & went with us to matinée. Tea with the players in Town hall. Met G.B.'s [Gertrude Bugler's] husband. Cockerell also went to eveng. p. . . . .
Dec. 11. Motored to Weymouth for performance of Tess . . . Obliged to attend 2nd performance . . .

In December Mrs Bugler was put at the receiving end of further tribulation from Florence, who sent her a letter, clearly angry, but not understandable by either Gertrude or her husband; this was followed by a telegram and another letter asking her to burn the previous one. All this should have been recognized as the behaviour of a sick woman, and on no account should Florence be 'blamed' for it. But her state of mind could hardly have escaped Tom, who was himself by now too old to deal with it adequately. It must have left its mark on him.

On 10 January 1923 Cockerell, he records, came again. On the next day, a Sunday, T.E. Lawrence dined. '12,' the diary continues, 'F's birthday. Mrs Gertrude Bugler lunched. Cockerell left.' So at some time he did remember Florence's birthday, although she claimed that he did not.

But much else had been happening about which he did not immediately know. Cockerell's own diary for 12 January reads:

Walked into Dorchester with F.H. in the morning. She told me she had been in such a fret in the night that she would go mad. It was her birthday (45) but he had not alluded to it in any way . . . Mrs Bugler

843

came to lunch . . . On the face of it there does not seem much harm in her . . . F.H. begged me to stay to make things easier, or I should have left in the morning.

She told him that Tom had 'spoken to her roughly', and that he was now closeted with the Haymarket Theatre manager, Frederick Harrison, arranging with him, and Mrs Bugler, about the *Tess* performances in London. As Bugler later said, if the matinées of *Tess* had been successful, then it would have gone 'into the evening bill' after a six-week season of John Barrymore as Hamlet. That Harrison (not to be confused with the old rationalist, whose first name lacked the final 'k'), a shrewd man, should have wanted this is some testimony to her skill. It was agreed that she should begin rehearsals in April.

That all the trouble was invented by Florence, clinically depressed though she may have been, is made all the more likely by the manner in which Tom had been treating her in recent months. As early as 7 June 1923 he had written to Yearsley about the 'gland' in Florence's neck. It was thought to be malignant. Would there be any danger in it, or 'risk of further complications', Tom had asked Yearsley in 1923. Both he and Florence, he anxiously told him, would be prepared to put up with the 'slight disfigurement it causes'. Yearsley replied that he had advised Florence not to have it removed for the time being. But by the autumn of 1924 it had grown larger, and she went to London to have the operation performed by another specialist surgeon. The surgery was successful, but Tom had been in a frenzy of worry, writing to her tenderly, almost daily, offering to come to London if she should wish it (she had felt that his own anxiety would further fuss her), and sending Henry in his new car, driven by Tilley's chauffeur Harold Voss, to bring her back. Thus it seems likely that she caused him to 'speak roughly' to her, if indeed he did so at all, by her own hysterical demeanour. She was also, in her weak state, judging Tom's behaviour with Bugler on the basis of his own past behaviour with her: if he had made her his mistress, why should he not now do the same with Bugler? All this was quite as 'mad' as any behaviour perpetrated by Emma.

His interest in Gertrude Bugler, though, was quite 'harmless': it was even good for him at his age; but Florence, judging by her previous behaviour and general lack of control, would probably have been unable to contain her jealousy and despair even had she been well. In January Cockerell had tried to convey the 'comic' side of it to her, but she had not forgotten the events of 26 November, at the first performance of

Tess, which had caused talk in the town on account of the attention which Tom had paid to Gertrude Bugler.

Although Bugler's own account of these events, given long afterwards, is decently reticent, she made it clear that initially Florence encouraged her to go to London: no doubt she wanted her out of the way. She wrote in 1959:

> I remember with extraordinary clarity my last visit to Max Gate during his lifetime . . . He was not a tall man, rather spare, quick in gesture and animated in conversation. His face was wrinkled and his hair was white when I knew him. They, Mr and Mrs Hardy, had been talking of my proposed stay in London and offered advice on this and that . . . Usually Mr and Mrs Hardy said 'Goodbye' to me in the porch, but that night – with something of the obstinacy of an old man, he insisted on seeing me to the car. We walked half-way down the short, winding drive in silence; then suddenly, he said 'If anyone asks you if you knew Thomas Hardy, say yes, he was my friend'.

This is moving, and quite obviously Tom, now in his eighty-fifth year, offered no threat whatever either to Bugler's marriage or to his own. But after this visit Florence changed her mind: it would not do, after all, to send Mrs Bugler off to London and out of the way of her husband. On 25 January she wrote to her and told her that to go would be a 'tragedy'. Mrs Bugler continued:

> Then Mrs Hardy came down to our Riverside Cottage in Beaminster. I have an idea that the visit was preceded by a telegram for I remember awaiting her arrival. She was somewhat agitated and said her husband did not know she had come to see me. Among other things, she said that Mr Hardy was very excited about the play going to London, he was in a nervous state. She feared he would want to go up to London to see it and, at his age, it would not be good for him, nor for his name. She asked me not to go to London, saying that I was still young and might have other chances later on. So, in the end, I wrote to Thomas Hardy and I wrote to Frederick Harrison saying that I had decided not to play Tess after all. How ungrateful they both must have thought me!

Florence actually said more than this. She said that if Tom came to London to see her in the theatre he would come to her dressing-room, and would thus create a scandal; and she told Mrs Bugler that Tom had written a poem in which he eloped with her on Toller Down. She had, Florence added, destroyed this. No trace of it has indeed ever been found; but it is unlikely that she would have dared to destroy any scrap written by him. She seems to have made the whole story up, although she may well have believed in it. The word 'paranoia' has been used in connection with Florence, and, although she was not actually paranoid, she was subject to occasional fleeting paranoid delusions when at her most vulnerable. So Mrs Bugler told Tom and Harrison that she could not, after all, bear to leave her husband and baby daughter, Diana. She did play Tess in London, in 1929, with success, but the opportunity came too late.

Florence's behaviour has been called 'enigmatic', but, apart from the plain fact that she was temporarily deranged, her motives are obvious. She felt sorry for herself, and was jealous of the attention which both the world and her husband were giving to the beautiful Mrs Bugler, who even had, as she herself had reminded her the previous December, a child. She was determined to see that Mrs Bugler would not enjoy any success in London as an actress: she could stay and enjoy what she, poor Florence, had never had – a child.

Gertrude Bugler, an eminently sensible and dignified woman, always believed that Tom's attention to her was based on the fact that she was the living incarnation of his Tess, and on the coincidence that her mother had been – or so he claimed – an inspiration for Hardy's character. This is borne out by everything that Tom ever said or wrote to her. It was not so much an 'infatuation' as a strong emotion on the part of a romantic poet: an emotion, moreover, which he had well under control. It is not silly or infatuated of an old man to tell a young woman that she is his *friend*, and it did not surprise or disturb Mrs Bugler (as, alas, the old Elgar disturbed the violinist Jelly d'Aranyi when he had a go at her in a taxi). Tom admitted that her performance was 'artless' (which is exactly what he liked about it), and at first opposed the idea of her going to London, feeling, he told J. W. Mackail, 'uneasy' about it. What he eventually did was entirely for her own sake, and, when he wrote on 7 February, in reply to her letter giving the part up, he thought it a 'wise conclusion', in spite of his belief that no actress would be as good. Eventually the part went to Gwen Ffrangçon-Davies, whom, he told Henry Arthur Jones in September 1925, he found to be 'free from the vanities one too often finds among stage people'. In December she and the cast came down to Max Gate to perform his *Tess* in the drawing-room.

Florence, though, still had cause for apprehension. She did not want Tom to meet Gertrude Bugler again, for she had by now represented to Barrie and others that the decision to abandon the London arrangement had been made entirely by Mrs Bugler. Ill or not, she had played her dishonest double game with consummate skill – a skill which she undoubtedly later regretted. On 3 August 1925, however, Tom wrote to the London producer:

> . . . if you have any difficulties in finding a good Tess you might write a line to
>
> Mrs Gertrude Bugler
> Riverside Cottage
> Beaminster.   Dorset
>
> telling her that as a matter of courtesy . . . you just put the question to her whether she will take it. You have seen what the *Times*, etc, said about her, and she is not altogether an amateur – only she wants a little drilling. The real trouble about it was her domestic arrangements till lately, as she had a young baby. But now there is no difficulty it seems.

Five days later Florence reported to Cockerell that Ridgeway had not taken up the offer: '*thank Heaven*'. But Tom, innocent of the decisive part that Florence had played in this, was simply looking after Mrs Bugler's interests. Had he known what Florence had done, he would have been disgusted and angry. But it may have been a good thing in the long run: Mrs Bugler probably had a happier life as a farmer's wife than she would have had as a professional actress. Tom, too, had initially felt that. His life, already a very long one, had now only slightly more than two years to run, and Florence was able to feel herself more securely in charge. The complaints diminished. She could with increasing reason regard him as infirm and helpless, an object of pity, a magnificent relic, no longer capable of 'full intercourse', under her close guard.

37

Good Things

There is little more to tell, except of poems which speak for themselves. In some ways Tom's life actually turned into those poems, or, perhaps more accurately, merged into his steady creation of them. He came to want to turn everything, from his most intimate memories to the death of his dog, into poetry. He worked at them persistently until his very last days. Many of the most important ones have been discussed along the way. There were four more collections after *Satires of Circumstance*, as well as the *Selected Poems* of 1916 in Macmillan's 'Golden Treasury' series, and the short play, *The Famous Tragedy of the Queen of Cornwall*.

Many of the poems in *Moments of Vision*, published on 30 November 1917, were of recent vintage. The collection is his largest, made so in part by the inclusion of the seventeen poems grouped together as 'Poems of War and Patriotism', a few of which (such as the sonnet about conscription, which had been commissioned, and which caused him difficulty), he might have chosen not to publish. But the war was still on, and he felt obliged not to suppress them. The 'Emma theme' continued, being celebrated in about thirty of the poems. It is as if, in these newer 'Emma' poems, he was still trying to make up for what he felt to be his lack of 'loving-kindness' – all too human though that lack had been, rather than peculiar to himself – by exploring Emma's past, and by seeing his own through her eyes. He continued to experiment. He comments directly upon one aspect of his poetic procedures in 'On a Midsummer Eve':

> I idly cut a parsley stalk,
> And blew therein towards the moon;
> I had not thought what ghosts would walk
> With shivering footsteps to my tune.
>
> I went, and knelt, and scooped my hand
> As if to drink, into the brook,

GOOD THINGS

> And a faint figure seemed to stand
> Above me, with the bygone look.
>
> I lipped rough rhymes of chance, not choice,
> I thought not what my words might be;
> There came into my ear a voice
> That turned a tenderer verse for me.

This, as Dennis Taylor suggests, echoes Blake's manner (although not, I think, as he claims, specifically the 'Introduction' to the *Songs of Innocence*). Like so many of Blake's, it is a more difficult poem than it seems to be. It is about the habit of love, and how the merely casual exercise of it leads to the sinister – but then, afterwards, perhaps, to the true. Midsummer's Eve is when girls hope, by spells, to get a glimpse of their future lovers. To cut parsley is to invite disaster in love; to blow it towards the moon also portends disaster. Here the process is reversed: the poet speaks in his own male voice; and what he sees when he goes to the brook to drink is not a future but a past (and now dead) lover. Tom is describing the process of falling in love with a ghost (the ghost of Emma, but perhaps, too, of any girl he had once loved). It is this ghost, now acting as muse, who puts the voice into his ear which enables him to be tender, to avoid generalizing, and to be as particular as love must be in order to transcend mere lust.

Tom had a way of opening and closing his collections with key poems. In *Satires* he had opened with 'In Front of the Landscape'; here it was the prime 'moment of vision', and gives the book its title:

> That mirror
> Which makes of men a transparency,
> Who holds that mirror
> And bids us such a breast-bare spectacle see
> Of you and me?
>
> That mirror
> Whose magic penetrates like a dart,
> Who lifts that mirror
> And throws our mind back on us, and our heart,
> Until we start?
>
> That mirror
> Works well in these night hours of ache;
> Why in that mirror
> Are tincts we never see ourselves once take

When the world is awake?

That mirror
Can test each mortal when unaware;
Yea, that strange mirror
May catch his last thoughts, whole life foul or fair,
Glassing it – where?

The mystery here addressed is that of the existence of conscience in an insensate universe: it is a religious one which cannot, however, be answered.

Florence was not in the least satisfied with Tom's inscription in her copy of *Moments*: 'From Thomas Hardy, this first copy of the first edition, to the first of women Florence Hardy'. Her jealousy of Emma would not allow her to be, and she whinged in a December letter to Owen that it must suggest that her own marriage to the author was a 'most disastrous one & that his sole wish is to find refuge in the grave with her with whom alone he found happiness' (this, though not happily phrased, was perhaps essentially true). The hoped-for happy sharing of the melancholy to which both were prone had not come about, for the melancholy of the one was profound, whereas that of the other was shallow and self-pitying. Those 'moments of vision' which Florence experienced, when she saw herself as she really was and could not help telling the truth, were too few and too far between. If Tom needed a certain amount of physical care, she needed more mental care than he was possibly now able to give.

Some idea of how life was lived at Max Gate in the early 1920s emerges from an anecdote related by a Mrs Adolphine Stanley, whose little boy, Oscar, was an unwelcome – because noisy – presence to Tom. Florence arranged with her mother to transfer her from Enfield, where she had long been maid-of-all-work, to Max Gate as cook. Florence always had trouble with cooks, and when she took some cookery lessons this only made the trouble worse. When interviewed, Mrs Stanley thought that she had worked at Max Gate from 1916 until 1918; but a note by Tom shows that she and her husband, who worked as their odd-job man, came on 7 November 1921. However, it may be that she had briefly worked there before. She tells this story:

While Mrs Hardy was out shopping in Dorchester a parcel arrived from a tradesman, addressed to her, and there was two or three pounds to pay. I went to Mr Hardy in his study and explained the situation and asked him for the the money, but he said: 'No, I shan't give you any. Tell them to take it back. And even if you have the money don't pay for it. Send it back.' So that is what I had to do, refuse to accept Mrs Hardy's parcel. When she returned she was a bit annoyed about it; but she didn't say much. She was very loyal to the old devil . . .

Mrs Stanley went on to say how unhappy Florence was: 'although fond of her husband, she was not happy really after her marriage to him'. Not a discerning woman, Mrs Stanley resented Tom (he was too mean, she expostulated, to buy himself a pair of trousers, and the ones he wore were frayed at the edges), and there are errors in her account. But her impression of Florence's unhappiness and her laboured efforts at loyalty is an interesting and confirmatory one. She had known Florence for some ten or more years, and had observed her when she was at home in Enfield.

The end of the war changed none of Tom's opinions, in part because he soon read Keynes' *Economic Consequences of the Peace* – and because, too, with his usual prescience, he did not believe in the efficacy of the newly formed League of Nations. Despite the state of the world at the end of this century, his so-called 'pessimism' and gloom about the future are usually deprecated – perhaps because he was so obviously right in his diagnosis. He told his liberal politician friend Pearce Edgcumbe, now knighted, that a magazine article he had written, surveying progress since 1860

> might be supplemented by a prophetic article on our probable retrogression during the next 60 years to the point from which we started (not to say further) – to turnpike-road travelling, high postage, scarce newspapers (for lack of paper to print them on), oppression of one class by another, etc., etc.

He was not so wrong: travelling in Britain has become almost impossible, and travel on our major highways will soon be charged for; postage is high and the service slower than it was then; few newspapers are worth reading; categories of people oppress one another; and only usurers, lawyers, accountants and munitions dealers prosper. The only members of society to speak of progress are politicians, and all the systems by which the 'civilized' world has lived, for better or worse, for centuries, are now rapidly breaking down.

But, for all his insistence upon the truth of the direction in which the world was going, he continued to be honoured. In 1920 Oxford awarded him a DCL, and the Oxford University Dramatic Society presented a performance of the Barker version of *The Dynasts*, which he witnessed. At Florence's request, the dramatist Charles Morgan wrote, for 'her' biography, a somewhat florid account of these and other proceedings.

Morgan spoke of how, when he was at Max Gate in 1922 for the Hardy Players' performance of *A Desperate Remedy*, Tom spoke of critics with 'a bitterness which surprised me': 'It was hard to believe that Hardy honestly thought that his genius was not recognised.' Robert Graves also met him on the Oxford visit and found him aphasic and confused in the strange surroundings; but he reversed this impression when, in the following August, he and his wife Nancy (daughter of William Nicholson, well known to Tom) called at Max Gate. Graves, less conventional than Morgan, could well understand Tom's disenchantment with critics, as well as his conviction that as a poet he was not well understood. Tom made a distinction between popular 'public' poems and those intended for fewer readers. His reply to Ezra Pound, who had sent him two volumes of poems at the end of 1920, is sympathetic and tolerant: he could tell that Pound was serious, even if more 'modern' than he could or wished to be. While he gently and teasingly upbraided him for deliberate obscurity, he referred to 'Homage to Sextus Propertius' as 'fine and striking', and to 'Hugh Selwyn Mauberley' as 'packed' and 'racy': he left him to the light of his own soul 'for guidance', and told him not to bother about his 'reactions'.

In 1920, when the aged positivist Frederic Harrison resentfully attacked him in the *Fortnightly* as having all that a man could wish, whose pessimism was 'not human, not social, not true', he was hurt and perturbed; the charge (as well as the disloyalty) so rankled with him that he eventually replied to it, two years later, in the long and well-reasoned 'Apology to *Late Lyrics and Earlier*'. This was published on 23 May 1922, and was intended to mark his first eighty years. The 'Apology' is one of his few ventures into literary criticism, a genre which in general he eschewed as inimical to the business of writing poetry. We are familiar with his arguments in defence of his so-called 'pessimism'. More interesting in this context are his general pronouncements, which today read as freshly as they did in 1922:

The thoughts of any man of letters concerned to keep poetry alive cannot but run uncomfortably on the precarious prospects of English verse at the present day. Verily the hazards and casualties surrounding the birth and setting forth of almost every modern creation in numbers are ominously like those of one of Shelley's paper-boats on a windy lake. And a forward conjecture scarcely permits the hope of a better time, unless men's tendencies should change. So indeed of all art, literature, and 'high thinking' nowadays. Whether owing to the barbarizing of taste in the younger minds by the dark madness of the late war, the unabashed cultivation of selfishness in all classes, the plethoric growth of knowledge simultaneously with the stunting of wisdom, 'a degrading thirst after outrageous stimulation' (to quote Wordsworth again), or from any other cause, we seem threatened with a new Dark Age.

He went on to write of the lack of 'whole-seeing in contemporary estimates of poetry and kindred work', and of 'the knowingness affected by junior reviewers'; but he did not think that these were the cause of the trouble, which was 'something of the deeper sort'.

Significantly, he equated poetry and 'pure literature in general' with religion 'in its essential and undogmatic sense': these were 'but different names for the same thing'. He ended with what he implied was a hopeless plea for 'an alliance between religion, which must be retained unless the world is to perish, and complete rationality, which must come, unless also the world is to perish, by means of the interfusing effect of poetry . . .'

However, here he retained a confusion persistent in his prose: for 'complete rationality' is not reconcilable with the poetry he wrote, and so he seems to have meant, but preferred not to say, that poetry gains its 'interfusing effect' by means of a certain irrationality – by means of its partaking in a mystery which he frequently acknowledged, if only in his poetry ('Moments of Vision', quoted above, provides an apt example). His poetry would have been nothing had it not been 'interfused' with this sense of puzzlement and mystery.

Late Lyrics is the collection which ends with the marvellously simple and naked 'Surview', but begins with the deliberately non-'pessimistic' and subtle lyric 'Weathers' – just to remind some of his more critical readers that he enjoyed the earth 'no less'. Many of the other poems come from the past or have been triggered by Tom's reading through of his old notebooks in preparation for the *Life*: a detritus which he would

853

destroy, but transform, before he did so, into a more meaningful form. There is also a graceful tribute to Florence, 'I Sometimes Think', as one who did 'care,/And, spiriting into my house, to, fro,/Like wind on the stair,/Cares still, heeds all, and will, even though/I may despair'. Read carefully, it may be less of a tribute than an admonition to her to behave in the best and most loving-kind manner possible, especially as he cannot tell her that she has in any way stopped him from despairing; but it is a real tribute, since it incorporates a recognition of her best impulses.

In April 1920, when they both stayed for two nights with Barrie, he made his last visit to London to attend the wedding of Harold Macmillan – an arrangement which was, ironically, to turn out more unhappily for the groom than either of Tom's own marriages. But, Macmillan having graduated from publisher to world statesman, public news of this was to be suppressed until after his death. When introducing a new beer called 'Hardy Ale' in the 1960s, Macmillan, the last prime minister who could honestly be called literate, remembered him as a man whose cheeks were as red as an apple.

There were more honours. An Honorary Fellowship of Queen's College, Oxford, in 1922, followed by a visit there in June 1923, the last occasion upon which he slept away from home. In 1925 a Litt. D from Bristol had to be awarded to him by a deputation. St Andrew's University had awarded him an Honorary LL.D in 1922. Closer to his heart was a presentation of a first edition of Keats' *Lamia* in 1921, accompanied by an address signed by over a hundred of his juniors: 'We thank you, sir, for all that you have written.'

The Famous Tragedy of the Queen of Cornwall – published, and performed by the Hardy Players, in late 1923 – was his last substantial work. It was important to him, and, while the verse in which it is written is deliberately subdued, it had been, as he told a reviewer, '53 years in contemplation'. He told Harold Child on 11 November that year that he had taken care to preserve the unities in it:

> My temerity in pulling together into the space of an hour events that in the traditional story covered a long time will doubtless be punished by reviewers of the book. But there are so many versions of the famous romance that I felt free to adapt it to my purposes in any way – as, in fact, the Greek dramatists did in their plays, notably Euripides.

The 'Chanters' he informed Child, fulfilled the purposes of a Greek chorus, but he had made them into ghosts. He would have liked, he added, to put Child up for the night when he came down in his capacity as *Times* reviewer, but 'our servants are in rebellion, and we are largely dependent on charwomen, added to which I am in a worse state of health than I have been in all the year, though it is nothing serious'. However, in a postscript he told Child that he could be put up 'without inconvenience' if he came down a day earlier, and that is what in fact he did. One of Florence's many desperate struggles with the servants, such as made her wish to be sent to an 'asylum,' seems to have been in progress.

What were his purposes in this strange play? It is, though not a major work, superior to the earlier efforts of Tennyson, Arnold and Swinburne to retell the legend. Tom's version, in which the language is a deliberate mixture of the archaic (he had quarried Malory most of all, in addition to his own *A Pair of Blue Eyes*) and the modern, resembles, as Bailey remarked, 'a macabre dream'. The amount of 'bickering' in it, much criticized, is the result of the bickering that he experienced in both his marriages – the two chief female characters, the original Iseult who married Mark, and Iseult the White Hand whom Tristram married, are in one sense Emma and Florence. The drunken and treacherous Mark seems not to be any particular person but rather the spirit of convention, a kind of cynical Mr Grundy. The play is dedicated to Emma, to Caddell Holder and his wife Helen, and to Florence (F.E.H.) 'in affectionate remembrance of those with whom I formerly spent many hours at the scene of the tradition who have now all passed away save one'. The events are seen as wholly fated, but there is certainly more of a hint of the spiteful but remorseful Florence in the speech of Iseult the White Hand in Scene XV:

> Have I done mischief? Maybe so, alas,
> To one I would not harm the littlest jot!

> *Re-enter TRISTRAM*

> I could not help it, O my husband! Yea
> I have dogged you close; I could not bear your rage;
> And heaven has favoured me! The sea smiled smooth
> The whole way over, and the sun shone kind . . .
> – Forgive me that I spoke untruly to you,
> And then to her, in my bruised brain's turmoil.
> But, in a way of saying, you were dead;
> You seemed so – in a dead drowse when she came.
> And I did send for her at your entreaty;

> But flesh is frail. Centred is woman's love,
> And knows no breadth.

Shades of Gertrude Bugler! Then, a few lines further on:

> Forgive me, do forgive, my lord, my husband!
> I love, have loved you so imperishably;
> Not with fleet flame at times, as some do use!
> Had I once been unfaithful, even perverse,
> I would have held some coldness fitly won;
> But I have ever met your wryest whim
> With ready-wrought acceptance, matched your moods,
> Clasped hands, touched lips, and smiled devotedly . . .

And later:

> I thought you loved my name for me myself,
> Not for another; or at the very least
> For sake of some dear sister or mother dead,
> And not, not –

When Tristram upbraids her for haunting 'another woman's house' she replies spiritedly (by her standards), 'O yes I can!' and tells him that if she goes away then something will happen of 'import dark to you'; she thus becomes even more like Florence, alternately threatening and pleading. The parallel is too close to ignore, but Tom makes no more of it. After all, his main motive in finishing the work had been to give the Hardy Players something of their very own – and to memorialize his 'own Iseult'. The drawing of Tintagel Castle he made as an illustration for the published volume was based on one that Emma herself had sketched. The composer Rutland Boughton, who spent two days at Max Gate in June 1924, failed to convert Tom or Florence to communism ('he was interested in his political views, although he could not share them'), but did produce an opera based on *The Queen of Cornwall* which pleased Tom, and which he attended at Glastonbury in the following August. He liked Boughton and said that he would have converted *him* had he had a few more hours with him; but to what he did not say.

The behaviour of Keir Hardie and the Labour Party during the war had irritated him, and Florence recorded him as voting against it at a municipal election in 1922 – this may, however, have been because of strictly local circumstances. Later, though, he became more sympathetic to socialism, and a Dorchester member of the party later confirmed, 'from personal knowledge', that he had been 'sympathetic to the Labour cause'. Certainly he never joined any party, although he was a nominal supporter of the Liberals until their virtual eclipse.

In the previous April Florence Henniker had died. This drew from him only the comment 'After a friendship of 30 years!' It had certainly been his closest and most successful friendship with any woman apart from Emma, and he must wryly have reflected that it had never been interrupted by a sexual encounter. Florence Dugdale apart, she was the only woman with whom he had unequivocally wanted to conduct an affair. She, too, though, had loved him in her way. Agnes Grove, to whom he had been less close, but of whom he had been fond, followed Mrs Henniker in 1926 and prompted the poem 'Concerning Agnes'.

In 1923 Tom managed to get through what might have been a trying ordeal: a visit from the Prince of Wales to Max Gate. The Prince was not actually scheduled to visit Dorchester on Hardy's account, but to open a new drill hall for the Dorset Territorials – a project upon which Tom was silent – but it had been felt on high that he might visit the man now acknowledged to be England's greatest author. Since the award of the Order of Merit in 1910 the Nobel Committe had neglected Hardy in favour of writers such as Maeterlinck, Romain Rolland (whose sister was his faithful translator), Anatole France, Jacinto Benavente and figures even more obscure. The truth is that the Nobel Prize for Literature was then usually awarded to Scandinavians or 'optimists'; those members of the Committee who were against Hardy argued not against his genius but against what they took to be his 'view of life'. The visit of the Prince might be seen to make up for this neglect, which was emphasized towards the end of the year when it was heard that the 1923 Prize had gone to W.B. Yeats (whose optimistic first reaction to the news was the question: 'How much?').

A huge lunch had to be provided by a caterer for, among others, a lord, an admiral and two stewards to the Duchy of Cornwall, which owned much of the land around Dorchester. Florence had been beside herself with worry; this shows in a photograph of her, sitting between the Prince and Tom, taken on the lawn at Max Gate. The Prince looks strained, bored and hot – it was a scorching day. Tom, on the other hand, looks as wise and pleased as a Cheshire Cat: his expression is a perfect comment upon such junketings. Later he told Florence that she had been 'cold', but may very well have been teasing her: he could hardly have agreed with the solemn spirit with which she described the event to Paul Lemperly, an American book collector: 'The eldest son of the sovereign has never before . . . paid such a compliment to literature.' It was the kind of day she lived for – and did not, therefore, enjoy at all. Wessex, much to his annoyance, must have been locked safely away: usually he was allowed to be on the dining-table itself ('contesting every forkful,' wrote Cynthia Asquith, at that time Barrie's secretary), expressing his master's unspoken comments upon the frequently pretentions proceedings.

Florence wrote in the *Life* of the Prince's 'simple and friendly manner' and 'easy informality'. But Tom, although he recognized the excellence of the Prince's training, knew him to be a philistine and told Sassoon, with some glee, of his now famous remark (and 'compliment to literature'): 'My mother tells me that you have written a book called [. . . er . . . er] *Tess of the d'Urbervilles*. I must try to read it some time.' The Gravesian addition to this story – notwithstanding his oath that he thus had it from Sassoon – that the Prince consulted a small slip of paper taken from his pocket just before pronouncing the title of the 'book' must, alas, be taken as apocryphal. But Tom did obtain for Florence a piece of adjoining (Duchy) land upon which she could keep chickens.

The sad Bugler affair apart, during which Tom's very best impulses were frustrated, there was not much more. He delighted in the company of Sassoon, Blunden and Lawrence, and in the calls of some local friends. There were occasional visits from such older friends as Gosse. His last public appearance (not that he had ever done less than make a point of avoiding these if he possibly could) was the laying of the foundation stone for the new Dorchester Grammar School, upon which occasion he made quite a long speech – reproduced in the *Life*. He received thousands of letters on each birthday, right up to the end: less pleasing, but attended to with compunction. There were performances on the lawn of Max Gate by the Balliol Players, from Oxford, of *The Curse of the House of Atreus* (1924) and then the *Hippolytus* (1926). The death of Wessex was deeply felt, because he had been a constant and faithful companion, fully deserving of the inscription on his tombstone:

THE

FAMOUS DOG

WESSEX

August 1913–27 Dec. 1926

Faithful. Unflinching.

GOOD THINGS

Wessex was much disliked by local people, and in much the same way that Tom himself was disliked by some of them. Attuned both to Tom's reveries and to his dislike of trivialities and pettiness, he wanted desperately (as May O'Rourke noted) to be human – and, she might have added, most of all he wanted to be Tom. He loved to listen to the radio, and, Tom told Graves, understood the quality of the programmes. Dogs, like cats, have perfectly developed and uncorrupted emotional faculties, so that Wessex shared in all his master's emotions. He knew who he liked (Lawrence, for example, whom he would never touch); but he was so well attuned to Tom's critical (if not necessarily unfriendly) faculties, and to his momentary irritations (natural and inevitable in a very old man), that he sometimes reacted, with a harmless enough nip, when he should not, by the highest standards, have done so. Thus an impertinent postman was slightly bitten, and some silly and gossiping maids, too, were threatened. In praising his 'great intelligence', Tom admitted that he had 'defects of temper'. What Wessex disliked above all – after insincere or specious writing, and foolishness – were unfriendliness and fear. He had tremendous courage, and endured a long battle with a stoat. There was talk, owing to town hostility, of having him put down before his time, but neither Tom nor Florence would allow this. His freedom from conventional notions of time – perhaps reflecting the emotional, if not the intellectual, impact of Einstein upon Tom – is nowhere better illustrated than in his compassionate and concerned behaviour towards William Watkins in the spring of 1925. Watkins was connected with the Society of Dorset Men in London, and had called on Tom to discuss certain matters:

> The dog, as was his wont, rushed into the hall and greeted his friend with vociferous barks. Suddenly these gave way to a piteous whine, and the change was so startling that Wessex's mistress went to see what had happened.
>
> Nothing, however, seemed amiss, and the dog returned to the room where Hardy was sitting and where he was joined by Mr Watkins. But even here Wessex seemed ill at ease, and from time to time went to the visitor and touched his coat solicitously with his paw, which he always withdrew giving a sharp cry of distress.
>
> Mr Watkins left a little after ten o'clock, apparently in very good spirits.

Early the next morning the telephone, recently put in for Florence, rang.

This was usually a signal for Wessex to bark loudly. But he knew what it was, and lay silent with his nose between his paws: Watkins had suddenly died at his hotel soon after returning from Max Gate.

Fear of being accused of sentimentality should not lead us to underestimate the importance of this magnificent creature, or the sharpness of his loss. Those who dislike dogs may no doubt like to be reminded yet again of Edmund Wilson's warning that the advantages of Philoctetes cannot be received without the endurance of his 'loathsome presence'. But Wessex's presence was anything but loathsome for Florence and for Tom, who was in fact never sentimental about animals and was well aware, as he told Florence Henniker when sympathizing with her over the loss of a cat, that attachment to pets was in a sense foolish. If he practised his love on animals as well as on human beings, that may be because the former are, as an experienced person once pronounced, 'more sensitive'. Florence gave him a Persian cat to replace Wessex, but he could not take it out with him for walks, and there is no doubt that the gap left by Wessex's departure made him more resigned to his own approaching end. To Granville Barker he wrote on 29 December 1926, in poignant strain:

> We have had a sad aftering to our Christmas. Our devoted (and masterful) dog Wessex died on the 27th, and last night had his bed outside the house under the trees for the first time for 13 years. We miss him greatly, but he was in such misery with swelling and paralysis that it was a relief when a kind breath of chloroform administered in his sleep by 2 good-natured doctors (not vets) made his sleep an endless one – A dog of such strong character required human doctors!

He now had, himself, less than a year before the onset of his last illness, which at first seemed an innocuous one. In June 1925 he had sent off the manuscript of the delightfully entitled *Human Shows, Far Phantasies, Songs and Trifles*, at first called just *Human Shows*. It was published on 20 November 1926. The least substantial of his single collections, it was more light-hearted in tone – as if for the time being he was still determined to reject the charges of pessimism and gloom which were so often made against him. The subject of the brilliantly laconic, beautifully observed, word-perfect and detached 'An East-End Curate' (which he left out of *Late Lyrics*, since it had appeared in the *London Mercury* in 1924) might once have been treated much more darkly:

GOOD THINGS

A small blind street off East Commercial Road;
  Window, door; window, door;
  Every house like the one before,
Is where the curate, Mr Dowle, has found a pinched abode.
Spectacled, pale, moustache straw-coloured, and with a long thin
    face,
Day or dark his lodgings' narrow doorstep does he pace.

A bleached pianoforte, with its drawn silk plaitings faded,
Stands in his room, its keys much yellowed, cyphering, and abraded,
'Novello's Anthems' lie at hand, and also a few glees,
And 'Laws of Heaven for Earth' in a frame upon the wall one sees.

He goes through his neighbours' houses as his own, and none
    regards,
And opens their back-doors off-hand, to look for them in their
    yards:
A man is threatening his wife on the other side of the wall,
But the curate lets it pass as knowing the history of it all.

Freely within his hearing the children skip and laugh and say:
  'There's Mister Dow-well! There's Mister Dow-well!' in their play;
  And the long, pallid, devoted face notes not,
But stoops along abstractedly, for good, or in vain, God wot!

Now, in almost his last year, he had only his last book to complete. In
the event, although he assembled it himself, it did not appear until 2
October 1928, some months after his death. Amazingly, most if not all
of the poems in it were written after he sent off *Human Shows*. Knowing
that it would be his last book, he no longer tried to conceal his feelings by
selection or omission. He had concluded his short 'Introductory Note'
with these words:

> This being probably my last appearance on the literary stage, I
> would say . . . that though, alas, it would be idle to pretend that
> the publication of these poems can have much interest for me, the
> track having been adventured so many times before today, the pieces
> themselves have been presented with reasonable care, if not quite with
> the zest of a young man new to print.
>   I also repeat what I have often stated on such occasions, that no
> harmonious philosophy is attempted in these pages – or in any bygone
> pages of mine, for that matter.

In *Winter Words* he has given up on everything in the public world except the poetry which he could never give up. On the last Good Friday of his life, that of 1927, he celebrated others who had suffered:

> There are many more Good Fridays
>   Than this, if we but knew
> The names, and could relate them,
>   Of men whom rulers slew
> For their goodwill, and date them
>   As runs the twelvemonth through . . .

Nor was the rest of the message much more hopeful in the usual conventional terms. But none of it was more than that full 'look at the Worst' which he, of all English-born poets of modern times, was the first, as he put it in 'In Tenebris', to 'exact'. There is, again amazingly, no sign of any flagging of energy – and perhaps in that connection he mentioned Verdi's music: how when he was young and 'enjoyed his life immensely' he listened to *Il Trovatore*.

On 27 October he told Florence of a strange experience he had had a 'few years ago'. During a tea party at Max Gate, when she had been present, he had seen a 'dark man' beside her. Possibly he did not want to upset Florence, and had in fact had the experience more recently, for it was Death he saw. 'This afternoon he said: "I can see his face now."'

From this time until he went to sleep for the last time he was busy revising poems and dwelling on the past. On Armistice Day he and Florence stood, when listening to the broadcast of the service from Canterbury, for the two minutes' silence. Later he told her that he had been thinking of Frank George; surely this disposes of the heartless charge that his grief for this young man had been 'extravagant' and 'factitious'?

He thought that he had done everything he had wanted to do, but still would have preferred to be 'a small architect in a country town'. He celebrated Emma's birthday and Mary's death, so close together in date, and Florence thought the better of her own addition to the *Life*, which she had recorded in her own diary, even at this stage in her husband's life: 'It is very pathetic – all the more so when one remembers what their married life was like.'

On 11 December he went into his study, but felt too weak to work. He went to bed. He talked about his will, read, and came downstairs for a few hours each day until Christmas Day. On that day he wrote his last letter, to Edmund Gosse: 'I am in bed on my back, living on butter-broth and beef-tea.' He did not come down after that. He became weaker, could no longer listen to prose being read, but asked Florence to read him both 'The Listeners' and 'Rabbi Ben Ezra'. By now Florence had procured the services of her sister Eva to nurse him. He seemed to be sinking, but then on 10 January made a 'strong rally', and certainly was well enough to go to the lavatory: the servants laid eiderdowns on the floor to ease his passage along the hall to it. On the next day the housemaid Nellie Titterington made him some 'kettle-broth': bacon, chopped parsley, onions and bread. He drank the broth but could not manage the bacon. Later, at dusk, while hopes for him were still high, he asked Florence to read him a verse from FitzGerald's *Rubaiyat*:

> Oh, Thou, who Man of baser Earth did make,
> And ev'n with Paradise devise the Snake:
> For all the Sin wherewith the Face of Man
> Is blackn'd – man's forgiveness give – and take!

He signalled that this was enough. Soon afterwards he 'had a sharp heart attack of a kind he had never had before', at which he may have uttered the words, 'Eva! Eva! What is this?' But those were not his last words. Florence's original sentence read: 'Hardy remained unconscious until a few minutes towards the end, when a few broken sentences, one of them heartrending in its poignancy, showed that his mind had reverted to a sorrow of the past. Shortly after nine he died.' The words were 'Em! Em!'

The immediate aftermath is sick and hateful farce. Cockerell and Barrie were in attendance, and between them took charge. He was wanted by the nation for a Westminster Abbey burial, but had directed that he be buried at Stinsford. So a ghastly compromise, possibly first suggested by the vicar of Stinsford in face of a Cockerell almost insane with officiousness, was reached: his heart was to be buried at Stinsford, and the rest in the Abbey. Florence did not like it, but was too ill to fight the others. Barrie, shamefully, did not defend her. A surgeon came to remove the heart, which was placed in a biscuit tin. The tale, which would have hugely amused Tom, that a cat prised off the lid and ate the heart, is possibly not true – although it is hardly unlikely. Tom was a poet, even if now a dead one, and strange things happened where he still was: a recent publication now arrived, by post, *Heart Burials and Some Purbeck Marble Heart-Shrines*, by G. Dru Henry.

There was mourning in two places: Stinsford and London. Somehow Cockerell and the grotesque Barrie, between them, had managed to make the event both macabre and farcical. What would Tom have thought? At least that it was a true *Satire of Circumstance*. But the absurd manner in which his funeral offices were conducted has not spoiled his life for us. Therefore we may give our priority to how his name and achievements live for us.

Those of good heart think of him as an English poet whose novels were as well done as a poet's novels could have been done; as a poet who could write poems as none of his time could write them; as a dramatist who saw what could be done in bad circumstances and did it incomparably better than anyone else. As a man we greet him, for all the calumnies that have been heaped upon him by envious moralists and their kind, with gratitude. No words are more appropriate for him than those 'incorrect' ones he put into the mouth of Marty South at the end of *The Woodlanders*: 'If ever I forget your name let me forget home and heaven! . . . But no, no, my love, I never can forget 'ee; for you was a good man, and did good things!'

Select Bibliography

What follows is a mere selection from some of the more useful of the thousands of books and articles that have been written about Thomas Hardy. Hardy's own works are best consulted either in the ongoing Clarendon Press edition, in which the poems and some novels are now available, or in the Wessex Edition (London, 1912–13). There is also a good edition of the *Complete Poems* by James Gibson (London, 1976), and a *Variorum Edition* of them, by the same editor (London, 1979). The *Literary Notebooks* were edited by Lennart Björk (two volumes, London, 1985). The *Collected Letters* were edited by R. L. Purdy and Michael Millgate (London, 1978–89). The *Personal Notebooks* were edited by Richard Taylor (London, 1979). *Thomas Hardy: A Bibliographical Study* was compiled by R. H. Purdy in 1954. The most complete bibliography was compiled by R. P. Draper and Martin S. Ray: *An Annotated Critical Bibliography of Thomas Hardy* (New York and London, 1989). The *Personal Writings* were edited by Harold Orel (London, 1966).

Archer, William, *Real Conversations*, New York, 1904.

Bailey, J. O., *The Poetry of Thomas Hardy: A Handbook and Commentary*, 1970.

Barber, D. F. (ed.), *Concerning Thomas Hardy*, 1968.

Baugner, Ulla, *A Study on the Use of Dialect in Thomas Hardy's Novels and Short Stories*, Stockholm, 1972.

Bayley, J., *An Essay on Thomas Hardy*, Cambridge, 1978.

Blunden, E., *Thomas Hardy*, London, 1942.

Boumbela, P., *Thomas Hardy and Women*, Brighton, 1982.

Clements, P., and Grindle, J. (eds), *The Poetry of Thomas Hardy*, London, 1980.

Collins, V. H., *Talks with Thomas Hardy at Max Gate*, London, 1928.

Cox, R. G. (ed.), *Thomas Hardy: The Critical Heritage*, 1970.

Cox, R. G. and G. S. (eds), *Thomas Hardy Yearbook*, St Peter Port, 1970 and onwards.

Cunningham, V., *Everywhere Spoken Against: Dissent in the Victorian Novel*, Oxford, 1975.

Davie, D., *Thomas Hardy and British Poetry*, London, 1973.

Dean, S., *Hardy's Poetic Vision in 'The Dynasts'*, 1977.

Drabble, M. (ed.), *The Genius of Thomas Hardy*, London, 1976.

Draper, R. P. (ed.), *Thomas Hardy: The Tragic Novels*, London, 1975.

Eliot, T. S., *After Strange Gods: A Primer of Modern Heresy*, 1934.

Firor, R., *Folkways in Thomas Hardy*, Philadelphia, 1931.

Gittings, R., *Young Thomas Hardy*, London, 1975.

Gittings, R., *The Older Hardy*, 1978.

Gittings, R., and Manton, J., *The Second Mrs Hardy*, London, 1979.

Goode, J., *Thomas Hardy: The Offensive Truth*, Oxford, 1988.

Gregor, I., *The Great Web: The Form of Hardy's Major Fiction*, London, 1974.

Griest, G. L., *Mudie's Circulating Library and the Victorian Novel*, Newton Abbot, 1970.

Grundy, J., *Hardy and the Sister Arts*, 1979.

Guerard, A. (ed.), *Hardy: A Collection of Critical Essays*, Engelwood Cliffs, New Jersey, 1963.

Hands, T., *Thomas Hardy: Distracted Preacher?*, London, 1989.

Hawkins, D., *Hardy: Novelist and Poet*, Newton Abbot, 1976.

Howe, I., *Thomas Hardy*, 1966.

Hynes, S., *The Pattern of Hardy's Poetry*, 1961.

Ingham, P., *Thomas Hardy*, Hemel Hempstead, 1989.

Johnson, L., *The Art of Thomas Hardy*, 1894 (revised, not by Johnson, 1923).

Kay-Robinson, D., *Hardy's Wessex Reappraised*, 1972.

Kay-Robinson, D., *The First Mrs Hardy*, 1979.

Kerr, Barbara, *Bound to the Soil: A Social History of Dorset 1750–1918*, Wakefield, 1975.

Kramer, D., *Thomas Hardy: The Forms of Tragedy*, London, 1975.

Kramer, D. (ed.), *Critical Approaches to the Fiction of Thomas Hardy*, London, 1979.

Jacobus, M. (ed.), *Women Writing and Writing about Women*, 1979.

Laird, J. T., *The Shaping of Tess of the d'Urbervilles*, Oxford, 1975.

Lawrence, D. H., *Phoenix*, 1936.

Lea, H., *Thomas Hardy's Wessex*, 1913.

Marsden, K., *The Poems of Thomas Hardy: A Critical Introduction*, London, 1969.

Miller, J. H., *Thomas Hardy: Distance and Desire*, Oxford, 1972.

SELECT BIBLIOGRAPHY

Millgate, M., *Thomas Hardy: His Career as a Novelist*, London, 1971.

Millgate, M., *Thomas Hardy: A Critical Biography*, London, 1982.

Morgan, R., *Women and Sexuality in the Novels of Thomas Hardy*, 1988.

Morrell, R., *Thomas Hardy: The Will and the Way*, Kuala Lumpur, 1965.

Orel, H., *Thomas Hardy's Epic Drama: A Study of 'The Dynasts'*, Kansas, 1963.

Orel, H., *The Final Years of Thomas Hardy 1912–1928*, London, 1976.

Paulin, T., *Thomas Hardy: The Poetry of Perception*, London, 1986.

Rutland, W., *Thomas Hardy: A Study of His Writings and Their Background*, 1938.

Smith, A. (ed.), *The Novels of Thomas Hardy*, London, 1979.

Springer, M., *Hardy's Use of Allusion*, London, 1983.

Stubbs, P., *Women and Fiction: Feminism and the Novel 1880–1920*, Brighton, 1979.

Zietlow, P., *Moments of Vision: The Poetry of Thomas Hardy*, Cambridge, Massachusetts, 1974.

Index

INDEX

INDEX

INDEX

INDEX

INDEX

INDEX

INDEX